COLLINS
POCKET
GREEK
DICTIONARY

COLLINS POCKET GREEK DICTIONARY

GREEK·ENGLISH ENGLISH·GREEK

Harry T. Hionides B.S., M.A. (Oxon)
Athens College

Collins
London and Glasgow

First published as Collins Contemporary Greek Dictionary 1977
First published in this edition 1982
© William Collins Sons and Company Limited 1977 1982
ISBN 0 00 433205 9

To Marjorie and Homer W. Davis

ISBN 0 00 433206 7 Special edition for Greece and Cyprus

Filmset by Oliver Burridge Filmsetting Limited, Crawley, Sussex
Printed and bound in Great Britain by William Collins Sons and
Company Limited

CONTENTS

Πρόλογος

Ἡ εὐρεῖα χρῆσις τῆς ἀγγλικῆς γλώσσης εἰς ὅλον τόν κόσμον κατέστησε λίαν αἰσθητήν τήν ἀνάγκην τῆς γνώσεως τῆς ἀκριβοῦς σημασίας τῆς ἀγγλικῆς ὁρολογίας. Τήν ἀνάγκην αὐτήν ζητεῖ νά πληρώσῃ τό νέον ἀνά χεῖρας Ἀγγλοελληνικόν καί Ἑλληνοαγγλικόν Λεξικόν, τό ὁποῖον προορίζεται κυρίως διά τούς, ἕλληνας μαθητάς τῆς ἀγγλικῆς καί διά τούς ἀγγλοφώνους ἐπισκέπτας τῆς Ἑλλάδος. Κατά τήν σύνταξιν τοῦ ἐπιτόμου Λεξικοῦ δύο στοιχεῖα ἐλήφθησαν ὑπ'ὄψιν, ἡ περιεκτικότης καί ἡ σαφήνεια. Κατά τήν περιεκτικότητα τό Λεξικόν εἶναι πλουσιώτατον διότι περιλαμβάνει τάς μᾶλλον προχείρους καί συνήθεις λέξεις καί φράσεις τῆς ἀγγλικῆς καί τῆς ἑλληνικῆς. Ὡς πρός τήν σαφήνειαν μεγάλη προσοχή κατεβλήθη εἰς τήν ἀπόδοσιν τῆς ἀκριβοῦς σημασίας ἑκάστης λέξεως. Ὅπου τυχόν μία λέξις ἔχει πλείονας σημασίας, ἀναγράφονται αὐται κατά σειράν συχνότητος χρησιμοποιήσεως. Ἐκτός τούτου προσεπάθησα νά ἀποδώσω εἰς τήν ἑλληνικήν πλείστας ὅσας λαϊκάς καί ἰδιωματικάς ἐκφράσεις τῆς ἀγγλικῆς.

Περιλαμβάνει ὅλας τάς ἐν χρήσει λέξεις τῆς ἀγγλικῆς καί τῆς ἑλληνικῆς γλώσσης μέ τάς κυριωτέρας σημασίας ἑκάστης, ὅσον ἐπιτρέπει ὁ χῶρος, ὡς καί τούς πλέον συνήθεις τεχνικούς καί ἐπιστημονικούς ὅρους τῶν δύο γλωσσῶν. Πλεῖσται νέαι λέξεις ἔχουν περιληφθῆ τάς ὁποίας δέν θά εὕρῃ τις εἰς ἄλλα ὀγκωδέστερα λεξικά.

Οὕτω τό Ἀγγλοελληνικόν καί Ἑλληνοαγγλικόν Λεξικόν ἀποτελεῖ δύο κεχωρισμένα μέν ἀλλά ἀλληλοσυμπληρούμενα τμήματα ἑνός ἀρτίου συνόλου, τό ὁποῖον τίθεται εἰς τήν διάθεσιν τῶν μαθητῶν καί τῶν γνωριζόντων τήν ἀγγλικήν.

Χάρης Χιονίδης

Foreword

Of all publications issuing from the press, a dictionary is certainly the last to require a long preface. The user has only to glance at a few pages to find out the system followed and to gauge the value of the work as a whole.

The aim of this Greek-English, English-Greek dictionary is to be a work of practical utility within convenient size in which are met the needs of Greek students of English and of English-speaking travellers in Greece. Completeness, as far as practicable, conciseness and accuracy have been the guide lines for the compilation. The vocabularies have been carefully sifted and compiled to embrace most words in current use including many scientific and technical terms which have become a part of everyday speech. Idiomatic and slang expressions as well as Americanisms are also included.

That bane of the Greek language, 'diglossia', has been resolved by preference for the popular and colloquial rather than the learned usage whenever this has been practicable. Every effort has been made not to give a mere string of terms on the chance of hitting the right one among them, but to find the exact and generally received equivalent of the word or phrase under consideration. And no effort has been spared to produce a comprehensive, yet concise, lucid and safe guide for those users of the dictionary whether they be students or travellers.

I wish here to express my gratitude to the numerous friends and colleagues who have in one way or another encouraged me to undertake this compilation. Among these I mention W. Lee Pierson, E. Glassmeyer, G. Savvides, Richard Thomas, Carol Purdon, and Iseabail Macleod.

Harry T. Hionides

Pronunciation of Modern Greek

Greek has nineteen consonant sounds and only five vowel sounds. Some of them are exactly as in English, some resemble their English counterparts very closely, and there are two for which no English equivalent exists. The system adopted here is to transcribe simply into Latin letters the sounds of Greek. The pronunciation is very simple. Each letter has the same phonetic sound with few exceptions. There are no variations in the pronunciation of Greek letters as in English, no silent characters or long or short vowel sounds. And there are only two letters without English equivalents—γ and χ.

Modern Greeks pronounce the following consonants like the English:

$$\beta, \zeta, \kappa, \lambda, \mu, \nu, \xi, \pi, \rho, \sigma, \tau, \varphi, \psi$$
$$v \quad z \quad k \quad l \quad m \quad n \quad ks \quad p \quad r \quad s \quad t \quad f \quad ps$$

Other consonant sounds:

Greek letter(s)	*Symbols*	
μπ	b (when initial)	b as in *b*oy
	mb, mp (when medial)	
ντ	d	d as in *d*ay. *d*o
	nd (when medial)	
	nt	
γκ or γγ	ng	g as in *g*o and
		ng as in E*ng*land
θ	th	as in *th*in
δ	δ	as in *th*is
γ	γ	as in *y*es

The following three sounds are the most troublesome:

ρ	r	as in ro*l*l (rolled like the Scottish *r*)
γ	γ	To produce this sound make a continuous *g* sound without withdrawing the tongue.
χ	h	There are two *h* sounds. One resembles the *ch* of the Scottish lo*ch* and it is how χ is generally pronounced. The other is like the *ch* sound of the German *ich*.

The υ of the groups αυ, ευ, ηυ is generally pronounced *v*. Before θ, κ, ξ, π, σ, τ, φ, χ, ψ it is pronounced *f*.

The three genders of *nouns* only are distinguished by the articles ὁ (masculine), ἡ (feminine) and τό (neuter).

Ἐπεξήγησις Προφορᾶς

Key to Pronunciation of English

Δέν ἀναφέρομεν παραδείγματα διά τά ἀκόλουθα φωνητικά σύμβολα διότι εἶναι γνωστά ὡς γράμματα τοῦ ἀλφαβήτου

p, b, d, t, k, m, n, l, r, f, v, s, z, h.

Ἐφιστῶμεν τήν προσοχήν τοῦ μαθητοῦ ἐπί τῶν κάτωθι συμβόλων, τά ὁποῖα εἴτε δέν ἀπαντοῦν εἰς τό ἀλφάβητον, εἴτε χρησιμοποιοῦνται πρός δήλωσιν φθόγγου ὁ ὁποῖος συχνά διαφέρει ἀπό τήν φωνήν τοῦ γράμματος τοῦ ἀλφαβήτου.

I Σύμφωνα

1.	g	leg	6. ʒ	régime
2.	ŋ	finger	7. j	your
3.	θ	thumb	8. w	water
4.	δ	this	9. tʃ	chest
5.	ʃ	ship	10. dʒ	danger

Κατάταξις τῶν Συμφώνων ἀναλόγως τῆς φωνῆς των καί τρόπου προφορᾶς

Ἄηχα	Ἠχηρά	
p	b	
t	d	} Στιγμιαῖα
k	g	
f	v	
θ	δ	
s	z	} Τριβόμενα
ʃ	ʒ	
	r	
	m	
	n	} Ρινικά
	ŋ	
	l	} Γλωσσικά
h	j	} Ἡμίφωνα
	w	

Τά 24 Σύμφωνα κατά σειράν

b, d, f, g, h, k, l, m, n, p, r, s, t, v, w, z

θ, δ, ŋ, j, ʃ, ʒ, tʃ, dʒ

II Φωνήεντα

'Εμπρόσθια

1	2	3	4
iː	i	e	æ
see	chin	leg	hand

'Οπίσθια

5	6	7	8	9
ɑː	ɔ	ɔː	u	uː
arm	on	your	foot	food

Κεντρικά

10	11	12
ʌ	əː	ə
thumb	girl	bitter

III Δίφθογγοι

13	14	15	16	17	18	19	20	21	22
ei	ou	ai	au	ɔi	iə	ɛə	uə	aiə	auə
face	nose	eye	mouth	boy	ear	there	poor	fire	power

English and Greek Abbreviations

a	adjective	ἐπίθετον
abbr	abbreviation	σύντμησις
ad	adverb	ἐπίρρημα
agr	agriculture	γεωργία
anat	anatomy	ἀνατομία
arch	archeology	ἀρχαιολογία
archit	architecture	ἀρχιτεκτονική
art	art	τέχνη
astr	astronomy	ἀστρονομία
attr	attributive	ἐπίθετον
aut	automobile	αὐτοκίνητον
aviat	aviation	ἀεροπορία
bibl	biblical	βιβλικός
biol	biology	βιολογία
bot	botany	βοτανική
Brit	British usage	Ἀγγλισμός
carp	carpentry	ξυλουργική
chem	chemistry	χημεία
cine	cinema	κινηματογράφος
col	colloquial	κοινός
collect	collective	περιληπτικός
comm	commercial	ἐμπορικός
comp	comparative	συγκριτικός
compd	compound, compound element	σύνθετος
cj	conjunction	σύνδεσμος
dim	diminutive	ὑποκοριστικός
dip	diplomacy	διπλωματική
eccl	ecclesiastical	ἐκκλησιαστικόν
econ	economics	οἰκονομία
elec	electricity	ἠλεκτρισμός
esp	especially	εἰδικῶς
excl	exclamation	ἐπιφώνημα
f	feminine noun	θηλυκόν
fig	figuratively	μεταφορικῶς
fin	finance	οἰκονομία
geog	geography	γεωγραφία
geol	geology	γεωλογία
gram	grammar	γραμματική
hunt	hunting	κυνήγι
impers	impersonal	ἀπρόσωπον
infin	infinitive	ἀπαρέμφατος

interj	interjection	ἐπιφώνημα
irreg	irregular	ἀνώμαλον
law	law	νομική
ling	linguistics	γλωσσολογία
lit	literal	κυριολεκτικός
liter	literature	λογοτεχνία
m	masculine noun	ἀρσενικόν
math	mathematics	μαθηματικά
mech	mechanism	μηχανισμός
med	medicine	ἰατρική
mil	military	στρατιωτικός
mus	music	μουσική
n	(neuter) noun	οὐδέτερον
naut	nautical, naval	ναυτικός
num	numeral	ἀριθμός
old	old-fashioned	ἀπηρχαιωμένος
o.s.	oneself	ἑαυτόν
parl	Parliament	κοινοβούλιον
part	participle	μετοχή
pej	pejorative	ὑποτιμητικός
pers	personal	προσωπικός
phil	philosophy	φιλοσοφία
phon	phonetics	φωνητική, φωνολογία
phot	photography	φωτογραφία
phys	physics	φυσική
pl	plural	πληθυντικός
poet	poetry	ποίησις
pol	politics	πολιτική
poss	possessive	κτητικός
pp	past participle	παθητική μετοχή, μετοχή ἀορίστου
pred	predicative	κατηγορούμενον
prep	preposition	πρόθεσις
print	printing/typography	τυπογραφία
pron	pronoun	ἀντωνυμία
pt	past tense	ἀόριστον, παρατατικόν
rad	radio	ραδιοφωνία
rail	railways	σιδηρόδρομος
rel	religion	θρησκεία
sch	school	σχολεῖον
sing	singular	ἑνικός
sl	slang	λαϊκός
s.o.	someone, somebody	κάποιος
sport	sport	ἀθλητικά
sth	something	κάτι
sup	superlative	ὑπερθετικός
tech	technical	τεχνικός
tel	telephone	τηλέφωνον
tex	textiles	ὑφαντά
theat	theatre	θέατρον
TV	television	τηλεόρασις
univ	university	πανεπιστήμιον
US	American usage	Ἀμερικανισμός
v	verb	ρῆμα

xii

vi	intransitive verb	ῥῆμα ἀμετάβατον
vt	transitive verb	ῥῆμα μεταβατικόν
vti	transitive and	ῥῆμα μεταβατικόν καί
	intransitive verb	ἀμετάβατον
zool	zoology	ζωολογία

ἀθλητ	ἀθλητικά	athletics, sport
ἀερο	ἀεροπορία	aviation
ἀμ, ἀμετ,	ῥῆμα ἀμετάβατον	intransitive verb
ἀμετάβ		
ἀνατ	ἀνατομία	anatomy
ἀρχιτεκ	ἀρχιτεκτονική	architecture
ἀστρον	ἀστρονομία	astronomy
βλ	βλέπε	see (cross-reference)
βοτ	βοτανική	botany
γεωγρ	γεωγραφία	geography
γεωμ	γεωμετρία	geometry
γραμμ	γραμματική	grammar
ἐκκλ	θρησκεία	religion
ἐμπορ	ἐμπόριον	commerce
ἐπίθ	ἐπίθετον	adjective
ἐπίρ	ἐπίρρημα	adverb
ἐπιφ	ἐπιφώνημα	exclamation
ζωολ	ζωολογία	zoology
ἠλεκ, ἠλεκτ	ἠλεκτρισμός	electricity
ἰατρ	ἰατρική	medicine
κτλ	καί τά λοιπά	et cetera
μαθημ	μαθηματικά	mathematics
μηχαν	μηχανισμός	mechanism
μεταφ	μεταφορικῶς	figuratively
μουσ	μουσική	music
ναυτ	ναυτικόν	nautical, naval
νομ	νομική	law
οἰκ, οἰκον,	οἰκονομικά	economics
οἰκονομ		
ὄνομ, οὐσ	ὄνομα, οὐσιαστικόν	noun
πλ	πληθυντικός	plural
πολιτ	πολιτική	politics
προθ	πρόθεσις	preposition
π.χ.	παραδείγματος χάριν	e.g. (for example)
στρατ	στρατιωτικός	military
σύνδ	σύνδεσμος	conjunction
τεχν	τεχνολογία	technical
τηλεφ	τηλέφωνον	telephony
τυπογρ	τυπογραφία	printing, typography
φιλοσ	φιλοσοφία	philosophy
φωτογρ	φωτογραφική	photography
χημ	χημεία	chemistry

Greek—English

A, α

ἀ-, ἀν- (negative particle) in-, un-, il-, ir-, -less.

ἀβαθής [avathees] shallow.

ἀβάντα, ἡ [avanta] advantage.

ἀβάπτιστος [avapteestos] unbaptised.

ἀβασίλευτος [avaseeleftos] without a king ‖ (ἥλιος κτλ) not set.

ἀβάσιμος [avaseemos] groundless ‖ unfounded.

ἀβάστακτος [avastaktos] unbearable ‖ (δύναμις) uncontrollable.

ἄβατος [avatos] inaccessible ‖ untrodden.

ἄβγαλτος [avγaltos] inexperienced.

ἀβγό, τό [avγo] egg.

ἀβγολέμονο, τό [avγolemono] sauce or soup with eggs and lemon.

ἀβέβαιος [aveveos] doubtful ‖ uncertain.

ἀβίαστος [aveeastos] unforced, natural.

ἀβίωτος [aveeotos] unbearable, intolerable.

ἀβλαβής [avlavees] unhurt, unharmed.

ἀβλεψία, ἡ [avlepseea] inadvertence.

ἀβοήθητος [avoeetheetos] without help, helpless.

ἄβολος [avolos] inconvenient ‖ (κάθισμα κτλ) uncomfortable.

ἄβραστος [avrastos] unboiled ‖ undercooked.

ἄβυσσος, ἡ [aveesos] abyss.

ἀγαθός [aγathos] good, kind ‖ (ἀφελῆς) naive ‖ (τίμιος) honest.

ἀγάλια [aγaleea] slowly, softly, gently.

ἄγαλμα, τό [aγalma] statue.

ἄγαμος [aγamos] unmarried, single.

ἀγανακτῶ [aγanakto] be indignant, be angry.

ἀγανάκτησις, ἡ [aγanakteesees] indignation, anger.

ἀγάπη, ἡ [aγapee] love, affection.

ἀγαπημένος [aγapeemenos] dear, beloved ‖ favourite.

ἀγαπητικός, ὁ [aγapeeteekos] lover, sweetheart.

ἀγαπητός [aγapeetos] βλ ἀγαπημένος.

ἀγαπῶ [aγapo] love ‖ (μοῦ ἀρέσει) like.

ἀγγαρεία, ἡ [angareea] chore ‖ drudgery.

ἀγγεῖον, τό [angeeon] vase ‖ pot ‖ (ἀνατ) blood vessel.

ἀγγειοπλαστική, ἡ [angeeoplasteekee] pottery.

ἀγγελία, ἡ [angeleea] announcement ‖ (ἐμπορ) advertisement.

ἀγγελιαφόρος, ὁ, ἡ [angeleeaforos] messenger ‖ orderly.

ἀγγελικός [angeleekos] angelic(al).

ἀγγέλω [angello] announce, declare.

ἄγγελμα, τό [angelma] message, notice.

ἄγγελος, ὁ [angellos] angel.

ἀγγίζω [angeezo] touch.

ἄγγιχτος [angeehtos] untouched ‖ (ἄθικτος) intact.

Ἀγγλία, ἡ [angleea] England.

ἀγγλικά, τά [angleeka] English (language).

ἀγγλικός [angleekos] English.

Ἀγγλίς, ἡ [anglees] Englishwoman.

Ἄγγλος, ὁ [anglos] Englishman.

ἀγγούρι, τό [angouree] cucumber.

ἀγελάδα, ἡ [aγelaδa] cow ‖ (μεταφ). big fat woman, old cow (col).

ἀγέλαστος [aγelastos] morose, sullen undeceived.

ἀγέλη, ἡ [aγelee] herd ‖ (προβάτων) flock ‖ (λύκων) pack.

ἀγέμιστος [aγemeestos] empty ‖ (στρῶμα κτλ) unstuffed.

ἀγένεια, ἡ [aγeneea] impoliteness.

ἀγενής [aγenees] rude, impolite.

ἀγέραστος [aγerastos] ever young.

ἀγέρωχος [aγerohos] haughty, arrogant.

ἀγιάζι [aγeeazi] hoarfrost, cold.

ἀγιάζω [aγeeazo] (γίνομαι ἅγιος) become a saint.

ἀγιασμός, ὁ [aγeeasmos] blessing of holy water.

ἀγιάτρευτος [aγeeatreftos] incurable ‖ (μή γιατρευθείς) uncured.

ἀγίνωτος [aγeenotos] (φροῦτο) unripe, raw ‖ (φαγητό) uncooked.

ἁγιογραφία, ἡ [aγeeoγrafeea] icon, hagiography.

ἅγιος [aγeeos] holy ‖ (πρόσωπον) saint.

ἀγκαζάρω [angazaro] reserve, book ‖ hire.

ἀγκαζέ [angaze] arm in arm ‖ (πιασμένο) engaged, taken, occupied.

ἀγκάθι, τό [angathee] thorn, prickle.

ἀγκαλιά, ἡ [angalia] embrace ‖ (ἐπιρ) armful.

ἀγκαλιάζω [angaliazo] embrace, hug.

ἀγκίδα, ἡ [angeeδa] splinter, thorn.

ἀγκινάρα, ἡ [angeenara] artichoke.

ἀγκίστρι, τό [angeestri] hook.

ἀγκομαχῶ [angomaho] gasp, pant.

ἀγκύλαι, αἱ [angeele] brackets.

ἀγκυλωτός [angeelotos] crooked, bent

ἄγκυρα, ἡ [angeera] anchor ‖ σηκώνω ~ weigh anchor.

ἀγκυροβολία, ἡ [angeerovoleea] anchoring, mooring.

ἀγκυροβολῶ [angeerovolo] anchor, drop anchor.

ἀγκών, ὁ [angon] elbow.

ἀγλαΐζω [aylaeezo] embellish, adorn, decorate.

ἀγναντεύω [aynantevo] see from a distance.

ἄγνοια, ἡ [ayneea] ignorance.

ἁγνός [aynos] chaste, modest.

ἀγνοῶ [aynoo] be ignorant of ‖ (περιφρονῶ) ignore.

ἀγνωμοσύνη, ἡ [aynomoseenee] ungratefulness.

ἀγνώμων [aynomon] ungrateful, unthankful.

ἀγνώριστος [aynoreestos] unrecognizable.

ἄγνωστος [aynostos] not known, obscure.

ἄγονος [ayonos] infertile, barren ‖ (μεταφ) vain ‖ ~ γραμμή unprofitable shipping line.

ἀγορά, ἡ [ayora] (τό μέρος) market ‖ (ἡ πρᾶξις) purchase.

ἀγοράζω [ayorazo] purchase, buy.

ἀγοραῖος [ayoreos] for hire ‖ (μεταφ) vulgar, common.

ἀγορανομία, ἡ [ayoranomeea] market inspection police.

ἀγοραπωλησία, ἡ [ayorapoleeseea] buying and selling.

ἀγοραστής, ὁ [ayorastees] buyer, purchaser.

ἀγορεύω [ayorevo] make a speech, harangue.

ἀγόρι, τό [ayoree] boy, lad.

ἀγουρίδα, ἡ [ayourida] sour grape.

ἄγουρος [ayouros] unripe, green, sour.

ἄγρα, ἡ [ayra] chase, hunting.

ἀγράμματος [ayrammatos] illiterate, ignorant.

ἄγραφος [ayrafos] unwritten.

ἀγριάδα, ἡ [ayriada] fierceness, savageness.

ἀγριάνθρωπος, ὁ [ayrianthropos] savage.

ἀγριεύω [ayrievo] be infuriated, become angry.

ἀγρίμι, τό [ayreemee] wild animal ‖ (μεταφ) rude fellow.

ἄγριος [ayreeos] wild, furious, harsh.

ἀγροῖκος [ayreekos] coarse, unrefined, ill-bred.

ἀγρόκτημα, τό [ayrokteema] farmland.

ἀγρός, ὁ [ayros] field ‖ country.

ἀγρότης, ὁ [ayrotees] farmer, peasant.

ἀγροφυλακή, ἡ [ayrofeelakee] agrarian police.

ἀγρυπνῶ [ayreepno] keep awake, lie awake ‖ be watchful.

ἀγυάλιστος [ayeealistos] unpolished, tarnished.

ἀγύμναστος [ayeemnastos] untrained, unexercised.

ἀγύρτης, ὁ [ayeertees] charlatan, imposto·.

ἀγχιστεία, ἡ [anghisteea] affinity by marriage.

ἀγχόνη, ἡ [anghonee] gallows, hanging.

ἄγχος, τό [anghos] anxiety.

ἄγω [ayo] lead, conduct, guide.

ἀγωγή, ἡ [ayoyee] breeding, conduct ‖ (νομ) lawsuit.

ἀγώγι, τό [ayoyee] fare, carriage.

ἀγωγιάτης, ὁ [ayoyeeatees] driver, guide.

ἀγωγός, ὁ [ayoyos] conductor ‖ pipe, conduit.

ἀγών, ὁ [ayon] struggle, fight ‖ (ἀθλητ) game, contest ‖ ~ ες πλ games, sports events.

ἀγωνία, ἡ [ayoneea] agony, anxiety.

ἀγωνίζομαι [ayoneezome] struggle, fight, strive.

ἀγωνιστής, ὁ [ayoneestees] contestant, fighter ‖ war veteran.

ἀγωνιῶ [ayoneeo] be in agony, be anxious.

ἀγωνιώδης [ayoneeodees] anxious, troubled.

ἀδαής [adaees] inexperienced, unfamiliar (with).

ἀδαμάντινος [adamanteenos] diamond .‖ (χαρακτήρ) indomitable.

ἀδάμας, ὁ [adamas] diamond.

ἀδάμαστος [adamastos] untamed ‖ (λαός) unconquered ‖ (θάρρος) unbroken.

ἀδάπανος [adapanos] free, inexpensive.

ἄδεια, ἡ [adeea] leave, permission ‖ (γάμου κτλ) licence, permit.

ἀδειάζω [adeeazo] empty ‖ (εὐκαιρῶ) have time, have leisure.

ἄδειος [adeeos] empty, unoccupied ‖ at leisure.

ἀδέκαστος [adekastos] incorruptible ‖ (ἀμερόληπτος) equitable, unbiased.

ἀδελφή, ἡ [adelfee] sister.

ἀδέλφια, τά [adelfeea] πλ brothers, brother and sister.

ἀδελφικός [adelfeekos] brotherly, dear.

ἀδελφός, ὁ [adelfos] brother.

ἄδενδρος [adendros] treeless.

ἀδέξιος [adekseeos] awkward, clumsy.

ἀδέσμευτος [adesmeftos] (μεταφ) under no obligation.

ἀδέσποτος [adespotos] stray, without owner.

ἄδετος [adetos] (βιβλίο) unbound ‖ (λυμένος) loose, untied.

ἄδηλος [adeelos] uncertain, doubtful ‖ ἄδηλοι πόροι invisible income.

ἀδήλωτος [adeelotos] undeclared.

ἀδημονῶ [adeemono] be anxious, fret.

ἀδήν, ὁ [adeen] gland.

Ἅδης, ὁ [adees] Hell ‖ Hades.

ἀδηφάγος [adeefayos] voracious ‖ greedy.

ἀδιάβαστος [adeeavastos] (βιβλίο) unread ‖ (μαθητής) unprepared.

ἀδιάβατος [adeeavatos] impassable, impenetrable.

ἀδιάβροχον, τό [adeeavrohon] raincoat.

ἀδιάθετος [aδeeathetos] (ὑγεία) unwell ‖ (κεφάλαιον) unspent.

ἀδιαίρετος [aδieretos] indivisible ‖ undivided.

ἀδιάκοπος [aδeeakopos] uninterrupted, ceaseless.

ἀδιάκριτος [aδeeakreetos] imperceptible ‖ (χαρακτήρ) indiscreet.

ἀδιάλλακτος [aδeealaktos] irreconcilable, uncompromising.

ἀδιάλυτος [aδeealeetos] indissoluble, undissolved.

ἀδιάντροπος [aδeeantropos] brazen ‖ (ἐνέργεια) impudent.

ἀδιαπέραστος [aδeeaperastos] impenetrable, impermeable.

ἀδιάρρηκτος [aδeeareektos] unbreakable ‖ (μεταφ) indissoluble.

ἀδιάσπαστος [aδeeaspastos] unbroken, inseparable.

ἀδιάφορος [aδeeaforos] apathetic ‖ of no interest.

ἀδιαχώριστος [aδeeahoreestos] inseparable.

ἀδίδακτος [aδeeδaktos] untaught.

ἀδιέξοδος, ἡ [aδieksoδos] impasse ‖ (δρόμος) cul-de-sac, dead end.

ἀδικία, ἡ [aδeekeea] injustice, wrongdoing, offence.

ἄδικος [aδeekos] unjust, unfair ‖ ἔχω ἄδικον I'm in the wrong.

ἀδικῶ [aδeeko] do wrong, be unjust.

ἀδιόρατος [aδeeoratos] imperceptible.

ἀδιόρθωτος [aδeeorthotos] irreparable ‖ (χαρακτήρ) incorrigible.

ἀδίσταχτος [aδeestahtos] unhesitating, resolute.

ἄδολος [aδolos] guileless, innocent.

ἄδοξος [aδoksos] inglorious.

ἀδούλευτος [aδouleftos] unwrought, raw ‖ (ἀγρός) uncultivated.

ἀδράνεια, ἡ [aδraneea] inertness ‖ (μεταφ) inactivity, apathy.

ἀδράχτι, τό [aδrahtee] spindle.

ἀδρός [aδros] plentiful, generous.

ἀδύνατος [aδeenatos] feeble, thin ‖ (δέν γίνεται) impossible.

ἀδυναμία, ἡ [aδeenamea] (πνεύματος) deficiency ‖ (σώματος) weakness.

ἀδυνατῶ [aδeenato] be unable to, cannot.

ἀδυσώπητος [aδeesopeetos] relentless, implacable.

ἄδυτον, τό [aδeeton] (ἐκκλ) sanctuary.

ᾄδω [aδo] sing.

ἀεί [aee] always ‖ ἐς ~ forever.

ἀειθαλής [aeethalees] evergreen.

ἀεικίνητος [aeekeeneetos] of perpetual motion.

ἀείμνηστος [aeemneestos] of blessed memory

ἀεράμυνα, ἡ [aerameena] air defence.

ἀεράγημα, τό [aerayeema] airborne troops.

ἀεραγωγός, ἡ [aerayoyos] air duct.

ἀέρας, ὁ [aeras] air, wind.

ἄεργος [aeryos] unemployed, idle.

ἀερίζω [aereezo] ventilate, fan.

ἀερισμός, ὁ [aereesmos] ventilation, airing.

ἀέριον, τό [aereeon] gas.

ἀεριοῦχος [aereeouhos] aerated, gaseous.

ἀεριστήρ, ὁ [aereesteer] ventilator.

ἀεροδρόμιον, τό [aeroδromeeon] aerodrome.

ἀερόλιθος, ὁ [aeroleethos] meteorite.

ἀερολιμήν, ὁ [aeroleemeen] airport.

ἀεροπλάνον, τό [aeroplanon] aeroplane.

ἀεροπορία, ἡ [aeroporeea] air force.

ἀεροπορικῶς [aeroporeekos] by air.

ἀερόστατον, τό [aerostaton] balloon.

ἀετός, ὁ [aetos] eagle ‖ (μεταφ) clever person ‖ (χαρταετός) kite.

ἀζήτητος [azeeteetos] unclaimed ‖ (ἐμπορ) not sought after, not demanded.

ἄζυμος [azeemos] unleavened.

ἄζωτον, τό [azoton] nitrogen.

ἀηδής [aeeδees] loathsome, sickening.

ἀηδία, ἡ [aeeδeea] disgust, loathing odiousness.

ἀηδιάζω [aeeδeeazo] feel disgust for loathe.

ἀηδόνι, τό [aeeδonee] nightingale.

ἀήρ, ὁ [aeer] air.

ἀήττητος [aeeteetos] undefeated, unbeatable.

ἀθανασία, ἡ [athanaseea] immortality, eternity.

ἀθάνατος [athanatos] immortal, deathless.

ἀθέατος [atheatos] invisible, unseen.

ἄθελα [athela] unintentionally.

ἀθέμιτος [athemeetos] illegal, unlawful.

ἄθεος [atheos] godless ‖ (οὐσ) atheist.

ἀθεόφοβος [atheofovos] impious ‖ (οὐσ) rogue.

ἀθεράπευτος [atherapevtos] incurable, incorrigible.

ἀθετῶ [atheto] break one's word, violate.

ἄθικτος [atheektos] untouched, unharmed.

ἀθλητής, ὁ [athleetees] athlete.

ἀθλητικός [athleeteekos] athletic, robust.

ἀθλητισμός, ὁ [athleeteesmos] athletics.

ἄθλιος [athleeos] wretched, miserable.

ἆθλος, ὁ [athlos] feat, exploit.

ἀθόρυβος [athoreevos] quiet, silent.

ἄθραυστος [athravstos] unbroken ‖ unbreakable.

ἄθρησκος [athreeskos] irreligious.

ἀθροίζω [athreezo] add up, count ‖ (στρατ) gather, assemble.

ἄθροισμα, τό [athreesma] sum, total.

ἀθυμία, ἡ [atheemeea] dejection, depression.

ἀθυρόστομος [atheerostomos] indiscreet, impertinent.

ἀθῶος [athoos] innocent, guileless.

ἀθωώνω [athoono] acquit, exonerate.

αἰγιαλός, ὁ [eyeealos] seashore, coast.

αἴγλη, ἡ [eylee] splendour ‖ (ὀνόματος κτλ) grandeur, glory.

αἰγόκλημα, τό [eyokleema] honeysuckle.

αἰδέσιμος [edeseemos] reverend, venerable.

αἰδήμων [edeemon] modest, chaste.

αἰθέριος [ethereeos] ethereal, essential.

αἰθήρ, ὁ [etheer] ether, air.

αἴθουσα, ἡ [ethousa] room, hall ǁ (σχολική) schoolroom.

αἴθριος [ethreeos] clear, bright, fair.

αἷμα, τό [ema] blood.

αἱματηρός [emateeros] bloody, blood-stained.

αἱματοχυσία, ἡ [ematoheeseea] bloodshed.

αἱματώνω [ematono] besmear with blood ǁ bleed.

αἱμοβόρος [emovoros] bloodthirsty ǁ (μεταφ) ferocious, cruel.

αἱμοδοσία, ἡ [emoδoseea] blood donation.

αἱμομιξία, ἡ [emomeekseea] incest.

αἱμορραγία, ἡ [emoraγeea] haemorrhage.

αἱμοσφαίριον, τό [emosfereeon] blood corpuscle.

αἴνιγμα, τό [eneeγma] enigma, riddle.

ἄϊντε [aeede] (ἔπιφ) come now!, come on!

αἴξ, ἡ [eks] goat.

αἵρεσις, ἡ [eresees] heresy.

αἱρετικός [ereteekos] heretical.

αἴρω [erro] lift ǁ raise.

αἰσθάνομαι [esthanome] feel.

αἴσθημα, τό [estheema] sensation, feeling ǁ ~τα feelings.

αἰσθηματικός [estheemateekos] sentimental.

αἴσθησις, ἡ [estheesees] sense, sensation.

αἰσθητικός [estheeteekos] aesthetic, sensitive.

αἰσθητός [estheetos] perceivable, noticeable.

αἰσιόδοξος [eseeoδoksos] optimistic.

αἶσχος, τό [eshos] shame, disgrace.

αἰσχροκέρδεια, ἡ [eshrokerδeea] profiteering, sordid gain.

αἰσχρολογία, ἡ [eshroloγeea] obscenity, filthy talk.

αἰσχρός [eshros] shameful, infamous.

αἰσχύνη, ἡ [esheenee] shame, infamy.

αἴτησις, ἡ [eteesees] application, petition, request.

αἰτία, ἡ [eteea] cause, reason, motive.

αἰτιατική, ἡ [eteeatikee] (γραμμ) accusative (case).

αἰτιολογία, ἡ [eteeoloγeea] explanation ǁ (οἰκον) particulars.

αἴτιον, τό [eteeon] cause ǁ motive.

αἴτιος [eteeos] responsible, causing.

αἰτῶ [eto] request (κάτι) ǁ αἰτοῦμαι beg (κάτι).

αἴφνης [efnees] suddenly ǁ (π.χ.) for example.

αἰφνιδιασμός, ὁ [efneeδeeasmos] surprise.

αἰχμαλωτίζω [ehmaloteezo] capture ǁ (μεταφ) captivate. .

αἰχμάλωτος, ὁ [ehmalotos] captive, prisoner.

αἰχμή, ἡ [ehmee] (βελόνης) point ǁ (βέλους) head.

αἰών, ὁ [eon] age, century.

αἰώνιος [eoneeos] eternal ǁ perpetual.

ἀκαδημία, ἡ [akaδeemeea] academy.

ἀκαθαρσία, ἡ [akatharseea] filth, dirt.

ἀκάθαρτος [akathartos] dirty, filthy.

ἀκάθεκτος [akathektos] unbridled, impetuous, unchecked.

ἀκαθόριστος [akathoreestos] undefined.

ἄκαιρος [akeros] inopportune, untimely, unseasonable.

ἀκακία, ἡ [akakeea] (δένδρον) acacia.

ἄκακος [akakos] harmless, innocent.

ἀκαλαισθησία, ἡ [akalestheeseea] lack of taste.

ἀκάλεστος [akalestos] uninvited.

ἀκαλλιέργητος [akalierγeetos] uncultivated ǁ (ἄνθρωπος) uncultured.

ἀκαμάτης, ὁ [akamatees] lazy fellow, loafer.

ἄκαμπτος [akamptos] unbending.

ἀκάμωτος [akamotos] undone ǁ unripe.

ἄκανθα, ἡ [akantha] thorn, thistle.

ἀκανθώδης [akanthoδees] thorny, prickly.

ἀκανόνιστος [akanoneestos] unregulated ǁ (σχήμα) irregular ǁ (σφυγμός) uneven.

ἀκαριαῖος [akareeayos] in an instant, momentary.

ἄκαρπος [akarpos] unfruitful ǁ (μεταφ) fruitless.

ἀκατάβλητος [akatavleetos] indomitable ǁ (χρέη) unsettled, unpaid.

ἀκατάδεκτος [akataδektos] disdainful snobbish.

ἀκατάληπτος [akataleeptos] incomprehensible.

ἀκατάλληλος [akataleelos] unsuitable, unfit.

ἀκαταλόγιστος [akataloγeestos] not responsible (for) ǁ incalculable.

ἀκατανόητος [akatanoeetos] inconceivable, unintelligible.

ἀκατάπαυστος [akatapavstos] unceasing, endless.

ἀκατάστατος [akatastatos] untidy ǁ (καιρος) unstable, unsettled.

ἀκατέργαστος [akaterγastos] unwrought, raw.

ἀκατοίκητος [akateekeetos] uninhabited.

ἀκατόρθωτος [akatorthotos] infeasible, impossible.

ἀκέραιος [akereos] integral, whole ǁ (τίμιος) upright ǁ ~ ἀριθμός integer.

ἀκεφιά, ἡ [akefia] dejection, gloom.

ἀκίνδυνος [akeenδeenos] safe, harmless.

ἀκίνητος [akeeneetos] immovable ǁ (περιουσία) estate, property.

ἀκλείδωτος [akleeδotos] unlocked.

ἄκληρος [akleeros] childless, without an heir.

ἄκλιτος [akleetos] indeclinable.

ἀκμάζω [akmazo] flourish, thrive, be in full bloom.

ἀκμαῖος [akmeos] vigorous, sturdy || (γερός) robust.

ἀκμή, ἡ [akmee] height, peak, edge.

ἄκμων, ὁ [akmon] anvil.

ἀκοή, ἡ [akoee] hearing || ἐξ ἀκουῆς by hearsay.

ἀκοινώνητος [akeenoneetos] unsociable || (ἐκκλ) not having taken first communion.

ἀκολασία, ἡ [akolaseea] debauchery, excess.

ἀκόλαστος [akolastos] licentious || (διαγωγή) unprincipled, lawless.

ἀκολουθία, ἡ [akoloutheea] retinue, suite || (ἐκκλ) church service || κατ' ~ν in consequence.

ἀκόλουθος [akolouthos] (οὐσ) attendant || (στρατ) attaché || (ἐπίθ) following, next.

ἀκολουθῶ [akoloutho] follow || attend.

ἀκολούθως [akolouthos] consequently, afterwards || ὡς ~ as follows.

ἀκόμα [akoma] yet, more || ~ καί even if.

ἀκονίζω [akoneezo] sharpen, whet.

ἀκόντιον, τό [akonteeon] javelin, dart.

ἄκοπος [akopos] not cut || (εὔκολος) easy || (ξεκούραστα) untiring.

ἀκόρεστος [akorestos] insatiable, greedy.

ἄκοσμος [akosmos] indecent, improper.

ἀκουμπῶ [akoumbo] lean, stand || (ρ.ά.) rest.

ἀκούμπωτος [akoumbotos] unbuttoned.

ἀκούραστος [akourastos] indefatigable, unwearied.

ἀκούρδιστος [akourdeestos] not tuned, not wound up.

ἀκούσιος [akouseeos] unintentional || involuntary.

ἀκουστικόν, τό [akousteekon] (τηλεφ) receiver.

ἀκουστικός [akousteekos] acoustic.

ἀκουστός [akoustos] famous, celebrated.

ἀκούω [akouo] hear, listen to, learn || (εἰσακούω) obey.

ἄκρα, ἡ [akra] end, tip, extremity.

ἀκραιφνής [akrefnees] sincere, pure.

ἀκρατής [akratees] intemperate, incontinent.

ἀκράτητος [akrateetos] impetuous, rash, unrestrained.

ἄκρη, ἡ [akree] βλ ἄκρα.

ἀκριβά [akreeva] dearly.

ἀκρίβεια, ἡ [akreeveea] (ὡρολογίου) accuracy, precision || (μεταφράσεως κτλ) exactness || (τιμῆς) costliness, dearness.

ἀκριβής [akreevees] exact || (ὡρολόγιον κτλ) accurate || (ὑπολογισμός) correct || (σὲ ραντεβού) punctual.

ἀκριβός [akreevos] dear || expensive.

ἀκριβῶς [akreevos] precisely, accurately.

ἀκρίδα; ἡ [akreeda] locust, grasshopper.

ἄκριτος [akreetos] thoughtless.

ἀκρόασις, ἡ [akroasees] hearing, listening || (συνάντησις) audience, interview.

ἀκροατήριον, τό [akroateereeon] audience || auditorium.

ἀκροατής, ὁ [akroatees] listener || (πανεπιστημίου) auditor.

ἀκροβάτης, ὁ [akrovatees] acrobat.

ἀκρογιάλι, τό [akroyeealee] seashore.

ἄκρον, τό [akron] extremity, end, tip.

ἀκρόπολις, ἡ [akropolees] acropolis || citadel.

ἄκρος [akros] extreme, utmost, excessive, outermost.

ἀκροσφαλής [akrosfalees] precarious, dangerous.

ἀκρωτηριάζω [akroteereeazo] maim || amputate.

ἀκρωτήριον, τό [akroteereeon] cape, promontory.

ἀκτή, ἡ [aktee] shore, beach, coast.

ἀκτινοβολία, ἡ [akteenovoleea] radiation, brilliancy.

ἀκτινογραφία, ἡ [akteenоyrafeea] X-ray.

ἀκτινοθεραπεία, ἡ [akteenotherapeea] radiotherapy.

ἀκτίς, ἡ [aktees] ray, beam || (ἐλπίδος) gleam || (ἐνεργείας) range || (τροχοῦ) spoke || (κύκλου) radius.

ἀκτοπλοΐα, ἡ [aktoploeea] coastal shipping, coasting.

ἄκυρος [akeeros] invalid, void, null.

ἀκυρώνω [akeerono] nullify, invalidate, cancel.

ἀλάβαστρον, τό [alavastron] alabaster.

ἀλάδωτος [aladotos] unanointed with oil || (μεταφ) not bribed.

ἀλαζονεία, ἡ [alazoneea] arrogance, boastfulness.

ἀλάθευτος [alathevtos] infallible, unerring.

ἀλάθητος [alatheetos] certain, sure, infallible.

ἄλαλος [alalos] speechless, dumb, mute.

ἀλάνθαστος [alanthastos] infallible, certain.

ἀλάργα [alarya] afar, apart, off.

ἅλας [alas] βλ ἁλάτι.

ἁλάτι, τό [alatee] salt || ἁλατιέρα saltcellar.

ἁλατίζω [alateezo] salt.

ἄλγεβρα, ἡ [alyevra] algebra.

ἄλγος, τό [alyos] pain, grief, suffering.

ἀλέθω [aletho] grind.

ἀλείβω [aleevo] coat, smear, rub.

ἀλείφω [aleefo] βλ ἀλείβω.

ἀλέκτωρ, ὁ [alektor] cock, rooster.

ἀλεξίβροχον, τό [alekseevrohon] umbrella.

ἀλεξικέραυνον, τό [alekseekeravnon] lightning conductor.

ἀλεξιπτωτιστής, ὁ [alekseeptoteestees] parachutist.

ἀλεξίπτωτον, τό [alekseeptoton] parachute.

ἀλεποῦ, ἡ [alepou] fox || (μεταφ) sly person.

ἄλεσμα, τό [alesma] grinding.

ἀλέστα [alesta] quickly.
ἀλέτρι, τό [aletree] plough.
ἀλεύρι, τό [alevri] flour.
ἀλήθεια, ἡ [aleetheea] truth ‖ (ἐπιρ) really, indeed.
ἀληθεύω [aleethevo] be true, be right.
ἀληθινός [aleetheenos] true, truthful ‖ real, genuine.
ἀλησμόνητος [aleesmoneetos] unforgettable.
ἀλήτης, ὁ [aleetees] vagabond, vagrant.
ἁλιεία, ἡ [alieea] fishing, fishery.
ἁλιεύς, ὁ [alievs] fisherman.
ἁλιεύω [alievo] fish (for).
ἁλισίβα, ἡ [aleeseeva] lye.
ἄλκιμος [alkeemos] strong, sturdy, robust.
ἀλκοολικός [alkooleekos] alcoholic.
ἀλκυών, ἡ [alkeeon] kingfisher, halcyon.
ἀλλά [alla] but, however, yet.
ἀλλαγή, ἡ [allayee] change ‖ variation.
ἀλλάζω [allazo] change, alter.
ἀλλαντικά, τά [allanteeka] πλ sausages.
ἀλλαχοῦ [allahou] elsewhere.
ἀλλεπάλληλος [allepaleelos] repeated, successive.
ἀλλεργία, ἡ [alleryeea] allergy.
ἀλληλεγγύη, ἡ [alleelengiee] mutual help solidarity.
ἀλληλένδετος [alleelendetos] interdependent, bound together.
ἀλληλογραφία, ἡ [alleeloyrafeea] correspondence.
ἀλλοδαπή, ἡ [allodapee] foreign country.
ἀλλοδαπός, ὁ [allodapos] foreigner, alien
ἀλλοίθωρος [alleethoros] cross-eyed.
ἀλλοίμονο [alleemono] (ἐπιφ) alas! oh dear!
ἀλλοιώνω [alleeono] alter, change.
ἀλλοιῶς [aleeos] otherwise, in a different way.
ἀλλοίωσις, ἡ [aleeosees] change alteration ‖ (τροφίμων) adulteration.
ἀλλοιωτικός [aleeoteekos] different unlike ‖ (πρόσωπον) odd, strange.
ἀλλόκοτος [alokotos] queer, strange, odd.
ἄλλος [allos] (an)other, else ‖ (ἑπόμενος) next ‖ (διαφορετικός) different ‖ (ἐπὶ πλέον) more ‖ κάθε ἄλλο! anything but!
ἄλλοτε [allote] formerly ‖ sometime.
ἀλλοῦ [allou] elsewhere.
ἀλλόφρων [allofron] beside o.s. mad, frantic.
ἄλλως [allos] otherwise, else, differently in other words ‖ οὕτως ἤ ~ anyway.
ἄλλωστε [alloste] besides, on the other hand.
ἅλμα, τό [alma] jump, leap ‖ ~τώδης by leaps and bounds.
ἅλμη, ἡ [almee] brine, pickle.
ἁλμυρός [almeeros] salty ‖·(μεταφ) costly.
ἀλόγιστος [aloyeestos] thoughtless, inconsiderate, irrational.

ἄλογο, τό [aloyo] horse ‖ ἀλογόμυγα horsefly.
ἄλογος [aloyos] irrational, unreasoned.
ἀλόη, ἡ [aloee] aloe.
ἀλοιφή, ἡ [aleefee] ointment.
ἀλουμίνιον, τό [aloumeeneeon] aluminium.
ἄλουστος [aloustos] unwashed, unbathed.
ἄλσος, τό [alsos] grove, thicket.
ἄλτης, ὁ [altees] (ἀθλητ) jumper.
ἀλύγιστος [aleeyeestos] inflexible.
ἀλύπητος [aleepeetos] pitiless, cruel, unmerciful.
ἁλυσίδα, ἡ [aleeseeda] chain.
ἄλυτος [aleetos] (πού δέν ἐλύθη) unsolved ‖ (δέν μπορεῖ νά λυθῇ) unsolvable.
ἄλφα, τό [alfa] the letter A.
ἀλφαβητάριον, τό [alfaveetareeon] primer, ABC-book.
ἀλφάβητον, τό [alfaveeton] alphabet.
ἀλφάδι, τό [alfadee] level, plumbline.
ἁλώνι, τό [allonee] threshing floor ‖ ἁλωνίζω thresh ‖ (σκορπῶ) scatter.
ἀλώπηξ, ἡ [alopeeks] fox.
ἅλωσις, ἡ [alosees] fall, capture, conquest.
ἅμα [ama] as soon as ‖ (ἐάν) if ‖ ~ ἔπος ἅμ' ἔργον no sooner said than done.
ἀμαζών, ἡ [amazon] amazon.
ἀμάθεια, ἡ [amatheea] ignorance, illiteracy.
ἀμαθής [amathees] ignorant, illiterate.
ἀμάν [aman] (ἐπιφ) for heaven's sake!
ἀμανάτι, τό [amanatee] pawn, security, pledge.
ἅμαξα, ἡ [amaksa] coach, carriage ‖ (μέ ἄλογο) horse cab.
ἁμαξᾶς, ὁ [amaksas] coachman, cab driver.
ἁμάξι, τό [amaksee] horse cab ‖ (αὐτοκίνητο) car.
ἁμαξοστοιχία, ἡ [amaksosteeheea] train.
ἁμαρτάνω [amartano] sin.
ἁμαρτία, ἡ [amarteea] sin ‖ εἶναι ~ ἀπ' τό Θεό it's a pity!
ἀμαυρώνω [amavrono] darken, obscure ‖ (μεταφ) sully.
ἄμαχος [amahos] non-combatant.
ἀμβλύς [amvlees] blunt ‖ (γεωμ) obtuse.
ἄμβων, ὁ [amvon] pulpit.
ἀμέ [amme] (ἐπιφ) why not? ‖ of course!
ἀμείβω [ameevo] reward, compensate.
ἀμείλικτος [ameeleektos] implacable, inexorable.
ἀμείωτος [ameeotos] undiminished.
ἀμέλγω [amelyo] milk.
ἀμέλεια, ἡ [ameleea] negligence, carelessness.
ἀμελέτητα [ameleteeta] πλ testicles.
ἀμελής [amelees] negligent ‖ (μαθητής) lazy.
ἀμελῶ [amelo] neglect.
ἄμεμπτος [amemptos] irreproachable, blameless.
ἀμερικάνικος [amereekaneekos] American
Ἀμερικανός, ὁ [amereekanos] American.
ἀμέριμνος [amereemnos] carefree, heedless.

ἀμέριστος [amereestos] indivisible ‖ undivided.

ἀμερόληπτος [ameroleeptos] impartial.

ἄμεσος [amesos] direct, immediate.

ἀμέσως [amesos] at once, immediately.

ἀμετάβλητος [ametavleetos] unchanged ‖ immutable.

ἀμετάκλητος [ametakleetos] irrevocable.

ἀμεταχείριστος [ametaheereestos] unused, new.

ἀμέτοχος [ametohos] exempt, not participating in.

ἀμέτρητος [ametreetos] countless, immeasurable.

ἀμήχανος [ameehanos] perplexed, embarrassed.

ἀμηχανία [ameehaneea] perplexity, confusion.

ἀμίαντος [ameeantos] undefiled ‖ (οὐσ) asbestos.

ἀμίλητος [ameeleetos] silent, quiet.

ἄμιλλα, ἡ [ameela] emulation, rivalry.

ἀμίμητος [ameemeetos] inimitable.

ἄμισθος [ameesthos] unsalaried, without pay.

ἀμμοκονία, ἡ [ammokoneea] cement, mortar.

ἄμμος, ἡ [ammos] sand.

ἀμμουδιά, ἡ [amoudia] sandy beach.

ἀμμώδης [amodees] sandy.

ἀμμωνία, ἡ [amoneea] ammonia.

ἀμνάς, ἡ [amnas] ewe, lamb.

ἀμνημόνευτος [amneemonevtos] immemorial ‖ unmentioned.

ἀμνησία, ἡ [amneeseea] amnesia.

ἀμνηστία, ἡ [amneesteea] amnesty.

ἀμνός, ὁ [amnos] lamb.

ἀμοιβάδες, αἱ [ameevades] πλ amoebic dysentery.

ἀμοιβαῖος [ameeveyos] mutual, reciprocal.

ἀμοιβή, ἡ [ameevee] reward, recompense.

ἄμοιρος [ameeros] unfortunate, destitute.

ἀμόνι, τό [amonee] anvil.

ἄμορφος [amorfos] shapeless.

ἀμόρφωτος [amorfotos] uneducated, unrefined.

ἀμπαζούρ, τό [ambazour] lampshade.

ἀμπάρα, ἡ [ambara] bolt, bar.

ἀμπάρι, τό [ambari] storeroom ‖ (ναυτ) hold.

ἀμπέλι, τό [ambelee] vine ‖ vineyard.

ἀμπελών, ὁ [ambelon] vineyard.

ἄμποτε(ς) [ambote(s)] (ἐπιφ) would that! ‖ would to God!

ἀμπραγιάζ, τό [ambrayeaz] clutch.

ἄμπωτις, ἡ [ambotees] ebb tide.

ἀμυγδαλές, αἱ [ameeγdales] πλ tonsils.

ἀμύγδαλο, τό [ameeγdalo] almond.

ἀμυδρός [ameedros] dim, faint.

ἄμυλον, τό [ameelon] starch.

ἄμυνα, ἡ [ameena] defence.

ἄμφια, τά [amfeea] πλ vestments

ἀμφιβάλλω [amfeevalo] doubt

ἀμφίβιος [amfeeveeos] amphibious.

ἀμφίβολος [amfeevolos] doubtful, dubious.

ἀμφίεσις, ἡ [amfiesees] dress, attire, clothing.

ἀμφιθέατρον, τό [amfeetheatron] amphitheatre.

ἀμφίρροπος [amfeeropos] undecided, in the balance, wavering.

ἀμφισβητῶ [amfeesveeto] dispute.

ἀμφορεύς, ὁ [amforevs] amphora, pitcher.

ἀμφότεροι [amfoteree] πλ both.

ἄν [an] if, whether ‖ ~ καί although, though.

ἀνά [ana] along, over ‖ ~ εἰς one by one ‖ ~ τήν πόλιν through the city.

ἀναβαίνω [anaveno] ascend, climb, go up.

ἀναβάλλω [anavalo] put off, postpone, delay.

ἀνάβασις, ἡ [anavasees] going up, ascension.

ἀναβολή, ἡ [anavolee] postponement, adjournment.

ἀναβρασμός, ὁ [anavrasmos] agitation, excitement ‖ fermentation.

ἀνάβω [anavo] light ‖ (φῶς κτλ) turn on, switch on ‖ (θυμώνω) get provoked.

ἀναγγέλλω [anangelo] announce, make known.

ἀναγγελία, ἡ [anangeleea] announcement. notice.

ἀναγέννησις, ἡ [anayeneesees] revival, renaissance.

ἀναγινώσκω [anayeenosko] read.

ἀναγκάζω [anangazo] force, compel.

ἀναγκαῖος [anangeyos] necessary, essential, needed.

ἀναγκασμός, ὁ [anangasmos] constraint, necessity.

ἀναγκαστικός [anangasteekos] compulsory ‖ (προσγείωσις κτλ) forced.

ἀνάγκη, ἡ [anangee] need, necessity, want.

ἀνάγλυφον, τό [anaγleefon] bas-relief.

ἀναγνώρησις, ἡ [anaγnoreesees] recognition, acknowledgement.

ἀναγνωρίζω [anaγnoreezo] recognize ‖ (παραδέχομαι) admit.

ἀνάγνωσις, ἡ [anaγnosees] reading.

ἀναγνώστης, ὁ [anaγnostees] reader.

ἀναγνωστικόν, τό [anaγnosteekon] primer, reader.

ἀναγούλα, ἡ [anaγoula] nausea, disgust.

ἀνάγω [anaγo] raise ‖ (μετατρέπω) reduce, convert.

ἀνάγωγος [anaγoγos] ill-bred, ill-mannered.

ἀναδάσωσις, ἡ [anadasosees] reafforestation.

ἀναδεικνύομαι [anadeekneeome] be distinguished.

ἀναδιοργανώνω [anadeeorγanono] reorganize.

ἀναδιπλασιασμός, ὁ [anadeeplaseeasmos] (γραμμ) reduplication.

ἀνάδοχος, ὁ [anaδohos] godparent, sponsor.

ἀναδρομικός [anaδromeekos] retroactive, retrospective.

ἀναδύομαι [anaδeeome] emerge.

ἀναζητῶ [anazeeto] search for, seek.

ἀναζωογονῶ [anazoogono] revive, invigorate.

ἀναζωπυρῶ [anazopeero] relight, rekindle ‖ (μεταφ) revive.

ἀναθαρρεύω [anatharevo] regain courage, cheer up.

ἀνάθεμα, τό [anathema] curse ‖ (ἐκκλ) excommunication.

ἀναθέτω [anatheto] commission, entrust ‖ (ἀφιερώνω) dedicate.

ἀναθεώρησις, ἡ [anatheoreesees] revision, review.

ἀναθυμίασις, ἡ [anatheemeeasees] stench, exhalation, fumes.

ἀναίδεια, ἡ [aneδeea] impudence.

ἀναιδής [aneδees] impudent, shameless.

ἀναίμακτος [anemaktos] bloodless.

ἀναιμία, ἡ [anemeea] anaemia.

ἀναίρεσις, ἡ [aneresees] refutation ‖ (ἐπί ἀνθρωποκτονία) manslaughter.

ἀναισθησία, ἡ [anestheeseea] unconsciousness ‖ (μεταφ) insensibility.

ἀναισθητικόν, τό [anestheeteekon] anaesthetic.

ἀναίσθητος [anestheetos] insensitive ‖ (στούς πόνους) unconscious, insensible ‖ (ἀσυγκίνητος) unmoved.

ἀναίσχυντος [anesheentos] shameless, impudent.

ἀναίτιος [aneteeos] innocent, blameless.

ἀνακαινίζω [anakeneezo] renovate, renew.

ἀνακαλύπτω [anakaleepto] discover, detect.

ἀνακαλῶ [anakalo] recall ‖ (ἄδεια, διέταγμα) repeal, abrogate ‖ (διαταγήν κτλ) cancel, withdraw ‖ (ὑπόσχεσιν) retract.

ἀνακατώνω [anakatono] mix, stir ‖ (συγχέω) confuse.

ἀνακάτωμα, τό [anakatoma] mixing ‖ (φασαρία) confusion ‖ (στομάχου) nausea.

ἀνακεφαλαίωσις, ἡ [anakefaleosees] recapitulation.

ἀνακηρύσσω [anakeereeso] proclaim, declare.

ἀνακινῶ [anakeeno] stir up ‖ (μεταφ) bring up, raise.

ἀνάκλησις, ἡ [anakleesees] revocation, recalling.

ἀνάκλιντρον, τό [anakleentron] reclining chair.

ἀνακοινῶ [anakeeno] announce.

ἀνακοινωθέν, τό [anakeenothen] communiqué, notification.

ἀνακολουθία, ἡ [anakoloutheea] incoherence, inconsistency.

ἀνακοπή, ἡ [anakopee] checking ‖ (νομ) reprieve.

ἀνακουφίζω [anakoufeezo] relieve, alleviate, lighten.

ἀνακριβής [anakreevees] inaccurate.

ἀνάκρισις, ἡ [anakreesees] interrogation, inquiry.

ἀνακριτής, ὁ [anakreetees] examining magistrate.

ἀνάκτορον, τό [anaktoron] palace ‖ πλ palace.

ἀνακωχή, ἡ [anakohee] armistice, truce.

ἀναλαμβάνω [analamvano] undertake ‖ recover.

ἀναλαμπή, ἡ [analambee] flash, glare.

ἀνάλατος [analatos] without salt ‖ (μεταφ) dull.

ἀνάληψις, ἡ [analeepsees] (ἐργασίας) resumption, undertaking ‖ (τοῦ Χριστοῦ) ascension.

ἀναλλοίωτος [analeeotos] unchanging, constant, unaltered.

ἀναλογία, ἡ [analoyeea] relation, proportion, ratio ‖ portion.

ἀναλογίζομαι [analoyeezome] call to mind reflect on.

ἀναλογικός [analoyeekos] proportionate.

ἀνάλογος [analoyos] proportionate ‖ (μαθημ) proportional.

ἀναλόγως [analoyos] proportionately, according to.

ἀνάλυσις, ἡ [analeesees] analysis.

ἀναλυτικός [analeeteekos] analytical ‖ detailed.

ἀναλφάβητος [analfaveetos] illiterate, ignorant.

ἀναμένω [anameno] wait for, expect.

ἀνάμεσα [anamesa] in between, among.

ἀναμεταξύ [anametaksee] between, among ‖ στό ~ in the meantime, meanwhile.

ἀναμετρῶ [anametro] weigh up, estimate, consider.

ἀναμιγνύω [anameeyneeo] mix, blend implicate.

ἀνάμικτος [anameektos] mixed.

ἀνάμιξις, ἡ [anameeksees] mixing, interfering.

ἄναμμα, τό [anama] lighting ‖ (προσώπου) inflammation ‖ (ἔξαψις) excitement ‖ (μοτέρ κτλ) ignition.

ἀναμμένος [anamenos] alight, burning.

ἀνάμνησις, ἡ [anamneesees] recollection, remembrance.

ἀναμονή, ἡ [anamonee] expectation, waiting.

ἀναμφισβήτητος [anamfeesveeteetos] indisputable, unquestionable.

ἀνανᾶς, ὁ [ananas] pineapple.

ἀνανεώνω [ananeono] renew, renovate.

ἀνανέωσις, ἡ [ananeosees] renewal, renovation.

ἀναντίρρητος [ananteereetos] incontrovertible, incontestable.

ἄναξ, ὁ [anaks] sovereign, king, ruler.

ἀναξιοπρεπής [anakseeoprepees] (συμπεριφορά) unseemly ‖ (ἄτομον) ill-bred, uncouth ‖ (βίος) disreputable.

ἀνάξιος [anakseeos] unworthy, unfit, inefficient.

ἀνάπαλιν [anapaleen] conversely, vice versa.

ἀναπαράστασις, ἡ [anaparastasees] representation ‖ (ἐγκλήματος) reconstruction.

ἀνάπαυλα, ἡ [anapavla] respite, rest.

ἀνάπαυσις, ἡ [anapavsees] rest, repose ‖ (στρατ) stand easy!

ἀναπαυτικός [anapavteekos] comfortable, restful.

ἀναπαύομαι [anapavome] rest, relax.

ἀναπέμπω [anapembo] give forth, emit.

ἀναπηδῶ [anapeedo] jump up, leap up, start.

ἀνάπηρος [anapeeros] disabled ‖ (διανοητικῶς) deficient.

ἀνάπλασις, ἡ [anaplasees] reforming, remodelling.

ἀναπληρώνω [anapleerono] replace ‖ substitute ‖ refill.

ἀναπνέω [anapneo] breathe.

ἀναπνοή, ἡ [anapnoee] breath, breathing, respiration.

ἀνάποδα [anapoda] backwards ‖ (μέσα ἔξω) inside out, topsy-turvy.

ἀνάποδη, ἡ [anapodee] wrong side ‖ inside out.

ἀναποδιά, ἡ [anapodia] reverse, bad luck ‖ contrariness.

ἀναποδογυρίζω [anapodoyeereezo] turn upside down.

ἀνάποδος [anapodos] reversed ‖ (ἄνθρωπος) difficult, cantankerous.

ἀναπολῶ [anapolo] recollect, remember.

ἀναπόφευκτος [anapofevktos] inevitable, unavoidable.

ἀναπτήρ, ὁ [anapteer] cigarette lighter.

ἀνάπτυξις, ἡ [anapteeksees] development ‖ (ἐξήγησις) explanation.

ἀναπτύσσω [anapteeso] unfold, develop ‖ (λόγον) expound, explain.

ἀνάπτω [anapto] βλ ἀνάβω.

ἀναρίθμητος [anareethmeetos] countless, innumerable.

ἀναρμόδιος [anarmodeeos] not competent, unqualified.

ἀνάρμοστος [anarmostos] (διαγωγή) improper, unbecoming ‖ (γλῶσσα) unsuitable.

ἀνάρπαστος [anarpastos] quickly bought up.

ἀναρριχῶμαι [anareehome] climb up, mount.

ἀνάρρωσις, ἡ [anarrosees] convalescence, recovery.

ἀναρτῶ [anarto] hang up, suspend.

ἀναρχία, ἡ [anarheea] anarchy.

ἀναρχικός [anarheekos] anarchical ‖ (οὐσ) anarchist.

ἀναρωτιέμαι [anarotieme] ask o.s., wonder.

ἀνάσα, ἡ [anasa] breath, breathing ‖ rest, respite.

ἀνασηκώνω [anaseekono] lift up, raise.

ἀνασκάπτω [anaskapto] dig, excavate.

ἀνασκαφή, ἡ [anaskafee] excavation.

ἀνάσκελα [anaskela] on one's back.

ἀνασκευάζω [anaskevazo] refute, disprove.

ἀνασκόπησις, ἡ [anaskopeesees] review, weighing up.

ἀνασταίνω [anasteno] revive, restore to life.

ἀνασταλτικός [anastalteekos] restraining, holding back.

ἀνάστασις, ἡ [anastasees] resurrection, rising.

ἀνάστατος [anastatos] in disorder, agitated, excited.

ἀναστατώνω [anastatono] disturb, upset.

ἀναστέλλω [anastelo] stop, stay, suspend.

ἀναστενάζω [anastenazo] sigh, groan.

ἀναστηλώνω [anasteelono] restore, erect.

ἀναστήλωσις, ἡ [anasteelosees] restoration, erection.

ἀνάστημα, τό [anasteema] height, stature.

ἀναστολή, ἡ [anastolee] reprieve ‖ suspension ‖ restraint.

ἀναστρέφω [anastrefo] turn back, reverse, invert.

ἀνασυγκρότησις, ἡ [anaseengroteesees] rehabilitation.

ἀνασύρω [anaseero] raise, pull out, pull up, draw up.

ἀνασφάλιστος [anasfaleestos] uninsured.

ἀναταράσσω [anataraso] stir up, upset.

ἀνατείνω [anateeno] extend, hold up, lift up, stretch up.

ἀνατέλλω [anatelo] rise ‖ appear.

ἀνατέμνω [anatemno] dissect, cut.

ἀνατίμησις, ἡ [anateemeesees] rise in price ‖ revaluation.

ἀνατινάζω [anateenazo] blow up ‖ spring up.

ἀνατίναξις, ἡ [anateenaksees] explosion, blowing up.

ἀνατοκισμός, ὁ [anatokeesmos] compound interest.

ἀνατολή, ἡ [anatolee] east ‖ Ἄπω Ἀ~ Far East ‖ Μέση Ἀ~ Middle East.

ἀνατολικός [anatoleekos] eastern ‖ oriental.

ἀνατομία, ἡ [anatomeea] anatomy.

ἀνατρέπω [anatrepo] upset ‖ (βάρκα κτλ) overturn, capsize.

ἀνατρέφω [anatrefo] rear, bring up, raise.

ἀνατρέχω [anatreho] refer back to, go back to.

ἀνατριχιάζω [anatreeheeazo] shiver, shudder.

ἀνατριχιαστικός [anatreeheeasteekos] terrifying, hair-raising.

ἀνατροπή, ἡ [anatropee] upset, overthrow ‖ (νομ) refutation, reversal.

ἀνατροφή, ἡ [anatrofee] upbringing, breeding.

ἀνάτυπον, τό [anateepon] offprint, reprint.

ἄναυδος [anavðos] speechless, dumbfounded.

ἀναφαίνομαι [anafenome] appear, rise, emerge.

ἀναφανδόν [anafanðon] manifestly, openly.

ἀναφέρω [anafero] mention, cite ‖ report ‖ relate.

ἀναφλέγω [anafleyo] inflame, ignite.

ἀνάφλεξις, ἡ [anafleksees] combustion, conflagration, ignition.

ἀναφορά, ἡ [anafora] report, relation ‖ (αἴτησις) petition.

ἀναφορικός [anaforeekos] relative ‖ to referring to.

ἀναφωνῶ [anafono] cry out, exclaim.

ἀναχαιτίζω [anaheteezo] check, restrain.

ἀναχρονισμός, ὁ [anahroneesmos] anachronism.

ἀνάχωμα, τό [anahoma] mound, bank, dyke.

ἀναχώρησις, ἡ [anahoreesees] departure.

ἀναχωρῶ [anahoro] leave, depart, go.

ἀναψυκτικά, τά [anapseekteeka] πλ refreshments.

ἀναψυχή, ἡ [anapseehee] recreation.

ἀνδραγάθημα, τό [anðrayatheema] heroic feat, exploit.

ἀνδράποδον, τό [anðrapoðon] slave.

ἀνδρεία, ἡ [anðreea] bravery, valour.

ἀνδρείκελον, τό [anðreekelon] puppet, manikin.

ἀνδρεῖος [anðreeos] brave, courageous.

ἀνδριάς, ὁ [anðrias] statue.

ἀνδρικός [anðreekos] manly, virile, male.

ἀνεβάζω [anevazo] carry up, lift up ‖ (θέατρον) put on ‖ (οἰκονομία) raise, put up.

ἀνεβαίνω [aneveno] βλ ἀναβαίνω.

ἀνέβασμα, τό [anevasma] going up ‖ lifting ‖ (ἔργου) production.

ἀνεβοκατεβαίνω [anevokateveno] go up and down ‖ (τιμές) fluctuate.

ἀνέγγιχτος [anengeehtos] untouched, new.

ἀνεγείρω [aneyeero] raise, erect, build.

ἀνέγερσις, ἡ [aneyersees] erection ‖ (σήκωμα) getting up.

ἀνεγνωρισμένος [aneynoreesmenos] recognized.

ἀνειλικρινής [aneeleekreenees] insincere ‖ false.

ἀνέκαθεν [anekathen] always, ever, from the beginning.

ἀνεκδιήγητος [anekðieeyeetos] defying description, ineffable.

ἀνέκδοτον, τό [anekðoton] anecdote, story.

ἀνεκμετάλλευτος [anekmetalevtos] not exploited.

ἀνεκπλήρωτος [anekpleerotos] unfulfilled.

ἀνεκτικός [anekteekos] tolerant, patient, indulgent.

ἀνεκτίμητος [anekteemeetos] priceless, inestimable.

ἀνεκτός [anektos] bearable, tolerable.

ἀνέκφραστος [anekfrastos] inexpressible, indescribable ‖ (ἠθοποιός) expressionless ‖ (βλέμμα) vacant.

ἀνελεύθερος [aneleftheros] servile, illiberal.

ἀνελκυστήρ, ὁ [anelkeesteer] lift, elevator.

ἀνελλιπής [aneleepees] flawless ‖ (ὀργάνωσις) complete ‖ (φοίτησις) continuous.

ἀνέλπιστος [anelpeestos] unexpected ‖ (γεγονός) unforeseen.

ἀνεμίζω [anemeezo] ventilate, air ‖ (σῖτον) winnow.

ἀνεμιστήρ, ὁ [anemeesteer] fan, ventilator.

ἀνεμοβλογιά, ἡ [anemovloyia] chickenpox.

ἀνεμοδείκτης, ὁ [anemoðeektees] weathercock, wind indicator.

ἀνεμόμυλος, ὁ [anemomeelos] windmill.

ἄνεμος, ὁ [anemos] wind.

ἀνεμοστρόβιλος, ὁ [anemostroveelos] whirlwind.

ἀνεμπόδιστος [anemboðeestos] unhindered, unimpeded.

ἀνεμώδης [anemoðees] windy.

ἀνεμώνη, ἡ [anemonee] anemone.

ἀνενδοίαστος [anenðeeastos] unhesitating, unhesitant.

ἀνένδοτος [anenðotos] unyielding, inflexible.

ἀνενόχλητος [anenohleetos] undisturbed.

ἀνεξαίρετος [anekseretos] without exception ‖ not exempted.

ἀνεξάντλητος [aneksantleetos] inexhaustible.

ἀνεξαρτησία, ἡ [aneksarteeseea] independence.

ἀνεξάρτητος [aneksarteetos] independent.

ἀνεξέλεγκτος [anekselengtos] not confirmed, unchecked ‖ (δαπάνη κτλ) unexamined.

ἀνεξήγητος [anekseeyeetos] inexplicable.

ἀνεξίκακος [anekseekakos] forbearing, meek.

ἀνεξίτηλος [anekseeteelos] indelible.

ἀνέξοδος [aneksoðos] inexpensive, cheap.

ἀνεξόφλητος [aneksofleetos] unpaid.

ἀνεπαίσθητος [anepestheetos] imperceptible, slight.

ἀνεπαρκής [aneparkees] insufficient, inadequate.

ἄνέπαφος [anepafos] untouched, intact.

ἀνεπηρέαστος [anepeereastos] unaffected, uninfluenced.

ἀνεπιθύμητος [anepeetheemeetos] undesirable.

ἀνεπίσημος [anepeeseemos] unofficial.

ἀνεπιτήδειος [anepeeteeðeeos] unskilful, unfit.

ἀνεπιτυχής [anepeeteehees] unsuccessful.

ἀνεπιφύλακτος [anepeefeelaktos] unreserved.

ἀνεπτυγμένος [anepteeγmenos] (ἄνθρωπος) cultured ‖ (σωματικῶς) developed.

ἄνεργος [anerγos] unemployed, idle.

ἀνέρχομαι [anerhome] ascend, climb ‖ (λογαριασμός) amount to.

ἄνεσις, ἡ [annesees] ease, comfort ‖ μέ ἄνεσιν at leisure.

ἀνεστραμμένος [anestramenos] reversed, inverted.

ἀνέτοιμος [aneteemos] unprepared, not ready.

ἄνετος [anetos] comfortable, easy.

ἄνευ [anev] without.

ἀνεύθυνος [anevtheenos] not accountable, not responsible.

ἀνευλαβής [anevlavees] disrespectful, irreverent.

ἀνευρίσκω [anevreesko] find out, discover, recover.

ἀνεφάρμοστος [anefarmostos] inapplicable ‖ (μή ἐφαρμοσθείς) unapplied.

ἀνέφικτος [anefeektos] unattainable, impossible.

ἀνεφοδιάζω [anefodeeazo] provision, restock.

ἀνέχεια [aneheea] poverty, want.

ἀνέχομαι [anehome] tolerate.

ἀνεψιά, ἡ [anepsia] niece.

ἀνεψιός, ὁ [anepsios] nephew.

ἀνήθικος [aneetheekos] immoral, corrupt.

ἄνηθο, τό [aneetho] dill, anise.

ἀνήκουστος [aneekoustos] unheard of, incredible.

ἀνήκω [aneeko] belong (to), pertain.

ἀνηλεής [aneeleyees] pitiless, cruel.

ἀνήλικος [aneeleekos] under age ‖ minor.

ἀνήμερα [aneemera] on the same day.

ἀνήμπορος [aneemboros] indisposed.

ἀνήρ, ὁ [aneer] man.

ἀνησυχία, ἡ [aneeseeheea] uneasiness, concern.

ἀνήσυχος [aneeseehos] uneasy, anxious.

ἀνησυχῶ [aneeseeho] be anxious, be worried.

ἀνήφορος, ὁ [aneeforos] uphill road ‖ ascent.

ἀνθεκτικός [anthekteekos] endurable, resistant.

ἀνθηρός [antheeros] flourishing, blooming.

ἄνθησις, ἡ [antheesees] flowering, blossoming.

ἀνθίζω [antheezo] blossom, flourish.

ἀνθίσταμαι [antheestame] resist, oppose.

ἀνθοδέσμη, ἡ [anthodesmee] bouquet, nosegay.

ἀνθοδοχεῖον, τό [anthodoheeon] flowerpot, vase.

ἀνθολογία, ἡ [antholoγeea] anthology.

ἀνθόνερο, τό [anthonero] orange-flower water, rose water.

ἀνθοπώλης, ὁ [anthopolees] florist.

ἄνθος, τό [anthos] flower.

ἀνθρακιά, ἡ [anthrakia] glowing embers.

ἀνθρακικός [anthrakeekos] carbonic.

ἀνθρακωρυχεῖον, τό [anthrakorreeheeon] coalmine.

ἄνθραξ, ὁ [anthraks] coal ‖ (ἰατρ) anthrax.

ἀνθρωπιά, ἡ [anthropia] civility ‖ good breeding.

ἀνθρώπινος [anthropeenos] human.

ἀνθρωπιστής, ὁ [anthropeestees] humanist.

ἀνθρωποκτονία, ἡ [anthropoktoneea] homicide.

ἀνθρωπολόγος, ὁ [anthropoloγos] anthropologist.

ἄνθρωπος, ὁ [anthropos] man, person.

ἀνθρωπότης, ἡ [anthropotees] mankind humanity.

ἀνθυγιεινός [antheeγeeinos] unhealthy, unwholesome.

ἀνθυπασπιστής, ὁ [antheepaspeestees] warrant officer ‖ sergeant-major.

ἀνθυπολοχαγός, ὁ [antheepolohaγos] second lieutenant.

ἀνθυποσμηναγός, ὁ [antheeposmeenaγos] pilot officer.

ἀνθυποπλοίαρχος, ὁ [antheepopleearhos] sub-lieutenant.

ἀνθῶ [antho] βλ ἀνθίζω.

ἀνία, ἡ [aneea] boredom, weariness, ennui.

ἐνίατος [aneeatos] incurable.

ἀνίδεος [aneedeos] unsuspecting ‖ ignorant.

ἀνιδιοτελής [aneedeeotelees] disinterested.

ἀνικανοποίητος [aneekanopieetos] unsatisfied.

ἀνίκανος [aneekanos] incapable, unable, unfit ‖ impotent.

ἀνισόρροπος [aneesoropos] unbalanced.

ἄνισος [aneesos] unequal, uneven.

ἀνιστορῶ [aneestoro] relate, recollect.

ἀνίσχυρος [aneesheeros] powerless, weak feeble.

ἀνίχνευσις, ἡ [aneehnevsees] tracking, searching.

ἄνοδος, ἡ [anodos] ascent, accession.

ἀνοησία, ἡ [anoeeseea] folly, foolishness, nonsense.

ἀνόητος [anoeetos] foolish, silly, absurd.

ἀνόθευτος [anothevtos] unadulterated pure.

ἄνοιγμα, τό [aneeγma] opening, aperture.

ἀνοίγω [aneeγo] open ‖ (βρύση) turn on ‖ (σύρτη) draw ‖ (ὀμπρέλλα) put up ‖ (φῶτα κτλ) turn on, switch on ‖ (συζήτησις) open, broach ‖ (χάρτη) unfold ‖ (χορό) lead, open ‖ (πηγάδι) dig ‖ (κουρτίνες) draw back ‖ (γιά χρῶμα) fade.

ἀνοίκειος [aneekeeos] unbecoming, improper.

ἀνοίκιαστος [aneekeeastos] unlet, unrented

ἀνοικοδομῶ [aneekodomo] rebuild.

ἀνοικονόμητος [aneekonomeetos] intractable, unmanageable.

ἀνοικτός [aneektos] open ‖ (ἐπί χρωμάτων) light.

ἀνοιξιάτικος [aneekseeateekos] spring.

άνοιξις, ή [aneeksees] spring, springtime.

άνοιχτόκαρδος [aneehtokarδos] open-hearted, cheerful.

άνοιχτοχέρης [aneehtoherees] open-handed, magnanimous.

άνομβρία, ή [anomvreea] drought, scarcity of rain.

άνόμοιος [anomeeos] dissimilar, unlike.

άνοξείδωτος [anokseeδotos] stainless, rust-proof.

άνοργάνωτος [anoryanotos] unorganized.

άνορεξία, ή [anorekseea] loss of appetite ‖ (μεταφ) half-heartedness.

άνορθογραφία, ή [anorthoyrafeea] misspelling.

άνορθώνω [anorthono] raise, stand upright ‖ restore.

άνοσία, ή [anoseea] immunity from disease.

άνοστος [anostos] insipid, unsavoury ‖ (μεταφ) ugly, disagreeable.

άνοχή, ή [anohee] forbearance, tolerance ‖ οίκος .~ς brothel.

άνταγωνίζομαι [antayoneezome] compete, vie with.

άνταγωνισμός, ό [antayoneesmos] competition, contest, rivalry.

άνταλλαγή, ή [antallayee] exchange, barter.

άντάλλαγμα, τό [antallayma] thing exchanged, recompense.

άνταλλακτικόν, τό [antallakteekon] spare part, refill.

άνταλλάξιμος [antalakseemos] exchangeable.

άνταλλάσσω [antalaso] exchange.

άντάμα [antama] together.

άνταμείβω [antameevo] reward, recompense.

άνταμώνω [antamono] meet, join.

άντάμωση [antamosee]: καλή ~ goodbye, farewell.

άντανάκλασις, ή [antanaklasees] reflection.

άντανακλῶ [antanaklo] reflect.

άντάξιος [antakseeos] worthy, deserving.

άνταποδίδω [antapoδeeδo] return, repay.

άνταποκρίνομαι [antapokreenome] be like, correspond to, respond, suit.

άνταπόκρισις, ή [antapokreesees] correspondence ‖ (έφημερίδος) dispatch.

άνταποκριτής, ό [antapokreetees] correspondent, reporter.

άντάρα, ή [antara] tumult, uproar, storm.

άνταρσία, ή [antarseea] rebellion, revolt, mutiny.

άντάρτης, ό [antartees] rebel, insurgent, guerrilla.

άντε [annte] (έπιφ) come on!, get a move on!

άντένα, ή [antena] aerial, antenna.

άντεπανάστασις, ή [antepanastasees] counter-revolution.

άντεπίθεσις, ή [antepeethesees] counter-attack.

άντεπιτίθεμαι [antepeeteetheme] counter-attack

άντεραστής, ό [anterastees] rival.

άντερο, τό [antero] intestine.

άντέχω [anteho] endure, hold firm, last.

άντζούγια, ή [antzouyeea] anchovy.

άντηλιά, ή [anteelia] glare, reflected sunlight.

άντηχῶ [anteeho] resound, re-echo.

άντί [antee] instead of, in exchange for ‖ (τιμή) for ‖ ~ γιά instead of ‖ ~ νά instead of.

άντιαεροπορικός [anteeaeroporeekos] anti-aircraft.

άντιβαίνω [anteeveno] be against, be contrary to, be opposed to.

άντιβασιλεύς [anteevaseelevs] regent, viceroy.

άντιγραφή, ή [anteeyrafee] copy, copying.

άντίγραφον, τό [anteeyrafon] copy, transcript.

άντιγράφω [anteeyrafo] copy, imitate .(στό σχολείο) crib.

άντίδι, τό [anteeδee] endive.

άντίδικος, ό [anteeδeekos] opponent.

άντίδοτον, τό [anteeδoton] antidote.

άντίδρασις, ή [anteeδrasees] reaction, opposition.

άντιδραστικός [anteeδrasteekos] reactionary, reactive.

άντιδρῶ [anteeδro] react, counteract, oppose.

άντίδωρον [anteeδoron] (έκκλ) holy bread

άντίζηλος [anteezeelos] rival.

άντίθεσις, ή [anteethesees] contrast opposition.

άντίθετος [anteethetos] contrary, opposite

άντίκα, ή [anteeka] antique.

άντικαθιστῶ [anteekatheesto] replace, substitute ‖ relieve.

άντικανονικός [anteekanoneekos] irregular, not according to rules.

άντικατάστασις, ή [anteekatastasees] replacement ‖ substitution.

άντικαταστάτης, ό [anteekatastatees] sub stitute ‖ successor.

άντίκειμαι [anteekeeme] be opposed to.

άντικειμενικός [anteekeemeneekos] objective.

άντικείμενον, τό [anteekeemenon] object thing ‖ topic.

άντικλείδι, τό [anteekleeδee] passkey.

άντικοινωνικός [anteekeenoneekos] un social.

άντικρούω [anteekrouo] oppose, refute.

άντίκρυ [anteekree] opposite, face to face.

άντικρύζω [anteekreezo] face, front ‖ meet.

άντικρυνός [anteekreenos] opposite, facing.

άντίκτυπος, ό [anteekteepos] repercussion, effect, result.

άντίλαλος, ό [anteelalos] echo.

άντιλαμβάνομαι [anteelamvanome] understand ‖ perceive, notice.

άντιλέγω [anteeleyo] object, contradict.

ἀντιληπτός [anteeleeptos] perceptible ‖ understandable.

ἀντίληψις, ἡ [anteeleepsees] understanding, opinion ‖ quickness of mind.

ἀντιλυσσικός [anteeleeseekos] anti-rabies.

ἀντιμετωπίζω [anteemetopeezo] confront, face.

ἀντιμέτωπος [anteemetopos] face to face, facing.

ἀντιμισθία, ἡ [anteemeestheea] reward ‖ (ἐργάτου) daily wage.

ἀντιμόνιον, τό [anteemoneeon] antimony.

ἀντιναύαρχος, ὁ [anteenavarhos] vice-admiral.

ἀντίο [anteeo] (ἐπιφ) goodbye!

ἀντιπάθεια, ἡ [anteepatheea] antipathy, aversion.

ἀντιπαθητικός [anteepatheeteekos] repulsive, repugnant.

ἀντιπαθῶ [anteepatho] dislike, feel aversion for.

ἀντίπαλος, ὁ [anteepalos] adversary, opponent ‖ (στρατ) enemy.

ἀντιπαρέρχομαι [anteeparerhome] go by, pass ‖ (μεταφ) escape, elude.

ἀντιπειθαρχικός [anteepeetharheekos] undisciplined.

ἀντίπερα [anteepera] on the other side, opposite.

ἀντιπερισπασμός, ὁ [anteepereespasmos] distraction ‖ (στρατ) diversion.

ἀντιπλοίαρχος, ὁ [anteepleearhos] commander.

ἀντίποινα, τά [anteepeena] πλ reprisals.

ἀντιπολίτευσις, ἡ [anteepoleetevsees] opposition.

ἀντίπραξις, ἡ [anteepraksees] opposition, thwarting.

ἀντιπρόεδρος, ὁ [anteeproedros] vice-president, deputy chairman.

ἀντιπροσωπεία, ἡ [anteeprosopeea] representation ‖ delegation.

ἀντιπροσωπεύω [anteeprosopevo] represent, stand for.

ἀντιπρόσωπος, ὁ [anteeprosopos] representative ‖ (ἐμπορικός) agent.

ἀντίρρησις, ἡ [anteereesees] objection, contradiction.

ἀντισηπτικός [anteeseepteekos] antiseptic.

ἀντίσκηνον, τό [anteeskeenon] army tent.

ἀντισμήναρχος, ὁ [anteesmeenarhos] wing commander.

ἀντισταθμίζω [anteestathmeezo] balance ‖ (μηχανική) compensate.

ἀντίστασις, ἡ [anteestasees] resistance, opposition.

ἀντιστέκομαι [anteestekome] resist, oppose.

ἀντίστοιχος [anteesteehos] corresponding, equivalent.

ἀντιστράτηγος, ὁ [anteestrateeyos] lieutenant-general.

ἀντιστρέφω [anteestrefo] invert, reverse.

ἀντίστροφος [anteestrofos] reverse, inverse.

ἀντισυνταγματάρχης, ὁ [anteeseentaymatarhees] lieutenant-colonel.

ἀντισυνταγματικός [anteeseentaymateekos] unconstitutional.

ἀντιτάσσω [anteetaso] oppose ‖ array (against).

ἀντιτίθεμαι [anteeteetheme] be opposed.

ἀντίτιμον, τό [anteeteemon] value, price.

ἀντιτορπιλλικόν, τό [anteetorpeeleekon] destroyer.

ἀντίτυπον, τό [anteeteepon] copy.

ἀντίφασις, ἡ [anteefasees] contradiction, discrepancy.

ἀντιφάσκω [anteefasko] contradict o.s.

ἀντίχειρ, ὁ [anteeheer] thumb.

ἄντλησις, ἡ [antleesees] pumping, drawing up of water.

ἀντλία, ἡ [antleea] pump.

ἀντλῶ [antlo] pump, draw up water ‖ derive.

ἀντοχή, ἡ [antohee] endurance, strength, resistance.

ἄντρας, ὁ [antras] man ‖ husband.

ἀντρίκιος [antreekeeos] βλ ἀνδρικός.

ἀντρόγυνο, τό [antroyeeno] married couple.

ἄντρον, τό [antron] cave, cavern, grotto.

ἀντωνυμία, ἡ [antoneemeea] pronoun.

ἄνυδρος [aneeδros] waterless, dry, arid

ἀνύμφευτος [aneemfevtos] unmarried.

ἀνύπανδρος [aneepanδros] unmarried, single.

ἀνύπαρκτος [aneeparktos] non-existent.

ἀνυπαρξία, ἡ [aneeparkseea] non-existence, lack.

ἀνυπέρβλητος [aneepervleetos] insuperable ‖ incomparable.

ἀνυπόληπτος [aneepoleeptos] not esteemed, not respected.

ἀνυπολόγιστος [aneepoloyeestos] incalculable.

ἀνυπόμονος [aneepomonos] impatient, anxious.

ἀνύποπτος [aneepoptos] not suspecting ‖ not suspect.

ἀνυπόστατος [aneepostatos] groundless, unfounded ‖ unsubstantial.

ἀνυπότακτος [aneepotaktos] insubordinate ‖ (λαός) not subdued ‖ (παιδί) disobedient.

ἀνυπόφορος [aneepoforos] intolerable.

ἀνυψώνω [aneepsono] raise ‖ (μεταφ) praise, elevate, extol.

ἄνω [ano] up, above ‖ ~ κάτω in confusion, upset ‖ (μέ γεν) above, over.

ἀνώγι, τό [anoyee] upper floor, upper storey.

ἀνώδυνος [anoδeenos] painless.

ἀνωμαλία, ἡ [anomaleea] irregularity, unevenness ‖ anomaly.

ἀνώμαλος [anomalos] (ἐπιφάνεια) irregular, uneven ‖ (ἄνθρωπος) erratic, eccentric.

ἀνώνυμος [anoneemos] anonymous ‖ ~ ἑταιρεία limited company.

ἀνώτατος [anotatos] supreme, uppermost ‖ ~ ὄροφος top floor.

ἀνώτερος [anoteros] superior, higher, upper ‖ ~ χρημάτων above money ‖ ἀνωτέρα κοινωνία upper class.

ἀνωφελής [anofelees] fruitless, futile, vain.

ἄξαφνα [aksafna] βλ ἔξαφνα.

ἀξέγνοιαστος [akseγneeastos] unconcerned ‖ without worries.

ἄξενος [aksenos] inhospitable.

ἄξεστος [aksestos] uncouth, rough, unpolished.

ἀξέχαστος [aksehastos] unforgotten ‖ unforgettable.

ἀξία, ἡ [akseea] worth, value, price.

ἀξιαγάπητος [akseeaγapeetos] amiable, lovable.

ἀξιέπαινος [aksiepenos] praiseworthy, laudable.

ἀξίζω [akseezo] be worth, cost ‖ merit ‖ ἀξίζει νά τιμωρηθῇ he deserves to be punished.

ἀξίνα, ἡ [akseena] pickaxe.

ἀξιοθαύμαστος [akseeothavmastos] wonderful, admirable.

ἀξιοθέατος [akseeotheatos] worth seeing ‖ τά ἀξιοθέατα the sights.

ἀξιοθρήνητος [akseeothreeneetos] lamentable, deplorable.

ἀξιόλογος [akseeoloγos] remarkable ‖ distinguished.

ἀξιόπιστος [akseeopeestos] trustworthy, reliable.

ἀξιοπρεπής [akseeoprepees] dignified, decent.

ἄξιος [akseeos] capable ‖ deserving ‖ worthy, worth.

ἀξιοσημείωτος [akseeoseemeeotos] noteworthy, notable, remarkable.

ἀξιότιμος [akseeoteemos] estimable, honourable.

ἀξιῶ [akseeo] claim, expect.

ἀξιωματικός, ὁ [akseeomateekos] officer.

ἀξιώνομαι [akseeonome] manage.

ἀξίωσις, ἡ [akseeosees] claim, pretension.

ἀξύριστος [akseereestos] unshaven.

ἄξων, ὁ [akson] axis ‖ axle, pivot, shaft.

ἄοκνος [aoknos] tireless ‖ indefatigable.

ἀόμματος [aomatos] blind.

ἄοπλος [aoplos] unarmed.

ἀόριστος [aoreestos] invisible, indefinite ‖ (γραμμ) aorist.

ἄοσμος [aosmos] odourless, scentless.

ἀπαγγελία, ἡ [apangeleea] recitation, declamation ‖ diction.

ἀπαγόρευσις, ἡ [apaγorevsees] prohibition.

ἀπαγορεύω [apaγorevo] prohibit, forbid.

ἀπαγχονίζω [apanghoneezo] hang.

ἀπαγωγή, ἡ [apaγoγee] abduction ‖ (παιδιοῦ) kidnapping.

ἀπάθεια, ἡ [apatheea] indifference, apathy.

ἀπαίδευτος [apedevtos] uneducated, unskilled illiterate.

ἀπαισιόδοξος [apeseeodoksos] pessimist.

ἀπάίσιος [apeseeos] frightful, sinister horrible.

ἀπαίτησις, ἡ [apeteesees] claim ‖ demand.

ἀπαιτητικός [apeteeteekos] demanding, exacting, importunate.

ἀπαιτῶ [apeto] claim, demand, require.

ἀπαλλαγή, ἡ [apallaγee] deliverance ‖ release ‖ dismissal.

ἀπαλλάσσω [apallasso] deliver, free ‖ (καθήκοντα) relieve.

ἀπαλλοτριῶ [apallotreeo] expropriate, alienate.

ἀπαλός [apalos] soft ‖ gentle.

ἀπάνθρωπος [apanthropos] inhuman, cruel.

ἄπαντα, τά [apanta] πλ complete works.

ἀπάντημα, τό [apanteema] encounter.

ἀπάντησις, ἡ [apanteesees] reply, answer, response.

ἀπαντῶ [apanto] answer, reply ‖ meet.

ἀπάνω [apano] up, above ‖ upstairs ‖ ~ κάτω approximately ‖ ἀπό πάνω on top, from above ‖ ἕως ~ to the top ‖ ~ πού at the moment when ‖ ~ ἀπό above, more than ‖ ~ σέ at the moment of.

ἅπαξ [apaks] once, inasmuch as.

ἀπαξίωσις, ἡ [apakseeosees] disdain, contempt.

ἀπαράβατος [aparavatos] inviolable ‖ inviolate.

ἀπαράδεκτος [aparadektos] unacceptable, inadmissible.

ἀπαραίτητος [apareteetos] indispensable.

ἀπαράλλακτος [aparalaktos] identical ‖ unchanged.

ἀπαράμιλλος [aparameelos] unrivalled, incomparable, peerless.

ἀπαρατήρητος [aparateereetos] unnoticed, unobserved.

ἀπαρέμφατον, τό [aparemfaton] (γραμμ) infinitive.

ἀπαρηγόρητος [apareeγoreetos] inconsolable.

ἀπαριθμῶ [apareethmo] enumerate, count.

ἀπαρνοῦμαι [aparnoume] renounce, deny, disavow, disown.

ἀπαρτίζω [aparteezo] form, constitute.

ἀπαρχή, ἡ [aparhee] beginning, outset.

ἅπας [apas] all, whole, entire ‖ ἐξ ἅπαντος without fail.

ἀπασχόλησις, ἡ [apasholeesees] occupation.

ἀπασχολῶ [apasholo] occupy, busy.

ἀπατεών, ὁ [apateon] cheat, deceiver, swindler.

ἀπάτη, ἡ [apatee] deceit, fraud ‖ illusion.

ἀπατηλός [apateelos] deceptive, false, fraudulent.

ἀπάτητος [apateetos] untrodden.

ἀπατῶ [apato] deceive, cheat, defraud.

ἀπαυδῶ [apavdo] tire, become tired.

ἀπεγνωσμένος [apeγnosmenos] desperate.

ἀπειθαρχία, ἡ [apeetharheea] insubordination, lack of discipline.

ἀπειθής [apeethees] disobedient.

ἀπεικονίζω [apeekoneezo] represent, portray, depict.

ἀπειλή, ἡ [apeelee] threat, menace.

ἀπειλητικός [apeeleeteekos] threatening.

ἀπείραχτος [apeerahtos] untouched, untroubled.

ἀπειρία, ἡ [apeereea] inexperience ‖ (μέτρον) infinity, immensity.

ἄπειρος [apeeros] inexperienced ‖ (ἀριθμός) infinite, boundless.

ἀπέλασις, ἡ [apelasees] deportation, expulsion.

ἀπελευθερώνω [apeleftherono] set free, emancipate.

ἀπελευθέρωσις, ἡ [apeleftherosees] liberation, emancipation.

ἀπελπίζομαι [apelpeezome] despair.

ἀπελπισία, ἡ [apelpeeseea] despair ‖ εἶναι ~ it's hopeless!

ἀπέναντι [apenantee] opposite, across the way ‖ (πληρωμή) towards, against.

ἀπεναντίας [apenanteeas] on the contrary.

ἀπένταρος [apentaros] penniless, broke.

ἀπέραντος [aperantos] immense, boundless, endless.

ἀπέραστος [aperastos] impassable, unbeatable ‖ (κλωστή) not threaded.

ἀπεργία, ἡ [apergeea] strike.

ἀπερίγραπτος [apereegraptos] indescribable.

ἀπεριόριστος [apereeoreestos] unlimited.

ἀπεριποίητος [apereepeeetos] neglected, untidy.

ἀπερίσκεπτος [apereeskeptos] thoughtless, foolish, heedless.

ἀπερίσπαστος [apereespastos] undistracted.

ἀπέριττος [apereetos] simple, plain, concise.

ἀπέρχομαι [aperhome] depart, go away, leave.

ἀπεσταλμένος, ὁ [apestalmenos] envoy, minister, delegate.

ἀπευθύνομαι [apeftheenome] apply, appeal, address.

ἀπεύχομαι [apevhome] do not wish, deprecate.

ἀπεχθάνομαι [apehthanome] detest, abhor.

ἀπεχθής [apehthees] odious, repulsive, detestable.

ἀπέχω [apeho] abstain ‖ be distant, be far from.

ἀπηγορευμένος [apeegorevmenos] forbidden, prohibited.

ἀπηνής [apeenees] merciless, cruel, ferocious

ἀπήχησις, ἡ [apeeheesees] effect ‖ echo.

ἀπηχῶ [apeeho] echo, resound.

ἄπιαστος [apeeastos] not caught ‖ intact, intangible.

ἀπίδι, τό [apeedee] pear.

ἀπίθανος [apeethanos] unlikely, improbable.

ἀπίστευτος [apeestevtos] unbelievable, incredible.

ἀπιστία, ἡ [apeesteea] infidelity ‖ incredulity.

ἄπιστος [apeestos] unbelieving, unfaithful ‖ faithless, infidel.

ἀπιστῶ [apeesto] disbelieve ‖ be unfaithful.

ἄπλα, ἡ [apla] spaciousness.

ἁπλά [apla] simply.

ἀπλανής [aplanees] fixed.

ἄπλετος [apletos] abundant.

ἀπλήρωτος [apleerotos] unfilled ‖ unpaid.

ἀπλησίαστος [apleeseeastos] unapproachable.

ἄπληστος [apleestos] insatiable, greedy, avid.

ἁπλοϊκός [aploeekos] naive, simple.

ἁπλός [aplos] simple ‖ (εἰσητήριον) single ‖ (ντύσιμο) plain.

ἁπλότης, ἡ [aplotees] simplicity, naïvety, plainness.

ἁπλούστατα [aploustata] simply.

ἁπλοχέρης [aploherees] open-handed, liberal.

ἀπλόχωρος [aplohoros] spacious, roomy.

ἄπλυτος [apleetos] unwashed ‖ τά ἄπλυτα dirty linen.

ἅπλωμα, τό [aploma] spreading, unfolding ‖ (χεριῶν) stretching ‖ (ρούχων) hanging out.

ἁπλώνω [aplono] spread, stretch ‖ (ρούχα) hang out.

ἁπλῶς [aplos] simply, merely, plainly.

ἄπνοια, ἡ [apneea] lack of wind.

ἄπνους [apnous] lifeless, breathless.

ἀπό [apo] from, of ‖ ~ καιροῦ εἰς καιρόν from time to time ‖ ~ φόβο out of fear ‖ by ‖ ~ μνήμης by heart ‖ ~ τόν ἴδιο δρόμο by the same road ‖ through ‖ ~ τό παράθυρο through the window ‖ than ‖ ξέρω περισσότερα ~ σένα I know more than you ‖ (προθ) μέσα ~ out of ‖ πρίν ~ before.

ἀποβάθρα, ἡ [apovathra] pier, wharf ‖ (σιδηροδρομική) platform.

ἀποβάλλω [apovalo] reject, expel, dismiss ‖ (μωρό) miscarry.

ἀπόβασις, ἡ [apovasees] disembarkation, landing.

ἀποβιβάζω [apoveevazo] disembark, unload.

ἀποβλέπω [apovlepo] consider ‖ aim at look forward to ‖ regard.

ἀποβολή, ἡ [apovolee] dismissal, turning out ‖ (μωροῦ) miscarriage, abortion.

ἀποβραδίς [apovradees] yesterday evening since last night.

ἀπόβρασμα, τό [apovrasma] scum, refuse dregs.

ἀπόγειος [apoyeeos] offshore, land.

ἀπογειοῦμαι [apoyeeoume] take off.

ἀπογείωσις, ἡ [apogeeoosees] takeoff.

ἀπόγεμα, τό [apogema] afternoon.

ἀπογίνομαι [apogeenome] become, happen.

ἀπόγνωσις, ἡ [apoɣnosees] despair, desperation.

ἀπογοήτευσις [apoɣoeetevsees] disappointment, disillusionment.

ἀπογοητεύω [apoɣoeetevo] disappoint, disillusion.

ἀπόγονος, ὁ [apoɣonos] offspring, descendant.

ἀπογραφή, ἡ [apoɣrafee] (πληθυσμοῦ) census || (ἐμπορ) inventory.

ἀπογυμνώνω [apoɣeemnono] strip, plunder || unclothe.

ἀποδεικνύω [apoδeekneeo] prove, demonstrate.

ἀποδεικτικόν, τό [apoδeekteekon] certificate.

ἀπόδειξις, ἡ [apoδeeksees] proof || receipt.

ἀποδεκατίζω [apoδekateezo] decimate.

ἀποδέκτης, ὁ [apoδektees] addressee, receiver, consignee.

ἀποδεκτός [apoδektos] acceptable || accepted.

ἀποδέχομαι [apoδehome] accept || admit.

ἀποδημία, ἡ [apoδeemeea] migration, travel.

ἀπόδημος [apoδeemos] living abroad.

ἀποδίδω [apoδeeδo] give back, return || (τιμάς) grant, award || (κάτι σέ κάτι) attribute || (ἐλευθερίαν) restore || (μετάφρασιν) express || (ἔργον) produce.

ἀποδοκιμάζω [apoδokeemazo] disapprove of || demonstrate against.

ἀποδοκιμασία, ἡ [apoδokeemaseea] disapproval, rejection || booing.

ἀπόδοσις, ἡ [apoδosees] (ἐπιστροφή) return, repaying || (μηχανῆς κτλ) efficiency, capacity || (ἐργοστασίου) output || (τῆς γῆς) yield, produce || (ἔργου) rendering.

ἀποδοχή, ἡ [apoδohee] acceptance || acceptation || ἀποδοχαί πλ salary, fees.

ἀπόδρασις, ἡ [apoδrasees] escape.

ἀποδύομαι [apoδeeome] undress || (μεταφ) ~ στόν ἀγῶνα roll up one's sleeves.

ἀποδυτήριον, τό [apoδeeteereeon] changing room.

ἀποζημιώνω [apozeemeeono] compensate, indemnify.

ἀποζημίωσις, ἡ [apozeemeeosees] compensation, indemnity.

ἀποθανών [apothanon] deceased, late.

ἀποθαρρύνω [apothareeno] discourage.

ἀπόθεμα, τό [apothema] deposit || stock, reserve.

ἀποθέωσις, ἡ [apotheosees] apotheosis || (μεταφ) rousing reception.

ἀποθηκάριος, ὁ [apotheekareeos] storehouse keeper.

ἀποθηκεύω [apotheekevo] store up.

ἀποθήκη, ἡ [apotheekee] storage room, storehouse, warehouse.

ἀποθνήσκω [apothneesko] die, pass away.

ἀποθρασύνομαι [apothraseenome] become arrogant.

ἀποθυμῶ [apotheemo] miss || wish for.

ἀποικία, ἡ [apeekeea] colony, settlement.

ἀποκαθιστῶ [apokatheesto] rehabilitate, restore || (κόρη) marry.

ἀποκαλύπτω [apokaleepto] disclose, unveil, reveal.

ἀποκάλυψις, ἡ [apokaleepsees] revelation || (θρησκεία) Apocalypse.

ἀποκάμω [apokamo] get tired || (τελειώνω) finish off.

ἀποκαρδιωτικός [apokarδeeoteekos] disheartening.

ἀποκατάστασις, ἡ [apokatastasees] restoration, resettlement || (κόρης) marriage.

ἀποκατινός [apokateenos] underneath, below.

ἀπόκειμαι [apokeeme] it is up to, it depends on || σέ σένα ἀπόκειται it's up to you.

ἀπόκεντρος [apokentros] outlying, remote, out-of-the-way.

ἀποκέντρωσις, ἡ [apokentrosees] decentralization.

ἀποκεφαλίζω [apokefaleezo] decapitate, behead.

ἀποκήρυξις, ἡ [apokeereeksees] denunciation, proscription.

ἀποκηρύσσω [apokeereeso] renounce, disavow || proscribe, outlaw.

ἀποκλεισμός, ὁ [apokleesmos] exclusion, blockade, boycott.

ἀποκλειστικός [apokleesteekos] exclusive.

ἀποκλείω [apokleeo] exclude || debar || boycott || ἀποκλείεται it's out of the question.

ἀποκληρώνω [apokleerono] disinherit.

ἀποκλίνω [apokleeno] lean, diverge, incline.

ἀποκοιμίζω [apokeemeezo] lull to sleep.

ἀποκοιμοῦμαι [apokeemoume] fall asleep.

ἀποκομίζω [apokomeezo] carry away || derive.

ἀπόκομμα, τό [apokoma] press cutting || (κομμάτι) bit.

ἀποκοπή, ἡ [apokopee] cutting off || amputation.

ἀπόκοτος [apokotos] bold.

ἀποκούμπι, τό [apokoumbee] prop.

ἀπόκρημνος [apokreemnos] precipitous, steep, abrupt.

ἀποκριές, οἱ [apokries] πλ carnival.

ἀποκρίνομαι [apokreenome] answer, reply.

ἀπόκρισις, ἡ [apokreesees] reply, answer.

ἀπόκρουσις, ἡ [apokrousees] repulsion || (κατηγορίας) refutation.

ἀποκρούω [apokrouo] repulse || reject.

ἀποκρύπτω [apokreepto] conceal, hide, cover.

ἀπόκρυφος [apokreefos] secret || (ἐκκλ) apocryphal.

ἀπόκτησις, ἡ [apokteesees] acquisition.

ἀποκτῶ [apokto] obtain, get ‖ (παιδί) have (a child).

ἀπολαβή, ἡ [apolavee] gain, profit, income.

ἀπολαμβάνω [apolamvano] gain, earn ‖ (διασκεδάζω) enjoy.

ἀπόλαυσις, ἡ [apolavsees] enjoyment.

ἀπολήγω [apoleeyo] terminate, finish, end up in.

ἀπολίθωμα, τό [apoleethoma] fossil.

ἀπολλύω [apoleeo] lose.

ἀπολογία, ἡ [apoloyeea] defence, plea, excuse.

ἀπολογισμός, ὁ [apoloyeesmos] financial statement, account, report.

ἀπολογοῦμαι [apoloyoume] justify o.s., apologize.

ἀπολύμανσις, ἡ [apoleemansees] disinfection.

ἀπόλυσις, ἡ [apoleesees] release ‖ dismissal.

ἀπολυτήριον, τό [apoleeteereeon] discharge certificate ‖ (σχολείου) school leaving certificate, diploma.

ἀπόλυτος [apoleetos] absolute ‖ (ἀριθμός) cardinal.

ἀπολυτρώνω [apoleetrono] ransom ‖ redeem.

ἀπολύτως [apoleetos] absolutely ‖ entirely.

ἀπολύω [apoleeo] untie ‖ release ‖ (διώχνω) dismiss.

ἀπομακρύνω [apomakreeno] remove, send away, keep off.

ἀπόμαχος [apomahos] veteran, pensioner.

ἀπομεινάρια [apomeenaria] πλ remains, left-overs, remnants.

ἀπομένω [apomeno] remain, be left ‖ (κατάπληκτος) be left speechless.

ἀπομίμησις, ἡ [apomeemeesees] imitation, copy.

ἀπομνημονεύματα, τά [apomneemonevmata] πλ memoirs.

ἀπομονώνω [apomonono] isolate ‖ (ἠλεκτ) insulate.

ἀπονέμω [aponemo] bestow, allot ‖ confer, award.

ἀπονομή, ἡ [aponomee] award, bestowal.

ἀποξενώνω [apoksenono] alienate, estrange.

ἀποξήρανσις, ἡ [apokseeransees] draining, drying.

ἀπόπατος, ὁ [apopatos] W.C., toilet.

ἀπόπειρα, ἡ [apopeera] attempt, trial.

ἀποπεράτωσις, ἡ [apoperatosees] completion.

ἀποπλάνησις, ἡ [apoplaneesees] seduction ‖ (φωτός) aberration.

ἀποπλέω [apopleo] set sail, sail away.

ἀποπλύνω [apopleeno] wash, rinse.

ἀπορία, ἡ [aporeea] doubt ‖ uncertainty, perplexity.

ἄπορος [aporos] needy, poor.

ἀπορρέω [aporeo] flow, stem (from), emanate.

ἀπόρρητος [aporeetos] secret

ἀπορρίματα, τά [aporeemata] πλ rubbish, refuse.

ἀπορρίπτω [aporeepto] cast off ‖ (προσφοράν κτλ) reject, refuse ‖ (στίς ἐξετάσεις) fail.

ἀπορροφητικός [aporofeeteekos] absorbent, sucking.

ἀπορροφῶ [aporofo] absorb.

ἀπορρυπαντικόν, τό [aporeepanteekon] detergent.

ἀπορῶ [aporo] be at a loss, wonder, be surprised.

ἀπόσβεσις, ἡ [aposvesees] extinguishing ‖ (χρέους) liquidation (of debt).

ἀποσείω [aposeeo] shake off.

ἀποσιωπητικά, τά [aposeeopeeteeka] πλ points of omission.

ἀποσιωπῶ [aposeeopo] hush up, pass in silence.

ἀποσκοπῶ [aposkopo] aim, have in view.

ἀπόσπασμα, τό [apospasma] extract, excerpt ‖ (στρατ) detachment.

ἀποσπῶ [apospo] detach, tear out ‖ (στρατ) detach.

ἀπόσταξις, ἡ [apostaksees] distillation ‖ trickling.

ἀποστασία, ἡ [apostaseea] revolt, defection ‖ apostasy.

ἀπόστασις, ἡ [apostasees] distance ‖ remoteness.

ἀποστειρῶ [aposteero] sterilize.

ἀποστέλλω [apostelo] dispatch, send, transmit.

ἀποστεροῦμαι [aposteroume] be deprived of, lose.

ἀποστερῶ [apostero] deprive.

ἀποστηθίζω [aposteetheezo] learn by heart.

ἀπόστημα, τό [aposteema] abscess.

ἀποστολεύς, ὁ [apostolevs] sender, shipper.

ἀποστολή, ἡ [apostolee] sending, consignment ‖ (ἐμπορική κτλ) mission.

ἀποστομώνω [apostomono] silence.

ἀποστράτευσις, ἡ [apostratevsees] demobilization.

ἀπόστρατος, ὁ [apostratos] retired officer, ex-serviceman, veteran.

ἀποστρέφομαι [apostrefome] detest, abhor, despise.

ἀποστρέφω [apostrefo] avert, turn away.

ἀποστροφή, ἡ [apostrofee] repugnance, aversion, abhorrence.

ἀπόστροφος, ὁ [apostrofos] apostrophe.

ἀποσύνθεσις, ἡ [aposeenthesees] decay, decomposition ‖ disorganization.

ἀποσύρω [aposeero] withdraw ‖ retract.

ἀποσώνω [aposono] complete, finish off.

ἀπότακτος [apotaktos] discharged (dishonourably).

ἀποταμιεύω [apotamievo] save, put aside ‖ (τρόφιμα) lay up.

ἀποτείνομαι [apoteenome] apply, inquire

ἀποτελειώνω [apoteleeono] complete ‖ finish off.

ἀποτέλεσμα [apotelesma] result, effect ‖ ἀποτελεσματικός effective.

ἀποτελοῦμαι [apoteloume] consist of, be composed of.

ἀποτεφρώνω [apotefrono] reduce to ashes, burn down.

ἀποτίνω [apoteeno] pay off ‖ (ποινήν) serve ‖ (εὐγνωμοσύνην) repay.

ἀπότομος [apotomos] sudden, abrupt ‖ (στροφή)· steep, sheer ‖ (τρόπος) curt, gruff.

ἀποτραβιέμαι [apotravieme] withdraw, give up.

ἀποτρέπω [apotrepo] avert, turn aside, ward off. ·

ἀποτρόπαιος [apotropeos] abominable, hideous, horrible.

ἀποτροπή [apotropee] averting, warding off, dissuasion.

ἀποτρώγω [apotroyo] finish eating.

ἀποτσίγαρο, τό [apotseeyaro] cigarette end, stub, fag end. ·

ἀποτυγχάνω [apoteenghano] fail, fall through, miss.

ἀποτυπώνω [apoteepono] impress, imprint.

ἀποτυφλώνω [apoteeflono] blind

ἀποτυχία, ή [apoteeheea] failure, reverse.

ἀπουσία, ή [apouseea] absence ‖ ἀπουσιάζω be absent.

ἀποφάγια, τά [apofayeea] πλ scraps of food, remnants of a meal.

ἀποφασίζω [apofaseezo] decide, resolve, determine.

ἀπόφασις, ή [apofasees] decision, resolution ‖ (νομ) verdict ‖ τό παίρνω ~ν make up one's mind.

ἀποφασιστικός [apofaseesteekos] decisive, determined.

ἀποφέρω [apofero] yield, bring in ‖ produce.

ἀποφεύγω [apofevyo] avoid, keep clear of ‖ (κάπνισμα κτλ) abstain from.

ἀπόφθεγμα, τό [apoftheyma] maxim, apothegm.

ἀπόφοιτος [apofeetos] school leaver ‖ university graduate.

ἀποφορά, ή [apofora] stink, emanation.

ἀποφυγή, ή [apofeeyee] avoidance, evasion.

ἀποφυλακίζω [apofeelakeezo] release from prison.

ἀπόφυσις, ή [apofeesees] excrescence ‖ protuberance.

ἀποχαιρετίζω [apohereteezo] wish goodbye, bid farewell.

ἀποχαιρετισμός, ὁ [apohereteesmos] farewell, goodbye.

ἀποχέτευσις, ή [apohetevsees] draining, drainage.

ἀπόχρωσις, ή [apohrosees] shade, tone ‖ (χρώματος) fading.

ἀποχώρησις, ή [apohoreesees] withdrawal, retirement, departure.

ἀποχωρητήριον, τό [apohoreeteerion]

W.C., lavatory ‖ (στρατ) latrine.

ἀποχωρίζομαι [apohoreezome] part with, be separated.

ἀποχωρισμός, ὁ [apohorreesmos] separation, parting.

ἀποχωρῶ [apohoro] withdraw, retire, leave.

ἀπόψε [apopse] tonight, this evening.

ἀποψινός [apopseenos] tonight's.

ἄποψις, ή [apopsees] view, sight ‖ (μεταφ) view, idea.

ἀπραγματοποίητος [apraymatopieetos] unrealizable ‖ unfulfilled.

ἄπρακτος [apraktos] unsuccessful ‖ unachieved.

ἀπραξία, ή [aprakseea] inactivity ‖ (οἰκ) stagnation, standstill.

ἀπρέπεια, ή [aprepeea] indecency, oad manners.

ἀπρεπής [aprepees] indecent, improper, unbecoming.

'Ἀπρίλης, ὁ [apreelees] April.

ἀπρόβλεπτος [aprovleptos] unforeseen, unexpected.

ἀπροετοίμαστος [aproeteemastos] unprepared, unready.

ἀπροθυμία, ή [aprotheemeea] reluctance, hesitancy.

ἀπρόθυμος [aprotheemos] unwilling, reluctant, hesitant.

ἀποκάλυπτος [aprokaleeptos] undisguised, unfeigned, frank.

ἀπρόκλητος [aprokleetos] unprovoked, uncalled-for, unchallenged.

ἀπρομελέτητος [apromeleteetos] unpremeditated.

ἀπρονοησία, ή [apronoeeseea] improvidence, imprudence.

ἀπρόοπτος [aprooptos] unforeseen, unexpected.

ἀπρόσβλητος [aprosvleetos] unassailable ‖ invulnerable.

ἀπροσδόκητος [aprosdokeetos] unexpected, unforeseen, sudden.

ἀπρόσεκτος [aprosektos] inattentive, careless, remiss.

ἀπροσεξία, ή [aprosekseea] inattention, inadvertence.

ἀπρόσιτος [aproseetos] inaccessible, unapproachable.

ἀπροσποίητος [aprospieetos] frank, unaffected, open, sincere.

ἀπροστάτευτος [aprostatevtos] unprotected ‖ forlorn.

ἀπρόσωπος [aprosopos] impersonal.

ἀπροχώρητον, τό [aprohoreeton] limit, dead end.

ἄπταιστος [aptestos] faultless, perfect, correct.

ἄπτερος [apteros] wingless.

ἀπτόητος [aptoeetos] undaunted, intrepid.

ἄπτομαι [aptome] touch, feel, finger.

ἀπτός [aptos] tangible, palpable, evident.

ἀπύθμενος [apeethmenos] bottomless.

ἀπωϑῶ [apotho] repel, repulse, thrust back ‖ (μεταφ) reject.

ἀπώλεια, ἡ [apoleea] loss ‖ (ϑάνατος) bereavement.

ἀπώλητος [apoleetos] unsold.

ἀπών [apon] absent, missing.

ἀπώτατος [apotatos] furthest, remotest, most distant.

ἀπώτερος [apoteros] farther, further ‖ ~ σκοπός ulterior motive.

ἄρα [ara] so, thus, therefore, consequently.

ἆρα [ara] I wonder if, can it be that?

ἀρά [ara] curse, imprecation.

ἀραβικός [araveekos] Arabian, Arabic.

ἀραβόσιτος, ὁ [aravoseetos] maize, corn.

ἄραγε [arage] is it?, can it be?, I wonder if.

ἄραγμα, τό [arayma] anchoring, mooring.

ἀράδα, ἡ [arada] line, row, file, rank ‖ (ἐπίρ) continuously ‖ τῆς ~ς common.

ἀραδιάζω [aradeeazo] put in a row, line up ‖ (ὀνόματα κτλ) enumerate.

ἀράζω [arazo] moor, anchor, drop anchor.

ἀράθυμος [aratheemos] irascible, irritable, testy.

ἀραιός [areos] sparse, scattered ‖ (ἐπισκέψεις) infrequent, rare.

ἀραιώνω [areono] (σάλτσα κτλ) thin down ‖ (γραμμές κτλ) spread out ‖ (ἐπισκέψεις) lessen, cut down.

ἀρακᾶς, ὁ [arakas] common pea.

ἀραμπᾶς, ὁ [arambas] two-wheeled cart.

ἀράπης, ὁ [arapees] negro, dark person ‖ (φόβητρον) bogey.

ἀραπίνα, ἡ [arapeena] negress, dark woman.

ἀράχνη, ἡ [arahnee] spider ‖ cobwèb.

Ἄραψ, ὁ [araps] Arab.

ἀρβύλα, ἡ [arveela] boot.

ἀργά [arya] slowly ‖ late.

ἀργαλειός, ὁ [aryalios] loom.

ἄργητα, ἡ [aryeeta] delay.

ἀργία, ἡ [aryeea] holiday, closing day ‖ idleness.

ἄργιλλος, ἡ [aryeelos] clay.

ἀργοκίνητος [aryokeeneetos] slow-moving, sluggish.

ἀργομισϑία, ἡ [aryomeestheea] sinecure.

ἀργοπορία, ἡ [aryoporeea] slowness, delay.

ἀργός [aryos] slow ‖ idle, inactive.

ἀργόσχολος [aryosholos] idle, unoccupied.

ἀργότερα [aryotera] later, then.

ἀργυραμοιβός, ὁ [aryierameevos] money-changer.

ἄργυρος, ὁ [aryieros] silver.

ἀργῶ [aryo] be late ‖ (μαγαζί) be closed.

ἄρδευσις, ἡ [ardevsees] irrigation.

ἄρδην [ardeen] entirely, from top to bottom, wholly.

ἀρειμάνιος [areemaneeos] bellicose, pugnacious.

Ἄρειος [areeos]: ~ Πάγος Supreme Court.

ἀρέσκεια, ἡ [areskeea] taste, pleasure ‖ κατ' ~ν as much as I like.

ἀρεστός [arestos] agreeable, pleasing, gratifying.

ἀρέσω [areso] please, delight, like ‖ μοῦ ἀρέσει I like it.

ἀρετή, ἡ [aretee] virtue.

ἀρετσίνωτος [aretseenotos] unresinated.

ἀρθρῖτις, ἡ [arthreetees] arthritis.

ἀρθρογράφος, ὁ [arthroyrafos] journalist.

ἄρθρον, τό [arthron] article, clause, term.

ἄρθρωσις, ἡ [arthrosees] articulation, joint ‖ pronouncing distinctly.

ἀρίθμησις, ἡ [areethmeesees] numbering, counting, pagination.

ἀριθμητής, ὁ [areethmeetees] numerator ‖ (μηχάνημα) adding machine.

ἀριθμητική, ἡ [areethmeeteekee] arithmetic.

ἀριθμός, ὁ [areethmos] number.

ἀριθμῶ [areethmo] count, enumerate.

ἄριστα [areesta] very well ‖ (βαϑμολογία) excellent.

ἀριστεῖον, τό [areesteeon] first prize, medal.

ἀριστερά [areestera] left hand ‖ (ἐπιρ) on the left, to the left.

ἀριστερός [areesteros] left, left-handed ‖ (σπόρ) left-wing.

ἀριστοκρατία, ἡ [areestokrateea] aristocracy.

ἀριστούργημα, τό [areestouryeema] masterpiece.

ἀρκετά [arketa] enough, sufficiently.

ἀρκετός [arketos] enough, sufficient, adequate.

ἀρκούδα, ἡ [arkouda] bear.

ἀρκούντως [arkountos] βλ ἀρκετά.

ἀρκτικός [arkteekos] Arctic, northern.

ἄρκτος, ἡ [arktos] bear.

ἀρκῶ [arko] be enough, suffice ‖ ἀρκεῖ νά as long as.

ἀρλούμπα, ἡ [arloumba] foolish talk, nonsense.

ἅρμα, τό [arma] chariot ‖ (στρατ) ~ μάχης tank.

ἁρμαϑιά, ἡ [armathia] bunch ‖ string.

ἁρμάρι, τό [armaree] cupboard ‖ wardrobe.

ἅρματα, τά [armata] πλ weapons.

ἁρματώνω [armatono] arm ‖ equip.

ἁρμέγω [armeyo] milk ‖ (μεταφ) fleece.

Ἀρμένης, ὁ [armenees] Armenian.

ἀρμενίζω [armeneezo] set sail, sail.

ἅρμη, ἡ [armee] brine, pickling brine.

ἁρμόδιος [armodeeos] qualified, competent ‖ propitious.

ἁρμοδιότης, ἡ [armodeeotees] competency, province, jurisdiction.

ἁρμόζω [armozo] fit ‖ befit, be becoming, be proper.

ἁρμονία, ἡ [armoneea] harmony, concord.

ἁρμός, ὁ [armos] joint.

ἁρμοστής, ὁ [armostees] high commisioner governor.

ἅρμυρα, ἡ [armeera] saltiness.

ἁρμυρός [armeeros] salty.

ἀρνάκι, τό [arnakee] baby lamb.
ἀρνησίθρησκος [arneeseethreeskos] renegade, apostate.
ἄρνησις, ἡ [arneesees] refusal ‖ denial ‖ negation.
ἀρνί, τό [arnee] lamb ‖ (μεταφ) docile person.
ἀρνοῦμαι [arnoume] refuse, deny, decline ‖ disown.
ἄροτρον, τό [arotron] plough.
ἀρουραῖος, ὁ [aroureos] field mouse, rat.
ἅρπα, ἡ [arpa] harp.
ἁρπαγή, ἡ [arpayee] rapine ‖ rape ‖ stealing.
ἁρπάγη, ἡ [arpayee] hook, harpoon, grapnel.
ἁρπάζω [arpazo] grab, snatch ‖ steal, pinch ‖ (εὐκαιρία) seize ‖ (λέξεις) catch, pick up.
ἁρπάζομαι [arpazome] take hold of ‖ come to blows.
ἁρπακτικός [arpakteekos] greedy ‖ (ζῶον) rapacious, predatory.
ἅρπαξ, ὁ [arpaks] plunderer ‖ (σφετεριστής) usurper.
ἀρραβῶνες, οἱ [aravones] engagement, betrothal (old).
ἀρραβωνιάζω [arravoneeazo] betroth (old), engage.
ἀρραβωνιαστικιά, ἡ [aravoneeasteekia] fiancée.
ἀρραβωνιαστικός, ὁ [aravoneeasteekos] fiancé.
ἀρράγιστος [arrayeestos] uncracked ‖ (φιλία) strong, firm.
ἄρρεν, τό [aren] son, boy.
ἀρρενωπός [arrenopos] manly, masculine.
ἄρρηκτος [areektos] unbreakable ‖ unbroken.
ἄρρην [arreen] male.
ἄρρητος [arreetos] unsaid ‖ unspeakable ‖ indescribable.
ἀρρωσταίνω [arrosteno] make sick ‖ fall ill.
ἀρρώστια, ἡ [arrosteea] illness, sickness.
ἄρρωστος [arrostos] ill, sick, unwell.
ἀρσενικός [arseneekos] male ‖ (γραμμ) masculine.
ἄρσις, ἡ [arsees] removal, lifting ‖ (μεταφ) raising, abrogation.
ἀρτηρία, ἡ [arteereea] artery ‖ (ὁδός) thoroughfare.
ἄρτι [artee] recently, lately, just now.
ἀρτιγενής [arteeyenees] newborn.
ἄρτιος [arteeos] whole, entire ‖ (ἀριθμός) even.
ἀρτοποιεῖον, τό [artopieeon] bakery, baker's shop.
ἀρτοπωλεῖον, τό [artopoleeon] baker's shop.
ἄρτος, ὁ [artos] bread.
ἄρτυμα, τό [arteema] seasoning, sauce.
ἀρτύ(ν)ω [artee(n)o] season.
ἀρχαιοκαπηλία, ἡ [arheokapeeleea] illicit trade in antiquities.

ἀρχαιολόγος, ὁ [arheoloyos] archeologist.
ἀρχαιολογία, ἡ [arheoloyeea] archeology.
ἀρχαῖος [arheos] ancient ‖ antiquated.
ἀρχαιότης, ἡ [arheotees] antiquity ‖ (στά γραφεῖα) seniority.
ἀρχαιρεσίαι, αἱ [arheresie] πλ election.
ἀρχάριος [arhareeos] beginner, novice, apprentice.
ἀρχέγονος [arheyonos] primitive, primordial, original.
ἀρχεῖον, τό [arheeon] archives, records.
ἀρχέτυπον, τό [arheteepon] archetype, original.
ἀρχή, ἡ [arhee] beginning, start ‖ (φιλοσ) principle ‖ (διοίκ) authority ‖ κατ᾽ ἀρχήν in principle.
ἀρχηγεῖον, τό [arheeyeeon] headquarters.
ἀρχηγία, ἡ [arheeyeea] command, leadership.
ἀρχηγός, ὁ [arheeyos] commander, leader, chief ‖ (οἰκογενείας) head.
ἀρχιεπίσκοπος, ὁ [arhiepeeskopos] archbishop.
ἀρχιεργάτης, ὁ [arhieryatees] leading workman, foreman.
ἀρχιερεύς, ὁ [arhierevs] prelate, high priest.
ἀρχίζω [arheezo] begin, start, commence.
ἀρχικός [arheekos] initial, first, original.
ἀρχινῶ [arheeno] begin, start.
ἀρχιστράτηγος, ὁ [arheestrateeyos] commander-in-chief, generalissimo.
ἀρχισυντάκτης, ὁ [arheeseentaktees] chief editor.
ἀρχιτέκτων, ὁ [arheetekton] architect.
ἄρχοντας, ὁ [arhontas] notable, lord, master, elder.
ἀρχοντιά, ἡ [arhontia] distinction, nobility ‖ wealth.
ἀρχοντικός [arhonteekos] fine, of distinction, lordly.
ἄρχων, ὁ [arhon] chief, lord, prince ‖ (στήν ἀρχαιότητα) archon.
ἀρωγή, ἡ [aroyee] help, assistance, aid.
ἄρωμα, τό [aroma] aroma, perfume, odour ‖ ἀρωματικός scented.
ἅς [as] let, may ‖ ~ εἶναι be it so, let it be.
ἀσανσέρ, τό [asanser] lift, elevator.
ἀσαφής [asafees] obscure, vague.
ἀσβέστης, ὁ [asvestees] lime.
ἀσβεστώνω [asvestono] whitewash.
ἀσέβεια, ἡ [aseveea] disrepect ‖ impiety.
ἀσεβής [asevees] disrespectful ‖ impious.
ἀσέλγεια, ἡ [aselyeea] lewdness, debauchery.
ἀσελγής [aselyees] licentious, lewd.
ἄσεμνος [asemnos] indecent, obscene, immodest.
ἀσήκωτος [aseekotos] unraised ‖ (βαρύς) impossible to lift.
ἀσήμαντος [aseemantos] insignificant, unimportant.
ἀσημένιος [aseemeneeos] silver(y).

ἀσήμι, τό [aseemee] silver ‖ ~κά πλ silver-ware.

ἄσημος [aseemos] obscure, insignificant, unimportant.

ἀσθένεια, ἡ [astheneea] sickness, illness ‖ (θελήσεως) weakness.

ἀσθενής [asthenees] ill, weak ‖ (ὁ ἄρρωστος) patient.

ἀσθενικός [astheneekos] sickly.

ἀσθενῶ [astheno] be ill, fall sick, get sick.

ἄσθμα, τό [asthma] asthma.

ἀσθμαίνω [asthmeno] pant, gasp, be out of breath.

ἀσιτία, ἡ [aseeteea] undernourishment, fasting.

ἀσκεπής [askepees] uncovered, bareheaded.

ἀσκέρι, τό [askeree] army, crowd.

ἄσκησις, ἡ [askeesees] exercise, practice ‖ drill.

ἀσκητής, ὁ [askeetees] hermit.

ἄσκοπος [askopos] pointless, aimless, purposeless.

ἀσκός, ὁ [askos] (skin) bag ‖ wineskin.

ἀσκοῦμαι [askoume] exercise, practise.

ἀσκῶ [asko] exercise, practise.

ἄσμα, τό [asma] song, air.

ἀσμένως [asmenos] gladly.

ἀσπάζομαι [aspazome] kiss, embrace ‖ (μεταφ) adopt, espouse.

ἀσπασμός, ὁ [aspasmos] embrace, kiss ‖ greeting.

ἄσπαστος [aspastos] unbroken ‖ unbreakable.

ἄσπιλος [aspeelos] immaculate, spotless.

ἀσπιρίνη, ἡ [aspeereenee] aspirin.

ἀσπίς, ἡ [aspees] shield ‖ (ὄφις) asp.

ἄσπλαγχνος [asplanghnos] hard-hearted, pitiless, unmerciful.

ἄσπονδος [aspondos] irreconcilable, relentless.

ἀσπούδαστος [aspoudastos] uneducated, ignorant.

ἀσπράδα, ἡ [asprada] whiteness.

ἀσπράδι, τό [aspradee] white spot ‖ (ματιοῦ, αὐγοῦ) white.

ἀσπρειδερός [aspreederos] whitish.

ἀσπρίζω [aspreezo] whiten, bleach ‖ (γίνομαι ἄσπρος) turn white.

ἀσπρομάλλης [aspromalees] white-haired.

ἀσπροπρόσωπος [asproprosopos] clean-faced, uncorrupted ‖ successful.

ἀσπρόρουχα, τά [asprorouha] πλ underclothes, linen.

ἄσπρος [aspros] white.

ἀσπρόχωμα, τό [asprohoma] white clay.

ἄσσος, ὁ [assos] ace.

ἀστάθεια, ἡ [astatheea] instability, inconstancy, fickleness.

ἀσταθής [astathees] unsteady, fickle, unstable.

ἀστακός, ὁ [astakos] lobster.

ἄστατος [astatos] fickle, unstable.

ἄστεγος [asteyos] homeless ‖ roofless.

ἀστειεύομαι [astievome] joke, jest.

ἀστεῖο, τό [asteeo] joke, pleasantry.

ἀστεῖος [asteeos] humorous, funny.

ἀστείρευτος [asteerevtos] inexhaustible, limitless.

ἀστέρι, τό [asteree] star.

ἀστερισμός, ὁ [astereesmos] constellation.

ἀστεροσκοπεῖον, τό [asteroskopeeon] observatory.

ἀστήρικτος [asteereektos] unsupported ‖ (μεταφ) untenable.

ἀστιγματισμός, ὁ [asteeymateesmos] astigmatism.

ἀστικός [asteekos] urban ‖ civic ‖ ~ κῶδιξ civil code.

ἄστικτος [asteektos] unspotted, unblemished.

ἀστοιχείωτος [asteeheeotos] unlearned, ignorant.

ἀστοργία, ἡ [astoryeea] lack of affection.

ἀστόχαστος [astohastos] thoughtless, imprudent.

ἀστοχία, ἡ [astoheea] failure ‖ carelessness.

ἀστοχῶ [astoho] miss the mark, fail ‖ (λησμονῶ) forget.

ἀστράγαλος, ὁ [astrayalos] anklebone ‖ (παιγνίδι) knucklebone.

ἀστραπή, ἡ [astrapee] lightning.

ἀστραπιαῖος [astrapieos] lightning, quick.

ἀστράπτω [astrapto] lighten ‖ flash, glitter.

ἀστρικός [astreekos] stellar, astral.

ἄστριφτος [astreeftos] not twisted.

ἄστρο, τό [astro] star.

ἀστρολογία, ἡ [astroloyeea] astrology.

ἀστρολόγος, ὁ [astroloyos] astrologer.

ἀστρονομία, ἡ [astronomeea] astronomy.

ἀστρονόμος, ὁ [astronomos] astronomer.

ἀστροπελέκι, τό [astropelekee] thunderbolt.

ἀστροφεγγιά, ἡ [astrofengia] starlight.

ἄστρωτος [astrotos] (κρεββάτι) not made ‖ (τραπέζι) unlaid ‖ (πάτωμα) bare ‖ (δρόμος) unpaved.

ἄστυ, τό [astee] city.

ἀστυνομία, ἡ [asteenomeea] police.

ἀστυνομικός [asteenomeekos] policeman, of the police.

ἀστυνόμος, ὁ [asteenomos] police officer.

ἀστυφύλαξ, ὁ [asteefeelaks] police constable.

ἀσυγκίνητος [aseengkeeneetos] unmoved, unfeeling.

ἀσυγκράτητος [aseengkrateetos] unsuppressible.

ἀσύγκριτος [aseengkreetos] incomparable.

ἀσύγχυστος [aseeyeereestos] untidy, disarranged.

ἀσυγχώρητος [aseenghoreetos] inexcusable, unforgivable.

ἀσυδοσία, ἡ [aseedoseea] immunity, exemption.

ἀσύδοτος [aseedotos] enjoying immunity.

ἀσυζήτητος [aseezeeteetos] unquestionable, incontrovertible.

ἀσυλία, ἡ [aseeleea] asylum, immunity, inviolability.

ἀσύλληπτος [aseeleeptos] elusive, not caught || (μεταφ) inconceivable.

ἀσυλλόγιστος [aseeloyeestos] rash, thoughtless.

ἄσυλον, τό [aseelon] shelter, refuge, asylum.

ἀσυμβίβαστος [aseemveevastos] irreconcilable, incompatible.

ἀσύμμετρος [aseemetros] disproportionate.

ἀσυμπλήρωτος [aseembleerotos] uncompleted, incomplete.

ἀσύμφορος [aseemforos] disadvantageous, not profitable.

ἀσυναγώνιστος [aseenayoneestos] unbeatable, unrivalled.

ἀσυναίσθητος [aseenestheetos] unconscious, inconsiderate.

ἀσυναρτησία, ἡ [aseenarteeseea] incoherence, inconsistency.

ἀσυνάρτητος [aseenarteetos] incoherent || inconsistent.

ἀσυνείδητος [aseeneedeetos] unscrupulous, unconscionable.

ἀσυνέπεια, ἡ [aseenepeea] inconsequence, inconsistency.

ἀσυνεπής [aseenepees] inconsistent.

ἀσύνετος [aseenetos] imprudent, unwise.

ἀσυνήθιστος [aseeneetheestos] unusual, uncommon.

ἀσυνταξία, ἡ [aseentakseea] (γραμμ) grammatical mistake.

ἀσυρματιστής, ὁ [aseermateestees] wireless operator.

ἀσύρματος, ὁ [aseermatos] wireless || σταθμός ἀσυρμάτου wireless station.

ἀσύστατος [aseestatos] not recommended || (ἰσχυρισμός) groundless, unsupported.

ἀσύστολος [aseestolos] impudent, brazen.

ἄσφαιρος [asferos] blank.

ἀσφάλεια, ἡ [asfaleea] security, safety || (ζωῆς κτλ) insurance || (ἀστυνομία) police || (ἠλεκτ) fuse || (ὅπλου) safety catch.

ἀσφαλής [asfalees] safe, secure, sure.

ἀσφαλίζω [asfaleezo] secure, assure || (ζωήν κτλ) insure.

ἀσφαλιστήριον, τό [asfaleesteereeon] insurance policy.

ἀσφάλιστρον, τό [asfaleestron] insurance premium.

ἄσφαλτος, ἡ [asfaltos] asphalt || (δρόμος) tarred road.

ἀσφαλῶς [asfalos] surely, certainly || safely.

ἀσφυκτικός [asfeekteekos] suffocating.

ἀσφυξία, ἡ [asfeekseea] suffocation, asphyxia.

ἄσχετος [ashetos] irrelevant, unrelated, unconnected.

ἀσχημία, ἡ [asheemeea] ugliness, deformity.

ἀσχημίζω [asheemeezo] make ugly || (μεταφ) spoil, mar.

ἀσχημονῶ [asheemono] offend modesty, misbehave.

ἄσχημος [asheemos] ugly || unsightly || bad.

ἀσχολία, ἡ [asholeea] occupation, business, job.

ἀσχολοῦμαι [asholoume] be occupied with, keep busy.

ἀσώματος [asomatos] incorporeal.

ἀσωτία, ἡ [asoteea] dissipation, prodigality.

ἄσωτος [asotos] dissolute || prodigal, wasteful.

ἀταίριαστος [atereeastos] incompatible || dissimilar.

ἄτακτος [ataktos] irregular || disorderly || (παιδί) naughty, unruly.

ἀταξία, ἡ [atakseea] confusion, disorder || unruliness.

ἀτάραχος [atarahos] calm, composed, quiet.

ἀταραξία, ἡ [atarakseea] composure, calmness, serenity.

ἀτάσθαλος [atasthalos] disorderly || improper, rude.

ἄταφος [atafos] unburied.

ἄτεκνος [ateknos] childless.

ἀτέλεια, ἡ [ateleea] defect || (δασμοῦ) exemption || (χαρακτῆρος) imperfection.

ἀτελείωτος [ateleeotos] endless || unfinished, incomplete.

ἀτελεσφόρητος [atelesforeetos] ineffectua, fruitless.

ἀτελεύτητος [atelevteetos] endless, interminable.

ἀτελής [atelees] incomplete || defective || (φόρου) tax-free.

ἀτελώνιστος [ateloneestos] duty-free || not cleared through customs.

ἀτενής [atenees] fixed, steadfast.

ἀτενίζω [ateneezo] gaze, stare at, look fixedly on.

ἄτεχνος [atehnos] unskilful, badly made.

ἀτζαμής [atzamees] unskilled || awkward, clumsy.

ἀτζέμ-πιλάφι, τό [atzempeelafee] lamb with rice.

ἄτι, τό [atee] steed, horse.

ἀτίθασος [ateethasos] stubborn || (ἄλογο) difficult to tame.

ἀτιμάζω [ateemazo] dishonour, disgrace || (βιάζω) defile, ravish.

ἀτίμητος [ateemeetos] inestimable, priceless, invaluable.

ἀτιμία, ἡ [ateemeea] dishonour, disgrace, infamy.

ἄτιμος [ateemos] dishonest, infamous, disreputable || (συμπεριφορά) disgraceful.

ἀτιμώρητος [ateemoreetos] unpunished.

ἀτλάζι, τό [atlazee] satin.

ἀτμάκατος, ἡ [atmakatos] small steamboat.

ἀτμάμαξα, ἡ [atmamaksa] locomotive.

ἀτμοκίνητος [atmokeeneetos] steam-driven.

άτμομηχανή, ή [atmomeehanee] steam engine, locomotive.

άτμοπλοΐα, ή [atmoploeea] steam navigation.

άτμόπλοιον, τό [atmopleeon] steamship.

άτμός, ὁ [atmos] steam, vapour || (κρασιοῦ) fume.

άτμόσφαιρα, ή [atmosfera] atmosphere.

άτοκος [atokos] without interest.

άτολμος [atolmos] timid, faint-hearted.

άτομικιστής [atomeekeestees] egoist.

άτομικός [atomeekos] personal || (ἐνέργεια κτλ) atomic.

άτομικότης, ή [atomeekotees] individuality.

άτομον, τό [atomon] (Φυσική) atom || (ἄνθρωπος) individual, person.

άτονία, ή [atoneea] languor, weakness, dejection.

άτονος [atonos] languid, dull || (γραμμ) unaccented.

άτοπος [atopos] improper, unbecoming, indecent || ridiculous.

άτοῦ, τό [atoo] trump.

άτόφυος [atofeeos] solid, massive.

άτραπός, ἡ [atrapos] path, track.

άτριφτος [atreeftos] not rubbed, not grated.

άτρόμητος [atromeetos] bold, dauntless, daring.

άτροφία, ή [atrofeea] atrophy.

άτροφικός [atrofeekos] atrophied, emaciated.

άτρύγητος [atreeyeetos] ungathered, unharvested.

άτρωτος [atrotos] unwounded, unhurt || invulnerable.

άτσαλένιος [atsaleneeos] of steel, steely.

άτσάλι, τό [atsalee] steel.

άτσαλος [atsalos] untidy, disorderly, unkempt || (ζωή) riotous, lawless.

άτσίγγανος, ὁ [atseenganos] gypsy.

άτσίδα, ή [atseeδa] alert person, wideawake person.

άτύχημα, τό [ateeheema] mishap, accident, misfortune, injury.

άτυχής [ateehees] unfortunate, unlucky, wretched.

άτυχος [ateehos] βλ άτυχής.

άτυχία, ή [ateeheea] misfortune, bad luck.

άτυχῶ [ateeho] fail, have bad luck, meet with misfortune.

αὐγερινός, ὁ [avyereenos] morning star.

αὐγή, ή [avyee] dawn, daybreak.

αὐγό, τό [avyo] egg.

αὐγολέμονο, τό [avyolemono] lemon and egg sauce or soup.

αὐγοτάραχο, τό [avyotaraho] botargo.

αὐγουλιέρα, ή [avyouliera] eggcup.

Αὔγουστος, ὁ [avyoustos] August.

αὐθάδεια, ή [anthaδeea] audacity, insolence.

αὐθάδης [anthaδees] impertinent, saucy.

αὐθαιρεσία, ή [avthereseea] high-handed act.

αὐθαίρετος [avtheretos] arbitrary, highhanded.

αὐθεντία, ή [avthenteea] authority, authenticity.

αὐθεντικός [avthenteekos] authentic, authoritative.

αὐθημερόν [avtheemeron] on the very same day.

αὐθίς [avthees] once more, again.

αὐθόρμητος [avthormeetos] spontaneous.

αὐθυποβολή, ή [avtheepovolee] autosuggestion.

αὐθωρεί [avthoree] immediately, instantly, at once.

αὐλαία, ή [avlea] curtain.

αὐλάκι, τό [avlakee] channel, ditch, trench || (ξύλου κτλ) groove.

αὐλακωτός [avlakotos] grooved, furrowed, scored.

αὐλάρχης, ὁ [avlarhees] Lord High Chamberlain.

αὐλή, ή [avlee] yard, courtyard || (βασιλέως) court.

αὐλικός [avleekos] of the court.

αὐλόγυρος, ὁ [avloyeeros] enclosure, surrounding wall.

αὐλός, ὁ [avlos] pipe, flute, reed.

ἄϋλος [aeelos] immaterial, incorporeal.

αὐξάνω [avksano] increase, augment || (ταχύτητα) accelerate.

αὔξησις, ή [avkseesees] increase || (γραμμ) augment.

αὐξομείωσις, ή [avksomeeosees] fluctuation, variation.

αὔξων [avkson] increasing || ~ ἀριθμός serial number.

άϋπνία, ή [aeepneea] sleeplessness, insomnia.

ἄϋπνος [aeepnos] sleepless, wakeful.

αὔρα, ή [avra] breeze.

αὐριανός [avreeanos] of tomorrow.

αὔριον [avreeon] tomorrow.

αὐστηρός [avsteeros] severe, rigorous, austere.

αὐστηρότης, ή [avsteerotees] severity, strictness, austerity.

αὔτανδρος [avtanδros] with all hands.

αὐταπάρνησις, ή [avtaparneesees] selfabnegation.

αὐταπάτη, ή [avtapatee] self-delusion, selfdeception.

αὐταρέσκεια, ή [avtareskeea] complacency.

αὐτάρκεια, ή [avtarkeea] contentment, selfcontent.

αὐτάρκης [avtarkees] self-sufficient, satisfied.

αὐταρχικός [avtarheekos] authoritative, dictatorial.

αὐτεξούσιος [avteksouseeos] independent, free.

αὐτί, τό [avtee] ear.

αὐτοβιογραφία, ή [avtoveeoyrafeea] autobiography.

αὐτόβουλος [avtovoulos] of one's own free will, unconstrained.

αὐτόγραφον, τό [avtoyrafon] autograph.

αὐτόδηλος [avtodeelos] self-evident.

αὐτοδημιούργητος [avtodeemeeouryeetos] self-made.

αὐτοδιάθεσις, ἡ [avtodeeathesees] self-determination.

αὐτοδικαίως [avtodeekeos] of right, de jure.

αὐτοδιοίκησις, ἡ [avtodieekeesees] self-government.

αὐτόθι [avtothee] in the same place, there.

αὐτοθυσία, ἡ [avtotheeseea] self-sacrifice.

αὐτοκαλούμενος [avtokaloumenos] self-styled.

αὐτοκέφαλος [avtokefalos] independent ‖ (ἐκκλ) autocephalous.

αὐτοκινητάμαξα, ἡ [avtokeeneetamaksa] railcar.

αὐτοκινητιστής, ὁ [avtokeeneeteestees] motorist, rallyist.

αὐτοκίνητο, τό [avtokeeneeto] car ‖ (US) automobile.

αὐτοκρατορία, ἡ [avtokratoreea] empire.

αὐτοκράτωρ, ὁ [avtokrator] emperor.

αὐτοκτονία, ἡ [avtoktoneea] suicide.

αὐτοκτονῶ [avtoktono] commit suicide.

αὐτολεξεί [avtoleksee] word for word, verbatim.

αὐτόματος [avtomatos] automatic.

αὐτονόητος [avtonoeetos] self-explanatory, obvious.

αὐτοπεποίθησις, ἡ [avtopepeetheesees] self-confidence, self-reliance.

αὐτοπροαίρετος [avtoproeretos] voluntary.

αὐτοπροσώπως [avtoprosopos] personally.

αὐτόπτης, ὁ [avtoptees] eyewitness.

αὐτός [avtos] he ‖ ὁ ~ the same.

αὐτοστιγμεί [avtosteeymee] instantly, immediately.

αὐτοσυντήρησις [avtoseenteereesees] self-preservation.

αὐτοσυντήρητος [avtoseenteereetos] self-supporting.

αὐτοσχεδιάζω [avtoshedeeazo] improvise, extemporize.

αὐτοσχέδιος [avtoshedeeos] improvised, impromptu, makeshift.

αὐτοτελής [avtotelees] self-sufficient independent.

αὐτοῦ [avtou] there.

αὐτουργός, ὁ [avtouryos] perpetrator.

αὐτοφυής [avtofiees] indigenous, self-growing, natural.

αὐτόφωρος [avtoforos] in the very act, red-handed.

αὐτόχειρ, ὁ [avtoheer] suicide.

αὐτόχθων, ὁ [avtohthon] indigenous, aboriginal, native.

αὐτόχρημα [avtohreema] wholly, entirely, indeed.

αὐτοψία, ἡ [avtopseea] (ἰατρ) autopsy ‖ (νομ) local inspection.

αὐχήν, ὁ [avheen] nape (of neck) ‖ (μεταφ) neck, pass.

αὐχμηρός [avhmeeros] dry, arid, barren.

ἀφάγωτος [afayotos] uneaten ‖ not having eaten ‖ untouched.

ἀφαίμαξις, ἡ [afemaksees] bloodletting.

ἀφαίρεσις, ἡ [aferesees] deduction, subtraction ‖ (φιλοσ) abstraction.

ἀφαιροῦμαι [aferoume] be absent-minded.

ἀφαιρῶ [afero] deduct, subtract ‖ (κλέβω) steal, rob.

ἀφαλός, ὁ [afalos] navel.

ἀφάνεια, ἡ [afaneea] obscurity, oblivion.

ἀφανής [afanees] obscure, unknown ‖ invisible.

ἀφανίζω [afaneezo] ruin, destroy.

ἀφάνταστος [afantastos] unimaginable.

ἄφαντος [afantos] invisible, unseen.

ἀφαρπάζομαι [afarpazome] lose one's temper.

ἀφασία, ἡ [afaseea] muteness, aphasia.

ἄφατος [afatos] inexpressible, unspeakable.

ἀφειδής [afeedees] lavish, extravagant.

ἀφελής [afelees] simple, ingenuous, guileless.

ἀφέντης, ὁ [afentees] master, boss ‖ owner.

ἀφεντικό, τό [afenteeko] governor, boss, employer.

ἀφερέγγυος [aferengeeos] insolvent.

ἄφεσις, ἡ [afesees] remission ‖ discharge.

ἀφετηρία, ἡ [afeteereea] starting point ‖ beginning.

ἄφευκτος [afevktos] inevitable, unavoidable.

ἀφή, ἡ [afee] sense of touch ‖ (αἴσθησις) feeling.

ἀφήγησις, ἡ [afeeyeesees] narration, account.

ἀφηγοῦμαι [afeeyoume] narrate, relate, tell.

ἀφηνιάζω [afeeneeazo] bolt ‖ (ἐπί ἀνθρώπων) run amok.

ἀφήνω [afeeno] let, permit ‖ (μόνος) let alone ‖ (ἐλευθερώνω) let go of ‖ (ἐγκαταλείπω) abandon.

ἀφηρημάδα, ἡ [afeereemaδa] absent-mindedness.

ἀφηρημένος [afeereemenos] absent-minded ‖ (φιλοσ) abstract.

ἀφθαρσία, ἡ [aftharseea] indestructibility, incorruptibility.

ἄφθαρτος [afthartos] incorruptible, indestructible.

ἄφθαστος [afthastos] unsurpassed, incomparable, unexcelled.

ἀφθονία, ἡ [afthoneea] abundance, profusion.

ἄφθονος [afthonos] abundant, plentiful, profuse.

ἀφθονῶ [afthono] abound with, teem with, be plentiful.

ἀφιέρωμα, τό [afieroma] offering, dedication.

ἀφιερώνω [afierono] dedicate, devote ‖ (βιβλίο κτλ) inscribe.

ἀφιέρωσις, ἡ [afierosees] dedication, devotion.

ἀφικνοῦμαι [afeeknoume] arrive, come.

ἀφιλοκερδής [afeelokerδees] disinterested, selfless.

ἀφιλότιμος [afeeloteemos] wanting in self-respect, mean.

ἀφίνω [afeeno] βλ ἀφήνω.

ἄφιξις, ἡ [afeeksees] arrival, coming.

ἀφιόνι, τό [afeeonee] poppy ‖ opium.

ἀφίσταμαι [afeestame] stand away from ‖ (διαφέρω) differ, vary.

ἄφλεκτος [aflektos] non-inflammable.

ἄφοβος [afovos] intrepid, fearless, bold.

ἀφομοιώνω [afomeeono] assimilate.

ἀφομοίωσις, ἡ [afomeeosees] assimilation.

ἀφοπλίζω [afopleezo] disarm ‖ (φρούριο κτλ) dismantle.

ἀφοπλισμός, ὁ [afopleesmos] disarmament.

ἀφόρετος [aforetos] unworn, new.

ἀφόρητος [aforeetos] intolerable, insufferable.

ἀφορίζω [aforeezo] excommunicate.

ἀφορισμός, ὁ [aforeesmos] excommunication.

ἀφορμή, ἡ [aformee] motive, pretext, cause.

ἀφορολόγητος [aforoloyeetos] untaxed, free from taxation.

ἀφορῶ [aforo] concern ‖ regard ‖ ὅσον ἀφορᾷ as regards.

ἀφοσιοῦμαι [afoseeoume] devote o.s., be attached to.

ἀφοσίωσις, ἡ [afoseeosees] devotion, attachment, affection.

ἀφότου [afotou] since, as long as.

ἀφοῦ [afou] since, after.

ἄφρακτος [afraktos] without a fence or wall.

ἀφρᾶτος [afratos] light and crisp ‖ frothy, foamy ‖ (δέρμα) soft.

ἀφρίζω [afreezo] foam ‖ (μεταφ) be furious.

ἀφρόγαλα, τό [afroyala] cream.

ἀφροδισιολόγος, ὁ [afroδeesioloyos] venereal disease specialist.

ἀφροδίσιος [afroδeesios] venereal.

ἀφρόντιστος [afronteestos] neglected, uncared for.

ἀφρός, ὁ [afros] foam ‖ (κοινωνίας) cream ‖ (σαπουνιοῦ) lather.

ἀφροσύνη, ἡ [afroseenee] foolishness, rashness.

ἀφρώδης [afroδees] frothy, foamy.

ἄφρων [afron] foolish, thoughtless, rash.

ἀφυδάτωσις, ἡ [afeeδatosees] dehydration.

ἀφύπνισις, ἡ [afeepneesees] awakening ‖ (μεταφ) dawning.

ἀφύσικος [afeeseekos] unnatural ‖ (προσποιητός) affected.

ἄφωνος [afonos] mute, speechless, silent.

ἀφώτιστος [afoteestos] dark ‖ (ἄνθρωπος) unenlightened.

ἄχ [ah] (ἐπιφ) ah!, oh!, alas!

ἀχαΐρευτος [ahaeerevtos] scoundrel.

ἀχάλαστος [ahalastos] unspoilt ‖ indestructible, intact.

ἀχαλίνωτος [ahaleenotos] unbridled ‖ (μεταφ) unmanageable.

ἀχαμνός [ahamnos] skinny, thin, lean.

ἀχανής [ahanees] immense, enormous, vast.

ἀχαρακτήριστος [aharakteereestos] unprincipled, hard to describe.

ἄχαρις [aharees] ungraceful, awkward, unsightly.

ἀχαριστία, ἡ [ahareesteea] ingratitude.

ἀχάριστος [ahareestos] ungrateful.

ἄχαρος [aharos] unsightly ‖ unpleasant.

ἀχηβάδα, ἡ [aheevaδa] cockle, sea shell, shellfish.

ἄχθος, τό [ahthos] weight, burden, load.

ἀχθοφόρος, ὁ [ahthoforos] porter.

ἀχινός, ὁ [aheenos] sea urchin.

ἀχλάδι, τό [ahlaδee] pear.

ἄχνα, ἡ [ahna] βλ ἀχνός.

ἀχνάρι, τό [ahnaree] footprint ‖ (μεταφ) pattern.

ἄχνη, ἡ [ahnee] mist, evaporation ‖ (χημ) corrosive sublimate.

ἀχνίζω [ahneezo] evaporate ‖ steam.

ἀχνός, ὁ [ahnos] vapour, steam ‖ (χρῶμα) pale, colourless.

ἀχόρταγος [ahortayos] insatiable, greedy ‖ (ζῶον) voracious.

ἄχου [ahoo] (ἐπιφ) oh!, damn it!

ἀχούρι, τό [ahouree] stable, stall.

ἀχρείαστος [ahreeastos] unnecessary, needless.

ἀχρεῖος [ahreeos] wicked, vile.

ἀχρησιμοποίητος [ahreeseemopieetos] unused.

ἀχρηστεύω [ahreestevo] make useless.

ἀχρηστία, ἡ [ahreesteea] obsoleteness, uselessness.

ἄχρηστος [ahreestos] useless, worthless.

ἄχρι [ahree] till, until.

ἀχρονολόγητος [ahronoloyeetos] undated.

ἄχρους [ahrous] colourless, uncoloured.

ἀχρωμάτιστος [ahromateestos] unpainted uncoloured, plain.

ἄχτι, τό [ahtee] yearning, longing.

ἀχτίδα, ἡ [ahteeδa] ray, beam.

ἀχτένιστος [ahteneestos] uncombed, unkempt ‖ (λόγος κτλ) unpolished.

ἄχυρον, τό [aheeron] straw, hay.

ἀχυρών, ὁ [aheeron] barn, hayloft.

ἀχώνευτος [ahonevtos] undigested ‖ indigestible.

ἀχώριστος [ahoreestos] inseparable.

ἄψητος [apseetos] not cooked, underdone.

ἀψηφῶ [apseefo] disregard, disdain, scorn.

ἀψιδωτός [apseeδotos] arched, vaulted.

ἀψιμαχία, ἡ [apseemaheea] skirmish.

άψίς, ή [apsees] arch, vault ‖ apse.

άψογος [apsoγos] faultless, irreproachable.

άψυχολόγητος [apseeholoγeetos] ill-considered, impolitic.

άψυχος [apseehos] lifeless ‖ (δειλός) cowardly, timid.

άωρος [aoros] (καρπός) unripe ‖ (σκέψις) premature.

άωτον, τό [aoton]: άκρον ~ acme, height of.

B, β

Βαβυλωνία, ή [vaveeloneea] Babylonia ‖ (μεταφ) chaos, confusion.

βαγένι, τό [vaγenee] βλ βαρέλι.

βαγόνι, τό [vaγonee] carriage ‖ (έμπορικόν) wagon, truck ‖ (βαγκόν-λί) sleeping car.

βάδην [vadeen] at a walking pace.

βαδίζω [vadeezo] walk ‖ (στρατ) march ‖ (πηγαίνω) go.

βάδισμα, τό [vadeesma] step, walk, gait.

βαζελίνη, ή [vazeleenee] vaseline.

βάζο, τό [vazo] vase.

βάζω [vazo] put, set, place ‖ (φορῶ) put on ‖ (φόρους κτλ) impose, lay ‖ ~ έμπρός start, begin ‖ ~ χέρι lay hands on ‖ ~ τά δυνατά μου do my best.

βαθαίνω [vatheno] deepen ‖ βλ καί βαθύνω.

βαθειά [vatheea] deep(ly), profoundly.

βαθμηδόν [vathmeedon] by degrees, gradually.

βαθμιαῖος [vathmieos] gradual, progressive.

βαθμίς, ή [vathmees] step, stair ‖ (μεταφ) rank.

βαθμολογία, ή [vathmoloγeea] (όργάνου) graduation ‖ (μαθήματος) grades, marks.

βαθμός, ό [vathmos] degree ‖ (στρατ) grade, rank ‖ (μαθήματος) mark.

βάθος, τό [vathos] depth, bottom ‖ (φόντο) back, background.

βαθούλωμα, τό [vathouloma] hollow, depression.

βαθουλώνω [vathoulono] hollow out ‖ become hollow.

βάθρον, τό [vathron] (βάσις) basis, foundation ‖ (άγάλματος κτλ) pedestal ‖ (γεφύρας) pillar ‖ έκ βάθρων radically, entirely.

βαθύνους [vatheenous] sagacious, perspicacious.

βαθύνω [vatheeno] deepen, hollow out, become deeper.

βαθύπλουτος [vatheeploutos] opulent.

βαθύς [vathees] deep ‖ (σκότος κτλ) heavy, deep ‖ (ύπνος) sound ‖ (αίσθημα) profound ‖ (πνεύμα) penetrating, sagacious.

βαθύτης, ή [vatheetees] depth, profundity, deepness.

βαθύφωνος [vatheefonos] bass, deep-voiced.

βαίνω [veno] (βαδίζω) walk, go ‖ (στηρί-

ζομαι) rest on ‖ (μεταφ) be on the way, progress.

βάϊον, τό [vaeeon] palm branch.

βακαλάος, ό [vakalaos] cod.

βάκιλλος, ό [vakeelos] bacillus.

βακτηρία, ή [vakteereea] walking stick ‖ (δεκανίκι) crutch.

βακτηρίδιον, τό [vakteereedeeon] bacillus.

βαλανίδι, τό [valaneedee] acorn ‖ βαλανιδιά oak tree.

βάλανος, ό [valanos] acorn.

βαλάντιον, τό [valanteeon] purse.

βαλβίς, ή [valvees] valve.

βαλές, ό [vales] knave (in cards).

βαλίτσα, ή [valeetsa] suitcase, (hand)bag.

βαλκάνια, τά [valkaneea] πλ the Balkans.

βάλλω [valo] fire, shoot, hurl ‖ (μεταφ) launch an attack.

βάλς, τό [vals] waltz.

βάλσαμον, τό [valsamon] balsam, balm ‖ (μεταφ) consolation.

βαλσαμώνω [valsamono] embalm ‖ (μεταφ) console, comfort.

βάλσιμο, τό [valseemo] placing, setting, laying.

βάλτος, ό [valtos] marsh, fen, bog.

βαλτός [valtos] instigated, planted.

βαμβακερός [vamvakeros] of cotton.

βαμβάκι, τό [vamvakee] cotton.

βάμβαξ, ό [vamvaks] cotton.

βάμμα, τό [vamma] tincture, dye.

βαμμένος [vamenos] dyed, painted.

βανάνα, ή [vanana] βλ μπανάνα.

βάναυσος [vanavsos] rough, coarse, rude.

βάνδαλος, ό [vandalos] vandal.

βανίλ(λ)ια, ή [vaneeleea] vanilla.

βάνω [vano] βλ βάλλω.

βαπόρι, τό [vaporee] steamship.

βαπτίζω [vapteezo] baptize, christen ‖ dip, plunge.

βάπτισις, ή [vapteesees] βλ βάπτισμα.

βάπτισμα, τό [vapteesma] baptism, christening.

βαπτιστικός [vapteesteekos] baptismal ‖ (ούσ) godchild.

βάπτω [vapto] (χάλυψ) temper ‖ (μπογιά) paint ‖ (παπούτσια) polish.

βάραθρον, τό [varathron] abyss, gulf, chasm.

βαραίνω [vareno] weigh down, make heavier ‖ (κουράζω) weary ‖ (αίσθάνομαι βάρος) feel heavy ‖ (μεταφ) carry weight.

βαράω [varao] βλ βαρώ.

βαρβαρικός [varvareekos] barbaric.

βάρβαρος [varvaros] barbarous, brutal, savage.

βαρβάτος [varvatos] (άλογο) stallion ‖ (μεταφ) robust, vigorous.

βάρδια, ή [vardeea] watch, duty, shift.

βαρεία, ή [vareea] (γραμμ) grave accent.

βαρέλι, τό [varelee] barrel, cask.

βαρετός [varetos] annoying, boring, tedious.

βαρέως [vareos] badly, severely (φορ τωμένος) heavily.

βαρήκοος [vareekoos] hard of hearing.

βαριά, ή [varia] (σφυρί) hammer | (επιρ) seriously.

βαρίδι, τό [vareedee] (counter)weight.

βαριέμαι [varieme] be bored, be tired (of) | (δέν θέλω) not want (to) | δέν **βαριέσαι** never mind!, don't bother!

βάρκα, ή [varka] small boat, rowing boat, dinghy.

βαρκάρης, ό [varkarees] boatman.

βαρόμετρον, τό [varometron] barometer.

βάρος, τό [varos] weight, load, burden | εἰς ~ του at his expense.

βαροῦλκον, τό [varoulkon] winch, windlass.

βαρύθυμος [vareetheemos] sad, depressed.

βαρύνω [vareeno] weigh down, lie heavy | βλ καί **βαραίνω**.

βαρύς [varees] heavy (ποινή) severe, harsh | (σφάλμα) serious | (ὕπνος) deep, heavy | (ζυγός) oppressive | (εὐθύνη) grave | (ἄνθρωπος) slow, dull-witted.

βαρυσήμαντος [vareeseemantos] significant, grave, momentous.

βαρύτιμος [vareeteemos] precious, costly, valuable.

βαρύτονος [vareetonos] baritone (γραμμ) with a grave accent.

βαρύφωνος [vareefonos] deep-voiced, bass.

βαρῶ [varo] beat, hit, shoot | (σάλπιγγα) sound | (καμπάνα) toll.

βασανίζω [vasaneezo] torture, torment (ἕνα θέμα κτλ) examine thoroughly, go into | (τό μυαλό) rack.

βασανιστήριον, τό [vasaneesteereeon] torture rack, torture chamber.

βάσανο, τό [vasano] pain, trial, ordeal (μεταφ) nuisance.

βάσανος, ή [vasanos] torture scrutiny, proof.

βασίζω [vaseezo] base.

βασικός [vaseekos] primary, basic, fundamental.

βασιλεία, ή [vaseeleea] kingdom | reign.

βασίλειον, τό [vaseeleeon] kingdom.

βασιλεύς, ό [vaseelevs] king.

βασιλεύω [vaseelevo] reign, rule.

βασιλιᾶς, ό [vaseelias] βλ **βασιλεύς**.

βασιλική, ή [vaseeleekee] basilica.

βασιλικός [vaseeleekos] royal, royalist (οὐσ) basil.

βασίλισσα, ή [vaseeleesa] queen.

βασιλομήτωρ, ή [vaseelomeetor] queen mother.

βασιλόπηττα, ή [vaseelopeeta] New Year's cake.

βασιλόφρων [vaseelofron] royalist.

βάσιμος [vaseemos] sound, trustworthy.

βάσις, ή [vasees] base, foundation (βαθμῶν) pass mark.

βασκανία, ή [vaskaneea] evil eye

βαστάζω [vastazo] βλ **βαστῶ**.

βαστῶ [vasto] (φέρω) bear, hold, support | (συγκρατῶ) hold, control | (ὕφασμα κτλ) keep, wear | (κρατῶ) carry, hold.

βάτ(τ), τό [vat] watt.

βατόμουρο, τό [vatomouro] blackberry.

βάτος, ό [vatos] bush, bramble.

βατός [vatos] (δρόμος) passable | (ποτάμι) fordable | (ὕψωμα) accessible.

βάτραχος, ό [vatrahos] frog, toad.

βαυκαλίζω [vavkaleezo] lull to sleep (μεταφ) lull.

βαφή, ή [vafee] dyeing | shoe polish | dye.

βάφομαι [vafome] make up.

βαφτίσια, τά [vafteeseea] πλ christening.

βαφτισμιός, ό [vafteeseemios] godson.

βάφω [vafo] βλ **βάπτω**.

βάψιμο, τό [vapseemo] painting, make-up.

βγάζω [vyazo] take off, raise, draw out (ἐξαλείφω) get out, wash out | (λάδι, χυμό κτλ) press out of, squeeze | (πόδι, χέρι) dislocate | (καπνό κτλ) give off | (παράγω) produce | (χρήματα) make, earn | (βουλευτάς κτλ) elect | (διακρίνω) make out, read | (δίδω ὄνομα) name, call | (ἀποδεικνύω) prove | (ἀφαιρῶ) take from | (ἐφημερίδα κτλ) publish (περίπατο) take for a walk.

βγαίνω [vyeno] go out, come out, get out | (ἀνατέλλω) rise | (κυκλοφορῶ) be out | (ἐκλέγομαι) be elected | (ἐξαλείφομαι) fade, come out | (ἄγω) lead.

βγαλμένος [vyalmenos] taken off, removed.

βγάλσιμο, τό [vyalseemo] extraction removal | (κοκκάλου) dislocation.

βδέλλα, ή [vδella] leech.

βδέλυγμα, τό [vδeleeyma] abomination, detestable object

βδελυρός [vδeleeros] repugnant, loathsome.

βέβαιος [veveos] certain, sure, convinced.

βεβαιώνω [veveono] confirm, affirm, assure | certify.

βεβαίως [veveos] certainly, surely.

βεβαίωσις, ή [veveoses] confirmation (χαρτί) certificate.

βεβαρημένος [vevareemenos] marked (συνείδησις) heavy.

βέβηλος [veveelos] profane, sacrilegious, impious.

βεβιασμένος [veviasmenos] forced.

βεζίρης, ό [vezeerees] vizier.

βέης, ό [vayees] bey.

βελάζω [velazo] bleat.

βελανίδι, τό [velaneeδee] acorn.

βέλο, τό [velo] veil.

βελόνα, ή [velona] needle.

βελονιά, ή [velonia] stitch.

βέλος, τό [velos] arrow, dart.

βελοῦδο, τό [velouδo] velvet.

βέλτιστος [velteestos] the best.

βελτίων [velteeon] better.

βελτιώνω [velteeono] improve, better.

βελτίωσις, ή [velteeoses] improvement.

βενζινάκατος, ἡ [venzeenakatos] small motorboat.

βενζίνη, ἡ [venzeenee] petrol.

βεντάλια, ἡ [ventaleea] fan.

βεντέττα, ἡ [venteta] vendetta || (ἠθοποιός) star.

βεντούζα, ἡ [ventouza] cupping glass.

βέρα, ἡ [vera] wedding ring.

βεράντα, ἡ [veranta] veranda, porch.

βερβερίτσα, ἡ [ververeetza] squirrel.

βέργα, ἡ [verga] stick, rod, switch, twig.

βερεσέ [verese] on credit, on trust.

βερίκοκκο, τό [vereekoko] apricot.

βερμούτ, τό [vermout] vermouth.

βερνίκι, τό [verneekee] varnish, polish || (μεταφ) veneer.

βέρος [veros] genuine, true, real.

βέτο, τό [veto] veto.

βῆμα, τό [veema] step, pace || (βίδας) pitch, thread || (ἕλικος) twist || (ἕδρα) rostrum, tribune.

βηματίζω [veemateezo] step, pace, walk.

βῆτα, τό [veeta] the letter B.

βήχας, ὁ [veehas] cough.

βήχω [veeho] cough.

βία, ἡ [veea] force, violence || hurry || μετά ~ς with difficulty.

βιάζομαι [veeazome] be in haste, be rushed.

βιάζω [veeazo] force, compel || (παραβιάζω) break open || (παραβαίνω) violate || (ἀσελγῶ) rape, ravish.

βιαιοπραγία, ἡ [vieeoprayeea] bodily assault, outrage.

βίαιος [vieos] violent, forcible || fiery, passionate.

βιαιότητες [vieoteetěs] πλ acts of violence.

βιαίως [vieos] violently, forcibly.

βιασμός, ὁ [veeasmos] rape, violation.

βιαστής, ὁ [veeastees] ravisher.

βιαστικός [veeasteekos] urgent, pressing, hurried.

βιασύνη, ἡ [veeaseenee] haste, urgency.

βιβλιάριον, τό [veevleeareeon] booklet, card, bank-book.

βιβλικός [veevleekos] biblical.

βιβλιογραφία, ἡ [veevleeoyrafeea] bibliography.

βιβλιοδέτης, ὁ [veevleeodetees] bookbinder.

βιβλιοθηκάριος, ὁ [veevleeotheekareeos] librarian.

βιβλιοθήκη, ἡ [veevleeotheekee] bookcase || library.

βιβλιοκρισία, ἡ [veevleeokreeseea] book review.

βιβλίον, τό [veevleeon] book.

βιβλιοπώλης, ὁ [veevleeopolees] bookseller.

βίβλος, ἡ [veevlos] Bible.

βίγλα, ἡ [veeyla] lookout post, watch.

βίδα, ἡ [veeda] screw || (μεταφ) whim, caprice.

βιδέλο, τό [veedelo] calf || veal.

βιδολόγος, ὁ [veedoloyos] screwdriver, turn-screw.

βιδώνω [veedono] screw.

βίζα, ἡ [veeza] visa.

βίζιτα, ἡ [veezeeta] visit, call || visitor.

βίλλα, ἡ [veela] villa.

βιογραφία, ἡ [veeoyrafeea] biography.

βιολέττα, ἡ [veeoleta] violet.

βιολί, τό [veeolee] violin, fiddle || ἀλλάζω ~ change one's tune.

βιολιτζῆς, ὁ [veeoleetzees] fiddler, violinist

βιολόγος, ὁ [veeoloyos] biologist.

βιομηχανία, ἡ [veeomeehaneea] industry | manufacture.

βιομηχανικός [veeomeehaneekos] industrial.

βιοπαλαιστής, ὁ [veeopalestees] breadwinner, toiler.

βιοπάλη, ἡ [veeopalee] working hard to make a living.

βίος, ὁ [veeos] life || διά βίου for life.

βιός, τό [veeos] wealth, property.

βιοτεχνία, ἡ [veeotehneea] handicraft.

βιοχημεία, ἡ [veeoheemeea] biochemistry

βιταμίνη, ἡ [veetameenee] vitamin.

βιτρίνα, ἡ [veetreena] shop window, showcase.

βίτσιο, τό [veetseeo] bad habit.

βιώσιμος [veeoseemos] viable, feasible.

βλαβερός [vlaveros] harmful || (ἔντομον) noxious || (ἐνέργεια) injurious.

βλάβη, ἡ [vlavee] harm, damage || (μηχανῆς) motor trouble, breakdown.

βλάκας, ὁ [vlakas] βλ βλάξ.

βλακεία, ἡ [vlakeea] nonsense, silliness.

βλακώδης [vlakodees] stupid, silly.

βλάξ, ὁ, ἡ [vlaks] blockhead, fool, idiot.

βλάπτω [vlapto] harm, injure, damage.

βλαστάρι, τό [vlastaree] sprout, bud | (οἰκογενείας) scion.

βλάστησις, ἡ [vlasteesees] sprouting | (φυτεία) vegetation.

βλαστός, ὁ [vlastos] shoot, sprout || (μεταφ) scion, offspring.

βλασφημία, ἡ [vlasfeemeea] blasphemy curse.

βλασφημῶ [vlasfeemo] curse, revile.

βλάφτω [vlafto] βλ βλάπτω.

βλάχος, ὁ [vlahos] (μεταφ) rustic fellow boor.

βλέμμα, τό [vlemma] look, glance, eye.

βλεννόρροια, ἡ [vlenoreea] gonorrhoea.

βλέπω [vlepo] see, look at || (ἐπί ἀψύχων) face, command.

βλεφαρίς, ἡ [vlefarees] eyelash.

βλέφαρον, τό [vlefaron] eyelid.

βλέψις, ἡ [vlepses] aim, purpose || πλ aspirations, designs, intentions.

βλῆμα, τό [vleema] projectile.

βλητική, ἡ [vleeteekee] ballistics.

βλογιά, ἡ [vloyia] smallpox.

βλοσυρός [vloseeros] fierce, stern, grim.

βόας, ὁ [voas] boa.

βογγητό, τό [vongeeto] groan, moan.

βογγῶ [vongo] moan, groan || roar.

βόδι, τό [vodee] ox.
βοδινό, τό [vodeeno] beef.
βοή, ή [voee] shout, cry, humming, roaring ‖ (όχλου) clamour.
βοήθεια, ή [voeetheea] help, aid, assistance.
βοήθημα, τό [voeetheema] help, assistance, relief.
βοηθητικός [voeetheeteekos] auxiliary ‖ (άνεμος) favourable, fair.
βοηθός, ό [voeethos] assistant, helper, collaborator.
βοηθώ [voeetho] help, aid, relieve, give a hand.
βόθρος, ό [vothros] cesspool, ditch.
βολά, ή [vola] (upon a) time.
βολάν, τό [volan] steering wheel, driving wheel.
βολβός, ό [volvos] bulb, kind of onion ‖ (ματιού) eyeball.
βολετός [voletos] possible, convenient.
βολεύομαι [volevome] get comfortable ‖ get fixed up.
βολεύω [volevo] accommodate, fit in, suit ‖ τά ~ get along, do well.
βολή, ή [volee] throw, blow, stroke, shot ‖ (άπόστασις) range.
βόλι, τό [volee] ball, bullet.
βολιδοσκοπώ [voleedoskopo] sound.
βολικός [voleekos] convenient, easy, handy.
βολίς, ή [volees] sounding lead ‖ (άστρον) meteor ‖ (σφαίρα) bullet, ball.
βόλτα, ή [volta] walk ‖ (στροφή) revolution ‖ (κοχλίου) thread ‖ κόβω βόλτες I stroll about.
βόμβα, ή [vomva] bomb.
βομβαρδίζω [vomvardeezo] bomb, bombard ‖ (μεταφ) assail.
βομβαρδισμός, ό [vomvardeesmos] bombing.
βομβαρδιστικόν, τό [vomvardeesteekon] (άερο) bomber.
βόμβος, ό [vomvos] hum, buzz, buzzing noise.
βόμβυξ, ό [vomveeks] silkworm.
βομβώ [vomvo] buzz, hum.
βορά, ή [vora] prey ‖ (μεταφ) food.
βόρβορος, ό [vorvoros] mire, mud, dirt.
βορειοανατολικός [voreeoanatoleekos] north-east(ern).
βορειοδυτικός [voreeodeeteekos] north-west(ern).
βόρειος [voreeos] north(ern).
βορείως [voreeos] northwards, to the north, on the north.
βοριάς, ό [vorias] βλ βορράς.
βορράς, ό [vorras] north (wind).
βοσκή, ή [voskee] pasture, pasturage.
βοσκοπούλα, ή [voskopoula] shepherdess.
βοσκός, ό [voskos] shepherd.
βοσκοτόπι, τό [voskotopee] pasture land.
βόσκω [vosko] graze ‖ (μεταφ) drift.
βόστρυχος, ό [vostreehos] curl, lock of hair.
βοτάνι, τό [votanee] plant, herb.

βοτανικός [votaneekos] botanic(al).
βότανο, τό [votano] herb, plant.
βοτανολόγος, ό [votanologos] botanist.
βότρυς, ό [votrees] bunch of grapes.
βότσαλο, τό [votsalo] pebble.
βουβαίνω [vouveno] make mute.
βουβάλι, τό [vouvalee] buffalo.
βουβός [vouvos] dumb, mute.
βουβών, ό [vouvon] groin.
βουδδιστής, ό [voudeestees] Buddhist.
βουερός [voueros] noisy.
βουή [vouee] βλ βοή.
βουΐζω [voueezo] buzz, hum.
βουκόλος, ό [voukolos] cowherd, herdsman.
βούλευμα, τό [voulevma] decision, ordinance, decree.
βουλεύομαι [voulevome] deliberate.
βουλευτήριον, τό [voulevteereeon] parliament, chamber (of deputies).
βουλευτής, ό [voulevtees] member of parliament, deputy.
βουλή, ή [voulee] parliament, chamber ‖ (θέλησις) will, volition.
βούλησις, ή [vouleesees] desire, will ‖ κατά βούλησιν at will.
βούλιαγμα, τό [vouleeagma] sinking, submergence ‖ collapse.
βουλιάζω [vouleeazo] sink ‖ (μεταφ) ruin, be ruined.
βουλιμία, ή [vouleemeea] insatiable appetite.
βοϋλλα, ή [voula] seal, stamp.
βουλλοκέρι, τό [voulokeree] sealing wax.
βούλλωμα, τό [vouloma] sealing, stamping ‖ (τό άντικείμενον) cork, stopper.
βουλλώνω [voulono] seal ‖ (πωματίζω) stop, choke up, fill.
βούλομαι [voulome] will, wish, intend.
βουνήσιος [vouneeseeos] mountainous ‖ (ούσ) highlander.
βουνό, τό [vouno] mountain.
βουρδουλάς, ό [vourdoulas] whip, lash.
βούρκος, ό [vourkos] mud, mire ‖ (μεταφ) mire, gutter.
βουρκώνω [vourkono] fill with tears ‖ (ό ούρανός) become overcast.
βοϋρλο, τό [vourlo] (bul)rush.
βούρτσα, ή [vourtsa] (hair)brush ‖ (ρούχων) clothes brush ‖ (όδόντων) toothbrush.
βουρτσίζω [vourtseezo] brush, brush down.
βοϋς, ό [vous] ox, bullock.
βουστάσιον, τό [voustaseeon] ox stall, cowshed.
βούτηγμα, τό [vouteegma] plunging, dipping ‖ (μεταφ) plundering, stealing.
βούτημα, τό [vouteema] hard biscuit.
βουτηχτής, ό [vouteehtees] diver ‖ (μεταφ) thief.
βουτιά, ή [voutia] dive ‖ (μεταφ) snatching, stealing.
βουτσί, τό [voutsee] cask, barrel.
βούτυρο, τό [vouteero] butter.

βουτῶ [vouto] plunge, dip ‖ (κλέβω) steal, snatch.

βοῶ [voo] yell, cry out.

βραβεῖον, τό [vraveeon] prize.

βραβεύω [vravevo] award, reward.

βράγχια, τά [vrangheea] πλ gills ‖ (ἰατρ) branchiae.

βραδέως [vradeos] slowly, gradually.

βραδιά, ἡ [vradia] evening.

βραδιάζω [vradeeazo]: βραδιάζει it's getting dark.

βραδινός [vradeenos] evening.

βράδυ, τό [vradee] evening.

βραδύνω [vradeeno] be late, be slow.

βραδύς [vradees] slow, sluggish, tardy.

βραδύτης, ἡ [vradeetees] slowness, tardiness.

βράζω [vrazo] boil, ferment, seethe.

βράκα, ἡ [vraka] large breeches.

βρακί, τό [vrakee] trousers ‖ underpants.

βράσιμο, τό [vraseemo] boiling, fermentation.

βράσις, ἡ [vrasees] boiling ‖ (μούστου κτλ) fermentation.

βρασμός, ὁ [vrasmos] boiling ‖ (μεταφ) agitation, excitement.

βραστός [vrastos] boiled ‖ boiling, hot.

βραχιόλι, τό [vraheeolee] bracelet.

βραχίων, ὁ [vraheeon] arm, forearm ‖ branch.

βραχνάδα, ἡ [vrahnaδa] hoarseness.

βραχνᾶς, ὁ [vrahnas] nightmare.

βραχνιάζω [vrahneeazo] become hoarse.

βραχνός [vrahnos] hoarse.

βράχος, ὁ [vrahos] rock.

βραχυκύκλωμα, τό [vraheekeekloma] short circuit.

βραχύνω [vraheeno] shorten ‖ (βῆμα) slow down.

βραχυπρόθεσμος [vraheeprothesmos] short-dated ‖ short-termed.

βραχύτης, ἡ [vraheetees] shortness, brevity, conciseness.

βραχώδης [vrahoδees] rocky.

βρέ [vre] (ἐπιφ) you there!, hey, you!

βρεγμένος [vreymenos] wet, moist.

βρέξιμο, τό [vrekseemo] wetting, watering, moistening.

βρεφοκομεῖον, τό [vrefokomeeon] foundling hospital, public nursery.

βρέφος, τό [vrefos] baby, infant.

βρέχω [vreho] water, wet, dampen, rain.

βρίζω [vreezo] abuse, swear at, insult ‖ outrage.

βρίθω [vreetho] teem with, swarm with.

βρισιά, ἡ [vreesia] abuse, insult, outrage.

βρισίδι, τό [vreeseeδee] stream of abuse.

βρίσκομαι [vreeskome] be, find o.s.

βρίσκω [vreesko] find ‖ (τυχαίως) come across, discover ‖ (σκέπτομαι) think, deem ‖ (παίρνω) get, procure ‖ (μαντεύω) guess.

βρογχῖτις, ἡ [vrongheetees] bronchitis.

βροντερός [vronteros] thundering, noisy.

βροντή, ἡ [vrontee] thunder.

βρόντος, ὁ [vrontos] noise, roar ‖ heavy fall ‖ στὸ βρόντο in vain.

βροντῶ [vronto] (μεταφ) knock, make a noise.

βροντώδης [vrontoδees] thundering, loud.

βροχερός [vroheros] wet, rainy.

βροχή, ἡ [vrohee] rain ‖ ~ ψιλή drizzle.

βρόχι, τό [vrohee] net, snare.

βρόχος, ὁ [vrohos] noose, loop, lasso.

βρυκόλακας, ὁ [vreekolakas] vampire, ghost.

βρύον, τό [vreeon] moss ‖ seaweed.

βρύση, ἡ [vreesee] fountain, spring ‖ (μεταλλική) tap.

βρυχῶμαι [vreehome] roar, bellow.

βρύω [vreeo] teem with.

βρῶμα, ἡ [vroma] filth, stink ‖ (γιά πρόσωπο) hussy, bitch, slut.

βρωμερός [vromeros] stinky, smelly ‖ (ὑπόθεσις) nasty, odious, vile ‖ (ἄτομον) stinking, dirty, slovenly.

βρώμη, ἡ [vromee] oats.

βρωμιά, ἡ [vromia] filth, dirt ‖ (μεταφ) nasty business, corruption.

βρωμίζω [vromeezo] stink, dirty, sully.

βρώμικος [vromeekos] dirty, grubby ‖ (μεταφ) nasty, odious, vile.

βρωμῶ [vromo] give off a stench, smell badly, stink.

βύζαγμα, τό [veezayma] nursing, lactation ‖ sucking.

βυζαίνω [veezeno] suckle ‖ (μεταφ) suck.

βυζαντινός [veezanteenos] Byzantine.

βυζί, τό [veezee] breast.

βυθίζω [veetheezo] sink, plunge, dip.

βύθισις, ἡ [veetheesees] sinking, submersion.

βύθισμα, τό [veetheesma] (ναυτ) draught ‖ sinking.

βυθοκόρος, ἡ [veethokoros] dredger, dredge.

βυθός, ὁ [veethos] bottom of the sea.

βυρσοδεψεῖον, τό [veersoδepseeon] tannery.

βύσσινο, τό [veeseeno] sour cherry.

βυτίον, τό [veeteeon] cask, barrel.

βωβός [vovos] dumb, mute, silent.

βωλοκοπῶ [volokopo] harrow.

βῶλος, ὁ [volos] clod ‖ βῶλοι πλ marbles.

βωμολοχία, ἡ [vomoloheea] obscenity scurrility.

βωμός, ὁ [vomos] altar.

βώτριδα, ἡ [votreeδa] moth.

Γ, γ

γαβάθα, ἡ [yavatha] earthenware vessel ‖ wooden bowl.

γάγγλιον, τό [yangleeon] ganglion.

γάγγραινα, ἡ [yangrena] gangrene ‖ (μεταφ) canker.

γάδος, ὁ [yados] cod(fish).
γάζα, ἡ [yaza] gauze.
γαζί, τό [yazee] stitch ‖ (τῆς χειρός) hand-stitch ‖ (τῆς μηχανῆς) machine-stitch.
γάζωμα, τό [yazoma] stitching.
γαῖα, ἡ [yea] earth, land.
γαιανθρακωρυχεῖον, τό [yeanthrakoree-heeon] coalmine, coalpit.
γαιάνθραξ, ὁ [yeanthraks] coal.
γάϊδαρος, ὁ [yaeedaros] ass, donkey ‖ (μεταφ) boor, ass.
γαϊδουράγκαθο, τό [yaeedourangatho] thistle.
γαϊδουριά, ἡ [yaeedouria] rudeness.
γαιοκτήμων, ὁ [yeokteemon] landowner.
γάλα, τό [yala] milk.
γαλάζιος [yalazeeos] azure, blue.
γαλαζοαίματος [yalazoematos] blue-blooded.
γαλαζόπετρα, ἡ [yalazopetra] turquoise.
γαλακτερός [yalakteros] milky, of milk.
γαλακτικός [yalakteekos] lactic.
γαλακτοκομεῖον, τό [yalaktokomeeon] dairy farm.
γαλακτοπωλεῖον, τό [yalaktopoleeon] dairy.
γαλακτοπώλης, ὁ [yalaktopolees] milkman.
γαλακτώδης [yalaktodees] milky, milk-white.
γαλάκτωμα, τό [yalaktoma] emulsion.
γαλανόλευκος, ἡ [yalanolevkos] the Greek flag.
γαλανομμάτης [yalanomatees] blue-eyed.
γαλανός [yalanos] blue.
Γαλαξίας, ὁ [yalakseeas] Milky Way.
γαλαρία, ἡ [yalareea] gallery.
γαλατᾶς, ὁ [yalatas] milkman.
γαλβανίζω [yalvaneezo] galvanize ‖ (μεταφ) electrify, rouse, stimulate.
γαλέρα, ἡ [yalera] galley.
γαλέττα, ἡ [yaleta] hard tack.
γαληνεύω [yaleenevo] calm, quieten down.
γαλήνη, ἡ [yaleenee] calm, peace, serenity.
γαλήνιος [yaleeneeos] calm, composed, serene.
γαληνός [yaleenos] βλ γαλήνιος.
γαλιφίζω [yaleefeezo] flatter, fawn.
Γαλλία, ἡ [yaleea] France.
γαλλικός [yaleekos] French.
γαλλοπούλα, ἡ [yalopoula] turkey hen.
Γάλλος, ὁ [yalos] Frenchman.
γαλόνι, τό [yalonee] (μέτρον) gallon ‖ (στρατ) stripe, pip.
γαλούχημα, τό [yalouheema] suckling ‖ (μεταφ) education, upbringing.
γαλουχῶ [yalooho] suckle, nurse ‖ (μεταφ) bring up.
γάμα, τό [yama] the letter Γ.
γαμβρός, ὁ [yamvros] bridegroom ‖ son-in-law ‖ brother-in-law.
γαμήλιος [yameeleeos] nuptial, bridal ‖ γαμήλιον ταξίδι honeymoon.
γάμπα, ἡ [yamba] calf, leg.

γαμψός [yampsos] hooked, crooked
γάντζος, ὁ [yantzos] hook, grapple
γαντζώνω [yantzono] hook.
γάντι, τό [yantee] glove.
γανώνω [yanono] tin, pewter.
γαργαλίζω [yaryalizo] tickle ‖ (μεταφ) tempt, allure.
γαργάρα, ἡ [yaryara] gargle.
γαργαρίζω [yaryareezo] gargle.
γαρδένια, ἡ [yardeneea] gardenia.
γαρίδα, ἡ [yareeda] shrimp, prawn.
γαρνίρισμα, τό [yarneereesma] adornment, garnishing, decoration.
γαρνίρω [yarniro] garnish, trim.
γαρνιτούρα, ἡ [yarneetoura] garniture, trimming.
γαρυφαλιά, ἡ [yareefalia] carnation ‖ (μπαχαρικοῦ) clove tree.
γαρύφαλλο, τό [yareefalo] carnation ‖ (μπαχαρικό) clove.
γαστήρ, ἡ [yasteer] belly.
γαστραλγία, ἡ [yastralyeea] stomach ache
γαστρικός [yastreekos] gastric.
γαστρῖτις, ἡ [yastreetees] gastritis.
γαστροεντερικός [yastroentereekos] gastro-intestinal.
γαστρονομία, ἡ [yastronomeea] gastron-omy.
γάτα, ἡ [yata] cat.
γαυγίζω [yavyeezo] bark.
γαύγισμα, τό [yavyeesma] barking, baying.
γδάρσιμο, τό [ydarseemo] (πρᾶξις) flaying ‖ (ἀποτέλεσμα) scratch.
γδέρνω [yderno] flay, skin ‖ (μεταφ) fleece
γδύνομαι [ydeenome] get undressed, strip
γδύνω [ydeeno] undress ‖ (μεταφ) rob.
γεγονός, τό [yeyonos] event, fact.
γειά, ἡ [yia] health ‖ ~ σας hello ‖ so long, goodbye.
γεῖσον, τό [yeeson] (ἀρχιτεκ) eaves ‖ cornice ‖ (κασκέτου) peak.
γειτνιάζω [yeetneeazo] βλ γειτονεύω.
γειτονεύω [yeetonevo] be close to, be adjoining.
γειτονιά, ἡ [yeetonia] neighbourhood, vicinity.
γέλασμα, τό [yelasma] (ἀπάτη) deceit ‖ laughing stock.
γελαστός [yelastos] smiling, pleasant, cheerful.
γελάω [yelao] βλ γελῶ.
γελέκι, τό [yelekee] waistcoat.
γελιέμαι [yelieme] be deceived, be mistaken
γέλιο, τό [yeleeo] laugh, laughter.
γελοιογραφία, ἡ [yeleeoyrafeea] caricature, cartoon.
γελοιοποίησις, ἡ [yeleeopieesees] ridicule, derision.
γελοιοποιοῦμαι [yeleeopeeoume] make o.s. ridiculous.
γελοιοποιῶ [yeleeopeeo] make ridiculous, ridicule.
γελοῖος [yeleeos] ludicrous, ridiculous.

γελῶ [yelo] laugh ‖ (μάτια κτλ) smile, twinkle ‖ (ἐξαπατῶ) deceive, take in.

γέλως, ὁ [yelos] βλ γέλιο.

γεμᾶτος [yematos] full ‖ (δρόμος κτλ) crowded, swarming ‖ (ὅπλο, δένδρο κτλ) loaded ‖ (δωμάτιος κτλ) packed, crammed ‖ (παχύς) stout, plump.

γεμίζω [yemeezo] fill up ‖ (πλοῖο) load ‖ (μαξιλάρι κτλ) stuff ‖ (συμπληρώνω) fill out.

γέμισμα, τό [yemeesma] filling ‖ (στρώματος) stuffing ‖ (φεγγαριοῦ) waxing ‖ (ὅπλου) charging, loading.

γεμιστός [yemeestos] stuffed.

γέμω [yemo] be full (of), abound.

γενάκι, τό [yenaki] small beard.

Γενάρης [yenarees] βλ Γεννάρης.

γενεά, ἡ [yenea] race, generation, breed.

γενεαλογία, ἡ [yenealoyeea] genealogy, lineage, pedigree.

γενέθλια, τά [yenethleea] πλ birthday, anniversary.

γενειάς, ἡ [yenias] beard.

γενειοφόρος, ὁ [yeneeoforos] bearded.

γενεσιουργία, ἡ [yeneseeouryeea] creation.

γένεσις, ἡ [yeneses] origin, birth ‖ (ἐκκλ) Genesis.

γενέτειρα, ἡ [yeneteera] native country, birthplace.

γενετή, ἡ [yenetee]: ἐκ ~ς from birth.

γενετήσιος [yeneteeseeos] productive, generative, sexual.

γενίκευσις, ἡ [yeneekevsees] generalization.

γενικεύω [yeneekevo] generalize.

γενική [yeneekee] general, universal, wide ‖ (γραμμ) genitive (case) ‖ βλ καί γενικός.

γενικός [yeneekos] general ‖ βλ καί γενική.

γενικότης, ἡ [yeneekotees] generality.

γέννα, ἡ [yenna] birth, childbirth ‖ (μεταφ) breed.

γενναιοδωρία, ἡ [yenneodoreea] generosity.

γενναιόδωρος [yenneodoros] generous, magnanimous.

γενναῖος [yenneos] courageous, brave.

γενναιότης, ἡ [yenneotees] courage, bravery.

γενναίως [yenneos] bravely.

γενναιοφροσύνη, ἡ [yenneofroseenee] generosity, liberality.

γενναιόφρων, ὁ [yenneofron] magnanimous, liberal.

γενναιόψυχος [yenneopsyhos] generous, brave.

Γεννάρης, ὁ [yennarees] January.

γέννημα, τό [yenneema] offspring, product ‖ (μωρό) progeny ‖ ~ τα cereals.

γέννησις, ἡ [yenneesees] birth.

γεννητικός [yenneeteekos] genital, sexual.

γεννήτρια, ἡ [yenneetrea] generator.

γεννήτωρ, ὁ [yenneetor] father.

γεννῶ [yenno] (γιά γυναῖκα) give birth to,

bring forth ‖ (γιά ἄλογα) drop a foal ‖ (γιά κουνέλια, γουρούνια) litter ‖ (γιά πτηνά) lay ‖ (μεταφ) create, breed, cause.

γεννῶμαι [yennome] be born.

γένος, τό [yenos] race, family, line ‖ τό ἀνθρώπινον ~ mankind ‖ (ζώων, φυτῶν) kind, species ‖ (γραμμ) gender.

γερά [yera] strongly, hard, vigorously.

γεράκι, τό [yerakee] hawk.

γεράματα, τά [yeramata] πλ old age.

γεράνιον, τό [yeraneeon] geranium.

γερανός, ὁ [yeranos] (πτηνό) crane ‖ (μηχάνημα) crane, winch.

γέρας, τό [yeras] prize, reward.

γερατειά [yeratia] βλ γεράματα.

Γερμανία, ἡ [yermaneea] Germany.

γερμανικός [yermaneekos] German.

Γερμανός, ὁ [yermanos] German.

γέρνω [yerno] lean, bend ‖ (γιά βάρκα κτλ) lean, tilt ‖ (γιά ἥλιο κτλ) go down, sink.

γερνῶ [yerno] βλ γηράσκω.

γεροντικός [yeronteekos] senile.

γεροντοκόρη, ἡ [yerontokoree] old maid, spinster.

γεροντοπαλήκαρο, τό [yerontopaleekaro] old bachelor.

γέρος, ὁ [yeros] old man.

γερός [yeros] (ἄνθρωπος) vigorous, sturdy ‖ (κρᾶσις) sound, healthy ‖ (τροφή) solid, substantial, hearty ‖ (ξύλο) sound ‖ (πάτωμα) solid, firm ‖ (τοῖχος) strong ‖ (ἐπιχείρημα) strong, valid.

γερουσία, ἡ [yerousea] senate.

γερουσιαστής, ὁ [yerouseeastees] senator.

γέρων, ὁ [yeron] old man.

γεῦμα, τό [yevma] meal, dinner.

γεύομαι [yevome] taste, try.

γεῦσις, ἡ [yevsees] taste, flavour.

γέφυρα, ἡ [yeffera] bridge.

γεφυρώνω [yefeerono] bridge ‖ build a bridge.

γεωγραφία, ἡ [yeoyrafeea] geography.

γεωγραφικός [yeoyrafeekos] geographic.

γεωγράφος, ὁ [yeoyrafos] geographer.

γεωδαισία, ἡ [yeodeseea] geodesy.

γεώδης [yeodees] earthy.

γεωλογία, ἡ [yeoloyeea] geology.

γεωλόγος, ὁ [yeoloyos] geologist.

γεωμετρία, ἡ [yeometreea] geometry.

γεωμετρικός [yeometreekos] geometric(al).

γεώμηλον, τό [yeomeelon] potato.

γεωπονία, ἡ [yeoponeea] agriculture.

γεωργία, ἡ [yeoryeea] agriculture, farming.

γεωργικός [yeoryeekos] agricultural.

γεωργός, ὁ [yeoryos] farmer.

γεώτρησις, ἡ [yeotreesees] drilling.

γεωτρύπανον, τό [yeotreepanon] drill.

γῆ, ἡ [yee] earth, land, ground.

γηγενής [yeeyenees] native, indigenous.

γήινος [yeeinos] earthly, terrestrial.

γήλοφος, ὁ [yeelofos] hillock, mound.

γήπεδον, τό [yeepedon] ground, sports-ground.

γῆρας, τό [yeeras] old age.

γηράσκω [yeerasko] age, grow old.

γιά [yea] for, because of, on behalf of ‖ γι' αὐτό therefore ‖ ~ καλά for certain, for good ‖ ~ τήν ὥρα for the time being ‖ ~ ποῦ whither? ‖ ~ τό Θεό for God's sake ‖ (ἐπίρ) as, for ‖ (συνδ) ~ νά in order to ‖ ~ φαντάσου! fancy that! ‖ ~ πές μου tell me.

γιαγιά, ἡ [yeeayia] grandmother.

γιακᾶς, ὁ [yeeakas] collar.

γιαλός, ὁ [yeealos] seashore.

γιαούρτι, τό [yeeaourtee] yoghurt.

γιασεμί, τό [yeeasemee] jasmine.

γιατί [yeeatee] why? ‖ (συνδ) because.

γιατρεύω [yeeatrevo] cure, heal, treat.

γιατρός, ὁ [yeeatros] doctor.

γιαχνί, τό [yeeahnee] ragout.

γιγάντιος [yeeyanteeos] gigantic.

γιγαντομαχία, ἡ [yeeyantomaheea] battle of the giants.

γιγαντόσωμος [yeeyantosomos] huge (in size).

γίγας, ὁ [yeeyas] giant.

γιγνώσκω [yeeynosko] βλ γνωρίζω.

γίδα, ἡ [yeeδa] goat.

γιδοβοσκός, ὁ [yeeδovoskos] goatherd.

γιλέκο, τό [yeeleko] waistcoat.

γινάτι, τό [yeenatee] obstinacy, stubbornness ‖ spite.

γίνομαι [yeenome] be done, become ‖ (μεγαλώνω) grow ‖ (στρέφω) turn ‖ (γεγονός κτλ) happen, occur ‖ (ὡριμάζω) ripen ‖ ~καλά recover ‖ τί γίνεσαι; how are you?

γινόμενον, τό [yeenomenon] product.

γινώσκω [yeenosko] βλ γνωρίζω.

γιουβαρλάκια, τά [yeeouvarlakeea] πλ meatballs with rice.

γιοῦχα [yeeouha] boo.

γιουχαΐζω [yeeouhaeezo] hoot, jeer.

γιρλάντα, ἡ [yeerlanta] garland, wreath.

γιώτ, τό [yeeot] yacht.

γκαβός [ngavos] cross-eyed ‖ (κατ' ἐπέκτασιν) blind.

γκάζι, τό [ngazee] gas ‖ πατῶ ~ step on the gas.

γκαζιέρα, ἡ [ngaziera] cooking stove, primus stove.

γκαζόζα, ἡ [ngazoza] lemonade.

γκάιδα, ἡ [ngaeeδa] bagpipe.

γκαρίζω [ngareezo] bray.

γκαρσόν, τό [ngarson] waiter.

γκαρσονιέρα, ἡ [ngarsoniera] bachelor flat.

γκάφα, ἡ [ngafa] blunder.

γκέμι, τό [ngemee] bridle, reins.

γκέττα, ἡ [ngetta] gaiter, legging.

γκίνια, ἡ [ngeenea] bad luck.

γκιώνης, ὁ [ngeeonees] (scops) owl.

γκουβερνάντα, ἡ [ngouvernanta] governess.

γκρεμίζω [ngremeezo] βλ κρημνίζω.

γκρεμνός [ngremnos] βλ κρημνός.

γκρίζος [ngreezos] grey.

γκρίνια, ἡ [ngreeneea] grumble, murmur, nag.

γκρινιάζω [ngreeneeazo] complain, nag, grumble.

γλάρος, ὁ [ylaros] seagull.

γλάστρα, ἡ [ylastra] flowerpot.

γλαυκός [ylavkos] blue, azure.

γλαύκωμα, τό [ylavkoma] glaucoma.

γλαῦξ, ἡ [ylafks] owl.

γλαφυρός [ylafeeros] elegant, graceful.

γλαφυρότης, ἡ [ylafeerotees] smoothness, elegance.

γλείφω [yleefo] lick.

γλεντζές, ὁ [ylentzes] fun-loving person, reveller.

γλέντι, τό [ylentee] party, feast.

γλεντῶ [ylento] amuse ‖ (ἀπολαμβάνω) enjoy ‖ (ἐπί χρημάτων) squander.

γλεῦκος, τό [ylevkos] must.

γλιστερός [yleesteros] slippery.

γλίστρημα, τό [yleestreema] slide, slip ‖ (μεταφ) blunder, mistake.

γλιστρῶ [yleestro] slide, slip ‖ (μεταφ) slip away.

γλίσχρος [yleeshros] niggardly, paltry, meagre.

γλοιῶδες [yleeoδees] slimy, sticky ‖ (μεταφ) oily (person).

γλόμπος, ὁ [ylombos] globe.

γλουτός, ὁ [yloutos] buttock, rump.

γλύκα, ἡ [yleeka] sweetness.

γλυκά, τά [yleeka] πλ pastries, confectionery.

γλυκάδι, τό [yleekaδee] vinegar.

γλυκαίνω [yleekeno] sweeten, make mild, soften.

γλυκάνισον, τό [yleekaneeson] anise.

γλύκισμα, τό [yleekeesma] cake, pastry.

γλυκοκυττάζω [yleekokeetazo] look at tenderly.

γλυκομίλητος [yleekomeeleetos] soft-spoken, affable.

γλυκομιλῶ [yleekomeelo] speak tenderly, speak kindly.

γλυκόν, τό [yleekon] jam, sweetmeat.

γλυκόξινος [yleekokseenos] bitter-sweet.

γλυκοτραγουδῶ [yleekotrayouδo] sing sweetly.

γλυκοχάραγμα, τό [yleekoharayma] daybreak, twilight.

γλυκύς [yleekees] affable, sweet ‖ (καιρός) mild ‖ (φῶς) subdued, mellow ‖ (χρῶμα) delicate ‖ (ἦχος) soft, sweet ‖ (κρασί) sweet ‖ (ὄνειρα) pleasant.

γλύπτης, ὁ [yleeptees] sculptor.

γλυπτική, ἡ [yleepteekee] sculpture.

γλυπτός [yleeptos] sculptured, carved.

γλυτωμός, ὁ [yleetomos] deliverance, escape.

γλυτώνω [yleetono] save, deliver ‖ (ἀμεταβ) escape.

γλύφω [γleefo] βλ γλείφω.

γλῶσσα, ἡ [γlossa] tongue, language || (ψάρι) sole.

γλωσσᾶς, ὁ [γlossas] chatterbox, gossip.

γλωσσίδι, τό [γlosseeδee] tongue, clapper.

γλωσσικός [γlosseekos] lingual || linguistic.

γλωσσολογία, ἡ [γlossoloγeea] linguistics.

γλωσσολόγος, ὁ [γlossoloγos] linguist.

γλωσσομαθής [γlossomathees] polyglot, linguist.

γλωσσοτρώγω [γlossotroγo] backbite, slander.

γνάθος, ὁ [γnathos] jaw.

γνέθω [γnetho] spin.

γνήσιος [γneeseeos] genuine, real || (τέκνον) legitimate.

γνησίως [γneeseeos] genuinely, authentically.

γνωμάτευσις, ἡ [γnomatevsees] opinion, adjudication.

γνωματεύω [γnomatevo] express an opinion.

γνώμη, ἡ [γnomee] opinion, mind, view.

γνωμικόν, τό [γnomeekon] maxim, saying, adage.

γνωμοδότης, ὁ [γnomoδotees] adviser, councillor.

γνωμοδοτῶ [γnomoδoto] give one's opinion, judge.

γνώμων, ὁ [γnomon] set square, level || (μεταφ) criterion, model.

γνωρίζω [γnoreezo] let it be known, inform || (ἔχω γνῶσιν) know, be aware of || (ἀναγνωρίζω) discern, distinguish || (ἔχω σχέσεις) know, be acquainted with || (παρουσιάζω κάποιον) introduce.

γνωριμία, ἡ [γnoreemeea] acquaintance, familiarity.

γνώριμος [γnoreemos] known, intimate.

γνώρισμα, τό [γnoreesma] sign, mark, indication.

γνῶσις, ἡ [γnosees] knowledge, notion || πλ knowledge, learning.

γνώστης, ὁ [γnostees] expert, connoisseur, specialist.

γνωστικός [γnosteekos] prudent.

γνωστοποίησις, ἡ [γnostopieesees] notification, announcement.

γνωστοποιῶ [γnostopeeo] notify, inform, advise.

γνωστός [γnostos] known || (φίλος) acquaintance.

γογγύζω [γongeezo] groan, grumble, moan, complain.

γογγυσμός, ὁ [γongeesmos] grumbling, groan.

γογγύλη, ἡ [γongeelee] turnip.

γοερός [γoeros] plaintive, woeful.

γόης, ὁ [γoees] charmer.

γοητεία, ἡ [γoeeteea] charm attractiveness.

γοητευτικός [γoeetevteekos] charming, captivating.

γοητεύω [γoeetevo] charm, attract.

γόητρον, τό [γoeetron] prestige, reputation.

γομάρι, τό [γomaree] load || (μεταφ) simpleton, beast.

γόμμα, ἡ [γomma] gum || (σβυσήματος) indiarubber, eraser.

γόμφος, ὁ [γomfos] peg, bolt, pin || (κοκκάλων) joint.

γόμωσις, ἡ [γomosees] stuffing || (ὅπλου) charge.

γονατίζω [γonateezo] (make to) kneel || (μεταφ) humble || (ἀμεταβ) kneel down || (μεταφ) give way, yield.

γονατιστά [γonateesta] on the knees, kneeling.

γόνατο, τό [γonato] knee.

γονεύς, ὁ [γonevs] father || πλ parents.

γονιμοποίησις, ἡ [γoneemopieesees] fertilization, impregnation.

γονιμοποιῶ [γoneemopeeo] fecundate, fertilize.

γόνιμος [γoneemos] fertile, prolific || (μεταφ) inventive.

γονιμότης, ἡ [γoneemotees] fecundity, fertility.

γονίμως [γoneemos] fruitfully, productively.

γόνος, ὁ [γonos] child, offspring || (σπέρμα) sperm, seed.

γόνυ, τό [γonee] knee.

γόπα, ἡ [γopa] bogue (fish).

γοργός [γorγos] rapid, quick.

γοργότης, ἡ [γorγotees] quickness, promptness.

γορίλλας, ὁ [γoreelas] gorilla.

γούβα, ἡ [γouva] cavity, hole.

γουδί, τό [γouδee] mortar.

γουδοχέρι, τό [γuδoheree] pestle.

γουλί, τό [γoulee] stalk, stump || (μεταφ) bald.

γουλιά, ἡ [γoulia] mouthful, drop.

γούμενα, ἡ [γoumena] cable.

γούνα, ἡ [γouna] fur.

γουναρικόν, τό [γounareekon] fur.

γουργουρητό, τό [γourγoureeto] rumbling, rumble.

γούρι, τό [γouree] good luck.

γουρλομάτης, ὁ [γourlomatees] person with bulging eyes, goggle-eyed person.

γουρλώνω [γourlono] open wide, goggle.

γουρούνα, ἡ [γourouna] sow, piglet.

γουρούνι, τό [γourounee] pig, hog.

γουρσούζης, ὁ [γoursouzees] luckless person, unlucky person.

γουρσουζιά, ἡ [γoursoozia] bad luck.

γουστάρω [γoustaro] desire, feel like || (εὐχαριστοῦμαι) delight in, enjoy.

γουστέρα, ἡ [γoustera] lizard.

γοῦστο, τό [γousto] taste || (φιλοκαλία) good taste || γιά ~ for the hell of it.

γοφός, ὁ [γofos] haunch, hip.

γραῖα, ἡ [γrea] old woman.

γραῖγος, ὁ [γreγos] north-east (wind).

Γραικός, ὁ [yrekos] Greek.

γράμμα, τό [yramma] letter, character.

γραμμάριον, τό [yrammareeon] gram(me).

γραμματεία, ἡ [yrammateea] secretariat, secretary's office.

γραμματεύς, ὁ [yrammatevs] secretary.

γραμματική, ἡ [yrammateekee] grammar.

γραμματικῶς [yrammateekos] grammatically.

γραμμάτιον, τό [yrammateeon] bill of exchange ‖ (χρεωστικόν) promissory note.

γραμματισμένος [yrammateesmenos] well-read, learned.

γραμματοκιβώτιον, τό [yrammatokeevoteeon] letterbox, postbox.

γραμματολογία, ἡ [yrammatoloyeea] literature.

γραμματόσημον, τό [yrammatoseemon] (postage) stamp.

γραμμένος [yrammenos] written ‖ (μεταφ) destined.

γραμμή, ἡ [yrammee] line, row ‖ (ἐπιρ) straight, in a row ‖ πρώτης ~ς first-class.

γραμμικός [yrameekos] linear.

γραμμόφωνον, τό [yrammofonon] gramophone.

γραμμωτός [yrammotos] lined, ruled ‖ (ὕφασμα) striped.

γρανίτης, ὁ [yraneetees] granite.

γραπτός [yraptos] written.

γραπτῶς [yraptos] in writing.

γραπώνω [yrapono] seize, snatch.

γρασίδι, τό [yraseedee] grass.

γρατσουνίζω [yratsouneezo] scratch.

γρατσούνισμα, τό [yratsouneesma] scratch.

γραφειοκράτης, ὁ [yrafeeokratees] bureaucrat.

γραφειοκρατία, ἡ [yrafeeokrateea] bureaucracy.

γραφεῖον, τό [yrafeeon] desk, bureau ‖ (δωμάτιον) study ‖ (ἴδρυμα) office, bureau.

γραφεύς, ὁ [yrafevs] clerk, copyist.

γραφικός [yrafeekos] of writing, clerical ‖ (μεταφ) picturesque, colourful.

γραφικότης, ἡ [yrafeekotees] picturesqueness, vividness.

γραφίς, ἡ [yrafees] nib, pen.

γραφίτης, ὁ [yrafeetees] graphite.

γραφομηχανή, ἡ [yrafomeehanee] typewriter.

γράφω [yrafo] write, record, compose ‖ enrol.

γράψιμο, τό [yrapseemo] writing.

γρήγορα [yreeyora] quickly, promptly.

γρηγορῶ [yreeyoro] watch, be alert ‖ be awake.

γρίλλια, ἡ [yreeleea] grille.

γρῖπος, ὁ [yreepos] dragnet.

γρίππη, ἡ [yreepee] influenza.

γρῖφος, ὁ [yreefos] riddle, puzzle, enigma.

γριφώδης [yreefodees] enigmatic(al), obscure.

γρονθοκόπημα, τό [yronthokopeema] boxing, punch.

γρονθοκοπῶ [yronthokopo] punch, pound on.

γρόνθος, ὁ [yronthos] fist ‖ punch.

γρουσούζης [yroosoozees] βλ γουρσούζης.

γρῦ [yree] not a word ‖ absolutely nothing.

γρυλισμός, ὁ [yreeleesmos] grunting, snorting.

γρυλλίζω [yreeleezo] grunt, squeal.

γρύλλος, ὁ [yreelos] piglet ‖ (ἔντομον) cricket ‖ (μηχάνημα) jack.

γρυπός [yreepos] hooked, crooked.

γρύψ, ὁ [yreeps] griffin.

γυάλα, ἡ [yeeala] glass, jar ‖ (ψαριῶν) bowl.

γυαλάδα, ἡ [yeealaδa] brilliance, shine, gloss.

γυαλάδικο, τό [yeealaδeeko] glassware ‖ glass works.

γυαλένιος [yeealeneeos] glass.

γυαλί, τό [yeealee] glass ‖ πλ spectacles, glasses.

γυαλίζω [yeealeezo] polish, shine.

γυάλισμα, τό [yeealeesma] polishing, glazing.

γυαλιστερός [yeealeesteros] polished, glossy.

γυαλόχαρτον, τό [yeealoharton] glasspaper, sandpaper.

γυιός, ὁ [yeeos] son.

γυλιός, ὁ [yeeleeos] knapsack ‖ (ἐργάτου) toolbag.

γυμνάζομαι [yeemnazome] train o.s., exercise, practise.

γυμνάζω [yeemnazo] exercise, train, drill.

γυμνασιάρχης, ὁ [yeemnaseearhees] director of a secondary school, headmaster.

γυμνάσια, τά [yeemnaseea] πλ manoeuvres.

γυμνάσιον, τό [yeemnaseeon] secondary school, high school.

γύμνασις, ἡ [yeemnasees] exercise, training.

γύμνασμα, τό [yeemnasma] exercise, task, theme.

γυμναστήριον, τό [yeemnasteereeon] gymnasium.

γυμναστής, ὁ [yeemnastees] P.T. instructor

γυμναστική, ἡ [yeemnasteekee] πλ gymnastics ‖ exercise.

γύμνια, ἡ [yeemneea] nudity, nakedness ‖ poverty.

γυμνιστής, ὁ [yeemneestees] nudist.

γυμνός [yeemnos] naked, bare, nude.

γυμνώνω [yeemnono] bare, expose ‖ (μεταφ) strip.

γύμνωσις, ἡ [yeemnosees] disrobing ‖ denudation ‖ fleecing.

γυναῖκα, ἡ [yeeneka] woman ‖ (σύζυγος) wife.

γυναικαδέλφη, ἡ [yeenekaδelfee] sister-in-law.

γυναικάδελφος, ὁ [yeenekaδelfos] brother-in-law.

γυναικάρα, ἡ [yeenekara] virago.

γυναικᾶς, ὁ [yeenekas] woman-chaser, rake.

γυναικείος [yeenekeeos] womanly, feminine.

γυναικολογία, ἡ [yeenekoloyeea] gynaecology.

γυναικολόγος, ὁ [yeenekoloyos] gynaecologist.

γυναικόπαιδα, τά [yeenekopeda] πλ women and children.

γυναικοπρεπής [yeenekoprepees] womanly, effeminate, womanish.

γυναικωνίτης, ὁ [yeenekoneetees] harem.

γυνή [yeenee] βλ γυναῖκα.

γυρεύω [yeerevo] ask for, call for || (ἐλεημοσύνη) beg for || (νά εὕρω κάτι) look for, seek || (ἀποζημίωσι κτλ) claim || (διαζύγιο) apply for || (βοήθεια) request.

γυρίζω [yeereezo] turn, rotate, revolve || (σβοῦρα) spin || (στρέφω) turn || (ἀναστρέφω) turn || (ἐπιστρέφω) return || (ἁμετάβ) turn, rotate || (ταινία) shoot || (ὁ ἥλιος) sink.

γύρισμα, τό [yeereesma] turn, revolution || (δρόμου, ποταμοῦ) turn, twist, winding || (ἐπιστροφή) return.

γυρισμός, ὁ [yeereesmos] return, coming back.

γυριστός [yeereestos] curved, turned up, crooked.

γυρνάω [yeernao] βλ γυρίζω.

γυρολόγος, ὁ [yeeroloyos] hawker, pedlar.

γῦρος, ὁ [yeeros] circle, circumference || (φορέματος) hem || (περιστροφή) turn, revolution || (περπάτημα) walk || (βαρελιοῦ) hoop.

γυρτός [yeertos] bent, inclined, curved.

γύρω [yeero] round, around, about, round about.

γυφτιά, ἡ [yeeftia] stinginess, avarice, shabbiness.

γύφτος, ὁ [yeeftos] gipsy || blacksmith.

γύψ, ὁ [yeeps] vulture.

γύψινος [yeepseenos] plaster.

γύψος, ὁ [yeepsos] plaster of Paris.

γυψώνω [yeepsono] plaster.

γύψωσις, ἡ [yeepsoseos] plastering.

γωνία, ἡ [yoneea] angle, corner || (ἐργαλεῖο) square, set square || (ἀπόμερος τόπος) nook, den || (ψωμιοῦ) crust of bread.

γωνιακός [yoneeakos] angular || (τῆς γωνίας) corner.

γωνιόλιθος, ὁ [yoneeoleethos] cornerstone.

γωνιώδης [yoneeodees] angular.

Δ, δ

δά [da] (indeclinable particle) ὄχι ~ certainly not! || τόσος ~ only so tall, so small.

δάγκωμα, τό [dangoma] bite.

δαγκώνω [dangono] bite.

δαδί, τό [dadee] pinewood, firewood.

δαίδαλος [dedalos] labyrinthine, intricate, complicated.

δαιμονίζω [demoneezo] enrage, infuriate.

δαιμονισμένος [demoneesmenos] (μεταφ) mischievous || possessed.

δαιμόνιον, τό [demoneeon] genius || (διάβολος) demon, fiend.

δαιμόνιος [demoneeos] very clever, marvellous, divine.

δαίμων, ὁ [demon] demon, devil, fiend.

δάκρυ, τό [dakree] tear.

δακρύζω [dakreezo] shed tears, weep || (ἐπί φυτῶν) sweat || (ἐπί ἀγγείων) ooze.

δακτυλήθρα, ἡ [dakteeleethra] thimble.

δακτυλίδι, τό [dakteeleedee] ring.

δακτυλικός [dakteeleekos] digital, dactylic.

δάκτυλο, τό [dakteelo] βλ δάκτυλος.

δακτυλογράφος, ὁ, ἡ [dakteeloyrafos] typist.

δάκτυλος, ὁ [dakteelos] finger || (ποδιοῦ) toe || (μονάς μήκους) inch || (ποίησις) dactyl.

δαμάζω [damazo] tame, subdue.

δαμαλίζω [damaleezo] vaccinate.

δαμαλισμός, ὁ [damaleesmos] vaccination.

δαμάσκηνον, τό [damaskeenon] plum || (ξηρό) prune.

δανείζομαι [daneezome] borrow.

δανείζω [daneezo] lend, loan.

δάνειον [daneeon] loan.

δανειστής, ὁ [daneestees] lender, creditor.

Δανία, ἡ [daneea] Denmark.

δαντέλλα, ἡ [dantella] lace.

δαπάνη, ἡ [dapanee] expenditure, expense, cost.

δαπανηρός [dapaneeros] costly, expensive.

δαπανῶ [dapano] spend, consume.

δάπεδον, τό [dapedon] floor || ground.

δαρμός, ὁ [darmos] βλ δάρσιμο.

δάρσιμο, τό [darseemo] beating || (γάλακτος) churning.

δασεῖα, ἡ [daseea] rough breathing (in Greek grammar).

δασκάλα, ἡ [daskala] βλ διδασκάλισσα.

δασκαλεύω [daskalevo] coach, teach.

δάσκαλος, ὁ [daskalos] βλ διδάσκαλος.

δασμολόγιον, τό [dasmoloyeeon] tariff.

δασμός, ὁ [dasmos] tax, (customs) duty.

δάσος, τό [dasos] forest, woodland.

δασύλλιον, τό [daseeleeon] thicket, grove.

δασύς, ὁ [dasees] thick, bushy, hairy.

δασύτης, ἡ [daseetees] thickness, density.

δασώδης [dasodees] wooded, woody.

δαυλί, τό [davlee] torch, firebrand.

δάφνη, ἡ [dafnee] laurel, bay tree, bay.

δαψίλεια, ἡ [dapseeleea] abundance.

δαψιλής [dapseelees] abundant, profuse.

δέ [de]: ὁ μέν ... ὁ ~ the one ... the other || and || but || on the other hand.

δεδομένα, τά [dedomena] πλ data, facts.

δεδουλεμένος [dedoulemenos]: ~ τόκος accrued interest.

δέησις, ή [deisees] prayer, supplication.

δεῖ [dee] there is need, it is necessary.

δεῖγμα, τό [deeyma] sample, specimen || (ἐνδείξις) token, sign.

δειγματολόγιον, τό [deeymatoloyeeón] sample, collection.

δεικνύω [deekneeo] show, point out || (ἐπὶ ὀργάνων) mark, indicate.

δείκτης, ὁ [deektees] indicator || (χειρός) forefinger || (φρολογίου) hand || (ζυγοῦ) index, cock || (πυξίδος) needle.

δεικτικός [deekteekos] indicative || (γραμμι) demonstrative.

δειλά [deela] timidly, faint-heartedly.

δείλι, τό [deelee] (late) afternoon.

δειλία, ή [deeleea] timidity, cowardice.

δειλιάζω [deeleeazo] lose courage, be afraid.

δειλινό, τό [deeleeno] afternoon.

δειλός [deelos] timid || cowardly, faint-hearted.

δεινός [deenos] horrid || (ἰκανός) able, clever, expert.

δεισιδαιμονία, ή [deeseedemoneea] superstition.

δεισιδαίμων [deeseedemon] superstitious.

δείχνω [deehno] βλ δεικνύω.

δέκα [deka] ten.

δεκάγωνον, τό [dekayonon] decagon.

δεκαδικός [dekadeekos] decimal.

δεκαεννέα [dekaenea] nineteen.

δεκαέξ [dekaeks] sixteen.

δεκαεπτά [dekaepta] seventeen.

δεκαετηρίς, ή [dekaeteerees] decade || (ἐορτή) tenth anniversary.

δεκαετής, ὁ, ή [dekaetees] ten-year-old.

δεκαετία, ή [dekaeteea] ten years, decade.

δεκάζω [dekazo] corrupt, bribe.

δεκάκις [dekakees] tenfold.

δεκάλογος, ὁ [dekaloyos] decalogue, Ten Commandments.

δεκανεύς, ὁ [dekanevs] corporal.

δεκανίκι, τό [dekaneekee] crutch.

δεκαπενθήμερον, τό [dekapentheemeron] fortnight.

δεκαπέντε [dekapente] fifteen.

δεκαπλάσιος [dekaplaseeos] tenfold.

δεκάρα [dekara] one tenth of a drachma.

δεκάρι, τό [dekaree] ten-drachma piece || (στὰ χαρτιά) ten.

δεκάς, ή [dekas] set of ten.

δεκασμός, ὁ [dekasmos] bribery, corruption.

δεκατέσσαρες [dekatessares] fourteen.

δέκατος [dekatos] tenth.

δεκατρεῖς [dekatrees] thirteen.

Δεκέμβριος, ὁ [dekemvreeos] December.

δέκτης, ὁ [dektees] receiver.

δεκτικός [dekteekos] capable of, susceptible to, receptive.

δεκτός [dektos] accepted || (γνώμη) admissible.

δελεάζω [deleazo] tempt, entice, bait.

δέλεαρ, τό [delear] lure, bait.

δελεαστικός [deleasteekos] tempting, attractive.

δέλτα, τό [delta] (γράμμα) delta || (ποταμοῦ) delta.

δελτάριον, τό [deltareeon] postcard, card || bulletin.

δελτίον, τό [delteeon] bulletin || (ὑγείας) report || (ψηφοδέλτιον) ballot.

δελφίν, ὁ [delfeen] dolphin.

δέμα, τό [dema] (ἱμάς, κορδόνι) cord, ribbon || (πάκο) bale, bundle || (ταχυδρομικόν) parcel.

δεμάτι, τό [dematee] bundle || (καρότων κτλ) bunch || (φρυγάνων) faggot.

δέ(ν) [de(n)] (negative particle) no, not.

δενδράκι, τό [dendrakee] small tree, shrub.

δενδρολίβανον, τό [dendroleevanon] rosemary.

δένδρον, τό [dendron] tree.

δενδρόφυτος [dendrofeetos] full of trees, wooded.

δενδρύλλιον, τό [dendreeleeon] young tree, shrub.

δένω [deno] bind, tie || (μὲ ἁλυσίδα) chain, link || (γραβάτα κτλ) tie || (βιβλίο) bind || (προσδένω) fasten, fix || (καράβι) moor, berth || (γλυκό κτλ) thicken || (μεταφ) bind.

δεξαμενή, ή [deksamenee] tank, reservoir || (ναυτ) dock, basin.

δεξιά, ή [deksia] right hand || (σπόρ) right wing || (ἐπιρ) to the right.

δεξιός [dekseeos] right || right-handed || (σπόρ) right-wing || (ἐπιτήδειος) clever.

δεξιόστροφος [dekseeostrofos] clockwise (movement).

δεξιότης, ή [dekseeotees] skilfulness, cleverness.

δεξιόχειρ, ὁ [dekseeoheer] right-handed (person).

δεξιώνομαι [dekseeonome] receive, welcome.

δεξίωσις, ή [dekseeoseos] reception.

δέομαι [deome] have need of || (προσεύχομαι) pray, beg, beseech.

δέον, τό [deon] what is needful.

δεόντως [deontos] suitably, fitly, properly.

δέος, τό [deos] awe, fear, fright.

δέρας, τό [deras]: τὸ χρυσόμαλλον ~ the golden fleece.

δέρμα, τό [derma] skin, pelt || leather.

δερμάτινος [dermateenos] of leather.

δερματῖτις, ή [dermateetees] dermatitis.

δερματοπώλης, ὁ [dermatopolees] leather merchant.

δέρνω [derno] beat, flog || (γάλα) churn.

δέσιμον, τό [deseemon] tying, binding || bandage.

δεσμά, τά [desma] πλ chains, fetters, bonds.

δέσμευσις, ή [desmevsees] tying, binding.

δεσμεύω [desmevo] bind by a promise, pledge.

δέσμη, ή [desmee] bunch ‖ (φύλλων) bundle ‖ (παιγνιοχάρτων) pack.

δεσμιος, ό [desmeeos] prisoner, captive.

δεσμίς, ή [desmees] (χάρτου) ream of paper.

δεσμός, ό [desmos] tie, bond.

δεσμοφύλαξ, ό [desmofeelaks] prison warder.

δεσπόζω [despozo] dominate, rule ‖ (ύπέρκειμαι) tower above, overlook ‖ (μεταφ) rise above.

δέσποινα, ή [despeena] mistress, madame.

δεσποινίς, ή [despeenees] young lady ‖ Miss.

δεσπότης, ό [despotees] ruler, master ‖ (έκκλ) (arch)bishop.

δεσποτικός [despoteekos] despotic.

δέστρα, ή [destra] stake.

δετός [detos] tied, bound.

δεύτε [devte] (έπιφ) come!

Δευτέρα, ή [devtera] Monday.

δευτερεύων [devterevon] secondary ‖ sub-ordinate.

δευτέρι, τό [devteree] account book.

δευτεροβάθμιος [devterovathmeeos] second-degree.

δευτεροετής [devteroetees] of the second year.

δευτερόλεπτον, τό [devterolepton] second.

δεύτερος [devteros] second ‖ (σέ ποιότητα) inferior.

δευτερότοκος [devterotokos] second-born.

δέχομαι [dehome] accept, receive ‖ (παρα-δέχομαι) approve ‖ (δεξιούμαι) welcome, greet ‖ (ύφίσταμαι) receive ‖ (άνέχομαι) tolerate

δήγμα, τό [deegma] bite ‖ (έρπετού) sting.

δήθεν [deethen] apparently, so called, as if.

δηκτικός [deekteekos] biting, scathing.

δηλαδή [deeladee] that is to say, namely, viz.

δηλητηριάζω [deeleeteereeazo] poison ‖ (μεταφ) corrupt, taint.

δηλητηρίασις [deeleeteereeasees] poisoning ‖ (μεταφ) corruption.

δηλητήριον, τό [deeleeteereeon] poison, venom.

δηλοποιώ [deelopeeo] βλ δηλώνω.

δήλος [deelos] manifest, obvious.

δηλώνω [deelono] declare, state ‖ (γέν-νησιν κτλ) register, give notice ‖ (έμπό-ρευμα) enter (goods).

δήλωσις, ή [deelosees] declaration, state-ment ‖ (γέννησις κτλ) register.

δημαρχείον, τό [deemarheeon] town hall ‖ (US) city hall.

δήμαρχος, ό [deemarhos] mayor.

δήμευσις, ή [deemevsees] confiscation.

δημεύω [deemevo] confiscate, seize.

δημηγορία, ή [deemeegoreea] harangue.

δημητριακός [deemeetreeakos]: τά δημη-τριακά cereals, crops.

δήμιος, ό [deemeeos] executioner, hang-man

δημιουργία, ή [deemeeouryeea] creation.

δημιουργικός [deemeeouryeekos] creative.

δημιουργός, ό [deemeeouryos] creator.

δημιουργώ [deemeeouryo] create ‖ establish.

δημογέρων, ό [deemoyeron] elder.

δημοδιδάσκαλος, ό [deemodeedaskalos] primary schoolteacher.

δημοκοπία, ή [deemokopeea] demagogy.

δημοκράτης, ό [deemokratees] democrat.

δημοκρατία, ή [deemokrateea] democracy ‖ republic.

δημοκρατικός [deemokrateekos] demo-cratic, republican.

δημοπρασία, ή [deemopraseea] auction.

δήμος, ό [deemos] municipality.

δημοσία [deemosea] (έπιρ) publicly.

δημοσίευμα, τό [deemosievma] newspaper article, publication.

δημοσίευσις, ή [deemosievsees] publication.

δημοσιεύω [deemosievo] publish, make known.

δημοσιογράφος, ό [deemoseeoyrafos] journalist, reporter.

δημόσιον, τό [deemoseeon] the state, the public.

δημόσιος [deemoseeos] public ‖ (κρατικός) national.

δημοσιότης, ή [deemoseeotees] publicity.

δημότης, ό [deemotees] citizen.

δημοτική, ή [deemoteekee] demotic (Greek).

δημοτικός [deemoteekos] municipal ‖ (δημοφιλής) popular.

δημοτικότης, ή [deemoteekotees] popu-larity.

δημοφιλής [deemofeelees] popular, well-liked.

δημοψήφισμα, τό [deemopseefeesma] plebi-scite.

δημώδης [deemodees] popular, folk.

δηώνω [deeono] ravage, plunder.

διά [dia] for, by, with, about ‖ (μετά γενικής) through, across, by means of ‖ ~ παντός forever ‖ ~ μιάς at one go ‖ ~ θαλάσσης by sea.

διαβάζω [deeavazo] read, study ‖ (μετά προσοχής) peruse.

διαβάθμισις, ή [deeavathmeesees] grading, graduation.

διαβαίνω [deeaveno] pass, go across, pass through.

διαβάλλω [deeavalo] slander, defame, calumniate.

διάβασις, ή [deeavasees] crossing, passage ‖ (στενόν) pass, ford.

διάβασμα, τό [deeavasma] reading, lecture ‖ studying.

διαβασμένος [deeavasmenos] learned, pre-pared (for examination).

διαβατήριον, τό [deeavateereeon] passport.

διαβάτης, ό [deeavatees] passer-by.

διαβατικός [deeavateekos] passing by, transient.

διαβατός [deeavatos] passable || (ποταμός) fordable.

διαβεβαιώνω [deeaveveono] assure, assert, affirm.

διαβεβαίωσις, ή [deeaveveosees] assurance, affirmation.

διάβημα, τό [deeaveema] step, measure, move.

διαβήτης, ό [deeaveetees] pair of compasses || (ιατρ) diabetes.

διαβιβάζω [deeaveevazo] transmit, forward, convey.

διαβίβασις, ή [deeaveevasees] transmission, forwarding.

διαβιβρώσκω [deeaveevrosko] corrode || (σκώληξ) eat into || (θάλασσα κτλ) erode.

διαβίωσις, ή [deeaveeosees] living.

διαβλέπω [deeavlepo] discern, penetrate, foresee.

διαβόητος [deeavoeetos] notorious.

διαβολάκι, τό [deeavolakee] little devil.

διαβολεμένος [deeavolemenos] shrewd, cunning || (μεταφ) devilish.

διαβολή, ή [deeavolee] slander, calumny.

διαβολικός [deeavoleekos] satanic, diabolical.

διάβολος, ό [deeavolos] devil, satan || (φασαρίας) noisy, boisterous.

διαβουλεύομαι [deeavoulevome] deliberate, confer || (μηχανορραφώ) plot.

διαβρέχω [deeavreho] wet, soak, steep.

διάβροχος [deeavrohos] drenched.

διάβρωσις, ή [deeavrosees] corrosion.

διαγγέλλω [deeangelo] announce, notify.

διαγινώσκω [deeayeenosko] discern, distinguish || (ιατρ) diagnose.

διάγνωσις, ή [deeayeenosees] diagnosis.

διάγραμμα, τό [deeayrama] diagram, drawing, plan.

διαγραφή, ή [deeayrafee] cancellation.

διαγράφω [deeayrafo] trace out || (σβήνω) efface, cancel || (περιγράφω) depict, picture.

διάγω [deeayo] live, pass one's time.

διαγωγή, ή [deeayoyee] behaviour, conduct, deportment.

διαγωνίζομαι [deeayoneezome] compete, contend.

διαγώνιος [deeayonees] diagonal.

διαγωνισμός, ό [deeayoneesmos] competition || (εξετάσεις) examination.

διαδέχομαι [deeadehome] succeed, follow.

διάδηλος [deeadeelos] manifest, evident.

διαδήλωσις, ή [deeadeelosees] demonstration, manifestation.

διάδημα, τό [deeadeema] crown, diadem.

διαδίδω [deeadeedo] spread, circulate, propagate.

διαδικασία, ή [deeadeekaseea] procedure, legal inquiry.

διάδικος, ό, ή [deeadeekos] litigant.

διάδοσις, ή [deeadosees] spreading || rumour.

διαδοχή, ή [deeadohee] succession.

διάδοχος, ό, ή [deeadohos] successor, crown prince.

διαδραματίζω [deeadramateezo] play (a role), act.

διαδρομή, ή [deeadromee] course, distance || (εμβόλου) stroke.

διάδρομος, ό [deeadromos] passage, corridor, hall.

διαζευγνύω [deeazevyneeo] separate || (ξεζεύω) unyoke.

διαζευκτικός [deeazevkteekos] (γραμμ) disjunctive.

διάζευξις, ή [deeazevksees] separation, severance.

διαζύγιον, τό [deeazeeyeeon] divorce.

διάζωμα, τό [deeazoma] frieze.

διαθέσιμος [deeatheemos] available, free.

διάθεσις, ή [deeatheesees] arrangement, disposal || (κέφι) mood, humour.

διαθέτω [deeatheto] dispose, arrange || (χρησιμοποιώ) employ, use, make available || (διανέμω) allot.

διαθήκη, ή [deeatheekee] will, testament.

διάθλασις, ή [deeathlasees] refraction.

διαίρεσις, ή [dieresees] division, separation || (μεταφ) discord, difference.

διαιρέτης, ό [dieretees] divisor, divider.

διαιρώ [diero] divide, separate.

διαισθάνομαι [diesthanome] feel, have a presentiment.

διαίσθησις, ή [diestheesees] presentiment.

δίαιτα, ή [dieta] diet.

διαιτησία, ή [dieteeseea] arbitration.

διαιτητής, ό [dieteetees] arbiter || (ποδοσφαίρου) referee || umpire.

διαιωνίζω [dieoneezo] perpetuate || protract.

διαιώνισις, ή [dieoneesees] perpetuation.

διακαής [diakaees] ardent, fervent, eager.

διακανονίζω [diakanoneezo] regulate, adjust, settle.

διακατέχω [deeakateho] possess.

διακαώς [deeakaos] ardently.

διάκειμαι [deeakeeme] be disposed, be inclined.

διακεκριμένος [deeakekreemenos] distinguished, eminent.

διάκενος [deeakenos] empty, hollow, vacant || τό διάκενον void, vacuum.

διακήρυξις, ή [deeakeereeksees] declaration, proclamation.

διακηρύττω [deeakeereeto] declare, proclaim, announce.

διακινδυνεύω [deeakeendeenevo] risk, endanger, hazard.

διακλάδωσις, ή [deeaklaδosees] branching off, fork || (δρόμου κτλ) branch.

διακοίνωσις, ή [deeakeenosees] communication, diplomatic note.

διακομίζω [deeakomeezo] transport, carry.

διακονιάρης, ό [deeakoneearees] beggar.

διάκονος, ό [deeakonos] deacon.

διακοπή, ἡ [δeeakopee] suspension, interruption, recess || (ρεύματος) cut.

διακόπτης, ὁ [δeeakoptees] switch, stopcock.

διακόπτω [δeeakopto] suspend, cut off, interrupt, discontinue.

διακορεύω [δeeakorevo] deflower.

διάκος, ὁ [δeeakos] deacon.

διακόσια [δeeakoseea] two hundred.

διακόσμησις, ἡ [δeeakosmeesees] decoration, embellishment.

διακοσμητής, ὁ [δeeakosmeetees] decorator.

διάκοσμος, ὁ [δeeakosmos] ornamentation, decoration.

διακοσμῶ [δeeakosmo] decorate, adorn.

διακρίνω [δeeakreeno] discern, discriminate.

διάκρισις, ἡ [δeeakreesees] distinction || (κρίσις) discretion.

διακύμανσις, ἡ [δeeakeemansees] fluctuation, undulation.

διακωμωδῶ [δeeakomodo] ridicule, satirize.

διαλαλῶ [δeealalo] proclaim, broadcast, cry out.

διαλαμβάνω [δeealamvano] contain, include.

διαλάμπω [δeealambo] shine, glitter.

διαλανθάνω [δeealanthano] escape unnoticed.

διαλεγμένος [δeealeymenos] selected, chosen.

διαλέγομαι [δeealeyome] converse, hold a discourse.

διαλέγω [δeealeyo] choose, select, pick out.

διάλειμμα, τό [δeealeema] interval, recess || intermission.

διάλειψις, ἡ [δeealeepsees] irregularity.

διαλεκτική, ἡ [δeealekteekee] dialectics.

διαλεκτός [δeealektos] chosen, select.

διάλεκτος, ἡ [δeealektos] dialect, idiom.

διάλεξις [δeealeksees] lecture || conversation.

διαλεύκανσις, ἡ [δeealevkansees] elucidation.

διαλλακτικός [δeeallakteekos] conciliatory.

διαλογή, ἡ [δeealoyee] sorting.

διαλογίζομαι [δeealoyeezome] meditate, consider.

διαλογισμός, ὁ [δeealoyeesmos] reflection, thought.

διάλογος, ὁ [δeealoyos] dialogue, conversation.

διάλυμα, τό [δeealeema] solution.

διάλυσις, ἡ [δeealeesees] dissolution, decomposition || (ἐντός ὑγροῦ) solution || (ἑταιρείας κτλ) liquidation || (στρατ) disbanding.

διαλυτός [δeealeetos] soluble, dissolvable.

διαλύω [δeealeeo] dissolve || (ἑταιρείαν) liquidate || (συμβόλαιον κτλ) annul, cancel || (ἐχθρόν) disband, defeat, scatter || (ἀμφιβολίαν κτλ) dispel.

διαμάντι, τό [δeeamantee] diamond ||

διαμαντικά πλ jewellery, gems.

διαμαρτύρομαι [δeeamarteerome] protest.

διαμαρτυρόμενος [δeeamarteeromenos] Protestant.

διαμαρτυρῶ [δeeamarteero] protest.

διαμάχη, ἡ [δeeamahee] dispute, fight.

διαμελίζω [δeeameleezo] dismember.

διαμένω [δeeameno] reside, live, stay.

διαμέρισμα, τό [δeeamereesma] region, constituency, district || (οἰκία) apartment, flat.

διάμεσος [δeeamesos] intermediary, intermediate.

διαμετακομίζω [δeeametakomizo] convey, transport, carry.

διαμέτρημα, τό [δeeametreema] bore, calibre.

διάμετρος, ἡ [δeeametros] diameter || gauge.

διαμηνύω [δeeameeneeo] inform, apprise.

διαμοιράζω [δeeameerazo] distribute, share.

διαμονή, ἡ [δeeamonee] stay, residence, sojourn.

διαμορφώνω [δeeamorfono] model, shape, form.

διαμφισβήτησις, ἡ [δeeamfeesveeteesees] contestation, calling into question.

διαμφισβητῶ [δeeamfeesveeto] question, contest, dispute.

διανέμω [δeeanemo] distribute || divide.

διανόησις, ἡ [δeeanoeesees] thought || intelligence.

διανοητικῶς [δeeanoeeteekos] intellectually.

διάνοια, ἡ [δeeaneea] intellect, mind.

διανοίγω [δeeaneeyo] open (up).

διανομεύς, ὁ [δeeanomevs] distributor || (ταχυδρομικός) postman.

διανομή, ἡ [δeeanomee] distribution.

διανοούμενοι, οἱ [δeeanooumenee] πλ intellectuals.

διανυκτερεύω [δeeaneekterevo] spend the night || stay open all night.

διανύω [δeeaneeo] go through, cover, terminate.

διαξιφισμός, ὁ [δeeakseefeesmos] sword thrust || fencing.

διαπασῶν, ἡ, τό [δeeapason] tuning fork || (μουσ) octave.

διαπεραιώνω [δeeapereono] ferry over.

διαπεραστικός [δeeaperasteekos] piercing, sharp || (βροχή) drenching.

διαπερῶ [δeeapero] pierce, penetrate, pass through.

διαπιστευτήριον, τό [δeeapeestevteereeon]: τά διαπιστευτήρια credentials.

διαπιστώνω [δeeapeestono] ascertain, find out, confirm.

διαπίστωσις, ἡ [δeeapeestosees] ascertainment.

διάπλασις, ἡ [δeeaplasees] (con)formation || moulding.

διαπλάσσω [δeeaplaso] form, shape || (μεταφ) educate, train.

διάπλατα [δeeaplata] wide open.

διαπλάτυνσις, ή [δeeaplateensees] widening.
διάπλευσις, ή [δeeaplevsees] crossing.
διαπλέω [δeeapleo] cross over, sail through.
διαπληκτισμός, ὁ [δeeapleekteesmos] dispute, quarrel.
διαπνοή, ή [δeeapnoee] respiration.
διαποικίλλω [δeeapeekeelo] embellish, diversify, vary.
διαπόρθμευσις, ή [δeeaporthmevsees] ferrying across.
διαποτίζω [δeeapoteezo] soak, saturate.
διαπραγματεύομαι [δeeapraɣmatevome] negotiate ǁ discuss.
διαπραγμάτευσις, ή [δeeapraɣmatevsees] negotiation.
διαπράττω [δeeaprato] perpetrate, commit.
διαπρεπής [δeeaprepees] eminent, distinguished.
διαπρέπω [δeeaprepo] excel.
διάπυρος [δeeapeeros] red-hot ǁ (μεταφ) fervent, eager.
διάρθρωσις, ή [δeearthrosees] articulation, joint, structure.
διάρκεια, ή [δeearkeea] duration.
διαρκῶ [δeearko] last, endure ǁ continue.
διαρκῶς [δeearkos] continually, constantly, always.
διαρπάζω [δeearpazo] pillage, plunder, loot.
διαρρέω [δeeareo] traverse ǁ (δοχεῖον) leak ǁ (ὑγροῦ, νέα κτλ) leak out ǁ (χρόνος) elapse, pass.
διαρρηγνύω [δeeareeɣneeo] tear, burst open, break.
διαρρήδην [δeeareeδeen] flatly, frankly, categorically.
διάρρηξις, ή [δeeareeksees] breaking, rupture ǁ (κλοπή) burglary.
διαρροή, ή [δeearoee] flow ǁ (σωλῆνος) leakage.
διάρροια, ή [δeeareea] diarrhoea.
διαρρυθμίζω [δeeareethmeezo] arrange, regulate.
διαρρύθμισις, ή [δeeareethmeesees] arrangement, regulation.
διασάλευσις, ή [δeeasalevsees] disturbance, agitation.
διασαφηνίζω [δeeasafeeneezo] clarify, elucidate.
διασαφήνισις, ή [δeeasafeeneesees] clarification, elucidation.
διασάφησις, ή [δeeasafeesees] βλ διασαφήνισις.
διάσεισις, ή [δeeaseesees] concussion, shock
διάσελο, τό [δeeaselo] pass, saddle (in hills).
διάσημον, τό [δeeaseemon]: τά διάσημα insignia.
διάσημος [δeeaseemos] famous, celebrated, renowned.
διασκεδάζω [δeeaskeδazo] scatter, dispel ǁ (ψυχαγωγῶ) divert, amuse ǁ (ἀμεταβ) amuse o.s.

διασκέδασις, ή [δeeaskeδasees] dispersion ǁ (ψυχαγωγία) entertainment.
διασκεδαστικός [δeeaskeδasteekos] diverting, entertaining.
διασκευάζω [δeeaskevazo] arrange, modify, alter.
διασκευή, ή [δeeaskevee] arrangement, adaptation, modification.
διάσκεψις, ή [δeeaskepsees] deliberation ǁ conference.
διασκορπίζω [δeeaskorpeezo] scatter, disperse ǁ (χρῆμα) waste.
διασπαθίζω [δeeaspatheezo] waste, squander.
διάσπασις, ή [δeeaspasees] distraction ǁ (ἀτόμου) splitting.
διασπείρω [δeeaspeero] disseminate, disperse, scatter ǁ (μεταφ) circulate.
διασπορά, ή [δeeaspora] dispersion, scattering.
διασπῶ [δeeaspo] sever, separate with violence, rupture.
διασταλτικός [δeeastalteekos] dilating, dilative.
διάστασις, ή [δeeastasees] separation, disagreement ǁ (μέτρον) dimension.
διασταυρώνω [δeeastavrono] cross ǁ meet.
διασταύρωσις, ή [δeeastavrosees] crossing ǁ (δρόμων) intersection.
διαστέλλω [δeeastelo] distinguish ǁ (διανοίγω) distend, expand.
διάστημα, τό [δeeasteema] space, interval, period ǁ κατά διαστήματα from time to time ǁ at intervals.
διάστικτος [δeeasteektos] spotted, stippled ǁ tattooed.
διαστολή, ή [δeeastolee] distinction ǁ (καρδιᾶς) diastole ǁ (γραμμ) comma.
διαστρεβλώνω [δeeastrevlono] twist, bend ǁ (μεταφ) alter, distort.
διαστρέφω [δeeastrefo] twist, bend ǁ (μεταφ) pervert, corrupt.
διαστροφή, ή [δeeastrofee] perversion, distortion.
διασύρω [δeeaseero] (μεταφ) defame, slander, backbite.
διασχίζω [δeeasheezo] tear ǁ (μεταφ) cross, travel through.
διάσχισις, ή [δeeasheesees] crossing, traversing.
διασώζω [δeeasozo] preserve, rescue deliver.
διάσωσις, ή [δeeasosees] deliverance, rescue, preservation.
διαταγή, ή [δeeataɣee] order, command instruction.
διάταγμα, τό [δeeataɣma] order, decree, edict.
διάταξις, ή [δeeataksees] arrangement ǁ (νόμου κτλ) provision.
διατάραξις, ή [δeeataraksees] disturbance upheaval.
διαταράσσω [δeeataraso] disturb, agitate.

διατάσσω [deeataso] arrange ‖ order, command.

διατείνομαι [deeateenome] maintain, declare.

διατείνω [deeateeno] stretch, tighten.

διατελῶ [deeatelo] be, stand.

διατέμνω [deeatemno] intersect, split.

διατήρησις [deeateereesees] maintenance, preservation, conservation.

διατηρῶ [deeateero] hold, maintain ‖ preserve, conserve ‖ (ψυχραιμίαν) keep.

διατί [deeatee] why? ‖ τό ~ cause, reason.

διατίμησις, ἡ [deeateemeesees] tariff, rate, price list.

διατιμῶ [deeateemo] fix the price of, regulate the sale of.

διατομή [deeatomee] cross-cut, cut.

διατράνωσις, ἡ [deeatranosees] manifestation.

διατρέφω [deeatrefo] keep, feed, support.

διατρέχω [deeatreho] run through ‖ (ἀπόστασιν) cover, traverse.

διάτρησις, ἡ [deeatreesees] perforation, drilling, cutting.

διάτρητος [deeatreetos] perforated, holed, drilled.

διατριβή, ἡ [deeatreevee] stay ‖ (μελέτη) study, thesis ‖ (ἀσχολία) pastime.

διατροφή, ἡ [deeatrofee] feeding, board ‖ (ἐπί διαζυγίου) alimony.

διατρυπῶ [deeatreepo] pierce, bore through.

διάττων, ὁ [deeaton] shooting star.

διατυμπανίζω [deeateembaneezo] divulge, let out, give away.

διατυπώνω [deeateepono] formulate, state.

διαύγεια, ἡ [deeavgeea] clearness, transparency.

διαφαίνομαι [deeafenome] show through, appear, come in sight.

διαφανής [deeafanees] clear, transparent.

διαφέρω [deeafero] be different from, differ.

διαφεύγω [deeafevgo] escape, get away, evade.

διαφημίζω [deeafeemeezo] advertise.

διαφήμισις, ἡ [deeafeemeesees] advertisement, advertising.

διαφημιστής, ὁ [deeafeemeestees] advertiser.

διαφθείρω [deeaftheero] spoil, damage, (μεταφ) corrupt ‖ (κορίτσι) deflower.

διαφθορά, ἡ [deeafthora] corruption, depravity.

διαφιλονεικῶ [deeafeeloneeko] dispute, quarrel.

διαφορά, ἡ [deeafora] difference ‖ dissension, contention.

διαφορετικός [deeaforeteekos] different, dissimilar.

διαφορικόν, τό [deeaforeekon] differential.

διαφορικός [deeaforeekos] differential.

διάφορο, τό [deeaforo] profit, interest, gain.

διαφοροποίησις, ἡ [deeaforopieesees] differentiation.

διάφορος [deeaforos] different, various, mixed ‖ τά διάφορα miscellaneous.

διαφοροτρόπως [deeaforotropos] diversely, variously.

διάφραγμα, τό [deeafraγma] partition ‖ (ἀνατ) diaphragm.

διαφυγή, ἡ [deeafeeγee] escape, evasion ‖ (ὑγροῦ κτλ) leak, leakage.

διαφύλαξις, ἡ [deeafeelaksees] preservation, protection.

διαφυλάσσω [deeafeelaso] preserve, protect, keep.

διαφωνία, ἡ [deeafoneea] discord, disagreement.

διαφωνῶ [deeafono] disagree, differ.

διαφωτίζω [deeafoteezo] clear up ‖ enlighten.

διαφώτισις, ἡ [deeafoteesees] enlightenment.

διαχαράσσω [deeaharaso] trace, mark out.

διαχειρίζομαι [deeaheereezome] administer, manage, handle.

διαχείρισις, ἡ [deeaheereesees] management, handling, administration.

διαχειριστής, ὁ [deeaheereestees] administrator ‖ (στρατ) pay corps officer.

διαχέω [deeaheo] diffuse, give out.

διάχυσις, ἡ [deeaheesees] diffusion ‖ (μεταφ) effusiveness, gaiety.

διαχυτικός [deeaheeteekos] effusive, gushing, demonstrative.

διάχυτος [deeaheetos] diffuse.

διαχωρίζω [deeahoreezo] separate, divide.

διαχώρισις, ἡ [deeahoreesees] separation.

διαψεύδομαι [deeapsevdome] contradict o.s., fail.

διαψεύδω [deeapsevdo] deny, give the lie to ‖ disappoint.

διάψευσις, ἡ [deeapsevsees] denial, contradiction ‖ disappointment.

διγαμία, ἡ [deeγameea] bigamy.

δίγαμος, ὁ [deeγamos] bigamist.

δίγλωσσος [deeγlosos] bilingual.

οιδαγμα, τό [deeδaγma] teaching, moral ‖ (ἐκκλ) lesson.

διδακτήριον, τό [deeδakteereeon] institute, school.

διδακτικός [deeδakteekos] instructive, didactic.

διδακτορία, ἡ [deeδaktoreea] doctorate.

δίδακτρα, τά [deeδaktra] πλ tuition fees.

διδάκτωρ, ὁ [deeδaktor] doctor.

διδασκαλεῖον, τό [deeδaskaleeon] teacher's training college.

διδασκαλία, ἡ [deeδaskaleea] teaching, instruction ‖ (θέατρου) production.

διδασκάλισσα, ἡ [deeδaskaleesa] schoolmistress.

διδάσκαλος, ὁ [deeδaskalos] teacher, schoolmaster.

διδάσκω [deeδasko] teach, instruct.

διδαχή, ἡ [deeδahee] teaching ‖ (ἐκκλ) sermon.

δίδυμος [δeedeemos] twin.

δίδω [δeeδo] give, grant ‖ (τιμή) offer ‖ (παράγω) produce, yield ‖ (μάχην) give battle ‖ (γροθιάν) deal a blow to.

διεγείρω [δieγeero] excite, rouse, incite.

διέγερσις, ή [δieγersees] excitation, stimulation.

διεζευγμένος [δiezevγmenos] divorced.

διεθνής [δiethnees] international.

διείσδυσις, ή [δieesδeesees] penetration, piercing.

διεισδύω [δieesδeeo] penetrate, enter, advance.

διεκδίκησις, ή [δiekδeekeesees] claim, vindication.

διεκδικῶ [δiekδeeko] claim, contest.

διεκπεραιώνω [δiekpereono] finish off, forward.

διεκπεραίωσις, ή [δiekpereosees] forwarding, consignment.

διεκφεύγω [δiekfevγo] slip away, escape.

διελαύνω [δielavno] drive through ‖ (μεταφ) run through.

διέλευσις, ή [δielevsees] crossing, passing.

διένεξις, ή [δieneksees] dispute, quarrel.

διενεργῶ [δienerγo] operate, effect, hold.

διεξάγω [δieksaγo] conduct, accomplish, carry out.

διεξέρχομαι [δiekserhome] traverse, travel through ‖ (μεταφ) look into.

διεξοδικός [δieksoδeekos] lengthy, extensive, detailed.

διέξοδος, ή [δieksoδos] issue, outlet ‖ (μεταφ) way out, alternative.

διέπω [δiepo] govern, rule.

διερεθίζω [δieretheezo] irritate.

διερεύνησις [δierevneesees] investigation, research.

διερευνητικός [δierevneeteekos] searching, exploratory.

διερευνῶ [δierevno] search, explore, examine.

διερμηνεύς, ό [δiermeenevs] interpreter, translator.

διερμηνευτής, ό [δiermeenevtees] interpreter, explainer.

διερμηνεύω [δiermeenevo] interpret, translate.

διέρχομαι [δierhome] pass by, cross ‖ (χρόνον) spend.

διερωτῶμαι [δierotome] ask o.s., wonder.

διεσπαρμένος [δiesparmenos] dispersed.

διεστραμμένος [δiestramenos] perverse, wicked.

διετής [δietees] lasting two years ‖ (ἐπὶ φυτῶν) biennial.

διετία, ή [δieteea] (space of) two years.

διευθέτης, ό [δievthetees] adjuster.

διευθέτησις, ή [δievtheteesees] arrangement, settlement.

διευθετῶ [δievtheto] arrange, settle ‖ adjust.

διεύθυνσις, ή [δievtheensees] address ‖ direction ‖ (ἑταιρείας) management.

διευθυντής, ό [δivtheentees] director ‖ (σχολῆς) principal ‖ (μουσ) conductor ‖ (θεάτρου) manager ‖ (ἐφημερίδος) editor ‖ (φυλακῶν) governor, warden ‖ (σωματείου) president ‖ (προσωπικοῦ) personnel manager.

διευθύνω [δivtheeno] direct, guide ‖ (ἐπιχείρησιν) manage ‖ (ἐφημερίδα) edit ‖ (βιομηχανίαν) handle, manage, direct ‖ (ἔργα) superintend, oversee ‖ (ὀρχήστραν) lead, conduct.

διευκόλυνσις, ή [δievkoleensees] easing, help.

διευκολύνω [δievkoleeno] facilitate, help forward.

διευκρίνησις, ή [δievkreeneesees] elucidation, explanation.

διευκρινίζω [δievkreeneezo] clear up, explain.

διεύρυνσις, ή [δievreensees] widening, broadening, enlargement.

διεφθαρμένος [δieftharmenos] corrupt, immoral, dissolute.

δίζυγον, τό [δeezeeγon] πλ parallel bars.

διήγημα, τό [δieeγeema] story, tale.

διήγησις, ή [δieeγeesees] narration.

διηγοῦμαι [δieeγoume] narrate, relate, tell.

διήθησις, ή [δieetheesees] filtration, percolation.

διηθῶ [δieetho] filter, percolate.

διημέρευσις, ή [δieemerevsees] spending the day, staying all day.

διηνεκής [δieenekees] unceasing, incessant.

διηνεκῶς [δieenekos] continually.

διηρημένος [δieereemenos] divided, separated.

διθύραμβος, ό [δeetheeramvos] dithyramb ‖ (μεταφ) bombast.

διΐσταμαι [δieestame] (μεταφ) stand apart ‖ (μεταφ) disagree.

διϊσχυρίζομαι [δieesheereezome] maintain.

δικάζω [δeekazo] try, judge.

δικαιόγραφον, τό [δeekeoγrafon] title deed.

δικαιοδοσία, ή [δeekeoδoseea] jurisdiction, province.

δικαιολόγησις, ή [δeekeoloγeesees] justification, excuse.

δικαιολογητικά, τά [δeekeoloγeeteeka] πλ supporting vouchers.

δικαιολογία, ή [δeekeoloγeea] justification, excuse.

δικαιολογῶ [δeekeoloγo] justify, excuse ‖ vindicate.

δίκαιον, τό [δeekeon] justice, right ‖ law.

δίκαιος [δeekeos] fair, just, righteous.

δικαιοσύνη, ή [δeekeoseenee] justice, fairness.

δικαιοῦχος, ό [δeekeouhos] beneficiary.

δικαιώνω [δeekeono] side with ‖ justify, vindicate.

δικαίωμα, τό [δeekeoma] right, claim.

δικαίωσις, ή [δeekeosees] justification, vindication.

δίκανον, τό [δeekanon] double-barrelled shotgun.

δικάσιμος, ἡ [δeekaseemos] day of trial.

δικαστήριον, τό [δeekasteereeon] court of justice, tribunal.

δικαστής, ὁ [δeekastees] judge, justice, magistrate.

δικαστικός [δeekasteekos] judicial, judiciary.

δικέλλα, ἡ [δeekela] two-pronged fork.

δικέφαλος [δeekefalos] two-headed.

δίκη, ἡ [δeekee] trial, suit, lawsuit, case.

δικηγόρος, ὁ, ἡ [δeekeeyoros] lawyer, barrister, attorney.

δικηγορῶ [δeekeeyoro] practise as a lawyer, plead.

δίκην [δeekeen] (ἐπιρ) after the manner of, like.

δικλείς, ἡ [δeeklees] valve.

δικογραφία, ἡ [δeekoyrafeea] file of proceedings ‖ (δικηγόρου) brief.

δικονομία, ἡ [δeekonomeea] procedure.

δίκοχον, τό [δeekohon] forage cap.

δίκρανον, τό [δeekranon] pitchfork.

δίκταμο, τό [δeektamo] dittany.

δικτατορία, ἡ [δeektatoreea] dictatorship.

δικτατορικός [δeektatoreekos] dictatorial.

δίκτυον, τό [δeekteeon] net, network ‖ (μεταφ) snare, trap.

δικτυωτόν, τό [δeekteeoton] wire netting, lattice, grille, trellis.

δίλημμα, τό [δeeleema] dilemma.

διμερής [δeemerees] bipartite.

διμοιρία, ἡ [δeemeereea] platoon, section.

δίνη, ἡ [δeenee] whirlpool, whirlwind.

δίνω [δeeno] βλ δίδω.

διό [δio] therefore, hence.

διογκώνω [δeeongono] swell, inflate.

διόγκωσις, ἡ [δeeongosees] swelling, inflation.

διόδια, τά [δeeodeea] πλ toll ‖ (ναυτ) port toll.

δίοδος, ἡ [δeeodos] passage, pass, defile.

διοίκησις, ἡ [δieekeesees] administration, command.

διοικητήριον, τό [δieekeeteereeon] prefecture, commissioner's office.

διοικητής, ὁ [δieekeetees] governor, commandant, commissioner.

διοικητικός [δieekeeteekos] administrative.

διοικῶ [δieeko] administer, govern, rule, command.

διολισθαίνω [δeeoleestheno] slip through.

διόλου [δeeolou] (ἐπιρ) not at all ‖ ὅλως ~ entirely, quite.

διομολογῶ [δeeomoloyo] stipulate, agree.

διονυχίζω [δeeoneeheezo] scrutinize, sift.

διοξείδιον, τό [δeeokseedeeon] dioxide.

διόπερ [δeeoper] wherefore, hence.

διοπτεύω [δeeoptevo] observe with field glasses ‖ (ναυτ) take bearings of.

δίοπτρα, τά [δeeoptra] πλ spectacles, glasses.

διόπτρα, ἡ [δeeoptra] binoculars.

διόρασις, ἡ [δeeorasees] perspicuity.

διορατικός [δeeorateekos] clear-sighted ‖ (πνεῦμα) shrewd, keen.

διορατικότης, ἡ [δeeorateekotees] perspicacity.

διοργανώνω [δeeoryanono] organize, form, arrange.

διοργάνωσις, ἡ [δeeoryanosees] organization, arrangement.

διορθώνω [δeeorthono] correct, put straight ‖ (πανταλόνι) patch, mend ‖ (μεταφ) remedy, make good.

διόρθωσις, ἡ [δeeorthosees] correction putting right.

διορθωτής, ὁ [δeeorthotees] (τυπογρ) proofreader.

διορία, ἡ [δeeoreea] time limit, term, delay

διορίζω [δeeoreezo] appoint ‖ order, fix.

διορισμός, ὁ [δeeoreesmos] appointment.

διόρυξις, ἡ [δeeoreeksees] digging, excavation.

διορρύσσω [δeeoreeso] dig out, scoop out excavate.

διορῶ [δeeoro] βλ διαβλέπω.

διότι [δeeotee] because.

διουρητικός [δeeoureeteekos] diuretic.

διοχέτευσις, ἡ [δeeohetevsees] (ἡλεκ) conduct ‖ (ὕδατος) conveyance.

διοχετεύω [δeeohetevo] conduct, convey ‖ (μεταφ) transmit, divert.

δίπατος [δeepatos] two-storeyed.

δίπλα, ἡ [δeepla] fold, pleat, wrinkle.

δίπλα [δeepla] (ἐπιρ) by, near, next door, close.

διπλά [δeepla] twice as much.

διπλανός [δeeplanos] nearby, next-door adjacent.

διπλαρώνω [δeeplarono] accost ‖ (ναυτ) come alongside.

διπλασιάζω [δeeplaseeazo] double.

διπλασιασμός, ὁ [δeeplaseeasmos] reduplication.

διπλάσιος [δeeplaseeos] double, twice as much.

διπλόγραφον, τό [δeeployrafon] duplicate.

διπλότυπον, τό [δeeploteepon] duplicate, stub.

διπλοῦς [δeeplous] double.

δίπλωμα, τό [δeeploma] diploma, degree ‖ (τύλιγμα) folding, wrapping.

διπλωμάτης, ὁ [δeeplomatees] diplomat.

διπλωματία, ἡ [δeeplomateea] diplomacy.

διπλωματικός [δeeplomateekos] diplomatic.

διπλωματοῦχος [δeeplomatouhos] possessing a diploma, holding a degree.

διπλώνω [δeeplono] fold.

δίπλωσις, ἡ [δeeplosees] folding, wrapping.

δίπους [δeepous] two-legged, two-footed.

διπρόσωπος [δeeprosopos] two-faced, deceitful.

διπυρίτης, ἡ [δeepeereetees] hard tack.

δίς [δees] twice.

δισάκκι, τό [deesakee] saddlebag, travelling bag.

δισέγγονος, ό, ή [deesengonos] great-grandchild.

δισεκατομμύριον, τό [deesekatomeereeon] billion.

δίσεκτον, τό [deesekton]: ~ έτος leap year.

δισκίον, τό [deeskeeon] tray || (ιατρ) tablet.

δισκοβόλος, ό [deeskovolos] discus thrower.

δισκοπότηρον, τό [deeskopoteeron] chalice.

δίσκος, ό [deeskos] tray || (ζυγοῦ) pan, scale || (ἀθλητ) discus || (ἡλίου κτλ) disk || (ἐκκλ) collection plate || (φωνογράφου) record.

δισταγμός, ό [deestaymos] hesitation, doubt.

διστάζω [deestazo] hesitate, doubt.

διστακτικός [deestaktikos] hesitant, irresolute.

δίστηλος [deesteelos] two-columned.

δίστιχον, τό [deesteehon] distich, couplet.

δισύλλαβος [deeseelavos] of two syllables.

δισχιδής [deesheedees] bifurcated.

δισχίλιοι [deesheeliee] two thousand.

δίτροχος [deetrohos] two-wheeled.

διττανθρακικός [deetanthrakeekos] bicarbonate.

διττῶς [deetos] doubly.

διϋλίζω [dieeleezo] filter, distil, strain.

διΰλισις [dieeleesees] filtering, straining.

διϋλιστήριον, τό [dieeleesteereeon] filter, strainer || (πετρελαίου) refinery.

διφθερῖτις, ή [deefthereetees] diphtheria.

δίφθογγος, ή [deefthongos] diphthong.

διφορούμενος [deeforoumenos] ambiguous || τό διφορούμενον ambiguity.

δίφραγκο, τό [deefrango] two-drachma piece.

δίφυλλος [deefeelos] two-leaved.

διχάζομαι [deehazome] (μεταφ) become disunited, disagree.

διχάζω [deehazo] divide, split || (μεταφ) estrange, disunite.

διχάλη, ή [deehalee] pitchfork.

διχαλωτός [deehalotos] forked, cloven.

διχασμός, ό [deehasmos] division || disagreement.

διχογνωμία, ή [deehoynomeea] dissent, disagreement.

διχόνοια, ή [deehoneea] dissension, discord.

δίχορδος [deehordos] two-stringed.

διχοτομία, ή [deehotomeea] bisection.

διχοτόμος [deehotomos] bisector.

διχοτομῶ [deehotomo] bisect.

δίχρονος [deehronos] (μηχανή) two-stroke (engine).

δίχως [deehos] without || ~ ἄλλο without fail.

δίψα, ή [deepsa] thirst.

διψασμένος [deepsasmenos] thirsty, eager (for).

διψῶ [deepso] feel thirsty || thirst for, be eager for.

διωγμός [deeoymos] persecution.

διώκω [deeoko] pursue, chase, expel, persecute || (μεταφ) banish, dispel.

διώνυμον, τό [deeoneemon] binomial.

δίωξις, ή [deeoksees] persecution, hunting.

διωρισμένος [deeoreesmenos] appointed.

διώροφος [deeorofos] two-storeyed.

δίθρυξ, ή [deeoreeks] canal.

διωστήρ, ό [deeosteer] connecting rod.

διώχνω [deeohno] βλ διώκω.

δόγμα, τό [doyma] dogma, creed, doctrine.

δογματικός [doymateekos] dogmatic(al).

δοθιήν, ό [dothieen] boil.

δόκανον, τό [dokanon] trap || (μεταφ) lure, snare.

δοκάρι, τό [dokaree] beam, rafter, girder.

δοκιμάζω [dokeemazo] taste, try out || (αὐτοκίνητο) test, try || (ἐνδυμασία) fit || (ὑποφέρω) undergo, suffer.

δοκιμασία, ή [dokeemaseea] suffering.

δοκιμαστικός [dokeemasteekos] trial, test || ~ σωλήν test tube.

δοκιμή, ή [dokeemee] trial, test, testing || (θέατρον) rehearsal || (ροῦχα) fitting.

δοκίμιον, τό [dokeemeeon] treatise || (τυπογρ) printer's proof.

δόκιμος [dokeemos] esteemed, first-rate || ό ~ cadet.

δοκός, ή [dokos] girder, beam.

δοκοῦν, τό [dokoon]: κατά τό ~ at pleasure, at will.

δόλιος [doleeos] fraudulent, crafty.

δόλιος [doleeos] wretched, unlucky, poor.

δολιότης, ή [doleeotees] deceit, fraudulence, fraud.

δολοπλόκος [doloplokos] treacherous, artful.

δόλος, ό [dolos] fraud, deceit, guile.

δολοφονία, ή [dolofoneea] murder.

δολοφονικός [dolofoneekos] murderous.

δολοφόνος, ό, ή [dolofonos] assassin, murderer.

δολοφονῶ [dolofono] murder, assassinate.

δόλωμα, τό [doloma] bait, decoy.

δόνησις, ή [doneesees] vibration || (σεισμός) tremor, shock.

δόντι, τό [dontee] tooth || (ἐλέφαντος) tusk || (μηχαν) cog.

δοντιά, ή [dontia] bite.

δονῶ [dono] vibrate, shake.

δόξα, ή [doksa] glory.

δοξάζω [doksazo] glorify, celebrate, extol.

δοξάρι, τό [doksaree] (μουσ) bow.

δοξασία, ή [doksaseea] belief.

δοξολογία, ή [doksoloyeea] doxology, Te Deum.

δοξομανής [doksomanees] ambitious, pretentious.

δορά, ή [dora] skinning || skin, hide.

δορκάς, ή [dorkas] roebuck.

δόρυ, τό [doree] spear.

δορυφόρος, ό [doreeforos] satellite.

δοσίλογος [doseeloyos] quisling.

δόσις, ἡ [dosees] portion ‖ dose ‖ (πληρωμή) instalment.

δοσοληψία, ἡ [dosoleepseea] transaction.

δοτική, ἡ [doteekee] (γραμμ) dative (case).

δουκάτον, τό [doukaton] duchy ‖ (νόμισμα) ducat.

δούκισσα, ἡ [doukeesa] duchess.

δούλα, ἡ [doula] servant girl, maidservant.

δουλεία, ἡ [douleea] slavery, servitude.

δουλειά, ἡ [doulia] work, affair, business.

δούλεμα, τό [doulema] teasing.

δουλευτής, ὁ [doulevtees] hard worker, industrious worker.

δουλεύω [doulevo] work, operate ‖ (ἔχω δουλειά) have a job ‖ (φρολόγι κτλ) work, operate ‖ (περιπαίζω) tease.

δούλη, ἡ [doulee] slave.

δουλικός [douleekos] servile, slavish.

δουλοπάροικος, ὁ [doulopareekos] serf.

δουλοπρεπής [douloprepees] servile, mean.

δοῦλος, ὁ [doulos] slave ‖ servant.

δουλώνω [doulono] enslave, subjugate.

δοῦναι, τό [doune] (ἐμπορ) debit.

δούξ, ὁ [douks] duke.

δοῦπος, ὁ [doupos] thump, bump.

δοχεῖον, τό [doheeon] receptacle, vessel, pot.

δρακόντειος [drakonteeos] (μεταφ) severe, harsh.

δράκος, ὁ [drakos] ogre, dragon.

δράμα, τό [drama] drama ‖ (μεταφ) trouble.

δραματική, ἡ [dramateekee] πλ dramatics.

δραματικός [dramateekos] dramatic, tragic.

δράμιον, τό [drameeon] dram ‖ (μεταφ) tiny amount.

δράξ, ἡ [draks] handful.

δραπετεύω [drapetevo] escape.

δραπέτης [drapetees] fugitive.

δρᾶσις, ἡ [drasees] activity, action ‖ ἄμεσος ~ flying squad.

δραστήριος [drasteereeos] active, energetic, vigorous.

δραστηριότης, ἡ [drasteereeotees] activity, energy, effectiveness.

δράστης, ὁ [drastees] perpetrator, culprit.

δραστικός [drasteekos] efficacious, drastic, effective.

δράττομαι [dratome] seize, grasp ‖ (μεταφ) avail o.s. of ‖ ~ τῆς εὐκαιρίας take the opportunity.

δραχμή, ἡ [drahmee] drachma.

δρεπάνι, τό [drepanee] βλ δρέπανον.

δρέπανον, τό [drepanon] sickle.

δριμέως [dreemeos] acutely, harshly.

δριμύς [dreemees] sharp, bitter, severe, keen.

δρομαῖος [dromeos] precipitate, hasty.

δρομάς, ἡ [dromas] dromedary.

δρομεύς, ὁ [dromevs] runner.

δρομίσκος, ὁ [dromeeskos] narrow street, lane.

δρομολόγιον, τό [dromologeeon] itinerary timetable.

δρόμος, ὁ [dromos] road, street ‖ (ἀθλητ) race ‖ (ἀπόστασι) distance.

δροσερός [droseros] cool, fresh.

δροσερότης, ἡ [droserotees] coolness, freshness.

δροσιά, ἡ [drosia] freshness ‖ dew.

δροσίζομαι [droseezome] refresh o.s., cool down.

δροσίζω [droseezo] cool, refresh ‖ get cool.

δροσιστικός [droseesteekos] refreshing.

δρόσος, ἡ [drosos] dew.

δρύϊνος [drieenos] oak(en).

δρυμός, ὁ [dreemos] forest, wood.

δρυοκολάπτης, ὁ [dreeokolaptees] woodpecker.

δρῦς, ἡ [drees] oak.

δρύφρακτον, τό [dreefrakton] balustrade, barrier.

δρῶ [dro] act, do, take effect.

δυαδικός [deeadeekos] binary ‖ dual.

δυάρι, τό [deearee] (στά χαρτιά) deuce.

δυάς, ἡ [deeas] couple, pair.

δυϊκός [dieekos] (γραμμ) dual (number).

δύναμαι [deename] can, may ‖ be able to.

δυναμική, ἡ [deenameekee] dynamics.

δυναμικός [deenameekos] energetic, dynamic.

δύναμις, ἡ [deenamees] strength, might, power, force.

δυναμίτις, ἡ [deenameetees] dynamite.

δυναμό, τό [deenamo] dynamo.

δυνάμωμα, τό [deenamoma] intensification, strengthening.

δυναμώνω [deenamono] strengthen, make stronger ‖ (ὑγείαν) become stronger.

δυναμωτικός [deenamoteekos] fortifying, strengthening ‖ (ἰατρ) tonic.

δυναστεία, ἡ [deenasteea] dynasty, regime, rule.

δυνάστης, ὁ [deenastees] ruler, potentate ‖ (μεταφ) oppressor, despot.

δυνατά [deenata] strongly, hard ‖ loudly.

δυνατός [deenatos] strong, powerful ‖ (κυβέρνησις) powerful ‖ (φωνή) loud ‖ (ἄνοδος) possible ‖ δυνατόν! possibly!, maybe!

δυνατότης, ἡ [deenatotees] possibility.

δυνητική, ἡ [deeneeteekee] (γραμμ) conditional (mood).

δύο [deeo] two.

δυόσμος, ὁ [deeosmos] mint, spearmint.

δυσανάγνωστος [deesanagnostos] illegible.

δυσανάλογος [deesanalogos] disproportionate.

δυσανασχετῶ [deesanasheto] be anxious, be indignant, get angry.

δυσαρέσκεια, ἡ [deesareskeea] displeasure, discontent.

δυσάρεστος [deesarestos] unpleasant, disagreeable.

δυσαρεστημένος [deeasaresteemenos] displeased, dissatisfied.

δυσαρεστῶ [δeesaresto] displease, dissatisfy.

δυσαρμονία, ή [δeesarmoneea] disharmony, discord.

δυσβάστακτος [δeesvastaktos] unbearable, heavy, overwhelming.

δύσβατος [δeesvatos] inaccessible, rough.

δυσειδής [δeeseeδees] ugly, unsightly.

δυσεντερία, ή [δeesentereea] dysentery.

δυσεξίτηλος [δeesekseeteelos] difficult to remove.

δισεπίλυτος [δeesepeeleetos] difficult to solve.

δισεύρετος [δeesevretos] difficult to find.

δυσήνιος [δeeseeneeos] insubordinate, refractory.

δυσθυμία, ή [δeestheemeea] sadness, depression.

δύσθυμος [δeestheemos] depressed, sad.

δύσις, ή [δeesees] west | (ήλίου) setting (μεταφ) decline.

δύσκαμπτος [δeeskamptos] rigid, stiff, hard to bend.

δυσκινησία, ή [δeeskeeneeseea] sluggishness.

δυσκοιλιότης, ή [δeeskeeleeotees] constipation.

δυσκολεύομαι[δeeskolevome] find difficult, find hard, be hard put.

δυσκολεύω [δeeskolevo] make difficult, make hard.

δυσκολία, ή [δeeskoleea] difficulty.

δυσκολο- [δeeskolo] (first component) difficult, hard.

δύσκολος [δeeskolos] difficult | (άνθρωπος) hard to please.

δυσκόλως [δeeskolos] with difficulty.

δύσληπτος [δeesleeptos] difficult to understand, hard to catch.

δυσμένεια, ή [δeesmeneea] disfavour, disgrace.

δυσμενής [δeesmenees] adverse, unfavourable.

δύσμοιρος [δeesmeeros] ill-fated, unlucky.

δύσμορφος [δeesmorfos] deformed, ugly.

δυσνόητος [δeesnoeetos] difficult to understand.

δυσοίωνος [δeeseeonos] inauspicious, ill-omened.

δυσοσμία, ή [δeesosmeea] bad smell, stench, offensive odour.

δύσπεπτος [δeespeptos] difficult to digest.

δυσπιστία [δeespeesteea] mistrust, incredulity.

δύσπιστος [δeespeestos] incredulous, distrustful, unbelieving.

δυσπιστῶ [δeespeesto] distrust, mistrust.

δύσπνοια, ή [δeespneea] difficult breathing.

δυσπρόσιτος [δeesproseetos] inaccessible.

δύστηνος [δeesteenos] wretched, unfortunate.

δυστοκία, ή [δeestokeea] difficult birth | (μεταφ) indecision.

δύστροπος [δeestropos] perverse, peevish.

δυστροπῶ [δeestropo] behave peevishly.

δυστύχημα, τό [δeesteeheema] accident stroke of bad luck.

δυστυχής [δeesteehees] unhappy, unfortunate.

δυστυχία, ή [δeesteeheea] unhappiness adversity, poverty.

δυστυχισμένος [δeesteeheesmenos] βλ δυστυχής.

δυστυχῶ [δeesteeho] be unhappy, be unfortunate, be poor.

δυσφημίζω [δeesfeemeezo] defame, slander.

δυσφήμισις, ή [δeesfeemeesees] calumny, slander.

δυσφόρητος [δeesforeetos] hard to endure.

δυσφορῶ [δeesforo] be displeased | (μέ κάτι) be discontented.

δυσχεραίνω [δeeshereno] impede make difficult.

δυσχέρεια, ή [δeeshereea] difficulty | hardship.

δυσχερής [δeesherees] difficult.

δύσχρηστος [δeeshreestos] unwieldy, inconvenient, awkward.

δυσώδης [δeesoδees] stinking, malodorous fetid.

δυσωδία, ή [δeesoδeea] stench, stink.

δυσώνυμος [δeesoneemos] ill-famed, notorious.

δύτης, ό [δeetees] diver.

δυτικός [δeeteekos] west(ern).

δύω [δeeo] set | (μεταφ) decline, wane.

δυωδία, ή [δeeoδeea] duet.

δώδεκα [δoδeka] twelve.

δωδεκάγωνον, τό [δoδekaγonon] dodecagon.

δωδεκαδάκτυλον, τό [δoδekaδakteelon] duodenum.

δωδεκαετής [δoδekaetees] twelve years old.

δωδεκαπλάσιος [δoδekaplaseeos] twelvefold.

δωδεκάς, ή [δoδekas] dozen.

δωδέκατος [δoδekatos] twelfth.

δῶμα, τό [δoma] flat roof, terrace | apartment.

δωμάτιον, τό [δomateeon] room | (ΰπνου) bedroom.

δωρεά, ή [δorea] bequest, present, gift ~ν (έπιρ) gratis, free, for nothing.

δωροδοκία, ή [δoroδokeea] bribery, corruption.

δωροδοκῶ [δoroδoko] bribe, corrupt.

δῶρον, τό [δoron] gift, present.

δωσίλογος [δoseeloγos] responsible answerable.

Ε, ε

έ [e] (έπιφ) well!, hey!, hallo!

έάν [ean] βλ άν.

έαρ, τό [ear] spring.

ἑαυτός [eaftos] oneself ‖ καθ᾽ἑαυτοῦ really, exactly, precisely.

ἑβδομάδα, ἡ [evdomaða] week.

ἑβδομαδιαῖος [evdomaðieos] weekly.

ἑβδομήντα [evdomeenta] seventy.

ἕβδομος [evdomos] seventh.

ἑβραϊκός [evraeekos] Jewish.

Ἑβραῖος, ὁ [evreos] Hebrew, Jew.

ἔγγαμος [engamos] married.

ἐγγίζω [engeezo] draw near (μεταφ) touch.

ἔγγιστα [engeesta]: ὡς ~ approximately, nearly.

ἐγγλέζικος [englezeekos] English.

Ἐγγλέζος, ὁ [englezos] Englishman.

ἐγγόνι, τό [engonee] grandchild.

ἐγγονός, ὁ [engonos] grandson.

ἐγγράμματος [engramatos] learned, lettered.

ἐγγραφή, ἡ [engrafee] registration, record, entry.

ἔγγραφον, τό [engrafon] document.

ἐγγράφω [engrafo] register, enrol (μαθημ) inscribe.

ἐγγύησις, ἡ [engieesees] security, guarantee, bail.

ἐγγύς [engees] near, at hand.

ἐγγυῶμαι [engeeome] guarantee, vouch for.

ἐγείρομαι [eyeerome] rise ‖ (ἐκ τοῦ ὕπνου) awake.

ἐγείρω [eyeero] raise, build.

ἔγερσις, ἡ [eyersees] raising, building ‖ (ἀπό ὕπνου) awakening.

ἐγκαθίσταμαι [engkatheestame] settle, put up, settle o.s.

ἐγκαθιστῶ [engkatheesto] set up, settle, establish.

ἐγκαίνια, τά [engkeneea] πλ inauguration, opening.

ἔγκαιρος [engkeros] timely, opportune.

ἐγκάρδιος [engkarðeeos] cordial, affectionate.

ἐγκάρσιος [engkarseeos] transversal, slanting, oblique.

ἐγκαταλείπω [engkataleepo] abandon, desert.

ἐγκατάστασις, ἡ [engkatastasees] installation, establishing.

ἔγκαυμα, τό [engkavma] burn.

ἔγκειται [engkeete]: εἰς ὑμᾶς ~ it rests with you.

ἐγκέφαλος, ὁ [engkefalos] brain.

ἐγκλείστως [engkleestos] enclosed (herein), herewith.

ἐγκλείω [engkleeo] enclose ‖ confine ‖ lock up.

ἔγκλημα, τό [engkleema] crime ‖ sin ‖ ~τίας, ὁ criminal ‖ ~τικός criminal ‖ ~τικότης, ἡ delinquency, wrongdoing, crime.

ἔγκλισις, ἡ [engkleesees] inclination ‖ (γραμμ) mood.

ἐγκόλπιον, τό [engkolpeeon] (φυλακτό) amulet ‖ manual.

ἐγκοπή, ἡ [engkopee] incision, notch, groove.

ἐγκόσμιος [engkosmeeos] mundane, worldly ‖ social.

ἐγκράτεια, ἡ [engkrateea] sobriety, moderation, temperance.

ἐγκρίνω [engkreeno] approve, ratify.

ἔγκρισις, ἡ [engkreesees] approval, sanction.

ἐγκύκλιος, ἡ [engkeekleeos] circular letter.

ἐγκυκλοπαιδεία, ἡ [engkeeklopeðeea] encyclopaedia.

ἔγκυος [engkeeos] pregnant.

ἔγκυρος [engkeeros] valid, sound, well-grounded.

ἐγκώμιον, τό [engkomeeon] praise, encomium.

ἔγνοια, ἡ [eyneea] care, anxiety, concern.

ἐγχείρησις, ἡ [engheereesees] operation.

ἐγχειρίδιον, τό [engheereeðeeon] manual ‖ (στιλέττο) dagger.

ἔγχρωμος [enghromos] coloured.

ἐγχώριος [enghoreeos] local, native, domestic.

ἐγώ [eyo] Ι ‖ (οὐσ) τό ~ ego ‖ ἐγωισμός, ὁ pride, conceit, selfishness.

ἐδάφιον, τό [eðafeeon] paragraph, passage.

ἔδαφος, τό [eðafos] ground, earth, soil.

ἕδρα, ἡ [eðra] seat, chair ‖ (ἀνατ) bottom ‖ (ἐκκλ) see.

ἑδραιώνω [eðreono] establish, strengthen, make firm.

ἑδρεύω [eðrevo] reside, have one's seat.

ἐδῶ [eðo] here ‖ ~ καί τρία χρόνια three years ago.

ἐδώλιον, τό [eðoleeon] bench, seat.

ἐθελοντής, ὁ [ethelontees] volunteer.

ἐθελουσίως [ethelouseeos] voluntarily.

ἔθιμον, τό [etheemon] custom, tradition ‖ habit.

ἐθιμοτυπία, ἡ [etheemoteepeea] formality etiquette.

ἐθνάρχης, ὁ [ethnarhees] national leader.

ἐθνικισμός, ὁ [ethneekeesmos] nationalism.

ἐθνικός [ethneekos] national.

ἐθνικότης, ἡ [ethneekotees] nationality.

ἐθνικόφρων [ethneekofron] patriotic nationalistic.

ἔθνος, τό [ethnos] nation.

εἰ [ee] if ‖ ~ δέ if not ‖ ~ δέ μή otherwise.

εἰδάλλως [eeðalos] if not, otherwise.

εἰδεχθής [eeðehthees] hideous, horrible repulsive.

εἰδήμων [eeðeemon] expert, skilled, well-informed.

εἰδήσεις, οἱ [eeðeesees] πλ news.

εἰδικός [eeðeekos] special, particular ‖ (ἄνθρωπος) specialist.

εἰδοποίησις, ἡ [eeðopieesees] notification, notice.

εἰδοποιῶ [eeðopeeo] notify, inform, advise.

εἶδος, τό [eeðos] sort, kind, type ‖ (βοτ) species ‖ τά εἴδη goods, wares ‖ kinds.

εἰδύλλιον, τό [eedeeleeon] love affair ‖ idyll.

εἰδωλολάτρης, ὁ [eedololatrees] pagan, heathen.

εἴδωλον, τό [eedolon] idol ‖ image.

εἰθισμένα, τά [eetheesmena]: κατά τά ~ as is the practice.

εἴθισται [eetheeste] it is the custom.

εἰκασία, ἡ [eekaseea] conjecture, guess.

εἰκαστικός [eekasteekos] conjectural ‖ εἰκαστικαί τέχναι fine arts.

εἰκόνα [eekona] βλ εἰκών.

εἰκονίζω [eekoneezo] portray, depict, represent.

εἰκονικός [eekoneekos] figurative ‖ (ἐπίθεσις) sham ‖ (πρᾶξις) bogus ‖ (τιμή) conventional.

εἰκόνισμα, τό [eekoneesma] portrait ‖ (ἁγιογραφία) icon.

εἰκονογραφία, ἡ [eekonoγrafeea] illustration ‖ (ἐκκλ) iconography.

εἰκονοστάσι(ον), τό [eekonostasee(on)] (ἐκκλ) shrine, screen.

εἴκοσι [eekosee] twenty.

εἰκοστός [eekostos] twentieth.

εἰκών, ἡ [eekon] image, picture ‖ (ἐκκλ) icon.

εἰλικρίνεια, ἡ [eeleekreeneea] sincerity, frankness.

εἰλικρινής [eeleekreenees] sincere, candid.

εἶμαι [eeme] I am, I'm.

εἰμή [eemee] unless, except, but.

εἶναι [eene] be, is, it is ‖ τό ~ being.

εἰρήνη, ἡ [eereene] peace.

εἰρηνικός [eereeneekos] peaceful.

εἰρηνοδικεῖον, τό [eereenoδeekeeon] magistrate's court.

εἱρμός, ὁ [eermos] train of thought, continuity.

εἰρωνεύομαι [eeronevome] speak derisively, speak ironically.

εἰρωνεία, ἡ [eeroneea] irony, mockery.

εἰς [ees] one ‖ (ἄρθρον) a, an.

εἰς [ees] in, among, at ‖ (χρόνος) within ‖ to, into, on.

εἰσαγγελεύς, ὁ [eesangelevs] public prosecutor ‖ (US) district attorney.

εἰσάγω [eesaγo] import ‖ (νομοσχέδιον) introduce ‖ (φέρω πρῶτα) introduce for the first time ‖ (παρουσιάζω) present ‖ εἰσαγωγεύς, ὁ importer ‖ εἰσαγωγή, ἡ importation ‖ (παρουσίασις) introduction ‖ εἰσαγωγικά, τά inverted commas.

εἰσβάλλω [eesvalo] invade ‖ (ποταμός) flow into.

εἰσβολή, ἡ [eesvolee] invasion.

εἰσδύω [eesδeeo] penetrate, slip in.

εἰσέρχομαι [eeserhome] come in, enter, go in.

εἰσέτι [eesetee] still, (not) yet, up to now.

εἰσήγησις, ἡ [eeseeγeesees] report ‖ suggestion.

εἰσηγοῦμαι [eeseeγoume] propose, move ‖ introduce.

εἰσιτήριον, τό [eeseeteereeon] ticket.

εἰσιτήριος [eeseeteereeos] of entry, of admission.

εἰσόδημα, τό [eesoδeema] income, revenue.

εἴσοδος, ἡ [eesoδos] entry, entrance ‖ admission.

εἰσπνέω [eespneo] inhale, breathe in.

εἰσπράκτωρ, ὁ [eespraktor] conductor ‖ collector.

εἴσπραξις, ἡ [eespraksees] collection ‖ receipt.

εἰσπράττω [eesprato] collect.

εἰσφορά, ἡ [eesfora] contribution.

εἰσχωρῶ [eeshoro] penetrate, intrude, get in.

εἶτα [eeta] then ‖ afterwards.

εἴτε [eete]: ~ . . . ~ either . . . or, whether . . . or.

ἐκ [ek] from, out of, by, of ‖ ἐξ ἀνάγκης of necessity ‖ ~ νέου again ‖ ἐξ ἴσου equally.

ἐκ-, ἐξ- [ek, eks] out, off ‖ completely, wholly.

ἔκαστος [ekastos] each, every one ‖ καθ' ἑκάστην every day ‖ τά καθ' ἕκαστα the details.

ἑκάστοτε [ekastote] each time.

ἑκατέρωθεν [ekaterothen] on both sides, mutually.

ἑκατομμύριον, τό [ekatomeereeon] million.

ἑκατομμυριοῦχος, ὁ [ekatomeereeouhos] millionaire.

ἑκατό(ν) [ekato(n)] hundred ‖ τά ~ per cent.

ἑκατονταετηρίς, ἡ [ekatontaeteerees] century ‖ centenary.

ἑκατονταπλάσιος [ekatontaplaseeos] hundredfold.

ἑκατοντούτης, ὁ [ekatontoutees] centenarian.

ἑκατοστάρι, τό [ekatostaree] hundreddrachma note.

ἑκατοστόμετρον, τό [ekatostometron] centimetre.

ἑκατοστός [ekatostos] hundredth.

ἐκβάλλω [ekvalo] take out, extract ‖ (ἀπομακρύνω) repudiate ‖ (ἐχθρόν) drive out ‖ (ἐπί ποταμῶν) flow into.

ἔκβασις [ekvasees] issue, outcome, result.

ἐκβιάζω [ekveeazo] (κάποιον) force, compel ‖ blackmail ‖ (διάβασιν κτλ) force.

ἐκβολή, ἡ [ekvolee] ejection ‖ (ποταμοῦ) mouth, estuary.

ἐκγυμνάζω [ekγeemnazo] exercise, train, drill.

ἔκδηλος [ekδeelos] manifest, evident, obvious.

ἐκδηλώνω [ekδeelono] show, reveal, evince.

ἐκδίδω [ekδeeδo] issue, publish ‖ (ἀπόφασιν) pronounce ‖ (συναλλαγματικήν) draw ‖ (ἐγκληματίαν κτλ) extradite.

ἐκδίκησις, ἡ [ekdeekeesees] vengeance, revenge.

ἐκδικητικός [ekdeekeeteekos] revengeful, vindictive.

ἐκδικοῦμαι [ekdeekoume] take revenge on, get even with.

ἐκδιώκω [ekdeeoko] expel, oust ‖ (στρατ) dislodge, drive out.

ἐκδορά, ἡ [ekdora] abrasion ‖ skinning.

ἔκδοσις, ἡ [ekdosees] publication, edition ‖ (χαρτονομίσματος) issue ‖ (παραλλαγή) version, story ‖ (ἐγκληματίου κτλ) extradition.

ἐκδότης, ὁ [ekdotees] publisher, editor.

ἐκδοτικός [ekdoteekos] publishing.

ἐκδοχή, ἡ [ekdohee] interpretation, version.

ἐκδρομή, ἡ [ekdromee] excursion, outing, trip.

ἐκεῖ [ekee] there ‖ ~ πού instead of, while, whereas ‖ ~ θεν thence, from there.

ἐκεῖνος [ekeenos] he, that one there.

ἐκεχειρία, ἡ [ekeheereea] truce, armistice.

ἔκθαμβος [ekthamvos] dazzled, astounded.

ἔκθεμα, τό [ekthema] exhibit.

ἔκθεσις, ἡ [ekthesees] (στό ὕπαιθρον) exposure ‖ (ἀνθέων κτλ) exhibition ‖ (ἐμπορευμάτων) display, exposition ‖ (γραπτή) composition.

ἐκθέτης, ὁ [ekthetees] exhibitor ‖ (μαθημ) exponent.

ἔκθετον, τό [ektheton] abandoned baby.

ἔκθετος [ekthetos] exposed.

ἐκθέτω [ektheto] expose, display, exhibit ‖ (τήν ζωήν) expose, imperil ‖ (τέκνον) abandon ‖ (σχέδια) state, expose, disclose ‖ (μεταφ) lay bare, expose.

ἐκθρονίζω [ekthroneezo] dethrone.

ἐκκαθαρίζω [ekathareezo] clear out, clean ‖ (λογαριασμόν) liquidate, settle.

ἐκκεντρικός [ekentreekos] eccentric.

ἐκκενῶ [ekeno] empty out, vacate ‖ (ποτήρι κτλ) drain ‖ (ὅπλον) fire ‖ (οἰκίαν) leave.

ἐκκένωσις, ἡ [ekenosees] evacuation, emptying ‖ (ἠλεκ) discharge.

ἐκκίνησις, ἡ [ekeeneesees] departure, starting off.

ἐκκλησία, ἡ [ekleeseea] church ‖ ἐκκλησιαστικός ecclesiastic(al).

ἔκκλησις, ἡ [ekleesees] appeal.

ἐκκλίνω [ekleeno] deviate ‖ (μεταφ) go astray, become corrupted.

ἐκκρεμής [ekremees] unsettled, pending.

ἐκκωφαντικός [ekofanteekos] deafening.

ἐκλαμβάνω [eklamvano] construe, interpret, take (for).

ἐκλέγω [ekleyo] choose, pick out ‖ elect.

ἔκλειψις, ἡ [ekleepsees] eclipse ‖ (μεταφ) disappearance.

ἐκλεκτικός [eklekteekos] choosy, selective.

ἐκλεκτός [eklektos] choice, select, picked ‖ οἱ ἐκλεκτοί élite.

ἐκλιπαρῶ [ekleeparo] entreat, implore

ἐκλογεύς, ὁ [ekloyevs] elector, voter.

ἐκλογή, ἡ [ekloyee] choice, selection ‖ election.

ἐκλογές, οἱ [ekloyes] πλ elections.

ἐκλογικός [ekloyeekos] electoral.

ἐκμαγεῖον, τό [ekmayeeon] (plaster) cast

ἐκμαιεύω [ekmeyevo] extract, elicit.

ἐκμεταλλεύομαι [ekmetalevome] exploit.

ἐκμηδενίζω [ekmeedeneezo] annihilate.

ἐκμίσθωσις, ἡ [ekmeesthosees] leasing, lease.

ἐκμισθωτής, ὁ [ekmeesthotees] lessor, hirer.

ἐκμυζῶ [ekmeezo] suck out, drain ‖ (μεταφ) exploit.

ἐκμυστηρεύομαι [ekmeesteerevome] confide a secret, confess.

ἐκνευρίζω [eknevreezo] annoy, exasperate.

ἑκούσιος [ekouseeos] voluntary ‖ willing.

ἐκπαίδευσις, ἡ [ekpedevsees] education, training.

ἐκπαιδευτήριον, τό [ekpedevteereeon] school, institute.

ἐκπαιδευτικός [ekpedevteekos] educational ‖ (διδάσκων) schoolteacher.

ἐκπαιδεύω [ekpedevo] educate, train, instruct.

ἔκπαλαι [ekpale] from time immemorial, long ago.

ἐκπατρίζω [ekpatreezo] expatriate.

ἐκπέμπω [ekpembo] send forth, emit ‖ (διά ραδιοφώνου) broadcast.

ἐκπίπτω [ekpeepto] decline, fall ‖ (μεταφ) deduct, reduce, lower.

ἐκπληκτικός [ekpleekteekos] astonishing, surprising.

ἔκπληξις, ἡ [ekpleeksees] surprise, astonishment.

ἐκπληρῶ [ekpleero] fulfil, perform.

ἐκπλήσσω [ekpleeso] surprise, astonish.

ἔκπλους, ὁ [ekplous] departure of ship.

ἐκπνέω [ekpneo] exhale ‖ (πεθαίνω) die ‖ (μεταφ) expire, terminate.

ἐκποιῶ [ekpeeo] sell, dispose of.

ἐκπομπή, ἡ [ekpombee] emission ‖ (ραδιοφώνου) broadcast.

ἐκπρόθεσμος [ekprothesmos] overdue.

ἐκπρόσωπος, ὁ [ekprosopos] representative.

ἐκπροσωπῶ [ekprosopo] represent.

ἔκπτωσις, ἡ [ekptosees] decline, fall ‖ (δικαιωμάτων) loss ‖ (τιμῆς κτλ) reduction, rebate, discount, deduction.

ἐκρήγνυμαι [ekreeyneeme] explode, erupt, burst.

ἐκρηκτικός [ekreekteekos] explosive.

ἔκρηξις, ἡ [ekreeksees] explosion, eruption, outburst.

ἔκρυθμος [ekreethmos] irregular, abnormal, unusual.

ἐκσκαφή, ἡ [ekskafee] excavation, cutting.

ἔκστασις, ἡ [ekstasees] ecstasy, rapture.

ἐκστομίζω [ekstomeezo] utter, launch.

ἐκστρατεία, ἡ [ekstrateea] expedition, campaign.

ἐκσφενδονίζω [eksfendoneezo] fling, throw, hurl.

ἔκτακτος [ektaktos] temporary, emergency ‖ (εἰδικός) special, exceptional, excellent.

ἐκτάκτως [ektaktos] temporarily ‖ extraordinarily, unusually.

ἔκτασις, ἡ [ektasees] extent, stretch.

ἐκτεθειμένος [ektetheemenos] exposed ‖ compromised.

ἐκτείνω [ekteeno] stretch, extend, prolong.

ἐκτέλεσις, ἡ [ektelesees] execution ‖ performance, fulfilment.

ἐκτελεστικός [ektelesteekos] executive.

ἐκτελῶ [ektelo] execute ‖ perform, carry out.

ἐκτενής [ektenees] extensive, lengthy, prolix.

ἐκτεταμένος [ektetamenos] extensive, long.

ἐκτίθεμαι [ektetheme] be embarrassed ‖ display ‖ (γιά ἐκλογές) run for office.

ἐκτίμησις, ἡ [ekteemeesees] esteem, estimation, appreciation.

ἐκτιμῶ [ekteemo] esteem, value, appreciate, estimate.

ἐκτοξεύω [ektoksevo] shoot, cast, hurl.

ἐκτοπίζω [ektopeezo] displace, dislodge ‖ (ἐξορίζω) exile.

ἐκτόπισμα, τό [ektopeesma] displacement.

ἕκτος [ektos] sixth.

ἐκτός [ektos] outside, save ‖ ~ τῆς πόλεως outside the city ‖ ~ ἀπό apart from, besides, except for ‖ ~ τοῦ Γεώργου except George ‖ ~ ἄν unless ‖ ~ κινδύνου out of danger.

ἔκτοτε [ektote] ever since, since then.

ἐκτρέπομαι [ektrepome] deviate from ‖ (μεταφ) go astray.

ἐκτρέπω [ektrepo] deflect, turn aside, divert.

ἔκτροπος [ektropos] improper, devious.

ἐκτροχιάζομαι [ektroheeazome] become derailed ‖ (μεταφ) go astray.

ἔκτρωμα, τό [ektroma] monster, freak.

ἔκτρωσις, ἡ [ektrosees] abortion, miscarriage.

ἐκτυλίσσομαι [ekteeleesome] develop, evolve.

ἐκτυπώνω [ekteepono] print ‖ engrave in relief.

ἐκτυφλωτικός [ekteéfloteekos] blinding.

ἐκφέρω [ekfero] express.

ἐκφοβίζω [ekfoveezo] intimidate, frighten.

ἐκφορά, ἡ [ekfora] funeral, burial.

ἐκφορτωτής, ὁ [ekfortotees] unloader, docker.

ἐκφράζω [ekfrazo] express, reveal.

ἔκφρασις, ἡ [ekfrasees] expression.

ἐκφραστικός [ekfrasteekos] expressive.

ἐκφυλισμός, ὁ [ekfeeleesmos] degeneration.

ἐκφωνῶ [ekfono] deliver a speech ‖ read aloud.

ἐκχύλισμα, τό [ekheeleesma] extract.

ἐκχωρῶ [ekhoro] transfer, assign, cede ‖ (θέσιν) make way.

ἑκών [ekon] willing ‖ voluntary ‖ ~ ἄκων willy-nilly.

ἔλα [ela] (ἐπιφ) come!, come now!

ἐλαία, ἡ [elea] olive tree.

ἐλαιογραφία, ἡ [eleoγrafeea] oil painting.

ἐλαιόλαδον, τό [eleoladon] olive oil.

ἔλαιον, τό [eleon] olive oil, oil.

ἐλαιοτριβεῖον, τό [eleotreeveeon] olive press.

ἐλαιόχρωμα, τό [eleohroma] oil paint.

ἐλαιώνας, ὁ [eleonas] olive grove.

ἔλασμα, τό [elasma] metal plate, sheet iron.

ἐλάσσων [elason] less, smaller ‖ (μουσ) minor.

ἐλαστικόν, τό [elasteekon] tyre ‖ rubber, elastic.

ἐλαστικός [elasteekos] flexible, elastic.

ἐλατήριον, τό [elateereeon] spring ‖ (μεταφ) incentive, motive.

ἔλατο, τό [elato] fir, fir tree.

ἐλάττωμα, τό [elatoma] defect, fault.

ἐλαττώνω [elatono] diminish, lessen, decrease.

ἐλάττωσις, ἡ [elatosees] decrease, curtailment.

ἐλαύνω [elavno] drive, press on, push on.

ἐλάφι, τό [elafee] deer.

ἐλαφρόπετρα, ἡ [elafropetra] pumice stone.

ἐλαφρός [elafros] light, slight ‖ (καφές κτλ) mild, thin, weak.

ἐλαφρώνω [elafrono] reduce, lighten ‖ feel relieved.

ἐλάχιστα [elaheesta] very little.

ἐλάχιστος [elaheestos] least, very little ‖ τ' οὐλάχιστον at least.

Ἑλβετία, ἡ [elveteea] Switzerland.

Ἑλβετικός [elveteekos] Swiss.

Ἑλβετός, ὁ [elvetos] Swiss (person).

ἐλεγκτής, ὁ [elengtees] inspector, auditor.

ἔλεγχος, ὁ [elenghos] inspection, examination ‖ (λογαριασμοῦ) verification, control, auditing ‖ (μηχανῆς) testing, overhauling ‖ (μεταφ) censure, check, reproach.

ἐλέγχω [elengho] check, control, test.

ἐλεεινός [eleeenos] pitiful, wretched, vile.

ἐλεημοσύνη, ἡ [eleyemoseenee] alms, charity.

ἔλεος, τό [eleos] mercy, pity.

ἐλευθερία, ἡ [elefthereea] liberty, freedom.

ἐλεύθερος [eleftheros] free ‖ (ἐργένης) unmarried.

ἐλευθερώνω [elefthrono] redeem, set free, release, rid.

ἐλεφαντόδους, ὁ [elefantodous] tusk ‖ ivory.

ἐλεφαντοστοῦν, τό [elefantostoun] ivory.

ἐλέφας, ὁ [elefas] elephant.

ἐλεῶ [eleo] give alms to, commiserate with ‖ Κύριε ἐλέησον (ἐπιφ) Lord have mercy!, for Heaven's sake!

ἐλιά, ἡ [elia] olive, olive tree ‖ (προσώπου κτλ) mole.

ἐλιγμός, ὁ [eleeymos] twisting, winding ‖ (στρατ) manoeuvre, movement.

ἑλικόπτερον, τό [eleekopteron] helicopter.

ἕλιξ, ἡ, ὁ [eleeks] coil, spiral ‖ (προπέλλα) screw, propeller ‖ (βοτ) tendril.

ἑλίσσομαι [eleesome] wind, coil, twist ‖ (στρατ) manoeuvre.

ἕλκηθρον, τό [elkeethron] sledge, sled.

ἑλκυστικός [elkeesteekos] attractive, winsome.

ἑλκύω [elkeeo] charm, attract ‖ draw, pull.

ἕλκω [elko] draw, pull, haul.

Ἑλλάδα, ἡ [elaða] Greece.

ἑλλανοδίκης, ὁ [elanoðeekees] judge, referee.

Ἑλλάς, ἡ [elas] Greece.

ἔλλειμμα, τό [eleema] deficit, shortage.

ἔλλειψις, ἡ [eleepsees] lack, want, deficiency ‖ (μαθημ) ellipse.

Ἕλλην(ας), ὁ [eleen(as)] Greek (person).

ἑλληνικά, τά [eleeneeka] πλ Greek (language).

ἑλληνικός [eleeneekos] Greek.

ἑλληνισμός, ὁ [eleeneesmos] the Greek race.

ἑλληνιστί [eleeneestee] in Greek.

ἐλλιπής [eleepees] defective, wanting.

ἕλξις, ἡ [elksees] pull, traction, drawing, attraction.

ἑλονοσία, ἡ [elonoseea] malaria.

ἕλος, τό [elos] marsh, swamp, morass.

ἐλπίδα, ἡ [elpeeða] hope, expectation ‖ παρ' ~ contrary to expectation.

ἐλπίς [elpees] βλ ἐλπίδα.

ἑλώδης [eloðees] marshy, swampy.

ἐμβαδόν, τό [emvaðon] area.

ἐμβαθύνω [emvatheeno] (μεταφ) examine thoroughly, probe deeply.

ἐμβάλλω [emvallo] insert, get into, put in.

ἔμβασμα, τό [emvasma] remittance of money.

ἐμβατήριον, τό [emvateereeon] march.

ἔμβλημα, τό [emvleema] emblem, crest, symbol.

ἐμβολιάζω [emvoleeazo] (φυτόν) graft ‖ (ἄνθρωπον) vaccinate, inoculate.

ἐμβόλιον, τό [emvoleeon] vaccine ‖ (φυτόν) graft.

ἔμβολον, τό [emvolon] piston, rod ‖ (πλοίου) ram.

ἐμβριθής [emvreethees] erudite ‖ grave, serious.

ἐμβρόντητος [emvronteetos] thunderstruck, stupefied.

ἔμβρυον, τό [emvreeon] embryo, foetus.

ἐμένα [emena] me.

ἐμεῖς [emees] we.

ἐμετικός [emeteekos] emetic.

ἐμετός, ὁ [emetos] vomiting.

ἐμμένω [emeno] adhere to ‖ persist, insist.

ἔμμεσος [emesos] indirect.

ἔμμετρος [emetros] in moderation ‖ (ποίησις) in verse, metrical.

ἔμμηνα, τά [emeena] πλ menstruation, monthlies.

ἔμμισθος [emeesthos] salaried, paid.

ἔμμονος [emonos] persistent, obstinate, persevering.

ἐμός [emos] my, mine.

ἐμπάθεια, ἡ [empatheea] animosity, ill feeling.

ἐμπαίζω [empezo] tease, mock, deceive.

ἐμπειρία, ἡ [embeereea] experience, skill.

ἐμπειρογνώμων, ὁ, ἡ [embeeroγnomon] expert, specialist.

ἔμπειρος [embeeros] experienced, skilled in, able.

ἐμπιστεύομαι [embeestevome] (en)trust, confide.

ἐμπιστευτικός [embeestevteekos] confidential.

ἔμπιστος [embeestos] trustworthy, reliable, faithful ‖ ἐμπιστοσύνη, ἡ trust, confidence.

ἔμπλαστρον, τό [emblastron] plaster.

ἐμπλοκή, ἡ [emblokee] (στρατ) engagement ‖ (μηχανῆς) jamming ‖ gear of car.

ἐμπλουτίζω [emblouteezo] enrich.

ἔμπνευσις, ἡ [embnevsees] inspiration.

ἐμπνέομαι [embneome] feel inspired.

ἐμπνέω [embneo] inspire.

ἐμποδίζω [emboðeezo] hinder, obstruct prevent ‖ hold back, impede.

ἐμπόδιον, τό [emboðeeon] obstacle, impediment, obstruction.

ἐμπόλεμος [embolemos] belligerent.

ἐμπόρευμα, τό [emborevma] merchandise, article of commerce.

ἐμπορεύομαι [emborevome] engage in commerce ‖ deal in, trade in.

ἐμπορικόν, τό [emboreekon] shop, store, haberdashery.

ἐμπορικός [emboreekos] commercial, mercantile.

ἐμπόριον, τό [emboreeon] trade, commerce.

ἔμπορος, ὁ [emboros] merchant, trader, vendor.

ἐμποροϋπάλληλος, ὁ, ἡ [emboroeepaleelos] shop assistant, shopgirl ‖ (US) clerk.

ἐμπρησμός, ὁ [embreesmos] arson.

ἐμπρηστικός [embreesteekos] incendiary ‖ (μεταφ) fiery.

ἐμπρόθεσμος [embrothesmos] within the time limit.

ἐμπρός [embros] forward(s), before, in front of ‖ ~ σέ compared with ‖ πηγαίνω ~ succeed ‖ ~ ἀπό in front of ‖ τό ρολόϊ πάει ~ the clock is fast ‖ ~ μου in front of me ‖ ~! hallo!, come in! ‖ βάζω ~ start.

ἔμπροσθεν [embrosthen] in front ‖ (προηγουμένως) previously ‖ (ἐπίθ) in front, previous.

ἐμπρόσθιος [embrostheeos] front, fore, anterior.

έμπυο, τό [embeeo] pus, matter.

ἐμφανής [emfanees] apparent, obvious, clear.

ἐμφανίζομαι [emfaneezome] appear, present o.s., make an appearance.

ἐμφανίζω [emfaneezo] exhibit, reveal ‖ (φωτογρ) develop.

ἐμφάνισις, ἡ [emfaneesees] appearance, presentation ‖ (φωτογρ) development.

ἔμφασις, ἡ [emfasees] stress, emphasis.

ἐμφύλιος [emfeeleeos]: ~ πόλεμος civil war.

ἔμφυτον, τό [emfeeton] instinct, intuition.

ἔμφυτος [emfeetos] innate, inherent, intuitive.

ἐμψυχώνω [empseehono] encourage, stimulate.

ἐν [en] in, at, within ‖ ~ τούτοις however, nevertheless ‖ ~ τάξει all right.

ἕν(α), τό [en(a)] one ‖ a, an.

ἐναγκαλίζομαι [enangaleezome] embrace, hug.

ἐναγόμενος [enayomenos] defendant.

ἐνάγω [enayo] sue, bring action against.

ἐναγωνίως [enayoneeos] anxiously, with anguish.

ἐναέριος [enaereeos] aerial, overhead, airy.

ἐναλλαγή, ἡ [enalayee] permutation, exchange, interchange.

ἐναλλάξ [enallaks] alternately, in turn.

ἐναλλάσσω [enalaso] alternate, exchange.

ἔναντι [enantee] towards, against ‖ βλ καί ἀπέναντι.

ἐνάντια [enanteea] adversely, contrarily ‖ ~ σέ against.

ἐναντίον [enanteeon] against ‖ contrary to.

ἐναντίον, τό [enanteeon] the contrary.

ἐνάντιος [enanteeos] adverse, contrary, opposite ‖ ἀπ' ἐναντίας on the contrary.

ἐναπόκειται [enapokeete]: σέ σένα ~ it's up to you.

ἐναργής [enaryees] clear, obvious, manifest.

ἐνάρετος [enaretos] virtuous, upright.

ἔναρθρος [enarthros] articulate, jointed.

ἐναρκτήριος [enarkteereeos] inaugural.

ἐναρμονίζω [enarmoneezo] harmonize.

ἔναρξις, ἡ [enarksees] opening, beginning, inauguration.

ἕνας, ὁ [enas] one ‖ a, an ‖ ~ ~ one by one ‖ ~ κι ~ especially good, very bad ‖ ὁ ~ τόν ἄλλον one another.

ἐνασχόλησις, ἡ [enasholeesees] occupation, employment.

ἔνατος [enatos] ninth.

ἔνδεια, ἡ [endeea] deficiency ‖ poverty.

ἐνδεικνύομαι [endeekneeome] be called for, be necessary.

ἐνδεικνύω [endeekneeo] indicate.

ἐνδεικτικόν, τό [endeekteekon] certificate.

ἐνδεικτικός [endeekteekos] indicative.

ἔνδειξις, ἡ [endeeksees] indication, sign.

ἕνδεκα [endeka] eleven.

ἐνδέχεται [endehete] it is possible, it is likely.

ἐνδεχόμενον, τό [endehomenon] eventuality, possibility.

ἐνδιάμεσος [endeeamesos] intermediate, in between.

ἐνδιαφέρομαι [endeeaferome] be interested in.

ἐνδιαφέρον, τό [endeeaferon] interest, concern.

ἐνδιαφέρω [endeeafero] concern, interest ‖ ~ν interesting.

ἐνδίδω [endeedo] give way to ‖ give way, bend.

ἔνδικος [endeekos] legal, judicial.

ἐνδοιάζω [endeeazo] hesitate, waver.

ἐνδόμυχος [endomeehos] intimate, inward, inmost, secret.

ἔνδον [endon] within, in.

ἔνδοξος [endoksos] celebrated, glorious, illustrious.

ἐνδότερος [endoteros] inner, interior.

ἐνδοχώρα, ἡ [endohora] hinterland.

ἔνδυμα, τό [endeema] dress, garment, clothes ‖ ~σία, ἡ suit, dress, garb.

ἐνδύομαι [endeeome] dress o.s., put on one's clothes.

ἐνέδρα, ἡ [enedra] ambush, ambuscade.

ἕνεκα [eneka] on account of, because of.

ἐνενήντα [enenenta] ninety.

ἐνέργεια, ἡ [eneryeea] energy, action ‖ (φαρμάκου) efficacy.

ἐνεργητικός [eneryeeteekos] energetic, active ‖ (φάρμακον) effective.

ἐνεργός [eneryos] active ‖ effective.

ἐνεργοῦμαι [eneryoume] move the bowels ‖ take place.

ἐνεργῶ [eneryo] act, take steps ‖ (φάρμακον κτλ) take effect, work ‖ (καθαρτικόν) purge.

ἔνεσις, ἡ [enesees] injection.

ἐνεστώς, ὁ [enestos] (γραμμ) present tense.

ἐνετικός [eneteekos] Venetian.

ἐνεχυροδανειστής, ὁ [eneheerodaneestees] pawnbroker.

ἐνηλικιοῦμαι [eneeleekeeoume] come of age, reach majority.

ἐνῆλιξ [eneeleeks] of age, adult.

ἐνήμερος [eneemeros] aware, informed.

ἐνημερώνω [eneemerono] inform, bring up to date.

ἔνθα [entha] where.

ἐνθάδε [enthade] here, hither.

ἐνθάρρυνσις, ἡ [enthareensees] encouragement, cheering up.

ἐνθαρρύνω [enthareeno] encourage, cheer up, hearten.

ἔνθεν [enthen] from here ‖ ~ καί ~ on each side.

ἔνθερμος [enthermos] ardent, warm, hearty.

ἐνθουσιάζομαι [enthouseeazome] be enthusiastic about.

ἐνθουσιασμός, ὁ [enthouseeasmos] enthusiasm.

ἐνθυμίζω [entheemeezo] call to mind ‖ remind.

ἐνθύμιον, τό [entheemeeon] keepsake, souvenir, memento.

ἐνθυμοῦμαι [entheemoume] recall, remember, recollect.

ἐνιαῖος [enieos] single, uniform.

ἑνικός [eneekos] (γραμμ) singular (number).

ἔνιοι [eniee] πλ some.

ἐνίοτε [eneeote] sometimes, now and then.

ἐνίσχυσις, ἡ [eneesheesees] reinforcement, strengthening ‖ (ἠλεκ) amplification.

ἐνισχύω [eneesheeo] support, reinforce, assist.

ἐννέα [ennea] nine ‖ ~κόσιοι nine hundred.

ἐννιά [ennia] nine.

ἔννοια, ἡ [enyeea] sense, concept, meaning, interpretation.

ἔννοια, ἡ [enyeea] concern, worry ‖ (σκοτούρα) anxiety ‖ ~ σου (ἐπιφ) take care!, don't worry!

ἔννομος [ennomos] lawful, legal, legitimate.

ἐννοεῖται [ennoeete] it is understood, certainly.

ἐννοῶ [ennoo] understand, mean, intend.

'ἐνοικιάζεται' [eneekeeazete] 'to let', 'for rent'.

ἐνοικιάζω [eneekeeazo] rent, let, hire.

ἐνοικιαστής, ὁ [eneekeeastees] tenant ‖ (νομ) lessee.

ἐνοίκιον, τό [eneekeeon] rent.

ἔνοικος, ὁ [eneekos] tenant, lodger.

ἔνοπλος [enoplos] armed, in arms.

ἐνόρασις, ἡ [enorasees] intuition.

ἐνορία, ἡ [enoreea] parish.

ἐνόρκως [enorkos] under oath, on oath.

ἐνόσω [enoso] as long as.

ἑνότης, ἡ [enotees] unity, concord.

ἐνοχή, ἡ [enohee] guilt, culpability.

ἐνόχλησις, ἡ [enohleesees] trouble, annoyance, inconvenience.

ἐνοχλητικός [enohleeteekos] troublesome, inconvenient, annoying.

ἐνοχλῶ [enohlo] trouble, annoy, pester, inconvenience.

ἐνσάρκωσις, ἡ [ensarkosees] incarnation, embodiment.

ἔνσημον, τό [enseemon] stamp.

ἐνσκήπτω [enskeepto] happen suddenly, break out ‖ break into.

ἐνσπείρω [enspeero] sow, spread, inspire.

ἔνστασις, ἡ [enstasees] objection.

ἐνστερνίζομαι [ensterneezome] embrace ‖ adopt, accept ‖ (μία ἰδέα) borrow.

ἔνστικτον, τό [ensteekton] instinct.

ἔνταλμα, τό [entalma] warrant, writ.

ἔντασις, ἡ [entasees] strain, tension ‖ intensity, intensification.

ἐντατικός [entateekos] intensive.

ἐνταῦθα [entavtha] here ‖ (ἔνδειξι, ἐπιστολῆς) in town, local

ἐντείνω [enteeno] stretch ‖ (τάς προσπαθείας) intensify ‖ (τάς σχέσεις) overstrain.

ἕντεκα [enteka] eleven.

ἐντέλεια, ἡ [enteleea] perfection.

ἐντέλλομαι [entelome] order, command, be ordered.

ἐντελῶς [entelos] completely, entirely, totally.

ἐντερικός [entereekos] intestinal.

ἔντερον, τό [enteron] intestine.

ἐντεταλμένος [entetalmenos] responsible for, charged with ‖ (οὐσ) delegate.

ἐντεῦθεν [entevthen] hence, from here.

ἔντεχνος [entehnos] skilful, artistic, ingenious.

ἔντιμος [enteemos] honest ‖ (οἰκογένεια κτλ) respectable, honourable.

ἔντοκος [entokos] with interest.

ἐντολή, ἡ [entolee] order, mandate ‖ authorization, commission.

ἐντομή [entomee] incision, groove.

ἐντομοκτόνον, τό [entomoktonon] insecticide.

ἔντομον, τό [entomon] insect.

ἔντονος [entonos] (προσπάθεια) strenuous, intense ‖ (φῶς) strong ‖ (χρῶμα) bright, deep.

ἐντοπίζω [entopeezo] localize ‖ (πυρκαϊάν) restrict, confine.

ἐντόπιος [entopeeos] local, native, indigenous.

ἐντός [entos] within, inside, in, into ‖ ~ ὀλίγου soon.

ἐντόσθια, τά [entostheea] πλ entrails, intestines.

ἐντριβή, ἡ [entreevee] massage ‖ (μηχανική) friction.

ἐντροπή, ἡ [entropee] shame, modesty.

ἔντυπον, τό [enteepon] printed matter.

ἔντυπος [enteepos] printed.

ἐντυπωσιακός [enteeposeeakos] impressive, striking.

ἐντύπωσις, ἡ [enteeposees] impression, sensation, feeling.

ἐνῶ [eno] while, whereas, since.

ἐνώνω [enono] unite, join, connect.

ἐνώπιον [enopeeon] in the presence of, in front of.

ἐνωρίς [enorees] early, in good time.

ἕνωσις, ἡ [enosees] union ‖ (ἠλεκτ) short circuit.

ἐξ [eks] βλ ἐκ.

ἐξαγοράζω [eksayorazo] buy off, redeem, ransom, obtain by bribery.

ἐξαγριώνω [eksayreeono] infuriate, enrage.

ἐξάγω [eksayo] take out, extract ‖ (ἐμπόριον) export ‖ (φιλοσ) deduce.

ἐξαγωγή, ἡ [eksayoyee] export ‖ (ὀδόντος) extraction.

ἐξάδελφος, ὁ [eksadelfos] cousin.

ἐξαερίζω [eksaereezo] ventilate, air.

ἐξαεριστήρ, ὁ [eksaereesteer] ventilator.

ἐξαίρεσις, ἡ [ekseresees] exception, exemption from, immunity (from).

ἐξαιρετικά [eksereteeka] exceptionally, unusually.

ἐξαιρετικός [eksereteekos] exceptional, unusual, excellent, remarkable.

ἐξαίρετος [ekseretos] excellent, remarkable.

ἐξαίρω [eksero] elevate, lift up || (μεταφ) exalt, extol, praise.

ἐξαιρῶ [eksero] except, exempt || (ἀποσπῶ) extract.

ἐξαίσιος [ekseseeos] excellent, splendid.

ἐξαίφνης [eksefnees] all of a sudden.

ἐξακολουθῶ [eksakoloutho] continue.

ἐξακόσιοι [eksakosiee] six hundred.

ἐξακριβώνω [eksakreevono] verify, ascertain, establish, clear up.

ἐξαλείφω [eksaleefo] efface, rub out, remove, obliterate.

ἔξαλλος [eksalos] beside o.s., frenzied.

ἐξάμβλωμα, τό [eksamvloma] monstrosity.

ἐξάμετρον, τό [eksametron] hexameter.

ἐξαμηνία, ἡ [eksameeneea] six months || pay for such period.

ἐξαναγκάζω [eksanangazo] compel, force, coerce.

ἐξάνθημα, τό [eksantheema] rash, pimples.

ἐξανίσταμαι [eksaneestame] rebel, protest.

ἐξαντλῶ [eksantlo] exhaust.

ἐξάπαντος [eksapantos] without fail, by all means.

ἐξαπατῶ [eksapato] cheat, deceive, delude || be unfaithful to.

ἐξαπίνης [eksapeenees] unexpectedly, suddenly.

ἐξάπλωσις, ἡ [eksaplosees] spreading out, extension.

ἐξαπολύω [eksapoleeo] let loose, hurl.

ἐξάπτω [eksapto] excite, provoke || (περιέργειαν κτλ) rouse, stir.

ἐξαργυρώνω [eksaryeerono] cash, turn into money.

ἐξάρθρωσις, ἡ [eksarthrosees] dislocation.

ἔξαρσις, ἡ [eksarsees] (μεταφ) elevation, exaltation.

ἐξαρτήματα, τά [eksarteemata] πλ gear, tackle, rigging, accessories.

ἐξάρτησις, ἡ [eksarteesees] dependence.

ἐξαρτῶμαι [eksartome] depend on, turn on.

ἐξασθένησις, ἡ [eksastheneesees] weakening, enfeeblement.

ἐξάσκησις, ἡ [eksaskeesees] exercise, practice, training.

ἐξασκῶ [eksasko] exercise, practise || (πίεσιν) exert.

ἐξασφαλίζω [eksasfaleezo] assure || (θέσιν) book, reserve.

ἐξατμίζω [eksatmeezo] evaporate || (μεταφ) vanish, melt away.

ἐξάτμισις, ἡ [eksatmeesees] evaporation || (αὐτοκινήτου) exhaust.

ἐξαφανίζομαι [eksafaneezome] disappear, vanish.

ἐξαφανίζω [eksafaneezo] eliminate, wipe out, destroy.

ἔξαφνα [eksafna] all of a sudden || (π.χ.) for instance.

ἔξαφνος [eksafnos] unexpected.

ἔξαψις, ἡ [eksapsees] fit of anger || excitement, elation.

ἐξεγείρομαι [ekseyeerome] rise, rebel.

ἐξέδρα, ἡ [eksedra] platform, stand || (λιμανιοῦ) pier.

ἐξελιγμένος [ekseleeyemenos] developed, evolved.

ἐξέλιξις, ἡ [ekseleeksees] evolution, development.

ἐξελίσσομαι [ekseleesome] unfold, evolve, develop.

ἐπίτηδες [eksepeeteedes] deliberately.

ἐξερευνητής, ὁ [ekserevneetees] explorer.

ἐξερευνῶ [ekserevno] investigate, explore.

ἐξέρχομαι [ekserhome] go out, leave || βλ καί βγαίνω.

ἐξετάζω [eksetazo] examine, interrogate, investigate.

ἐξέτασις, ἡ [eksetasees] examination, inspection.

ἐξεύρεσις, ἡ [eksevresees] discovery, finding out, invention.

ἐξευτελίζω [eksevteleezo] cheapen, lower, humiliate.

ἐξέχω [ekseho] stand out, project || excel.

ἐξήγησις, ἡ [ekseeyeesees] explanation, interpretation.

ἐξηγοῦμαι [ekseeyoume] explain, make clear, give an explanation.

ἐξηγῶ [ekseeyo] explain || interpret.

ἐξή(κο)ντα [eksee(ko)nta] sixty.

ἐξημερώνω [ekseemerono] tame.

ἐξηντλημένος [ekseentleemenos] exhausted, used up.

ἑξῆς [eksees]: ὡς ~ as follows || τά ~ the following || εἰς τό ~ henceforth || καί οὕτω καθ' ~ and so on.

ἐξιλεώνω [ekseeleono] appease, pacify || atone for.

ἕξις, ἡ [eksees] habit, custom, use.

ἐξίσταμαι [ekseestame] be astonished, wonder at.

ἐξίσωσις, ἡ [ekseesosees] balancing, equalizing || (μαθημ) equation.

ἐξόγκωμα, τό [eksongoma] swelling, tumour, bulge.

ἐξογκώνω [eksongono] swell || (μεταφ) exaggerate, overcolour.

ἐξόγκωσις, ἡ [eksongosees] swelling || exaggeration.

ἐξοδεύω [eksodevo] spend, use up, consume.

ἔξοδον, τό [eksodon] expense.

ἔξοδος, ἡ [eksodos] opening, emergence | (πόρτα) exit || (στρατ) sortie || (ἐκκλ) exodus.

ἐξοικειώνω [ekseekeeono] familiarize, accustom.

ἐξοκέλλω [eksokelo] run aground, go astray.

ἐξολοθρεύω [eksolothrevo] exterminate, destroy.

ἐξομαλύνω [eksomaleeno] smooth down ‖ level.

ἐξομοιώνω [eksomeeono] assimilate to, liken to, rank together.

ἐξομολόγησις, ἡ [eksomoloγeesees] confession, acknowledgement.

ἐξομολογῶ [eksomoloγo] confess.

ἐξόν [ekson] besides, except ‖ ~ ἄν unless.

ἐξοντῶ [eksonto] annihilate, exterminate.

ἐξοπλίζω [eksopleezo] arm, equip.

ἐξοργίζω [eksorγeezo] enrage, make angry.

ἐξορία, ἡ [eksoreea] banishment, exile.

ἐξορίζω [eksoreezo] exile, banish.

ἐξορκίζω [eksorkeezo] conjure, exorcise.

ἐξουδετερώνω [eksoυdeterono] neutralize.

ἐξουθενίζω [eksoυtheneezo] debase, degrade.

ἐξουσία, ἡ [eksouseea] power, authority, government.

ἐξουσιοδοτῶ [eksouseeoδoto] give authority to, authorize, empower.

ἐξόφθαλμος [eksofthalmos] obvious, plain.

ἐξοφλῶ [eksoflo] (λογαριασμόν) pay off, liquidate ‖ (μεταφ) fulfil.

ἐξοχή, ἡ [eksohee] countryside ‖ (ἐδαφική) eminence, protrusion ‖ κατ' ~ ν preeminently, par excellence.

ἐξοχικός [eksoheekos] country, rural, rustic.

ἔξοχος [eksohos] excellent, eminent, notable.

ἐξοχότης, ἡ [eksohotees] excellence ‖ ἡ αὐτοῦ ~ His Excellency.

ἐξύβρισις, ἡ [ekseevreesees] abuse, insult, offence.

ἐξυμνῶ [ekseemno] praise, celebrate.

ἐξυπακούεται [ekseepakouete] it is understood, it follows.

ἐξυπηρέτησις, ἡ [ekseepeereteesees] assistance, service, attendance.

ἐξυπηρετικός [ekseepeereteekos] helpful, useful.

ἐξυπηρετῶ [ekseepeereto] serve, assist, attend upon.

ἐξυπνάδα, ἡ [ekseepnaδa] cleverness, shrewdness.

ἔξυπνος [ekseepnos] clever, intelligent, smart, witty.

ἐξυπνῶ [ekseepno] wake up, awake.

ἐξυφαίνω [ekseefeno] weave ‖ (κίνημα) hatch, plot, contrive.

ἐξυψώνω [ekseepsono] elevate, raise ‖ (μεταφ) exalt, extol, glorify.

ἔξω [ekso] out, outside, without, abroad ‖ ἀπ' ~ from outside ‖ (μάθημα) by heart ‖ ~ ἀπό outside, except for ‖ μιά καί ~ at one go

ἐξώγαμος [eksoγamos] illegitimate, bastard.

ἔξωθεν [eksothen] from outside, from without.

ἐξώθυρα, ἡ [eksotheera] outside door, gateway.

ἐξωθῶ [eksotho] drive, push, force.

ἐξωκκλήσιον, τό [eksokleeseeon] chapel, country church.

ἐξωμότης, ὁ [eksomotees] renegade, apostate.

ἐξώπορτα, ἡ [eksoporta] βλ ἐξώθυρα.

ἐξωραΐζω [eksoraeezo] beautify, decorate, embellish.

ἔξωσις, ἡ [eksosees] eviction, expulsion.

ἐξώστης, ὁ [eksostees] balcony.

ἐξωτερικόν, τό [eksotereekon] exterior foreign country.

ἐξωτερικός [eksotereekos] external foreign.

ἐξωτικό, τό [eksoteeko] spook, spectre, wraith.

ἐξωτικός [eksoteekos] exotic ‖ outlandish.

ἐξωφρενικός [eksofreneekos] crazy ‖ maddening ‖ unreasonable, absurd.

ἐξώφυλλον, τό [eksofeelon] cover, flyleaf ‖ (παραθύρου) shutter.

ἑορτάζω [eortazo] celebrate.

ἑορτή, ἡ [eortee] holiday ‖ name day ‖ festival.

ἐπάγγελμα, τό [epangelma] profession, vocation ‖ ἐπαγγελματίας, ὁ craftsman, businessman.

ἐπαγγέλομαι [epangelome] practise ‖ (παριστάνω) pretend.

ἔπαθλον, τό [epathlon] prize, trophy.

ἔπαινος, ὁ [epenos] praise.

ἐπαινῶ [epeno] praise, speak highly of.

ἐπαισθητός [epestheetos] perceptible, noticeable.

ἐπαίσχυντος [epesheentos] shameful.

ἐπαίτης, ὁ [epetees] beggar.

ἐπακόλουθα, τά [epakoloutha] πλ consequences.

ἐπακολουθῶ [epakoloutho] follow, come after.

ἔπακρον, τό [epakron]: εἰς τό ~ extremely, to the extreme.

ἐπαλείφω [epaleefo] smear, anoint (with).

ἐπαληθεύω [epaleethevo] establish, verify.

ἐπάλληλος [epaleelos] successive, one after another.

ἐπάναγκες [epananges] essential, necessary.

ἐπανάγω [epanaγo] bring back (again).

ἐπανακάμπτω [epanakampto] return.

ἐπανακτῶ [epanakto] recover.

ἐπαναλαμβάνω [epanalamvano] repeat, resume.

ἐπανάληψις, ἡ [epanaleepsees] resumption, repetition.

ἐπανάστασις, ἡ [epanastasees] revolution.

ἐπαναστάτης, ὁ [epanastatees] revolutionary, rebel.

ἐπαναστατικός [epanastateekos] revolutionary.

ἐπαναστατῶ [epanastato] revolt, rebel.

ἐπαναφέρω [epanafero] restore, bring back.

ἐπανειλημμένος [epaneeleemenos] repeatedly.

ἐπανέρχομαι [epanerhome] return.

ἐπάνοδος, ἡ [epanodos] return.

ἐπανόρθωσις, ἡ [epanorthosees] reparation, restoration.

ἐπανωφόρι, τό [epanoforee] overcoat.

ἐπαξίως [epakseeos] deservedly, worthily.

ἐπάρατος [eparatos] (μεταφ) hateful, abominable.

ἐπάρκεια, ἡ [eparkeea] sufficiency, adequacy.

ἔπαρσις, ἡ [eparsees] conceit, haughtiness.

ἐπαρχία, ἡ [eparheea] province, district.

ἐπαρχιώτης, ὁ [eparheeotees] provincial.

ἔπαυλις, ἡ [epavlees] villa || country house.

ἐπαύριον [epavreeon]: ἡ ~ the following day, tomorrow.

ἐπαφή, ἡ [epafee] contact, touch.

ἐπαχθής [epahthees] oppressive || tedious.

ἐπείγομαι [epeeyome] be in a hurry, make haste.

ἐπειγόντως [epeeyontos] urgently.

ἐπείγων [epeeyon] urgent, pressing.

ἐπειδή [epeedee] because, as, for, since.

ἐπεισόδιον, τό [epeesodeeon] episode, incident || (καυγάς) quarrel, dispute.

ἔπειτα [epeeta] next, then, afterwards || moreover || ~ ἀπό after.

ἐπέκτασις, ἡ [epektasees] extension.

ἐπεκτείνω [epekteeno] extend, prolong.

ἐπεμβαίνω [epemveno] interfere, intervene.

ἐπέμβασις, ἡ [epemvasees] intervention, interference || (ἰατρ) operation.

ἐπένδυσις, ἡ [ependeesees] lining, covering || (οἶκον) investment.

ἐπεξεργασία, ἡ [epekseryaseea] processing, elaboration.

ἐπεξήγησις, ἡ [epekseeyeesees] explanation, elucidation.

ἐπέρχομαι [eperhome] come suddenly. occur, happen.

ἐπέτειος, ἡ [epeteeos] anniversary.

ἐπετηρίς, ἡ [epeteerees] anniversary.

ἐπευφημῶ [epefeemo] cheer, applaud.

ἐπηρεάζω [epeereazo] influence, affect.

ἐπί [epee] on, upon, over, above || (διαρκείας) for || ~ πλέον furthermore || ~ τέλους at last.

ἐπιβαίνω [epeeveno] go aboard || mount.

ἐπιβάλλομαι [epeevalome] assert o.s. || be indispensable.

ἐπιβάλλω [epeevalo] impose, inflict.

ἐπιβαρύνω [epeevareeno] burden.

ἐπιβατηγόν, τό [epeevateeyon] passenger ship.

ἐπιβάτης, ὁ [epeevatees] passenger.

ἐπιβατικόν, τό [epeevateekon] passenger vehicle, passenger ship.

ἐπιβεβαιώνω [epeeveveono] confirm, corroborate.

ἐπιβιβάζομαι [epeeveevazome] embark, go on board.

ἐπιβιβάζω [epeeveevazo] put aboard.

ἐπιβλαβής [epeevlavees] harmful.

ἐπιβλέπω [epeevlepo] supervise.

ἐπιβλητικός [epeevleeteekos] imposing.

ἐπιβολή, ἡ [epeevolee] imposition, infliction.

ἐπιβουλεύομαι [epeevoulevome] plot against.

ἐπίβουλος [epeevoulos] insidious, malicious.

ἐπιβραδύνω [epeevradeeno] retard, delay.

ἐπίγειος [epeeyeeos] earthly, worldly.

ἐπίγνωσις, ἡ [epeeynosees] knowledge, understanding.

ἐπίγονος, ὁ [epeeyonos] descendant.

ἐπίγραμμα, τό [epeeyrama] epigram.

ἐπιγραφή, ἡ [epeeyrafee] inscription || (βιβλίου) title.

ἐπιγραφική, ἡ [epeeyrafeekee] epigraphy.

ἐπιδεικνύομαι [epeedeekneeome] show off, be pompous.

ἐπιδεικνύω [epeedeeikneeo] display || show off.

ἐπιδεικτικός [epeedeeikteekos] showy.

ἐπιδείνωσις, ἡ [epeedeenosees] aggravation.

ἐπίδειξις, ἡ [epeedeeksees] display || showing off.

ἐπιδέξιος [epeedekseeos] skilful.

ἐπιδερμίδα, ἡ [epeedermeeδa] complexion || epidermis.

ἐπίδεσμος, ὁ [epeedesmos] bandage.

ἐπιδέχομαι [epeedehome] allow, be susceptible, tolerate.

ἐπιδημία, ἡ [epeedeemeea] epidemic.

ἐπιδίδω [epeedeeδo] present || deliver || serve.

ἐπιδιόρθωσις, ἡ [epeedeeorthosees] repair, mending.

ἐπιδιώκω [epeedeeoko] aim at, pursue, seek.

ἐπιδοκιμάζω [epeedokeemazo] approve.

ἐπίδομα, τό [epeedoma] allowance, extra pay.

ἐπίδοσις, ἡ [epeedosees] presentation, delivery || (νομ) deposit || (μεταφ) progress, development || (ἀθλητ) record.

ἐπίδρασις, ἡ [epeedrasees] effect, influence.

ἐπιδρομή, ἡ [epeedromee] invasion, raid.

ἐπιδρῶ [epeeδro] influence, act upon.

ἐπιεικής [epieekees] lenient, indulgent.

ἐπιζήμιος [epeezeemeeos] harmful, injurious.

ἐπιζῶ [epeezo] survive, outlive.

ἐπίθεσις, ἡ [epeethesees] attack, application.

ἐπιθετικός [epeetheteekos] aggressive || (γραμμ) adjectival.

ἐπίθετον, τό [epeetheton] adjective || surname.

ἐπιθανάτιος [epeethanateeos] of death mortal.

ἐπιθεώρησις, ἡ [epeetheoreesees] inspection ‖ (περιοδικόν) review ‖ (θέατρον) revue.

ἐπιθυμία, ἡ [epeetheemeea] desire, wish.

ἐπιθυμῶ [epeetheemo] wish for, desire.

ἐπίκαιρος [epeekeros] timely, opportune topical.

ἐπικαλοῦμαι [epeekaloume] invoke.

ἐπίκειμαι [epeekeeme] be imminent ‖ impend.

ἐπικερδής [epeekerðees] profitable.

ἐπικεφαλίς, ἡ [epeekefalees] headline title.

ἐπικίνδυνος [epeekeenðeenos] dangerous, hazardous.

ἐπικλινής [epeekleenees] sloping, inclined.

ἐπικοινωνία, ἡ [epeekeenoneea] contact, communication.

ἐπικοινωνῶ [epeekeenono] communicate.

ἐπικός [epeekos] epic.

ἐπικουρία, ἡ [epeekoureea] help ‖ (στρατ) relief, reinforcements.

ἐπικράτεια, ἡ [epeekrateea] state, dominion.

ἐπικρατῶ [epeekrato] prevail, predominate.

ἐπικρίνω [epeekreeno] criticize, censure.

ἐπικροτῶ [epeekroto] approve.

ἐπικυρώνω [epeekeerono] ratify, confirm, sanction.

ἐπιλαχών, ὁ [epeelahon] runner-up.

ἐπίλεκτος [epeelektos] select, chosen.

ἐπιληψία, ἡ [epeeleepseea] epilepsy.

ἐπιλογή, ἡ [epeeloyee] selection, choice.

ἐπίλογος, ὁ [epeelogos] epilogue ‖ conclusion.

ἐπιλοχίας, ὁ [epeeloheeas] sergeant-major.

ἐπίμαχος [epeemahos] disputed ‖ controversial.

ἐπιμελής [epeemelees] diligent, industrious, careful.

ἐπιμελητήριον, τό [epeemeleeteereeon] (ἐμπορικόν) chamber of commerce.

ἐπιμελητής, ὁ [epeemeleetees] superintendent ‖ (university) tutor.

ἐπιμελοῦμαι [epeemeloume] take care of.

ἐπιμένω [epeemeno] insist, persist.

ἐπιμήκης [epeemeekees] oblong, elongated.

ἐπιμονή, ἡ [epeemonee] insistence, perseverance.

ἐπίμονος [epeemonos] persistent, stubborn ‖ obstinate.

ἐπινοῶ [epeenoo] invent, contrive, devise

ἐπιοῦσα, ἡ [epeeousa] the next day.

ἐπίπαγος, ὁ [epeepagos] crust.

ἐπίπεδον, τό [epeepeðon] plane.

ἐπίπεδος [epeepeðos] plane, level, flat even.

ἐπιπίπτω [epeepeepto] fall upon.

ἔπιπλα, τά [epeepla] πλ furniture.

ἐπίπλαστος [epeeplastos] feigned, fictitious.

ἐπιπλέω [epeepleo] float ‖ (μεταφ) keep afloat

ἐπίπληξις, ἡ [epeepleeksees] reproach, rebuke.

ἐπιπλήττω [epeepleeto] reproach, chide.

ἐπιπλοκή, ἡ [epeeplokee] complication.

ἐπιπλώνω [epeeplono] furnish.

ἐπίπλωσις, ἡ [epeeplosees] furnishing.

ἐπιπόλαιος [epeepoleos] superficial frivolous.

ἐπίπονος [epeeponos] laborious, toilsome.

ἐπιπροσθέτως [epeeprosthetos] in addition, furthermore.

ἐπίρρημα, τό [epeereema] adverb.

ἐπιρροή, ἡ [epeeroee] influence.

ἐπίσημος [epeeseemos] official, formal.

ἐπίσης [epeesees] likewise, also, too.

ἐπισιτισμός, ὁ [epeeseeteesmos] provisioning, victualling, provisions.

ἐπισκεπτήριον, τό [epeeskepteereeon] visiting card.

ἐπισκέπτης, ὁ [epeeskeptees] visitor.

ἐπισκέπτομαι [epeeskeptome] visit, call upon.

ἐπισκευάζω [epeeskevazo] repair, mend.

ἐπισκευή, ἡ [epeeskevee] repairing, mending.

ἐπίσκεψις, ἡ [epeeskepsees] visit, call.

ἐπίσκοπος, ὁ [epeeskopos] bishop.

ἐπισμηναγός, ὁ [epeesmeenayos] squadron leader.

ἐπισπεύδω [epeespevðo] hasten, rush.

ἐπιστάτης, ὁ [epeestatees] supervisor overseer ‖ attendant.

ἐπιστήθιος [epeesteetheeos]: ~ φίλος bosom friend.

ἐπιστήμη, ἡ [epeesteemee] science.

ἐπιστημονικός [epeesteemoneekos] scientific.

ἐπιστήμων, ὁ, ἡ [epeesteemon] scientist, professional (man) ‖ expert.

ἐπιστολή, ἡ [epeestolee] letter.

ἐπιστόμιον, τό [epeestomeeon] mouthpiece ‖ valve, plug.

ἐπιστράτευσις, ἡ [epeestratevsees] mobilization, call-up.

ἐπιστρέφω [epeestrefo] return.

ἐπιστροφή, ἡ [epeestrofee] return.

ἐπίστρωμα, τό [epeestroma] covering (κρεββατιοῦ) blanket.

ἐπισύρω [epeeseero] attract, draw, catch one's eye.

ἐπισφαλής [epeesfalees] precarious, risky unstable.

ἐπισωρεύω [epeesorevo] accumulate, pile up.

ἐπιταγή, ἡ [epeetayee] order ‖ chequé.

ἐπιτακτικός [epeetakteekos] imperative.

ἐπίταξις, ἡ [epeetaksees] requisition.

ἐπιτάφιος, ὁ [epeetafeeos] Good Friday procession.

ἐπιταχύνω [epeetaheeno] accelerate, speed up.

ἐπιτελάρχης, ὁ [epeetelarhees] chief of staff.

ἐπιτελεῖον, τό [epeeteleeon] (general) staff.

ἐπιτετραμμένος, ὁ [epeetetramenos] chargé d'affaires.

ἐπίτευγμα, τό [epeetevyma] achievement.

ἐπίτευξις, ἡ [epeetevksees] attainment ‖ obtaining.

ἐπιτήδειος [epeeteedeeos] suitable for ‖ clever, skilful.

ἐπίτηδες [epeeteedes] on purpose, purposely.

ἐπιτηδευμένος [epeeteedevmenos] affected.

ἐπιτηρῶ [epeeteero] supervise, oversee, watch.

ἐπιτίθεμαι [epeeteetheme] attack, assail, assault.

ἐπίτιμος [epeeteemos] honorary.

ἐπιτόκιον, τό [epeetokeeon] compound interest.

ἐπιτομή, ἡ [epeetomee] summary, abridgement.

ἐπίτομος [epeetomos] abridged, shortened, condensed.

ἐπιτόπιος [epeetopeeos] local.

ἐπιτρέπω [epeetrepo] allow, permit.

ἐπιτροπή, ἡ [epeetropee] committee, commission.

ἐπίτροπος, ὁ [epeetropos] guardian, trustee ‖ agent.

ἐπιτυγχάνω [epeeteenghano] attain, get ‖ get right ‖ (κατά τύχην) meet, find ‖ (στήν δουλειά) succeed.

ἐπιτυχής [epeeteehees] successful.

ἐπιτυχία, ἡ [epeeteeheea] success.

ἐπιφάνεια, ἡ [epeefaneea] surface.

ἐπιφανής [epeefanees] eminent, prominent.

Ἐπιφάνια, τά [epeefaneea] πλ Epiphany.

ἐπιφέρω [epeefero] bring about, cause.

ἐπίφοβος [epeefovos] dangerous, alarming.

ἐπιφυλακή, ἡ [epeefeelakee]: ἐν ~ at the ready, on the alert.

ἐπιφύλαξις, ἡ [epeefeelaksees] circumspection ‖ reservation.

ἐπιφυλάσσομαι [epeefeelasome] reserve, intend.

ἐπιφώνημα, τό [epeefoneema] (γραμμ) interjection.

ἐπιχείρημα, τό [epeeheereema] argument ‖ attempt.

ἐπιχειρηματίας, ὁ [epeeheereemateeas] businessman.

ἐπιχείρησις, ἡ [epeeheereesees] undertaking ‖ (οἶκον) enterprise, business ‖ (στρατ) operation.

ἐπιχρίω [epeehreeo] coat, paint, daub.

ἐπιχρυσώνω [epeehreesono] gild.

ἐποικοδομητικός [epeekoδomeeteekos] constructive, edifying.

ἔπομαι [epome] follow.

ἐπόμενος [epomenos] next, following.

ἐπομένως [epomenos] consequently, therefore.

ἐπονομάζω [eponomazo] surname, name.

ἐποπτεύω [epoptevo] supervise, oversee, inspect.

ἐπουλώνω [epoulono] heal.

ἐποφθαλμιῶ [epofthalmeeo] covet.

ἐποχή, ἡ [epohee] epoch, era ‖ (τοῦ ἔτους) season.

ἑπτά [epta] seven.

ἑπτακόσιοι [eptakosiee] seven hundred.

ἐπώδυνος [epoδeenos] painful.

ἐπωμίζομαι [epomeezome] shoulder (a burden).

ἐπωμίς, ἡ [epomees] epaulette.

ἐπωνυμία, ἡ [eponeemeea] (nick)name surname ‖ (ἑταιρείας) title.

ἐπώνυμον, τό [eponeemon] surname, family name.

ἐπωφελής [epofelees] profitable, beneficial, useful.

ἐπωφελοῦμαι [epofeloume] take advantage, avail o.s., profit.

ἔρανος, ὁ [eranos] fund, collection.

ἐρασιτέχνης, ὁ [eraseetehnees] amateur.

ἐραστής, ὁ [erastees] lover.

ἐργάζομαι [eryazome] work ‖ function.

ἐργαλεῖον, τό [eryaleeon] tool, implement.

ἐργασία, ἡ [eryaseea] work, job, business ‖ (ἐπιδεξιότης) workmanship.

ἐργαστήριον, τό [eryasteereeon] laboratory ‖ studio ‖ workshop.

ἐργάτης, ὁ [eryatees] labourer, worker ‖ (ναυτ) windlass.

ἐργατιά, ἡ [eryatea] working class.

ἐργατικός [eryateekos] industrious, of the working class.

ἐργένης, ὁ [eryenees] bachelor.

ἐργοδηγός, ὁ [eryoδeeγos] foreman.

ἐργοδότης, ὁ [eryoδotees] employer.

ἐργολάβος, ὁ [eryolavos] contractor ‖ (γλυκό) macaroon.

ἔργον, τό [eryon] work ‖ act, deed ‖ (βιβλίον) book ‖ (σινεμά) film.

ἐργοστάσιον, τό [eryostaseeon] factory works.

ἐργόχειρον, τό [eryoheeron] handiwork ‖ (κέντημα) embroidery.

ἐρεθίζω [eretheezo] irritate, excite.

ἐρεθισμός, ὁ [eretheesmos] irritation.

ἐρείπιον, τό [ereepeeon] ruin, wreck.

ἔρεισμα, τό [ereesma] prop, support.

ἔρευνα, ἡ [erevna] (re)search, investigation.

ἐρευνητής, ὁ [erevneetees] researcher ‖ explorer.

ἐρευνῶ [erevno] search, investigate.

ἐρημία, ἡ [ereemeea] solitude ‖ wilderness.

ἔρημος, ἡ [ereemos] desert ‖ (ἐπίθ) desolate, deserted.

ἐρημώνω [ereemono] lay waste, devastate.

ἔριον, τό [ereeon] wool, fleece.

ἔρις, ἡ [erees] dispute, quarrel.

ἔριφι, τό [ereefee] kid.

ἕρμαιον, τό [ermaeon] prey ‖ victim.

ἑρμάριον, τό [ermareeon] cupboard, closet.

ἑρμηνεία, ἡ [ermeeneea] interpretation.

ἑρμηνεύω [ermeenevo] interpret.

ἑρμητικός [ermeeteekos] hermetic.

ἑρπετόν, τό [erpeton] reptile.
ἕρπω [erpo] crawl, creep.
ἐρυθριῶ [ereethreeo] blush.
ἐρυθρόδερμος, ὁ [ereethroδermos] redskin.
ἐρυθρός [ereethros] red.
ἔρχομαι [erhome] come.
ἐρχόμενος [erhomenos] coming, next.
ἐρχομός, ὁ [erhomos] coming, arrival.
ἐρωμένη, ἡ [eromenee] mistress.
ἐρωμένος, ὁ [eromenos] lover.
ἔρωτας, ὁ [erotas] love, passion.
ἐρωτευμένος [erotevmenos] in love.
ἐρωτεύομαι [erotevome] fall in love.
ἐρώτημα, τό [eroteema] question, problem.
ἐρωτηματικόν, τό [eroteemateekon] question mark.
ἐρωτηματολόγιον, τό [eroteematoloyeeon] questionnaire.
ἐρώτησις, ἡ [eroteesees] question, query.
ἐρωτικός [eroteekos] erotic ‖ amatory.
ἐρωτοτροπία, ἡ [erototropeea] flirtation.
ἐρωτύλος [eroteelos] amorous.
ἐρωτῶ [eroto] ask, inquire ‖ question.
ἐσκεμμένος [eskemenos] premeditated ‖ deliberately.
ἐσοδεία, ἡ [esoδeea] crop, harvest.
ἔσοδον, τό [esoδon] income, revenue, receipt.
ἐσοχή, ἡ [esohee] recess, indentation.
ἑσπέρα, ἡ [espera] evening.
ἑσπεριδοειδῆ, τά [espereeδoeeδee] πλ citrus fruits.
ἑσπερινός [espereenos] evening.
ἑσπερινός, ὁ [espereenos] vespers.
ἐσπευσμένος [espevsmenos] hasty, hurried.
ἑστία, ἡ [esteea] hearth, fireplace ‖ (σπίτι) home ‖ (λίκνος) cradle ‖ (σόμπας) burner.
ἑστιατόριον, τό [esteeatoreeon] restaurant.
ἔστω [esto] so be it ‖ ~ καί even, even if.
ἐσύ [esee] you.
ἐσχάρα, ἡ [eshara] grill, gridiron, grid.
ἔσχατος [eshatos] extreme, utmost, last.
ἐσχάτως [eshatos] recently, lately.
ἔσω [eso] within, inside.
ἐσωκλείω [esokleeo] enclose.
ἐσώρουχα, τά [esorouha] πλ underclothes, underwear.
ἐσωτερικός [esotereekos] interior, inner, internal ‖ domestic.
ἑταιρεία, ἡ [etereea] company, society, firm, partnership.
ἑτερογενής [eteroyenees] heterogeneous.
ἕτερος [eteros] (an)other ‖ ἀφ' ἑτέρου on the other hand.
ἐτήσιος [eteeseeos] annual, yearly.
ἔτι [etee] moreover, still, yet.
ἐτικέττα, ἡ [eteeketa] label, price tag.
ἑτοιμάζομαι [eteemazome] get ready, prepare.
ἑτοιμάζω [eteemazo] prepare, make ready.
ἑτοιμασία, ἡ [eteemaseea] preparation.
ἕτοιμος [eteemos] ready.
ἔτος, τό [etos] year.

ἔτσι [etsee] thus, so, like this, like that, in this way ‖ ~ κι' ~ middling ‖ in any case ‖ ~ κι' ἀλλοιῶς in any case, either way.
ἐτυμηγορία, ἡ [eteemeeyoreea] verdict.
ἐτυμολογία, ἡ [eteemoloyeea] etymology.
εὖ [ev] well.
εὐ— [ev] well, easily.
εὐαγγέλιον, τό [evangeleeon] gospel.
Εὐαγγελισμός, ὁ [evangeleesmos] Annunciation.
εὐάερος [evaeros] well-ventilated, airy.
εὐαισθησία, ἡ [evestheeseea] sensitivity.
εὐαίσθητος [evestheetos] sensitive.
εὐανάγνωστος [evanaynostos] legible.
εὐάρεστος [evarestos] agreeable, pleasant.
εὐαρεστοῦμαι [evarestoume] be pleased, be willing.
εὖγε [evye] (ἐπιφ) bravo!, good show!
εὐγένεια, ἡ [evyeneea] courtesy, politeness.
εὐγενικός [evyeneekos] polite, courteous.
εὐγενής [evyenees] βλ εὐγενικός.
εὔγευστος [evyevstos] palatable, tasty.
εὐγλωττία, ἡ [evyloteea] eloquence.
εὐγνωμοσύνη, ἡ [evynomoseenee] gratitude.
εὐγνώμων [evynomon] grateful, thankful.
εὐδαιμονία, ἡ [evδemoneea] prosperity ‖ happiness.
εὐδιάθετος [evδeeathetos] in good humour.
εὐδιάκριτος [evδeeakreetos] discernible, distinct.
εὐδοκιμῶ [evδokeemo] succeed ‖ thrive ‖ prosper.
εὐδοκῶ [evδoko] be pleased to, deign, consent.
εὔελπις [evelpees] hopeful, promising ‖ (στρατ) cadet.
εὐέξαπτος [eveksaptos] irritable, excitable.
εὐεργέτης, ὁ [everyetees] benefactor.
εὐεργετικός [everyeteekos] beneficial, beneficent, charitable.
εὔζωνας, ὁ [evzonas] evzone.
εὐήλιος [eveeleeos] sunny.
εὐημερῶ [eveemero] prosper.
εὔηχος [eveehos] melodious, tuneful.
εὐθεῖα, ἡ [evtheea] straight line ‖ κατ' ~ direct, straight.
εὔθετος [evthetos] suitable, proper, convenient.
εὔθικτος [evtheektos] touchy, sensitive.
εὔθραυστος [evthravstos] fragile, brittle.
εὐθύγραμμος [evtheeyramos] straight, rectilinear.
εὐθυμία, ἡ [evtheemeea] gaiety, cheerfulness.
εὔθυμος [evtheemos] merry, gay, cheerful.
εὐθύνη, ἡ [evtheenee] responsibility.
εὐθύνομαι [evtheenome] be responsible, be accountable.
εὐθύς [evthees] (ἐπιρ) immediately, at once.
εὐθύς [evthees] straight, upright ‖ (τίμιος) honest, straightforward.

εὐκαιρία, ἡ [evkereea] opportunity, chance || (ἐμπόριον) bargain.

εὔκαιρος [evkeros] opportune || (ἐλεύθερος) available, free.

εὐκάλυπτος [evkaleeptos] eucalyptus.

εὔκαμπτος [evkamptos] flexible, pliable.

εὐκατάστατος [evkatastatos] well-to-do, well-off.

εὐκίνητος [evkeeneetos] agile, nimble.

εὐκοιλιότης, ἡ [evkeeleeotees] diarrhoea.

εὐκολία, ἡ [evkoleea] ease, convenience || (χάρις) favour.

εὔκολος [evkolos] easy || convenient.

εὐκολύνω [evkoleeno] facilitate.

εὐκρατής [evkratees] temperate, mild.

εὐκρινής [evkreenees] clear, distinct, lucid.

εὐκτική, ἡ [evkteekee] (γραμμ) optative (mood).

εὐλαβής [evlavees] devout, pious.

εὐλογία, ἡ [evloyeea] blessing, benediction.

εὐλογιά, ἡ [evloyia] smallpox.

εὔλογος [evloyos] reasonable, fair.

εὐλογῶ [evloyo] bless.

εὐλύγιστος [evleeyeestos] flexible, supple, pliant.

εὐμενής [evmenees] benevolent, kind, well-disposed.

εὐμετάβλητος [evmetavleetos] changeable, inconstant.

εὔμορφος [evmorfos] βλ ὄμορφος.

εὐνόητος [evnoeetos] easily understood || intelligible.

εὔνοια, ἡ [evneea] favour, goodwill.

εὐνοϊκός [evnoeekos] propitious, favourable.

εὐνοούμενος [evnooumenos] favourite.

εὐνοῶ [evnoo] favour.

εὐοδοῦμαι [evodoume] succeed, gο well.

εὐοίωνος [eveeonos] auspicious.

εὐπαθής [evpathees] sensitive, delicate.

εὐπαρουσίαστος [evparouseeastos] presentable, imposing.

εὐπειθής [evpeethees] obedient.

εὔπιστος [evpeestos] credulous, gullible.

εὔπορος [evporos] well-off, prosperous.

εὐπρέπεια, ἡ [evprepeea] propriety || decency.

εὐπρεπίζω [evprepeezo] put in order || adorn, embellish.

εὐπρόσδεκτος [evprosdektos] welcome, acceptable.

εὐπρόσιτος [evproseetos] accessible, approachable.

εὔρεσις, ἡ [evresees] discovery.

εὐρετήριον, τό [evreteereeon] index, catalogue.

εὐρέως [evreos] widely, largely.

εὕρημα, τό [evreema] find, discovery.

εὑρίσκομαι [evreeskome] find o.s., be.

εὑρίσκω [evreesko] find, obtain || (τυχαίως) come across.

εὐρύνω [evreeno] widen, broaden, enlarge.

εὐρύς [evrees] wide, extended, broad.

εὐρύχωρος [evreehoros] spacious, roomy.

εὐρωπαϊκός [evropaeekos] European.

Εὐρώπη, ἡ [evropee] Europe.

εὔρωστος [evrostos] robust, vigorous.

εὐσέβεια, ἡ [evseveea] piety, devoutness.

εὐσεβής [evsevees] pious, devout.

εὐσπλαγχνία, ἡ [evsplanghneea] compassion, pity.

εὐστάθεια, ἡ [evstatheea] stability, firmness.

εὔστοχος [evstohos] well-aimed, proper.

εὔστροφος [evstrofos] agile, nimble, versatile.

εὐσυνείδητος [evseeneedeetos] conscientious || scrupulous.

εὔσωμος [evsomos] well-built, stout, sturdy.

εὐτέλεια, ἡ [evteleea] meanness, baseness, cheapness.

εὐτελής [evtelees] cheap, mean, worthless.

εὐτράπελος [evtrapelos] humorous, witty.

εὐτύχημα, τό [evteeheema] good luck, lucky thing.

εὐτυχής [evteehees] lucky, fortunate, happy.

εὐτυχία, ἡ [evteeheea] happiness, good fortune.

εὐτυχισμένος [evteeheesmenos] βλ εὐτυχής.

εὐτυχῶς [evteehos] luckily, happily, fortunately.

εὐυπόληπτος [eveepoleeptos] reputable, esteemed.

εὔφλεκτος [evflektos] inflammable.

εὐφορία, ἡ [evforeea] fruitfulness, fertility.

εὐφραδής [evfradees] fluent, eloquent.

εὐφραίνω [evfreno] delight, rejoice, gladden.

εὐφυής [evfiees] intelligent, witty, clever.

εὐφυΐα, ἡ [evfieea] intelligence, wit, ingenuity.

εὐχαρίστησις, ἡ [evhareesteesees] satisfaction, pleasure.

εὐχαριστίες, οἱ [evhareesties] πλ thanks.

εὐχάριστος [evhareestos] pleasant, agreeable.

εὐχαρίστως [evhareestos] gladly, with pleasure.

εὐχαριστῶ [evhareesto] thank || please, gratify.

εὐχέρεια, ἡ [evhereea] ease, facility.

εὐχή, ἡ [evhee] prayer || wish || blessing.

εὔχομαι [evhome] wish, hope.

εὔχρηστος [evhreestos] useful, handy || in general use.

εὐώδης [evodees] fragrant.

ἐφ'- [ef] βλ ἐπί.

ἐφάμιλλος [efameelos] equal to, on a par with, a match for.

ἐφάπαξ [efapaks] in a lump sum, once only.

ἐφαπτομένη, ἡ [efaptomenee] tangent.

ἐφαρμογή, ἡ [efarmoyee] application, fitting.

ἐφαρμόζω [efarmozo] fit || apply || enforce.

ἔφεδρος, ὁ [efedros] reservist.

ἐφεκτικός [efekteekos] reserved, guarded.

ἐφεξῆς [efeksees] henceforth, hereafter.

ἔφεσις, ἡ [efesees] (νομ) appeal.
ἐφετεῖον, τό [efeteeon] court of appeal.
ἐφετεινός [efeteenos] of this year.
ἐφέτος [efetos] this year.
ἐφεύρεσις, ἡ [efevresees] invention.
ἐφευρετικός [efevreteekos] inventive, ingenious.
ἔφηβος, ὁ [efeevos] youth, adolescent.
ἐφηβικός [efeeveekos] of youth, of puberty
‖ ἐφηβική ἡλικία adolescence.
ἐφημερεύω [efeemerevo] be on duty.
ἐφημερίδα, ἡ [efeemereeδa] newspaper,
journal, gazette.
ἐφιάλτης, ὁ [efeealtees] nightmare ‖ bug-
bear:
ἐφικτός [efeektos] possible, attainable,
feasible.
ἐφιστῶ [efeesto]: ~ τήν προσοχήν draw
attention to.
ἐφόδια, τά [efoδeea] πλ supplies, equipment
‖ ἐφοδιάζω supply, equip, furnish.
ἔφοδος [efoδos] charge, assault, attack.
ἐφοπλιστής, ὁ [efopleestees] shipowner.
ἐφορεία, ἡ [eforeea] tax office, revenue
department ‖ trustees.
ἐφορμῶ [eformo] attack, fall upon.
ἔφορος, ὁ [eforos] inspector, director,
keeper, curator.
ἐφτά [efta] βλ ἑπτά.
ἐφτακόσιοι [eftakosiee] βλ ἑπτακόσιοι.
ἐχέγγυον, τό [ehengeeon] guarantee,
pledge.
ἐχεμύθεια, ἡ [ehemeetheea] secrecy, discretion ‖ ὑπό ~ ν under pledge of secrecy.
ἐχθές [ehthes] yesterday.
ἔχθρα, ἡ [ehthra] enmity, hostility.
ἐχθρεύομαι [ehthrevome] hate, dislike.
ἐχθρικός [ehthreekos] hostile, (of the)
enemy, inimical.
ἐχθρικότης, ἡ [ehthreekotees] hostility.
ἐχθροπραξίες, οἱ [ehthropraksies] πλ hostilities.
ἐχθρός, ὁ [ehthros] enemy, foe.
ἔχιδνα, ἡ [eheeδna] viper, adder.
ἐχῖνος, ὁ [eheenos] sea urchin.
ἔχω [eho] have, keep ‖ consider ‖ cost, be
worth ‖ ~ δίκιο I am right ‖ τί ἔχεις;
what's wrong?, what's the matter?
ἐψές [epses] yesterday.
ἔψιλον, τό [epseelon] the letter E.
ἑωθινός [eotheenos] morning.
ἕως [eos] till, until, to ‖ as far as.
Ἑωσφόρος, ὁ [eosforos] Lucifer.

Z, ζ

ζαβολιά, ἡ [zavolia] cheating, trickery.
ζαβός [zavos] crooked, perverse ‖ clumsy.
ζακέτα, ἡ [zaketa] jacket.
ζαλάδα, ἡ [zalaδa] giddiness, dizziness
headache.
ζάλη, ἡ [zalee] dizziness

ζαλίζομαι [zaleezome] become dizzy, become confused.
ζαλίζω [zaleezo] make dizzy, confuse, daze,
stun.
ζαμπόν, τό [zambon] ham.
ζάπλουτος [zaploutos] very rich, opulent.
ζάρα, ἡ [zara] crease, wrinkle.
ζάρια, τά [zareea] πλ dice.
ζαρκάδι, τό [zarkaδee] roe(buck).
ζάρωμα, τό [zaroma] creasing, wrinkling ‖
crease, wrinkle.
ζαρώνω [zarono] crease, wrinkle ‖ shrink.
ζαφείρι, τό [zafeeree] sapphire.
ζαχαρένιος [zahareneeos] sugary ‖ (μεταφ)
honeyed.
ζάχαρη, ἡ [zaharee] sugar.
ζαχαροκάλαμο, τό [zaharokalamo] sugar
cane.
ζαχαροπλαστεῖο, τό [zaharoplasteeo] confectioner's shop, pastry shop.
ζαχαρωτά, τά [zaharota] πλ sweets.
ζεματίζω [zemateezo] scald ‖ be very hot.
ζεματιστός [zemateestos] scalding, boiling.
ζεμπίλι, τό [zembeelee] straw basket, straw
bag.
ζενίθ, τό [zeneeth] zenith.
ζερβά [zerva] on the left ‖ (μεταφ) awry.
ζερβός [zervos] left-handed ‖ left.
ζέσις, ἡ [zesees] boiling ‖ (μεταφ) warmth,
fervour.
ζεσταίνομαι [zestenome] get warm, feel hot.
ζεσταίνω [zesteno] heat up, warm.
ζεστασιά, ἡ [zestasia] warmth, heat.
ζέστη, ἡ [zestee] heat, warmth ‖ κάνει ~
it's hot, it's warm.
ζεστός [zestos] hot, warm.
ζευγαράκι, τό [zevgarakee] pair (of lovers).
ζευγάρι, τό [zevgaree] pair, couple ‖ (βοδιῶν)
yoke ‖ (ἄροσις) ploughing, tilling.
ζευγνύω [zevgneeo] yoke, harness, link.
ζεῦγος, τό [zevgos] pair, couple.
ζεῦξις, ἡ [zevksees] yoking ‖ bridging,
junction.
ζέφυρος, ὁ [zefeeros] light breeze.
ζέω [zeo] boil.
ζήλεια, ἡ [zeeleea] envy, jealousy.
ζηλευτός [zeelevtos] enviable, desirable ‖
much desired.
ζηλεύω [zeelevo] envy, be jealous of.
ζηλιάρης [zeeleearees] envious, jealous.
ζῆλος, ὁ [zeelos] zeal, ardour, eagerness.
ζηλότυπος [zeeloteepos] βλ ζηλιάρης.
ζημία, ἡ [zeemeea] damage, loss, injury ‖
harm.
ζημιώνω *[zeemeeono] damage, cause a
loss, injure.
ζῆτα, τό [zeeta] the letter Z.
ζήτημα, τό [zeeteema] question, subject,
matter ‖ εἶναι ~ it's doubtful (whether).
ζήτησις, ἡ [zeeteesees] demand ‖ search,
pursuit.
ζητιανεύω [zeeteeanevo] beg, ask for alms
ζητιάνος, ὁ [zeeteeanos] beggar.

ζήτω [zeeto] (ἐπιφ) long live!, up with!
ζητῶ [zeeto] seek, ask for, look for, demand ‖ beg.
ζητωκραυγή, ἡ [zeetokravyee] cheer.
ζιζάνιον, τό [zeezaneeon] (μεταφ) naughty person.
ζόρι, τό [zoree] force, violence ‖ difficulty ‖ μέ τό ~ against one's will.
ζορίζω [zoreezo] force, exert pressure on.
ζόρικος [zoreekos] hard, difficult ‖ (ἐπί ἀνθρώπων) hard to please, irksome.
ζούγκλα, ἡ [zoungla] jungle.
ζουζούνι, τό [zouzounee] insect.
ζούλισμα, τό [zouleesma] squeezing, crushing.
ζουμερός [zoumeros] juicy, succulent.
ζουμί, τό [zoumee] juice ‖ broth ‖ (ψητοῦ) gravy.
ζουμπούλι, τό [zoumboulee] hyacinth.
ζούρλα, ἡ [zourla] lunacy, folly.
ζουρλομανδύας, ὁ [zourlomandeeas] strait jacket.
ζουρλός [zourlos] crazy, insane.
ζοφερός [zoferos] dark, gloomy.
ζοχάδα, ἡ [zohada] peevishness, sourness, sullenness.
ζοχάδες, οἱ [zohades] πλ piles, haemorrhoids.
ζυγαριά, ἡ [zeeyaria] pair of scales, balance.
ζυγίζομαι [zeeyeezome] hover over.
ζυγίζω [zeeyeezo] weigh.
ζυγός, ὁ [zeeyos] yoke ‖ (παλάντζας) scale, beam.
ζυγός [zeeyos] even (number) ‖ μονά ζυγά odd or even.
ζυγώνω [zeeyono] draw near.
ζῦθος, ὁ [zeethos] beer, ale.
ζυμάρι, τό [zeemaree] dough ‖ ζυμαρικά pastry, pies, cakes.
ζύμη, ἡ [zeemee] leaven, dough ‖ (μεταφ) quality, nature.
ζύμωμα, τό [zeemoma] kneading.
ζυμώνομαι [zeemonome] ferment.
ζυμώνω [zeemono] knead ‖ ferment.
ζύμωσις, ἡ [zeemosees] fermentation.
ζῶ [zo] live, experience ‖ lead a life.
ζωάριον, τό [zoareeon] small animal (μεταφ) worthless fellow.
ζωγραφιά, ἡ [zoyrafia] painting, drawing.
ζωγραφική, ἡ [zoyrafeekee] painting.
ζωγραφιστός [zoyrafeestos] painted (μεταφ) very beautiful.
ζωγράφος, ὁ [zoyrafos] painter, artist.
ζώδιον, τό [zodeeon] sign of the zodiac (μεταφ) fate, lot.
ζωέμπορος, ὁ [zoemboros] cattle dealer.
ζωή, ἡ [zoee] life, living ‖ lifetime.
ζωηρεύω [zoeerevo] become lively ‖ brighten up.
ζωηρός [zoeeros] lively, vivid ‖ (θερμός) warm, animated ‖ (χρώματος) bright (εὔθυμος) gay, full of life.
ζωηρότης, ἡ [zoeerotees] heat, warmth

(κινήσεως) quickness, promptness (βλέμματος) vivacity, brightness.
ζωικός [zoeekos] animal ‖ vital, necessary.
ζωμός, ὁ [zomos] broth, soup.
ζωνάρι, τό [zonaree] belt, sash, girdle, waistband.
ζώνη, ἡ [zonee] zone ‖ βλ καί ζωνάρι.
ζώνομαι [zonome] put on.
ζωντανεύω [zontanevo] revive, return to life.
ζωντάνια, ἡ [zontaneea] liveliness, alertness.
ζωντανός [zontanos] living, live, vivid ‖ lively.
ζωντοχήρα, ἡ [zontoheera] divorced woman, divorcee.
ζωντοχήρος, ὁ [zontoheeros] divorced man, divorcee.
ζωογονῶ [zooyono] animate ‖ (μεταφ) stimulate, excite.
ζωοδόχος [zoodohos]: ~ πηγή source of life.
ζωοκλοπή, ἡ [zooklopee] cattle rustling, sheep stealing.
ζωολογία, ἡ [zooloyeea] zoology.
ζῶον, τό [zoon] animal ‖ (μεταφ) fool, ass.
ζωοτροφίες, οἱ [zootrofies] πλ animal fodder, provisions.
ζωόφιλος [zoofeelos] fond of animals.
ζωοφόρος, ἡ [zooforos] frieze.
ζωπυρῶ [zopeero] rekindle, revive.
ζωστήρ, ὁ [zosteer] belt, sash ‖ (ἰατρ) shingles.
ζωτικός [zoteekos] vital.
ζωτικότης, ἡ [zoteekotees] vitality ‖ (μεταφ) vital importance.
ζωύφιον, τό [zoeefeeon] insect, louse ‖ πλ vermin.

H, η

ἡ [ee] the.
ἤ [ee] or ‖ ~ . . . ~ either . . . or (συγκριτικός) than.
ἥβη, ἡ [eevee] puberty.
ἡγεμών, ὁ [eeyemon] prince, sovereign ‖ governor.
ἡγεσία, ἡ [eeyeseea] leadership.
ἡγέτης, ὁ [eeyetees] leader, chief.
ἡγοῦμαι [eeyoume] lead, command.
ἡγούμενος, ὁ [eeyoumenos] abbot.
ἡδέως [eedeos] sweetly, pleasingly.
ἤδη [eedee] already, even now.
ἡδονή, ἡ [eedonee] delight, sensual pleasure, lust.
ἡδονικός [eedoneekos] delightful ‖ sensual.
ἡδύς [eedees] sweet, agreeable, pleasant.
ἠθική, ἡ [eetheekee] ethics ‖ morality.
ἠθικόν, τό [eetheekon] morale ‖ morality, morals.
ἠθικός [eetheekos] ethical, moral ‖ virtuous ‖ modest.

ήθικότης, ή [eetheekotees] morality, modesty.

ήθογραφία, ή [eethoyrafeea] folk customs, folklore.

ήθοποιία, ή [eethopieea] acting.

ήθοποιός, ό, ή [eethopeeos] actor, actress.

ήθη, τά [eethee] πλ manners, habits, customs.

ήθος, τό [eethos] character, nature, manner.

ήκιστα [eekeesta] not at all, least || in the least.

ήλεκτρίζω [eelektreezo] electrify.

ήλεκτρικόν, τό [eelektreekon] electricity.

ήλεκτρικός [eelektreekos] electric.

ήλεκτρισμός, ό [eelektreesmos] electricity.

ήλεκτρολόγος, ό [eelektroloyos] electrician.

ήλεκτρονική, ή [eelektroneekee] πλ electronics.

ήλεκτρόνιον, τό [eelektroneeon] electron.

ήλεκτροπληξία, ή [eelektropleekseea] electric shock.

ήλιακός [eeleeakos] of the sun, solar.

ήλίασις, ή [eeleeasees] sunstroke.

ήλίθιος [eeleetheeos] idiotic, stupid, silly.

ήλικία, ή [eeleekeea] age.

ήλικιωμένος [eeleekeeomenos] aged, advanced in years.

ήλιοβασίλεμα, τό [eeleeovaseelema] sunset.

ήλιοθεραπεία, ή [eeleeotherapeea] sunbathing.

ήλιοκαμένος [eeleeokamenos] sunburnt, tanned.

ήλιος, ό [eeleeos] sun || (φυτόν) sunflower.

ήλος, ό [eelos] nail || (μεταφ) corn.

ήμεῖς [eemees] we.

ήμέρα, ή [eemera] day || τῆς ~ς fresh, today's.

ήμερεύω [eemerevo] tame, domesticate || calm down, appease.

ήμερήσιος [eemereeseeos] daily, everyday.

ήμερολόγιον, τό [eemeroloyeeon] calendar, almanac || (πλοίου) logbook || (άτόμου) diary.

ήμερομηνία, ή [eemeromeeneea] date.

ήμερομίσθιον, τό [eemeromeestheeon] daily wage.

ήμερος [eemeros] domesticated || tame, gentle.

ήμερώνω [eemerono] tame || calm down, pacify.

ήμέτερος [eemeteros] our, ours.

ήμι- [eemee] half.

ήμιαργία, ή [eemeearyeea] half-day (holiday).

ήμιεπίσημος [eemiepeeseemos] semiofficial.

ήμιδανής [eemeethanees] half-dead.

ήμίθεος, ό [eemeetheos] demigod.

ήμικύκλιον, τό [eemeekeekleeon] semicircle.

ήμιμαθής [eemeemathees] half-learned (person), having a smattering of learning.

ήμίμετρα, τά [eemeemetra] πλ half-measures

ήμίονος, ό, ή [eemeeonos] mule.

ήμιπληγία, ή [eemeepleeyeea] stroke, paralysis.

ήμισέληνος, ή [eemeeseleenos] crescent.

ήμισυ, τό [eemeesee] half.

ήμισφαίριον, τό [eemeesfereeon] hemisphere.

ήμιτελής [eemeetelees] half-finished.

ήμίφωνον, τό [eemeefonon] (γραμμ) semivowel.

ήμίφως, τό [eemeefos] twilight || dim light.

ήμιχρόνιον, τό [eemeehroneeon] (άθλητ) half-time.

ήμίωρον, τό [eemeeoron] half-hour.

ήμπορῶ [eemboro] be able, be in a position to || may.

ήνίον, τό [eeneeon] rein, bridle.

ήνίοχος, ό [eeneeohos] charioteer.

ήνωμένος [eenomenos] united, joint.

ήξεύρω [eeksevro] βλ ξέρω.

ήπαρ, τό [eepar] liver.

ήπειρος, ή [eepeeros] continent || mainland, land.

ήπειρωτικός [eepeeroteekos] continental.

ήπιος [eepeeos] mild, indulgent || (άσθένεια) benign.

ήρέμως [eeremos] quietly, calmly.

ήρεμία, ή [eeremeea] quietness, tranquility, serenity.

ήρεμος [eeremos] calm, tranquil, peaceful, still.

ήρεμῶ [eeremo] be calm || keep quiet, keep still.

ήρωικός [eeroeekos] heroic.

ήρωίνη, ή [eeroeenee] heroin.

ήρῶον, τό [eeroon] war memorial, hero's tomb.

ήρωας, ό [eeroas] hero.

ήρωίς, ή [eeroees] heroine.

ήρωισμός, ό [eeroeesmos] heroism.

ήσυχάζω [eeseehazo] grow quiet, rest, calm down.

ήσυχία, ή [eeseeheea] quietness, peace, serenity.

ήσυχος [eeseehos] quiet, peaceful, composed.

ήτα, τό [eeta] the letter H.

ήτοι [eetee] that is, namely.

ήττα, ή [eeta] defeat, beating.

ήττοπάθεια, ή [eetopatheea] defeatism.

ήττον [eeton] less || ούχ ~ nevertheless, nonetheless.

ήττῶμαι [eetome] be defeated, succumb.

ήφαίστειον, τό [eefesteeon] volcano.

ήχηρός [eeheeros] loud, ringing, resonant.

ήχητικός [eeheeteekos] producing sound, resounding.

ήχος, ό [eehos] sound.

ήχώ, ή [eeho] echo, sound || (μεταφ) repercussion.

ήχῶ [eeho] ring, sound, strike, reverberate.

ήώς, ή [eeos] dawn, daybreak.

Θ, θ

θά [tha] shall, will, should, would.

θάβω [thavo] βλ θάπτω.

θαλαμηγός, ή [thalameeyos] yacht.

θάλαμος, ό [thalamos] room | (νοσοκομείου) ward | (ποδηλάτου κτλ) inner tube || (ὅπλου) chamber.

θάλασσα, ή [thalassa] sea | τά κάνω ~ mess up, fail.

θαλασσινά, τά [thalaseena] πλ shellfish.

θαλασσοδέρνω [thalassoδerno] buffet | (μεταφ) struggle against (adversity).

θαλασσόλυκος, ό [thalasoleekos] sea dog, mariner.

θαλασσοπόρος, ό [thalasoporos] navigator, seafarer.

θαλασσώνω [thalasono]: τά ~ turn things topsy-turvy, mess it up.

θαλερός [thaleros] green, in bloom | (μεταφ) fresh, vigorous.

θάμβος, τό [thamvos] astonishment, wonder.

θάμνος, ό [thamnos] bush, shrub, scrub.

θαμπός [thambos] (χρῶμα) lifeless, without lustre || dim, cloudy.

θάμπωμα, τό [thamboma] dazzle || astonishment || (ματιοῦ) dimness || (μυαλοῦ) confusion.

θαμπώνω [thambono] dazzle || tarnish, blur, dim || grow dim.

θαμών, ό [thamon] habitué, regular customer, frequent visitor.

θανάσιμος [thanaseemos] deadly, fatal.

θανατηφόρος [thanateeforos] deadly, murderous.

θανατικός [thanateekos] capital, of death.

θάνατος, ό [thanatos] death.

θανατώνω [thanatono] execute.

θανή, ή [thanee] death || funeral.

θάπτω [thapto] bury, inter || (μεταφ) hide.

θαρραλέος [tharaleos] plucky, daring, bold.

θαρρετός [tharetos] βλ θαρραλέος.

θαρρεύω [tharevo] venture, dare, hazard.

θάρρος, τό [tharos] daring, courage, spunk, mettle.

θαρρῶ [tharo] believe, think.

θαῦμα, τό [thavma] miracle, wonder.

θαυμάζω [thavmazo] wonder at, admire, be amazed.

θαυμάσιος [thavmaseeos] admirable, marvellous, superb.

θαυμασμός, ό [thavmasmos] wonder, admiration, astonishment.

θαυμαστής [thavmastees] admirer, fan.

θαυμαστικόν, τό [thavmasteekon] exclamation mark.

θαυμαστικός [thavmasteekos] admiring.

θαυμαστός [thavmastos] admirable, astonishing.

θαυματουργός [thavmatouryos] wondrous, miracle-making, miraculous.

θάψιμο, τό [thapseemo] burial.

θεά, ή [thea] goddess.

θέα, ή [thea] view, sight, aspect.

θέαμα, τό [theama] spectacle, show θεαματικός spectacular, wonderful.

θεάρεστος [thearestos] pleasing.

θεατής, ό [theatees] spectator, onlooker.

θεατός [theatos] visible, perceptible.

θεατρικός [theatreekos] theatrical | (μεταφ) pompous, showy.

θεατρῖνος, ό [theatreenos] actor.

θέατρο, τό [theatro] theatre, stage.

θεία, ή [theea] aunt.

θειάφι, τό [theeafee] sulphur.

θεϊκός [theyeekos] divine.

θεῖον, τό [theeon] βλ θειάφι.

θεῖος, ό [theeos] uncle.

θεῖος [theeos] divine, holy, sacred.

θέλγητρον, τό [thelyeetron] charm, enchantment, attraction.

θέλγω [thelyo] charm, enchant, fascinate.

θέλημα, τό [theleema] will, wish, desire | θεληματικός voluntary | willing.

θέλησις, ή [theleesees] will, volition, will power.

θελκτικός [thelkteekos] seductive, attractive, captivating.

θέλω [thelo] wish, want, require, need || be willing || ~ νά πῶ I mean to say | θέλει δέν θέλει whether he likes it or not.

θέμα, τό [thema] subject, point, topic | (γραμμ) stem, theme.

θεμέλιον, τό [themeleeon] foundation | (μεταφ) basis, groundwork.

θεμιτός [themeetos] lawful, legal || permissible.

θεόγυμνος [theoyeemnos] stark naked.

θεοκρατία, ή [theokrateea] theocracy.

θεολογία, ή [theoloyeea] theology.

θεολογικός [theoloyeekos] theological.

θεολόγος, ό [theoloyos] theologian.

θεομηνία, ή [theomeeneea] natural disaster, calamity.

θεοποιῶ [theopeeo] (μεταφ) idolize, praise, laud.

θεόρατος [theoratos] enormous, colossal.

θεός, ό [theos] god.

θεοσεβής [theosevees] pious, devout.

θεότης, ή [theotees] deity.

θεοτόκος, ή [theotokos] the Virgin Mary.

θεοφάνεια, τά [theofaneea] πλ the Epiphany.

θεοφοβούμενος [theofovoumenos] godly, pious.

θεραπεία, ή [therapeea] cure, treatment | recovery.

θεραπευτήριον, τό [therapevteereeon] hospital, clinic || (σχολῆς) infirmary.

θεραπευτικός [therapevteekos] curative.

θεραπεύω [therapevo] cure, treat | (μεταφ) satisfy.

θεράπων, ό [therapon] servant || attendant.

θέρετρον, τό [theretron] resort | country house.

θερίζω [thereezo] mow, cut ‖ reap ‖ (μεταφ) annihilate.

θερινός [thereenos] summer, summery.

θεριό, τό [therio] beast.

θερισμός, ὁ [thereesmos] reaping, mowing, cutting.

θεριστής, ὁ [thereestees] reaper, mower.

θεριστικός [thereesteekos] of reaping, for mowing ‖ sweeping.

θέρμαι, οἱ [therme] πλ hot springs.

θερμαίνομαι [thermenome] be feverish.

θερμαίνω [thermeno] heat up, warm up ‖ (μεταφ) revive.

θέρμανσις, ἡ [thermansees] heating, warming.

θερμαστής, ὁ [thermastees] stoker.

θερμάστρα, ἡ [thermastra] heating stove, furnace.

θέρμη, ἡ [thermee] fever ‖ (μεταφ) ardour, zeal.

θερμίς, ἡ [thermees] calorie.

θερμόαιμος [thermoemos] hot-blooded, irritable, touchy.

θερμοκήπιον, τό [thermokeepeeon] hothouse, greenhouse.

θερμοκρασία, ἡ [thermokraseea] temperature.

θερμόμετρον, τό [thermometron] thermometer.

θερμός [thermos] warm ‖ (μεταφ) passionate, fervent, heated.

θερμοσίφων, ὁ [thermoseefon] water heater.

θερμοστάτης, ὁ [thermostatees] thermostat.

θερμότης, ἡ [thermotees] heat, warmth ‖ (μεταφ) zeal, earnestness.

θερμοφόρος, ἡ [thermoforos] hot-water bottle.

θέρος, ὁ [theros] harvest.

θέρος, τό [theros] summer.

θέσις, ἡ [thesees] place, seat ‖ (τάξις) position ‖ (στρατ) emplacement, location ‖ (ἐργασίαν) employment, job, office ‖ (χῶρος) room, space ‖ (ταξιδιοῦ) class.

θεσμός, ὁ [thesmos] institution, law, decree.

θεσπίζω [thespeezo] decree, legislate, enact (laws).

θετικός [theteekos] positive, real, actual ‖ (πληροφορία) definite.

θετός [thetos] adopted ‖ foster.

θέτω [theto] put, set ‖ impose.

θεῶμαι [theome] see, behold ‖ be seen.

θεωρεῖον, τό [theoreeon] (θεάτρου) box (τύπου κτλ) gallery.

θεώρημα, τό [theoreema] theorem.

θεώρησις, ἡ [theoreesees] visa ‖ (ἐγγράφου) certification.

θεωρητικός [theoreeteekos] theoretical imposing.

θεωρία, ἡ [theoreea] theory ‖ (ὄψις) appearance, air.

θεωρῶ [theoro] consider, regard, look at ‖ certify, visa

θηκάρι, τό [theekaree] scabbard, sheath.

θήκη, ἡ [theekee] box, case ‖ (ἐργαλείων) toolbag.

θηλάζω [theelazo] suckle, nurse.

θηλαστικόν, τό [theelasteekon] mammal.

θηλειά, ἡ [theelia] noose, loop, slipknot ‖ buttonhole.

θηλή, ἡ [theelee] nipple, teat.

θηλυκό, τό [theeleeko] female.

θηλυκός [theeleekos] female ‖ (γραμμ) feminine.

θηλυκότης, ἡ [theeleekotees] femininity.

θηλυκώνω [theeleekono] button up, fasten, clasp.

θηλυπρεπής [theeleeprepees] effeminate, womanish.

θῆλυς [theelees] female, feminine.

θημωνιά, ἡ [theemonia] stack, pile ‖ (σανοῦ) haystack.

θήρα, ἡ [theera] chase, hunt ‖ (κυνήγι) (hunting) game, quarry.

θήραμα, τό [theerama] game, prey.

θηρεύω [theerevo] hunt, shoot ‖ (μεταφ) seek, search.

θηρίον, τό [theereeon] wild beast, brute ‖ (μεταφ) monster, fiend.

θηριώδης [theereeodees] fierce, savage, brutal, bestial.

θησαυρίζω [theesavreezo] hoard up, accumulate ‖ become wealthy.

θησαυρός, ὁ [theesavros] treasure ‖ (μεταφ) storehouse, thesaurus.

θησαυροφυλάκειον, τό [theesavrofeelakeeon] treasury.

θῆτα, τό [theeta] the letter Θ.

θητεία, ἡ [theeteea] military service ‖ term of office.

θιασάρχης, ὁ [theeasarhees] manager, impresario.

θίασος, ὁ [theeasos] cast, troupe.

θιασώτης, ὁ [theeasotees] adherent, supporter, devotee.

θίγω [theego] touch (upon) ‖ (μεταφ) offend, insult.

θλάσις, ἡ [thlasees] breaking ‖ (ἰατρ) fracture, bruise.

θλιβερός [thleeveros] sad ‖ (γεγονότα) deplorable, painful.

θλίβω [thleevo] press, crush ‖ (μεταφ) afflict, distress.

θλιμμένος [thleemenos] distressed, afflicted ‖ in mourning.

θλῖψις, ἡ [thleepsees] crushing ‖ (μεταφ) grief, sorrow.

θνησιμότης, ἡ [thneeseemotees] death rate, mortality.

θνήσκω [thneesko] βλ ἀποθνήσκω.

θνητός [thneetos] mortal.

θόλος [tholos] (ἀρχιτεκ) vault, dome ‖ (οὐρανίσκου) roof.

θολός [tholos] dull, blurred ‖ (κρασί) turbid ‖ (κατάστασις) confused.

θολώνω [tholono] make dull ‖ (τό μυαλό)

confuse, disturb ‖ (νερό κτλ) make muddy ‖ (ουρανός) get overcast.

θολωτός [tholotos] vaulted.

θόρυβος, ὁ [thoreevos] noise, turmoil, clamour.

θορυβοῦμαι [thoreevoume] worry, be uneasy.

θορυβῶ [thoreevo] create a disturbance ‖ disturb.

θορυβώδης [thoreevodees] noisy, boisterous.

θρανίον, τό [thraneeon] (school) desk, bench, seat.

θράσος, τό [thrasos] impudence, insolence.

θρασύς [thrasees] impudent, brazen, saucy, bold.

θραῦσις, ἡ [thravsees] fracture ‖ destruction, ruin.

θραῦσμα, τό [thravsma] fragment ‖ (λίθου) splinter.

θραύω [thravo] break, smash, crack.

θρεμμένος [thremenos] well-fed.

θρεπτικός [threpteekos] nourishing, nutritious.

θρέφω [threfo] βλ τρέφω.

θρέψις, ἡ [threpsees] feeding, nourishing.

θρῆνος, ὁ [threnos] lamentation, wailing.

θρηνῶ [threeno] lament, mourn ‖ complain.

θρησκεία, ἡ [threeskeea] religion.

θρησκευτικός [threeskevteekos] religious ‖ (ἀκρίβεια) scrupulous.

θρησκόληπτος [threeskoleeptos] fanatically religious.

θρῆσκος [threeskos] religious.

θριαμβευτικός [threeamvefteekos] triumphant, triumphal.

θριαμβεύω [threeamvevo] triumph ‖ (μεταφ) excel, prevail.

θρίαμβος, ὁ [threeamvos] triumph, victory.

θρίξ, ἡ [threeks] hair ‖ (βούρτσας) bristle.

θρόισμα, τό [throeesma] rustle.

θρόμβωσις, ἡ [thromvosees] thrombosis.

θρόνος, ὁ [thronos] throne.

θρούμπα, ἡ [throumba] ripe olive.

θρυαλλίς, ἡ [threealees] wick.

θρυλεῖται [threeleete] people are saying.

θρυλικός [threeleekos] legendary♦

θρῦλος, ὁ [threelos] legend ‖ rumour.

θρύμμα, τό [threema] fragment, scrap ‖ **θρυμματίζω** break to pieces, shatter.

θυγατέρα, ἡ [theeyatera] daughter.

θύελλα, ἡ [thiela] storm.

θυελλώδης [thielodees] stormy.

θυλάκιον, τό [theelakeeon] pocket.

θύλαξ, ὁ [theelaks] satchel, pouch.

θῦμα, τό [theema] victim.

θυμᾶμαι [theemame] βλ θυμοῦμαι.

θυμάρι, τό [theemaree] thyme.

θυμηδία, ἡ [theemeedeea] gaiety, levity.

θύμηση, ἡ [theemeesee] memory, remembrance.

θυμητικό, τό [theemeeteeko] memory.

θυμίαμα, τό [theemeeama] incense.

θυμιατό, τό [theemeeato] censer.

θυμίζω [theemeezo] remind, recall.

θυμός, ὁ [theemos] anger, rage.

θυμοῦμαι [theemoume] remember, recall.

θυμώνω [theemono] make angry, infuriate ‖ get angry, flare up.

θύρα, ἡ [theera] door, gate, doorway.

θυρίς, ἡ [theerees] small window ‖ (θεάτρου) box office ‖ (τραπέζης) counter.

θυρόφυλλον, τό [theerofeelon] leaf of a door, shutter.

θυρωρός, ὁ [theeroros] hall porter, concierge.

θύσανος, ὁ [theesanos] crest, tuft ‖ tassel.

θυσία, ἡ [theeseea] sacrifice ‖ **θυσιάζω** sacrifice.

θύω [theeo] offer up a sacrifice.

θωπεία, ἡ [thopeea] petting, patting, stroking, caress(ing).

θωπεύω [thopevo] caress, fondle ‖ (μεταφ) make much of, fawn upon.

θωρακίζω [thorakeezo] plate with steel.

θώραξ, ὁ [thoraks] cuirass, breastplate thorax.

θωρηκτόν, τό [thoreekton] battleship.

θωριά, ἡ [thoria] air, appearance ‖ colour, complexion.

θωρῶ [thoro] see, look.

Ι, ι

ιαματικός [eeamateekos] curative, medicinal.

ίαμβος, ὁ [eeamvos] iambus.

Ἰανουάριος, ὁ [eeanouareeos] January.

Ἰαπωνία, ἡ [eeaponeea] Japan.

Ἰάπων, ὁ [eeapon] Japanese (person).

ιαπωνικός [eeaponeekos] Japanese.

ιάσιμος [eeaseemos] curable.

ίασις, ἡ [eeasees] cure, healing, recovery.

ιατρεῖον, τό [eeatreeon] doctor's surgery, clinic ‖ infirmary.

ιατρεύω [eeatrevo] βλ θεραπεύω.

ιατρική, ἡ [eeatreekee] medicine.

ιατρικόν, τό [eeatreekon] medicine ‖ remedy.

ιατρικός [eeatreekos] medical.

ιατρός, ὁ, ἡ [eeatros] doctor, physician.

ιβίσκος, ὁ [eeveeskos] hibiscus.

ιδανικόν, τό [eedaneekon] ideal.

ιδανικός [eedaneekos] ideal.

ιδέα, ἡ [eedea] idea ‖ notion, thought.

ιδεαλιστής, ὁ [eedealeestees] idealist.

ιδεολογία, ἡ [eedeoloyeea] ideology.

ιδεολόγος, ὁ, ἡ [eedeoloyos] idealist.

ιδεώδης [eedeodees] ideal.

ιδία [eedeea] specially, especially, chiefly, primarily.

ιδιάζων [eedeeazon] typical, singular.

ιδιαίτερος [eedieteros] special, characteristic ‖ ὁ ~ private secretary ‖ τά ιδιαίτερα private affairs.

ἰδιαιτέρως [eeδieteros] in particular ‖ privately.

ἰδικός [eeδeekos] my, my own, mine.

ἰδιοκτησία, ἡ [eeδeeokteeseea] ownership ‖ property, estate.

ἰδιοκτήτης, ὁ [eeδeeokteetees] owner, proprietor ‖ landlord.

ἰδιόκτητος [eeδeeokteetos] privately owned.

ἰδιοποιοῦμαι [eeδeeopeeoume] appropriate, usurp.

ἰδιόρρυθμος [eeδeeoreethmos] peculiar, original, eccentric.

ἴδιος [eeδeeos] same ‖ own, oneself ‖ particular ‖ ~ μέ same as ‖ ἐγώ ὁ ~ I myself.

ἰδιοσυγκρασία, ἡ [eeδeeoseengkraseea] temperament, idiosyncrasy.

ἰδιοτελής [eeδeeotelees] selfish, self-centred.

ἰδιότης, ἡ [eeδeeotees] property, quality, characteristic.

ἰδιότροπος [eeδeeotropos] peculiar, eccentric ‖ singular.

ἰδιοφυής [eeδeeofiees] talented, gifted.

ἰδιόχειρος [eeδeeoheeros] handwritten, with one's own hand.

ἰδίωμα, τό [eeδeeoma] idiom, dialect ‖ property, characteristic ‖ ἰδιωματικός idiomatic.

ἰδιωματισμός, ὁ [eeδeeomateesmos] idiom.

ἰδίως [eeδeeos] specially, especially, particularly.

ἰδιωτεύω [eeδeeotevo] lead a private life, live in retirement.

ἰδιωτικός [eeδeeoteekos] private, particular.

ἰδιώτης, ὁ [eeδeeotees] individual, layman.

ἰδού [eeδou] (ἐπιφ) look!, behold!, here it is!

ἵδρυμα, τό [eeδreema] institution, foundation ‖ establishment.

ἵδρυσις, ἡ [eeδreesees] establishment, founding.

ἱδρυτής, ὁ [eeδreetees] founder.

ἱδρύω [eeδreevo] found, establish.

ἱδρώνω [eeδrono] perspire, sweat.

ἱδρώτας, ὁ [eeδrotas] sweat.

ἱέραξ, ὁ [ieraks] falcon, hawk.

ἱεραπόστολος, ὁ [ierapostolos] missionary.

ἱερεύς, ὁ [ierevs] priest.

ἱερόδουλος, ἡ [ieroδoulos] prostitute.

ἱεροκήρυξ, ὁ [ierokeereeks] preacher, missionary.

ἱερόν, τό [ieron] sanctuary, holy of holies.

ἱερός [ieros] holy, sacred.

ἱεροσυλία, ἡ [ieroseeleea] sacrilege.

ἵζημα, τό [eezeema] sediment.

ἰθαγένεια, ἡ [eethayeneea] nationality, citizenship.

ἰθαγενής [eethayenees] native, indigenous.

ἰθύνω [eetheeno] direct, manage, rule ‖ (ἰσιώνω) straighten.

ἱκανοποίησις, ἡ [eekanopieesees] satisfaction, contentment.

ἱκανοποιητικός [eekanopieeteekos] satisfactory, satisfying.

ἱκανοποιῶ [eekanopeeo] satisfy, please ‖ (τά πάθη) satiate ‖ (πεῖνα) appease.

ἱκανός [eckanos] capable, able ‖ sufficient ‖ (ἐργάτης) skilful.

ἱκανότης, ἡ [eekanotees] capacity, competence, skill.

ἱκετεύω [eeketevo] implore, beg.

ἱκρίωμα, τό [eekreeoma] scaffold(ing) ‖ (γιά θεατάς) platform, stand.

ἴκτερος, ὁ [eekteros] jaundice.

ἰλαρά, ἡ [eelara] measles.

ἰλιγγιώδης [eeleengeeoδees] giddy, dizzy.

ἴλιγγος, ὁ [eeleengos] giddiness, dizziness.

ἰλύς, ἡ [eelees] mud, sediment, deposit.

ἰμάμ μπαϊλντί [eemam mbaeelndee] aubergines with oil.

ἱμάς, ὁ [eemas] strap ‖ (μηχανῆς) belt, band.

ἱματιοθήκη, ἡ [eemateeotheekee] wardrobe ‖ cloakroom.

ἱμάτιον, τό [eemateeon] garment, dress.

ἴνα, ἡ [eena] fibre, filament.

ἵνα [eena] (in order) to, so that.

ἴνδαλμα, τό [eenδalma] ideal ‖ illusion, fancy.

ἰνδιάνος, ὁ [eenδeeanos] turkey.

ἰνδικός [eenδeekos] Indian.

ἰνδοκάλαμος, ὁ [eenδokalamos] bamboo.

ἰνστιτοῦτον, τό [eensteetouton] institute ‖ ~ καλλονῆς beauty salon.

ἴντσα, ἡ [eentsa] inch.

ἰνώδης [eenoδees] fibrous ‖ (κρέας) stringy.

ἰξώδης [eeksoδees] glutinous, sticky, gummy.

ἰοβόλος [eeovolos] venomous, poisonous.

ἴον, τό [eeon] violet.

ἰός, ὁ [eeos] venom ‖ (ἰατρ) virus ‖ (μεταφ) malice, spite.

Ἰουδαῖος, ὁ [eeouδeeos] Jew.

Ἰούλιος, ὁ [eeouleeos] July.

Ἰούνιος, ὁ [eeouneeos] June.

ἱππασία, ἡ [eepaseea] horsemanship ' riding.

ἱππεύς, ὁ [eepevs] rider, horseman ‖ (σκακιοῦ) knight.

ἱππικόν, τό [eepeekon] cavalry.

ἱπποδρομίες, οἱ [eepoδromies] πλ races.

ἱπποδρόμιον, τό [eepoδromeeon] racecourse ‖ hippodrome.

ἱπποδύναμις, ἡ [eepoδeenamees] horsepower.

ἱπποπόταμος, ὁ [eepopotamos] hippopotamus.

ἵππος, ὁ [eepos] horse ‖ ὀχτώ ἵππων eight horsepower.

ἱππότης, ὁ [eepotees] knight, chevalier.

ἵπταμαι [eeptame] fly, soar.

ἱπταμένη, ἡ [eeptamenee] air hostess.

ἱπτάμενος, ὁ [eeptamenos] flyer.

ἰριδισμός, ὁ [eereeδeesmos] iridescence.

ἶρις, ἡ [eerees] rainbow ‖ (ματιοῦ) iris.

ἴς, ἡ [ees] fibre, sinew.

ἴσα [eesa] equally, as far as ‖ straight,

directly | ~ ~ exactly, precisely | ~ μέ up to, until.
ισάζω [eesazo] straighten | adjust | fix.
ίσαμε [eesame] βλ ίσα μέ.
ισάξιος [eesakseeos] equivalent (to).
ισάριθμος [eesareethmos] equal in number.
ισημερία, ή [eeseemereea] equinox.
ισημερινός [eeseemereenos] equinoctial | (ούσ) equator.
ισθμός, ό [eesthmos] isthmus.
ίσια [eeseea] βλ ίσα.
ίσιο, τό [eeseeo] justice, right.
ίσιος [eeseeos] straight, erect | honest | equal to.
ισ(ι)ώνω [ees(ee)ono] straighten | make even, smooth.
ίσκιος, ό [eeskeeos] shade, shadow.
ισόβιος [eesoveeos] for life, lifelong.
ισόγειον, τό [eesoyeeon] ground floor.
ισοδύναμος [eesodeenamos] equivalent | equal in force.
ισοδυναμώ [eesodeenamo] be equivalent to.
ισοζύγιον, τό [eesozeeyeeon] balancing balance.
ισολογισμός, ό [eesoloyeesmos] balance sheet.
ισόπαλος [eesopalos] evenly matched, of equal strength.
ισοπεδώνω [eesopedono] level up, level down, smooth.
ισόπλευρος [eesoplevros] equilateral.
ισορροπημένος [eesoropeemenos] well-balanced.
ισορροπία, ή [eesoropeea] balance, equilibrium.
ισορροπώ [eesoropo] balance.
ίσος [eesos] equal to, the same as | έξ ίσου likewise.
ισοσκελής [eesoskelees] (γεωμ) isosceles.
ισότης, ή [eesotees] equality.
ισότιμος [eesoteemos] equal in rank | equal in value.
ισοφαρίζω [eesofareezo] equal, make equal | be equal to.
Ισπανία, ή [eespaneea] Spain.
ισπανικός [eespaneekos] Spanish.
Ισπανός, ό [eespanos] Spaniard.
ίσταμαι [eestame] stand.
ιστίον, τό [eesteeon] sail.
ιστιοπλοΐα, ή [eesteeoploeea] sailing.
ιστιοφόρον, τό [eesteeoforon] sailing ship.
ιστορία, ή [eestoreea] history | story, tale.
ιστορίες, οι [eestories] πλ trouble, scene, quarrel.
ιστορικός [eestoreekos] historic(al) | (ούσ) historian.
ιστός, ό [eestos] mast, pole | (βιολ) tissue.
ισχιαλγία, ή [eesheealyeea] sciatica.
ισχίον, τό [eesheeon] hip.
ισχνός [eeshnos] lean, thin | (βλάστησις) scanty, sparse.
ισχυρίζομαι [eesheereezome] assert, maintain, declare.

ισχυρισμός, ό [eesheereesmos] assertion contention, allegation.
ισχυρογνώμων [eesheeroγnomon] stubborn, headstrong, obstinate.
ισχυρός [eesheeros] strong, sturdy | (φωνή) loud | (άνεμος) stiff, strong.
ισχύς, ή [eeshees] strength, power, force | (νόμου κτλ) validity.
ισχύω [eesheeo] have validity | be in force.
ισώνω [eesono] βλ ισ(ι)ώνω.
ίσως [eesos] perhaps, probably, naybe.
Ιταλία, ή [eetaleea] Italy.
ιταλικός [eetaleekos] Italian.
Ιταλός, ό [eetalos] Italian (person).
ιταμός [eetamos] impudent, shameless.
ιτιά, ή [eetia] willow tree.
ιχθυοπωλείον, τό [eehtheeopoleeon] fish monger's shop.
ιχθύς, ό [eehthees] fish.
ιχνογράφημα, τό [eehnoγrafeema] sketch drawing, design.
ιχνογραφία, ή [eehnoγrafeea] sketching, drawing.
ίχνος, τό [eehnos] footprint, track | trace, vestige | (μεταφ) mark, sign.
ιωβηλαίον, τό [eeoveeleon] jubilee, anniversary.
ιώδιον, τό [eeodeeon] iodine.
ιωνικός [eeoneekos] Ionic, Ionian.
ιώτα, τό [eeota] the letter I.

Κ, κ

κάβα, ή [kava] wine cellar.
καβαλιέρος, ό [kavalieros] escort, partner.
καβάλλα, ή [kavala] riding | (έπιρ) on horseback | (σέ τοίχο κτλ) astride.
καβαλλάρης, ό [kavalarees] rider, horseman | (έγχόρδου) bridge.
καβαλλέτο, τό [kavaleto] easel.
καβαλλικεύω [kavaleekevo] mount a horse | (μεταφ) dominate.
καβαλλώ [kavalo] βλ καβαλλικεύω.
καβγαδίζω [kavγadeezo] quarrel, wrangle, squabble.
καβγάς, ό [kavγas] row, quarrel.
καβγατζής, ό [kavγatzees] grouch, wrangler.
κάβος, ό [kavos] cape, headland | (ναυτ) cable.
καβούκι, τό [kavoukee] shell.
κάβουρας, ό [kavouras] crab | crawfish.
καβουρδίζω [kavourdeezo] roast, brown | scorch.
καβούρι, τό [kavouree] βλ κάβουρας.
καγκελάριος, ό [kangelareeos] chancellor.
κάγκελο, τό [kangelo] (παραθύρου κτλ) bar | (σκάλας) balustrade | (κήπου) railings | (δικτυωτό) grille.
καγχάζω [kanghazo] guffaw.
καδής, ό [kadees] Turkish judge.

κάδος, ὁ [kados] bucket, vat, tub, small barrel

κάδρο, τό [kadro] (πλαίσιον) frame || (πίνακος) frame || (χάρτου) border || (φωτογραφία) framed picture.

καημένος [kaeemenos] (μεταφ) miserable, wretched.

καημός, ὁ [kaeemos] longing, yearning, mental anguish.

καθαίρεσις, ἡ [katheresees] dismissal, degradation.

καθαιρῶ [kathero] dismiss, discharge || (ἱερέα) unfrock.

καθαρεύουσα, ἡ [katharevousa] formal Greek (language).

καθαρίζω [kathareezo] clean, clear || (κουκιά, φρούτα) peel, pare, shell || (μετάλλινα εἴδη) burnish || (ποτήρια) polish || (ἐξηγῶ) explain, clarify || (λογαριασμούς) settle, clear up.

καθαριότης, ἡ [kathareeotees] cleanness, cleanliness || brightness.

καθάρισμα, τό [kathareesma] cleaning || peeling || polishing.

καθαριστήριον, τό [kathareesteereeon] dry cleaner's.

καθαρίστρια, ἡ [kathareestria] charwoman, cleaning lady.

κάθαρμα, τό [katharma] (μεταφ) rogue, rascal, scamp.

καθαρόαιμος [katharoemos] thoroughbred.

καθαρός [katharos] (πρόσωπον κτλ) neat, tidy || (φωνή) clear, distinct || (χρυσός) pure || (οὐρανός) clear || (ἀπάντησις) plain, straightforward || (ἰδέα) clear, distinct || (κέρδος) clear, net || (ἔννοια) obvious, manifest, evident.

καθαρότης, ἡ [katharotees] cleanness, purity || clearness.

καθάρσιον, τό [katharseeon] cathartic, purge.

κάθαρσις, ἡ [katharsees] cleansing, refining || catharsis || quarantine.

καθαυτό [kathavto] exactly, precisely || really.

κάθε [kathe] each, every || ~ ἄλλο far from it || τό ~ τι everything.

κάθειρξις, ἡ [katheerksees] βλ φυλάκισις.

καθείς [kathees] everyone, each one, everybody.

καθέκαστα, τά [kathekasta] πλ details, particulars.

καθελκύω [kathelkeeo] (ναυτ) launch.

καθένας [kathenas] βλ καθείς.

καθεξῆς [katheksees] so forth, so on.

καθεστώς, τό [kathestos]: τό ~ regime, status quo.

κάθετος [kathetos] vertical, perpendicular, upright.

καθηγητής, ὁ [katheeyeetees] professor, teacher.

καθήκι, τό [katheekee] chamberpot || (μεταφ) rogue, vicious person.

καθῆκον, τό [katheekon] duty, task || ~ τα πλ functions, duties.

καθηλώνω [katheelono] pin down, fix || immobilize.

καθημερινός [katheemereenos] daily, everyday.

καθημερινῶς [katheemereenos] daily.

καθησυχάζω [katheeseehazo] (ἕνα φόβο) calm, reassure, pacify || become calm.

καθιερώνω [kathierono] consecrate, dedicate || establish, validate.

καθίζησις, ἡ [katheezeesees] subsidence, landslide.

καθίζω [katheezo] seat, place || (πλοῖον) run aground.

καθισιό, τό [katheesio] idleness, unemployment, inactivity.

κάθισμα, τό [katheesma] chair, seat || (πλοῖον) stranding.

καθίσταμαι [katheestame] become, get, grow.

καθιστός [katheestos] sitting (down).

καθιστῶ [katheesto] (ἐγκαθιστῶ) establish, install || (κάποιον) make, render || (διορίζω) appoint.

καθό [katho] as, inasmuch as, insofar as.

καθοδηγῶ [kathodeeyo] instruct, guide, lead.

κάθοδος, ἡ [kathodos] descent || alighting || (ἐξ ἵππου) dismounting.

καθολικόν, τό [katholeekon] ledger || (ἐκκλ) nave.

καθολικός [katholeekos] catholic || (γνώμη) unanimous || universal.

καθόλου [katholou] generally || (διόλου) not at all, no way.

κάθομαι [kathome] be seated, sit down, sit.

καθομιλουμένη, ἡ [kathomeeloumenee] the spoken language.

καθορίζω [kathoreezo] determine, define, fix, decide.

καθορισμός, ὁ [kathoreesmos] defining, fixing, determination.

καθόσον [kathoson] as || according to what || being.

καθρέφτης, ὁ [kathreftees] mirror, looking-glass.

καθρεφτίζω [kathrefteezo] reflect, mirror.

καθυστερημένος [katheestereemenos] backward || late.

καθυστέρησις, ἡ [katheestereesees] delay, lateness.

καθυστερούμενα, τά [katheesteroumena] πλ arrears.

καθώς [kathos] as well as, like, as || ~ πρέπει proper.

καί [ke] and, also, too || ~ .. ~ both and || ~ νά even if.

καΐκι, τό [kaeekee] caique, sailing vessel.

καϊμάκι, τό [kaeemakee] cream || (τοῦ καφέ) froth.

καινοτομία, ἡ [kenotomeea] innovation.

καινούργιος [kenouryeeos] new, fresh.

καίπερ [keper] though, although.
καιρικός [kereekos] of the weather.
καίριος [kereeos] timely ‖ (πλῆγμα) deadly, mortal ‖ (σημεῖον) vital, important.
καιρός, ὁ [keros] time, period ‖ weather ‖ μέ τόν καιρό in course of time.
καιροσκοπῶ [keroskopo] wait for an opportunity, be an opportunist.
καισαρικός [kesareekos] Caesarean.
καίτοι [ketee] though, although.
καίομαι [keome] be on fire.
καίω [keo] burn.
κακά [kaka] badly, ill ‖ bad things.
κακάο, τό [kakao] cocoa.
κακαρίζω [kakareezo] cluck, gobble.
κακαρώνω [kakarono] perish from cold, die, kick the bucket (col).
κακεντρέχεια, ἡ [kakentreheea] malevolence, spite.
κακία, ἡ [kakeea] wickedness, malice.
κακίζω [kakeezo] reproach, blame, reprimand.
κακοβαλμένος [kakovalmenos] untidy, badly placed.
κακόβουλος [kakovoulos] malicious.
κακογλωσσιά, ἡ [kakoyloseea] slander, calumny ‖ gossip.
κακοδαιμονία, ἡ [kakodemoneea] misfortune, adversity.
κακοήθης [kakoeethees] dishonest, vile ‖ (ἰατρ) malignant, serious.
κακόηχος [kakoeehos] dissonant, unpleasant to hear.
κακοκαιρία, ἡ [kakokereea] bad weather.
κακοκεφιά, ἡ [kakokefia] depression, bad mood.
κακομαθαίνω [kakomatheno] (μωρό κτλ) spoil ‖ acquire bad habits.
κακομαθημένος [kakomatheemenos] ill-bred, spoilt, rude.
κακομεταχειρίζομαι [kakometaheereezome] maltreat, abuse.
κακομοίρης [kakomeerees] hapless, wretched.
κακό(ν), τό [kako(n)] evil, harm, wrong, bad, mischief.
κακοπέραση, ἡ [kakoperasee] privation, hardship.
κακοπερνῶ [kakoperno] lead a hard life, suffer.
κακοπιστία, ἡ [kakopeesteea] perfidy, faithlessness.
κακοποιός [kakopeeos] criminal, ill-doer.
κακοποιῶ [kakopeeo] maltreat ‖ rape.
κακορρίζικος [kakoreezeekos] βλ κακομοίρης.
κακός [kakos] bad, wicked ‖ (παιδί) mischievous ‖ nasty, serious.
κακοσμία, ἡ [kakosmeea] stench, stink.
κακοσυνηθίζω [kakoseeneetheezo] βλ κακομαθαίνω.
κακοτυχία, ἡ [kakoteeheea] misfortune, bad luck.

κακούργημα, τό [kakouryeema] crime, villainy, felony.
κακουργιοδικεῖον, τό [kakouryiodeekeeon] criminal court.
κακοῦργος, ὁ [kakouryos] criminal ‖ (μεταφ) villain, rogue.
κακουχία, ἡ [kakouheea] hardship, privation.
κακοφαίνεται [kakofenete]: μοῦ ~ it displeases me, it offends me.
κακοφέρνομαι [kakofernome] behave badly.
κακοφτιαγμένος [kakofteeaymenos] badly made, badly wrought.
κακόφωνος [kakofonos] discordant, dissonant.
κάκτος, ὁ [kaktos] cactus.
κακῶς [kakos] badly, wrongly.
κάκωσις, ἡ [kakosees] ill treatment ‖ (ἀποτέλεσμα) suffering, hardship.
καλά [kala] well, all right ‖ properly, thoroughly.
καλάθι, τό [kalathee] basket.
κάλαθος, ὁ [kalathos]: ~ ἀχρήστων waste-paper bin.
καλάϊ, τό [kalaee] solder, pewter.
καλαισθησία, ἡ [kalestheeseea] good taste, elegance.
καλαμαράς, ὁ [kalamaras] writer, scholar.
καλαμάρι, τό [kalamaree] inkstand, inkpot ‖ (ψάρι) cuttlefish, squid.
καλαματιανός [kalamateeanos] (dance) of Kalamata.
καλάμι, τό [kalamee] reed, cane ‖ (ψαρέματος) fishing rod ‖ (ἀνατ) shinbone.
κάλαμος, ὁ [kalamos] cane, reed ‖ pen.
καλαμοσάκχαρον, τό [kalamosakharon] cane sugar.
καλαμπόκι, τό [kalambokee] maize, corn.
καλαμπούρι, τό [kalambouree] pun.
κάλαντα, τά [kalanta] πλ carols.
καλαπόδι, τό [kalapodee] (shoemaker's) last, shoe last.
καλαφατίζω [kalafateezo] caulk.
κάλεσμα, τό [kalesma] invitation.
καλεσμένος [kalesmenos] invited ‖ (οὐσ) guest.
καλημαύκι, τό [kaleemavkee] priest's high hat.
καλημέρα [kaleemera] (ἐπιφ) good morning.
καληνύχτα [kaleeneehta] (ἐπιφ) good night.
καληνυχτίζω [kaleeneehteezo] bid good night.
καλησπέρα [kaleespera] (ἐπιφ) good afternoon ‖ good evening.
καλησπερίζω [kaleespereezo] wish good evening.
κάλι, τό [kalee] potash.
καλιακούδα, ἡ [kaleeakouda] crow.
καλλιέργεια, ἡ [kalieryeea] cultivation, tilling ‖ (μεταφ) cultivation.
καλλιεργῶ [kalieryo] cultivate, till, grow

καλλικάντζαρος, ὁ [kaleekantzaros] sprite, spook, goblin.

κάλλιστα [kaleesta] very well.

καλλιστεῖα, τά [kaleesteea] πλ beauty competition.

κάλλιστος [kaleestos] best, perfect, exquisite, excellent.

καλλιτέχνης, ὁ [kaleetehnees] artist.

καλλιτεχνικός [kaleetehneekos] of art, of artists, artistic.

καλλονή, ἡ [kalonee] beauty.

κάλλος, τό [kalos] beauty, charm.

καλλυντικά, τά [kaleenteeka] πλ cosmetics, make-up.

καλλωπίζω [kalopeezo] beautify, decorate, adorn.

καλμάρω [kalmaro] become calm, relax.

καλντερίμι, τό [kalntereemee] cobbled street, paving stone.

καλοαναθρεμμένος [kaloanathremenos] well brought up.

καλοβαλμένος [kalovalmenos] well turned out, well-groomed, tidy.

καλόβολος [kalovolos] accommodating, easy-going, complaisant.

καλόγερος, ὁ [kaloyeros] monk || (σπυρί) boil, carbuncle || (παιχνίδι) hopscotch.

καλόγηρος, ὁ [kaloyeros] βλ **καλόγερος.**

καλόγνωμος [kaloynomos] well-disposed, good-natured.

καλόγρια, ἡ [kaloyreea] nun.

καλοζῶ [kalozo] live well || support comfortably.

καλοήθης [kaloeethees] moral, virtuous || (ἐπί νόσου) benign.

καλοθρεμμένος [kalothremenos] well-nourished || well-bred.

καλοκάγαθος [kalokayathos] kind-natured, good.

καλοκαίρι, τό [kalokeree] summer || **καλοκαιρία** fine weather || **καλοκαιρινός** summer, summery.

καλοκαμωμένος [kalokamomenos] well-made || handsome.

καλόκαρδος [kalokardos] good-hearted, cheerful.

καλοκοιτάζω [kalokeetazo] look closely at || look after well || ogle.

καλομαθαίνω [kalomatheno] spoil, pamper, pet || develop good habits.

καλομαθημένος [kalomatheemenos] pampered.

καλό(ν), τό [kalo(n)] good, benefit || favour || blessing || στό ~ ! so long!

καλοντυμένος [kalonteemenos] well-dressed.

καλοπέραση, ἡ [kaloperasee] comfort, happy life, good life.

καλοπερνῶ [kaloperno] lead a pleasant life || be well treated.

καλοπιάνω [kalopeeano] coax, treat gently.

καλοπροαίρετος [kaloproeretos] well-disposed, obliging.

καλοριφέρ, τό [kaloreefer] central heating || radiator, heater.

καλορρίζικος [kaloreezeekos] lucky.

κάλος, ὁ [kalos] corn.

καλός [kalos] (ἄνθρωπος) kind, good || (ἐργάτης) skilful || (ὑπάλληλος) able, efficient || (νέα) good, favourable || (τροφή) wholesome || (καρδιά) kind.

καλοσυνηθίζω [kaloseeneetheezo] βλ **καλομαθαίνω.**

καλούπι, τό [kaloupee] form, mould.

καλούτσικος [kaloutseekos] not bad, passable, adequate.

καλπάζω [kalpazo] gallop || walk fast, run.

κάλπη, ἡ [kalpee] ballot box.

κάλπικος [kalpeekos] counterfeit, false || (μεταφ) worthless.

κάλτσα, ἡ [kaltsa] sock, stocking.

καλύβι, τό [kaleevee] hut, cabin, hovel.

κάλυμμα, τό [kaleema] wrapper, cover || (κρεββατιοῦ) blanket, coverlet || (κεφαλῆς) cap, headdress || (τραπεζιτικό) margin, cover.

κάλυξ, ὁ [kaleeks] (βοτ) calyx || (στρατ) cartridge || (ἀνατ) calix.

καλύπτω [kaleepto] cover, veil, hide || (προθέσεις) cloak, mask, conceal.

καλύτερα [kaleetera] better.

καλυτερεύω [kaleeterevo] improve || get better.

καλύτερος [kaleeteros] better.

κάλυψις, ἡ [kaleepsees] covering.

καλῶ [kalo] call, beckon, name || (σέ δεῖπνο) invite || (νομ) summon.

καλώδιον, τό [kalodeeon] rope || cable.

καλῶς [kalos] well || rightly, properly || ἔχει ~ good, agreed || ~ ὡρίσατε (ἐπιφ) welcome!

καλωσορίζω [kalosoreezo] welcome.

καλωσύνη, ἡ [kaloseenee] goodness, kindness || (καιρός) fine weather.

καμάκι, τό [kamakee] harpoon, fish spear.

κάμαρα, ἡ [kamara] room.

καμάρα, ἡ [kamara] arch, archway, arcade || (θόλου) vault.

καμάρι, τό [kamaree] pride, boast.

καμαριέρα, ἡ [kamariera] chambermaid, parlourmaid.

καμαρότος, ὁ [kamarotos] steward, cabin boy.

καμαρώνω [kamarono] take pride in, glory in.

καμαρωτά [kamarota] proudly, haughtily.

καμαρωτός [kamarotos] (ἀρχιτεκ) arched, vaulted || (ὑπερηφάνεια) proud, haughty.

κάματος, ὁ [kamatos] fatigue || (ἀροτρίασις) tilling.

καμέλια, ἡ [kameleea] camellia.

καμήλα, ἡ [kameela] camel.

καμηλοπάρδαλις, ἡ [kameelopardalees] giraffe.

καμινάδα, ἡ [kameenada] chimney, smokestack || funnel.

καμινέτο, τό [kameeneto] spirit lamp.
καμίνι, τό [kameenee] furnace, kiln.
καμιόνι, τό [kameeonee] lorry, truck.
καμμιά [kamia] βλ κανένας.
κάμνω [kamno] make, do, create, build.
καμουτσίκι, τό [kamoutseekee] whip.
καμουφλάζ, τό [kamouflaz] camouflage, disguise.
καμουφλάρω [kamouflaro] camouflage, disguise.
καμπάνα, ἡ [kambana] bell.
καμπαναρειό, τό [kambanario] belfry, steeple.
καμπανιά, ἡ [kambania] bell ringing.
καμπαρντίνα, ἡ [kambarndeena] gabardine.
καμπή, ἡ [kambee] bend, turn || (σωλῆνος κτλ) elbow, knee.
κάμπια, ἡ [kambeea] caterpillar.
καμπίνα, ἡ [kambeena] cabin.
καμπινές, ὁ [kambeenes] toilet, rest room, W.C.
κάμπος, ὁ [kambos] plain, flat country.
καμπόσος [kambosos] considerable, some.
καμπούρα, ἡ [kamboura] hump, hunch.
καμπούρης, ὁ [kambourees] hunchback.
καμπουριάζω [kamboureeazo] hunch || stoop.
κάμπτομαι [kamptome] bow || yield, sag || (τιμές) go down.
κάμπτω [kampto] bend, turn, curve.
καμπύλη, ἡ [kambeelee] curve, bend.
καμπύλος [kambeelos] curved, rounded || crooked.
καμτσίκι, τό [kamtseekee] whip.
καμφορά, ἡ [kamfora] camphor.
κάμψις, ἡ [kampsees] bending, flexion || (τιμῶν) fall, drop.
καμώματα, τά [kamomata] πλ affected manners, antics.
καμωμένος [kamomenos] done, made || ripe.
καμώνομαι [kamonome] pretend, feign.
κἄν [kan] at least, even || οὔτε ~ not even || ~ ... ~ either ... or.
κανακάρης [kanakarees] petted, spoilt || (οὐσ) only child.
κανάλι, τό [kanalee] channel, canal.
καναπές, ὁ [kanapes] sofa.
καναρίνι, τό [kanareenee] canary.
κανάτα, ἡ [kanata] jug, pitcher.
κανείς [kanees] someone, anyone || no one, nobody.
κανέλλα, ἡ [kanela] cinnamon.
κανένας [kanenas] anyone, one, some || no, no one.
κάνθαρος, ὁ [kantharos] beetle.
κανναβάτσο, τό [kanavatso] canvas, pack cloth.
καννάβι, τό [kanavee] hemp.
κάννη, ἡ [kanee] barrel of a gun.
καννίβαλος, ὁ [kaneevalos] cannibal.
κανόνας, ὁ [kanonas] rule.
κανόνι, τό [kanonee] cannon.

κανονίζω [kanoneezo] regulate || (ὑποθέσεις) settle, arrange || (λογαριασμούς) settle, close, pay off.
κανονικός [kanoneekos] regular, usual, ordinary ||' (ἐκκλ) canonical.
κανονισμός, ὁ [kanoneesmos] regulation, rule(s), by-laws.
κάνουλα, ἡ [kanoula] tap || (US) faucet.
καντάδα, ἡ [kantada] serenade.
καντήλι, τό [kanteelee] small olive-oil light, nightlight.
καντίνα, ἡ [kanteena] canteen.
κάνω [kano] do, make, create, build || (ὑποκρίνομαι) play, sham || τά ~ θάλασσα (ἤ σαλάτα) make a mess of it || ~ παιδί have a child || ~ νερά leak || (μεταφ) hedge || ~ πῶς pretend that || τί κάνετε; how are you?
κανών, ὁ [kanon] rule || (ἐκκλ) canon.
κάπα, ἡ [kapa] peasant's cloak.
κapάκι, τό [kapakee] lid, cover.
καπάρο, τό [kaparo] deposit.
καπαρώνω [kaparono] give a deposit || book, engage.
καπαρτίνα, ἡ [kaparteena] gabardine.
κάπελας, ὁ [kapelas] tavern-keeper.
καπέλλο, τό [kapelo] hat.
καπετάνιος, ὁ [kapetaneeos] captain, skipper, chief.
καπηλεία, ἡ [kapeeleea] (μεταφ) huckstering, exploiting.
καπηλειό, τό [kapeelio] wine shop, taverna.
καπίστρι, τό [kapeestree] bridle, halter.
κapλαμάς, ὁ [kaplamas] veneer.
καπνέμπορος, ὁ [kapnemboros] tobacco dealer, tobacconist.
καπνιά, ἡ [kapnia] soot, lampblack.
καπνίζω [kapneezo] smoke || cure.
κάπνισμα, τό [kapneesma] smoking.
καπνιστής, ὁ [kapneestees] smoker || (κρέατος) curer.
καπνιστός [kapneestos] smoked, smoke-cured.
καπνοδόχος, ἡ [kapnodohos] chimney || (πλοίου) funnel.
καπνοπώλης, ὁ [kapnopolees] tobacconist.
καπνός, ὁ [kapnos] smoke || tobacco || (μεταφ) ἔγινε ~ he vanished (into thin air).
κάποιος [kapeeos] someone || a certain.
καπόνι, τό [kaponee] capon.
καπότα, ἡ [kapota] shepherd's cloak || prophylactic, rubber.
κάποτε [kapote] from time to time, now and again, sometimes || once.
κάπου [kapou] somewhere || ~ ~ once in a while || ~ δέκα about ten.
κάππα, τό [kappa] the letter K.
κάππαρη, ἡ [kapparee] caper.
καπρίτσιο, τό [kapreetseeo] caprice, whim fancy.
κάπρος, ὁ [kapros] wild boar.

κάπως [kapos] somehow, somewhat.

κάρα, ή [kara] head, skull.

καραβάνα, ή [karavana] mess tin ‖ platter.

καραβάνι, τό [karavanee] caravan.

καράβι, τό [karavee] ship, boat, vessel.

καραβίδα, ή [karaveeda] crawfish ‖ crab.

καραβοκύρης, ό [karavokeerees] owner of a vessel ‖ captain.

καραγκιόζης, ό [karangeeozees] (μεταφ) comical person, comedian.

καραδοκώ [karodoko] watch for, look out for ‖ waylay.

καρακάξα, ή [karakaksa] magpie.

καραμέλα, ή [karamela] sweet ‖ caramel.

καραμούζα, ή [karamouza] toy flute (αὐτοκινήτου) horn.

καραμπίνα, ή [karambeena] carbine.

καραντίνα, ή [karanteena] quarantine.

καράτι, τό [karatee] carat.

καρατομῶ [karatomo] behead, decapitate.

καράφα, ή [karafa] carafe ‖ (κρασιοῦ) decanter.

καράφλα, ή [karafla] baldness.

καρβέλι, τό [karvelee] (round) loaf.

καρβουνιάρης, ό [karvouneearees] coal merchant ‖ coalman.

κάρβουνο, τό [karvouno] coal, charcoal.

κάργα [karya] quite full ‖ tightly, closely.

κάρδαμον, τό [kardamon] cress.

καρδιά, ή [kardia] heart ‖ (φροῦτου) core, centre.

καρδιακός [kardiakos] affected with heart disease.

καρδιολόγος, ό [kardioloyos] heart specialist.

καρδιοχτύπι, τό [kardiohteepee] heartbeat ‖ (μεταφ) anxiety.

καρέκλα, ή [karekla] chair, seat.

καρίνα, ή [kareena] keel.

καριοφίλι, τό [kareeofeelee] flintlock, carabine.

καρκινοβατῶ [karkeenovato] make no progress, get nowhere.

καρκίνος, ό [karkeenos] cancer ‖ crab.

καρκίνωμα, τό [karkeenoma] carcinoma.

καρμανιόλα, ή [karmaneeola] guillotine (στά χαρτιά) dishonest card game.

καρμπόν, τό [karbon] carbon paper.

καρναβάλι, τό [karnavalee] carnival.

καρότο, τό [karoto] carrot.

καρούλι, τό [karoulee] reel, spool ‖ pulley.

καφούμπαλο, τό [karoumbalo] bump (on the head).

καρπαζιά, ή [karpazia] clout on the head.

καρπός, ό [karpos] fruit ‖ (ἀνατ) wrist.

καρπούζι, τό [karpouzee] watermelon.

καρπούμαι [karpoume] reap the fruits of ‖ (μεταφ) benefit by.

καρποφόρος [karpoforos] fruitful , effective ‖ lucrative.

καρποφορῶ [karpoforo] produce fruit ‖ (μεταφ) succeed.

καρρέ, τό [karre] (στα χαρτιά) foursome ‖

(φουστανιοῦ) open neck of dress.

καρρό, τό [karo] (στά χαρτιά) diamond ‖ (σχεδίου) check.

κάρρο, τό [karo] cart, wagon.

καρροτσάκι, τό [karotsakee] handcart, barrow ‖ (μωροῦ) pram.

καρσί [karsee] opposite.

κάρτα, ή [karta] postcard ‖ visiting card.

καρτέρι, τό [karteree] βλ ἐνέδρα.

καρτερῶ [kartero] persevere, persist ‖ wait for, expect.

καρύδι, τό [kareedee] walnut ‖ Adam's apple ‖ καρυδιά, ή walnut tree, walnut (wood).

καρύκευμα, τό [kareekevma] seasoning ‖ (τό μπαχαρικό) condiment, spice.

καρυοθραύστης, ό [kareeothravstees] nutcracker.

καρυοφύλλι, τό [kareeofeelee] clove ‖ (ὅπλου) flintlock.

καρφί, τό [karfee] nail.

καρφίτσα, ή [karfeetsa] pin ‖ (κόσμημα) brooch.

καρφώνω [karfono] nail, pin ‖ (μεταφ) fix.

καρχαρίας, ό [karhareeas] shark.

κασετίνα, ή [kaseteena] (σχολική) pencil box ‖ (κοσμημάτων) jewellery box.

κάσ(σ)α, ή [kasa] case, box ‖ (χρηματοκιβώτιον) safe ‖ (μεταφ) coffin, bier.

κασ(σ)έλα, ή [kasela] wooden chest, trunk.

κασκέτο, τό [kasketo] cap.

κασμήρι, τό [kasmeeree] cashmere.

κασ(σ)όνι, τό [kasonee] packing case.

κασσίτερος, ό [kaseeteros] tin.

καστανιά, ή [kastania] chestnut tree.

κάστανο, τό [kastano] chestnut.

καστανός [kastanos] chestnut-coloured maroon.

καστόρι, τό [kastoree] beaver ‖ felt.

κάστρο, τό [kastro] castle, fortress.

κατά [kata] against, upon, during, according to, by, about ‖ ~ ξηράν by land ‖ ~ τύχην by chance ‖ ~ βάθος at bottom ‖ καθ' ἑκάστην every day ‖ ~ διαβόλου to the devil, to hell.

καταβαίνω [kataveno] βλ κατεβαίνω.

καταβάλλω [katavalo] overthrow, overcome, exhaust ‖ (προσπαθείας) strive, endeavour ‖ (χρήματα) pay, put down.

κατάβασις, ή [katavasees] descent, alighting, getting off.

καταβιβάζω [kataveevazo] let down, take down ‖ (ὕψος) lower, reduce.

καταβολή, ή [katavolee] (χρημάτων) paying in, deposit.

καταβρέχω [katavreho] sprinkle, soak, water.

καταβροχθίζω [katavrohtheezo] devour, eat ravenously, gulp down.

καταγγελία, ή [katangeleea] denunciation, accusation ‖ annulment, revocation.

καταγέλαστος [katayelastos] ridiculous ludicrous.

καταγῆς [katayees] on the ground, on the floor.

καταγίνομαι [katayeenome] busy o.s. with, see to.

κάταγμα, τό [katayma] fracture.

κατάγομαι [katayome] be descended from, come from.

καταγωγή, ή [katayoyee] descent, origin, lineage.

καταγώγιον, τό [katayoyeeon] hovel, hideout, den of vice.

καταδεικνύω [katadeekneeo] demonstrate, show clearly.

καταδέχομαι [katadehome] deign, condescend.

κατάδηλος [katadeelos] evident, clear.

καταδίδω [katadeedo] denounce, betray.

καταδικάζω [katadeekazo] condemn, sentence || (μεταφ) doom, proscribe.

καταδίκη, ή [katadeekee] sentence, conviction || censure, blame.

κατάδικος, ό, ή [katadeekos] prisoner, condemned person.

καταδιωκτικόν, τό [katadeeokteekon] fighter (plane).

καταδιώκω [katadeeoko] pursue, chase || (πολιτικῶς) persecute, oppress.

κατάδοσις, ή [katadosees] betrayal, denunciation.

καταδρομή, ή [katadromee] pursuit || (μεταφ) bad luck, bad streak.

καταδρομικόν, τό [katadromeekon] cruiser.

καταδυναστεύω [katadeenastevo] oppress.

καταδύομαι [katadeeome] dive, plunge.

καταζητῶ [katazeeto] pursue, chase.

καταθέτω [katatheto] deposit, lay down || (ὡς μάρτυρας) give evidence || (ὅπλα) lay down || (σχέδιον) introduce.

καταθλιπτικός [katathleepteekos] crushing, overwhelming.

καταιγίδα, ή [kateyeeda] tempest, storm, hurricane.

καταΐφι, τό [kataeefee] kind of oriental cake.

κατακάθι, τό [katakathee] residue, sediment, dregs.

κατάκειμαι [katakeeme] lie flat, lie down.

κατάκαρδα [katakarda] deeply, seriously, profoundly, to heart.

κατακέφαλα [katakefala] headlong, on the head.

κατακλίνομαι [katakleenome] lie down, go to bed.

κατακλύζω [katakleezo] flood, inundate || (μεταφ) invade, overrun.

κατακλυσμός, ό [katakleesmos] flood.

κατάκοιτος [katakeetos] bedridden.

κατάκοπος [katakopos] exhausted, deadbeat, dog-tired.

κατακόβω [katakovo] cut to pieces, cut up, lacerate.

κατακόρυφον, τό [katakoreefon] zenith || (μεταφ) acme

κατακόρυφος [katakoreefos] vertical, perpendicular.

κατακρατῶ [katakrato] withhold, keep illegally.

κατακραυγή, ή [katakravyee] outcry || protestation.

κατακρεουργῶ [katakreouryo] butcher, massacre.

κατακρημνίζω [katakreemneezo] demolish, pull down.

κατακρίνω [katakreeno] blame, criticize, condemn.

κατάκτησις, ή [katakteesees] conquest, subjugation.

κατακτῶ [katakto] conquer, subjugate.

καταλαβαίνω [katalaveno] βλ καταλαμβάνω.

καταλαμβάνω [katalamvano] take, lay hold of, seize || (χῶρο) take up || (τό νόημα) understand.

καταλείπω [kataleepo] leave behind, abandon, forsake.

καταλεπτῶς [kataleptos] in detail, minutely.

καταλήγω [kataleeyo] end in, come to, result in, come to an end.

κατάληξις, ή [kataleeksees] termination, ending.

καταληπτός [kataleeptos] comprehensible, intelligible, clear.

κατάληψις, ή [kataleepsees] occupation, capture || (ἰδέας) understanding, comprehension.

κατάλληλος [kataleelos] suitable, appropriate, fit, proper.

καταλογίζω [kataloyeezo] attribute, impute, ascribe.

κατάλογος, ό [kataloyos] catalogue, list || (φαγητῶν) menu || (τιμῶν) inventory, register, roll.

κατάλυμα, τό [kataleema] lodging, housing || (στρατ) barracks, billeting.

κατάλυσις, ή [kataleesees] abolition || (χημ) catalysis.

καταλύω [kataleeo] abolish, do away with || take up lodging.

καταμερίζω [katamereezo] share out, distribute, apportion.

καταμεσῆς [katamesees] in the very middle.

κατάμεστος [katamestos] quite full, crowded.

καταμετρῶ [katametro] measure, survey, gauge.

κατάμουτρα [katamoutra] point-blank.

καταναλίσκω [katanaleesko] consume, spend, use up || (ποτά) drink.

κατανάλωσις, ή [katanalosees] consumption || drinking.

καταναλωτής, ό [katanalotees] consumer customer.

κατανέμω [katanemo] distribute || (εὐθύνας) allot, assign, share.

κατανόησις, ή [katanoeesees] understanding, comprehension.

κατανοῶ [katanoo] understand, comprehend.

κατάντημα, τό [katanteema] wretched state.

καταντῶ [katanto] be reduced to, bring to, end up as.

κατάνυξις, ἡ [kataneeksees] compunction, piety.

καταπακτή, ἡ [katapaktee] trap, pitfall.

καταπατῶ [katapato] violate, encroach upon.

κατάπαυσις, ἡ [katapavsees] cessation, stopping, halting.

καταπέλτης, ὁ [katapeltees] catapult.

καταπέτασμα, τό [katapetasma]: τρώω τό ~ eat to bursting point.

καταπιάνομαι [katapeeanome] undertake, enter upon, engage upon.

καταπιέζω [katapiezo] oppress, crush, harass.

καταπίνω [katapeeno] swallow, gobble up || (ἐπί κυμάτων) engulf.

καταπίπτω [katapeepto] fall down, come down || collapse || (ὀλιγοστεύω) diminish.

καταπλακώνω [kataplakono] flatten, crush.

κατάπλασμα, τό [kataplasma] poultice.

καταπλέω [katapleo] sail in, sail down.

καταπληκτικός [katapleekteekos] amazing, wonderful, marvellous, astonishing.

κατάπληκτος [katapleektos] stupefied, amazed.

κατάπληξις, ἡ [katapleeksees] surprise, astonishment.

καταπλήσσω [katapleeso] astonish, surprise, amaze, stupefy.

καταπνίγω [katapneego] strangle, throttle, suffocate || (στάσιν) suppress, put down.

καταπονάω [kataponao] strain, weary, exhaust || (ἵππον) override.

καταποντίζομαι [kataponteezome] go down, sink.

καταπότιον, τό [katapoteeon] pill, tablet.

καταπραΰνω [katapraeeno] pacify, mollify, appease, calm, assuage.

κατάπτυστος [katapteestos] despicable, abject, low, villainous.

κατάπτωσις, ἡ [kataptosees] downfall || (ἐδάφους) landslide || (μεταφ) prostration, exhaustion || dejection, depression.

κατάρα, ἡ [katara] curse, imprecation || (μεταφ) hell, woe, damnation.

καταραμένος [kataramenos] cursed, damned.

καταργῶ [kataryo] abolish, annul, cancel || (κάπνισμα) cut out.

καταριέμαι [katarieme] curse, damn, call down curses on.

καταρράκτης, ὁ [kataraktees] cascade, waterfall || (τεχν) sluice.

καταρρέω [katarreo] collapse, fall down || (μεταφ) give out.

καταρρίπτω [katareepto] (κάποιον) knock down || (τοῖχον) pull down, demolish ||

(ἐπιχείρημα) prove to be wrong || (ρεκόρ) beat, break || (ἄερο) shoot down.

καταρροή, ἡ [kataroee] catarrh, head cold.

κατάρτι, τό [katartee] mast.

καταρτίζω [katarteezo] organize, establish, form, prepare, construct.

καταρῶμαι [katarome] βλ **καταριέμαι.**

κατάσβεσις, ἡ [katasvesees] extinction, blowing out || (μεταφ) suppression || (δίψας) slaking, quenching.

κατασκευάζω [kataskevazo] construct, make, erect, build || (ἱστορία κτλ) invent, concoct, fabricate || (ἔργον τέχνης) fashion, model.

κατασκεύασμα, τό [kataskevasma] fabrication, concoction || construction, creation.

κατασκευή, ἡ [kataskevee] making, construction || (ἔργον) structure, edifice, building || (ἐφεύρεσις) invention, fabrication.

κατασκήνωσις, ἡ [kataskeenosees] camp, encampment || camping.

κατάσκοπος, ὁ [kataskopos] spy, secret agent.

κατασκοτώνομαι [kataskotonome] make a great effort || overwork.

κάτασπρος [kataspros] pure white, white as a sheet.

κατασταλάζω [katastalazo] (μεταφ) end in, conclude, settle on.

κατάστασις, ἡ [katastasees] situation, condition, state || (περιουσία) wealth, property || (ὀνομαστική) register, list.

καταστατικόν, τό [katastateekon] (ἑταιρείας) statute.

καταστέλλω [katastelo] suppress, overcome || curb, control, contain.

κατάστημα, τό [katasteema] establishment, institution || shop, store || **καταστηματάρχης** shopkeeper.

κατάστικτος [katasteektos] spotted, dotted, speckled || tattooed.

κατάστιχον, τό [katasteehon] accounts book || register.

καταστολή, ἡ [katastolee] suppression || checking, bridling, controlling.

καταστρεπτικός [katastrepteekos] destructive, devastating, ruinous.

καταστρέφω [katastrefo] destroy, ruin, devastate || spoil, damage.

καταστροφή, ἡ [katastrofee] destruction, ruin, disaster, catastrophe.

κατάστρωμα, τό [katastroma] deck.

καταστρώνω [katastrono] draw up, make up, frame || lay down.

κατάσχεσις, ἡ [katasheesees] seizure, confiscation || (λόγω χρέους) attachment.

κατάταξις, ἡ [katataksees] classification, sorting, grading || (στρατ) induction.

κατατάσσομαι [katatasome] enlist.

κατατομή, ἡ [katatomee] profile || vertical section, cutoff.

κατατόπια, τά [katatopeea] πλ locality, every nook and cranny.

κατατοπίζομαι [katatopeezome] find one's bearings.

κατατοπίζω [katatopeezo] direct, explain, inform.

κατατρέχω [katatreho] persecute, harass.

κατατρίβω [katatreevo] pulverize ‖ abrade, powder.

καταφανής [katafanees] obvious, evident, manifest.

καταφατικός [katafateekos] affirmative, positive.

καταφέρνω [kataferno] persuade, convince, manage, accomplish, succeed ‖ τά ~ succeed, manage.

καταφέρω [katafero] deal, strike ‖ βλ καί **καταφέρνω**.

καταφθάνω [katafthano] arrive ‖ overtake, catch up, overhaul.

κατάφορτος [katafortos] overloaded.

καταφρονώ [katafrono] scorn, despise.

καταφύγιον, τό [katafeeyeeon] refuge, hiding place.

κατάφυτος [katafeetos] covered with vegetation.

κατάφωρος [kataforos] manifest, flagrant, evident.

κατάφωτος [katafotos] profusely illuminated.

καταχάμα [katahama] on the ground, on the floor.

καταχθόνιος [katahthoneeos] infernal, fiendish, devilish.

καταχνιά [katahneea] mist, fog.

καταχραστής, ὁ [katahrastees] embezzler, defaulter.

κατάχρεως [katahreos] deep in debt.

κατάχρησις, ἡ [katahreesees] abuse, misuse, breach of trust.

καταχρηστικῶς [katahreesteekos] abusively, excessively, unduly.

καταχρῶμαι [katahrome] abuse, take advantage of, presume upon.

καταχωρῶ [katahoro] enter in a register, insert, register, record.

καταψηφίζω [katapseefeezo] vote against, oppose.

κατάψυξις, ἡ [katapseeksees] refrigeration.

κατεβάζω [katevazo] let down ‖ (ἀπο-σκευές) take or bring down ‖ (θερμο-κρασία κτλ) lower, reduce ‖ (κόστος) lessen, decrease ‖ (αὐλαίαν) drop.

κατεβαίνω [kateveno] come down, go down, descend.

κατέβασμα, τό [katevasma] descent, lowering, taking down.

κατεβασμένος [katevasmenos] (τιμή) reduced ‖ (κατηφής) depressed.

κατεδαφίζω [katedafeezo] demolish, pull-down, raze.

κατειλημμένος [kateeleemenos] occupied, reserved.

κατέναντι [katenantee] right opposite.

κατεργάζομαι [kateryazome] elaborate, work out, shape, fashion.

κατεργάρης, ὁ [kateryarees] rascal, rogue ‖ (ἐπίθ) cunning, tricky.

κατέρχομαι [katerhome] βλ **κατεβαίνω**.

κατεύθυνσις, ἡ [kateftheensees] direction, line, course.

κατευθύνομαι [kateftheenome] turn, head (for).

κατευθύνω [kateftheeno] direct, guide, aim, turn.

κατευνάζω [katevnazo] calm, pacify, appease, mollify.

κατευόδιον, τό [katevodeeon] (a) good journey, (a) bon voyage.

κατέχω [kateho] possess, own, have, hold ‖ (θέσιν) occupy ‖ (γνωρίζω) know.

κατεψυγμένος [katepseeymenos] frozen, icy, frigid, polar.

κατηγορηματικός [kateeyoreemateekos] categorical, explicit.

κατηγορητήριον, τό [kateeyoreeteereeon] indictment.

κατηγορία, ἡ [kateeyoreea] accusation, charge ‖ category, class, division.

κατήγορος, ὁ [kateeyoros] plaintiff, accuser ‖ δημόσιος ~ public prosecutor.

κατηγορούμενον, τό [kateeyoroumenon] (γραμμ) complement ‖ attribute.

κατηγορούμενος [kateeyoroumenos] the accused ‖ defendant.

κατηγορῶ [kateeyoro] accuse, charge ‖ blame, criticize.

κατηφής [kateefees] gloomy, depressed.

κατήφορος, ὁ [kateeforos] descent, slope.

κατηχῶ [kateeho] (ἐκκλ) catechize ‖ (σὲ ὀργάνωσι) initiate.

κάτι [katee] something ‖ some.

κατιών [kateeon] descending, falling.

κατοικία, ἡ [kateekeea] dwelling, residence, home.

κατοικίδιος [kateekeedeeos] domesticated.

κατοικῶ [kateeko] live in, dwell in, inhabit, reside.

κατολίσθησις, ἡ [katoleestheesees] landslide.

κατόπιν [katopeen] after, close after ‖ then ‖ behind ‖ ~ ἀπό after.

κατοπτεύω [katoptevo] keep an eye on, observe, survey.

κατοπτρίζω [katoptreezo] reflect, mirror ‖ (μεταφ) represent.

κάτοπτρον, τό [katoptron] mirror, looking-glass.

κατόρθωμα, τό [katorthoma] achievement, feat.

κατορθώνω [katorthono] succeed in, perform well.

κατορθωτός [katorthotos] feasible, possible, practicable.

κατουρλιό, τό [katourlio] urine, piss (col).

κατουρῶ [katouro] piss (col), urinate.

κατοχή, ή [katohee] possession ‖ (στρατ) occupation ‖ (νομ) detention.

κάτοχος, ό [katohos] possessor, occupier ‖ experienced person ‖ ~ τῆς Ἀγγλικῆς one whose English is good.

κατοχυρώνω [katoheerono] fortify ‖ (μεταφ) secure, safeguard.

κατρακυλῶ [katrakeelo] bring down, tumble down, come down.

κατράμι, τό [katramee] tar, asphalt.

κατσαβίδι, τό [katsaveedee] screwdriver.

κατσάδα, ή [katsada] scolding, dressing-down, reprimand.

κατσαρίδα, ή [katsareeda] cockroach.

κατσαρόλα, ή [katsarola] saucepan.

κατσαρός [katsaros] curly, curled, fuzzy.

κατσίκα, ή [katseeka] goat.

κατσικήσιος [katseekeeseeos] of a goat.

κατσίκι, τό [katseekee] kid.

κατσουφιάζω [katsoufeeazo] look sour, look sullen, frown.

κάτω [kato] down, under, underneath, below ‖ on the ground ‖ στό ~ ~ after all ‖ ἀπάνω ~ approximately, about ‖ ἄνω ~ upset, in a turmoil.

κατώγειον, τό [katoyeeon] basement, cellar.

κάτωθεν [katothen] from below ‖ below.

κατώτατος [katotatos] lowest, least, undermost.

κατώτερος [katoteros] lower ‖ poorer (quality), inferior.

κατώφλι, τό [katoflee] threshold, doorstep ‖ (μεταφ) eve.

καυγάς, ό [kavyas] quarrel, wrangle, squabble, argument.

καύκαλο, τό [kavkalo] skull ‖ shell, carapace.

καϋμα, τό [kavma] burn ‖ burning heat.

καύσιμα, τά [kavseema] πλ fuel.

καύσιμος [kavseemos] combustible, inflammable.

καῦσις, ή [kavsees] burning ‖ (χημ) combustion.

καυστικός [kavsteekos] caustic.

καύσων, ό [kavson] heatwave.

καυτερός [kavteros] hot ‖ (ὑγρό) scalding ‖ (μεταφ) caustic, biting.

καυτηριάζω [kavteereeazo] cauterize ‖ (ζῶα) brand ‖ (μεταφ) stigmatize.

καυτός [kavtos] scalding, boiling, hot.

καύχημα, τό [kavheema] boast, pride, glory.

καυχηματίας, ό [kavheemateeas] braggart.

καυχιέμαι [kavhieme] boast of, be proud.

καφάσι, τό [kafasee] trellis, lattice ‖ (γιά φροῦτα) crate.

καφενεῖον, τό [kafeneeon] coffee house.

καφές, ό [kafes] coffee.

καφετζῆς, ό [kafetsees] coffee-house keeper.

καφετιέρα, ή [kafetiera] coffee pot.

καφετής [kafetees] coffee-coloured.

καχεκτικός [kahekteekos] sickly (person), weakly (person).

καχύποπτος [kaheepoptos] suspicious, distrustful.

κάψα, ή [kapsa] excessive heat.

καψαλίζω [kapsaleezo] singe, broil ‖ toast.

κάψιμο, τό [kapseemo] burning ‖ scald.

καψούλι, τό [kapsoulee] (ἰατρ) capsule.

κέδρος, ή [keδros] cedar tree, cedar (wood).

κεῖμαι [keeme] lie ‖ be situated.

κείμενον, τό [keemenon] text.

κειμήλιον, τό [keemeeleeon] heirloom, treasure.

κέκτημαι [kekteeme] possess, own, occupy.

κελαϊδῶ [kelaeeδo] sing, warble, chirp.

κελεπούρι, τό [kelepouree] bargain ‖ windfall, godsend.

κελευστής, ό [kelevstees] petty officer.

κελλάρι, τό [kelaree] cellar ‖ larder.

κελλί(ον), τό [kelee(on)] cell ‖ honeycomb.

κέλυφος, ό [keleefos] shell, husk, bark.

κενόδοξος [kenoδoksos] conceited, self-satisfied, vainglorious.

κενόν, τό [kenon] void, empty space, vacuum ‖ (μεταφ) gap.

κενός [kenos] empty ‖ (οἰκία) unoccupied, vacant.

κέντημα, τό [kenteema] sting, bite ‖ embroidery ‖ (μεταφ) exhortation.

κεντητός [kenteetos] embroidered.

κεντρί, τό [kentree] sting ‖ thorn.

κεντρίζω [kentreezo] (βόδι) prick, goad ‖ (ἄλογο) spur ‖ (δένδρον) graft ‖ (μεταφ) rouse, stir up.

κεντρικός [kentreekos] central, middle ‖ principal.

κεντρομόλος [kentromolos] centripetal.

κέντρον, τό [kentron] sting, goad, spur ‖ (πόλεως) centre ‖ (γεωμ) centre ‖ (διασκεδάσεως) (night) club, taverna ‖ τηλεφωνικόν ~ telephone exchange.

κεντρόφυξ [kentrofeeks] centrifugal.

κεντρώνω [kentrono] βλ **κεντρίζω.**

κεντῶ [kento] embroider ‖ (μεταφ) incite, rouse, awaken, stir up.

κενώνω [kenono] empty ‖ (δρόμο) drain ‖ (συρτάρι) clean out ‖ (σπίτι) evacuate.

κένωσις, ή [kenoses] emptying, clearing out ‖ bowel movement.

κεραία, ή [kerea] antenna, feeler ‖ (ἀσυρμάτου) aerial.

κεραμίδι, τό [kerameeδee] tile, slate ‖ πλ roof.

κεραμική, ή [kerameekee] ceramics.

κέρας, τό [keras] horn.

κεράσι, τό [kerasee] cherry ‖ **κερασιά, ή** cherry tree.

κέρασμα, τό [kerasma] treat.

κερατᾶς, ό [keratas] cuckold.

κέρατο, τό [kerato] horn ‖ (ἐπί ἀνθρώπου) obstinate, perverse.

κεραυνοβόλος [keravnovolos] blitzkrieg-like, like lightning.

κεραυνός, ό [keravnos] thunderbolt.

κερδίζω [kerdeezo] win, earn ‖ get, gain ‖ profit by.

κέρδος, τό [kerdos] earnings, winnings ‖ advantage.

κερδοσκοπῶ [kerdoskopo] speculate.

κερένιος [kereneeos] wax, waxen.

κερί, τό [keree] wax ‖ taper, wax candle.

κερκίδα, ἡ [kerkeeda] tier of seats.

κέρμα, τό [kerma] fragment ‖ coin ‖ (διά μηχάνημα) token.

κερνῶ [kerno] treat ‖ stand or buy a drink.

κεσές, ὁ [keses] shallow dish.

κετσές, ὁ [ketses] felt.

κεφαλαιοκρατία, ἡ [kefaleokrateea] capitalism.

κεφάλαια, τά [kefalea] πλ funds, capital.

κεφάλαιον, τό [kefaleon] capital, funds ‖ (βιβλίου) chapter.

κεφαλαῖον, τό [kefaleon] capital (letter).

κεφαλαιώδης [kefaleodees] essential, fundamental.

κεφαλαλγία, ἡ [kefalalyeea] headache.

κεφαλή, ἡ [kefalee] head ‖ leader, chief.

κεφάλι, τό [kefalee] head ‖ (μεταφ) brains.

κέφαλος, ὁ [kefalos] mullet.

κεφᾶτος [kefatos] well-disposed, merry, jovial.

κέφι, τό [kefee] good humour, gaiety ‖ στό ~ merry, mellow.

κεφτές, ὁ [keftes] meatball, rissole.

κεχρί, τό [kehree] millet.

κεχριμπάρι, τό [kehreembaree] amber.

κηδεία, ἡ [keedeea] funeral (procession).

κηδεμών, ὁ [keedemon] guardian ‖ curator.

κήλη, ἡ [keelee] hernia, rupture.

κηλιδώνω [keeleedono] stain, dirty ‖ (μεταφ) sully, tarnish.

κηλίς, ἡ [keelees] spot, stain ‖ (μεταφ) slur, blemish.

κῆπος, ὁ [keepos] garden.

κηπουρική, ἡ [keepoureekee] gardening, horticulture.

κηπουρός, ὁ [keepouros] gardener.

κηρήθρα, ἡ [keereethra] honeycomb.

κηρίον, τό [keereeon] βλ κερί.

κηροπήγιον, τό [keeropeeyeeon] candlestick, taper-stand.

κηρός, ὁ [keeros] wax.

κήρυγμα, τό [keereeyma] proclamation ‖ (ἐκκλ) sermon, preaching.

κῆρυξ, ὁ [keereeks] herald ‖ (ἐκκλ) preacher.

κηρύσσω [keereeso] proclaim, announce ‖ (ἐκκλ) preach.

κῆτος, τό [keetos] cetacean, whale.

κηφήν, ὁ [keefeen] drone ‖ (μεταφ) idler, loafer.

κιάλια, τά [kialea] πλ binoculars, opera glasses.

κίβδηλος [keevdeelos] adulterated, counterfeit ‖ (μεταφ) fraudulent.

κιβώτιον, τό [keevoteeon] chest, box ‖ ~ ταχυτήτων gearbox.

κιγκλίδωμα, τό [keengleedoma] (φράκτης) barrier, fence ‖ (σιδηροῦν) grating ‖ (ξύλινον) lattice work ‖ (παραθύρου) bar.

κιθάρα, ἡ [keethara] guitar.

κιλό, τό [keelo] kilogram.

κιμᾶς, ὁ [keemas] minced meat.

κιμωλία, ἡ [keemoleea] chalk.

Κίνα, ἡ [keena] China.

κινδυνεύω [keendeenevo] endanger ‖ be in danger, risk, venture.

κίνδυνος, ὁ [keendeenos] danger, peril, hazard, jeopardy.

κινέζικα, τά [keenezeeka] πλ Chinese language.

Κινέζος, ὁ [keenezos] Chinese, Chinaman.

κίνημα, τό [keeneema] movement ‖ (μεταφ) rebellion, revolt.

κινηματογράφος, ὁ [keeneematoyrafos] cinema.

κίνησις, ἡ [keeneesees] movement (κυκλοφορίας) flow of traffic ‖ (ἀξιῶν) transactions.

κινητήρ, ὁ [keeneeteer] motor.

κινητός [keeneetos] movable.

κίνητρον, τό [keeneetron] motive.

κινίνη, ἡ [keeneenee] quinine.

κινοῦμαι [keenoume] move.

κινῶ [keeno] set in motion, move, rouse ‖ make go, set going.

κιόλα(ς) [keeola(s)] already, also, even.

κιονόκρανον, τό [keeonokranon] capital (archit).

κιονοστοιχία, ἡ [keeonosteeheea] colonnade.

κιόσκι, τό [keeoskee] kiosk.

κίσσα, ἡ [keesa] magpie.

κισσός, ὁ [keesos] ivy.

κιτρινάδα, ἡ [keetreenada] paleness ‖ (ἀρρώστεια) jaundice.

κιτρινίζω [keetreeneezo] go yellow, make yellow, pale.

κίτρινος [keetreenos] yellow ‖ sallow, pale

κίτρον, τό [keetron] citron.

κίων, ὁ [keeon] pillar, column.

κλαγγή, ἡ [klangee] clanking of arms, clashing.

κλαδευτήρι, τό [kladevteeree] pruning hook, pruning scissors.

κλαδεύω [kladevo] prune, trim.

κλάδος, ὁ [klados] branch, arm.

κλαίομαι [kleome] complain, gripe.

κλαίω [kleo] cry, weep ‖ feel sorry for weep for.

κλάμα, τό [klama] crying, wailing, weeping

κλάνω [klano] break wind, fart (col).

κλαρί, τό [klaree] small branch.

κλάσις, ἡ [klasees] class, age group, category ‖ breaking.

κλάσμα, τό [klasma] fraction ‖ fragment.

κλασσικός [klaseekos] classic(al) ‖ (μεταφ) standard, standing.

κλαυθμηρός [klafthmeeros] tearful, mournful, plaintive.

κλαψιάρης [klapseearees] given to complaining || tearful, plaintive.

κλαψιάρικος [klapseeareekos] always whining || always beefing.

κλάψιμο, τό [klapseemo] crying, grumbling.

κλέβω [klevo] βλ κλέπτω.

κλειδαριά, ἡ [kleedaria] lock || (ἀσφαλείας) safety lock || (κρεμαστή) padlock.

κλειδαρότρυπα, ἡ [kleedarotreepa] keyhole.

κλειδί, τό [kleedee] key.

κλειδώνω [kleedono] lock up || (περιορίζω) confine, coop up.

κλείδωσις, ἡ [kleedosees] joint.

κλεῖθρον, τό [kleethron] lock || bar.

κλείνω [kleeno] close, shut, shut up, seal || (μέ σύρτη) bolt || (βρύση) turn off || ~ τό μάτι wink || ~ τά ἐξῆντα I'm nearing sixty.

κλείς, ἡ [klees] key.

κλείσιμο, τό [kleeseemo] closing, locking up || (μεταφ) conclusion.

κλεισούρα, ἡ [kleesoura] pass || mustiness.

κλειστός [kleestos] shut, closed.

κλέπτης, ὁ [kleptees] thief, burglar || (πορτοφολιῶν) pickpocket.

κλέπτω [klepto] (κάτι) steal || (κάποιον) rob || (μέ ἀπάτη) cheat, swindle.

κλεφτά [klefta] furtively, stealthily || hurriedly.

κλέφτης, ὁ [kleftees] thief || klepht.

κλεφτοπόλεμος, ὁ [kleftopolemos] guerrilla warfare.

κλεφτός [kleftos] stolen || furtive, stealthy.

κλεψιά, ἡ [klepseea] βλ κλοπή.

κλέψιμο, τό [klepseemo] theft, robbery, burglary.

κλεψύδρα, ἡ [klepseedra] water clock, sandglass.

κλήθρα, ἡ [kleethra] alder.

κλῆμα, τό [kleema] vine || κληματαριά, ἡ vine arbour, climbing vine || bower || κληματόφυλλο, τό vine leaf.

κληρικός [kleereekos] clerical, of the clergy.

κληροδότημα, τό [kleerodoteema] legacy, bequest.

κληρονομιά, ἡ [kleeronomeea] inheritance || heritage, legacy.

κληρονομικός [kleeronomeekos] hereditary.

κληρονόμος, ὁ, ἡ [kleeronomos] heir, heiress.

κληρονομῶ [kleeronomo] inherit, come into an estate.

κλῆρος, ὁ [kleeros] lot, fate || (ἐκκλ) clergy || (μεταφ) lot, fortune.

κλήρωσις, ἡ [kleerosees] drawing of lottery, prize drawing.

κλῆσις, ἡ [kleesees] call, calling || writ of summons.

κλητήρας, ὁ [kleeteeras] usher || (δικαστικός) bailiff.

κλητική, ἡ [kleeteekee] (γραμμ) vocative (case).

κλίβανος, ὁ [kleevanos] oven, kiln, furnace.

κλίμα, τό [kleema] climate || (μεταφ) atmosphere.

κλιμάκιον, τό [kleemakeeon] detachment, gang || (στρατ) echelon || small scale.

κλιμακωτός [kleemakotos] graduated.

κλίμαξ, ἡ [kleemaks] staircase, stairs, ladder || scale || (μουσ) gamut, scale.

κλιματισμός, ὁ [kleemateesmos] air conditioning.

κλινάμαξα, ἡ [kleenamaksa] sleeper (rail).

κλίνη, ἡ [kleenee] bed || (ἐκστρατείας) campbed || (μωροῦ) cot, crib.

κλινήρης [kleeneerees] bedridden.

κλινική, ἡ [kleeneekee] clinic, (private) hospital.

κλινοσκέπασμα, τό [kleenoskepasma] blanket, coverlet.

κλίνω [kleeno] lean, bend || (ἔχω τάσιν πρός) tend || (γραμμ) decline, conjugate.

κλίσις, ἡ [kleesees] inclination, slope || proneness, tendency || (γραμμῆς) slope || (γραμμ) declension, conjugation || (στέγης) slant.

κλιτύς, ἡ [kleetees] slope (of mountain), declivity.

κλονίζομαι [kloneezome] stagger || (μεταφ) hesitate, falter, waver.

κλονίζω [kloneezo] shake, unsettle || (ὑγείαν) damage, ruin.

κλονισμός, ὁ [kloneesmos] shaking, concussion || (μεταφ) hesitation, wavering.

κλοπή, ἡ [klopee] theft, robbery, burglary.

κλοπιμαῖος [klopeemeos] stolen || furtive, stealthy.

κλουβί, τό [klouvee] cage.

κλούβιος [klouveeos] bad, rotten || (μεταφ) empty-headed, stupid.

κλύσμα, τό [kleesma] enema.

κλωβός, ὁ [klovos] cage.

κλώθω [klotho] spin.

κλωνάρι, τό [klonaree] branch (of tree) || shoot.

κλώσιμο, τό [kloseemo] spinning.

κλῶσσα, ἡ [klosa] (brooding) hen.

κλωστή, ἡ [klostee] thread, string.

κλωτσιά, ἡ [klotsia] kick.

κλωτσῶ [klotso] kick.

κνήμη, ἡ [kneemee] shin || leg.

κόβομαι [kovome] cut o.s.

κόβω [kovo] (ψωμί) cut, slice || (μαλλιά) cut, trim || (νύχια) pare || (κρέας) carve || (νομίσματα) coin, mint || (νερό) turn off || (καφέ, σιτάρι) grind, mill || (κεφάλι) behead || (ἐρόδια) cut off || ~ μονέδα make money || ~ εἰσιτήριο buy a ticket || ~ δεξιά turn right.

κόγχη, ἡ [konghee] marine shell || (ματιοῦ) eye socket || (ἀρχιτεκ) niche.

κογχύλι, τό [kongheelee] sea shell || shellfish.

κοιλάδα, ἡ [keelada] valley, vale.

κοιλαρᾶς [keelaras] pot-bellied, portly.

κοιλιά, ή [keelia] belly, abdomen || (τοίχου) bulge.

κοιλόπονος, ό [keeloponos] stomach ache.

κοῖλος [keelos] hollow, sunken.

κοιλότης, ή [keelotees] hollowness || concavity.

κοιμᾶμαι [keemame] sleep, be asleep.

κοίμησις, ή [keemeesees] (ἐκκλ) Assumption || sleeping.

κοιμητήριον, τό [keemeeteereeon] cemetery, graveyard.

κοιμίζω [keemeezo] put to sleep || quiet, lull, beguile.

κοιμισμένος [keemeesmenos] (μεταφ) sluggish, stupid, dull.

κοιμοῦμαι [keemoume] βλ **κοιμᾶμαι**.

κοινοβουλευτικός [keenovoulevteekos] parliamentary, parliamentarian.

κοινοβούλιον, τό [keenovouleeon] parliament || (εἰς 'Αγγλίαν) Houses of Parliament.

κοινόν, τό [keenon] the public.

κοινοποιῶ [keenopeeo] notify, inform, announce || serve (a notice).

κοινοπολιτεία, ή [keenopoleeteea] commonwealth.

κοινός [keenos] common || ordinary, vulgar || (ἐργασιά κτλ) collective || (γραμμ) common (noun) || **κοινή γνώμη** public opinion || **ἀπό κοινοῦ** in common, together.

κοινότης, ή [keenotees] community || parish || **Βουλή τῶν Κοινοτήτων** House of Commons.

κοινοτοπία, ή [keenotopeea] commonplace || banality.

κοινωνία, ή [keenoneea] society, community, association || (ἐκκλ) Holy Communion.

κοινωνικός [keenoneekos] social, sociable.

κοινωνῶ [keenono] receive Holy Communion || administer Holy Communion.

κοιτάζομαι [keetazome] look after o.s.

κοιτάζω [keetazo] look at, pay attention to || consider, see || attend.

κοίτασμα, τό [keetasma] layer, deposit, stratum.

κοίτη, ή [keetee] bed || (ζώων) lair || (πτηνῶν) nest.

κοιτίς, ή [keetees] cradle || (μεταφ) origin, birthplace.

κοιτών, ό [keeton] bedroom || dormitory.

κοκεταρία, ή [koketareea] smartness, coquetry, stylishness.

κόκκαλο, τό [kokalo] bone || (παπουτσιοῦ) shoehorn || **ἔμεινε ~** he was astounded.

κοκκινάδι, τό [kokeenadee] rouge.

κοκκινέλι, τό [kokeenelee] red wine.

κοκκινίζω [kokeeneezo] redden, blush, turn red.

κοκκινογούλι, τό [kokeenogoulee] beet-root, beet.

κοκκινομάλλης [kokeenomalees] red-haired.

κόκκινος [kokeenos] red, scarlet || (μάγουλα) ruddy, rosy.

κόκκος, ό [kokos] grain || (καφέ) bean || (σκόνης) speck.

κοκκύτης, ό [kokeetees] whooping cough.

κόκορας, ό [kokoras] cock, rooster.

κοκορέτσι, τό [kokoretsee] sheep's entrails.

κολάζω [kolazo] punish, chastise.

κολακεία, ή [kolakeea] flattery, soft-soaping.

κολακευτικός [kolakevteekos] complimentary.

κολακεύω [kolakevo] flatter, fawn upon.

κόλακας, ό [kolakas] flatterer, wheedler

κόλασις, ή [kolasees] hell.

κολατσίζω [kolatseezo] have a snack.

κολατσιό, τό [kolatsio] snack.

κολικός, ό [koleekos] colic.

κολιός, ό [kolios] kind of mackerel.

κόλλα, ή [kola] glue, gum, paste || (κολλαρίσματος) starch || (χαρτιοῦ) sheet of paper.

κολλάρο, τό [kolaro] collar.

κολλέγιον, τό [kole·yeeon] college.

κόλλημα, τό [koleema] glueing, sticking || soldering.

κολλητικός [koleeteekos] contagious, infectious.

κολλητός [koleetos] soldered || close-fitting ||.(ἐφαπτόμενος) contiguous.

κολλητσίδα, ή [koleetseeda] burdock || (μεταφ) pest.

κολλιέ, τό [kolie] necklace.

κόλλυβα, τό [koleeva] boiled wheat.

κολλῶ [kolo] glue, stick, paste || solder, fuse || (ἀρρώστεια) get, catch || (σέ κάποιον) stick to, attach to.

κολοβός, ό [kolovos] truncated, mutilated || deficient.

κολοκύθι, τό [kolokeethee] vegetable marrow, pumpkin.

κολόνα, ή [kolona] βλ **κολώνα**.

κολόνια, ή [koloneea] eau de Cologne.

κολοσσιαῖος [kolosieos] colossal, enormous.

κολοσσός, ό [kolosos] colossus, giant.

κολοφών, ό [kolofon] summit || (μεταφ) height, acme.

κόλπο, τό [kolpo] trick, artifice, deceit.

κόλπος, ό [kolpos] breast, bosom || (γεωγραφικός) gulf, bay.

κολυμβήθρα, ή [koleemveethra] font.

κολυμβητής, ό [koleemveetees] swimmer.

κολύμπι, τό [koleembee] swimming.

κολυμπῶ [koleembo] swim.

κολώνα, ή [kolona] pillar, column.

κομβίον, τό [komveeon] button.

κομβολόγιον, τό [komvoloyeeon] string of beads, worry beads.

κόμβος, ό [komvos] knot || junction.

κόμη, ή [komee] hair.

κόμης, ὁ [komees] count, earl.
κομητεία, ἡ [komeeteea] county, shire.
κομήτης, ὁ [komeetees] comet.
κομίζω [komeezo] bring, carry, convey.
κομιστής, ὁ [komeestees] carrier, bearer.
κόμιστρα, τά [komeestra] πλ carriage fees.
κόμμα, τό [koma] (πολιτικόν) party || (γραμμ) comma || (μαθημ) decimal point.
κομματάρχης, ὁ [komatarhees] party leader.
κομμάτι, τό [komatee] piece || (ψωμί) slice || (ζάχαρις) lump || fragment, chip || (ὡς ἐπιρ) a bit.
κομματιάζομαι [komateeazome] try hard.
κομματιάζω [komateeazo] cut up, parcel out, tear, break.
κομμένος [komenos] sliced, cut || (κουρασμένος) exhausted.
κομ(μ)ό, τό [komo] chest of drawers.
κομ(μ)οδίνο, τό [komodeeno] bedside table.
κομμουνιστής, ὁ [komouneestees] communist.
κόμμωσις, ἡ [komosees] hairdressing, hair style.
κομμωτήριον, τό [komoteereeon] hairdressing salon.
κομπάζω [kombazo] brag of, boast (about).
κομπιάζω [kombeeazo] (μεταφ) hesitate.
κομπίνα, ἡ [kombeena] racket (col).
κομπιναιζόν, τό [kombeenezon] slip, petticoat.
κομπογιαννίτης, ὁ [komboyeeaneetees] impostor, charlatan.
κομπόδεμα, τό [kombodema] hoard of money, savings.
κόμπος, ὁ [kombos] βλ κόμβος.
κομπόστα, ἡ [kombosta] compote.
κομπρέσσα, ἡ [kompresa] compress.
κομφόρ, τά [komfor] πλ home comforts, necessities.
κομψός [kompsos] fashionable, stylish, smart.
κονδύλιον, τό [konδeeleeon] item, entry.
κονδυλοφόρος, ὁ [konδeeloforos] penholder.
κονιάκ, τό [koneeak] cognac, brandy.
κονίαμα, τό [koneeama] mortar || plaster.
κούνικλος, ὁ [koneeklos] rabbit.
κονιορτός, ὁ [koneeortos] dust.
κόνις, ἡ [konees] powder, dust.
κονίστρα, ἡ [koneestra] arena || (μεταφ) political lists.
κονσέρβα, ἡ [konserva] tinned food, canned food, preserve(s).
κονσέρτο, τό [konserto] concert.
κοντά [konta] close to, close by, near || almost, nearly || ~ σέ near, next to || ~ στά ἄλλα moreover.
κονταίνω [konteno] shorten, curtail || get shorter.
κοντάρι, τό [kontaree] pole || (σημαίας) staff || (ναυτ) mast.

κοντεύω [kontevo] be about to, be nearly finished, be on the verge (of) || (πλησιάζω) approach, come near, draw near.
κόντημα, τό [konteema] shortening, shrinking.
κοντινός [konteenos] neighbouring, near-(by) || (δρόμος) short, quick.
κοντοζυγώνω [kontozeeyono] approach, come near.
κοντολογῆς [kontoloyees] in short, in a few words.
κοντός [kontos] short || (οὐσ) pole, post, stake.
κοντοστέκω [kontosteko] pause || hesitate, waver.
κοντούλης [kontoulees] short.
κόντρα [kontra] against, opposite.
κοπάδι, τό [kopaδee] flock || herd, drove || (λύκων) pack || (ἀνθρώπων) crowd, throng.
κοπάζω [kopazo] calm down, grow quiet, subside.
κοπανίζω [kopaneezo] beat, pound, grind || (μεταφ) reprimand, rebuke.
κόπανος, ὁ [kopanos] pestle, crusher || (μεταφ) fool, idiot.
κοπέλλα, ἡ [kopela] girl || (ὑπηρεσίας) servant, maid.
κοπή, ἡ [kopee] cutting || stoppage.
κόπια, ἡ [kopeea] copy, transcript.
κοπιάζω [kopeeazo] labour, toil || take the trouble (to).
κοπιαστικός [kopeeasteekos] wearisome, hard, fatiguing, troublesome.
κοπίδι, τό [kopeeδee] chisel.
κοπιώδης [kopeeoδees] βλ κοπιαστικός.
κόπος, ὁ [kopos] fatigue, toil, labour, trouble, effort.
κόπρανα, τά [koprana] πλ excrement.
κοπριά, ἡ [kopreea] dung, manure.
κόπρος, ἡ [kopros] βλ κοπριά.
κοπρόσκυλο, τό [koproskeelo] (μεταφ) worthless person, scoundrel.
κοπτήρ, ὁ [kopteer] incisor || (χαρτοκοπτήρ) cutter.
κοπτική, ἡ [kopteekee] cutting, tailoring.
κόπτω [kopto] βλ κόβω.
κόπωσις, ἡ [koposees] fatigue, weariness, toil.
κόρακας, ὁ [korakas] crow, raven.
κοράλλιον, τό [koraleeon] coral.
κόραξ, ὁ [koraks] βλ κόρακας.
κοράσιον, τό [koraseeon] little girl.
κορδέλλα, ἡ [korδela] ribbon, band, tape || (μεταφ) zigzag, twist and turn.
κορδόνι, τό [korδonee] cord, string.
κορδώνομαι [korδonome] strut, swagger, put on airs.
κορδώνω [korδono] tighten, stretch, extend.
κορεσμός, ὁ [koresmos] satisfaction, satiety.
κόρη, ἡ [koree] girl || (παρθένα) virgin ||

(παιδί) daughter ‖ (ὀφθαλμοῦ) pupil.
κορινθιακός [koreentheeakos] Corinthian.
κοριός, ὁ [korios] bedbug.
κοριτσάκι, τό [koreetsakee] little girl.
κορίτσι, τό [koreetsee] girl ‖ virgin.
κορμί, τό [kormee] body ‖ trunk.
κορμός, ὁ [kormos] trunk.
κορμοστασιά, ἡ [kormostasia] stature, bearing, figure.
κορνάρω [kornaro] sound one's horn, hoot.
κορνίζα, ἡ [korneeza] frame ‖ cornice.
κοροϊδεύω [koroeedevo] scoff at, laugh at, ridicule ‖ deceive.
κορόϊδο, τό [koroeedo] laughing stock, butt, scapegoat.
κορόμηλο, τό [koromeelo] plum.
κόρος, ὁ [koros] satiety.
κορσές, ὁ [korses] corset.
κορτάρω [kortaro] flirt, court.
κορυδαλλός, ὁ [koreedalos] skylark, lark.
κορυφαῖος, ὁ [koreefeos] leader, chief.
κορυφή, ἡ [koreefee] top ‖ (ὄρους) top, peak ‖ (γωνίας) vertex ‖ (μεταφ) leading person, outstanding person.
κορφή, ἡ [korfee] βλ **κορυφή**.
κόρφος, ὁ [korfos] bosom ‖ (γεωγραφικός) bay, inlet.
κορώνα, ἡ [korona] crown, coronet ‖ ~ γράμματα heads or tails.
κοσκινίζω [koskeeneezo] sift, screen ‖ (μεταφ) sift carefully.
κόσκινο, τό [koskeeno] sieve, sifter.
κοσμάκης, ὁ [kosmakees] the man in the street.
κόσμημα, τό [kosmeema] decoration, jewel ‖ ~τα πλ jewellery.
κοσμήτωρ, ὁ [kosmeetor] dean (univ).
κοσμικός [kosmeekos] lay ‖ mundane ‖ (γεγονός) social.
κόσμιος [kosmeeos] decent, modest, proper.
κόσμος, ὁ [kosmos] universe, world ‖ (ἄνθρωποι) people ‖ (στόλισμα) embellishment.
κοσμῶ [kosmo] adorn, embellish.
κοστίζω [kosteezo] cost, be expensive.
κόστος, τό [kostos] cost (price).
κοστούμι, τό [kostoumee] suit.
κότερο, τό [kotero] sailboat ‖ (ναυτ) cutter.
κοτέτσι, τό [kotetsee] hen coop.
κοτολέττα, ἡ [kotoleta] cutlet.
κοτόπουλο, τό [kotopoulo] chicken.
κοτρώνι, τό [kotronee] large stone, boulder.
κοτσάνι, τό [kotsanee] stem, stalk.
κότσι, τό [kotsee] anklebone.
κότσια, τά [kotseea] πλ guts, strength.
κοτσίδα, ἡ [kotseeda] tress, braid, pigtail.
κότσυφας, ὁ [kotseefas] blackbird.
κότ(τ)α, ἡ [kota] hen ‖ fowl.
κοτῶ [koto] dare, venture.
κουβαλῶ [kouvalo] carry, bring, transport.
κουβάρι, τό [kouvaree] ball.

κουβαριάζω [kouvareeazo] wind into a ball ‖ crumple ‖ (μεταφ) cheat.
κουβαρίστρα, ἡ [kouvareestra] bobbin, spool.
κουβᾶς, ὁ [kouvas] bucket, pail.
κουβέντα, ἡ [kouventa] conversation, chat.
κουβεντιάζω [kouventeeazo] converse, discuss, chat.
κουβέρ, τό [kouver] service charge, cover charge.
κουβερνάντα, ἡ [kouvernanta] governess.
κουβέρτα, ἡ [kouverta] blanket, coverlet ‖ (ναυτ) deck.
κουδούνι, τό [koudounee] bell ‖ (εἰσόδου) doorbell.
κουδουνίζω [koudouneezo] ring, tinkle, jingle.
κουδουνίστρα, ἡ [koudouneestra] rattle.
κουζίνα, ἡ [kouzeena] kitchen ‖ (γιά μαγείρευμα) stove.
κουκέτα, ἡ [kouketa] berth.
κουκί, τό [koukee] broad bean ‖ grain.
κούκλα, ἡ [koukla] doll ‖ (ράφτη) dummy ‖ (καλαμποκιοῦ) corn cob ‖ (μεταφ) lovely child ‖ pretty woman.
κούκ(κ)ος, ὁ [koukos] cuckoo ‖ bonnet, cap.
κουκουβάγια, ἡ [koukouvayea] owl.
κουκούλα, ἡ [koukoula] cowl, hood ‖ (τσαϊοῦ) tea cosy.
κουκούλι, τό [koukoulee] cocoon.
κουκουλώνω [koukoulono] keep secret ‖ bury ‖ wrap warmly.
κουκουνάρι, τό [koukounaree] pine cone ‖ seed of pine cone.
κουκούτσι, τό [koukoutsee] stone, kernel, pip ‖ (μεταφ) morsel, scrap.
κουλούρα, ἡ [kouloura] roll, French roll ‖ (ναυτ) lifebuoy.
κουλούρι, τό [koulouree] ring-shaped biscuit.
κουλουριάζω [kouloureeazo] coil, roll up, fold.
κουμάντο, τό [koumanto] order, control, direct.
κουμάρι, τό [koumaree] jug, crock, pitcher.
κουμπάρα, ἡ [koumbara] godmother ‖ matron of honour.
κουμπαρᾶς, ὁ [koumbaras] moneybox, piggy bank.
κουμπάρος, ὁ [koumbaros] godfather ‖ (σέ γάμο) best man.
κουμπί, τό [koumbee] button, stud ‖ (φώτων) switch.
κουμπότρυπα, ἡ [koumbotreepa] buttonhole.
κουμπώνω [koumbono] button up, fasten.
κουνάβι, τό [kounavee] marten, ferret.
κουνέλι, τό [kounelee] rabbit.
κούνημα, τό [kouneema] shaking, swinging, wagging ‖ (μεταφ) swaying.
κούνια, ἡ [kouneea] cradle, cot, crib ‖ (κήπου) swing.

κουνιάδα, ή [kouneeaδa] sister-in-law.

κουνιάδος, ό [kouneeaδos] brother-in-law.

κουνιστός [kouneestos] rocking || (μεταφ) swaying.

κουνούπι, τό [kounoupee] mosquito.

κουνουπίδι, τό [kounoupeeδee] cauliflower.

κουνουπιέρα, ή [kounoupiera] mosquito net.

κουνιέμαι [kounieme] move, shake || get moving.

κουνῶ [kouno] move, shake || (μαντήλι) wave || (οὐράν) wag || (μωρό) rock || (κεφάλι) toss.

κούπα, ή [koupa] cup, bowl, glass || (σέ χαρτιά) heart.

κουπί, τό [koupee] oar || τραβῶ ~ row.

κουπόνι, τό [kouponee] coupon.

κούρα, ή [koura] cure || medical attendance.

κουράγιο, τό [kourayeeo] bravery, fearlessness.

κουράζομαι [kourazome] get tired, tire o.s.

κουράζω [kourazo] tire, weary || bore || (ὅρασιν) strain.

κουραμάνα, ή [kouramana] army bread.

κουραμπιές, ὁ [kourambies] bun.

κούραση, ή [kourasee] weariness, fatigue || (μηχανῆς) wear and tear.

κουρασμένος [kourasmenos] tired, weary || (πρόσωπον) drawn.

κουραστικός [kourasteekos] tiresome, trying, troublesome.

κουραφέξαλα, τά [kourafeksala] πλ bullshit (col), balls (col).

κουρδίζω [kourδeezo] wind up || (βιολί) tune || (μεταφ) stir up, incite.

κουρέας, ὁ [koureas] barber.

κουρεῖον, τό [koureeon] barber's shop.

κουρελιάρης, ὁ [koureleearees] person in rags || vagabond.

κουρέλι, τό [kourelee] rag, tatter, shred.

κούρε(υ)μα, τό [koure(v)ma] haircut || shearing, clipping.

κουρεύω [kourevo] cut the hair of, trim, clip || (πρόβατον) shear || (χλόη) mow.

κουρκούτι, τό [kourkoutee] batter || pap.

κούρσα, ή [koursa] race || (διαδρομή) ride || (ἀμάξι) car.

κουρσάρος, ὁ [koursaros] pirate.

κουρσεύω [koursevo] plunder, raid.

κουρτίνα, ή [kourteena] curtain.

κουσούρι, τό [kousouree] defect, fault.

κουτάβι, τό [koutavee] puppy.

κουτάλι, τό [koutalee] spoon.

κουταμάρα, ή [koutamara] foolishness, nonsense.

κούτελο, τό [koutelo] forehead.

κουτί, τό [koutee] box, case || (σπίρτων) matchbox || (κονσέρβας) tin.

κουτός [koutos] silly, foolish, slow-witted.

κουτουλῶ [koutoulo] nod drowsily || butt.

κουτουρού [koutourou] στά ~ heedlessly, haphazardly, by chance.

κουτρουβάλα, ή [koutrouvala] somersault.

κουτρούλης [koutroulees] bald.

κούτσα, ή [koutsa] lameness.

κουτσαίνω [koutseno] limp || cripple.

κουτσομπολεύω [koutsombolevo] gossip, spread reports, tittle-tattle.

κουτσομπολιό, τό [koutsombolio] gossip, tittle-tattle.

κουτσός [koutsos] crippled, limping.

κούτσουρο, τό [koutsouro] log, stump.

κουφαίνομαι [koufenome] go deaf.

κουφαίνω [koufeno] deafen, make deaf.

κουφαμάρα, ή [koufamara] deafness.

κουφάρι, τό [koufaree] body.

κουφέτο, τό [koufeto] sugared almond.

κούφιος [koufeeos] hollow, empty || (δόντι) decayed || (ἦχο) muffled || (ἄνθρωπος) not serious, frivolous.

κουφόβραση, ή [koufovrasee] sweltering heat.

κοῦφος [koufos] lightweight.

κουφός [koufos] hard of hearing.

κούφωμα, τό [koufoma] hollow, cavity || opening.

κοφίνι, τό [kofeenee] basket, hamper, pannier.

κοφτά [kofta]: ὀρθά ~ frankly, categorically.

κοφτερός [kofteros] sharp, cutting.

κόφτω [kofto] βλ **κόβω**.

κόχη, ή [kohee] βλ **κόχη**.

κοχλάζω [kohlazo] boil, bubble || (μεταφ) seethe.

κοχλιάριον, τό [kohleeareeon] spoon.

κοχλίας, ὁ [kohleeas] snail || (ἦλος) screw.

κοχύλι, τό [koheelee] sea shell.

κόψη, ή [kopsee] cutting, slicing, clipping || edge.

κόψιμο, τό [kopseemo] cut, gash || cutting || (ἀσθένεια) bellyache (col).

κραγιόν, τό [krayion] crayon || lipstick.

κραδαίνω [kraδeno] flourish, wave, vibrate.

κράζω [krazo] croak, caw || cry out || call.

κραιπάλη, ή [krepalee] riot, orgy || drunkenness.

κράμα, τό [krama] mixture, blend || alloy, amalgam.

κράμβη, ή [kramvee] cabbage.

κρανίον, τό [kraneeon] cranium || skull.

κράνος, τό [kranos] helmet || (ἀποικιῶν) topee, sun helmet.

κράξιμο, τό [krakseemo] crowing, cawing.

κρασάτος [krasatos] cooked in wine.

κρασί, τό [krasee] wine.

κρᾶσις, ή [krasees] (σώματος) temperament, make-up.

κράσπεδον, τό [kraspeδon] (φορέματος) hem, border || (λόφου) foot || (πεζοδρομίου) kerb || (US) curb.

κρατήρ, ὁ [krateer] crater.

κράτησις, ή [krateesees] confinement, arrest || (μισθοῦ) deduction(s).

κρατιέμαι [kratieme] hold one's own, be well preserved.

κρατικοποίησις, ή [krateekopieesees] nationalization.

κρατικός [krateekos] national.

κράτος, τό [kratos] influence, power, authority ‖ the state.

κρατῶ [krato] last, keep ‖ (ἐπιβάλλομαι) hold in check, rule ‖ (κατάγομαι) be descended from ‖ (βαστῶ) have, hold ‖ (ὑποβαστῶ) support.

κραυγάζω [kravyazo] cry, howl, shout, scream.

κραυγή, ή [kravyee] shout, cry, outcry.

κρέας, τό [kreas] meat, flesh.

κρεατόμυγα, ή [kreotomeeya] bluebottle.

κρεατόπηττα, ή [kreatopeeta] meat pie.

κρεββάτι, τό [krevatee] bed.

κρεββατοκάμαρα, ή [krevatokamara] bedroom.

κρεββατώνω [krevatono] confine to bed, lay up.

κρέμα, ή [krema] cream.

κρεμάζω [kremazo] hang, suspend.

κρεμάλα, ή [kremala] gallows, gibbet.

κρέμασμα, τό [kremasma] suspension, hooking on ‖ hanging.

κρεμαστός [kremastos] suspended.

κρεμάστρα, ή [kremastra] hanger ‖ hat rack ‖ portmanteau.

κρεμιέμαι [kremieme] hang, be suspended.

κρεμμύδι, τό [kremeedee] onion.

κρεμ(ν)ῶ [krem(n)o] hang, hook up, suspend.

κρεοπώλης, ὁ [kreopolees] butcher.

κρεουργῶ [kreouryo] butcher ‖ massacre.

κρέπ, τό [krep] crêpe rubber ‖ crape.

κρεπάρω [kreparo] split, burst ‖ grieve, mourn.

κρημνίζομαι [kreemneezome] fall, crumble, collapse.

κρημνίζω [kreemneezo] hurl down, pull down, wreck.

κρημνός [kreemnos] sheer drop, crag.

κρήνη, ή [kreenee] fountain.

κρηπίδωμα, τό [kreepeedoma] foundation, base, groundwork ‖ (ναυτ) breakwater ‖ (σταθμοῦ) railway platform.

κρησφύγετον, τό [kreesfeeyeton] hideaway, retreat.

κριάρι, τό [kreearee] ram.

κριθαράκι, τό [kreetharakee] barley-shaped noodle ‖ (ματιοῦ) sty.

κριθάρι, τό [kreetharee] barley.

κρίκος, ὁ [kreekos] link, buckle, ring ‖ (ἀνυψώσεως) jack.

κρῖμα, τό [kreema] sin, guilt ‖ pity, misfortune ‖ τί ~ ! what a pity!, what a shame!

κρίνος, ὁ [kreenos] lily.

κρίνω [kreeno] judge, consider ‖ (ἀποφασίζω) decide.

κριός, ὁ [krios] ram.

κρίσιμος, ὁ [kreeseemos] critical, grave, momentous ‖ trying.

κρίσις, ή [kreesees] judgment, view ‖ (οἰκο-

νομική) crisis, depression ‖ (ἔλλειψις) deficiency, shortage ‖ (πνεύματος) judgment.

κριτήριον, τό [kreeteereeon] criterion, test.

κριτής, ὁ [kreetees] judge.

κριτική, ή [kreeteekee] criticism, review.

κριτικός [kreeteekos] discerning, critical ‖ (οὐσ) critic.

κροκάδι, τό [krokadee] yolk.

κροκόδειλος, ὁ [krokodeelos] crocodile.

κρόκος, ὁ [krokos] crocus ‖ (αὐγοῦ) yolk.

κρομμύδι, τό [kromeedee] onion.

κρόσσι, τό [krosee] fringe.

κρόταλον, τό [krotalon] rattle.

κρόταφος, ὁ [krotafos] temple (anat).

κρότος, ὁ [krotos] crash, bang, noise ‖ (μεταφ) sensation.

κρουαζιέρα, ή [krouaziera] cruise.

κρουνός, ὁ [krounos] source, spring ‖ tap, cock ‖ (US) faucet.

κροῦσις, ή [krousees] striking, sounding ‖ (στρατ) encounter.

κροῦσμα, τό [krousma] case (law, med).

κρούστα, ή [krousta] crust, rind ‖ scab.

κρούω [krouo] strike, sound ‖ knock on ‖ (κουδούνι) ring.

κρυάδα, ή [kreeaδa] cold, chill.

κρύβομαι [kreevome] go into hiding.

κρύβω [kreevo] βλ κρύπτω.

κρυμμένος [kreemenos] concealed.

κρύο, τό [kreeo] cold.

κρυολόγημα, τό [kreeoloyeema] cold (med).

κρυοπάγημα, τό [kreeopayeema] frostbite.

κρύος [kreeos] cold ‖ indifferent, phlegmatic, cool.

κρύπτω [kreepto] hide, conceal ‖ cover, screen ‖ (μεταφ) withhold, hold back.

κρυστάλλινος [kreestaleenos] like crystal, very clear.

κρύσταλλον, τό [kreestalon] crystal (glass).

κρυφά [kreefa] secretly, clandestinely, stealthily.

κρύφιος [kreefeeos] βλ κρυφός.

κρυφός [kreefos] private, secluded ‖ (χαρά) secret, inner ‖ (ἄνθρωπος) discreet, reticent.

κρυφτός [kreeftos] hidden.

κρύψιμο, τό [kreepseemo] concealing, hiding.

κρυψίνους [kreepseenous] deceitful, underhand, sneaky.

κρυψώνας, ὁ [kreepsonas] hideout, lurking place.

κρυώνω [kreeono] grow cold, feel cold ‖ cool down, chill.

κτένι, τό [ktenee] comb ‖ (τσουγκράνα) rake ‖ κτενίζω comb ‖ (μεταφ) brush up, finish in detail ‖ ~σμα combing ‖ hairdressing.

κτῆμα, τό [kteema] estate, land ‖ κτηματίας, ὁ landowner, proprietor.

κτηνίατρος, ὁ [kteeneeatros] veterinary surgeon.

κτῆνος, τό [kteenos] brute, beast, animal ‖ πλ cattle.

κτηνοτροφία, ή [kteenotrofeea] stock-breeding.

κτηνώδης [kteenoδees] beastly, bestial ‖ (ὄρεξις) hoggish.

κτῆσις, ή [kteesees] acquisition, occupation, occupancy.

κτητικός [kteeteekos] (γραμμ) possessive ‖ acquisitive.

κτίζω [kteezo] construct, erect, build.

κτίριον, τό [kteereeon] building, edifice.

κτίσιμον, τό [kteeseemon] building, erection.

κτίστης, ὁ [kteestees] builder, mason.

κτυπῶ [kteepo] beat, strike, flog, thrash.

κύαμος, ὁ [keeamos] bean.

κυάνιον, τό [keeaneeon] cyanide.

κυανόλευκος [keeanolevkos] blue and white.

κυανοῦς [keeanous] blue, azure.

κυβέρνησις, ή [keeverneesees] government, management.

κυβερνήτης, ὁ [keeverneetees] governor ‖ (ναυτ) commander.

κυβερνητικός [keeverneeteekos] governmental.

κυβερνῶ [keeverno] govern ‖ (πλοῖο) steer ‖ (σπίτι) manage, direct.

κύβος, ὁ [keevos] cube ‖ die.

κυδώνι, τό [keeδonee] quince ‖ (ὄστρακο) kind of shellfish.

κύησις, ή [kieesees] pregnancy ‖ gestation.

κυκεών, ὁ [keekeon] confusion, anarchy, chaos, disorder.

κυκλάμινο, τό [keeklameeno] cyclamen.

κυκλικός [keekleekos] circular.

κύκλος, ὁ [keeklos] circle ‖ (ἡλιακός κτλ) cycle, period ‖ (προσώπων) set.

κυκλοτερής [keekloterees] circular.

κυκλοφορία, ή [keekloforeea] circulation ‖ (αὐτοκινήτων) traffic flow.

κυκλοφορῶ [keekloforo] put into circulation, spread ‖ go about.

κύκλωμα, τό [keekloma] electric circuit ‖ encirclement.

κυκλών, ὁ [keeklon] cyclone.

κυκλώνω [keeklono] surround, encircle, envelop.

κύκνος, ὁ [keeknos] swan.

κυλάω [keelao] roll.

κυλιέμαι [keelieme] roll over ‖ (χοῖρος) wallow.

κυλικεῖον, τό [keeleekeeon] buffet, sideboard ‖ refreshment room.

κύλινδρος, ὁ [keeleenδros] cylinder ‖ roller, barrel.

κυλίω [keeleeo] roll, trundle, push.

κυλότα, ή [keelota] panties.

κῦμα, τό [keema] wave.

κυμαίνομαι [keemenome] undulate, wave, ripple ‖ (μεταφ) fluctuate, waver, hesitate.

κυματίζω [keemateezo] wave, flutter ‖ ripple.

κυματοθραύστης, ὁ [keematothravstees] breakwater.

κύμινον, τό [keemeenon] cumin.

κυνήγι, τό [keeneeyee] hunting, shooting, chase ‖ game.

κυνηγός, ὁ [keeneeyos] hunter, shooter.

κυνηγῶ [keeneeyo] hunt, chase, run after ‖ go shooting.

κυνικός [keeneekos] cynic(al).

κυοφορῶ [keeoforo] be pregnant.

κυπαρίσσι, τό [keepareesee] cypress tree.

κύπελλον, τό [keepelon] cup, goblet, tumbler.

κυπρῖνος, ὁ [keepreenos] carp.

κύπτω [keepto] bend, bow ‖ slant ‖ (μεταφ) give way.

κυρά, ή [keera] missus (col).

κυρία, ή [keereea] lady, mistress ‖ Mrs.

κυριακάτικος [keereeakateekos] Sunday (attr).

Κυριακή, ή [keereeakee] Sunday.

κυριαρχία, ή [keereearheea] sovereignty, dominion.

κυριαρχῶ [keereearho] dominate, exercise authority ‖ be sovereign.

κυριεύω [keerievo] subjugate, capture, dominate ‖ (ἐπί πάθους) seize, possess.

κυριολεκτικῶς [keereeolekteekos] exactly, precisely, to the letter.

κύριος, ὁ [keereeos] master, sir, gentleman ‖ Mr.

κύριος [keereeos] essential, vital ‖ main, chief, leading.

κυριότης, ή [keereeotees] ownership.

κυρίως [keereeos] principally, chiefly mainly, especially.

κῦρος, τό [keeros] authority, power ‖ validity, weight.

κυρτός [keertos] bent, crooked ‖ convex, bulging.

κυρώνω [keerono] confirm ‖ (νόμον) sanction, approve ‖ (ἀπόφασιν) ratify, validate.

κύρωσις, ή [keerosees] confirmation, sanction ‖ penalty.

κύστις, ή [keestees] bladder, cyst.

κυτίον, τό [keeteeon] small box, case.

κύτος, τό [keetos] (ναυτ) hold.

κυττάζω [keetazo] βλ κοιτάζω.

κύτταρον, τό [keetaron] cell.

κυφός [keefos] hunchbacked, humpbacked.

κυψέλη, ή [keepselee] swarm (of bees) ‖ beehive ‖ (αὐτιοῦ) earwax.

κύων, ὁ, ή [keeon] dog, bitch.

κώδιξ, ὁ [koδeeks] code ‖ codex.

κώδων, ὁ [koδon] bell.

κωδωνοκρουσία, ή [koδonokrouseea] chiming, ringing, pealing.

κωδωνοστάσιον, τό [koδonostaseeon] belfry, church steeple.

κώκ, τό [kok} coke.

κῶλον, τό [kolon] (γραμμ) colon.

κῶλος, ὁ [kolos] arse (col), bottom, back-side (col) ‖ ~ καί βρακί intimate.

κωλοφωτιά, ή [kolofotia] glow-worm.

κώλυμα, τό [koleema] obstacle, impediment.

κωλυσιεργῶ [koleesiergo] obstruct, hinder.

κωλύω [koleeo] stop, prevent, hinder.

κῶμα, τό [koma] coma.

κωματώδης [komatoδees] comatose, lethargic.

κώμη, ή [komee] small market town, hamlet.

κωμικός [komeekos] comic(al), funny ‖ (ούσ) comedian.

κωμόπολις, ή [komopolees] market town.

κωμωδία, ή [komoδeea] comedy.

κώνειον, τό [koneeon] hemlock.

κῶνος, ὁ [konos] cone.

κώνωψ, ὁ [konops] mosquito.

κώπη, ή [kopee] oar.

κωπηλασία, ή [kopeelaseea] rowing.

κωπηλάτης, ὁ [kopeelatees] rower.

κωφάλαλος [kofalalos] deaf-and-dumb.

κωφός [kofos] deaf.

κώχη, · ή [kohee] corner, nook, recess ‖ (πανταλονιού) crease.

Λ, λ

λάβα, ή [lava] lava.

λαβαίνω [laveno] βλ λαμβάνω.

λάβαρον, τό [lavaron] banner, standard.

λαβεῖν, τό [laveen] credit ‖ δοῦναι καί ~ debit and credit.

λαβή, ή [lavee] handle, grip ‖ pretext, excuse, reason.

λαβίς, ή [lavees] grip, nippers, hold ‖ (χειρουργική) forceps.

λάβρα, ή [lavra] excessive heat, suffocating heat.

λαβράκι, τό [lavrakee] bass fish.

λαβύρινθος, ὁ [laveereenthos] labyrinth.

λαβωματιά, ή [lavomatia] wound.

λαβώνω [lavono] wound.

λαγάνα, ή [laγana] unleavened bread.

λαγήνι, τό [laγeenee] pitcher, jug, crock.

λαγκάδι, τό [langaδee] ravine, narrow valley, defile.

λάγνος [laγnos] lewd, lascivious, wanton.

λαγόνες, οί [laγones] πλ loins ‖ flanks.

λαγός, ὁ [laγos] hare.

λαγωνικό, τό [laγoneeko] hunting dog ‖ greyhound, pointer.

λαδερός [laδeros] oily, greasy ‖ cooked with oil.

λάδι, τό [laδee] olive oil.

λαδομπογιά, ή [laδomboyia] oil paint.

λαδόχαρτο, τό [laδoharto] greaseproof paper.

λαδώνω [laδono] apply oil ‖ lubricate ‖ (μεταφ) bribe.

λαδωτήρι, τό [laδoteeree] cruet stand.

λάθος, τό [lathos] error, mistake, slip, fault ‖ κατά ~ by mistake.

λαθραῖος [lathreos] furtive, clandestine secret.

λαθραίως [lathreos] secretly, furtively, stealthily.

λαθρεμπόριο, τό [lathremboreeo] smuggling ‖ contraband.

λαθρέμπορος, ὁ [lathremboros] smuggler, contrabandist.

λαθρεπιβάτης, ὁ [lathrepeevatees] stow-away.

λαίδη, ή [leδee] lady.

λαϊκός [laeekos] popular, familiar, vulgar ‖ current, common ‖ lay.

λαίλαψ, ή [lelaps] hurricane, tempest.

λαίμαργος [lemarγos] gluttonous, greedy ‖ (ούσ) gourmand.

λαιμητόμος, ή [lemeetomos] guillotine.

λαιμοδέτης, ὁ [lemoδetees] necktie, cravat.

λαιμός, ὁ [lemos] neck, throat, gullet ‖ (μεταξύ βουνῶν) gorge, pass.

λακέρδα, ή [lakerδa] salted tunny fish.

λακές, ὁ [lakes] lackey, flunkey.

λακκάκι, τό [lakakee] dimple.

λάκκος, ὁ [lakos] hole, pit ‖ grave.

λακκούβα, ή [lakouva] βλ λάκκος.

λακτίζω [lakteezo] kick, boot, lash out.

λακωνικός [lakoneekos] laconic, terse, brief.

λαλιά, ή [lalia] voice ‖ speech ‖ (ἐπί πτηνῶν) singing, warbling.

λαλῶ [lalo] speak, talk ‖ crow ‖ sing.

λάμα, ή [lama] sheet, thin plate (μαχαιριοῦ) blade.

λαμαρίνα· ή [lamareena] sheet iron, iron plate.

λαμβάνω [lamvano] take hold of, take receive, obtain ‖ ~ τήν τιμήν I have the honour ‖ ~ χώραν take place, occur.

λάμβδα, τό [lamδa] the letter Λ.

λάμια, ή [lameea] ogress ‖ (μεταφ) greedy eater, glutton.

λάμπα, ή [lamba] lamp ‖ (ἠλεκτρική) electric lamp, bulb.

λαμπάδα, ή [lambaδa] torch ‖ candle, taper.

λαμπίκος, ὁ [lambeekos] distilling apparatus ‖ (μεταφ) very clean, clear.

λαμποκοπῶ [lambokopo] shine, gleam.

Λαμπρή, ή [lambree] Easter.

λαμπρός [lambros] brilliant, splendid, excellent, superb.

λαμπρῶς [lambros] (ἐπιφ) splendid!, excellent! ‖ (ἐπίρ) brilliantly.

λαμπτήρ, ὁ [lambteer] βλ λάμπα.

λαμπυρίς, ή [lambeerees] glow-worm.

λάμπω [lambo] shine, glitter, gleam ‖ (μεταφ) excel.

λάμψις, ή [lampsees] brightness, brilliance ‖ glaze.

λανθάνομαι [lanthanome] deceive o.s., be mistaken, err.

λανθάνω [lanthano] be latent ‖ escape notice.

λανθασμένος [lanthasmenos] mistaken, wrong.

λανσάρω [lansaro] launch, advertise, present.

λαξεύω [laksevo] hew, chisel, carve.

λαογραφία, ή [laoɣrafeea] folklore.

λαός, ό [laos] people, multitude, masses.

λαοῦτο, τό [laouto] lute.

λαπᾶς, ό [lapas] pap, boiled rice ‖ poultice ‖ (μεταφ) indolent person.

λαρδί, τό [larδee] lard, fat.

λαρύγγι, τό [lareengee] throat, larynx, windpipe, gullet.

λαρυγγῖτις, ή [lareengeetees] laryngitis.

λαρυγγολόγος, ό [lareengoloɣos] throat specialist.

λάρυγξ, ό [lareenks] βλ λαρύγγι.

λασκάρω [laskaro] slacken, loosen ‖ (ναυτ) cast off.

λάσπη, ή [laspee] mud, mire ‖ mortar ‖ τὄκοψε ~ he escaped ‖ he disappeared.

λασπώνω [laspono] cover with mud, dirty, soil.

λαστιχένιος [lasteeheneeos] rubber ‖ elastic.

λάστιχο, τό [lasteeho] rubber ‖ elastic ‖ rubber band ‖ (αὐτοκινήτου) tyre ‖ (παιδιοῦ) catapult, sling.

λατέρνα, ή [laterna] barrel organ.

λατινικά, τά [lateeneeka] πλ Latin.

λατινικός [lateeneekos] Latin.

λατομεῖον, τό [latomeeon] quarry.

λατρεία, ή [latreea] adoration, worship ‖ (ἀγάπη) fervent love.

λατρευτός [latrevtos] adorable, adored.

λατρεύω [latrevo] adore ‖ idolize.

λάτρης, ό [latrees] worshipper ‖ fan.

λάφυρον, τό [lafeeron] booty, spoils, loot.

λαχαίνω [laheno] meet, come across ‖ (συμβαίνω) happen, occur ‖ (στό κλῆρο) fall to, win.

λαχαναγορά, ή [lahanaɣora] vegetable market.

λαχανιάζω [lahaneeazo] pant, gasp.

λαχανικόν, τό [lahaneekon] vegetable, green.

λάχανον, τό [lahanon] cabbage.

λαχεῖον, τό [laheeon] lottery, raffle.

λαχνός, ό [lahnos] lot, chance ‖ prize, share.

λαχτάρα, ή [lahtara] anxiety ‖ (ἐπιθυμία) yearning ‖ (φόβος) dread, fright.

λαχταρῶ [lahtaro] be impatient ‖ (ἐπιθυμῶ) yearn, desire ‖ (φοβᾶμαι) be frightened.

λέαινα, ή [layena] lioness.

λεβάντα, ή [levanta] lavender.

λεβαντίνος, ό [levanteenos]·Levantine.

λεβέντης, ό [leventees] fine man, gentleman ‖ brave man.

λεβεντιά, ή [leventia] manliness.

λέβης, ό [levees] kettle, cauldron ‖ boile.

λεβιές, ό [levies] lever.

λεγάμενος [leɣamenos]: ό ~ you know who ‖ the so-called.

λεγεών, ό, ή [leɣeon] legion ‖ great number.

λέγω [leɣo] say, tell, speak ‖ (πιστεύω) think ‖ (ἐννοῶ) mean ‖ δέν σοῦ ~ I do not deny it, but ‖ τί λές (ἐπιφ) you don't say!, fancy that! ‖ πού λές well! ‖ λές καί as if.

λεηλασία, ή [leyeelaseea] plundering, looting, pillage.

λεηλατῶ [leyeelato] plunder, loot.

λεία, ή [leea] prey ‖ booty, loot.

λειαίνω [lieno] smooth, level, plane, polish.

λειβάδι, τό [leevaδee] pasture land, meadow.

λειμών, ό [leemon] βλ λειβάδι.

λεῖος [leeos] smooth, even, level.

λείπω [leepo] be absent, be missing, want, lack ‖ μοῦ λείπει I am missing, I lack ‖ μᾶς ἔλειπες we missed you ‖ λίγο ἔλειψε νά he nearly, he almost.

λειρί, τό [leeree] cockscomb, crest.

λειτουργία, ή [leetourɣeea] function, operation ‖ (ἐκκλ) mass, liturgy.

λειτουργός, ό, ή [leetourɣos] officer, official, civil servant.

λειτουργῶ [leetourɣo] function, work ‖ (ἐκκλ) celebrate mass.

λειχήν, ό [leeheen] lichen.

λείχω[leeho] lick.

λείψανα, τά [leepsana] πλ remnants, remains ‖ (ἐκκλ) relics.

λειψός [leepsos] deficient, defective.

λειώνω [leeono] melt, liquefy ‖ (συνθλίβω) crush, smash ‖ (διαλύω) dissolve ‖ (παθαίνω φθορά) wear out, spoil.

λεκάνη, ή [lekanee] basin, washbowl ‖ pan.

λεκές, ό [lekes] stain, splash, spot ‖ (μελάνης) blot.

λεκιάζω [lekeeazo] stain, soil, spot.

λελέκι, τό [lelekee] stork.

λεμβοδρομία, ή [lemvoδromeea] regatta, boat race.

λέμβος, ή [lemvos] rowboat ‖ launch.

λεμβοῦχος, ό [lemvouhos] boatman, rower

λεμονάδα, ή [lemonaδa] lemonade.

λεμόνι, τό [lemonee] lemon ‖ λεμονιά lemon tree.

λεξικογραφία, ή [lekseekoɣrafeea] lexicography.

λεξικό(ν), τό [lekseeko(n)] lexicon, dictionary.

λεξιλόγιον, τό [lekseeloɣeeon] vocabulary ‖ glossary.

λέξις, ή [leksees] word.

λεοντάρι, τό [leontaree] lion.

λεοπάρδαλις, ή [leoparδalees] leopard.

λέπι, τό [lepee] (ψαριοῦ) scale (of fish).

λεπίς, ή [lepees] blade.

λέπρα, ή [lepra] leprosy.

λεπρός [lepros] leprous.

λεπτά, τά [lepta] πλ money.

λεπταίνω [lepteno] thin, make slender ‖ refine.

λεπτοκαμωμένος [leptokamomenos] delicate, frail ‖ thin, slim.
λεπτολογῶ [leptoloyo] scrutinize, examine
carefully, sift.
λεπτομέρεια [leptomereea] detail, particular ‖ λεπτομερειακός detailed, of detail.
λεπτομερής [leptomerees] detailed, minute,
scrupulous, close.
λεπτομερῶς [leptomeros] minutely, closely,
in detail.
λεπτόν, τό [lepton] (τῆς ὥρας) minute ‖
(νόμισμα) lepton (one hundredth of a
drachma).
λεπτός [leptos] thin, fine, slight, slim ‖
(στὴν σκέψιν) subtle ‖ (ρουχισμόν) light
‖ (τῶν αἰσθήσεων) keen.
λεπτότης, ἡ [leptotees] delicacy, weakness
‖ tactfulness, tact ‖ subtlety.
λεπτύνω [lepteeno] βλ λεπταίνω.
λέρα, ἡ [lera] dirt, filth ‖ (ἄνθρωπος) rogue,
rascal.
λερωμένος [leromenos] dirty, filthy, grubby,
grimy.
λερώνομαι [leronome] get dirty.
λερώνω [lerono] dirty, soil, stain ‖ (μεταφ)
tarnish, taint.
λέσχη, ἡ [leshee] club ‖ casino.
λεύκα, ἡ [levka] poplar.
λευκαίνω [levkeno] whiten ‖ bleach ‖
(τοῖχο) whitewash.
λευκόλιθος, ὁ [levkoleethos] magnesite.
λευκός [levkos] white, clean ‖ blank.
λευκοσίδηρος [levkoseedeeros] tin.
λευκόχρυσος, ὁ [levkohreesos] platinum.
λεύκωμα, τό [levkoma] album ‖ (ἰατρ)
albumin.
λευτεριά, ἡ [levteria] freedom, liberty.
λευχαιμία, ἡ [levhemeea] leukaemia.
λεφτά [lefta] βλ λεπτά.
λεφτό [lefto] βλ λεπτό.
λεχώνα, ἡ [lehona] woman who has just
given birth.
λέω [leo] βλ λέγω.
λέων, ὁ [leon] lion.
λεωφορεῖον, τό [leoforeeon] bus, omnibus,
coach.
λεωφόρος, ἡ [leoforos] avenue, boulevard.
λήγω [leeyo] come to an end, terminate ‖
(οἶκον) mature, fall due.
λήθαργος, ὁ [leetharyos] lethargy, drowsiness, stupor.
λήθη, ἡ [lethee] forgetfulness, forgetting,
oversight.
λημέρι, τό [leemeree] retreat, hiding place,
hideout, den.
ληξιαρχεῖον, τό [leekseearheeon] registry
office, parish register.
ληξιπρόθεσμος [leekseeprothesmos] falling
due, expired (of terms).
λῆξις, ἡ [leeksees] termination, conclusion
‖ expiration date.
λησμονῶ [leesmono] forget, neglect, omit.
λησταία, ἡ [leesteea] holdup, robbery.

ληστεύω [leestevo] rob, hold up.
ληστής, ὁ [leestees] brigand, bandit, robber.
ληστρικός [leestreekos] predatory ‖ pertaining to robbers.
λῆψις, ἡ [leepsees] receipt, receiving.
λιάζομαι [leeazome] sunbathe, lie in the
sun.
λιακάδα, ἡ [leeakaδa] sunshine.
λίαν [leean] much, very much, too.
λιανίζω [leeaneezo] cut to pieces, mince
λιανικός [leeaneekos] retail.
λιανός [leeanos] thin, slender.
λιβάδι, τό [leevaδee] βλ λειβάδι.
λιβάνι, τό [leevanee] incense, frankincense.
λιβανίζω [leevaneezo] burn incense ‖
(μεταφ) flatter basely.
λίβελλος, ὁ [leevelos] libel ‖ lampoon.
λίβρα, ἡ [leevra] pound.
λιγάκι [leeyakee] a little, a bit.
λίγδα, ἡ [leeyδa] fat, grease ‖ dirt, stain.
λιγνίτης, ὁ [leeyneetees] lignite.
λιγνός [leeynos] skinny, thin, slim.
λίγο [leeyo] a little, a bit ‖ ~ πολύ more
or less.
λίγος [leeyos] a little, a bit ‖ παρά λίγο
nearly, almost.
λιγοστεύω [leeyostevo] lessen, decrease.
λιγοστός [leeyostos] very little, hardly
enough.
λιγότερος [leeyoteros] less.
λιγούρα, ἡ [leeyoura] nausea ‖ faintness
from hunger.
λιγοψυχία, ἡ [leeyopseeheea] fainthearted-
ness ‖ faintness.
λιγώνομαι [leeyonome] long for, be impatient ‖ be faint from desire.
λιγώνω [leeyono] nauseate ‖ make faint.
λιθάρι, τό [leetharee] stone.
λίθινος [leetheenos] of stone.
λιθοβολῶ [leethovolo] pelt with stones,
stone.
λιθογραφία, ἡ [leethoyrafeea] lithography.
λιθοδομή, ἡ [leethoδomee] stonework,
masonry.
λιθοκόπος, ὁ [leethokopos] stone-breaker.
λιθόκτιστος [leethokteestos] built in stone.
λιθοξόος, ὁ [leethoksoos] stone-cutter
marble worker.
λίθος, ὁ, ἡ [leethos] stone ‖ (ἰατρ) calculus.
λιθόστρωτον, τό [leethostroton] pavement,
paved way.
λιθόστρωτος [leethostrotos] paved with
stones.
λικέρ, τό [leeker] liqueur.
λικνίζω [leekneezo] rock, lull to sleep ‖
swing.
λίκνον, τό [leeknon] cradle, cot, crib.
λίμα, ἡ [leema] (ἐργαλεῖον) file ‖ (μεταφ)
talkativeness, tiresome chatter.
λιμάνι, τό [leemanee] port, harbour.
λιμάρω [leemaro] file ‖ chatter, gossip.
λιμενάρχης, ὁ [leemenarhees] harbour
master.

λιμενικός [leemeneekos] of the port, of the harbour.

λιμήν, ὁ [leemeen] βλ λιμάνι.

λίμνη, ἡ [leemnee] lake.

λιμνοθάλασσα, ἡ [leemnothalasa] lagoon.

λιμοκτονῶ [leemoktono] starve, famish.

λιμός, ὁ [leemos] famine.

λινάρι, τό [leenaree] flax.

λινάτσα, ἡ [leenatsa] sacking.

λινέλαιον, τό [leeneleon] linseed oil.

λίνον, τό [leenon] βλ λινάρι.

λινός [leenos] linen.

λιοντάρι, τό [leeontaree] lion.

λιπαίνω [leepeno] lubricate, grease || (μέ λίπασμα) manure, fertilize.

λιπαρός [leeparos] greasy, fatty || (γόνιμος) fat, rich.

λίπασμα, τό [leepasma] fertilizer, manure.

λιποθυμία, ἡ [leepotheemeea] faint(ing), swooning.

λιποθυμῶ [leepotheemo] faint, lose consciousness.

λίπος, τό [leepos] fat, lard || grease.

λιποτάκτης, ὁ [leepotaktees] deserter.

λίρα, ἡ [leera] pound, sovereign.

λιρέττα, ἡ [leereta] Italian lira.

λίστα, ἡ [leesta] list, catalogue.

λιτανεία, ἡ [leetaneea] religious procession.

λιτός [leetos] temperate, frugal || plain.

λιτότης, ἡ [leetotees] temperance, moderation.

λίτρα, ἡ [leetra] (βάρος) pound || litre.

λίτρον, τό [leetron] βλ λίτρα.

λιχνίζω [leehneezo] winnow, sift.

λιχουδιά, ἡ [leehoudia] titbit || appetizer.

λοβός, ὁ [lovos] lobe || husk || (ἀρχιτεκ) foil.

λογαριάζω [loyareeazo] count, measure, compute || rely on, look to || (λαμβάνω ὑπ' ὄψιν) consider || (πρόθεσις νά) count on, aim to, mean to.

λογαριασμός, ὁ [loyareeasmos] count, calculation, computation || bill || accounts

λογάριθμος, ὁ [loyareethmos] logarithm.

λογᾶς, ὁ [loyas] gossip, babbler, long-winded talker.

λόγγος, ὁ [longos] thicket.

λόγια, τά [loyeea] πλ words.

λογιάζω [loyeeazo] take into consideration.

λογίζομαι [loyeezome] calculate, consider || think o.s., deem o.s.

λογική, ἡ [loyeekee] logic.

λογικός [loyeekos] rational, logical, sensible || right, fair.

λόγιος, ὁ [loyeeos] scholar, man of letters.

λογισμός, ὁ [loyeesmos] reasoning, thought || reckoning || (μαθημ) calculus.

λογιστήριον, τό [loyeesteereeon] bursar's office || bursary.

λογιστής, ὁ [loyeestees] accountant, bookkeeper || (ναυτ) purser.

λογιστική, ἡ [loyeesteekee] accountancy.

λογοδιάρροια, ἡ [loyodeeareea] unrestrained talkativeness, chattering.

λογοδοτῶ [loyodoto] give an account, account for.

λογοκρισία, ἡ [loyokreeseea] censorship.

λογομαχία, ἡ [loyomaheea] dispute, wrangle, controversy.

λογοπαίχνιον, τό [loyopehneeon] pun.

λόγος, ὁ [loyos] (ὁμιλία) speech || (φράσις κτλ) word, saying || (μνεία) mention || rumour || (αἴτιον) cause, reason, purpose || (παράδειγμα) instance, supposition || (ἀγόρευσις) speech, discourse || (λογοδοσία) explanation, account || (ὑπόσχεσις) promise || (ἀναλογία) ratio, proportion.

λογοτέχνης, ὁ [loyotehnees] author, writer.

λογοτεχνία, ἡ [loyotehneea] literature.

λόγχη, ἡ [longhee] bayonet || spear, lance.

λοιδορῶ [leedoro] insult, abuse, outrage, ridicule.

λοιμός, ὁ [leemos] pestilence, pest, plague.

λοιμώδης [leemodees] pestilential.

λοιπόν [leepon] then, thus, and so || well!, what then!

λοιπός [leepos] left, remaining || καί τά λοιπά and so forth, and so on || τοῦ λοιποῦ henceforth, from now on.

λόξα, ἡ [loksa] (γιά μόδα κτλ) whim, mania, fancy.

λοξά [loksa] on the slant, obliquely || in an underhand way.

λοξοδρομῶ [loksodromo] shift course || deviate || (ναυτ) tack || (μεταφ) go astray.

λοξός [loksos] oblique, slanting, inclined.

λόξυγγας, ὁ [lokseengas] hiccup.

λόρδος, ὁ [lordos] lord.

λοσιόν, ἡ [losion] lotion.

λοστός, ὁ [lostos] crowbar, iron bar.

λοστρόμος, ὁ [lostromos] boatswain.

λούζομαι [louzome] have a bath.

λούζω [louzo] wash, bathe || (μεταφ) reproach severely.

λουκάνικο, τό [loukaneeko] sausage, hot dog, frankfurter.

λουκέτο, τό [louketo] padlock.

λούκι, τό [loukee] pipe, conduit || gutter.

λουκούμι, τό [loukoumee] Turkish delight || (μεταφ) delicious (attr).

λουλάκι, τό [loulakee] indigo.

λουλούδι, τό [louloudee] flower, blossom.

λούξ [louks] luxurious, posh.

λουρί, τό [louree] strap || (μηχανῆς) belt, band.

λουρίδα, ἡ [loureeda] strip, belt, band.

λούσιμο, τό [louseemo] bathing, washing || (μεταφ) reprimanding.

λοῦσο, τό [louso] smart clothes || sumptuousness, luxury.

λουστράρω [loustraro] gloss, glaze || (παπούτσια) polish.

λουστρίνια, τά [loustreeneea] πλ patent leather shoes.

λοῦστρος, ὁ [loustros] shoeblack, bootblack.

λουτρά, τά [loutra] πλ baths, hot springs.

λουτρόν, τό [loutron] bath | (δωμάτιον) bathroom.

λουτρόπολις, ή [loutropolees] bathing resort, spa.

λουφάζω [loufazo] remain silent | cringe with fear.

λούω [louo] bathe, wash, give a bath to.

λοφίον, τό [lofeeon] plume | (πτηνού) tuft, crest | (στρατ) pompom.

λόφος, ὁ [lofos] hill, height.

λοχαγός, ὁ [lohaγos] captain.

λοχίας, ὁ [loheeas] sergeant.

λόχος, ὁ [lohos] company.

λυγερός [leeγeros] slim, lithe, graceful.

λυγίζω [leeγeezo] bend, curve | yield.

λυγμός, ὁ [leeγmos] sob, sobbing.

λύγξ, ὁ [leenks] lynx.

λυθρίνι, τό [leethreenee] kind of red mullet, gurnard.

λυκαυγές, τό [leekavγes] daybreak, dawn.

λύκειον, τό [leekeeon] private secondary school, lyceum.

λύκος, ὁ [leekos] wolf.

λυκόσκυλον, τό [leekoskeelon] wolfhound.

λυκόφως, τό [leekofos] evening twilight, dusk.

λυμαίνομαι [leemenome] ravage, devastate, lay waste.

λυντσάρω [leentsaro] lynch.

λύνω [leeno] βλ λύω.

λύομαι [leeome] come undone.

λυπᾶμαι [leepame] be sorry, regret | pity.

λύπη, ή [leepee] grief, chagrin, sorrow | pity, commiseration.

λυπημένος [leepeemenos] sad, grieved, distressed.

λυποῦμαι [leepoume] βλ λυπᾶμαι.

λύσιμο, τό [leeseemo] undoing, loosening | solution, solving | taking to pieces.

λύσις, ή [leesees] answer, solution | untying | dismantling.

λυσιτέλεια, ή [leeseeteleea] utility, usefulness, benefit.

λύσσα, ή [leesa] rabies | (μεταφ) rage, fury, wrath.

λυσσάζω [leesazo] rage, go mad.

λυσσῶ [leeso] (μεταφ) be furious.

λυσσώδης [leesodees] rabid | fierce, stubborn, desperate.

λυτός [leetos] loose, untied, unfastened.

λύτρα, τά [leetra] πλ ransom money.

λυτρώνω [leetrono] deliver, free, set free.

λυτρωτής, ὁ [leetrotees] liberator, redeemer, rescuer.

λυχνάρι, τό [leehnaree] small lamp, Chinese lantern.

λυχνία, ή [leehneea] lamp.

λύχνος, ὁ [leehnos] βλ λυχνάρι.

λύω [leeo] unloose | (δεσμόν κτλ) untie, unfasten | (διαλύω) dismantle | (εὑρίσκω λύσιν) resolve | (παύω) close, discharge | (καταργῶ) annul, break off.

λυώνω [leeono] βλ λειώνω.

λώβα, ὁ [lova] leprosy.

λωβός [lovos] leprous.

λωλαίνω [loleno] drive mad, bewilder.

λωλός [lolos] foolish, crazy, mad.

λωποδύτης, ὁ [lopoδeetees] thief, blackleg, sharper.

λωρίον [loreeon] βλ λουρί.

λωρίς, ή [lorees] strip, band, belt.

λωτός, ὁ [lotos] lotus.

λωφάζω [lofazo] βλ λουφάζω

Μ, μ

μά [ma] but | by | ~ τόν Θεό! by God!, God be witness!

μαγαζί, τό [maγazee] shop, store.

μαγγάνι, τό [manganee] (ἐργαλεῖον) tool, vice | (πηγαδιού) wheel | winch.

μαγγάνιον, τό [manganeeon] manganese.

μαγγανοπήγαδο, τό [manganopeeγaδo] wheel well (for water).

μαγγώνω [mangono] grip, squeeze, clip.

μαγεία, ή [maγeea] sorcery, witchcraft, magic | charm, fascination.

μάγειρας, ὁ [maγeeras] cook.

μαγειρεῖον, τό [maγeereeon] kitchen.

μαγειρεύω [maγeerevo] cook | (μεταφ) plot, manipulate.

μαγειρική, ή [maγeereekee] cooking, cookery.

μαγευτικός [maγevteekos] charming, enchanting, delightful.

μαγεύω [maγevo] charm, fascinate, delight, attract.

μάγια, τά [maγea] πλ witchcraft, spell, charm.

μαγιά, ή [maγia] yeast, leaven.

μαγικός [maγeekos] magic(al), fascinating, bewitching.

μαγιό, τό [maγio] bathing suit, swimsuit.

μαγιονέζα, ἡ [maγeeoneza] mayonnaise.

μάγισσα, ή [maγeesa] witch, enchantress.

μαγκάλι, τό [mangalee] brazier, firepan.

μάγκας, ὁ [mangas] urchin, rascal, bum.

μαγκούρα, ή [mangoura] crook, heavy stick.

μαγκούφης, ὁ [mangoufees] lonely person | miserable person.

μαγνήσιον, τό [maγneeseeon] magnesium.

μαγνήτης, ὁ [maγneetees] magnet.

μαγνητίζω [maγneeteezo] magnetize attract, captivate.

μαγνητικός [maγneeteekos] magnetic | attractive.

μαγνητισμός, ὁ [maγneeteesmos] magnetism.

μαγνητόφωνον, τό [maγneetofonon] tape recorder.

μάγος, ὁ [maγos] magician, wizard.

μαγουλήθρα, ή [maγouleethra] mumps parotitis.

μάγουλο, τό [maγoulo] cheek (of face).

μαδέρι, τό [maderee] thick plank, joist, beam.

μάδημα, τό [madeema] plucking, depilation || (μεταφ) fleecing.

μαδῶ [mado] pluck, pluck off, remove the hair || (μεταφ) fleece.

μαέστρος, ὁ [maestros] conductor || (μεταφ) authority.

μάζα, ἡ [maza] paste || lump || (ἐπί ἀνθρώπων) mass, crowd.

μάζεμα, τό [mazema] collecting, gathering || (ὑφάσματος) shrinking.

μαζεμένος [mazemenos] good-mannered || snuggling.

μαζεύομαι [mazevome] collect || nestle || settle down.

μαζεύω [mazevo] gather, collect || (μαλλί) wind || (γιά ροῦχα) shrink.

μαζί [mazee] together, with, in one lot, jointly.

μαζικός [mazeekos] of the mass, collective.

μαζώνω [mazono] βλ μαζεύω.

Μάης, ὁ [maees] May.

μαθαίνω [matheno] learn || teach, train || (νέα) hear || learn.

μάθημα, τό [matheema] lesson.

μαθηματικά, τά [matheemateeka] πλ mathematics.

μαθηματικός [matheemateekos] mathematical || (οὐσ) mathematician.

μαθημένος [matheemenos] used to.

μάθησις, ἡ [matheesees] learning, education.

μαθητεία, ἡ [matheeteea] apprenticeship.

μαθητευόμενος [matheetevomenos] apprentice, novice.

μαθητεύω [matheetevo] be a student, be an apprentice.

μαθητής, ὁ [matheetees] student, pupil || (φιλοσόφου) disciple.

μαῖα, ἡ [mea] midwife.

μαίανδρος, ὁ [meanðros] meander, in-and-out.

μαιευτήρ, ὁ [mayevteer] obstetrician.

μαιευτήριον, τό [mayevteereeon] maternity hospital.

μαιευτική, ἡ [mayevteekee] obstetrics.

μαϊμοῦ, ἡ [maeemou] monkey, ape.

μαίνομαι [menome] rage, be furious.

μαϊντανός, ὁ [maeentanos] parsley.

Μάιος, ὁ [maeeos] May.

μακάβριος [makavreeos] macabre, gruesome, ghastly.

μακάρι [makaree] (ἐπιφ) would to God!, may!

μακαρίζω [makareezo] regard as fortunate, envy.

μακάριος [makareeos] happy, fortunate, blessed || calm, serene.

μακαρίτης [makareetees] late, deceased.

μακαρόνια, τά [makaroneea] πλ macaroni.

μακελειό, τό [makelio] (μεταφ) slaughter, massacre.

μακέττα, ἡ [maketa] model, drawing, plan.

μακραίνω [makreno] make longer || grow taller.

μακράν [makran] (a)far, far off, at a distance.

μακριά [makria] βλ μακράν.

μακρινός [makreenos] far distant, far off || (ταξίδι) long.

μακρόβιος [makroveeos] long-lived.

μακρόθεν [makrothen] from a distance, from afar.

μάκρος, τό [makros] length || duration.

μακρός [makros] long, lengthy, extensive.

μακρύνω [makreeno] βλ μακραίνω.

μακρύς [makrees] βλ μακρός.

μάκτρον, τό [maktron] dishcloth || table napkin || rag.

μαλάζω [malazo] massage, knead || soften, mollify, pacify || (πόνον) alleviate.

μαλάκιον, τό [malakeeon] mollusc.

μαλακός [malakos] soft || mild, gentle || (κλίμα) genial.

μαλάκυνσις, ἡ [malakeensees] softening, enervation.

μαλακώνω [malakono] soften, get milder || assuage || become calmer.

μάλαμα, τό [malama] gold.

μαλάσσω [malaso] βλ μαλάζω.

μαλθακός [malthakos] soft, effeminate, delicate.

μάλιστα [maleesta] more especially, particularly || yes, indeed || even.

μαλλί, τό [malee] wool, fleece || hair.

μαλλιά, τά [malia] πλ hair (of the head) || ~ κουβάρια upside down.

μαλλιαρός [maleearos] hairy, long-haired || woolly.

μάλλινος [maleenos] woollen.

μᾶλλον [malon] more, better, rather || κατά τό ~ ἤ ἧττον more or less.

μαλώνω [malono] argue || chide, reprimand, rebuke.

μαμά, ἡ [mama] mother, mummy.

μάμμη, ἡ [mamee] grandmother.

μαμμή, ἡ [mamee] midwife.

μαμμούνι, τό [mamounee] small insect, grub.

μάνα, ἡ [mana] βλ μάννα.

μάνδαλος, ὁ [manðalos] latch, bolt, bar.

μανδύας, ὁ [manðeeas] mantle, cloak || (στρατ) greatcoat.

μανθάνω [manthano] βλ μαθαίνω.

μάνι μάνι [manee manee] quickly, in a jiffy.

μανία, ἡ [maneea] fury, passion, mania || whim, fancy || ἔχω ~ν μέ be crazy about.

μανιακός [maneeakos] raving, frenzied || (παίκτης) inveterate.

μανιβέλλα, ἡ [maneevela] starting handle || lever, bar.

μανικέτι, τό [maneeketee] cuff.

μανίκι, τό [maneekee] sleeve.

μανιτάρι, τό [maneetaree] mushroom

μανιώδης [maneeoδees] passionate, inveterate ‖ furious, raging.

μάν(ν)α, ἡ [mana] mother, mamma.

μαν(ν)ούλα, ἡ [manoula] mummy ‖ (US) mom.

μανουάλιον, τό [manoualeeon] candelabrum.

μανούβρα, ἡ [manouvra] manoeuvre.

μανούρι, τό [manouree] kind of white cheese.

μανταλάκι, τό [mantalakee] clothes peg.

μάνταλο, τό [mantalo] βλ μάνδαλος.

μανταλώνω [mantalono] latch, lock up, bolt.

μανταρίνι, τό [mantareenee] tangerine.

μαντάρισμα, τό [mantareesma] darning ‖ (ὑφάσματος) mending.

μαντάρω [mantaro] darn, mend.

μαντᾶτο, τό [mantato] information, news.

μαντεῖον, τό [manteeon] oracle.

μαντεύω [mantevo] foretell ‖ guess ‖ find out, fathom.

μαντήλι, τό [manteelee] handkerchief.

μαντινάδα, ἡ [manteenaδa] rhyming couplet.

μάντις, ὁ [mantees] wizard, prophet.

μαντολᾶτο, τό [mantolato] nougat.

μάντρα, ἡ [mantra] pen, fold, sty ‖ (περίφραγμα) enclosure, wall ‖ yard.

μαντράχαλος, ὁ [mantrahalos] lanky fellow.

μαντρόσκυλο, τό [mantroskeelo] sheepdog.

μαξιλλάρι, τό [makseelaree] pillow, cushion.

μάπ(π)α, ἡ [mapa] cabbage.

μάππας, ὁ [mapas] stupid fellow, imbecile.

μαραγκός, ὁ [marangos] carpenter ‖ joiner.

μαράζι, τό [marazee] pining, depression, languor.

μάραθ(ρ)o, τό [marath(r)o] fennel.

μαραίνομαι [marenome] fade, wither away, shrivel ‖ (μεταφ) waste away.

μαραίνω [mareno] wither, dry up, fade.

μαρασμός, ὁ [marasmos] withering, fading away ‖ (μεταφ) decay.

μαργαρίνη, ἡ [marγareenee] margarine.

μαργαρίτα, ἡ [marγareeta] daisy.

μαργαριτάρι, τό [marγareetaree] pearl.

μαργαρίτης, ὁ [marγareetees] βλ μαργαριτάρι.

μαρίδα, ἡ [mareeδa] whitebait, small fry.

μάρκα, ἡ [marka] (ἐμπορ) trademark, make ‖ (αὐτοκινήτου) model ‖ (νόμισμα) mark ‖ (μεταφ) cunning fellow.

μαρμαρένιος [marmareneeos] of marble.

μάρμαρον, τό [marmaron] marble.

μαρμελάδα, ἡ [marmelaδa] marmalade.

μαρούλι, τό [maroulee] lettuce.

Μάρτης, ὁ [Martees] March.

μαρτυρία, ἡ [marteereea] deposition, giving of evidence ‖ proof, token.

μαρτυρικός [marteereekos] insufferable, unbearable.

μαρτύριον, τό [marteereeon] torment, suffering.

μαρτυρῶ [marteero] give evidence, testify ‖ (προδίδω) betray, inform against ‖ (ἐνδεικνύω) show, indicate ‖ (γίνομαι μάρτυς) suffer martyrdom (for Christ).

μάρτυς, ὁ [martees] witness ‖ (ἐκκλ) martyr.

μᾶς, μας [mas] us ‖ our.

μασέλλα, ἡ [masela] false teeth.

μασιά, ἡ [masia] πλ tongs, fire-tongs ‖ pincers.

μάσκα, ἡ [maska] mask ‖ μασκαρᾶς, ὁ masquerader ‖ (μεταφ) impostor, rascal, scoundrel.

μασόνος, ὁ [masonos] freemason.

μασουλῶ [masoulo] chew, munch.

μασούρι, τό [masouree] spool, bobbin ‖ tube.

μαστάρι, τό [mastaree] udder.

μαστίγιον, τό [masteeyeeon] whip ‖ switch.

μαστιγώνω [masteeγono] whip, lash, flog.

μαστίζω [masteezo] infest, devastate, desolate.

μάστιξ, ἡ [masteeks] whip ‖ (μεταφ) curse, plague.

μαστίχα, ἡ [masteeha] mastic ‖ (ποτόν) mastic brandy.

μάστορας, ὁ [mastoras] artisan, workman ‖ (μεταφ) expert, skilful person.

μαστορεύω [mastorevo] work ‖ mend, repair.

μαστός, ὁ [mastos] breast ‖ (μεταφ) hillock.

μαστροπός, ὁ, ἡ [mastropos] procurer, procuress, pimp.

μασχάλη, ἡ [mashalee] armpit.

μασῶ [maso] chew, masticate ‖ (τά λόγια) stammer.

ματαιόδοξος [mateoδoksos] vain, selfconceited.

ματαιοπονῶ [mateopono] work in vain, labour uselessly.

μάταιος [mateos] vain, useless, unavailing ‖ conceited.

ματαιώνω [mateono] frustrate, foil, cancel, stop.

μάτην [mateen] to no purpose, uselessly, vainly.

μάτι, τό [matee] eye ‖ (φύλλου κτλ) bud ‖ αὐγό ~ fried egg (sunny-side up) ‖ βάζω στό ~ set one's heart on ‖ ἔχω στό ~ covet ‖ κλείνω τό ~ wink ‖ ~ μου! my darling!

ματιά, ἡ [matia] glance, gaze, eye, look ‖ ~ζω cast an evil eye on, bewitch.

ματίζω [mateezo] splice ‖ lengthen.

ματογυάλια, τά [matoγeealeea] πλ spectacles, glasses.

ματόκλαδο, τό [matoklaδo] eyelash, lash.

ματόφρυδο, τό [matofreeδo] eyebrow.

ματόφυλλο, τό [matofeelo] eyelid.

μάτσο, τό [matso] truss, bunch, bundle ‖ (ξύλων) faggot.

ματσούκα, ή [matsouka] club, cudgel.

ματώνω [matono] bleed.

μαυραγορίτης, ὁ [mavrayorectees] black marketeer.

μαυρειδερός [mavreeðeros] blackish || brown.

μαυρίζω [mavreezo] blacken, darken || (ἀπό ἥλιο) get sunburnt || (μεταφ) black-ball, vote against.

μαυρίλα, ή [mavreela] blackness, darkness, gloominess.

μαυροδάφνη, ή [mavroðafnee] kind of sweet wine.

μαυροπίναξ, ὁ [mavropeenaks] blackboard || blacklist.

μαυροπούλι, τό [mavropoulee] starling.

μαῦρος [mavros] black || brown || (νέγρος) negro || (μεταφ) miserable, luckless.

μαχαίρι, τό [maheree] knife || στά ~α at loggerheads.

μαχαιριά, ή [maheria] stab.

μαχαιροβγάλτης, ὁ [maherovyaltees] cut-throat || bully.

μαχαιροπήρουνα, τά [maheropeerouna] πλ cutlery.

μαχαιρώνω [maherono] stab.

μαχαλᾶς, ὁ [mahalas] quarter, district, neighbourhood.

μάχη, ή [mahee] battle, combat || struggle, fight.

μαχητής, ὁ [maheetees] combatant, fighter, soldier.

μαχητικός [maheeteekos] warlike, martial || combative, ready to fight.

μάχομαι [mahome] fight, combat, struggle || hate, abhor.

μέ [me] with, by, through, by means of, on, of || ~ τά πόδια on foot || ~ τό καλό God willing || ~ τό μῆνα by the month || δύο ~ τρία two by three (feet etc) || ~ τόν καιρό eventually, in the course of time || δύο ~ τρεῖς between two and three o'clock || ἔχω μανία ~ τό be mad on, be crazy about || γελῶ ~ laugh at || ~ τή σειρά in turn || λίρες ~ δραχμές pounds for drachmas || ἀναλόγως ~ according to whether.

μέ, με [me] me.

μεγάθυμος [meyatheemos] generous, magnanimous.

μεγαλεῖο [meyaleeo] first-rate!

μεγαλεῖον, τό [meyaleeon] splendour, grandeur || (μεταφ) splendid.

μεγαλειότης, ή [meyaleeotees] majesty, grandeur || ἡ Αὐτοῦ ~ His Majesty.

μεγαλειώδης [meyaleeoðees] magnificent, superb, majestic.

μεγαλέμπορος, ὁ [meyalemboros] whole-saler.

μεγαλεπήβολος [meyalepeevolos] gran-diose, imposing.

μεγάλη [meyalee]: ~ Ἑβδομάδα Holy Week.

μεγαλόδωρος [meyaloðoros] munificent, generous, bounteous.

μεγαλοποιῶ [meyalopeeo] magnify, exag-gerate, overdo.

μεγαλοπρεπής [meyaloprepees] majestic, stately, splendid, magnificent.

μεγάλος [meyalos] great, large, big, long.

μεγαλουργῶ [meyalouryo] achieve great things.

μεγαλόφρων [meyalofron] generous, mag-nanimous || boastful, arrogant.

μεγαλοφυής [meyalofiees] gifted, ingeni-ous.

μεγαλόψυχος [meyalopseehos] magnani-mous, generous.

μεγαλύνω [meyaleeno] magnify, exalt.

μεγαλώνω [meyalono] increase, enlarge || (ἀνατρέφω) bring up, raise || (μεγαλο-ποιῶ) magnify, exaggerate || grow up.

μέγαρον, τό [meyaron] mansion, palace, imposing building.

μέγας [meyas] βλ μεγάλος.

μεγάφωνον, τό [meyafonon] (ραδιοφώνου) loudspeaker || megaphone.

μέγγενη, ή [mengenee] (ἐργαλεῖον) vice.

μέγεθος, τό [meyethos] size, greatness, height, magnitude, extent, length.

μεγέθυνσις, ή [meyetheensees] enlarge-ment, increase, extension.

μεγιστάν, ὁ [meyeestan] magnate, seigneur.

μέγιστον, τό [meyeeston] maximum, greatest.

μέγιστος [meyeestos] greatest, largest || enormous, colossal.

μεδούλι, τό [meðoulee] marrow.

μέδουσα, ή [meðousa] kind of jellyfish.

μεζές, ὁ [mezes] titbit, snack.

μεζούρα, ή [mezoura] tape measure.

μεθαύριον [methavreeon] the day after tomorrow.

μέθη, ή [methee] intoxication, drunkenness || (μεταφ) enthusiasm.

μεθοδικός [methoðeekos] systematic, meth-odical.

μέθοδος, ή [methoðos] method, system, process.

μεθόριος, ή [methoreeos] boundary, fron-tier.

μεθύσι, τό [metheesee] βλ μέθη.

μεθύσκομαι [metheeskome] get drunk.

μεθύσκω [metheesko] intoxicate, make drunk.

μεθυσμένος [metheesmenos] drunk.

μεθύω [metheeo] βλ μεθύσκομαι.

μεθῶ [metho] make drunk || get drunk.

μειδίαμα, τό [meeðeeama] smile.

μειδιῶ [meeðeeo] smile.

μείζων [meezon] larger, greater || (μουσ) major.

μειλίχιος [meeleeheeos] mild, gentle, affable.

μειοδοτῶ [meeoðoto] bid the lowest price.

μεῖον [meeon] less, minus.

μειονέκτημα, τό [meeonekteema] disadvantage, inconvenience.

μειονότης, ή [meeonotees] minority.

μειοψηφία, ή [meeopseefeea] minority of votes.

μείων [meeon] lesser.

μειώνω [meeono] lesson, diminish, reduce, decrease.

μείωσις, ή [meeosees] decrease, reduction || (μεταφ) humiliation.

μελαγχολία, ή [melangholeea] melancholy, dejection, gloominess.

μελαγχολικός [melangholeekos] sad, depressed, gloomy.

μελαγχολῶ [melangholo] become sad.

μελάνη, ή [melanee] ink.

μελανιά, ή [melania] inkstain | bruise | ~ζω bruise || turn blue with cold.

μελανοδοχεῖον, τό [melanodoheeon] inkstand, inkpot.

μέλας [melas] black.

μελᾶτος [melatos] (αὐγό) soft-boiled (egg).

μελαχροινός [melahreenos] dark, brown, swarthy.

μελαψός [melapsos] dark-skinned, swarthy.

μέλει [melee]: δεν μέ ~ I don't care, I'm not interested.

μελέτη, ή [meletee] (πραγματεία) treatise || study || (κτιρίου) plan, design || meditation, contemplation.

μελετηρός [meleteeros] studious.

μελετῶ [meleto] study || (ἐρευνῶ) search, investigate || (σκοπεύω) have in mind, intend || (πιάνο) practise.

μέλημα, τό [meleema] concern, care, solicitude, duty.

μέλι, τό [melee] honey.

μελίγγι, τό [meleenghee] temple (anat).

μέλισσα, ή [meleesa] bee.

μελίσσι, τό [meleesee] beehive || swarm.

μελισσοκομία, ή [meleesokomeea] beekeeping.

μελιτζάνα, ή [meleetzana] eggplant.

μέλλον, τό [melon] future || outlook.

μελλόνυμφος, ὁ, ή [meloneemfos] husband-to-be, fiancé || fiancée.

μέλλω [melo] intend, be about to.

μέλλων [melon] future || ὁ ~ (γραμμ) future tense.

μελόδραμα, τό [melodrama] melodrama.

μέλος, τό [melos] member || (μουσ) melody, air || (τοῦ σώματος) member, limb.

μελτέμι, τό [meltemee] north wind, trade wind.

μελωδία, ή [melodeea] melody, tune.

μελωδικός [melodeekos] melodious, tuneful.

μεμβράνη, ή [memvranee] membrane | (χαρτί) parchment.

μεμονωμένος [memonomenos] isolated, lonely, alone.

μέμφομαι [memfome] reproach, blame, censure, find fault with.

μέν [men] on the one hand || οἱ ~ . . . οἱ δέ some . . . others.

μενεξές, ὁ [menekses] violet.

μένος, τό [menos] fervour, zeal, eagerness | wrath, anger, fury.

μέντα, ή [menta] mint, peppermint.

μένω [meno] remain, stop, stay || (ἀπομένω) be left, survive || (διαμένω) reside, live ~ ἀπό run out of, be short of.

μέρα, ή [mera] βλ ἡμέρα.

μεράκι, τό [merakee] ardent desire, yearning || (λύπη) regret, sorrow.

μεραρχία, ή [merarheea] division.

μερδικό, τό [merdeeko] portion, part, share.

μερί, τό [meree] thigh.

μεριά, ή [meria] place | side.

μερίδα, ή [mereeda] ration, portion, helping.

μερίδιον, τό [mereedeeon] share, portion.

μερικός [mereekos] partial, some, a few | μερικά πλ some, certain, a few.

μέριμνα, ή [mereemna] care, anxiety, solicitude, concern.

μεριμνῶ [mereemno] look after, care for, be anxious about.

μερίς, ή [merees] βλ μερίδα.

μέρισμα, τό [mereesma] dividend || allotment, part.

μερμήγκι, τό [mermeengee] ant.

μεροδούλι, τό [merodoulee] day's wages

μεροκάματο, τό [merokamato] day's wages.

μεροληπτῶ [meroleepto] take sides, be partial, be one-sided.

μέρος, τό [meros] part, party || (μερίς) portion, share || (τόπος) place, spot || (πλευρά) side || (ρόλος) role || (γραμμ) part of speech || (ἀποχωρητήριον) W.C. || κατά ~ aside, apart.

μέσα [mesa] in(to) || inside || within ~ among || (πολιτ) means || ~ σέ inside, within || in, into.

μεσάζω [mesazo] mediate, intercede.

μεσαῖος [meseos] middle.

μεσαίων, ὁ [meseon] Middle Ages || μεσαιωνικός medieval.

μεσάνυχτα, τά [mesaneehta] πλ midnight.

μέση, ή [mesee] middle || (σώματος) waist || ἀφίνω στή ~ leave incomplete, leave undone.

μεσῆλιξ [meseeleeks] middle-aged.

μεσημβρία, ή [meseemvreea] midday, noon || (νότος) south.

μεσημβρινός [meseemvreenos] of noon || (νότιος) southern || (οὐ) meridian.

μεσημέρι, τό [meseemeree] noon || μέρα ~ in broad daylight || μεσημεριανός midday || μεσημεριανός ὕπνος siesta.

μεσίστιος [meseesteeos] half-mast.

μεσιτεία, ή [meseeteea] mediation, agency || (ἐμπορ) brokerage.

μεσιτεύω [meseetevo] intercede, intervene || be a broker.

μεσίτης, ὁ [meseetees] mediator ‖ agent, broker.

μεσιτικό [meseeteeko]: ~ γραφεῖο house agency.

μεσογειακός [mesoyeeakos] Mediterranean. Μεσόγειος, ἡ [mesoyeeos] the Mediterranean.

μεσόκοπος [mesokopos] βλ μεσῆλιξ.

μεσολαβῶ [mesolavo] intercede, intervene ‖ (εἰς χρόνον) come between.

μέσον, τό [meson] middle, midst ‖ (τρόπος) method, means, way ‖ μέσα πλ influence, pull, power.

μέσος [mesos] middle ‖ medium ‖ (ὅρος) mean, average.

μεσοφόρι, τό [mesoforee] petticoat, underskirt.

μεστός [mestos] full, replete, crammed with ‖ (ὥριμος) ripe.

μεστώνω [mestono] mature, ripen, mellow.

μέσω [meso] through, via.

μετά [meta] with ‖ after, in ‖ (ἐπίρ) afterwards.

μεταβαίνω [metaveno] go, proceed.

μεταβάλλω [metavalo] change, convert, transform.

μετάβασις, ἡ [metavasees] going, passage, transference.

μεταβατικός [metavateekos] transitional, provisory ‖ (γραμμ) transitive (verb).

μεταβιβάζω [metaveevazo] (διαταγήν) transmit, hand on ‖ (μεταφέρω) transport ‖ (ἰδιοκτησίαν) transfer, hand over.

μεταβλητός [metavleetos] variable, unsettled, changeable.

μεταβολή, ἡ [metavolee] alteration, change ‖ (στρατ) about-turn, half-turn.

μετάγγισις, ἡ [metangeesees] transfusion, drawing off ‖ (κρασιοῦ κτλ) decanting.

μεταγενέστερος [metayenesteros] posterior, subsequent, later.

μεταγραφή, ἡ [metayrafee] transfer.

μεταγωγικόν, τό [metayoyeekon] (ναυτ) transport ship.

μεταγωγικός [metayoyeekos] of transport.

μεταδίδω [metadeedo] impart, transmit ‖ (ραδιοφωνία) broadcast ‖ (νόσον) infect.

μετάδοσις, ἡ [metadosees] transmission ‖ (νόσον) contagion, spreading ‖ ἁγία ~ Holy Communion.

μεταδοτικός [metadoteekos] contagious, infectious.

μετάθεσις, ἡ [metathesees] transfer, removal.

μεταθέτω [metatheto] transpose, transfer, remove, move.

μεταίχμιον, τό [metehmeeon] (μεταφ) halfway point ‖ turning point.

μετακινῶ [metakeeno] move, shift, displace.

μετακομίζω [metakomeezo] transport, transfer, remove ‖ (σπίτι) move, change residence, move out.

μεταλαμβάνω [metalamvano] take Holy Communion.

μεταλλεῖον, τό [metaleeon] mine.

μετάλλευμα, τό [metalevma] ore.

μεταλλικός [metaleekos] metallic ‖ mineral.

μετάλλινος [metaleenos] of metal.

μετάλλιον, τό [metaleeon] medal.

μέταλλον, τό [metalon] metal.

μεταμέλεια, ἡ [metameleea] repentance, regrets.

μεταμεσημβρινός [metameseemvreenos] afternoon.

μεταμόρφωσις, ἡ [metamorfosees] transformation, reformation ‖ (ἐκκλ) transfiguration.

μεταμόσχευσις, ἡ [metamoshevsees] transplantation.

μεταμφίεσις, ἡ [metamfieesees] disguise, masquerade.

μετανάστευσις, ἡ [metanastevsees] emigration, (im)migration.

μεταναστεύω [metanastevo] (e)migrate, immigrate.

μετανάστης, ὁ [metanastœs] (e)migrant, immigrant.

μετάνοια, ἡ [metaneea] repentance, regret ‖ (ἐκκλ) penance ‖ (γονυκλισιά) genuflexion.

μετανοῶ [metanoo] repent, regret, be sorry (for).

μετάξι, τό [metaksee] silk.

μεταξοσκώληξ, ὁ [metaksoskoleeks] silkworm.

μεταξύ [metaksee] between, among, amongst, amid(st) ‖ ~ μας between ourselves, between you and me ‖ ἐν τῷ ~ meanwhile.

μεταξωτόν, τό [metaksoton] silk material, silk stuff.

μεταπείθω [metapeetho] dissuade, prevail upon.

μεταποιῶ [metapeeo] transform, alter, convert.

μεταπολεμικός [metapolemeekos] postwar.

μετάπτωσις, ἡ [metaptosees] change, relapse.

μεταπωλῶ [metapolo] resell, sell again.

μεταρρυθμίζω [metareethmeezo] reform, rearrange.

μεταστάς [metastas] deceased, late.

μετασχηματιστής, ὁ [metasheemateestees] transformer.

μετατοπίζω [metatopeezo] shift, displace.

μετατόπισις, ἡ [metatopeesees] shifting ‖ displacement.

μετατρέπω [metatrepo] transform, turn, change, alter ‖ (ἐπί ποινῶν) commute.

μεταφέρω [metafero] transport, carry, convey ‖ (οἰκον) transfer, carry over.

μεταφορά, ἡ [metafora] transportation, conveyance ‖ (γραμμ) metaphor.

μεταφορικά, τά [metaforeeka] πλ carriage fees.

μεταφορικός [metaforeekos] transporting, transport ‖ (γραμμ) metaphoric(al).

μεταφράζω [metafrazo] translate.

μετάφρασις, ἡ [metafrasees] translation.

μεταφραστής, ὁ [metafrastees] translator.

μεταφυτεύω [metafeetevo] transplant.

μεταχειρίζομαι [metaheereezome] use, employ ‖ treat, behave towards.

μεταχειρισμένος [metaheereesmenos] worn, used ‖ (δεύτερο χέρι) secondhand.

μετεκπαίδευσις, ἡ [metekpedevsees] postgraduate study.

μετεξεταστέος [meteksetasteos] be re-examined (sch).

μετέπειτα [metepeeta] after, afterwards, subsequently ‖ oἱ ~ posterity, the descendants.

μετέχω [meteho] take part in, participate ‖ partake of.

μετέωρον, τό [meteoron] meteor, shooting star.

μετέωρος [meteoros] dangling, in the air ‖ (μεταφ) hesitant, undecided ‖ in suspense.

μετημφιεσμένος [meteemfiesmenos] disguised.

μετοικῶ [meteeko] emigrate ‖ (σπίτι) move house.

μετόπισθεν [metopeesthen]: τά ~ the rear.

μετοχή, ἡ [metohee] (οἴκον) stock, share ‖ (γραμμ) participle.

μετόχι, τό [metohee] dependency of a monastery.

μετοχικός [metoheekos] (οἴκον) of a share, of joint stock ‖ (γραμμ) participial.

μέτοχος, ὁ [metohos] participant, sharer ‖ (οἴκον) shareholder.

μέτρημα, τό [metreema] measuring, mensuration ‖ counting, numbering.

μετρημένος [metreemenos] measured, limited ‖ (ἄνθρωπος) temperate, discreet, moderate.

μετρητά, τά [metreeta] πλ: τά ~ cash, money ‖ τοῖς μετρητοῖς in cash, (for) ready money.

μετρητής, ὁ [metreetees] meter, counter, gauge.

μετρητός [metreetos] measurable, calculable.

μετριάζω [metreeazo] moderate, diminish, slacken, lessen.

μετρική, ἡ [metreekee] versification, prosody, metrics.

μετρικός [metreekos] metric(al).

μετριοπάθεια, ἡ [metreeopatheea] moderation, temperance.

μετριοπαθής [metreeopathees] moderate, sober, temperate.

μέτριος [metreeos] ordinary, moderate ‖ (καφές) medium ‖ mediocre.

μετριοφροσύνη, ἡ [metreeofroseenee] modesty, decency.

μετριόφρων [metreeofron] modest, unassuming, decent, retiring.

μετρα, τά [metra] πλ measurements ‖ proceedings, steps ‖ λαμβάνω ~ take measures.

μέτρον, τό [metron] measure, metre ‖ (μεταφ) measure, step ‖ (μουσική) bar, measure ‖ (ποιητικό) metre, foot.

μετρῶ [metro] measure, count, number, gauge.

μέτωπον, τό [metopon] forehead, brow ‖ (πρόσοψις) face, front, façade ‖ (μάχη) front, battlefront.

μέχρι(ς) [mehree(s)] till, until, down to, up to ‖ as far as ‖ ~ ἑνός to the last man ‖ ~ τοῦδε until now.

μή [mee] don't ‖ not, no ‖ lest.

μηδαμινός [meedameenos] worthless, of no account, insignificant, trivial.

μηδέ, μηδείς [meede, meedees] βλ οὐδείς.

μηδέν, τό [meeden] nothing ‖ zero ‖ cipher.

μηδενικό, τό [meedeneeko] zero ‖ cipher.

μηδενίζω [meedeneezo] nullify ‖ mark with a zero.

μηδενιστής [meedeneestees] nihilist.

μῆκος, τό [meekos] length ‖ (γεωγραφικόν) longitude ‖ κατά ~ in length, lengthwise.

μηκύνω [meekeeno] lengthen, elongate ‖ protract, prolong.

μηκῶμαι [meekome] roar ‖ bleat ‖ howl, yell.

μηλίγγι, τό [meeleengee] temple (anat).

μῆλον, τό [meelon] apple ‖ (τῶν παρειῶν) cheekbone ‖ μηλονίτης apple cider.

μηλόπηττα, ἡ [meelopeeta] apple pie.

μήν(ας), ὁ [meen(as)] month.

μηνιαῖος [meenieos] monthly ‖ month's.

μηνιάτικο, τό [meenieateeko] month's wages ‖ month's rent.

μηνίγγι, τό [meeneengee] βλ μηλίγγι.

μηνιγγῖτις, ἡ [meeneengeetees] meningitis.

μῆνις, ἡ [meenees] rage, anger, fury, wrath.

μήνυμα, τό [meeneema] message, notice, announcement.

μήνυσις, ἡ [meeneesees] summons, charge.

μηνυτής, ὁ [meeneetees] plaintiff, complainant.

μηνύω [meeneeo] give notice ‖ bring a charge against.

μηνῶ [meeno] send a message, send word, call for.

μήπως [meepos] lest in any way, in case ‖ I wonder if.

μηρός, ὁ [meeros] thigh, leg.

μηρυκάζω [meereekazo] chew the cud, ruminate.

μήτε [meete] βλ οὔτε.

μητέρα, ἡ [meetera] mother.

μήτρα, ἡ [meetra] uterus, womb ‖ (χυτηρίου) mould, matrix, form.

μητρική [meetreekee]: ~ γλῶσσα mother tongue, native language.

μητρόπολις, ἡ [meetropolees] metropolis, capital ‖ (ἐκκλ) cathedral.

μητροπολιτικός [meetropoleeteekos] metropolitan.

μητροπολίτης, ὁ [meetropolcetccs] metropolitan bishop.

μητρότης, ἡ [meetrotees] motherhood.

μητρυιά, ἡ [meetria] stepmother.

μητρυιός, ὁ [meetrios] stepfather.

μητρῷον, τό [meetroon] register, roll, official list of names.

μηχανεύομαι [meehanevome] contrive, engineer, plot, bring about.

μηχανή, ἡ [meehanee] machine, engine, works || (μεταφ) typewriter || camera.

μηχάνημα, τό [meehaneema] machine, apparatus, contrivance.

μηχανική, ἡ [meehaneekee] engineering, mechanics.

μηχανικόν, τό [meehaneekon] corps of engineers.

μηχανικός [meehaneekos] mechanical || (οὐσ) engineer || mechanic || architect.

μηχανισμός, ὁ [meehaneesmos] mechanism, machinery.

μηχανοδηγός, ὁ [meehanodeeyos] engine driver.

μηχανοκίνητος [meehanokeeneetos] motorized || machine-operated.

μηχανοποιῶ [meehanopeeo] mechanize.

μηχανορραφία, ἡ [meehanorafeea] machination || intrigue.

μία, μιά [meea, mia] one || a, an || ~ καί since, seeing that || ~ πού as, since.

μιαίνω [mieno] pollute, sully, soil || (ἱερόν) desecrate.

μιαρός [meearos] dirty, polluted || foul.

μίασμα, τό [meeasma] miasma, infection.

μιγάς, ὁ [meeyas] half-caste, mulatto || hybrid.

μίγμα, τό [meeyma] mixture, blend.

μίζα, ἡ [meeza] (μηχανῆς) self-starter || (στά χαρτιά) stake.

μιζέρια, ἡ [meezereea] misery, wretchedness || (τσιγγουνιά) meanness.

μικραίνω [meekreno] curtail, lessen || shorten, grow smaller.

μικρέμπορος, ὁ [meekremboros] retailer.

μικρόβιον, τό [meekroveeon] microbe.

μικρογραφία, ἡ [meekroyrafeea] miniature.

μικροπρά(γ)ματα, τά [meekropra(γ)mata] πλ trifles.

μικροπρεπής [meekroprepees] mean, base.

μικρός [meekros] small, little || short || young || (διαφορά) trivial.

μικροσκοπικός [meekroskopeekos] minute.

μικροσκόπιον, τό [meekroskopeeon] microscope.

μικρόφωνον, τό [meekrofonon] microphone.

μικρόψυχος [meekropseehos] faint-hearted.

μικρύνω [meekton] βλ μικραίνω.

μικτόν [meekton]: ~ βάρος gross weight.

μικτός [meektos] mixed, composite || (σχόλεῖον) coeducational.

μιλιά, ἡ [meelia] speech, word.

μίλι(ον), τό [meelee(on)] mile.

μιλῶ [meelo] speak.

μίμησις, ἡ [meemeesees] imitation.

μιμητής, ὁ [meemeetees] imitator.

μιμητικός [meemeeteekos] imitative.

μιμόζα, ἡ [meemoza] mimosa.

μῖμος, ὁ [meemos] mimic, jester.

μιμοῦμαι [meemoume] imitate, copy, mimic.

μιναρές, ὁ [meenares] minaret.

μινιατούρα, ἡ [meeneeatoura] miniature.

μίξις, ἡ [meeksees] mixing, mixture, blend.

μισαλλόδοξος [meesalodoksos] intolerant.

μισάνθρωπος, ὁ [meesanthropos] misanthrope.

μισεύω [meesevo] depart, leave.

μισητός [meeseetos] hated, hateful, odious.

μίσθαρνος [meestharnos] mercenary, venal.

μισθοδοτῶ [meesthodoto] pay a salary to, hire.

μισθολόγιον, τό [meestholoyeeon] payroll || rate of pay.

μισθός, ὁ [meesthos] salary, wages, pay.

μισθοφόρος, ὁ [meesthoforos] mercenary, hired man.

μισθώνω [meesthono] hire, rent || let out, hire out.

μισθωτής, ὁ [meesthotees] tenant || hirer.

μισθωτός [meesthotos] salaried, paid.

μισό, τό [meeso] half || στά μισά halfway, in the middle.

μισογύνης, ὁ [meesoyeenees] woman-hater, misogynist.

μῖσος, τό [meesos] hatred, aversion.

μισός [meesos] half.

μισοφέγγαρο, τό [meesofengaro] halfmoon, crescent.

μίσχος, ὁ [meeshos] stalk (of leaf).

μισῶ [meeso] hate, detest, loathe.

μίτος, ὁ [meetos] thread, woof.

μίτρα, ἡ [meetra] mitre.

μνεία, ἡ [mneea] mention.

μνῆμα, τό [mneema] grave, tomb, sepulchre.

μνημεῖον, τό [mneemeeon] monument, cenotaph.

μνήμη, ἡ [mneemee] memory, mind, recollection.

μνημονεύω [mneemonevo] celebrate, commemorate || quote, mention || learn by heart.

μνημονικόν, τό [mneemoneekon] βλ μνήμη.

μνημόσυνον, τό [mneemoseenon] requiem.

μνήμων [mneemon] mindful.

μνησίκακος [mneeseekakos] spiteful, vindictive.

μνηστεία, ἡ [mneesteea] engagement.

μνηστεύομαι [mneestevome] get engaged.

μνηστεύω [mneestevo] affiance.

μνηστή, ἡ [mneestee] fiancée.

μνηστήρ, ὁ [mneesteer] fiancé || (μεταφ) claimant.

μόδα, ἡ [moδa] fashion, custom, habit, way ‖ **τῆς ~ς** fashionable.

μοδίστρα, ἡ [moδeestra] dressmaker, seamstress.

μοιάζω [meeazo] look like.

μοῖρα, ἡ [meera] fate, destiny, fortune ‖ **(ἀερο)** squadron ‖ **(γεωμ)** degree.

μοιράζομαι [meerazome] share with.

μοιράζω [meerazo] share out, divide, distribute ‖ **(ρόλους)** allot, assign ‖ **(διανέμω)** deliver ‖ **(χαρτιά)** deal ‖ **~ τή διαφορά** split the difference.

μοιραῖος [meeros] unavoidable ‖ fatal, deadly.

μοιραίως [meeros] inevitably, fatally.

μοίραρχος, ὁ [meerarhos] captain of the gendarmerie.

μοιρολατρία, ἡ [meerolatreea] fatalism.

μοιρολόγι, τό [meerologee] dirge, lamentation.

μοιρολογῶ [meerologo] lament, mourn.

μοιχεία, ἡ [meeheea] adultery.

μολαταῦτα [molatavta] nevertheless, yet, still.

μόλις [molees] barely, hardly, scarcely ‖ as soon as.

μολονότι [molonotee] although, though.

μολοσσός, ὁ [molosos] large sheepdog.

μόλυβδος, ὁ [moleevδos] lead.

μολύβι, τό [moleevee] lead ‖ pencil.

μόλυνσις, ἡ [moleensees] contamination, infection, pollution.

μολύνω [moleeno] infect, contaminate, pollute.

μόλυσμα, τό [moleesma] infection, contagion.

μομφή, ἡ [momfee] blame, reproach, reprimand.

μοναδικός [monaδeekos] unique, singular, only.

μοναξιά, ἡ [monaksia] solitude, isolation, loneliness.

μονάρχης, ὁ [monarhees] monarch, sovereign.

μοναρχία, ἡ [monarheea] monarchy.

μοναρχικός, ὁ [monarheekos] monarchist.

μονάς, ἡ [monas] unit.

μοναστήρι, τό [monasteeree] monastery.

μονάχα [monaha] only.

μοναχή, ἡ [monahee] nun.

μοναχικός [monaheekos] monastic ‖ **(ἐρημικός)** isolated, solitary, lonely.

μοναχοπαίδι, τό [monahopeδee] only child.

μοναχός [monahos] alone, single, only, sole ‖ real, authentic.

μοναχός, ὁ [monahos] monk.

μονέδα, ἡ [moneδa] money.

μονή, ἡ [monee] βλ **μοναστήρι**.

μονήρης [moneerees] solitary, isolated, lonely.

μόνιμος [moneemos] permanent, lasting, durable, fixed.

μονογαμία, ἡ [monoγameea] monogamy.

μονογενής [monoγenees] one and only.

μονόγραμμα, τό [monoγrama] monogram, initials.

μονογραφή, ἡ [monoγrafee] initials.

μονογραφία, ἡ [monoγrafeea] monograph, treatise.

μονόδρομος, ὁ [monoδromos] one-way street.

μονοιάζω [moneeazo] agree with, get on well with ‖ reconcile.

μονοκατοικία, ἡ [monokateekeea] one-family house.

μονοκόμματος [monokomatos] in one piece ‖ stiff ‖ forthright ‖ massive.

μονομανία, ἡ [monomaneea] obsession ‖ whim, fancy.

μονομαχία, ἡ [monomaheea] duel.

μονομερής [monomerees] one-sided, partial.

μονομιάς [monomias] all at once.

μόνο(ν) [mono(n)] only, alone, solely, merely, nothing but ‖ **~ πού** except that ‖ **~ νά** provided that.

μονοπάτι, τό [monopatee] footpath, pathway.

μονόπλευρος [monoplevros] one-sided, partial.

μονοπώλιον, τό [monopoleeon] monopoly.

μονοπωλῶ [monopolo] monopolize.

μόνος [monos] alone, single, by o.s., apart ‖ **~ μου** of my own accord, by myself.

μονός [monos] single ‖ simple ‖ **(ἀριθμός)** odd.

μονότονος [monotonos] monotonous, unvaried ‖ **(μεταφ)** wearisome.

μονόφθαλμος [monofthalmos] one-eyed.

μοντέλο, τό [montelo] model.

μοντέρνος [monternos] modern, up-to-date.

μονόκελος, ὁ [monielos] monocle.

μονώνω [monono] set apart, cut off ‖ insulate.

μόνωσις, ἡ [monosees] insulation ‖ solitude, isolation.

μονωτικός [monoteekos] insulating.

μορέα, ἡ [morea] mulberry tree.

μόριον, τό [moreeon] particle ‖ molecule.

μόρτης, ὁ [mortees] hooligan, blackguard.

μορφάζω [morfazo] grimace, make faces ‖ **(ἀπό πόνο)** wince.

μορφασμός, ὁ [morfasmos] grimace ‖ wince.

μορφή, ἡ [morfee] shape, form ‖ look, face, aspect ‖ phase.

μορφίνη, ἡ [morfeenee] morphine.

μορφολογία, ἡ [morfoloγeea] morphology.

μορφώνω [morfono] shape, form ‖ **(ἐκπαιδεύω)** train, educate, teach.

μόρφωσις, ἡ [morfosees] education, learning.

μορφωτικός [morfoteekos] cultural ‖ instructive.

μόστρα, ἡ [mostra] shop window, display ‖ specimen, sample.

μοσχάρι, τό [mosharee] calf ‖ veal.

μοσχάτο, τό [moshato] muscatel.
μοσχοβολῶ [moshovolo] smell sweetly, be fragrant.
μοσχοκάρυδο, τό [moshokareedo] nutmeg.
μοσχοκάρφι, τό [moshokarfee] clove.
μοσχολίβανο, τό [mosholeevano] frankincense.
μόσχος, ὁ [moshos] βλ μοσχάρι.
μοτοσυκλέτα, ἡ [motoseekleta] motorbike, motorcycle.
μοῦ, μου [mou] me || my.
μουγγός [moungos] dumb, mute.
μουγγρίζω [moungreezo] roar, bellow || (ἄνεμος) howl, wail || (ἀπό πόνο) moan, groan.
μουδιάζω [moudeeazo] become numb.
μουλάρι, τό [moularee] mule.
μοῦλος, ὁ [moulos] bastard, crossbreed.
μούμια, ἡ [moumeea] mummy || shrivelled person.
μουνουχίζω [mounouheezo] castrate.
μουντζούρα, ἡ [mountzoura] smudge, stain, smear || (μεταφ) blemish.
μουντός [mountos] dull, dim.
μούρη, ἡ [mouree] face || snout.
μούρλια, ἡ [mourleea] madness || εἶναι ~ it's perfect!, it's a dream!
μουρλός [mourlos] mad, insane || bewildered.
μουρμουρητό, τό [mourmoureeto] murmuring || grumbling.
μουρμουρίζω [mourmoureezo] mutter, murmur || (μεταφ) whisper || babble.
μοῦρο, τό [mouro] mulberry.
μουρούνα, ἡ [mourouna] codfish.
μοῦσα, ἡ [mousa] muse.
μουσακᾶς, ὁ [mousakas] moussaka, minced meat with vegetables.
μουσαμᾶς, ὁ [mousamas] oilcloth, linoleum || mackintosh.
μουσαφίρης, ὁ [mousafeerees] guest, visitor.
μουσεῖον, τό [mouseeon] museum.
μούσι, τό [mousee] goatee.
μουσική, ἡ [mouseekee] music.
μουσικός [mouseekos] musical || (οὐσ) musician.
μούσκεμα, τό [mouskema] wetting, soaking || τά κάνω ~ make a mess of.
μουσκεύω [mouskevo] soak, wet, damp || get wet.
μούσμουλο, τό [mousmoulo] loquat.
μουσουργός, ὁ, ἡ [mousouryos] composer.
μουστάκι, τό [moustakee] moustache.
μουσταλευριά, ἡ [moustalevria] must-jelly.
μουστάρδα, ἡ [moustarda] mustard.
μοῦστος, ὁ [moustos] must.
μοῦτρα, τά [moutra] πλ: ἔχω ~ νά I dare to || πέφτω μέ τά ~ apply o.s. enthusiastically || tuck in.
μοῦτρο [moutro]: εἶναι ~ he's a thief, he's deceitful.
μοῦτσος, ὁ [moutsos] cabin boy.

μούχλα, ἡ [mouhla] mould, mildew.
μουχλιάζω [mouhleeazo] make mouldy || become mouldy.
μοχθηρός [mohtheeros] wicked, mischievous, malicious.
μόχθος, ὁ [mohthos] pains, fatigue, trouble.
μοχλός, ὁ [mohlos] lever, (crow)bar || (μεταφ) promoter, instigator.
μπαγιάτικος [mbayeeateekos] (ψωμί) stale || rancid.
μπάγκος, ὁ [mbangos] bench || counter.
μπάζ(ι)α, τά [mbaz(i)a] πλ debris, rubble.
μπάζω [mbazo] usher in, thrust || (συμμαζεύομαι) shrink.
μπαίνω [mbeno] go into, get in, enter || (ὑφάσματος) shrink || (μεταφ) catch on, understand || ~ μέσα fall into debt || ~ σέ μιά σειρά settle down, fall into line.
μπακάλης, ὁ [mbakalees] grocer.
μπακάλικο, τό [mbakaleeko] grocer's shop || (US) grocery.
μπακαλιάρος, ὁ [mbakaleearos] salted codfish.
μπακίρι, τό [mbakeeree] copper.
μπακλαβᾶς, ὁ [mbaklavas] pastry of almonds and honey.
μπαλαντέρ, ὁ [mbalander] (στά χαρτιά) joker.
μπαλάντζα, ἡ [mbalantza] balance, pair of scales.
μπαλκόνι, τό [mbalkonee] balcony.
μπάλλα, ἡ [mbala] ball || bullet.
μπαλλέτο, τό [mbaleto] ballet.
μπαλλόνι, τό [mbalonee] balloon.
μπαλντᾶς, ὁ [mbaldas] axe, hatchet.
μπάλωμα, τό [mbaloma] mending, patching, repairing.
μπαλώνομαι [mbalonome] benefit, profit.
μπαλώνω [mbalono] patch, mend, repair || τά ~ make excuses || make up.
μπάμιες, οἱ [mbamies] πλ okra, gumbo, lady's fingers.
μπαμπάκι, τό [mbambakee] cotton.
μπαμπᾶς, ὁ [mbambas] daddy, papa.
μπαμπέσης [mbambesees] perfidious, treacherous, fraudulent.
μπάμπουρας, ὁ [mbambouras] hornet.
μπανάνα, ἡ [mbanana] banana.
μπανιέρα, ἡ [mbaniera] bathtub.
μπανιερό, τό [mbaniero] swimsuit, bathing suit.
μπάνιο, τό [mbaneeo] bath || bathing, swimming || (λεκάνη) tub || (δωμάτιο) bathroom.
μπάντα, ἡ [mbanta] (ἥσυχη γωνιά) corner || (πλευρά) side || (μουσική) band || (συμμορία) gang, band || βάζω στή ~ save || κάνε στή ~ make room, stand aside.
μπαντιέρα, ἡ [mbantiera] banner, standard.
μπαξές, ὁ [mbakses] garden.
μπαοῦλο, τό [mbaoulo] trunk, chest.
μπαρκάρω [mbarkaro] go on board || ship.

μπάρμπας, ὁ [mbarbas] old man ‖ uncle.

μπαρμπούνι, τό [mbarbounee] red mullet.

μπαρούτι, τό [mbaroutee] gunpowder ‖ ἔγινε ~ he got furious.

μπάρρα, ἡ [mbara] bar, crowbar.

μπασμένος [mbasmenos] aware ‖ knowledgeable ‖ shrunk.

μπάσταρδος, ὁ [mbastarðos] bastard.

μπαστούνι, τό [mbastounee] walking stick, cane ‖ (χαρτιά) club.

μπαταρία, ἡ [mbatareea] battery.

μπατζανάκης, ὁ [mbatzanakees] brother-in-law.

μπάτσος, ὁ [mbatsos] slap, smack.

μπαχαρικό, τό [mbahareeko] spice.

μπέζ [mbez] beige.

μπεκάτσα, ἡ [mbekatsa] woodcock.

μπεκιάρης, ὁ [mbekiarees] bachelor.

μπεκρῆς, ὁ [mbekrees] drunkard, tippler, boozer.

μπελᾶς, ὁ [mbelas] trouble, embarrassment, annoyance.

μπελντές, ὁ [mbelntes] tomato purée ‖ (φρούτων) jelly.

μπέμπης, ὁ [mbembees] baby.

μπενζίνα, ἡ [mbenzeena] petrol ‖ (πλοιάριον) motorboat.

μπέρδεμα, τό [mberðema] tangle, entanglement, confusion, disorder.

μπερδεύομαι [mberðevome] get implicated, become entangled ‖ be confused.

μπερδεύω [mberðevo] involve ‖ confuse, make a muddle of ‖ entangle.

μπερμπάντης, ὁ [mbermbantees] rascal, scoundrel.

μπετόν, τό [mbeton] concrete.

μπετούγια, ἡ [mbetouyeea] latch, catch.

μπήζω [mbeezo] drive in, hammer in ‖ (βελόνην) stick in, thrust in.

μπιζέλι, τό [mbeezelee] pea.

μπιλιέτο, τό [mbeelieto] visiting card ‖ ticket.

μπίρα, ἡ [mbeera] beer.

μπισκότο, τό [mbeeskoto] biscuit.

μπίτ(ι) [mbeet(ee)] entirely ‖ not in the least.

μπιφτέκι, τό [mbeeftekee] steak.

μπλάστρι, τό [mblastree] plaster.

μπλέ [mble] blue.

μπλέκω [mbleko] complicate, perplex ‖ get implicated.

μπλέξιμο, τό [mblekseemo] entanglement, involvement, complication.

μπλοκάρω [mblokaro] blockade ‖ block.

μπλούζα, ἡ [mblouza] blouse.

μπλόφα, ἡ [mblofa] bluff, deception.

μπογιά, ἡ [mboyia] paint, dye ‖ (παπουτσιῶν) boot-polish.

μπόγιας, ὁ [mboyeas] dog-catcher ‖ hangman.

μπογιατζῆς, ὁ [mboyeeatzees] painter ‖ polisher.

μπογιατίζω [mboyeeateezo] paint, colour, coat ‖ polish.

μπόϊ, τό [mboee] height, size.

μπόλι, τό [mbolee] graft ‖ μπολιάζω vaccinate, inoculate ‖ graft.

μπόλικος [mboleekos] plentiful, abundant, numerous.

μπόμπα, ἡ [mbomba] bomb.

μπομπότα, ἡ [mbombota] maize flour, bread of maize.

μποναμᾶς, ὁ [mbonamas] New Year's gift ‖ present.

μποξᾶς, ὁ [mboksas] shawl.

μπόρα, ἡ [mbora] rain squall, shower, storm.

μπορετός [mboretos] possible, practicable.

μπορῶ [mboro] can, be able, may.

μπόσικος [mboseekos] loose, slack ‖ (μεταφ) trifling ‖ unreliable.

μποστάνι, τό [mbostanee] melon field.

μποτίλια, ἡ [mboteeleea] bottle ‖ μποτιλιάρω bottle ‖ (μεταφ) block up, jam.

μπότα, ἡ [mbota] boot.

μπουγάδα, ἡ [mbouyaða] family wash, washing.

μπουζί, τό [mbouzee] spark plug.

μπουζούκι, τό [mbouzoukee] kind of mandolin, bouzouki.

μπούκα, ἡ [mbouka] hole, mouth, entrance ‖ muzzle.

μπουκάλα, ἡ [mboukala] big bottle ‖ ἔμεινε ~ he was left in the lurch.

μπουκάλι, τό [mboukalee] bottle.

μπουκιά, ἡ [mboukia] mouthful.

μπούκλα, ἡ [mboukla] curl, lock (of hair).

μπουκώνω [mboukono] fill the mouth ‖ (μεταφ) bribe.

μπουλούκι, τό [mbouloukee] crowd ‖ band, troop.

μπουμπούκι, τό [mboumboukee] bud, sprout.

μπουμπουνητό, τό [mboumbouneeto] thundering, roll of thunder, rumble.

μπουνάτσα, ἡ [mbounatsa] fine weather ‖ calm sea.

μπουνιά, ἡ [mbounia] punch, blow with the fist.

μπούρδα, ἡ [mbourða] rubbish, hot air.

μπουρμπουλήθρα, ἡ [mbourmbouleethra] bubble.

μπουσουλῶ [mbousoulo] crawl.

μπούστος, ὁ [mboustos] bust.

μπούτι, τό [mboutee] thigh ‖ (ἀρνήσιο) leg of lamb.

μπουφές, ὁ [mboufes] sideboard ‖ buffet.

μπούφος, ὁ [mboufos] horned owl ‖ (μεταφ) booby.

μπουχτίζω [mbouhteezo] have enough of ‖ eat one's fill.

μπόχα, ἡ [mboha] stink, foul smell.

μπράβο [mbravo] (ἐπιφ) good show! bravo!, good for you!

μπράτσο, τό [mbratso] arm.

μπριγιαντίνη, ἡ [mbreeyeeanteenee] brilliantine.

μπριζόλα, ἡ [mbreezola] chop, cutlet.

μπρίκι, τό [mbreekee] coffee pot.

μπρός [mbros] forward(s), in front of ‖ βλ καί ἐμπρός.

μπροστινός [mbrosteenos] in front ‖ former.

μπρούμυτα [mbroumeeta] flat on one's face.

μπρούντζος, ὁ [mbrountzos] bronze, brass.

μπύρα, ἡ [mbeera] βλ μπίρα.

μῦ, τό [mee] the letter M.

μυαλό, τό [meealo] brain(s) ‖ (γνώση) mind, intellect.

μυαλωμένος [meealomenos] learned, wise.

μῦγα, ἡ [meeya] fly.

μύδι, τό [meeδee] mussel.

μυδραλλιοβόλον, τό [meeδraleeovolon] machine gun.

μυελός, ὁ [mielos] marrow (of bone).

μυζήθρα, ἡ [meezeethra] kind of white soft cheese.

μυζῶ [meezo] suck.

μύησις, ἡ [mieesees] initiation.

μυθικός [meetheekos] mythical, legendary ‖ incredible.

μυθιστόρημα, τό [meetheestoreema] novel, romance, story.

μυθιστοριογράφος, ὁ [meetheestoreeoyrafos] novelist.

μυθολογία, ἡ [meetholoyeea] mythology.

μῦθος, ὁ [meethos] fable ‖ myth ‖ legend.

μυθώδης [meethoδees] fabled, legendary ‖ untrue ‖ incredible.

μυῖα, ἡ [meea] fly.

μυϊκός [mieekos] muscular.

μυκηθμός, ὁ [meekeethmos] bellowing, howling ‖ lowing.

μύκης, ὁ [meekees] fungus, mushroom.

μυκτηρίζω [meekteereezo] scoff, mock at, sneer.

μυκῶμαι [meekome] bellow, roar ‖ low.

μῦλος, ὁ [meelos] mill ‖ (ἀνεμόμυλος) windmill.

μυλωνᾶς, ὁ [meelonas] miller.

μύξα, ἡ [meeksa] snot ‖ mucus.

μυριάκις [meereeakees] infinitely, often.

μυρίζω [meereezo] smell.

μύριοι [meeriee] ten thousand ‖ (μεταφ) numberless.

μυρμήγκι, τό [meermeengee] ant.

μύρμηξ, ὁ [meermeeks] βλ μυρμήγκι.

μυροβόλος [meerovolos] fragrant, scented.

μύρον, τό [meeron] aromatic oil ‖ perfume ‖ ἅγιον ~ holy oil, unction.

μυροπωλεῖον, τό [meeropoleeon] perfumery.

μυρσίνη, ἡ [meerseenee] βλ μυρτιά.

μυρτιά, ἡ [meertia] myrtle.

μυρτόν, τό [meerton] myrtle bough.

μυρωδᾶτος [meeroδatos] aromatic, fragrant.

μυρωδιά, ἡ [meeroδia] smell, scent, odour

‖ (ἀρωματικό) fragrance, perfume ‖ παίρνω ~ get wind of.

μυρώνω [meerono] anoint, administer the holy oil.

μῦς, ὁ [mees] muscle ‖ (ποντικός) mouse.

μυσαρός [meesaros] abominable, detestable, odious.

μυσταγωγία, ἡ [meestayoyeea] initiation ‖ holy ceremony.

μύσταξ, ὁ [meestaks] moustache ‖ (γάτας) whiskers.

μυστήριον, τό [meesteereeon] mystery, secret.

μυστήριος [meesteereeos] mysterious, inexplicable.

μυστηριώδης [meesteereeoδees] mysterious, dark.

μύστης, ὁ [meestees] initiate ‖ (μεταφ) adept, expert.

μυστικιστής, ὁ [meesteekeestees] mystic.

μυστικόν, τό [meesteekon] secret.

μυστικός [meesteekos] secret(ive) ‖ reticent, discreet ‖ (ἀστυνόμος) undercover man ‖ ~ δεῖπνος Last Supper.

μυστικότης, ἡ [meesteekotees] secrecy, discretion.

μυστρί, τό [meestree] trowel.

μυτερός [meeteros] pointed.

μύτη, ἡ [meetee] nose ‖ (ἄκρη) tip ‖ (παπουτσιοῦ) toe ‖ (πέννας) nib ‖ (βελόνας) point.

μύχιος [meeheeos] intimate, secret, internal.

μυχός, ὁ [meehos] recess, corner ‖ creek, bay.

μυῶ [meeo] initiate into, admit into.

μυώδης [meeoδees] muscular, brawny, powerful.

μυών, ὁ [meeon] muscle, muscular flesh.

μύωψ [meeops] near-sighted, short-sighted.

μωαμεθανός, ὁ [moamethanos] Mohammedan.

μώβ [mov] mauve.

μῶλος, ὁ [molos] mole, jetty, pier.

μωλωπίζω [molopeezo] bruise, contuse.

μώλωψ, ὁ [molops] bruise, contusion.

μωραίνω [moreno] make stupid, become dull, stupefy.

μωρέ [more] (ἐπιφ) hey you!, you!, I say!

μωρία, ἡ [moreea] stupidity, foolishness.

μωρό, τό [moro] baby, infant.

μωρολόγος, ὁ [moroloyos] babbler, dotard, driveller.

μωρός [moros] silly, stupid, idiotic.

μωσαϊκόν, τό [mosaeekon] mosaic.

N, ν

νά [na] that, to, in order to, so as to ‖ here it is!

ναί [ne] yes, indeed, certainly.

νάϊλον, τό [naeelon] nylon.

ναΐσκος, ὁ [naeskos] chapel, small church.

νάνος, ὁ [nanos] dwarf.

νανουρίζω [nanoureezo] lull to sleep | (στήν κούνια) rock | (στήν ἀγκάλη) nurse.

νανούρισμα, τό [nanoureesma] lullaby | rocking to sleep.

ναός, ὁ [naos] church | temple.

ναργιλές, ὁ [naryeeless] hubble-bubble, hookah.

νάρθηξ, ὁ [nartheeks] (ἐκκλ) nave, narthex | (βοτ) fennel.

ναρκαλιευτικόν, τό [narkalievteekon] minesweeper.

νάρκη, ἡ [narkee] numbness, torpor | (ναυτ) mine | (πνεύματος) sluggishness.

νάρκισσος, ὁ [narkeesos] narcissus.

ναρκοθέτις, ἡ [narkothetees] minelayer.

ναρκώνω [narkono] numb | (μεταφ) dull, stupefy.

νάρκωσις, ἡ [narkosees] numbness | torpidity, sluggishness.

ναρκωτικά, τά [narkoteeka] πλ drugs, narcotics.

νάτριον, τό [natreeon] sodium.

ναυάγιον, τό [navayeeon] shipwreck | (μεταφ) wreck.

ναυαγός, ὁ [navayos] shipwrecked person.

ναυαρχεῖον, τό [navarheeon] admiralty.

ναύαρχος, ὁ [navarhos] admiral.

ναύκληρος, ὁ [navkleeros] boatswain.

ναῦλα, τά [navla] πλ fare, passage money.

ναυλώνω [navlono] charter, freight.

ναυμαχία, ἡ [navmaheea] sea battle, naval action.

ναυπηγεῖον, τό [navpeeyeeon] shipyard, dockyard.

ναῦς, ἡ [navs] ship, vessel.

ναυσιπλοΐα, ἡ [navseeploeea] sailing, shipping | navigation.

ναύσταθμος, ὁ [navstathmos] dockyard, naval arsenal.

ναύτης, ὁ [navtees] sailor, seaman, mariner.

ναυτία, ἡ [navteea] seasickness | nausea.

ναυτική, ἡ [navteekee] seamanship, art of navigation.

ναυτικόν, τό [navteekon] navy

ναυτικός [navteekos] maritime | nautical | (ἄνδρας) seafarer.

ναυτιλία, ἡ [navteeleea] navigation | shipping | ναυτιλιακός marine, naval, nautical.

ναυτολογῶ [navtoloyo] enlist a crew, muster seamen.

ναυτόπαις, ὁ [navtopes] ship's boy, cabin boy.

νέα, ἡ [nea] girl | τά ~ news.

νεανίας, ὁ [neaneeas] young man, lad, youth.

νεανικός [neaneekos] youthful, juvenile.

νεᾶνις, ἡ [neanees] girl, lass.

νεαρός [nearos] young | youthful, juvenile.

νέγρος, ὁ [neyros] negro.

νέκρα, ἡ [nekra] dead silence, stagnation.

νεκρικός [nekreekos] of death funeral gloomy.

νεκροθάπτης, ὁ [nekrothaptees] gravedigger | (μεταφ) killjoy.

νεκροκεφαλή, ἡ [nekrokefalee] skull.

νεκρολογία, ἡ [nekroloyeea] obituary.

νεκρός [nekros] dead, lifeless | (οὐσ) ὁ ~ dead person.

νεκροταφεῖον, τό [nekrotafeeon] cemetery graveyard.

νεκροτομεῖον, τό [nekrotomeeon] mortuary.

νεκροφόρα, ἡ [nekrofora] hearse.

νεκροψία, ἡ [nekropseea] autopsy, post-mortem.

νεκρώνω [nekrono] deaden | (τά πάθη) subdue.

νεκρώσιμος [nekroseemos] funeral.

νέκρωσις, ἡ [nekrosees] stagnation.

νέκταρ, τό [nektar] nectar.

νέμομαι [nemome] enjoy something, reap the profit from.

νέμω [nemo] distribute, share.

νέο, τό [neo] piece of news.

νεογέννητος [neoyeenetos] newborn.

νεογνόν, τό [neoynon] newborn animal | newborn baby.·

νεόδμητος [neodmeetos] newly constructed.

νεοελληνικά, τά [neoeleeneeka] πλ modern Greek (language).

νεοελληνικός [neoeleeneekos] of modern Greece.

νεόκτιστος [neokteestos] βλ νεόδμητος.

νεολαία, ἡ [neolea] youth.

νεόνυμφος, ὁ, ἡ [neoneemfos] recently married man or woman.

νεόπλουτος [neoploutos] nouveau riche, parvenu.

νέος [neos] young | (καινούριο) new, fresh | (ἐπιπρόσθετο) further, additional | (σύγχρονος) modern | (οὐσ) ὁ ~ a young man.

νεοσσός, ὁ [neosos] nestling, chick.

νεοσύλλεκτος, ὁ [neoseelektos] recruit.

νεοσύστατος [neoseestatos] newly-established, newly-founded.

νεότης, ἡ [neotees] βλ νεολαία.

νεράϊδα, ἡ [neraeeda] fairy, Nereid.

νεράντζι, τό [nerantzee] bitter orange.

νερό, τό [nero] water | urine.

νερόβραστος [nerovrastos] boiled in water | (μεταφ) insipid, tasteless.

νερομπογιά, ἡ [neromboyia] watercolour.

νερόμυλος, ὁ [neromeelos] water mill.

νεροποντή, ἡ [neropontee] shower of rain downpour.

νερουλός [neroulos] watery, thin.

νερόχιονο, τό [neroheeono] sleet.

νεροχύτης, ὁ [neroheetees] kitchen sink.

νερώνω [nerono] mix with water.

νέτα σκέτα [netasketa] frankly, flatly.

νέτος [netos] net | (μεταφ) done, finished completed.

N

νεῦμα, τό [nevma] sign, nod, wink, beckoning.

νευραλγία, ἡ [nevralyeea] neuralgia.

νευραλγικός [nevralyeekos]: νευραλγικὸν σημεῖον weak spot.

νευριάζω [nevreeazo] make angry, irritate, vex || become angry.

νευρικός [nevreekos] nervous || excitable, highly strung.

νεῦρον, τό [nevron] nerve || muscle || vigour.

νευρόσπαστον, τό [nevrospaston] marionette || (μεταφ) weak-willed person.

νευρώδης [nevroδees] sinewy || nervous || (μεταφ) strong, spirited.

νευρωτικός [nevroteekos] neurotic.

νεύω [nevo] nod, make a sign, beckon, wink.

νεφέλη, ἡ [nefelee] cloud.

νεφελώδης [nefeloδees] cloudy, nebulous || (μεταφ) vague, hazy.

νέφος, τό [nefos] cloud || (μεταφ) gloom, shadow.

νεφοσκεπής [nefoskepees] cloudy, overcast.

νεφρόν, τό [nefron] kidney.

νέφτι, τό [neftee] turpentine, turps.

νεωκόρος, ὁ [neokoros] sacristan, verger.

νεώριον, τό [neoreeon] dry dock, dockyard.

νεωστί [neostee] lately, recently, newly.

νεωτερισμός, ὁ [neotereesmos] innovation || novelty, fashion.

νεώτερα, τά [neotera] πλ latest news.

νεώτερος [neoteros] younger || (γεγονός) recent, later || (νέα) fresh.

νῆμα, τό [neema] thread || (βαμβακερόν) linen thread || (μάλλινο) yarn.

νηνεμία, ἡ [neenemeea] calmness, stillness.

νηολόγιον, τό [neeoloyeeon] register of merchant shipping.

νηοπομπή, ἡ [neeopombee] convoy, escort of ships.

νηοψία, ἡ [neeopseea] inspection or searching of ship.

νηπιαγωγεῖον, τό [neepeeayoyeeon] kindergarten.

νήπιον, τό [neepeeon] infant, baby, new-born child.

νησί, τό [neesee] island.

νησιώτης, ὁ [neeseeotees] islander.

νῆσος, ἡ [neesos] βλ νησί.

νῆσσα, ἡ [neesa] duck.

νηστεία, ἡ [neesteea] fast, fasting || Lent.

νηστεύω [neestevo] fast, keep Lent.

νηστήσιμος [neesteeseemos] Lenten (food).

νηστικός [neesteekos] hungry.

νηφάλιος [neefaleeos] sober || (μεταφ) calm, cool, composed.

νιαουρίζω [neeaoureezo] miaow, mew

νιάτα, τά [neeata] πλ youth.

νίβω [neevo] βλ νίπτω.

νικέλιον, τό [neekeleeon] nickel.

νίκη, ἡ [neekee] victory, triumph.

νικητής, ὁ [neekeetees] victor || (σέ παιχνίδι) winner.

νικηφόρος [neekeeforos] victorious, triumphant.

νικῶ [neeko] (τόν ἐχθρόν) defeat, vanquish || (ἀνταγωνιστήν) beat, surpass || (ἐμπόδια κτλ) surmount, overcome.

νίλα, ἡ [neela] practical joke || calamity, ruin.

νιπτήρ, ὁ [neepteer] washbasin, washstand.

νίπτω [neepto] wash || (μεταφ) wash out.

νισάφι, τό [neesafee] mercy, compassion, pity.

νίτρον, τό [neetron] nitre, saltpetre.

νιφάς, ἡ [neefas] snowflake.

Νοέμβρης, ὁ [noemvrees] November.

νοερός [noeros] mental, intellectual.

νόημα, τό [noeema] reflection, thought || (ἔννοια) sense, meaning || (νεῦμα) sign, wink.

νοημοσύνη, ἡ [noeemoseenee] intelligence, intellect.

νοήμον [noeemon] intelligent, smart.

νόησις, ἡ [noeesees] understanding, intellect || mind, wit.

νοητός [noeetos] comprehensible, conceivable.

νοθεία, ἡ [notheea] falsification, adulteration.

νόθευσις, ἡ [nothevsees] adulteration, forgery.

νοθεύω [nothevo] falsify, forge, adulterate.

νόθος [nothos] bastard || (ἐπί ζώων κτλ) hybrid || (μεταφ) unstable.

νοιάζει [neeazee]: μέ ~ I care, I am anxious about.

νοιάζομαι [neeazome] care about, look after || be anxious about.

νοίκι, τό [neekee] rent || νοικιάζω rent, hire, let out || νοικάρης, ὁ tenant.

νοικοκυρά, ἡ [neekokeera] housewife, mistress of the house || landlady.

νοικοκύρης, ὁ [neekokeerees] landlord || owner || (αὐτεξούσιος) independent || wise.

νοικοκυριό, τό [neekokeerio] housekeeping.

νοιώθω [neeotho] understand || feel, perceive || know.

νομαδικός [nomaδeekos] nomadic, roving.

νομαρχεῖον, τό [nomarheeon] prefecture.

νομάρχης, ὁ [nomarhees] prefect, governor.

νομάς, ὁ [nomas] nomad, rover.

νομή, ἡ [nomee] pasture.

νομίζω [nomeezo] believe, think || suppose, presume.

νομικά, τά [nomeeka] πλ law studies, jurisprudence.

νομική, ἡ [nomeekee] law.

νομικός [nomeekos] of the law, legal, lawful.

νομιμοποιῶ [nomeemopeeo] legitimize, legalize, validate.

νόμιμος [nomeemos] legal, lawful, rightful.

νομιμότης, ή [nomeemotees] legitimacy, legality.

νομιμόφρων [nomeemofron] law-abiding, obedient, loyal.

νόμισμα, τό [nomeesma] money, coin, currency.

νομισματολογία, ή [nomeesmatoloyeea] numismatics.

νομοθεσία, ή [nomotheseea] legislation, law-making.

νομοθέτης, ὁ [nomothetees] legislator, lawgiver.

νομομαθής, ὁ [nomomathees] jurist, legist.

νομός, ὁ [nomos] prefecture, province.

νόμος, ὁ [nomos] law, act (of Parliament), enactment.

νομοσχέδιον, τό [nomoshedeeon] bill, draft of a law.

νομοταγής [nomotayees] law-abiding, loyal.

νονά, ή [nona] godmother, sponsor.

νονός, ὁ [nonos] godfather, sponsor.

νοοτροπία, ή [nootropeea] mentality, mental character.

νοσηλεία, ή [noseeleea] nursing, treatment, care of the sick.

νοσηλεύω [noseelevo] treat, tend, nurse.

νόσημα, τό [noseema] sickness, illness, disease, malady.

νοσηρός [noseeros] unhealthy, sickly, weakly || (περιέργεια) morbid.

νοσοκομείον, τό [nosokomeeon] hospital, infirmary.

νοσοκόμος, ὁ, ή [nosokomos] nurse || (στρατ) hospital orderly.

νόσος, ή [nosos] illness, disease, sickness.

νοσταλγία, ή [nostalyeea] nostalgia || homesickness.

νοσταλγικός [nostalyeekos] nostalgic || homesick.

νοσταλγῶ [nostalyo] feel nostalgic for || crave for || be homesick.

νοστιμάδα, ή [nosteemaδa] tastiness || prettiness || piquancy.

νοστιμεύω [nosteemevo] flavour, make tasty || make attractive.

νόστιμος [nosteemos] tasty || attractive, charming.

νοσῶ [noso] be sick, be ill.

νότα, ή [nota] (διπλωματική) note || (μουσ) note (mus).

νοτιά, ή [notia] south || south wind.

νοτίζω [noteezo] moisten, dampen || become damp.

νοτιοανατολικός [noteeoanatoleekos] south-eastern.

νοτιοδυτικός [noteeoδeeteekos] south-western.

νότιος [noteeos] southern.

νότος, ὁ [notos] south.

νουθεσία, ή [noutheseea] admonition, advice, counsel.

νουθετῶ [noutheto] admonish, advise, give advice to.

νούμερο, τό [noumero] number || (θεάτρου) act || odd character.

νουνεχής [nounehees] prudent, careful, wary.

νουνός, ὁ [nounos] godfather, sponsor.

νοῦς, ὁ [nous] mind, wit, intelligence, sense.

νούφαρο, τό [noufaro] water lily.

νοῶ [noo] comprehend, understand || think, reflect.

νταβάς, ὁ [ndavas] kind of baking tin or tray.

νταής, ὁ [ndaees] bully, hector, ruffian.

ντάλια, ή [ndaleea] dahlia.

ντάμα, ή [ndama] lady || partner || (στά χαρτιά) queen || (παιχνίδι) game of draughts.

νταμιτζάνα, ή [ndameetzana] demijohn.

νταμπλᾶς, ὁ [ndamblas] apoplexy || (μεταφ) amazement, stupefaction.

νταντά, ή [ndanda] child's nurse, nanny.

νταντέλλα, ή [ndantela] lace.

νταούλι, τό [ndaoulee] drum.

νταραβέρι, τό [ndaraveree] relation, dealing || (φασαρία) fuss, trouble.

ντέ [nde]: ἔλα ~ (ἐπιφ) come on!, hurry up!

ντεπόζιτο, τό [ndepozeeto] cistern || tank.

ντέρτι, τό [ndertee] regret, pain, sorrow || longing, yearning.

ντιβάνι, τό [ndeevanee] divan.

ντολμᾶς, ὁ [ndolmas] stuffed vine || stuffed cabbage.

ντομάτα, ή [ndomata] tomato.

ντόμπρος [ndombros] sincere, candid, frank, honest.

ντόπιος [ndopeeos] local, native.

ντόρος, ὁ [ndoros] trouble, din || (μεταφ) sensation.

ντουβάρι, τό [ndouvaree] wall || (μεταφ) fool.

ντουέτο, τό [ndoueto] duet.

ντουζίνα, ή [ndouzeena] dozen.

ντουλάπα, ή [ndoulapa] wardrobe.

ντουλάπι, τό [ndoulapee] cupboard.

ντουνιᾶς, ὁ [ndounias] people, mankind, humanity.

ντοῦρος [ndouros] hard, firm || obstinate.

ντούς, τό [ndous] shower bath.

ντρέπομαι [ndrepome] be bashful || be ashamed.

ντροπαλός [ndropalos] shy, modest, timid.

ντροπή, ή [ndropee] shame || modesty, bashfulness.

ντροπιάζω [ndropeeazo] shame.

ντυμένος [ndeemenos] dressed.

ντύνομαι [ndeenome] get dressed.

ντύνω [ndeeno] dress || (ἔπιπλα) upholster.

ντύσιμο, τό [ndeeseemo] dressing || attire, outfit, dress.

νῦ, τό [nee] the letter N.

νυγμός, ὁ [neeymos] bite, prick || (μεταφ) hint, allusion.

νυκτερινός [neektereenos] of night, nocturnal.

νυκτόβιος [neektoveeos] living by night.

νυκτοφύλαξ, ὁ [neektofeelaks] night watchman.

νύκτωρ [neektor] by night.

νυμφεύω [neemfevo] marry, wed.

νύμφη, ἡ [neemfee] bride || (μυθολογία) nymph || (ζωολ) larva.

νῦν [neen] now, at present.

νύξ, ἡ [neeks] night, darkness.

νύξις, ἡ [neeksees] βλ νυγμός.

νύστα, ἡ [neesta] sleepiness, drowsiness.

νυστάζω [neestazo] be sleepy, feel sleepy.

νυσταλέος [neestaleos] sleepy || (μεταφ) dull, sluggish.

νύφη, ἡ [neefee] βλ νύμφη.

νυφικός [neefeekos] bridal, nuptial.

νυφίτσα, ἡ [neefeetsa] weasel.

νυχθημερόν [neehtheemeron] day and night.

νύχι, τό [neehee] nail || (ποδιῶν) toenail || (ζώου) claw, talon || ~ α, τά clutches.

νυχιά, ἡ [neehia] scratch.

νύχτα, ἡ [neehta] night, darkness || (ἐπιρ) at night, by night.

νυχτερίδα, ἡ [neehtereeda] bat.

νυχτικό, τό [neehteeko] nightgown.

νυχτώνω [neehtono]: νυχτώνει night falls.

νωθρός [nothros] sluggish, lazy, slothful.

νωματάρχης, ὁ [nomatarhees] sergeant.

νωπός [nopos] fresh, new, recent || (γιά ροῦχα) still damp.

νωρίς [norees] early.

νῶτα, τά [nota] πλ back || (στρατ) rear.

νωχελής [nohelees] indolent, idle, slothful.

Ξ, ξ

ξαγρυπνῶ [ksaγreepno] stay awake || watch over || burn the midnight oil.

ξαδέρφη, ἡ [ksaderfee] cousin.

ξάδερφος, ὁ [ksaderfos] cousin.

ξαίρω [ksero] know, know how to.

ξακουστός [ksakoustos] renowned, celebrated, famous.

ξαλαφρώνω [ksalafrono] lighten the load of, help || (μεταφ) relieve || relieve one's mind.

ξανά [ksana] again, afresh, anew.

ξαναβάζω [ksanavazo] put back again, replace.

ξανάβω [ksanavo] irritate || become annoyed, get furious.

ξαναγυρίζω [ksanaγeereezo] return, send back || turn again.

ξαναδίνω [ksanadeeno] return, restore.

ξανακάνω [ksanakano] redo, remake, repeat.

ξαναλέω [ksanaleo] repeat, reiterate.

ξανανιώνω [ksananeeono] rejuvenate || become young again.

ξαναπαθαίνω [ksanapatheno] be taken in again || suffer again.

ξαναπαίρνω [ksanaperno] take again || (θάρρος) pluck up again || (ὑπάλληλος) take on again, rehire || (θέσι) go back to.

ξαναπαντρεύομαι [ksanapandrevome] remarry.

ξαναρχῆς [ksanarhees] from the beginning, again.

ξανασαίνω [ksanaseno] recover, refresh o.s., relax.

ξαναφορτώνω [ksanafortono] reload.

ξανθίζω [ksantheezo] become fairer.

ξανθομάλλης [ksanthomalees] fair-haired.

ξανθός [ksanthos] blond, fair, light || (στάχυς) yellow, golden.

ξάνοιγμα, τό [ksaneeγma] clearing up, brightening || launching out.

ξανοίγομαι [ksaneeγome] confide one's secrets || spend freely.

ξανοίγω [ksaneeγo] (μεταφ) look, see || clear up.

ξάπλα, ἡ [ksapla] sprawling around || lying down.

ξάπλωμα, τό [ksaploma] lying down || stretching out, spreading.

ξαπλώνομαι [ksaplonome] spread || lie down.

ξαπλώνω [ksaplono] spread out || lie down.

ξαπλωτός [ksaplotos] reclining, lying down.

ξαποσταίνω [ksaposteno] rest, relax.

ξαποστέλνω [ksapostelno] send off, forward || dismiss.

ξασπρίζω [ksaspreezo] whiten || blanch, pale, fade.

ξάστερα [ksastera] frankly, flatly, categorically.

ξάστερος [ksasteros] cloudless, bright || (μεταφ) lucid, clear.

ξαφνιάζομαι [ksafneeazome] be taken by surprise, be frightened.

ξαφνίζω [ksafneeazo] startle, surprise, frighten, scare.

ξαφνικά [ksafneeka] all of a sudden.

ξαφνικό, τό [ksafneeko] surprise || accident, mishap.

ξαφνικός [ksafneekos] unexpected.

ξάφνου [ksafnou] βλ ξαφνικά.

ξαφρίζω [ksafreezo] skim || (μεταφ) steal.

ξάφρισμα, τό [ksafreesma] skimming || frothing.

ξεβάφω [ksevafo] fade || lose colour, discolour.

ξεβγάζω [ksevγazo] wash out || (προπέμπω) show out, get rid of.

ξεβρακώνω [ksevrakono] take off the trousers.

ξεβράκωτος [ksevrakotos] trouserless || (μεταφ) penniless.

ξεβρωμίζω [ksevromeezo] disinfect || clean, remove the dirt.

ξεγελῶ [kseγelo] cheat, dupe, deceive.

ξεγεννῶ [kseyeno] deliver a child be delivered of.

ξεγνοιάζω [kseyneeazo] be free from care.

ξεγράφω [kseyrafo] efface, strike out (μεταφ) wipe out | write off.

ξεδιαλέγω [ksedeealeyo] select, choose, sort.

ξεδιαλύνω [ksedeealeeno] get to the bottom of, unravel.

ξεδιάντροπος [ksedeeantropos] immodest, brazen.

ξεδιπλώνω [ksedeeplono] unfurl, open out, spread.

ξεδιψῶ [ksedeepso] quench one's thirst refresh.

ξεθαρρεύω [ksetharevo] become too bold.

ξεθεώνω [ksetheono] wear out, exhaust, harass, worry.

ξεθυμαίνω [ksetheemeno] escape, leak out | (μεταφ) calm down, abate.

ξεθωριάζω [ksethoreeazo] fade lose colour, discolour.

ξεκαθαρίζω [ksekathareezo] liquidate, settle accounts | elucidate | kill off.

ξεκάνω [ksekano] sell off | kill, exterminate.

ξεκαρδίζομαι [ksekardeezome] burst out laughing.

ξεκάρφωτος [ksekarfotos] (μεταφ) unconnected, irrelevant.

ξεκινῶ [ksekeeno] set off, start, depart | drive off.

ξεκοκκαλίζω [ksekokaleezo] eat to the bone | (μεταφ) spend foolishly.

ξεκομμένα [ksekomena] to the point, frankly.

ξεκομμένη [ksekomenee]: τιμή ~ fixed price.

ξεκούμπωτος [ksekoumbotos] unfastened, unbuttoned.

ξεκουμπώνω [ksekoumbono] unbutton, unfasten.

ξεκουράζομαι [ksekourazome] relax, rest.

ξεκουράζω [ksekourazo] rest, relieve, refresh, repose.

ξεκουφαίνω [ksekoufeno] deafen, stun.

ξελιγωμένος [kseleeyomenos] be hungry for, hunger for.

ξελιγώνω [kseleeyono] (μεταφ) wear o.s. out, tire.

ξελογιάζω [kseloyeeazo] seduce, lead astray, fascinate.

ξεμαλλιασμένος [ksemaleeasmenos] dishevelled.

ξεμοναχιάζω [ksemonaheeazo] take aside.

ξεμπαρκάρω [ksembarkaro] land || unload.

ξεμπερδεύω [ksemberdevo] unravel, disentangle || get clear of, get rid of.

ξεμπλέκω [ksembleko] free o.s. || ~ ἀπό get free of.

ξεμυαλίζω [ksemeealeezo] infatuate, turn the head of, lead astray.

ξένα, τά [ksena] πλ foreign parts.

ξεναγός, ὁ, ἡ [ksenayos] tourist guide.

ξενητειά, ἡ [kseneetia] foreign parts' foreign country.

ξενητεύομαι [kseneetevome] live abroad.

ξενίζομαι [kseneezome] be astonished.

ξενίζω [kseneezo] surprise, astonish.

ξενικός [kseneekos] foreign, alien, outlandish.

ξεν(ν)οιάζω [kseneeazo] be free from cares

ξενοδοχεῖον, τό [ksenoδoheeon] hotel.

ξενοδόχος, ὁ [ksenoδohos] hotelie, innkeeper.

ξενοικιάζομαι [kseneekeeazome] become vacant.

ξένος [ksenos] foreign, strange, unfamiliar (οὐς) ὁ ~ foreigner, stranger | visitor

ξενοφοβία, ἡ [ksenofoveea] xenophobia.

ξενόφωνος [ksenofonos] foreign-speaking.

ξεντύνω [ksenteeno] undress, disrobe.

ξενυχτῶ [kseneehto] stay up late, stay out all night.

ξενών, ὁ [ksenon] spare room, guest room.

ξεπαγιάζω [ksepayeeazo] freeze | get frozen.

ξεπαστρεύω [ksepastrevo] exterminate, wipe out.

ξεπατώνω [ksepatono] (μεταφ) exhaust tire, overwork.

ξεπερασμένος [kseperasn enos] out-of-date old-fashioned.

ξεπερνῶ [kseperno] surpass, overtake (σέ δρόμο) outrun | (σέ ὕψος) be taller.

ξεπεσμός, ὁ [ksepesmos] decay, decline | (τιμῶν) fall || (νομίσματος) depreciation.

ξεπετιέμαι [ksepetieme] jump up suddenly. shoot up.

ξεπέφτω [ksepefto] reduce, abate |, (ἐπί τιμῶν) fall || (μεταφ) fall into disrepute.

ξεπηδῶ [ksepeeδo] jump out suddenly.

ξεπλένω [ksepleno] rinse.

ξεπληρώνω [kspleerono] pay off, dis charge (a debt).

ξέπλυμα, τό [ksepleema] rinsing.

ξεπούλημα, τό [ksepouleema] sale, sellout liquidation || (US) fire sale.

ξεπουλῶ [ksepoulo] sell off | sell out liquidate.

ξεπροβοδίζω [kseprovoδeezo] escort off say goodbye to.

ξέρα, ἡ [ksera] (θαλάσσης) rock, reef | (καιροῦ) drought, dryness.

ξεραΐλα, ἡ [kseraeela] aridity, dryness drought.

ξεραίνομαι [kserenome] dry up, wither get parched.

ξεραίνω [ksereno] dry up | parch, bake (φυτά) wither.

ξερακιανός [kserakeeanos] thin, lean skinny.

ξέρασμα, τό [kserasma] vomiting.

ξερνῶ [kserno] vomit, bring up || belch out

ξερόβηχας, ὁ [kseroveehas] dry cough

ξεροβούνι, τό [kserovounee] bare moun tain, naked mountain.

ξεροκαταπίνω [kserokatapeeno] swallow with embarrassment.

ξεροκέφαλος [kserokefalos] thickheaded ‖ obstinate, stubborn.

ξερονήσι, τό [kseroneesee] barren island, desert island.

ξερός [kseros] arid, dry, barren ‖ (γλῶσσα) parched ‖ (ὕφος) curt, snappish ‖ ἔμεινε ~ he was stumped ‖ he dropped dead ‖ ἔπεσε ~ στόν ὕπνο he dropped off to sleep.

ξερ(ρ)ιζώνω [ksereezono] pull up, uproot ‖ root out, wipe out.

ξέρω [ksero] know how to, understand, be aware of.

ξεσηκώνω [kseseekono] rouse, excite ‖ (σχέδιο) transfer, copy.

ξεσκάζω [kseskazo] refresh o.s., relax.

ξεσκεπάζω [kseskepazo] unveil, uncover ‖ reveal, disclose, let out.

ξεσκίζω [kseskeezo] rip up.

ξεσκονίζω [kseskoneezo] dust, give a dusting to.

ξεσκονιστήρι, τό [kseskoneesteeree] feather duster.

ξεσκονόπανο, τό [kseskonopano] duster, dust rag.

ξεσκούφωτος [kseskoufotos] bare-headed.

ξεσπάζω [ksespazo] (μεταφ) burst into, burst out.

ξεσπαθώνω [ksespathono] unsheathe one's sword.

ξεστομίζω [ksestomeezo] utter, launch, hurl.

ξεστραβώνω [ksestravono] straighten out ‖ become straight.

ξεστρώνω [ksestrono] take up, remove ‖ (τραπέζι) clear away.

ξέστρωτος [ksestrotos] unmade ‖ unpaved.

ξεσχίζω [kssheezo] tear to pieces, lacerate.

ξετινάζω [kseteenazo] toss, shake, beat ‖ (μεταφ) reduce to poverty.

ξετρελλαίνω [ksetreleno] drive mad, bewilder ‖ (ἀπό ἔρωτα) bewitch.

ξετρυπώνω [ksetreepono] appear suddenly, crop up.

ξετσίπωτος [ksetseepotos] shameless.

ξεύρω [ksevro] βλ ξέρω.

ξεφαντώνω [ksefantono] live fast, feast, revel.

ξεφεύγω [ksefevgo] elude ‖ slip out.

ξεφλουδίζω [ksefloudeezo] peel ‖ pare ‖ shell ‖ (τό δέρμα) lose the skin.

ξεφορτώνομαι [ksefortonome] get rid of, shake off.

ξεφορτώνω [ksefortono] unload ‖ (μεταφ) get rid of.

ξεφτέρι, τό [ksefteree] sharp person, witty person.

ξεφτίζω [ksefteezo] fray out ‖ (νῆμα) pull out, unweave.

ξεφυλλίζω [ksefeeleezo] skim over, run through ‖ strip the leaves, plück.

ξεφυτρώνω [ksefeetrono] sprout, shoot up ‖ appear suddenly.

ξεφωνητό, τό [ksefoneeto] yell, shout, outcry, scream.

ξεφωνίζω [ksefoneezo] shout, bawl, yell, scream.

ξεχαρβαλωμένος [kseharvalomenos] shaky, loose, falling apart.

ξεχασμένος [ksehasmenos] forgotten.

ξεχειλίζω [kseheeleezo] overflow, run over.

ξεχειμωνιάζω [kseheemoneeazo] pass the winter, winter.

ξεχνῶ [ksehno] forget, leave out, neglect.

ξεχρεώνω [ksehreono] pay up, discharge ‖ settle, fulfil.

ξεχύνομαι [kseheenome] overflow.

ξεχύνω [kseheeno] pour out, overflow.

ξέχωρα [ksehora] apart, separately ‖ ~ ἀπό apart from.

ξεχωρίζω [ksehoreezo] separate ‖ single out ‖ distinguish, discern ‖ make one's mark.

ξεχωριστά [ksehoreesta] separately.

ξεχωριστός [ksehoreestos] separate ‖ distinct, peculiar ‖ distinguished, exceptional.

ξεψυχῶ [ksepseeho] die, expire, give up the ghost.

ξέω [kseo] scratch, scrape ‖ erase.

ξηλώνω [kseelono] take apart, unstitch.

ξημερώματα [kseemeromata] πλ daybreak, dawn.

ξημερώνομαι [kseemeronome] stay awake till morning.

ξηρά, ἡ [kseera] dry land, mainland.

ξηραίνομαι [kseerenome] dry up, get parched, wither.

ξηραίνω [kseereno] dry, drain.

ξηραντήριον, τό [kseeranteereeon] drier.

ξηρασία, ἡ [kseeraseea] aridity ‖ drought.

ξηροί [kseeree]: ~ καρποί πλ dried fruit and nuts.

ξῖ, τό [ksee] the letter Ξ.

ξινάρι, τό [kseenaree] pickaxe.

ξινίζω [kseeneezo] turn sour, get sour.

ξινίλα, ἡ [kseeneela] bitterness, acidity, tartness, sharpness.

ξινό, τό [kseeno] citric acid.

ξινός [kseenos] sour, acid, sharp ‖ (ἐπί φρούτων) unripe, green.

ξιππασμένος [kseepasmenos] vain, conceited.

ξιππάζω [kseepazo] frighten ‖ impress.

ξιφασκία, ἡ [kseefaskia] fencing, swordplay.

ξιφίας, ὁ [kseefeeas] swordfish.

ξιφολόγχη, ἡ [kseefolonghee] bayonet.

ξιφομαχῶ [kseefomaho] fence.

ξίφος, τό [kseefos] sword ‖ (ξιφομαχίας) foil.

ξόβεργα, ἡ [ksoverga] lime twig.

ξοδεύομαι [ksodevome] spend, incur expenses.

ξοδεύω [ksoðevo] spend, use up, consume, expend.

ξόμπλι, τό [ksomblee] pattern for embroidery.

ξόρκι, τό [ksorkee] exorcism || entreaty.

ξουρίζω [ksoureezo] βλ ξυρίζω.

ξύγκι, τό [kseengee] fat, lard, grease, tallow.

ξυδάτος [kseeðatos] pickled.

ξύδι, τό [kseeðee] vinegar.

ξυλάδικο, τό [kseelaðeeko] timberyard, woodyard.

ξυλάνθραξ, ό [kseelanthraks] charcoal.

ξυλεία, ή [kseeleea] timber, lumber.

ξύλινος [kseeleenos] wooden, wood.

ξύλο, τό [kseelo] wood || τρώω ~ receive a beating || έπεσε ~ there was a fight.

ξυλογράφημα, τό [kseeloγrafeema] woodcut, wood engraving.

ξυλοκάρβουνο, τό [kseelokarvouno] charcoal.

ξυλοκέρατο, τό [kseelokerato] carob.

ξυλοκόπος, ό [kseelokopos] woodcutter, lumberjack.

ξυλοκοπῶ [kseelokopo] thrash, beat soundly.

ξυλοκρέββατο, τό [kseelokrevato] wooden bedstead || (μεταφ) coffin.

ξυλοπόδαρο, τό [kseelopoðaro] stilt.

ξυλοστάτης, ό [kseelostatees] jamb.

ξυλουργική, ή [kseelourγeekee] joinery, carpentry.

ξυλουργός, ό [kseelourγos] joiner, carpenter.

ξυλοφορτώνω [kseelofortono] thrash, leather, lick.

ξύνομαι [kseenome] scratch (o.s.).

ξύνω [kseeno] scratch, scrape || (μολύβι) sharpen || scrape off.

ξύπνημα, τό [kseepneema] awakening, waking up.

ξυπνητήρι, τό [kseepneeteeree] alarm clock.

ξύπνιος [kseepneeos] wakeful, awake || (μεταφ) alert, clever, intelligent.

ξυπνῶ [kseepno] wake up, rouse.

ξυπόλυτος [kseepoleetos] barefooted, shoeless.

ξυράφι, τό [kseerafee] razor.

ξυραφάκι, τό [kseerafakee] razor blade.

ξυρίζομαι [kseereezome] shave, get shaved, have a shave.

ξυρίζω [kseereezo] shave.

ξύρισμα, τό [kseereesma] shave, shaving.

ξυριστική [kseereesteekee]: ~ μηχανή safety razor.

ξύσιμο, τό [kseeseemo] scratching, scraping || rubbing, erasing || sharpening.

ξυστήρ, ό [kseesteer] βλ ξύστρα.

ξυστός [kseestos] grated, scratched.

ξύστρα, ή [kseestra] grater, scraper, rasp || pencil sharpener.

ξύω [kseeo] βλ ξύνω.

ξωκκλήσι, τό [ksokleesee] country chapel.

ξωτικιά, ή [ksoteekia] fairy, sprite.

ξωτικό, τό [ksoteeko] ghost, spirit, goblin

ξώφυλλο, τό [ksofeelo] book cover || (παραθύρου) outside shutter.

Ο, ο

ό [o] the.

όασις [oasees] oasis.

όβελίας, ό [oveleeas] lamb on the spit.

όβελίσκος, ό [oveleeskos] small spit || (στήλη) obelisk.

όβίδα, ή [oveeða] shell.

όβίς, ή [ovees] βλ όβίδα.

όβολός, ό [ovolos] mite, contribution.

ογδοήκοντα [oγðoeekonta] eighty.

ογδοηκοστός [oγðoeekostos] eightieth.

ογδοντάρης, ό [oγðontarees] octogenarian

όγδοος [oγðoos] eighth.

ογκηθμός, ό [ongeethmos] braying.

ογκόλιθος, ό [ongoleethos] block of stone

όγκος, ό [ongos] volume, mass, bulk, lump || (ιατρ) tumour.

όγκούμαι [ongoume] swell, grow fatter || (μεταφ) increase, swell.

όγκώδης [ongoðees] voluminous, massive || (άτομον) stout, portly.

όδαλίσκη, ή [oðaleeskee] odalisque.

όδε [oðe] this.

όδεύω [oðevo] walk, tramp, trudge || accompany || (πρός) proceed, advance.

όδηγητής, ό [oðeeγeetees] guide.

όδηγία, ή [oðeeγeea] direction, guidance || instruction, directions, orders.

όδηγός, ό [oðeeγos] guide, conductor || (αύτοκινήτου) driver, chauffeur.

όδηγῶ [oðeeγo] guide, lead || (αύτοκίνητον κτλ) drive || show how to, instruct.

όδογέφυρα, ή [oðoγefeera] viaduct.

όδοιπορία, ή [oðeeporeea] walk, journey || march.

όδοιπορικά, τά [oðeeporeeka] πλ: ~ έξοδα travelling expenses.

όδοιπόρος, ό, ή [oðeeporos] traveller, voyager.

όδοιπορῶ [oðeeporo] walk, tramp || march || travel.

όδοκαθαριστής, ό [oðokathareestees] street sweeper.

όδόμετρον, τό [oðometron] pedometer.

όδονταλγία, ή [oðontalγeea] toothache.

όδοντιατρεῖον, τό [oðonteeatreeon] dentist's surgery, dental clinic.

όδοντιατρική, ή [oðonteeatreekee] dentistry.

όδοντίατρος, ό, ή [oðonteeatros] dentist.

όδοντόβουρτσα, ή [oðontovourtsa] toothbrush.

όδοντογλυφίδα, ή [oðontoγleefeeða] toothpick.

όδοντόκονις, ή [oðontokonees] dentifrice, tooth powder.

όδοντόπονος, ὁ [odontoponos] toothache.
όδοντοστοιχία, ἡ [odontosteeheea] (set of) false teeth.
όδοντόφωνος [odontofonos] (γραμμ) dental.
όδοντωτός [odontotos] toothed, jagged, cogged ‖ ~ σιδηρόδρομος funicular railway.
όδοποιΐα, ἡ [odopieea] road construction, roadmaking.
όδός, ἡ [odos] street ‖ (εὐρεῖα) main street, thoroughfare ‖ (ἐθνική) state highway ‖ (ἐμπορική) trade route ‖ καθ' ὁδόν on the way, along the road.
όδόστρωμα, τό [odostroma] road surface.
όδοστρωτήρ, ὁ [odostroteer] steamroller.
όδούς [odous] βλ δόντι.
όδόφραγμα, τό [odofrayma] barricade, roadblock, barrier.
όδύνη, ἡ [odeenee] pain, suffering ‖ (ἠθική) grief ‖ affliction.
όδυνηρός [odeeneeros] (πληγή) painful ‖ (μέρος) sore ‖ (θέαμα) harrowing.
όδυρμός, ὁ [odeermos] lamentation, wailing.
όδύρομαι [odeerome] lament, complain, moan.
όζον, τό [ozon] ozone.
όζος, ὁ [ozos] knot ‖ (τῶν δακτύλων) knuckles.
όζώδης [ozodees] knotty, gnarled.
όθεν [othen] whence, thence, then, therefore.
όθενδήποτε [othendeepote] from any place, from anywhere.
όθόνη, ἡ [othonee] linen ‖ (τραπέζης) table linen ‖ (κλίνης) linen sheet ‖ (κινηματογράφου) screen.
'Οθωμανός, ὁ [othomanos] Ottoman.
οἰακίζω [eeakeezo] steer, pilot.
οἴαξ, ὁ [eeaks] tiller, helm.
οἴδημα, τό [eedeema] swelling.
οἴκαδε [eekade] at home ‖ homeward.
οἰκειοθελῶς [eekeeothelos] (ὑπακούω) voluntarily ‖ (κάνω κάτι) purposely, wilfully.
οἰκειοποίησις, ἡ [eekeeopieesees] appropriation.
οἰκειοποιοῦμαι [eekeeopeeoume] appropriate to o.s., usurp.
οἰκεῖος [eekeeos] intimate, familiar ‖ sociable, affable ‖ οἱ οἰκεῖοι relatives, close relations.
οἰκειότης, ἡ [eekeeotees] familiarity, closeness.
οἰκείως [eekeeos] intimately, closely.
οἴκημα, τό [eekeema] dwelling, lodging, habitation.
οἴκησις, ἡ [eekeesees] inhabiting, habitation.
οἰκία, ἡ [eekeea] house, home.
οἰκιακός [eekeeakos] domestic, home ‖ (ζῷο) domesticated.
οἰκίζω [eekeezo] inhabit, colonize, settle.
οἰκίσκος, ὁ [eekeeskos] cottage ‖ (σκύλου)

dog kennel ‖ (ξυλοκόπου) cabin, hut ‖ (φύλακος) lodge.
οἰκισμός, ὁ [eekeesmos] settling, colonizing.
οἰκιστής, ὁ [eekeestees] settler, colonist.
οἰκογένεια, ἡ [eekoyeneea] family.
οἰκογενειακός [eekoyeneeakos] of the family.
οἰκογενειακῶς [eekoyeneeakos] with the entire family.
οἰκοδέσποινα, ἡ [eekodespeena] lady of the house, hostess.
οἰκοδεσπότης, ὁ [eekodespotees] master of the house, host.
οἰκοδομή, ἡ [eekodomee] construction, act of building ‖ building under construction.
οἰκοδόμημα, τό [eekodomeema] building, structure.
οἰκοδόμησις, ἡ [eekodomeesees] construction, building, erection.
οἰκοδομική, ἡ [eekodomeekee] building.
οἰκοδομικός [eekodomeekos] constructive.
οἰκοδομῶ [eekodomo] build, construct, raise.
οἴκοθεν [eekothen]: ~ ἐννοεῖται it is obvious.
οἴκοι [eekee] at home.
οἰκοκυρά [eekokeera] βλ νοικοκυρά.
οἰκοκύρης [eekokeerees] βλ νοικοκύρης.
οἰκονομία, ἡ [eekonomeea] economy, husbandry, thrift ‖ saving.
οἰκονομικά, τά [eekonomeeka] πλ finances ‖ (ἐπιρ) reasonably, cheaply.
οἰκονομικός [eekonomeekos] economic, financial ‖ (φθηνά) reasonable, cheap.
οἰκονόμος, ὁ, ἡ [eekonomos] steward, stewardess ‖ (μεταφ) thrifty person.
οἰκονομῶ [eekonomo] save, economize ‖ find, get hold of ‖ τά ~ make ends meet, make money.
οἰκόπεδον, τό [eekopedon] building site, plot.
οἴκον [eekon]: κατ' ~ at home.
οἶκος, ὁ [eekos] house ‖ business house.
οἰκοτροφεῖον, τό [eekotrofeeon] boarding school.
οἰκότροφος, ὁ, ἡ [eekotrofos] boarder.
οἰκουμένη, ἡ [eekoumenee] world, universe.
οἰκουμενική [eekoumeneekee]: ~ κυβέρνησις coalition government.
οἰκουρῶ [eekouro] be confined by illness, keep indoors.
οἰκτείρω [eekteero] feel compassion for, pity ‖ despise, scorn.
οἶκτος, τό [eektos] compassion, pity ‖ contempt, scorn.
οἰκτρός [eektros] deplorable ‖ wretched, miserable.
οἴμοι [eemee] (ἐπιφ) alas!, woe is me!
οἰμωγή, ἡ [eemoyee] lamentation, wailing, moaning.
οἰνόπνευμα, τό [eenopnevma] alcohol ‖ οἰνοπνευματώδης alcoholic.
οἶνος, ὁ [eenos] wine.

οἶον [eeon] such as, for example.
οἰονεί [eeonee] as if, as it were.
οἶος [eeos] such as, who, which, what.
οἱοσδήποτε [eeosdeepote] any(body) ‖ any kind of, whoever, whichever.
οἰσοφάγος, ὁ [eesofagos] oesophagus.
οἶστρος, ὁ [eestros] gadfly ‖ (μεταφ) inspiration, goading.
οἰωνός, ὁ [eeonos] omen, presage, portent.
ὀκνηρός [okneeros] lazy, idle, sluggish.
ὀκνός [oknos] nonchalant, languid, slack.
ὀκρίβας, ὁ [okreevas] easel.
ὀκτάγωνος [oktagonos] octagonal.
ὀκτακόσιοι [oktakosiee] eight hundred.
ὀκταπόδι, τό [oktapodee] octopus.
ὀκτώ [octo] eight.
Ὀκτώβριος, ὁ [oktovreeos] October.
ὅλα, τά [ola] πλ everything ‖ ~ κι’ ~ anything else but.
ὁλάκερα [olakera] entirely, completely, wholly.
ὁλάκερος [olakeros] whole, entire, total, complete.
ὄλβιος [olveeos] happy, blissful ‖ wealthy, rich.
ὀλέθριος [oletlreeos] ominous, disastrous, destructive.
ὄλεθρος, ὁ [olethros] calamity, destruction, ruin.
ὁλημερίς [oleemerees] all day long.
ὀλιγάκις [oleeyakees] seldom, rarely.
ὀλιγάριθμος [oleeyareethmos] few in number, a few.
ὀλιγαρκής [oleeyarkees] temperate, frugal, moderate.
ὀλιγαρχία, ἡ [oleeyarheea] oligarchy.
ὀλίγιστος [oleeyeestos] very little, tiny.
ὀλιγόλογος [oleeyologos] concise, succinct ‖ taciturn.
ὀλίγον [oleeyon] (a) little.
ὀλίγος [oleeyos] short, a little, a few ‖ ὀλίγον κατ’ ὀλίγον gradually ‖ παρ’ ὀλίγον νά nearly, almost.
ὀλιγοστεύω [oleeyostevo] diminish, decrease, lessen.
ὀλιγοστός [oleeyostos] scarcely enough, scanty, inconsiderable.
ὀλιγοψυχία, ἡ [oleeyopseeheea] timidity.
ὀλιγωρία, ἡ [oleeyoreea] negligence, neglect, indifference.
ὁλικός [oleekos] total, whole, complete.
ὁλικῶς [oleekos] totally, utterly.
ὀλισθαίνω [oleestheno] slip, slide ‖ (μεταφ) lapse into, slip into.
ὀλίσθημα, τό [oleestheema] slip(ping), slide ‖ mistake, fault.
ὀλισθηρός [oleestheeros] slippery, greasy.
ὁλκή, ἡ [olkee] attraction, pull, weight ‖ calibre, bore.
ὄλμος, ὁ [olmos] mortar.
ὅλο [olo] all ‖ ~ καί (περισσότερο) more and more, always.
ὁλογράφως [oloyrafos] written in full.

ὁλόγυρα [oloyeera] all round, in a circle.
ὁλοέν(α) [oloen(a)] incessantly, constantly.
ὁλοήμερος [oloeemeros] lasting a whole day.
ὁλοΐδιος [oloeedeeos] the spitting image.
ὁλόΐσιος [oloeeseeos] direct, straight ‖ upright.
ὁλοκαύτωμα, τό [olokavtoma] holocaust ‖ sacrifice.
ὁλόκληρος [olokleeros] entire, whole, full, complete.
ὁλοκληρῶ [olokleero] complete, finish , (μαθημ) integrate.
ὁλοκληρωτικός [olokleeroteekos] full, entire, complete ‖ totalitarian ‖ (μαθημ) integral.
ὀλολύζω [ololeezo] lament, howl, bewail.
ὁλόμαλλος [olomalos] all wool, pure wool.
ὁλομέλεια, ἡ [olomeleea] total membership, all members present.
ὁλομερής [olomerees] entire, whole, complete.
ὁλομόναχος [olomonahos] quite alone.
ὁλονέν [olonen] always.
ὁλονυχτίς [oloneehtees] the whole night long.
ὁλόρθος [olorthos] straight, upright, standing.
ὅλος [olos] all, whole ‖ ὅλοι everyone, everybody ‖ ὅλοι μας all of us, altogether ‖ ὅλα ὅλα altogether, the total.
ὁλοσχερής [olosherees] utter complete, full, entire.
ὁλοταχῶς [olotahos] at full speed, at top speed.
ὁλότελα [olotela] entirely, altogether, completely.
ὁλότης, ἡ [olotees] entirety, totality.
ὁλοῦθε [olouthe] from all sides, everywhere, from all directions.
ὁλοφάνερος [olofaneros] obvious, plain, clear.
ὁλοφύρομαι [olofeerome] βλ ὀλολύζω.
ὁλόχαρος [oloharos] joyful, happy.
ὁλοχρονίς [olohronees] throughout the year.
ὁλόχρυσος [olohreesos] all gold, solid gold.
ὁλόψυχος [olopseehos] wholeheartedly.
Ὀλυμπιακός [oleembeeakos] Olympic.
ὅλως [olos] wholly, altogether, totally ‖ ~ διόλου completely, wholly ‖ ~ ὑμέτερος yours truly.
ὁμάδα, ἡ [omada] βλ ὁμάς.
ὁμάδι [omadee] together.
ὁμαδικός [omadeekos] collective, en masse.
ὁμαδικῶς [omadeekos] in a body, collectively.
ὁμαλός [omalos] even ‖ level ‖ smooth, regular ‖ (βίος) uneventful ‖ flat.
ὁμαλότης, ἡ [omalotees] regularity, smoothness, evenness.
ὁμάς, ἡ [omas] group, company, band, gang ‖ (ἀθλητική) team.

ὄμβριος [omvreeos] of rain.
ὀμελέτα, ἡ [omeleta] omelet.
ὁμήγυρις, ἡ [omeeyeerees] party, meeting, assembly, circle.
ὁμῆλιξ, ὁ, ἡ [omeeleeks] person of the same age.
ὄμηρος, ὁ [omeeros] hostage.
ὄμικρον, τό [omeekron] the letter Ο.
ὁμιλητής, ὁ [omeeleetees] speaker, lecturer.
ὁμιλητικός [omeeleeteekos] sociable, affable.
ὁμιλία, ἡ [omeeleea] talk, conversation || speech, lecture.
ὅμιλος, ὁ [omeelos] company, group, club
ὁμιλῶ [omeelo] speak, talk.
ὁμίχλη, ἡ [omeehlee] fog, mist.
ὁμιχλώδης [omeehlodees] foggy, misty.
ὄμμα, τό [oma] eye, look.
ὀμματοϋάλια, τά [omatoeealeea] πλ spectacles.
ὀμνύω [omneeo] swear, affirm.
ὀμοβροντία, ἡ [omovronteea] salvo, volley.
ὁμογένεια, ἡ [omoyeneea] homogeneity || fellow Greeks.
ὁμογενής [omoyenees] similar || of the same race || expatriate Greek.
ὁμογνώμων [omoynomon] of the same opinion.
ὁμοεθνής [omoethnees] of the same nation, fellow (countryman).
ὁμοειδής [omoeedees] of the same kind || uniform, similar.
ὁμόθρησκος [omothreeskos] of the same religion.
ὁμόθυμος [omotheemos] unanimous.
ὁμοιάζω [omeeazo] resemble, look like || be like.
ὁμοιογενής [omeeoyenees] homogeneous || uniform.
ὁμοιοκαταληξία, ἡ [omeeokataleekseea] rhyme, rime.
ὁμοιόμορφος [omeeomorfos] uniform, unvarying.
ὁμοιοπαθής [omeeopathees] fellow (sufferer), in the same boat.
ὅμοιος [omeeos] similar, (a)like, same, in conformity with.
ὁμοιότης, ἡ [omeeotees] resemblance, similarity, likeness.
ὁμοιοτρόπως [omeeotropos] likewise, similarly.
ὁμοίωμα, τό [omeeoma] likeness, image || effigy.
ὁμοιωματικά, τά [omeeomateeka] πλ ditto marks.
ὁμόκεντρος [omokentros] concentric.
ὁμολογία, ἡ [omoloyeea] confession, avowal, acknowledgement, admission || (οἶκον) bond, share.
ὁμόλογον, τό [omoloyon] bond, promissory note, obligation.
ὁμολογουμένως [omoloyoumenos] avowedly, admittedly.

ὁμολογῶ [omoloyo] acknowledge, confess, admit.
ὁμόνοια, ἡ [omoneea] concord, agreement accord, peace.
ὁμόρρυθμος [omoreethmos]: ~ ἑταιρεία partnership (in business).
ὁμορφαίνω [omorfeno] beautify || become beautiful.
ὁμορφιά, ἡ [omorfia] beauty, handsomeness.
ὄμορφος [omorfos] handsome, beautiful nice.
ὁμοσπονδία, ἡ [omospondeea] federation, confederacy.
ὁμότιμος [omoteemos]: ~ καθηγητής professor emeritus.
ὁμοῦ [omou] together, jointly, in one lot.
ὁμόφρων [omofron] having the same ideas, thinking alike.
ὁμοφυλοφιλία, ἡ [omofeelofeeleea] homosexuality.
ὁμοφωνία, ἡ [omofoneea] unanimity.
ὁμόφωνος [omofonos] unanimous.
ὀμπρέλλα, ἡ [ombrella] umbrella.
ὀμφαλός, ὁ [omfalos] navel || (μεταφ) centre.
ὁμώνυμος [omoneemos] having the same name.
ὅμως [omos] yet, nevertheless, but, however.
ὄν, τό [on] creature, being.
ὄναγρος, ὁ [onayros] wild ass.
ὄναρ, τό [onar] dream, vision.
ὄνειδος, τό [oneedos] disgrace, shame, infamy || blame, reproach.
ὀνειρεύομαι [oneerevome] dream, have visions.
ὀνειροκρίτης, ὁ [oneerokreetees] dream interpreter.
ὄνειρον, τό [oneeron] dream || vision, imagination.
ὀνειροπολῶ [oneeropolo] daydream || dream of, build castles in the air.
ὀνειρώδης [oneerodees] dreamlike, fantastic || grand.
ὀνηλάτης, ὁ [oneelatees] donkey driver.
ὄνομα, τό [onoma] name || (γραμμ) noun || fame, reputation || βγάζω ~ gain renown, become famous || ~ καί πρᾶμα in every sense || ὀνόματι by name of.
ὀνομάζω [onomazo] name, call || appoint.
ὀνομασία, ἡ [onomasea] name, appellation || designation, appointment.
ὀνομαστί [onomastee] by name, namely.
ὀνομαστική, ἡ [onomasteekee] (γραμμ) nominative (case) || ~ ἑορτή name day.
ὀνομαστικός [onomasteekos] nominal.
ὀνομαστός [onomastos] famous, famed, celebrated.
ὀνοματεπώνυμον, τό [onomateponeemon] name and surname.
ὀνοματολογία, ἡ [onomatoloyeea] nomenclature, terminology.

όνος, ό, ή [onos] ass, donkey.

όντότης, ή [ontotees] entity, being ‖ personality.

όντως [ontos] really, truly, in truth.

όνυξ, ό [oneeks] nail ‖ (ζώου) claw ‖ (όρνέου) talon ‖ (λίθος) onyx.

όξαποδώ, ό [oksapodo] the devil, satan.

όξεία, ή [okseea] (γραμμ) acute accent.

όξείδιον, τό [okseedeeon] oxide.

όξείδωσις, ή [okseedosees] oxidation corrosion, rusting.

όξικός [okseekos] acetic.

όξινος [okseenos] sour, bitter, acid.

όξος, τό [oksos] vinegar.

όξύ, τό [oksee] acid.

όξυά, ή [oksia] beech tree ‖ beech.

όξυγονοκόλλησις, ή [okseeyonokoleesees] oxyacetylene welding.

όξυγόνον, τό [okseeyonon] oxygen.

όξυδέρκεια, ή [okseederkeea] perspicacity, acumen ‖ (μεταφ) discernment.

όξύθυμος [okseetheemos] irritable, touchy.

όξύνους [okseenous] sagacious, acute, keen, clever.

όξύνω [okseeno] sharpen, whet ‖ (τόν νοῦν) sharpen ‖ (αίσθήματα) stir up, arouse, provoke.

όξύς [oksees] sharp, pointed ‖ piercing, shrill ‖ (γεῦσις) sour, strong.

όξύτης, ή [okseetees] sharpness ‖ keenness, acuteness.

όξύφωνος, ό [okseefonos] (μουσ) tenor.

όξω [okso] βλ έξω.

όπαδός, ό, ή [opados] adherent, partisan, supporter.

όπερ [oper] which, what.

όπερα, ή [opera] opera.

όπή, ή [opee] opening, aperture, hole, gap.

όπιον, τό [opeeon] opium.

όπισθεν [opeesthen] behind, in the rear ‖ κάνω ~ go backwards, put in reverse.

όπίσθιος [opeestheeos] hind, posterior, back.

όπισθογραφῶ [opeesthoyrafo] endorse (a cheque).

όπισθοδρομικός [opeesthodromeekos] retrogressive ‖ (στάς άπόψεις) reactionary.

όπισθοφυλακή, ή [opeesthofeelakee] rearguard.

όπισθοχώρησις, ή [opeesthohoreesees] retreat, withdrawal.

όπίσω [opeeso] behind, back ‖ again.

όπλα, τά [opla] πλ arms.

όπλή, ή [oplee] hoof.

όπλίζω [opleezo] arm ‖ (μεταφ) reinforce, strengthen.

όπλισμός, ό [opleesmos] armament, equipment ‖ (καλωδίου) sheathing.

όπλιταγωγόν [opleetayoyon] troopship.

όπλίτης, ό [opleetees] soldier.

όπλον, τό [oplon] arm, weapon ‖ rifle ‖ (άμύνης) branch of army.

όπλοπολυβόλον, τό [oplopoleevolon] light machine gun.

όπλοστάσιον, τό [oplostaseeon] arsenal, armoury.

όπλοφορία, ή [oploforeea] carrying of arms.

όπόθεν [opothen] whence, from where.

όποιος [opeeos] whoever, whichever ‖ ~ κι' whosoever, anybody.

όποιοσδήποτε [opeeosdeepote] whoever, whatsoever.

όποῖος [opeeos] of what kind ‖ ό ~ who, which.

όπόταν [opotan] whenever, when.

όπότε [opote] whenever, at any time.

όπότε [opote] at which time, when.

όπου [opou] where, wherever.

όποῦ [opou] he who ‖ whom, which.

όπουδήποτε [opoudeepote] wheresoever, wherever.

όπτασία, ή [optaseea] vision, apparition.

όπτική, ή [opteekee] optics.

όπτικός [opteekos] optic(al) ‖ (ούσ) optician.

όπτός [optos] roast, baked.

όπωρικά, τά [oporeeka] πλ fruit.

όπωροπωλεῖον [oporopoleeon] fruit market.

όπωροφόρος [oporoforos] bearing fruit, fruit-producing.

όπως [opos] as, like ‖ ~ ~ somehow or other, after a fashion ‖ (συνδ) in order that, so as.

όπωσδήποτε [oposdeepote] howsoever, anyway, without fail ‖ definitely.

όπωσοῦν [oposoun] somewhat, rather.

όραμα, τό [orama] vision ‖ ~ τίζομαι have visions, visualize.

όρασις, ή [orasees] sense of sight, vision.

όρατός [oratos] visible, perceptible.

όρατότης, ή [oratotees] visibility.

όργανικός [oryaneekos] organic.

όργανισμός, ό [oryaneesmos] organism ‖ organization.

όργανον, τό [oryanon] organ ‖ (μουσ) instrument ‖ implement, tool ‖ (κατασκοπείας) agent.

όργανώνω [oryanono] organize, constitute, form.

όργάνωσις, ή [oryanosees] organization, arranging.

όργασμός, ό [oryasmos] orgasm, heat ‖ (μεταφ) feverish activity.

όργή, ή [oryee] anger, rage ‖ νά πάρη ή ~ damn it!, damnation!

όργια, τά [oryeea] πλ orgies ‖ (μεταφ) corrupt practices ‖ όργιάζω revel, debauch.

όργίζω [oryeezo] anger, enrage, irritate.

όργίλος [oryeelos] irate, angry ‖ irascible, wrathful.

όργυιά, ή [oryia] fathom.

όργωμα, τό [oryoma] ploughing, tilling, tillage.

ὀργώνω [oryono] plough, till, furrow.

ὀρδή, ἡ [orðee] horde, host, rabble.

ὀρέγομαι [oreyome] envy, covet, desire.

ὀρειβασία, ἡ [oreevaseea] mountain climbing.

ὀρειβάτης, ὁ [oreevatees] mountain climber.

ὀρειβατικός [oreevateekos] of climbing, of mountaineering.

ὀρεινός [oreenos] mountainous, hilly ‖ of the mountains.

ὀρείχαλκος, ὁ [oreehalkos] brass, bronze.

ὀρεκτικόν, τό [orekteekon] appetizer, titbit ‖ drink.

ὀρεκτικός [orekteekos] appetizing, savoury ‖ tempting.

ὄρεξις, ἡ [oreksees] appetite ‖ desire, liking.

ὀρθά [ortha] right, rightly ‖ upright ‖ ~ κοφτά flatly, frankly.

ὀρθάνοιχτος [orthaneehtos] wide open.

ὄρθιος [ortheeos] on end, upright, erect, standing.

ὀρθογραφία, ἡ [orthoyrafeea] spelling, orthography ‖ dictation.

ὀρθογώνιον, τό [orthoyoneeon] rectangle.

ὀρθογώνιος [orthoyoneeos] right-angled ‖ rectangular.

ὀρθοδοξία, ἡ [orthoðokseea] orthodoxy.

ὀρθόδοξος [orthoðoksos] orthodox.

ὀρθολογισμός, ὁ [ortholoyeesmos] rationalism.

ὀρθοπεδική, ἡ [orthopeðeekee] orthopaedics.

ὀρθοποδῶ [orthopoðo] walk straight ‖ stand on sure ground, thrive.

ὀρθός [orthos] right ‖ correct ‖ proper ‖ upright, erect, standing.

ὀρθοστασία, ἡ [orthostaseea] standing.

ὀρθότης, ἡ [orthotees] accuracy ‖ soundness ‖ aptness.

ὄρθρος, ὁ [orthros] (ἐκκλ) matins ‖ dawn, daybreak.

ὀρθώνομαι [orthonome] rise, get up ‖ (ἄλογο) rear up.

ὀρθώνω [orthono] raise, pull up, lift up ‖ redress.

ὀρθῶς [orthos] βλ ὀρθά.

ὁριζόντιος [oreezonteeos] horizontal, level.

ὁρίζω [oreezo] mark, bound, delimit ‖ fix, settle, define ‖ rule, control, govern.

ὁρίστε [oreeste] I beg your pardon? ‖ come in, take a seat ‖ your pleasure, sir? ‖ καλῶς ὁρίσατε (ἐπιφ) welcome!

ὁρίζων, ὁ [oreezon] horizon.

ὅριον, τό [oreeon] boundary, limit, border ‖ (μεταφ) scope, boundary.

ὁρισμένος [oreesmenos] defined, fixed ‖ certain, special.

ὁρισμός, ὁ [oreesmos] designation, fixing ‖ definition ‖ order, instruction.

ὁριστική, ἡ [oreesteekee] (γραμμ) indicative (mood).

ὁριστικός [oreesteekos] definitive, final.

ὁρκίζομαι [orkeezome] swear, take the oath.

ὁρκίζω [orkeezo] put on oath, swear in.

ὅρκος, ὁ [orkos] oath ‖ vow.

ὁρκωμοσία, ἡ [orkomoseea] swearing (in).

ὁρκωτός [orkotos] sworn ‖ οἱ ὁρκωτοί the jury.

ὁρμαθός, ὁ [ormathos] string, chain, bunch.

ὁρμέμφυτον, τό [ormemfeeton] instinct.

ὁρμή, ἡ [ormee] vehemence ‖ impulse, impetus ‖ passion.

ὁρμητήριον, τό [ormeeteereeon] starting place ‖ motive.

ὁρμητικός [ormeeteekos] impetuous, hot-tempered, fiery.

ὁρμιά, ἡ [ormia] fishing line.

ὁρμόνη, ἡ [ormonee] hormone.

ὅρμος, ὁ [ormos] bay, inlet.

ὁρμῶ [ormo] dash, rush ‖ ~μαι be urged ‖ come from.

ὄρνεον, τό [orneon] bird of prey.

ὄρνιθα, ἡ [orneetha] hen, chicken, fowl.

ὀρνιθοσκαλίσματα, τά [orneethoskaleesmata] πλ scrawl, scribble.

ὀρνιθοτροφεῖον, τό [orneethotrofeeon] poultry farm.

ὀρνιθών, ὁ [orneethon] chicken coop, hen-house, hen roost.

ὄρνιο, τό [orneeo] bird of prey ‖ (μεταφ) dullard, dolt.

ὄρνις, ἡ [ornees] βλ ὄρνιθα.

ὁροθεσία, ἡ [orotheseea] fixing of boundaries.

ὁρολογία, ἡ [oroloyeea] terminology.

ὁροπέδιον, τό [oropeðeeon] plateau, table-land.

ὄρος, τό [oros] mountain.

ὅρος, ὁ [oros] term, condition, stipulation, proviso ‖ limit, end ‖ (ἐπιστημονικός) term, definition.

ὀρ(ρ)ός, ὁ [oros] serum.

ὀροσειρά, ἡ [oroseera] mountain range, mountain chain.

ὁρόσημον, τό [oroseemon] boundary mark, boundary stone.

ὀροφή, ἡ [orofee] ceiling, roof.

ὄροφος, ὁ [orofos] floor, storey.

ὀρτύκι, τό [orteekee] quail.

ὄρυγμα, τό [oreeyma] pit, trench, ditch, excavation.

ὄρυζα, ἡ [oreeza] rice.

ὀρυκτέλαιον, τό [oreekteleon] petroleum lubricant.

ὀρυκτολογία, ἡ [oreektoloyeea] mineralogy.

ὀρυκτόν, τό [oreekton] mineral, ore.

ὀρυκτός [oreektos] mineral, dug-up.

ὀρύσσω [oreeso] dig, excavate ‖ (φρέαρ) bore, sink.

ὀρυχεῖον, τό [oreeheeon] mine.

ὀρφανός [orfanos] orphan.

ὀρφανοτροφεῖον, τό [orfanotrofeeon] orphanage.

ὀρχήστρα, ἡ [orheestra] orchestra.

ὄρχις, ἡ [orhees] testicle ‖ (λουλούδι) orchid.

ὀρχοῦμαι [orhoume] dance.

ὀρῶ [oro] βλ βλέπω.

ὅς [os] who.

ὁσάκις [osakees] whenever, as often as.

ὅσιος [oseeos] holy, blessed ‖ saint.

ὀσμή, ἡ [osmee] odour, smell, scent.

ὅσο(ν) [oso(n)] as, as far as, as long as ‖ ~ γιά as for ‖ ~ ἀφορᾶ as regards, with regard to ‖ ἐφ᾽ ~ as long as, inasmuch as ‖ ~ νἄρϑη until he comes ‖ ~ νἄναι nevertheless.

ὁσονούπω [osonoupo] soon, in a while, before long.

ὅσος [osos] as much as, as many as, all.

ὄσπριον, τό [ospreeon] pulse (legume).

ὅστις [ostees] who(ever).

ὀστοῦν, τό [ostoun] bone.

ὀστρακιά, ἡ [ostrakia] scarlet fever.

ὄστρακον, τό [ostrakon] shell ‖ (ἀρχαιολογία) potsherd.

ὀσφραίνομαι [osfrenome] smell, scent ‖ (μεταφ) feel.

ὄσφρησις, ἡ [osfreesees] sense of smell.

ὀσφύς, ἡ [osfees] waist, loins, haunches.

ὅταν [otan] when, at the time when, whenever.

ὁτέ [ote] sometimes.

ὅτι [otee] (συνδ) that ‖ (ἐπίρ) as soon as ‖ just (now).

ὅ τι [otee] what(ever).

ὁτιδήποτε [oteedeepote] whatsoever ‖ anything at all.

ὅτου [otou]: ἕως ~ until ‖ μέχρις ~ until ‖ ἀφ᾽ ~ since.

οὐ [ou] not, no.

οὐγγιά, ἡ [oungia] ounce.

οὐδαμοῦ [oudamou] nowhere, not anywhere.

οὐδαμῶς [oudamos] not at all, not in any way, by no means.

οὐδέ [oude] βλ οὔτε.

οὐδείς [oudees] no(body), no one, none.

οὐδέποτε [oudepote] never.

οὐδέτερος [oudeteros] neither ‖ (ἐπίϑ) neutral ‖ (γραμμ) neuter.

οὐδόλως [oudolos] by no means, no wise, by no manner of means.

οὔζο, τό [ouzo] ouzo.

οὐκ [ouk] βλ οὐ.

οὐλή [oulee] scar.

οὖλον, τό [oulon] gum (anat).

οὖρα, τά [oura] πλ urine, piss (col).

οὐρά, ἡ [oura] tail ‖ train of dress ‖ queue ‖ (κατσαρόλας) handle ‖ (φάλαγγος) rear ‖ λεφτά μέ ~ loads of money.

οὐραγός, ὁ [ouragos] person bringing up the rear, the last one.

οὐρανής [ouranees] sky-blue.

οὐράνιον, τό [ouraneeon] uranium.

οὐράνιον [ouraneeon]: ~ τόξον rainbow.

οὐράνιος [ouraneeos] heavenly, celestial.

οὐρανίσκος, ὁ [ouraneeskos] palate.

οὐρανισκόφωνος [ouraneeskofonos] palatal.

οὐρανοκατέβατος [ouranokatevatos] heaven-sent ‖ (μεταφ) unexpected.

οὐρανοξύστης, ὁ [ouranokseestees] skyscraper.

οὐρανός, ὁ [ouranos] sky, heaven ‖ canopy.

οὐρητήριον, τό [oureeteereeon] urinal, john (col).

οὐρικός [oureekos] uric, urinary.

οὔριος [oureeos] tail (wind), favourable (wind), fair (wind).

οὐρλιάζω [ourleeazo] howl, roar ‖ (ἀπό πόνο) yell, scream ‖ (ἀπό θυμό) bellow.

οὔρλιασμα, τό [ourleeasma] howl(ing), bellowing, yelling.

οὐροδοχεῖον, τό [ouroδoheeon] chamberpot.

οὐρῶ [ouro] urinate.

οὖς, τό [ous] ear.

οὐσία, ἡ [ouseea] matter, substance ‖ essence ‖ (μεταφ) gist, main point.

οὐσιαστικόν, τό [ouseeasteekon] (γραμμ) substantive, noun.

οὐσιαστικός [ouseeasteekos] substantial, essential.

οὐσιώδης [ouseeoδees] essential, vital, indispensable, capital.

οὔτε [oute] not even ‖ ~ . . . ~ neither . . . nor.

οὐτιδανός [outeeδanos] worthless, useless, vile, base, abject.

οὐτοπία, ἡ [outopeea] Utopia.

οὗτος [outos] he, this one, that, it.

οὕτω(ς) [outo(s)] so, such, thus ‖ ~ ὥστε so that, in order that.

οὐχ [ouh] not ‖ ~ ἧττον nonetheless.

οὐχί [ouhee] βλ ὄχι.

ὀφειλέτης, ὁ [ofeeletees] debtor.

ὀφειλή, ἡ [ofeelee] debt, sum due ‖ (μεταφ) obligation, duty.

ὀφείλομαι [ofeelome] be due.

ὀφείλω [ofeelo] owe ‖ be obliged to ‖ ~ νά πάω I should go.

ὄφελος, τό [ofelos] profit, advantage, benefit.

ὀφθαλμαπάτη, ἡ [ofthalmapatee] optical illusion.

ὀφθαλμίατρος, ὁ, ἡ [ofthalmeeatros] eye specialist, oculist.

ὀφθαλμός, ὁ [ofthalmos] eye ‖ (βιολ) bud.

ὀφθαλμοφανής [ofthalmofanees] obvious, manifest, evident.

ὀφιοειδής [ofeeoeeδees] serpentine, meandering, winding.

ὄφις, ὁ [ofees] snake, serpent.

ὀφρύς, ἡ [ofrees] eyebrow ‖ (ὄρους) range ‖ (χάνδακος) edge.

ὀφφίς, τό [ofees] domestic office.

ὄχεντρα, ἡ [ohentra] βλ ὀχιά.

ὀχέτευσις, ἡ [ohetevsees] drainage.

C.G.D.—E

ὀχετός, ὁ [ohetos] drain, sewer ‖ conduit, pipe.

ὄχημα, τό [oheema] vehicle, carriage, coach.

ὄχθη, ἡ [ohthee] (ποταμοῦ) bank ‖ (λίμνης) shore.

ὄχι [ohee] no ‖ not.

ὀχιά, ἡ [ohia] viper.

ὀχλαγωγία, ἡ [ohlagogeea] disturbance, riot, tumult.

ὀχληρός [ohleeros] tiresome, unpleasant, burdensome.

ὀχλοβοή, ἡ [ohlovoee] uproar, din, hubbub.

ὀχλοκρατία, ἡ [ohlokrateea] mob rule.

ὄχλος, ὁ [ohlos] populace, mob, crowd, rabble.

ὀχυρόν, τό [oheeron] strong point, fort, stronghold.

ὀχυρώνομαι [oheeronome] (μεταφ) find an excuse, justify.

ὀχυρώνω [oheerono] fortify, entrench.

ὄψη [opsee] βλ ὄψις.

ὀψιγενής [opseeyenees] posthumous ‖ late, belated.

ὄψιμος [opseemos] tardy, late, of a late season.

ὄψις, ἡ [opsees] aspect, appearance, look ‖ view, sight ‖ countenance ‖ face ‖ λαμβάνω ὑπ' ὄψιν take into account ‖ ἐξ ὄψεως by sight ‖ ἐν ὄψει in view of ‖ in view.

ὀψοφυλάκιον, τό [opsofeelakeeon] larder, pantry.

ὀψώνια, τά [opsoneea] πλ purchases, supplies, shopping, provisions.

Π, π

παγάνα, ἡ [payana] trap, snare.

παγανισμός, ὁ [payaneesmos] paganism.

παγερός [payeros] icy cold, freezing ‖ (μεταφ) chilly, frigid.

παγετός, ὁ [payetos] frost.

παγετώδης [payetodees] icy, icy cold, freezing.

παγετών, ὁ [payeton] glacier.

παγίδα, ἡ [payeeda] trap, snare ‖ (τάφρος) pitfall.

παγίδευμα, τό [payeedevma] ensnaring, trapping.

παγιδεύω [payeedevo] snare, catch, entice.

πάγιος [payeeos] fixed, stable, firm ‖ (καθεστώς) secure, durable ‖ (δάνειον) consolidated loan ‖ (πρόσοδος) steady income.

παγίς, ἡ [payees] βλ παγίδα.

παγιώνω [payeeono] consolidate, make secure.

παγίως [payeeos] firmly, securely.

πάγκοινος [pangkeenos] common, universal, public.

πάγκος, ὁ [pangkos] bench, seat.

παγκόσμιος [pangkosmeeos] universal world-wide.

πάγκρεας, τό [pangkreas] pancreas.

παγόβουνον, τό [payovounon] iceberg.

παγόδα, ἡ [payoda] pagoda.

παγοδρομία, ἡ [payodromeea] skating.

παγοθραύστης, ὁ [payothravstees] icebreaker.

παγοπέδιλο, τό [payopedeelo] iceskate.

πάγος, ὁ [payos] ice, frost.

παγούρι, τό [payouree] can, tin, flask ‖ (στρατ) canteen.

παγωμένος [payomenos] frozen, frostbitten.

παγώνι, τό [payonee] peacock.

παγωνιά, ἡ [payonia] frost.

παγώνω [payono] freeze, congeal, frost.

παγωτό, τό [payoto] ice cream.

παζαρεύω [pazarevo] haggle over, bargain for.

παζάρι, τό [pazaree] market, bazaar ‖ bargaining, haggling.

παθαίνω [patheno] undergo, suffer, be injured.

πάθημα, τό [patheema] mishap, accident.

πάθησις, ἡ [patheesees] complaint, sickness, affliction.

παθητικός [patheeteekos] passive, submissive ‖ (γραμμ) passive (voice) ‖ charged with passion ‖ (οἰκ) debit.

παθολογία, ἡ [patholoyeea] pathology.

παθολογικός [patholoyeekos] pathological.

παθολόγος, ὁ [patholoyos] general practitioner.

πάθος, τό [pathos] illness, passion ‖ suffering ‖ (ἔχθρα) animosity.

παιγνίδι, τό [peyneedee] play, game, sport ‖ (γιά παιδιά) toy, plaything.

παιγνιδιάρης [peyneedeearees] playful, gay, mirthful.

παίγνιον, τό [peyneeon] βλ παιγνίδι.

παιγνιόχαρτον, τό [peyneeoharton] playing card.

παιδαγωγεῖον, τό [pedagoyeeon] children's school.

παιδαγωγία, ἡ [pedagoyeea] education, pedagogy.

παιδαγωγικός [pedagoyeekos] educational, pedagogical.

παιδαγωγός, ὁ, ἡ [pedagoyos] tutor, preceptor, pedagogue.

παιδαγωγῶ [pedagoyo] educate, instruct, teach.

παιδάκι, τό [pedakee] little child.

παιδαριώδης [pedareeodees] puerile, childish ‖ (εὔκολο) quite simple, trivial.

παιδεία, ἡ [pedeea] education, learning, instruction, culture.

παίδεμα, τό [pedema] torture, trial, ordeal.

παιδεύομαι [pedevome] try hard, struggle.

παιδευτήριον, τό [pedevteereeon] βλ ἐκπαιδευτήριον.

παιδεύω [pedevo] pester, torture, torment.

παιδί, τό [pedee] child, boy ‖ chap.

παιδιά, ή [peðia] game, sport ǁ amusement, distraction.

παιδιαρίζω [peðeeareezo] act like a child.

παιδίατρος, ὁ, ή [peðeeatros] paediatrician, child specialist.

παιδικός [peðeekos] child's, of children childish ǀ ~ σταθμός day nursery.

παιδίον, τό [peðeeon] βλ παιδί.

παιδίσκη, ή [peðeeskee] little girl, lassie.

παίζω [pezo] play ǀ (παιχνίδι) speculate, gamble ǀ (μεταφ) swing, sway.

παίκτης, ὁ [pektees] player ǀ gambler, gamester.

παινεύω [penevo] βλ ἐπαινῶ.

παίξιμο, τό [pekseemo] playing ǀ (μέ κάτι) toying with ǀ (θεάτρου) performance ǀ (παιχνίδι) gaming, gambling.

παίρνω [perno] receive, take hold of, get, contain ǀ (πόλιν κτλ) capture ǀ (διά τής βίας) wrench from ǀ (ὑπηρέτην) hire, take on ǁ (καφέ κτλ) take, have ǀ (κρύο κτλ) catch, get ǀ (ὡς παράδειγμα) take, draw ǀ (σημείωσι) take (a note) ǀ (κάτι γιά κάτι) take for, consider (as) ǀ (μέ κάποια ἔννοια) understand, interpret ǀ (χρήματα) be paid, draw, receive ǀ (γιά γυναίκα) marry, wed ǀ τόν ~ fall asleep ǀ ~ ἀπό πίσω follow closely.

παῖς, ὁ, ή [pes] βλ παιδί.

πακετάρω [paketaro] pack, box.

πακέτο, τό [paketo] pack, packet, parcel, box, bundle.

παλαβομάρα, ή [palavomara] madness, lunacy, foolish act.

παλαβός [palavos] mad, insane, stupid ǀ (παράτολμος) foolhardy.

παλάβρας, ὁ [palavras] braggart, windbag.

πάλαι [pale] of old.

παλαίμαχος [palemahos] veteran.

παλαιογραφία, ή [paleoγrafeea] pal(a)e-ography.

παλαιόθεν [paleothen] from olden times.

παλαιόκαστρον, τό [paleokastron] old castle, ruined castle.

παλαιοπωλεῖον, τό [paleopoleeon] second-hand shop, antique shop.

παλαιοπώλης, ὁ [paleopolees] secondhand dealer.

παλαιός [paleos] old ǀ (μνημεῖον κτλ) ancient, old ǀ (ἄλλοτε) former.

παλαιστής, ὁ [palestees] wrestler.

παλαίστρα, ή [palestra] arena, ring.

παλαίω [paleo] βλ παλεύω.

παλαιώνω [paleono] wear out, become anti-quated.

παλαμάκια, τά [palamakeea] πλ clapping, applause.

παλαμάρι, τό [palamaree] (ναυτ) cable, mooring line.

παλάμη, ή [palamee] palm ǀ (μέτρον) span.

παλαμίδα, ή [palameeða] kind of small tunny.

παλάτι, τό [palatee] palace ǀ mansion.

παλεύω [palevo] wrestle, struggle, fight.

πάλη, ή [palee] wrestling ǀ (μεταφ) struggle, strife, contest.

παλιανθρωπιά, ή [palianthropia] villainy, meanness, roguery.

παλιάνθρωπος, ὁ [palianthropos] rogue, rascal, scamp.

παλιάτσος, ὁ [paliatsos] clown, buffoon.

παλιγγενεσία, ή [paleengeneseea] revival, renaissance.

πάλι(ν) [pali(n)] again, once more, over again.

παλινδρομικός [paleenðromeekos] alter-nating, reciprocating, recoiling.

παλιν(ν)οστῶ [paleenosto] repatriate.

παλινόρθωσις, ή [paleenorthosees] restor-ation, re-establishment.

παλινωδῶ [paleenoðo] (μεταφ) retract, recant, take back.

παλιογύναικο, τό [palioγeeneko] street-walker, tart.

παλιοκόριτσο, τό [paliokoreetso] ill-bred girl ǀ prostitute.

παλιόμουτρο, τό [paliomoutro] villain, scoundrel, scamp.

παλιόπαιδο, τό [paliopeðo] bad boy, young scamp.

παλίρροια, ή [paleereea] tide, floodtide.

παλλακίς, ή [palakees] concubine, mistress.

πάλλευκος [palevkos] pure white, snow-white.

παλληκαρᾶς, ὁ [paleekaras] bully.

παλληκάρι, τό [paleekaree] young man, brave person ǀ (ἐργένης) bachelor.

παλληκαρίσια [paleekareeseea] boldly, bravely.

πάλλω [palo] throb, beat, palpitate ǀ (ἠλεκτ) vibrate.

παλμός, ὁ [palmos] oscillation, vibration palpitation, throbbing ǀ (ἐνθουσιασμοῦ) feeling, eagerness.

παλούκι, τό [paloukee] stake, pole ǀ (μεταφ) difficulty.

παλτό, τό [palto] overcoat.

παμμακάριστος [pamakareestos] most blessed.

παμπάλαιος [pampaleos] ancient ǀ out-of-date.

πάμπλουτος [pamploutos] extremely wealthy.

παμπόνηρος [pamponeeros] very cunning, very sly.

πάμπτωχος [pamptohos] very poor, very needy.

πάμφθηνος [pamftheenos] very cheap, ex-tremely cheap.

παμψηφεί [pampseefee] unanimously.

πᾶν, τό [pan] the whole world ǀ (τό κεφα-λαιῶδες) essentials, everything.

Πάν, ὁ [pan] Pan.

πανάγαθος [panaγathos] merciful ǀ ex-tremely virtuous.

Παναγία, ή [panaγeea] the Virgin Mary.

Π

παναγιότης, ἡ [panayeeotees] holiness.
πανάδα, ἡ [panada] brown patch, freckle.
πανάθλιος [panathleeos] wretched, miserable.
πανάκεια, ἡ [panakeea] panacea.
πανάρχαιος [panarheos] very ancient.
πανδαιμόνιον, τό [pandemoneeon] pandemonium.
πάνδεινος [pandeenos] disastrous, most terrible.
πάνδημος [pandeemos] public, of all the people.
πανδοχεῖον, τό [pandoheeon] inn.
πανδρειά, ἡ [pandria] marriage, matrimony.
πανδρεύω [pandrevo] marry.
πανελλήνιος [paneleeneeos] panhellenic.
πανεπιστημιακός [panepeesteemeeakos] of the university.
πανεπιστήμιον, τό [panepeesteemeeon] university.
πανέρι, τό [paneree] wide basket.
πανευτυχής [panefteehees] very happy.
πανηγυρίζω [paneeyeereezo] celebrate, fête.
πανηγυρικός [paneeyeereekos] festive (οὐσ) oration, panegyric.
πανήγυρις, ἡ [paneeyeerees] festival, festivity || (ἐμπορική) fair.
πανηγυρισμός, ὁ [paneeyeereesmos] celebration.
πάνθεον, τό [pantheon] pantheon.
πάνθηρ, ὁ [pantheer] panther.
πανί, τό [panee] cloth, linen || (ναυτ) sail.
πανιερότης, ἡ [panierotees] (ὡς τίτλος) His Grace.
πανικόβλητος [paneekovleetos] panic-stricken.
πανικός, ὁ [paneekos] panic.
πανίς, ἡ [panees] fauna.
πανίσχυρος [paneesheeros] all-powerful.
πάν(ν)ινος [paneenos] of cloth, of linen, of cotton.
πανόμοιος [panomeeos] similar, alike.
πανομοιότυπον, τό [panomeeoteepon] facsimile.
πανοπλία, ἡ [panopleea] arms, armour.
πανόραμα, τό [panorama] panorama.
πανοσιότης [panoseeotees] reverence.
πανοσιώτατος, ὁ [panoseeotatos] most reverend.
πανούκλα, ἡ [panoukla] plague, pestilence.
πανουργία, ἡ [panouryeea] ruse, trick, cunning.
πανούργος [panouryos] malicious, tricky, wily, cunning.
πανσέληνος, ἡ [panseleenos] full moon.
πανσές, ὁ [panses] pansy.
πάντα [panta] forever, always || anyway, in any case.
πανταλόνι, τό [pantalonee] trousers || pants, knickers.
παντάπασι [pantapasee] completely, fully, utterly.

πανταχόθεν [pantahothen] from all parts.
πανταχού [pantahoo] everywhere.
παντελής [pantelees] complete, absolute, entire.
παντελῶς [pantelos] utterly, absolutely, totally.
παντζάρι, τό [pantzaree] beetroot.
παντιέρα, ἡ [pantiera] banner, flag.
παντοδύναμος [pantodeenamos] omnipotent, all-powerful.
παντοειδῶς [pantoeedos] in every way.
παντοιοτρόπως [panteeotropos] in every way, by every means.
παντοκράτωρ, ὁ [pantokrator] the Almighty.
παντομίμα, ἡ [pantomeema] pantomime.
παντοπωλεῖον, τό [pantopoleeon] grocer's shop || (US) grocery.
παντοπώλης, ὁ [pantopolees] grocer.
πάντοτε [pantote] always, at all times, forever.
παντοτεινά [pantoteena] perpetually, everlastingly.
παντοῦ [pantou] everywhere.
παντούφλα, ἡ [pantoufla] slipper.
παντρειά, ἡ [pantria] βλ πανδρειά.
παντρεύω [pantrevo] βλ πανδρεύω.
πάντως [pantos] anyhow, in any case, at any rate.
πάνυ [panee] very much, a great deal.
πανωλεθρία, ἡ [panolethreea] heavy loss, total ruin.
πανώλης, ἡ [panolees] plague, pestilence.
πανώριος [panoreeos] very beautiful.
πανωφόρι, τό [panoforee] overcoat.
παξιμάδι, τό [pakseemadee] rusk || (γιά κοχλία) nut (of screw).
παπαγαλιστί [papayaleestee] parrot-like.
παπαδιά, ἡ [papadia] priest's wife.
παπάκι, τό [papakee] duckling.
παπαρούνα, ἡ [paparouna] poppy.
Πάπας, ὁ [papas] Pope.
παπᾶς, ὁ [papas] priest.
παπί, τό [papee] young duck || γίνομαι ~ get wet to the skin.
πάπια, ἡ [papeea] duck || bedpan || κάνω τήν ~ play the fool, keep mum.
παπικός [papeekos] papal.
πάπλωμα, τό [paploma] cotton quilt.
παπουτσάδικο, τό [papoutsadeeko] shoemaker's shop.
παπουτσῆς, ὁ [papoutsees] shoemaker, bootmaker.
παπούτσι, τό [papoutsee] shoe.
παππούς, ὁ [papoos] grandfather.
παρά [para] than || but || (πρόθ) near, close, by || (προσθήκην) in spite of, against my will || (ἀντίθεσιν) against, contrary to || (ἀφαίρεσιν) by, almost, nearly.
παραβαίνω [paraveno] break, violate, infringe.
παραβάλλω [paravalo] compare.
παραβάν, τό [paravan] (folding) screen.

παραβαρύνω [paravareeno] overload, overburden ‖ become very heavy.

παράβασις, ἡ [paravasees] violation, transgression, breach.

παραβάτης, ὁ [paravatees] violator, transgressor.

παραβιάζω [paraveeazo] (πόρτα κτλ) force entry, break open ‖ (νόμον) violate, infringe.

παραβλέπω [paravlepo] neglect, omit ‖ turn a blind eye (to), ignore.

παραβολή, ἡ [paravolee] comparison, collation ‖ (ἐκκλ) parable ‖ (μαθημ) parabola.

παράβολον, τό [paravolon] fee, deposit.

παραγάδι, τό [paragadee] large fishing net.

παραγγελία, ἡ [parangeleea] command, commission, order ‖ (μήνυμα) message ‖ ἐπί ~ made to order.

παραγγέλω [parangelo] order, command ‖ inform.

παραγεμίζω [parayemeezo] fill up ‖ become too full ‖ (μαγειρική) stuff ‖ cram.

παραγίνομαι [parayenome] grow too much ‖ go too far ‖ get overripe ‖ ~ χοντρός grow too fat.

παράγκα, ἡ [paranga] wooden hut, shack.

παραγκωνίζω [parangoneezo] elbow, thrust aside.

παραγνωρίζω [paraynoreezo] ignore ‖ misinterpret ‖ mistake identity of.

παραγραφή, ἡ [parayrafee] lapse of right, lapse of penalty.

παράγραφος, ὁ [parayrafos] paragraph.

παράγομαι [parayome] be derived from.

παράγω [parayo] produce, bear ‖ derive.

παραγωγή, ἡ [parayoyee] production ‖ output, generation ‖ (γραμμ) derivation.

παραγωγικός [parayoyeekos] productive.

παραγωγός, ὁ [parayoyos] producer, grower.

παράγων, ὁ [parayon] agent, factor ‖ (μαθημ) factor.

παράδειγμα, τό [paradeeyma] example ‖ ~ τος χάριν for example, for instance.

παραδειγματίζω [paradeeymateezo] set an example, exemplify.

παράδεισος, ὁ [paradeesos] paradise.

παραδεκτός [paradektos] admitted, accepted ‖ acceptable, admissible.

παραδέχομαι [paradehome] admit, acknowledge, confess, allow.

παραδίδομαι [paradeedome] surrender, submit, yield.

παραδίδω [paradeedo] hand over ‖ surrender ‖ (μάθημα) teach, give lessons.

παράδοξος [paradoksos] peculiar, odd, singular ‖ unusual.

παραδόπιστος [paradopeestos] greedy, extremely fond of money.

παράδοσις, ἡ [paradosees] delivery, surrender ‖ (τῆς χώρας) tradition ‖ (μαθήματος) teaching.

παραδοτέος [paradoteos] due for delivery.

παραδουλεύτρα, ἡ [paradoulevtra] charwoman.

παραδρομή, ἡ [paradromee] carelessness, oversight.

παραείμαι [paraeeme] be beyond measure, be too much.

παραζάλη, ἡ [parazalee] confusion, agitation, turmoil.

παραθαλάσσιος [parathalaseeos] by the sea, coastal.

παραθερίζω [parathereezo] spend the summer.

παραθεριστής, ὁ [parathereestees] summer holidaymaker.

παραθετικός [paratheteekos] comparative.

παραθέτω [paratheto] contrast, compare ‖ (ἀναφέρω) cite, quote ‖ (φαγητό) serve, offer.

παράθυρο, τό [paratheero] window.

παραθυρόφυλλο, τό [paratheerofeelo] shutter.

παραίνεσις, ἡ [parenesees] advice, counsel, admonition.

παραίσθησις, ἡ [parestheesees] hallucination, illusion.

παραίτησις, ἡ [pareteesees] resignation, renunciation ‖ abdication.

παραιτοῦμαι [paretoume] resign, give up ‖ (ἀποφεύγω) avoid.

παραιτῶ [pareto] give up, leave, desert.

παρακάθομαι [parakathome] overstay ‖ sit too long.

παράκαιρος [parakeros] unseasonable, inopportune, untimely.

παρακάλια, τά [parakaleea] πλ supplications, pleading.

παρακαλῶ [parakalo] ask, beg, entreat ‖ ~! don't mention it!, please!, a pleasure!

παρακάμ(ν)ω [parakam(n)o] exaggerate, go too far.

παρακάμπτω [parakampto] get round, surpass ‖ (ἕνα θέμα) evade.

παρακαταθήκη, ἡ [parakatatheekee] consignation, deposit ‖ stock ‖ provisions ‖ (παράδοσις) heritage.

παρακάτω [parakato] lower down ‖ at a lower price.

παρακείμενος [parakeemenos] adjoining, adjacent ‖ ὁ ~ (γραμμ) perfect tense.

παρακινῶ [parakeeno] exhort, urge ‖ instigate.

παρακλάδι, τό [parakladee] shoot, bough ‖ (ποταμοῦ) branch.

παράκλησις, ἡ [parakleesees] request, plea ‖ (ἐκκλ) prayer.

παρακμή, ἡ [parakmee] decay, decline.

παρακοή, ἡ [parakoee] disobedience, insubordination.

παρακολουθῶ [parakoloutho] follow, come behind ‖ watch ‖ go after ‖ (τήν ἔννοια) understand.

παρακούω [parakouo] hear wrongly ‖ (ἀπειθαρχῶ) disobey.

παρακρατῶ [parakrato] retain ‖ keep back ‖ (γιά χρόνο) last too long.

παράκτιος [parakteeos] coastal, inshore.

παραλαβή, ἡ [paralavee] receipt, receiving, delivery.

παραλαμβάνω [paralamvano] receive, take delivery of ‖ take possession of.

παραλείπω [paraleepo] leave out, miss, neglect, omit.

παράλειψις, ἡ [paraleepsees] omission, neglect(ing).

παραλέω [paraleo] exaggerate, overcolour.

παραλήπτης, ὁ [paraleeptees] payee, addressee, consignee.

παραλήρημα, τό [paraleereema] delirium, frenzy.

παραλία, ἡ [paraleea] seashore, shore, coast, beach ‖ παραλιακός of the seashore, of the coast.

παραλῆς [paralees] rich, wealthy.

παραλλαγή, ἡ [paralayee] change, variation ‖ (ἀστρον) deviation.

παράλληλος [paraleelos] parallel.

παραλογίζομαι [paraloyeezome] talk irrationally, rave.

παράλογος [paraloyos] illogical, absurd, foolish.

παραλυσία, ἡ [paraleeseea] palsy, paralysis ‖ dissoluteness, debauchery.

παράλυσις, ἡ [paraleesees] paralysis ‖ helplessness.

παράλυτος [paraleetos] paralytic, stiff, crippled ‖ (ἰατρ) paralyzed.

παραλύω [paraleeo] make loose, make shaky ‖ slacken, relax ‖ (ἰατρ) paralyze.

παραμάννα, ἡ [paramana] nurse, nanny ‖ (καρφίτσα) safety pin.

παραμελῶ [paramelo] neglect, leave undone, disregard.

παραμένω [parameno] stay by ‖ remain, continue to exist ‖ sojourn.

παράμερα [paramera] out of the way, apart.

παραμερίζω [paramereezo] set aside ‖ get out of the way ‖ fend off.

παράμερος [parameros] remote, outlying.

παραμιλῶ [parameelo] speak too much ‖ rave.

παραμονεύω [paramonevo] watch for, waylay.

παραμονή, ἡ [paramonee] stay ‖ eve.

παραμορφώνω [paramorfono] deform, disfigure, twist.

παραμύθι, τό [parameethee] fable, story, fairy tale.

παρανόησις, ἡ [paranoeesees] misunderstanding.

παρανομία, ἡ [paranomeea] illegality ‖ breach of the law.

παράνομος [paranomos] illegal, unlawful.

παρανομῶ [paranomo] transgress a law.

παρανοῶ [paranoo] misunderstand.

παράνυμφος, ὁ, ἡ [paraneemfos] best man ‖ bridesmaid.

παρανυχίδα, ἡ [paraneeheeda] hangnail.

παράξενα [paraksena] oddly, strangely.

παραξενεύομαι [paraksenevome] be astonished, be amazed (at).

παραξενιά, ἡ [paraksenia] caprice, fancy, whim.

παράξενος [paraksenos] peculiar, singular, odd.

παραξηλώνω [parakseelono] unsew, unstitch ‖ τό ~ I go too far, I exaggerate.

παραπανήσιος [parapaneeseeos] superfluous, to spare ‖ (τιμή) excess, overly much.

παραπάνω [parapano] higher up ‖ (ἐπιπρόσθετα) in addition ‖ μέ τό ~ enough and to spare ‖ ~ ἀπό over, more than, greater than.

παραπάτημα, τό [parapateema] false step ‖ (μεταφ) misconduct.

παραπατῶ [parapato] slip, stumble ‖ stagger.

παραπέμπω [parapembo] refer to ‖ send, hand over.

παραπέρα [parapera] further on, over there.

παραπεταμένος [parapetamenos] thrown away ‖ (μεταφ) disdained, scorned.

παραπέτασμα, τό [parapetasma] curtain.

παραπέτο, τό [parapeto] parapet, breastwork.

παραπέφτω [parapefto] βλ παραπίπτω.

παράπηγμα, τό [parapeeyma] wooden hut, shack, shanty.

παραπίπτω [parapeepto] be mislaid, get lost, go astray.

παραπλανῶ [paraplano] seduce, mislead, lead astray.

παραπλεύρως [paraplevros] next door ‖ next to, beside.

παραπλήρωμα, τό [parapleeroma] complement, supplement.

παραπλήσιος [parapleeseeos] next to, nearby ‖ (ὅμοιος) very like, similar.

παραποιῶ [parapeeo] counterfeit ‖ forge, tamper with.

παραπομπή, ἡ [parapombee] referring ‖ (σέ βιβλίο) reference, footnote.

παραπονετικός [paraponeteekos] doleful, whining.

παραπονιάρης [paraponeearees] grumbling, grousing.

παραπονιέμαι [paraponieme] complain, grumble.

παράπονον, τό [paraponon] complaint, grievance.

παραπόταμος, ὁ [parapotamos] tributary.

παράπτωμα, τό [paraptoma] fault, mistake ‖ breach.

παράρτημα, τό [pararteema] annexe, supplement ‖ outbuilding ‖ (τραπέζης) branch ‖ (ἐφημερίδος) special edition, extra.

παράς, ὁ [paras] money, cash.

παράστημον, τό [paraseemon] decoration, medal, order, insignia.

παρασημοφορῶ [paraseemoforo] decorate, invest with an order.

παράσιτα, τά [paraseeta] πλ atmospherics ‖ parasites.

παράσιτος, ὁ [paraseetos] sponger, hanger-on, parasite.

παρασιωπῶ [paraseeopo] pass over in silence.

παρασκευάζω [paraskevazo] prepare, get ready, arrange.

παρασκεύασμα, τό [paraskevasma] substance prepared, preparation.

παρασκευή, ἡ [paraskevee] preparation ‖ (ἡμέρα) Friday.

παρασκήνια, τά [paraskeeneea] πλ wings (theat) ‖ **παρασκηνιακός** behind the scenes.

παρασταίνω [parasteno] βλ **παριστάνω**.

παράστασις, ἡ [parastasees] representation, portrayal ‖ (παρουσία) presence, demeanour ‖ (θεάτρου) show performance ‖ (νομ) appearance.

παραστάτης, ὁ [parastatees] assistant, helper ‖ (πόρτας) jamb.

παραστατικός [parastateekos] expressive, descriptive, vivid.

παραστέκω [parasteko] assist, help, support.

παράστημα, τό [parasteema] carriage, bearing, figure.

παραστράτημα, τό [parastrateema] straying, misconduct.

παρασύνθημα, τό [paraseentheema] password.

παρασύρω [paraseero] drag along, sweep away ‖ run over ‖ (σέ σφάλμα) lead astray, carry away.

παράταξις, ἡ [parataksees] array, parade, order ‖ pomp, ceremony ‖ (πολιτική) political party.

παράτασις, ἡ [paratasees] extension, protraction ‖ renewal.

παρατάσσω [parataso] arrange, set in order, line up.

παρατατικός, ὁ [paratateekos] (γραμμ) imperfect tense.

παρατείνω [parateeno] prolong, lengthen ‖ extend, defer.

παρατήρησις, ἡ [parateereesees] observation, remark ‖ (κουβέντα) comment ‖ reproach, reprimand.

παρατηρητής, ὁ [parateereetees] observer, watcher, spotter.

παρατηρητικός [parateereeteekos] observing, keen ‖ reproachful.

παρατηρῶ [parateero] observe, perceive, notice ‖ (ἐπιτιμῶ) reproach, blame.

παράτολμος [paratolmos] reckless, audacious, bold.

παρατραβῶ [paratravo] draw out, prolong ‖ last too long ‖ (μεταφ) go too far.

παρατράγουδο, τό [paratragoudo] untoward incident.

παρατρέχω [paratreho] leave out, omit ‖ run back and forth.

παρατσούκλι, τό [paratsouklee] nickname.

παρατυγχάνω [parateenghano] chance to be present.

παρατυπία, ἡ [parateepeea] breach of formalities ‖ irregularity.

πάραντα [paravta] immediately, at once, forthwith.

παραφέρνω [paraferno] carry more than necessary ‖ resemble.

παραφέρομαι [paraferome] flare up, lose one's temper.

παραφθορά, ἡ [parafthora] alteration, corruption, change.

παραφορά, ἡ [parafora] frenzy, outburst ‖ rage.

παράφορος [paraforos] hotheaded, hasty, furious.

παραφορτώνομαι [parafortonome] become overburdened ‖ (ἐνοχλῶ) nag, annoy.

παραφορτώνω [parafortono] overload, overburden ‖ (μεταφ) drive too hard.

παράφρασις, ἡ [parafrasees] paraphrase, free translation.

παραφρονῶ [parafrono] become insane, go mad.

παραφροσύνη, ἡ [parafroseenee] madness, insanity, foolish act.

παράφρων [parafron] mad, frenzied.

παραφυάς, ἡ [parafias] sprout, shoot ‖ (οἰκογενείας) scion, offspring.

παραφυλάω [parafeelao] lie in wait for ‖ be on the watch for.

παραφωνία, ἡ [parafoneea] dissonance ‖ (μεταφ) discord, disagreement.

παραχαράκτης, ὁ [paraharaktees] forger, counterfeiter.

παραχειμάζω [paraheemazo] pass the winter, winter.

παραχρῆμα [parahreema] immediately, instantly.

παραχώνω [parahono] bury, hide ‖ (γεμίζω) stuff into.

παραχωρῶ [parahoro] grant, yield, concede ‖ (παραδίδω) surrender, resign.

παρδαλός [parδalos] spotted ‖ multicoloured, gaudy.

παρέα, ἡ [parea] company, set, party ‖ **κάνω ~ μέ** keep company with.

παρειά, ἡ [paria] cheek ‖ (μεταφ) wall.

παρείσακτος [pareesaktos] intrusive, intruding.

παρεκβαίνω [parekveno] digress, deviate.

παρέκβασις, ἡ [parekvasees] digression.

παρέκει [parekee] further on, a little further.

παρεκκλήσι(ον), τό [parekleesee(on)] chapel.

παρεκκλίνω [parekleeno] deviate from, turn aside from ‖ diverge.

παρεκτείνω [parekteeno] prolong, extend.

παρεκτός [parektos] except, save, besides.

παρεκτροπή, ή [parektropee] aberration, deviation || (ήθική) misconduct, dissoluteness.

παρέλασις, ή [parelasees] parade, march-past, procession.

παρελαύνω [parelavno] march past, parade.

παρέλευσις, ή [parelevsees] passage of time, passing.

παρελθών [parelthon] past, bygone.

παρελκύω [parelkeeo] drag out, protract, retard, delay.

παρεμβαίνω [paremveno] interfere, intervene, meddle with.

παρεμβάλλω [paremvalo] insert, interpose.

παρέμβασις, ή [paremvasees] intervention, mediation.

παρεμβολή, ή [paremvolee] insertion.

παρεμπιπτόντως [parempeeptontos] by the way.

παρεμφερής [paremferees] similar, of the same nature, resembling.

παρενέργεια, ή [pareneryeea] side effect.

παρένθεσις, ή [parenthesees] insertion || (γραμμ) parenthesis.

παρενθέτω [parentheto] insert, interpose.

παρενοχλῶ [parenohlo] inconvenience, trouble, harass.

παρεξήγησις, ή [parekseeyeesees] misunderstanding.

παρεξηγῶ [parekseeyo] misunderstand, misinterpret, misconstrue.

παρεπιδημῶ [parepeedeemo] live temporarily (abroad).

παρεπόμενα, τά [parepomena] πλ consequences, issues.

πάρεργον, τό [pareryon] sideline, hobby.

παρερμηνεία, ή [parermeeneea] misinterpretation.

παρέρχομαι [parerhome] elapse, pass || (τελείωνω) come to an end || (πηδῶ) pass over || omit.

παρεστῶτες, οἱ [parestotes] πλ those present, those attending.

παρευθύς [parevthees] βλ πάραυτα.

παρευρίσκομαι [parevreeskome] be present at, attend.

παρεφθαρμένος [pareftharmenos] defective (linguistically).

παρέχω [pareho] procure || give, supply || (εὐκαιρίαν) occasion, bring about.

παρηγορία, ή [pareeyoreea] consolation, comfort, solace.

παρηγορῶ [pareeyoro] console, comfort.

παρθεναγωγεῖον, τό [parthenayoyeeon] girls' school.

παρθενία, ή [partheneea] virginity, maidenhood || chastity.

παρθενικός [partheneekos] virginal || (μεταφ) pure || maiden.

παρθένος, ή [parthenos] virgin, maiden.

Παρθενών, ό [parthenon] Parthenon.

παρίσταμαι [pareestame] be present at, assist (at) || arise.

παριστάνω [pareestano] represent, portray, depict || (ρόλον) perform || pretend to be.

πάρκο, τό [parko] park.

παρντόν [parnton] pardon me!

παροδικός [parodeekos] passing, fleeting, momentary.

πάροδος, ή [parodos] side street || (χρόνον κτλ) passing, course.

παροικία, ή [pareekeea] colony, quarter.

παροιμία, ή [pareemeea] proverb, adage, saying.

παροιμιώδης [pareemeeodees] proverbial || famous, renowned.

παρομοιάζω [paromeeazo] compare, liken || resemble, be similar.

παρόμοιος [paromeeos] similar, alike.

παρόν, τό [paron] the present.

παρονομασία, ή [paronomaseea] play on words || (παρατσούκλι) nickname.

παρονομαστής, ό [paronomastees] (μαθημ) denominator.

παροξυσμός, ό [parokseesmos] fit, attack || incitement.

παροξύτονος [parokseetonos] accented on penultimate syllable.

παρόραμα, τό [parorama] mistake, blunder || erratum.

παροργίζω [paroryeezo] irritate, enrage, vex, annoy.

παρόρμησις, ή [parormeesees] prompting, instigation || stimulation, exhortation.

παροτρύνω [parotreeno] βλ παρακινῶ.

παρουσία, ή [parouseea] presence, attendance || δευτέρα ~ second coming, doomsday.

παρουσιάζομαι [parouseeazome] appear || introduce o.s.

παρουσιάζω [parouseeazo] present, show, introduce.

παρουσιαστικόν, τό [parouseeasteekon] presence, demeanour, bearing.

παροχή, ή [parohee] furnishing || contribution, donation || granting.

παρρησία, ή [pareeseea] frankness, candour.

πάρσιμο, τό [parseemo] capture, taking || (ἐλάττωσις) trimming, lessening.

παρτέρι, τό [parteree] flower bed.

παρτίδα, ή [parteeda] part, portion || (παιγνιδιοῦ) game (of cards).

παρυφή, ή [pareefee] hem || border, edge.

παρωδία, ή [parodeea] parody, farce, travesty.

παρών [paron] present, actual.

παρωνυμία, ή [paroneemeea] nickname || surname.

παρωνυχίς, ή [paroneehees] hangnail.

παρωπίς, ή [paropees] blinker, blind.

πάρωρα [parora] untimely, too late.

παρωχημένος [paroheemenos] past, gone by.

πᾶς [pas] any, all, every ‖ (οἱ πάντες) everybody, everyone.

πασαλείβομαι [pasaleevome] be smeared ‖ get a smattering of knowledge.

πασαλείβω [pasaleevo] smear, daub ‖ smudge.

πασᾶς, ὁ [pasas] pasha.

πασίγνωστος [paseeγnostos] well-known, notorious.

πασιέντζα, ἡ [pasientza] patience, solitaire (card game).

πασπαλίζω [paspaleezo] sprinkle, powder (with).

πασπατεύω [paspatevo] pry about, feel, finger.

πάσσαλος, ὁ [passalos] stake, post, pole.

πάσσο, τό [passo] stride, step ‖ πάω ~ (στά χαρτιά) pass (at cards).

πάστα, ἡ [pasta] dough, paste ‖ (γλυκό) pastry, cake ‖ (χαρακτήρ) character, sort.

παστέλι, τό [pastelee] concoction of honey and sesame.

παστίτσιο, τό [pasteetseeo] baked macaroni.

παστός [pastos] salted.

παστουρμᾶς, ὁ [pastourmas] seasoned cured meat.

παστρεύω [pastrevo] clean, cleanse ‖ (μεταφ) destroy, exterminate.

παστρικός [pastreekos] clean, neat ‖ (μεταφ) dishonest, depraved.

Πάσχα, τό [pasha] Easter.

πασχαλιά, ἡ [pashalia] lilac.

πασχίζω [pasheezo] try hard to, strive, endeavour.

πάσχω [pasho] be ill, suffer ‖ ὁ ~ν the patient, the sufferer.

πάταγος, ὁ [pataγos] din, noise, bang ‖ (μεταφ) sensation, stir.

παταγώδης [pataγoδees] uproarious, noisy, loud.

πατάρι, τό [pataree] loft, attic.

πατάσσω [patasso] strike, treat severely.

πατάτα, ἡ [patata] potato.

πατατάλευρον, τό [patatalevron] potato flour.

πατέρας, ὁ [pateras] βλ πατήρ.

πατερίτσα, ἡ [patereetsa] crook, crutch ‖ bishop's staff.

πατερό, τό [patero] beam, rafter ‖ floor.

πατηκώνω [pateekono] press down, crush, compress.

πάτημα, τό [pateema] step, footstep ‖ (ἴχνος) footprint ‖ (σταφυλιῶν) treading, pressing ‖ excuse.

πατημασιά, ἡ [pateemasia] footprint, trace, track.

πατήρ, ὁ [pateer] father.

πατινάρω [pateenaro] skate.

πάτος, ὁ [patos] bottom ‖ (ποδός) sole.

πατούσα, ἡ [patousa] sole (anat).

πατριάρχης, ὁ [patreearhees] patriarch.

πατριαρχεῖον, τό [patreearheeon] patriarchate.

πατρίδα, ἡ [patreeδa] native country, birthplace.

πατρικός [patreekos] paternal ‖ fatherly.

πάτριος [patreeos] paternal, ancestral ‖ native.

πατρίς, ἡ [patrees] native country, fatherland.

πατριώτης, ὁ [patreeotees] compatriot ‖ patriot.

πατριωτικός [patreeoteekos] patriotic.

πατριωτισμός, ὁ [patreeoteesmos] patriotism.

πατρογονικός [patroγoneekos] paternal, ancestral ‖ hereditary.

πατρόν, τό [patron] pattern (in dressmaking).

πατροπαράδοτος [patroparaδotos] usual, customary, traditional ‖ hereditary.

πατρυιός, ὁ [patreeos] stepfather.

πατσαβούρα, ἡ [patsavoura] dish cloth, rag ‖ (μεταφ) rag (newspaper) ‖ prostitute.

πατσᾶς, ὁ [patsas] (soup of) tripe.

πάτσι [patsee] even, quits.

πατῶ [pato] step on ‖ (κουδούνι κτλ) press ‖ press down ‖ ~ τόν πάτο touch bottom ‖ (μεταφ) violate ‖ run over ‖ ~ πόδι I put my foot down.

πάτωμα, τό [patoma] floor, ground ‖ storey.

πατώνω [patono] lay a floor ‖ touch bottom, reach bottom.

παῦλα, ἡ [pavla] dash (punctuation).

παῦσις, ἡ [pavsees] stoppage, cessation, discharge ‖ (μουσ) rest, pause.

παύω [pavo] cease, stop ‖ cause to cease ‖ (ἀπολύω) dismiss ‖ (σταματῶ) stop, finish, give up.

παφλασμός, ὁ [paflasmos] splashing, gushing ‖ bubbling up.

παχαίνω [paheno] βλ παχύνω.

παχιά [pahia] πλ: ~ λόγια empty words, empty promises.

πάχνη, ἡ [pahnee] hoarfrost, rime.

παχνί, τό [pahnee] manger, crib.

πάχος, τό [pahos] plumpness ‖ thickness ‖ (λίπος) fat, grease ‖ (στρώματος) depth.

παχουλός [pahoulos] plump, chubby.

παχύδερμος [paheeδermos] (μεταφ) insensitive.

παχύνω [paheeno] fatten ‖ grow fat.

παχύς [pahees] thick ‖ fleshy, fat ‖ (εἰς λίπος) rich in fat ‖ (λειβάδι) rich.

παχύσαρκος [paheesarkos] fat, stout, obese.

πάω [pao] go ‖ take ‖ carry ‖ τά ~ καλά I get along well with ‖ ~ περίπατο it's a washout ‖ I go for a walk ‖ ~ νά σκάσω I'm ready to burst.

πεδιάδα, ἡ [peδeeaδa] plain, flat country

πεδιάς, ἡ [peδias] βλ πεδιάδα.

πεδικλώνομαι [peδeeklonome] trip.

πεδικλώνω [peδeeklono] fetter ‖ hobble ‖ trip up.

πέδιλον, τό [peδeelon] sandal.

πεδινός [pedeenos] flat, level ‖ (ἔδαφος) even, smooth.

πεδίον, τό [pedeeon] plain, flat country, ground ‖ (μάχης) field of battle ‖ (ὀπτικόν) field.

πεζεύω [pezevo] dismount.

πεζή [pezee] on foot.

πεζικόν, τό [pezeekon] infantry.

πεζογραφία, ἡ [pezoγrafeea] prose.

πεζογράφος [pezoγrafos] prose writer, novelist.

πεζοδρόμιον, τό [pezoδromeeon] pavement ‖ (US) sidewalk.

πεζοναύτης, ὁ [pezonavtees] marine.

πεζοπορία, ἡ [pezoporeea] walking, walk ‖ (στρατ) march.

πεζός [pezos] pedestrian ‖ (τῆς πρόζας) in prose ‖ (μεταφ) banal, trivial, common.

πεζούλι, τό [pezoulee] parapet ‖ bench ‖ (σέ λόφο) terrace.

πεθαίνω [petheno] die ‖ (μεταφ) perish ‖ be fond of, be mad about.

πεθαμός, ὁ [pethamos] death ‖ (μεταφ) excessive hardship.

πεθερά, ἡ [pethera] mother-in-law.

πεθερικά, τά [pethereeka] πλ in-laws.

πεθερός, ὁ [petheros] father-in-law.

πειθαναγκάζω [peethanangazo] persuade by force, force, compel.

πειθαρχία, ἡ [peetharheea] discipline.

πειθαρχικός [peetharheekos] disciplinary ‖ (ὑπάκουος) obedient, docile, submissive.

πειθαρχῶ [peetharho] be obedient, obey one's superiors.

πειθήνιος [peetheeneeos] docile, obedient, submissive.

πείθω [peetho] convince, persuade.

πειθώ, ἡ [peetho] persuasion, conviction.

πείνα [peena] hunger, famine, starvation ‖ πειναλέος starving, famishing, ravenous ‖ πεινασμένος hungry, famished.

πεινῶ [peeno] be hungry, be starving.

πείρα, ἡ [peera] experience, background.

πείραγμα, τό [peeraγma] teasing ‖ annoyance ‖ (ἀσθένεια) malady.

πειραγμένος [peeraγmenos] hurt, offended ‖ (κρέας) tainted, spoilt.

πειράζει [peerazee]: ~ ; is it all right?, is it important?

πειράζω [peerazo] trouble, anger, annoy ‖ tease ‖ (τήν ὑγεία) upset, be bad for ‖ (ἐνοχλῶ) disturb.

πειρακτικός [peerakteekos] irritating, offensive, cutting.

πείραμα, τό [peerama] experiment ‖ trial, test ‖ πειραματικός experimental.

πειρασμός, ὁ [peerasmos] temptation.

πειρατής, ὁ [peeratees] pirate, corsair ‖ pirate taxi.

πείρος, ὁ [peeros] plug, peg.

πείσμα, τό [peesma] obstinacy, stubbornness ‖ πεισματάρης obstinate, stubborn ‖ πεισματώδης headstrong, stubborn ‖

πεισματώνομαι be unyielding ‖ πεισματώνω make obstinate, irritate ‖ become obdurate.

πείσμων [peesmon] βλ πεισματάρης.

πειστήριον, τό [peesteereeon] proof.

πειστήριος [peesteereeos] convincing, persuasive.

πειστικός [peesteekos] βλ πειστήριος.

πέλαγος, τό [pelaγos] open sea.

πελαγώνω [pelaγono] (μεταφ) lose one's way, be at a loss, feel at sea.

πελαργός, ὁ [pelarγos] stork.

πελατεία, ἡ [pelateea] clientèle, customers, patronage.

πελάτης, ὁ [pelatees] customer, patron, client ‖ (ξενοδοχείου) guest.

πελεκάνος, ὁ [pelekanos] pelican.

πελεκούδι, τό [pelekoudee] chip, paring, shaving.

πέλεκυς, ὁ [pelekees] axe, hatchet ‖ (μεταφ) punishment.

πελεκῶ [peleko] axe, hew, cut into shape, carve ‖ (μεταφ) thrash.

πελιδνός [peleednos] livid.

πέλμα, τό [pelma] sole (anat) ‖ (τεχνική) shoe, flange.

Πελοπόννησος, ἡ [peloponeesos] the Peloponnese.

πελότα, ἡ [pelota] pincushion.

πελτές [peltes] βλ μπελντές.

πελώριος [peloreeos] enormous, mammoth ‖ (σφάλμα) gross.

Πέμπτη, ἡ [pemptee] Thursday.

πέμπτος [pemptos] fifth.

πέμπω [pempo] send, send out ‖ forward.

πενήντα [peneenta] fifty.

πενηνταριά, ἡ [peeneentaria]: καμμιά ~ about fifty.

πένης, ὁ [penees] destitute or needy person.

πενθερά [penthera] βλ πεθερά.

πενθερός [pentheros] βλ πεθερός.

πενθήμερος [pentheemeros] of five days.

πένθιμος [pentheemos] sorrowful, mournful, dismal ‖ in mourning.

πένθος, τό [penthos] bereavement ‖ mourning.

πενθῶ [pentho] lament, mourn ‖ be in mourning.

πενία, ἡ [peneea] poverty, want.

πενιχρός [peneehros] poor, mean ‖ (γεῦμα) poor, scant ‖ paltry.

πέννα, ἡ [pena] pen ‖ (μουσικῆς) plectrum ‖ (νόμισμα) penny.

πεννάκι, τό [penakee] nib.

πένομαι [penome] be poverty-stricken, be needy.

πένσα, ἡ [pensa] tweezers, forceps ‖ (ραπτικῆς) dart.

πεντάγραμμον, τό [pentaγramon] (μουσ) stave, staff.

πεντακόσιοι [pentakosiee] five hundred.

πεντάμορφος [pentamorfos] extremely beautiful.

πεντάρα, ἡ [pantara] (μεταφ) farthing || (US) nickel.

πεντάρι, τό [pentaree] figure 5 || (στά χαρτιά) five (at cards).

πέντε [pente] five.

πεντήκοντα [penteekonta] βλ πενήντα.

Πεντηκοστή, ἡ [penteekostee] Whit Sunday.

πέος, τό [peos] penis.

πεπαιδευμένος [pepedevmenos] educated, learned, trained.

πεπειραμένος [pepeeramenos] experienced, versed in.

πεπεισμένος [pepeesmenos] convinced, certain, sure.

πέπλος, ὁ [peplos] veil.

πεποίθησις, ἡ [pepeetheesees] conviction, certainty, assurance.

πεπόνι, τό [peponee] melon.

πεπτικός [pepteekos] digestive, peptic.

πέρα [pera] beyond, over, on the other side, over there || ἐκεῖ ~ yonder || ~ γιά ~ through and through || ἐδῶ ~ here || ~ ἀπό beyond, across || τά βγάζω ~ manage, make out.

περαιτέρω [peretero] further || moreover.

πέραμα, τό [perama] passage, ford || ferry.

πέραν [peran] βλ πέρα.

πέρας, τό [peras] end, extremity || completion, close.

πέρασμα, τό [perasma] crossing, passage || (βελόνας) threading || (ἀσθενείας) passing || (τόπος) much-visited spot.

περασμένος [perasmenos] past, gone, last, by.

περαστικά [perasteeka]: ~! get well soon!

περαστικός [perasteekos] passing by || transient, transitory || (δρόμος) frequented, busy.

περατώνω [peratono] finish, bring to an end, complete.

περβάζι, τό [pervazee] doorframe, frame, cornice.

περγαμηνή, ἡ [peryameenee] parchment.

πέρδικα, ἡ [perdeeka] partridge.

περδικλώνομαι [perdeeklonome] βλ πεδικλώνομαι.

περδικλώνω [perdeeklono] βλ πεδικλώνω.

πέρδομαι [perdome] fart (col), break wind.

περηφάνεια, ἡ [pereefaneea] βλ ὑπερηφάνεια.

περηφανεύομαι [pereefanevome] βλ ὑπερηφανεύομαι.

περήφανος [pereefanos] βλ ὑπερήφανος.

περί [peree] about, concerning, regarding, of || (μέ αἰτ) round, near || round about, approximately || ~ τίνος πρόκειται· what's it all about?

περιαυτολογία, ἡ [pereeavtoloyeea] boasting, bragging.

περιαυτολογῶ [pereeavtoloyo] boast.

περιβάλλον, τό [pereevalon] environment, surroundings.

περιβάλλω [pereevalo] encircle, surround || (ροῦχα) clothe, dress.

περίβλημα, τό [pereevleema] wrapper (καρποῦ) shell, husk || casing.

περιβόητος [pereevoeetos] famous, renowned, infamous.

περιβολάρης, ὁ [pereevolarees] gardener.

περιβολή, ἡ [pereevolee] garment, dress || surrounding.

περιβόλι, τό [pereevolee] garden, orchard.

περίβολος, ὁ [pereevolos] enclosure, yard || (τοῖχος) surrounding wall || park.

περιβρέχω [pereevreho] bathe, wash.

περιγελῶ [pereeyelo] mock, ridicule, deride || dupe, trick.

περίγελως, ὁ [pereeyelos] laughing stock.

περιγιάλι, τό [pereeyialee] seashore, coast.

περιγραφή, ἡ [pereeyrafee] description, account.

περιγράφω [pereeyrafo] describe, portray.

περιδεής [pereedees] terrified, frightened.

περιδέραιον, τό [pereedereon] necklace.

περίδοξος [pereedoksos] illustrious, famous.

περιεκτικός [periekteekos] capacious || (τροφή) substantial || (λόγος) comprehensive, concise, succinct.

περιεργάζομαι [perieryazome] examine carefully.

περιέργεια, ἡ [perieryeea] curiosity.

περίεργος [perieryos] curious, strange, inquiring.

περιέρχομαι [perierhome] travel through, walk round || come into reach.

περιεχόμενον, τό [periechomenon] contents || (σημασία) meaning.

περιέχω [perieho] contain, hold.

περιζήτητος [pereezeeteetos] in great demand, greatly prized.

περιηγητής, ὁ [perieeyeetees] tourist, traveller.

περιθάλπω [pereethalpo] attend, look after, treat.

περίθαλψις, ἡ [pereethalpsees] attendance, care, relief.

περιθώριον, τό [pereethoreeon] margin, room.

περικάλυμμα, τό [pereekaleema] wrapper, covering, shell.

περικεφαλαία, ἡ [pereekefalea] helmet.

περικλείω [pereekleeo] enclose, include.

περικοκλάδα, ἡ [pereekoklada] climbing plant || convolvulus.

περικοπή, ἡ [pereekopee] cutting off, deduction || (ἀπό βιβλίο) extract, passage.

περικόχλιον, τό [pereekohleeon] nut (for screw).

περικυκλώνω [pereekeeklono] surround.

περιλαίμιον, τό [pereelemeeon] animal's collar || necklace.

περιλάλητος [pereelaleetos] celebrated, famous, renowned.

περιλαμβάνω [pereelamvano] contain, have, hold || (περιέχω) include, comprise.

περιληπτικός [pereeleepteekos] comprehensive || concise, succinct.

περίληψις, ή [pereeleepsees] summary, précis, résumé.

περίλυπος [pereeleepos] sad, sorrowful || (ἔκφρασις) gloomy, doleful.

περιμαζεύω [pereemazevo] gather up || (ἀπό τόν δρόμο) rescue, harbour || (περιορίζω) check, control.

περιμένω [pereemeno] wait || wait for, expect.

περίμετρος, ή [pereemetros] circumference, perimeter.

πέριξ [pereeks] about, round || τά ~ the environs, suburb.

περιοδεία, ή [pereeodeea] tour, travelling, trip.

περιοδικόν, τό [pereeodeekon] magazine, periodical.

περιοδικός [pereeodeekos] periodic(al).

περίοδος, ή [pereeodos] period, era, age || season || (γυναικῶν) monthlies.

περίοπτος [pereeoptos] overlooking, rising, conspicuous || noticeable.

περιορίζω [pereeoreezo] limit, restrict || (ἐλέγχω) control || (ἐλαττώνω) reduce, cut down, curtail.

περιορισμός, ὁ [pereeoreesmos] limitation || detention, restriction || (ἐλάττωσις) reduction.

περιουσία, ή [pereeouseea] property, estate || (πλούτη) fortune, wealth.

περιοχή, ή [pereeohee] area, region, district || extent, expanse.

περιπαθής [pereepathees] full of feeling, passionate, impetuous.

περιπαίζω [pereepezo] ridicule, mock || dupe, trick, take in.

περίπατο [pereepato]: πάω ~ go for a stroll || (μεταφ) be a failure.

περίπατος, ὁ [pereepatos] walk, ride, drive, spin.

περιπατῶ [pereepato] βλ περπατῶ.

περιπέτεια, ή [pereepeteea] misadventure, incident.

περιπέτειες, οἱ [pereepeties] πλ the ups and downs.

περιπετειώδης [pereepeteeodees] full of adventures || (ἱστορία) of adventure.

περιπίπτω [pereepeepto] fall into || be reduced to.

περιπλανῶ [pereeplano] send long way round || ~μαι wander, rove, lose one's way.

περιπλέκω [pereepleko] interlace, entangle || complicate, confuse, muddle.

περιπλέον [pereepleon] moreover, besides || τό ~ surplus, excess.

περιπλέω [pereepleo] circumnavigate.

περιπλοκή, ή [pereeplokee] complication, complexity, intricacy.

περίπλοκος [pereeplokos] complex, involved.

περιπόθητος [pereepotheetos] much loved, greatly desired.

περιποίησις, ή [pereepieesees] care, attendance, looking after.

περιποιητικός [pereepieeteekos] considerate, obliging.

περιποιοῦμαι [pereepeeoume] take care of || (ἀσθενῆ) nurse.

περίπολος, ή [pereepolos] patrol.

περίπου [pereepou] about, nearly, almost.

περίπτερον, τό [pereepteron] pavilion, kiosk.

περιπτώσει [pereeptosee]: ἐν πάσει ~ in any case, anyway.

περίπτωσις, ή [pereeptosees] case, condition, circumstance.

περισκελίς, ή [pereeskelees] pair of trousers, pants || (γυναικός) knickers, panties.

περίσκεψις, ή [pereeskepsees] prudence, caution, discretion.

περισπασμός, ὁ [pereespasmos] diversion, distraction || (μεταφ) embarrassment, perplexity.

περισπῶ [pereespo] distract, divert || (γραμμ) circumflex.

περισπωμένη, ή [pereespomenee] circumflex accent.

περίσσεια, ή [pereeseea] excess, superabundance.

περίσσευμα, τό [pereesevma] surplus, excess.

περισσεύω [pereesevo] be in excess, be left over.

περίσσιος [pereeseeos] (ἄφθονος) abundant || (περιττός) unnecessary.

περισσοῦ [pereesou]: ὡς ἐκ ~ without absolute necessity, moreover.

περισσότερον [pereesoteron] more.

περισσότερος [pereesoteros] more || ὁ ~ most.

περισταλτικός [pereestalteekos] checking, repressive || (ἰατρ) peristaltic.

περίστασις, ή [pereestasees] circumstance, event, fact, occasion, situation.

περιστατικόν, τό [pereestateekon] incident, event.

περιστέλλω [pereestelo] repress, check, restrain, reduce.

περιστερώνας, ὁ [pereesteronas] dovecote.

περιστέρι, τό [pereesteree] pigeon, dove.

περιστοιχίζω [pereesteeheezo] surround, encircle.

περιστολή, ή [pereestolee] limitation, decrease, restriction, checking.

περιστρέφομαι [pereestrefome] revolve, spin, turn.

περιστρέφω [pereestrefo] (ρόδα κτλ) turn, rotate || (κλειδί) turn, twist.

περιστροφή, ή [pereestrofee] revolution, turn, rotation.

περίστροφον, τό [pereestrofon] revolver.

περισυλλέγω [pereeseelego] collect, gather.

περισφίγγω [pereesfingo] hug, embrace, clasp in one's hand.

περιτειχίζω [pereeteeheezo] build a wall round.

περιτομή, ἡ [pereetomee] circumcision.

περίτρανος [pereetranos] obvious, clear, evident.

περιτριγυρίζω [pereetreeyeereezo] surround, encircle, border.

περίτρομος [pereetromos] terrified, frightened.

περιτροπή, ἡ [pereetropee]: ἐκ περιτροπῆς by turns, in turn.

περιττός [pereetos] (προσπάθεια) useless, unavailing ‖ superfluous, unnecessary, needless ‖ ~ ἀριθμός odd number.

περιτύλιγμα, τό [pereeteeleeyma] wrapper, wrapping.

περιτυλίσσω [pereeteeleeso] wrap up ‖ roll up.

περιφανής [pereefanees] manifest, obvious ‖ (ἄνθρωπος) eminent, distinguished.

περιφέρεια, ἡ [pereefereea] (δένδρου) girth ‖ (γεωμ) circumference ‖ (χῶρος) district, region.

περιφέρομαι [pereeferome] stroll, walk up and down, hang about ‖ (ἡ γῆ κτλ) turn round, rotate.

περιφέρω [pereefero] turn, revolve, rotate.

περίφημος [pereefeemos] famous, admirable, celebrated.

περιφορά, ἡ [pereefora] turn, rotation ‖ (ἐκκλ) procession.

περίφραγμα, τό [pereefrayma] enclosure, hedge, fencing.

περίφραξις, ἡ [pereefraksees] enclosing, fencing.

περιφραστικός [pereefrasteekos] periphrastic(al).

περιφρόνησις, ἡ [pereefroneesees] contempt, scorn.

περιφρονητικός [pereefroneeteekos] disdainful, contemptuous, haughty.

περίφροντις [pereefrontees] full of care, concerned.

περιφρονῶ [pereefrono] hold in contempt, despise, spurn.

περιχαρής [pereeharees] cheerful, merry, joyful, gay.

περίχωρα, τά [pereehora] πλ neighbourhood, environs ‖ (πόλεως) suburb, outskirts.

περιώνυμος [pereeoneemos] celebrated, illustrious.

περιωπή, ἡ [pereeopee] eminence ‖ (μεταφ) importance ‖ ἀπό περιωπῆς with detachment.

περνῶ [perno] (ποτάμι, γέφυρα κτλ) pass, cross, go over ‖ (κάτι σέ κάποιον) pass, hand over ‖ (κάτι μέσα σέ κάτι) pass through ‖ (τόν καιρό) spend ‖ (βελόνη) thread (a needle) ‖ (ὑγρό ἀπό φίλτρο) filter, strain ‖ (νόμον) get voted, pass ‖

(στό δρόμο) pass, leave behind ‖ ~ γιά mistake for ‖ ~ ἀπό call at, go via.

περονιάζω [peroneeazo] pierce, go through.

περονόσπορος, ὁ [peronosporos] mildew.

περούκα, ἡ [perouka] wig.

περπάτημα, τό [perpateema] walking ‖ gait.

περπατῶ [perpato] walk ‖ go across ‖ (σκύλο κτλ) take for a walk.

πέρ(υ)σι [per(ee)see] last year ‖ περ(υ)σινός of last year.

πέσιμο, τό [peseemo] falling, fall.

πεσμένος [pesmenos] fallen ‖ impaired, worsened.

πέστροφα, ἡ [pestrofa] trout.

πέταγμα, τό [petayma] flying, flight ‖ throwing away, casting.

πετάγομαι [petayome] fly up ‖ rush ‖ butt in.

πετάλι, τό [petalee] pedal.

πεταλίδα, ἡ [petaleeda] limpet.

πέταλο, τό [petalo] petal ‖ (ἀλόγου) horseshoe.

πεταλούδα, ἡ [petalouda] butterfly (λαιμοδέτου) bow, bow tie.

πεταλώνω [petalono] shoe (a horse).

πέταμα [petama] βλ πέταγμα.

πεταχτά [petahta]: στά ~ hastily, hurriedly, quickly.

πεταχτός [petahtos] nimble ‖ sticking out.

πετεινός, ὁ [peteenos] cock ‖ (ὅπλου) hammer.

πετ(ι)μέζι, τό [pet(ee)mezee] must turned into syrup.

πετονιά, ἡ [petonia] fishing line.

πέτρα, ἡ [petra] stone, rock ‖ precious stone.

πετράδι, τό [petradee] pebble ‖ precious stone.

πετραχήλι, τό [petraheelee] (ἐκκλ) stole.

πετρέλαιον, τό [petreleon] petroleum, oil ‖ (ἀκάθαρτο) crude oil.

πετρελαιοπηγή, ἡ [petreleopeeyee] oil well.

πετρελαιοφόρον, τό [petreleoforon] oil tanker.

πέτρινος [petreenos] made of stone.

πετροβολῶ [petrovolo] pelt with stones.

πέτσα, ἡ [petsa] skin ‖ (ψωμιοῦ) crust ‖ (γάλακτος) cream.

πετσέτα, ἡ [petseta] table napkin ‖ towel.

πετσί, τό [petsee] skin, pelt, hide ‖ leather, dressed skin.

πέτσινος [petseenos] leather.

πετσοκόβω [petsokovo] cut up, carve ‖ cut badly, butcher.

πέττο, τό [peto] lapel.

πετυχαίνω [peteeheno] βλ ἐπιτυγχάνω.

πετῶ [peto] fly ‖ (ἀπό χαρά) jump for joy ‖ (στά σκουπίδια) throw away ‖ ~ ἔξω throw out ‖ kick out (col).

πεύκο, τό [pefko] pine.

πέφτει [peftee]: δέν σοῦ ~ λόγος you've got no say in the matter.

πέφτω [pefto] tumble, fall ‖ drop, come

down, subside ‖ come off ‖ occur ‖ ~ στό
κρεββάτι I go to bed ‖ ~ ἔξω make a
mistake ‖ (ναυτ) run aground ‖ ~ δίπλα
make up to ‖ ~ μέ τά μοῦτρα apply o.s.,
take up eagerly.

πέψις, ἡ [pepsees] digestion.

πηγάδι, τό [peeγαδee] well.

πηγάζω [peeγazo] spring from, originate,
emanate.

πηγαινοέλα, τό [peeγenoela] toing and
froing.

πηγαινοέρχομαι [peeγenoerhome] go to
and fro.

πηγαίνω [peeγeno] go ‖ escort, take ‖ βλ
καί κάω.

πηγή, ἡ [peeγee] spring, source ‖ (μεταφ)
origin, cause.

πηγούνι, τό [peeγounee] chin.

πηδάλιον, τό [peeδaleeon] rudder ‖ helm ‖
wheel.

πηδαλιοῦχος, ὁ [peeδaleeouhos] helmsman.

πήδημα, τό [peeδeema] jump(ing), spring
‖ sudden rise.

πηδῶ [peeδo] leap, jump, vault ‖ jump over
‖ (παραλείπω) skip, leave out.

πήζω [peezo] coagulate, thicken, curdle.

πηκτός [peektos] coagulated, thick,
curdled.

πηλάλα, ἡ [peelala] quick running ‖ (ἐπίρ)
at full speed.

πηλαλῶ [peelalo] run (quickly, at full speed).

πηλήκιον, τό [peeleekeeon] cap.

πηλίκον, τό [peeleekon] quotient.

πήλινος [peeleenos] earthen, of clay.

πηλός, ἡ [peelos] clay ‖ mud, slime, sludge.

πηνίον, τό [peeneeon] bobbin, spool ‖
(ἠλεκ) coil.

πήξις, ἡ [peeksees] coagulation, congealing
‖ sticking in.

πηρούνι, τό [peerounee] fork.

πήττα, ἡ [peeta] kind of cake, pie.

πήχη, ἡ [peehee] measure of length (0.46 m).

πηχτή, ἡ [peehtee] galantine.

πηχτός [peehtos] coagulated, jellied ‖ thick.

πήχυς, ὁ [peehees] cubit ‖ ell.

πῖ, τό [pee] the letter Π ‖ στό ~ καί φῖ in
two shakes of a lamb's tail.

πιά [pia] not any longer ‖ now, finally, at
last, at long last.

πιάνο, τό [peeano] piano.

πιάνομαι [peeanome] be caught at, be
paralyzed ‖ (τσακώνομαι) quarrel with ‖
(κατάγομαι) be related to.

πιάνω [peeano] take hold of, catch ‖ occupy
‖ (συζήτηση) engage ‖ (περιέχω) contain,
hold ‖ (λιμάνι) land ‖ ~ σπίτι rent a
house ‖ ~ τόπο come in useful ‖ ~ κουβέντα get into conversation ‖ ~ δουλειά
start a job, find a job.

πιάσιμο, τό [peeaseemo] hold, grasp ‖
catching ‖ (ἀφή) feeling, touch ‖ (φυτοῦ
κτλ) taking root ‖ (σώματος) stiffness,
paralysis.

πιασμένος [peeasmenos] occupied, taken ‖
(στό σῶμα) paralyzed, (feeling) stiff,
crippled.

πιατάκι, τό [peeatakee] small plate ‖
saucer.

πιατέλλα, ἡ [peeatela] large dish, flat dish.

πιατικά, τά [peeateeka] πλ crockery,
earthenware.

πιάτσα, ἡ [peeatsa] market ‖ (ταξί) taxi
rank.

πίδαξ, ὁ [peeδaks] jet of water, gush, spirt,
fountain.

πιέζω [piezo] press, squeeze, compress ‖
oppress, force.

πίεσις, ἡ [piesees] pressure, oppression ‖
(αἵματος) blood pressure.

πιεστήριον, τό [piesteereeon] press ‖
(ἐλαιῶν) oil-press.

πιεστικός [piesteekos] pressing, oppressive
‖ urgent.

πιέτα, ἡ [pieta] pleat.

πιθαμή, ἡ [peethamee] span of hand.

πιθανός [peethanos] probable, likely.

πιθανότης, ἡ [peethanotees] likelihood,
probability.

πιθανῶς [peethanos] probably, likely, in
all likelihood.

πίθηκος, ὁ [peetheekos] ape.

πιθάρι, τό [peetharee] jar.

πίθος, ὁ [peethos] βλ πιθάρι.

πίκα, ἡ [peeka] umbrage, pique ‖ (στά
χαρτιά) spade.

πικάντικος [peekanteekos] piquant, spicy.

πίκρα, ἡ [peekra] grief, bitterness, affliction.

πικράδα, ἡ [peekraδa] bitterness ‖ (μεταφ)
sorrow, chagrin.

πικραίνομαι [peekrenome] be grieved, be
embittered.

πικραίνω [peekreno] render bitter ‖ grieve,
distress.

πικροδάφνη, ἡ [peekroδafnee] oleander.

πικρός [peekros] bitter ‖ biting, harsh.

πικρότης, ἡ [peekrotees] bitterness.

πικρόχολος [peekroholos] (μεταφ) touchy,
irritable, snappy.

πιλάφι, τό [peelafee] pilaf, rice dish.

πῖλος, ὁ [peelos] hat.

πιλότος, ὁ [peelotos] pilot.

πινάκιον, τό [peenakeeon] dish, plate ‖ list,
roll, register.

πινακίς, ἡ [peenakees] nameplate ‖ (αὐτοκινήτου) licence plate, number plate.

πινακοθήκη, ἡ [peenakotheekee] picture
gallery, art gallery.

πίνακας, ὁ [peenakas] βλ πίναξ.

πίναξ, ὁ [peenaks] list, table ‖ (τοῦ τείχου)
notice board ‖ (σχολείου) blackboard ‖
(περιεχομένων) table of contents.

πινέζα, ἡ [peeneza] drawing pin.

πινέλο, τό [peenelo] artist's paintbrush.

πίνω [peeno] drink, take in ‖ (τσιγάρο)
smoke.

πιό [pio] more, greater.

πιοτό, τό [pioto] drinking || drink, liquor.

πίπα, ἡ [peepa] pipe || cigarette holder.

πιπεράτος [peeperatos] peppery || biting, caustic, piquant.

πιπέρι, τό [peeperee] pepper.

πιπεριά, ἡ [peeperia] pepper || (δένδρον) pepper tree.

πιπιλίζω [peepeeleezo] suck, sip.

πίπτω [peepto] βλ πέφτω.

πισίνα, ἡ [peeseena] swimming pool.

πισινός [peeseenos] back, posterior || ὁ ~ backside (col), arse (col), bum (col).

πίσσα, ἡ [peesa] pitch, tar, asphalt.

πισσόχαρτο, τό [peesoharto] roofing felt.

πισσώνω [peesono] tar, pitch.

πίστα, ἡ [peesta] ring || racetrack || (χοροῦ) dance floor.

πιστευτός [peestevtos] trustworthy || credible.

πιστεύω [peestevo] believe, have faith in || suppose, fancy, think.

πίστις, ἡ [peestees] faith, confidence, trust || fidelity || (οἴκον) credit, trustworthiness.

πιστόλι, τό [peestolee] pistol.

πιστοποιητικόν, τό [peestopieeteekon] certificate, testimonial.

πιστοποιῶ [peestopeeo] certify, guarantee, vouch for.

πιστός [peestos] faithful, loyal, devoted || accurate.

πιστώνω [peestono] (οἴκον) credit with, give credit.

πίστωσις, ἡ [peestosees] credit, trust.

πιστωτής, ὁ [peestotees] creditor.

πίσω [peeso] behind || back || over again || πάει ~ τὸ ρολόϊ the clock is slow || κάνω ~ move back || ~ μου behind me || ~ ἀπό behind, following.

πίτουρο, τό [peetouro] bran.

πιτσιλάδα, ἡ [peetseelaδa] freckle.

πιτσιλίζω [peetseeleezo] splash, sprinkle, dash (with).

πιτσιρίκος, ὁ [peetseereekos] small boy || kid (col).

πιτσούνι, τό [peetsounee] young pigeon, squab.

πίττα [peeta] βλ πήττα.

πιτυρίδα, ἡ [peeteereeδa] scurf, dandruff.

πίτυρον, τό [peeteeron] βλ πίτυρο.

πιωμένος [piomenos] drunk, tipsy.

πλά(γ)ι, τό [pla(γ)ee] side || στό ~ close by, near, beside.

πλαγιά, ἡ [playia] slope of hill, hillside.

πλαγιάζω [playiazo] go to bed || lie down || put to bed.

πλαγιαστός [playiastos] lying down, reclining.

πλάγιος [playeeos] oblique || indirect || crooked, dishonest.

πλαγίως [playeeos] indirectly || next door.

πλαδαρός [plaδaros] flabby, soft || (προσπάθεια) feeble, ineffective.

πλάζ, ἡ [plaz] bathing beach.

πλάθω [platho] mould, create, fashion.

πλάϊ [plaee] alongside, next door || ~ ~ side by side || ~ σέ next to, along with.

πλαϊνός [plaeenos] adjoining, next door.

πλαίσιον, τό [pleseeon] frame, framework || chassis || (μεταφ) scope, range.

πλαισιώνω [pleseeono] border, surround, frame, encircle.

πλάκα, ἡ [plaka] slab, plate, paving stone || plaque || (σχολική) slate || (σαπούνι) cake || (γραμμοφώνου) record || (φωτογραφική) plate || σπάσαμε ~ we had a lot of fun || ἔχει ~ it's funny, it's hilarious.

πλακάκι, τό [plakakee] floor tile, wall tile.

πλακόστρωτος [plakostrotos] paved, laid with tiles.

πλάκωμα, τό [plakoma] pressure, crush || unexpected arrival.

πλακώνω [plakono] crush, press down || happen unexpectedly || come suddenly.

πλακωτός [plakotos] flat(tened), in layers.

πλάνη, ἡ [planee] mistake, delusion || (ἐργαλεῖον) plane.

πλάνης, ὁ [planees] wanderer, vagrant.

πλανήτης, ὁ [planeetees] planet.

πλανίζω [planeezo] plane, smooth down.

πλανόδιος [planoδeeos] travelling || ~ ἔμπορος pedlar, hawker.

πλαντάζω [plantazo] be furious, fume, be enraged.

πλανῶμαι [planome] ramble, wander || (κάνω λάθος) be mistaken, delude o.s.

πλάξ, ἡ [plaks] βλ πλάκα.

πλασιέ, ὁ [plasie] commercial traveller, salesman.

πλάσις, ἡ [plasees] foundation, creation || moulding, formation.

πλάσμα, τό [plasma] creature, being || invention, fiction || beauty.

πλάστιγξ, ἡ [plasteengks] weighing machine, balance.

πλαστικός [plasteekos] plastic || comely.

πλαστογραφῶ [plastoγrafo] counterfeit || falsify.

πλαστός [plastos] false, forged || artificial, fictitious.

πλαταίνω [plateno] βλ πλατύνω.

πλάτανος, ὁ [platanos] plane tree.

πλατεῖα, ἡ [plateea] town square || (θεάτρου) pit.

πλάτη, ἡ [platee] back || shoulder blade.

πλατιά [platia] widely.

πλάτος, τό [platos] width, broadness, breadth || (γεωγραφικόν) latitude.

πλάττω [plato] βλ πλάθω.

πλατύνω [plateeno] make wider, stretch, let out || become wider, broaden.

πλατύς [platees] wide, broad, large, ample || (μεταφ) far-reaching.

πλέγμα, τό [pleγma] network || (μαλλιῶν) tress, braid.

πλειοδοτῶ [pleeoδoto] make highest offer or bid.

πλεῖον [pleeon] more.

πλειονότης, ἡ [pleeonotees] majority.

πλειο(νο)ψηφία, ἡ [pleeo(no)pseefeea] majority (of votes).

πλειστάκις [pleestakees] many times, often.

πλειστηριασμός, ὁ [pleesteereeasmos] auction.

πλεῖστος [pleestos] most, very much.

πλεκτός [plektos] knitted, plaited, woven.

πλέκω [pleko] plait, weave ‖ (κάλτσες) knit.

πλεμόνι, τό [plemonee] lung.

πλένω [pleno] βλ πλύνω.

πλέξιμο, τό [plekseemo] knitting ‖ braiding ‖ (σέ ὑπόθεσι) involvement.

πλεξοῦδα, ἡ [pleksouda] plait, braid, tress.

πλέον [pleon] more ‖ ἐπί ~ in addition ‖ not any longer ‖ moreover ‖ now.

πλεονάζω [pleonazo] abound, be plentiful ‖ exceed, be superfluous.

πλεόνασμα, τό [pleonasma] surplus, excess ‖ (βάρους) overweight.

πλεονέκτημα, τό [pleonekteema] advantage, benefit ‖ gift, quality, merit.

πλεονέκτης, ὁ [pleonektees] greedy person, covetous person.

πλεονεκτῶ [pleonekto] have the advantage ‖ be greedy.

πλεονεξία, ἡ [pleonekseea] cupidity, greed, avidity.

πλέριος [plereeos] full.

πλευρά, ἡ [plevra] side ‖ rib ‖ (ὄρους) slope, declivity ‖ (μεταφ) point of view.

πλευρίζω [plevreezo] (ναυτ) come alongside.

πλευρῖτις, ἡ [plevreetees] pleurisy.

πλευρόν, τό [plevron] side ‖ rib ‖ (στρατ) flank.

πλεχτό, τό [plehto] pullover ‖ knitted article.

πλέω [pleo] navigate, sail ‖ float ‖ (μεταφ) wade, wallow.

πληγή, ἡ [pleeyee] wound, injury, sore ‖ (μεταφ) plague, evil, sore.

πλήγμα, τό [pleeyma] blow ‖ wound.

πληγώνω [pleeyono] wound, injure ‖ offend, hurt.

πλήθη, τά [pleethee] πλ the masses.

πλῆθος, τό [pleethos] crowd ‖ mass ‖ great number.

πληθυντικός, ὁ [pleetheenteekos] (γραμμ) plural.

πληθύνω [pleetheeno] multiply, increase ‖ augment.

πληθυσμός, ὁ [pleetheesmos] population.

πληθώρα, ἡ [pleethora] abundance, excess, plenitude.

πληθωρισμός, ὁ [pleethoreesmos] inflation ‖ plenitude.

πληκτικός, ὁ [pleekteekos] boring, tiresome, irksome, dull, trying.

πλῆκτρον, τό [pleektron] (πιάνο κτλ) key ‖ plectrum ‖ drumstick.

πλημμελειοδικεῖον, τό [pleemeleeodeekeeon] (νομ) magistrate's court.

πλημμέλημα, τό [pleemeleema] misdemeanour, offence.

πλημμελής [pleemelees] faulty, inadequate, defective.

πλημμύρα, ἡ [pleemeera] flood, inundation ‖ (μεταφ) plenitude.

πλημμυρίζω [pleemeereezo] inundate, overflow ‖ (μεταφ) swarm.

πλήν [pleen] except, save ‖ (ἐπίρ) unless, except that ‖ (σύνδ) but ‖ (μαθημ) minus ‖ ~ τούτου besides, moreover.

πλῆξις, ἡ [pleeksees] tedium, weariness, boredom.

πληρεξούσιον, τό [pleereksouseeon] power of attorney.

πληρεξούσιος, ὁ, ἡ [pleereksouseeos] representative, proxy ‖ plenipotentiary, deputy.

πλήρης [pleerees] full, complete, whole ‖ swarming, teeming, packed.

πληροφορία, ἡ [pleeroforeea] information, report.

πληροφορίες, οἱ [pleerofories] πλ information.

πληροφοροῦμαι [pleeroforoume] learn, discover.

πληροφορῶ [pleeroforo] inform, notify.

πληρῶ [pleero] fill ‖ fulfil, perform.

πλήρωμα, τό [pleeroma] crew ‖ fullness ‖ filling, completion.

πληρωμή, ἡ [pleeromee] payment, reward ‖ salary, wages.

πληρώνω [pleerono] pay, settle ‖ (μεταφ) pay up, discharge.

πληρωτέος [pleeroteos] payable.

πληρωτής [pleerotees] payer.

πλησιάζω [pleeseeazo] approach, go near, put near, draw near.

πλησιέστερος [pleesiesteros] closer ‖ ὁ ~ the nearest.

πλησίον [pleeseeon] near, close by ‖ ὁ ~ neighbour.

πλησμονή, ἡ [pleesmonee] abundance, plenitude ‖ satiety.

πλήττω [pleeto] strike, hit, wound, afflict ‖ (παθαίνω πλήξι) be bored, be weary.

πλιάτσικο, τό [pleeatseeko] booty, pillage, loot.

πλίθ(ρ)α, ἡ [pleeth(r)a] brick.

πλινθόκτιστος [pleenthokteestos] built of bricks.

πλίνθος, ἡ [pleenthos] brick, firebrick.

πλοηγός, ὁ [ploeeyos] (ναυτ) pilot.

πλοιάριον, τό [pleeareeon] small boat, launch.

πλοίαρχος, ὁ [pleearhos] (ναυτ) captain ‖ (ἐμπορικοῦ) master, skipper.

πλοῖον, τό [pleeon] ship, vessel, boat.

πλόκαμος, ὁ [plokamos] tress, braid, plait ‖ (κινέζων) pigtail ‖ (ὀκταποδιοῦ) tentacle.

πλοκή, ἡ [plokee] plot (of play).
πλουμίδι, τό [ploumeeδee] embroidery, ornamentation.
πλοῦς, ὁ [plous] sailing, passage || navigating.
πλουσιοπάροχος [plouseeoparohos] copious, generous, abundant.
πλούσιος [plouseeos] rich, wealthy || splendid, magnificent.
πλουταίνω [plouteno] get rich, become wealthy.
πλουτίζω [plouteezo] make rich || get rich.
πλούτη, τά [ploutee] πλ riches, wealth.
πλοῦτος, ὁ [ploutos] opulence, wealth · richness || (ἐδάφους) fertility.
πλυντήριον, τό [pleenteereeon] laundry room || washing machine.
πλύνω [pleeno] wash, clean || brush || scrub.
πλύσιμο, τό [pleeseemo] wash(ing).
πλυσταριό, τό [pleestario] laundry room.
πλύστρα, ἡ [pleestra] washerwoman || washboard.
πλώρη, ἡ [ploree] prow || βάζω ~ set sail (for).
πλωτάρχης, ὁ [plotarhees] lieutenant-commander.
πλωτός [plotos] navigable || floating || (γέφυρα) pontoon bridge.
πνεῦμα, τό [pnevma] ghost, soul, breath of life || mind || genius, spirit || (γραμμ) breathing || Ἅγιον ~ Holy Ghost.
πνευματικός [pnevmateekos] spiritual || intellectual, mental || pneumatic.
πνευμονία, ἡ [pnevmoneea] pneumonia.
πνεύμων, ὁ [pnevmon] lung.
πνευστός [pnevstos] blown, wind (instrument).
πνέω [pneo] blow || ~ τά λοίσθια I breathe my last.
πνιγηρός [pneeyeeros] stifling, suffocating, choking.
πνιγμός, ὁ [pneeymos] suffocation, choking || drowning || throttling.
πνίγω [pneeyo] drown || stifle, suffocate || choke, throttle.
πνικτικός [pneekteekos] suffocating, choking.
πνίξιμο, τό [pneekseemo] drowning || strangulation.
πνοή, ἡ [pnoee] breath(ing) || (μεταφ) inspiration.
ποδάγρα, ἡ [poδayra] gout.
ποδάρι, τό [poδaree] βλ πόδι.
ποδήλατον, τό [poδeelaton] bicycle.
ποδηλατῶ [poδeelato] cycle, pedal.
πόδι, τό [poδee] foot, leg || (ποτηριού) stem || στό ~ standing || on the go || σηκώνω στό ~ cause a commotion.
ποδιά, ἡ [poδia] apron, overall || (παραθύρου) windowsill.
ποδόγυρος, ὁ [poδoyeeros] border, hem || (μεταφ) the fair sex.

ποδοπατῶ [poδopato] tread on, trample on trample underfoot.
ποδόσφαιρα, ἡ [poδosfera] football.
ποδοσφαιριστής, ὁ [poδosfereestees] football player.
ποδόσφαιρον, τό [poδosferon] game of football.
πόζα, ἡ [poza] pose, affectation.
ποζάρω [pozaro] pose, sit for || put on.
πόθεν [pothen] whence, from where, from what.
πόθος, ὁ [pothos] desire, wish, yearning.
ποθῶ [potho] desire, long for, wish, be eager for.
ποίημα, τό [pieema] poem.
ποίησις, ἡ [pieesees] poetry, poesy.
ποιητής, ὁ [pieetees] poet || creator, maker.
ποιητικός [pieeteekos] poetic.
ποικιλία, ἡ [peekeeleea] variety, diversity, assortment.
ποικίλλω [peekeelo] embellish, adorn || vary, change.
ποικίλος [peekeelos] varied, diverse, different || miscellaneous.
ποιμενικός [peemeneekos] pastoral, bucolic.
ποιμήν, ὁ [peemeen] shepherd, herdsman.
ποίμνιον, τό [peemneeon] flock, herd, drove || (ἐκκλ) flock.
ποινή, ἡ [peenee] penalty, punishment, pain.
ποινικός [peeneekos] penal, criminal, felonious.
ποιόν, τό [peeon] quality, property, attribute, nature.
ποῖος [peeos] who?, which?, what?
ποιότης, ἡ [peeotees] quality, property.
ποιῶ [peeo] create, make || do.
πολεμικόν, τό [polemeekon] warship.
πολεμικός [polemeekos] warlike, bellicose || of war, martial.
πολέμιος [polemeeos] unfriendly, hostile || ὁ ~ enemy, adversary.
πολεμιστής, ὁ [polemeestees] fighter, warrior, combatant.
πόλεμος, ὁ [polemos] war, warfare.
πολεμοφόδια, τά [polemofoδeea] πλ munitions, ammunition.
πολεμῶ [polemo] fight, make war against || contend, strive (to).
πολεοδομία, ἡ [poleoδomeea] town planning.
πολικός [poleekos] polar.
πολιορκία, ἡ [poleeorkeea] siege, blockade.
πολιορκῶ [poleeorko] besiege, surround || invest.
πόλις, ἡ [polees] city, town.
πολιτεία, ἡ [poleeteea] state, government || country, nation || town.
πολίτευμα, τό [poleetevma] system of government, regime.
πολιτεύομαι [poleetevome] go into politics, meddle in politics.

πολιτευτής, ὁ ʻʋ∪leetevteesⳂ politician, statesman.

πολιτικά, τά [poleeteeka] πλ politics.

πολίτης, ὁ [poleetees] citizen ‖ civilian.

πολιτική, ἡ [poleeteekee] politics ‖ policy ‖ (μεταφ) cunning, shrewdness.

πολιτικός [poleeteekos] civic, civilian ‖ political ‖ (οὐσ) politician.

πολιτισμένος [poleeteesmenos] civilized, cultured.

πολιτισμός, ὁ [poleeteesmos] civilization, culture.

πολιτογραφῶ [poleetoɣrafo] naturalize (as citizen).

πολιτοφυλακή, ἡ [poleetofeelakee] militia, civil guard ‖ (US) national guard.

πολίχνη, ἡ [poleehnee] large village, small market town.

πολλάκις [polakees] often, many times, frequently.

πολλαπλασιάζω [polaplaseeazoⳘ multiply ‖ propagate, increase.

πολλαπλασιασμός, ὁ [polaplaseeasmos] multiplication ‖ increase.

πολλαπλάσιον, τό [polaplaseeon] multiple.

πολλοί [polee] πλ many.

πόλο, τό [polo] polo.

πόλος, ὁ [polos] pole.

πολτός, ὁ [poltos] pap ‖ purée ‖ rag pulp.

πολύ [polee] much ‖ numerous, several ‖ great, lot ‖ τό ~ at the most.

πολυάνθρωπος [poleeanthropos] populous, crowded.

πολυάριθμος [poleeareethmos] numerous.

πολυάσχολος [poleeasholos] very busy, very occupied.

πολυβόλον, τό [poleevolon] machine gun.

πολυγαμία, ἡ [poleeɣameea] polygamy.

πολύγλωσσος [poleeɣlosos] polyglot.

πολυγράφος, ὁ [poleeɣrafos] duplicator.

πολυέλαιος, ὁ [polieleos] chandelier.

πολυζήτητος [poleezeeteetos] much sought-after.

πολυθρόνα, ἡ [poleethrona] armchair.

πολυκατοικία, ἡ [poleekateekeea] block of flats, apartment building.

πολυκοσμία, ἡ [poleekosmeea] crowds of people.

πολύκροτος [poleekrotos] causing a commotion.

πολυλογᾶς, ὁ [poleeloɣas] chatterbox, babbler, gossip.

πολυλογία, ἡ [poleeloɣeea] loquacity, garrulity, babble.

πολυμάθεια, ἡ [poleematheea] erudition, learning.

πολυμελής [poleemelees] having many members, numerous.

πολυμερής [poleemerees] varied, diversified.

πολυμήχανος [poleemeehanos] very ingenious ‖ cunning, crafty.

πολυπαθής [poleepathees] sorely tried, much afflicted.

πολυπληθής [poleepleethees] very numerous, crowded.

πολύπλοκος [poleeplokos] intricate, complicated, very involved.

πολύπους, ὁ [poleepous] polyp ‖ (ἰατρ) polypus.

πολυπράγμων [poleepraɣmon] meddlesome, inquisitive ‖ fussy.

πολύπτυχος [poleepteehos] with many folds, many-pleated.

πολύς [polees] much, numerous, many, great ‖ (χρόνος) long.

πολυσήμαντος [poleeseemantos] very significant, very important.

πολυσύνθετος [poleeseenthetos] very complex ‖ compound.

πολυτέλεια, ἡ [poleeteleea] luxury.

πολυτελής [poleetelees] sumptuous, splendid, rich.

πολυτεχνεῖον, τό [poleetehneeon] Polytechnic, National Technical School.

πολύτιμος [poleeteemos] valuable, precious, priceless.

πολυφαγία, ἡ [poleefaɣeea] gluttony, voracity, greediness.

πολύφωτον, τό [poleefoton] chandelier, candelabrum.

πολύχρωμος [poleehromos] multicoloured, variegated.

πολύωρος [poleeoros] lasting many hours, long-drawn-out.

πόμολο, τό [pomolo] door knob, handle.

πομπή, ἡ [pompee] procession, parade ‖ shame, stigma.

πομπός, ὁ [pompos] transmitter.

πομπώδης [pompodees] pompous, bombastic.

πονεμένος [ponemenosⳂ ɪn distress ‖ sad, hurt.

πονηρεύομαι [poneerevomeⳂ employ cunning, use wiles ‖ become suspicious.

πονηρεύω [poneerevo] rouse suspicions of ‖ make suspicious ‖ become cunning.

πονηρία, ἡ [poneereea] ruse, trick, guile ‖ suspicion, slyness.

πονηρός [poneeros] cunning, wily, crafty ⵉ suspicious, distrustful ‖ diabolical.

πονόδοντος, ὁ [ponodontos] toothache.

πονοκέφαλος, ὁ [ponokefalos] headache.

πονόλαιμος, ὁ [ponolemos] sore throat.

πόνος, ὁ [ponos] suffering, pain ‖ (τόκετοῦ) labour ‖ compassion, pity, sympathy.

ποντάρω [pontaro] punt ‖ back, bet on.

ποντικός, ὁ [ponteekos] mouse, rat ‖ (ἀνατ) muscle.

ποντοπόρος, ὁ [pontoporos] seafarer, navigator.

πόντος, ὁ [pontos] sea ‖ (παιχνιδιοῦ) poin ‖ (μέτρον) centimetre ‖ (στή πλεκτική stitch ‖ Εὔξεινος ~ Black Sea.

πονῶ [pono] feel compassion for, sympathize with ‖ hurt, pain ‖ (ἀμετ) feel pain, suffer.

πορδή, ή [pordee] fart (col).

πορεία, ή [poreea] march, route || course, run.

πορεύομαι [porevome] proceed, go, walk, march.

πορθμείον, τό [porthmeeon] ferry(boat).

πορθμός, ό [porthmos] strait, sound, channel.

πορθώ [portho] sack, pillage || take, capture.

πόρισμα, τό [poreesma] deduction, inference, conclusion || finding || (μαθημ) corollary.

πορνείον, τό [porneeon] brothel || (US) whorehouse.

πόρνη, ή [pornee] prostitute, whore.

πόρος, ό [poros] passage, ford || (τοῦ δέρματος) pore || πλ means, income, resources.

πόρπη, ή [porpee] buckle, clasp, brooch.

πόρρω [poro] far off, far away, at a distance.

πορσελάνη, ή [porselanee] china, porcelain.

πόρτα, ή [porta] door, gate, doorway, gateway.

πορτοκαλάδα, ή [portokalada] orangeade.

πορτοκάλι, τό [portokalee] orange.

πορτοκαλιά, ή [portokalia] orange tree.

πορτοφολάς, ό [portofolas] pickpocket.

πορτοφόλι, τό [portofolee] wallet.

πορτραίτο, τό [portreto] portrait.

πορφύρα, ή [porfeera] purple.

πορώδης [porodees] porous.

ποσάκις [posakees] how often?

πόσιμο [poseemo]: ~ νερό drinking water.

πόσιμος [posemos] drinkable.

ποσόν, τό [poson] quantity, amount || (χρήματος) sum.

πόσο(ν) [poso(n)] how much.

πόσος [posos] how much?, how many?, how large?, how great?

ποσοστόν, τό [pososton] percentage, share, quota.

ποσότης, ή [posotees] quantity, amount.

πόστα [posta]: τόν ἔβαλα ~ I berated him.

πόστο, τό [posto] strategic position.

ποσῶς [posos] not at all, in no way, by no means.

ποταμηδόν [potameedon] in torrents, in gushes.

ποτάμι, τό [potamee] river.

ποταμός, ό [potamos] βλ ποτάμι.

ποταπός [potapos] vile, base, abject.

πότε [pote] when? || ~ ~ sometimes, from time to time || ~ ... ~ sometimes ... sometimes.

ποτέ [pote] once, formerly || ever || (μετά ἀπό ἀρνητ) never || ~ πλέον never again.

ποτήρι(ον), τό [poteeree(on)] drinking glass.

πότης, ό [potees] heavy drinker, boozer.

ποτίζω [poteezo] water, irrigate || become damp, become saturated.

πότισμα, τό [poteesma] watering, irrigation.

ποτιστήρι, τό [poteesteeree] watering can.

ποτόν, τό [poton] drink, beverage.

ποῦ [pou] where?, whither? || γιά ~ where are you going? || ~ νά ξέρω how should I know? || ~ καί ~ once in a while, now and then.

πού [pou] who, whom, which, that || when || (συνδ) that || (ἐπίρ) somewhere, where.

πουγγί, τό [poungee] purse, bag || money.

πούδρα, ή [poudra] powder.

πούθε [pouthe] βλ πόθεν.

πουθενά [pouthena] not anywhere || nowhere.

πουκάμισο, τό [poukameeso] shirt.

πουλάδα, ή [poulada] young hen, pullet.

πουλάκι, τό [poulakee] little bird || ~ μου my darling, my pet.

πουλάρι, τό [poularee] foal, colt.

πουλερικά, τά [poulereeka] πλ poultry.

πούλημα, τό [pouleema] βλ πώλησις.

πουλί, τό [poulee] bird.

πούλμαν, τό [poulman] (motor) coach.

πουλῶ [poulo] βλ πωλῶ.

πούντα, ή [pounda] cold, pleurisy.

πουντιάζω [pounteeazo] cool, chill || feel very cold.

πούπουλο, τό [poupoulo] down, plume, feather.

πουρές, ό [poures] purée.

πουρμπουάρ, τό [pourmbouar] gratuity, tip.

πουρνάρι, τό [pournaree] evergreen oak.

πούρο, τό [pouro] cigar.

πούς, ό [pous] foot, leg || (μέτρον) foot.

πούσι, τό [pousee] mist, fog.

πούστης, ό [poustees] bugger, queen (col), queer (col).

πουτάνα, ή [poutana] whore.

πουτίγγα, ή [poutinga] pudding.

ποώδης [poodees] mossy.

πράγμα, τό [prayma] thing, object || matter, business, affair || (προϊόντα) goods || (ὕφασμα) cloth.

πράγματι [praymatee] in fact, actually.

πραγματεύομαι [praymatevome] deal with, treat, handle || negotiate.

πραγματευτής, ό [praymatevtees] tradesman, dealer || pedlar.

πραγματικός [praymateekos] real, actual, substantial, authentic.

πραγματικότης, ή [praymateekotees] reality, fact, truth.

πραγματογνώμων, ό [praymatoynomon] assessor, valuer || expert.

πραγματοποιῶ [praymatopeeo] carry out, realize, fulfil, work out.

πρακτέον, τό [prakteon] what should be done.

πρακτικά, τά [prakteeka] πλ records, minutes, proceedings.

πρακτικός [prakteekos] useful, practical || vocational.

πρακτορείον, τό [praktoreeon] agency travel agency.

πράκτωρ, ὁ [praktor] agent.

πραμάτεια, ἡ [pramateea] goods, commodities.

πραματευτής, ὁ [pramatevtees] βλ πραγματευτής.

πραξικόπημα, τό [prakseekopeema] coup d'état.

πρᾶξις, ἡ [praksees] action, act || practice, experience || (γεννήσεως κτλ) certificate, registration || (οίκον) deal, transaction || (μαθημ) operation.

πρᾶος [praos] affable, gentle, kind.

πρασιά, ἡ [prasia] flower bed or lawn round house.

πρασινάδα, ἡ [praseenada] verdure, greenery || green colour.

πράσινος [praseenos] green, verdant || unripe.

πράσο, τό [praso] leek.

πρατήριον, τό [prateereeon] specialist shop || ~ βενζίνης petrol station.

πράττω [prato] perform, act || do.

πραΰνω [praeeno] appease, calm, soothe, pacify.

πρέζα, ἡ [preza] pinch.

πρέπει [prepee] it is necessary, it is proper that || ~ νά πάω I must go || καθώς ~ decent, honourable, a gentleman.

πρεπόντως [prepontos] properly, suitably, fitly || correctly.

πρέπων [prepon] suitable, fitting, proper || decent, correct.

πρεσβεία, ἡ [presveea] embassy, legation || delegation.

πρεσβευτής, ὁ [presvevtees] ambassador, minister || representative.

πρεσβεύω [presvevo] profess, avow, affirm, represent.

πρεσβύτερος [presveeteros] elder, senior, older.

πρεσβυωπία, ἡ [presveeopeea] long-sightedness.

πρέφα, ἡ [prefa] card game || τό πῆρε ~ he smelt a rat.

πρήζομαι [preezome] become swollen, swell.

πρήζω [preezo] (μεταφ) infuriate.

πρηνής [preenees] prostrate, prone.

πρήξιμο, τό [preekseemo] swelling, tumour.

πρήσκω [preesko] swell up, become swollen || infuriate.

πρίγκηπας, ὁ [preengkeepas] prince.

πρίζα, ἡ [preeza] plug, socket.

πρίν [preen] before, previously, prior to || ~ ἀπό μένα ahead of me, in front of me || ~ τόν πόλεμο before the war.

πριναρι, τό [preenaree] evergreen oak holm oak.

πριόνι, τό [preeonee] saw, handsaw, hacksaw.

πριονίζω [preeoneezo] saw.

πρίσμα, τό [preesma] prism.

πριχοῦ [preehou] before.

πρό [pro] before, in front of, ahead of, in the face of || ~ ἡμερῶν a few days ago || ~ παντός especially, above all.

προαγγέλλω [proangelo] predict, prophesy.

προάγω [proago] put forward, promote, advance || speed up, further ι προαγωγή (οὐσ) advancement, promotion || προαγωγός (οὐσ) pimp, pander.

προαίρεσις, ἡ [proereesees] intention, purpose || bent, bias.

προαιρετικός [proereteekos] optional voluntary.

προαίσθησις, ἡ [proestheesees] presentiment, foreboding.

προάλλες [proales]: τίς ~ just the other day, recently.

προανάκρουσμα, τό [proanakrousma] prelude, preliminary.

προαναφερθείς [proanafenthees] abovementioned.

προασπίζω [proaspeezo] defend, protect, guard.

προάστειον, τό [proasteeon] suburb.

προαύλιον, τό [proavleeon] forecourt, courtyard.

πρόβα, ἡ [prova] fitting of clothes || trial, rehearsal.

προβάδισμα, τό [provadeesma] precedence, priority.

προβαίνω [proveno] advance, move forward || proceed, make || ~ εἰς carry out, make.

προβάλλω [provalo] project, further || (σκιά) cast || (φίλμ) project, show || (ἀντίστασι) offer resistance || (ἀντίρρησι) raise || (δικαιολογία) put forward an excuse || (ἀμετ) appear suddenly in view.

προβάρω [provaro] try on, go for a fitting.

προβατίνα, ἡ [provateena] ewe, lamb.

πρόβατον, τό [provaton] sheep.

προβιά, ἡ [provia] animal's skin.

προβιβάζω [proveevazo] promote, push forward.

πρόβιος [proveeos] of a sheep.

προβλέπω [provlepo] foresee, forecast || prepare for, provide.

πρόβλεψις, ἡ [provlepsees] forecast, anticipation.

πρόβλημα, τό [provleema] problem || (μεταφ) riddle, puzzle.

προβλής, ἡ [provlees] jetty, mole.

προβολεύς, ὁ [provolevs] searchlight, headlight || (σινεμά) projector.

προβολή, ἡ [provolee] projection || (προϊόντος) promotion.

προβοσκίς, ἡ [provoskees] trunk || (ἐντόμου) proboscis.

προγενέστεροι, οἱ [proyenesteree] πλ predecessors.

προγενέστερος [proyenesteros] anterior, previous, former || (οὐσ) precursor.

πρόγευμα, τό [proyevma] breakfast.

προγεφύρωμα, τό [proyefeeroma] bridge-head.

προγνωστικόν, τό [proynosteekon] prediction, forecast || tip.

πρόγονος, ὁ [proyonos] ancestor, forefather, forbear.

προγονός, ὁ, ἡ [proyonos] stepson, stepdaughter.

πρόγραμμα, τό [proyrama] programme, plan, schedule.

προγραφή, ἡ [proyrafee] proscription.

προγράφω [proyrafo] proscribe, outlaw.

προγυμνάζω [proyeemnazo] exercise, train || tutor.

πρόδηλος [prodeelos] obvious, evident, manifest, plain.

προδιαγράφω [prodeeayrafo] prearrange.

προδιάθεσις, ἡ [prodeeathesees] predisposition, liability (to), prejudice (against).

προδιαθέτω [prodeeatheto] predispose, forewarn, influence, prejudice.

προδίδω [prodeedo] reveal, betray || denounce, inform.

προδοσία, ἡ [prodoseea] betrayal || treachery.

προδότης, ὁ [prodotees] traitor, informer.

πρόδρομος, ὁ [prodromos] forerunner, precursor || herald.

προεδρεία, ἡ [proedreea] presidency, chairmanship.

προεδρεύω [proedrevo] preside, chair.

πρόεδρος, ὁ, ἡ [proedros] president, chairman || presiding judge.

προειδοποίησις, ἡ [proeedopieesees] previous warning, premonition.

προειδοποιῶ [proeedopeeo] let know || warn.

προειρημένος [proeereemenos] aforesaid.

προεισαγωγή, ἡ [proeesayoyee] introduction, preface.

προεκλογικός [proekloyeekos] pre-election.

προέκτασις, ἡ [proektasees] extension, prolongation.

προέλασις, ἡ [proelasees] advance, forward movement.

προελαύνω [proelavno] advance, move forward.

προέλευσις, ἡ [proelevsees] provenance, place of origin.

προεξέχω [proekseho] jut out, project, protrude.

προεξοφλῶ [proeksoflo] (χρέος) pay off in advance || receive in advance || take for granted, rely on.

προεξοχή, ἡ [proeksohee] projection, protrusion, prominence.

προεργασία, ἡ [proeryaseea] preliminary work.

προέρχομαι [proerhome] originate, come from, issue from.

προεστώς [proestos] notable, elder || chief.

προετοιμάζω [proeteemazo] prepare, fit for, train for.

προετοιμασία, ἡ [proeteemaseea] preparation.

προέχω [proeho] jut out || surpass || predominate.

πρόζα, ἡ [proza] prose.

προζύμι, τό [prozeemee] leaven, yeast.

προηγοῦμαι [proeeyoume] surpass, be ahead || precede, come before.

προηγούμενα, τά [proeeyoumena]: ἔχουν ~ they have a grudge.

προηγούμενον, τό [proeeyoumenon] precedent.

προηγούμενος [proeeyoumenos] preceding, previous, earlier.

προηγουμένως [proeeyoumenos] previously, beforehand.

προθάλαμος, ὁ [prothalamos] anteroom, antechamber, waiting room.

πρόθεσις, ἡ [prothesees] purpose, design, intention || (γραμμ) preposition, prefix.

προθεσμία, ἡ [prothesmeea] time limit, delay, term, option.

προθήκη, ἡ [protheekee] shop window || showcase.

προθυμία, ἡ [protheemeea] eagerness, readiness, alacrity.

πρόθυμος [protheemos] eager, willing, ready || obliging.

πρόθυρα, τά [protheera] πλ gates, approach || (μεταφ) verge, eve, threshold.

προίκα, ἡ [preeka] dowry, marriage portion.

προικίζω [preekeezo] dower || endow (with), equip (with).

προικοθήρας, ὁ [preekotheeras] fortune hunter, dowry hunter.

προικοσύμφωνον, τό [preekoseemfonon] marriage contract

προϊόν, τό [proeeon] product, production || proceeds.

προϊόντα, τά [proeeonta] πλ produce, articles, products.

προΐσταμαι [proeestame] direct, manage, supervise.

προϊστάμενος, ὁ [proeestamenos] superior, chief, supervisor.

πρόκα, ἡ [proka] nail, tack.

προκαλύπτω [prokaleepto] hide, screen, cover.

προκαλῶ [prokalo] challenge || provoke, incite.

προκάνω [prokano] catch, overtake || arrive on time || have the time to.

προκαταβολή, ἡ [prokatavolee] prepayment, advance payment || deposit.

προκαταβολικῶς [prokatavoleekos] in advance, beforehand.

προκαταλαμβάνω [prokatalamvano] forestall, occupy beforehand.

προκατάληψις, ἡ [prokataleepsees] bias, prejudice.

προκαταρκτικός [prokatarkteekos] preliminary, preparatory.

προκατειλημμένος [prokateeleemenos] biased, prejudiced.

προκάτοχος, ὁ [prokatohos] predecessor || previous holder, previous occupant.

πρόκειται [prokeete] it's a matter of || it's a question of || **περί τίνος ~** ; what's it all about? || **~ νά ἔλθω** I am due to come.

προκήρυξις, ἡ [prokeereeksees] proclamation, announcement || manifesto.

πρόκλησις, ἡ [prokleesees] affront, challenge || provocation, instigation.

προκλητικός [prokleeteekos] provocative, provoking || seductive.

προκόβω [prokovo] progress, succeed, prosper, make good.

προκομμένος [prokomenos] hard-working, diligent.

προκοπή, ἡ [prokopee] progress || industry || success.

προκρίνω [prokreeno] prefer, choose || predetermine.

πρόκριτος [prokreetos] notable.

προκυμαία, ἡ [prokeemea] quay, pier, jetty.

προκύπτω [prokeepto] arise || result, ensue.

προλαβαίνω [prolaveno] get a start on, forestall || catch, overtake || (σέ χρόνον) be on time, manage || have enough time for.

προλαμβάνω [prolamvano] βλ **προλαβαίνω**.

προλεγόμενα, τά [proleyomena] πλ preface, foreword.

προλέγω [proleyo] forecast, predict || say previously.

προλετάριος [proletareeos] proletarian.

προληπτικός [proleepteekos] precautionary, preventive || superstitious.

πρόληψις, ἡ [proleepsees] avertion, prevention || superstition.

πρόλογος, ὁ [proloyos] prologue, preface, preamble.

προμάμμη, ἡ [promamee] great-grandmother.

προμαντεύω [promantevo] prophesy, foretell, predict.

πρόμαχος, ὁ [promahos] champion, defender, protector.

προμαχών, ὁ [promahon] bastion, bulwark, rampart.

προμελέτη, ἡ [promeletee] preliminary study || premeditation || **ἐκ ~ς** deliberately || premeditated.

προμεσημβρία, ἡ [promeseemvreea] forenoon, morning.

προμήθεια, ἡ [promeetheea] supply, provision, supplying, victualling || (ποσοστόν) commission, brokerage.

προμηθευτής, ὁ [promeethevtees] provider, purveyor, supplier.

προμηθεύομαι [promeethevome] get, supply o.s. with.

προμηθεύω [promeethevo] supply, provide, furnish

προμηνύω [promeeneeo] portend, presage, foretell.

προνοητικός [pronoeeteekos] having foresight, provident, careful.

πρόνοια, ἡ [proneea] care, concern, precaution || providence, welfare.

προνόμιον, τό [pronomeeon] privilege, advantage || gift, talent.

προνομιοῦχος [pronomeeouhos] privileged, favoured.

προνοῶ [pronoo] foresee, forecast || provide for, think of.

προξενεῖον, τό [prokseneeon] consulate.

προξενητής, ὁ [prokseneetees] intermediary, matchmaker.

προξενιά, ἡ [proksenia] matchmaking.

πρόξενος, ὁ [proksenos] author, perpetrator, cause || (διπλωμάτης) consul.

προξενῶ [prokseno] cause, occasion, inflict, bring about.

προοδευτικός [prooodevteekos] progressive, forward || (φορολογία) graduated.

προοδεύω [prooodevo] progress, make headway || develop.

πρόοδος, ἡ [prooodos] advance, progress || development, improvement || (μαθημ) progression.

προοίμιον, τό [prooeemeeon] preface, prelude, preamble.

προοπτική, ἡ [proopteekee] perspective || prospect in view.

προορίζω [prooreezo] destine, intend, foreordain.

προορισμός, ὁ [prooreesmos] end, intention || destination.

προπαγάνδα, ἡ [propayanda] propaganda.

πρόπαππος, ὁ [propapos] great-grandfather.

προπαρασκευή, ἡ [proparaskevee] preparation || coaching.

προπάτορες, οἱ [propatores] πλ forefathers, ancestors.

προπέλλα, ἡ [propela] propeller.

προπέμπω [propembo] see off, accompany, go along with.

πρόπερσι [propersee] two years ago.

προπέτασμα [propetasma] screen || **~ καπνοῦ** smoke screen.

προπέτεια, ἡ [propeteea] insolence, arrogance.

προπίνω [propeeno] drink to s.o.'s health || toast.

προπληρώνω [propleerono] pay in advance.

πρόποδες, οἱ [propodes] πλ foot of mountain.

προπολεμικός [propolemeekos] prewar.

προπόνησις, ἡ [proponeesees] training, coaching.

πρόποσις, ἡ [proposees] toast (drink).

προπύλαια, τά [propeelea] πλ propylaea.

προπύργιον, τό [propeeryeeon] rampart, bulwark, bastion.

πρός [pros] towards || (γιά) for || at || in || **~ ὄφελός μου** to my advantage, to my good || ~ τιμήν του in his honour, for his sake || ~ τό παρόν for the present || ἕνα ~ ἕνα one by one || ὡς ~ ἐμέ as far as I am concerned || ~ Θεοῦ! for God's sake! || ~ τούτοις moreover || ~ δέ in addition, furthermore.

προσαγορεύω [prosayorevo] address, harangue, greet.

προσάγω [prosayo] put forward, exhibit, produce.

προσάναμα, τό [prosanama] tinder, firewood || fuel.

προσανατολίζομαι [prosanatoleezome] find one's bearings.

προσανατολίζω [prosanatoleezo] orientate || direct, guide.

προσαράσσω [prosaraso] run aground, be stranded.

προσαρμογή, ἡ [prosarmoyee] adaptation, accommodation || adjustment.

προσαρμόζω [prosarmozo] fit to || adapt, adjust, apply.

προσάρτημα, τό [prosarteema] accessory, annexe, addition.

προσάρτησις, ἡ [prosarteesees] annexation.

προσαρτῶ [prosarto] append, attach || annex.

προσβάλλω [prosvalo] assail, attack || (ὑγείαν) harm, injure || (δυσαρεστῶ) hurt, offend || (διαθήκην) challenge.

προσβλητικός [prosvleeteekos] offensive, abusive, insolent.

προσβολή, ἡ [prosvolee] onset, attack || (ὑγείας) fit, stroke || offence, insult.

προσγειοῦμαι [prosyeeoume] make a landing.

προσγείωσις, ἡ [prosyeeosees] landing, alighting.

προσδένω [prosdeno] tie, attach, fasten.

προσδίδω [prosdeedo] lend, add to, give.

προσδιορίζω [prosdeeoreezo] determine, define, fix || allocate, assign.

προσδοκώ [prosdoko] hope, expect, anticipate.

προσεγγίζω [prosengeezo] put near || approach, come near || (κατά προσέγγισιν) approximate || (ναυτ) put in at, land at.

προσεκτικός [prosekteekos] attentive, heedful, mindful || careful.

προσέλευσις, ἡ [proselevsees] arrival, approach.

προσελκύω [proselkeeo] (προσοχήν) attract, win, draw, catch || (ὑποστηρικτές) gain, win over.

προσέρχομαι [proserhome] attend, present o.s. || apply for.

προσέτι [prosetee] also, besides, in addition to, more.

προσευχή, ἡ [prosevhee] prayer.

προσεύχομαι [prosevhome] pray, say one's prayers.

προσεχής [prosehees] next || forthcoming.

προσέχω [proseho] pay attention to, notice || be attentive, be mindful || (κάποιον) take care of.

προσεχῶς [prosehos] shortly, soon, in a short time.

προσηκόντως [proseekontos] becomingly, properly.

προσηλυτίζω [proseeleeteezo] convert, proselytize.

προσηλωμένος [proseelomenos] attached to, devoted to, absorbed in.

προσηλώνω [proseelono] nail, fix || (μεταφ) look fixedly (at).

προσηνής [proseenees] affable, kind, mild, gentle.

πρόσθεσις, ἡ [prosthesees] addition, increase.

πρόσθετος [prosthetos] additional, extra.

προσθέτω [prostheto] add, sum up || mix with.

προσθήκη, ἡ [prostheekee] addition, increase.

πρόσθιος [prostheeos] front, fore.

προσιτός [proseetos] attainable, accessible || (τιμή) reasonable, within one's means.

πρόσκαιρος [proskeros] transitory, passing, momentary.

προσκαλῶ [proskalo] call, send for || (νομ) summon, subpoena || (εἰς γεῦμα κτλ) invite.

προσκεκλημένος [proskekleemenos] invited.

προσκέφαλον, τό [proskefalon] pillow, cushion.

πρόσκλησις, ἡ [proskleesees] call, summons || (τηλεφώνου) telephone call || (εἰς δεξίωσιν κτλ) invitation || (στρατ) calling up || (εἰσιτήριον δωρεάν) complimentary ticket.

προσκλητήριον, τό [proskleeteereeon] invitation (card) || (στρατ) call, roll call || (ναυτ) muster roll.

προσκόλλησις, ἡ [proskoleesees] adherence, attaching || fidelity.

προσκολλῶ [proskolo] stick, attach, paste on || second (attach).

προσκομίζω [proskomeezo] bring forward, bring || offer.

πρόσκομμα, τό [proskoma] obstacle, impediment, hindrance.

πρόσκοπος, ὁ [proskopos] scout || boy scout.

προσκόπτω [proskopto] stumble over || (εἰς ἐμπόδιον) meet with difficulties.

προσκρούω [proskrouo] crash || strike (against) || be opposed to.

προσκύνημα, τό [proskeeneema] adoration || submission || place of pilgrimage.

προσκυνητής, ὁ [proskeeneetees] pilgrim.

προσκυνῶ [proskeeno] adore, worship || pay homage to, yield.

προσλαμβάνω [proslamvano] take on, engage, employ || (ὕφος) put on.

προσμένω [prosmeno] wait for, hope for.

πρόσμειξις, ἡ [prosmeeksees] blending, mixing.

πρόσοδος, ἡ [prosodos] income, revenue ‖ (ἐμπόριον) profit ‖ yield.

προσοδοφόρος [prosodoforos] productive, profitable, lucrative.

προσοικειοῦμαι [proseekeeoume] become familiar with ‖ (συνηθίζω) get accustomed to.

προσόν, τό [proson] aptitude, fitness, qualification ‖ advantage.

προσορμίζομαι [prosormeezome] moor, come to, land.

προσοχή, ἡ [prosohee] attention, notice ‖ caution, precaution, care.

προσόψι(ον), τό [prosopsee(on)] towel.

πρόσοψις, ἡ [prosopsees] façade, front(age).

προσπάθεια, ἡ [prospatheea] endeavour, effort, attempt, labour.

προσπαθῶ [prospatho] try, attempt.

προσπερνῶ [prosperno] overtake ‖ (μεταφ) surpass.

προσποίησις, ἡ [prospieesees] pretence, sham.

προσποιητός [prospieetos] affected, assumed, feigned.

προσποιοῦμαι [prospeeoume] affect, put on ‖ pretend.

προσταγή, ἡ [prostayee] order, ordering, command.

προστάζω [prostazo] order, direct, command.

προστακτική, ἡ [prostakteekee] (γραμμ) imperative (mood).

προστασία, ἡ [prostaseea] protection, defence.

προστατευόμενος, ὁ [prostatevomenos] protégé.

προστατευτικός [prostatevteekos] protecting ‖ condescending.

προστατεύω [prostatevo] defend, protect ‖ extend patronage to.

προστάτης, ὁ [prostatees] protector, patron ‖ (ἀνατ) prostate.

προστίθεμαι [prosteetheme] be added, be mixed (with).

πρόστιμον, τό [prosteemon] fine, penalty.

προστρέχω [prostreho] rush up, run up ‖ resort to, turn to.

προστριβή, ἡ [prostreevee] friction, rubbing ‖ (μεταφ) dispute.

προστυχαίνω [prosteeheno] make vulgar, coarsen ‖ grow vulgar.

προστυχιά, ἡ [prosteehia] vulgarity, rudeness, contemptible act.

πρόστυχος [prosteehos] vile, rude, ill-mannered ‖ of bad quality.

προσύμφωνον, τό [proseemfonon] preliminary agreement, draw-up agreement.

προσφά(γι)ι, τό [prosfa(γ)ee] anything eaten with bread.

πρόσφατος [prosfatos] recent, new ‖ (μόδα) modern.

προσφέρομαι [prosferome] offer ‖ be appropriate, be fitting.

προσφέρω [prosfero] offer, present, give.

προσφεύγω [prosfevγo] have recourse to, turn (to).

προσφιλής [prosfeelees] dear, loved, precious.

προσφορά, ἡ [prosfora] offer, offering, proposal, bid ‖ thing offered ‖ (ἐκκλ) consecrated bread.

πρόσφορος [prosforos] convenient, opportune, suitable.

πρόσφυγας, ὁ [prosfeeγas] refugee.

προσφυγή, ἡ [prosfeeγee] recourse, resort ‖ (νομ) legal redress, appeal.

προσφυής [prosfiees] suitable, well-adapted, fitting.

πρόσφυξ, ὁ, ἡ [prosfeeks] βλ πρόσφυγας.

προσφωνῶ [prosfono] address, greet.

πρόσχαρος [prosharos] cheerful, lively, merry, gay.

προσχέδιον, τό [prosheδeeon] rough draft, sketch.

πρόσχημα, τό [prosheema] pretext, excuse.

προσχωρῶ [proshoro] join, go over (to) ‖ cleave (to), adhere (to).

πρόσω [proso] forwards, ahead.

προσωδία, ἡ [prosoδeea] prosody.

προσωνυμία, ἡ [prosoneemeea] nickname, name.

προσωπάρχης, ὁ [prosoparhees] personnel officer, staff manager.

προσωπεῖον, τό [prosopeeon] mask.

προσωπικόν, τό [prosopeekon] personnel, staff ‖ (σπιτιοῦ) servants.

προσωπικός [prosopeekos] personal.

προσωπικότης, ἡ [prosopeekotees] personality, individuality.

προσωπικῶς [prosopeekos] personally.

προσωπίς, ἡ [prosopees] mask.

προσωπογραφία, ἡ [prosopoγrafeea] portrait painting, portrait.

πρόσωπον, τό [prosopon] face, visage ‖ person ‖ (θεάτρου) role, character, part.

προσωποποίησις, ἡ [prosopopieesees] personification ‖ impersonation.

προσωρινός [prosoreenos] provisional, passing, fleeting.

πρότασις, ἡ [protasees] proposal, suggestion, offer, motion ‖ (γραμμ) sentence ‖ clause.

προτείνω [proteeno] extend, stretch out, put forward ‖ propose, suggest.

προτελευταῖος [protelevteos] last but one.

προτεραία, ἡ [proterea] the preceding day.

προτεραιότης, ἡ [protereotees] priority, primacy.

προτέρημα, τό [protereema] gift, faculty, advantage, talent.

πρότερος [proteros] earlier, previous to, prior (to).

προτέρων [proteron]: ἐκ τῶν ~ beforehand.

προτεσταντισμός, ὁ [protestanteesmos] Protestantism.

προτίθεμαι [proteetheme] intend, propose, mean, think.

προτίμησις, ἡ [proteemeesees] preference, predilection.

προτιμότερος [proteemoteros] preferable to.

προτιμῶ [proteemo] prefer, like better.

προτομή, ἡ [protomee] bust.

προτοῦ [protou] before ‖ previously.

προτρέπω [protrepo] exhort, instigate, incite.

προτρέχω [protreho] run in advance of ‖ (περνῶ) outrun, overtake.

προτροπή, ἡ [protropee] exhortation, prompting.

πρότυπον, τό [proteepon] original, pattern, model, example ‖ mould.

πρότυπος [proteepos] model.

προϋπαντῶ [proeepanto] go to meet s.o.

προϋπάρχω [proeeparho] pre-exist ‖ (εἰς χρόνον) come before.

προϋπόθεσις, ἡ [proeepothesees] assumption, presumption.

προϋποθέτω [proeepotheto] presuppose, presume.

προϋπολογίζω [proeepoloyeezo] estimate, compute beforehand.

προϋπολογισμός, ὁ [proeepoloyeesmos] estimate ‖ budget.

προὔχων, ὁ [prouhon] notable.

προφανής [profanees] obvious, evident, plain, clear.

προφανῶς [profanos] obviously, evidently, manifestly.

πρόφασις, ἡ [profasees] pretext, excuse, pretence.

προφέρ(ν)ω [profer(n)o] pronounce, utter, articulate.

προφητεία, ἡ [profeeteea] prophecy, prophetic utterance.

προφητεύω [profeetevo] prophesy, predict.

προφήτης, ὁ [profeetees] prophet.

προφητικός [profeeteekos] prophetic.

προφθάνω [profthano] anticipate, forestall ‖ catch, overtake, overhaul ‖ (εἰς χρόνον) be in time for, have the time to.

προφορά, ἡ [profora] pronunciation, accent.

προφτάνω [proftano] βλ προφθάνω.

προφυλακή, ἡ [profeelakee] vanguard, outpost.

προφυλακίζω [profeelakeezo] hold in custody, detain.

προφυλακτήρ, ὁ [profeelakteer] bumper (aut).

προφυλακτικός [profeelakteekos] wary, careful ‖ precautionary, preventive.

προφύλαξις, ἡ [profeelaksees] precaution, cautiousness.

προφυλάσσομαι [profeelasome] take precautions, protect o.s.

προφυλάσσω [profeelaso] protect, preserve (from), defend.

πρόχειρος [proheeros] ready, handy ‖ impromptu.

προχθές [prohthes] the day before yesterday.

πρόχωμα, τό [prohoma] earthwork ‖ dam, dyke.

προχωρῶ [prohoro] go forward, advance ‖ progress, gain ground.

προωθῶ [prootho] impel ‖ push forward, urge on.

πρόωρος [prooros] premature, untimely hasty.

πρύμ(ν)η, ἡ [preem(n)ee] stern, poop.

πρυτανεύω [preetanevo] (μεταφ) predominate, prevail, get the better of.

πρύτανις, ὁ [preetanees] head of university dean.

πρώην [proeen] former, ex-.

πρωθυπουργός, ὁ [protheepouryos] prime minister, premier.

πρωί [proee] in the morning ‖ (οὐσ) morning.

πρωία, ἡ [proeea] morning, forenoon.

πρώιμος [proeemos] untimely, premature ‖ (γιά φυτά) precocious, early.

πρωινός [proeenos] morning ‖ rising early.

πρωινό, τό [proeeno] morning ‖ (πρόγευμα) breakfast.

πρωκτός, ὁ [proktos] anus.

πρώρα, ἡ [prora] prow, bows.

πρῶτα [prota] first, at first ‖ before, formerly, once.

πρωταγωνιστής, ὁ [protayoneestees] protagonist, hero.

πρωτάθλημα, τό [protathleema] championship.

πρωταίτιος, ὁ [proteteeos] ringleader, perpetrator ‖ cause.

πρωτάκουστος [protakoustos] unheard-of, unprecedented.

πρωταρχικός [protarheekos] most important.

πρωτεῖα, τά [proteea] πλ first place, primacy, precedence.

πρωτεργάτης, ὁ [proteryatees] perpetrator pioneer, cause.

πρωτεύουσα, ἡ [protevousa] capital, metropolis.

πρωτεύω [protevo] be first, lead, surpass, triumph (over).

πρωτεύων [protevon] primary, foremost, first.

πρωτίστως [proteestos] essentially, principally.

πρωτοβάζω [protovazo] wear for the first time.

πρωτοβάθμιος [protovathmeeos] of the first degree.

πρωτόβγαλτος [protovyaltos] inexperienced, unskilful, uninitiated.

πρωτοβουλία, ἡ [protovouleea] initiative.

πρωτοβρόχια, τά [protovroheea] πλ first rains in autumn.

πρωτογέννητος [protoyeneetos] first-born.

πρωτόγονος [protoyonos] primitive || (ἤδη) rough, rude, unpolished.

πρωτοδικεῖον, τό [protodeekeeon] court of first instance.

πρωτοετής [protoetees] first-year.

πρωτόκολλον, τό [protokolon] register, record || protocol, etiquette.

πρωτοκολλῶ [protokolo] enter in register, record.

Πρωτομαγιά, ἡ [protomayia] May Day.

πρωτομηνιά, ἡ [protomeenia] first day of month.

πρῶτον [proton] first, firstly, in the first place, to start with.

πρωτοπορεία, ἡ [protoporeea] vanguard.

πρωτοπόρος, ὁ [protoporos] pioneer, forerunner, innovator.

πρῶτος [protos] first, foremost || best, top || initial, elementary || (ἀριθμός) prime

πρωτοστατῶ [protostato] lead.

πρωτότοκος [prototokos] first born, oldest.

πρωτοτυπία, ἡ [prototeepeea] originality || eccentricity.

πρωτότυπον, τό [prototeepon] original, pattern, model.

πρωτότυπος [prototeepos] original, novel, singular.

πρωτοφανής [protofanees] new, fresh || astonishing.

Πρωτοχρονιά, ἡ [protohronia] New Year's Day.

πρωτύτερα [proteetera] earlier on, at first, before.

πταῖσμα, τό [ptesma] misdemeanour, violation || fault, error.

πταισματοδικεῖον, τό [ptesmatodeekeeon] police court.

πταίω [pteo] be at fault, be responsible.

πτέρνα, ἡ [pterna] heel.

πτερνιστήρ, ὁ [pterneesteer] spur.

πτερόν, τό [pteron] wing || feather, plume || (προπέλλας) blade, vane.

πτερύγιον, τό [ptereeyeeon] fin || aileron, wing flap.

πτέρυξ, ἡ [ptereeks] wing.

πτέρωμα, τό [pteroma] plumage, feathers.

πτερωτός [pterotos] winged.

πτηνόν, τό [pteenon] bird, fowl.

πτηνοτροφία, ἡ [pteenotrofeea] poultry farming.

πτῆσις, ἡ [pteesees] flight, flying.

πτίλον, τό [pteelon] down, plume.

πτοῶ [ptoo] intimidate, frighten, browbeat.

πτύελον, τό [ptielon] spittle, spit, sputum.

πτυχή, ἡ [pteehee] fold, pleat || wrinkle || (πανταλονιοῦ) crease.

πτυχίον, τό [pteeheeon] diploma, certificate.

πτυχιοῦχος [pteeheeouhos] graduate, holding a diploma.

πτύω [pteeo] spit out || expectorate.

πτῶμα, τό [ptoma] corpse, dead body || (ζώου) carcase.

πτῶσις, ἡ [ptosees] fall, tumble || collapse || drop || (γραμμ) case.

πτώχευσις, ἡ [ptohevsees] bankruptcy, failure, insolvency.

πτωχεύω [ptohevo] go bankrupt || become poor.

πτωχοκομεῖον, τό [ptohokomeeon] poorhouse.

πτωχός [ptohos] poor, needy.

πυγμαῖος, ὁ [peeymeos] pygmy.

πυγμαχία, ἡ [peengmaheea] boxing, pugilism.

πυγμή, ἡ [peeymee] fist || (μεταφ) vigour, determination.

πυγολαμπίς, ἡ [peeyolampees] glow-worm, firefly.

πυθμήν, ὁ [peethmeen] bottom.

πύθων, ὁ [peethon] python.

πυκνά [peekna] closely, densely, thickly.

πυκνός [peeknos] thick, dense, closely-packed, close || (γένεια) bushy.

πυκνότης, ἡ [peeknotees] density, compactness, thickness || (κυμάτων) frequency.

πυκνώνω [peeknono] thicken, condense, grow thick || make more frequent.

πυκνωτής, ὁ [peeknotees] (ἠλεκ) condenser.

πύλη, ἡ [peelee] gate, gateway.

πυλών, ὁ [peelon] gateway, portal, gate, entrance way.

πυνέζα, ἡ [peeneza] drawing pin.

πυξίς, ἡ [peeksees] (mariner's) compass box.

πύξος, ἡ [peeksos] box tree.

πύον, τό [peeon] pus, matter.

πῦρ, τό [peer] fire, firing.

πυρά, ἡ [peera] fire || (μεταφ) sensation of burning.

πυρακτώνω [peeraktono] make red-hot, glow.

πυραμίς, ἡ [peeramees] pyramid.

πύραυλος, ὁ [peeravlos] rocket.

πύραυνον, τό [peeravnon] brazier.

πυργίσκος, ὁ [peeryeeskos] turret.

πύργος, ὁ [peeryos] tower || castle, palace || (ναυτ) bridge house.

πυρεῖον, τό [peereeon] match (for lighting), lucifer.

πυρετός, ὁ [peeretos] high temperature, fever || (μεταφ) activity, energy.

πυρετώδης [peeretodees] feverish || (μεταφ) restless, feverish.

πυρήν, ὁ [peereen] stone, pip || centre, core || nucleus.

πυρηνικός [peereeneekos] nuclear.

πυρηνέλαιον, τό [peereeneleon] oil from stones || seed oil.

πύρινος [peereenos] burning, fiery, red-hot || (μεταφ) ardent, fervent.

πυρῖτις, ἡ [peereetees] pyrites, flint.

πυριτιδαποθήκη, ἡ [peereeteedapotheekee] powder magazine.

πυρῖτις, ἡ [peereetees] gunpowder, powder.

πυρκαϊά, ή [peerkaeea] fire, burning, conflagration.

πυροβολείον, τό [peerovoleeon] gun emplacement, gun position.

πυροβολητής, ὁ [peerovoleetees] gunner.

πυροβολικόν, τό [peerovoleekon] artillery.

πυροβολισμός, ὁ [peerovoleesmos] firing, shot.

πυροβολῶ [peerovolo] fire || shoot at || shell.

πυρομαχικά, τά [peeromaheeka] πλ munitions || ammunition.

πυροσβέστης, ὁ [peerosvestees] fireman.

πυροσβεστική [peerosvesteekee]: ~ ὑπηρεσία fire brigade.

πυροτέχνημα, τό [peerotehneema] firework, cracker.

πυρπολικόν, τό [peerpoleekon] fire ship.

πυρπολῶ [peerpolo] set on fire, burn down, consume by fire.

πυρρός [peeros] red-haired || russet, carroty.

πυρσός, ὁ [peersos] torch, brand || beacon.

πυρώνω [peerono] get red-hot, heat.

πυτζάμα, ή [peetzama] pyjamas.

πυώδης [peeodees] full of pus.

πώγων, ὁ [pogon] beard || chin.

πωλεῖται [poleete]: ' ~ ' 'for sale'.

πώλησις, ἡ [poleesees] sale, selling.

πωλητής, ὁ [poleetees] seller || salesman || shop assistant.

πωλήτρια, ή [poleetreea] seller || saleswoman.

πῶλος, ὁ [polos] foal, colt.

πωλῶ [polo] sell || (μεταφ) sell, betray.

πῶμα, τό [poma] stopper, plug || (μποτίλιας) cork || lid, cover.

πωρόλιθος, ὁ [poroleethos] porous stone.

πώρωσις, ἡ [poroses] hardening || (μεταφ) insensibility, callousness.

πῶς [pos] how?, what? || ~ ὄχι; and why not? || ~ ! yes, certainly.

πώς [pos] that.

πως [pos] somewhat, somehow, in any way.

Ρ, ρ

ραβαῖσι, τό [ravaeesee] banqueting, carousal || uproar.

ραββίνος, ὁ [raveenos] rabbi.

ραβδί, τό [ravdee] cane, stick.

ραβδίζω [ravdeezo] flog, thrash, cane.

ραβδισμός, ὁ [ravdeesmos] flogging.

ράβδος, ή [ravdos] stick, staff || (μαγική) wand || (ἐκκλ) pastoral staff || (σιδηροδρομική) rail.

ραβδώσεις, αἱ [ravdosees] πλ fluting, grooves || stripes.

ράβδωσις, ἡ [ravdosees] stripe || (ἀρχιτεκτονική) fluting || groove.

ραβδωτός [ravdotos] striped || fluted || lined, ruled.

ράβω [ravo] sew up, sew on || stitch || (κοστούμι) have a suit made.

ράγα, ή [raya] grape, berry || nipple.

ραγάδα, ή [rayada] crack, fissure, chink

ραγδαῖος [raydeos] violent, turbulent || (πτῶσις) rapid, headlong || (πρόοδος) rapid, speedy.

ραγδαίως [raydeos] violently, impetuously, swiftly.

ραγιᾶς, ὁ [rayias] slave, bondsman

ραγίζω [rayeezo] crack, split

ράγισμα, τό [rayeesma] crack, fissure, split

ραγού, τό [rayou] ragout.

ραδιενέργεια, ἡ [radieneryeea] radio activity.

ραδιενεργός [radieneryos] radioactive

ραδίκι, τό [radeekee] chicory, dandelion

ραδιογραφία, ἡ [radeeoyrafeea] Χ-ray photography.

ραδιοθεραπεία, ἡ [radeeotherapeea] Χ-ray treatment.

ραδιολογία, ἡ [radeeoloyeea] radiology

ράδιον, τό [radeeon] radium.

ράδιος [radeeos] easy, not difficult

ραδιοτηλεγράφημα, τό [radeeoteeleyrafeema] radiotelegram.

ραδιοτηλεγραφία, ἡ [radeeoteeleyrafeea] radiotelegraphy

ραδιοτηλεφωνία, ἡ [radeeoteelefoneea] radiotelephony.

ραδιουργία, ἡ [radiouryeea] intrigue. machination.

ραδιοῦργος [radiouryos] scheming, intriguing, plotting.

ραδιόφωνον, τό [radeeofonon] radio

ραδίως [radeeos] easily.

ράθυμος [ratheemos] languid, listless, lazy

ραιβοποδία, ἡ [revopodeea] bandy-legged-ness.

ραίνω [reno] sprinkle, scatter, spread

ράϊσμα [raeesma] βλ **ράγισμα**.

ρακένδυτος [rakendeetos] in rags, tattered.

ρακί, τό [rakee] kind of spirit.

ράκος, ὁ [rakos] rag, tatters || (μεταφ) physical wreck.

ράμμα, τό [rama] stitch, thread.

ραμμένος [ramenos] sewn.

ράμνος, ή [ramnos] boxthorn.

ραμολής, ὁ [ramolees] imbecile, half-wit

ραμφίζω [ramfeezo] peck at, pick up.

ράμφος, τό [ramfos] (μεγάλων πουλιῶν) bill, beak || (μεταφ) burner, jet.

ρανίς, ή [ranees] drop, blob.

ραντεβοῦ, τό [rantevou] meeting, engagement, rendezvous.

ραντίζω [ranteezo] sprinkle, spray, water.

ράντισμα, τό [ranteesma] sprinkling, watering.

ραντιστήρι, τό [ranteesteeree] watering can || (ἐκκλ) sprinkler.

ράντσο, τό [rantso] campbed.

ράξ, ή [raks] βλ **ράγα**.

ραπάνι, τό [rapanee] radish.

ραπίζω [rapeezo] slap or smack s.o. in the face.

ράπισμα, τό [rapeesma] clout, slap.
ραπτάδικο, τό [raptadeeko] βλ ραφτάδικο.
ράπτης, ὁ [raptees] tailor.
ραπτικά, τά [rapteeka] πλ fees for tailoring,
fees for sewing.
ραπτική, ἡ [rapteekee] βλ ραφτική.
ραπτομηχανή, ἡ [raptomeehanee] sewing
machine.
ράπτρια, ἡ [raptreea] dressmaker ||
(ἀσπρορρούχων) seamstress.
ράπτω [rapto] βλ ράβω.
ράσον, τό [rason] frock, cassock.
ρασοφόρος, ὁ [rasoforos] priest, monk.
ράσπα, ἡ [raspa] rasp.
ράτσα, ἡ [ratsa] race, generation, breed ||
ἀπό ~ thoroughbred.
ραφεῖον, τό [rafeeon] tailor's shop.
ραφή, ἡ [rafee] dressmaking || stitching,
seam.
ράφι, τό [rafee] shelf || (τοίχου) bracket ||
μένω στό ~ be left on the shelf, be an old
maid.
ραφινάρισμα, τό [rafeenareesma] refinement.
ραφινάρω [rafeenaro] refine || purify, polish.
ραφίς, ἡ [rafees] sewing needle.
ραφτάδικο, τό [raftadeeko] tailor's shop.
ράφτης [raftees] βλ ράπτης.
ραφτικά [rafteeka] βλ ραπτικά.
ραφτική, ἡ [rafteekee] dressmaking, sewing,
tailoring.
ραχάτι, τό [rahatee] lazing about, idling,
leisure.
ράχη, ἡ [rahee] back, backbone || (βιβλίου)
spine || (βουνοῦ) crest, ridge.
ράχις [rahees] βλ ράχη.
ραχιτικός [raheeteekos] suffering from
rickets.
ραχοκοκκαλιά, ἡ [rahokokalia] backbone,
spine.
ράψιμο, τό [rapseemo] sewing, stitching ||
tailoring, dressmaking.
ραψωδία, ἡ [rapsodeea] rhapsody.
ρεαλισμός, ὁ [realeesmos] realism.
ρεαλιστής, ὁ [realeestees] realist.
ρεβεγιόν, τό [reveyion] midnight supper.
ρεβίθι, τό [reveethee] chickpea.
ρεγάλο, τό [reyalo] tip, gratuity, present,
gift.
ρέγγα, ἡ [renga] herring.
ρεγούλα, ἡ [reyoula] order, regular arrange-
ment || moderation, measure.
ρεζέρβα, ἡ [rezerva] stock || (λάστιχου κτλ)
spare part.
ρεζές, ὁ [rezes] hinge.
ρεζιλεύω [rezeelevo] ridicule, make a fool
of || humiliate.
ρεζίλι, τό [rezeelee] shame, derision, object
of ridicule || γίνομαι ~ become a laughing
stock.
ρεζιλίκι [rezeeleekee] βλ ρεζίλι.
ρεῖθρον, τό [reethron] watercourse, rivulet
|| ditch, gutter (of street).

ρεκλάμα, ἡ [reklama] advertisement || show,
display.
ρεκλαμάρω [reklamaro] advertise.
ρεκόρ, τό [rekor] record.
ρέκτης, ὁ [rektees] pushing person, enterprising person.
ρεμάλι, τό [remalee] worthless person.
ρεματιά, ἡ [rematia] ravine, torrent, river-
bed.
ρεμβάζω [remvazo] muse, daydream, be in
a reverie.
ρεμβασμός, ὁ [remvasmos] musing, reverie.
ρεμούλα, ἡ [remoula] plunder, pillage ||
thieving, graft.
ρέμπελος [rembelos] lazy, sluggish || dis-
orderly.
ρεμπούμπλικα, ἡ [remboumpleeka] trilby,
homburg.
ρεπάνι, τό [repanee] radish.
ρεπερτόριον, τό [repertoreeon] repertoire.
ρεπό, τό [repo] time off, break, rest period,
rest.
ρέπω [repo] lean, incline, slope || (μεταφ)
tend towards.
ρεσιτάλ, τό [reseetal] recital.
ρέστα, τά [resta] πλ change.
ρετάλι, τό [retalee] remnant.
ρετσέτα, ἡ [retseta] prescription.
ρετσίνα, ἡ [retseena] resinated wine.
ρετσινόλαδο, τό [retseenolado] castor oil.
ρεύγομαι [revyome] belch.
ρεῦμα, τό [revma] current, stream, flow ||
(ἀέρος) draught.
ρευματισμός, ὁ [revmateesmos] rheumatism.
ρεύομαι [revome] βλ ρεύγομαι.
ρεῦσις, ἡ [revsees] outflow, flowing || emis-
sion.
ρευστοποιῶ [revstopeeo] liquefy.
ρευστός [revstos] fluid, liquid || (μεταφ)
fickle, inconstant, changeable.
ρευστότης, ἡ [revstotees] fluidity || (μεταφ)
inconstancy.
ρεφενές, ὁ [refenes] share, quota.
ρεφορμιστής, ὁ [reformeestees] reformist.
ρέψιμο, τό [repseemo] belching || decay.
ρέω [reo] flow, stream || (στάγδην) trickle
|| (δάκρυα) shed.
ρήγας, ὁ [reeyas] king.
ρῆγμα, τό [reeyma] crack, breach, fissure
hole || (μεταφ) rupture.
ρηθείς [reethees] (the) said.
ρῆμα, τό [reema] word, saying || (γραμμ)
verb.
ρημάδι, τό [reemadee] ruin || wreckage,
derelict || κλεῖσ' τό ~ shut the blooming
thing!
ρημάζω [reemazo] ruin, destroy || fall into
ruins.
ρηξικέλευθος [reekseekelefthos] innovat-
ing, modernist.
ρῆξις, ἡ [reeksees] rupture, breach || con
flict, quarrel, dispute.

ρῆσις, ἡ [reesees] saying, word.
ρητίνη, ἡ [reeteenee] resin.
ρητόν, τό [reeton] maxim, saying, motto.
ρητορεύω [reetorevo] make speeches, harangue.
ρητορική, ἡ [reetoreekee] oratory.
ρητός [reetos] formal, explicit, flat, positive.
ρήτρα, ἡ [reetra] clause, proviso, provision.
ρήτωρ, ὁ [reetor] orator.
ρητῶς [reetos] explicitly, expressly, flatly.
ρηχά, τά [reeha] πλ shallows.
ρίγα, ἡ [reega] ruler, measuring rule ‖ line, stripe.
ρίγανη, ἡ [reeganee] origanum.
ριγέ [reeye] striped.
ρῖγος, τό [reeyos] shiver ‖ thrill.
ριγῶ [reeyo] shiver, tremble, thrill.
ριγώνω [reeyono] draw lines, rule lines (on).
ριγωτός [reeyotos] (χάρτης) lined, ruled ‖ (ύφασμα) striped.
ρίζα, ἡ [reeza] root ‖ (βουνοῦ) foot, base ‖ (μεταφ) origin, source, cause.
ριζικό, τό [reezeeko] destiny, fortune, lot, fate.
ριζικός [reezeekos] radical, fundamental.
ριζόγαλο, τό [reezoyalo] rice pudding.
ριζόνερο, τό [reezonero] rice water.
ριζοσπάστης, ὁ [reezospastees] radical.
ριζοσπαστικός [reezospasteekos] radical.
ριζώνω [reezono] become established, become fixed, take root, grow.
ρικνός [reeknos] wrinkled, shrivelled, warped.
ρίμα, ἡ [reema] rhyme.
ρίνη, ἡ [reenee] file.
ρινίζω [reeneezo] file.
ρινικός [reeneekos] nasal.
ρινίσματα, τά [reeneesmata] πλ filings.
ρινόκερος, ὁ [reenokeros] rhinoceros.
ριξιά, ἡ [reeksia] throw, cast(ing) ‖ (ὅπλου) charge ‖ shot, firing.
ρίξιμο, τό [reekseemo] casting, throwing ‖ dropping ‖ (ὅπλου) firing, shooting.
ριπή, ἡ [reepee] burst of firing, throwing ‖ (ἀνέμου) gust, blast.
ριπίδιον, τό [reepeedeeon] fan.
ρίπτω [reepto] βλ ρίχνω.
ρίς, ἡ [rees] nose.
ρίχνομαι [reehnome] fling o.s., rush ‖ (στό νερό) plunge.
ρίχνω [reehno] throw, fling, cast ‖ (βόμβα) drop ‖ (ὅπλου) shoot, fire ‖ (ἀνατρέπω) overthrow, defeat ‖ (τοῖχο) pull down, demolish ‖ (δένδρο) hew, fell ‖ ρίχνει βροχή it's raining.
ριψοκινδυνεύω [reepsokeendeenevo] risk, endanger ‖ take risks.
ροβολῶ [rovolo] roll down, rush down.
ρόγχος, ὁ [ronghos] rattle, blowing ‖ death rattle.
ρόδα, ἡ [roda] wheel.
ροδάκινον, τό [rodakeenon] peach.
ροδαλός [rodalos] rosy, light pink.

ροδάνθη, ἡ [rodanthee] roseola.
ροδάνι, τό [rodanee] spinning wheel.
ροδέλαιον, τό [rodeleon] attar of roses.
ροδέλλα, ἡ [rodela] washer.
ρόδι, τό [rodee] pomegranate.
ρόδινος [rodeenos] rosy ‖ (μεταφ) rose-coloured, bright.
ροδίτης, ὁ [rodeetees] kind of pink grape.
ροδοδάφνη, ἡ [rododafnee] oleander.
ροδόδενδρον, τό [rododendron] rhododendron.
ροδοκόκκινος [rodokokeenos] ruddy, rose-red.
ρόδον, τό [rodon] rose.
ροδόστα(γ)μα, τό [rodosta(γ)ma] rose water.
ροδόχρους [rodohrous] rosy, rose-hued.
ρόζ [roz] pink.
ροζιάρικος [rozeeareekos] gnarled.
ρόζος, ὁ [rozos] knot, node ‖ (δακτύλων) knuckle.
ροή, ἡ [roee] flow, flood ‖ (πύου) discharge running.
ροῖδι, τό [roeedee] pomegranate.
ρόκα, ἡ [roka] distaff ‖ (χόρτο) rocket.
ροκάνα, ἡ [rokana] (παιχνίδι) rattle.
ροκάνι, τό [rokanee] plane.
ροκανίδι, τό [rokaneedee] chip, shaving.
ροκανίζω [rokaneezo] plane ‖ (μεταφ) gnaw, crunch.
ροκέτ(τ)α, ἡ [roketa] rocket.
ρολό, τό [rolo] cylindrical roll ‖ shutter.
ρολογᾶς, ὁ [roloyas] watchmaker, clockmaker.
ρολόϊ, τό [roloee] (τοίχου) clock ‖ (χεριοῦ) watch ‖ (μετρητής) meter ‖ πάει ~ it's going smoothly.
ρόλος, ὁ [rolos] roll ‖ (θεατρικός) part, role ‖ (μεταφ) part ‖ δέν παίζει ρόλο it's not important.
ρομάντζο, τό [romantzo] romance.
ρόμβος, ὁ [romvos] rhombus ‖ (ὄργανον παιδιᾶς) spinning top.
ρόμπα, ἡ [romba] dressing gown.
ρομφαία, ἡ [romfea] sword.
ρόπαλον, τό [ropalon] club.
ροπή, ἡ [ropee] inclination, propensity ‖ (μηχανῆς) momentum.
ρούβλιον, τό [rouvleeon] rouble.
ρούζ, τό [rouz] rouge.
ρουθούνι, τό [routhounee] nostril.
ρουθουνίζω [routhouneezo] snort, sniff, snuffle.
ρουκέτ(τ)α [rouketa] βλ ροκέτ(τ)α.
ρουλεμάν, τό [rouleman] ball bearings, roller bearings.
ρουλέττα, ἡ [rouleta] roulette.
ρουμάνι, τό [roumanee] dense forest, thicket.
Ρουμανία, ἡ [roumaneea] Rumania.
ρούμι, τό [roumee] rum.
ρουμπίνι, τό [roumbeenee] ruby.
ρούπι, τό [roupee] measure of length (.08 m) ‖ δέν τό κουνάω ~ I refuse to move.

ρούς, ὁ [rous] βλ ροή.

ρουσφέτι, τό [rousfetee] favour, string pulling, political favour.

ρουτίνα, ἡ [routeena] routine.

ρούφη(γ)μα, τό [roufee(γ)ma] noisy sipping, gulp, sucking in.

ρουφηξιά, ἡ [roufeeksia] mouthful, sip ‖ (πίπας κτλ) puff.

ρουφήχτρα, ἡ [roufeehtra] whirlpool.

ρουφιάνος, ὁ [roufeeanos] pimp ‖ schemer.

ρουφῶ [roufo] draw in, suck up, absorb, sip.

ρουχικά, τά [rouheeka] πλ clothing, garments.

ρούχο, τό [rouho] cloth, stuff, material ‖ (φόρεμα) dress, attire.

ρόφημα, τό [rofeema] hot drink.

ροφῶ [rofo] βλ ρουφῶ.

ροχαλητό, τό [rohaleeto] snore, snoring.

ροχαλίζω [rohaleezo] snore.

ροχάλισμα, τό [rohaleesma] βλ ροχαλητό.

ρόχαλο, τό [rohalo] phlegm, spit.

ρόχθος, ὁ [rohthos] (κυμάτων) roaring, hissing.

ρύαξ, ὁ [reeaks] stream, brook, rivulet.

ρύγχος, ὁ [reenghos] muzzle, nose, snout ‖ nozzle.

ρύζι, τό [reezee] rice.

ρυζόγαλο, τό [reezoγalo] rice pudding.

ρυθμίζω [reethmeezo] (ὡρολόγι) regulate, set right ‖ (τά τοῦ οἴκου) manage ‖ (ὑποθέσεις) settle ‖ (λογαριασμούς) close, make up.

ρυθμικός [reethmeekos] rhythmical.

ρύθμισις, ἡ [reethmeesees] regulating, adjusting.

ρυθμιστής, ὁ [reethmeestees] regulator.

ρυθμός, ὁ [reethmos] rhythm, rate ‖ (μουσ) cadence ‖ (ἀρχιτεκτονική) order, style.

ρύμη, ἡ [reemee] force, momentum ‖ (φορά) course.

ρυμοτομία, ἡ [reemotomeea] street plan, roadmaking.

ρυμούλκα, ἡ [reemoulka] trailer.

ρυμούλκησις, ἡ [reemoulkeesees] towing, dragging.

ρυμούλκιον, τό [reemoulkeeon] towrope.

ρυμουλκόν, τό [reemoulkon] tugboat, steam tug ‖ (τρακτέρ) tractor.

ρυμουλκῶ [reemoulko] tow, tug, drag, pull ‖ (μεταφ) drag by the nose.

ρυπαίνω [reepeno] make dirty, soil ‖ (μεταφ) defile, tarnish.

ρύπανσις, ἡ [reepansees] dirtying, blemishing, defiling.

ρυπαρός [reeparos] dirty, filthy ‖ (μεταφ) odious, vile.

ρύπος, ὁ [reepos] filth, dirt ‖ ((μεταφ) disgrace, shame.

ρυτίδα, ἡ [reeteeδa] wrinkle, seam, line ‖ (τῆς θαλάσσας) ripple.

ρυτιδώνω [reeteeδono] wrinkle, line ‖ get wrinkled.

ρυτίς, ἡ [reetees] βλ ρυτίδα.

ρῶ, τό [ro] the letter P.

ρώγα, ἡ [roγa] nipple.

ρωγμή, ἡ [roγmee] crack, split, cleft, crevice.

ρωγοβύζι, τό [roγoveezee] feeding bottle.

ρώθων, ὁ [rothon] βλ ρουθούνι.

ρωμαίϊκα, τά [romeïka] modern Greek, demotic Greek ‖ μίλα ~! come to the point!

ρωμαίϊκο, τό [romeïko] modern Greece.

ρωμαίϊκος [romeïkos] of modern Greece.

ρωμαϊκός [romaeekos] Roman.

Ρωμαῖος, ὁ [romeos] Roman.

ρωμαλέος [romaleos] robust, strong, vigorous, sturdy.

ρωμάντζα, ἡ [romantza] romantic background, romantic setting.

ρωμαντικός [romanteekos] romantic.

ρωμαντικότης, ἡ [romanteekotees] romanticism.

ρώμη, ἡ [romee] vigour, strength, force, robustness.

Ρώμη, ἡ [romee] Rome.

Ρωμιός, ὁ [romios] modern Greek.

Ρωμιοσύνη, ἡ [romioseenee] the modern Greek people.

Ρωσία, ἡ [roseea] Russia.

Ρῶσος, ὁ [rosos] Russian (person).

ρώτημα, τό [roteema] βλ ἐρώτημα.

ρωτῶ [roto] βλ ἐρωτῶ.

Σ, σ

σά [sa] βλ σάν.

σάβανον, τό [savanon] winding sheet, shroud.

σαββατοκύριακο, τό [savatokeereeako] weekend.

σάββατον, τό [savaton] Saturday.

σαβούρα, ἡ [savoura] rubbish, junk, trash ‖ ballast.

σαγανάκι, τό [saγanakee] frying pan ‖ (φαγητό) dish of fried cheese.

σαγή, ἡ [saγee] harness.

σαγηνεύω [saγeenevo] seduce, charm, attract.

σαγήνη, ἡ [saγeenee] fascination, enchantment.

σάγμα, τό [saγma] packsaddle.

σαγματοποιός, ὁ [saγmatopeeos] packsaddle maker.

σαγόνι, τό [saγonee] chin.

σαδισμός, ὁ [saδeesmos] sadism.

σαδιστής, ὁ [saδeestees] sadist.

σαθρός [sathros] rotted, decayed, rotten ‖ (μεταφ) groundless.

σαθρότης, ἡ [sathrotees] rottenness, decay.

σαιζόν, ἡ [sezon] season.

σαΐτα, ἡ [saeeta] arrow, dart ‖ weaver's shuttle.

σακαράκα, ἡ [sakaraka] (μεταφ) tin

lizzie (col), old motorcar, old bike.
σακατεύω [sakatevo] cripple, mutilate, maim ‖ (μεταφ) wear out, exhaust.
σακάτης, ό [sakatees] cripple, maimed person.
σάκκα, ή [saka] (μαθητική) satchel ‖ (κυνηγού) game pouch, gamebag ‖ briefcase.
σακκάκι, τό [sakakee] jacket, coat.
σακκί, τό [sakee] sack, bag.
σακκίδιον, τό [sakeedeeon] haversack, satchel, small bag.
σακκοράφα, ή [sakorafa] sack needle, packing needle.
σάκκος, ό [sakos] sack, bag, sackful (ταχυδρομικός) mailbag ‖ kitbag.
σακκούλα, ή [sakoula] sack, bag ‖ paper bag.
σακκούλι, τό [sakoulee] sack, small bag.
σακκουλιάζω [sakouleeazo] put into a bag, put into a sack, pocket ‖ (ἐπί ἐνδυμασίας) be loose-fitting, not fit well.
σάκχαρις, ή [sakharees] sugar.
σακχαροκάλαμον, τό [sakharokalamon] sugar cane.
σάκχαρον, τό [sakharon] sugar.
σαλαμάνδρα, ή [salamandra] salamander (θερμάστρα) combustion stove.
σαλάμι, τό [salamee] sausage, salami.
σαλαμούρα, ή [salamoura] brine.
σαλάτα, ή [salata] salad ‖ τά κάνω ~ make a muddle of it, foul up the works.
σαλατιέρα, ή [salatiera] salad bowl.
σάλεμα, τό [salema] moving, stirring, shaking.
σαλέπι, τό [salepee] salep.
σαλεύω [salevo] move, stir, shake ‖ budge.
σάλι, τό [salee] shawl.
σάλιαγκας, ό [saleeangas] snail.
σαλιάζω [saleeazo] salivate.
σαλιάρα, ή [saleeara] baby's bib.
σαλιάρης, ό [saleearees] (μεταφ) babbler, gossip.
σαλιαρίζω [saleeareezo] chatter, prattle.
σαλιγκάρι [saleengaree] βλ **σάλιαγκας.**
σαλιέρα, ή [saliera] saltcellar.
σάλιο, τό [saleeo] saliva, spittle.
σαλιώνω [saleeono] lick, moisten, dampen, wet.
σαλόνι, τό [salonee] drawing room (πλοίου) saloon.
σάλος, ό [salos] swell, surge (πλοίου) rolling ‖ (μεταφ) disturbance ‖ tumult.
σαλπάρω [salparo] weigh anchor.
σάλπιγξ, ή [salpeenks] trumpet, bugle (ἀνατ) tube.
σαλπίζω [salpeezo] sound the trumpet.
σάλπισμα, τό [salpeesma] trumpet call.
σαλτάρω [saltaro] jump, leap.
σαλτιμπάγκος, ό [salteembangos] fairground acrobat (μεταφ) charlatan, buffoon.
σάλτος, ό [saltos] jump, leap, bound.

σάλτσα, ή [saltsa] gravy, sauce.
σαμάρι, τό [samaree] packsaddle.
σαμαρώνω [samarono] saddle, pack.
σαματάς, ό [samatas] (φασαρία) noise, din roar ‖ fight.
σάματι(ς) [samatee(s)] as though.
σαμόλαδο, τό [samolaδo] sesame oil.
σαμούρι, τό [samouree] sable.
σαμπάνια, ή [sampaneea] champagne.
σαμποτάζ, τό [sampotaz] sabotage.
σαμποτάρω [sampotaro] sabotage.
σαμπρέλλα, ή [sambrela] inner tube.
σάμπως [sambos] as though   it appears that.
σάν [san] when, as soon as, if ‖ like, as if
  ~ σήμερα πέρσυ about a year ago today
  ~ τί; like what? ‖ ~ νά as though.
σανατόριον, τό [sanatoreeon] sanatorium.
σανδάλιον, τό [sanδaleeon] sandal.
σανδαλοποιός, ό [sanδalopeeos] sandal maker.
σανίδα, ή [saneeδa] board, beam, plank (σιδερώματος) ironing board.
σανιδόσκαλα, ή [saneeδoskala] gangplank.
σανιδώνω [saneeδono] floor, plank, cover with board.
σανίδωσις, ή [saneeδosees] flooring, planking, boarding.
σανίς, ή [sanees] βλ **σανίδα.**
σανός, ό [sanos] hay, fodder.
σαντιγύ, τό [santeeyee] chantilly.
σάντουϊτς, τό [santoueets] sandwich.
σαντούρι, τό [santouree] kind of string instrument.
σαπίζω [sapeezo] rot, spoil, decompose, decay.
σαπίλα, ή [sapeela] decay, putridity (μεταφ) corruption, dishonesty.
σάπιος [sapeeos] decomposed, rotten corrupt, depraved, wicked.
σαπουνάδα, ή [sapounaδa] soapsuds, lather.
σαπούνι, τό [sapounee] soap (ξυρίσματος) shaving soap.
σαπουνίζω [sapouneezo] soap ‖ lather.
σαπουνόφουσκα, ή [sapounofouska] soap bubble.
σαπρός [sapros] βλ **σάπιος.**
σάπφειρος, ό [sapfeeros] sapphire.
σάπων, ό [sapon] βλ **σαπούνι.**
σαπωνοποιός, ό [saponopeeos] soap manufacturer.
σάρα, ή [sara]: ή ~ καί ή μάρα rabble.
σαράβαλο, τό [saravalo] ruin, wreck ‖ sickly person.
σαράκι, τό [sarakee] woodworm (μεταφ) remorse, prick of conscience.
σαρακοστή, ή [sarakostee] Lent.
σαράντα [saranta] forty.
σαραντάμερο, τό [sarantamero] Advent.
σαρανταποδαρούσα, ή [sarantapoδarousa] centipede.
σαρανταριά, ή [sarantaria] forty.

Σ

σαραντίζω [saranteezo] become forty ‖ be forty days since.
σαράφης, ὁ [sarafees] moneychanger.
σαρδέλλα, ἡ [sarðela] anchovy ‖ sardine.
σαρδόνιος [sarðoneeos] sardonic, sarcastic.
σαρίδι, τό [sareeðee] sweepings, garbage, refuse.
σαρίκι, τό [sareekee] turban.
σάρκα, ἡ [sarka] flesh.
σαρκασμός, ὁ [sarkasmos] derision, raillery, sarcasm.
σαρκαστικός [sarkasteekos] sarcastic, jeering, mocking.
σαρκικός [sarkeekos] carnal, fleshy, sensual.
σαρκοβόρος [sarkovoros] βλ σαρκοφάγος.
σαρκοφάγος [sarkofayos] carnivorous, flesh-eating ‖ ἡ ~ sarcophagus.
σαρκώδης [sarkoðees] fleshy, ‖ (φροῦτο) pulpy.
σάρκωμα, τό [sarkoma] sarcoma, fleshy growth.
σάρξ, ἡ [sarks] βλ σάρκα.
σάρπα, ἡ [sarpa] scarf.
σάρωθρον, τό [sarothron] broom.
σάρωμα, τό [saroma] sweeping.
σαρώνω [sarono] (δωμάτιο) sweep ‖ (δρόμο) scavenge ‖ (μεταφ) rake.
σᾶς, σας [sas] you ‖ your.
σασ(σ)ί, τό [sasee] chassis.
σαστίζω [sasteezo] disconcert, embarrass, confuse ‖ get disconcerted.
σατανᾶς, ὁ [satanas] Satan ‖ (μεταφ) devilish person.
σατανικός [sataneekos] devilish, satanical, fiendish.
σατέν, τό [saten] satin.
σατίρι, τό [sateeree] meat cleaver.
σατράπης, ὁ [satrapees] satrap ‖ (μεταφ) tyrant.
σάτυρα, ἡ [sateera] satire, skit, lampoon.
σατυρίζω [sateereezo] satirize, ridicule.
σατυρικός [sateereekos] satirical.
σάτυρος, ὁ [sateeros] satyr ‖ (μεταφ) debauchee.
σαύρα, ἡ [savra] lizard.
σαφήνεια, ἡ [safeeneea] clearness, distinctness, lucidity.
σαφηνίζω [safeeneezo] clarify, elucidate, explain.
σαφής [safees] clear, obvious, plain.
σαφῶς [safos] clearly, obviously.
σαχάνι, τό [sahanee] shallow frying pan.
σάχης, ὁ [sahees] Shah.
σάχλα, ἡ [sahla] insipid talk ‖ stupidity.
σαχλαμάρα, ἡ [sahlamara] nonsense, rubbish.
σαχλός [sahlos] flat, flabby ‖ stupid.
σβάρνα, ἡ [svarna] harrow.
σβέλτος [sveltos] nimble ‖ slim, slender.
σβέρκος, ὁ [sverkos] nape of neck, scruff.
σβέσις, ἡ [svesees] (φωτιᾶς κτλ) extinguishing ‖ (κεριοῦ) blowing out ‖ (ἀσβέστου) slaking.

σβήνω [sveeno] extinguish, quench, put out ‖ (γράμματα) erase ‖ (διά τριβῆς) rub out ‖ (μέ πέννα κτλ) strike out ‖ (φωτιά) die out ‖ (χρῶμα) fade ‖ (ἐνθουσιασμός) subside, die down.
σβήσιμο, τό [sveeseemo] extinction ‖ erasure, rubbing out.
σβηστός [sveestos] put out, extinguished, switched off.
σβίγγος, ὁ [sveengos] fritter.
σβουνιά, ἡ [svounia] ox dung.
σβούρα, ἡ [svoura] spinning top.
σβύνω [sveeno] βλ σβήνω.
σβῶλος, ὁ [svolos] lump (of earth) ‖ ball, clod.
σγάρα, ἡ [syara] bird's crop.
σγουραίνω [syoureno] curl ‖ become curly.
σγουρός [syouros] curly, fuzzy, curled ‖ curly-haired.
σέ [se] you ‖ to, at, in.
σέβας, τό [sevas] regard, reverence, deference.
σεβασμός, ὁ [sevasmos] βλ σέβας.
σεβάσμιος [sevasmeeos] venerable, respectable, reverend.
σεβασμιώτης, ἡ [sevasmeeotees]: ἡ ἡμετέρα ~ Your Reverence.
σεβαστός [sevastos] respected ‖ respectable, considerable.
σέβη, τά [sevee] πλ respects.
σεβντᾶς, ὁ [sevntas] love, yearning.
σέβομαι [sevome] respect, venerate, admire, esteem.
σειρά, ἡ [seera] series, succession ‖ row, line, rank ‖ (στήν τάξι) turn ‖ sequence, order ‖ μέ τήν ~ in turn, in order ‖ μπαίνω σέ ~ settle down.
σειρήν, ἡ [seereen] siren, enchantress ‖ hooter, buzzer, alarm.
σειρήτι, τό [seereetee] stripe, ribbon, braid.
σεισμικός [seesmeekos] seismic.
σεισμογράφος, ὁ [seesmoyrafos] seismograph.
σεισμόπληκτος [seesmopleektos] struck by earthquake.
σεισμός, ὁ [seesmos] earthquake.
σείω [seeo] move, shake, wave.
σεκλέτι, τό [sekletee] nuisance ‖ worry ‖ sorrow, distress.
σελαγίζω [selayeezo] shine, gleam.
σέλας, τό [selas] brightness, brilliance, radiance ‖ βόρειον ~ northern lights, aurora borealis.
σελάχι, τό [selahee] gun belt ‖ (ψάρι) ray.
σελέμης, ὁ [selemees] sponger, parasite.
σελεμίζω [selemeezo] beg, sponge, cadge.
σελήνη, ἡ [seleenee] moon.
σεληνιασμός, ὁ [seleeneeasmos] epilepsy.
σεληνόφως, τό [seleenofos] moonlight.
σελίδα, ἡ [seleeða] page (of book).
σελίνι, τό [seleenee] shilling.
σέλινον, τό [seleenon] celery.
σελίς, ἡ [selees] βλ σελίδα.

σέλλα, ή [sela] saddle.

σελλώνω [selono] saddle.

σεμινάριον, τό [semeenareeon] seminary.

σεμνοπρεπής [semnoprepees] dignified, decent, modest, proper.

σεμνός [semnos] decent, unassuming, modest ‖ (ἐνδυμασία) simple, plain.

σεμνότης, ή [semnotees] dignity, modesty, decency.

σεμνότυφος [semnoteefos] prudish, demure, priggish.

σένα [sena] you.

σεντόνι, τό [sentonee] sheet.

σεντούκι, τό [sentoukee] linen closet ‖ box, chest.

σέξ, τό [seks] sex.

σεξουαλισμός, ό [seksoualeesmos] sexual instinct, sexuality.

Σεπτέμβρης, ό [septemvrees] September.

σεπτός [septos] august, venerable, revered.

σερβίρισμα, τό [serveereesma] waiting on, serving.

σερβίρω [serveero] wait at table, serve.

σερβιτόρα, ή [serveetora] waitress.

σερβιτόρος, ό [serveetoros] waiter.

σερβίτσιο, τό [serveetseeo] dinner service ‖ place setting.

σεργιάνι, τό [seryeeanee] walk, promenade.

σεργιανίζω [seryeeaneezo] take for a walk, go for a walk ‖ wander about.

σερμπέτι, τό [sermbetee] sherbet, syrup.

σέρνομαι [sernome] creep, crawl, drag | drag o.s. along.

σέρνω [serno] draw, pull, drag ‖ (βαρύ πράγμα) haul ‖ (χορό) lead ‖ ~ φωνή scream, shriek, cry out.

σέρρα, ή [sera] greenhouse, glasshouse.

σεσημασμένος [seseemasmenos] criminal.

σέσουλα, ή [sesoula] scoop, ladle ‖ (ναυτ) skeet.

σεφτές, ό [seftes] first sale (of a day).

σήκαλη, ή [seekalee] rye.

σηκός, ό [seekos] shrine ‖ enclosure.

σήκωμα, τό [seekoma] raising, lifting ‖ getting out of bed.

σηκωμός, ό [seekomos] rising, rebellion.

σηκώνομαι [seekonome] rise, stand up, get up ‖ (ἐπαναστατῶ) rebel.

σηκώνω [seekono] raise, hoist, pick up, lift up ‖ (μεταφέρω) carry ‖ (ἀφυπνίζω) get up ‖ (ἀνέχομαι) bear, tolerate ‖ ~ τό τραπέζι clear the table ‖ ~ στό πόδι incite, rouse, disturb ‖ ~ κεφάλι become arrogant, rebel.

σηκώτι, τό [seekotee] liver.

σήμα, τό [seema] signal, sign, mark, badge ‖ ~ κατατεθέν trademark, registration mark.

σημαδεμένος [seemaδemenos] marked ‖ maimed, scarred.

σημαδεύω [seemaδevo] mark ‖ aim at, take aim at.

σημάδι, το [seemaδee] trace, scar, spot

‖ (ἔνδειξις) sign, mark, indication.

σημαδούρα, ή [seemaδoura] buoy.

σημαία, ή [seemea] flag, ensign, colours, standard.

σημαίνω [seemeno] mean, be a sign of, signify ‖ (καμπάνα κτλ) ring, strike, sound, signal ‖ (ἔχων σημασία) matter, be of consequence.

σημαιοφόρος, ό [seemeoforos] standard bearer ‖ (ναυτ) ensign, sub-lieutenant ‖ (μεταφ) leader.

σήμανσις, ή [seemansees] marking, stamping ‖ noting of details.

σημαντήρ, ό [seemanteer] buoy.

σημαντικός [seemanteekos] important, significant ‖ (πρόσωπον) remarkable, considerable ‖ momentous.

σήμαντρον, τό [seemantron] stamp, seal ‖ (ἐκκλ) special monastery bell.

σημασία, ή [seemaseea] sense, meaning ‖ importance, gravity, significance.

σηματοφόρος, ό [seematoforos] semaphore, signal station.

σημεῖον, τό [seemeeon] sign, mark, proof, indication ‖ (θέσις, βαθμοῦ) stage, point ‖ (μάθημ) symbol, sign ‖ ~ τοῦ ὁρίζοντος point of the compass.

σημείωμα, τό [seemeeoma] written note, memorandum, record.

σημειωματάριον, τό [seemeeomatareeon] notebook, agenda, diary.

σημειωμένος [seemeeomenos] noted ‖ scarred.

σημείωσις, ή [seemeeosees] written note ‖ remark, comment.

σημειωτέος [seemeeoteos] to be noted ‖ noticeable, noteworthy.

σήμερα [seemera] today ‖ ~ τό ἀπόγευμα this evening, this afternoon.

σήμερον [seemeron] βλ σήμερα.

σημύδα, ή [seemeeδa] birch tree

σηπία, ή [seepeea] cuttlefish.

σήπομαι [seepome] rot, decay, decompose.

σηπτικός [seepteekos] septic, putrefactive.

σήπω [seepo] putrefy, rot.

σήραγξ, ή [seeranks] tunnel.

σηροτροφία, ή [seerotrofeea] sericulture.

σησάμι, τό [seesamee] sesame.

σήστρον, τό [seestron] sieve, sifter.

σηψαιμία, ή [seepsemeea] septicaemia, blood poisoning.

σῆψις, ή [seepsees] decay, putrefaction ‖ (ἰατρ) sepsis.

σθεναρός [sthenaros] sturdy, strong, vigorous, powerful, robust.

σθένος, τό [sthenos] vigour, strength, energy ‖ courage, pluck.

σιαγών, ή [seeayon] jaw ‖ (ἀνατ) jawbone.

σιάζω [seeazo] arrange, set in order, straighten, tidy ‖ (ἐπισκευάζω) repair, mend, patch.

σίαλος, ό [seealos] saliva, spittle.

σιάξιμον, τό [seeakseemon] tidying,

setting in order, arranging ‖ mending.

σιγά [seeya] softly, lightly, gently, slowly ‖ ~ ~ carefully, by degrees.

σιγαλός [seeyalos] silent, quiet, gentle, still ‖ slowly.

σιγανός [seeyanos] βλ σιγαλός.

σιγαρέττον, τό [seeyareton] cigarette.

σιγαροθήκη, ή [seeyarotheekee] cigarette case.

σιγάρον, τό [seeyaron] (πούρο) cigar ‖ (τσιγάρο) cigarette.

σιγαρόχαρτον, τό [seeyaroharton] cigarette paper ‖ tissue paper.

σιγή, ή [seeyee] silence, hush.

σιγηλός [seeyeelos] quiet, silent, noiseless.

σίγμα, τό [seeyma] the letter Σ.

σιγοβράζω [seeyovrazo] simmer.

σίγουρα [seeyoura] for certain, for sure.

σίγουρος [seeyouros] certain, assured, sure ‖ (φάρμακο) infallible.

σιγῶ [seeyo] keep quiet, remain silent ‖ die down.

σίδερα, τά [seedera] πλ ironwork ‖ (γραμμές) railway lines ‖ (φυλακή) irons, fetters.

σιδεράς, ὁ [seederas] blacksmith, iron-monger.

σιδερένιος [seedereneeos] of iron.

σιδερικά, τά [seedereeka] πλ scrap iron ‖ ironware.

σίδερο, τό [seedero] iron ‖ (σιδερώματος) flatiron ‖ (μαλλιών) curling tongs.

σιδέρωμα, τό [seederoma] ironing, pressing.

σιδερώνω [seederono] iron.

σιδηροδρομικός [seedeeroδromeekos] of railways.

σιδηροδρομικώς [seedeeroδromeekos] by rail, by train.

σιδηρόδρομος, ὁ [seedeeroδromos] railway, railroad.

σιδηροπυρίτης, ὁ [seedeeropeereetees] pyrites.

σίδηρος, ὁ [seedeeros] iron.

σιδηροτροχιά, ή [seedeerotrohia] railway track.

σιδηρουργείον, τό [seedeerouryeeon] forge, smithy.

σιδηρουργός, ὁ [seedeerouryos] blacksmith.

σιδηρούς [seedeerous] iron, made of iron.

σιδηρούχος [seedeerouhos] ferruginous.

σιδηρωτής, ὁ [seedeerotees] one who irons, one who presses.

σιδηρωρυχείον, τό [seedeeroreeheeon] iron mine.

σίελος, ὁ [sielos] βλ σίαλος.

σίκ [seek] (οὖσ) chic, stylishness ‖ (ἐπίθ) smart, stylish.

σίκαλις, ή [seekalees] rye.

σιλό, τό [seelo] silo.

σιλουέττα, ή [seeloueta] silhouette, figure.

σιμά [seema] near, close by.

σιμιγδάλι, τό [seemeeyδalee] semolina.

σιμός [seemos] snub-nosed ‖ (μύτη) snub, flat.

σίμωμα, τό [seemoma] drawing near, approaching.

σιμώνω [seemono] approach, draw near.

σινάπι, τό [seenapee] mustard, mustard seed.

σινδόνη, ή [seenδonee] bed sheet.

σινιάλο, τό [seeneealo] βλ σήμα.

σινικός [seeneekos]: σινική μελάνη India ink.

σιντριβάνι, τό [seentreevanee] fountain.

σιρόκος, ὁ [seerokos] south-east wind.

σιρόπι, τό [seeropee] syrup.

σιταρένιος [seetareneeos] wheaten, of wheat.

σιτάρι, τό [seetaree] wheat, grain.

σιτεύω [seetevo] fatten ‖ (τό κρέας) hang, make tender.

σιτηρά, τά [seeteera] πλ cereals.

σιτηρέσιον, τό [seeteereseeon] ration, portion, allowance.

σιτίζω [seeteezo] feed, nurture, nourish.

σιτιστής, ὁ [seeteestees] quartermaster sergeant.

σιτοβολών, ὁ [seetovolon] granary, barn.

σιτοδεία, ή [seetoδeea] scarcity, shortage, famine.

σῖτος, ὁ [seetos] βλ σιτάρι.

σιφόνι, τό [seefonee] siphon.

σιφονιέρα, ή [seefoniera] chest of drawers.

σίφουνας, ὁ [seefounas] waterspout, whirl-wind.

σίφων, ὁ [seefon] siphon ‖ (σωλήνας) pipe, tube, conduit ‖ (μετεωρολογικός) whirl-wind.

σιχαίνομαι [seehenome] loathe, detest, feel disgust for.

σιχαμένος [seehamenos] loathsome, sicken-ing.

σιχαμερός [seehameros] disgusting, repul-sive.

σιωπή, ή [seeopee] silence.

σιωπηλός [seeopeelos] silent, quiet, noise-less.

σιωπηρός [seeopeeros] tacit.

σιωπῶ [seeopo] remain silent ‖ hold one's tongue.

σκάβω [skavo] βλ σκάπτω.

σκάγι, τό [skayee] small shot, pellet.

σκάζω [skazo] burst, open, split, crack ‖ (ξύλο κτλ) split, splinter ‖ (ὀβίδα) burst, explode ‖ be exasperated, be infuriated (by) ‖ τό ~ make off ‖ σκάσε! shut up!

σκαθάρι, τό [skatharee] scarab(ee).

σκαιός [skeos] rough, blunt, abrupt, rude coarse.

σκαιώς [skeos] rudely, coarsely, roughly.

σκά(κ)κι, τό [skakee] chess.

σκάλα, ή [skala] stairs, staircase, flight, ladder ‖ (ὑπηρεσίας) backstairs ‖ (ἀπο-βάθρα) landing stage ‖ (λιμάνι) port ‖ (πρός ἵππευσιν) stirrup ‖ (μουσ) scale ‖ (μαλλιών) wave.

σκάλεθρον, τό [skalethron] poker.

σκαληνός [skaleenos] oblique || (γεωμ) scalene.

σκαλί, τό [skalee] step, flight, rung || grade.

σκαλίζω [skaleezo] hoe, weed, dig || (μέταλλο) chisel || (πέτρα κτλ) sculpture || (ξύλο) carve || (φωτιά) stir, poke || (βιβλιοθήκη κτλ) rummage, seek, search.

σκάλισμα, τό [skaleesma] weeding, hoeing || searching || carving, sculpting.

σκαλιστήρι, τό [skaleesteeree] hoe, weeding fork.

σκαλιστής, ὁ [skaleestees] carver, engraver, chiseller.

σκαλιστός [skaleestos] engraved, carved, chiselled, sculptured.

σκαλοπάτι, τό [skalopatee] step, rung.

σκάλωμα, τό [skaloma] scaling || (μεταφ) hitch, impediment.

σκαλώνω [skalono] climb, mount || (μεταφ) get held up, meet with an obstacle.

σκαλωσιά, ἡ [skalosia] scaffolding.

σκαμνί, τό [skamnee] stool || chair.

σκαμπίλι, τό [skambeelee] slap, smack.

σκαμπιλίζω [skambeeleezo] slap.

σκανδάλη, ἡ [skandalee] trigger.

σκανδαλιάρης, ὁ [skandaliarees] unruly or muddled or mischievous person.

σκανδαλίζομαι [skandaleezome] be tempted, be shocked.

σκανδαλίζω [skandaleezo] intrigue, allure || scandalize, shock, offend.

σκάνδαλον, τό [skandalon] scandal || intrigue.

σκανδαλώδης [skandaloδees] scandalous, disgraceful.

σκαντζόχοιρος, ὁ [skantzoheeros] hedgehog.

σκαπανεύς, ὁ [skapanevs] sapper || pioneer || digger.

σκαπάνη, ἡ [skapanee] mattock, pickaxe, pick.

σκαπουλάρω [skapoularo] escape from, elude, give the slip.

σκάπτω [skapto] dig up, scoop out || (τάφρον) excavate || (χαράσσω) engrave, carve, chisel.

σκάρα [skara] βλ ἐσχάρα.

σκαρδαμύσσω [skarδameeso] flicker, twinkle.

σκαρί, τό [skaree] slipway || (μεταφ) character, make-up, idiosyncrasy.

σκαρίφημα, τό [skareefeema] sketch, rough outline.

σκαρλατίνα, ἡ [skarlateena] scarlet fever.

σκαρπίνι, τό [skarpeenee] lace-up shoe.

σκάρτος [skartos] defective, useless, unserviceable.

σκαρφάλωμα, τό [skarfaloma] climbing up, scrambling up.

σκαρφαλώνω [skarfalono] climb, clamber up, scramble up.

σκάρωμα, τό [skaroma] (μεταφ) fabrication, invention

σκαρώνω [skarono] (μεταφ) fabricate, invent, lay on.

σκασίλα, ἡ [skaseela] chagrin, spite, vexation, distress.

σκάσιμο, τό [skaseemo] fissure, cracking || (δέρματος) chap || (διαφυγή) desertion, escape || (μαθήματος) playing truant.

σκασμός, ὁ [skasmos] suffocation || resentment || ~! shut up!, hold your tongue!

σκατά, τά [skata] πλ shit (col).

σκαστός [skastos] noisy || loud || (στρατιώτης) AWOL || (μαθητής) playing truant.

σκάφανδρον, τό [skafanδron] diving suit.

σκαφεύς, ὁ [skafevs] digger, labourer.

σκάφη, ἡ [skafee] trough, tub.

σκαφή, ἡ [skafee] digging.

σκάφος, τό [skafos] hull || ship, vessel, boat.

σκάφτω [skafto] βλ σκάπτω.

σκάψιμο, τό [skapseemo] digging, ploughing || carving.

σκάω [skao] βλ σκάζω.

σκεβρός [skevros] crooked, warped, deformed.

σκεβρώνω [skevrono] warp, twist || get warped.

σκέλεθρο, τό [skelethro] βλ σκελετός.

σκελετός, ὁ [skeletos] skeleton || framework, shape || (αὐτοκινήτου) chassis.

σκελετώδης [skeletoδees] bony, emaciated.

σκελίδα, ἡ [skeleeδa] clove of garlic.

σκέλος, τό [skelos] leg || side.

σκεπάζω [skepazo] cover || protect || hide.

σκεπάρνι, τό [skeparnee] adze.

σκέπασμα, τό [skepasma] roofing, covering || blanket || lid.

σκεπαστά [skepasta] secretly, on the quiet.

σκεπαστός [skepastos] covered in, veiled, roofed || (μεταφ) secret.

σκέπαστρον, τό [skepastron] cover, screen, shelter.

σκέπη, ἡ [skepee] shelter, cover || (μεταφ) protection.

σκεπή, ἡ [skepee] roof.

σκεπτικιστής, ὁ [skepteekeestees] sceptic doubtful person.

σκεπτικός [skepteekos] sceptical || pensive, engrossed.

σκέπτομαι [skeptome] think, reflect || contemplate (doing).

σκέρτσα, τά [skertsa] πλ flirtatious ways.

σκέρτσο, τό [skertso] charm || jesting, playfulness.

σκέτος [sketos] plain, simple || (καφές) without sugar.

σκευασία, ἡ [skevaseea] preparation, composition, disposition.

σκεῦος, τό [skevos] utensil, implement || (ἐκκλ) vessel.

σκευοφόρος, ὁ [skevoforos] luggage van, baggage cart.

σκευωρία, ἡ [skevoreea] scheme, machination, intrigue.

σκέψις, ή [skepsees] thought, consideration ‖ concern.

σκηνή, ή [skeenee] scene, trouble, quarrel ‖ (θεάτρου) action, stage ‖ (τέντα) tent.

σκηνικά, τά [skeeneeka] πλ (stage) scenery.

σκηνικός [skeeneekos] of the stage, theatrical.

σκηνογραφία, ή [skeenoyrafeea] stage designing.

σκηνοθεσία, ή [skeenotheseea] stage production ‖ (μεταφ) fabrication.

σκηνοθέτης, ὁ [skeenothetees] stage manager.

σκήνωμα, τό [skeenoma] (μεταφ) corpse.

σκήπτρα, τά [skeeptra] πλ: κατέχω τά ~ bear the palm.

σκῆπτρον, τό [skeeptron] sceptre ‖ (μεταφ) superiority, prevalence.

σκήτη, ή [skeetee] small monastery, cloister.

σκιά, ή [skia] shade, shadow ‖ phantom.

σκιαγραφῶ [skeeayrafo] sketch, line.

σκιάδι, τό [skeeadee] straw hat ‖ sunshade.

σκιάζομαι [skeeazome] be scared of, take fright (at).

σκιάζω [skeeazo] shade ‖ conceal the sun ‖ veil, hide ‖ (φοβίζω) frighten ‖ (μεταφ) overshadow.

σκιάχτρο, τό [skeeahtro] scarecrow ‖ bogey.

σκιερός [skieros] shady, shadowy.

σκίζα, ή [skeeza] splinter, shaving.

σκίζομαι [skeezome] struggle.

σκίζω [skeezo] split, cleave, tear, rip ‖ ~ τά ρούχα μου I swear I'm innocent.

σκίουρος, ὁ [skeeouros] squirrel.

σκιόφως, τό [skeeofos] partial shadow ‖ twilight, dusk.

σκιρτῶ [skeerto] bound, leap, bounce, hop.

σκίσιμο, τό [skeeseemo] tear, rent, laceration ‖ crack.

σκίτσο, τό [skeetso] sketch, cartoon.

σκιώδης [skeeodees] βλ σκιερός.

σκλαβιά, ή [sklavia] servitude, slavery ‖ (μεταφ) obligation, drudgery.

σκλάβος, ὁ [sklavos] slave ‖ captive.

σκλαβώνω [sklavono] subjugate, enslave ‖ (μεταφ) put under obligation.

σκλήθρος, ὁ [skleethros] alder.

σκληραγωγῶ [skleerayoyo] accustom to hardship, season, toughen.

σκληραίνω [skleereno] harden, make hard ‖ become callous.

σκληρός [skleeros] hard, tough ‖ cruel, heartless.

σκληροτράχηλος [skleerotraheelos] opinionated, headstrong, obstinate.

σκληρύνω [skleereeno] βλ σκληραίνω.

σκνίπα, ή [skneepa] gnat, midge ‖ (μεταφ) drunk as a lord.

σκοινί, τό [skeenee] βλ σχοινί(ον).

σκολειό, τό [skolio] βλ σχολείον.

σκόλη, ή [skolee] holiday, feast day.

σκολιανά, τά [skoleeana] Sunday best.

σκολιός [skolios] tortuous, crooked (ἄνθρωπος) difficult, wicked, perverse.

σκολίωσις, ή [skoleeoses] scoliosis.

σκολνῶ [skolno] repose ‖ get off (work), leave.

σκολόπενδρα, ή [skolopenðra] centipede.

σκόνη, ή [skonee] dust, powder ‖ (γιά δόντια) tooth powder.

σκονίζω [skoneezo] coat with dust.

σκοντάφτω [skontafto] knock against, stumble ‖ come up against an obstacle.

σκόντο, τό [skonto] discount, deduction.

σκόπελος, ὁ [skopelos] reef, rock, shoal ‖ (μεταφ) stumbling block, danger.

σκοπευτήριον, τό [skopevteereeon] shooting gallery, shooting range.

σκοπεύω [skopevo] take aim at ‖ (μέ ὅπλον) take aim ‖ (ἔχω σκοπόν) intend, propose, plan.

σκοπιά, ῆ [skopia] lookout ‖ sentry box ‖ (σιδηροδρομική) signal box.

σκόπιμος [skopeemos] opportune, convenient, expedient ‖ intentional, deliberate.

σκοπίμως [skopeemos] intentionally, deliberately.

σκοποβολή, ή [skopovolee] target practice, shooting.

σκοπός, ὁ [skopos] purpose, intent, intention ‖ aim, goal ‖ (φρουρός) sentinel ‖ (στόχος) mark, target ‖ (ἦχος) tune, air.

σκοπῶ [skopo] βλ σκοπεύω.

σκορβοῦτον, τό [skorvouton] scurvy.

σκορδαλιά, ή [skorðalia] garlic sauce.

σκόρδο, τό [skorðo] garlic.

σκόρος, ὁ [skoros] βλ σκῶρος.

σκοροφαγωμένος [skorofayomenos] motheaten.

σκορπίζω [skorpeezo] scatter, disperse ‖ (περιουσίαν) dissipate, waste ‖ (φῶς) shed, spread ‖ disintegrate, melt away.

σκόρπιος [skorpeeos] dispersed.

σκορπιός, ὁ [skorpios] scorpion.

σκορπῶ [skorpo] βλ σκορπίζω.

σκοτάδι, τό [skotaðee] darkness, obscurity ‖ gloom.

σκοτεινιάζει [skoteeneeazee] it's getting dark.

σκοτεινιάζω [skoteeneeazo] darken, become overcast ‖ cloud over.

σκοτεινός [skoteenos] dark, dismal, gloomy ‖ (οὐρανός) overcast ‖ (νύχτα) murky ‖ (χαρακτήρ) sombre, melancholy ‖ (προθέσεις) underhand, sinister ‖ (λόγια) obscure, abstruse.

σκοτίζομαι [skoteezome] worry, trouble o.s. ‖ care for.

σκοτίζω [skoteezo] darken, obscure ‖ worry, annoy, vex.

σκοτοδίνη, ή [skotoðeenee] dizziness, vertigo.

σκότος, τό [skotos] darkness, obscurity, gloom.

σκοτούρα, ή [skotoura] (μεταφ) care, nuisance ‖ dizziness.

σκοτωμός, ὁ [skotomos] massacre, killing ‖ (μεταφ) hustle, jostle.

σκοτώνομαι [skotonome] hurt o.s. seriously ‖ (μεταφ) work o.s. to death.

σκοτώνω [skotono] kill ‖ while away (the time), kill time.

σκούζω [skouzo] howl, yell, scream.

σκουλαρίκι, τό [skoulareekee] earring.

σκουλήκι, τό [skouleekee] worm ‖ maggot, mite.

σκουντουφλῶ [skountouflo] stumble, bump against.

σκουντῶ [skounto] push, jostle, shove.

σκούπα, ή [skoupa] broom.

σκουπιδαρειό, τό [skoupeedario] rubbish dump.

σκουπίδι, τό [skoupeedee] rubbish, garbage, refuse.

σκουπιδιάρης, ὁ [skoupeedeearees] dustman, garbage collector.

σκουπίζω [skoupeezo] sweep, wipe, mop, dust, clean.

σκούρα [skoura]: τά βρῆκα ~ I found things difficult.

σκουραίνω [skoureno] darken ‖ deteriorate.

σκουριά, ή [skouria] rust ‖ ~ζω rust, corrode.

σκοῦρος [skouros] dark-coloured, brown.

σκούφια, ή [skoufeea] cap, baby's bonnet.

σκοῦφος, ὁ [skoufos] cap, beret, bonnet.

σκύβαλα, τά [skeevala] πλ (μεταφ) sweepings ‖ grain siftings.

σκύβω [skeevo] bend, lean, bow, incline.

σκυθρωπός [skeethropos] sullen, sulky, surly ‖ (ὕφος) morose.

σκύλα, ή [skeela] bitch ‖ (μεταφ) cruel woman.

σκυλεύω [skeelevo] despoil, rob ‖ plunder.

σκυλήσιος [skeeleeseeos] of a dog, like a dog.

σκυλί, τό [skeelee] dog ‖ ἔγινε ~ he got furious.

σκυλιάζω [skeeleeazo] infuriate ‖ become enraged.

σκυλοβρίζω [skeelovreezo] berate rudely.

σκυλολόι, τό [skeeloloee] rabble, mob, riffraff.

σκυλομούρης [skeelomourees] dog-faced ‖ (μεταφ) impudent, without shame.

σκύλος, ὁ [skeelos] βλ σκυλί.

σκυλόψαρο, τό [skeelopsaro] dogfish ‖ shark.

σκύμνος, ὁ [skeemnos] lion cub.

σκύρα, τά [skeera] πλ gravel ‖ macadam.

σκυταλοδρομία, ή [skeetalodromeea] relay race.

σκυφτός [skeeftos] bending, stooping.

σκωληκόβρωτος [skoleekovrotos] worm-eaten

σκωληκοειδῖτις, ή [skoleekoeedeetees] appendicitis.

σκώληξ, ὁ [skoleeks] βλ σκουλήκι.

σκῶμμα, τό [skoma] scoff, gibe ‖ mockery.

σκώπτω [skopto] mock, deride, jeer, taunt.

σκωρία, ή [skoreea] βλ σκουριά.

σκῶρος, ὁ [skoros] moth.

σκώτι, τό [skotee] βλ σηκώτι.

σλέπι, τό [slepee] lighter.

σμάλτον, τό [smalton] enamel.

σμαράγδι, τό [smaraɣdee] emerald.

σμάρι, τό [smaree] βλ σμῆνος.

σμέουρο, τό [smeouro] raspberry.

σμηναγός, ὁ [smeenaɣos] (ἀερο) flight lieutenant.

σμήναρχος, ὁ [smeenarhos] group captain ‖ (US) colonel.

σμηνίας, ὁ [smeeneeas] sergeant.

σμηνίτης, ὁ [smeeneetees] airman.

σμῆνος, τό [smeenos] swarm ‖ (ἀερο) flight, squadron ‖ crowd.

σμίγω [smeeɣo] mingle, mix ‖ meet, come face to face with ‖ join.

σμίκρυνσις, ή [smeekreensees] reduction, diminution, decrease.

σμιλάρι, τό [smeelaree] chisel.

σμίλη, ή [smeelee] chisel.

σμίξιμο, τό [smeekseemo] mixing, meeting, mating, joining.

σμιχτοφρύδης [smeehtofreedees] with eyebrows that meet.

σμόκιν, τό [smokeen] dinner jacket.

σμπαράλια, τά [smbaraleea] πλ tiny pieces.

σμπάρο, τό [smbaro] shot.

σμύρις, ή [smeerees] emery.

σνομπαρία, ή [snombareea] snobbishness.

σοβαρεύομαι [sovarevome] look serious, speak seriously.

σοβαρόν [sovaron]: ~ ποσόν a substantial sum.

σοβαρός [sovaros] serious, grave, solemn.

σοβᾶς, ὁ [sovas] wall plaster.

σοβατίζω [sovateezo] plaster.

σοβῶ [sovo] be near, be at hand.

σόδα, ή [soδa] soda water ‖ bicarbonate of soda.

σοδειά, ή [soδia] βλ ἐσοδεία.

σόι [soee] lineage, breed ‖ sort, kind ‖ ἀπό ~ from a good family.

σοκάκι, τό [sokakee] narrow street, lane, alley.

σοκάρω [sokaro] shock, upset.

σόκιν [sokeen] shocking, suggestive.

σοκολάτα, ή [sokolata] chocolate.

σόλα, ή [sola] sole (of shoe).

σόλοικος [soleekos] incorrect, ungrammatical ‖ (μεταφ) improper.

σολομός, ὁ [solomos] salmon.

σόμπα, ή [somba] heater, heating stove.

σορόκος, ὁ [sorokos] βλ σιρόκος.

σορός, ή [soros] bier, coffin ‖ the dead (person).

σός [sos] your.

σοσιαλιστής, ὁ [soseealeestees] socialist.

σου [sou] your.

σούβλα, ἡ [souvla] skewer.

σουβλάκια, τά [souvlakeea] πλ meat on a skewer.

σουβλερός [souvleros] sharp, pointed.

σουβλί, τό [souvlee] awl ‖ spit.

σουβλιά, ἡ [souvlia] injury from a pointed object ‖ (πόνος) acute pain.

σουβλίζω [souvleezo] run through, pierce ‖ (ψήνω) skewer ‖ (πονῶ) cause pain.

σουγιάς, ὁ [souyias] penknife.

σούζα [souza]: στέκομαι ~ obey blindly ‖ (μεταφ) fawn.

σουλατσάρω [soulatsaro] wander about, loaf.

σουλούπι, τό [souloupee] outline, cut, contour.

σουλτανίνα, ἡ [soultaneena] sort of seedless grape.

σουλτάνα, ἡ [soultana] Sultana.

σουλτάνος, ὁ [soultanos] Sultan.

σουμάδα, ἡ [soumada] orgeat (of almonds).

σουμιές, ὁ [soumies] spring mattress.

σούπα, ἡ [soupa] soup.

σουπιά, ἡ [soupia] cuttlefish ‖ (μεταφ) sneaky person.

σούρα, ἡ [soura] fold, wrinkle, crease, pleat.

σουραύλι, τό [souravlee] pipe, reed, flute.

σουρομαδῶ [souromado] tug by the hair.

σούρουπο, τό [souroupo] dusk, nightfall.

σουρούπωμα, τό [souroupoma] nightfall.

σουρτούκης, ὁ [sourtoukees] gadabout.

σουρωμένος [souromenos] intoxicated.

σουρώνω [sourono] strain, filter ‖ fold, pleat, crease ‖ (ἀδυνατίζω) lose weight, grow thin ‖ get drunk.

σουρωτήρι, τό [souroteeree] strainer.

σουσάμι, τό [sousamee] sesame.

σουσουράδα, ἡ [sousourada] wagtail.

σούσουρο, τό [sousouro] noise, din ‖ rustle ‖ (μεταφ) scandal.

σούστα, ἡ [sousta] spring (of seat) ‖ (ὄχημα) cart ‖ clasp, clip.

σούτ [sout] (ἐπιφ) hush!, shut up!

σουτζούκι, τό [soutzoukee] type of sausage.

σουτζουκάκια, τά [soutzoukakeea] πλ meatballs.

σουτιέν, τό [soutien] bra(ssière).

σούφρα, ἡ [soufra] pleat, crease, fold ‖ (μεταφ) theft.

σουφρώνω [soufrono] fold, pleat, crease ‖ (μεταφ) pinch, steal.

σοφία, ἡ [sofeea] wisdom, learning ‖ erudition.

σοφίζομαι [sofeezome] devise.

σοφιστεία, ἡ [sofeesteea] sophistry, subtlety.

σοφίτα, ἡ [sofeeta] attic, garret.

σοφός [sofos] wise ‖ learned, lettered.

σπαγγοραμένος [spangoramenos] mean, tight-fisted.

σπάγγος, ὁ [spangos] twine, string ‖ (μεταφ) mean person.

σπάζω [spazo] break, shatter, smash ‖ ~ τό κεφάλι μου think hard ‖ ~ στό ξύλο beat.

σπαθάτος [spathatos] sword-bearing ‖ (μεταφ) slim, slender.

σπάθη, ἡ [spathee] sword.

σπαθί, τό [spathee] sabre, sword ‖ (στά χαρτιά) spade.

σπαθιά, ἡ [spathia] sword stroke.

σπανάκι, τό [spanakee] spinach.

σπανίζω [spaneezo] become rare, be exceptional, be scarce.

σπάνιος [spaneeos] few and far between, uncommon.

σπανιότης, ἡ [spaneeotees] rarity, rareness, scarcity.

σπάνις, ἡ [spanees] rarity, shortage.

σπανίως [spaneeos] rarely.

σπανός [spanos] smooth-faced, beardless ‖ raw, very young.

σπάνω [spano] βλ σπάζω.

σπαράγγι, τό [sparangee] asparagus ‖ (US) sparrow grass.

σπαραγμός, ὁ [sparaymos] tearing ‖ heartbreak, anguish.

σπαρακτικός [sparakteekos] heartbreaking, agonizing ‖ (θέαμα) harrowing.

σπαράσσω [sparaso] tear ‖ (μεταφ) cut to the heart.

σπάραχνα, τά [sparahna] πλ gills.

σπάργανα, τά [sparyana] πλ swaddling clothes.

σπαρμένος [sparmenos] spread ‖ strewn, sown.

σπαρτά, τά [sparta] πλ crops.

σπαρταριστός [spartareestos] (ψάρι) fresh ‖ (κορίτσι) beautiful ‖ vivid, very descriptive.

σπαρταρῶ [spartaro] throb, palpitate, jump.

σπαρτός [spartos] βλ σπαρμένος.

σπάσιμο, τό [spaseemo] break, fracture.

σπασμός, ὁ [spasmos] convulsion, twitching.

σπασμωδικός [spasmodeekos] spasmodic ‖ hasty.

σκατάλη, ἡ [spatalee] lavishness, extravagance, waste.

σπάταλος [spatalos] wasteful, extravagant.

σπαταλῶ [spatalo] waste, lavish, squander.

σπάτουλα, ἡ [spatoula] spatula.

σπεῖρα, ἡ [speera] coil, spiral ‖ (ὁμάδα) band, gang, clique.

σπείρω [speero] sow ‖ propagate.

σπεκουλάρω [spekoularo] speculate.

σπέρμα, τό [sperma] seed, germ ‖ semen, sperm ‖ (μεταφ) offspring ‖ cause, motive.

σπερμολογία, ἡ [spermoloyeea] spreading of rumours.

σπέρνω [sperno] βλ σπείρω.

σπεύδω [spevdo] hurry, make haste.

σπήλαιον, τό [speeleon] cave, cavern, lair.

σπηλιά, ή [speelia] βλ σπήλαιον.
σπίθα, ή [speetha] spark, flash.
σπιθαμή, ή [speethamee] span.
σπιθοβολῶ [speethovolo] sparkle, spark ‖ gleam, glitter.
σπιθούρι, τό [speethouree] pimple.
σπιλῶ [speelo] soil, dirty ‖ (μεταφ) tarnish.
σπινθήρ [speentheer] (αὐτοκινήτου) ignition spark.
σκίνος, ὁ [speenos] finch.
σπιοῦνος, ὁ [speeounos] spy ‖ stool pigeon.
σπιρούνι, τό [speerounee] spur.
σπιρτάδα, ἡ [speertaδa] pungency ‖ (μεταφ) wit, intelligence.
σπίρτο, τό [speerto] alcohol ‖ (πυρεῖον) match.
σπιρτόζος [speertozos] witty, clever, ingenious.
σπιτήσιος [speeteeseeos] home-made, domestic.
σπίτι, τό [speetee] house, home ‖ (μεταφ) family ‖ ἀπό ~ well-born.
σπιτικό, τό [speeteeko] βλ σπίτι.
σπιτικός [speeteekos] βλ σπιτήσιος.
σπιτονοικοκύρης, ὁ [speetoneekokeerees] householder, landlord.
σπιτώνω [speetono] lodge, house ‖ (μεταφ) keep (a woman).
σπλά(γ)χνα, τά [splan(g)hna] πλ entrails, innards ‖ (μεταφ) feelings ‖ offspring.
σπλα(γ)χνικός [splan(g)hneekos] merciful, sympathetic.
σπλά(γ)χνο, τό [splan(g)hno] offspring, child.
σπλήν, ὁ [spleen] spleen.
σπλήνα, ἡ [spleena] βλ σπλήν.
σπληνάντερο, τό [spleenantero] sheep's intestines.
σπληνιάρης [spleeneearees] irritable, hypochondriac.
σπογγαλιεία, ἡ [spongalieea] sponge fishing.
σπογγαλιεύς, ὁ [spongalievs] sponge fisher.
σπογγίζω [spongeezo] sponge up ‖ mop up, wipe away.
σπόγγος, ὁ [spongos] sponge.
σπογγώδης [spongoδees] spongy.
σποδός, ἡ [spoδos] cinders, ashes.
σπονδή, ἡ [sponδee] libation.
σπονδυλική [sponδeeleekee]: ~ στήλη spine, backbone.
σπονδυλικός [sponδeeleekos] vertebral.
σπόνδυλος, ὁ [sponδeelos] vertebra ‖ (κίονος) drum.
σπονδυλωτός [sponδeelotos] vertebrate.
σπόρ, τό [spor] sport, games, pastime.
σπορά, ἡ [spora] sowing ‖ seed time ‖ (μεταφ) generation.
σποράδην [sporaδeen] sporadically.
σποραδικός [sporaδeekos] dispersed, scanty.
σπορέλαιον, τό [sporeleon] seed oil.
σπόρια, τά [sporeea] πλ seeds.

σπόρος, ὁ [sporos] seed, germ ‖ semen.
σπουδάζω [spouδazo] study, attend school.
σπουδαῖος [spouδeos] serious, important ‖ exceptional.
σπουδασμένος [spouδasmenos] learned, educated.
σπουδαστής, ὁ [spouδastees] student.
σπουδή, ἡ [spouδee] haste, keenness ‖ (μελέτη) study.
σπουργίτης, ὁ [spourγeetees] sparrow.
σπρωξιά, ἡ [sproksia] push, hustle, jostle, shoving.
σπρώξιμο, τό [sprokseemo] pushing ‖ encouraging.
σπρώχνω [sprohno] push, thrust, shove ‖ encourage, incite.
σπυρί, τό [speeree] grain ‖ (κολλιέ) bead ‖ (βάρος) grain ‖ (ἐξάνθημα) pimple ‖ boil.
σπυρωτός [speerotos] granular, granulated.
στάβλος, ὁ [stavlos] stable ‖ cowshed.
στάγδην [staγδeen] in drops.
σταγόνα, ἡ [staγona] βλ σταγών.
σταγονόμετρον, τό [staγonometron] dropper ‖ μέ τό ~ in small doses, little by little.
σταγών, ἡ [staγon] drop, dash.
σταδιοδρομία, ἡ [staδeeoδromeea] career, course.
στάδιον, τό [staδeon] stadium, athletic ground ‖ (μεταφ) career, vocation.
στάζω [stazo] trickle, dribble, drip, leak.
σταθεροποίησις, ἡ [statheropieesees] stabilization, steadying down.
σταθερός [statheros] stable, firm, steadfast, secure.
σταθμά, τά [stathma] πλ weights.
σταθμάρχης, ὁ [stathmarhees] station master.
στάθμευσις, ἡ [stathmevsees] stopping, waiting, parking ‖ stationing.
σταθμεύω [stathmevo] stop, wait, stand, camp, park.
στάθμη, ἡ [stathmee] level, plumbline ‖ (νεροῦ) water level ‖ (τοῦ βίου) standard (of living).
σταθμίζω [stathmeezo] weigh, level ‖ (μεταφ) appreciate, calculate.
σταθμός, ὁ [stathmos] station, halting place ‖ (αὐτοκινήτου) garage ‖ (US) parking lot ‖ (ταξί) taxi rank ‖ stop, stay, wait ‖ (στήν ἱστορία) landmark, stage.
στάκτη, ἡ [staktee] ash, ashes, cinders.
σταλα(γ)ματιά, ἡ [stala(γ)matia] drop, dash.
σταλάζω [stalazo] drip, dribble, trickle.
σταλακτίτης, ὁ [stalakteetees] stalactite.
στάλσιμο, τό [stalseemo] sending.
σταμάτημα, τό [stamateema] stop, halting, checking ‖ pause ‖ block.
σταματῶ [stamato] stop (working), check.
στάμνα, ἡ [stamna] pitcher, jug.
στάμπα, ἡ [stampa] stamp, seal ‖ impression.

στάνη, ή [stanee] sheepfold, pen.

στανιό, τό [stanio]: μέ τό ~ against one's will, involuntarily.

στάξιμο, τό [stakseemo] dripping, trickling.

στασιάζω [staseeazo] mutiny, rebel.

στασίδι, τό [staseedee] pew, stall.

στάσιμος [staseemos] motionless, stationary || (ὕδωρ) stagnant.

στάσις, ή [stasees] halt, stop, bus stop, station || (ἐργασίας) suspension, stoppage || (τρόπος) posture, position || (ἰατρ) retention || (ἐξέγερσις) revolt, rebellion || (μεταφ) behaviour, attitude.

στατήρ, ὁ [stateer] hundredweight.

στατική, ή [stateekee] statics.

στατικός [stateekos] static(al).

στατιστική, ή [stateesteekee] statistics.

σταυλάρχης, ὁ [stavlarhees] stable master.

στάβλος, ὁ [stavlos] stable || cowshed || (χοίρων) pigsty.

σταυροδρόμι, τό [stavrodromee] crossroads || crossing.

σταυροειδής [stavroeedees] cruciform, crosslike.

σταυροειδῶς [stavroeedos] crosswise.

σταυροκοπιέμαι [stavrokopieme] cross o.s. over and over again.

σταυρόλεξο, τό [stavrolekso] crossword puzzle.

σταυροπόδι [stavropodee] cross-legged.

σταυρός, ὁ [stavros] cross, crucifix || stake, pale.

σταυροφορία, ή [stavroforeea] crusade.

σταυρώνω [stavrono] crucify || (τά χέρια) cross || (διασταυροῦμαι) cross, meet and pass, cut across.

σταυρωτός [stavrotos] crossways, cross-wise || (σακκάκι) double-breasted.

σταφίδα, ή [stafeeda] raisin || κορινθιακή ~ currant || (σμυρναίϊκη) sultana || γίνομαι ~ get intoxicated.

σταφυλή, ή [stafeelee] grapes || (ἀνατ) uvula.

σταφύλι, τό [stafeelee] grape.

σταφυλόκοκκος, ὁ [stafeelokokos] staphylococcus.

στάχι, τό [stahee] ear of corn, ear of wheat.

στάχτη, ή [stahtee] βλ στάκτη.

σταχτής [stahtees] ashen, pale.

σταχτόνερο, τό [stahtonero] lye.

Σταχτοπούτα, ή [stahtopouta] Cinderella.

σταχυολόγημα, τό [staheeologeema] gleaning || (μεταφ) selection, selecting.

στεατοκήριον, τό [steatokeereeon] tallow candle.

στεγάζω [stegazo] roof || cover, house, shelter.

στεγανόπους [steganopous] webfooted.

στεγανός [steganos] airtight, hermetical, waterproof.

στέγασις, ή [stegasees] housing, sheltering.

στέγασμα, τό [stegasma] roof || cover, shelter.

στέγη, ή [stegee] roof || (μεταφ) house, dwelling.

στεγνός [stegnos] dry || (μεταφ) skinny, spare.

στεγνώνω [stegnono] dry, become dry.

στειλιάρι, τό [steeleearee] helve || cudgel.

στεῖρος [steeros] barren, unproductive || (προσπάθεια) vain.

στέκα, ή [steka] billiard cue || (μεταφ) woman as thin as a rake.

στέκει [stekee]: ~ καλά he is well-off || he is fit and well.

στέκομαι [stekome] stand up | come to a standstill, stop || (μεταφ) prove to be || happen.

στέκω [steko] stand, stand still, come to a stop || it is fit to be.

στελέχη, τά [stelehee] πλ cadres.

στέλεχος, τό [stelehos] stalk, stem || shank, rod || (τσέκ) counterfoil || (χερούλι) handle.

στέλλω [stelo] send, direct, dispatch, forward.

στέλνω [stelno] βλ στέλλω.

στέμμα, τό [stema] crown, diadem.

στεναγμός, ὁ [stenagmos] sigh, sighing || moan, groan.

στενάζω [stenazo] sigh, heave a sigh || (μεταφ) moan.

στενεύω [stenevo] narrow down, take in, tighten || shrink, get narrow.

στενογραφία, ή [stenografeea] shorthand, stenography.

στενοδακτυλογράφος, ὁ, ή [stenodakteeloyrafos] shorthand typist.

στενόκαρδος [stenokardos] apt to worry.

στενοκέφαλος [stenokefalos] narrow-minded, strait-laced.

στενόμακρος [stenomakros] long and narrow, oblong.

στενόν, τό [stenon] strait || (δροσειράς) pass, gorge.

στενός [stenos] narrow || tight-fitting || (μεταφ) close, intimate || (φίλος) dear (friend).

στενότης, ή [stenotees] tightness, closeness || narrowness || ~ χρήματος lack of money.

στενοχωρημένος [stenohoreemenos] hard-up || ill at ease.

στενοχωρία, ή [stenohoreea] lack of room || (δυσκολία) difficulty, inconvenience, discomfort.

στενόχωρος [stenohoros] narrow, limited, tight || troublesome.

στενοχωρῶ [stenohoro] worry, embarrass, annoy.

στενωπός, ή [stenopos] narrow street, back street || defile, pass.

στέργω [steryo] content o.s. with, allow, agree to.

στερεά, ή [sterea] mainland || ~ Ἑλλάς central Greece.

στερεοποιῶ [stereopeeo] solidify.

στερεός [stereos] firm, compact, well-built ‖ solid, substantial ‖ (χρῶμα) fast.

στερεότυπος [stereoteepos] stereotyped, invariable.

στερεύω [sterevo] dry up ‖ stop, cease.

στερέωμα, τό [stereoma] consolidation ‖ support, fastening ‖ (οὐρανός) firmament.

στερεώνω [stereono] consolidate ‖ make secure ‖ ~ σέ μιά δουλειά settle down to one job.

στερήσεις, οἱ [stereesees] πλ privation, want, loss.

στέρησις, ἡ [stereesees] deprivation ‖ shortage, absence.

στεριά, ἡ [steria] terra firma.

στεριανός, ὁ [stereeanos] mainlander.

στερλίνα, ἡ [sterleena] pound sterling.

στέρνα, ἡ [sterna] cistern, tank.

στέρνον, τό [sternon] breastbone, chest.

στερνός [sternos] later, last.

στεροῦμαι [steroume] go without, lack ‖ (πένομαι) be needy.

στερῶ [stero] deprive of, take away.

στέφανα, τά [stefana] πλ marriage wreaths.

στεφάνη, ἡ [stefanee] crown ‖ (ἀγγείου) brim ‖ (βαρελιοῦ) hoop ‖ (ἄνθους) corolla ‖ ring, band ‖ (τροχοῦ) tyre.

στεφάνι, τό [stefanee] garland, wreath ‖ (βαρελιοῦ) hoop, band.

στέφανος, ὁ [stefanos] garland, wreath crown.

στεφανώνομαι [stefanonome] marry, get married.

στεφανώνω [stefanono] crown ‖ be the best man at a wedding.

στέψις, ἡ [stepsees] coronation ‖ wedding ceremony.

στηθαῖον, τό [steetheon] parapet.

στηθικός [steetheekos] of the chest ‖ consumptive.

στηθόδεσμος, ὁ [steethodesmos] βλ σουτιέν.

στῆθος, τό [steethos] chest, breast ‖ (γυναικός) bosom.

στηθοσκοπῶ [steethoskopo] examine with a stethoscope.

στήλη, ἡ [steelee] staff, pillar, column ‖ (μπαταρία) electric battery ‖ (ἐφημερίδος) column.

στηλιτεύω [steeleetevo] defame, slander.

στηλώνω [steelono] prop up, support ‖ bolster up.

στημόνι, τό [steemonee] warp.

στήνω [steeno] raise, hold up, erect, put up ‖ ~ παγίδα lay a trap.

στήριγμα, τό [steereegma] prop, support, stay.

στηρίζομαι [steereezome] lean on, rely on ‖ be based on.

στηρίζω [steereezo] support ‖ prop ‖ base on, reckon on.

στητός [steetos] standing, upright.

στιβάλι, τό [steevalee] ankle boot, laced boot.

στιβαρός [steevaros] strong, robust, steady, firm.

στιβάς, ἡ [steevas] pile, heap, mass.

στίβος, ὁ [steevos] track, ring, racetrack.

στίγμα, τό [steegma] spot, brand, stain, stigma ‖ disgrace ‖ position, fix.

στιγμή, ἡ [steegmee] instant, moment ‖ (τυπογραφικό) dot, point ‖ τελεία ~ full stop ‖ ἄνω ~ colon.

στιγμιαῖος [steeymieos] instantaneous ‖ momentary, temporary.

στιγμιότυπον, τό [steeymeeoteepon] snapshot, snap.

στικτός [steektos] spotted, dotted, stippled ‖ tattooed.

στίλβω [steelvo] shine, glitter, sparkle.

στιλβώνω [steelvono] polish, varnish, burnish.

στιλβωτήριον, τό [steelvoteereeon] shoe black's.

στιλέττο, τό [steeleto] stiletto, dagger.

στιλπνός [steelpnos] brilliant, polished, bright.

στίξις, ἡ [steeksees] punctuation ‖ dot, spot, speckle.

στιφάδο, τό [steefado] meat stew with onions.

στῖφος, τό [steefos] crowd, horde, throng ‖ rabble, gang.

στιχομυθία, ἡ [steehomeetheea] vivid dialogue.

στίχος, ὁ [steehos] line, row, file ‖ verse.

στιχουργός, ὁ [steehouryos] rhymester, versifier.

στοά, ἡ [stoa] colonnade, portico, arcade ‖ passage ‖ (ὀρυχείου) gallery ‖ (μασωνική) (masonic) lodge.

στοίβα, ἡ [steeva] pile, stack, mass.

στοιβάζω [steevazo] stack, pile up ‖ crowd, squeeze.

στοιχεῖα, τά [steeheea] πλ elements, rudiments ‖ (τυπογραφείου) printing types.

στοιχειό, τό [steehio] ghost, phantom.

στοιχειοθεσία, ἡ [steeheeotheseea] typesetting.

στοιχεῖον, τό [steeheeon] component, element ‖ (νομ) piece of evidence ‖ (ἀλφαβήτου) letter ‖ (ἠλεκτ) cell ‖ (μεταφ) factor.

στοιχειώδης [steeheeodees] elementary, rudimentary ‖ essential, capital.

στοιχειωμένος [steeheeomenos] haunted.

στοιχειώνω [steeheeono] become haunted, haunt.

στοίχημα, τό [steeheema] bet, wager ‖ stake ‖ βάζω ~ lay a bet, wager.

στοιχηματίζω [steeheemateezo] bet, wager.

στοιχίζω [steeheezo] cost ‖ (μεταφ) pain, grieve.

στοῖχος, τό [steehos] row, line, rank.

στόκος, ὁ [stokos] putty, stucco.

στολή, ή [stolee] uniform || costume.
στολίδι, τό [stoleedee] jewellery || (στόλισμα) adornment, decoration.
στολίζω [stoleezo] adorn, decorate, deck, trim, embellish.
στολίσκος, ό [stoleeskos] flotilla || flight.
στολισμός, ό [stoleesmos] ornamenting, decoration, embellishing.
στόλος, ό [stolos] navy, fleet.
στόμα, τό [stoma] mouth || lips.
στομάχι, τό [stomahee] stomach.
στομαχιάζω [stomaheeazo] suffer from indigestion.
στόμαχος, ό [stomahos] βλ στομάχι.
στόμιον, τό [stomeeon] mouth, opening, aperture, entrance || muzzle.
στόμφος, ό [stomfos] boast, declamation.
στομώνω [stomono] blunt || temper, harden.
στόρ(ι), τό [stor(ee)] blind, roller blind.
στοργή, ή [storyee] affection, tenderness, love.
στουμπίζω [stoumbeezo] pound, grind, crush || beat s.o. mercilessly.
στουμπώνω [stoumbono] stuff, pad, plug || become stuffed.
στουπί, τό [stoupee] oakum, wad, tow || (μεταφ) drunk as a fiddler.
στουπόχαρτο, τό [stoupoharto] blotting paper.
στουπώνω [stoupono] stop, choke up || be choked up.
στουρνάρι, τό [stournaree] flint, gun flint.
στοχάζομαι [stohazome] think, meditate (on) || consider.
στοχασμός, ό [stohasmos] thought, meditation.
στοχαστικός [stohasteekos] thoughtful || discreet, wise.
στόχαστρον, τό [stohastron] front sight (of gun).
στόχος, ό [stohos] mark, target, objective || aim, end.
στραβά [strava] obliquely, crookedly || wrongly, amiss || τόβαλε ~ he doesn't give a damn.
στραβισμός, ό [straveesmos] squinting.
στραβοβλέπω [stravovlepo] look askance at, leer at.
στραβοκάνης [stravokanees] bandy-legged.
στραβομάρα, ή [stravomara] blindness || (κακοτυχία) bad luck, mischance || (μεταφ) blunder, gross mistake, howler.
στραβόξυλο, τό [stravokseelo] obstinate person, contrary fellow.
στραβοπάτημα, τό [stravopateema] staggering || false step.
στραβός [stravos] crooked, awry, twisted || (λοξός) slanting || (ἐλαττωματικός) faulty || (τυφλός) blind.
στραβώνομαι [stravonome] go blind.
στραβώνω [stravono] bend, distort || make a mess of || spoil || (τυφλώνω) blind || (λυγίζω) become twisted.

στραγάλια, τά [strayaleea] πλ roasted chickpeas.
στραγγαλίζω [strangaleezo] strangle, throttle || stifle.
στραγγαλιστής, ό [strangaleestees] strangler.
στραγγίζω [strangeezo] drain, filter, press out, wring out || (κουράζομαι) get exhausted.
στραγγιστήρι, τό [strangeesteeree] strainer, filter, colander.
στραγγουλίζω [strangouleezo] sprain, twist, wrench.
στράκα, ή [straka] crack || (πυροτέχνημα) cracker.
στραμπουλίζω [strambouleezo] sprain, twist.
στραπατσάρω [strapatsaro] harm, damage || ruffle || (ταπεινώνω) humiliate.
στραπάτσο, τό [strapatso] maltreatment || humiliation.
στράτα, ή [strata] way, street, road.
στρατάρχης, ό [stratarhees] (field) marshal.
στράτευμα, τό [stratevma] army, troops, forces.
στρατεύματα, τά [stratevmata] πλ troops.
στρατεύομαι [stratevome] serve in the army, take the field.
στρατεύσιμος [stratevseemos] subject to conscription.
στρατηγείον, τό [strateeyeeon] headquarters.
στρατήγημα, τό [strateeyeema] stratagem || trick, ruse.
στρατηγία, ή [strateeyeea] generalship.
στρατηγική, ή [strateeyeekee] strategy.
στρατηγικός [strateeyeekos] strategic.
στρατηγός, ό [strateeyos] general.
στρατί, τό [stratee] βλ στράτα.
στρατιά, ή [stratia] army, force.
στρατιώτης, ό [strateeotees] soldier, private || warrior.
στρατιωτικό, τό [strateeoteeko] military service.
στρατιωτικός [strateeoteekos] military || ~ νόμος martial law.
στρατοδικείον, τό [stratodeekeeon] court-martial.
στρατοκρατία, ή [stratokrateea] militarism, military government.
στρατολογία, ή [stratoloyeea] conscription, call-up.
στρατόπεδον, τό [stratopeδon] camp, encampment || side, party.
στρατός, ό [stratos] army, troops, forces.
στρατόσφαιρα, ή [stratosfera] stratosphere.
στρατώνας, ό [stratonas] barracks.
στρεβλός [strevlos] crooked, deformed, twisted || (μεταφ) rough, difficult.
στρείδι, τό [streeδee] oyster.
στρέμμα, τό [strema] (approx) quarter of an acre.
στρέφομαι [strefome] turn, rotate || revolve.

στρέφω [strefo] turn, turn about ‖ rotate, revolve.

στρεψοδικία, ἡ [strepsodeekeea] chicanery, quibbling, pettifoggery.

στρίβω [streevo] twist, rotate, turn ‖ τό ~ slip away, slip off.

στρίγ(γ)λα, ἡ [stree(n)gla] witch, sorceress, shrew.

στριγ(γ)λιά, ἡ [stree(n)glia] wickedness, shrewishness ‖ (κραυγή) shrill cry, shriek.

στριμμένος [streemenos] twisted ‖ ill-humoured, wicked, malicious.

στρίποδο, τό [streepodo] trestle, tripod.

στριφογυρίζω [streefoγeereezo] move round, turn round ‖ whirl, spin.

στρίφωμα, τό [streefoma] hemming.

στρίψιμο, τό [streepseemo] twisting, turning.

στροβιλίζω [stroveeleezo] whirl, turn round, twirl.

στρόβιλος, ὁ [stroveelos] spinning top, peg top ‖ (ἄνεμος) whirlwind ‖ (χιόνος) eddying, swirling (snow) ‖ (μηχανή) turbine ‖ (σκόνης) whirling cloud.

στρογγυλεύω [strongelevo] make round ‖ grow plump, get stout.

στρογγυλός [strongeelos] round(ed) ‖ (πρόσωπο) full ‖ (ἀριθμός) round, even.

στρούγγα, ἡ [strounga] sheepfold, enclosure.

στρουθίον, τό [stroutheeon] sparrow.

στρουθοκάμηλος, ἡ [strouthokameelos] ostrich.

στρουμπουλός [stroumboulos] dumpy.

στρόφαλος, ὁ [strofalos] crank, handle ‖ (αὐτοκινήτου) starting handle.

στροφεῖον, τό [strofeeon] winch.

στροφεύς, ὁ [strofevs] hinge, pivot.

στροφή, ἡ [strofee] turn, revolution ‖ (ὁδοῦ) twist, bend ‖ (κατευθύνσεως) detour, change of direction ‖ (ποίηση) stanza ‖ (μους) ritornello.

στρόφιγξ, ἡ [strofeenks] hinge, pivot ‖ tap.

στρυμώ(χ)νω [streemo(h)no] squeeze, crowd, cram ‖ press hard, oppress, annoy.

στρυφνός [streefnos] harsh ‖ peevish ‖ (χαρακτήρ) crabbed ‖ (ὕφος κτλ) obscure, difficult ‖ (εἰς γεῦσιν) sharp, biting.

στρῶμα, τό [stroma] couch, bed, mattress ‖ (γεωλογίας) bed, layer, stratum ‖ στό ~ ill in bed.

στρώνομαι [stronome] apply o.s. ‖ install o.s.

στρώνω [strono] spread, lay ‖ (κρεββάτι) make ‖ (δρόμο) pave ‖ (μεταφ) be well under way ‖ τό κρεββάτι make the bed.

στρώση, ἡ [strosee] layer ! strewing ‖ paving, flooring.

στρωσίδι, τό [stroseedee] carpet ‖ bedding.

στρωτός [strotos] strewn / paved ‖ (ζωή) even, normal, regular.

στύβω [steevo] squeeze, wring, press ‖

(μεταφ) rack one's brains ‖ (στειρεύω) dry up, run dry.

στυγερός [steeγeros] abominable, heinous, horrible.

στυγνός [steeγnos] doleful, despondent, gloomy.

στυλό, τό [steelo] fountain pen.

στυλοβάτης, ὁ [steelovatees] pedestal, base ‖ (μεταφ) pillar, founder.

στυλογράφος, ὁ [steeloγrafos] βλ στυλό.

στῦλος, ὁ [steelos] pillar, column, pole ‖ (μεταφ) prop, mainstay, breadwinner.

στυλώνω [steelono] support, prop up ‖ fix.

στυπτηρία, ἡ [steepteereea] βλ στύψη.

στυπτικός [steepteekos] binding, styptic.

στυφός [steefos] sour, acrid, bitter.

στύψη, ἡ [steepsee] alum.

στύψιμο, τό [steepseemo] squeezing, pressing, wringing.

στωϊκός [stoeekos] stoic(al).

στωμύλος [stomeelos] eloquent, fluent.

σύ [see] you.

συβαρίτης, ὁ [seevareetees] sybarite.

σύγγαμβρος, ὁ [seengamvros] brother-in-law.

συγγένεια, ἡ [seengeneea] relationship, kinship ‖ affinity, relation, connection.

συγγενής [seengenees] connected, related ‖ (οὐσ) relation, kinsman.

συγγενολό(γ)ι, τό [seengenolo(γ)ee] relations, relatives, kindred.

συγγνώμη, ἡ [seeγnomee] pardon, excuse ‖ forgiveness.

σύγγραμμα, τό [seengrama] work (of writing), treatise.

συγγραφεύς, ὁ [seengrafevs] author, writer.

συγγράφω [seengrafo] write a work, compose.

σύγκαιρα [seengkera] in time ‖ simultaneously.

συγκαίομαι [seengkeome] be chafed, be galled.

σύγκαλα, τά [seengkala] πλ: στά ~ μου normal, in good health.

συγκαλύπτω [seengkaleepto] hide, cloak, hush up, cover.

συγκάλυψις, ἡ [seengkaleepsees] cloaking, masking, suppression.

συγκαλῶ [seengkalo] convene, convoke ‖ (πρόσωπα) assemble, call together.

συγκαταβατικός [seengkatavateekos] accommodating ‖ (τιμή) moderate, reasonable.

συγκατάθεσις, ἡ [seengkatathesees] assent, consent, acquiescence.

συγκαταλέγω [seengkataleγo] include, number among ‖ consider, regard.

συγκατανεύω [seengkatanevo] consent, assent, adhere to.

συγκατατίθεμαι [seengkatateetheme] βλ συγκατανεύω.

συγκατοικῶ [seengkateeko] cohabit, live together.

σύγκειμαι [seengkeeme] be composed of, consist of.

συγκεκαλυμμένος [seengkekaleemenos] disguised, indirect.

συγκεκριμένος [seéngkekreemenos] concrete, positive, clear, specific.

συγκεκριμένως [seengkekreemenos] plainly, concretely, actually.

συγκεντρώνομαι [seengkentronome] concentrate.

συγκεντρώνω [seengkentrono] collect, bring together, concentrate || centralize.

συγκέντρωσις, ή [seengkentrosees] crowd, gathering, . assembly || concentration || centralization.

συγκερασμός, ό [seengkerasmos] mixing, mingling || compromise.

συγκεφαλαιώνω [seengkefaleono] summarize, sum up.

συγκεχυμένος [seengkeheemenos] confused, jumbled || (ήχος) indistinct || (φήμες) vague || (ἰδέες) hazy, dim || (λόγοι) imprecise, obscure.

συγκίνησις, ή [seengkeeneesees] emotion, sensation.

συγκινητικός [seengkeeneeteekos] moving, touching, stirring.

συγκινούμαι [seengkeenoume] be excited || be touched.

συγκινῶ [seengkeeno] move, affect, touch || excite.

σύγκλησις, ή [seengkleesees] convocation, calling together.

σύγκλητος, ή [seengkleetos] senate.

συγκλίνω [seengkleeno] converge, concentrate.

συγκλονίζω [seengkloneezo] shake, excite, stir up, shock.

συγκοινωνία, ή [seengkeenoneea] communications || means of transport.

συγκοινωνῶ [seengkeenono] communicate, be connected.

συγκολλῶ [seengkolo] glue, join together || (μέταλλα) weld, solder || ~ σαμπρέλα mend a puncture.

συγκομιδή, ή [seengkomeeδee] harvest, crop.

συγκοπή, ή [seengkopee] syncopation || (ἰατρ) heart failure || (γραμμ) contraction.

συγκράτησις, ή [seengkrateesees] containing, bridling, restraining.

συγκρατούμαι [seengkratoume] control o.s., contain o.s.

συγκρατῶ [seengkrato] check || (πάθη) govern || (θυμόν) contain, control, suppress || (τά πλήθη) restrain.

συγκρίνω [seengkreeno] compare (with), liken (to).

σύγκρισις, ή [seengkreesees] comparison, parallel.

συγκριτικός [seengkreeteekos] comparative, compared (to).

συγκρότημα, τό [seengkroteema] group, cluster.

συγκροτῶ [seengkroto] form, compose || convoke, convene.

συγκρούομαι [seengkrouome] bump into, collide || clash, come to blows.

σύγκρουσις, ή [seengkrousees] collision, clash, fight, engagement.

σύγκρυο, τό [seengkreeo] shivering, trembling.

συγκυρία, ή [seengkeereea] coincidence, occurrence, chance.

συγυρίζω [seeyeereezo] tidy up, arrange || (μεταφ) ill-treat.

συγχαίρω [seenghero] congratulate, compliment.

συγχαρητήρια, τά [seenghareeteereea] πλ congratulations.

συγχέω [seengheo] confound, confuse, perplex.

συγχορδία, ή [seenghorδeea] harmony of sounds, accord.

συγχρονίζω [seenghroneezo] modernize, bring up to date.

σύγχρονος [seenghronos] contemporary || simultaneous || contemporaneous.

συγχύζω [seengheezo] get mixed up || worry, confound, harass.

σύγχυσις, ή [seengheesees] confusion, disorder || chaos, commotion.

συγχωνεύω [seenghonevo] amalgamate, blend, merge.

συγχώρησις, ή [seenghoreesees] remission, pardon.

συγχωρητέος [seenghoreeteos]. pardonable, excusable.

συ(γ)χωρεῖτε [see(ng)horeete]: μέ ~ excuse me, I beg your pardon.

συγχωρῶ [seenghoro] pardon, forgive, excuse || tolerate, permit.

συζήτησις, ή [seezeeteesees] discussion, debate || οὔτε ~ it's out of the question.

συζητῶ [seezeeto] discuss, argue, debate.

συζυγία, ή [seezeeyeea] conjugation || union.

συζυγικός [seezeeyeekos] conjugal, marital.

σύζυγος, ὁ, ή [seezeeyos] consort, spouse, husband, wife.

συζῶ [seezo] live together, cohabit.

συθέμελα [seethemela] to the very roots.

συκιά, ή [seekia] fig tree.

σῦκον, τό [seekon] fig.

συκοφάντης, ὁ [seekofantees] slanderer, calumniator.

συκοφαντῶ [seekofanto] slander, calumniate.

συκώτι, τό [seekotee] liver.

σύλησις, ή [seeleesees] spoliation, sacking.

συλητής, ὁ [seeleetees] despoiler || looter, pilferer.

συλλαβή, ή [seelavee] syllable.

συλλαλητήριον, τό [seelaleeteereeon] mass meeting, demonstration.

συλλαμβάνω [seelamvano] catch, lay hold of, capture, seize, arrest ‖ (ἰδέες) conceive.

συλλέγω [seelego] collect, gather.

συλλέκτης, ὁ [seelektees] collector.

συλλήβδην [seeleevdeen] collectively, in one word, as a whole.

σύλληψις, ἡ [seeleepsees] capture, arrest. seizure ‖ (ἰδέας) conception.

συλλογή, ἡ [seelogee] set, assortment, collection ‖ (σκέψις) thought, concern.

συλλογίζομαι [seelogeezome] think out reflect about, consider, reason.

συλλογικός [seelogeekos] collective.

συλλογισμένος [seelogeesmenos] pensive, thoughtful, absorbed (in).

συλλογισμός, ὁ [seelogeesmos] thought, reflexion ‖ reasoning, syllogism.

σύλλογος, ὁ [seelogos] society, club, association.

συλλυπητήρια, τά [seeleepeeteereea] πλ condolences, sympathy.

συλλυποῦμαι [seeleepoume] offer condolence ‖ feel sorry for.

συλῶ [seelo] plunder, despoil, loot.

συμβαδίζω [seemvadeezo] keep up with ‖ go together, coexist.

συμβαίνω [seemveno] happen, take place, come about.

συμβάλλομαι [seemvalome] contract, enter into an agreement.

συμβάλλω [seemvalo] contribute to, pay one's share ‖ (ποτάμι) meet, join, unite.

συμβάν, τό [seemvan] event, accident, occurrence.

σύμβασις, ἡ [seemvasees] agreement, contract, treaty, pact.

συμβεβηκός, τό [seemveveekos] βλ συμβάν.

συμβία, ἡ [seemveea] wife, consort.

συμβιβάζομαι [seemveevazome] compromise, agree with ‖ be compatible with.

συμβιβάζω [seemveevazo] reconcile, arrange, adjust.

συμβιβασμός, ὁ [seemveevasmos] compromise, accommodation, adjustment, settlement.

συμβίωσις, ἡ [seemveeosees] living together, cohabitation.

συμβολαιογράφος, ὁ [seemvoleografos] notary public.

συμβόλαιον, τό [seemvoleon] contract, agreement.

συμβολή, ἡ [seemvolee] contribution ‖ (ποταμῶν) confluence, junction.

συμβολίζω [seemvoleezo] symbolize, represent.

σύμβολον, τό [seemvolon] symbol, mark, sign, emblem, token ‖ ~ τῆς πίστεως Apostles' Creed.

συμβουλεύομαι [seemvoulevome] consult, refer to, take s.o.'s advice.

συμβουλεύω [seemvoulevo] advise, recommend.

συμβουλή, ἡ [seemvoulee] advice, counsel.

συμβούλιον, τό [seemvouleeon] council, board, committee.

σύμβουλος, ὁ [seemvoulos] adviser, counsellor ‖ councillor.

συμμαζεύω [seemazevo] tidy up, collect, assemble, gather together ‖ (ἐλέγχω) restrain, check, hold.

συμμαχία, ἡ [seemaheea] alliance, coalition.

σύμμαχος [seemahos] allied ‖ (οὐσ) ally.

συμμερίζομαι [seemereezome] share, have a part (in).

συμμετέχω [seemeteho] participate in, take part in, be a party to.

συμμετοχή, ἡ [seemetohee] participation ‖ sharing.

συμμετρία, ἡ [seemetreea] symmetry, proportion.

συμμετρικός [seemetreekos] symmetrical ‖ well-proportioned.

συμμιγδην [seemeegdeen] pell-mell, in confusion.

συμμορία, ἡ [seemoreea] gang, band, body.

συμμορφώνομαι [seemorfonome] comply, conform, agree with, adapt to.

συμμορφώνω [seemorfono] adapt, conform ‖ bring to heel.

συμπαγής [seembayees] solid, firm, compact, close.

συμπάθεια, ἡ [seembatheea] compassion, sympathy ‖ weakness (for) ‖ favourite.

συμπαθής [seembathees] likeable, lovable.

συμπαθητικός [seembatheeteekos] likeable, lovable ‖ sympathetic.

συμπάθιο, τό [seembatheeo]: μέ τό ~ begging your pardon.

συμπαθῶ [seembatho] feel compassion for ‖ have a liking for.

συμπαιγνία, ἡ [seembegneea] collusion.

σύμπαν, τό [seempan] universe ‖ everything, all, everybody.

συμπατριώτης, ὁ [seembatreeotees] compatriot, fellow countryman.

συμπεθεριά, ἡ [seempetheria] relationship by marriage.

συμπεθεριό, τό [seempetherio] βλ συμπεθεριά.

συμπέθεροι, οἱ [seempetheree] πλ fathers-in-law ‖ relations by marriage.

συμπεπυκνωμένος [seempepeeknomenos] condensed.

συμπεραίνω [seempereno] conclude, presume, infer, surmise.

συμπέρασμα, τό [seemperasma] conclusion, inference, end.

συμπεριλαμβάνω [seempereelamvano] include, contain, comprise.

συμπεριφέρομαι [seempereeferome] behave, conduct o.s.

συμπεριφορά, ἡ [seempereefora] behaviour, conduct.

σύμπηξις, ἡ [seempeeksees] forming ‖ coagulation, curdling.

συμπίεσις, ή [seempiesees] compression, squeezing.

συμπίπτω [seempeepto] coincide, concur, converge || happen, chance.

σύμπλεγμα, τό [seempleyma] tangle || cluster || network.

συμπλέκομαι [seemplekome] come to blows, quarrel || fight.

συμπλέκω [seempleko] interlace, interweave, entwine.

συμπλήρωμα, τό [seempleeroma] complement || supplement, addition.

συμπληρωματικός [seempleeromateekos] complementary, further || supplementary.

συμπληρώνω [seempleerono] complete, complement, finish || (θέσιν) fill || (φόρμα) fill in.

συμπλήρωσις, ή [seempleerosees] completion, filling, achievement.

συμπλοκή, ή [seemplokee] fight, engagement, clash, brawl.

σύμπνοια, ή [seempneea] harmony, agreement, understanding.

συμπολιτεία, ή [seempoleeteea] confederation, confederacy.

συμπολίτης, ό [seempoleetees] fellow citizen, fellow countryman.

συμπονώ [seempono] feel compassion for, sympathize with.

συμπόσιον, τό [seemposeeon] banquet, feast.

συμποσοῦμαι [seemposoume] come to, run (to).

σύμπραξις, ή [seempraksees] cooperation, contribution.

συμπτύσσομαι [seempteesome] fall back, shorten.

συμπτύσσω [seempteeso] shorten, abridge, abbreviate, cut short.

σύμπτωμα, τό [seemptoma] symptom || sign, indication.

σύμπτωσις, ή [seemptosees] coincidence, accident, chance.

συμπυκνώ [seempeekno] condense, compress.

συμπυκνωτής, ό [seempeeknotees] condenser.

συμφέρει [seemferee] it's worth it, it's to one's advantage.

συμφέρον, τό [seemferon] advantage, interest, profit, benefit.

συμφεροντολογία, ή [seemferontoloyeea] self-interest.

συμφιλιώνω [seemfeeleeono] reconcile, restore friendship, make up.

συμφορά, ή [seemfora] calamity, disaster, misfortune.

συμφόρησις, ή [seemforeesees] traffic jam, congestion || (ιατρ) stroke.

σύμφορος [seemforos] advantageous, profitable, useful.

συμφυής [seemfiees] innate, inborn, inherent

συμφυρμός, ό [seemfeermos] mixing, blending, jumbling.

συμφύρομαι [seemfeerome] get mixed up with.

συμφύρω [seemfeero] confuse, mingle, mix, jumble.

σύμφωνα [seemfona]: ~ μέ according to, in conformity (with).

συμφωνητικόν, τό [seemfoneeteekon] agreement, deed of contract.

συμφωνία, ή [seemfoneea] agreement, convention || accord, consent || (μουσ) symphony.

σύμφωνον, τό [seemfonon] consonant || compact, agreement, pact.

σύμφωνος [seemfonos] in accord, in conformity with.

συμφωνώ [seemfono] concur, agree || match, go well together.

συμφώνως [seemfonos] according to || ~ πρός in accordance with.

συμψηφίζω [seempseefeezo] counterbalance, make up for.

σύν [seen] together, with || (μάθημ) plus || ~ τῷ χρόνω in time, gradually, eventually || ~ τοῖς ἄλλοις moreover, in addition.

συναγερμός, ό [seenayermos] alarm, call to arms, alert || (πολιτικός) rally, mass meeting.

συναγρίδα, ή [seenayreeδa] kind of sea bream.

συνάγω [seenayo] assemble, collect, bring together || (συμπεραίνω) infer, conclude, deduce.

συναγωγή, ή [seenayoyee] collection, gathering, assembly || (Εβραίων) synagogue.

συναγωνίζομαι [seenayoneezome] rival, compete || fight together.

συναγωνιστής, ό [seenayoneestees] rival, competitor || (συμπολεμιστής) brother in arms || (ἀνταγωνιστής) rival.

συνάδελφος, ό [seenaδelfos] colleague, fellow member.

συνάζω [seenazo] collect, assemble || gather || heap up.

συναθροίζω [seenathreezo] βλ **συνάζω**.

συναινώ [seeneno] consent to, agree to, acquiesce.

συναίρεσις, ή [seeneresees] (γραμμ) contraction.

συναισθάνομαι [seenesthanome] become aware of, be conscious of, feel.

συναίσθημα, τό [seenestheema] sentiment, feeling, sensation.

συναισθήματα, τά [seenestheemata] πλ emotions, feelings.

συναισθηματικός [seenestheemateekos] emotional, sentimental.

συναίσθησις, ή [seenestheesees] feeling, sense, appreciation, consciousness.

συναλλαγή, ή [seenalayee] exchange, dealings, trade || ἐλευθέρα ~ free trade.

συνάλλαγμα, τό [seenalayma] foreign currency || draft, bill || τιμή ~τος rate of exchange.

συναλλαγματική, ή [seenalaymateekee] bill of exchange.

συναλλάσσομαι [seenalasome] deal, trade, traffic || (συναναστρέφομαι) associate with.

συνάμα [seenama] together, in one lot, at the same time, at once.

συναναστρέφομαι [seenanastrefome] consort with, mix with.

συναναστροφή, ή [seenanastrofee] association, company || party, reception.

συνάντησις, ή [seenanteesees] falling in with, meeting || encounter.

συναντῶ [seenanto] meet, happen (upon), run across.

συναντῶμαι [seenantome] meet, come together.

σύναξις, ή [seenaksees] concentration, meeting || collecting, receipts.

συναπτός [seenaptos] consecutive, successive || annexed, tied, appended.

συνάπτω [seenapto] annex, attach || (συμμαχίαν) contract, form || (δάνειον) incur || (εἰρήνην) conclude || (μάχην) join, give battle || ~ σχέσεις make friends.

συναρμολογῶ [seenarmoloyo] fit together || join || make up, piece together.

συναρπάζω [seenarpazo] carry away, enrapture, entrance.

συνάρτησις, ή [seenarteesees] attachment, connection || cohesion.

συνασπισμός, ό [seenaspeesmos] coalition, alliance, league.

συναυλία, ή [seenavleea] concert.

συνάφεια, ή [seenafeea] connection, link, reference.

συναφής [seenafees] adjacent (to) || linked, connected || like.

συνάχι, τό [seenahee] cold (in the head), catarrh.

σύναψις, ή [seenapsees] conclusion, arrangement || contraction || joining.

συνδαιτυμών, ό [seendeteemon] table guest, dinner guest, fellow diner.

συνδαυλίζω [seendavleezo] poke a fire || stir up.

συνδεδεμένος [seendedemenos] closely associated, having ties with.

σύνδεσις, ή [seendesees] joining, binding together.

σύνδεσμος, ό [seendesmos] bond, union || (στρατ) liaison || relationship, affinity || (γραμμ) conjunction.

συνδετήρ, ό [seendeteer] clip, paper clip.

συνδετικός [seendeteekos] joining, connective || (γραμμ) copulative.

συνδέω [seendeo] bind together, unite || (μεταφ) join, link, bind.

συνδιαλέγομαι [seendeealeyome] converse (with), talk to.

συνδιαλλαγή, ή [seendeealayee] reconciliation.

συνδιάσκεψις, ή [seendeeaskepsees] deliberation || conference.

συνδικᾶτον, τό [seendeekaton] syndicate || (ἐργατῶν) trade union.

συνδράμω [seendramo] support, help || contribute to.

συνδρομή, ή [seendromee] coincidence, conjunction || (ἀρωγή) help, assistance || subscription, contribution || (ἰατρ) syndrome.

συνδρομητής, ό [seendromeetees] subscriber.

συνδυάζομαι [seendeeazome] harmonize, go together, match.

συνδυάζω [seendeeazo] unite, combine || match, pair || arrange.

συνδυασμός, ό [seendeeasmos] combination, arrangement || matching.

σύνεγγυς [seenengees]: ἐκ τοῦ ~ very close, from close to.

συνεδριάζω [seenedreeazo] meet, be in session.

συνέδριον, τό [seenedreeon] congress, convention, council.

σύνεδρος, ό [seenedros] delegate || councillor || (δικαστηρίου) judge.

συνείδησις, ή [seeneedeesees] conscience.

συνειδητός [seeneedeetos] conscious, wilful.

συνειρμός, ό [seeneermos] coherence, order, sequence.

συνεισφέρω [seeneesfero] contribute, subscribe.

συνεκτικός [seenekteekos] cohesive, binding, tenacious.

συνέλευσις, ή [seenelevsees] meeting, assembly.

συνεννόησις, ή [seenenoeesees] understanding, concert, concord, agreement || exchange of views.

συνεννοοῦμαι [seenenooume] agree, come to an agreement || exchange views.

συνενοχή, ή [seenenohee] complicity, abetment, connivance.

συνέντευξις, ή [seenentevksees] interview, appointment, rendezvous.

συνενῶ [seeneno] unite, join together.

συνεπάγομαι [seenepayome] lead to, involve, have as consequence, call for.

συνεπαίρνω [seeneperno] transport, carry away.

συνέπεια, ή [seenepeea] result, outcome, consequence || consistency.

συνεπής [seenepees] true, in keeping with consistent || punctual.

συνεπῶς [seenepos] consequently, accordingly.

συνεπτυγμένος [seenepteeymenos] compact, succinct, brief.

συνεργάζομαι [seeneryazome] cooperate, collaborate || contribute.

συνεργάτης, ὁ [seeneryatees] collaborator ‖ contributor.

συνεργατική, ἡ [seeneryateekee] cooperative.

συνεργεῖον, τό [seeneryeeon] workroom, workshop ‖ gang, shift, team of workers ‖ repair shop.

συνεργία, ἡ [seeneryeea] complicity, abetment, confederacy.

σύνεργο, τό [seeneryo] implement, tool, instrument.

συνεργός, ὁ [seeneryos] accessary, accomplice, abettor, party (to).

συνερίζομαι [seenereezome] heed, take into account, keep up rivalry with.

συνέρχομαι [seenerhome] get over, recover ‖ come together, meet, assemble.

σύνεσις, ἡ [seenesees] caution, good sense, prudence, judgment.

συνεσταλμένος [seenestalmenos] shy, modest, timid, circumspect.

συνεταιρισμός, ὁ [seenetereesmos] cooperative, association.

συνέταιρος, ὁ [seeneteros] partner, associate, colleague, copartner.

συνετός [seenetos] wise, discreet, prudent, sensible, cautious.

συνεφέρνω [seeneferno] revive, bring s.o. round ‖ come to.

συνέχεια, ἡ [seeneheea] continuity ‖ continuation, outcome ‖ (ἐπίρ) continuously, successively.

συνεχής [seenehees] continuous, incessant, unceasing, continual ‖ successive ‖ adjacent.

συνεχίζω [seeneheezo] continue, keep on, go on.

συνέχομαι [seenehome] be communicating, be contiguous, adjoin.

συνέχω [seeneho] possess, seize, curb, control, check ‖ adjoin.

συνεχῶς [seenehos] continually, endlessly.

συνήγορος, ὁ [seeneeyoros] advocate, defender, counsel.

συνήθεια, ἡ [seeneetheea] habit, custom, practice, use.

συνήθειο, τό [seeneetheeo] βλ συνήθεια.

συνήθης [seeneethees] habitual, customary, usual, common, ordinary.

συνηθίζεται [seeneetheezete] it is usual, it is the fashion.

συνηθίζω [seeneetheezo] accustom to ‖ get accustomed to ‖ be in the habit of.

συνηθισμένος [seeneetheesmenos] accustomed, familiar with ‖ habitual, customary.

συνημμένος [seeneemenos] attached, connected, annexed, enclosed.

σύνθεσις, ἡ [seenthesees] mixture, composition ‖ collocation ‖ structure, synthesis.

συνθέτης, ο [seenthetees] compose· ‖ compositor

συνθετικόν, τό [seentheteekon] component, constituent.

συνθετικός [seentheteekos] constituent, component ‖ artificial, synthetic.

σύνθετον, τό [seentheton] (γραμμ) compound (word).

σύνθετος [seenthetos] compound, composite ‖ intricate.

συνθέτω [seentheto] compose, make up.

συνθῆκες, οἱ [seentheekes] πλ conditions, circumstances, situation.

συνθήκη, ἡ [seentheekee] treaty, agreement, pact ‖ convention.

συνθηκολογῶ [seentheekoloyo] surrender, capitulate ‖ negotiate a treaty.

σύνθημα, τό [seentheema] signal, sign, password, watchword.

συνθηματικός [seentheemateekos] symbolic ‖ in code.

συνθλίβω [seenthleevo] squeeze, compress, crush.

συνίζησις, ἡ [seeneezeesees] synizesis ‖ (χώματος) subsidence.

συνίσταμαι [seeneestame] consist of, be composed of.

συνιστῶ [seeneesto] advise, recommend ‖ (ἐπιτροπήν) establish, set up, form ‖ (γνωρίζω) introduce.

συννεφιά, ἡ [seenefia] cloudy weather ‖ ~ζω become cloudy ‖ (μεταφ) look sullen.

σύννεφο, τό [seenefo] cloud.

συννυφάδα, ἡ [seeneefaδa] wife of one's brother-in-law.

συνοδ(ε)ία, ἡ [seenoδeea] escort, retinue, suite, convoy, procession ‖ (μους) accompaniment.

συνοδεύω [seenoδevo] accompany, go with, escort ‖ (ναυτ) convoy.

συνοδοιπόρος, ὁ, ἡ [seenoδeeporos] fellow traveller.

σύνοδος, ἡ [seenoδos] congress, sitting, assembly ‖ (ἐκκλ) synod.

συνοδός, ὁ, ἡ [seenoδos] steward, escort ‖ ἱπταμένη ~ air hostess.

συνοικέσιον, τό [seeneekeseeon] arranged marriage, match.

συνοικία, ἡ [seeneekeea] quarter, neighbourhood, ward.

συνοικιακός [seeneekeeakos] local, suburban.

συνοικισμός, ὁ [seeneekeesmos] settlement ‖ colonization ‖ quarter.

συνολικός [seenoleekos] total, whole.

σύνολον, τό [seenolon] total, entirety.

συνόλω [seenolo] ἐν ~ in all, totally.

συνομήλικος [seenomeeleekos] of the same age.

συνομιλητής, ὁ [seenomeeleetees] interlocutor.

συνομιλία, ἡ [seenomeeleea] conversation, chat, talk ‖ interview.

συνομολογῶ [seenomoloyo] conclude ‖ acknowledge, admit.

συνομοταξία, ή [seenomotakseea] branch, group, class.

συνονόματος [seenonomatos] namesake, having the same name.

συνοπτικός [seenopteekos] summary, brief, synoptic, concise.

σύνορα, τά [seenora] πλ frontier, boundaries.

συνορεύω [seenorevo] have a common frontier, border on.

σύνορον, τό [seenoron] boundary, border, frontier.

συνουσία, ή [seenouseea] coition, intercourse, copulation.

συνοφρυοῦμαι [seenofreeoume] frown, scowl || look sullen.

συνοχή, ή [seenohee] coherence, cohesion || (ἰδεῶν) sequence, chain.

σύνοψις, ή [seenopsees] summary, compendium, synopsis || (ἐκκλ) prayer book, breviary.

συνταγή, ή [seentayee] formula, prescription || recipe.

σύνταγμα, τό [seentayma] constitution, charter || (στρατ) regiment.

συνταγματάρχης, ὁ [seentaymatarhees] colonel.

συνταγματικός [seentaymateekos] constitutional.

συντάκτης, ὁ [seentaktees] author, writer |, (ἐφημερίδος) editor || (συνθήκης) drawer-up, framer.

συντακτικόν, τό [seentakteekon] syntax, book of syntax.

συντακτικός [seentakteekos] component, constituent || (ἐφημερίδος) editorial || (γραμμ) syntactic(al).

συνταξιοῦχος, ὁ, ἡ [seentaksiouhos] pensioner || retired officer.

σύνταξις, ή [seentaksees] compilation || wording, writing || organization || (ἐφημερίδος) editing, editorial staff || pension || (γραμμ) construction, syntax.

συνταράσσω [seentaraso] agitate, shake, disturb, trouble || (μεταφ) disconcert.

συντάσσομαι [seentasome] take sides with, fall in with || (γραμμ) govern.

συντάσσω [seentaso] arrange, compile || write, draft, draw up || (γραμμ) construe || constitute, form, organize || (νόμον) frame || (ἐφημερίδα) edit.

συνταυτίζω [seentavteezo] identify, regard as the same.

συντείνω [seenteeno] contribute to, concur.

συντέλεια, ή [seenteleea]: ~ τοῦ κόσμου end of the world.

συντελεστής, ὁ [seentelestees] factor, component, contributor || (μαθημ) coefficient.

συντελεστικός [seentelesteekos] contributory, conductive.

συντελῶ [seentelo] finish, complete || contribute to, conduce to.

συντέμνω [seentemno] shorten, curtail, abridge.

συντεταγμένη, ή [seentetaymenee] coordinate.

συντετριμμένος [seentetreemenos] deeply afflicted, crushed.

συντεχνία, ή [seentehneea] guild, fellowship, confraternity || trade union.

συντήρησις, ή [seenteereesees] preservation, conservation || (μηχανῆς) maintenance.

συντηρητικός [seenteereeteekos] conservative, preserving.

συντηρῶ [seenteero] preserve, conserve || keep up, maintain || (διατρέφω) maintain, support.

συντίθεμαι [seenteetheme] be composed of, be made up of.

σύντομα [seentoma] in short, briefly || soon, at once, immediately.

συντομεύω [seentomevo] shorten, curtail, abridge.

συντομία, ή [seentomeea] shortness, brevity || terseness.

σύντομος [seentomos] short, succinct, brief.

συντόμως [seentomos] in a word, in short || (χρονικῶς) soon.

συντονίζω [seentoneezo] coordinate, harmonize, tune together.

σύντονος [seentonos] unremitting, constant, incessant.

συντρέχω [seentreho] help || meet, converge || contribute.

συντριβή, ή [seentreevee] ruin || crushing, smashing.

συντρίβω [seentreevo] shatter, break, crush, smash || ruin, wear out.

σύντριμμα, τό [seentreema] fragment, debris, wreck.

συντρίμματα, τά [seentreemata] πλ debris, fragments, wreckage.

συντριπτικός [seentreepteekos] (μεταφ) crushing, overwhelming.

συντροφιά, ή [seentrofia] companionship, company || gathering, society || (ἐπίρ) together.

σύντροφος, ὁ, ἡ [seentrofos] companion, mate, comrade || (ἐμπορ) associate, partner.

συντυχαίνω [seenteeheno] happen, chance || converse with.

συνύπαρξις, ή [seeneeparksees] coexistence

συνυπάρχω [seeneeparho] coexist.

συνυπεύθυνος [seeneepevtheenos] jointly liable.

συνυφαίνω [seeneefeno] entwine || (μεταφ) conspire, intrigue.

συνωθοῦμαι [seenothoume] jostle, push

συνωμοσία, ή [seenomoseea] conspiracy, plot.

συνωμοτῶ [seenomoto] conspire, plot.

συνώνυμον, τό [seenoneemon] synonym.

συνώνυμος [seenoneemos] synonymous.

συνωστισμός, ὁ [seenosteesmos] jostle, crush, scramble.

σύξυλος [seekseelos] with crew and cargo ‖ ἔμεινε ~ he was amazed, he was speechless.

σύριγξ, ἡ [seereenks] Pan's pipe ‖ syringe, tube.

συρίζω [seereezo] hiss, whistle, whizz, whir, wheeze.

σύρμα, τό [seerma] wire.

συρματόπλεγμα, τό [seermatopleyma] barbed wire ‖ wire netting.

συρμός, ὁ [seermos] railway train ‖ (μόδα) fashion, manner, habit.

σύρραξις, ἡ [seeraksees] clash, collision, shock, conflict.

συρρέω [seereo] crowd, throng, flock ‖ flow into.

σύρριζα [seereeza] by the root, root and branch ‖ very closely.

συρροή, ἡ [seerooee] crowd, throng ‖ inflow, influx ‖ abundance, profusion.

συρτάρι, τό [seertaree] drawer.

συρτή, ἡ [seertee] dragnet, trail net.

σύρτης, ὁ [seertees] bolt, bar.

σύρτις, ἡ [seertees] sandbank.

συρτός [seertos] dragged ‖ listless, drawling ‖ (πόρτα) sliding ‖ (οὐσ) kind of circular dance.

συρφετός, ὁ [seerfetos] mob, populace, common people.

σύρω [seero] βλ σέρνω.

συσκέπτομαι [seeskeptome] confer, deliberate, take counsel.

συσκευάζω [seeskevazo] pack, box, wrap, parcel.

συσκευασία, ἡ [seeskevaseea] wrapping up, packing ‖ (φαρμακευτική) preparation.

συσκευή, ἡ [seeskevee] apparatus, contrivance.

σύσκεψις, ἡ [seeskepsees] discussion, deliberation ‖ conference, consultation.

συσκοτίζω [seeskoteezo] obscure, darken, black out ‖ (μεταφ) confuse.

συσκότισις, ἡ [seeskoteesees] blackout ‖ confusion.

σύσπασις, ἡ [seespasees] contraction, writhing, shrinking.

συσπειρούμαι [seespeeroume] roll into a ball, coil ‖ (μεταφ) snuggle.

συσσίτιον, τό [seeseeteeon] mess, common meal ‖ soup kitchen.

σύσσωμος [seesomos] all together, entire, united, in a body.

συσσωρευτής, ὁ [seesorevtees] accumulator.

συσσωρεύω [seesorevo] accumulate, collect, pile up ‖ amass.

συστάδην [seestaδen]: ἐκ τοῦ ~ hand-to-hand, at close quarters.

συσταίνω [seesteno] βλ συνιστῶ.

συστάς, ἡ [seestas] clump of trees, cluster, grove.

συστάσεις, οἱ [seestasees] πλ references,

advice ‖ recommendation, introductions.

σύσταση, ἡ [seestasee] address.

σύστασις, ἡ [seestasees] composition, structure ‖ (πάχος) consistency ‖ (σχηματισμός) formation, creation, setting up ‖ (πρότασις) recommendation, recommending ‖ (συμβουλή) advice, counsel.

συστατικά, τά [seestateeka] πλ component parts, ingredients ‖ references, recommendations.

συστατική [seestateekee]: ~ ἐπιστολή letter of introduction, letter of reference.

συστατικός [seestateekos] component, essential, constituent.

συστέλλομαι [seestelome] shrink, contract ‖ feel shy, be timid.

συστέλλω [seestelo] contract, shrink, shrivel.

σύστημα, τό [seesteema] method, system, plan ‖ custom, habitude.

συστηματικός [seesteemateekos] systematic, methodical.

συστημένο [seesteemeno]: ~ γράμμα registered letter.

συστήνω [seesteeno] βλ συνιστῶ.

συστολή, ἡ [seestolee] shrinking, contraction ‖ modesty, shame, bashfulness.

συσφίγγω [seesfeengo] tighten, constrict, draw tighter, grasp.

συσχετίζω [seesheteezo] compare, relate, put together.

σύφιλις, ἡ [seefeelees] syphilis.

συχνά [seehna] often, frequently ‖ ~κις often, many times.

συχνάζω [seehnazo] frequent, haunt, resort.

συχνός [seehnos] frequent, repeated.

συχνότης, ἡ [seehnotees] frequency.

συχωράω [seehorao] forgive, tolerate.

σφαγεῖον, τό [sfayeeon] slaughterhouse ‖ butchery, slaughter.

σφαγή, ἡ [sfayee] slaughter, carnage, massacre.

σφαγιάζω [sfayeeazo] massacre, slaughter ‖ sacrifice ‖ (μεταφ) violate, transgress.

σφάγιον, τό [sfayeeon] victim, animal for slaughter.

σφαδάζω [sfaδazo] writhe, jerk, squirm.

σφάζω [sfazo] slaughter, kill, massacre, murder.

σφαῖρα, ἡ [sfera] globe, sphere ‖ ball ‖ (ὅπλου) bullet ‖ (μεταφ) sphere, field.

σφαιρίδιον, τό [sfereeδeeon] small shot ‖ (αἵματος) globule.

σφαιριστήριον, τό [sfereesteereeon] billiard table, billiard room ‖ (US) poolroom.

σφαλερός [sfaleros] mistaken, erroneous ‖ (ἐπικίνδυνος) unsafe, unsound, dangerous.

σφαλιάρα, ἡ [sfaleeara] slap in the face ‖ smack.

σφαλίζω [sfaleezo] enclose, shut in ‖ (κλείνω) close, lock, bolt.

σφαλιστός [sfaleestos] shut ‖ sealed, locked.

σφάλλομαι [sfalome] be wrong, make a mistake ‖ misfire.

σφάλλω [sfalo] βλ σφάλλομαι.

σφάλμα, τό [sfalma] wrong act, fault ‖ error, blunder, slip.

σφάξιμο, τό [sfakseemo] butchering.

σφάχτης, ὁ [sfahtees] twinge, sharp pain

σφένδαμνος, ὁ [sfendamnos] maple tree.

σφενδόνη, ἡ [sfendonee] sling.

σφερδούκλι, τό [sferdouklee] asphodel.

σφετερίζομαι [sfetereezome] purloin, embezzle ‖ appropriate, usurp.

σφή(γ)κα, ἡ [sfee(ng)ka] wasp.

σφήν(α), ἡ [sfeen(a)] wedge.

σφηνώνω [sfeenono] push in, thrust in between ‖ wedge.

σφήξ, ὁ [sfeeks] βλ σφή(γ)κα.

σφίγγομαι [sfeengome] squeeze together ‖ endeavour, try hard.

σφίγγω [sfeengo] squeeze, press ‖ tighten, pull tighter ‖ (σκληρύνω) become tight, stick.

σφίγξ, ἡ [sfeenks] sphinx ‖ (μεταφ) enigmatic.

σφίξη, ἡ [sfeeksee] urgency, necessity.

σφίξιμο, τό [sfeekseemo] pressing, tightening, squeezing ‖ pressure, squeeze.

σφιχτός [sfeehtos] tight, hard, thick ‖ stingy, tight-fisted.

σφόδρα [sfodra] extremely, very, greatly, excessively.

σφοδρός [sfodros] violent, wild, strong, severe, sharp.

σφοδρότης, ἡ [sfodrotees] violence, vehemence, wildness.

σφουγγαράς, ὁ [sfoungaras] sponge fisherman, sponge seller.

σφουγγάρι, τό [sfoungaree] sponge.

σφουγγαρόπανο, τό [sfoungaropano] mop, floorcloth.

σφουγγάτο, τό [sfoungato] omelet.

σφουγγίζω [sfoungeezo] wipe off, sponge ‖ (πιάτα) dry.

σφραγίζω [sfrageezo] set one's seal to, stamp ‖ (μπουκάλι) cork ‖ (δόντι) fill (tooth).

σφραγίδα, ἡ [sfrageeda] seal, signet, stamp ‖ (μεταφ) impression.

σφραγίς, ἡ [sfragees] βλ σφραγίδα.

σφρίγος, τό [sfreeyos] youthful exuberance, vigour, pep.

σφυγμός, ὁ [sfeeymos] pulse ‖ (μεταφ) caprice, whim.

σφύζω [sfeezo] throb, beat violently, pulsate.

σφύξις, ἡ [sfeeksees] pulsation, throbbing, throb.

σφύρα, ἡ [sfeera] hammer.

σφυρηλατῶ [sfeereelato] hammer, batter, forge, pound away ‖ trump up.

σφυρί, τό [sfeeree] βλ σφύρα.

σφύριγμα, τό [sfeereeyma] whistling, hissing.

σφυρίδα, ἡ [sfeereeda] kind of fish.

σφυρίζω [sfeereezo] whistle, hiss, boo.

σφυρίχτρα, ἡ [sfeereehtra] whistle ‖ (ναυτ) pipe.

σφυροκοπῶ [sfeerokopo] hammer ‖ pound away.

σφυρόν, τό [sfeeron] ankle.

σχεδία, ἡ [shedeea] raft, float.

σχεδιάγραμμα, τό [shedeeayrama] sketch outline, draft.

σχεδιάζω [shedeeazo] sketch, outline, design, draw ‖ plan, intend, mean.

σχεδιαστής, ὁ [shedeeastees] draughtsman, designer.

σχέδιον, τό [shedeeon] plan, design ‖ sketch, outline ‖ scheme ‖ ~ πόλεως town planning.

σχεδόν [shedon] almost, nearly, all but ‖ not much, scarcely.

σχέσις, ἡ [shesees] relation, connection reference ‖ intercourse, relations.

σχετίζομαι [sheteezome] be intimate with, get acquainted, make friends with.

σχετίζω [sheteezo] put side by side, connect, compare.

σχετικά [sheteeka] relative to, relatively ‖ ~ μέ with reference to, regarding, referring to.

σχετικός [sheteekos] relative, pertinent.

σχετικότης, ἡ [sheteeckotees] relativity.

σχετικῶς [sheteekos] βλ σχετικά.

σχετλιασμός, ὁ [shetleeasmos] complaining, lamenting ‖ grumble, complaint.

σχῆμα, τό [sheema] form, shape ‖ (μέγεθος) format, size ‖ (ἱερατικόν) cloth ‖ gesture ‖ ~ λόγου figure of speech.

σχηματίζω [sheemateezo] form, model, shape ‖ create, produce ‖ constitute.

σχηματισμός, ὁ [sheemateesmos] forming, formation, fashioning, construction.

σχίζα, ἡ [sheeza] split wood, splinter, shaving.

σχίζομαι [sheezome] crack, tear ‖ fork.

σχίζω [sheezo] split, cleave ‖ tear, rend fissure.

σχῖνος, ἡ [sheenos] lentisk (bush).

σχίσμα, τό [sheesma] crack ‖ schism, dissension, breach.

σχισμάδα, ἡ [sheesmada] crack, split, fissure.

σχισμή, ἡ [sheesmee] crack, fissure, split.

σχιστόλιθος, ὁ [sheestoleethos] schist, slate.

σχιστός [sheestos] split, slit, torn, open.

σχοινάκι, τό [sheenakee] skipping rope.

σχοινί(ον), τό [sheenee(on)] rope, cord ‖ clothes line.

σχοινοβάτης, ὁ [sheenovatees] acrobat ropedancer.

σχοινοτενής [sheenotenees] long-drawn-out, long-winded, wordy.

σχολάζω [sholazo] stop work ‖ rest, be on vacation ‖ (ἀπό σχολεῖον) let out ‖ (ἀπό ἐργασίαν) dismiss, discharge.

σχολαστικός [sholasteekos] pedantic, scholastic.

σχολεῖον, τό [sholeeon] school.

σχολή, ἡ [sholee] free time, leisure ‖ school, academy.

σχόλη, ἡ [sholee] holiday, feast day.

σχολιάζω [sholeeazo] comment on, pass remarks, criticize ‖ annotate, edit.

σχολιαστής, ὁ [sholeeastees] commentator ‖ editor, annotator, scholiast.

σχολικός [sholeekos] of school, scholastic, educational.

σχόλιον, τό [sholeeon] comment, commentary, annotation.

σώβρακο, τό [sovrako] pants, drawers.

σώζομαι [sozome] escape ‖ remain in existence.

σώζω [sozo] save, rescue ‖ preserve, keep.

σωθικά, τά [sotheeka] πλ entrails, bowels, intestines, innards.

σωλήν, ὁ [soleen] pipe, tube, conduit ‖ hose.

σωληνάριον, τό [soleenareeon] small tube.

σῶμα, τό [soma] body, corpse, corps ‖ ~ στρατοῦ army corps, armed force, army.

σωματάρχης, ὁ [somatarhees] corps commander.

σωματεῖον, τό [somateeon] guild, association.

σωματεμπορία, ἡ [somatemboreea] white slave traffic ‖ slave trade.

σωματέμπορος, ὁ [somatemboros] white slaver ‖ pimp.

σωματικός [somateekos] of the body, physical.

σωματοφυλακή, ἡ [somatofeelakee] bodyguard.

σωματώδης [somatoδees] corpulent, stout, portly.

σώνει [sonee]: ~ καί καλά with stubborn insistence.

σώνω [sono] save, rescue, preserve ‖ use up, consume ‖ attain, reach ‖ be enough, be sufficient.

σῶος [soos] safe, entire, whole, unharmed ‖ intact.

σωπαίνω [sopeno] keep silent, say nothing.

σωρεία, ἡ [soreea] heap, pile ‖ abundance of, great number.

σωρηδόν [soreeδon] by heaps ‖ in heaps, in piles ‖ in crowds.

σωριάζομαι [soreeazome] collapse, fall in.

σωρός, ὁ [soros] heap, mass, pile ‖ a lot of, stack of.

σωσίας, ὁ [soseeas] liying image, double ‖ stand-in.

σωσ(σ)ίβιον, τό [soseeveeon] lifebelt, life jacket.

σώσιμο, τό [soseemo] saving ‖ finishing up, eating.

σωστά [sosta]: μέ τά ~ του in his senses, in earnest.

σωστά [sosta] correctly, precisely, rightly, exactly, absolutely.

σωστός [sostos] correct, just, right ‖ whole, entire ‖ absolute.

σωτήρ, ὁ [soteer] saviour, liberator, rescuer.

σωτηρία, ἡ [soteereea] safety, security ‖ salvation, deliverance, saving.

σωφάρω [sofaro] drive a car.

σωφέρ, ὁ [sofer] chauffeur, driver.

σωφρονίζω [sofroneezo] reform, chastise, correct, bring to reason, render wise.

σωφρονιστήριον, τό [sofroneesteereeon] reformatory, house of correction.

σωφροσύνη, ἡ [sofroseenee] wisdom, prudence, sense, judgment ‖ moderation, composure.

σώφρων [sofron] wise, sensible, prudent ‖ moderate, sober, temperate.

Τ, τ

τά [ta] πλ the ‖ them.

ταβάνι, τό [tavanee] ceiling.

ταβέρνα, ἡ [taverna] tavern, inn, eating house.

τάβλα, ἡ [tavla] board, plank ‖ table ‖ ~ στό μεθύσι dead drunk.

τάβλι, τό [tavlee] backgammon.

ταγάρι, τό [tayaree] bag, sack, wallet.

ταγγίζω [tangeezo] grow rancid.

ταγγός [tangos] rancid, rank.

ταγή, ἡ [tayee] fodder.

ταγιέρ, τό [tayier] woman's suit.

ταγίζω [tayeezo] feed ‖ (μωρό) nurse.

τάγμα, τό [tayma] order ‖ (στρατ) battalion.

ταγματάρχης, ὁ [taymatarhees] major.

ταγμένος [taymenos] under a vow.

τάδε [taδe] as follows, the following, this, that ‖ ὁ ~ Mr so and so ‖ such.

τάζομαι [tazome] make a vow, promise.

τάζω [tazo] promise, dedicate, vow.

ταΐζω [taeezo] βλ ταγίζω.

ταινία, ἡ [teneea] band, stretch, strip, ribbon ‖ (κινηματογράφου) strip, film ‖ (μηχανῆς) tape, ribbon ‖ (ἰατρ) tapeworm ‖ (μετρήσεως) tape measure.

ταίρι, τό [teree] helpmate, partner, mate ‖ one of two ‖ match, equal.

ταιριάζει [tereeazee]: δέν ~ it's not fitting, it's not proper.

ταιριάζω [tereeazo] match, pair, suit, harmonize.

ταιριαστός [tereeastos] well-suited, matched.

τάκος, ὁ [takos] wooden fixing block, stump.

τακούνι, τό [takounee] heel.

τάκτ, τό [takt] tact.

τακτικά [takteeka] regularly, frequently.

τακτική, ή [takteekee] tactics, strategy method, regularity.

τακτικός [takteekos] regular ǀ orderly, settled, quiet ‖ fixed ‖ (ἀριθμός) ordinal.

τακτικῶς [takteekos] regularly, often.

τακτοποίησις, ή [taktopieesees] arrangement, accommodation ‖ compromise.

τακτοποιῶ [taktopeeo] arrange, set in order ‖ settle, fix up.

τακτός [taktos] fixed, appointed, settled.

ταλαιπωρία, ή [taleporeea] torment, hardship, pain, adversity.

ταλαίπωρος [taleporos] miserable, wretched, unfortunate.

ταλαιπωροῦμαι [taleporoume] suffer, toil, labour.

ταλαιπωρῶ [taleporo] harass, pester, torment.

ταλαντεύομαι [talantevome] swing, sway, rock ‖ waver, hesitate.

τάλαντον, τό [talanton] talent, gift, faculty.

τάλας [talas] βλ **ταλαίπωρος**.

ταλέντο, τό [talento] βλ **τάλαντον**.

τάλ(λ)ηρον, τό [taleeron] coin of five drachmas.

τάμα, τό [tama] βλ **τάξιμο**.

ταμεῖον, τό [tameeon] cashier's office, booking office, cashdesk ‖ treasury, pension fund.

ταμίας, ὁ [tameeas] cashier, teller, treasurer.

ταμιευτήριον, τό [tamievteereeon] savings bank.

ταμπακιέρα, ή [tambakiera] cigarette case ǀ snuffbox.

ταμπάκος, ὁ [tambakos] snuff.

ταμπέλα, ή [tambela] nameplate, bill ǀ registration plate.

ταμπλό, τό [tamblo] painting, picture ǀ (αὐτοκινήτου) dashboard ‖ switchboard ‖ instrument panel.

ταμπούρι, τό [tambouree] fortification.

ταμπούρλο, τό [tambourlo] drum ‖ (παιδικό) side drum.

τανάλια, τά [tanaleea] πλ pliers, tongs, tweezers.

τανάπαλιν [tanapaleen] inversely, conversely, vice versa.

τάνκ, τό [tank] tank.

τανύζομαι [taneezome] stretch o.s., reach out.

τανύζω [taneezo] stretch, extend.

ταξείδιον, τό [takseedeeon] βλ **ταξίδι(ον)**.

ταξί, τό [taksee] taxi(cab).

ταξιάρχης, ὁ [takseearhees] brigadier ǀ (ἐκκλ) archangel.

ταξιαρχία, ή [takseearheea] brigade.

ταξίαρχος, ὁ [takseearhos] brigadier general.

ταξιδεύω [takseedevo] travel, journey.

ταξίδι(ον), τό [takseedee(on)] trip, journey, travel, voyage.

ταξιδιώτης, ὁ [takseedeeotees] traveller.

ταξιθέτις, ή [takseethetees] theatre attendant, usher.

ταξικός [takseekos] class.

ταξίμετρον, τό [takseemetron] taximeter.

τάξιμο, τό [takseemo] vow, promise.

ταξινομῶ [takseenomo] classify, class, arrange ‖ grade.

τάξις, ή [taksees] order, succession, regularity ǀ class, rank, grade ǀ (σχολείου) form ‖ ἐν τάξει O.K., all right ǀ τάξεις πλ ranks ‖ πρώτης τάξεως first-rate, first-class.

τάπα, ή [tapa] plug, cork, stopper ǀ ~ στό μεθύσι dead drunk.

ταπεινός [tapeenos] modest, humble ǀ abject, vile, base.

ταπεινοφροσύνη, ή [tapeenofroseenee] humility, modesty.

ταπεινώνομαι [tapeenonome] be humiliated ‖ lower o.s.

ταπεινώνω [tapeenono] humble, humiliate mortify, embarrass.

ταπέτο, τό [tapeto] carpet, rug.

ταπετσαρία, ή [tapetsareea] tapestry, wall covering ‖ upholstery.

τάπης, ὁ [tapees] βλ **ταπέτο**.

ταπητουργία, ή [tapeetouryeea] carpet-making.

τάραγμα, τό [tarayma] agitation, shaking.

ταράζω [tarazo] shake ǀ disturb, upset.

ταραμᾶς, ὁ [taramas] preserved roe.

ταραξίας, ὁ [tarakseeas] rowdy person, agitator, noisy person.

ταράσσω [tarasso] βλ **ταράζω**.

ταράτσα, ή [taratsa] flat roof, terrace.

ταραχή, ή [tarahee] agitation, disturbance ‖ upset.

ταραχοποιός, ὁ [tarahopeeos] βλ **ταραξίας**.

ταραχώδης [tarahodees] turbulent, unruly, stormy, disturbed, disorderly.

ταρίφα, ή [tareefa] scale of charges, price list, rates.

ταριχεύω [tareehevo] embalm ǀ preserve, cure, smoke.

ταρσανᾶς, ὁ [tarsanas] boatbuilder's yard.

τάρταρα, τά [tartara] πλ bowels of the earth.

τασάκι, τό [tasakee] saucer ‖ ashtray.

τάσι, τό [tasee] shallow bowl, goblet.

τάσις, ή [tasees] tension, strain ǀ (ἠλεκτ) voltage ‖ (μεταφ) inclination, proclivity, tendency.

τάσσομαι [tasome] place o.s. ǀ (μεταφ) support.

τάσσω [taso] place, put ǀ post, set ǀ marshal ‖ assign, fix.

ταῦ, τό [tav] the letter T.

ταυρομαχία, ή [tavromaheea] bullfight.

ταυρομάχος, ὁ [tavromahos] matador.

ταῦρος, ὁ [tavros] bull.

ταῦτα [tavta] πλ these ǀ μετά ~ afterwards.

ταυτίζω [tavteezo] identify, regard as same.

ταυτόσημος [tavtoseemos] equivalent to, synonymous.

ταυτότης, ή [tavtotees] identity, sameness ‖ identity card.

ταυτόχρονος [tavtohronos] simultaneous.

ταφή, ή [tafee] burial, interment.

τάφος, ὁ [tafos] grave, tomb, vault.

τάφρος, ὁ [tafros] ditch, trench, drain ‖ (ὀχυροῦ) moat.

ταφτᾶς, ὁ [taftas] taffeta.

τάχα(τες) [taha(tes)] perhaps, apparently, supposedly ‖ as if.

ταχεῖα, ή [taheea] express train.

ταχέως [taheos] quickly, rapidly ‖ soon ‖ ὡς τάχιστα as soon as possible.

ταχιά [tahia] tomorrow.

ταχίνι, τό [taheenee] ground sesame.

ταχύ [tahee] tomorrow morning.

ταχυδακτυλουργία, ή [taheedakteelourγeea] conjuring trick, juggling.

ταχυδρομεῖον, τό [taheedromeeon] post, mail ‖ post office.

ταχυδρομικά, τά [taheedromeeka] πλ postage.

ταχυδρομικῶς [taheedromeekos] by post, by mail.

ταχυδρόμος, ὁ [taheedromos] postman.

ταχυδρομῶ [taheedromo] mail, post.

ταχύνους [taheenous] quick-thinking, alert, quick-witted.

ταχύνω [taheeno] quicken, speed up, accelerate ‖ hasten, push forward.

ταχυπαλμία, ή [taheepalmeea] palpitation.

ταχύς [tahees] quick, brisk, rapid, fleet, swift, fast ‖ prompt, speedy.

ταχύτης, ή [taheetees] swiftness, speed, rapidity ‖ promptness ‖ velocity, rate.

ταψί, τό [tapsee] large shallow baking pan.

ταώς, ὁ [taos] peacock.

τέζα [teza] stretched, spread, tight ‖ ἔμεινε ~ he kicked the bucket (col) ‖ ~ στό μεθύσι dead drunk.

τεθλασμένη, ή [tethlasmenee] zigzag line, broken line.

τεθλασμένος [tethlasmenos] broken.

τεθλιμμένος [tethleemenos] grief-stricken, heartbroken.

τείνω [teeno] tighten, stretch out ‖ strain ‖ τεηδ (το), lead (to), be inclined (to).

τεῖον, τό [teyon] tea.

τεῖχος, τό [teehos] wall, high wall.

τεκμήριον, τό [tekmeereeon] sign, token, mark, clue, indication.

τέκνον, τό [teknon] child, infant, offspring.

τεκτονισμός, ὁ [tektoneesmos] freemasonry.

τέκτων, ὁ [tekton] bricklayer, mason ‖ freemason.

τελάρο, τό [telaro] embroidery frame ‖ (θύρας) doorframe ‖ (πίνακος) frame.

τελεία, ή [teleea] full stop ‖ ἄνω ~ semicolon.

τελειοποιῶ [teleeopeeo] perfect, improve, make better.

τέλειος [teleeos] perfect, faultless ‖ ideal ‖ accomplished.

τελειότης, ή [teleeotees] perfection, faultlessness.

τελειόφοιτος [teleeofeetos] final-year (student) ‖ graduate.

τελειωμό [teleeomo]: ~ δέν ἔχει it is interminable, it is inexhaustible.

τελειωμός, ὁ [teleeomos] ending, finishing ‖ exhaustion of supply.

τελειώνω [teleeono] exhaust, finish up ‖ end, conclude, finish ‖ ((μεταφ) die, be exhausted.

τελείως [teleeos] faultlessly, perfectly ‖ completely, fully, entirely, utterly.

τελειωτικός [teleeoteekos] definitive, de-. cisive, final, conclusive.

τελεσίγραφον, τό [teleseeγrafon] ultimatum.

τελεσίδικος [teleseedeekos] final, irrevocable, decisive.

τέλεσις, ή [telesees] ceremony ‖ perpetration ‖ completion.

τελεσφορῶ [telesforo] end in success, meet with success.

τελετάρχης, ὁ [teletarhees] master of ceremonies.

τελετή, ή [teletee] celebration, rite ‖ feast, festival.

τελετουργῶ [teletourγo] officiate, celebrate, solemnize.

τελευταῖος [televteos] last ‖ most recent.

τελευταίως [televteos] of late, recently.

τελευτή, ή [televtee] end ‖ (μεταφ) death.

τελεύω [televo] βλ τελειώνω.

τέλι, τό [telee] thin wire.

τελικά [teleeka] in the end, finally.

τελικῶς [teleekos] βλ τελικά.

τέλμα, τό [telma] swamp, marsh, bog.

τέλος, τό [telos] end ‖ (φόρος) tax, duty ‖ expiration, close ‖ ~ πάντων after all, at all events, finally ‖ ἐπί τέλους at last, at long last ‖ στό ~ at the end, finally ‖ ἐν τέλει in the end, finally.

τελοῦμαι [teloume] happen, take place.

τελῶ [telo] perform, celebrate ‖ achieve, accomplish.

τελωνεῖον, τό [teloneeon] customs house.

τελώνης, ὁ [telonees] customs officer.

τεμαχίζω [temaheezo] cut in pieces, separate, break up.

τεμάχιον, τό [temaheeon] piece, parcel, bit, fragment, chunk.

τέμενος, τό [temenos] temple, shrine, mosque, house of worship.

τέμνουσα, ή [temnousa] secant.

τέμνω [temno] cut, divide, open.

τεμπέλης ῆ [tembelees] lazy, indolent, idle.

τεμπελιάζω [tembeleeazo] loaf, get lazy, idle.

τέμπλο, τό [templo] iconostasis, reredos.

τέναγος, τό [tenaγos] shoal ‖ fen ‖ lagoon.

τενεκεδένιος [tenekedeneeos] made of tin.

τενεκές, ὁ [tenekes] tin ‖ large can ‖ (μεταφ) good-for-nothing.

τενεκετζῆς, ὁ [teneketzees] tinsmith.

τέννις, τό [tenees] tennis.

τενόρος, ὁ [tenoros] tenor.

τέντα, ἡ [tenta] tent ‖ marquee.

τέντζερες, ὁ [tentzeres] cooking pot, kettle, casserole.

τεντώνω [tentono] stretch, tighten, bend ‖ (μεταφ) strain.

τένων, ὁ [tenon] tendon.

τέρας, τό [teras] monster, abortion, freak ‖ (μεταφ) terror.

τεράστιος [terasteeos] prodigious, enormous, huge, vast.

τερατολογία, ἡ [teratoloγeea] extravagant tale, fishy story.

τερατόμορφος [teratomorfos] monstrous, hideous.

τερατούργημα, τό [teratouryeema] monstrosity ‖ atrocious deed.

τερατώδης [teratodees] prodigious, monstrous ‖ ugly, frightful.

τερεβινθέλαιον, τό [terevintheleon] turpentine.

τερετίζω [tereteezo] chirp, warble, twitter.

τέρμα, τό [terma] extremity, terminus, end ‖ (ἀθλητ) goal.

τερματίζω [termateezo] finish, put an end to, terminate, end.

τερματοφύλαξ, ὁ [termatofeelaks] goalkeeper.

τερπνός [terpnos] delightful, agreeable, pleasing.

τέρπω [terpo] delight, please, amuse.

τερτίπι, τό [terteepee] trick.

τέρψις, ἡ [terpsees] delight, pleasure, amusement.

τέσσαρα [tessara] four ‖ μέ τά ~ on all fours.

τεσσαράκοντα [tessarakonta] forty.

τέσσερις [tesserees] four.

τεταγμένος [tetaγmenos] placed, set ‖ determined.

τεταμένος [tetamenos] stretched, extended, strained.

τέτανος, ὁ [tetanos] tetanus.

Τετάρτη, ἡ [tetartee] Wednesday.

τέταρτον, τό [tetarton] quarter of an hour ‖ quarto.

τέταρτος [tetartos] fourth.

τετελεσμένος [telelesmenos] accomplished, achieved, done ‖ τετελεσμένον γεγονός fait accompli ‖ ~ μέλλων (γραμμ) future perfect tense.

τέτοιος [teteeos] similar, alike, such ‖ ὁ ~ what's-his-name ‖ (US) whatchacallit.

τετραγωνικός [tetraγoneekos] square, quadrangular ‖ (μεταφ) frank, outspoken.

τετράγωνον, τό [tetraγonon] (γεωμ) square, quadrangle ‖ (πόλεως) block.

τετράγωνος [tetraγonos] square ‖ (μεταφ) well-grounded, reasonable.

τετράδιον, τό [tetradeeon] exercise book, copybook.

τετράκις [tetrakees] four times.

τετρακόσιοι [tetrakosiee] four hundred.

τετράπαχος [tetrapahos] very stout, very fat, corpulent.

τετραπέρατος [tetraperatos] very clever, shrewd.

τετραπλάσιος [tetraplaseeos] four times as much.

τετραπλοῦς [tetraplous] βλ τετραπλάσιος.

τετράποδο, τό [tetrapodo] quadruped ‖ (μεταφ) beast, brute.

τετράπους [tetrapous] fourfooted.

τετράς, ἡ [tetras] set of four.

τετράτροχος [tetratrohos] four-wheeled.

τετριμμένος [tetreemenos] worn-out ‖ (μεταφ) hackneyed.

τέττιξ, ὁ [teteeks] cicada ‖ grasshopper.

τεῦτλον, τό [tevtlon] beetroot, beet.

τεῦχος, τό [tevhos] instalment, number, part, issue.

τέφρα, ἡ [tefra] ashes, cinders.

τεφρόχρους [tefrohrous] ashen ‖ grey, grizzled.

τεφτέρι, τό [tefteree] notebook ‖ account book.

τεχνάζομαι [tehnazome] contrive, hatch, think up, invent ‖ imagine.

τέχναι, αἱ [tehne] πλ: καλαί ~ fine arts.

τέχνασμα, τό [tehnasma] ruse, artifice, trick, device.

τέχνη, ἡ [tehnee] art ‖ profession ‖ dexterity ‖ (πολεμική) stratagem.

τεχνηέντως [tehnientos] skilfully, artfully, cleverly.

τεχνητός [tehneetos] sham, false, artificial ‖ simulated, affected.

τεχνική, ἡ [tehneekee] technique, means.

τεχνικός [tehneekos] technical, professional ‖ (οὐσ) technician.

τεχνίτης, ὁ [tehneetees] professional, craftsman ‖ technician, mechanic ‖ (μεταφ) specialist, expert.

τεχνοκρίτης, ὁ [tehnokreetees] art critic.

τεχνολογία, ἡ [tehnoloγeea] technology ‖ (γραμμ) grammatical analysis.

τεχνοτροπία, ἡ [tehnotropeea] artistic style.

τέως [teos] formerly, former, late ‖ ὁ ~ πρόεδρος ex-president.

τζάκι, τό [tzakee] fireplace ‖ heating range.

τζαμαρία, ἡ [tzamareea] glass panelling.

τζάμι, τό [tzamee] window pane, pane of glass.

τζαμί, τό [tzamee] mosque.

τζαμόπορτα, ἡ [tzamoporta] glazed door, glass door.

τζάμπα [tzamba] free, gratis, for nothing ‖ to no purpose, wantonly.

τζαναμπέτης, ὁ [tzanambetees] peevish person ‖ wicked person.

τζάνερο, τό [tzanero] plum ‖ prune.

τζελατίνα, ή [tzelateena] gelatine ‖ celluloid holder.

τζίβα, ή [tzeeva] vegetable fibre.

τζίγκος, ό [tzeengos] βλ. τσίγκος.

τζίρος, ό [tzeeros] business turnover.

τζίτζικας, ό [tzeetzeekas] βλ. τέττιξ.

τζιτζιφιά, ή [tzeetzeefia] jujube tree.

τζίφρα, ή [tzeefra] cipher ‖ initial, monogram.

τζόγος, ό [tzoyos] gambling.

τζόκεϋ, ό [tzokey] jockey.

τζούτα, ή [tzouta] jute.

τήβεννος, ή [teevenos] toga ‖ gown, robe.

τηγανητός [teeyaneetos] fried.

τηγάνι, τό [teeyanee] frying pan.

τηγανίζω [teeyaneezo] fry.

τηγανίτα, ή [teeyaneeta] fritter, pancake.

τήκομαι [teekome] thaw, melt ‖ wither, pine, languish.

τήκω [teeko] melt, thaw.

τηλεβόας, ό [teelevoas] loudhailer, loudspeaker.

τηλεβόλον, τό [teelevolon] cannon.

τηλεγραφείον, τό [teeleyrafeeon] telegraph office.

τηλεγράφημα, τό [teeleyrafeema] telegram, cable.

τηλέγραφος, ό [teeleyrafos] telegraph.

τηλεγραφώ [teeleyrafo] telegraph, wire.

τηλεόρασις, ή [teeleoraseess] television.

τηλεπάθεια, ή [teelepatheea] telepathy.

τηλεπικοινωνία, ή [teelepeekeenoneea] telecommunications.

τηλεσκόπιον, τό [teeleskopeeon] telescope.

τηλεφώνημα, τό [teelefoneema] telephone call.

τηλεφωνητής, ό [teelefoneetees] telephone operator.

τηλέφωνον, τό [teelefonon] telephone, phone.

τηλεφωνώ [teelefono] telephone, call up.

τῆξις, ή [teeksees] melting, thawing ‖ casting.

τήρησις, ή [teereesees] observance ‖ maintenance, keeping.

τηρώ [teero] keep, observe, follow, maintain.

τηρῶ [teero] see, look at ‖ watch.

τί [tee] what? ‖ what, how.

τι [tee] something ‖ a bit.

τίγρις, ή [teeyrees] tiger, tigress.

τιθασ(σ)εύω [teethasevo] tame, domesticate.

τίθεμαι [teetheme] be arranged, be placed, be imposed.

τίκτω [teekto] give birth ‖ give rise to.

τίλιο, τό [teeleeo] infusion of lime flowers.

τίλλω [teelo] pluck, pull out ‖ card wool, unweave.

τιμαλφῆ, τά [teemalfee] πλ jewellery, jewels.

τιμαλφής [teemalfees] precious, valuable.

τιμάριθμος, ό [teemareethmos] cost of living.

τιμάριον, τό [teemareeon] fief, manor.

τιμή, ή [teemee] respect, honour ‖ rate, price ‖ value, worth.

τίμημα, τό [teemeema] cost, price ‖ value.

τιμητικός [teemeeteekos] honorary ‖ honouring.

τίμιος [teemeeos] honest, upright ‖ precious, valuable.

τιμιότης, ή [teemeeotees] honesty.

τιμοκατάλογος, ό [teemokataloyos] price list, tariff.

τιμολόγιον, τό [teemoloyeeon] invoice, bill.

τιμόνι, τό [teemonee] helm, rudder ‖ tiller, wheel ‖ (αὐτοκινήτου) steering wheel ‖ (ποδηλάτου) handlebars.

τιμονιέρης, ό [teemonierees] steersman, helmsman.

τιμῶ [teemo] honour, respect, venerate, do honour to.

τιμῶμαι [teemome] cost, be worth ‖ be honoured.

τιμωρία, ή [teemoreea] punishment, chastisement, penalty.

τιμωρῶ [teemoro] punish, chastise ‖ fine.

τίναγμα, τό [teenayma] shake, shaking ‖ jerk, jolt, start.

τινάζομαι [teenazome] leap, spring, start ‖ brush one's clothes.

τινάζω [teenazo] shake off, shake ‖ (πετῶ) hurl, toss ‖ (φτερουγίζω) flap ‖ ~ στόν ἀέρα blow up.

τίποτα [teepota] any, anything ‖ nothing ‖ ~! don't mention it!, forget it!

τιποτένιος [teepoteneeos] mean, trivial, trifling, worthless.

τιράντες, οἱ [teerantes] πλ pair of braces.

τιρμπουσόν, τό [teermbouson] corkscrew.

τίς [tees] who?, what?, which?

τις [tees] someone, somebody ‖ anybody, one ‖ a certain.

τίτλος, ό [teetlos] title, right, claim ‖ certificate.

τιτλοφορῶ [teetloforo] entitle, confer a title.

τμῆμα, τό [tmeema] part, segment, section ‖ (ὑπουργείου) branch, department ‖ (ἀστυνομίας) police station.

τμηματάρχης, ό [tmeematarhees] chief of a department.

τμηματικῶς [tmeemateekos] partially, bit by bit, by instalments.

τό [to] the ‖ it.

τοιοῦτος [teeoutos] such ‖ (μεταφ) homosexual.

τοιουτοτρόπως [teeoutotropos] thus, in this way, in this manner.

τοιχογραφία, ή [teehoyrafeea] fresco, wall painting.

τοιχοκόλλησις, ή [teehokoleesees] bill posting, bill sticking.

τοῖχος, ό [teehos] wall.

τοίχωμα, τό [teehoma] inner wall, partition wall ‖ inner surface.

τοκετός, ὁ [toketos] childbirth, confinement.

τοκίζω [tokeezo] lend at interest, invest (money).

τοκογλύφος, ὁ [tokoγleefos] usurer.

τοκομερίδιον, τό [tokomereeδeeon] dividend coupon.

τόκος, ὁ [tokos] interest, rate.

τόλμη, ἡ [tolmee] daring ‖ audacity.

τολμηρός [tolmeeros] bold, courageous, daring, venturesome.

τολμῶ [tolmo] dare, risk, hazard.

τολύπη, ἡ [toleepee] ball of raw wool ‖ (μεταφ) flake.

τομάρι, τό [tomaree] hide, skin, leather.

τομάτα, ἡ [tomata] tomato.

τομεύς, ὁ [tomevs] sector ‖ incisor, chiseι.

τομή, ἡ [tomee] cut, gash, incision ‖ (διαγράμματος) section.

τόμος, ὁ [tomos] volume, tome.

τονίζω [toneezo] accent ‖ accentuate, stress, lay emphasis on ‖ tone up.

τονισμός, ὁ [toneesmos] accentuation ‖ emphasizing.

τόννος, ὁ [tonos] ton ‖ (ψάρι) tunny.

τόνο [tono]: μιλῶ μὲ ~ raise one's voice δίνω ~ σὲ brighten up.

τόνος, ὁ [tonos] tone ‖ (μεταφ) force, energy ‖ (γραμμ) accent ‖ (μουσ) key.

τονώνω [tonono] fortify, invigorate, brace up.

τονωτικός [tonoteekos] bracing, invigorating, tonic.

τοξεύω [toksevo] shoot with bow, throw a dart.

τοξικομανής, ὁ, ἡ [tokseekomanees] drug addict.

τοξικός [tokseekos] toxic ‖ poisonous.

τοξοειδής [toksoeeδees] bowed, archeα, curved, bow-shaped.

τόξον, τό [tokson] bow ‖ (κτιρίου) arch ‖ (γεωμ) arc, curve.

τοξότης, ὁ [toksotees] archer, bowman.

τοπ(ε)ίον, τό [topeeon] landscape ‖ site, locality.

τόπι, τό [topee] ball ‖ (ὑφάσματος) roll of cloth ‖ (κανονιοῦ) cannonball.

τοπικισμός, ὁ [topeekeesmos] localism.

τοπικός [topeekos] local.

τοπιογραφία, ἡ [topeeoγrafeea] landscape painting.

τοπογραφία, ἡ [topoγrafeea] topography

τοποθεσία, ἡ [topotheseea] locality, situation, site, position, place.

τοποθέτησις, ἡ [topotheteesees] putting, placing ‖ (οἴκον) investment, investing.

τοποθετῶ [topotheto] place, set, put ‖ (οἰκ) invest.

τόπος, ὁ [topos] place, position, site ‖ (χῶρα) country ‖ (χῶρο) space, room ‖ (μαθημ) locus ‖ πιάνω τόπο have effect, be of use ‖ ἔμεινε στόν τόπο he died suddenly.

τοπούζι, τό [topouzee] club.

τοπωνυμία, ἡ [toponeemeea] place-name.

τορνευτής, ὁ [tornevtees] turner.

τορνευτός [tornevtos] well-turned, turned.

τορνεύω [tornevo] turn a lathe, work a lathe ‖ (μεταφ) give fine shape to.

τόρνος, ὁ [tornos] lathe.

τορπίλλη, ἡ [torpeelee] torpedo.

τορπιλλίζω [torpeeleezo] torpedo.

τορπιλλοβόλον, τό [torpeelovolon] torpedo boat.

τος [tos]: νά ~ here he is, here he comes.

τοσάκις [tosakees] so many times, so often.

τόσο(ν) [toso(n)] so much ‖ ~ ... ὅσο(ν) as much ... as, both ... and ‖ ὄχι καί ~ not so much.

τόσος [tosos] so big, so large, so great ‖ so much, so many ‖ ~ δά very little, very small, only so small ‖ ἄλλοι τόσοι as many again ‖ κάθε τόσο every now and again ‖ ἑκατόν τόσα a hundred odd.

τοσοῦτος [tosoutos] so large, so much ‖ ἐν τοσούτω nevertheless, yet, still ‖ τοσούτω μᾶλλον with all the more reason.

τότε [tote] then, at that time ‖ in that case, therefore, thereupon ‖ ~ πού when.

τουαλέττα, ἡ [toualeta] toilet ‖ (γυναικός) dress ‖ (αἴθουσα) dressing room ‖ (τραπέζι) dressing table ‖ (ἀποχωρητήριον) lavatory.

τούβλο, τό [touvlo] brick ‖ (μεταφ) simpleton.

τουλάχιστον [toulaheeston] at least, at all events.

τούλι, τό [toulee] tulle.

τουλίπα, ἡ [touleepa] tulip.

τουλούμι, τό [touloumee] goatskin bottle ‖ βρέχει μέ τό ~ it's raining cats and dogs,

τουλούμπα, ἡ [touloumba] pump.

τουλ(ου)πάνι, τό [toul(ou)panee] muslin ‖ veil, small shawl.

τούμπα, ἡ [toumba] somersault, fall ‖ mound ‖ κάνω τούμπες kowtow ‖ fall head over heels.

τούμπανο, τό [toumbano] drum.

τουμπάρω [toumbaro] overturn, upset ‖ (μεταφ) persuade ‖ reverse.

τουναντίον [tounanteeon] on the contrary.

τουπέ, τό [toupe] cheek, audacity, nerve.

τουρισμός, ὁ [toureesmos] tourism, touring

τουρίστας, ὁ [toureestas] tourist.

Τουρκάλα, ἡ [tourkala] Turkish woman.

τουρκεύω [tourkevo] (μεταφ) fly into a rage.

Τουρκία, ἡ [tourkeea] Turkey.

τουρκικός [tourkeekos] Turkish.

τουρκοκρατία, ἡ [tourkokrateea] Turkish domination of Greece.

Τοῦρκος, ὁ [tourkos] Turk ‖ γίνομαι ~ get angry.

τούρλα, ἡ [tourla] mound ‖ (ἐπίρ) piled up.

τουρλώνω [tourlono] pile up ‖ swell out, become round.

τουρλωτός [tourlotos] piled up ‖ rounded, bulging.

τουρνέ, ή [tourne] theatrical tour.

τουρσί, τό [toursee] pickle, brine.

τούρτα, ή [tourta] gateau, layer cake, tart.

τουρτουρίζω [tourtoureezo] shiver, tremble, shudder.

τουτέστι [toutestee] that is, in other words, i.e.

τοῦτος [toutos] this one.

τοῦφα, ή [toufa] tuft, bunch, cluster.

τουφέκι, τό [toufekee] rifle, musket, gun.

τουφεκιά, ή [toufekia] gunshot, rifle shot.

τουφεκίζω [toufekeezo] shoot, fire ‖ execute.

τράβηγμα, τό [traveeyma] pulling, dragging, tug ‖ (ύγροῦ) drawing off.

τραβηξιά, ή [traveeksia] sip ‖ (πίπας) pull.

τραβῶ [travo] pull, drag, heave, haul ‖ ~ τό δρόμο μου go my own way ‖ (ὅπλο, χρήματα κτλ) draw ‖ τό τραβάει he imbibes ‖ (άπορροφάω) absorb ‖ (τυφεκιά) fire, shoot ‖ (ταχύτητα) reach distance of ‖ (προσελκύω) entice, attract ‖ δέν μέ τραβάει it doesn't attract me ‖ (ζητῶ) ask for, want ‖ ό καιρός τραβάει πανωφόρι the weather calls for a coat ‖ ή καρδιά μου ~ τσιγάρο I need a smoke ‖ (ύποφέρω) undergo, endure, bear ‖ (άμετ) make towards, head for ‖ move on ‖ (συνεχίζω) last, go on ‖ (τσιμπούκι κτλ) suck, draw ‖ τραβιέμαι (άμετ) draw back, leave ‖ (έμπόριον) be in demand ‖ (δέν ύποφέρεται) it's unbearable.

τραγανίζω [trayaneezo] crunch, munch, grind.

τραγανό, τό [trayano] cartilage, grist.

τραγανός [trayanos] crisp, brittle.

τραγέλαφος, ό [trayelafos] monstrosity, freak, mix-up.

τραγήσιος [trayeeseeos] of a goat.

τραγί, τό [trayee] kid.

τραγικός [trayeekos] calamitous, tragic ‖ (ποιητής) tragic poet.

τράγος, ό [trayos] goat.

τραγούδι, τό [trayoudee] song, air, tune.

τραγουδιστής, ό [trayoudeestees] singer, vocalist.

τραγουδιστός [trayoudeestos] sung ‖ (φωνή) tuneful.

τραγουδῶ [trayoudo] sing, chant ‖ (σιγά) hum.

τραγωδία, ή [trayodeea] tragedy.

τραγωδός, ό, ή [trayodos] tragic actor, tragedian, tragic actress.

τραῖνο, τό [treno] railway train ‖ (ἐπιβατηγό) passenger train.

τράκ, τό [trak] stage fright.

τρακάρισμα, τό [trakareesma] crash, collision ‖ unexpected meeting.

τρακάρω [trakaro] knock against, collide with ‖ meet by accident ‖ (μεταφ) touch for (a loan), bum (col) (a cigarette).

τρακατρούκα, ή [trakatrouka] firecracker.

τράκο(ς), τό (ό) [trako(s)] collision ‖ (μεταφ) attack, assault.

τρακτέρ, τό [trakter] farm tractor.

τράμ, τό [tram] tram, tramcar, tramway.

τραμουντάνα, ή [tramountana] north wind.

τραμπαλίζομαι [trambaleezome] seesaw ‖ go up and down.

τραμπούκος, ό [tramboukos] out-and-out rascal, scoundrel, rotter.

τρανεύω [tranevo] grow, augment.

τρανός [tranos] powerful ‖ large, grand ‖ important, weighty.

τράνταγμα, τό [trantayma] jolting, shake, shaking ‖ jolt, jerk.

τραντάζω [trantazo] jolt, shake up and down.

τρανταχτός [trantahtos] spectacular, dramatic.

τράπεζα, ή [trapeza] table ‖ (ἐμπορ) bank ‖ άγία ~ altar.

τραπεζαρία, ή [trapezareea] dining room.

τραπέζι, τό [trapezee] table ‖ dinner ‖ στρώνω ~ set the table ‖ τούς εἴχαμε ~ we invited them to dinner.

τραπέζιον, τό [trapezeeon] small table ‖ (τσίρκου) trapeze ‖ (γεωμ) trapezium, trapezoid.

τραπεζίτης, ό [trapezeetees] banker ‖ (δόντι) molar.

τραπεζιτικός [trapezeeteekos] banking ‖ (ύπάλληλος) bank employee.

τραπεζογραμμάτιον, τό [trapezoyramateeon] banknote.

τραπεζομάντηλο, τό [trapezomanteelo] tablecloth.

τράπουλα, ή [trapoula] pack of cards.

τράτα, ή [trata] seine ‖ fishing boat ‖ (χορός) circular dance.

τρατάρω [trataro] regale ‖ pay for, offer.

τραυλίζω [travleezo] stammer, stutter, lisp.

τραυλός [travlos] stammering, stuttering.

τραῦμα, τό [travma] wound, hurt, injury ‖ (μεταφ) wound, sore.

τραυματίας, ό [travmateeas] casualty ‖ wounded person.

τραυματίζω [travmateezo] wound, hurt, injure.

τραχανᾶς, ό [trahanas] kind of home-made noodles.

τραχεία, ή [traheea] trachea, windpipe.

τραχέως [traheos] harshly, rudely.

τραχηλιά, ή [traheelia] collar, collaret ‖ bib.

τράχηλος, ό [traheelos] neck.

τραχύνω [traheeno] make harsh, make rough ‖ irritate.

τραχύς [trahees] harsh, rough ‖ (τήν γεύσιν) tart, sharp ‖ (τήν άκοήν) harsh, grating ‖ (χαρακτήρ) sour, crabbed.

τρεῖς [trees] three.

τρέλλα, ή [trela] madness, insanity ‖ folly ‖ (ίατρ) mania ‖ (μεταφ) anything pleasing.

τρελλαίνομαι [trelenome] go insane ‖ be driven mad ‖ be mad about.

τρελλαίνω [treleno] drive mad, bewilder.

τρελλοκομείο, τό [trelokomeeo] madhouse.

τρελλός [trelos] insane, mad ‖ (ούς) madman ‖ (μωρό) mischievous.

τρεμοσβήνω [tremosveeno] flicker, sparkle.

τρεμούλα, ή [tremoula] shivering, trembling ‖ (φωνής) quiver ‖ (άπό κρύο) shivering ‖ scare.

τρεμουλιάζω [tremouleeazo] tremble, shiver, shudder.

τρέμω [tremo] tremble ‖ (άπό κρύο) shiver ‖ (άπό φόβο) shake ‖ (τό φώς) flicker, waver ‖ (φωνή) quiver.

τρεξίματα, τά [trekseemata] πλ bustle, running around.

τρέξιμο, τό [trekseemo] running ‖ (ύγρού) flowing ‖ (αίματος) flow, gush.

τρέπομαι [trepome] turn to, turn into.

τρέπω [trepo] change, convert ‖ turn, translate ‖ ~ είς φυγήν put to flight.

τρέφω [trefo] nourish, feed, nurture ‖ (έλπίδα) cherish, foster ‖ (γένεια) grow ‖ support, keep.

τρεχάλα, ή [trehala] running ‖ (ώς έπίρ) at full speed.

τρεχάματα, τά [trehamata] πλ running about ‖ (μεταφ) cares.

τρεχάμενος [trehamenos] running.

τρεχαντήρι, τό [trehanteeree] small sailing boat.

τρεχάτος [trehatos] running, hasty.

τρέχω [treho] run, race, hurry ‖ (έπί ύγρών) flow ‖ leak ‖ τί τρέχει; what's happening?, what's the matter?

τρέχων [trehon] current, present, contemporary.

τρία [treea] three.

τριάδα, ή [treeaδa] trinity ‖ trio.

τρίαινα, ή [triena] trident.

τριάκοντα [treeakonta] thirty.

τριακόσιοι [treeakosiee] three hundred.

τριακοστός [treeakostos] thirtieth.

τριανδρία, ή [treeanδreea] triumvirate.

τριάντα [treeanta] thirty.

τριαντάφυλλο, τό [treeantafeelo] rose.

τριάρι, τό [treearee] figure 3 ‖ three at cards.

τριάς, ή [treeas] trinity ‖ trio.

τριβέλι, τό [treevelee] drill.

τριβή, ή [treevee] friction, chafing, rubbing ‖ wear and tear ‖ (μεταφ) practice, use, experience.

τρίβολος, ό [treevolos] caltrop, thistle.

τρίβομαι [treevome] wear out ‖ disintegrate ‖ (μεταφ) get experienced, get practice in.

τρίβω [treevo] rub ‖ polish up ‖ grate ‖ (τό σώμα) massage.

τρίγλυφον, τό [treeyleefon] triglyph.

τριγμός, ό [treeymos] crackling, creaking ‖ (όδόντων) grinding, gnashing.

τριγυρίζω [treeyeereezo] encircle ‖ roam, hang about.

τριγυρίστρα, ή [treeyeereestra] whitlow ‖ (γυναίκα) gadabout.

τριγυρνώ [treeyeerno] βλ **τριγυρίζω.**

τριγωνικός [treeyoneekos] triangular

τριγωνομετρία, ή [treeyonometreea] trigonometry.

τρίγωνον, τό [treeyonon] triangle.

τρίγωνος [treeyonos] three-cornered.

τρίδιπλος [treeδeeplos] triple, three times.

τρίδυμα, τά [treeδeema] πλ triplets.

τριετής [trietees] of three years ‖ (ήλικία) three years old ‖ (φοιτητής) third-year.

τρίζω [treezo] crackle, crack, creak, squeak ‖ (δόντια) grind, gnash, grit.

τριήρης, ή [trieerees] trireme.

τρικαντό, τό [treekanto] three-cornered hat, cocked hat.

τρικλίζω [treekleezo] stagger, totter, wobble, reel.

τρίκλωνος [treeklonos] three-stranded thread.

τρικούβερτος [treekouvertos] (μεταφ) splendid, terrific, wonderful.

τρικυμία, ή [treekeemeea] storm, tempest, hurricane.

τρικυμιώδης [treekeemeeoδees] stormy, tempestuous, rough.

τρίκωχο, τό [treekoho] βλ **τρικαντό.**

τρίλλια, ή [treeleea] trill.

τριμελής [treemelees] of three members.

τριμερής [treemerees] tripartite.

τριμηνία, ή [treemeeneea] quarter of a year ‖ quarter's rent.

τριμηνιαίος [treemeenieos] of three months, quarterly.

τρίμηνο, τό [treemeeno] βλ **τριμηνία.**

τρίμηνος [treemeenos] βλ **τριμηνιαίος.**

τρίμμα, τό [treema] fragment, morsel, chip, particle.

τριμμένος [treemenos] showing signs of wear and tear ‖ ground.

τρίξιμο, τό [treekseemo] gnashing, grinding.

τρίπατος [treepatos] three-storeyed.

τριπλασιάζω [treeplaseeazo] treble, triple, triplicate.

τριπλάσιος [treeplaseeos] threefold, triple, treble.

τριπλός [treeplos] βλ **τριπλάσιος.**

τριποδίζω [treepoδeezo] trot.

τρίποδο, τό [treepoδo] tripod ‖ easel ‖ three-legged support.

τρίπτυχον, τό [treepteehon] triptych.

τρίς [trees] thrice, three times.

τρισάγιον, τό [treesayeeon] canticle ‖ Te Deum.

τρισδιάστατος [treesδeeastatos] three-dimensional.

τρισέγγονο, τό [treesengono] great-great-grandchild.

τρισκατάρατος [treeskataratos] thrice cursed ‖ abominable.

τριτεύω [treetevo] come third.

Τρίτη, ή [treetee] Tuesday.

τρίτον, τό [treeton] third || (ἐπίρ) thirdly.
τρίτος [treetos] third || third-party.
τρίφτης, ὁ [treeftees] grater, rasp.
τριφύλλι, τό [treefeelee] clover, trefoil.
τρίχα, ἡ [treeha] hair || bristle || fur || στήν ~ spruced up || παρά ~ nearly.
τρίχες, οἱ [treehes] πλ nonsense, rubbish.
τριχιά, ἡ [treehia] rope.
τριχοειδής [treehoeeδees] capillary.
τρίχρωμος [treehromos] three-coloured.
τρίχωμα, τό [treehoma] fur || (σώματος) hair.
τριχωτός [treehotos] hairy, shaggy.
τρίψιμο, τό [treepseemo] chafing, massage, rubbing, friction || (στίλβωμα) polishing || grating, grinding, crushing.
τρίωρος [treeoros] of three hours.
τρόλλεϋ, τό [troley] trolley bus.
τρόμαγμα, τό [tromayma] fright, scare.
τρομάζω [tromazo] terrify, frighten || get scared.
τρομακτικός [tromakteekos] fearful, awful, frightening || (μεταφ) terrific.
τρομάρα, ἡ [tromara] dread, fright, fear.
τρομερός [tromeros] terrible, dreadful, frightful || (μεταφ) terrific, astonishing.
τρομοκρατία, ἡ [tromokrateea] terrorism || terror.
τρομοκρατῶ [tromokrato] terrorize.
τρόμος, ὁ [tromos] trembling, shaking || dread, fright.
τρόμπα, ἡ [trompa] pump.
τρομπέτα, ἡ [trompeta] trumpet.
τρομπόνι, τό [tromponee] trombone.
τρόπαιον, τό [tropeon] trophy || triumph.
τροπαιοῦχος [tropeouhos] triumphant, victorious.
τροπάριον, τό [tropareeon] (ἐκκλ) hymn || (μεταφ) same old refrain.
τροπή, ἡ [tropee] change || turn || (μαθημ) conversion.
τροπικός [tropeekos] tropical || (γραμμ) of manner.
τρόπις, ἡ [tropees] keel, bottom.
τροπολογία, ἡ [tropoloyeea] amendment, alteration, change, modification.
τροποποίησις, ἡ [tropopieesees] modification, alteration, change.
τρόποι, οἱ [tropee] πλ manners, behaviour.
τρόπος, ὁ [tropos] way, manner, method || behaviour, conduct || (μουσ) mode || ~ τοῦ λέγειν so to speak.
τροῦλλος, ὁ [troulos] dome, cupola.
τρουλλωτός [troulotos] domed, dome-shaped.
τροφή, ἡ [trofee] food, nutrition || (ζώων) pasture, fodder || sustenance.
τρόφιμα, τά [trofeema] πλ provisions, food, victuals.
τρόφιμος, ὁ, ἡ [trofeemos] lodger, boarder || paying guest || inmate || (μεταφ) nursling.
τροφοδοσία, ἡ [trofoδoseea] provisioning, supplying || supply, provisions.

τροφοδότης, ὁ [trofoδotees] caterer, purveyor, provider, supplier.
τροφοδοτῶ [trofoδoto] feed, provision, keep supplied, supply, serve.
τροφός, ἡ [trofos] wet-nurse.
τροχάδην [trohaδen] hurriedly, hastily, at full speed || (μεταφ) fluently.
τροχαία [trohea]: ~ κίνησις traffic || ἡ ~ traffic police.
τροχαῖον [troheon]: ~ ὑλικόν rolling stock.
τροχαῖος, ὁ [troheos] trochee || (ἐπιϑ) wheeled, rolling.
τροχαλία, ἡ [trohaleea] pulley, block.
τροχιά, ἡ [trohia] track, groove, rut || (σιδηροδρόμου) track, rail || (δορυφόρου κτλ) orbit, trajectory.
τροχίζω [troheezo] sharpen, whet, grind (knife) || (μεταφ) train, exercise.
τροχιόδρομος, ὁ [troheeoδromos] tramway.
τρόχισμα, τό [troheesma] sharpening, whetting, grinding || (μεταφ) exercising.
τροχονόμος, ὁ [trohonomos] traffic policeman.
τροχοπέδη, ἡ [trohopeδee] brake, skid, wheel brake.
τροχοπέδιλον, τό [trohopeδeelon] roller skate || scooter.
τροχός, ὁ [trohos] wheel || grindstone, whetstone.
τροχοφόρον, τό [trohoforon] vehicle.
τροχοφόρος [trohoforos] wheeled.
τρυγητής, ὁ [treeyeetees] grape harvester, vintager.
τρυγητός, ὁ [treeyeetos] grape harvest, vintage.
τρυγόνι, τό [treeyonee] turtledove.
τρύγος, ὁ [treeyos] βλ τρυγητός.
τρυγῶ [treeyo] gather grapes || (μεταφ) loot, fleece.
τρύπα, ἡ [treepa] hole || (βελόνης) eye || (μεταφ) den, lair.
τρυπάνι, τό [treepanee] drill, drilling machine.
τρυπανίζω [treepaneezo] bore, drill, pierce || (ιατρ) trepan.
τρύπανον, τό [treepanon] βλ τρυπάνι.
τρύπημα, τό [treepeema] perforating, boring, piercing || prick, punch.
τρυπητήρι, τό [treepeeteeree] awl, punch, drill.
τρυπητό, τό [treepeeto] strainer, colander.
τρυπητός [treepeetos] perforated, holed, riddled.
τρύπιος [treepeeos] with holes, perforated, holed, riddled
τρυπῶ [treepo] bore, make a hole, pierce || prick, punch.
τρυπώνω [treepono] hide, conceal || squeeze in || take refuge.
τρυφερός [treeferos] tender, soft || affectionate, affable, mild.
τρυφερότης, ἡ [treeferotees] tenderness, softness || affection, kindness.

τρωγαλίζω [troyaleezo] gnaw, nibble.

τρώγλη, ή [troylee] hole, lair, den || hovel, shack.

τρωγλοδύτης, ὁ [troyloδeetees] troglodyte.

τρώγομαι [troyome] be edible || (μεταφ) be tolerable || τρώγονται they are quarrelling.

τρώγω [troyo] eat, bite || μὲ τρώει it itches || ~ ξύλο get a beating || ~ τόν κόσμο look everywhere.

τρωκτικόν, τό [trokteekon] rodent.

Τρωϊκός [troeekos] Trojan.

τρωτόν, τό [troton] shortcoming, weak point.

τρωτός [trotos] vulnerable.

τσάγαλο, τό [tsayalo] green almond.

τσαγγός [tsangos] βλ ταγγός.

τσαγιέρα, ή [tsayiera] teapot.

τσαγιερό, τό [tsayiero] βγ τσαγιέρα.

τσαγκάρης, ὁ [tsangarees] shoemaker.

τσάϊ, τό [tsaee] tea.

τσακάλι, τό [tsakalee] jackal.

τσακίζομαι [tsakeezome] strive, struggle || (διπλώνω) fold.

τσακίζω [tsakeezo] break, shatter, smash | (μεταφ) weaken, wear out, enfeeble.

τσάκιση, ή [tsakeesee] crease, pleat.

τσάκισμα, τό [tsakeesma] breaking, shattering, smashing.

τσακμάκι, τό [tsakmakee] tinderbox || cigarette lighter.

τσάκωμα, τό [tsakoma] seizing, catching || quarrelling, dispute.

τσακώνομαι [tsakonome] quarrel.

τσακώνω [tsakono] catch in the act.

τσαλαβουτῶ [tsalavouto] flounder, wallow, splash about || (μεταφ) do a sloppy job.

τσαλακώνω [tsalakono] crease, crumple, wrinkle.

τσαλαπατῶ [tsalapato] trample underfoot, tread over.

τσάμι, τό [tsamee] Aleppo pine.

τσάμικος, ὁ [tsameekos] kind of circular dance.

τσάμπα [tsamba] βλ τζάμπα.

τσαμπί, τό [tsambee] bunch (of grapes), cluster.

τσάμπουρο, τό [tsambouro] grape stalk.

τσανάκι, τό [tsanakee] shallow bowl, earthenware plate.

τσάντα, ή [tsanta] pouch || handbag || briefcase || (ψωνίσματος) shopping bag || (ταχυδρόμου) satchel.

τσαντίρι, τό [tsanteeree] tent.

τσάπα, ή [tsapa] hoe, pickaxe.

τσαπατσούλης [tsapatsoulees] untidy in one's work.

τσαπέλλα, ή [tsapela] string of dried figs.

τσαπί, τό [tsapee] βλ τσάπα.

τσάρκα, ή [tsarka] walk, promenade, stroll.

τσάρος, ὁ [tsaros] czar.

τσαρούχι, τό [tsarouhee] rustic shoe with pompom.

τσατσάρα, ή [tsatsara] comb.

τσαχπινιά, ή [tsahpeenia] coquetry, roguery, trickery.

τσέκ, τό [tsek] cheque || (US) check.

τσεκούρι, τό [tsekouree] axe, hatchet.

τσεκουρώνω [tsekourono] cut with an axe.

τσέλιγκας, ὁ [tseleengas] chief shepherd.

τσεμπέρι, τό [tsemberee] kerchief, veil.

τσέπη, ή [tsepee] pocket || pocketful.

τσεπώνω [tsepono] pocket || (μεταφ) filch, swipe.

τσέρι, τό [tseree] cherry brandy.

τσέρκι, τό [tserkee] hoop || stirrup.

τσέτουλα, ή [tsetoula] tally.

τσευδίζω [tsevδeezo] lisp, stammer, falter.

τσευδός [tsevδos] lisping, stammering.

τσιγαρίζω [tseeyareezo] fry lightly, brown, roast brown.

τσιγάρο, τό [tseeyaro] cigarette.

τσιγαροθήκη, ή [tseeyarotheekee] cigarette case.

τσιγαρόχαρτο, τό [tseeyaroharto] tissue paper.

τσιγγάνος, ὁ [tseenganos] gipsy.

τσιγγούνης [tseengounees] miserly, stingy || (οὐσ) miser.

τσιγκέλι, τό [tseengelee] meat hook.

τσιγκλῶ [tseenglo] goad, prick, spur.

τσίγκος, ὁ [tseengos] zinc.

τσίκνα, ή [tseekna] smell of burning meat.

τσικνίζω [tseekneezo] scorch, burn || have burnt smell.

τσικουδιά, ή [tseekouδia] terebinth || (ποτόν) kind of spirit.

τσίμα [tseema]: ~ ~ scarcely || on the brink of.

τσιμέντο, τό [tseemento] cement.

τσιμουδιά, ή [tseemouδia]: δέν ἔβγαλε ~ he remained speechless || ~ ! not a word!, mum's the word!

τσίμπημα, τό [tseembeema] prick, sting, pinch || bite, peck.

τσιμπιά, ή [tseembia] pinch.

τσιμπίδα, ή [tseembeeδa] nippers, tongs, forceps, pincers.

τσιμπιδάκι, τό [tseembeeδakee] tweezers || hairclip.

τσιμπίδι, τό [tseembeeδee] tweezers || clothes peg.

τσίμπλα, ή [tseembla] mucus of eyes.

τσιμπούκι, τό [tseemboukee] tobacco pipe.

τσιμπούρι, τό [tseembouree] (ἔντομον) tick || (μεταφ) troublesome or bothersome person, pest.

τσιμπούσι, τό [tseembousee] spread, repast, regalement, feast.

τσιμπῶ [tseembo] prick, pinch, sting || (δαγκώνω) bite, peck || (φαγητό) nibble || (μεταφ) cadge || (συλλαμβάνω) seize, collar.

τσίνουρο, τό [tseenouro] eyelash.

τσίπα, ή [tseepa] thin skin, crust || (μεταφ) shame.

τσιπούρα, ή [tseepoura] gilthead.

τσίπουρο, τό [tseepouro] kind of spirit.
τσιράκι, τό [tseerakee] apprentice, boy, novice.
τσιρίζω [tseereezo] screech, shriek, scream.
τσιρίσι, τό [tseereesee] glue.
τσίρκο, τό [tseerko] circus.
τσίρλα, ἡ [tseerla] diarrhoea.
τσίρος, ὁ [tseeros] dried mackerel || (μεταφ) skinny person.
τσιρότο, τό [tseeroto] sticking plaster.
τσίτα [tseeta] very tight || ~ ~ scarcely.
τσίτι, τό [tseetee] calico.
τσιτσίδι [tseetseeδee] stark naked.
τσιτσιμπύρι, τό [tseetseembeeree] ginger beer.
τσιτσιρίζω [tseetseereezo] sizzle.
τσιτώνω [tseetono] stretch, tighten, strain.
τσιφλίκι, τό [tseefleekee] large country estate, farm, ranch.
τσιφούτης, ὁ [tseefoutees] miser.
τσίχλα, ἡ [tseehla] thrush || (ἀδύνατος) skinny person.
τσόκαρο, τό [tsokaro] wooden shoe.
τσοκολάτα, ἡ [tsokolata] chocolate.
τσολιᾶς, ὁ [tsolias] evzone, kilted soldier.
τσο(μ)πάνης, ὁ [tso(m)panees] shepherd.
τσοντάρω [tsontaro] join on.
τσότρα, ἡ [tsotra] gourd, flask.
τσουβάλι, τό [tsouvalee] sackful || sack.
τσουγκράνα, ἡ [tsoungrana] rake.
τσουγκρανίζω [tsoungraneezo] scratch, rake.
τσουγκρίζω [tsoungreezo] strike against || clink glasses, touch glasses.
τσούζω [tsouzo] smart, sting, hurt.
τσουκάλι, τό [tsoukalee] jug, pot || chamberpot.
τσουκνίδα, ἡ [tsoukneeδa] nettle.
τσούλα, ἡ [tsoula] loose-living woman, whore.
τσουλάω [tsoulao] slip along, slide along || (ὄχημα) push.
τσουλί, τό [tsoulee] doormat.
τσουλίστρα, ἡ [tsouleestra] slide.
τσουλούφι, τό [tsouloufee] lock of hair.
τσουράπι, τό [tsourapee] woollen sock, stocking.
τσουρέκι, τό [tsourekee] bun, brioche.
τσούρμο, τό [tsourmo] throng || band, troop.
τσουρουφλίζω [tsouroufleezo] grill brown, scorch.
τσουχτερός [tsouhteros] keen, smart, sharp || (κρύο) biting || harsh.
τσούχτρα, ἡ [tsouhtra] jellyfish.
τσόφλι, τό [tsoflee] shell || rind.
τσόχα, ἡ [tsoha] felt.
τυγχάνω [teenghano] happen to be || obtain, attain.
τύλιγμα, τό [teeleeghma] winding, rolling, coiling, wrapping.
τυλίγω [teeleeyo] roll up, wind, coil || wrap up, fold round, twist.
τυλίσσω [teeleeso] βλ τυλίγω.

τύλος, ὁ [teelos] callus || corn.
τυλώνω [teelono] fill up.
τύμβος, ὁ [teemvos] grave, tomb.
τυμβωρύχος, ὁ [teemvoreehos] graverobber.
τύμπανον, τό [teembanon] drum, tambour || (αὐτιοῦ) eardrum || tympanum.
τυπικόν, τό [teepeekon] (γραμμ) morphology || formality, ritual.
τυπικός [teepeekos] usual, conventional || typical.
τυπικότης, ἡ [teepeekotees] formality.
τύπο [teepo]: γιά τόν ~ for the sake of form.
τυπογραφεῖον, τό [teepoyrafeeon] printing press, printer's.
τυπογραφία, ἡ [teepoyrafeea] printing.
τυπογράφος, ὁ [teepoyrafos] printer.
τύποι, οἱ [teepee] πλ conventions, form.
τυποποίησις, ἡ [teepopieesees] standardization.
τύπος, ὁ [teepos] print, imprint, stamp || (καλούπι) mould, matrix, form || (ὑπόδειγμα) model, type || (συμπεριφορᾶς) formality, rule of procedure || (οἰκίας) type, kind of || (μαθημ) formula || (ἐφημερίδες) the press || (γιά ἄνθρωπο) figure, character.
τύπτω [teepto] beat, strike.
τυπώνω [teepono] print, stamp.
τυραννία, ἡ [teeraneea] tyranny, oppression || torment, torture.
τύραννος, ὁ [teeranos] oppressor, tyrant.
τυραννῶ [teerano] oppress || torture, harass.
τυρί, τό [teeree] cheese.
τυροκομία, ἡ [teerokomeea] cheese-making.
τυρόπηττα, ἡ [teeropeeta] cheese pie, cheesecake.
τυρός, ὁ [teeros] βλ τυρί.
τύρφη, ἡ [teerfee] peat.
τύφλα, ἡ [teefla] blindness || ~ στό μεθύσι dead drunk.
τυφλόμυγα, ἡ [teeflomeeya] blind man's buff.
τυφλοπόντικας, ὁ [teefloponteekas] mole.
τυφλός [teeflos] blind.
τυφλώνομαι [teeflonome] grow blind, blind o.s.
τυφλώνω [teeflono] blind || (φῶς) dazzle || (μεταφ) deceive, hoodwink.
τυφοειδής [teefoeeδees]: ~ πυρετός typhoid fever.
τύφος, ὁ [teefos]: ἐξανθηματικός ~ typhus || κοιλιακός ~ typhoid fever.
τυφών, ὁ [teefon] typhoon, hurricane, cyclone.
τυχαίνω [teeheno] βλ τυγχάνω.
τυχαῖος [teeheos] casual, fortuitous, chance.
τυχαίως [teeheos] by chance, by accident.
τυχερά [teehera] πλ casual profits, tips, perks.
τυχερό, τό [teehero] fortune, destiny.
τυχερός [teeheros] fortunate, lucky.

τύχη, ή [teehee] destiny, chance, fortune, lot, fate ‖ (καλή) good luck ‖ στήν ~ haphazard, at random.
τυχηρός [teeheeros] βλ τυχερός.
τυχοδιώκτης, ὁ [teehoδeeoktees] adventurer, opportunist.
τυχόν [teehon] by chance ‖ τά ~ ἔξοδα incidental expenses.
τυχών [teehon]: ὁ ~ the first comer, anyone.
τύψις, ή [teepsees] remorse, prick of conscience.
τωόντι [toontee] in fact, actually, in effect, indeed.
τώρα [tora] nowadays, at present, now ‖ this minute ‖ at once.
τωρινός [toreenos] present-day, contemporary, of today.

Y, υ

ὕαινα, ή [iena] hyena.
ὑάκινθος, ὁ [eeakeenthos] hyacinth.
ὑαλοπίναξ, ὁ [eealopeenaks] window pane.
ὕαλος, ή [eealos] glass.
ὑαλουργία, ή [eealouryeea] glassmaking.
ὑαλουργός, ὁ [eealouryos] glassmaker.
ὑαλόφρακτος [eealofraktos] glazed.
ὑαλόχαρτον, τό [eealoharton] emery paper, sandpaper.
ὑαλώδης [eealoδees] glassy ‖ vitreous.
ὑάρδα, ή [eearδa] yard.
ὕβος, ὁ [eevos] hump.
ὑβρεολόγιον, τό [eevreoloyeeon] volley of abuse, tirade.
ὑβρίζω [eevreezo] insult, abuse, swear at.
ὕβρις, ή [eevrees] insult, injury ‖ oath.
ὑβριστικός [eevreesteekos] insulting, rude.
ὑγεία, ή [eeyeea] health.
ὑγειονομικός [eeyeeonomeekos] sanitary.
ὑγιαίνω [eeyieno] be healthy.
ὑγιεινός [eeyieenos] healthy ‖ wholesome.
ὑγιής [eeyiees] healthy ‖ (μεταφ) sound.
ὑγραίνω [eeyreno] moisten, dampen, wet.
ὑγρασία, ή [eeyraseea] moisture, moistness, humidity.
ὑγροποιῶ [eeyropeeo] liquefy.
ὑγρός [eeyros] fluid, liquid ‖ humid, damp ‖ watery.
ὑδαρής [eeδarees] watery, aqueous.
ὕδατα, τά [eeδata] πλ waters.
ὑδαταγωγός, ὁ [eeδatagoyos] water pipe.
ὑδατάνθραξ, ὁ [eeδatanthraks] carbohydrate.
ὑδατογραφία, ή [eeδatoyrafeea] watercolour, aquarelle.
ὑδατοπτώσεις, οἱ [eeδatoptoςees] πλ waterfalls.
ὑδατοστεγής [eeδatosteyees] watertight, waterproof.
ὑδατοφράκτης, ὁ [eeδatofraktees] dam, weir.

ὑδραγωγεῖον, τό [eeδragoyeeon] aqueduct.
ὑδραντλία, ή [eeδrantleea] water pump.
ὑδράργυρος, ὁ [eeδraryeeros] mercury, quicksilver.
ὑδρατμός, ὁ [eeδratmos] vapour, steam.
ὑδραυλική, ή [eeδravleekee] hydraulics.
ὑδραυλικός [eeδravleekos] hydraulic ‖ (ούσ) plumber.
ὑδρεύομαι [eeδrevome] draw water.
ὕδρευσις, ή [eeδrevsees] water supply, drawing of water.
ὑδρία, ή [eeδreea] pitcher, water jar, jug.
ὑδρόβιος [eeδroveeos] aquatic.
ὑδρόγειος, ή [eeδroyeeos] earth.
ὑδρογόνον, τό [eeδroyonon] hydrogen.
ὑδρογραφία, ή [eeδroyrafeea] hydrography.
ὑδροηλεκτρικός [eeδroeelektreekos] hydroelectric.
ὑδροκέφαλος [eeδrokefalos] hydrocephalous.
ὑδροκίνητος [eeδrokeeneetos] waterpowered.
ὑδροκυάνιον, τό [eeδrokeeaneeon] prussic acid.
ὑδρολήπτης, ὁ [eeδroleeptees] water consumer, receiver of water.
ὑδρόμυλος, ὁ [eeδromeelos] water mill.
ὑδρονομεύς, ὁ [eeδronomevs] water distributor ‖ water key.
ὑδροπλάνον, τό [eeδroplanon] seaplane.
ὑδρορρόη, ή [eeδroroee] gutter of roof.
ὑδροσκόπος, ὁ [eeδroskopos] water diviner.
ὑδροστάθμη, ή [eeδrostathmee] water level.
ὑδροστατικός [eeδrostateekos] hydrostatic.
ὑδροστρόβιλος, ὁ [eeδrostroveelos] water turbine ‖ whirlpool.
ὑδροσωλήν, ὁ [eeδrosoleen] water pipe, conduit.
ὑδροφοβία, ή [eeδrofoveea] rabies, hydrophobia.
ὑδροφόρος [eeδroforos] water-carrying ‖ (ούσ) water carrier.
ὑδροφράκτης, ὁ [eeδrofraktees] dam, lock.
ὑδροχαρής [eeδroharees] water-loving.
ὑδροχλωρικός [eeδrohloreekos] hydrochloric.
ὑδρόχρωμα, τό [eeδrohroma] whitewash.
ὑδρόψυκτος [eeδropseektos] water-cooled.
ὑδρωπικία, ή [eeδropeekeea] dropsy.
ὕδωρ, τό [eeδor] water.
ὑετός, ὁ [ietos] shower, downpour ‖ rains.
υἱοθεσία, ή [ieotheseea] adoption.
υἱοθετῶ [ieotheto] adopt, accept, support.
υἱός, ὁ [ieos] son.
ὑλακή, ή [eelakee] barking, baying.
ὑλακτῶ [eelakto] bark, bay.
ὕλη, ή [eelee] material, matter, stuff.
ὑλικόν, τό [eeleekon] material, stuff ‖ element, ingredient.
ὑλικός [eeleekos] material, real.
ὑλισμός, ὁ [eeleesmos] materialism.
ὑλιστής, ὁ [eeleestees] materialist.

ὑλιστικός [eeleesteekos] materialistic.

ὑλοτομία, ἡ [eelotomeea] woodcutting, timber-felling.

ὑμεῖς [eemees] you.

ὑμέτερος [eemeteros] your, yours.

ὑμήν, ὁ [eemeen] membrane || tissue, hymen.

ὑμνητής, ὁ [eemneetees] eulogist, praiser, panegyrist.

ὕμνος, ὁ [eemnos] hymn || anthem.

ὑμνῶ [eemno] celebrate, praise, eulogize.

ὑνί, τό [eenee] ploughshare.

ὑπάγομαι [eepayome] belong to, be dependent || be answerable.

ὑπαγόρευσις, ἡ [eepayorevsees] dictation || (μεταφ) suggestion.

ὑπαγορεύω [eepayorevo] dictate || (μεταφ) inspire, suggest.

ὑπάγω [eepayo] go || go under, rank.

ὑπαίθριος [eepethreeos] outdoor, in the open air || field.

ὕπαιθρον, τό [eepethron] open air, open country.

ὕπαιθρος [eepethros]: ἡ ~ χώρα countryside.

ὑπαινιγμός, ὁ [eepeneeymos] hint, allusion, intimation.

ὑπαινίσσομαι [eepeneesome] hint at, allude to.

ὑπαίτιος [eepeteeos] responsible, culpable.

ὑπακοή, ἡ [eepakoee] obedience || submission.

ὑπάκουος [eepakouos] obedient || submissive.

ὑπακούω [eepakouo] obey.

ὑπάλληλος, ὁ, ἡ [eepaleelos] employee, clerk || (ὑπουργείου) official, functionary || δημόσιος ~ civil servant, government employee.

ὑπαναχωρῶ [eepanahoro] withdraw || recant.

ὑπανδρεία, ἡ [eepandreea] marriage.

ὑπανδρεύω [eepandrevo] marry.

ὕπανδρος [eepandros] married.

ὑπαξιωματικός, ὁ [eepakseeomateekos] non-commissioned officer.

Ὑπαπαντή, ἡ [eepapantee] Candlemas.

ὑπαρκτός [eeparktos] existent || subsisting || real.

ὕπαρξις, ἡ [eeparksees] existence || being, life.

ὑπαρχή, ἡ [eeparhee] very beginning || ἐξ ὑπαρχῆς from the very beginning.

ὑπαρχηγός, ὁ [eeparheeyos] deputy commander.

ὑπάρχω [eeparho] exist, be || live || ὑπάρχει there is || τά ὑπάρχοντά μου my possessions, my things.

ὑπασπιστής, ὁ [eepaspeestees] aide-decamp || (στρατ) adjutant.

ὕπατος, ὁ [eepatos] consul || (ἐπίθ) highest, supreme.

ὑπέδαφος, τό [eepedafos] subsoil.

ὑπείκω [eepeeko] succumb to, obey.

ὑπεισέρχομαι [eepeeserhome] enter secretly || glide into.

ὑπεκμισθώνω [eepekmeesthono] sublet, rent from a tenant.

ὑπεκφεύγω [eepekfevyo] escape, avoid || slip away.

ὑπεκφυγή, ἡ [eepekfeeyee] escape, subterfuge || evasion.

ὑπενθυμίζω [eepentheemeezo] remind of, call to mind || allude to.

ὑπενοικιάζω [eepeneekeeazo] βλ ὑπεκμισθώνω.

ὑπεξαίρεσις, ἡ [eepekseresees] pilfering, taking away.

ὑπέρ [eeper] over, upwards, above || (γιά) for, on behalf of || τά ~ καί τά κατά pros and cons, for and against.

ὑπεράγαν [eeperayan] too much, exceedingly.

ὑπεραιμία, ἡ [eeperemeea] excess of blood.

ὑπεραμύνομαι [eeperameenome] defend, support.

ὑπεράνθρωπος [eeperanthropos] superhuman || (οὐσ) superman.

ὑπεράνω [eeperano] above, beyond, over.

ὑπεράριθμος [eeperareethmos] supernumerary, redundant.

ὑπερασπίζομαι [eeperaspeezome] defend o.s.

ὑπερασπίζω [eeperaspeezo] defend, protect || maintain.

ὑπεράσπισις, ἡ [eeperaspeesees] defence || protection || the defendants.

ὑπεραστικός [eeperasteekos] long-distance.

ὑπερβαίνω [eeperveno] cross, surmount || exceed, go beyond, overdo.

ὑπερβαλλόντως [eepervalontos] excessively, exceedingly || too, deeply.

ὑπερβάλλω [eepervalo] surpass, outdo, exceed || exaggerate, overdo, magnify.

ὑπέρβασις, ἡ [eepervasees] exceeding || (traffic) violation || trespass.

ὑπερβολή, ἡ [eepervolee] exaggeration || (γεωμ) hyperbola.

ὑπερβολικός [eepervoleekos] excessive || exaggerated, exaggerating.

ὑπέργηρος [eeperyeeros] extremely old, very old.

ὑπερδιέγερσις, ἡ [eeperdieyersees] overexcitement.

ὑπερέντασις, ἡ [eeperentasees] overstrain, overstress.

ὑπερευαίσθητος [eeperevestheetos] oversensitive, hypersensitive.

ὑπερέχω [eepereho] excel, surpass, exceed.

ὑπερήλιξ, ὁ, ἡ [eepereeleeks] elderly person, very old person.

ὑπερηφάνεια, ἡ [eepereefaneea] pride || haughtiness.

ὑπερηφανεύομαι [eepereefanevome] pride o.s. || be proud.

ὑπερήφανος [eepereefanos] proud ‖ haughty.

ὑπερθεματίζω [eeperthemateezo] make higher bid ‖ (μεταφ) outdo.

ὑπερθετικός [eepertheteekos] superlative.

ὑπερίπταμαι [eepereeptame] fly over, fly above.

ὑπερισχύω [eepereesheeo] predominate, prevail over ‖ overcome, triumph.

ὑπεριώδης [eepereeoδees] ultraviolet.

ὑπερκέρασις, ἡ [eeperkerasees] outflanking.

ὑπερκόπωσις, ἡ [eeperkoposees] overwork, breakdown.

ὑπέρμαχος, ὁ, ἡ [eepermahos] champion, defender.

ὑπέρμετρος [eepermetros] excessive, huge.

ὑπερνικῶ [eeperneeko] overcome ‖ subdue, master.

ὑπέρογκος [eeperongos] colossal, enormous ‖ outrageous.

ὑπεροπλία, ἡ [eeperopleea] superiority in arms.

ὑπεροπτικός [eeperopteekos] haughty, presumptuous, arrogant.

ὑπεροχή, ἡ [eeperohee] superiority, predominance.

ὑπέροχος [eeperohos] superior, excellent, eminent.

ὑπεροψία, ἡ [eeperopseea] arrogance, disdain, haughtiness.

ὑπερπέραν, τό [eeperperan] the beyond, afterlife.

ὑπερπηδῶ [eeperpeeδo] surmount ‖ jump over.

ὑπερπόντιος [eeperponteeos] overseas ‖ transmarine.

ὑπέρποτε [eeperpote] more than ever.

ὑπερσυντέλικος [eeperseenteleekos] (γραμμ) pluperfect (tense).

ὑπέρτασις, ἡ [eepertasees] high blood pressure.

ὑπέρτατος [eepertatos] highest, greatest, supreme.

ὑπέρτερος [eeperteros] superior to.

ὑπερτερῶ [eepertero] excel, exceed, surpass ‖ outnumber.

ὑπερτίμησις, ἡ [eeperteemeesees] overestimation ‖ (οἰκ) rise in price, increase in value.

ὑπερτιμῶ [eeperteemo] overvalue, overestimate ‖ (οἰκ) raise price of.

ὑπερτροφία, ἡ [eepertrofeea] (ἰατρ) hypertrophy.

ὑπέρυθροι [eepereethree] πλ: ~ ἀκτίνες infrared rays.

ὑπέρυθρος [eepereethros] reddish.

ὑπερύψηλος [eepereepseelos] very high, exceedingly high.

ὑπερυψῶ [eepereepso] raise up ‖ exalt.

ὑπερφαλάγγισις, ἡ [eeperfalangeesees] outflanking.

ὑπερφίαλος [eeperfeealos] overweening, arrogant, insolent.

ὑπερφυσικός [eeperfeeseekos] supernatural ‖ (μεταφ) extraordinary, prodigious.

ὑπερῴα, ἡ [eeperoa] palate.

ὑπερωκεάνειον, τό [eeperokeaneeon] liner.

ὑπερῷον, τό [eeperoon] attic, garret ‖ (θεάτρου) gallery.

ὑπερωρία, ἡ [eeperoreea] overtime.

ὑπεύθυνος [eepevtheenos] responsible, answerable.

ὑπέχω [eepeho] bear.

ὑπήκοος [eepeekoos] submissive, obedient ‖ (οὐσ) subject of state.

ὑπηκοότης, ἡ [eepeekootees] nationality, citizenship.

ὑπήνεμος [eepeenemos] (ναυτ) leeward.

ὑπηρεσία, ἡ [eepeereseea] service, attendance ‖ duty, employ ‖ (οἰκίας) domestic servant.

ὑπηρεσιακή [eepeereseeakee]: ~ κυβέρνησις caretaker government.

ὑπηρεσιακός [eepeereseeakos] of service.

ὑπηρέτης, ὁ [eepeeretees] servant.

ὑπηρέτρια, ἡ [eepeeretreea] maid.

ὑπηρετῶ [eepeereto] serve ‖ do one's military service.

ὑπναλέος [eepnaleos] drowsy, sleepy.

ὑπναρᾶς, ὁ [eepnaras] person who enjoys sleeping.

ὑπνοβάτης, ὁ [eepnovatees] sleepwalker.

ὕπνος, ὁ [eepnos] sleep.

ὕπνωσις, ἡ [eepnosees] hypnosis.

ὑπνωτίζω [eepnoteezo] hypnotize.

ὑπνωτικόν, τό [eepnoteekon] soporific drug, sleeping pill.

ὑπνωτισμός, ὁ [eepnoteesmos] hypnotism.

ὑπό [eepo] below, beneath ‖ (μέσον) by, with.

ὑπόβαθρον, τό [eepovathron] base, pedestal, stand.

ὑποβάλλω [eepovalo] submit, hand in ‖ (ὑποτάσσω) subject ‖ suggest, propose.

ὑποβαστάζω [eepovastazo] support, prop up, bear.

ὑποβιβάζω [eepoveevazo] lower ‖ reduce, diminish ‖ demote.

ὑποβλέπω [eepovlepo] suspect ‖ cast glances at, leer.

ὑποβλητικός [eepovleeteekos] evocative.

ὑποβοηθῶ [eepovoeetho] assist, back up, support.

ὑποβολεύς, ὁ [eepovolevs] prompter ‖ instigator.

ὑποβολή, ἡ [eepovolee] submission, presentation ‖ prompting, instigation.

ὑποβολιμαῖος [eepovoleemeos] spurious ‖ interposed, inserted.

ὑποβόσκω [eepovosko] smoulder ‖ lie hidden.

ὑποβρύχιον, τό [eepovreeheeon] submarine ‖ (μεταφ) kind of sweet.

ὑπογεγραμμένη, ἡ [eepoyeyramenee] (iota) subscript.

ὑπόγειον, τό [eepoyeeon] basement, cellar.

ὑπόγειος [eepoyeeos] underground.

ὑπόγλυκος [eepoyleekos] sweetish.

ὑπογραμμίζω [eepoyrameezo] underline, emphasize.

ὑπογραφή, ἡ [eepoyrafee] signature.

ὑπογράφω [eepoyrafo] sign || (μεταφ) approve, subscribe.

ὑπογράψας, ὁ [eepoyrapsas] signatory.

ὑποδαυλίζω [eepodavleezo] fan the flame || (μεταφ) foment, excite.

ὑποδεέστερος [eepodeesteros] inferior, lower.

ὑπόδειγμα, τό [eepodeeyma] model, example, specimen || sample.

ὑποδειγματικός [eepodeeymateekos] exemplary, representative.

ὑποδεικνύω [eepodeekneeo] indicate || suggest, propose.

ὑπόδειξις, ἡ [eepodeeksees] indication || recommendation.

ὑποδέχομαι [eepodehome] receive, welcome, greet.

ὑποδηλῶ [eepodeelo] convey, indicate, hint at.

ὑπόδημα, τό [eepodeema] shoe, boot.

ὑποδηματοποιεῖον, τό [eepodeematopieeon] shoemaker's shop.

ὑπόδησις, ἡ [eepodeesees] footgear, footwear.

ὑποδιαίρεσις, ἡ [eepodieresees] subdivision.

ὑποδιαιρῶ [eepodiero] subdivide.

ὑποδιαστολή, ἡ [eepodeeastolee] decimal point || (γραμμ) comma.

ὑποδιευθυντής, ὁ [eepodieftheentees] assistant director, vice-principal, deputy manager.

ὑπόδικος, ὁ [eepodeekos] the accused.

ὑπόδουλος [eepodoulos] enslaved.

ὑποδουλώνω [eepodoulono] subjugate, enslave, subdue.

ὑποδοχή, ἡ [eepodohee] reception.

ὑποδύομαι [eepodeeome] play the part of, assume a role.

ὑποζύγιον, τό [eepozeeyeeon] beast of burden.

ὑποθάλπω [eepothalpo] foment || protect, maintain || entertain, harbour.

ὑπόθεμα, τό [eepothema] suppository.

ὑπόθεσις, ἡ [eepothesees] conjecture, supposition || matter, affair, business || (δικαστηρίου) case, action || (θεατρικοῦ ἔργου κτλ) subject, plot, matter, theme.

ὑποθετικός [eepotheteekos] hypothetical, speculative || imaginary || (γραμμ) conditional.

ὑποθέτω [eepotheto] suppose, assume.

ὑποθηκεύω [eepotheekevo] mortgage.

ὑποθήκη, ἡ [eepotheekee] mortgage.

ὑποθηκοφυλακεῖον, τό [eepotheekofeelakeeon] mortgage office.

ὑποκαθιστῶ [eepokatheesto] replace, substitute.

ὑποκάμισον, τό [eepokameeson] shirt.

ὑποκατάστασις, ἡ [eepokatastasees] replacement, substitution.

ὑποκατάστημα, τό [eepokatasteema] branch office || (US) chain store.

ὑποκάτω [eepokato] below, beneath, under.

ὑπόκειμαι [eepokeeme] be subject to, be liable || lie under.

ὑποκειμενικός [eepokeemeneekos] subjective.

ὑποκείμενον, τό [eepokeemenon] subject || individual || seamp.

ὑποκινῶ [eepokeeno] stir up, excite, incite.

ὑποκλέπτω [eepoklepto] purloin, pilfer.

ὑποκλίνομαι [eepokleenome] bow, bend || yield.

ὑπόκλισις, ἡ [eepokleesees] bow, curtsy.

ὑποκόμης, ὁ [eepokomees] viscount.

ὑποκόπανος, ὁ [eepokopanos] butt of weapon, butt-end.

ὑποκοριστικόν, τό [eepokoreesteekon] diminutive.

ὑπόκοσμος, ὁ [eepokosmos] underworld.

ὑποκρίνομαι [eepokreenome] act, play the part of, impersonate || dissemble.

ὑποκρισία, ἡ [eepokreeseea] hypocrisy.

ὑπόκρισις, ἡ [eepokreesees] pretending, acting || dissembling.

ὑποκριτής, ὁ [eepokreetees] actor || hypocrite.

ὑποκριτικός [eepokreeteekos] feigned, insincere.

ὑπόκρουσις, ἡ [eepokrousees] accompaniment.

ὑποκύπτω [eepokeepto] bend, submit, succumb || yield.

ὑπόκωφος [eepokofos] hollow, deep || smothered.

ὑπόλειμμα, τό [eepoleema] residue, remnant, rest.

ὑπολείπομαι [eepoleepome] be left || be inferior to.

ὑπόληψις, ἡ [eepoleepsees] esteem || credit, reputation.

ὑπολογίζω [eepoloyeezo] estimate, calculate || consider.

ὑπολογισμός, ὁ [eepoloyeesmos] calculation, estimate || account.

ὑπόλογος [eepoloyos] responsible, accountable, liable.

ὑπόλοιπον, τό [eepoleepon] left-over, remainder, balance.

ὑπόλοιπος [eepoleepos] remaining, rest of.

ὑπολοχαγός, ὁ [eepolohayos] lieutenant.

ὑπομένω [eepomeno] endure, tolerate.

ὑπομιμνήσκω [eepomeemneesko] remind.

ὑπομισθώνω [eepomeesthono] sublet.

ὑπόμνημα, τό [eepomneema] memorandum.

ὑπομνήματα, τά [eepomneemata] πλ commentary, memorabilia.

ὑπόμνησις, ἡ [eepomneesees] reminder suggestion.

ὑπομοίραρχος, ὁ [eepomeerarhos] lieutenant of gendarmerie.

ὑπομονεύω [eepomonevo] be patient ‖ endure.

ὑπομονή, ἡ [eepomonee] patience, endurance.

ὑπομονητικός [eepomoneeteekos] patient, enduring.

ὑποναύαρχος, ὁ [eeponavarhos] rear admiral.

ὑπόνοια, ἡ [eeponeea] suspicion ‖ surmise.

ὑπονομεύω [eeponomevo] undermine, sabotage.

ὑπόνομος, ὁ, ἡ [eeponomos] sewer ‖ (στρατ) mine.

ὑπονοῶ [eeponoo] infer, mean.

ὑποπίπτω [eepopeepto] commit, fall into ‖ come to s.o.'s notice.

ὑποπλοίαρχος, ὁ [eepopleearhos] lieutenant ‖ first mate.

ὑποπόδιον, τό [eepopodeeon] footstool.

ὑποπροϊόν, τό [eepoproeeon] by-product.

ὑποπρόξενος, ὁ [eepoproksenos] vice-consul.

ὑποπτεύομαι [eepoptevome] suspect, have an idea.

ὕποπτος [eepoptos] suspect, suspicious, suspected.

ὑποσημείωσις, ἡ [eeposeemeeosees] footnote, annotation.

ὑποσιτισμός, ὁ [eeposeeteesmos] undernourishment, malnutrition.

ὑποσκάπτω [eeposkapto] undermine, sabotage.

ὑποσκελίζω [eeposkeleezo] upset ‖ supplant.

ὑποσμηναγός, ὁ [eeposmeenayos] flight lieutenant.

ὑποστάθμη, ἡ [eepostathmee] dregs, sediment, residue.

ὑπόστασις, ἡ [eepostasees] existence ‖ foundation, basis ‖ (ιατρ) hypostasis.

ὑποστατικόν, τό [eepostateekon] property, farm.

ὑπόστεγον, τό [eeposteyon] shed, hangar ‖ shelter.

ὑποστέλλω [eepostelo] strike, lower ‖ slow down, reduce.

ὑποστήριγμα, τό [eeposteereeyma] support, prop.

ὑποστηρίζω [eeposteereezo] prop up, support ‖ second, back ‖ maintain.

ὑποστήριξις, ἡ [eeposteereeksees] prop, support ‖ backing.

ὑποστράτηγος, ὁ [eepostrateeyos] major-general.

ὑπόστρωμα, τό [eepostroma] substratum ‖ saddlecloth.

ὑποσυνείδητον, τό [eeposeeneedeeton] subconscious.

ὑπόσχεσις, ἡ [eeposheesees] promise, pledge, engagement.

ὑπόσχομαι [eeposhome] promise, pledge.

ὑποταγή, ἡ [eepotayee] obedience, subjection, submission.

ὑποτακτική, ἡ [eepotakteekee] subjective.

ὑποτακτικός [eepotakteekos] obedient, submissive.

ὑπότασις, ἡ [eepotasees] low blood pressure.

ὑποτάσσομαι [eepotasome] submit, give in.

ὑποτάσσω [eepotaso] subjugate, subdue.

ὑποτείνουσα, ἡ [eepoteenousa] hypotenuse.

ὑποτελής [eepotelees] subordinate, tributary, vassal.

ὑποτίθεμαι [eepoteetheme] be supposed / suppose, consider.

ὑποτίμησις, ἡ [eepoteemeesees] reduction in price, depreciation ‖ underestimation.

ὑποτιμῶ [eepoteemo] underestimate ‖ lower the price of, depreciate.

ὑποτονθορύζω [eepotonthoreezo] murmur, mumble, hum.

ὑποτροπή, ἡ [eepotropee] relapse, deterioration.

ὑποτροφία, ἡ [eepotrofeea] scholarship.

ὑποτυπώδης [eepoteepodees] sketchy, imperfectly formed.

ὕπουλος [eepoulos] shifty, underhand, cunning.

ὑπουργεῖον, τό [eepouryeeon] ministry.

ὑπουργικός [eepouryeekos] ministerial.

ὑπουργός, ὁ [eepouryos] minister ‖ (US) secretary.

ὑποφαινόμενος [eepofenomenos]: ὁ ~ the undersigned.

ὑποφερτός [eepofertos] tolerable ‖ passable.

ὑποφέρω [eepofero] bear, support, endure ‖ feel pain, suffer.

ὑποφώσκω [eepofosko] dawn, glimmer.

ὑποχείριος [eepoheereeos] under the power of, subject.

ὑποχθόνιος [eepohthoneeos] infernal, subterranean.

ὑποχονδρία, ἡ [eepohonδreea] hypochondria ‖ obsession.

ὑπόχρεος [eepohreos] obliged.

ὑποχρεώνω [eepohreono] oblige ‖ compel.

ὑποχρέωσις, ἡ [eepohreosees] obligation, duty.

ὑποχρεωτικός [eepohreoteekos] obligatory ‖ compulsory.

ὑποχώρησις, ἡ [eepohoreesees] withdrawal, yielding ‖ subsidence.

ὑποχωρῶ [eepohoro] withdraw, give way ‖ fall in, cave in.

ὑποψήφιος, ὁ [eepopseefeeos] candidate, applicant.

ὑποψηφιότης, ἡ [eepopseefeeotees] candidature, application.

ὑποψία, ἡ [eepopseea] suspicion, misgiving

ὑποψιάζομαι [eepopseeazome] suspect, have suspicions.

ὕπτιος [eepteeos] lying on one's back.

ὑπώρεια, ἡ [eeporeea] foot of mountain.

ὕσκα, ἡ [eeska] tinder, touchwood.

ὕστατος [eestatos] last, final.

ὕστερα [eestera] afterwards, then, later

furthermore ‖ ~ **άπό** after, following (this).

ύστέρημα, τό [eestereema] shortage, deficiency ‖ small savings.

ύστερία, ή [eestereea] hysteria.

ύστερικός [eestereekos] hysterical.

ύστερισμός, ό [eestereesmos] hysteria, hysterics.

ύστερ(ι)νός [eester(ee)nos] later, ultimate, last.

ύστεροβουλία, ή [eesterovouleea] afterthought ‖ deceit.

ύστερόγραφον, τό [eesteroyrafon] postscript.

ύστερον [eesteron] βλ **ύστερα**.

ύστερος [eesteros] later ‖ inferior ‖ **έκ τών ύστέρων** on second thought, looking back.

ύστερῶ [eestero] come after ‖ be inferior ‖ deprive.

ύφάδι, τό [eefadee] weft, woof.

ύφαίνω [eefeno] weave, spin ‖ (μεταφ) plot.

ύφαλα, τά [eefala] πλ beam ‖ part below waterline.

ύφαλος, ή [eefalos] reef, shoal.

ύφανσις, ή [eefansees] weaving ‖ weave.

ύφαντός [eefantos] woven.

ύφαντουργία, ή [eefantouryeea] textile industry, weaving industry.

ύφαρπάζω [eefarpazo] obtain by fraud.

ύφασμα, τό [eefasma] cloth, fabric, stuff, material ‖ ~ **τα** textiles.

ύφεσις, ή [eefesees] decrease, abatement ‖ (βαρομέτρου) depression ‖ (μουσ) flat (note).

ύφή, ή [eefee] texture, web, weave.

ύφηγητής, ό [eefeeyeetees] lecturer ‖ (US) assistant professor.

ύφήλιος, ή [eefeeleeos] earth, world, globe.

ύφίσταμαι [eefeestame] bear, undergo, sustain ‖ (είμαι) exist, be in force.

ύφιστάμενος, ό [eefeestamenos] subordinate, inferior.

ύφος, τό [eefos] style ‖ air, look, tone.

ύφυπουργός, ό [eefeepouryos] undersecretary of state.

ύψηλός [eepseelos] high, towering, tall ‖ (μεταφ) lofty, great.

ύψηλότης, ή [eepseelotees] Highness ‖ **ή A.B.** ~ Her Royal Highness.

ύψηλόφρων [eepseelofron] generous ‖ highminded, haughty.

ύψικάμινος, ή [eepseekameenos] blast furnace.

ύψιλον, τό [eepseelon] the letter Y.

ύψίπεδον, τό [eepseepedon] plateau.

ύψιστος [eepseestos] highest ‖ (ούσ) God.

ύψίφωνος, ό, ή [eepseefonos] tenor ‖ soprano.

ύψόμετρον, τό [eepsometron] altitude.

ύψος, τό [eepsos] height, altitude ‖ (μουσ) pitch.

ύψωμα, τό [eepsoma] height, elevation ‖ hillock.

ύψωμός, ό [eepsomos] lifting ‖ rise in price.

ύψώνω [eepsono] raise, elevate increase ‖ hoist.

ύψωσις, ή [eepsosees] raising, lifting, elevation ‖ rise in price.

Φ, φ

φάβα, ή [fava] yellow pea ‖ pea purée.

φαγάνα, ή [fayana] dredger.

φαγᾶς, ό [fayas] glutton, gourmand.

φαγγρί, τό [fangree] sea bream.

φαγέδαινα, ή [fayedena] canker, cancerous sore.

φαγητόν, τό [fayeeton] meal, dish, food dinner.

φαγί, τό [fayee] food, meal.

φαγκότο, τό [fangoto] bassoon.

φαγοπότι, τό [fayopotee] revel, eating and drinking.

φαγούρα, ή [fayoura] itching, irritation.

φάγωμα, τό [fayoma] corrosion, disintegration ‖ (τσακωμός) quarrel, dispute, wrangling.

φαγωμάρα, ή [fayomara] itch, irritation (τσακωμός) discord, arguing, dispute.

φαγωμένος [fayomenos] eaten ‖ eroded ‖ **είμαι** ~ I've eaten.

φαγώσιμα, τά [fayoseema] πλ provisions, victuals.

φαγώσιμος [fayoseemos] eatable, edible.

φαεινή [faeenee]: ~ **ιδέα** brainwave, bright idea.

φαΐ, τό [faee] food, meal.

φαιδρός [fedros] merry, cheerful ‖ (μεταφ) ridiculous.

φαιδρύνω [fedreeno] cheer up, gladden, enliven.

φαίνομαι [fenome] appear, come in sight seem, look ‖ show o.s. to be.

φαινόμενα, τά [fenomena] πλ: **κατά τά** ~ judging by appearances.

φαινομενικώς [fenomeneekos] apparently, outwardly.

φαινόμενον, τό [fenomenon] wonder, prodigy ‖ phenomenon.

φαιός [feos] grey ‖ brown, dun.

φάκα, ή [faka] mousetrap ‖ snare.

φάκελλος, ό [fakelos] envelope ‖ file, cover, dossier, record.

φακή, ή [fakee] lentils.

φακίδα, ή [fakeeda] freckle.

φακιόλι, τό [fakeeolee] kerchief, neckerchief.

φακίρης, ό [fakeerees] fakir.

φακός, ό [fakos] lens ‖ magnifying glass, magnifier.

φάλαγξ, ή [falanks] phalanx ‖ (στρατ) column ‖ (στοίχος) row.

φάλαινα, ή [falena] whale.

φαλάκρα, ή [falakra] baldness ‖ bald head.

φαλακραίνω [falakreno] go bald.

φαλακρός [falakros] bald(-headed) ׀ bare.

φαλ(λ)ίρω [faleero] go bankrupt, fail, break.

φαλλός, ὁ [falos] phallus.

φαλτσέτα, ἡ [faltseta] shoemaker's knife, paring knife.

φαλτσάρω [faltsaro] be out of tune ׀ make a mistake.

φάλτσο, τό [faltso] wrong note, dissonance ׀ (μεταφ) mistake, fault, error.

φαμελίτης, ὁ [fameleetees] family man, head of the family.

φαμίλια, ἡ [fameeleea] family.

φάμπρικα, ἡ [fambreeka] factory ׀ fabrication, device, artifice.

φαμπρικάρω [fambreekaro] manufacture (μεταφ) fabricate, concoct, forge, invent.

φανάρι, τό [fanaree] lamp, light, lantern ׀ (αὐτοκινήτου) headlamp ׀ (φάρου) lighthouse.

φαναρτζῆς, ὁ [fanartzees] tinsmith ׀ lampmaker.

φανατίζω [fanateezo] make fanatical, fanaticize.

φανατικός [fanateekos] overzealous, fanatical ׀ (οὐσ) fanatic, zealot.

φανατισμός, ὁ [fanateesmos] fanaticism.

φανέλλα, ἡ [fanela] flannel ׀ vest ׀ woollen cloth.

φανερός [faneros] clear, plain, evident, certain.

φανερώνω [fanerono] reveal, make plain.

φανός, ὁ [fanos] lamp, lantern, street lamp.

φαντάζομαι [fantazome] imagine, fancy, think ׀ (πιστεύω) believe.

φαντάζω [fantazo] make an impression, stand out ׀ look glamorous.

φαντάρος, ὁ [fantaros] infantryman ׀ (US) buck private.

φαντασία, ἡ [fantaseea] imagination ׀ illusion ׀ (ὑπερηφάνεια) vanity, pride ׀ (μουσ) fantasia.

φαντασιοκόπος [fantasiokopos] dreamer, visionary.

φαντασιοπληξία, ἡ [fantaseeopleekseea] extravagant notion ׀ caprice, whim.

φαντασιώδης [fantaseeoδees] illusory, imaginary ׀ fictitious ׀ beyond imagination.

φάντασμα, τό [fantasma] phantom, ghost, spirit.

φαντασμαγορία, ἡ [fantasmaγoreea] phantasmagoria.

φαντασμένος [fantasmenos] presumptuous, vain.

φανταστικός [fantasteekos] illusory, imaginary ׀ fantastic, extravagant.

φανταχτερός [fantahteros] showy, bright ׀ gaudy, glaring.

φάντης, ὁ [fantees] (στά χαρτιά) knave.

φανφαρόνος, ὁ [fanfaronos] braggart, boaster, blusterer.

φάπα, ἡ [fapa] slap, box on the ear, smack.

φάρα, ἡ [fara] race, progeny, breed ׀ crew.

φαράγγι, τό [farangee] βλ. **φάραγξ**.

φάραγξ, ἡ [faranks] gorge, gully, precipice, ravine.

φαράσι, τό [farasee] dustpan.

φαρδαίνω [farδeno] widen, broaden, become wider ׀ stretch, extend.

φάρδος, τό [farδos] width, breadth.

φαρδύνω [farδeeno] βλ **φαρδαίνω**.

φαρδύς [farδees] wide, large, broad, ample.

φαρέτρα, ἡ [faretra] quiver.

φαρί, τό [faree] steed.

φαρμακεῖον, τό [farmakeeon] chemist shop.

φαρμακέμπορος, ὁ [farmakemboros] chemist ׀ (US) druggist.

φαρμακερός [farmakeros] venomous ׀ spiteful, bitter.

φαρμάκι, τό [farmakee] poison ׀ (μεταφ) anything bitter.

φαρμακίλα, ἡ [farmakeela] bitter taste.

φάρμακον, τό [farmakon] drug, medicine, remedy.

φαρμακοποιός, ὁ [farmakopeeos] pharmacist, chemist ׀ (US) druggist.

φαρμακώνω [farmakono] poison ׀ (μεταφ) cause grief ׀ mortify.

φάρος, ὁ [faros] lighthouse, beacon.

φάρσα, ἡ [farsa] trick, farce ׀ practical joke.

φάρυγξ, ὁ [fareenks] pharynx, windpipe.

φαρφουρί, τό [farfouree] porcelain, china.

φασαρία, ἡ [fasareea] disturbance ׀ fuss, noise, bustle.

φασιανός, ὁ [faseeanos] pheasant.

φάσις, ἡ [fasees] phase ׀ change, turn ׀ aspect.

φασισμός, ὁ [faseesmos] fascism.

φασιστικός [faseesteekos] fascist.

φασκιά, ἡ [faskia] swaddling band, swaddling clothes.

φασκόμηλο, τό [faskomeelo] three-lobed sage, wild mountain tea.

φάσκω [fasko]: ~ καί ἀντιφάσκω contradict o.s.

φάσμα, τό [fasma] ghost, spirit ׀ (φυσική) spectrum.

φασματοσκόπιον, τό [fasmatoskopeeon] spectroscope.

φασόλι, τό [fasolee] haricot bean, kidney bean.

φασο(υ)λάδα, ἡ [faso(u)laδa] bean soup.

φασο(υ)λάκια, τά [faso(u)lakeea] πλ green beans.

φασούλι, τό [fasoulee] βλ **φασόλι**.

φασουλῆς, ὁ [fasoulees] Jack and the Beanstalk ׀ Punch.

φάτνη, ἡ [fatnee] manger, crib, stall.

φατνίον, τό [fatneeon] (ἀνατ) alveolus.

φατρία, ἡ [fatreea] faction, clique, gang.

φατριάζω [fatreeazo] form factions, be factious.

φάτσα, ἡ [fatsa] face ׀ front ׀ (ἐπίρ) opposite.

Φ

φαυλόβιος [favloveeos] licentious, debauched.

φαυλοκρατία, ή [favlokrateea] political corruption.

φαῦλος [favlos] wicked, depraved || ~ **κύκλος** vicious circle.

φαφλατᾶς, ὁ [faflatas] chatterer, mumbler.

φαφούτης, ὁ [fafoutees] toothless man, very old man.

Φεβρουάριος, ὁ [fevrouareeos] February.

φεγγάρι, τό [fengaree] moon.

φεγγίτης, ὁ [fengeetees] skylight, fanlight, garret window.

φεγγοβολῶ [fengovolo] shine brightly.

φέγγος, τό [fengos] light, gleam, splendour.

φέγγω [fengo] shine, give light.

φείδομαι [feedome] save, spare || be sparing of, be stingy.

φειδώ, ή [feedo] thrift, economy, frugality.

φειδωλός [feedolos] sparing, thrifty || stingy, mean, niggardly.

φελλός, ὁ [felos] cork.

φέλπα, ή [felpa] velveteen, plush.

φενάκη, ή [fenakee] false hair, wig || (μεταφ) deceit, deception.

φεουδαρχικός [feoudarheekos] feudal.

φέουδον, τό [feoudon] fief.

φερέγγυος [ferengeeos] solvent, trustworthy.

φέρελπις [ferelpees] full of promise || hopeful.

φερετζές, ὁ [feretzes] veil (of a Moslem woman).

φέρετρον, τό [feretron] coffin, bier.

φερμένος [fermenos] arrived, brought, imported.

φερμουάρ, τό [fermouar] zip fastener.

φέρνω [ferno] βλ **φέρω**.

φέρομαι [ferome] conduct, behave || be reputed, be held as.

φέρσιμο, τό [ferseemo] behaviour, conduct.

φέρω [fero] bring, carry, support || (στέλλω) fetch || (ἔχω πάνω μου) carry, have || (προξενῶ) cause || (παράγω) bear, bring forth, bring in, yield || (φορῶ) wear || (κατευθύνω) lead, conduct || ~ **ἀντιρρήσεις** protest || **φερ'εἰπεῖν** for example.

φέσι, τό [fesee] fez || **γίνομαι** ~ get dead drunk.

φέτα, ή [feta] slice || (τυρί) kind of white cheese.

φετινός [feteenos] of this year.

φέτος [fetos] this year.

φεῦ [fev] alas!, ah!, woe!

φευγάλα, ή [fevgala] flight, escape, stampede.

φευγαλέος [fevgaleos] fleeting.

φευγατίζω [fevgateezo] help to escape.

φευγάτος [fevgatos] gone, fled, run away, left.

φεύγω [fevgo] leave, depart, get away || escape, flee || run away from, shun.

φευκτέος [fevkteos] avoidable.

φήμη, ή [feemee] report, rumour || reputation || renown, repute || fame.

φημίζομαι [feemeezome] be well-known.

φηρίκι, τό [feereekee] kind of apple.

φθάνω [fthano] catch, overtake, attain || (μεταφ) equal, be equal to || arrive, reach || draw near || ~ **σέ** reach the point of, be reduced to || **φθάνει νά** provided that.

φθαρτός [fthartos] perishable, destructible, liable to decay.

φθείρ, ὁ, ή [ftheer] louse.

φθείρομαι [ftheerome] decay, wash away || (μεταφ) lose importance.

φθείρω [ftheero] damage, spoil || corrupt, pervert, taint.

φθινόπωρον, τό [ftheenoporon] autumn.

φθίνω [ftheeno] pine away || decay || decline, fail.

φθισικός [ftheeseekos] consumptive, tubercular.

φθίσις, ή [ftheesees] consumption || decline.

φθόγγος, ὁ [fthongos] voice, sound || (μουσ) note.

φθογγόσημον, τό [fthongoseemon] (musical) note.

φθονερός [fthoneros] envious of, jealous.

φθόνος, ὁ [fthonos] malicious envy, jealousy.

φθονῶ [fthono] be envious of, begrudge.

φθορά, ή [fthora] deterioration, damage, destruction || decay || loss.

φθορεύς, ὁ [fthorevs] seducer, corrupter || destroyer.

φθορισμός, ὁ [fthoreesmos] fluorescence.

φί, τό [fee] the letter Φ.

φιάλη, ή [feealee] bottle, flagon, flask.

φιγούρα, ή [feegoura] figure, image || (μεταφ) expression, air || **κάνω** ~ cut a fine figure.

φιγουράρω [feegouraro] show off, appear.

φιδές, ὁ [feedes] vermicelli.

φίδι, τό [feedee] snake, serpent.

φιδωτός [feedotos] winding, twisting.

φίλαθλος, ὁ, ή [feelathlos] sports fan.

φιλαλήθης [feelaleethees] truthful.

φιλάνθρωπος, ὁ, ή [feelanthropos] philanthropist, charitable person.

φιλαράκος, ὁ [feelarakos] beau || chum, pal || scoundrel, rascal.

φιλάργυρος [feelaryeeros] niggardly, miserly || (οὐσ) miser.

φιλάρεσκος [feelareskos] coquettish, spruce.

φιλαρμονική, ή [feelarmoneekee] (musical) band.

φιλαρχία, ή [feelarheea] love of authority.

φιλάσθενος [feelasthenos] sickly, weakly, puny.

φιλαυτία, ή [feelavteea] egoism, vanity, conceit.

φιλέκδικος [feelekdeekos] vindictive, revengeful.

φιλελευθερισμός, ὁ [feelelevthereesmos] liberalism.

φιλελεύθερος, ὁ [feelelevtheros] liberal.

φιλέλλην, ὁ, ἡ [feeleleen] philhellene.

φιλενάδα, ἡ [feelenaδa] girlfriend ‖ (μεταφ) mistress.

φίλεργος [feeleryos] hard-working, fond of work.

φίλερις [feelerees] quarrelsome, contentious.

φιλές, ὁ [feeles] hairnet.

φιλέτο, τό [feeleto] fillet of meat ‖ (ὕφασμα) piping ‖ (διακόσμηση) strip, border.

φιλεύω [feelevo] make a present ‖ entertain.

φίλη, ἡ [feelee] friend.

φιλήδονος [feeleeδonos] sensual, voluptuous.

φίλημα, τό [feeleema] kiss.

φιλήσυχος [feeleeseehos] peace-loving, calm, quiet, serene.

φιλί, τό [feelee] βλ **φίλημα**.

φιλία, ἡ [feeleea] friendship.

φιλικός [feeleekos] friendly ‖ of a friend.

φίλιππος, ὁ, ἡ [feeleepos] horse lover ‖ racegoer.

φιλιστρίνι, τό [feeleestreenee] porthole.

φιλιώνω [feeleeono] reconcile ‖ be reconciled.

φίλμ, τό [feelm] film.

φίλντισι, τό [feelnteesee] mother-of-pearl ‖ ivory.

φιλόδικος [feeloδeekos] litigious.

φιλόδοξυς [feeloδoksos] ambitious ‖ pretentious, showy.

φιλοδοξῶ [feeloδokso] be ambitious ‖ aspire to, desire strongly.

φιλοδώρημα, τό [feeloδoreema] tip ‖ gratuity.

φιλοκερδής [feelokerδees] greedy, covetous, eager for gain.

φιλολογία, ἡ [feeloloyeea] literature ‖ philology.

φιλόλογος, ὁ [feeloloyos] man of letters, philologist ‖ scholar.

φιλομαθής [feelomathees] fond of learning.

φιλόμουσος [feelomousos] lover of music ‖ fond of learning.

φιλον(ε)ικία, ἡ [feeloneekeea] dispute, wrangle.

φιλόν(ε)ικος [feeloneekos] contentious.

φιλον(ε)ικῶ [feeloneeko] quarrel, wrangle.

φιλοξενία, ἡ [feelokseneea] hospitality.

φιλόξενος [feeloksenos] hospitable.

φιλοξενῶ [feelokseno] entertain, give hospitality, receive.

φιλοπαίγμων [feelopeymon] playful, frolicsome.

φιλοπατρία, ἡ [feelopatreea] patriotism.

φιλοπόλεμος [feelopolemos] warlike, martial.

φιλόπονος [feeloponos] assiduous, diligent, industrious

φιλοπονῶ [feelopono] prepare assiduously.

φιλοπράγμων [feelopraymon] curious, inquiring, inquisitive.

φίλος, ὁ [feelos] friend ‖ (ἐπιθ) dear, friendly.

φιλοσοφία, ἡ [feelosofeea] philosophy.

φιλοσοφικός [feelosofeekos] philosophical.

φιλόσοφος, ὁ, ἡ [feelosofos] philosopher.

φιλόστοργος [feelostoryos] loving, affectionate.

φιλοτελισμός, ὁ [feeloteleesmos] philately.

φιλοτέχνημα, τό [feelotehneema] work of art.

φιλότεχνος [feelotehnos] art lover ‖ artistic, skilful.

φιλοτιμία, ἡ [feeloteemeea] sense of honour, pride, self-respect, dignity.

φιλότιμο, τό [feeloteemo] βλ **φιλοτιμία**.

φιλότιμος [feeloteemos] eager to excel ‖ obliging ‖ having sense of pride and honour ‖ generous.

φιλοτιμοῦμαι [feeloteemoume] make it a point of honour.

φιλοτιμῶ [feeloteemo] put s.o. on his dignity.

φιλοφρόνησις, ἡ [feelofroneesees] compliment, courtesy.

φιλόφρων [feelofron] courteous, affable, kindly, polite.

φίλτατος [feeltatos] dearest, most beloved.

φίλτρον, τό [feeltron] filter ‖ philtre.

φιλύποπτος [feeleepoptos] distrustful, suspicious.

φιλύρα, ἡ [feeleera] lime tree.

φιλῶ [feelo] kiss, embrace.

φιμώνω [feemono] muzzle, gag ‖ (μεταφ) silence, hush.

φίμωτρον, τό [feemotron] muzzle, gag.

φίνος [feenos] fine.

φιόγκος, ὁ [feeongos] knot, bow.

φιρίκι, τό [feereekee] kind of small apple.

φίρμα, ἡ [feerma] firm ‖ trade name.

φίσα, ἡ [feesa] filing slip ‖ gambling chip.

φίσκα [feeska] brimming over.

φιστίκι, τό [feesteekee] pistachio nut ‖ ~ ἀράπικο monkey nut ‖ peanut.

φιτίλι, τό [feeteelee] wick ‖ (δυναμίτιδος) fuse.

φκιάρι, τό [f'keearee] βλ **φτυάρι**.

φλαμούρι, τό [flamouree] lime wood ‖ lime blossom infusion.

φλάμπουρο, τό [flambouro] pennon standard.

φλάουτο, τό [flaouto] flute.

φλέβα, ἡ [fleva] vein ‖ (μεταλλεύματος) lode ‖ (μεταφ) talent.

Φλεβάρης, ὁ [flevarees] February.

φλέγμα, τό [fleyma] phlegm, mucus ‖ (μεταφ) coolness, unconcern.

φλεγματικός [fleymateekos] phlegmatic ‖ stolid.

φλεγμονή, ἡ [fleymonee] inflammation soreness.

φλέγομαι [fleyome] burn, ignite ‖ (μεταφ) flare up.

φλέγον [fleyon]: ~ ζήτημα topical problem.

φλερτάρω [flertaro] flirt with.

φλέψ, ή [fleps] βλ **φλέβα**.

φληναφῶ [fleenafo] prate, babble, prattle.

φλιτζάνι, τό [fleetzanee] cup(ful).

φλόγα, ή [floya] flame, blaze ‖ (μεταφ) passion, ardour.

φλογέρα, ή [floyera] shepherd's pipe, reed.

φλογερός [floyeros] burning, flaming ‖ (μεταφ) ardent, fervent.

φλογίζω [floyeezo] inflame, kindle.

φλογοβόλον, τό [floyovolon] flamethrower.

φλόγωσις, ή [floyosees] inflammation, soreness.

φλοιός, ὁ [fleeos] peel, rind ‖ (φυστικοῦ) shell ‖ (δένδρου) bark ‖ (γῆς) crust.

φλοῖσβος, ὁ [fleesvos] rippling of waves ‖ babbling.

φλοκάτη, ή [flokatee] thick blanket, peasant's cape.

φλόκος, ὁ [flokos] jib.

φλομώνω [flomono] stun ‖ grow wan.

φλόξ, ή [floks] βλ **φλόγα**.

φλούδα, ή [flouda] βλ **φλοιός**.

φλουρί, τό [flouree] gold coin.

φλυαρία, ή [fleearea] gossiping, chatter, prattle.

φλύαρος [fleearos] talkative.

φλυαρῶ [fleearo] chatter, tattle, prattle.

φλύκταινα, ή [fleektena] blister ‖ pustule.

φλυτζάνι, τό [fleetzanee] cup(ful).

φοβᾶμαι [fovame] be afraid (of).

φοβέρα, ή [fovera] threat, menace, intimidation.

φοβερίζω [fovereezo] threaten, menace, intimidate.

φοβερός [foveros] terrible, frightful ‖ amazing, formidable.

φόβητρον, τό [foveetron] scarecrow ‖ bogey ‖ fright.

φοβητσιάρης [foveetseearees] fearful, timid, timorous.

φοβία, ή [foveea] fear, phobia.

φοβίζω [foveezo] frighten ‖ menace, threaten, intimidate.

φόβος, ὁ [fovos] fear, dread, fright.

φοβοῦμαι [fovoume] βλ **φοβᾶμαι**.

φόδρα, ή [fodra] lining.

φοίνιξ, ὁ [feeneeks] palm tree ‖ (καρπός) date ‖ (bird) phoenix.

φοίτησις, ή [feeteesees] attendance (at school) ‖ frequenting.

φοιτητής, ὁ [feeteetees] student.

φοιτῶ [feeto] be a student, attend a course of studies ‖ frequent.

φόλα, ἡ [fola] dog poison ‖ (παπουτσιοῦ) patch.

φολίς, ή [folees] scale.

φονεύς, ὁ [fonevs] murderer, assassin.

φονεύω [fonevo] murder, kill.

φονιᾶς, ὁ [fonias] murderer.

φονικό, τό [foneeko] murder, homicide, carnage.

φόνος, ὁ [fonos] murder, homicide.

φόντο, τό [fonto] bottom, base, back ‖ (ζωγραφιᾶς) background ‖ (κεφάλαιο) capital.

φόρα, ή [fora] impulse, impetus ‖ force ‖ βγάζω στή ~ bring into the open, uncover.

φορά, ή [fora] force ‖ course, run, impetus ‖ (κατεύθυνσις) direction ‖ (εὐκαιρία) time ‖ ἄλλη ~ another time ‖ ἄλλη μιά ~ once again ‖ μιά ~ once, only once.

φοράδα, ή [forada] mare.

φορατζῆς, ὁ [foratzees] tax collector.

φορβάς, ή [forvas] βλ **φοράδα**.

φορβή, ή [forvee] fodder, forage.

φορεῖον, τό [foreeon] stretcher, litter.

φόρεμα, τό [forema] dress, garment.

φορεσιά, ή [foresia] dress, suit of clothes ‖ attire.

φορεύς, ὁ [forevs] carrier, porter.

φορητός [foreetos] portable, easy to carry.

φόρμα, ή [forma] form, shape ‖ mould, matrix ‖ (ἐργάτου) overall ‖ (ντοκουμέντο) form, document ‖ σέ ~ in good form, in tiptop shape.

φοροδιαφυγή, ή [forodeeafeeyee] tax evasion.

φορολογία, ή [foroloyeea] taxation ‖ tax, rate.

φορολογούμενος, ὁ [foroloyoumenos] taxpayer, ratepayer.

φορολογῶ [foroloyo] tax, put a tax on.

φόρος, ὁ [foros] tax, rate, duty.

φορτηγόν, τό [forteeyon] lorry ‖ (US) truck ‖ (ναυτ) cargo vessel.

φορτηγός [forteeyos] freight-carrying, of transport.

φορτίζω [forteezo] charge with electricity.

φορτικός [forteekos] intrusive, importunate ‖ troublesome.

φορτίον, τό [forteeon] cargo, load ‖ burden, charge, weight.

φορτοεκφορτωτής, ὁ [fortoekfortotees] stevedore.

φόρτος, ὁ [fortos] burden, heavy load.

φορτσάρω [fortsaro] force ‖ intensify ‖ (ἀνέμου) increase, strengthen.

φόρτωμα, τό [fortoma] loading ‖ (μεταφ) burden, care.

φορτώνομαι [fortonome] pester, annoy, bother.

φορτώνω [fortono] load, pile (on) ‖ take on cargo.

φορτωτική, ή [fortoteekee] bill of lading.

φορῶ [foro] wear ‖ put on, get into ‖ carry.

φουγάρο, τό [fouyaro] funnel, flue, tall chimney, smokestack.

φουκαράς, ὁ [foukaras] poor devil ‖ unfortunate fellow.

φούμαρα, τά [foumara] πλ boasting ‖ pie in the sky.

φουμάρω [foumaro] smoke.

φοῦμος, ὁ [foumos] soot ‖ lampblack.

φούντα, ἡ [founta] tassel ‖ tuft, crest.

φουντάρω [fountaro] (ναυτ) sink ‖ cast anchor.

φουντούκι, τό [fountoukee] hazelnut.

φουντώνω [fountono] become bushy ‖ stretch out, spread ‖ expand.

φουντωτός [fountotos] bushy, thick.

φούξια, ἡ [foukseea] fuchsia.

φούρια, ἡ [foureea] haste.

φούρκα, ἡ [fourka] rage, anger ‖ (κρεμάλα) gallows, gibbet.

φουρκέτα, ἡ [fourketa] hairpin.

φουρκίζω [fourkeezo] vex, harass ‖ (κρεμῶ) hang.

φούρναρης, ὁ [fournarees] baker.

φουρνάρικο, τό [fournareeko] bakery, baker's shop.

φουρνέλο, τό [fournelo] grid ‖ blasting charge.

φουρνιά, ἡ [fournia] ovenful ‖ (μεταφ) batch.

φοῦρνος, ὁ [fournos] oven ‖ bakery ‖ kiln, furnace.

φουρτούνα, ἡ [fourtouna] tempest, storm ‖ rough sea ‖ (μεταφ) calamity, misfortune.

φούσκα, ἡ [fouska] bladder ‖ (παιχνίδι) balloon ‖ blister ‖ soap bubble.

φουσκάλα, ἡ [fouskala] blister ‖ bubble.

φουσκί, τό [fouskee] manure, dung.

φουσκοθαλασσιά, ἡ [fouskothalasia] surge of sea.

φούσκωμα, τό [fouskoma] inflation, swelling ‖ swaggering.

φουσκωμένος [fouskomenos] swollen, inflated, puffed up.

φουσκώνω [fouskono] swell, inflate, blow up ‖ (λάστιχο) pump ‖ (μεταφ) exaggerate ‖ (ἐνοχλῶ) irritate ‖ (ζύμην) rise ‖ (ἀναπνοή) puff, pant ‖ (μεταφ) puff o.s. up.

φουσκωτός [fouskotos] puffed, inflated ‖ curved.

φούστα, ἡ [fousta] skirt.

φουστανέλλα, ἡ [foustanela] kilt.

φουστάνι, τό [foustanee] gown, dress, frock.

φούχτα, ἡ [fouhta] handful ‖ hollow of hand.

φραγγέλιον, τό [frangeleeon] whip, lash.

Φράγκικος [frangeekos] Frankish ‖ Roman Catholic ‖ West European.

Φράγκος, ὁ [frangos] Frank ‖ Roman Catholic.

φράγκο, τό [frango] franc ‖ drachma.

Φραγκολεβαντίνος, ὁ [frangolevanteenos] Levantine.

φραγκόπαππας, ὁ [frangopapas] Roman Catholic priest.

φραγκοστάφυλο, τό [frangostafeelo] red currant.

φραγκόσυκο, τό [frangoseeko] prickly pear.

φράγμα, τό [frayma] enclosure, fence ‖ barrage, dam ‖ barrier.

φραγμός, ὁ [fraymos] fence, barrier ‖ (στρατ) barrage.

φράζω [frazo] surround, hedge ‖ bar, block up, stop, obstruct.

φράκο, τό [frako] dress coat, tails.

φράκτης, ὁ [fraktees] fence, enclosure, fencing.

φραμπαλᾶς, ὁ [frambalas] furbelow.

φράντζα, ἡ [frantza] fringe.

φραντζόλα, ἡ [frantzola] long loaf.

φράξιμο, τό [frakseemo] enclosing, fencing ‖ stopping up, blockage.

φράουλα, ἡ [fraoula] strawberry.

φράπα, ἡ [frapa] kind of large citrus fruit grapefruit.

φρασεολογία, ἡ [fraseoloyeea] phraseology

φράσις, ἡ [frasees] phrase ‖ period.

φράσσω [fraso] βλ **φράζω.**

φράχτης, ὁ [frahtees] fence, enclosure, fencing, hedge.

φρέαρ, τό [frear] well ‖ (μεταλλεῖον) pit, shaft.

φρεάτιον, τό [freateeon] small well.

φρεγάδα, ἡ [freyada] frigate.

φρένα, τά [frena] πλ reason, senses ‖ brakes.

φρενάρισμα, τό [frenareesma] braking.

φρενάρω [frenaro] brake ‖ (μεταφ) check.

φρένες, οἱ [frenes] πλ mind, reason, wits ‖ ἔξω φρενῶν off one's head, enraged ‖ unbelievable.

φρενιάζω [freneeazo] get furious, fret and fume.

φρενῖτις, ἡ [freneetees] fury, frenzy ‖ insanity.

φρένο, τό [freno] brake.

φρενοβλαβής [frenovlavees] mentally disturbed.

φρενοκομεῖον, τό [frenokomeeon] madhouse, lunatic asylum.

φρενολογία, ἡ [frenoloyeea] phrenology.

φρενοπαθής [frenopathees] βλ **φρενοβλαβής.**

φρεσκάδα, ἡ [freskada] freshness ‖ coolness, chilliness.

φρεσκάρω [freskaro] freshen, cool ‖ (ὁ καιρός) become worse.

φρέσκο, τό [fresko] fresco ‖ coolness, freshness, chilliness ‖ στό ~ in quod, in prison.

φρέσκος [freskos] fresh, new, recent ‖ cool.

φρικαλέος [freekaleos] horrible, hideous, ghastly.

φρικαλεότης, ἡ [freekaleotees] atrocity, savagery.

φρίκη, ἡ [freekee] terror, horror ‖ (ἐπιφ) frightful!

φρικίασις, ἡ [freekeeasees] shuddering, shivering.

φρικιῶ [freekeeo] shiver, shudder ‖ be disgusted.

φρικτός [freektos] (θέαμα) horrible

ghastly ‖ (ἐμφάνισις) hideous ‖ (καιρός) horrid, vile ‖ awful.

φρικώδης [freekoðees] βλ **φρικτός**.

φρίσσω [freeso] quiver, rustle ‖ shudder ‖ be horrified.

φρόκαλο, τό [frokalo] sweepings, rubbish ‖ broom.

φρόνημα, τό [froneema] opinion, sentiment, morale ‖ ~τα political convictions.

φρονηματίζω [froneemateezo] inspire self-confidence, render self-confident.

φρόνησις, ἡ [froneesees] prudence, wariness, circumspection.

φρόνιμα [froneema] (ἐπιφ) behave yourself!

φρονιμάδα, ἡ [froneemaða] wisdom, prudence ‖ moderation ‖ (παιδιοῦ) quietness, good behaviour ‖ (γυναικός) modesty, chastity.

φρονιμεύω [froneemevo] become prudent, grow wise, be well-behaved.

φρονιμίτης, ὁ [froneemeetees] wisdom tooth.

φρόνιμος [froneemos] reasonable, sound, well-behaved ‖ virtuous, wise.

φροντίζω [fronteezo] look after, care for ‖ see to.

φροντίδα, ἡ [fronteeða] concern, care, anxiety.

φροντίδες, οἱ [fronteeðes] πλ things to do, cares.

φροντίς, ἡ [frontees] βλ **φροντίδα**.

φροντιστήριον, τό [fronteesteereeon] coaching school ‖ prep school.

φρονῶ [frono] think, suppose, believe, consider.

φροῦδος [frouðos] vain, useless, futile.

φρουρά, ἡ [froura] lookout, guard ‖ garrison.

φρούραρχος, ὁ [frourarhos] garrison commander.

φρούριον, τό [froureeon] fortress, stronghold.

φρουρός, ὁ [frouros] guard, sentinel, sentry ‖ (μεταφ) guardian.

φρουρῶ [frouro] guard, keep watch, stand sentry.

φροῦτο, τό [frouto] fruit, dessert.

φρυάττω [freeato] be furious, fume.

φρύγανα, τά [freeyana] πλ dry firewood, twigs.

φρυγανιά, ἡ [freeyania] toast.

φρύδι, τό [freeðee] eyebrow.

φταίξιμο, τό [ftekseemo] fault, error, mistake, blame.

φταίχτης, ὁ [ftehtees] person responsible, culprit.

φταίω [fteo] be responsible, be to blame ‖ make a mistake.

φτάνω [ftano] βλ **φθάνω**.

φτελιά, ἡ [ftelia] elm (tree).

φτέρη, ἡ [fteree] fern.

φτέρνα, ἡ [fterna] heel

φτερνίζομαι [fterneezome] sneeze.

φτέρνισμα, τό [fterneesma] sneeze, sneezing.

φτερό, τό [ftero] feather, plume ‖ wing ‖ (ξεσκονίσματος) feather duster ‖ (αὐτοκινήτου) mudguard ‖ (US) fender.

φτερούγα, ἡ [fterouya] wing.

φτερουγίζω [fterouyeezo] flutter, flap.

φτηναίνω [fteeneno] cheapen, become cheaper, go down.

φτήνεια, ἡ [fteeneea] cheapness, low price.

φτηνός [fteenos] cheap.

φτιά(χ)νομαι [fteea(h)nome] make up one's face ‖ look better.

φτιά(χ)νω [fteea(h)no] arrange, tidy up, correct ‖ (κατασκευάζω) make ‖ have made ‖ do.

φτιασίδι, τό [fteeaseeðee] rouge, cosmetic ‖ make-up.

φτιαχτός [fteeahtos] fabricated, affected.

φτυάρι, τό [fteearee] shovel, spade, scoop.

φτύνω [fteeno] spit, expectorate ‖ spit out.

φτύσιμο, τό [fteeseemo] spitting.

φτυστός [fteestos]: ~ ὁ πατέρας του the spitting image of his father.

φτωχαίνω [ftoheno] impoverish, make poor ‖ become poor.

φτώχεια, ἡ [ftoheea] poverty, destitution.

φτωχεύω [ftohevo] become poor ‖ go bankrupt.

φτωχικό, τό [ftoheeko] humble abode (of a person).

φτωχικός [ftoheekos] poor, mean, scant ‖ shabby.

φτωχός [ftohos] poor, needy, penniless.

φυγαδεύω [feeyaðevo] facilitate s.o.'s escape.

φυγάς, ὁ, ἡ [feeyas] runaway, deserter, fugitive, renegade.

φυγή, ἡ [feeyee] escape, fleeing, flight.

φυγοδικία, ἡ [feeyoðeekeea] default.

φυγόδικος, ὁ, ἡ [feeyoðeekos] defaulter.

φυγόκεντρος [feeyokentros] centrifugal.

φυγόπονος [feeyoponos] lazy ‖ (οὐσ) slacker, shirker.

φυγόστρατος, ὁ [feeyostratos] defaulting conscript, deserter.

φύκια, τά [feekeea] πλ seaweed.

φυλάγομαι [feelayome] take precautions, take care.

φυλάγω [feelayo] guard, protect ‖ mind, tend ‖ (ἀντικείμενον) keep, lay aside ‖ lie in wait for.

φύλακας, ὁ [feelakas] keeper, guardian, watchman, guard, caretaker.

φυλακεῖον, τό [feelakeeon] guardhouse, post.

φυλακή, ἡ [feelakee] prison, jail.

φυλακίζω [feelakeezo] incarcerate, imprison.

φυλάκισις, ἡ [feelakeesees] imprisonment.

φυλακισμένος, ὁ [feelakeesmenos] prisoner.

φύλαξ, ὁ [feelaks] βλ φύλακας.
φυλά(σσ)ω [feela(s)o] βλ φυλάγω.
φυλάττω [feelato] βλ φυλάγω.
φύλαρχος, ὁ [feelarhos] tribal chief.
φυλαχτό, τό [feelahto] talisman, amulet, charm.
φυλετικός [feeleteekos] tribal, racial.
φυλή, ἡ [feelee] race, tribe, line.
φυλλάδα, ἡ [feelaδa] booklet, pamphlet, brochure.
φυλλάδιον, τό [feelaδeeon] pamphlet || instalment, issue, part.
φυλλοκάρδια, τά [feelokarδeea] πλ bottom of one's heart.
φυλλομετρῶ [feelometro] turn pages of, skim over, run through.
φύλλον, τό [feelon] leaf || (λουλουδιοῦ) petal || (χαρτιοῦ κτλ) sheet || (σελίς) page || (πόρτας κτλ) shutter, leaf || (χαρτοπαιξίας) (playing) card || (ἐφημερίς) newspaper || ~ πορείας marching orders.
φυλλοξήρα, ἡ [feelokseera] phylloxera.
φυλλορροῶ [feeloroo] shed leaves, shed petals || (μεταφ) fade (of hope).
φύλλωμα, τό [feeloma] foliage, leafage.
φῦλον, τό [feelon] sex || race.
φυματικός [feemateekos] consumptive, tubercular.
φυματίωσις, ἡ [feemateeosees] tuberculosis, consumption.
φύομαι [feeome] grow, bud, sprout.
φύρα, ἡ [feera] loss of weight, waste.
φυραίνω [feereno] shorten, shrink || lose weight, lose volume.
φύραμα, τό [feerama] paste, dough || blend || (μεταφ) character, sort.
φύρδην [feerδeen]: ~ μίγδην pell-mell, helter-skelter.
φυρός [feeros] cracked, shrunken || lacking in weight.
φυσαλ(λ)ίς, ἡ [feesalees] bubble || blister.
φυσαρμόνικα, ἡ [feesarmoneeka] accordion || mouth organ.
φυσέκι, τό [feesekee] cartridge || roll (of coins).
φυσερό, τό [feesero] bellows.
φύση, ἡ [feesee] nature.
φύσημα, τό [feeseema] breath || puff || breathing.
φυσίγγιον, τό [feeseengeeon] cartridge.
φῦσιγξ, ἡ [feeseenks] ampoule for serum.
φυσικά, τά [feeseeka] πλ physics.
φυσικά [feeseeka] naturally, as a matter of fact || φυσικῶ τῶ λόγω naturally, of course.
φυσική, ἡ [feeseekee] physics, natural philosophy.
φυσικό, τό [feeseeko] custom, habit.
φυσικός [feeseekos] natural || physical || (οὐσ) physicist.
φυσικότης, ἡ [feeseekotees] naturalness, artlessness.
φυσιογνωμία, ἡ [feeseeognomeea] cast of

features || countenance || well-known person.
φυσιοδίφης, ὁ [feeseeoδeefees] naturalist.
φυσιολάτρης, ὁ [feeseeolatrees] lover of nature.
φυσιολογία, ἡ [feeseeologeea] physiology.
φυσιολογικός [feeseeologeekos] physiological || (μεταφ) normal.
φύσις, ἡ [feesees] nature || character temper || φύσει by nature.
φυσομανῶ [feesomano] rage.
φυσῶ [feeso] blow up || puff, blow out || pant || φυσάει it's windy.
φυτεία, ἡ [feeteea] plantation || vegetation bed of vegetables.
φύτε(υ)μα, τό [feete(v)ma] planting.
φυτευτός [feetevtos] planted, cultivated.
φυτεύω [feetevo] plant, lay out || (μεταφ) lodge, stick.
φυτικός [feeteekos] vegetable.
φυτοζωῶ [feetozoo] live in poverty, scrape through.
φυτοκομία, ἡ [feetokomeea] horticulture.
φυτολογία, ἡ [feetologeea] botany.
φυτόν, τό [feeton] plant, vegetable.
φύτρα, ἡ [feetra] germ, embryo || (μεταφ) lineage, origin.
φυτρώνω [feetrono] grow, germinate, sprout.
φυτώριον, τό [feetoreeon] nursery, plantation, seedbed.
φώκια, ἡ [fokeea] seal.
φωλεά, ἡ [folea] nest, den, lair, hole || (μεταφ) hovel.
φωλιάζω [foleeazo] nestle, nest.
φωνάζω [fonazo] shout, call, summon || cry, scream, shriek.
φωνακλᾶς, ὁ [fonaklas] loud talker, noisy talker.
φωνασκῶ [fonasko] bawl, shout.
φωνή, ἡ [fonee] sound || voice || cry, shout, scream.
φωνῆεν, τό [fonien] vowel.
φωνητική, ἡ [foneeteekee] phonetics.
φωνητικός [foneeteekos] vocal || phonetic phonic.
φωνοληψία, ἡ [fonoleepseea] recording.
φωνοταινία, ἡ [fonoteneea] talkie.
φωρῶμαι [forome] be caught red-handed || be shown up.
φῶς, τό [fos] light || (μεταφ) sight || knowledge, illumination.
φωστήρ(ας), ὁ [fosteer(as)] luminary || (μεταφ) learned, erudite person.
φωσφόρος, ὁ [fosforos] phosphorus.
φῶτα, τά [fota] πλ lights || (μεταφ) knowledge, learning || (ἐκκλ) Epiphany.
φωταγωγός, ὁ [fotayoyos] light well, skylight.
φωταγωγῶ [fotayoyo] illuminate.
φωταέριον, τό [fotaereeon] gas(lighting).
φωταυγής [fotavyees] bright, brilliant luminous.

φωταψία, ή [fotapseea] illumination.

φωτεινός [foteenos] luminous, light, bright ‖ clear, lucid.

φωτιά, ή [fotia] fire ‖ (καπνιστοῦ) light ‖ (μεταφ) great heat ‖ fury ‖ (σέ τιμή) costliness.

φωτίζω [foteezo] illuminate, light up, light ‖ enlighten, inform.

φώτιση, ή [foteesee] βλ φώτισις.

φώτισις, ή [foteesees] enlightenment ‖ inspiration.

φωτισμός, ὁ [foteesmos] lighting, illumination.

φωτοβολία, ή [fotovoleea] brightness, luminosity.

φωτοβολίς, ή [fotovolees] flare.

φωτογενής [fotoyenees] photogenic.

φωτογραφεῖον, τό [fotoyrafeeon] photographic studio.

φωτογραφία, ή [fotoyrafeea] photograph ‖ photography.

φωτογραφική, ή [fotoyrafeekee] photography ‖ ~ μηχανή camera.

φωτογραφικός [fotoyrafeekos] photographic.

φωτογράφος, ὁ [fotoyrafos] photographer.

φωτόμετρον, τό [fotometron] light meter.

φωτοσκίασις, ή [fotoskeeasees] shading, light and shade.

φωτοστέφανος, ὁ [fotostefanos] halo ‖ (μεταφ) glory, prestige.

φωτοτυπία, ή [fototeepeea] photostatic copy.

φωτοχυσία, ή [fotoheeseea] illumination.

Χ, χ

χαβάνι, τό [havanee] (brass) mortar.

χαβᾶς, ὁ [havas] tune, air, melody.

χαβιάρι, τό [haviaree] caviar.

χαβούζα, ή [havouza] cistern, reservoir.

χαγιάτι, τό [hayiatee] upper gallery round courtyard.

χάδια, τά [hadeea] πλ petting, cajolery.

χαζεύω [hazevo] gape ‖ idle about, loiter.

χάζι, τό [hazee] pleasure, delight ‖ τό κάνω ~ it entertains me.

χαζός [hazos] stupid, silly, foolish.

χαϊβάνι, τό [haeevanee] beast ‖ (μεταφ) jackass.

χάϊδεμα, τό [haeedema] caressing, pat, stroke ‖ (μεταφ) cajolery.

χαϊδευτικός [haeedevteekos] caressing, affectionate ‖ (άνεμος) soft.

χαϊδεμένος [haeedemenos] spoilt.

χαϊδεύομαι [haeedevome] nuzzle, cuddle ‖ seek attention.

χαϊδεύω [haeedevo] caress, fondle, pat ‖ pet, spoil ‖ fawn upon.

χαϊδιάρης [haeedeearees] fond of being caressed.

χαίνω [heno] gape, be wide open.

χαιρέκακος [herekakos] malicious, mischievous.

χαίρετε [herete] (ἐπιφ) hello!, good day! ‖ be seeing you!

χαιρετίζω [hereteezo] hail, greet ‖ salute.

χαιρέτισμα, τό [hereteesma] salute, greeting, salutation, bow.

χαιρετισμός, ὁ [hereteesmos] βλ χαιρέτισμα.

χαιρετῶ [hereto] βλ χαιρετίζω.

χαίρομαι [herome] be happy ‖ enjoy.

χαίρω [hero] be pleased ‖ ~ ἄκρας ὑγείας be in tiptop shape.

χαίτη, ή [hetee] mane, shock of hair.

χακί, τό [hakee] khaki.

χάλαζα, ή [halaza] βλ χαλάζι.

χαλάζι, τό [halazee] hail.

χαλαζίας, ὁ [halazeeas] quartz.

χαλάλι [halalee]: ~ σου you merit it, you can have it.

χαλαρός [halaros] relaxed, slack, loose.

χαλαρώνω [halarono] unbend ‖ (σχοινί) loosen, slacken ‖ (μεταφ) relax ‖ (προσπάθειαν) abate, ease up ‖ (ζῆλον) cool.

χάλασμα, τό [halasma] ruin, demolition ‖ (μηχανῆς) putting out of order ‖ ruin.

χαλασμένος [halasmenos] rotten, turned bad ‖ broken, not working ‖ damaged, demolished.

χαλασμός, ὁ [halasmos] demolition, destruction ‖ (μεταφ) disturbance, storm, excitement ‖ catastrophe.

χαλάστρα, ή [halastra]: μοῦ κάναν ~ they foiled my plans, they cramped my style.

χαλβᾶς, ὁ [halvas] halva ‖ (μεταφ) indolent person, silly fellow.

χαλεπός [halepos] arduous, difficult, wearisome.

χαλί, τό [halee] carpet, rug.

χάλια, τά [haleea] πλ bad condition, sad plight.

χαλίκι, τό [haleekee] pebble, small stone, gravel.

χαλιμά, ή [haleema]: τά παραμύθια τῆς ~ς Arabian Nights.

χαλιναγωγῶ [haleenayoyo] lead by the bridle ‖ (μεταφ) check, curb ‖ (πάθη) control, curb.

χαλινάρι, τό [haleenaree] bridle, bit, rein ‖ (μεταφ) curbing, holding back.

χαλινός, ὁ [haleenos] βλ χαλινάρι.

χαλκᾶς, ὁ [halkas] ring, link.

χαλκεῖον, τό [halkeeon] coppersmith's forge ‖ (μεταφ) fabrication, concoction.

χαλκεύω [halkevo] work copper ‖ (μεταφ) fabricate.

χαλκιᾶς, ὁ [halkeeas] coppersmith ‖ tinsmith.

χάλκινος [halkeenos] of copper.

χαλκογραφία, ή [halkoyrafeea] copper plate engraving, art of copperplating.

χαλκομανία, ή *[halkomaneea] transfer design.

χαλκός, ὁ [halkos] copper, brass, bronze.
χαλκωματᾶς, ὁ [halkomatas] βλ χαλκιᾶς.
χαλνῶ [halno] βλ χαλῶ.
χαλύβδινος [haleevdenos] made of steel.
χάλυψ, ὁ [haleeps] steel.
χαλῶ [halo] demolish, break, ruin, spoil |
(φθείρω) wear out | (νεῦρα) fret |
(ὑγείαν) break down | (δαπανῶ) spend,
consume ‖ (διαφθείρω) corrupt, pervert
| (νόμισμα) change ‖ (δόντι) decay |
(κρέας) taint, go bad ‖ | ~ τόν κόσμον
move heaven and earth, make a fuss.
χαμαί [hame] down, on the ground.
χαμαιλέων, ὁ [hameleon] chameleon |
(βοτ) ground thistle.
χαμαιπετής [hamepetees] creeping |
(μεταφ) grovelling, servile.
χαμαιτυπεῖον, τό [hameteepeeon] brothel,
whorehouse.
χαμάλης, ὁ [hamalees] porter ‖ (μεταφ)
vulgar fellow, scoundrel.
χαμαλίκι, τό [hamaleekee] hard work,
arduous labour.
χαμάμι, τό [hamamee] Turkish bath.
χαμένα [hamena]: τά ἔχω ~ be mixed up,
be bewildered.
χαμένος [hamenos] lost, disappeared |
(στά χαρτιά) loser | (μεταφ) scoundrel,
rascal ‖ scatterbrain.
χαμερπής [hamerpees] vile, mean, crawl-
ing, low.
χαμηλός [hameelos] low | (φωνή) gentle,
soft, subdued.
χαμηλοφώνως [hameelofonos] in an
undertone, softly.
χαμηλώνω [hameelono] lower, reduce,
bring down | subside.
χαμίνι, τό [hameenee] street urchin, mischievous youngster.
χαμόγελο, τό [hamoyelo] smile.
χαμογελῶ [hamoyelo] smile.
χαμόκλαδο, τό [hamoklado] shrub.
χαμομήλι, τό [hamomeelee] camomile.
χαμός, ὁ [hamos] loss, destruction, ruin
death.
χάμουρα, τά [hamoura] πλ harness, trappings.
χαμπάρι, τό [hambaree] piece of news
παίρνω ~ become aware, perceive.
χαμψί, τό [hampsee] anchovy.
χάμω [hamo] βλ χαμαί.
χάνδαξ, ὁ [handaks] ditch, drain, trench
(ὀχυροῦ) moat.
χάνδρα, ἡ [handra] bead.
χάνι, τό [hanee] country inn, lodging house.
χανούμισσα, ἡ [hanoumeesa] Turkish lady.
χαντάκι, τό [hantakee] βλ χάνδαξ.
χαντακώνω [hantakono] (μεταφ) destroy,
ruin.
χάντρα, ἡ [hantra] βλ χάνδρα.
χάνομαι [hanome] lose o.s., ruin o.s., get
lost ‖ νά χαθῆς go to hell! | χάσου get
out of my sight!

χάνω [hano] lose, go astray | (εὐκαιρίαν)
let slip | (καιρόν) waste time | (τραῖνο)
lose, miss | become disconcerted, get
confused.
χάος, τό [haos] chaos, wild disorder
bottomless pit.
χάπι, τό [hapee] pill.
χαρά, ἡ [hara] joy | (ὑπερβολική) delight,
glee ‖ pleasure, enjoyment | ~ Θεοῦ
delight ‖ μιά ~ very well, splendidly |
γειά ~ so long!, good-bye! | hello! | ~ στό
πρᾶμα wonderful!, it's nothing! (ironic).
χαραγή, ἡ [harayee] tracing, engraving |
incision, cut.
χάραγμα, τό [harayma] βλ χαραγή.
χαράδρα, ἡ [haradra] ravine, gorge, gully.
χαράζω [harazo] cut, engrave | rule lines ‖
trace ‖ (δρόμον κτλ) mark out, lay out.
χάρακας, ὁ [harakas] straight edge, ruler.
χαρακιά, ἡ [harakia] scratch, incision
mark ‖ groove ‖ (γραμμή) line, stroke.
χαρακτήρ, ὁ [harakteer] character, letter
temper, nature.
χαρακτηρίζω [harakteereezo] define, qual-
ify ‖ characterize.
χαρακτηριστικά, τά [harakteereesteeka] πλ
person's features.
χαρακτηριστικός [harakteereesteekos] typical, distinctive, characteristic.
χαράκτης, ὁ [haraktees] engraver, carver.
χαρακτική, ἡ [harakteekee] art of engraving.
χαράκωμα, τό [harakoma] trench | (γραμ-
μῶν) ruling.
χαρακώνω [harakono] rule lines, line
scratch, incise.
χαραμάδα, ἡ [haramada] fissure, crack
crevice.
χαράματα, τά [haramata] πλ dawn daybreak.
χαραματιά, ἡ [haramatia] incision, crack |
(ἐπιφανείας) scratch, trace, engraving.
χαραμίζω [harameezo] waste, spend uselessly.
χάραξις, ἡ [haraksees] engraving, tracing
incision | (δρόμου) laying out.
χαράσσω [harasso] engrave, carve |
(γραμμές) rule | map out, trace | (δρόμον)
lay out.
χαράτσι, τό [haratsee] (μεταφ) oppressive
tax.
χαρατσώνω [haratsono] exact money from
| tax oppressively.
χαραυγή, ἡ [haravyee] daybreak, dawn.
χάρβαλο, τό [harvalo] ruin, dilapidated
building.
χαρέμι, τό [haremee] harem.
χάρη, ἡ [haree] grace, charm | good point
| favour ‖ gratitude | ~ σέ σένα thanks
to you | λόγου ~ for instance.
χαρίεις [hariees] graceful, charming,
delightful.
χαριεντίζομαι [harienteezome] be in a

teasing mood, jest ‖ become very charming.

χαρίζομαι [hareezome] be indulgent ‖ favour.

χαρίζω [hareezo] give, donate, present ‖ (χρέος κτλ) remit.

χάρις, ή [harees] grace, delightfulness ‖ (ποινής) remittance, pardon ‖ ~ εἰς thanks to ‖ χάριν τοῦ for, on behalf of ‖ παραδείγματος χάριν for example, for instance ‖ πρός χάριν σου for your sake, on your behalf.

χάρισμά, τό [hareesma] talent, gift ‖ accomplishment ‖ (ἐπίρ) free, gratis, for nothing.

χαριστική [hareesteekee]: ~ βολή coup de grâce.

χαριστικός [hareesteekos] prejudiced, partial.

χαριτολογῶ [hareetoloγo] jest, speak wittily, speak amusingly.

χαριτωμένος [hareetomenos] charming, enchanting.

χάρμα, τό [harma] delight, source of joy.

χαρμάνι, τό [harmanee] mixture, blend.

χαρμόσυνος [harmoseenos] cheerful, glad.

χαροκόπος, ὁ [harokopos] pleasure-loving person, rake.

χάρος, ὁ [haros] death.

χαρούμενος [haroumenos] cheerful, joyful, happy.

χαρούπι, τό [haroupee] carob.

χαρταετός, ὁ [hartaetos] kite.

χαρτένιος [harteneeos] of paper.

χαρτζιλίκι, τό [hartzeeleekee] pocket money.

χάρτης, ὁ [hartees] paper ‖ (γεωγραφικός) map ‖ (συνταγματικός) charter ‖ ~ ὑγείας toilet paper.

χαρτί, τό [hartee] paper ‖ (χαρτοπαιξίας) playing card.

χάρτινος [harteenos] βλ χαρτένιος.

χαρτόδετος [hartoδetos] paper-bound.

χαρτοκοπτήρας, ὁ [hartokopteeras] paper knife.

χαρτόνι, τό [hartonee] cardboard, pasteboard.

χαρτονόμισμα, τό [hartonomeesma] banknote ‖ (US) bill ‖ paper money.

χαρτοπαίκτης, ὁ [hartopektees] gambler, card player.

χαρτοπαιξία, ή [hartopekseea] gambling, card playing.

χαρτοπόλεμος, ὁ [hartopolemos] confetti throwing.

χαρτοπώλης, ὁ [hartopolees] stationer, paper merchant.

χαρτόσημον, τό [hartoseemon] stamp tax.

χαρτοφυλάκιον, τό [hartofeelakeeon] letter-case, briefcase ‖ (μεταφ) portfolio.

χαρτοφύλαξ, ὁ [hartofeelaks] briefcase ‖ (ἐκκλ) archivist.

χαρωπός [haropos] cheerful, happy.

χασάπης, ὁ [hasapees] butcher.

χασάπικο, τό [hasapeeko] butcher's shop.

χασάπικος, ὁ [hasapeekos] kind of circular dance.

χασές, ὁ [hases] cotton cloth.

χάση, ή [hasee]: στή ~ καί στή φέξη once in a blue moon.

χάσιμο, τό [haseemo] loss.

χασίσι, τό [haseesee] hashish.

χάσκω [hasko] yawn, gape ‖ stand ajar.

χάσμα, τό [hasma] abyss, pit ‖ lacuna, gap.

χασμούρημα, τό [hasmoureema] yawning, yawn.

χασμουριέμαι [hasmourieme] yawn.

χασμωδία, ή [hasmoδeea] hiatus ‖ disorder, confusion.

χασομερῶ [hasomero] be idle ‖ hang around, linger.

χασούρα, ή [hasoura] loss.

χαστούκι, τό [hastoukee] slap, smack, clout.

χατζής, ὁ [hatzees] pilgrim, hadji.

χατίρι, τό [hateeree] favour, good turn ‖ γιά τό ~ σου for your sake.

χαυλιόδους, ὁ [havleeoδous] tusk.

χαῦνος [havnos] slack, indolent ‖ faint-hearted.

χαφιές, ὁ [hafies] stool, nark, agent, informer.

χάφτω [hafto] swallow, gobble down ‖ (μεταφ) take in.

χαχανίζω [hahaneezo] burst into laughter, laugh loudly.

χάχας, ὁ [hahas] moron, idiot.

χαψιά, ή [hapsia] mouthful.

χαώδης [haoδees] chaotic, confused.

χέζομαι [hezome] be in a fright, be scared ‖ χέστηκα I don't give a damn.

χέζω [hezo] defecate ‖ send to the devil.

χείλι, τό [heelee] lip ‖ (μεταφ) brink, verge ‖ (ποτηριοῦ) brim, rim.

χειλικός [heeleekos] labial.

χεῖλος, τό [heelos] βλ χείλι.

χειμάζομαι [heemazome] undergo hardship.

χείμαρρος, ὁ [heemaros] torrent, torrent bed.

χειμαρρώδης [heemaroδees] torrential, impetuous.

χειμερινός [heemereenos] winter, wintry.

χειμών(ας), ὁ [heemon(as)] winter.

χειμωνιάζει [heemoneeazee] winter approaches.

χειμωνιάτικος [heemoneeateekos] βλ χειμερινός.

χείρ, ή [heer] βλ χέρι.

χειραγωγῶ [heeraγoγo] lead by the hand ‖ (μεταφ) lead, conduct.

χειράμαξα, ή [heeramaksa] handbarrow, wheelbarrow.

χειραφετῶ [heerafeto] liberate, emancipate ‖ manumit.

χειραψία, ή [heerapseea] shake of the hand.

χειρίζομαι [heereezome] handle, manipulate, manage ‖ (μηχανήν) drive.

χειρισμός, ὁ [heereesmos] manipulation, working, driving ‖ (ὑποθέσεως) handling, management.

χειριστήρια, τά [heereesteereea] πλ controls of a machine.

χειριστής, ὁ [heereestees] operator ‖ pilot.

χείριστος [heereestos] worst.

χειροβομβίς, ή [heerovomvees] grenade.

χειρόγραφον, τό [heeroyrafon] manuscript.

χειροθετῶ [heerotheto] ordain.

χειροκίνητος [heerokeeneetos] hand-operated.

χειροκρότημα, τό [heerokroteema] clapping, applause.

χειροκροτῶ [heerokroto] applaud, cheer, clap.

χειρόκτιον, τό [heerokteeon] glove, gauntlet.

χειρόμακτρον, τό [heeromaktron] towel, napkin.

χειρομαντεία, ή [heeromanteea] palm-reading.

χειρονομία, ή [heeronomeea] flourish, gesture ‖ gesticulation.

χειροπέδη, ή [heeropedee] pair of hand-cuffs.

χειροπιαστός [heeropeeastos] tangible.

χειροπόδαρα [heeropodara] hand and foot.

χειροποίητος [heeropieetos] handmade.

χειρότερα [heerotera] worse.

χειροτερεύω [heeroterevo] worsen, deteriorate.

χειρότερος [heeroteros] worse ‖ ὁ ~ the worst.

χειροτεχνία, ή [heerotehneea] handicraft.

χειροτονία, ή [heerotoneea] ordination, consecration (of a bishop).

χειρουργεῖον, τό [heerouryeeon] operating theatre.

χειρουργική, ή [heerouryeekee] surgery.

χειρουργικός [heerouryeekos] surgical.

χειρουργός, ὁ [heerouryos] surgeon.

χειροφίλημα, τό [heerofeeleema] kissing of the hand.

χειρωνακτικός [heeronakteekos] manual.

χέλι, τό [helee] eel.

χελιδόνι, τό [heleedonee] βλ χελιδών.

χελιδών, ή [heleedon] swallow.

χελώνα, ή [helona] tortoise, turtle.

χεράκι, τό [herakee] tiny hand.

χέρι, τό [heree] hand ‖ arm ‖ (χειρολαβή) handle ‖ (μπογιᾶς) coat ‖ (στὸ πλύσιμο) treatment, going-over ‖ ~ ~ hand-in-hand ‖ ~ μέ ~ quickly, directly ‖ βάζω ἕνα ~ give a hand ‖ βάζω ~ lay hands on, fondle ‖ ἀπό πρῶτο ~ at first hand.

χερούλι, τό [heroulee] handle, haft ‖ (στάμνας) ear.

χερσαῖος [herseos] terrestrial ‖ (κλίμα) continental

χερσόνησος, ή [hersoneesos] peninsula.

χέρσος [hersos] uncultivated (land), fallow, waste.

χέσιμο, τό [heseemo] defecation ‖ (μεταφ) fright, terror ‖ volley of abuse.

χηλή, ή [heelee] hoof.

χημεία, ή [heemeea] chemistry.

χημικός [heemeekos] chemical ‖ (οὐσ) chemist.

χήν, ὁ [heen] gander.

χήνα, ή [heena] goose.

χήρα, ή [heera] widow.

χηρεύω [heerevo] become widowed (θέσεως) be unoccupied, be vacant.

χῆρος, ὁ [heeros] widower.

χθές [hthes] yesterday.

χθεσινός [htheseenos] of yesterday (πρόσφατος) latest, recent.

χθόνιος [hthoneeos] infernal.

χί, τό [hee] the letter X.

χιαστί [heeastee] crossways, crosswise, diagonally.

χίλια [heeleea]: ~ δύο a hundred and one.

χιλιάρικο, τό [heeleeareeko] note of a thousand drachmas.

χιλιάς, ή [heeleeas] thousand.

χιλιετηρίς, ή [heelieteerees] βλ χιλιετία.

χιλιετία, ή [heelieteea] millenium.

χιλιόγραμμον, τό [heelioyramon] kilo-gramme.

χίλιοι [heeliee] thousand.

χιλιόμετρον, τό [heelieometron] kilometre.

χιλιοστημόριον, τό [heelieosteemoreeon] thousandth part.

χιλιοστόν, τό [heeleeoston] millimetre ‖ thousandth part.

χιλιοστός [heeleeostos] thousandth.

χίμαιρα, ή [heemera] chimera ‖ (μεταφ) illusion.

χιμαιρικός [heemereekos] fanciful, visionary.

χιμπαντζῆς, ὁ [heempantzees] chimpanzee.

χιονάνθρωπος, ὁ [heeonanthropos] snow-man.

χιονᾶτος [heeonatos] snow-white, snowy.

χιόνι, τό [heeonee] snow.

χιονιά, ή [heeonia] snowy weather ‖ snow-ball.

χιονίζει [heeoneezee] it is snowing.

χιονίστρα, ή [heeoneestra] chilblain.

χιονοδρομία, ή [heeonodromeea] skiing.

χιονοθύελλα, ή [heeonothiela] snowstorm, blizzard.

χιονόνερο, τό [heeononero] sleet, melted snow.

χιονοπέδιλον, τό [heeonopedeelon] snow-shoe.

χιονοστιβάς, ή [heeonosteevas] avalanche snowdrift.

χιοῦμορ, τό [heeoumor] wit, humour ‖ ~ιστικός humorous, humoristic.

χιτών, ὁ [heeton] robe, tunic ‖ (ματιοῦ) cornea.

χιτώνιον, τό [heetoneeon] tunic || jacket.

χιών, ή [heeon] βλ χιόνι.

χλαίνη, ή [hlenee] greatcoat || (ναυτ) duffel coat || cloak, capote.

χλαμύς, ή [hlamees] mantle.

χλευάζω [hlevazo] mock, scoff at, make fun of.

χλευαστικός [hlevasteekos] mocking, sarcastic, derisive.

χλιαίνω [hlieno] make tepid || become luke-warm.

χλιαρός [hleearos] tepid, lukewarm |, (άνεμος) mild || (μεταφ) weak, lax.

χλιδή, ή [hleeδee] luxury, voluptuousness

χλιμιντρίζω [hleemeentreezo] neigh, whinny.

χλοερός [hloeros] green, fresh, verdant.

χλόη, ή [hloee] grass, turf, lawn || green-ness, verdure.

χλωμάδα, ή [hlomaδa] paleness.

χλωμιάζω [hlomeeazo] (go) pale || blanch.

χλωμός [hlomos] pale, pallid, wan.

χλώριον, τό [hloreeon] chlorine, chloride.

χλωρίς, ή [hlorees] flora.

χλωρός [hloros] green, unseasoned || fresh.

χλωροφόρμιον, τό [hloroformeeon] chloro-form.

χλωροφύλλη, ή [hlorofeelee] chlorophyll.

χνάρι, τό [hnaree] pattern, model || track.

χνότα, τά [hnota] βλ χνώτο.

χνούδι, τό [hnouδee] down, fuzz, fluff.

χνουδωτός [hnouδotoς] downy, fluffy.

χνώτο, τό [hnoto] breath.

χοάνη, ή [hoanee] crucible, melting pot || horn.

χόβολη, ή [hovolee] embers, burning charcoal.

χοίρειον [heereeon]: ~ λίπος lard.

χοιρίδιον, τό [heereeδeeon] young pig, piglet.

χοιρινό, τό [heereeno] pork.

χοιρομέρι, τό [heeromeree] ham, bacon.

χοῖρος, ὁ [heeros] pig, hog, swine.

χολέρα, ή [holera] cholera.

χολή, ή [holee] bile || (ζώου) gall || (μεταφ) rancour, bitterness.

χολιάζω [holeeazo] get irritated || irritate || lose one's temper.

χολόλιθος, ὁ [hololeethos] gallstone.

χολοσκάνω [holoskano] afflict, grieve, exasperate || get riled.

χολώδης [holoδes] bilious || (μεταφ) irascible.

χονδρικός [honδreekos] wholesale.

χονδροειδής [honδroeeδees] rough, clumsy, coarse || (ψεῦδος) flagrant || vulgar.

χόνδρος, τό [honδros] cartilage || grit.

χονδρός [honδros] big, fat, stout, thick || (εἰς τρόπους) vulgar, unpolished || (ἀστεῖον) coarse.

χονδρύνω [honδreeno] βλ χοντραίνω.

χοντραίνω [hontreno] become fat, make thicker, put on weight.

χοντροκέφαλος [hontrokefalos] stupid, thickheaded || obstinate, headstrong.

χοντροκοπιά, ή [hontrokopia] clumsy job of work.

χόντρος, τό [hontros] thickness, stoutness.

χοντρός [hontros] βλ χονδρός.

χορδή, ή [horδee] chord, string || (ἀνατ) cord.

χορδίζω [horδeezo] wind up, key, tune.

χορεία, ή [horeea] clique, group, body, clan.

χορευτής, ὁ [horevtees] dancer || partner.

χορευτικός [horevteekos] for dancing, of dancing.

χορεύω [horevo] dance || dance with.

χορήγησις, ή [horeeyeesees] granting, giving, supplying.

χορηγός, ὁ [horeeyos] purveyor, furnisher, supplier || donor.

χορηγῶ [horeeyo] provide, allocate, supply, grant.

χορογραφία, ή [horoγrafeea] choreography.

χοροδιδάσκαλος, ὁ [horoδeeδaskalos] dancing master.

χοροεσπερίς, ή [horoesperees] ball, dancing party.

χοροπηδῶ [horopeeδo] leap about, gambol, caper.

χορός, ὁ [horos] dancing, dance || chorus, choir.

χοροστατῶ [horostato] conduct divine service.

χόρτα, τά [horta] πλ green vegetables, wild greens.

χορταίνω [horteno] have enough, satiate || satisfy || (βαριέμαι) get bored with.

χορτάρι, τό [hortaree] grass.

χορταρικά, τά [hortareeka] πλ vegetables, greens.

χορτασμός, ὁ [hortasmos] satisfaction, satiety.

χορταστικός [hortasteekos] satisfying, sub-stantial, filling || abundant.

χορτάτος [hortatos] satisfied, satiated.

χόρτον, τό [horton] grass, herb || (ἄγριον) weed.

χορτόσουπα, ή [hortosoupa] vegetable soup.

χορτοφάγος [hortofaγos] vegetarian || (ζῶον) herbivorous.

χορωδία, ή [horoδeea] choir, chorus.

χουζούρι, τό [houzouree] rest, idleness, leisure.

χουλιάρα, ή [houleeara] ladle.

χουλιάρι, τό [houleearee] spoon.

χουμᾶς, ὁ [hourmas] date.

χοῦς, ὁ [hous] dust, earth.

χούφτα, ή [houfta] handful || hollow of hand.

χουφτιά, ή [houftia] handful.

χοχλακίζω [hohlakeezo] boil, simmer.

χράμι, τό [hramee] handwoven sheet, woollen coverlet.

χρεία, ἡ [hreea] necessity, lack ‖ indigence, poverty.

χρειάζομαι [hreeazome] lack, want, require ‖ be necessary, be useful.

χρειώδης [hreeodees] necessary, useful.

χρεμετίζω [hremeteezo] neigh, whinny.

χρεόγραφον, τό [hreoyrafon] security, debenture, bond.

χρέος, τό [hreos] debt ‖ obligation.

χρεωκοπία, ἡ [hreokopeea] bankruptcy, failure.

χρεωκοπῶ [hreokopo] go bankrupt, break.

χρεωλυσία, ἡ [hreoleeseea] amortization, sinking fund.

χρεώνομαι [hreonome] get into debt.

χρεώνω [hreono] debit, charge.

χρεωστάσιον, τό [hreostaseeon] moratorium.

χρεώστης, ὁ [hreostees] debtor.

χρεωστῶ [hreosto] be in debt, owe, be indebted (to) ‖ be obliged.

χρῆμα(τα) [hreema(ta)] πλ money.

χρηματίζομαι [hreemateezome] take bribes ‖ hoard up money.

χρηματίζω [hreemateezo] serve as, be.

χρηματικός [hreemateekos] of money, monetary.

χρηματιστήριον, τό [hreemateesteereeon] stock exchange.

χρηματιστής, ὁ [hreemateestees] stockbroker.

χρηματοδοτῶ [hreematodoto] finance, invest.

χρηματοκιβώτιον, τό [hreematokeevotteeon] safe, strongbox, cashbox.

χρησιμεύω [hreeseemevo] be useful ‖ be good for, serve.

χρησιμοποίησις, ἡ [hreeseemopieesees] employment, utilization.

χρησιμοποιῶ [hreeseemopeeo] use, utilize, make use of.

χρήσιμος [hreeseemos] useful, handy.

χρησιμότης, ἡ [hreeseemotees] usefulness, utility, benefit.

χρῆσις, ἡ [hreesees] use, usage, employment ‖ enjoyment ‖ application ‖ (οἰκ) financial year ‖ πρός χρῆσιν for the use ‖ ἐν χρήσει in use, used.

χρησμός, ὁ [hreesmos] oracle, divination.

χρηστοήθης [hreestoeethees] honest, moral, honourable, upright.

χρηστός [hreestos] honourable, upright, virtuous.

χρίζω [hreezo] βλ χρίω.

χρίσμα, τό [hreesma] chrism, unction ‖ anointing.

χριστιανικός [hreesteeaneekos] Christian.

χριστιανισμός, ὁ [hreesteeaneesmos] Christianity.

χριστιανός, ὁ [hreesteeanos] Christian.

χριστιανοσύνη, ἡ [hreesteeanoseenee] Christendom.

Χριστός, ὁ [hreestos] Christ.

Χριστούγεννα, τά [hreestouyena] πλ Christmas.

χρίω [hreeo] anoint ‖ plaster.

χροιά, ἡ [hreea] complexion, colour ‖ shade, tone, nuance.

χρονιά, ἡ [hroneea] year.

χρονιάτικο, τό [hroneeateeko] year's payment.

χρονίζω [hroneezo] linger on ‖ be persistent ‖ be one year dead.

χρονικά, τά [hroneeka] πλ annals.

χρονικογράφος, ὁ [hroneekoyrafos] chronicler.

χρονικόν, τό [hroneekon] chronicle.

χρονικός [hroneekos] of time, temporal.

χρόνιος [hroneeos] chronic, enduring, lasting.

χρονογράφημα, τό [hronoyrafeema] newspaper column, topical comment.

χρονογράφος, ὁ [hronoyrafos] writer of newspaper articles (special features).

χρονολογία, ἡ [hronoloyeea] date ‖ chronology.

χρονολογοῦμαι [hronoloyoume] date from, be dated.

χρονόμετρον, τό [hronometron] chronometer.

χρόνος, ὁ [hronos] time, duration ‖ age, period ‖ (γραμμ) tense, quantity ‖ ὁ ~ year ‖ πρό χρόνων some years ago ‖ τοῦ χρόνου next year ‖ χρόνια πολλά! happy name day!, happy birthday!, many happy returns!

χρονοτριβῶ [hronotreevo] linger, loiter.

χρυσαλλίς, ἡ [hreesalees] chrysalis.

χρυσάνθεμον, τό [hreesanthemon] chrysanthemum.

χρυσάφι, τό [hreesafee] gold.

χρυσαφικά, τά [hreesafeeka] πλ jewellery

χρυσή, ἡ [hreesee] jaundice.

χρυσικός, ὁ [hreeseekos] goldsmith ‖ jeweller.

χρυσίον, τό [hreeseeon] wealth, riches.

χρυσόδετος [hreesodetos] mounted in gold

χρυσοθήρας, ὁ [hreesotheeras] gold digger prospector.

χρυσοκέντητος [hreesokenteetos] embroidered with gold.

χρυσόμαλλον [hreesomalon]: ~ δέρας golden fleece.

χρυσοπωλεῖον, τό [hreesopoleeon] βλ χρυσοχοεῖον.

χρυσός, ὁ [hreesos] gold ‖ (ἐπίθ) golden ‖ (μεταφ) kind-hearted, adorable.

χρυσοῦς [hreesous] golden, of gold.

χρυσοχοεῖον, τό [hreesohoeeon] jeweller s shop, goldsmith's shop.

χρυσοχόος, ὁ [hreesohoos] goldsmith ‖ jeweller.

χρυσόψαρο, τό [hreesopsaro] goldfish

χρυσώνω [hreesono] gild, gold-plate.

χρυσωρυχεῖον, τό [hreesoreeheeon] gold mine.

χρῶμα, τό [hroma] colour, tint, hue ‖ (μπογιά) paint, dye ‖ complexion.

χρωματίζω [hromateezo] colour, paint, dye, tint.

χρωματικός [hromateekos] chromatic ‖ of colour.

χρωματισμός, ὁ [hromateesmos] colouring, painting.

χρωματιστός [hromateestos] coloured.

χρώμιον, τό [hromeeon] chromium, chrome.

χρωστήρ, ὁ [hrosteer] paintbrush.

χρωστικός [hrosteekos] colouring.

χρωστῶ [hrosto] βλ χρεωστῶ.

χταπόδι, τό [htapodee] octopus.

χτένα, ἡ [htena] βλ χτένι.

χτένι, τό [htenee] comb.

χτενίζω [hteneezo] comb ‖ (ὁμιλίαν κτλ) polish up.

χτένισμα, τό [hteneesma] combing ‖ hairstyle.

χτές [htes] βλ χθές.

χτεσινός [hteseenos] βλ χθεσινός.

χτῆμα, τό [hteema] βλ κτῆμα.

χτίζω [hteezo] βλ κτίζω.

χτικιάρης, ὁ [hteekeearees] consumptive person.

χτικιό, τό [hteekio] tuberculosis ‖ (μεταφ) torture, anguish.

χτίριο, τό [hteereeo] βλ κτίριον.

χτίσιμο, τό [hteeseemo] βλ κτίσιμον.

χτίστης, ὁ [hteestees] bricklayer, builder.

χτυπάω [hteepao] βλ χτυπῶ.

χτύπημα, τό [hteepeema] blow, punch, kick, hit, knock ‖ bruise, wound.

χτυπητό, τό [hteepeeto] βλ χτυπητός.

χτυπητός [hteepeetos] beaten ‖ tawdry, garish, loud, striking.

χτυποκάρδι, τό [hteepokardee] rapid beating of the heart.

χτύπος, ὁ [hteepos] blow, stroke ‖ (καρδιᾶς) throb, beat ‖ (ὡρολογιοῦ) tick(ing).

χτυπῶ [hteepo] knock, thrash, hit, beat, strike ‖ (χέρια) clap ‖ (πόδια) stamp ‖ (χρόνον) beat ‖ (αὐγά κτλ) whisk ‖ (ὡρολογίου κτλ) peal, strike, sound ‖ hurt o.s. ‖ χτυπάει ἄσχημα it jars, it looks bad ‖ μοῦ χτυπάει στά νεῦρα it gets on my nerves ‖ χτυπιέμαι come to blows ‖ feel sorry, repent.

χυδαιολογῶ [heedeologo] speak crudely, swear.

χυδαῖος [heedeos] vulgar, trivial, crude, rude, coarse.

χυδαιότης, ἡ [heedeotees] vulgarity, coarseness, foul language.

χυλόπιττα, ἡ [heepoleeta] kind of macaroni ‖ (μεταφ) failure in love.

χυλός, ὁ [heelos] pap, liquid paste.

χύμα [heema] confusedly, pell-mell ‖ loose, unpacked, unbottled.

χυμός, ὁ [heemos] sap, juice.

χυμώδης [heemodees] juicy, sappy.

χυμῶ [heemo] rush upon, charge.

χύνομαι [heenome] overflow, pour out ‖ flow out ‖ (μεταφ) charge against, rush upon.

χύνω [heeno] spill, tip over, pour out ‖ (δάκρυα) shed ‖ (μέταλλον) cast.

χύσιμο, τό [heeseemo] discharge, pouring out, spilling ‖ casting, moulding.

χυτήριον, τό [heeteereeon] foundry, smelting works.

χυτός [heetos] moulded, cast ‖ (σκορπισμένος) dispersed, scattered ‖ (μαλλιά) flowing, loose ‖ (ροῦχα) perfect (fit).

χυτοσίδηρος, ὁ [heetoseedeeros] castiron.

χύτρα, ἡ [heetra] cooking pot, pot, porridge pot.

χώλ, τό [hol] hall.

χωλαίνω [holeno] limp, be lame ‖ (μεταφ) halt, hobble, move slowly.

χωλός [holos] lame, limping.

χῶμα, τό [homa] soil, dust, earth ‖ ground.

χωματένιος [homateneeos] earthen.

χώνευσις, ἡ [honevsees] digestion ‖ (μετάλλων) casting, founding.

χωνευτήριον, τό [honevteereeon] crucible, melting pot.

χωνευτικός [honevteekos] digestible, digestive.

χωνευτός [honevtos] cast ‖ fusible ‖ hidden.

χωνεύω [honevo] digest ‖ (μέταλλον) cast, smelt ‖ (μεταφ) tolerate, endure.

χωνί, τό [honee] funnel, horn ‖ (παγωτοῦ) cone.

χώνομαι [honome] squeeze in ‖ hide ‖ (μεταφ) interfere.

χώνω [hono] thrust, force ‖ bury ‖ (κρύβω) hide.

χώρα, ἡ [hora] country, place ‖ chief town ‖ (ἀνατ) region ‖ λαμβάνω ~ν happen.

χωρατό, τό [horato] joke, jest, witticism.

χωρατεύω [horatevo] joke (in a pleasant way).

χωράφι, τό [horafee] field, land.

χωράω [horao] βλ χωρῶ.

χωρητικότης, ἡ [horeeteekotees] volume, capacity ‖ (ναυτ) tonnage.

χώρια [horeea] βλ χωριστά.

χωριανός, ὁ [horeeanos] fellow villager countryman.

χωριάτης, ὁ [horeeatees] peasant, villager, countryman ‖ (μεταφ) ill-mannered person, unpolished person.

χωριάτικος [horeeateekos] peasant, of the village ‖ rustic.

χωρίζομαι [horeezome] leave, part from.

χωρίζω [horeezo] separate, disconnect, part, split ‖ (δρόμοι) branch off ‖ (ζεῦγος) get a divorce ‖ ~ μέ break up with, part from.

χωρικός [horeekos] village, rural, country ‖ (οὐσ) peasant, villager.

χωριό, τό [horio] village, hamlet ‖ (μεταφ) hometown.

χωρίον, τό [horeeon] village ‖ (βιβλίου) passage.

χωρίς [horees] without, apart from ‖ not including ‖ ~ άλλο without fail ‖ μέ ~ without.

χώρισμα, τό [horeesma] sorting, separation ‖ (δωματίου) wall, partition ‖ compartment.

χωρισμένος [horeesmenos] divided ‖ separated, divorced.

χωρισμός, ὁ [horeesmos] separation ‖ partition ‖ separating ‖ divorce.

χωριστά [horeesta] apart, individually ‖ (προϑ) not counting, apart from, not including.

χωριστός [horeestos] separate, different, distinct, isolated. ◥

χωρίστρα, ἡ [horeestra] parting of hair.

χῶρος, ὁ [horos] space, area, room ‖ interval, distance.

χωροστάϑμησις, ἡ [horostathmeesees] levelling.

χωροφύλαξ, ὁ [horofeelaks] gendarme.

χωροφυλακή, ἡ [horofeelakee] gendarmerie.

χωρῶ [horo] move forward ‖ fit into, get into.

χωρ(ά)ῶ [hor(a)o] fit into, have room ‖ (περιέχω) hold, contain ‖ δέν χωράει ἀμφιβολία there's no doubt, undoubtedly.

χώσιμο, τό [hoseemo] driving in, burying ‖ hiding.

χωστός [hostos] driven in, deep, penetrating.

Ψ, ψ

ψάϑα, ἡ [psatha] straw, cane ‖ (χαλί) rush mat ‖ (καπέλλο) straw hat ‖ στήν ~ penniless.

ψαϑάκι, τό [psathakee] man's boater, straw hat.

ψάϑινος [psatheenos] made of straw.

ψαλίδα, ἡ [psaleeδa] shears ‖ centipede.

ψαλίδι, τό [psaleeδee] scissors, pruning scissors ‖ curling tongs.

ψαλιδίζω [psaleeδeezo] cut, trim ‖ (μεταφ) reduce, cut down.

ψαλιδωτός [psaleeδotos] swallow-tailed.

ψάλλω [psalo] sing, chant ‖ extol, celebrate.

ψαλμός, ὁ [psalmos] psalm, chant.

ψαλμωδία, ἡ [psalmoδeea] chanting of psalms ‖ monotonous delivery.

ψαλτήριον, τό [psalteereeon] psalter, psalm book.

ψάλτης, ὁ [psaltees] chorister, singer, chanter.

ψαμμίασις, ἡ [psamccasces] gravel.

ψαμμίτης, ὁ [psameetees] sandstone.

ψάξιμο, τό [psakseemo] searching, quest, search.

ψαράδικο, τό [psaraδeeko] fishing boat ‖ fishmonger's shop.

ψαράδικος [psaraδeekos] of a fisherman.

ψαράς, ὁ [psaras] fisherman ‖ fishmonger.

ψάρε(υ)μα, τό [psare(v)ma] fishing, angling, netting.

ψαρεύω [psarevo] fish ‖ sound, fish for information.

ψαρής [psarees] grey-haired, grey, grizzled.

ψάρι, τό [psaree] fish.

ψαρόβαρκα, ἡ [psarovarka] fishing boat.

ψαροκόκκαλο, τό [psarokokalo] fish bone ‖ (σχέδιο) herringbone.

ψαρόκολλα, ἡ [psarokola] fish glue.

ψαρομάλλης, ὁ [psaromalees] grey-haired person.

ψαρονέφρι, τό [psaronefree] fillet of meat.

ψαροπούλα, ἡ [psaropoula] fishing boat, smack.

ψαρός [psaros] βλ ψαρής.

ψαῦσις, ἡ [psavsees] touching, feeling, light touch.

ψαύω [psavo] touch, feel, finger.

ψαχνό, τό [psahno] lean meat.

ψάχνομαι [psahnome] look through one's pockets.

ψάχνω [psahno] search for, look for ‖ seek, rummage.

ψαχουλεύω [psahoulevo] search, grope for, fumble around.

ψεγάδι, τό [pseγaδee] fault, failing, shortcoming.

ψέγω [pseγo] blame, reprove, censure.

ψείρα, ἡ [pseera] louse ‖ vermin.

ψειριάζω [pseereeazo] get lousy.

ψειρίζω [pseereezo] delouse ‖ (μεταφ) rob.

ψεκάζω [psekazo] spray.

ψεκαστήρ, ὁ [psekasteer] spray, vapourizer ‖ scent sprayer.

ψελλίζω [pseleezo] stammer, stutter.

ψέλνω [pselno] βλ ψάλλω.

ψέμα, τό [psema] βλ ψεῦδος.

ψές [pses] yesterday.

ψευδαίσϑησις, ἡ [psevδestheesees] delusion, hallucination.

ψευδάργυρος, ὁ [psevδarγeeros] zinc.

ψευδής [psevδees] untrue, false ‖ artificial, sham, fictitious ‖ deceptive.

ψευδίζω [psevδeezo] βλ ψελλίζω.

ψευδολογῶ [psevδoloγo] tell lies, tell stories, fib.

ψεύδομαι [psevδome] lie, fib.

ψευδομαρτυρῶ [psevδomarteero] give false witness, commit perjury.

ψευδομάρτυς, ὁ, ἡ [psevδomartees] false witness, perjurer.

ψευδορκία, ἡ [psevδorkeea] perjury.

ψευδορκῶ [psevδorko] commit perjury, perjure.

ψεῦδος, τό [psevδos] lie, falsehood, fib.

ψευδός [psevδos] lisping, stammering, stuttering.

ψευδώνυμον, τό [psevdoneemon] pseudonym, assumed name.

ψεῦμα, τό [psevma] βλ **ψεῦδος**.

ψεύ(σ)της, ὁ [psev(s)tees] liar, fibber ‖ cheat, impostor.

ψευτιά, ἡ [psevtia] untruth, lie.

ψευτίζω [psevteezo] · adulterate ‖ become adulterated.

ψεύτικος [psevteekos] false, untrue ‖ artificial ‖ (σέ ποιότητα) inferior.

ψῆγμα, τό [pseeyma] filings, shavings, chips.

ψῆκτρα, ἡ [pseektra] brush ‖ (μαλλιῶν) hairbrush.

ψηλά [pseela] high up, aloft.

ψηλαφητός [pseelafeetos] tangible, palpable ‖ (μεταφ) obvious, manifest, evident.

ψηλαφῶ [pseelafo] feel, touch, finger ‖ (ψάχνω) feel one's way, grope.

ψηλομύτης [pseelomeetees] haughty, overbearing.

ψηλός [pseelos] high, tall, lofty, great.

ψήλωμα, τό [pseeloma] eminence, elevation ‖ making taller, growing.

ψηλώνω [pseelono] make taller, make higher ‖ grow taller.

ψήνομαι [pseenome] become very hot ‖ (στήν δουλειά) become broken in.

ψήνω [pseeno] bake, roast, cook ‖ (μεταφ) torture, worry, pester.

ψησιά, ἡ [pseesia] potful.

ψήσιμο, τό [pseeseemo] baking, broiling, roasting, cooking, frying.

ψησταριά, ἡ [pseestaria] barbecue apparatus.

ψητό, τό [pseeto] roast meat, grilled meat ‖ (μεταφ) the main point.

ψητός [pseetos] roast, baked, roasted.

ψηφιδωτόν, τό [pseefeedoton] mosaic.

ψηφίζω [pseefeezo] vote ‖ (νόμον) pass, carry.

ψηφίον, τό [pseefeeon] cipher, figure ‖ (ἀλφαβήτου) letter, character.

ψήφισμα, τό [pseefeesma] decree, enactment, edict.

ψηφοδέλτιον, τό [pseefodelteeon] ballot paper.

ψηφοδόχος, ἡ [pseefodohos] ballot box.

ψηφοθηρῶ [pseefotheero] solicit votes, canvass for votes.

ψῆφος, ὁ, ἡ [pseefos] vote, voting, suffrage.

ψηφοφορία, ἡ [pseefoforeea] voting, ballot(ting). ·

ψηφῶ [pseefo] take into account, consider ‖ appreciate.

ψί, τό [psee] the letter Ψ.

ψίαθος, ὁ [pseeathos] straw, cane.

ψίδι, τό [pseedee] vamp of shoe, upper part of boot.

ψιθυρίζω [pseetheereezo] mutter, murmur, whisper

ψιθύρισμα, τό [pseetheereesma] whisper(ing), muttering, murmuring.

ψιθυρισμός, ὁ [pseetheereesmos] βλ **ψιθύρισμα**.

ψίθυρος, ὁ [pseetheeros] murmur, whisper ‖ mutter, growl.

ψιλά, τά [pseela] πλ small change ‖ (μεταφ) cash, money.

ψιλαίνω [pseeleno] thin down ‖ become thinner.

ψιλή, ἡ [pseelee] smooth (soft) breathing.

ψιλικά, τά [pseeleeka] πλ haberdashery ‖ small wares.

ψιλικαντζήδικον, τό [pseeleekantzeedeekon] haberdashery.

ψιλολογῶ [pseeloloyo] examine carefully, sift.

ψιλός [pseelos] fine, slender, thin ‖ shrill.

ψιλοτραγουδῶ [pseelotrayoudo] hum.

ψιμάρι, τό [pseemaree] late-born lamb ‖ (μεταφ) easily-duped fellow.

ψιμύθιον, τό [pseemeetheeon] rouge, make-up.

ψιττακίζω [pseetakeezo] parrot, jabber.

ψιττακός, ὁ [pseetakos] parrot.

ψίχα, ἡ [pseeha] kernel, crumb ‖ (καρυδιοῦ) edible part of nut ‖ (μεταφ) bit, scrap.

ψιχάλα, ἡ [pseehala] drizzle.

ψιχαλίζει [pseehaleezei] it's drizzling.

ψίχουλο, τό [pseehoulo] crumb.

ψιχίον, τό [pseeheeon] βλ **ψίχουλο**.

ψόγος, ὁ [psoyos] blame, reproach.

ψοφίμι, τό [psofeemee] carcass, carrion.

ψόφιος [psofeeos] (περί ζώων) dead ‖ (μεταφ) worn-out ‖ ~ στήν κούραση dead tired.

ψόφος, ὁ [psofos] noise, tumult ‖ (θάνατος) death ‖ (μεταφ) freezing cold.

ψοφῶ [psofo] die, kick the bucket (col) ‖ (μεταφ) ~ γιά yearn for, be mad on.

ψυγεῖον, τό [pseeyeeon] refrigerator, icebox ‖ (αὐτοκινήτου) radiator.

ψυκτικός [pseekteekos] cooling.

ψύλλος, ὁ [pseelos] flea ‖ (μεταφ) trifle.

ψῦξις, ἡ [pseeksees] refrigeration ‖ chill, chilling.

ψυχαγωγία, ἡ [pseehayoyeea] recreation, amusement, diversion, entertainment.

ψυχαγωγικός [pseehayoyeekos] recreational, entertaining.

ψυχανάλυσις, ἡ [pseechanaleeseees] psychoanalysis.

ψυχή, ἡ [pseehee] soul, ghost ‖ heart, core ‖ (θάρρος) energy, spirit.

ψυχιατρεῖον, τό [pseeheeatreeon] mental hospital, asylum.

ψυχιατρική, ἡ [pseeheeatreekee] psychiatry.

ψυχίατρος, ὁ [pseeheeatros] psychiatrist.

ψυχικό, τό [pseeheeko] act of charity ‖ alms, charity.

ψυχικός [pseeheekos] psychical ‖ **ψυχική διάθεσις** humour, mood, disposition ‖ **ψυχική ὀδύνη** mental stress.

ψυχογιός, ὁ [pseehoyios] adopted son.

ψυχοκόρη, ἡ [pseehokoree] adopted daughter.

ψυχολογία, ἡ [pseeholoyeea] psychology.

ψυχολογικός [pseeholoyeekos] psychological.

ψυχολόγος, ὁ [pseeholoyos] psychologist.

ψυχολογῶ [pseeholoyo] read mind of | psychoanalyse.

ψυχομαχῶ [pseehomaho] be at the last gasp.

ψυχοπαθής [pseehopathees] psychopath.

ψυχοπαίδι, τό [pseehopedee] adopted child.

ψυχοπόνια, ἡ [pseehoponeea] commiseration, pity.

ψυχορραγῶ [pseehorayo] βλ ψυχομαχῶ.

ψῦχος, τό [pseehos] cold, chilliness.

ψυχοσάββατο, τό [pseehosavato] All Souls' Day.

ψυχοσύνθεσις, ἡ [pseehoseenthesees] person's psychological make-up.

ψύχρα, ἡ [pseehra] chilly weather, cold.

ψυχραιμία, ἡ [pseehremeea] self-control, sangfroid, coolness.

ψύχραιμος [pseehremos] cool, cool-headed.

ψυχραίνομαι [pseehrenome] be on bad terms with.

ψυχραίνω [pseehreno] cool, chill, make cold | (μεταφ) cool off.

ψυχρολουσία, ἡ [pseehrolouseea] (μεταφ) telling off, rebuke.

ψυχρός [pseehros] cold | (μεταφ) indifferent, apathetic.

ψυχρότης, ἡ [pseehrotees] coldness | indifference.

ψυχρούλα, ἡ [pseehroula] freshness of weather, coolness.

ψύχω [pseeho] freeze, chill, make cold.

ψύχωσις, ἡ [pseehosees] psychosis | craze, complex.

ψωμάκι, τό [psomakee] roll, piece of bread.

ψωμάς, ὁ [psomas] baker.

ψωμί, τό [psomee] bread | loaf (μεταφ) living.

ψωμοζῶ [psomozo] eke out one's living, live scantily.

ψωμοτύρι, τό [psomoteeree] bread and cheese.

ψώνια, τά [psoneea] πλ provisions, shopping, purchases.

ψωνίζω [psoneezo] buy, purchase | go shopping | τήν ~ become queer, go mad.

ψώνιο, τό [psoneeo] purchase (μεταφ) mania.

ψώρα, ἡ [psora] scabies, itch, mange | (μεταφ) pest.

ψωριάζω [psoreeazo] become itchy, be mangy.

ψωριάρης [psoreearees] mangy | (μεταφ) beggar, ragamuffin.

ψωρίασις, ἡ [psoreeasees] psoriasis, itch(ing).

ψωριῶ [psoreeo] be itchy, have scabies.

ψωροκώσταινα, ἡ [psorokostena] poverty-stricken Greece, poor Greece!

ψωροπερηφάνεια, ἡ [psoropereefaneea] pretensions, stupid pride.

Ω, ω

ὤ [o] (ἐπιφ) oh!, ah!, aha!

ὠάριον, τό [oareeon] ovum.

ὧδε [οδe] thus, so | here, in this place.

ὠδεῖον, τό [οδeeon] conservatory.

ὠδή, ἡ [οδee] ode, song.

ὠδική, ἡ [οδeekee] singing lesson | art of singing.

ὠδικός [οδeekos] singing, melodious.

ὠδῖνες, οἱ [οδenes] πλ childbirth pains (μεταφ) difficulties.

ὤθησις, ἡ [otheesees] push, pushing, thrust, impulsion.

ὠθῶ [otho] push, thrust, impel | incite, urge.

ὠϊμέ(να) [oeeme(na)] alas!, woe is me!

ὠκεανός, ὁ [okeanos] ocean.

ὠκύπους [okeepous] swift-footed, nimble.

ὠλένη, ἡ [olenee] forearm.

ὠμέγα, τό [omeya] the letter Ω.

ὠμοπλάτη, ἡ [omoplatee] shoulder blade.

ὤμορφος [omorfos] βλ ὄμορφος.

ὦμος, ὁ [omos] shoulder.

ὠμός [omos] uncooked, raw | hard, cruel, unrelenting.

ὠμότης, ἡ [omotees] cruelty, ferocity.

ὠμότητες, οἱ [omoteetes] πλ outrages, atrocities.

ὄν [on] being, existing.

ὤνια, τά [oneea] πλ commodities, goods, provisions.

ὠνοῦμαι [onoume] buy, purchase.

ὠοειδής [οoeeδees] oval, egg-shaped.

ὠοθήκη, ἡ [ootheekee] ovary | eggcup.

ὠόν, τό [oon] egg.

ὠοτόκος [ootokos] oviparous, egg-laying.

ὥρα, ἡ [ora] hour, time | μέ τήν ~ on the hour | ~ μέ τήν ὥρα any minute | μέ τίς ὥρες for hours | στήν ~ at the right time, on the dot, on time | τῆς ὥρας fresh, cooked to order.

ὡραία [orea] beautiful | very well, perfectly, good.

ὡραῖος [oreos] handsome, comely, lovely | fine, good.

ὡραιότης, ἡ [oreotees] beauty, good looks.

ὡράριον, τό [orareeon] working hours, timetable.

ὡριαῖος [orieos] hourly | lasting an hour.

ὡριμάζω [oreemazo] become ripe, mature, mellow.

ὡρίμανσις, ἡ [oreemansees] ripening, maturity.

ὥριμος [oreemos] ripe, mature, mellow.

ὡριμότης, ἡ [oreemotees] ripeness, maturity, full growth.

ὡρισμένος [oreesmenos] fixed, settled, determined, definite ‖ certain.

ὡρισμένως [oreesmenos] definitely, positively, without fail.

ὡροδείκτης, ὁ [orodeektees] hourhand.

ὡρολογᾶς, ὁ [oroloyas] watch repairer clockmaker.

ὡρολόγιον, τό [oroloyeeon] clock, watch ‖ (ἐργασίας) timetable, schedule ‖ (ἐκκλ) breviary.

ὡρολογοποιός, ὁ [oroloyopeeos] watchmaker, clockmaker.

ὡροσκόπιον, τό [oroskopeeon] horoscope.

ὡρυγή, ἡ [oreeyee] howling, roar.

ὡρύομαι [oreeome] howl, roar ‖ yell, scream.

ὡς [os] until, till, down to, up to, as far as ‖ (ἐπίρ) about ‖ ~ ὅτου νά until.

ὡς [os] as, for, like, just as, such as ‖ (συνδ) as, while, as soon as ‖ βλ καί ὡς.

ὡσάν [osan] as if, as, like, when.

ὡσαύτως [osavtos] also, too, likewise, in like manner.

ὡσεί [osee] as though, as if ‖ about, nearly.

ὡσότου [osotou] until, by the time.

ὥσπερ [osper] like, as, such as.

ὥσπου [ospou] until.

ὥστε [oste] thus, and so, so, accordingly therefore ‖ that ‖ οὕτως ~ thereby.

ὡστόσο [ostoso] nevertheless ‖ meanwhile.

ὠτακουστής, ὁ [otakoustees] eavesdropper.

ὠτίον, τό [oteeon] ear.

ὠτομοτρίς, ἡ [otomotrees] railcar.

ὠτορινολαρυγγολόγος, ὁ [otoreenolareengoloyos] ear, nose and throat doctor.

ὠφέλεια, ἡ [ofeleea] benefit, utility, usefulness, profit, advantage ‖ εἶδα ~ I benefited.

ὠφέλημα, τό [ofeleema] benefit, gain, particular profit, advantage.

ὠφέλιμος [ofeleemos] beneficial, useful, of use, advantageous.

ὠφελοῦμαι [ofeloume] benefit, profit from, turn to good account.

ὠφελῶ [ofelo] do good to, be useful to, benefit, aid.

ὤχρα, ἡ [ohra] ochre.

ὠχραίνω [ohreno] βλ ὠχριῶ.

ὠχριῶ [ohreeo] become pale, make wan.

ὠχρός [ohros] pallid, pale ‖ (μεταφ) indistinct, dim.

ὠχρότης, ἡ [ohrotees] pallor, paleness.

English—Greek

A, a

a, an [ei, æn] *indefinite article* ἕνας, μιά, ἕνα.
aback [ə'bæk] *ad*: **to be taken ~** ξαφνιάζομαι, σαστίζω.
abandon [ə'bændən] *vt* ἐγκαταλείπω, ἀφήνω.
abash [ə'bæʃ] *vt* ξεφτελίζω, ντροπιάζω.
abate [ə'beit] *vi* μειώνομαι, κοπάζω, καταργοῦμαι.
abbess ['æbis] *n* ἡγουμένη.
abbey ['æbi] *n* μονή, μοναστήρι.
abbot ['æbət] *n* ἡγούμενος, ἀββᾶς.
abbreviate [ə'bri:vieit] *vt* συντομεύω.
abbreviation [əbri:vi'eiʃən] *n* σύντμησις, συντετμημένη λέξις.
abdicate ['æbdikeit] *vi* παραιτοῦμαι, ἐγκαταλείπω.
abdication [æbdi'keiʃən] *n* παραίτησις.
abdomen ['æbdəmən] *n* κοιλιά.
abdominal [æb'dəminl] *a* κοιλιακός.
abduction [æb'dʌkʃən] *n* ἀπαγωγή.
aberration [æbə'reiʃən] *n* παρέκκλισις, παρεκτροπή.
abet [ə'bet] *vt* ὑποκινῶ, παρακινῶ.
abeyance [ə'beiəns] *n*: **in ~** ἐκκρεμῶ, ἀχρηστεύομαι.
abhor [əb'hɔ:*] *vt* ἀπεχθάνομαι, σιχαίνομαι ‖ **~rence** ἡ ἀπέχθεια ‖ **~rent** *a* ἀπεχθής.
abide [ə'baid] (*irreg v*) *vt* ἀνέχομαι, ἀντέχω ‖ *vi* ἐμμένω, τηρῶ ‖ **to ~ by** τηρῶ, συμμορφοῦμαι.
ability [ə'biliti] *n* ἱκανότης, ἐπιδεξιότης, δύναμη.
abject ['æbʒekt] *a* ἀπαίσιος, ἄθλιος, ἀξιοθρήνητος.
ablaze [ə'bleiz] *a* φλεγόμενος, λάμπων.
able ['eibl] *a* ἱκανός, ἐπιτήδειος.
ably ['eibli] *ad* ἐπιδεξίως, προκομμένα.
abnormal [æb'nɔ:məl] *a* ἀνώμαλος ‖ **~ity** *n* ἀνωμαλία ‖ (*biol*) τερατωδία, δυσμορφία.
aboard [ə'bɔ:d] *ad*: **to go ~** ἐπιβιβάζομαι ‖ **to be ~** εὑρίσκομαι ἐπί.
abode [ə'bəud] *n* διαμονή, κατοικία.
abolish [ə'bɔliʃ] *vt* καταργῶ.
abolition [æbə'liʃən] *n* κατάργησις.
abominable [ə'bɔminəbl] *a* ἀποτρόπαιος, ἀπεχθής, ἀπαίσιος.
abominably [ə'bɔminəbli] *ad* ἀπαισίως, ἀπεχθῶς.
aborigines [æbə'ridʒini:z] *npl* ἰθαγενεῖς.
abort [ə'bɔ:t] *vt* ἀποβάλλω, διακόπτω ‖ *vi* ἀποβάλλομαι, ματαιοῦμαι.
abortion [ə'bɔ:ʃən] *n* ἔκτρωσι, ἀποβολή ‖ (*col*) ἔκτρωμα, τέρας.
abortive [ə'bɔ:tiv] *a* ἀποτυχών, πρόωρος, ἀνεπιτυχής.
abound [ə'baund] *vi* ἀφθονῶ, βρίθω.

about [ə'baut] *prep* περί, γύρω ἀπό, κοντά ‖ *ad* (τριγύρω), κοντά ‖ (*estimate*) περίπου ‖ **to be ~ to** μόλις πρόκειται νά.
above [ə'bʌv] *prep* πάνω ἀπό, πέρα ἀπό ‖ (*in rank*) ἀνώτερος ἀπό, μεγαλύτερος ἀπό ‖ *ad* ὑπεράνω, ἐπάνω, στούς οὐρανούς ‖ **the ~** τά προαναφερθόμενα, τά ὡς ἄνω ‖ **~board** *a* τίμια καί εἰλικρινή, ἄψογα ‖ **~ ground** ἐπιφανειακός.
abrade [ə'breid] *vt* ξύνω, ἐκτρίβω.
abrasion [ə'breiʒən] *n* ἀπόξεσις, (ἐκ)τριβή.
abrasive [ə'breiziv] *a,n* ἀποξεστικός ‖ **~ material** μέσον λειάνσεως.
abreast [ə'brest] *ad* παραπλεύρως, μαζύ.
abridge [ə'bridʒ] *vt* συντομεύω, συντέμνω.
abroad [ə'brɔ:d] *ad* στό ἐξωτερικό, στά ξένα ‖ (*widely*) εὐρέως, πλατιά.
abrupt [ə'brʌpt] *a* ἀπότομος, ξαφνικός, ἀγενής.
abscess ['æbsis] *n* ἀπόστημα.
abscond [əb'skɔnd] *vi* φυγοδικῶ, δραπετεύω, φεύγω κρυφά.
absence ['æbsəns] *n* ἀπουσία ‖ (*lack of*) ἔλλειψις, ἀνυπαρξία ‖ (*of mind*) ἀφηρημάδα ‖ **leave of ~** ἄδεια.
absent ['æbsənt] *a* ἀπών, ἀπουσιάζων ‖ [æb'sent] *vt*: **he ~ed himself** ἀπουσίαζε ‖ **~ee** *n* ἀπών, ἀπουσιάζων ‖ **~eeism** *n* ἀπουσία ‖ **~-minded** *a* ἀφηρημένος.
absolute ['æbsəlu:t] *a* ἀπόλυτος, τέλειος, ἀπεριόριστος ‖ **~ly** *ad* τελείως.
absolve [əb'zɔlv] *vt* ἀπαλλάσσω, ἀθωώνω.
absorb [əb'zɔ:b] *vt* ἀπορροφῶ.
absorbent [əb'zɔ:bənt] *a,n* ἀπορροφητικός ‖ **~ cotton** (*US*) ἀπορροφητικόν βάμβαξ.
absorbing [əb'zɔ:biŋ] *a* ἀπορροφῶν.
abstain [əb'stein] *vi* ἀπέχω, συγκρατοῦμαι ‖ **~er** *n* ὁ μή πίνων ποτά ‖ **to ~ from** ἀποφεύγω.
abstemious [əb'sti:miəs] *a* ἐγκρατής, λιτοδίαιτος.
abstinence ['æbstinəns] *n* ἀποχή, ἐγκράτεια.
abstract ['æbstrækt] *a* ἀφηρημένος, δυσνόητος ‖ *n* τό ἀφηρημένον ‖ (*summary*) περίληψις ‖ (*excerpt*) ἀπόσπασμα ‖ [æb'strækt] *vt* (*remove*) ἀφαιρῶ.
abstruse [æb'stru:s] *a* ἀσαφής, δυσνόητος.
absurd [əb'sə:d] *a* γελοῖος, παράλογος ‖ **~ity** *n* παραλογισμός, μωρία.
abundance [ə'bʌndəns] *n* ἀφθονία, περίσσευμα.
abundant [ə'bʌndənt] *a* ἄφθονος, πλούσιος.
abuse [ə'bju:z] *vt* (*misuse*) κακομεταχειρίζομαι, καταχρῶμαι ‖ (*speak harshly*) βλαστημῶ, ὑβρίζω.
abuse [ə'bju:s] *n* κακομεταχείρησις, κατάχρησις ‖ (*swearing*) βλασφημία.

abusive [ə'bju:siv] *a* καταχρηστικός, ὑβριστικός.

abut [ə'bʌt] *vi* συνορεύω μέ.

abysmal [ə'bizml] *a* φοβερός, ἀπερίγραπτος.

abyss [ə'bis] *n* ἄβυσσος.

acacia [ə'keiʃə] *n* ἀκακία.

academic [ækə'demik] *a* (*unpractical*) σχολαστικός ‖ *n* ἀκαδημαϊκός.

academy [ə'kædəmi] *n* ἀκαδημία.

accede [æk'si:d] *vi* (*agree*) συμφωνῶ, προσχωρῶ ‖ (*to throne*) ἀνέρχομαι.

accelerate [æk'seləreit] *vt* ἐπιταχύνω, ἐπισπεύδω ‖ *vi* ἐπιταχύνομαι.

acceleration [ækselə'reiʃən] *n* ἐπιτάχυνσις.

accelerator [ək'seləreitə*] *n* (*aut*) ἀξελερατέρ.

accent ['æksent] *n* τόνος, τονισμός ‖ (*of speech*) προφορά.

accent [æk'sent] *vt* τονίζω ‖ ~uate *vt* τονίζω.

accept [ək'sept] *vt* (*gift etc*) δέχομαι, ἀποδέχομαι ‖ (*agree*) παραδέχομαι ‖ ~able *a* (ἀπο)δεκτός, εὐπρόσδεκτος, παραδεκτός ‖ ~ance *n* ἀποδοχή, παραδοχή ‖ ~ation *n* ἀποδοχή.

access ['ækses] *n* (*entrance*) εἴσοδος, μπάσιμο, πλησίασμα ‖ ~ible *a* προσιτός, εὐπρόσιτος ‖ ~ion *n* (*to throne, office*) προσχώρησις, ἄνοδος ‖ (*increase*) προσθήκη, αὔξησις.

accessories [æk'sesəriz] *npl* ἐξαρτήματα, συμπληρώματα ‖ (*toilet*) εἴδη τουαλέτας.

accessory [æk'sesəri] *a* βοηθητικός, συμπληρωματικός ‖ *n* (*to a crime etc*) συνένοχος ‖ (*part*) ἐξάρτημα.

accident ['æksidənt] *n* (*mishap*) δυστύχημα, ἀτύχημα ‖ (*chance*) συμβάν, τύχη ‖ by ~ κατά τύχην ‖ ~ally *ad* τυχαίως, ἐξ ἀπροσεξίας.

acclaim [ə'kleim] *vt* ἐπευφημῶ, ζητωκραυγάζω, ἀναφωνῶ ‖ *n* ζητωκραυγαί.

acclimatize [ə'klaimətaiz] *vt*: to become ~d to ἐγκλιματίζομαι.

accommodate [ə'kɔmədeit] *vt* (*be suitable for*) ἐξοικονομῶ, διευθετῶ, προσαρμόζω ‖ (*lodge*) στεγάζω, παρέχω κατάλυμα ‖ (*supply etc*) ἐξοικονομῶ, ἐφοδιάζω.

accommodating [ə'kɔmədeitiŋ] *a* ἐξυπηρετικός, πρόθυμος.

accommodation [əkɔmə'deiʃən] *n* (*lodging*) κατάλυμα, στέγασις ‖ (*loan*) δάνειον ‖ (*adjustment*) προσαρμογή, διευθέτησις.

accompaniment [ə'kʌmpənimənt] *n* συνοδεία, ἀκκομπανιαμέντο.

accompanist [ə'kʌmpənist] *n* ἀκκομπανιατέρ.

accompany [ə'kʌmpəni] *vt* συνοδεύω, συντροφεύω.

accomplice [ə'kʌmplis] *n* συνένοχος, συνεργός.

accomplish [ə'kʌmpliʃ] *vt* περατώνω, συμπληρώνω, φέρω εἰς πέρας ‖ ~ed *a*

(*skilled*) τέλειος, ὁλοκληρωμένος ‖ ~ment *n* (*ability*) ἱκανότης, προσόντα ‖ (*completion*) ἐκπλήρωσις.

accord [ə'kɔ:d] *n* συμφωνία, ὁμοφωνία ‖ of my own ~ αὐθόρμητα, ἐπειδή θέλω ‖ *vt* (*grant*) παρέχω, χορηγῶ ‖ (*agree with*) συμφωνῶ ‖ ~ance *n* συμφωνία ‖ in ~ance with σύμφωνα μέ ‖ ~ing *ad*, ~ing to *prep* σύμφωνα μέ, κατά τόν ‖ ~ingly *ad* ὅθεν, ἑπομένως.

accordion [ə'kɔ:diən] *n* ἀκκορντεόν.

accost [ə'kɔst] *vt* πλησιάζω, πλευρίζω.

account [ə'kaunt] *n* (*bill*) λογαριασμός, ὑπολογισμός ‖ (*credit*) λογαριασμός ‖ (*story*) ἀφήγησις, περιγραφή ‖ (*financial report*) ἀνάλυσις, ἔκθεσις ‖ on no ~ ἐπ'οὐδενί λόγω ‖ on ~ of ἕνεκα, χάριν τοῦ ‖ to ~ for *vt* ἐξηγῶ, λογοδοτῶ διά ‖ to take into ~ λαμβάνω ὑπ'ὄψιν ‖ ~able *a* ὑπόλογος, ὑπεύθυνος ‖ (*explicable*) εὐεξήγητος ‖ ~ant *n* λογιστής.

accredit [ə'kredit] *vt* διαπιστεύομαι, ἀποδίδω.

accredited [ə'kreditid] *a* διαπιστευμένος, παραδεδεγμένος.

accretion [ə'kri:ʃən] *n* ἐπαύξησις, προσαύξησις ‖ (*biol*) πρόσφυσις.

accrue [ə'kru:] *vi* προκύπτω, ἀπορρέω.

accumulate [ə'kju:mjuleit] *vt* συσσωρεύω, μαζεύω ‖ *vi* συσσωρεύομαι.

accumulation [əkju:mju'leiʃən] *n* συσσώρευσις, μάζεμα, ἄθροισις.

accuracy ['ækjurəsi] *n* ἀκρίβεια.

accurate ['ækjurit] *a* ἀκριβής, ὀρθός ‖ ~ly *ad* μέ ἀκρίβειαν, σωστά.

accusation [ækju:'zeiʃən] *n* κατηγορία.

accusative [ə'kju:zətiv] *n* (*gram*) αἰτιατική.

accuse [ə'kju:z] *vt* κατηγορῶ ‖ ~d *n* κατηγορούμενος ‖ ~r *n* ἐνάγων, μηνυτής, κατήγορος.

accustom [ə'kʌstəm] *vt* συνηθίζω, ἐθίζω ‖ ~ed *a* συνηθισμένος, μαθημένος εἰς.

ace [eis] *n* (*aviat*) ἄσσος ‖ (*cards*) ἄσσος.

ache [eik] *vi* πονῶ.

achieve [ə'tʃi:v] *vt* κατορθώνω, ἐπιτυγχάνω, φθάνω ‖ ~ment *n* κατόρθωμα, ἐπίτευξις.

acid ['æsid] *a* ὀξύς, ξινός ‖ *n* (*chem*) ὀξύ ‖ ~ test *n* ἀποφασιστική δοκιμασία, τελικόν κριτήριον ‖ ~ity *n* (*chem*) ὀξύτης, ξινίλα.

acknowledge [ək'nɔlidʒ] *vt* (*admit*) ἀναγνωρίζω, παραδέχομαι ‖ (*thank*) εἶμαι εὐγνώμων, ἀπαντῶ εἰς ‖ ~ment *n* ἀναγνώρισις, παραδοχή ‖ (*of letter etc*) βεβαίωσις ‖ ~ments *npl* εὐχαριστίαι.

acme ['ækmi] *n* ἀκμή, ἄκρον ἄωτον.

acne ['ækni] *n* ἀκμή, σπυράκια.

acorn ['eikɔ:n] *n* βαλανίδι.

acoustic [ə'ku:stik] *a* ἀκουστικός ‖ ~s *npl* ἀκουστική.

acquaint [ə'kweint] *vt* γνωρίζω, πληροφορῶ ‖ ~ance *n* (*person*) γνωριμία ‖ (*knowledge*) γνῶσις, ἐξοικείωσις.

acquiesce [ækwi'es] *vi* συναινῶ, συγκατα-τίθεμαι, δέχομαι.

acquire [ə'kwaiə*] *vt* ἀποκτῶ.

acquisition [ækwi'ziʃən] *n* ἀπόκτημα, ἀπόκτησις.

acquisitive [ə'kwizitiv] *a* πλεονέκτης, ἀρπακτικός.

acquit [ə'kwit] *vt* (*free from accusation*) ἀπαλλάσσω, ἀθωώνω ‖ (*conduct o.s.*) ἐκπληρῶ, καταφέρνω ‖ ~ **tal** *n* ἀθώωσις, ἀπαλλαγή.

acre ['eikə*] *n* ἄκρ (4 στρέμματα) ‖ ~ **age** *n* στρεμματική ἔκτασις.

acrimonious [ækri'məuniəs] *a* δηκτικός, πικρός.

acrobat ['ækrəbæt] *n* ἀκροβάτης.

across [ə'krɔs] *prep* (*through*) διά, διά μέσου ‖ *ad* (*crosswise*) ἐγκαρσίως, λοξά, σταυροειδῶς ‖ (*distance*) πλάτος, μῆκος ‖ ~ **the road** (στό δρόμο) ἀπέναντι.

act [ækt] *n* (*deed*) πρᾶξις, ἐνέργεια ‖ (*law or decree*) νόμος, νομοθέτημα ‖ (*of play*) πρᾶξις (ἔργου) ‖ *vti* (*take action*) ἐνεργῶ, πράττω ‖ (*part*) παίζω, παριστάνω, κάνω ‖ (*pretend*) προσποιοῦμαι, ὑποκρίνομαι, ὑποδύομαι ‖ ~ **ing** *n* (*theat*) ἠθοποιΐα, παίξιμο ‖ *a* ἐνεργῶν, ἀναπληρωματικός.

action ['ækʃən] *n* (*deed*) πρᾶξις ‖ (*motion*) λειτουργία, ἐνέργεια ‖ (*battle*) μάχη ‖ **to bring an** ~ **against** κάνω ἀγωγήν κατά ‖ **naval** ~ *n* ναυμαχία ‖ **to take** ~ ἐνεργῶ.

active ['æktiv] *a* (*lively*) ἐνεργητικός, ζωηρός ‖ (*working*) δραστήριος, ἐνεργός ‖ (*gram*) ἐνεργητικός ‖ **on** ~ **service** ἐν ἐνεργεία ‖ ~ **ly** *ad* ἐνεργῶς.

activity [æk'tiviti] *n* δραστηριότης, δρᾶσις.

actor ['æktə*] *n* ἠθοποιός.

actress ['æktris] *n* (ἡ) ἠθοποιός, θεατρίνα.

actual ['æktjuəl] *a* πραγματικός, ἀληθινός ‖ ~ **ly** *ad* πράγματι.

actuate ['æktjueit] *vt* (παρα)κινῶ, ὠθῶ.

acumen ['ækjumen] *n* ὀξύνοια, εὐφυΐα.

acute [ə'kju:t] *a* ὀξύς, διαπεραστικός ‖ ~ **ly** *ad* ἐντόνως ‖ ~ **accent** *n* ὀξεῖα.

Adam ['ædəm] *n* 'Ἀδάμ ‖ ~ **'s apple** *n* καρύδι τοῦ λαιμοῦ.

adamant ['ædəmənt] *a* ἀμετάπειστος, ἄκαμπτος.

adapt [ə'dæpt] *vt* προσαρμόζω, ἐναρμόζω ‖ *vi*: **to** ~ **to** προσαρμόζομαι ‖ ~ **able** *a* προσαρμόσιμος, εὐάρμοστος ‖ ~ **ation** *n* προσαρμογή ‖ (*of play etc*) διασκευή ‖ ~ **er** *n* (*elec*) προσαρμοστής.

add [æd] *vt* προσθέτω, ἀθροίζω ‖ **to** ~ **up** *vt* προσθέτω.

addendum [ə'dendəm] *n* προσθήκη, συμπλήρωμα.

adder ['ædə*] *n* (*snake*) ὀχιά, ὄχεντρα.

addict ['ædikt] *n* -μανής.

addict [ə'dikt] *vt* ἀφοσιώνω, παραδίδω ‖ ~ **ed** **to** ἐπιρρεπής εἰς ‖ ~ **ion** *n* ῥοπή πρός, ἐθισμός.

adding machine ['ædiŋməʃi:n] *n* ἀθροιστική μηχανή.

addition [ə'diʃən] *n* πρόσθεσις, προσθήκη ‖ **in** ~ ἐπί πλέον, ἐπιπροσθέτως, προσέτι ‖ ~ **al** *a* πρόσθετος.

address [ə'dres] *n* διεύθυνσις ‖ (*speech*) προσφώνησις, λόγος ‖ (*manners*) συμπεριφορά ‖ *vt* ἀπευθύνω ‖ (*speak*) προσφωνῶ ‖ (*envelope*) γράφω διεύθυνσι.

addressee [ædre'si:] *n* παραλήπτης.

addressograph [ə'dresəugra:f] *n* ἀντρεσσο-γράφος.

adduce [ə'dju:s] *vt* προσάγω, παραθέτω παρέχω.

adenoids ['ædinɔidz] *npl* κρεατάκια.

adept ['ædept] *a*: ~ **at** ἔμπειρος εἰς, ἱκανός εἰς.

adequacy ['ædikwəsi] *n* ἐπάρκεια, ὀρθότης.

adequate ['ædikwit] *a* ἐπαρκής, ἱκανός ~ **ly** *ad* δικαίως, ἐπαρκῶς.

adhere [əd'hiə*] *vi* (*stick to*) προσκολλῶμαι ‖ (*support*) ἐμμένω, προσχωρῶ ‖ **to** ~ **to** προσχωρῶ, ἐμμένω.

adhesion [əd'hi:ʒən] *n* προσκόλλησις πιάσιμο ‖ (*med*) σύμφυσις.

adhesive [əd'hi:ziv] *a* συγκολλητικός, κολλώδης ‖ *n* κολλητική οὐσία ‖ ~ **tape** *n* λευκοπλάστης.

adjacent [ə'dʒeisənt] *a* παρακείμενος γειτονικός, γειτνιάζων.

adjective ['ædʒektiv] *n* ἐπίθετον.

adjoin [ə'dʒɔin] *vi* γειτονεύω, συνορεύω μέ συνάπτω ‖ ~ **ing** *a* συνεχόμενος, παρα-κείμενος, γειτνιάζων.

adjourn [ə'dʒə:n] *vt* (*postpone*) ἀναβάλλω *vi* ἀναβάλλομαι, διακόπτομαι ‖ ~ **ment** *n* ἀναβολή, διακοπή.

adjudicator [ə'dʒu:dikeitə*] *n* διαιτητής, δικαστής.

adjunct ['ædʒʌŋkt] *n* παρεπόμενον, βοηθός ‖ *a* πρόσθετος.

adjust [ə'dʒʌst] *vt* (*put right*) ῥυθμίζω, κανονίζω ‖ (*to fit*) προσαρμόζω, ἐφαρ-μόζω ‖ ~ **able** *a* ῥυθμιζόμενος, ῥυθμιστός ‖ ~ **ment** *n* ῥύθμισις, τακτοποίησις.

adjutant ['ædʒətənt] *n* ὑπασπιστής.

ad lib [æd'lib] *ad* κατά βούλησιν ‖ **ad-lib** *vi* αὐτοσχεδιάζω.

administer [əd'ministə*] *v.* (*manage*) διευθύνω, διαχειρίζομαι, διοικῶ ‖ (*dispense*) ἀπονέμω ‖ (*medicine*) παρέχω δίδω.

administration [ədminis'treiʃən] *n* διοίκη-σις, διαχείρισις, διεύθυνσις ‖ ~ **of justice** *n* ἀπονομή δικαιοσύνης.

administrative [əd'ministrətiv] *a* διοικητι-κός.

administrator [əd'ministreitə*] *n* διευ-θυντής, διοικητής ‖ (*of will*) ἐκτελεστής.

admirable ['ædmərəbl] *a* θαυμαστός, θαυμάσιος.

admiral ['ædmərəl] *n* ναύαρχος ‖ ~ **ty** *n* ναυαρχεῖον.

admiration [ædmə'reiʃən] n θαυμασμός, κατάπληξις.

admire [əd'maiə*] vt θαυμάζω ‖ ~r n θαυμαστής.

admissible [əd'misəbl] a (παρα)δεκτός, ἐπιτρεπτός.

admission [əd'miʃən] n (entrance) εἴσοδος, εἰσαγωγή ‖ (fee) τιμή εἰσητηρίου ‖ (confession) παραδοχή, ἀναγνώρισις.

admit [əd'mit] vt (let in) ἀφήνω νά εἰσέλθῃ, εἰσέρχομαι ‖ (confess) παραδέχομαι, ἀναγνωρίζω ‖ (receive as true) (ἐπι)δέχομαι ‖ ~tance n εἰσδοχή, εἴσοδος ‖ ~tedly ad ὁμολογουμένως.

admonish [əd'mɔniʃ] vt (warn) προειδοποιῶ ‖ (reprove) ἐπιτιμῶ, ψέγω ‖ (advise) νουθετῶ, παραινῶ.

ado [ə'du:] n: without more ~ χωρίς περισσότερη φασαρία.

adolescence [ædəu'lesns] n ἐφηβική ἡλικία.

adolescent [ædəu'lesnt] a,n ἔφηβος.

adopt [ə'dɔpt] vt υἱοθετῶ ‖ (accept) παραδέχομαι, ἀποδέχομαι ‖ ~ed son n θετός ‖ ~ion n υἱοθεσία ‖ (of idea etc) ἀποχή, ἔγκρισις.

adorable [ə'dɔ:rəbl] a λατρευτός, ἀξιαγάπητος.

adoration [ædə'reiʃən] n λατρεία.

adore [ə'dɔ:*] vt λατρεύω, ὑπεραγαπῶ.

adorn [ə'dɔ:n] vt κοσμῶ, στολίζω, καλλωπίζω.

adrenalin [ə'drenəlin] n ἀδρεναλίνη.

Adriatic [eidri'ætik] n 'Αδριατική.

adrift [ə'drift] ad ἕρμαιον ‖ (col) τά ἔχω χαμένα.

adroit [ə'drɔit] a ἐπιδέξιος, ἐπιτήδειος.

adulation [ædju'leiʃən] n κολακεία, θωπεία.

adult ['ædʌlt] a,n ἐνῆλιξ, ἔφηβος ‖ (law) ἐνήλικος.

adulterate [ə'dʌltəreit] vt νοθεύω, ἀλλοιώνω, νερώνω.

adultery [ə'dʌltəri] n μοιχεία.

advance [əd'va:ns] n πρόοδος, προχώρησις ‖ (money) προκαταβολή, πίστωσις ‖ (in prices) αὔξησις, ὕψωσις ‖ vi προχωρῶ ‖ (mil) προελαύνω ‖ (price) ἀνατιμῶμαι, ἀνεβαίνω ‖ ~d a προχωρημένος ‖ (ideas) προοδευτικός ‖ (study etc) ἀνώτερος ‖ ~d ignition n προανάφλεξις, ἀβάνς ‖ in ~ προκαταβολικῶς ‖ in ~ of πρίν ἀπό, ἐνωρίτερα ‖ ~ booking n κλείνω θέσιν.

advantage [əd'va:ntidʒ] n πλεονέκτημα, προτέρημα ‖ to take ~ of (profit by) ἐπωφελοῦμαι ἀπό, ἐκμεταλλεύομαι ‖ (misuse) καταχρῶμαι ‖ ~ over ὑπεροχή. **·dvantageous** [ædvən'teidʒəs] a ἐπωφελής, λυσιτελής.

advent ['ædvənt] n ἔλευσις, ἐμφάνισις ‖ (rel) σαραντάμερο ‖ the Second A~ ἡ Δευτέρα Παρουσία.

adventure [əd'ventʃə*] n περιπέτεια ‖ (bold

undertaking) τόλμημα ‖ ~r n τολμηρός ‖ (in bad sense) τυχοδιώκτης.

adventurous [əd'ventʃərəs] a ριψοκίνδυνος, τυχοδιωκτικός.

·adverb ['ædvə:b] n ἐπίρρημα.

adversary ['ædvəsəri] n ἀντίπαλος, ἀνταγωνιστής.

adverse ['ædvə:s] a ἀντίθετος, ἐνάντιος, δυσμενής.

adversity [əd'və:siti] n ἀτυχία, ἀναποδιά.

advertise ['ædvətaiz] vt διαφημίζω, ρεκλαμάρω ‖ ~ment [əd'və:tismənt] n διαφήμησις, ρεκλάμα ‖ (poster) ἀφίσα ‖ ~r n διαφημιστής.

advertising ['ædvətaiziŋ] n διαφήμησις, ρεκλάμα ‖ ~ agency n διαφημιστικόν γραφεῖον.

advice [əd'vais] n συμβουλή ‖ (information) πληροφορία, εἴδησις.

advisability [ədvaizə'biliti] n σκοπιμότης, χρησιμότης.

advisable [əd'vaizəbl] a φρόνιμος, σκόπιμος.

advise [əd'vaiz] vt συμβουλεύω, συνιστῶ ‖ (apprise) εἰδοποιῶ ‖ ~dly ad ἐσκεμμένως ‖ (wisely) κατόπιν σκέψεως ‖ ~r n σύμβουλος.

advisory [əd'vaizəri] a συμβουλευτικός.

advocacy ['ædvəkəsi] n συνηγορία, ὑπεράσπισις.

advocate ['ædvəkit] n (law) δικηγόρος, συνήγορος ‖ (supporter) ὑποστηρικτής ['ædvəkeit] vt ὑποστηρίζω, συνιστῶ ‖ (law) συνηγορῶ.

aerated ['eəreitid] a ἀεριοῦχος ‖ ~ waters npl ἀεριοῦχα νερά, σόδα.

aerial ['eəriəl] a (ἐν)ἀέριος ‖ n κεραία ‖ ~ photograph n ἐναέριος φωτογραφία.

aerobatics [eərəu'bætiks] npl ἐναέριοι ἀκροβασίαι.

aeronautics [eərə'nɔ:tiks] n ἀεροναυτική.

aeroplane ['eərəplein] n ἀεροπλάνον.

aerosol ['eərəsɔl] n ἀεροζόλ.

aesthetic [i:s'θetik] a αἰσθητικός ‖ (artistic) καλαίσθητος ‖ ~s npl αἰσθητική.

afar [ə'fa:*] ad: from ~ ἀπό μακράν, μακρόθεν.

affable ['æfəbl] a προσηνής, γλυκομίλητος, καταδεκτικός.

affair [ə'feə*] n ὑπόθεσις, δουλειά ‖ (matter) πρᾶγμα.

affect [ə'fekt] vt (influence) θίγω, ἐπηρεάζω ‖ (feign) προσποιοῦμαι, κάνω τόν ‖ ~ation n προσποίησις ‖ ~ed a προσποιητός ‖ (moved) συγκινημένος ‖ (med) προσβεβλημένος ‖ ~ion n ἀγάπη, στοργή ‖ ~ionate a φιλόστοργος, ἀγαπῶν ‖ ~ionately ad στοργικά, μέ ἀγάπη.

affidavit [æfi'deivit] n ἔνορκος κατάθεσις, γραπτή βεβαίωσις.

affiliate [ə'filieit] vt εἰσάγω, συνεργάζομαι.

affiliation [əfili'eiʃən] n σύνδεσις, δεσμός.

affinity [ə'finiti] n συγγένεια.

affirm [ə'fə:m] vt ἐπιβεβαιῶ ‖ ~ation n
(δια)βεβαίωσις ‖ (assent) κατάφασις ‖
~ative a καταφατικός, βεβαιωτικός ‖ n
κατάφασις ‖ in the ~ative καταφατικῶς.

affix [ə'fiks] vt ἐπισυνάπτω, προσαρτῶ,
θέτω.

afflict [ə'flikt] vt θλίβω, πικραίνω ‖ (med)
προσβάλλω ‖ ~ion n θλῖψις, λύπη ‖
(misfortune) ἀτύχημα, συμφορά.

affluence ['æfluəns] n (abundance) ἀφθονία
‖ (wealth) πλοῦτος.

affluent ['æfluənt] a πλούσιος.

afford [ə'fɔːd] vt (have the means) δύναμαι,
ἔχω τά μέσα ‖ (provide) παρέχω,
προσφέρω.

affront [ə'frʌnt] vt προσβάλλω, ντροπιάζω
‖ n προσβολή, ὕβρις ‖ ~ed a προσβεβλημένος.

Afghanistan [æf'gænistæn] n Ἀφγανιστάν.

afield [ə'fiːld] ad: far ~ μακράν.

afloat [ə'fləut] ad: I am ~ ἐπιπλέω.

afoot [ə'fut] ad (astir) εἰς κίνησιν, κυκλοφορῶ.

afraid [ə'freid] a ἔμφοβος, φοβισμένος ‖
to be ~ of φοβοῦμαι ‖ to be ~ to δέν
τολμῶ ‖ ~ that φοβοῦμαι ὅτι.

afresh [ə'freʃ] ad ἐκ νέου, πάλιν.

Africa ['æfrikə] n Ἀφρική ‖ ~n n
Ἀφρικανός ‖ a ἀφρικανικός.

aft [aːft] ad πρός τήν πρύμνην, πρός τά
πίσω.

after ['aːftə*] prep μετά, κατόπιν, ὕστερα
ἀπό ‖ (according to) κατά ‖ ad ἔπειτα,
κατόπιν, ὕστερον ‖ a ὕστερος, ἑπόμενος
‖ cj ἀφοῦ ‖ some time ~ ὀλίγον ἀργότερα
‖ what is he ~? τί ζητᾶ ‖ τί ψάχνει; ‖
~ all τέλος πάντων, ἐπί τέλους ‖ ~ five
(o'clock) περασμένες πέντε ‖ ~ you, sir!
παρακαλῶ!, περάστε!

after- ['aːftə*] (in compds) a μετά, μέλλων,
ὀπίσθιος.

aftermath ['aːftəmæθ] n συνέπεια, ἐπακόλουθον.

afternoon ['aːftə'nuːn] n ἀπόγευμα ‖
good ~! χαίρετε!, καλό βράδυ!

afterthought ['aːftəθɔːt] n μεταγενεστέρα
σκέψις.

afterwards ['aːftəwədz] ad κατόπιν, ἔκτοτε,
ἐν συνεχείᾳ.

again [ə'gen] ad πάλιν, ξανά ‖ ~ and ~
ἐπανειλημμένως, πάλι καί πάλι.

against [ə'genst] prep κατά, ἐναντίον.

agape [ə'geip] a,ad μέ ἀνοιχτό στόμα.

age [eidʒ] n ἡλικία ‖ (generation) γενεά ‖
(period) ἐποχή ‖ (century) αἰώνας ‖ vti
γηράσκω, γηράζω ‖ (wine etc) ὡριμάζω ‖
of ~ ἐνηλικιωμένος, ἐνήλικος ‖ ~d a
ἡλικιωμένος, γέρος ‖ ~d 20 (years)
ἡλικίας 20 ἐτῶν ‖ ~less a ἀγέραστος,
αἰώνιος.

agency ['eidʒənsi] n,a (ἐπί)δρασις, ἐνέργεια ‖ (factor) παράγων, αἴτιον n (intervention) ὑπηρεσία, ὀργανισμός ‖ (office)
πρακτορεῖον, ἀντιπροσωπεία.

agenda [ə'dʒendə] n ἡμερησία διάταξις ‖
(notebook) ἀτζέντα, σημειωματάριον.

agent ['eidʒənt] n πράκτωρ, ἀντιπρόσωπος
‖ (cause) παράγων, συντελεστής.

aggravate ['ægrəveit] vt ἐπιδεινώνω.
χειροτερεύω ‖ (provoke) ἐντείνω
ἐρεθίζω.

aggregate ['ægrigit] n ἄθροισμα, σύνολον
a συνολικός.

aggression [ə'greʃən] n ἐπίθεσις, ἐπιδρομή.

aggressive [ə'gresiv] a ἐπιθετικός ‖ (US)
δραστήριος ‖ ~ly ad ἐπιθετικῶς ‖ ~ness
n ἐπιθετικότης.

aggressor [ə'gresə*] n ἐπιτιθέμενος.

aggrieved [ə'griːvd] a θλιμμένος, πικρα
μένος.

aghast [ə'gaːst] a κατάπληκτος, ἐμβρόντητος.

agile ['ædʒail] a εὐκίνητος, ἐλαφρός.

agility [ə'dʒiliti] n εὐκινησία, εὐκαμψία.

agitate ['ædʒiteit] vt (set in motion)
(ἀνα)ταράσσω ‖ (excite) ταράσσω,
ἀνησυχῶ ‖ (pol) κινοῦμαι, κάνω κίνησιν
‖ to ~ for δημιουργῶ κίνησιν γιά.

agitation [ædʒi'teiʃən] n ἀναταραχή.

agitator ['ædʒiteitə*] n ὑποκινητής,
ταραχοποιός.

agnostic [æg'nɔstik] a,n ἀγνωστικός.

agnosticism [æg'nɔstisizəm] n ἀγνωστικι-
σμός.

ago [ə'gəu] ad περασμένος, παρελθόν,
πρό, πρίν ‖ long ~ πρό πολλοῦ ‖ som
time ~ πρό καιροῦ.

agog [ə'gɔg] a ἀνυπόμονος.

agonizing ['ægənaizin] a σπαρακτικός
φρικτός.

agony ['ægəni] n ἀγωνία, βάσανο.

agree [ə'griː] vti (consent) συγκατατίθεμαι,
ἀποδέχομαι ‖ (have same opinion)
συμφωνῶ, εἶμαι σύμφωνος ‖ (of climate
etc) ταιριάζω, ὠφελῶ ‖ (come to an agreement) συμβιβάζομαι ‖ it does not ~
with me μέ πειράζει, μ' ἐνοχλεῖ, δέν μοῦ
ταιριάζει ‖ ~able a εὐχάριστος,
σύμφωνος ‖ ~ably ad εὐχαρίστως,
συμφώνως πρός ‖ ~d a (of persons) εἶμαι
σύμφωνος ‖ (of things) ἐγκρίνεται!,
σύμφωνοι! ‖ ~ment n συμφωνία
(formal) σύμβασις, συνθήκη.

agricultural [ægri'kʌltʃərəl] a γεωργικός.

agriculture ['ægrikʌltʃə*] n γεωργία.

aground [ə'graund] ad (naut) στήν ξέρα,
στήν στεριά ‖ to run ~ προσαράσσω,
καθίζω, ἐξοκέλλω.

ahead [ə'hed] ad ἐμπρός, πρό, πρόσω ‖ to
get ~ προχωρῶ, προηγοῦμαι ‖ ~ of
μπρός ἀπό.

ahoy [ə'hɔi] excl: boat ~! αἴ, τῆς λέμβου!,
ἔ, ἐσεῖς στή βάρκα!

aid [eid] n βοήθεια, συνδρομή ‖ (assistant)
βοηθός ‖ vt βοηθῶ, συντρέχω.

ailing ['eiliŋ] a πάσχων, ἀσθενής.

ailment ['eilmənt] n ἀδιαθεσία, ἀρρώστια.

aim [eim] n (point) σκόπευσις || (target) στόχος || (purpose) σκοπός, ἀντικείμενον || vti (throw) ρίχνω, κτυπῶ || (point) σκοπεύω || (intend) ἐπιδιώκω || ~less a ἄσκοπος, ἀσυνάρτητος.

air [ɛə*] n ἀέρας, ἀγέρας || (tune) μέλος, σκοπός, ἦχος || (appearance) παρουσιαστικό, ἀέρας, ὕφος || vt ἀερίζω || (question) ἐκθέτω, ἀνακινῶ || (opinions) ἐπιδεικνύω, ἀποκαλύπτω || ~borne a ἀεροφερόμενος || ~ conditioning n κλιματισμός || ~craft n ἀεροσκάφος, ἀεροπλάνο || ~craft carrier n ἀεροπλανοφόρο || ~field n ἀεροδρόμιον || ~force n (πολεμική) ἀεροπορία || ~ freight n ἀεροπορικόν φορτίον || ~gun n σφυρίον πεπιεσμένου ἀέρος || ~ hostess n ἱπταμένη συνοδός || ~ily ad εὔθυμα, ἐλαφρά || ~line n ἀεροπορική γραμμή || ~liner n ἐπιβατικόν ἀεροπλάνον || ~mail n: by ~mail ἀεροπορικῶς || ~plane n (US) ἀεροπλάνον || ~ pocket n κενόν ἀέρος || ~port n ἀερολιμήν || ~ pressure n ἀτμοσφαιρική πίεσις || ~ pump n ἀεραντλία || ~ raid n ἀεροπορική ἐπιδρομή || ~-raid shelter n καταφύγιον || ~tight a ἀεροστεγές, ἑρμητικός.

aisle [ail] n διάδρομος || (of church) πτέρυξ.

ajar [ə'dʒa:*] ad μισοανοιγμένος.

akimbo [ə'kimbəu] ad ἐπὶ τῶν ἰσχίων.

akin [ə'kin] a συγγενεύων.

à la carte [ælæ'ka:t] ad ἀ-λα-κάρτ.

alack [ə'læk] excl ἀλλοί!

alarm [ə'la:m] n (of danger) συναγερμός, κραυγὴ κινδύνου || (device) σύστημα εἰδοποιήσεως || (fright) φόβος, ἀναταραχή || vt τρομάζω, φοβίζω, ταράσσω || ~ clock n ξυπνητήρι || ~ing a ἀνησυχητικός || ~ist n διαδόσεις.

alas [ə'læs] excl ἀλλοίμονον!, φεῦ!

Albania [æl'beiniə] n 'Αλβανία || ~n a 'Αλβανός, 'Αρβανίτης.

album ['ælbəm] n λεύκωμα, ἄλμπουμ.

alcohol ['ælkəhɔl] n ἀλκοόλ, οἰνόπνευμα || ~ic a,n ἀλκοολικός.

alcove ['ælkəuv] n παστάς, ἀλκόβα || (of wall) σηκός, ἀγιβάδα.

alder ['ɔ:ldə*] n (σ)κλήθρα, σκλέθρος.

alderman ['ɔ:ldəmən] n δημοτικός σύμβουλος.

ale [eil] n μπύρα.

alert [ə'lɔ:t] a ἄγρυπνος, προσεκτικός || (nimble) εὐκίνητος, σβέλτος || n ἐπιφυλακή, συναγερμός || ~ness n ἐπαγρύπνησις || (cleverness) ἐξυπνάδα, εὐστροφία.

algebra ['ældʒibrə] n ἄλγεβρα.

alias ['eiliæs] ad ἄλλως, ἤ || n ψευδώνυμο, πλαστὸ ὄνομα.

alibi ['ælibai] n ἄλλοθι || (col) δικαιολογία.

alien ['eiliən] n,a ξένος, ἀλλοδαπός || ~ate

vt (turn away) ἀποσπῶ, ἀποξενῶ || ~ation n ἀποξένωσις.

alight [ə'lait] a ἀναμμένος, φλεγόμενος || vi κατέρχομαι, κατεβαίνω || (of birds) κάθομαι.

align [ə'lain] vt εὐθυγραμμίζω || ~ment n εὐθυγράμμισις.

alike [ə'laik] a ὅμοιος, παρόμοιος, ἴδιος || ad ὁμοίως, ἴδια.

alive [ə'laiv] a ζωντανός || (lively) ζωηρός || (teeming) βρίθων, γεμᾶτος.

alkali ['ælkəlai] n ἄλκαλι.

all [ɔ:l] a,pron πᾶς, ὅλος, ὅλοι, πάντες || ὅλον, σύνολον, ὁλότης || ad ἐντελῶς, τελείως, ὅλο || after ~ στὸ κάτω-κάτω || ~ in ~ ἐν συνόλω || above ~ πρὸ παντός.

all- ['ɔ:l] (in compds) a ὁλο-, παν-, παντο-, τελείως.

allay [ə'lei] vt καταπραΰνω, γλυκαίνω || (lessen) καθησυχάζω, ἀνακουφίζω.

allegation [æle'geiʃən] n ἰσχυρισμός, ὑπαινιγμός.

allege [ə'ledʒ] vt ἰσχυρίζομαι, ἐπικαλοῦμαι || ~dly ad δῆθεν.

allegiance [ə'li:dʒəns] n πίστις, ὑπακοή.

allegory ['æligəri] n ἀλληγορία.

alleluia [æli'lu:jə] n ἀλληλούϊα.

all-embracing [ɔ:lim'breisiŋ] a περιλαμβάνων τά πάντα.

allergic [ə'lə:dʒik] a ἀλλεργικός.

allergy ['ælədʒi] n ἀλλεργία.

alleviate [ə'li:vieit] vt ἐλαφρώνω, ἀνακουφίζω.

alleviation [əli:vi'eiʃən] n ἀνακούφισις, ἀλάφρωμα, ξαλάφρωμα.

alley ['æli] n δρομίσκος, πάροδος, δρομάκος || ~way n δρομίσκος, στενόν.

alliance [ə'laiəns] n συμμαχία || (marriage) ἐπιγαμία, συμπεθεριά.

allied ['ælaid] a: ~ to συγγενεύω μέ.

all-important ['ɔ:lim'pɔ:iənt] a σπουδαιότατος.

all-in ['ɔ:lin] a (exhausted) ἐξηντλημένος.

alliteration ['əlitə'reiʃən] n παρήχησις.

all-night ['ɔ:l'nait] a (cafe etc) ὁλονύκτιος, διανυκτερεύων.

allocate ['æləukeit] vt διαθέτω, παραχωρῶ || (for special purpose) κατανέμω, ἀναθέτω.

allocation [æləu'keiʃən] n ἐκχώρησις, ἀπονομή.

allot [ə'lɔt] vt παραχωρῶ, διαθέτω, κατανέμω || ~ment n (share) μερίδιον, τμῆμα.

all-out ['ɔ:l'aut] ad μέ ὅλες τίς δυνάμεις.

allow [ə'lau] vt ἐπιτρέπω || (grant) παρέχω, δίδω || (acknowledge) ἀναγνωρίζω, (παρα)δέχομαι || ~ to ~ for ἀφήνω περιθώριον γιά || ~able a δεκτός, ἐπιτρεπόμενος || ~ance n ἐπίδομα, εἰσόδημα.

alloy ['ælɔi] n κρᾶμα || vt ἀναμιγνύω, συντήκω || (fig) νοθεύω.

all-round ['ɔ:l'raund] a τελειότατος, ἀρτιώτατος.

all-rounder ['ɔːl'raundə*] n ἄνθρωπος γενικῆς μορφώσεως.
all-time ['ɔːl'taim] a παντοτινός.
allude [ə'luːd] vi: **to ~ to** ἐννοῶ, ὑπονοῶ,
ὑπαινίσσομαι.
alluring [ə'ljuəriŋ] a δελεαστικός, γοητευτικός.
allusion [ə'luːʒən] n ὑπαινιγμός, νύξις.
ally ['ælai] n σύμμαχος ‖ [ə'lai] vt συνδέω,
ἐνώνω ‖ vi συμμαχῶ, συνδέομαι.
almighty [ɔːl'maiti] a: **the A~** ὁ Παντοδύναμος.
almond · ['aːmənd] n ἀμύγδαλο ‖ (tree)
ἀμυγδαλιά.
almost ['ɔːlməust] ad σχεδόν, περίπου.
alms [aːmz] npl ἐλεημοσύνη, ψυχικό.
alone [ə'ləun] a μόνος, μονάχος, μοναχός
‖ ad μόνον.
along [ə'lɔŋ] ad: **move ~** προχωρῶ, βηματίζω ‖ ἐμπρός!, ἔλα λοιπόν! ‖ prep κατά
μῆκος ‖ **~side** ad,prep πλευρισμένες,
πλάϊ-πλάϊ ‖ **all ~** ἀπό καιρό, ἀπ' τήν
ἀρχή.
aloof [ə'luːf] a,ad μακράν, εἰς ἀπόστασιν.
aloud [ə'laud] ad μεγαλοφώνως, φωναχτά,
δυνατά.
alphabet ['ælfəbet] n ἀλφάβητον ‖ **~ical** a
ἀλφαβητικός ‖ **~ically** ad ἀλφαβητικῶς.
alpine ['ælpain] a ἀλπικός.
Alps [ælps] npl: **the ~** αἱ Ἄλπεις.
already [ɔːl'redi] ad ἤδη, κιόλας.
alright [ɔːl'rait] = **all right** ‖ see right.
also ['ɔːlsəu] ad ἐπίσης, ὡσαύτως, ἀκόμη
καί.
altar ['ɔltə*] n βωμός, θυσιαστήριον ‖
(church) Ἁγία Τράπεζα.
alter ['ɔltə*] vt μεταβάλλω, τροποποιῶ,
μεταποιῶ ‖ vi μεταβάλλομαι ‖ **~ation** n
μεταβολή, ἀλλαγή, ἀλλοίωσις.
alternate [ɔl'təːnit] a ἐναλλάσσων, ἐναλ-
λασσόμενος ‖ ['ɔltə:neit] vt ἐναλλάσσω,
χρησιμοποιῶ ἐναλλάξ ‖ vi ἐναλλάσσομαι
(with μέ) ‖ **~ly** ad ἐναλλάξ, ἀλληλοδια-
δόχως.
alternative [ɔl'təːnətiv] n ἐκλογή, λύσις ‖
~ly ad ἐναλλάξ.
alternator ['ɔltəːneitə*] n (elec) ἐναλλάκτης.
although [ɔːl'ðəu] cj ἄν καί, μόλον ὅτι,
καίτοι.
altitude ['æltitjuːd] n ὕψος, ὑψόμετρον.
alto ['æltəu] n (male) ὀξύφωνος ‖ (female)
κοντράλτο.
altogether [ɔːltə'geðə*] ad τελείως, ὁλοσχερῶς, ἐντελῶς.
altruistic [æltru'istik] a ἀλτρουϊστικός.
aluminium [ælju'miniəm], (US) **aluminum**
[ə'luːminəm] n ἀλουμίνιον, ἀργίλιον.
always ['ɔːlweiz] ad πάντα, πάντοτε,
διαρκῶς.
am [æm] see **be**.
amalgam [ə'mælgəm] n ἀμάλγαμα ‖ **~ate**
vti ἀμαλγαμώνω, συγχωνεύω, ἐνοῦμαι ‖
~ation n συγχώνευσις.

amass [ə'mæs] vt συσσωρεύω, μαζεύω.
amateur ['æmətə*] n ἐρασιτέχνης ‖ a ἐρα-
σιτεχνική ‖ **~ish** a ἐρασιτεχνικός.
amaze [ə'meiz] vt ἐκπλήσσω, καταπλήσσω,
θαμπώνω ‖ **~d** a ἔκπληκτος, κατάπληκτος ‖ **~ment** n κατάπληξις, ἔκπληξις, ξάφνιασμα.
amazing [ə'meiziŋ] a καταπληκτικός, ἀπίστευτος.
ambassador [æm'bæsədə*] n πρεσβευτής,
πρέσβυς.
ambiguity [æmbi'gjuiti] n ἀμφιλογία,
ἀσάφεια, διφορούμενον.
ambiguous [æm'bigjuəs] a ἀμφίλογος,
ἀβέβαιος, ἀσαφής.
ambition [æm'biʃən] n φιλοδοξία.
ambitious [æm'biʃəs] a φιλόδοξος.
amble ['æmbl] vi πηγαίνω ραχβάνι, βαδίζω
ἤρεμα.
ambulance ['æmbjuləns] n ἀσθενοφόρον
αὐτοκίνητον.
ambush ['æmbuʃ] n ἐνέδρα, καρτέρι ‖ vt
παρασύρω εἰς ἐνέδραν.
ameliorate [ə'miːliəreit] vt βελτιώνω, καλυτερεύω.
amelioration [ə'miːliə'reiʃən] n καλυτέ-
ρευσις, βελτίωσις.
amen ['aːmen] interj ἀμήν.
amenable [ə'miːnəbl] a ὑπάκουος, πρόθυμος.
amend [ə'mend] vt διορθώνω, τροποποιῶ ‖
vi διορθώνομαι ‖ **~ment** n τροποποίησις,
διόρθωσις ‖ **to make ~s** ἐπανορθώνω,
ἀποζημιώνω.
amenity [ə'miːniti] n χάρις, ὀμορφιά,
ἄνεσις.
America [ə'merikə] n Ἀμερική.
American [ə'merikən] a ἀμερικανικός ‖ n
Ἀμερικανός ‖ **~ize** vt ἐξαμερικανίζω.
amiable ['eimiəbl] a εὐγενικός, φιλόφρων,
γλυκύς.
amicable ['æmikəbl] a φιλικός ‖ **~ settlement** n συμβιβασμός.
amid(st) [ə'mid(st)] prep ἀνάμεσα, ἀναμεταξύ.
amiss [ə'mis] a,ad ἐσφαλμένος, κακά,
στραβά ‖ **to take ~** παίρνω στραβά
παρεξηγῶ.
ammeter ['æmitə*] n ἀμπερόμετρον.
ammunition [æmju'niʃən] n πολεμοφόδια,
πυρομαχικά.
amnesia [æm'niːziə] n ἀμνησία.
amnesty ['æmnisti] n ἀμνηστία.
among(st) [ə'mʌŋ(st)] prep μεταξύ, μέσα,
ἀνάμεσα.
amoral [æ'mɔrəl] a ἄσχετος μέ τήν ἠθικήν.
amorous ['æmərəs] a ἐρωτόληπτος, ἐρωτι-
άρης.
amorphous [ə'mɔːfəs] a ἄμορφος.
amount [ə'maunt] n ποσόν, σύνολον,
ποσότης ‖ vi ἀνέρχομαι, συμποσοῦμαι,
ἰσοδυναμῶ ‖ **to ~ to** ἀνέρχομαι, συμποσοῦμαι.

ampère ['æmpεə*] n ἀμπέρ.
amphibious [æm'fibiəs] a ἀμφίβιος.
amphitheatre ['æmfiθiətə*] n ἀμφιθέατρον.
ample ['æmpl] a (enough) ἀρκετός, πλήρης ‖ (big) εὐρύς, πλατύς ‖ (abundant) ἄφθονα, πλούσια.
amplifier ['æmplifaiə*] n ἐνισχυτής.
amputate ['æmpjuteit] vt ἀποκόπτω, ἀκρωτηριάζω.
amputation [æmpju'teiʃən] n ἐκτομή, ἀκρωτηριασμός.
amuck [ə'mʌk] ad: to run ~ παθαίνω ἀμόκ, παραφέρομαι.
amuse [ə'mju:z] vt διασκεδάζω, ξεκουράζω ‖ ~ment n διασκέδασις, θέαμα, ἀναψυχή.
amusing [ə'mju:ziŋ] a διασκεδαστικός, ξεκαρδιστικός.
an [æn] see a.
anachronism [ə'nækrənizəm] ι. ἀναχρονισμός.
anaemia [ə'ni:miə] n ἀναιμία
anaemic [ə'ni:mik] a ἀναιμικός.
anaesthetic [ænis'θetik] n ἀναισθητικόν.
anagram ['ænəgræm] n ἀναγραμματισμός.
analgesic [ænæl'dʒi:sik] a,n ἀναλγητικός.
analogous [ə'næləgəs] a ἀνάλογος.
analogy [ə'nælədʒi] n ἀναλογία.
analyse ['ænəlaiz] vt ἀναλύω.
analysis [ə'næləsis] n ἀνάλυσις.
anarchist ['ænəkist] n ἀναρχικός.
anarchy ['ænəki] n ἀναρχία.
anatomical [ænə'tɔmikəl] a ἀνατομικός.
anatomy [ə'nætəmi] n ἀνατομία.
ancestor ['ænsistə*] n πρόγονος, προπάτωρ.
ancestral [æn'sestrəl] a προγονικός, προπατορικός.
ancestry ['ænsistri] n καταγωγή.
anchor ['æŋkə*] n ἄγκυρα ‖ vi ἀγκυροβολῶ, ρίχνω ἄγκυραν, ἀράζω ‖ ~age n ἀγκυροβόλιον, ἀραξοβόλι.
anchovy ['æntʃəvi] n ἀντσούγια, χαμψί.
ancient ['einʃənt] a ἀρχαῖος, παλαιός.
and [ænd, ənd] cj καί.
anecdote ['ænikdəut] n ἀνέκδοτον.
anemone [ə'neməni] n ἀνεμώνη.
anew [ə'nju:] ad ἐκ νέου, πάλιν, ξανά.
angel ['eindʒəl] n ἄγγελος, ἀγγελούδι ‖ ~ic a ἀγγελικός.
anger ['æŋgə*] n ὀργή, θυμός, παραφορά ‖ vt ἐξοργίζω, θυμώνω.
angle ['æŋgl] n γωνία ‖ (viewpoint) ἄποψις ‖ vi ψαρεύω ‖ ~r n ψαρὰς (μέ καλάμι).
Anglican ['æŋglikən] n Ἀγγλικανός.
anglicize ['æŋglisaiz] vt χρησιμοποιῶ ἀγγλισμούς.
angling ['æŋgliŋ] n ψάρεμα.
Anglo- ['æŋgləu] prefix ἀγγλο-.
angrily ['æŋgrili] ad ὠργισμένα, θυμωμένα.
angry ['æŋgri] a ὠργισμένος, θυμωμένος.
anguish ['æŋgwiʃ] n ἀγωνία, ἀδημονία, πόνος.
angular ['æŋgjulə*] a γωνιακός, γωνιώδης.
animal ['æniməl] n ζῶον ‖ a ζωϊκός.

animate ['ænimit] a ἔμψυχος, ζωντανός ‖ ['ænimeit] vt ζωογονῶ, δίδω κίνησιν ‖ ~d a ζωντανός, ζωηρός.
animation [æni'meiʃən] n ζωηρότης, θέρμη, σφρῖγος.
animosity [æni'mɔsiti] n ἐχθρότης, ἔχθρα.
aniseed ['ænisi:d] n γλυκάνισον.
ankle ['æŋkl] n ἀστράγαλος, σφυρόν.
annex(e) ['æneks] n παράρτημα ‖ annex [ə'neks] vt προσαρτῶ.
annihilate [ə'naiəleit] vt ἐκμηδενίζω, ἐξαφανίζω.
anniversary [æni'və:səri] n ἐπέτειος.
annotate ['ænəuteit] vt σχολιάζω.
announce [ə'nauns] vt (ἀν)αγγέλλω, ἀνακοινῶ ‖ ~ment n ἀναγγελία, ἀνακοίνωσις ‖ ~r n ἐκφωνητής.
annoy [ə'nɔi] vt ἐνοχλῶ, πειράζω ‖ ~ance n ἐνόχλησις, μπελᾶς, στενοχωρία ‖ ~ing a ἐνοχλητικός, ὀχληρός.
annual ['ænjuəl] a ἐτήσιος, χρονιάρικος ‖ n (book) ἐπετηρίς, ἡμερολόγιον ‖ ~ly ad ἐτησίως.
annuity [ə'nju:iti] n πρόσοδος, ἐπίδομα.
annul [ə'nʌl] vt ἀκυρώνω, διαλύω, καταργέλλω ‖ ~ment n ἀκύρωσις, κατάργησις.
anoint [ə'nɔint] vt χρίω, ἀλείφω.
anomalous [ə'nɔmələs] a ἀνώμαλος.
anomaly [ə'nɔməli] n ἀνωμαλία.
anonymity [ænə'nimiti] n ἀνωνυμία.
anonymous [ə'nɔniməs] a ἀνώνυμος.
another [ə'nʌðə*] a, pron ἄλλος (ἕνας), ἀκόμη (ἕνας) ‖ one ~ ὁ ἕνας τόν ἄλλον.
answer ['a:nsə*] n ἀπάντησις ‖ (solution) λύσις ‖ vt ἀπαντῶ ‖ (suit) ἀνταποκρίνομαι ‖ to ~ for vt ἐγγυῶμαι διά ‖ ~able a ὑπεύθυνος, ὑπόλογος.
ant [ænt] n μυρμήκι.
antagonism [æn'tægənizəm] n ἀνταγωνισμός, ἀντιζηλία, ἐχθρότης.
antagonist [æn'tægənist] n ἀνταγωνιστής, ἀντίπαλος ‖ ~ic a ἐχθρικός, ἀνταγωνιστικός.
antagonize [æn'tægənaiz] vt προκαλῶ ἀνταγωνισμόν, προκαλῶ ἐχθρότητα.
Antarctic [ænt'a:ktik] a ἀνταρκτικός.
antecedent [ænti'si:dənt] n ἡγούμενον ‖ a προηγούμενος.
antelope ['æntiləup] n ἀντιλόπη.
antenatal ['ænti'neitl] a πρό τῆς γεννήσεως.
antenna [æn'tenə] n κεραία.
anthem ['ænθəm] n ὕμνος.
anthology [æn'θɔlədʒi] n ἀνθολογία.
anthropologist [ænθrə'pɔlədʒist] n ἀνθρωπολόγος.
anthropology [ænθrə'pɔlədʒi] n ἀνθρωπολογία.
anti-aircraft ['ænti'εəkra:ft] a ἀντιαεροπορικός.
antibiotic ['æntibai'ɔtik] n ἀντιβιοτικόν.
anticipate [æn'tisipeit] vt προλαμβάνω ‖ (foresee) προβλέπω, προσδοκῶ.

anticipation [æntisi'peiʃən] n πρόληψις, πρόβλεψις ‖ (*expectation*) προσδοκία.

anticlimax ['ænti'klaimæks] n ἀντικλῖμαξ, κατάπτωσις, παρακμή.

anticlockwise ['ænti'klɔkwaiz] ad = counterclockwise ‖ see counter.

antics ['æntiks] npl κόλπα, ἀστεῖα, φάρσες.

anticyclone ['ænti'saikloun] n ἀντικυκλών.

antidote ['æntidaut] n ἀντίδοτον.

antifreeze ['ænti'fri:z] n ἀντιψυκτικός, ἀντιπηκτικός.

antipathy [æn'tipəθi] n ἀντιπάθεια.

antiquarian [ænti'kweəriən] n ἀρχαιοδίφης, ἀρχαιόφιλος.

antiquated ['æntikweitid] a ἀρχαϊκός, ἀπηρχαιωμένος, πεπαλαιωμένος.

antique [æn'ti:k] n ἀρχαῖον, παλαιόν, ἀντίκα ‖ ~s npl ἀρχαιότητες, ἀντίκες.

antiquity [æn'tikwiti] n ἀρχαιότης.

antiseptic [ænti'septik] a,n ἀντισηπτικόν.

antisocial ['ænti'sɔuʃəl] a ἀντικοινωνικός.

antithesis [æn'tiθisis] n ἀντίθεσις.

antlers ['æntləz] npl κέρατα (ἐλάφου).

anus ['einəs] n δακτύλιος, ἕδρα.

anvil ['ænvil] n ἄκμων, ἀμόνι.

anxiety [æŋ'zaiəti] n ἀνησυχία, φόβος.

anxious ['æŋkʃəs] a ἀνήσυχος, στενοχωρημένος ‖ (*impatient*) ἀνυπόμονος ‖ ~ly ad ἀνήσυχα, ἀνυπόμονα.

any ['eni] pron,a κανείς, καμμιά, κανένα ‖ (*whosoever*) ὁποιοσδήποτε, κάθε ‖ ad καθόλου, πιά ‖ ~body pron κανείς, καμμιά, οἰοσδήποτε, καθένας ‖ ~how ad ὁπωσδήποτε, ὅπως κιάν εἶναι ‖ ~one pron ὁποιοσδήποτε, καθένας, ὅλοι ‖ ~thing pron τίποτε, κάτι, ὁτιδήποτε ‖ ~way ad ὁπωσδήποτε, κουτσά-στραβά ‖ cj ὁπωσδήποτε, ἐν πάση περιπτώσει ‖ ~where ad ὁπουδήποτε, πουθενά.

apace [ə'peis] ad γρήγορα, ταχέως.

apart [ə'pɑ:t] ad κεχωρισμένος, χωριστά, κατά μέρος ‖ ~ from ἐκτός τοῦ ὅτι.

apartheid [ə'pɑ:teit] n διαχωρισμός, φυλετική διάκρισις.

apartment [ə'pɑ:tmənt] n δωμάτιον ‖ (*flat*) διαμέρισμα.

apathetic [æpə'θetik] a ἀπαθής, ἀδιάφορος.

apathy ['æpəθi] n ἀπάθεια, ἀδιαφορία.

ape [eip] n πίθηκος, ματμοῦ ‖ vt μιμοῦμαι.

apéritif [ə'peritiv] n ὀρεκτικός.

aperture ['æpətʃjuə*] n ἄνοιγμα, ὀπή, σχισμή.

apex ['eipeks] n κορυφή.

apiece [ə'pi:s] ad ἕκαστος, καθένας.

Apollo [ə'pɔlou] n 'Απόλλων.

apologetic [əpɔlə'dʒetik] a ἀπολογητικός, τῆς συγγνώμης.

apologize [ə'pɔlədʒaiz] vi ζητῶ συγγνώμη.

apology [ə'pɔlədʒi] n ἀπολογία, συγγνώμη.

apoplexy ['æpəpleksi] n ἀποπληξία, συμφόρικός.

apostle [ə'pɔsl] n ἀπόστολος.

apostrophe [ə'pɔstrəfi] n ἀπόστροφος.

appal [ə'pɔ:l] vt τρομάζω, προκαλῶ φρίκην ‖ ~ling a τρομερός, φρικτός.

apparatus [æpə'reitɔs] n συσκευή, μηχάνημα.

apparel [ə'pærəl] n ἔνδυμα, ντύσιμο.

apparent [ə'pærənt] a φαινόμενος, ἐμφανής, φανερός ‖ ~ly ad προφανώς, ὅπως φαίνεται.

apparition [æpə'riʃən] n φάντασμα.

appeal [ə'pi:l] n (ἐκ)κλησις, προσφυγή ‖ (*law*) κλῆσις, ἔφεσις ‖ (*charm*) γοητευτική, ἑλκυστική ‖ vi προσφεύγω, ἀπευθύνομαι ‖ ~ing a συγκινητικός, συμπαθητικός.

appear [ə'piə*] vi φαίνομαι, ἐμφανίζομαι ‖ ~ance n ἐμφάνισις, παρουσία, παρουσιαστικό ‖ to put in or make an ~ance ἐμφανίζομαι, παρουσιάζομαι.

appease [ə'pi:z] vt κατευνάζω, ἱκανοποιῶ.

appendage [ə'pendidʒ] n προσάρτημα, παράρτημα ‖ (*anat*) ἀπόφυσις, ἐξάρτημα.

appendicitis [əpendi'saitis] n σκωληκοειδῖτις.

appendix [ə'pendiks] n παράρτημα, ἐξάρτημα ‖ (*anat*) σκωληκοειδής ἀπόφυσις.

appetite ['æpitait] n ὄρεξη ‖ loss of ~ n ἀνορεξία.

appetizer ['æpitaizə*] n ὀρεκτικόν, μεζές.

appetizing ['æpitaiziŋ] a ὀρεκτικός, ἑλκυστικός.

applaud [ə'plɔ:d] vt χειροκροτῶ, ἐπευφημῶ.

applause [ə'plɔ:z] n χειροκροτήματα, ἐπιδοκιμασία.

apple ['æpl] n μῆλον ‖ ~ pie n μηλόπητα ‖ ~ tree n μηλιά.

appliance [ə'plaiəns] n ὄργανον, μηχάνημα, ἐργαλεῖον.

applicable [ə'plikəbl] a ἐφαρμόσιμος, κατάλληλος.

applicant ['æplikənt] n αἰτῶν, ὑποψήφιος, αἰτητής.

application [æpli'keiʃən] n (*request*) αἴτησις, παράκλησις ‖ (*hard work*) ἐπιμέλεια, προσοχή, προσήλωσις ‖ (*putting into practice*) ἐφαρμογή, χρῆσις.

applied [ə'plaid] a προσηρμοσμένος, ἐφηρμοσμένος.

apply [ə'plai] vi ἐφαρμόζω ‖ (*place on*) ἐπιθέτω, βάζω ‖ (*for job etc*) ἀπευθύνομαι, ὑποβάλλω αἴτησιν ‖ to ~ the brake πατῶ φρένο, φρενάρω ‖ to ~ o.s. προσηλοῦμαι, ἀφοσιώνομαι.

appoint [ə'pɔint] vt (δι)ορίζω, ὀνομάζω ‖ ~ment n συνάντησις, ραντεβού, συνέντευξις.

apportion [ə'pɔ:ʃən] vt κατανέμω, διανέμω, μοιράζω.

appreciable [ə'pri:ʃəbl] a ὑπολογίσιμος, αἰσθητός.

appreciate [ə'pri:ʃieit] vt ἐκτιμῶ, ὑπολογίζω, ἀποδίδω σημασίαν ‖ vi (*econ*) ἀνατιμοῦμαι, ὑπερτιμοῦμαι.

appreciation [əpri:ʃi'eiʃən] *n* ἐκτίμησις ‖ (*econ*) ὑπερτίμησις, ἀνατίμησις, ὑπεραξία.

apprehend [æpri'hend] *vt* συλλαμβάνω, ἀντιλαμβάνομαι.

apprehension [æpri'henʃən] *n* (*fear*) φόβος, ἀνησυχία ‖ (*understanding*) ἀντίληψις, νόησις ‖ (*arrest*) σύλληψις, τσάκισμα.

apprehensive [æpri'hensiv] *a* (*worried*) ἀνήσυχος, ἔμφοβος, φοβισμένος.

apprentice [ə'prentis] *n* μαθητευόμενος ‖ *vt* τοποθετῶ ὡς μαθητευόμενον ‖ ~ship *n* μαθητεία, μαθήτευσις.

approach [ə'prəutʃ] *n* προσέγγισις, πλησίασμα ‖ (*path*) εἴσοδος, ὁδός ‖ (*golf*) κτύπημα ‖ *vti* πλησιάζω, προσεγγίζω ‖ ~able *a* εὐπρόσιτος, προσηνής, προσιτός.

approbation [æprə'beiʃən] *n* ἔγκρισις, ἐπιδοκιμασία.

appropriate [ə'prəupriit] *a* κατάλληλος, ἁρμόδιος, ταιριαστός ‖ [ə'prəuprieit] *vt* οἰκειοποιοῦμαι, ἰδιοποιοῦμαι, παίρνω.

appropriation [əprəupri'eiʃən] *n* (*pol*) πίστωσις, κονδύλιον ‖ (*setting apart*) διάθεσις, πρόβλεψις.

approval [ə'pru:vəl] *n* ἔγκρισις.

approve [ə'pru:v] *vti* ἐγκρίνω, ἐπιδοκιμάζω, ἐπικυρώνω ‖ ~d *a* ἐγκριθείς, ἐγκεκριμένος.

approximate [ə'prɔksimit] *a* κατά προσέγγισιν ‖ [ə'prɔksimeit] *vt* προσεγγίζω, πλησιάζω.

approximation [əprɔksi'meiʃən] *n* προσέγγισις, ἐγγύτης.

apricot ['eiprikɔt] *n* βερύκκοκο.

April ['eiprəl] *n* Ἀπρίλιος.

apron ['eiprən] *n* ποδιά, μπροστέλλα.

apse [æps] *n* κόγχη, ἁψίς.

apt [æpt] *a* (*suitable*) κατάλληλος, ἁρμόζων ‖ (*ready*) ὑποκείμενος εἰς.

aptitude ['æptitju:d] *n* ἱκανότης.

squalung ['ækwələη] *n* συσκευή καταδύσεως, ἀκουαλάγκ.

aquarium [ə'kwɛəriəm] *n* ἐνυδρεῖον, ἀκουάριον.

aquatic [ə'kwætik] *a* ὑδρόβιος ‖ ~ sports *npl* θαλάσσια σπόρ.

aqueduct ['ækwidʌkt] *n* ὑδραγωγεῖον.

Arab ['ærəb] *a* ἀραβικός ‖ ~ia [ə'reibiə] *n* Ἀραβία ‖ ~ian [ə'reibiən] *a* Ἄραψ, ἀραβικός ‖ *n* Ἄραψ, Ἀράπης ‖ ~ic *a* ἀραβικός ‖ *n* ἀραβική γλῶσσα.

arable ['ærəbl] *a* καλλιεργήσιμος.

arbiter ['a:bitə*] *n* διαιτητής, κριτής.

arbitrary ['a:bitrəri] *a* αὐθαίρετος.

arbitration [a:bi'treiʃən] *n* διαιτησία ‖ ~ court *n* διαιτητικόν δικαστήριον.

arbitrator ['a:bitreitə*] *n* διαιτητής.

arc [a:k] *n* τόξον.

arcade [a:'keid] *n* στοά, καμάρα.

arch [a:tʃ] *n* ἁψίς, καμάρα ‖ *a* (*chief*) ἀρχι- ‖ *vt* (*bend*) λυγίζω, καμπουριάζω.

archaeologist [a:ki'ɔlədʒist] *n* ἀρχαιολόγος.

archaeology [a:ki'ɔlədʒi] *n* ἀρχαιολογία.

archaic [a:'keiik] *a* ἀρχαϊκός.

archbishop ['a:tʃ'biʃəp] *n* ἀρχιεπίσκοπος.

arch-enemy ['a:tʃ'enimi] *n* μέγας ἐχθρός.

archer ['a:tʃə*] *n* τοξότης ‖ ~y *n* τοξοβολία.

archetype ['a:kitaip] *n* ἀρχέτυπον.

archimandrite ['a:ki'mændrait] *n* ἀρχιμανδρίτης.

archipelago [a:ki'peligəu] *n* ἀρχιπέλαγος, πολύνησον.

architect ['a:kitekt] *n* ἀρχιτέκτων ‖ ~ure *n* ἀρχιτεκτονική ‖ ~ural *a* ἀρχιτεκτονικός.

archives ['a:kaivz] *npl* ἀρχεῖα, ἔγγραφα.

archway ['a:tʃwei] *n* στοά, ἁψιδωτή εἴσοδος.

arc lamp ['a:klæmp] *n* λυχνία βολταϊκοῦ τόξου.

Arctic ['a:ktik] *a* Ἀρκτικός.

ardent ['a:dənt] *a* φλογερός, διακαής, ζωηρός.

ardour ['a:də*] *n* ζέσις, μανία, πόθος.

arduous ['a:djuəs] *a* τραχύς, δύσκολος, κοπιώδης.

are [a:*] *see* be.

area ['ɛəriə] *n* περιοχή, ἔκτασις, χῶρος ‖ (*math*) ἐμβαδόν.

arena [ə'ri:nə] *n* παλαίστρα, κονίστρα, ἀρένα.

aren't [a:nt] = **are not** ‖ *see* be.

argue ['a:gju:] *vti* (*discuss*) συζητῶ, πραγματεύομαι ‖ (*prove*) (ἀπο)δεικνύω ‖ (*reason*) φέρω ἐπιχειρήματα, παρατάσσω.

argument ['a:gjumənt] *n* ἐπιχείρημα, συζήτησις ‖ (*dispute*) φιλονεικία, λογομαχία ‖ (*of play*) σύνοψις, περίληψις ‖ ~ative *a* συζητητικός.

aria ['a:riə] *n* ἦχος, σκοπός, ἄρια.

arid ['ærid] *a* ξηρός, ἄνυδρος.

arise [ə'raiz] (*irreg v*) *vi* ἐγείρομαι, σηκώνομαι ‖ (*appear*) ἐμφανίζομαι, ἀπορρέω.

aristocracy [æris'tɔkrəsi] *n* ἀριστοκρατία.

aristocrat ['æristəkræt] *n* ἀριστοκράτης ‖ ~ic *a* ἀριστοκρατικός, ἀρχοντικός.

arithmetic [ə'riθmətik] *n* ἀριθμητική.

arm [a:m] *n* βραχίων, μπράτσο ‖ (*hand*) χέρι ‖ (*weapon*) ὅπλον ‖ *vt* (ἐξ)ὁπλίζω, ἁρματώνω ‖ ~s *npl* ὅπλα ‖ ~ed forces *npl* ἐνόπλοι δυνάμεις.

armchair ['a:mtʃeə*] *n* πολυθρόνα.

armful ['a:mful] *n* ἀγκαλιά.

armistice ['a:mistis] *n* ἀνακωχή.

armour, (US) armor ['a:mə*] *n* θωράκισις ‖ (*panoply*) ἁρματωσιά ‖ ~ed car *n* τεθωρακισμένο ἅρμα μάχης.

armoury ['a:məri] *n* ὁπλοστάσιον, ὁπλαποθήκη.

armpit ['a:mpit] *n* μασχάλη.

army ['a:mi] *n* στρατός ‖ (*of people etc*) πλῆθος.

aroma [ə'rəumə] *n* ἄρωμα, μυρωδιά ‖ ~**tic** *a* ἀρωματικός.

around [ə'raund] *ad* πέριξ, (τρι)γύρω, ὁλόγυρα ‖ (*about*) (*US*) περίπου ‖ *prep* περί, γύρω.

arouse [ə'rauz] *vt* διεγείρω, ἀφυπνίζω, ξυπνῶ.

arrange [ə'reindʒ] *vt* τακτοποιῶ, διαρρυθμίζω, διευθετῶ, κανονίζω ‖ ~**ment** *n* τακτοποίησις, ρύθμισις, διευθέτησις.

array [ə'rei] *n* (*in lines*) σειρά, παράταξις ‖ (*dress*) στολή.

arrears [ə'riəz] *npl* καθηστερούμενα, ἐκπρόθεσμος ‖ **in** ~ καθυστερούμενα ‖ ~ **of pay** *n* καθυστερούμενοι μισθοί.

arrest [ə'rest] *n* (*making prisoner*) σύλληψις, κράτησις ‖ (*halt*) ἀναχαίτησις, σταμάτημα ‖ *vt* σταματῶ, ἀναχαιτίζω ‖ (*law*) συλλαμβάνω.

arrival [ə'raivəl] *n* ἄφιξις, ἐρχομός ‖ **new** ~ *n* νεοαφιχθείς ‖ (*baby*) νεογέννητον.

arrive [ə'raiv] *vi* ἀφικνοῦμαι, φθάνω (*at* εἰς) ‖ (*at a conclusion*) καταλήγω.

arrogance ['ærəgəns] *n* ἀλαζονεία, ἔπαρσις, αὐθάδεια.

arrogant ['ærəgənt] *a* ἀλαζών, ὑπερόπτης, αὐθάδης.

arrow ['ærəu] *n* βέλος, σαΐτα.

arsenal ['aːsinl] *n* ὁπλοστάσιον.

arsenic ['aːsnik] *n* ἀρσενικόν.

arson ['aːsn] *n* ἐμπρησμός.

art [aːt] *n* τέχνη ‖ ~ **gallery** *n* πινακοθήκη.

artery ['aːtəri] *n* ἀρτηρία.

artesian well [aː'tiːziən'wel] *n* ἀρτεσιανόν φρέαρ.

artful [aːtful] *a* (*person*) ἐπιδέξιος, ἐφευρετικός ‖ (*crafty*) πονηρός, δόλιος.

arthritis [aː'θraitis] *n* ἀρθρῖτις.

artichoke ['aːtitʃəuk] *n* ἀγκινάρα.

article ['aːtikl] *n* (*of agreement etc*) ἄρθρον, ὅρος ‖ (*gram*) ἄρθρον ‖ (*newspaper etc*) ἄρθρον ‖ (*items*) εἶδος, ἀντικείμενον.

articulate [aː'tikjulit] *a* ἀρθρωτός, ἔναρθρος ‖ (*in expression*) σαφής, εὐκρινής ‖ ~**d** *a* ἔναρθρος.

artifice ['aːtifis] *n* τέχνασμα, κόλπο ‖ (*skill*) τέχνη, ἐπιδεξιότης.

artificial [aːti'fiʃəl] *a* τεχνητός, ψεύτικος ‖ ~ **respiration** *n* τεχνητή ἀναπνοή.

artillery [aː'tiləri] *n* πυροβολικόν.

artisan [aːti'zæn] *n* τεχνίτης, βιοτέχνης, ἐργάτης.

artist [aːtist] *n* καλλιτέχνης ‖ (*painter*) ζωγράφος ‖ ~**ic** *a* καλλιτεχνικός.

artless ['aːtlis] *a* ἄτεχνος ‖ (*natural*) ἀπέριττος, φυσικός ‖ (*naive*) ἀφελής, ἀπονήρευτος.

as [æz, əz] *ad* (*in main clause*) ἐπίσης, ἐξ ἴσου, τόσον . . . ὅσον ‖ ~ **regards** ὅσον γιά ‖ *cj* (*in subject clause*) ὅσον, τόσον . . . ὅσον, σάν ‖ (*time*) ἐνῶ, καθὼς ‖ (*because*) ἐπειδή ‖ (*manner*) **do** ~ **you**

like κάμετε ὅπως σᾶς ἀρέσει ‖ ~ **is** ὅπως εἶναι.

asbestos [æz'bestəs] *n* ἀμίαντος, ἄσβεστος.

ascend [ə'send] *vi* ἀνέρχομαι, ἀνεβαίνω ‖ ~**ant** *a* ἀνερχόμενος ‖ *n* ἄνοδος ‖ ~**ancy** *n* (*influence*) ἐπιρροή, ἐπιβολή ‖ (*rule*) ἡγεμονία, ὑπεροχή.

ascension [ə'senʃən] *n* ἀνάβασις, ἄνοδος, ἀνάληψις ‖ **A~ Day** *n* τῆς Ἀναλήψεως.

ascent [ə'sent] *n* ἄνοδος, ἀνάβασις ‖ (*incline*) ἀνήφορος, ἀνωφέρεια, κλίσις.

ascertain [æsə'tein] *vt* διαπιστώνω, ἐξακριβώνω.

ascetic [ə'setik] *a* ἀσκητικός.

ash [æʃ] *n* τέφρα, στάχτη ‖ (*tree*) μελία, φλαμούρι.

ashamed [ə'ʃeimd] *a*: **to be** ~ εἶμαι ντροπιασμένος, ντρέπομαι.

ashen ['æʃən] *a* σταχτής ‖ (*person*) ὠχρός, κίτρινος.

ashore [ə'ʃɔː*] *ad* στήν ξηρά, προσηραγμένος.

ashtray ['æʃtrei] *n* σταχτοδοχεῖο.

Asia ['eiʃə] *n* Ἀσία ‖ ~*n* *a* ἀσιατικός ‖ ~**tic** *a* ἀσιατικός ‖ ~ **Minor** *n* Μικρά Ἀσία.

aside [ə'said] *ad* κατά μέρος, πλάϊ, παράμερα ‖ ~ **from** ἐκτός, πέραν.

ask [aːsk] *vt* (ἐ)ρωτῶ, ζητῶ, προσκαλῶ ‖ **to** ~ **a question** ὑποβάλλω ἐρώτησιν.

askance [ə'skaːns] *ad*: **to look at s.o.** ~ κοιτάζω μέ δυσπιστίαν.

askew [ə'skjuː] *ad* λοξά, στραβά.

asleep [ə'sliːp] *a,ad* κοιμισμένος ‖ (*foot*) μουδιασμένος ‖ **to fall** ~ ἀποκοιμιέμαι.

asparagus [əs'pærəgəs] *n* σπαράγγι.

aspect ['æspekt] *n* θέα, ὄψις, προσανατολισμός.

asphalt ['æsfælt] *n* ἄσφαλτος ‖ ~ **road** *n* ἀσφαλτοστρωμένος (δρόμος).

asphyxiate [æs'fiksieit] *vt* πνίγω.

asphyxiation [æsfiksi'eiʃən] *n* ἀσφυξία.

aspirate ['æspəreit] *vt* δασύνω.

aspiration [æspə'reiʃən] *n* φιλοδοξία, βλέψις ‖ (*gram*) δασεῖα προφορά.

aspire [əs'paiə*] *vt*: **to** ~ **to** φιλοδοξῶ, ἐποφθαλμιῶ.

aspirin ['æsprin] *n* ἀσπιρίνη.

ass [æs] *n* γάϊδαρος.

assail [ə'seil] *vt* ἐπιτίθεμαι, προσβάλλω ‖ ~**ant** *n* ἐπιτιθέμενος.

assassin [ə'sæsin] *n* δολοφόνος ‖ ~**ate** *vt* δολοφονῶ ‖ ~**ation** *n* δολοφονία.

assault [ə'sɔːlt] *n* ἔφοδος, ἐπίθεσις ‖ *vt* ἐπιτίθεμαι, ἐξορμῶ ‖ (*person*) βιάζω.

assemblage [ə'semblidʒ] *n* σύνδεσις, συναρμολόγησις.

assemble [ə'sembl] *vt* συγκεντρώνω, συναθροίζω ‖ (*machine etc*) ἑνώνω, συναρμολογῶ ‖ *vi* συγκεντροῦμαι, συγκεντρώνομαι.

assembly [ə'sembli] *n* συνέλευσις, συγκέντρωσις ‖ (*machines*) συναρμολόγησις, συγκρότημα ‖ ~ line *n* τράπεζα συναρμολογήσεως, άλυσίδα.

assent [ə'sent] *n* συγκατάθεσις, έγκρισις ‖ *vi* συγκατατίθεμαι, συναινῶ, ἐπικυρῶ.

assert [ə'sə:t] *vt* ἐπιβάλλω, διεκδικῶ ‖ (*ascertain*) βεβαιῶ, ὑποστηρίζω ‖ ~ion *n* ἰσχυρισμός, ὑποστήριξις ‖ ~ive *a* κατηγορηματικός, θετικός.

assess [ə'ses] *vt* καταλογίζω, ὑπολογίζω, ἐπιβάλλω (φόρον) ‖ (*property*) ἐκτιμῶ, φορολογῶ ‖ ~ment *n* καταλογισμός, ἐκτίμησις ‖ (*tax*) φόρος ‖ ~or *n* ἐλεγκτής (ἐφοριακός).

asset ['æset] *n* περιουσιακόν στοιχεῖον ‖ (*qualities*) προσόν, ἀξία, ἀτού ‖ ~s *npl* περιουσία ‖ (*econ*) ἐνεργητικόν, λαβεῖν.

assiduity [æsi'djuəti] *n* ἐπιμονή, προσήλωσις, ἐπιμέλεια.

assiduous [ə'sidjuəs] *a* ἐπιμελής, προσεκτικός.

assign [ə'sain] *vt* προορίζω, παρέχω, παραχωρῶ, δίδω ‖ ~ ment *n* ἀνατιθεμένη ἐργασία.

assimilate [ə'simileit] *vt* ἐξομοιώνω ‖ (*food*) ἀφομοιώνω.

assimilation [əsimi'leifən] *n* ἀφομοίωσις.

assist [ə'sist] *vt* βοηθῶ, συντρέχω, μετέχω ‖ ~ance *n* βοήθεια, ἀρωγή ‖ ~ant *n* βοηθός ‖ *a* βοηθητικός, ἀναπληρωματικός.

assizes [ə'saiziz] *npl*: court of ~ ὁρκωτόν δικαστήριον.

associate [ə'səufiit] *n* ἑταῖρος, συνέταιρος, συνεργάτης ‖ [ə'səufieit] *vti*: to ~ with συνδέω, συνεταιρίζω, συνεργάζομαι, συναναστρέφομαι.

association [əsəusi'eifən] *n* (*club*) ἑταιρεία, ὀργανισμός, σωματεῖον ‖ (*keeping company*) συναναστροφή, σχέσις ‖ ~ football *n* ποδόσφαιρον.

assort [ə'sɔ:t] *vt* (*arrange*) ταξινομῶ, τακτοποιῶ ‖ (*match*) ταιριάζω, προσαρμόζω ‖ ~ed *a* ταιριασμένος, ἀσορτί ‖ ~ment *n* συλλογή, ἀσορτιμέντο ‖ (*arrangement*) τακτοποίησις, ταξινόμησις.

assuage [ə'sweidʒ] *vt* κατευνάζω, ἀνακουφίζω, καλμάρω.

assume [ə'sju:m] *vt* (*take for granted*) ὑποθέτω, θεωρῶ ‖ (*duty*) ἀναλαμβάνω, ἀναδέχομαι ‖ ~d name *n* ψευδώνυμον.

assumption [ə'sʌmpʃən] *n* (*supposition*) ὑπόθεσις, εἰκασία ‖ (*eccl*) Κοίμησις τῆς Θεοτόκου.

assurance [ə'ʃuərəns] *n* (*certainty*) βεβαιότης ‖ (*confidence*) διαβεβαίωσις, ὑπόσχεσις ‖ (*insurance*) ἀσφάλεια (ζωῆς).

assure [ə'ʃuə*] *vt* (δια)βεβαιῶ, ἐξασφαλίζω ‖ ~d *a* βέβαιος.

aster ['æstə*] *n* ἀστήρ, ἀστράκι.

asterisk ['æstərisk] *n* ἀστερίσκος.

astern [ə'stə:n] *ad* ὀπίσω, πρός τά ὀπίσω.

asthma ['æsmə] *n* ἄσθμα ‖ ~tic *a* ἀσθματικός.

astonish [ə'stɔnif] *vt* ἐκπλήσσω, καταπλήσσω ‖ ~ing *a* ἐκπληκτικός, καταπληκτικός ‖ ~ment *n* ἔκπληξις, κατάπληξις.

astound [ə'staund] *vt* καταπλήσσω, ξαφνίζω ‖ ~ing *a* καταπληκτικός, πρωτοφανής.

astray [ə'strei] *ad*: to go ~ περιπλανῶμαι, παραστρατίζω, ξεστρατίζω.

astride [ə'straid] *a,prep* καβάλλα, ἀσεβάλ.

astringent [əs'trindʒənt] *n* στυπτικόν ‖ *a* στυπτικός.

astrologer [əs'trɔlədʒə*] *n* ἀστρολόγος.

astrology [əs'trɔlədʒi] *n* ἀστρολογία.

astronaut ['æstrənɔ:t] *n* ἀστροναύτης.

astronomer [əs'trɔnəmə*] *n* ἀστρονόμος.

astronomy [əs'trɔnəmi] *n* ἀστρονομία.

astute [əs'tju:t] *a* ἔξυπνος, τετραπέρατος ‖ (*crafty*) πανούργος, πονηρός.

asunder [ə'sʌndə*] *ad* κεχωρισμένως, κομματιαστά.

asylum [ə'sailəm] *n* (*refuge*) ἄσυλον, καταφύγιον ‖ (*for insane*) ψυχιατρεῖον.

at [æt] *prep* (*of place*) εἰς ‖ (*of time*) εἰς, κατά, περί ‖ ~ six o'clock στίς ἕξι ‖ ~ first στήν ἀρχή ‖ ~ home στό σπίτι ‖ ~ least τουλάχιστο ‖ ~ last ἐπί τέλους ‖ (*of cause*) γιά ‖ ~ all καθόλου ‖ not ~ all οὐδόλως ‖ ~ sea (*col*) τά ἔχω χαμένα.

ate [eit] *pt of* eat.

atheism ['eiθiizm] *n* ἀθεϊσμός.

atheist ['eiθiist] *n* ἄθεος, ἀθεϊστής.

athlete ['æθli:t] *n* ἀθλητής.

athletic [æθ'letik] *a* ἀθλητικός ‖ ~s *n* ἀθλητισμός, σπόρ.

atlas ['ætləs] *n* ἄτλας.

atmosphere ['ætməsfiə*] *n* ἀτμόσφαιρα.

atmospheric [ætməs'ferik] *a* ἀτμοσφαιρικός ‖ ~s *npl* παράσιτα (ἀτμοσφαιρικά).

atoll ['ætɔl] *n* ἀτόλλη.

atom ['ætəm] *n* ἄτομον ‖ ~ic bomb *n* ἀτομική βόμβα ‖ ~ic energy *n* ἀτομική ἐνέργεια.

atonement [ə'təunmənt] *n* ἔκτισις, ἐπανόρθωσις.

atrocious [ə'trəuʃəs] *a* φρικτός, φρικώδης, φρικαλέος.

atrocity [ə'trɔsiti] *n* ἀγριότης, φρίκη (ἐγκλήματος).

attach [ə'tætʃ] *vt* συνδέω, προσαρτῶ, (ἐπι)συνάπτω ‖ to ~ importance to δίνω σημασίαν ‖ ~ed *a* ἀπεσπασμένος, προσηρτημένος ‖ ~ment *n* προσάρτησις, προσκόλλησις ‖ (*devotion to*) ἀφοσίωσις, στοργή.

attaché [ə'tæʃei] *n* ἀκόλουθος ‖ ~ case *n* χαρτοφύλαξ.

attack [ə'tæk] *n* ἐπίθεσις, προσβολή ‖ *vt* ἐπιτίθεμαι, προσβάλλω ‖ ~er *n* ἐπιτιθέμενος.

attain [ə'tein] *vt* φθάνω, ἀφικνοῦμαι,

κατορθώνω ‖ ~able *a* ἐφικτός, κατορθωτός ‖ ~ment *n* ἐπίτευξις, πραγματοποίησις ‖ (*learning*) γνῶσις, προσόν.

attempt [ə'tempt] *n* ἀπόπειρα, προσπάθεια, δοκιμή ‖ *vt* ἀποπειρῶμαι, προσπαθῶ.

attend [ə'tend] *vt* (*be present*) παρευρίσκομαι ‖ (*visit*) ἐπισκέπτομαι, συχνάζω ‖ (*wait on*) ὑπηρετῶ ‖ *vi* (*listen*) εἰσακούω ‖ (*look after*) ἀσχολοῦμαι ‖ to ~ to προσέχω, φροντίζω ‖ ~ance *n* (*presence*) συμμετοχή, παρουσία ‖ ~ant *n* ἀκόλουθος, ὑπηρέτης ‖ *a* συνοδεύων.

attention [ə'tenʃən] *n* προσοχή ‖ (*care*) περιποίησις, φροντίδα.

attentive [ə'tentiv] *a* προσεκτικός, περιποιητικός ‖ ~ly *ad* προσεκτικά.

attenuate [ə'tenjueit] *vt* μετριάζω, ἀμβλύνω, ἀραιώνω.

attest [ə'test] *vt* ἐπικυρῶ, (ἐπι)βεβαιῶ, καταθέτω ὡς μάρτυς.

attic ['ætik] *n* σοφίτα.

attire [ə'taiə*] *n* ἐνδυμασία, ἔνδυμα, ντύσιμο, φορεσιά ‖ *vt* ἐνδύομαι, στολίζομαι, ντύνομαι.

attitude ['ætitju:d] *n* στάσις.

attorney [ə'tə:ni] *n* δικηγόρος, πληρεξούσιος ‖ district ~ *n* εἰσαγγελεύς ‖ A~ general *n* γενικός εἰσαγγελεύς ‖ power of ~ *n* πληρεξούσιον.

attract [ə'trækt] *vt* ἑλκύω, ἕλκω, τραβῶ, γοητεύω ‖ ~ion *n* (*phys*) ἕλξις ‖ (*of person*) γοητεία, χάρες ‖ (*theat*) ἀτραξιόν ‖ ~ive *a* ἑλκυστικός, γοητευτικός.

attribute ['ætribju:t] *n* χαρακτηριστικόν γνώρισμα ‖ (*gram*) ἐπίθετον ‖ [ə'tribju:t] *vt*: to ~ to ἀποδίδω (εἰς).

attrition [ə'triʃən] *n* τριβή, φθορά, ξύσιμο.

auburn ['ɔ:bən] *a* πυρόξανθα.

auction [ɔ:kʃən] *n* πλειστηριασμός, δημοπρασία ‖ *vt* πλειστηριάζω, βγάζω στό σφυρί ‖ ~ room *n* αἴθουσα δημοπρασιῶν ‖ ~eer *n* προϊστάμενος δημοπρασιῶν.

audacious [ɔ:'deiʃəs] *a* τολμηρός, παράτολμος ‖ (*insolent*) θρασύς, ἀναιδής.

audacity [ɔ:'dæsiti] *n* τόλμη, θάρρος ‖ (*insolence*) ἀναίδεια, ἰταμότης.

audible ['ɔ:dibl] *a* ἀκουστός, ἀκουόμενος.

audience ['ɔ:diəns] *n* (*formal interview*) ἀκρόασις ‖ (*gathering*) ἀκροατήριον ‖ (*theat*) θέαται.

audit ['ɔ:dit] *n* ἔλεγχος, ἐπαλήθευσις ‖ *vt* ἐλέγχω ‖ ~or *n* ἐλεγκτής ‖ (*student*) ἀκροατής.

audition [ɔ:'diʃən] *n* ἀκρόασις (τραγουδιστοῦ κτλ).

auditorium [ɔ:di'tɔ:riəm] *n* αἴθουσα, θέατρον.

augment [ɔ:g'ment] *vt* (ἐπ)αυξάνω, μεγαλώνω.

augur ['ɔ:gə*] *vi* προοιωνίζομαι, προβλέπω.

augury ['ɔ:gjuri] *n* οἰωνός, προφητεία, προμήνυμα.

August ['ɔ:gəst] *n* Αὔγουστος.

august [ɔ:'gʌst] *a* σεβάσμιος, μεγαλοπρεπής.

aunt [a:nt] *n* θεία ‖ ~y, ~ie *n* θείτσα.

aura ['ɔ:rə] *n* αὔρα, φωτοστέφανος.

auspices ['ɔ:spisiz] *npl* αἰγίς ‖ (*omens*) οἰωνοί ‖ under the ~ of ὑπό τήν αἰγίδα τοῦ.

auspicious [ɔ:s'piʃəs] *a* εὐνοϊκός, εὐοίωνος.

austere [ɔs'tiə*] *a* αὐστηρός.

austerity [ɔs'teriti] *n* αὐστηρότης ‖ (*of habits etc*) λιτότης.

Australia [ɔs'treiliə] *n* Αὐστραλία ‖ ~n *a,n* Αὐστραλός, αὐστραλιακός.

Austria ['ɔstriə] *n* Αὐστρία ‖ ~n *a,n* Αὐστριακός.

authentic [ɔ:'θentik] *a* αὐθεντικός, γνήσιος ‖ ~ity *n* αὐθεντικότης.

authenticate [ɔ:'θentikeit] *vt* ἐπισημοποιῶ, βεβαιῶ.

author ['ɔ:θə*] *n* συγγραφεύς ‖ (*cause*) δημιουργός, πρωταίτιος.

authoritarian [ɔ:θɔri'teəriən] *a* ἀπολυταρχικός.

authority [ɔ:'θɔriti] *n* ἐξουσία, ἄδεια, ἐντολή ‖ (*specialist*) αὐθεντία ‖ (*pol*) ὑπηρεσία.

authorize ['ɔ:θəraiz] *vt* ἐξουσιοδοτῶ, ἐπιτρέπω.

auto ['ɔ:təu] *n* (*US*) — automobile.

autobiographical ['ɔ:təubaiəu'græfikəl] *a* αὐτοβιογραφικός.

autobiography [ɔ:təubai'ɔgrəfi] *n* αὐτοβιογραφία.

autocracy [ɔ:'tɔkrəsi] *n* μονοκρατορία, ἀπολυταρχία.

autocratic [ɔ:təu'krætik] *a* αὐτοκρατορικός, αὐταρχικός.

autograph ['ɔ:təgra:f] *n* αὐτόγραφον.

automatic [ɔ:tə'mætik] *a* αὐτόματος ‖ ~ally *ad* αὐτομάτως.

automation [ɔ:tə'meiʃən] *n* αὐτοματοποίησις.

automaton [ɔ:'tɔmətən] *n* αὐτόματον.

automobile ['ɔ:təməbi:l] *n* (*US*) αὐτοκίνητο, ἁμάξι.

autonomous [ɔ:'tɔnəməs] *a* αὐτόνομος.

autonomy [ɔ:'tɔnəmi] *n* αὐτονομία.

autopsy ['ɔ:tɔpsi] *n* αὐτοψία, νεκροψία.

autumn ['ɔ:təm] *n* φθινόπωρο.

auxiliary [ɔ:g'ziliəri] *a* βοηθητικός, ἐπικουρικός.

avail [ə'veil] *n* χρησιμότης, ὠφέλεια, ὄφελος ‖ *vti* ὠφελῶ, βοηθῶ, ἐξυπηρετῶ ‖ ~able *a* διαθέσιμος, προσιτός ‖ ~ability *n* διαθεσιμότης.

avalanche ['ævəla:nʃ] *n* χιονοστιβάδα (*fig*) συρροή, πλημμύρα.

avant-garde ['ævɑː̃gɑːd] *n* προφυλακή.

avarice ['ævəris] *n* τσιγγουνιά.

avaricious [ævə'riʃəs] *a* τσιγγούνης.

avenge [ə'vendʒ] *vt* ἐκδικοῦμαι.

avenue ['ævənju:] *n* λεωφόρος.

average ['ævəridʒ] n μέσον, μέσος όρος ‖ (naut) ἀβαρία ‖ a μέσος, μέτριος ‖ vti ἐξάγω τόν μέσον όρον.

averse [ə'vɔ:s] a ἀντίθετος, ἐνάντιος ‖ to be ~ to ἐναντιοῦμαι εἰς.

aversion [ə'vɔ:ʃən] n ἀποστροφή, ἀπέχθεια ‖ (col) ἀντιπάθεια.

avert [ə'vɔ:t] vt ἀποστρέφω ‖ (prevent) ἀποτρέπω, ἀπομακρύνω.

aviary ['eiviəri] n πτηνοτροφεῖον.

aviation [eivi'eiʃən] n ἀεροπορία.

avid ['ævid] a: ~ for ἄπληστος, ἀχόρταγος γιά ‖ ~ly ad ἀπλήστως.

avocado [ævə'ka:dəu] n ἀβοκάντο.

avoid [ə'vɔid] vt ἀποφεύγω ‖ ~able a φευκτέος ‖ ~ance n ἀποφυγή.

avow [ə'vau] vt ὁμολογῶ ‖ ~al n ὁμολογία.

await [ə'weit] vt ἀναμένω, περιμένω.

awake [ə'weik] (irreg v) vti ξυπνῶ, ἀφυπνίζω, ἐφυπνίζομαι ‖ a ξύπνιος, ἄγρυπνος.

awakening [ə'weikniŋ] n ἀφύπνησις, ξύπνημα.

award [ə'wɔ:d] n βραβεῖον ‖ (law) διαιτησία ‖ vt ἐπιδικάζω ‖ (reward) ἀπονέμω.

aware [ə'wɛə*] a: ~ (of) πληροφορημένος, γνώστης ‖ ~ness n συνείδησις.

away [ə'wei] ad μακράν, μακρυά ‖ (absent) ἀπουσιάζω, λείπω ‖ ~ with! πάρτο ἀπ' ἐδῶ!

awe [ɔ:] n φόβος, τρόμος ‖ (deep respect) σεβασμός ‖ vt τρομάζω ‖ ~-inspiring a ἐπιβλητικός.

awful ['ɔ:fəl] a (very bad) τρομερός, φοβερός ‖ ~ly ad τρομερά, τρομακτικά.

awhile [ə'wail] ad ὀλίγον, ἐπ' ὀλίγον, μιά στιγμή.

awkward ['ɔ:kwəd] a ἀδέξιος, ἀνεπιτήδειος ‖ ~ness n (embarrassment) στενοχώρια, ἀμηχανία.

awning ['ɔ:niŋ] n σκηνή, τέντα.

awoke [ə'wəuk] pt, pp of awake.

awry [ə'rai] ad λοξῶς, στραβῶς ‖ to go ~ πηγαίνω στραβά.

ax [æks] (US) = axe.

axe [æks] n τσεκούρι ‖ vt περιορίζω ‖ (dismiss) ἀπολύω.

axiom ['æksiəm] n ἀξίωμα ‖ ~atic a ἀξιωματικός, προφανής.

axis ['æksis] n ἄξων.

axle ['æksl] n ἄξων.

ay(e) [ai] interj (yes) the ~es npl τά ναί, τά ὑπέρ.

azure ['eiʒə*] a κυανοῦς, γαλανός.

B, D

babble ['bæbl] n μωρολογία, τραύλισμα ‖ vi τραυλίζω, φλυαρῶ.

babe [beib] n μωρό, μπέμπης.

baboon [bə'bu:n] n μπαμπουίνος.

baby ['beibi] n βρέφος, νήπιον, μωρό ‖

~ carriage n (US) καροτσάκι μωροῦ ‖ ~ish a μωρουδίστικος ‖ ~-sit vi μπέϊμπισιτ, φυλάω νήπιον, προσέχω μωρό ‖ ~-sitter n φύλακας νηπίων, μπέϊμπισιτερ.

bachelor ['bætʃələ*] n ἄγαμος, ἐργένης ‖ B~ of Arts n πτυχιοῦχος (φιλολογίας) ‖ B~ of Science n πτυχιοῦχος ἐπιστημῶν.

back [bæk] n (person, horse) ράχη, πλάτη, νῶτα ‖ (house etc) ὀπίσθιος, πισινός ‖ (sport) μπάκ ‖ vt (support) ὑποστηρίζω ‖ (movement) κάνω πίσω ‖ (sport) ποντάρω ‖ vi (go backwards) ὀπισθοχωρῶ, κάνω πίσω ‖ a ὀπίσθιος, πισινός ‖ ad (ὁ)πίσω, πρός τά πίσω ‖ (again) πάλι ‖ (in time) ἐδῶ καί λίγα χρόνια ‖ to ~ out vi ἀνακαλῶ, ξελέω ‖ (col) τό σκάω ‖ ~biting n κουτσομπολιό ‖ ~bone n ραχοκοκκαλιά ‖ (firmness) θάρρος, κουράγιο ‖ ~-cloth n φόντο ‖ ~er n (sport) παίκτης ‖ (comm) χρηματοδότης ‖ ~fire n πρόωρος ἔκρηξις ‖ ~ground n (scene) βάθος, φόντο ‖ (information) προϊστορία, τό ἱστορικό ‖ (education etc) προσόντα ‖ ~hand n (blow) ἀνάποδη καρπαζιά ‖ ~handed a ὕπουλον ‖ (compliment) διαφορούμενον κομπλιμέντο, διαφορούμενη φιλοφρόνησις ‖ ~ing n ὑποστήριξις ‖ (movement) ὀπισθοδρόμησις ‖ ~ number n (newspaper etc) παλαιόν φύλλον ‖ ~ pay n καθυστερούμενος μισθός ‖ ~side n (col) πισινός ‖ ~ward a ὀπίσθιος, πρός τά πίσω ‖ (child etc) καθυστερημένο ‖ ~wardness n καθυστέρησις ‖ (hesitation) δειλία, δισταγμός ‖ ~wards ad πρός τά πίσω ‖ (flow) ἀντίθετα ‖ ~yard n ὀπισθία αὐλή.

bacon ['beikən] n καπνιστό χοιρινό, μπέϊκον.

bacteria [bæk'tiəriə] npl μικρόβια.

bad [bæd] a κακός, ἄσχημος.

badge [bædʒ] n διακριτικό, σῆμα, ἔμβλημα.

badger ['bædʒə*] n ἀσβός ‖ vt παρενοχλῶ, βασανίζω.

badly ['bædli] ad κακῶς, ἄσχημα ‖ ~ off σέ δύσκολη θέση, φτωχός.

bad-tempered ['bæd'tempəd] a δύστροπος, γκρινιάρης.

baffle ['bæfl] vt (puzzle) ματαιώνω, τά χάνω.

bag [bæg] n σάκκος, σακκούλα ‖ (handbag) τσάντα ‖ vt σακκουλιάζω ‖ (capture etc) σκοτώνω, πιάνω ‖ ~ful n σακκουλιά ‖ ~gage n ἀποσκευές, βαλίτσες ‖ ~pipes npl γκάϊντα.

bail [beil] n ἐγγύησις ‖ vt (prisoner) ἐλευθερώνω μέ ἐγγύηση ‖ to ~ out (boat) βγάζω τά νερά, ἀδειάζω ‖ see also bale.

bailiff ['beilif] n δικαστικός κλητήρας.

bait [beit] n δόλωμα ‖ vt δελεάζω, δολώνω ‖ (harass) βασανίζω.

bake [beik] vt ψήνω σέ φοῦρνο ‖ vi ψήνομαι ‖ ~r n φούρναρης ‖ ~ry n φουρνάρικο.

baking ['beikiŋ] n ψήσιμο.

balance ['bæləns] n ζυγός, ζυγαριά || (*equilibrium*) ισορροπία || (*of account*) υπόλοιπον || (*econ*) ισολογισμός || vt ζυγίζω, σταθμίζω || (*counterbalance*) ισορροπώ, ισοζυγίζω || ~**d** a ισορροπημένος || (*equal*) ίσος, ισοδύναμος || ~ **sheet** n ισολογισμός.

balcony ['bælkəni] n εξώστης, μπαλκόνι.

bald [bɔːld] a φαλακρός, καραφλός || (*plain*) γυμνός, ξηρός.

bale [beil] n δέμα, μπάλλα, κόλος || **to ~ or bail out** (*aviat*) πηδώ μέ αλεξίπτωτο.

balk [bɔːk] vt ματαιώνω, ανατρέπω.

Balkan ['bɔːlkən] a Βαλκανικός.

ball [bɔːl] n σφαίρα, μπάλλα, τόπι || (*dance*) χοροεσπερίς, χορός.

ballad ['bæləd] n μπαλάντα.

ballast ['bæləst] n έρμα, σαβούρα.

ball bearing ['bɔːl'beəriŋ] n σφαιροτριβεύς, ρουλεμάν.

ballerina [bælə'riːnə] n μπαλλαρίνα.

ballet ['bælei] n μπαλλέτο.

balloon [bə'luːn] n αερόστατο, μπαλόνι.

ballot ['bælət] n ψηφοδέλτιον.

ballpoint (pen) ['bɔːlpɔint (pen)] n μπίκ, στυλό, πέννα διαρκείας.

ballroom ['bɔːlrum] n αίθουσα χορού.

balmy ['baːmi] a γλυκύς, κατευναστικός || (*col*) παλαβός.

balustrade [bæləs'treid] n κιγκλίδωμα, κάγκελλα.

bamboo [bæm'buː] n μπαμπού, καλάμι.

bamboozle [bæm'buːzl] vt εξαπατώ, κοροϊδεύω.

ban [bæn] n προγραφή || (*church*) αφορισμός || vt απαγορεύω.

banal [bə'naːl] a κοινός, χυδαίος.

banana [bə'naːnə] n μπανάνα.

band [bænd] n δεσμός, δέσιμο, στεφάνι || (*group*) ομάδα, συντροφιά || (*mus*) ορχήστρα, μπάντα || vi (+ *together*) συνασπίζομαι || vt (*tie*) δένω || ~**age** n επίδεσμος, φασκιά.

bandit ['bændit] n ληστής.

bandy ['bændi] vt ανταλλάσσω.

bandy-legged ['bændi'legd] a στραβοπόδης, στραβοκάνης.

bang [bæŋ] n (*blow*) κτύπημα || (*noise*) θόρυβος || vti κτυπάω, κρούω.

banish ['bæniʃ] vt εξορίζω, εκτοπίζω.

banister(s) ['bænistə*(z)] n(pl) κιγκλίδωμα, κάγκελλα.

banjo ['bændʒəu] n μπάντζο.

bank [bæŋk] n τράπεζα || (*ground*) ανάχωμα, ύψωμα || (*of river*) όχθη || vt (*tilt*) κλίνω, στρέφω || (*pile up*) σωριάζω || (*money*) καταθέτω, βάζω || ~ **account** n τραπεζιτικός λογαριασμός || ~**er** n τραπεζίτης || ~ **holiday** n αργία τραπεζών || ~**note** n τραπεζογραμμάτιον, μπανκνότα || ~**rupt** n πτωχεύσας, χρεωκοπημένος || vt πτωχεύω || ~**ruptcy** n πτωχεύσις, χρεωκοπία.

banner ['bænə*] n σημαία, μπαντιέρα.

banns [bænz] npl αι αγγελία γάμου.

banquet ['bæŋkwit] n συμπόσιο, γλέντι, τσιμπούσι.

banter ['bæntə*] n χαριτολόγημα, σκέρτσο.

baptism ['bæptizəm] n βάπτισμα.

Baptist ['bæptist] n βαπτιστής.

baptize [bæp'taiz] vt βαπτίζω.

bar [baː*] n (*rod*) ράβδος, κοντάρι || (*of soap etc*) κομμάτι, πλάκα || (*pub*) μπάρ, ποτοπωλείον || (*obstacle*) φραγμός, εμπόδιον || (*in court*) εδώλιον || (*mus*) μπάρα || vt (*fasten*) κλείνω, αμπαρώνω, κιγκλιδώνω || (*hinder*) φράσσω, εμποδίζω || (*exclude*) απαγορεύω, αποκλείω || **the B~** δικηγορικόν επάγγελμα.

barbarian [baː'beəriən] n βάρβαρος.

barbaric [baː'bærik] a βάρβαρος, αγροίκος.

barbarity [baː'bæriti] n βαρβαρότης, αγριότης.

barbarous ['baːbərəs] a βάρβαρος.

barbecue ['baːbikjuː] n σχάρα.

barbed wire ['baːbd'waiə*] n συρματόπλεγμα.

barber ['baːbə*] n κουρέας, μπαρμπέρης.

barbiturate [baː'bitjurit] n βαρβιτουρικόν.

bare [beə*] a γυμνός || (*living etc*) λιγοστός, μόλις || vt γυμνώνω || (*reveal*) αποκαλύπτω || ~**back** ad χωρίς σέλλα || ~**faced** a ξεδιάντροπος, αναιδής || ~**foot** a ξυπόλητος || ~**headed** a ξεσκούφωτος, ασκεπής || ~**ly** ad μόλις || ~**ness** n γύμνια.

bargain ['baːgin] n συναλλαγή, αγορά || (*bought cheaply*) ευκαιρία || **into the ~** επί πλέον, από πάνω.

barge [baːdʒ] n φορτηγίς, μαούνα || **to ~ in** vi επεμβαίνω.

baritone ['bæritəun] n βαρύτονος.

bark [baːk] n (*tree*) φλοιός, φλούδα || (*dog*) γαύγισμα || vi (*dog*) γαυγίζω.

barley ['baːli] n κριθάρι.

barmaid ['baːmeid] n σερβιτόρα του μπάρ.

barman ['baːmən] n μπάρμαν.

barn [baːn] n (σιτ)αποθήκη || (*US*) στάβλος.

barnacle ['baːnəkl] n ανατίφη, στρειδόνι.

barometer [bə'rɔmitə*] n βαρόμετρον.

baron ['bærən] n βαρώνος || ~**ess** n βαρώνη.

baroque [bə'rɔk] a μπαρόκ.

barracks ['bærəks] npl στρατώνας, μπαράκα.

barrage ['bæraːʒ] n (*dam*) φράγμα || (*mil*) πυρ φραγμού, μπαράζ.

barrel ['bærəl] n βυτίον, βαρέλι || (*measure*) βαρέλιον || (*gun*) κάννη || ~ **organ** n λατέρνα.

barren ['bærən] a στείρος, άγονος.

barricade [bæri'keid] n προπέτασμα, φράγμα || vt φράσσω.

barrier ['bæriə*] n φραγμός || (*obstruction*) εμπόδιον.

barrister ['bæristə*] n δικηγόρος.

barrow ['bærəu] *n* (*cart*) μονότροχον, χειραμάξιον.

bartender ['ba:tendə*] *n* (*US*) = barman.

base [beis] *n* βάσις ‖ *vt* βασίζω, στηρίζω ‖ *a* ταπεινός, πρόστυχος ‖ (*inferior*) φθηνός ‖ ~ball *n* μπέϊζ-μπώλ ‖ ~less *a* ἀβάσιμος, ἀστήρικτος ‖ ~ment *n* ὑπόγειον.

bash [bæʃ] *vt* (*col*) κτυπῶ, τσακίζω.

bashful ['bæʃful] *a* ντροπαλός.

basic ['beisik] *a* βασικός, θεμελιώδης ‖ ~ally *ad* βασικά.

basilica [bə'zilikə] *n* βασιλική.

basin ['beisn] *n* λεκάνη ‖ (*naut*) νεωδόχος, δεξαμενή.

basis ['beisis] *n* βάσις.

bask [ba:sk] *vi* λιάζομαι.

basket ['ba:skit] *n* καλάθι, πανέρι ‖ ~ball *n* καλαθόσφαιρα, μπάσκετ.

bass [bæs] *n* (*fish*) πέρκα ‖ [beis] (*mus*) βαθύφωνος, μπάσος.

bassoon [bə'su:n] *n* φαγκότο.

bastard ['ba:stəd] *n* νόθος, μπάσταρδος.

baste [beist] *vt* (*sewing*) παρραράβω, ξυλίζω, ραβδίζω ‖ (*cooking*) βουτυρώνω.

bastion ['bæstiən] *n* (*stronghold*) προμαχώνας.

bat [bæt] *n* (*sport*) ρόπαλον, μαγγούρα ‖ (*zool*) νυκτερίδα ‖ *vi* κτυπῶ μέ τό ρόπαλο ‖ off one's own ~ ἐξ ἰδίας πρωτοβουλίας.

batch [bætʃ] *n* φουρνιά (ψωμί) ‖ (*set*) σωρός, ὁμάδα.

bath [ba:θ] *n* λουτρό, μπάνιο ‖ (*tub*) λουτήρας, μπανιέρα ‖ *vt* λούω, μπανιαρίζω ‖ ~s *npl* δημόσια λουτρά, μπάνια, χαμάμ ‖ ~chair *n* καρροτσάκι (ἀναπήρων), ἀναπηρική καρέκλα.

bathe [beið] *vi* λούομαι, κάνω μπάνιο ‖ *vt* λούω, πλένω ‖ ~r *n* κολυμβητής, λουόμενος.

bathing ['beiðiŋ] *n* κολύμπι ‖ ~ cap *n* σκούφος τοῦ μπάνιου ‖ ~ costume *n* μπανιερό, μαγιό.

bathmat ['ba:θmæt] *n* ψάθα τοῦ μπάνιου.

bathroom ['ba:θrum] *n* λουτρόν.

bath towel ['ba:θtauəl] *n* πετσέτα τοῦ μπάνιου.

batman ['bætmən] *n* ὑπηρέτης, ὀρντινάντσα.

baton ['bætən] *n* ράβδος ‖ (*conductor's*) μπαγκέτα ‖ (*truncheon*) γκλόμπ.

battalion [bə'tæliən] *n* τάγμα.

batter ['bætə*] *n* κουρκούτι ‖ *vt* κτυπῶ, κοπανίζω.

battery ['bætəri] *n* (*mil*) πυροβολαρχία ‖ (*cell*) συστοιχία.

battle ['bætl] *n* μάχη ‖ *vi* μάχομαι, πολεμῶ ‖ ~field *n* πεδίον μάχης ‖ ~ments *npl* ἐπάλξεις, παραπέτο, πολεμίστρες ‖ ~ship *n* θωρηκτόν.

bawdy ['bɔ:di] *a* ἀσελγής, αἰσχρός.

bawl [bɔ:l] *vi* κραυγάζω, σκούζω.

bay [bei] *n* (*of sea*) κόλπος, κόρφος ‖ (*tree*)

δάφνη ‖ at ~ σέ δύσκολη θέσι, στά στενά.

bayonet ['beiənit] *n* ξιφολόγχη, μπαγιονέττα.

bay window ['bei'windəu] *n* σαχνισί, θολωτό παράθυρο.

bazaar [bə'za:*] *n* παζάρι ‖ (*for charity*) φιλανθρωπική ἀγορά.

bazooka [bə'zu:kə] *n* μπαζούκα.

be [bi:] (*irreg v*) *vi* (*exist*) εἶμαι, ὑπάρχω ‖ (*live*) εἶμαι, ζῶ, κατοικῶ ‖ (*stay*) εἶμαι, κάνω ‖ (*cost*) εἶμαι, κοστίζω ‖ (*location*) εἶμαι, εὑρίσκομαι ‖ (*visit*) εἶμαι, ἐπισκέπτομαι ‖ (*take place*) εἶμαι, γίγνομαι.

beach [bi:tʃ] *n* παραλία, ἀκρογιαλιά ‖ *vt* προσγιαλῶ, ἀράζω ‖ (*run aground*) προσαράσσω.

beacon ['bi:kən] *n* φάρος, φανάρι.

bead [bi:d] *n* χάντρα, πέρλα ‖ (*perspiration*) σταγονίδι.

beak [bi:k] *n* ράμφος, μύτη.

beaker ['bi:kə*] *n* ὑάλινο ποτήρι ζέσεως.

beam [bi:m] *n* δοκός, δοκάρι ‖ (*of balance*) ζυγοστάτης, μπράτσο ‖ (*of light*) ἀχτίδα, δέσμη ‖ (*smile*) λάμψη, ἀκτινοβολία ‖ *vi* ἀκτινοβολῶ, λάμπω.

bean [bi:n] *n* (*broad*) κουκί ‖ (*kidney*) φασόλι ‖ (*string*) φασολάκι.

bear [bεə*] (*irreg v*) *n* ἀρκούδα ‖ *vt* (*carry*) φέρω, βαστῶ, σηκώνω ‖ (*support*) ὑποβαστάζω, στηρίζω ‖ (*put up with*) ὑποφέρω, ἀντέχω, ἀνέχομαι ‖ (*produce*) γεννῶ, παράγω ‖ ~able *a* ὑποφερτός, ἀνεκτός.

beard [biəd] *n* γένι, μοῦσι ‖ ~ed *a* μέ γένεια.

bearer ['bεərə*] *n* (*person*) κομιστής, φορέας.

bearing ['bεəriŋ] *n* (*behaviour*) συμπεριφορά, ὕφος ‖ (*relation*) σχέσις, ἔννοια ‖ ~s *npl*: I lose my ~s χάνω τό μπούσουλα.

beast [bi:st] *n* ζῶον, κτῆνος, θηρίον ‖ (*person*) ζῶον, παλιάνθρωπος ‖ ~ly *ad* κτηνώδης, βρώμικος.

beat [bi:t] (*irreg. v*) *n* (*stroke*) κτύπημα ‖ (*pulsation*) σφυγμός, παλμός ‖ (*of policeman*) περιπολία ‖ (*mus*) χρόνος, μέτρον ‖ *vt* κτυπῶ, δέρνω, ματσουκώνω ‖ (*defeat*) ὑπερτερῶ, νικῶ ‖ to ~ about the bush χρονοτριβῶ, ταλαντεύομαι ‖ to ~ time κρατῶ τόν χρόνο ‖ to ~ off *vt* διώχνω, ἀπωθῶ ‖ to ~ up *vi* σπάζω στό ξύλο ‖ ~en track *n* πεπατημένη ‖ ~er *n* (*for eggs, cream*) κτυπητήρι.

beautiful ['bju:tiful] *a* ὡραῖος, ἐξαίσιος, ὑπέροχος ‖ ~ly *ad* θαυμάσια, ὑπέροχα.

beautify ['bju:tifai] *vt* ἐξωραΐζω, ὀμορφαίνω.

beauty ['bju:ti] *n* ὀμορφιά ‖ (*woman*) καλλονή.

beaver ['bi:və*] *n* κάστόρι, κάστορας.

becalm [bi'ka:m] *vt* ἀπαγκιάζω.

because [bi'kɔz] *ad,cj* διότι, γιατί, ἐπειδή.

beckon ['bekən] *vt* γνέφω, κάνω νόημα.

become [bi'kʌm] *vt* (*befit*) ἁρμόζω, ταιριάζω ‖ *vi* γίνομαι, καταντῶ.

becoming [bi'kʌmiŋ] *a* ἁρμόζων ‖ (*dress etc*) ταιριαστός, πού πηγαίνει.

bed [bed] *n* κρεββάτι ‖ (*of river*) κοίτη ‖ (*foundation*) στρῶμα, στρῶσις ‖ (*garden*) πρασιά ‖ ~ **and breakfast** *n* δωμάτιο μέ πρωϊνό ‖ ~**clothes** *npl* σεντόνια καί κουβέρτες ‖ ~**ding** *n* στρώματα.

bedlam ['bedləm] *n* (*uproar*) φασαρία, θόρυβος.

bedraggled [bi'drægld] *a* κουρελιασμένος.

bedridden ['bedridn] *a* κρεββατωμένος, κατάκοιτος.

bedroom ['bedrum] *n* ὑπνοδωμάτιο, κρεββατοκάμαρα.

bed-sitter ['bed'sitə*] *n* ὑπνοδωμάτιο.

bedtime ['bedtaim] *n* ὥρα γιά ὕπνο.

bee [bi:] *n* μέλισσα.

beech [bi:tʃ] *n* ὀξυά.

beef [bi:f] *n* βωδινό.

beehive ['bi:haiv] *n* κυψέλη.

beeline ['bi:lain] *n*: **to make a** ~ **for** πηγαίνω κατ' εὐθεῖαν.

been [bi:n] *pp of* **be**.

beer [biə*] *n* μπύρα.

beetle ['bi:tl] *n* σκαθάρι.

beetroot ['bi:ru:t] *n* πατζάρι, κοκκινογούλι.

befall [bi'fɔ:l] *vti* συμβαίνω, τυχαίνω.

before [bi'fɔ:*] *prep* (*in place*) πρό, ἐμπρός, ἐνώπιον ‖ (*of time*) πρίν, πρό ‖ *cj* πρό, πρίν, πρίν νά ‖ *ad* (*of place*) ἐμπρός, πρό, μπροστά ‖ (*of time*) πρίν, πρωτύτερα, προτοῦ.

befriend [bi'frend] *vt* βοηθῶ, προστατεύω.

beg [beg] *vi* ζητῶ, παρακαλῶ ‖ (*for alms*) ζητιανεύω ‖ ~**gar** *n* ζητιάνος, ἐπαίτης.

began [bi'gæn] *pt of* **begin**.

begin [bi'gin] (*irreg v*) *vi* ἀρχίζω, ἀρχινῶ, ἄρχομαι ‖ **to** ~ **with** *vt* πρῶτα-πρῶτα, πρίν ν'ἀρχίσουμε ‖ ~**ner** *n* ἀρχάριος, πρωτάρης ‖ ~**ning** *n* ἀρχή.

begrudge [bi'grʌdʒ] *vt* δίνω μέ τό ζόρι, λυποῦμαι.

begun [bi'gʌn] *pp of* **begin**.

behalf [bi'hɑ:f] *n* ἐκ μέρους, ὑπέρ ‖ **on** ~ **of** γιά λογαριασμό του, ἐκ μέρους.

behave [bi'heiv] *vi* (συμπερι)φέρομαι.

behaviour, (*US*) **behavior** [bi'heivjə*] *n* συμπεριφορά, φέρσιμο.

behead [bi'hed] *vt* ἀποκεφαλίζω.

behind [bi'haind] *prep* πίσω ἀπό ‖ (*time*) καθυστερημένος ‖ *ad* ὄπισθεν, ὀπίσω, πίσω ἀπό ‖ *n* πισινός.

behold [bi'həuld] *vt* βλέπω, ἀντικρύζω.

beige [beiʒ] *a* μπέζ.

being ['bi:iŋ] *n* ὕπαρξις, γέννησις ‖ (*person*) ὄν, εἶναι.

belch [beltʃ] *vti* ρεύομαι.

belfry ['belfri] *n* καμπαναριό

Belgium ['beldʒəm] *n* Βέλγιον.

belie [bi'lai] *vt* διαψεύδω, ξεγελῶ.

belief [bi'li:f] *n* (*trust*) πίστη ‖ (*idea*) γνώμη, δοξασία.

believable [bi'li:vəbl] *a* πιστευτός.

believe [bi'li:v] *vt* πιστεύω, δέχομαι ‖ *vi* πιστεύω, Ἔχω ἐμπιστοσύνη ‖ ~**r** *n* πιστός ὀπαδός.

belittle [bi'litl] *vt* ὑποτιμῶ, περιφρονῶ.

bell [bel] *n* καμπάνα ‖ (*in house*) κουδούνι.

belligerent [bi'lidʒərənt] *a* (*fig*) καυγατζῆς.

bellow ['beləu] *vti* μουγγρίζω, γκαρίζω ‖ *n* μουγκρητό.

bellows ['beləuz] *npl* φυσερό.

belly ['beli] *n* κοιλιά.

belong [bi'lɔŋ] *vi* ἀνήκω ‖ **it does not** ~ **here** δέν ἀνήκει ἐδῶ ‖ **to** ~ **to** *vt* ἀνήκω, μετέχω εἰς ‖ (*a place*) κατάγομαι ἀπό ‖ ~**ings** *npl* περιουσία, ὑπάρχοντα.

beloved [bi'lʌvid] *a* πολυαγαπημένος ‖ *n* ἀγαπητός.

below [bi'ləu] *prep* ὑπό, κάτω, κάτωθεν ‖ *ad* κάτω ἀπό, ἀπό κάτω.

belt [belt] *n* ζώνη, ταινία ‖ (*round waist*) ζωνάρι, λουρί ‖ *vt* ζώνω ‖ (*beat*) δέρνω μέ λουρί.

bench [bentʃ] *n* κάθισμα, μπάγκος ‖ (*workshop*) τεζάκι, μπάγκος ‖ (*of judge*) ἕδρα.

bend [bend] (*irreg v*) *n* καμπή, στροφή, γωνία ‖ *vt* κάμπτω, λυγίζω ‖ (*naut*) δένω ‖ *vi* (*stoop*) σκύβω.

beneath [bi'ni:θ] *prep* κάτωθεν, χαμηλότερα, ὑπό ‖ *ad* (ὑπο)κάτω.

benefactor ['benifæktə*] *n* εὐεργέτης, δωρητής.

beneficial [beni'fiʃəl] *a* ὠφέλιμος, χρήσιμος.

beneficiary [beni'fiʃəri] *n* δικαιοῦχος.

benefit ['benifit] *n* ὄφελος, ὠφέλεια ‖ *vt* ὠφελῶ ‖ *vi* ἐπωφελοῦμαι.

benevolent [bi'nevələnt] *a* ἀγαθοεργός, καλοπροαίρετος.

benign [bi'nain] *a* (*tumour etc*) καλοήθης.

bent [bent] *n* (*inclination*) κλίσις, ροπή ‖ *a*: **to be** ~ **on** ἀποφασισμένος νά ‖ *pt,pp of* **bend**.

bequeath [bi'kwi:ð] *vt* κληροδοτῶ, ἀφήνω.

bequest [bi'kwest] *n* κληροδότημα.

bereaved [bi'ri:vd] *n* (*person*) τεθλιμμένος.

bereavement [bi'ri:vmənt] *n* ἀπώλεια, πένθος.

beret ['berei] *n* μπερέ, σκοῦφος.

berry ['beri] *n* ρόγα, μοῦρο.

berserk [bə'sə:k] *a*: **to go** ~ γίνομαι ἔξω φρενῶν.

berth [bə:θ] *n* (*anchoring*) ὄρμος ‖ (*ship, train*) κλίνη, καμπίνα ‖ *vt* προσορμίζω, πλευρίζω ‖ *vi* ἀγκυροβολῶ, πλευρίζω.

beseech [bi'si:tʃ] (*irreg v*) *vt* ἱκετεύω, ἐκλιπαρῶ.

beset [bi'set] *vt* κυκλώνω, περισφίγγω.

beside [bi'said] *prep* πλάϊ, πλησίον, δίπλα ‖ **to be** ~ **o.s.** εἶμαι ἐκτός ἑαυτοῦ.

besides [bi'saidz] *prep* ἐκτὸς ἀπὸ ‖ *ad* ἐκτὸς αὐτοῦ, ἀκόμη, ἄλλωστε.

besiege [bi'si:dʒ] *vt* πολιορκῶ.

bespectacled [bi'spektikld] *a* μέ γυαλιά.

best [best] *a* καλύτερος ‖ *ad* καλύτερα ‖ **at ~** τό καλύτερον, ἀκόμα καί ‖ **to make the ~ of it** ὅσον μπορῶ καλύτερα ‖ **~ man** *n* παράνυμφος, κουμπάρος.

bestow [bi'stəu] *vt* παρέχω, ἀπονέμω.

bestseller ['best'selə*] *n* βιβλίον μεγάλης κυκλοφορίας.

bet [bet] (*irreg v*) *n* στοίχημα ‖ *vt* στοιχηματίζω, βάζω στοίχημα ‖ **you ~** ! ἀσφαλῶς!, ἔχεις δίκαιο!, σίγουρα!

betray [bi'trei] *vt* προδίδω, ἀποκαλύπτω ‖ (*be false*) ἀπατῶ ‖ **~al** *n* προδοσία.

better ['betə*] *a* καλύτερος ‖ *ad* καλύτερα ‖ *vt* καλυτερεύω, βελτιώνω ‖ *n*: **to get the ~** of νικῶ κάποιον, ὑπερέχω ‖ **he thought ~ of it** ἄλλαξε γνώμην ‖ **~ off** *a* (*richer*) πιό εὔπορος, πλουσιώτερος.

betting ['betiŋ] *n* στοίχημα(τα).

between [bi'twi:n] *prep* μεταξύ, ἀνάμεσα ‖ *ad* ἀνάμεσα.

bevel ['bevəl] *n* λοξά, φάλτσο.

beverage ['bevəridʒ] *n* ποτό.

beware [bi'weə*] *vt* προσέχω, φοβοῦμαι ‖ '**~ of the dog**' προσοχή, σκύλας.

bewildered [bi'wildəd] *a* ζαλισμένος, χαμένος.

bewildering [bi'wildəriŋ] *a* ἐκπληκτικός, κάτι πού ζαλίζει.

bewitching [bi'witʃiŋ] *a* γοητευτικός, μαγευτικός.

beyond [bi'jɒnd] *prep* (*of place*) πέρα ἀπό ‖ (*of time*) πέραν τοῦ ‖ (*in addition*) ἐκτὸς, πέραν ‖ *ad* πέραν, ἐκεῖθεν.

bias ['baiəs] *n* (*slant*) λοξότης, λοξά ‖ (*prejudice*) προκατάληψις, συμπάθεια ‖ **~(s)ed** *a* προκατειλημμένος, ἐπηρεασμένος.

bib [bib] *n* σαλιάρα, μποῦστος.

Bible ['baibl] *n* Βίβλος, Εὐαγγέλιον.

bibliography [bibli'ɔgrəfi] *n* βιβλιογραφία.

bicentenary [baisen'ti:nəri] *n* δισεκατονταετηρίδα.

biceps ['baiseps] *npl* δικέφαλος (μυς).

bicker ['bikə*] *vi* καυγαδίζω ‖ **~ing** *n* καυγάς.

bicycle ['baisikl] *n* ποδήλατο.

bid [bid] (*irreg v*) *n* προσφορά ‖ (*cards*) δήλωσις ‖ *vt* (*command*) διατάσσω, προστάζω ‖ (*offer*) προσφέρω, πλειοδοτῶ ‖ (*greeting*) καλημερίζω ‖ (*goodbye*) ἀποχαιρετῶ ‖ **~der** *n* (*person*) πλειοδότης ‖ **~ding** *n* (*order*) ἐντολή, παραγγελία ‖ (*offer*) πλειοδοσία.

bidet ['bi:dei] *n* μπιντέ.

big [big] *a* μεγάλος, σπουδαῖος.

bigamy ['bigəmi] *n* διγαμία.

big-hearted ['big'ha:tid] *a* μεγαλόψυχος, μέ χρυσή καρδιά.

bigot ['bigət] *n* στενοκέφαλος, φανατικός

‖ **~ed** *a* στενοκέφαλος ‖ **~ry** *n* μισαλλοδοξία.

bigwig ['bigwig] *n* σπουδαῖο πρόσωπο, μεγιστάνος, προσωπικότης.

bike [baik] *n* ποδήλατο.

bikini [bi'ki:ni] *n* μπικίνι.

bile [bail] *n* χολή.

bilingual [bai'liŋwəl] *a* δίγλωσσος.

bilious ['biliəs] *a* χολερικός ‖ (*peevish*) πικρόχολος.

bill [bil] *n* (*notice*) ἀγγελία, ἀφίσα ‖ (*account*) λογαριασμός ‖ (*law*) νομοσχέδιον ‖ (*note*) γραμμάτιον ‖ (*beak*) ράμφος, μύτη ‖ (*US*) χαρτονόμισμα.

billet ['bilit] *n* (*mil*) κατάλυμα ‖ (*job*) θέσι.

billfold ['bilfəuld] *n* (*US*) πορτοφόλι.

billiards ['biliədz] *n* μπιλλιάρδο.

billion ['biliən] *n* (*Brit*) τρισεκατομμύριο ‖ (*US*) δισεκατομμύριο.

billy goat ['biligəut] *n* τράγος.

bin [bin] *n* κασέλα, κασόνι, κιβώτιο.

bind [baind] (*irreg v*) *vt* (*tie*) δένω ‖ (*together*) προσδένω ‖ (*a book*) δένω ‖ (*oblige*) δεσμεύω, δένω ‖ **~ing** *n* (*σύν*)δεσις, δέσιμο ‖ (*book*) βιβλιοδεσία.

binoculars [bi'nɔkjuləz] *npl* κιάλια.

biochemistry ['baiəu'kemistri] *n* βιοχημεία.

biographer [bai'ɔgrəfə*] *n* βιογράφος.

biographic(al) [baiəu'græfik(əl)] *a* βιογραφικός.

biography [bai'ɔgrəfi] *n* βιογραφία.

biological [baiə'lɔdʒikəl] *a* βιολογικός.

biologist [bai'ɔlədʒist] *n* βιολόγος.

biology [bai'ɔlədʒi] *n* βιολογία.

birch [bə:tʃ] *n* (*tree*) σημύδα ‖ (*for whipping*) βέργα.

bird [bə:d] *n* πουλί ‖ **~'s-eye view** *n* κάτοψη.

birth [bə:θ] *n* γέννα, τοκετός ‖ (*beginning*) γέννησις ‖ **of good ~** καλῆς καταγωγῆς ‖ **~ certificate** *n* πιστοποιητικόν γεννήσεως ‖ **~ control** *n* ἔλεγχος γεννήσεων ‖ **~day** *n* γενέθλια ‖ **~ place** *n* τόπος γεννήσεως ‖ **~ rate** *n* γεννήσεις.

biscuit ['biskit] *n* παξιμάδι, μπισκότα.

bisect [bai'sekt] *vt* διχοτομῶ.

bishop ['biʃəp] *n* ἐπίσκοπος, δεσπότης.

bit [bit] *n* (*piece*) κομμάτι ‖ (*of tool*) τρυπάνι ‖ (*of horse*) στομίς, χαβιά, χαλινάρι.

bitch [bitʃ] *n* (*dog*) σκύλα ‖ (*unpleasant woman*) παλιοθήλυκο.

bite [bait] (*irreg v*) *n* δάγκωμα ‖ (*mouthful*) μπουκιά ‖ *vti* δαγκώνω ‖ (*insect*) τσιμπῶ ‖ **a ~ to eat** μπουκιά, λίγο φαγητό.

biting ['baitiŋ] *a* δηκτικός.

bitter ['bitə*] *a* πικρός ‖ (*feeling*) φαρμακερός, δηκτικός, πικρά ‖ *n* (*beer*) πικρή μπύρα ‖ **to the ~ end** μέχρι τέλους, μέχρις-ἐσχάτων ‖ **~ness** *n* πικρία, πίκρα ‖ **~sweet** *a* γλυκόπικρος.

bivouac ['bivuæk] *n* καταυλισμός.

bizarre [bi'za:*] *a* παράξενος, ἀλλόκοτος.

blab [blæb] *vti* τά λέω ὅλα, προδίδω.

black [blæk] *a* μαῦρος ‖ (*without light*)

σκοτάδι ‖ vt (shoes) βάφω, λουστράρω ‖ (eye) μαυρίζω τό μάτι ‖ ~ and blue γεμάτος σημάδια, καταμαυρισμένος ‖ ~berry n βατόμουρον ‖ ~bird n κότσυφας ‖ ~board n πίνακας, μαυροπίνακας ‖ ~currant n μαύρο φραγκοστάφυλλο ‖ ~en vt μαυρίζω, λερώνω ‖ ~guard n παλιάνθρωπος, μασκαράς ‖ ~leg n ἀπεργοσπάστης ‖ ~list n μαύρος πίνακας ‖ ~mail vt ἐκβιάζω ‖ ~mailer n ἐκβιαστής ‖ ~ market n μαύρη ἀγορά ‖ ~ness n μαυράδα, μαυρίλα ‖ ~out n (mil) συσκότησις ‖ (elec) διακοπή ρεύματος ‖ (faint) σκοτοδίνη, λιποθυμία ‖ ~ sheep n (fig) ζιζάνιον, ἄσωτος ‖ ~smith n σιδεράς.

bladder ['blædə*] n κύστις ‖ (of football etc) σαμπρέλλα.

blade [bleid] n (leaf etc) φύλλον ‖ (of tool etc) λεπίδα, λάμα ‖ (of oar etc) πτερύγιον, φτερό.

blame [bleim] n μομφή, ψόγος, φταίξιμο ‖ vt κατηγορῶ, ψέγω ‖ ~less a ἄψογος, ἀνεύθυνος.

bland [blænd] a ἤπιος, μειλίχιος.

blank [blæŋk] a (page) λευκός, ἄγραφος ‖ (vacant) ἀνέκφραστος, χαμένα, συγχισμένος ‖ n κενό ‖ (cartridge) ἄσφαιρο φυσίγγι.

blanket ['blæŋkit] n κλινοσκέπασμα, κουβέρτα.

blankly ['blæŋkli] ad μέ ἀνέκφραστον βλέμμα.

blare [bleə*] n ἰσχυρός ἦχος, οὐρλιασμα ‖ vi ἀντηχῶ, διασαλπίζω.

blarney ['blɑːni] n κολακεία, γαλιφιά.

blasé ['blɑːzei] a μπλαζέ.

blaspheme [blæs'fiːm] vi βλαστημῶ.

blasphemous ['blæsfiməs] a ἀσεβής, ἀπρεπής.

blasphemy ['blæsfimi] n βλαστήμια.

blast [blɑːst] n (gust) φύσημα, ριπή ‖ (naut) σφύριγμα ‖ (mining) φουρνέλο ‖ vt βάζω φουρνέλο ‖ ~off n (space) ἐκτόξευσις.

blatant ['bleitənt] a κραυγαλέος, φωνακλάδικος.

blaze [bleiz] n (fire) φλόγα, ἀνάφλεξις, φωτιά ‖ vi παίρνω φωτιά ‖ (person) ἐξάπτομαι ‖ vt: to ~ a trail χαράσσω δρόμον.

blazer ['bleizə*] n ἀθλητικό σακάκι.

bleach [bliːtʃ] n ἄσπρισμα, μπουγάδα ‖ vt ἀσπρίζω, ξεβάφω ‖ (hair) ἀποχρωματίζω.

bleak [bliːk] a ψυχρός, μελαγχολικός.

bleary-eyed ['bliəriaid] a μέ θολωμένα μάτια.

bleat [bliːt] n βέλασμα ‖ vi βελάζω.

bled [bled] pt,pp of **bleed**.

bleed [bliːd] (irreg v) vi χύνω αἷμα, χάνω αἷμα ‖ vt φλεβοτομῶ, παίρνω αἷμα.

bleeding ['bliːdiŋ] a αἱματηρός.

blemish ['blemiʃ] n ἐλάττωμα, κηλίδα ‖ vt κηλιδώνω ‖ (reputation) καταστρέφω.

blench [blentʃ] vi κιτρινίζω (ἀπό φόβο).

blend [blend] n χαρμάνι ‖ vt ἀνακατεύω, συγχωνεύω ‖ vi (colours etc) ταιριάζω.

bless [bles] vt εὐλογῶ, δοξάζω ‖ ~ing n εὐλογία, εὐτύχημα.

blew [bluː] pt of **blow**.

blight [blait] n (disease) ἐρυσίβη, συρίκι, συναπίδι ‖ (fig) πληγή ‖ vt καταστρέφω.

blimey ['blaimi] excl (col) νά μέ πάρη ὁ διάβολος!

blind [blaind] a τυφλός, στραβός ‖ (alley etc) ἀδιέξοδος ‖ n τέντα, περσίς ‖ (excuse) πρόσχημα, ὑποκρισία ‖ vt τυφλώνω, στραβώνω ‖ ~fold a μέ δεμένα μάτια ‖ vt δένω τά μάτια ‖ ~ly ad στά τυφλά, στά στραβά ‖ ~ness n τυφλότης, στραβομάρα.

blink [bliŋk] vti ἀνοιγοκλείνω τά μάτια, μισοκλείνω τά μάτια ‖ ~ers npl παρωπίδες.

blinking ['bliŋkiŋ] a (col) = **bloody**.

bliss [blis] n μακαριότητα, εὐδαιμονία ‖ ~fully ad εὐτυχισμένα.

blister ['blistə*] n (on skin) φυσαλίδα, φουσκάλα ‖ (on surfaces etc) φουσκάλα ‖ vti φουσκαλιάζω, φλυκταινούμαι.

blithe [blaið] a χαρούμενος, εὔθυμος ‖ ~ly ad φαιδρά, χαρούμενα.

blithering ['bliðəriŋ] a: ~ idiot τελείως βλάκας.

blitz [blits] n μπλίτς, βίαιη ἐπίθεσις.

blizzard ['blizəd] n χιονοθύελλα.

bloated ['bləutid] a φουσκωμένος, πρησμένος.

bloc [blɔk] n (pol) συνασπισμός, μπλόκ.

block [blɔk] n (piece) τεμάχι, μεγάλο κομμάτι ‖ (for chopping) ἐπικόπανον, πικόπι ‖ (traffic) συνωστισμός, διακοπή ‖ (obstacle) ἐμπόδιον ‖ (city) τετράγωνον ‖ vt φράσσω, ἐμποδίζω ‖ ~ade n ἀποκλεισμός, μπλόκο ‖ vt ἀποκλείω, μπλοκάρω ‖ ~age n ἔμφραξη, μπλοκάρισμα.

bloke [bləuk] n (col) ἄνθρωπος.

blond(e) [blɔnd] a ξανθός, ξανθή ‖ n ξανθός, ξανθιά.

blood [blʌd] n αἷμα ‖ (kinship) συγγένεια ‖ (descent) καταγωγή ‖ ~ donor n αἱμοδότης ‖ ~ group n ὁμάδα αἵματος ‖ ~less a (victory etc) ἀναίμακτος ‖ ~ poisoning n δηλητηρίασις αἵματος ‖ ~ pressure n πίεσις αἵματος ‖ ~shed n αἱματοχυσία ‖ ~shot a κόκκινο (μάτι) ‖ ~stained a αἱματοσταγής, ματωμένος ‖ ~stream n κυκλοφορικό σύστημα ‖ ~thirsty a αἱμοβόρος ‖ ~ transfusion n μετάγγισις αἵματος ‖ ~y a (col) παλιο-, βρωμο- ‖ (lit) αἱματηρός ‖ ~y-minded a τζαναμπέτης.

bloom [bluːm] n (flower) λουλούδι ‖ (perfection) ἄνθησις, ἀκμή ‖ vi ἀνθίζω ‖ in ~ στήν ἄνθησί του.

blossom ['blɔsəm] n ἄνθος ‖ vi ἀνθίζω.

blot [blɔt] n λεκές ‖ (disgrace) κηλίδα ‖ vt

(*stain*) λεκιάζω ‖ (*dry ink*) στυπώνω, τραβῶ ‖ to ~ out *vt* ἐξαφανίζω, σβήνω.
blotchy ['blɔtʃi] *a* γεμάτος κοκκινίλες.
blotting paper ['blɔtiŋpeipə*] *n* στυπόχαρτο.
blouse [blauz] *n* μπλούζα.
blow [bləu] (*irreg v*) *n* (*with fist*) κτύπημα, γρονθιά ‖ (*with stick*) ραβδισμός ‖ (*of air*) φύσημα ‖ (*of fate*) πλῆγμα ‖ *vt* φυσάω ‖ (*a fuse*) καίομαι ‖ (*col: squander*) σπαταλάω ‖ at a single ~ μ'ἕνα κτύπημα ‖ to ~ one's top ξεσπάω ‖ to ~ over *vi* περνῶ, ξεθυμαίνω ‖ to ~ up *vi* σκάω, ἀνατινάσσω ‖ *vt* (*tyre*) φουσκώνω ‖ ~lamp *n* καμινευτήρ ‖ ~-out *n* (*aut*) κλατάρισμα ‖ ~y *a* ἀνεμώδης.
blubber ['blʌbə*] *n* λίπος φάλαινας.
blue [blu:] *a* γαλάζιος, γαλανός ‖ (*paint*) μπλέ ‖ (*with cold etc*) μελανιασμένος ‖ *n*: to have the ~s μελαγχολῶ ‖ ~bell *n* ζυμπούλι ‖ ~-blooded *a* γαλαζοαίματος ‖ ~bottle *n* κρεατόμυγα ‖ ~print *n* κυανοτυπία, σχέδιον.
bluff [blʌf] *n* (*deception*) μπλόφα, ἀπάτη ‖ *vt* μπλοφάρω, ἐξαπατῶ ‖ *a* ντόμπρος.
bluish ['blu:iʃ] *a* γαλαζωπός.
blunder ['blʌndə*] *n* μεγάλο λάθος, χοντροκοπιά ‖ *vi* κάνω γκάφα.
blunt [blʌnt] *a* ἀμβλύς, στομωμένος ‖ (*person*) μονοκόμματος ‖ *vt* ἀμβλύνω, στομώνω ‖ ~ly *ad* ἀπότομα, ντόμπρα.
blur [blə:*] *n* θολούρα, θαμπάδα ‖ (*stain*) μουτζούρα ‖ *vti* θολώνω, θαμπώνω.
blurt [blə:t] to ~ out *vt* προδίδω, ἀποκαλύπτω.
blush [blʌʃ] *vi* κοκκινίζω ‖ *n* κοκκίνισμα ‖ ~ing *a* ντροπαλός.
bluster ['blʌstə*] *vi* (*of wind*) φυσῶ δυνατά ‖ (*of person*) κάνω φασαρία, κομπάζω.
boa ['bəuə] *n* βόας.
boar [bɔ:*] *n* γουρούνι ἀρσενικό, κάπρί.
board [bɔ:d] *n* (*of wood*) σανίδα, τάβλα ‖ (*notice*) πινακίδα, ταμπλό ‖ (*of paper*) χαρτόνι ‖ (*meal*) φαΐ ‖ (*of men*) συμβούλιον, ἐπιτροπή ‖ *vt* (*feed*) δίδω τροφήν ‖ (*ship, train*) ἐπιβαίνω, μπαρκάρω ‖ (*with planks*) σανιδώνω ‖ ~ and lodging φαΐ καί ὕπνος ‖ to ~ up *vt* (*περι*) φράσσω μέ σανίδες ‖ ~er *n* οἰκότροφος ‖ (*lodger*) ἔνοικος ‖ ~ing house *n* πανσιόν ‖ ~ing school *n* σχολή μέ οἰκοτροφεῖον ‖ ~ing school pupil *n* ἐσωτερικός.
boast [bəust] *vi* καυχῶμαι, κομπορρημονῶ ‖ *n* κομπασμός, καυχησιολογία ‖ ~ful *a* καυχησιάρης, φανφαρόνος ‖ ~fulness *n* κομπασμός.
boat [bəut] *n* βάρκα, καΐκι ‖ (*ship*) καράβι ‖ ~er *n* (*hat*) ναυτική ψάθα ‖ ~ing *n* λεμβοδρομία μέ βάρκα ‖ ~swain ['bəusən] *n* λοστρόμος.
bob [bɔb] *vi* ἀνεβοκατεβαίνω.
bobbin ['bɔbin] *n* πηνίον, κουβαρίστρα ‖ (*elec*) μπομπίνα.

bobsleigh ['bɔbslei] *n* μπόπ-σλέϊ, ἕλκηθρο.
bodice ['bɔdis] *n* στῆθος φορέματος, μπούστος.
bodily ['bɔdili] *ad* σωματικῶς ‖ (*together*) συλλογικῶς, ὅλοι μαζί.
body ['bɔdi] *n* σῶμα, κορμί ‖ (*legislative etc*) σῶμα, σωματεῖον ‖ (*collection*) μέγα πλῆθος, μᾶζα ‖ (*of car etc*) σῶμα, κύριον μέρος ‖ ~guard *n* σωματοφύλακας ‖ ~work *n* καρρότσα.
bog [bɔg] *n* ἕλος ‖ *vi*: to get ~ged down βουλιάζω.
boggle ['bɔgl] *vi* διστάζω.
bogie ['bəugi] *n* τροχοφορεύς.
bogus ['bəugəs] *a* ψευδής, ψεύτικος.
boil [bɔil] *vt* (*potatoes etc*) βράζω ‖ *vi* βράζω, κοχλάζω ‖ *n* (*med*) καλόγερος ‖ to come to the ~ παίρνω βράση ‖ ~er *n* λέβης, καζάνι ‖ ~ing point *n* σημεῖον βρασμοῦ.
boisterous ['bɔistərəs] *a* θορυβώδης, ταραχώδης.
bold [bəuld] *a* τολμηρός, θαρραλέος ‖ ~ly *ad* θαρραλέα, μέ τόλμην ‖ ~ness *n* τολμηρότης, θάρρος.
bollard ['bɔləd] *n* δέστρα.
bolster ['bəulstə*] *n* μαξιλάρα ‖ to ~ up *vt* (ὑπο)στηρίζω.
bolt [bəult] *n* (*of door etc*) σύρτης, μάνταλον ‖ (*rush away*) ἐξόρμησις, φυγή ‖ *vt* (*a door etc*) μανταλώνω, κλειδώνω ‖ (*food*) καταβροχθίζω ‖ *vi* (*rush away*) φεύγω, ἐξορμῶ ‖ (*escape*) δραπετεύω.
bomb [bɔm] *n* βόμβα ‖ *vt* βομβαρδίζω ‖ ~ard *vt* βομβαρδίζω, σφυροκοπῶ ‖ ~ardment *n* βομβαρδισμός ‖ ~er *n* (*person*) βομβαριστής ‖ (*aviat*) βομβαρδιστικό ‖ ~ing *n* βομβαρδισμός ‖ ~shell *n* (*fig*) κατάπληξις, σάν βόμβα.
bona fide ['bəunə'faidi] *a* καλῆς πίστεως.
bond [bɔnd] *n* (*link*) δεσμός, συνάφεια ‖ (*promise*) ὑπόσχεσις, σύμβασις ‖ (*econ*) ὁμολογία.
bone [bəun] *n* κόκκαλο ‖ *vt* ξεκοκκαλίζω ‖ ~-dry *a* ἐντελῶς ξηρός, κατάξερος ‖ ~r *n* (*US*) γκάφα.
bonfire ['bɔnfaiə*] *n* φωτιά.
bonnet ['bɔnit] *n* γυναικεῖο καπέλλο ‖ (*child's*) σκουφίτσα ‖ (*cap*) σκοῦφος, μπερές ‖ (*Brit: of car*) καπό.
bonus ['bəunəs] *n* ἐπιμίσθιον, ἐπίδομα.
bony ['bəuni] *a* κοκκαλιάρης.
boo [bu:] *vt* ἀποδοκιμάζω, γιουχαΐζω.
book [buk] *n* βιβλίον, κιτάπι ‖ *vt* (*ticket etc*) βγάζω εἰσιτήριο ‖ (*a room*) κλείνω δωμάτιο ‖ (*person*) πληρώνω, τιμωρούμαι ‖ ~case *n* βιβλιοθήκη ‖ ~ing office *n* πρακτορεῖον εἰσιτηρίων ‖ ~keeping *n* λογιστική ‖ ~let *n* φυλλάδιον, βιβλιαράκι ‖ ~maker *n* (*racing*) μπουκμέϊκερ ‖ ~seller *n* βιβλιοπώλης ‖ ~shop *n* βιβλιοπωλεῖον ‖ ~stall *n* πάγκος βιβλιοπώλου ‖ ~store *n* = ~shop.

boom [bu:m] *n* (*noise*) κρότος, βόμβος ‖ (*naut*) ἀπώστης ‖ (*port*) φράγμα ‖ (*busy period*) μπούμ, κῦμα εὐημερίας, αἰχμή εὐημερίας ‖ *vi* ἀνέρχομαι, ἀνεβαίνω.

boon [bu:n] *n* (*blessing*) ὄφελος.

boorish [ˈbuəriʃ] *a* ἄξεστος, ἀγροῖκος.

boost [bu:st] *n* προώθησις ‖ *vt* προωθῶ, διαφημίζω.

boot [bu:t] *n* μπόττα ‖ (*Brit: of car*) πόρτμπαγκάζ ‖ *vt* (*kick*) λακτίζω, κλωτσάω ‖ **to ~** (*in addition*) ἐπὶ πλέον.

booze [bu:z] *n* ποτόν ‖ *vi* ξεφαντώνω, μεθοκοπῶ.

border [ˈbɔːdə*] *n* (*frontier*) σύνορον, μεθόριος ‖ (*edge*) γῦρος, σειρίτι, μπορντούρα ‖ (*page etc*) πλαίσιον, βινιέτα ‖ **to ~ on** *vt* συνορεύω μέ ‖ **~line** *n* (*fig*) ἐγγίζων τά ὅρια.

bore [bɔː*] *pt of* **bear** ‖ *n* (*person or thing*) πληκτικός, ἐνοχλητικός, ἀφόρητος ‖ (*of gun etc*) διαμέτρημα ‖ *vt* τρυπῶ, ἀνοίγω ὀπήν ‖ (*weary*) πλήττω, λιμάρω ‖ **~dom** *n* πλῆξις, ἀνία.

boring [ˈbɔːriŋ] *a* ἀνιαρός, βαρετός.

born [bɔːn] *pp*: **to be ~** γεννιέμαι.

borough [ˈbʌrə] *n* (διοικητική) περιφέρεια.

borrow [ˈbɔːrəu] *vt* δανείζομαι.

bosom [ˈbuzəm] *n* στῆθος, κόρφος.

boss [bɔs] *n* κύφωμα, καμπούρα ‖ (*master*) τό ἀφεντικό ‖ *vt* διευθύνω, κάνω τὸν διευθυντῆ ‖ **~y** *a* κάνω τό δερβέναγα.

bosun [ˈbousn] *n* — **boatswain** ‖ *see* **boat**.

botanical [bəˈtænikəl] *a* βοτανικός.

botanist [ˈbɔtənist] *n* βοτανολόγος.

botany [ˈbɔtəni] *n* βοτανική.

botch [bɔtʃ] *vt* φτιάνω τσαπατσούλικα, κουτσοφτιάχνω ‖ (*patch*) κουτσομπαλώνω.

both [bəuθ] *a.pron* ἀμφότεροι, καί οἱ δύο ‖ *ad* καί . . . καί ‖ *cj* ὄχι μόνον . . . ἀλλά καί . . . .

bother [ˈbɔðə*] *n* ἐνόχλησις, μπελᾶς ‖ *vt* ἐνοχλῶ, πειράζω, σκοτίζω ‖ *vi* στεναχωριέμαι, νοιάζομαι.

bottle [ˈbɔtl] *n* φιάλη, μπουκάλι, μποτίλια ‖ *vt* ἐμφιαλώνω, μπουκαλάρω, μποτιλλιάρω ‖ **~neck** *n* (*production*) δυσχέρεια ‖ (*traffic*) συνωστισμός.

bottom [ˈbɔtəm] *n* κάτω μέρος, βάθος ‖ (*of sea etc*) πυθμήν, βυθός ‖ (*seat*) πισινός, ποπός ‖ (*ship*) πλοῖον ‖ *a* κάτω μέρος, κάτω-κάτω ‖ (*lowest*) κατώτατος ‖ **~less** *a* ἀπύθμενος.

bough [bau] *n* κλάδος, κλαδί.

bought [bɔːt] *pt,pp of* **buy**.

boulder [ˈbəuldə*] *n* λίθος, λιθάρι, ὀγκόλιθος.

bounce [bauns] *n* (*rebound*) ἀναπήδησις, γκέλ ‖ *vi* κάνω γκέλ, ἀναπηδῶ ‖ (*col: person*) μπαίνω—βγαίνω ξαφνικά ‖ *vt* κάνω μπάλλα νά κάνει γκέλ.

bound [baund] *pt,pp of* **bind** ‖ *n* ὅριον, σύνορον ‖ (*restriction*) ὅρια ‖ (*leap*) πήδημα ‖ *vi* (*spring, leap*) πηδῶ, σκιρτῶ ‖ (*limit*) περιορίζω ‖ *a* προοριζόμενον γιά, κατευθυνόμενον εἰς ‖ **~ary** *n* ὅριον σύνορον ‖ **~less** *a* ἀπεριόριστος.

bouquet [ˈbukei] *n* μπουκέτο.

bourgeois [ˈbuəʒwaː] *a* μπουρζουάζ, ἀστός.

bout [baut] *n* (*contest*) γῦρος, ἀγών, συνάντησις ‖ (*of illness*) προσβολή.

bow [bəu] *n* (*curve*) καμπή ‖ (*ribbon*) φιόγκος ‖ (*weapon*) τόξο, δοξάρι ‖ (*mus*) δοξάρι βιολιοῦ.

bow [bau] *vi* ὑποκλίνομαι, σκύβω τό κεφάλι ‖ *vt* κλίνω, κάμπτω ‖ (*submit*) ὑποκύπτω, ὑποτάσσομαι ‖ *n* ὑπόκλισις, κλίσις (τῆς κεφαλῆς) ‖ (*of ship*) πλώρη.

bowels [bauəlz] *npl* ἔντερα, σπλάχνα ‖ (*fig*) σπλάχνα.

bowl [bəul] *n* (*basin*) λεκάνη, γαβάθα ‖ (*of pipe*) λουλάς (τσιμπουκιοῦ) ‖ (*wooden ball*) σφαίρα ‖ *vti* παίζω μπάλλα, ρίχνω μπάλλα ‖ **~s** *npl* παιχνίδι τῆς μπάλλας.

bow-legged [ˈbəulegid] *a* στραβοπόδης, στραβοκάνης.

bowler [ˈbəulə*] *n* παίκτης τῆς μπάλλας ‖ (*hat*) μελόν.

bowling [ˈbəuliŋ] *n* (*game*) παιχνίδι τῆς μπάλλας, μπόλιγκ.

bow tie [ˈbəuˈtai] *n* παπιγιόν, πεταλούδα.

box [bɔks] *n* κιβώτιον ‖ (*small*) κουτί ‖ (*theat*) θεωρεῖον ‖ *vt* (*s.o.'s ears*) καρπαζώνω ‖ (*package*) πακετάρω ‖ *vi* πυγμαχῶ, παίζω μπόξ ‖ **~er** *n* (*person*) πυγμάχος, μποξέρ ‖ (*dog*) μπόξερ ‖ **~ing** *n* (*sport*) πυγμαχία, μπόξ ‖ **~ office** *n* ταμεῖον (θεάτρου) ‖ **~ room** *n* ἀποθήκη οἰκίας.

boy [bɔi] *n* ἀγόρι, παιδί.

boycott [ˈbɔikɔt] *n* μποϋκοττάρισμα ‖ *vt* ἀποκλείω, μποϋκοττάρω.

boyfriend [ˈbɔifrend] *n* φίλος, ἀγαπημένος.

boyish [ˈbɔiiʃ] *a* παιδιάστικος, ἀγορίστικος.

bra [braː] *n* σουτιέν, στηθόδεσμος.

brace [breis] *n* (*clamp*) δεσμός ‖ (*pair*) ζευγάρι ‖ (*support*) στύλωμα ‖ (*tool*) ματικάπι ‖ *vt* συνδέω, στερεώνω ‖ (*o.s.*) τονώνω, δυναμώνω ‖ **~s** *npl* τιράντες.

bracelet [ˈbreislit] *n* βραχιόλι.

bracing [ˈbreisiŋ] *a* τονωτικός.

bracken [ˈbrækən] *n* φτέρη.

bracket [ˈbrækit] *n* (*support*) ὑποστήριγμα, ὠτίς, κρεμάθρα ‖ (*round*) παρένθεσις ‖ (*square*) ἀγκύλη ‖ (*group*) ὁμάδα, ἰσάξιοι ‖ *vt* θέτω ἐν παρενθέσει ‖ (*associate*) συνδέω.

brag [bræg] *vi* κουχῶμαι.

braid [breid] *n* (*of hair*) πλεξίδα, πλεξούδα ‖ (*officer's etc*) σειρήτι, κορδόνι.

Braille [breil] *n* Μπράϊλ.

brain [brein] *n* ἐγκέφαλος, μυαλό ‖ (*person*) διάνοια, ‖ **~s** *npl* μυαλά ‖ **~less** *a* ἄμυαλος, βλάκας ‖ **~washing** *n* πλύσις ἐγκεφάλου ‖ **~wave** *n* ἔμπνευσις, ἐπινόησις ‖ **~y** *a* εὐφυής.

braise [breiz] *vt* ψήνω σιγά στήν κατσαρόλα.

brake [breik] n (on vehicle) τροχοπέδη, φρένο ‖ vti φρενάρω, πατώ φρένο.

bramble ['bræmbl] n βάτος.

branch [bra:ntʃ] n (of tree) κλάδος, κλαδί ‖ (division) κλάδος ‖ (office) ὑποκατάστημα ‖ vi διακλαδοῦμαι, χωρίζομαι.

brand [brænd] n (trademark) μάρκα ‖ (on cattle) σφράγισις μέ ἀναμμένο σίδηρο.

brand-new ['brænd'nju:] a κατακαίνουργος, ὁλοκαίνουργος, τοῦ κουτιοῦ.

brandy ['brændi] n κονιάκ.

brash [bræʃ] a ἀναιδής, ἀδιάντροπος.

brass [bra:s] n μπροῦτζος ‖ ~ band n μπάντα, φανφάρα.

brassière ['bræsiεə*] n σουτιέν, στηθόδεσμος.

brat [bræt] n κουτσούβελο, διαβολάκι.

bravado [brə'va:dəu] n παλληκαρισμός.

brave [breiv] a γενναῖος ‖ (show) περίφημος ‖ n ἐρυθρόδερμος πολεμιστής ‖ vt ἀψηφῶ ‖ ~ly ad γενναῖα, παλληκαρίσια ‖ ~ry n θάρρος, ἀνδρεία.

bravo [bra:'vəu] excl εὖγε!, μπράβο!

brawl [bro:l] n καυγάς ‖ vi καυγαδίζω.

brawn [bro:n] n μυϊκή δύναμις, δύναμι ‖ (cooking) πηχτή ‖ ~y a γεροδεμένος.

bray [brei] n γκάρισμα ‖ vi γκαρίζω.

brazen ['breizn] a (metal) μπροῦτζινος ‖ (shameless) ἀναιδής, ξετσίπωτος ‖ vt: to ~ it out καυχώμαι ξετσίπωτα.

brazier ['breiziə*] n μαγκάλι, φουφού.

Brazil [brə'zil] n Βραζιλία ‖ ~ian a βραζιλιανός ‖ n Βραζιλιάνος ‖ ~ nut n Βραζιλιανόν καρύδι.

breach [bri:tʃ] n (gap) ῥῆγμα, τρύπα ‖ (of trust, duty) παραβίασις, παράβασις ‖ (quarrel) ῥῆξις, τσάκωμα ‖ vt γκρεμίζω.

bread [bred] n ψωμί ‖ (living) καθημερινό ψωμί ‖ ~ and butter n μέσα συντηρήσεως ‖ ~crumbs npl ψύχουλα ‖ ~winner n στήριγμα τῆς οἰκογενείας.

break [breik] (irreg v) vt (crush) συντρίβω, τσακίζω ‖ (apart) σπάω ‖ (promise) ἀθετῶ ‖ (silence etc) διακόπτω ‖ (habit) κόβω ‖ (the law) παραβιάζω ‖ vi θραύομαι, τσακίζομαι ‖ (friendship etc) τά χαλῶ ‖ (dissolve) διαλύομαι ‖ n (gap) ῥῆξις, ἄνοιγμα, χάσμα ‖ (rest) διακοπή διάλειμμα ‖ (chance) εὐκαιρία, τύχη ‖ (fracture) ῥωγμή ‖ to ~ free or loose vi δραπετεύω, ἀπελευθερώνομαι ‖ to ~ in vt (a horse etc) δαμάζω ‖ (conversation) διακόπτω ‖ vi (burglar) κάνω διάρρηξι ‖ to ~ out vi ξεσπῶ ‖ (of prison) δραπετεύω ‖ to ~ up vi διαλύομαι ≠ vt χωρίζω, συντρίβω, τεμαχίζω ‖ ~able a εὔθραστος ‖ ~age n σπάσιμο, ῥάγισμα ‖ ~down n (in discussions) διακοπή ‖ (of health) κατάρρευσις ‖ (mental) χάσιμο τοῦ μυαλοῦ ‖ ~er n (naut) κῦμα ‖ ~fast n πρωϊνό, κολατσό ‖ ~through n δίοδος, ῥῆγμα ‖ ~water n κυματοθραύστης.

breast [brest] n (of woman) μαστός, βυζί ‖ (of man, animal) στῆθος ‖ ~-stroke n ἁπλωτή.

breath [breθ] n πνοή, ἀναπνοή ‖ out of ~ λαχανιασμένος.

breathe [bri:ð] vti ἀναπνέω ‖ ~r n ἀνάσα.

breathing ['bri:ðiŋ] n ἀναπνοή.

breathless ['breθlis] a λαχανιασμένος.

breathtaking ['breθteikiŋ] a καταπληκτικός, τρομακτικός.

bred [bred] pt,pp of breed.

breed [bri:d] (irreg v) n γενεά, ράτσα ‖ vti γεννῶ, φέρνω ‖ (animals) τρέφω ‖ vi ἀναπαράγομαι ‖ ~er n (person) ἀναπαραγωγός, τροφεύς ‖ ~ing n ἀνατροφή

breeze [bri:z] n αὔρα, ἀεράκι.

breezy ['bri:zi] a εὐάερος ‖ (person) γεμάτος ζωή.

brevity ['breviti] n βραχύτης, συντομία.

brew [bru:] vt (drinks) παρασκευάζω, μπύρα, ἀποστάζω ‖ (tea) βράζω ‖ (plot) μηχανορραφῶ ‖ vi βράζομαι ‖ (storm etc) ἔρχεται ‖ ~ery n ζυθοποιία, ποτοποιία.

bribe [braib] n δωροδοκία ‖ vt δωροδοκῶ, λαδώνω ‖ ~ry n δωροδοκία, μπούκωμα.

brick [brik] n πλίνθος, τοῦβλο ‖ ~layer n τουβλᾶς ‖ ~work n πλινθοδομή.

bridal ['braidl] a νυφικός, γαμήλιος.

bride [braid] n νύφη ‖ ~groom n γαμπρός ‖ ~smaid n παράνυφη.

bridge [bridʒ] n γεφύρι, γιοφύρι ‖ (naut) γέφυρα ‖ (cards) μπριτζ ‖ (of nose) ράχη τῆς μύτης ‖ vt γεφυρώνω.

bridle ['braidl] n χαλινάρι, γκέμι ‖ vt (a horse) χαλινώνω ‖ (control) χαλιναγωγῶ.

brief [bri:f] a σύντομος, βραχύς ‖ n (law) δικογραφία, φάκελλος ‖ vt δίδω ὁδηγίες, ἐνημερώνω ‖ ~s npl κοντή κυλόττα ‖ ~case n χαρτοφύλακας ‖ ~ing n καταρτισμός, ὁδηγίες ‖ ~ly ad σύντομα, μέ λίγα λόγια ‖ ~ness n βραχύτης, συντομία.

brigade [bri'geid] n (mil) ταξιαρχία ‖ see fire.

brigadier [brigə'diə*] n ταξίαρχος.

bright [brait] a (as light) φωτεινός, λαμπερός, γυαλιστερός ‖ (weather) φωτεινός, καθαρός ‖ (clever) ἔξυπνος, εὐφυής ‖ (colour) ζωηρός, λαμπρός ‖ ~en vti ζωηρεύω, φωτίζομαι, ἀστράφτω ‖ ~ly ad λαμπρά, λαμπερά.

brilliance ['briljəns] n λαμπρότης, ἐξυπνάδα ‖ (of surface etc) φωτεινότης ‖ (of style) ζωηρότης.

brilliant ['briljənt] a φωτεινός, λαμπρός ‖ (person) σπουδαῖος, λαμπρός ‖ (splendid) ἔξοχος ‖ ~ly ad λαμπρά.

brim [brim] n (of cup) χεῖλος ‖ (of hat) γῦρος, μπόρ ‖ vi ξεχειλίζω ‖ ~ful a ξέχειλος.

brine [brain] n σαλαμούρα, ἄρμη.

bring [briŋ] (irreg v) vt φέρω, φέρνω ‖ to ~ about vt ἐπιτυγχάνω, καταφέρνω ‖ to ~ off vt φέρω εἰς πέρας ‖ to ~ round or

to *vt* ἐπαναφέρω, συνεφέρω ‖ to ~ up *vt*
(*raise*) ἀνατρέφω, μεγαλώνω ‖ (*introduce*)
προβάλλω, θέτω.
brisk [brisk] *a* ζωηρός.
bristle ['brisl] *n* γουρουνότριχα ‖ *vi*
ἀνατριχιάζω ‖ **bristling with** γεμᾶτος μέ.
Britain ['britən] *n* Βρεττανία.
British ['britiʃ] *a* Βρεττανικός, Ἀγγλικός
‖ **the** ~ *npl* οἱ Ἄγγλοι ‖ ~ **Isles** *npl*
Βρεττανικαί Νῆσοι.
Briton ['britən] *n* Βρεττανός, Ἄγγλος.
brittle ['britl] *a* εὔθραυστος.
broach [brəutʃ] *vt* (*subject*) θίγω (ζήτημα).
broad [brɔːd] *a* εὐρύς, φαρδύς, πλατύς ‖
(*daylight*) στό φῶς τῆς ἡμέρας ‖ (*general*)
ἁπλό, γενικό ‖ (*accent*) χωρ/ατικη
προφορά ‖ ~**cast** *n* ἐκπομπή ‖ *vti*
μεταδίδω διά ραδιοφώνου ‖ ~**casting** *n*
ἐκπομπή, μετάδοσις ‖ ~**en** *vt* εὐρύνω,
πλαταίνω ‖ *vi* εὐρύνομαι, ἀνοίγω ‖ ~**ly**
ad εὐρέως, πλατειά ‖ ~**minded** *a* μέ
ἀνοικτό μυαλό, ἀνεκτικός, εὐρείας
ἀντιλήψεως.
brocade [brəu'keid] *n* μπροκάρ.
broccoli ['brɔkəli] *n* μπρόκολο.
brochure ['brəuʃjuə*] *n* φυλλάδιον,
μπροσούρα.
broiler ['brɔilə*] *n* ψησταριά.
broke [brəuk] *pt of* **break** ‖ *a* ἀπένταρος ‖
~**n** *pp of* **break** ‖ ~**n-hearted** *a* μέ
ραγισμένη καρδιά.
broker ['brəukə*] *n* μεσίτης, χρηματιστής.
bronchitis [brɔŋ'kaitis] *n* βρογχίτιδα.
bronze [brɔnz] *n* μπροῦντζος ‖ ~**d** *a* ἡλι-
ογημένος, μαυρισμένος.
brooch [brəutʃ] *n* καρφίτσα.
brood [bruːd] *n* κλώσσισμα, γενιά ‖ *vt*
κλωσσῶ ‖ (*meditate*) μελαγχολῶ ‖ ~**y**
a ἀφηρημένος.
brook [bruk] *n* (*stream*) ρυάκι, ρέμα.
broom [brum] *n* σκούπα ‖ ~**stick** *n* σκουπό
ξυλο.
broth [brɔθ] *n* ζουμί κρέατος, σούπα.
brothel ['brɔθl] *n* μπορντέλο, οἶκος ἀνοχῆς.
brother ['brʌðə*] *n* ἀδελφός ‖ ~**hood** *n*
ἀδελφοσύνη, ἀδελφότης ‖ ~**-in-law** *n*
γαμπρός, κουνιάδος ‖ ~**ly** *a* ἀδελφικός.
brought [brɔːt] *pt,pp of* **bring**.
brow [brau] *n* (*forehead*) κούτελο, μέτωπο
‖ (*eyebrow*) φρύδι ‖ (*of hill etc*) χεῖλος,
φρύδι ‖ ~**beat** *vt* φοβίζω, τρομάζω.
brown [braun] *a* καστανός, καφετής ‖ *n*
καφετής ‖ *vti* σκουραίνω, μαυρίζω ‖
(*cooking*) καβουρδίζω ‖ ~**ie** *n* (*girl guide*)
προσκοπίνα.
browse [brauz] *vi* (*examine casually*)
ξεφυλλίζω, βόσκω, τριγυρίζω.
bruise [bruːz] *n* μώλωψ, κτύπημα ‖ *vti*
κτυπῶ, κτυπιέμαι.
brunette [bruː'net] *n* μελαχροινή.
brunt [brʌnt] *n* ὁρμή, φόρα.
brush [brʌʃ] *n* βούρτσα ‖ (*paint*) πινέλο
‖ (*fight*) σύγκρουσις ‖ *vt* βουρτσίζω

(*lightly*) ξεσκονίζω ‖ **to** ~ **aside** *vt* παραμερίζω ‖ ~**wood** *n* θάμνοι, χαμόκλαδα.
brusque [bruːsk] *a* ἀπότομος, τραχύς.
Brussels sprout ['brʌslz'spraut] *n* (Βελγικό)
λαχανάκι, πετί-σού.
brutal ['bruːtl] *a* κτηνώδης ‖ ~**ity** *n*
κτηνωδία.
brute [bruːt] *n* κτῆνος, θηρίον.
brutish ['bruːtiʃ] *a* ἀποκτηνωμένος,
κτηνώδης.
bubble ['bʌbl] *n* μπουρμπουλήθρα, φουσκάλα ‖ *vi* κοχλάζω ‖ (-*iver, wine*) ἀφρίζω
‖ **to** ~ **over** (*fig*) ξεχειλίζω.
buck [bʌk] *n* ἐλάφι ἀρσενικό ‖ (*rabbit*)
κούνελος ‖ *vt* ἐνθαρρύνω, δίνω κουράγιο
‖ **to** ~ **up** *vi* ἐνθαρρύνομαι, (ξανα)παίρνω
κουράγιο.
bucket ['bʌkit] *n* κουβᾶς, κάδος.
buckle ['bʌkl] *n* πόρπη, φιούμπα ‖ *vt*
κουμπώνω, θηλυκώνω ‖ (*bend*) λυγίζω,
στραβώνω.
bud [bʌd] *n* μπουμπούκι.
Buddha ['budə] *n* Βούδδας.
Buddhism ['budizəm] *n* Βουδδισμός.
Buddhist ['budist] *n* βουδδιστής ‖ *a* βουδ-
δικός.
budding ['bʌdiŋ] *a* πού μπουμπουκιάζει.
buddy ['bʌdi] *n* φιλαράκος.
budge [bʌdʒ] *vti* κινοῦμαι, ὑποχωρῶ.
budgerigar ['bʌdʒərigaː*] *n* παπαγαλάκι.
budget ['bʌdʒit] *n* προϋπολογισμός.
buff [bʌf] *a* (*colour*) σαμουά, κρεατί.
buffalo ['bʌfələu] *n* βουβάλι.
buffer ['bʌfə*] *n* ἀπωσβεστήρ, ἀμορτισέρ.
buffet ['bʌfit] *n* πλῆγμα, κτύπημα ‖ ['bufei]
(*bar*) ἀναψυκτήριον ‖ (*food*) μπουφές ‖
vt πλήττω, κτυπῶ.
buffoon [bə'fuːn] *n* παλιάτσος, καραγκιόζης.
bug [bʌg] *n* (*insect*) κοριός ‖ (*US*) ζωΰφιον
‖ (*spy device*) κρυφό μικρόφωνο ‖ ~**bear**
n ἀντιπάθεια, φόβητρον.
buggy ['bʌgi] *n* ἁμαξάκι.
bugle ['bjuːgl] *n* σάλπιγγα.
build [bild] (*irreg v*) *vt* οἰκοδομῶ, χτίζω ‖
~**er** *n* οἰκοδόμος, κατασκευαστής ‖
~**ing** *n* χτίριο, οἰκοδομή ‖ ~**ing society**
n οἰκοδομικός συνεταιρισμός ‖ ~**-up** *n*
διαφήμησις.
built [bilt] *pt,pp of* **build** ‖ **well-**~ *a* (*person*)
γεροδεμένος ‖ ~**-in** *a* (*cupboard*)
ἐντοιχισμένος.
bulb [bʌlb] *n* (*bot*) βολβός ‖ (*elec*) λάμπα,
γλόμπος ‖ ~**ous** *a* βολβώδης.
Bulgaria [bʌl'gεəriə] *n* Βουλγαρία.
bulge [bʌldʒ] *n* διόγκωσις, φούσκωμα ‖ *vi*
προεξέχω, ἐξογκοῦμαι, φουσκώνω.
bulk [bʌlk] *n* μέγεθος, ὄγκος ‖ (*greater
part*) μέγιστον μέρος ‖ ~**head** *n* διάφραγμα ‖ ~**y** *a* ὀγκώδης, χονδρός.
bull [bul] *n* ταῦρος ‖ (*rubbish*) ψέμματα
ἀρλούμπες ‖ ~**dog** *n* μπουλντόγκ.
bulldozer ['buldəuzə*] *n* μπουλντόζα

bullet ['bulit] *n* σφαῖρα, βόλι.
bulletin ['bulitin] *n* δελτίον, ἀνακοινωθέν.
bullfight ['bulfait] *n* ταυρομαχία.
bullion ['buljən] *n* χρυσός (ἄργυρος) εἰς ράβδους.
bullock ['bulək] *n* βόδι, μοσχάρι.
bull's-eye ['bulzai] *n* κέντρον (στόχου).
bully ['buli] *n* τύραννος ‖ *vt* ἀπειλῶ, τρομοκρατῶ.
bum [bʌm] *n* (*col*) πισινός ‖ (*tramp*) ἀλήτης, ἀκαμάτης ‖ **to ~ around** *vi* κοπροσκυλιάζω.
bump [bʌmp] *n* (*blow*) κτύπημα, τίναγμα ‖ (*bruise*) πρήξιμο, καρούλα, καρούμπαλο ‖ *vti* κτυπῶ, σκοντάφτω ‖ **~er** *n* (*car*) προφυλακτήρας ‖ *a* πλουσία (ἐσοδεία).
bumptious ['bʌmpʃəs] *a* ψηλομύτης.
bumpy ['bʌmpi] *a* ἀνώμαλος (δρόμος).
bun [bʌn] *n* σταφιδόψωμο, κουλουράκι.
bunch [bʌntʃ] *n* μάτσο, φούχτα, χούφτα, δέμα.
bundle ['bʌndl] *n* δέμα, μπόγος ‖ *vt* πακετάρω, δένω ‖ (*also* **~ off**) ξεφορτώνομαι.
bung [bʌŋ] *n* πῶμα, τάπα ‖ *vt* (*throw*) ρίχνω, χώνω.
bungalow ['bʌŋgələu] *n* μπάγκαλο, ἐξοχικό σπίτι.
bungle ['bʌŋgl] *vt* τά κάνω θάλασσα, εἶμαι ἀδέξιος.
bunion ['bʌnjən] *n* κάλος.
bunk [bʌŋk] *n* κλίνη, κουκέτα.
bunker ['bʌŋkə*] *n* ἀποθήκη καυσίμων, καρβουνιέρα.
bunny ['bʌni] *n* κουνελάκι.
Bunsen burner ['bʌnsn'bə:nə*] *n* λυχνία Μποῦνσεν.
bunting ['bʌntiŋ] *n* σακκελίς, σημαιοστολισμός.
buoy [bɔi] *n* (*naut*) σημαδούρα ‖ (*lifebuoy*) σωσσίβιο ‖ **~ancy** *n* πλευστότης ‖ **~ant** *a* (*of person*) εὔθυμος, κεφάτος ‖ **to ~ up** *vt* ἐνισχύω, ἀναθαρρύνω, ἐνθαρρύνω.
burden ['bə:dn] *n* φόρτωμα, βάρος, δυσβάστακτον βάρος ‖ *vt* (ἐπι)βαρύνω, φορτώνω.
bureau [bjuə'rəu] *n* γραφεῖον πού κλείνει ‖ (*for information etc*) ὑπηρεσία πληροφοριῶν.
bureaucracy [bjuə'rɔkrəsi] *n* γραφειοκρατία.
bureaucrat ['bjuərəukræt] *n* γραφειοκράτης ‖ **~ic** *a* γραφειοκρατικός.
burglar ['bə:glə*] *n* διαρρήκτης ‖ **~ alarm** *n* κουδούνι ἀσφαλείας ‖ **~ize** *vt* (*US*) διαρρηγνύω ‖ **~y** *n* διάρρηξις.
burgle ['bə:gl] *vt* διαρρηγνύω.
burial ['beriəl] *n* ταφή ‖ **~ ground** *n* νεκροταφεῖον.
burlesque [bə:'lesk] *n* ἐπιθεώρησις, μπυρλέσκ.
burly ['bə:li] *a* γεροδεμένος.
burn [bə:n] (*irreg v*) *n* ἔγκαυμα ‖ *vt* καίω ‖ *vi* φλέγομαι ‖ **to ~ one's fingers** (*fig*)

βρίσκω τό μπελά μου ‖ **~ing question** φλέγον ζήτημα.
burnish ['bə:niʃ] *vt* στιλβώνω, γυαλίζω.
burnt [bə:nt] *pt,pp of* **burn** ‖ *a* καμένος, ψημένος.
burrow ['bʌrəu] *n* φωλιά, τρύπα, λαγούμι ‖ *vti* σκάβω λαγούμι, ἀνοίγω τρύπα.
burst [bə:st] (*irreg v*) *n* ἔκρηξις, ριπή ‖ *vt* (*explode*) προκαλῶ ἔκρηξιν ‖ (*break*) σπάζω ‖ (*break out*) διαρρηγνύω, σπάω ‖ *vi* (*tank etc*) διαρρηγνύομαι, σπάζω ‖ (*flower*) σκάζω, ἀνοίγω ‖ (*into pieces*) γίνομαι κομμάτια.
bury ['beri] *vt* (*inter*) θάβω ‖ (*hide*) κρύβομαι, χώνω, βυθίζομαι.
bus [bʌs] *n* λεωφορεῖον, μπούσι.
bush [buʃ] *n* θάμνος, χαμόκλαδο.
bushel ['buʃl] *n* μπούσελ (36 λίτρα).
bushy ['buʃi] *a* δασύς, πυκνός.
busily ['bizili] *ad* δραστηρίως.
business ['biznis] *n* ἐπιχείρησις, δουλειά ‖ (*concern*) ἐνδιαφέρον, δουλειά ‖ **~man** *n* ἐπιχειρηματίας.
bus stop ['bʌsstɔp] *n* στάσις λεωφορείου.
bust [bʌst] *n* (*statue*) προτομή, μπούστος ‖ (*of woman*) στῆθος.
bustle ['bʌsl] *n* (θορυβώδης) κίνησις, πάταγος ‖ *vi* πηγαινοέρχομαι, βιάζομαι.
bustling ['bʌsliŋ] *a* δραστήριος, πολυάσχολος.
bust-up ['bʌstʌp] *n* (*col*) χρεωκόπησις, ἀποτυχία.
busy ['bizi] *a* ἀπησχολημένος, πολυάσχολος ‖ *vt* ἀσχολοῦμαι, φροντίζω ‖ **~body** *n* πολυπράγμων, παπατρέχας.
but [bʌt] *cj* (*still, yet, besides*) ἀλλά, μά ‖ *ad* (*only, except, as*) μόνον, μόλις, δέν . . . παρά ‖ *prep* (*except*) ἐκτός, πλήν, παρά.
butane ['bju:tein] *n* βουτάνιον.
butcher ['butʃə*] *n* χασάπης ‖ (*savage*) σφαγεύς ‖ *vt* σφάζω.
butler ['bʌtlə*] *n* κελλάρης, μπάτλερ, ἀρχιϋπηρέτης.
butt [bʌt] *n* (*cask*) βαρέλι, βουτσί ‖ (*target*) στόχος ‖ (*of cigarette*) ἀποτσίγαρο, γόπα ‖ (*thick end*) χονδρόν ἄκρον ‖ *vt* κτυπῶ μέ τό κεφάλι.
butter ['bʌtə*] *n* βούτυρο ‖ *vt* βουτυρώνω ‖ (*fig*) **to ~ s.o. up** κολακεύω, ξεσκονίζω ‖ **~fly** *n* πεταλούδα.
buttocks ['bʌtəks] *npl* γλουτοί, τά ὀπίσθια.
button ['bʌtn] *n* κουμπί ‖ *vti* κουμπώνω ‖ **~hole** *n* κουμπότρυπα.
buttress ['bʌtris] *n* ἀντέρεισμα.
buy [bai] (*irreg v*) *vt* ἀγοράζω ‖ **to ~ up** *vt* ἀγοράζω χονδρικῶς ‖ **~er** *n* ἀγοραστής.
buzz [bʌz] *n* βούϊσμα ‖ *vi* βουΐζω.
buzzard ['bʌzəd] *n* ἰκτίνος.
buzzer ['bʌzə*] *n* βομβητής, ψιθυριστής.
by [bai] *prep* (*near, beside*) παρά, πλησίον, πλάϊ, δίπλα, κοντά ‖ (*through*) διά, ἀπό ‖

(with) ἀπό, μέ ‖ ~ **and large** κατά κανόνα ‖ ~-**election** n ἀναπληρωματικές ἐκλογές ‖ ~**gone** a περασμένος, παλιός ‖ n: **let** ~**gones be** ~**gones** περασμένα, ξεχασμένα ‖ ~ **far** κατά πολύ ‖ ~**pass** n βοηθητική δίοδος κατ᾽ ὄνομα ‖ ~-**product** n ὑποπροϊόν ‖ ~**stander** n παριστάμενος ‖ ~**word** n παροιμία ‖ (person) περίγελως, τό κορόϊδο.
Byzantine [bai'zæntain] a Βυζαντινός.

C, c

cab [kæb] n ἅμάξι, ταξί ‖ (of train, truck) θέσις ὁδηγοῦ.
cabaret ['kæbərei] n καμπαρέ.
cabbage ['kæbidʒ] n λάχανο.
cabin ['kæbin] n καλύβα ‖ (naut) καμπίνα ‖ ~ **cruiser** n θαλαμηγός χωρίς κατάρτια.
cabinet ['kæbinit] n κομό ‖ (pol) ὑπουργικόν συμβούλιον ‖ ~**maker** n ἐπιπλοποιός.
cable ['keibl] n καλώδιον ‖ (message) τηλεγράφημα ‖ vti τηλεγραφῶ ‖ ~**gram** n τηλεγράφημα ‖ ~ **railway** n κρεμαστός σιδηρόδρομος.
cache [kæʃ] n (place) κρύπτη ‖ (material) ἀποκρυπτόμενα εἴδη.
cackle ['kækl] n κακάρισμα ‖ vi κακαρίζω.
cactus ['kæktəs] n κάκτος.
caddie, caddy ['kædi] n κάντι.
cadet [kə'det] n (naut) δόκιμος ‖ (mil) εὔελπις ‖ (aviat) ἴκαρος.
cadge [kædʒ] vt ζητιανεύω, σελεμίζω.
Caesarean [si:'zeəriən] a: ~ (section) καισαρική (τομή).
cafe ['kæfei] n καφενεῖον ‖ (with food) καφεστιατόριον ‖ (bar) καφεμπάρ ‖ ~**teria** n καφετιρία.
cage [keidʒ] n κλουβί ‖ vt ἐγκλουβίζω.
cagey ['keidʒi] a (col) πονηρός.
cajole [kə'dʒəul] vt καλοπιάνω.
cake [keik] n κέϊκ, γλύκισμα ‖ (pie) πήττα ‖ (of soap etc) πλάκα.
calamitous [kə'læmitəs] a καταστρεπτικός.
calamity [kə'læmiti] n συμφορά, καταστροφή.
calcium ['kælsiəm] n ἀσβέστιον.
calculate ['kælkjuleit] vti ὑπολογίζω, λογαριάζω.
calculating ['kælkjuleitiŋ] a ὑπολογιστικός, ἐσκεμμένη.
calculation [kælkju'leiʃən] n ὑπολογισμός.
calculus ['kælkjuləs] n λογισμός.
calendar ['kæləndə*] n ἡμερολόγιον.
calf [ka:f] n (cow) μοσχάρι ‖ (skin) βιδέλο ‖ (anat) κνήμη, γάμπα.
calibre, (US) caliber ['kælibə*] n διαμέτρημα ‖ (fig) ἀξία, ἱκανότης.
call [kɔ:l] vt καλῶ, φωνάζω ‖ (meeting) συγκαλῶ ‖ (tel) κλῆσις, πρόσκλησις ‖ vi (visit) ἐπισκέπτομαι, ἔρχομαι ‖ n

(shout) φωνή, κραυγή ‖ (visit) ἐπίσκεψις ‖ ~**box** n τηλεφωνικός θάλαμος ‖ ~**er** n (visitor) ἐπισκέπτης ‖ ~ **girl** n κοκότα ‖ ~**ing** n (profession) ἐπάγγελμα ‖ **to** ~ **for** vt καλῶ, ζητῶ, ἔρχομαι ‖ **to** ~ **off** vt ἀκυρώνω, σταματῶ, διακόπτω ‖ **to** ~ **on** vt (visit) ἐπισκέπτομαι ‖ **to** ~ **up** vt (mil) (ἐπι)στρατεύω ‖ (tel) (πρόσ)καλῶ, τηλεφωνῶ.
callous ['kæləs] a σκληρός, ἄκαρδος ‖ ~**ly** ad σκληρά ‖ ~**ness** n ἀναισθησία.
calm [ka:m] n ἀταραξία ‖ vti καθησυχάζω ‖ a ἥρεμος, ἀτάραχος ‖ ~**ly** ad ἠρέμως ‖ ~**ness** n ἡσυχία, κάλμα ‖ **to** ~ **down** vi καταπραΰνω, καλμάρω ‖ vt ἠρεμῶ καθησυχάζω.
calorie ['kæləri] n θερμίδα.
calve [ka:v] vi γεννῶ ἀγελάδα.
cam [kæm] n ἔκκεντρον, κάμα.
camber ['kæmbə*] n καμπυλότης, κυρτότης.
came [keim] pt of **come**.
camel ['kæməl] n καμήλα.
camellia [kə'mi:liə] n καμέλια.
cameo ['kæmiəu] n καμέα.
camera ['kæmərə] n φωτογραφική μηχανή ‖ ~ **man** n ὀπερατέρ.
camouflage ['kæməfla:ʒ] n καμουφλάρισμα ‖ vt καμουφλάρω.
camp [kæmp] n κατασκήνωσις ‖ (mil) στρατόπεδον ‖ vi κατασκηνώνω ‖ (mil) στρατοπεδεύω.
campaign [kæm'pein] n ἐκστρατεία ‖ vi (also fig) ἐκστρατεύω, κάνω καμπάνια.
campbed ['kæmp'bed] n κρεββάτι ἐκστρατείας, ράντσο.
camper ['kæmpə*] n σκηνίτης, ἐκδρομεύς.
camping ['kæmpiŋ] n: **to go** ~ πηγαίνω εἰς κατασκήνωσιν.
campsite ['kæmpsait] n τόπος κατασκηνώσεως.
can [kæn] auxiliary v (be able) δύναμαι, μπορῶ ‖ (be allowed) ἐπιτρέπεται, μπορῶ ‖ (know how) γνωρίζω, ξέρω ‖ n τενεκές, κουτί ‖ vt κονσερβοποιῶ.
Canada ['kænədə] n Καναδάς.
Canadian [kə'neidiən] a καναδικός ‖ n Καναδός.
canal [kə'næl] n (waterway) διώρυγα, κανάλι ‖ (anat) σωλήν, πόρος.
canary [kə'neəri] n καναρίνι ‖ a καναρινί (χρῶμα).
cancel ['kænsəl] vt (check etc) ἀκυρώνω ‖ (strike out) διαγράφω ‖ (math) ἐξαλείφω ‖ ~**lation** n ἀκύρωσις, ματαίωσις.
cancer ['kænsə*] n καρκίνος.
candid ['kændid] a εἰλικρινής, ντρίτα ‖ ~**ly** ad εἰλικρινά.
candidate ['kændideit] n ὑποψήφιος.
candle ['kændl] n κερί ‖ ~**light** n φῶς κεριοῦ ‖ ~**stick** n κηροπήγιον.
candour ['kændə*] n εὐθύτης, ντομπροσύνη.

candy ['kændi] n καραμέλα.

cane [kein] n (bamboo etc) καλάμι ‖ (stick) μπαστούνι ‖ vt (beat) ραβδίζω.

canine ['kænain] a σκυλήσιος.

canister ['kænistə*] n τενεκεδάκι, κουτί.

cannabis ['kænəbis] n κάνναβις.

canned ['kænd] a (food) κονσερβοποιημένο.

cannibal ['kænibəl] n καννίβαλος, άνθρωποφάγος ‖ ~ism n άνθρωποφαγία.

cannon ['kænən] n (gun) πυροβόλον, κανόνι.

cannot ['kænɔt] = can not ‖ see can.

canoe [kə'nu:] n μονόξυλο, κανό ‖ ~ing n κανό ‖ ~ist n φίλος τοῦ κανό.

canon ['kænən] n κανών ‖ (criterion) κριτήριον ‖ (clergyman) κανονικός.

canonize ['kænənaiz] vt άγιοποιῶ.

can opener ['kænəupnə*] n άνοιχτήρι.

canopy ['kænəpi] n σκιάς, προστέγασμα.

can't [kænt] = can not ‖ see can.

cantankerous [kæn'tæŋkərəs] a διεστραμμένος, καυγατζῆς.

canteen [kæn'ti:n] n (shop) καντίνα ‖ (mil) παγούρι.

canter ['kæntə*] n τριποδισμός ‖ vi καλπάζω έλαφρῶς.

canvas ['kænvəs] n καννναβάτσο ‖ (naut) πανιά ‖ (art) μουσαμᾶς ‖ **under ~** εἰς σκηνάς.

canvass ['kænvəs] vt (election) ψηφοθηρῶ ‖ (discuss) συζητῶ, έρευνῶ.

canyon ['kænjən] n φαράγγι, χαράδρα.

cap [kæp] n (hat) σκούφος, τραγιάσκα ‖ (top) κάλυμμα ‖ vt στέφω, στεφανώνω ‖ (bottle etc) πωματίζω, σφραγίζω ‖ (outdo) ὑπερβάλλω.

capability [keipə'biləti] n ἱκανότης.

capable ['keipəbl] a ἱκανός ‖ **to be ~ of** ἱκανός νά.

capacity [kə'pæsiti] n (space) χωρητικότης ‖ (ability) ἱκανότης ‖ (position) ἰδιότης.

cape [keip] n (garment) κάπα, μπελερίνα ‖ (geog) ἀκρωτήρι.

capital ['kæpitl] n (city) πρωτεύουσα ‖ (econ) κεφάλαιον ‖ (letter) κεφαλαῖον γράμμα ‖ ~ism n καπιταλισμός, κεφαλαιοκρατία ‖ ~ist a καπιταλιστής ‖ ~ **punishment** n θανατική ποινή.

capitulate [kə'pitjuleit] vi συνθηκολογῶ.

capitulation [kəpitju'leiʃən] n συνθηκολόγησις.

capricious [kə'priʃəs] a ἰδιότροπος, ἀσταθής.

capsize [kæp'saiz] vti ἀνατρέπω, μπατάρω.

capstan ['kæpstən] n ἐργάτης.

capsule ['kæpsju:l] n (anat) κάψα ‖ (med) καψούλα.

captain ['kæptin] n (leader) ἀρχηγός ‖ (mil) λοχαγός ‖ (naut) πλοίαρχος ‖ vt ὁδηγῶ, διευθύνω.

caption ['kæpʃən] n ἐπικεφαλίς ‖ (of picture) λεζάντα.

captivate ['kæptiveit] vt γοητεύω, σαγηνεύω, δελεάζω.

captive ['kæptiv] n,a αἰχμάλωτος.

captivity [kæp'tiviti] n αἰχμαλωσία.

capture ['kæptʃə*] vt συλλαμβάνω, αἰχμαλωτίζω ‖ (fort etc) κυριεύω ‖ n σύλληψις ‖ (objective) κατάληψις.

car [ka:*] n (motor) αὐτοκίνητον, ἀμάξι ‖ (railway) βαγόνι.

carafe [kə'ræf] n καράφα.

caramel ['kærəməl] n καραμέλα.

carat ['kærət] n καράτι.

caravan ['kærəvæn] n καραβάνι ‖ (house on wheels) τροχοφόρον οἴκημα.

caraway ['kærəwei] ~ **seed** n κύμινο.

carbon ['ka:bən] n ἄνθραξ ‖ (paper) καρμπόν ‖ ~ **copy** n καρμπόν.

carburettor [ka:bju'retə*] n καρμπυρατέρ.

carcass ['ka:kəs] n πτῶμα, κουφάρι, ψοφίμι.

card [ka:d] n (playing) τραπουλόχαρτο ‖ (visiting) ἐπισκεπτήριον ‖ (general) δελτάριον ‖ ~**board** n χαρτόνι ‖ ~ **game** n χαρτοπαιξία.

cardiac ['ka:diæk] a καρδιακός.

cardigan ['ka:digən] n πλεκτό γιλέκο.

cardinal ['ka:dinl] a: ~ **number** ἀπόλυτος ἀριθμός.

care [kɛə*] n (worry, attention) φροντίδα, μέριμνα, προσοχή ‖ vi φροντίζω, μέ νοιάζει ‖ ~ **of** (abbr c/o) τῇ φροντίδι τοῦ ‖ **to ~ about** vt μέ ἐνδιαφέρει, μέ νοιάζει ‖ **to take ~** προσέχω ‖ **to take ~ of** vt ἐνδιαφέρομαι γιά, φροντίζω γιά ‖ **to ~ for** vt ἐνδιαφέρομαι ‖ (love) ἀγαπῶ, ἀρέσω.

career [kə'riə*] n σταδιοδρομία, καρριέρα ‖ vi τρέχω, ὁρμῶ.

carefree ['kɛəfri:] a ἀμέριμνος, ξένοιαστος.

careful ['kɛəful] a προσεκτικός, ἐπιμελής ‖ ~**ly** ad προσεχτικά.

careless ['kɛəlis] a ἀπρόσεκτος, ἀπερίσκεπτος ‖ ~**ly** ad ἀδιάφορα, ἀπρόσεκτα ‖ ~**ness** n ἀπροσεξία, ἀμέλεια.

caress [kə'res] n θωπεία, χάδι ‖ vt θωπεύω, χαϊδεύω.

caretaker ['kɛəteikə*] n ἐπιστάτης ‖ ~ **government** n ὑπηρεσιακή κυβέρνησις.

car-ferry ['ka:fɛri] n πορθμεῖον ὀχημάτων, φέρρυ-μπωτ.

cargo ['ka:gəu] n φορτίον.

caricature ['kærikətjuə*] n γελοιογραφία, καρικατούρα.

carnal ['ka:nl] a σαρκικός.

carnation [ka:'neiʃən] n γαρύφαλλο.

carnival ['ka:nivəl] n (public celebration) ἀποκρηές, καρναβάλι.

carob ['kærəb] n χαρούπι, ξυλοκέρατον.

carol ['kærəl] n (Christmas) κάλαντα.

carp [ka:p] n (fish) κυπρῖνος, σαζάνι ‖ **to ~ at** vt ἐπικρίνω, κατσαδιάζω, ἀντιλέγω.

car park ['ka:pa:k] n χῶρος παρκαρίσματος.

carpenter ['ka:pintə*] n μαραγκός.

carpentry ['ka:pintri] n ξυλουργική.

carpet ['ka:pit] n τάπης, χαλί ‖ vt στρώνω με χαλί.

carping ['ka:piŋ] a (critical) ἐπικριτικός.

carriage ['kæridʒ] n (vehicle) ἅμαξα, ὄχημα ‖ (carrying) μεταφορά ‖ (fees) μεταφορικά ‖ (bearing) συμπεριφορά, ὕφος ‖ ~way n (part of road) ἁμαξιτή ὁδός.

carrier ['kærɪə*] n (μετα)φορεύς, κομιστής ‖ ~bag n (μεγάλη χαρτοσακκούλα ‖ ~ pigeon n ταχυδρομική περιστερά.

carrot ['kærət] n καρότο.

carry ['kæri] vt (transport, hold) (μετα)φέρω, βαστάζω, κουβαλῶ ‖ (responsibility) ἔχω εὐθύνες ‖ **to be carried away** (fig) παρασύρομαι ‖ **to ~ on** vti συνεχίζω, ἐπιμένω ‖ **to ~ out** vt (orders) ἐκτελῶ.

cart [ka:t] n κάρρο ‖ vt μεταφέρω μέ κάρρο.

cartilage ['ka:tilidʒ] n χόνδρος, τραγανό.

carton ['ka:tən] n κουτί ἀπό χαρτόνι.

cartoon [ka:'tu:n] n (press) γελοιογραφία, σκίτσο ‖ (cine) κινούμεναι εἰκόνες, μίκυ-μάους.

cartridge ['ka:tridʒ] n (for gun) φυσίγγι, φυσέκι.

carve [ka:v] vti σκαλίζω, χαράσσω, κόβω.

carving ['ka:viŋ] n (in wood etc) γλυπτική, σκάλισμα ‖ ~ knife n μαχαίρι γιά κόψιμο.

car wash ['ka:wɔʃ] n πλύσιμο αὐτοκινήτου.

cascade [kæs'keid] n καταρράκτης.

case [keis] n (box) θήκη, κιβώτιο, κασόνι ‖ (instance) περίπτωσις ‖ (state) κατάστασις, ζήτημα ‖ (gram) πτῶσις ‖ (law) ὑπόθεσις ‖ **in ~** εἰς περίπτωσιν πού ‖ **in any ~** ἐν πάσει περιπτώσει.

cash [kæʃ] n μετρητά (χρήματα) ‖ vt ξαργυρώνω ‖ ~desk n ταμεῖον ‖ ~ier n ταμίας, κασιέρης ‖ ~ register n μηχανή ταμείου, ταμειακή μηχανή.

cashmere [kæʃ'miə*] n κασμήρι.

casing ['keisiŋ] n περίβλημα, πλαίσιον, θήκη.

casino [kə'si:nəu] n καζίνο.

cask [ka:sk] n βαρέλι.

casket ['ka:skit] n (box) κουτί, κασετίνα ‖ (US) φέρετρον.

casserole ['kæsərəul] n (pot) τσουκάλι, νταβᾶς ‖ (meal) γκιουβέτσι.

cassock ['kæsək] n ράσον.

cast [ka:st] (irreg v) vt (throw) ρίπτω, ρίφνω, πετῶ ‖ (shed) βγάζω, ἀπορρίπτω ‖ (theat) διανέμω ρόλους, ἀναθέτω ρόλον ‖ (metal) χύνω, καλουπώνω ‖ n (theat) θίασος ‖ **to ~ off** vti βγάζω ‖ (naut) ἀπωλέω.

castanets [kæstə'nets] npl καστανιέτες.

caste [ka:st] n κοινωνική τάξις, κάστα.

casting ['ka:stiŋ] a: ~ **vote** ἀποφασιστική ψῆφος.

castiron ['ka:st'aiən] n χυτοσίδηρος.

castle ['ka:sl] n (fortress) φρούριον ‖ (mansion) πύργος.

castor ['ka:stə*] n (wheel) καρούλι, ρόδα ‖ ~ oil n ρετσινόλαδο ‖ ~ sugar n ψιλή ζάχαρι.

castrate [kæs'treit] vt μουνουχίζω.

casual ['kæʒjul] a (occasional) τυχαία ‖ (work, attitude) τυχαῖος, ἀπερίσκεπτος ‖ (meeting) τυχαῖος ‖ ~ly ad παρεπιπτόντως.

casualty ['kæʒjulti] n τραυματίας.

cat [kæt] n γάτα.

catalogue, (US) catalog ['kætələɡ] n κατάλογος ‖ vt ἐγγράφω εἰς κατάλογον.

catalyst ['kætəlist] n καταλύτης.

catapult ['kætəpʌlt] n καταπέλτης.

cataract ['kætərækt] n (waterfall) καταρράκτης ‖ (med) καταρράκτης.

catarrh [kə'ta:*] n κατάρρους.

catastrophe [kə'tæstrəfi] n καταστροφή, συμφορά.

catastrophic [kætə'strɔfik] a καταστροφικός.

catch [kætʃ] (irreg v) n (for window etc) δόντι, μπετούγια, ἀσφάλεια ‖ (sport, breath) πιάσιμο ‖ (fish) πιάνω (πολλὰ ψάρια) ‖ (hunt) θήραμα ‖ vt(seize) πιάνω, ἁρπάζω ‖ (surprise) συλλαμβάνω ‖ (in time) (προ)φθάνω, πιάνω στὰ πράσα ‖ **to ~ a cold** ἁρπάζω κρύο.

catching ['kætʃiŋ] a (med) μεταδοτικό κολλητικός.

catch phrase ['kætʃfreiz] n σύνθημα.

catchy ['kætʃi] a (tune) ἑλκυστικό.

catechism ['kætikizəm] n (rel) κατήχησις.

categorical [kæti'ɡɔrikəl] a κατηγορηματικός ‖ ~ly ad κατηγορηματικῶς.

categorize ['kætiɡəraiz] vt κατατάσσω εἰς κατηγορίες.

category ['kætiɡəri] n κατηγορία, τάξις.

cater ['keitə*] vi (food) τροφοδοτῶ, σερβίρω ‖ ~ing n προμήθεια, τροφοδοσία ‖ **to ~ for** (fig) φροντίζω, ἱκανοποιῶ.

caterpillar ['kætəpilə*] n κάμπια ‖ ~ tread n ἑρπύστρια.

cathedral [kə'θi:drəl] n καθεδρικός ναός, μητρόπολις.

catholic ['kæθəlik] a καθολικός, παγκόσμιος, εὐρύς ‖ C~ n Καθολικός ‖ a καθολικός.

cattle ['kætl] npl κτήνη, ζῶα.

catty ['kæti] a δηκτικός, πονηρός.

cauliflower ['kɔliflauə*] n κουνουπίδι.

cause [kɔ:z] n (reason) αἰτία, ἀφορμή, λόγος ‖ (object) ὑπόθεσις, χάρις ‖ vt προξενῶ, κάνω νά.

causeway ['kɔ:zwei] n ὑψωμένος δρόμος.

caustic ['kɔ:stik] a (burning) καυστικός ‖ (sarcastic) σαρκαστικός.

cauterize ['kɔ:təraiz] vt καυτηριάζω.

caution ['kɔ:ʃən] n (care) προσοχή ‖ (warning) προειδοποίησις ‖ vt προειδοποιῶ.

cautious ['kɔ:ʃəs] a προσεκτικός ‖ ~ly ad προσεκτικά.

cavalcade [kævəl'keid] n ἔφιππος παρέλασις.

cavalier [kævə'liə*] a εὔθυμος, ξένοιαστος.

cavalry ['kævəlri] npl ἱππικόν.

cave [keiv] n σπηλιά ‖ ~man n τρωγλοδύτης ‖ to ~ in vi καταρρέω, σωριάζομαι.

cavern ['kævən] n σπηλιά ‖ ~ous a σπηλαιώδης.

caviar(e) ['kævia:*] n χαβιάρι.

cavity ['kæviti] n κοίλωμα, τρύπα.

cease [si:s] vti παύω, σταματῶ, τελειώνω ‖ ~fire n ἀνακωχή ‖ ~less a ἀκατάπαυστος, ἀδιάκοπος.

cedar ['si:də*] n κέδρος.

cede [si:d] vt παραχωρῶ, ἐκχωρῶ.

ceiling ['si:liŋ] n ταβάνι ‖ (fig) ἀνώτατον ὕψος.

celebrate ['selibreit] vt γιορτάζω ‖ (wedding etc) τελῶ ‖ ~d a διάσημος.

celebration [seli'breiʃən] n γιορτασμός, τέλεσις.

celebrity [si'lebriti] n (person) διασημότης.

celery ['seləri] n σέλινο.

celestial [si'lestiəl] a οὐράνιος.

celibacy ['selibəsi] n ἀγαμία.

cell [sel] n (in monastery) κελλί ‖ (in jail) φυλακή ‖ (elec) στοιχεῖον ‖ (biol) κύτταρον.

cellar ['selə*] n ὑπόγειον, κελλάρι ‖ (wine) κάβα.

'cellist ['tʃelist] n βιολοντσελλίστας.

'cello ['tʃeləu] n βιολοντσέλλο.

cellophane ['seləfein] n ® σελλοφάν.

cellular ['seljulə*] a κυτταρικός, κυψελοειδής.

cellulose ['seljuləus] n κελλουλόζη, κυτταρίνη.

Celtic ['keltik, 'seltik] a Κελτικός.

cement [sə'ment] n τσιμέντο ‖ vt (lit) συγκολλῶ μέ τσιμέντο ‖ (fig) στερεώνω, κατοχυρώνω.

cemetery ['semitri] n νεκροταφεῖον.

cenotaph ['senəta:f] n κενοτάφιον.

censer ['sensə*] n θυμιατήρι, λιβανιστήρι.

censor ['sensə*] n λογοκριτής, ἐλεγκτής ‖ ~ship n λογοκρισία.

censure ['senʃə*] vt ἐπικρίνω, ψέγω.

census ['sensəs] n ἀπογραφή.

cent [sent] n σέντ ‖ (col) πεντάρα.

centenary [sen'ti:nəri] n ἑκατονταετηρίς.

center ['sentə*] n (US) = centre.

centigrade ['sentigreid] a ἑκατονταβάθμιος.

centilitre, (US) ~liter ['sentili:tə*] n ἑκατοστόλιτρον.

centimetre, (US) ~meter ['sentimi:tə*] n ἑκατοστόμετρον.

centipede ['sentipi:d] n σαρανταποδαρούσα.

central ['sentrəl] a κεντρικός ‖ ~ heating n κεντρική θέρμανσις ‖ ~ize vt συγκεντρώνω.

centre ['sentə*] n κέντρον.

centrifugal [sen'trifjugəl] a φυγόκεντρος.

century ['sentjuri] n αἰώνας.

ceramic [si'ræmik] a κεραμικός.

cereal ['siəriəl] n (any grain) δημητριακά, σιτηρά.

ceremonial [seri'məuniəl] a ἐθιμοτυπικός.

ceremony ['seriməni] n ἐθιμοτυπία ‖ (religious) τελετή.

certain ['sə:tən] a (sure) βέβαιος, σίγουρος, ἀσφαλής ‖ (some, one) ὡρισμένος, κάποιος ‖ for ~ σίγουρα ‖ ~ly ad ἀσφαλῶς, σίγουρα ‖ ~ty n βεβαιότης, σιγουριά.

certificate [sə'tifikit] n πιστοποιητικόν, βεβαίωσις.

certify ['sə:tifai] vti πιστοποιῶ, βεβαιῶ, κυρώνω.

cessation [se'seiʃən] n κατάπαυσις, λῆξις.

chafe [tʃeif] vti τρίβω, ἐρεθίζομαι, φθείρομαι.

chaffinch ['tʃæfintʃ] n σπίνος.

chagrin ['ʃægrin] n λύπη, πικρία.

chain [tʃein] n ἁλυσίδα, καδένα ‖ (mountains) σειρά ‖ vt (also ~ up) δένω μέ ἁλυσίδες, δεσμεύω ‖ ~ reaction n ἁλυσωτή ἀντίδρασις ‖ ~ smoker n μεγάλος καπνιστής ‖ ~ store n ὑποκατάστημα.

chair [tʃeə*] n καρέκλα ‖ (univ etc) ἕδρα ‖ vt (preside) προεδρεύω ‖ ~man n πρόεδρος ‖ (director) διευθυντής.

chalet ['ʃælei] n σαλέ.

chalice ['tʃælis] n δισκοπότηρο.

chalk [tʃɔ:k] n (geol) ἀσβεστόλιθος ‖ (crayon) κιμωλία.

challenge ['tʃælindʒ] n πρόκλησις ‖ vt προκαλῶ ‖ (dispute) ἀμφισβητῶ ‖ ~r n διεκδικητής.

challenging ['tʃælindʒiŋ] a προκλητικό.

chamber ['tʃeimbə*] n (compartment) δωμάτιον ‖ (of gun etc) θαλάμη (ὅπλου) ‖ ~ of commerce n 'Εμπορικόν 'Επιμελητήριον ‖ ~maid n καμαριέρα ‖ ~ music n μουσική δωματίου ‖ ~pot n καθίκι.

chamois ['ʃæmwa:] n: ~ leather n σαμουά.

champagne [ʃæm'pein] n σαμπάνια.

champion ['tʃæmpiən] n (sport) πρωταθλητής ‖ (of cause) πρόμαχος ‖ ~ship n πρωτάθλημα.

chance [tʃa:ns] n (opportunity) εὐκαιρία ‖ (possibility) ἐλπίδα, πιθανότης ‖ a τυχαῖος ‖ vt: to ~ it διακινδυνεύω, παίζω στήν τύχη ‖ to take a ~ δοκιμάζω.

chancel ['tʃa:nsəl] n ἱερόν (ναοῦ).

chancellor ['tʃa:nsələ*] n (univ) πρύτανις ‖ C~ of the Exchequer n Ὑπουργός Οἰκονομικῶν.

chandelier [ʃændə'liə*] n πολύφωτο, πολυέλαιο.

change [tʃeindʒ] vt ἀλλάζω, τροποποιῶ ‖ (exchange) ἀνταλλάσσω ‖ (trains) ἀλλάζω

‖ *vi* ἀλλάζω, μεταβάλλομαι ‖ *n* (*alteration*) ἀλλαγή, μεταβολή ‖ (*coins*) ψιλά ‖ (*balance*) ρέστα ‖ ~**able** *a* (*weather*) ἄστατος ‖ ~**over** *n* (*to new system*) ἀλλαγή συστήματος.

changing ['tʃeindʒiŋ] *a* εὐμετάβλητος, ἀλλάζων ‖ ~-**room** *n* (*in shop*) βεστιάριον.

channel ['tʃænl] *n* (*of stream*) κοίτη ‖ (*of bay etc*) δίαυλος, μπούκα ‖ (*strait*) πορθμός, στενόν ‖ (*of communication*) ὁδός, δρόμος ‖ (*rad etc*) ζώνη συχνοτήτων ‖ (*TV*) κανάλι ‖ *vt* αὐλακώνω ‖ **the (English) C~** ἡ Μάγχη ‖ **C~ Islands** *npl* νησιά τῆς Μάγχης.

chant [tʃɑ:nt] *n* τραγοῦδι ‖ (*church*) ψαλμός ‖ *vt* τραγουδῶ ‖ (*church*) ψάλλω.

chaos ['keiɔs] *n* χάος.

chaotic [kei'ɔtik] *a* χαώδης.

chap [tʃæp] *n* ρωγμή, σκάσιμο ‖ (*skin*) σκάζω ἀπό τό κρύο.

chapel ['tʃæpəl] *n* παρεκκλήσι.

chaperon ['ʃæpərəun] *n* συνοδός κοριτσιοῦ ‖ *vt* συνοδεύω.

chaplain ['tʃæplin] *n* ἐφημέριος.

chapter ['tʃæptə*] *n* (*of book*) κεφάλαιον.

char [tʃɑ:*] *vt* (*burn*) μαυρίζω μέ κάψιμο ‖ *n* (*cleaner*) παραδουλεύτρα.

character ['kæriktə*] *n* (*qualities*) χαρακτήρ ‖ (*liter, theat etc*) πρόσωπον, χαρακτήρ ‖ (*peculiar person*) τύπος, χαρακτήρας ‖ (*letter, sign*) χαρακτήρ, στοιχεῖον, γράμμα ‖ ~**istic** *a* χαρακτηριστικός ‖ *n* χαρακτηριστικόν γνώρισμα ‖ ~**ize** *vt* χαρακτηρίζω.

charade [ʃə'rɑ:d] *n* συλλαβόγριφος.

charcoal ['tʃɑ:kəul] *n* ξυλοκάρβουνο.

charge [tʃɑ:dʒ] *n* (*price*) τίμημα, τιμή ‖ (*accusation*) κατηγορία ‖ (*load for gun*) γόμωσις ‖ (*attack*) ἔφοδος, προσβολή ‖ *vt* (*fill, load*) γεμίζω, φορτίζω ‖ (*a price*) ζητῶ (τιμήν), χρεώνω ‖ (*a battery*) ἐπιφορτίζω ‖ (*attack*) ἐφορμῶ ‖ (*accuse*) κατηγορῶ ‖ *vi* ἐπιπίπτω, προσβάλλω ‖ **in** ~ **of** φροντίζω, πού φροντίζει ‖ **to take** ~ ἀναλαμβάνω, εἶμαι ὑπεύθυνος.

chariot ['tʃæriət] *n* ἅρμα.

charitable ['tʃæritəbl] *a* φιλάνθρωπος, ἐλεήμων.

charity ['tʃæriti] *n* (*institution*) φιλανθρωπικόν ἵδρυμα ‖ ἀγαθοεργία.

charlady ['tʃɑ:leidi] *n* παραδουλεύτρα.

charlatan ['ʃɑ:lətən] *n* ἀγύρτης, τσαρλατάνος.

charm [tʃɑ:m] *n* (*attractiveness*) γοητεία ‖ (*for luck*) φυλαχτό ‖ *vt* μαγεύω, γοητεύω ‖ ~**ing** *a* γοητευτικός.

chart [tʃɑ:t] *n* (*of information*) γραφική παράστασις, διάγραμμα ‖ (*naut*) χάρτης.

charter ['tʃɑ:tə*] *vt* ναυλώνω ‖ *n* καταστατικός χάρτης ‖ ~ **flight** *n* ναυλωμένη πτῆσις ‖ ~**ed accountant** *n* λογιστής.

charwoman ['tʃɑ:wumən] *n* = **charlady**.

chase [tʃeis] *vt* (*run after*) κυνηγῶ, (κατα)-

διώκω ‖ *n* (*act of chasing*) κυνήγι, καταδίωξις.

chasm ['kæzəm] *n* χάσμα, κενόν.

chassis ['ʃæsi] *n* σασσί.

chaste [tʃeist] *a* ἁγνός.

chastity ['tʃæstiti] *n* ἁγνότης, παρθενία.

chat [tʃæt] *vi* κουβεντιάζω ‖ *n* (*friendly, casual talk*) φιλική κουβεντούλα.

chatter ['tʃætə*] *vi* φλυαρῶ ‖ (*of teeth*) τρέμω, κτυπῶ ‖ *n* φλυαρία, τερετισμός ‖ ~**box** *n* (*esp child*) φλύαρος.

chatty ['tʃæti] *a* (*style*) ὁμηλιτικός, πολυλογᾶς.

chauffeur ['ʃəufə*] *n* ὁδηγός, σωφέρ.

cheap [tʃi:p] *a* (*joke*) ἄνοστο (ἀστεῖο) ‖ (*poor quality*) φτηνός, πρόστυχος, μικρᾶς ἀξίας ‖ ~**en** *vi* (*person*) ὑποτιμῶ, ξευτελίζω ‖ ~**ly** *ad* φτηνά.

cheat [tʃi:t] *vti* (ἐξ)ἀπατῶ, κοροϊδεύω ‖ *n* ἀγύρτης, κατεργάρης ‖ ~**ing** *n* (*at cards*) κλέψιμο ‖ (*general*) παγανοντιά.

check [tʃek] *vt* (*examine*) ἐλέγχω ‖ (*halt*) σταματῶ, ἀναχαιτίζω ‖ *n* (*examination*) ἔλεγχος, ἐπαλήθευσις ‖ (*restraint*) περιορισμός ‖ (*restaurant bill*) λογαριασμός ‖ (*pattern*) καρρώ ‖ (*US*) = **cheque** ‖ ~**ers** *npl* (*US*) ντάμα ‖ ~**list** *n* κατάλογος ἐλέγχου ‖ ~**mate** *n* μάτ ‖ ~**point** *n* σημεῖον ἐλέγχου ‖ ~**up** *n* (*med*) γενική ἐξέτασις.

cheek [tʃi:k] *n* παρειά, μάγουλο ‖ (*impudence*) ἀναίδεια ‖ ~**bone** *n* μῆλον (παρειᾶς) ‖ ~**y** *a* ἀναιδής.

cheer [tʃiə*] *n* (*joy*) εὐθυμία ‖ (*shout*) ζητωκραυγή ‖ *vt* (*shout*) ἐπευφημίζω, ζητωκραυγάζω ‖ (*comfort*) χαροποιῶ ‖ (*encourage*) ἐνθαρρύνω ‖ *vi*: **to** ~ **up** κάνω κέφι ‖ **good** ~ *n* φαγητά ‖ ~**ful** *a* χαρωπός, καλόκεφος ‖ ~**fulness** *n* εὐθυμία ‖ (*of fireplace etc*) ζεστασιά ‖ ~**ing** *n* ζητοκραυγαί, χειροκροτήματα ‖ *a* ἐνθαρρυντικός, προκαλῶν τό κέφι ‖ ~**io** *interj* (*in departure*) γειά χαρά! ‖ (*greeting*) γειά σου ‖ ~**less** *a* μελαγχολικός, κακόκεφος.

cheese [tʃi:z] *n* τυρί.

chef [ʃef] *n* ἀρχιμάγειρας.

chemical ['kemikəl] *a* χημικός.

chemist ['kemist] *n* (*med*) φαρμακοποιός ‖ (*scientist*) χημικός ‖ ~**ry** *n* χημεία ‖ ~**'s (shop)** *n* φαρμακεῖον.

cheque [tʃek] *n* ἐπιταγή ‖ ~ **book** *n* βιβλιάριον ἐπιταγῶν.

chequered ['tʃekəd] *a* (*fig*) περιπετειώδης.

cherish ['tʃeriʃ] *vt* (*a hope*) τρέφω ‖ (*love*) λατρεύω ‖ (*look after*) περιποιοῦμαι.

cheroot [ʃə'ru:t] *n* εἶδος φτηνοῦ πούρου.

cherry ['tʃeri] *n* (*tree*) κερασιά ‖ (*fruit*) κεράσι.

chess [tʃes] *n* σκάκι ‖ ~**board** *n* σκακιέρα ‖ ~**man** *n* πιόνι, πεσσός ‖ ~**player** *n* σκακιστής.

chest [tʃest] *n* (*anat*) στῆθος ‖ (*box*)

κιβώτιον, μπαούλο ‖ **to get sth off one's ~**
ξελαφρώνω ‖ **~ of drawers** n σιφονιέρα,
κομό.

chestnut ['tʃesnʌt] n κάστανο ‖ **~ (tree)** n
καστανιά.

chew [tʃuː] vti μασῶ ‖ **~ing gum** n τσίχλα.

chic [ʃiːk] a κομψός, σίκ.

chicanery [ʃi'keinəri] n στρεψοδικία,
κατεργαριά.

chick [tʃik] n πουλάκι ‖ **~en** n (bird, food)
κοτόπουλο ‖ **~enpox** n ανεμοβλογιά.

chicory ['tʃikəri] n κιχώρι, αντίδι, ραδίκι.

chief [tʃiːf] n αρχηγός, διευθυντής ‖ a
κύριος, πρωτεύων, πρῶτος ‖ **~ly** ad
κυρίως, προπάντων.

chiffon ['ʃifɔn] n σιφφόν.

chilblain ['tʃilblein] n χιονίστρα.

child [tʃaild] n παιδί ‖ **~birth** n τοκετός,
γέννα ‖ **~hood** n παιδικά χρόνια ‖ **~ish**
a παιδαριώδης, παιδιάστικος ‖ **~like** a
άφελής, παιδιάστικος ‖ **~ren** ['tʃildrən]
npl of **child** παιδιά, παιδάκια.

chill [tʃil] n (coldness) ψυχρότης, κρυάδα ‖
(cold) κρυολόγημα ‖ a ψυχρός, κρύος ‖
~y a ψυχρός, κρύος.

chime [tʃaim] n κωδωνοκρουσία ‖ vi ηχῶ
αρμονικῶς.

chimney ['tʃimni] n καπνοδόχος, καμινάδα.

chimpanzee [tʃimpæn'ziː] n χιμπαντζής.

chin [tʃin] n πηγούνι.

china ['tʃainə] n πορσελάνη ‖ (dishes, cups)
πιάτα.

China ['tʃainə] n Κίνα.

Chinese ['tʃai'niːz] a Κινέζικος ‖ n (person)
Κινέζος ‖ (language) κινεζική.

chink [tʃiŋk] n (opening) ρωγμή, σκάσιμο ‖
(noise) ήχος (μετάλλου κτλ).

chintz [tʃints] n τσίτι.

chip [tʃip] n απόκομμα, θρύμμα ‖ vt τραύω,
θρυμματίζω, αποκόπτω ‖ **to ~ in** vi
(cards) ποντάρω ‖ (interrupt) παρεμβαίνω
‖ συνεισφέρω.

chiropodist [ki'rɔpədist] n πεντικιουρίστας.

chirp [tʃəːp] n τερετισμός, τιτίβισμα,
κελάδημα ‖ vi τερετίζω, τιτιβίζω,
κελαϊδῶ.

chisel ['tʃizl] n σμίλη.

chit [tʃit] n σημείωμα, γραπτή άδεια ‖
~chat n κουβέντα.

chivalrous ['ʃivəlrəs] a ιπποτικός, ευγε-
νικός.

chivalry ['ʃivəlri] n (knighthood) ιπποτισμός
‖ (courtesy) ευγένεια.

chloride ['klɔːraid] n χλωρίδιον.

chlorine ['klɔːriːn] n χλώριον.

chloroform ['klɔrəfɔːm] n χλωροφόρμιον.

chock [tʃɔk] n μόρσος, τάκος ‖ **~-a-block**
a παραγεμισμένος.

chocolate ['tʃɔklit] n σοκολάτα.

choice [tʃɔis] n εκλογή, προτίμησις ‖
(variety) ποικιλία ‖ a εκλεκτός.

choir ['kwaiə*] n χορός ‖ **~boy** n παιδί
χορωδίας.

choke [tʃəuk] vi (be unable to breathe)
πνίγομαι ‖ vt (stop breathing of) ασφυ-
κτιῶ, στραγγαλίζω ‖ (block) εμφράσσω ‖
n (aut) διαχύτης, εμφράκτης.

cholera ['kɔlərə] n χολέρα.

choose [tʃuːz] (irreg v) vt διαλέγω, προτιμῶ
‖ (decide) αρέσω, προτιμῶ.

chop [tʃɔp] vt (cut with a blow) κόπτω,
αποκόπτω ‖ (into pieces) κατακόπτω,
διαμελίζω, λιανίζω ‖ vi: **to ~ and change**
πωλῶ καί αγοράζω ‖ n (blow) κτύπημα ‖
(meat) μπριζολάκι ‖ **~py** a ταραγμένος,
κυματώδης ‖ **~sticks** npl ξυλαράκια
(γιά τό πιλάφι), κινέζικο πηρούνι.

choral ['kɔːrəl] a χορικός.

chord [kɔːd] n χορδή.

chore [tʃɔə*] n βαρετή δουλειά.

choreographer [kɔri'ɔgrəfə*] n χορογράφος.

chorister ['kɔristə*] n ψάλτης.

chortle ['tʃɔːtl] vi καγχάζω, κακαρίζω.

chorus ['kɔːrəs] n (choir etc) χορός, χορωδία ‖ (many voices) τραγούδι ἐν χορῷ ‖
~ of praise n (fig) συναυλία επαίνων.

chose [tʃəuz] pt of **choose** ‖ **~n** pp of **choose**.

chow [tʃau] n (dog) τσάου (είδος πεκινουά).

Christ [kraist] n Χριστός ‖ **c~en** ['krisn] vt
βαπτίζω ‖ **c~ening** n βάπτισμα ‖ **~ian**
['kristiən] n Χριστιανός ‖ a χριστιανικός
‖ **~ian name** n μικρόν όνομα ‖ **~ianity** n
χριστιανισμός ‖ **~mas** ['krisməs] n
Χριστούγεννα ‖ **~mas card** n χριστου-
γεννιάτικη κάρτα ‖ **~mas tree** n
χριστουγεννιάτικο δένδρο.

chrome [krəum] n = **chromium plating** ‖
see **chromium**.

chromium ['krəumiəm] n χρώμιον ‖
~-plating n επιχρωμίωσις.

chronic ['krɔnik] a (med) χρόνιος.

chronicle ['krɔnikl] n χρονικόν, χρονογράφημα.

chronological [krɔnə'lɔdʒikəl] a χρονολο-
γικός.

chrysalis ['krisəlis] n χρυσαλλίς, νύμφη.

chrysanthemum [kri'sænθəməm] n χρυσάνθεμον.

chubby ['tʃʌbi] a παχουλός, στρουμπουλός.

chuck [tʃʌk] vt πετῶ, ρίπτω ‖ n σφιγκτήρ,
τσόκ.

chuckle ['tʃʌkl] vi γελῶ χαμηλοφώνως.

chum [tʃʌm] n στενός φίλος.

chunk [tʃʌŋk] n χονδρό κομμάτι.

church [tʃəːtʃ] n (building) εκκλησία, ναός
‖ **~ service** n λειτουργία ‖ **~yard** n
αυλόγυρος εκκλησίας, νεκροταφείον.

churlish ['tʃəːliʃ] a άξεστος, δύστροπος.

churn [tʃəːn] n (for butter) βουτίνα,
καρδάρα, ντουρβάνι.

chute [ʃuːt] n τσουλήθρα.

chutney ['tʃʌtni] n τσάτνυ (αρωματικόν).

cicada [si'kɑːdə] n τζίτζικας.

cider ['saidə*] n μηλίτης (οίνος).

cigar [si'gɑː*] n πόυρο ‖ **~ette** n τσιγάρο,
σιγαρέττο ‖ **~ette case** n τσιγαροθήκη,

ταμπακιέρα ‖ ~ette end n γόπα, ἀποτσίγαρο ‖ ~ette holder n πίπα.
cinch [sintʃ] n (sl) σιγουριά.
cinder ['sində*] n ἀνθρακιά, θράκα, στάκτη.
Cinderella [sində'relə] n Σταχτοπούτα.
cine ['sini] n ~-camera n κινηματογραφική
μηχανή ‖ ~-film n κινηματογραφική
ταινία.
cinema ['sinəmə] n (theat) σινεμά ‖ (motion
pictures) κινηματογράφος.
cine-projector [siniprə'dʒektə*] n κινημα-
τογραφικὸς προβολεύς.
cinnamon ['sinəmən] n κανέλλα.
cipher ['saifə*] n (zero) μηδενικόν ‖ (code)
κρυπτογράφησις ‖ (person) μηδενικός.
circle ['sə:kl] n (ring, figure) κύκλος, γύρος
‖ (of friends) κύκλος, συντροφιά ‖ vi
περιστρέφομαι, στριφογυρίζω ‖ vt
(surround) περικυκλώνω ‖ vi (move in a
circle) κάνω τόν κύκλον, κάνω κύκλους.
circuit ['sə:kit] n (moving around) κυκλικός
δρόμος, περιστροφή ‖ (tour by judges)
περιοδεία (δικαστοῦ) ‖ (elec) κύκλωμα ‖
~ous a κυκλικός, ἔμμεσος.
circular ['sə:kjulə*] a κυκλικός ‖ (in a circle)
κυκλοτερής ‖ n ἐγκύκλιος, διαφημιστικόν γράμμα.
circulate ['sə:kjuleit] vi κυκλοφορῶ ‖ vt
θέτω εἰς κυκλοφορίαν.
circulation [sə:kju'leiʃən] n κυκλοφορία.
circumcise ['sə:kəmsaiz] vt περιτέμνω.
circumference [sə'kʌmfərəns] n περιφέρεια.
circumflex ['sə:kəmfleks] n περισπωμένη.
circumspect ['sə:kəmspekt] a προσεκτικός,
μετρημένος.
circumstances ['sə:kəmstənsiz] npl (facts
connected with sth) περιστάσεις, συνθῆκες, συμβάντα ‖ (financial condition)
οἰκονομική κατάστασις.
circus ['sə:kəs] n τσίρκο.
cistern ['sistən] n δεξαμενή, ντεπόσιτο.
cite [sait] vt (mention, quote) ἀναφέρω,
παραπέμπω.
citizen ['sitizn] n (city dweller) ἀστός ‖
πολίτης ‖ ~ship n πολιτικά δικαιώματα.
citrus ['sitrəs] ~ fruit n ἑσπεριδοειδῆ.
city ['siti] n πόλις ‖ the C~ τό Ἐμπορικόν
κέντρον Λονδίνου.
civic ['sivik] a ἀστικός, πολιτικός.
civil ['sivl] a πολιτικός ‖ (polite) εὐγενικός
‖ ~ engineer n πολιτικός μηχανικός ‖
~ engineering n πολιτική μηχανική ‖
~ian n πολίτης, ἰδιώτης ‖ a πολιτικός
‖ ~ization n πολιτισμός ‖ ~ized a πολιτισμένος ‖ ~ law n ἀστικόν δίκαιον ‖
~ servant n δημόσιος ὑπάλληλος ‖ C~
Service n Δημόσιαι Ὑπηρεσίαι ‖ ~ war
n ἐμφύλιος πόλεμος.
claim [kleim] vt ἀπαιτῶ, ζητῶ, διεκδικῶ ‖
n αἴτησις, ἀπαίτησις, ἀξίωσις ‖ ~ant
ἀπαιτητής ‖ (law) ἐνάγων, δικαιοῦχος.
clam [klæm] n ἀχιβάδα.
clamber ['klæmbə*] vi σκαρφαλώνω.

clammy ['klæmi] a ἱδρωμένος, κολλώδης.
clamp [klæmp] n σφιγκτήρ, σύνδεσμος ‖ vt
(συσ)σφίγγω.
clan [klæn] n φυλή, πατριά.
clang [klæŋ] n κλαγγή, κρότος ‖ vti ἀντηχῶ,
κροτῶ.
clap [klæp] vti κτυπῶ, χειροκροτῶ ‖ ~ping
n χειροκρότημα.
claret ['klærət] n μαῦρο κρασί, μπορντώ.
clarification [klærifi'keiʃən] n (fig) διευκρί-
νισις.
clarify ['klærifai] vt διευκρινίζω.
clarinet [klæri'net] n κλαρίνο.
clarity ['klæriti] n διαύγεια.
clash [klæʃ] n σύγκρουσις, ἀντίθεσις ‖
(sound) ἰσχυρόν καί ἠχηρόν κτύπημα ‖
vi συγκρούομαι.
clasp [kla:sp] n πόρπη, κόπιτσα ‖ vt ἐναγκα-
λιάζω, σφίγγω.
class [kla:s] n (rank) τάξις ‖ (sort) τάξις,
εἶδος, κατηγορία ‖ (sch) τάξις ‖ vt ταξινομῶ, βαθμολογῶ.
classic ['klæsik] n κλασσικός ‖ a (traditional) κλασσικός, ἀκαδημαϊκός ‖ ~al a
κλασσικός ‖ (mus) κλασσική (μουσική).
classification [klæsifi'keiʃən] n ταξινόμησις, κατάταξις.
classify ['klæsifai] vt ταξινομῶ, κατατάσσω.
classroom ['kla:srum] n αἴθουσα παραδό-
σεων, τάξις.
classy ['kla:si] a (posh) καλῆς τάξεως.
clatter ['klætə*] n θόρυβος, γδοῦπος ‖ vi
κροτῶ, θορυβῶ.
clause [klɔ:z] n (of contract etc) ὅρος,
ἄρθρον, διάταξις ‖ (gram) πρότασις.
claustrophobia [klɔ:strə'fəubiə] n κλειστο-
φοβία.
claw [klɔ:] n νύχι ‖ (of quadrupeds) χηλή,
ὀπλή ‖ vt νυχιάζω, γρατσουνίζω.
clay [klei] n ἄργιλος, πηλός.
clean [kli:n] a (free from dirt) καθαρός,
παστρικός ‖ (guiltless) καθαρός, τίμιος ‖
(lines) καθαρές (γραμμές), σαφές περίγραμμα ‖ vt καθαρίζω, παστρεύω ‖ ~er
n (person) καθαριστής ‖ ~ing n καθαρ-
σις, καθάρισμα ‖ ~liness n καθαριότης,
πάστρα ‖ ~ly ad καθαρά, παστρικά ‖
~se [klenz] vt ἀποκαθαίρω, καθαρίζω,
πλένω ‖ ~-shaven a φρεσκοξυρισμένος
‖ ~up n καθαρισμός ‖ to ~ out vt καθαρίζω ‖ (col) ξεπεντιαρίζω ‖ to ~ up vt
κάνω καθαρισμόν, σιάζω ‖ (col) κερδίζω.
clear [kliə*] a (water etc) καθαρό, διαυγές ‖
(sound) καθαρό (ἦχο) ‖ (meaning) σαφής,
καθαρή ‖ (certain) σαφής ‖ (road) ἀνοικτός ‖ vt καθαρίζω, ξεκαθαρίζω ‖ vi
(become clear) διευκρινίζεται ‖ ~ance n
(sale) ἐκποίησις, ξεπούλημα ‖ (free
space) ἀπελευθέρωσις, ἐκκένωσις ‖ (permission) ἄδεια ‖ ~-cut a σαφής, συγκεκριμένος ‖ ~ing n καθάρισμα ‖ ~ly ad
σαφῶς, προφανῶς, ἀσφαλῶς ‖ ~way n
(Brit) ἐθνική ὁδός ἄνευ σταθμεύσεως ‖

to ~ up *vi* διαλύω, ξεκαθαρίζω ‖ *vt* τακτοποιῶ, στάζω ‖ ξεκαθαρίζω.

clef [klef] *n* κλειδί.

clematis ['klemətis] *n* κληματίς, ἀμπελίνα.

clench [klentʃ] *vt* (*teeth etc*) σφίγγω.

clergy ['klə:dʒi] *n* κλῆρος, ἱερατεῖον ‖ **~man** *n* κληρικός, ἱερωμένος, παπᾶς.

clerical ['klerikəl] *a* κληρικός, ἱερατικός ‖ τοῦ γραφείου ‖ **~ error** *n* λάθος ἀντιγραφῆς.

clerk [klɑ:k, (*US*) klə:rk] *n* (*US*) (*salesman*, *woman*) ὑπάλληλος ‖ (*in office*) γραφεύς.

clever ['klevə*] *a* (*with hands*) ἐπιδέξιος, καπάτσος ‖ (*in mind*) εὐφυής, σπιρτόζος ‖ **~ly** *ad* εὐφυῶς, ἔξυπνα.

cliché ['kli:ʃei] *n* στερεότυπον, κλισέ.

click [klik] *vi* κτυπῶ, κάνω τίκ-τάκ ‖ *n* κλίκ, ξηρός κρότος.

client ['klaiənt] *n* πελάτης ‖ **~ele** [kli:ɑ̃:n'tel] *n* πελατεία.

cliff [klif] *n* γκρεμός.

climate ['klaimit] *n* κλῖμα.

climax ['klaimæks] *n* ἀποκορύφωμα.

climb [klaim] *vti* ἀνέρχομαι, ἀνεβαίνω, σκαρφαλώνω ‖ *n* ἀνέβασμα, ἀνηφοριά ‖ **~er** *n* (*of mountains*) ὀρειβάτης ‖ **~ing**: **to go ~ing** κάνω ὀρειβασία.

clinch [klintʃ] *vt* (*fig: decide*) συνάπτω, κλείνω.

cling [kliŋ] *vi* προσκολλῶμαι, πιάνομαι.

clinic ['klinik] *n* κλινική ‖ **~al** *a* κλινικός.

clink [kliŋk] *n* κτύπημα (ποτηριῶν) ‖ *vti* κτυπῶ, ἠχῶ.

clip [klip] *n* συνδετήρ, τσιμπιδάκι ‖ *vt* (*papers*) συνδέω ‖ (*hair*) κουρέβω, ψαλιδίζω ‖ (*hedge*) κόβω ‖ **~pers** *npl* (*instrument*) κουρευτική μηχανή.

clique [kli:k] *n* κλίκα, φάρα.

cloak [kləuk] *n* πανωφόρι ‖ (*fig*) κάλυμμα, πέπλον ‖ **~room** *n* (*for coats etc*) γκαρνταρόπα ‖ (*W.C.*) ἀποχωρητήριο, μέρος, καμπινέτο.

clock [klɔk] *n* ὡρολόγι, ρολόϊ ‖ **~wise** *ad* δεξιόστροφος ‖ **~work** *n* μηχανισμός ὡρολογιοῦ.

clog [klɔg] *n* (*shoe*) τσόκαρο ‖ *vti* ἐμποδίζω, κωλύω, φράσσω.

close [kləus] *a* (*near*) πλησίον, ἐγγύς, διπλανός ‖ (*atmosphere etc*) ἀσφυκτικός, πνιγηρός, στενός ‖ (*mean*) σφιχτός ‖ (*weather*) κλειστός, βαρύς ‖ *ad* (*near*) κοντά, ἀπό κοντά, σφιχτά ‖ **~ly** *ad* προσεκτικά, στενά, κατά πόδας ‖ **~ shave** *n* (*fig*) γλυτωμός παρά τρίχα ‖ **~-up** *n* λεπτομέρεια.

close [kləuz] *vt* (*shut*) κλείνω ‖ (*end*) τελειώνω, τερματίζω ‖ *vi* κλείνομαι ‖ (*end*) τερματίζομαι ‖ *n* (*end*) τέλος ‖ **to ~ down** *vti* κλείνω, διακόπτω ‖ **~d** *a* (*road*) 'ἀπαγορεύεται ἡ διάβασις' ‖ **~d shop** *n* κλειστόν κατάστημα.

closet ['klɔzit] *n* μικρό δωμάτιο ‖ (*storeroom*) ἀποθήκη.

closure ['kləuzə*] *n* κλείσιμο, τερματισμός.

clot [klɔt] *n* (*esp blood*) θρόμβος, σβῶλος ‖ *vi* θρομβοῦμαι, πήζω.

cloth [klɔθ] *n* (*material*) ὕφασμα, πανί ‖ (*for cleaning*) πατσαβούρα.

clothe [kləud] *vt* ντύνω, καλύπτω ‖ **~s** *npl* ροῦχα ‖ **~sbrush** *n* βούρτσα ‖ **~s line** *n* σχοινί ἁπλώματος ρούχων ‖ **~s peg** *n* μανταλάκι.

clothing ['kləudiŋ] *n* = **clothes** ‖ *see* **clothe**.

cloud [klaud] *n* σύννεφο ‖ (*of dust etc*) νέφος, σύννεφο ‖ **~burst** *n* μπόρα ‖ **~y** *a* συνεφιασμένος ‖ (*wine etc*) θολωμένο.

clout [klaut] *n* κτύπημα ‖ *vt* κτυπῶ, καρπαζώνω.

clove [kləuv] *n* γαρύφαλο.

clover ['kləuvə*] *n* τριφύλλι ‖ **~leaf** *n* τριφύλλι.

clown [klaun] *n* παλιάτσος, κλάουν ‖ *vi* κάνω τόν παλιάτσο.

club [klʌb] *n* (*stick*) ρόπαλο, ματσούκα ‖ (*society*) λέσχη ‖ (*golf*) κλόμπ ‖ (*cards*) σπαθί ‖ *vt* κτυπῶ μέ ρόπαλο, μέ κλόμπ ‖ *vi*: **to ~ together** συνεισφέρω, βάζω ρεφενέ ‖ **~house** *n* λέσχη.

cluck [klʌk] *vi* κακαρίζω.

clue [klu:] *n* νύξις, ἔνδειξις ‖ **he hasn't a ~** δέν ἔχει ἰδέα.

clump [klʌmp] *n* συστάς (δένδρων), μεγάλο κομμάτι.

clumsy ['klʌmzi] *a* (*person*) ἀδέξιος, ἀτζαμῆς ‖ (*object*) βαρύς, ἄκομψος.

clung [klʌŋ] *pt,pp* of **cling**.

cluster ['klʌstə*] *n* συστάς, ὁμάς ‖ (*of grapes*) τσαμπί ‖ (*of stars*) σύμπλεγμα ‖ *vi* φύομαι βοτρηδόν, μαζεύομαστε.

clutch [klʌtʃ] *n* (*grip, grasp*) ἅρπαγμα, σφιχτό πιάσιμο ‖ (*aut*) ἀμπραγιάζ, συμπλέκτης ‖ *vt* ἁρπάζω, πιάνω σφιχτά.

clutter ['klʌtə*] *vt* παραγεμίζω, κάνω ἄνωκάτω.

coach [kəutʃ] *n* (*bus*) λεωφορεῖον, πούλμαν ‖ (*teacher*) φροντιστής ‖ (*rail*) ἅμαξα, βαγόνι ‖ (*trainer*) προγυμναστής ‖ *vt* προγυμνάζω.

coagulate [kəu'ægjuleit] *vti* πηγνύω, πήζω.

coal [kəul] *n* ἄνθραξ, κάρβουνο, γαιάνθραξ.

coalfield ['kəulfi:ld] *n* ἀνθρακοφόρος περιοχή.

coalition [kəuə'liʃən] *n* συνασπισμός.

coalmine ['kəulmain] *n* ἀνθρακωρυχεῖον.

coarse [kɔ:s] *a* (*lit*) τραχύς, ἀκατέργαστος ‖ (*fig*) ἄξεστος, χυδαῖος.

coast [kəust] *n* παραλία, ἀκτή ‖ **~al** *a* παράκτιος, παραλιακός ‖ **~er** *n* ἀκτοπλοϊκόν ‖ **~guard** *n* ἀκτοφυλακή ‖ **~line** *n* ἀκτή, παραλία.

coat [kəut] *n* (*garment*) σακάκι ‖ (*of animal*) προβειά ‖ (*layer etc*) στρῶμα, χέρι ‖ *vt* (*with paint etc*) ἐπιχρίω ‖ **~ of arms** *n* οἰκόσημον ‖ **~ hanger** *n* κρεμαστάρι ‖ **~ing** *n* ἐπίστρωμα, χέρι.

coax [kəuks] *vt* καλοπιάνω, καταφέρνω.

cobbler ['kɔblə*] n μπαλωματῆς.
cobble(stone)s ['kɔbl(stəun)z] npl βότσαλα, καλντερίμι.
cobra ['kəubrə] n κόμπρα.
cobweb ['kɔbweb] n ἱστός ἀράχνης, ἀράχνη.
cocaine [kə'kein] n (med) κοκαΐνη.
cock [kɔk] n (poultry) κόκκορας, πετεινός || (bird etc) ἀρσενικό πουλί || (tap, faucet etc) κρουνός, κάνουλα || vt σηκώνω, βάζω στραβά (τό καπέλλο) || (a gun) σηκώνω τόν λύκο || ~erel n κοκκοράκι || ~eyed a (fig) στραβός, λοξός.
cockle ['kɔkl] n κοχύλι.
cockney ['kɔkni] n Λονδρέζος κατωτέρας τάξεως, κόκνυ.
cockpit ['kɔkpit] n (aviat) θέσις χειριστοῦ.
cockroach ['kɔkrəutʃ] n κατσαρίδα.
cocktail ['kɔkteil] n (drink) κοκτέϊλ || ~ cabinet n μπάρ || ~ party n πάρτυ κοκτέϊλ || ~ shaker n κτυπητήρι τοῦ κοκτέϊλ, σαίκερ.
cocoa ['kəukəu] n κακάο.
coconut ['kəukənʌt] n καρύδα.
cocoon [kə'ku:n] n κουκούλι.
cod [kɔd] n μουρούνα.
code [kəud] n (of laws) κώδιξ || (signals) σύστημα κρυπτογραφίας.
codify ['kəudifai] vt κωδικοποιῶ.
coeducational ['kəuedju'keiʃənl] a (school) μικτόν σχολεῖον.
coerce [kəu'ɔ:s] vt πιέζω, ἀναγκάζω.
coercion [kəu'ɔ:ʃən] n καταπίεσις.
coexistence ['kəuig'zistəns] n συνύπαρξις.
coffee ['kɔfi] n καφές || ~ bar n καφέ-μπάρ.
coffin ['kɔfin] n φέρετρον, κάσα.
cog [kɔg] n (of wheel etc) δόντι.
cogent ['kəudʒənt] a πειστικός.
cognac ['kɔnjæk] n κονιάκ.
coherent [kəu'hiərənt] a (consistent) συναφής, συνεπής.
coil [kɔil] n κουλούρα, σπείρωμα || (elec) μπομπίνα || vt συσπειρώνω, τυλίγω, κουλουριάζω.
coin [kɔin] n νόμισμα, κέρμα || ~age n (system) νομισματικόν σύστημα || νόμισμα.
coincide [kəuin'said] vi συμπίπτω, συμφωνῶ || ~nce [kəu'insidəns] n σύμπτωσις || ~ntal [kəuinsi'dentl] a συμπτωματικός.
coke [kəuk] n κώκ.
colander ['kʌləndə*] n τρυπητό, σουρωτήρι.
cold [kəuld] a ψυχρός, κρύος || n ψύχος, κρύο || (illness) κρυολόγημα || to have ~ feet (γ)κιοτέβω || to give s.o. the ~ shoulder φέρομαι ψυχρά || ~ly a ψυχρά, κρύα.
coleslaw ['kəulslɔ:] n λαχανοσαλάτα.
colic ['kɔlik] n κωλικόπονος.
collaborate [kə'læbəreit] vi (+ with) συνεργάζομαι μέ.
collaboration [kəlæbə'reiʃən] n συνεργασία.

collaborator [kə'læbəreitə*] n συνεργάτης.
collapse [kə'læps] vi καταρρέω || n κατάρρευσις.
collapsible [kə'læpsəbl] a πτυσσόμενος, διπλωτός.
collar ['kɔlə*] n (of coat, shirt) κολλάρο, γιακάς || ~bone n κλειδί τοῦ ὤμου.
collate [kɔ'leit] vt (ἀντι)παραβάλλω.
colleague ['kɔli:g] n συνάδελφος, συνεργάτης.
collect [kə'lekt] vt συλλέγω, μαζεύω || vi συναθροίζομαι || ~ed a συγκεντρωμένος || (fig) ἀτάραχος || ~ion n συλλογή || (money) εἰσπράξις || ~ive a συλλογικός || (pol) κολλεκτίβο || ~or n (of art etc) συλλέκτης || (of money) εἰσπράκτωρ.
college ['kɔlidʒ] n (non-specialized) κολλέγιον || (esp Oxford and Cambridge) πανεπιστήμιον.
collide [kə'laid] vi συγκρούομαι, τρακάρω.
collie ['kɔli] n κόλι.
colliery ['kɔliəri] n ἀνθρακωρυχεῖον.
collision [kə'liʒən] n σύγκρουσις.
colloquial [kə'ləukwiəl] a τῆς καθομιλουμένης.
collusion [kə'lu:ʒən] n συμπαιγνία.
colon ['kəulən] n (gram) διπλῆ στιγμή.
colonel ['kə:nl] n συνταγματάρχης.
colonial [kə'ləuniəl] a ἀποικιακός.
colonize ['kɔlənaiz] vt ἀποικίζω.
colonnade [kɔlə'neid] n περιστύλιον, κιονοστοιχία.
colony ['kɔləni] n ἀποικία || (of immigrants etc) παροικία.
color ['kʌlə*] n (US) = colour.
colossal [kə'lɔsl] a κολοσσιαῖος.
colour ['kʌlə*] n χρῶμα || (paints etc) βαφή, μπογιά || (of skin) χρῶμα || vt χρωματίζω, βάφω || (news) χρωματίζω, γαρνίρω || ~s npl χρώματα || (naut) σημαία || ~ bar n φυλετική διάκρισις || ~-blind a δαλτωνικός || ~ed a χρωματιστός, ἔγχρωμος || (fig) ἐξογκωμένος || ~ed man n νέγρος || ~ film n (for camera) ἔγχρωμο φίλμ || ~ful a ζωντανός || ~ television n ἔγχρωμη τηλεόραση.
colt [kəult] n πῶλος, πουλάρι.
column ['kɔləm] n (pillar) κίων, στύλος, κολώνα || (of troops) φάλαγγα || (of page) στήλη || ~ist n ἀρθρογράφος.
coma ['kəumə] n κῶμα, λήθαργος.
comb [kəum] n (for hair) κτένι, χτένα || (of cock) λειρί || (honey) κηρήθρα || vt (hair) κτενίζω || (search) ἐρευνῶ, ψάχνω.
combat ['kɔmbæt] n πάλη, διαμάχη || vt (κατα)πολεμῶ.
combination [kɔmbi'neiʃən] n συνδυασμός, ἔνωσις.
combine [kəm'bain] vti συνδυάζω, συνεργάζομαι, ἑνοῦμαι || ['kɔmbain] n συνδυασμός, ἑταιρεία, συνδικᾶτον || ~ harvester n θεριστική καί ἁλωνιστική μηχανή.

combustible [kəm'bʌstibl] *a* καύσιμος, εύφλεκτος.

combustion [kəm'bʌstʃən] *n* καῦσις, ἀνάφλεξις.

come [kʌm] (*irreg v*) *vi* (*approach*) ἔρχομαι, φθάνω ‖ (*reach*) τελειώνω, φθάνω, βρίσκομαι ‖ (*become*) γίνομαι, συμβαίνω ‖ (*result*) καταλήγω ‖ **to ~ about** *vi* συμβαίνω, γίνομαι ‖ **to ~ across** *vt* συναντῶ ‖ **to ~ by** *vt* (*visit*) περνῶ ‖ (*find*) βρίσκω, ἀποκτῶ ‖ **to ~ in for** *vt* ἔχω μερίδιον, μετέχω ‖ **to ~ into** *vt* (*enter*) μπαίνω μέσα, ἐμφανίζομαι ‖ (*inherit*) κληρονομῶ ‖ (*fashion*) γίνομαι τῆς μόδας ‖ **to ~ out with** *vt* βγαίνω, βγάζω ‖ **to ~ to** *vt* (*bill*) φθάνω ‖ (*grief*) μοῦ συμβαίνει δυστύχημα ‖ (*nothing*) ἀποτυγχάνω ‖ (*notice*) ἀντιλαμβάνομαι ‖ **to ~ up to** *vt* ἀνεβαίνω ‖ (*amount*) φθάνω ‖ **to ~ up with** *vt* προφθάνω ‖ **~back** *n* ἐπάνοδος.

comedian [kə'mi:diən] *n* κωμικός.

comedown [ˈkʌmdaun] *n* ξεπεσμός.

comedy [ˈkɔmidi] *n* κωμωδία.

comet [ˈkɔmit] *n* κομήτης.

comfort [ˈkʌmfət] *n* (*of body*) ἄνεσις ‖ (*of mind*) παρηγοριά ‖ *vt* παρηγορῶ ‖ **~s** *npl* ἀνέσεις, ἀπολαύσεις ‖ **~able** *a* ἀναπαυτικός, ἄνετος ‖ **~ station** *n* (*US*) ἀποχωρητήριο.

comic [ˈkɔmik] *n* (*actor*) κωμικός ‖ (*magazine*) κόμικς ‖ *a* (*also* **~al**) κωμικός, ἀστεῖος.

comma [ˈkɔmə] *n* (*gram*) κόμμα.

command [kə'ma:nd] *n* (*order*) διαταγή ‖ (*control*) ἐξουσία, κυριαρχία, διοίκησις ‖ *vt* (*order*) διατάσσω ‖ (*be in charge*) διοικῶ, ἐξουσιάζω, ἐλέγχω ‖ (*be able to get*) κατέχω, διαθέτω ‖ *vi* προστάζω ‖ **~eer** [kɔmən'diə*] *vt* ἐπιτάσσω ‖ **~er** *n* (*mil*) διοικητής ‖ (*naut*) πλωτάρχης ‖ **~ing officer** *n* διοικητής ‖ **~ment** *n* ἐντολή ‖ **~o** *n* κομμάντο, καταδρομεύς.

commemorate [kə'meməreit] *vt* ἑορτάζω.

commemoration [kəmeməˈreiʃən] *n*: **in ~ of** εἰς μνήμην τοῦ.

commemorative [kə'memərətiv] *a* ἀναμνηστικός.

commence [kə'mens] *vti* ἀρχίζω.

commend [kə'mend] *vt* συνιστῶ, ἐπαινῶ ‖ **~able** *a* ἀξιέπαινος ‖ **~ation** [kɔmən'deiʃən] *n* ἔπαινος.

commensurate [kə'menʃərit] *a* (*+with*) ἀνάλογος.

comment [ˈkɔment] *n* σχόλιον, ἐξήγησις ‖ *vi* (*+on*) σχολιάζω, ἐπεξηγῶ ‖ **~ary** *n* (*sport*) ρεπορτάζ ‖ σχόλιον ‖ **~ator** *n* σχολιαστής.

commerce [ˈkɔmə:s] *n* ἐμπόριον.

commercial [kə'mə:ʃəl] *a* ἐμπορικός ‖ (*TV*) διαφήμισις ‖ **~ize** *vt* ἐμπορεύομαι ‖ **~ vehicle** *n* δημοσίας χρήσεως.

commiserate [kə'mizəreit] *vi* (*+with*) συμπονῶ, συλλυποῦμαι.

commission [kə'miʃən] *n* (*duty*) ἐντολή, παραγγελία ‖ (*fee*) προμήθεια ‖ (*mil*) βαθμὸς ἀξιωματικοῦ ‖ (*reporting body*) ἐπιτροπή ‖ *vt* ἐντέλλομαι, ἐπιφορτίζω ‖ **out of ~** ἐκτὸς ἐνεργείας, χαλασμένο ‖ **~aire** *n* θυρωρός ‖ **~er** *n* μέλος ἐπιτροπῆς, ἁρμοστής.

commit [kə'mit] *vt* (*a crime*) διαπράττω (ἔγκλημα) ‖ (*to paper*) καταγράφω ‖ (*to memory*) ἀπομνημονεύω ‖ (*entrust*) ἐμπιστεύομαι, ἀναθέτω ‖ **~ment** *n* δέσμευσις, ὑποχρέωσις.

committee [kə'miti] *n* ἐπιτροπή.

commodious [kə'məudiəs] *a* εὐρύχωρος.

commodity [kə'mɔditi] *n* ἐμπόρευμα.

common [ˈkɔmən] *a* (*shared*) κοινός ‖ (*knowledge etc*) κοινός, συνήθης ‖ (*ordinary, usual*) συνήθης, συνηθισμένος ‖ (*mean, low*) χυδαῖος, πρόστυχος ‖ (*frequent*) συνήθης ‖ *n*: **in ~** ἀπὸ κοινοῦ ‖ **~ly** *ad* συνήθως ‖ **C~ Market** *n* Κοινή Ἀγορά ‖ **~place** *a* κοινοτοπία, πεζός ‖ **~room** *n* αἴθουσα καθηγητῶν ‖ **~sense** *n* κοινὸς νοῦς ‖ **the C~wealth** *n* Κοινοπολιτεία.

commotion [kə'məuʃən] *n* ταραχή.

communal [ˈkɔmju:nl] *a* κοινοτικός.

commune [ˈkɔmju:n] *n* (*group of people living communally*) κοινότης ‖ [kə'mju:n] *vi* (*+with*) συναναστρέφομαι.

communicate [kə'mju:nikeit] *vt* (*transmit*) ἀνακοινώνω, μεταδίδω ‖ *vi* (*connect*) συγκοινωνῶ ‖ (*be in touch*) (*+with*) ἐπικοινωνῶ.

communication [kəmju:ni'keiʃən] *n* ἀνακοίνωσις, μετάδοσις ‖ συγκοινωνία, ἐπικοινωνία ‖ **~s** *npl* (*transport etc*) συγκοινωνία ‖ **~ cord** *n* κώδων κινδύνου.

communion [kə'mju:niən] *n* κοινότης ‖ (*rel*) θρησκευτικὴ ὁμάς ‖ (**Holy**) **C~** *n* (Ἁγία) Μετάληψις.

communiqué [kə'mju:nikei] *n* ἀνακοινωθέν.

communism [ˈkɔmjunizəm] *n* κομμουνισμός.

communist [ˈkɔmjunist] *n* κομμουνιστής ‖ *a* κομμουνιστικός.

community [kə'mju:niti] *n* κοινότης ‖ (*the public*) κοινωνία, τό κοινόν ‖ **~ centre** *n* αἴθουσα ἀναψυχῆς ‖ **~ chest** *n* (*US*) φιλανθρωπικόν ταμεῖον.

commutation ticket [kɔmju'teiʃəntikit] *n* (*US*) εἰσιτήριον διαρκείας.

compact [kəm'pækt] *a* συμπαγής, σφικτός ‖ [ˈkɔmpækt] *n* (*agreement*) σύμβασις, συμφωνία ‖ (*powder*) πουδριέρα.

companion [kəm'pæniən] *n* σύντροφος, συνάδελφος, ταῖρι ‖ **~ship** *n* συντροφιά.

company [ˈkʌmpəni] *n* (*business*) ἑταιρεία ‖ (*of people*) παρέα, συντροφιά ‖ (*mil*) λόχος ‖ (*guests*) κόσμο ‖ **to keep s.o. ~** κάνω παρέα.

comparable [ˈkɔmpərəbl] *a* συγκρίσιμος, ἀνάλογος, παραβλητός.

comparative [kəm'pærətiv] *a* συγκριτικός, σχετικός ‖ ~**ly** *ad* συγκριτικῶς.

compare [kəm'pɛə*] *vt* συγκρίνω, παραβάλλω ‖ (+*with*) παρομοιάζω ‖ *vi* συγκρίνομαι.

comparison [kəm'pærisn] *n* σύγκρισις ‖ παρομοίωσις ‖ **in** ~ (**with**) συγκρινόμενος (μέ).

compartment [kəm'pɑ:tmənt] *n* (*naut*) διαμέρισμα ‖ (*rail*) βαγκόν-λί.

compass ['kʌmpəs] *n* (*instrument*) πυξίς ‖ ~**es** *npl* διαβήτης.

compassion [kəm'pæʃən] *n* εὐσπλαχνία, οἶκτος ‖ ~**ate** *a* φιλεύσπλαχνος.

compatible [kəm'pætibl] *a* συμβιβάσιμος, σύμφωνος.

compel [kəm'pel] *vt* ἀναγκάζω, ὑποχρεώνω.

compendium [kəm'pendiəm] *n* σύνοψις, ἐπιτομή.

compensate ['kɔmpenseit] *vt* ἀμείβω, ἀποζημιώνω ‖ *vi*: **to** ~ **for** ἀντισταθμίζω.

compensation [kɔmpen'seiʃən] *n* ἀμοιβή ‖ (*money*) ἀποζημίωσις ‖ (*satisfaction*) ἱκανοποίησις.

compere ['kɔmpɛə*] *n* κομπέρ.

compete [kəm'pi:t] *vi* συναγωνίζομαι, ἀνταγωνίζομαι ‖ (*for prize*) διαγωνίζομαι.

competence ['kɔmpitəns] *n* ἱκανότης, ἐπιδεξιότης.

competent ['kɔmpitənt] *a* ἱκανός, ἐπιδέξιος ‖ (*office etc*) ἁρμόδιος.

competition [kɔmpi'tiʃən] *n* ἅμιλλα ‖ (*rivalry*) ἀνταγωνισμός, συναγωνισμός.

competitive [kəm'petitiv] *a* ἀνταγωνιστικός, συναγωνιστικός.

competitor [kəm'petitə*] *n* ἀνταγωνιστής, ἀντίπαλος.

compile [kəm'pail] *vt* συλλέγω, συναθροίζω.

complacency [kəm'pleisnsi] *n* αὐταρέσκεια.

complacent [kəm'pleisənt] *a* αὐτάρεσκος, ἐπηρμένος.

complain [kəm'plein] *vi* παραπονιέμαι, γκρινιάζω ‖ ~**t** *n* παράπονο, γκρίνια ‖ (*illness*) ἀρρώστια.

complement ['kɔmplimənt] *n* πληρότης ‖ (*math*) συμπλήρωμα ‖ (*esp ship's crew etc*) πλῆρες ‖ ~**ary** *a* συμπληρωματικός.

complete [kəm'pli:t] *a* πλήρης, συμπληρωμένος, τέλειος ‖ *vt* συμπληρώνω, ἀποτελειώνω ‖ ~**ly** *ad* πλήρως, ἐντελῶς.

completion [kəm'pli:ʃən] *n* συμπλήρωσις, ἀποπεράτωσις.

complex ['kɔmpleks] *a* πολύπλοκος, πολυσύνθετος ‖ *n* (*mental*) σύμπλεγμα, κόμπλεξ ‖ (*of buildings*) σύμπλεγμα.

complexion [kəm'plekʃən] *n* χρῶμα, χροιά.

complexity [kəm'pleksiti] *n* περιπλοκή.

complicate ['kɔmplikeit] *vt* περιπλέκω ‖ ~**d** *a* μπλεγμένος.

complication [kɔmpli'keiʃən] *n* περιπλοκή.

compliment ['kɔmplimənt] *n* φιλοφρόνησις, κομπλιμέντο ‖ ['kɔmpliment] *vt* κομπλι-

μεντάρω, συγχαίρω ‖ ~**s** *npl* εὐχές, χαιρετισμοί ‖ ~**ary** *a* φιλοφρονητικός, κομπλιμεντόζος.

comply [kəm'plai] *vi*: **to** ~ **with** συμφωνοῦμαι, ἐνδίδω, ἐκπληρῶ.

component [kəm'pəunənt] *a* συνθετικός, συστατικός ‖ *n* συστατικόν ‖ (*phys*) συνιστῶσα δύναμις.

compose [kəm'pəuz] *vt* συντάσσω, γράφω ‖ (*mus*) μελοποιῶ, συνθέτω ‖ (*calm*) ἠρεμῶ ‖ ~**d** *a* ἀτάραχος, ἤρεμος ‖ ~**r** *n* (*mus*) μουσουργός, συνθέτης.

composite ['kɔmpəzit] *a* σύνθετος, μικτός.

composition [kɔmpə'ziʃən] *n* σύνθεσις ‖ (*structure*) σύστασις.

compost ['kɔmpɔst] *n* (*fertilizer*) φουσκί.

composure [kəm'pəuʒə*] *n* ἠρεμία, ἀταραξία.

compound ['kɔmpaund] *n* (*gram*) σύνθετος λέξις ‖ (*enclosure*) κλειστός χῶρος ‖ *a* σύνθετος ‖ (*chem*) ἕνωσις ‖ ~ **fracture** *n* τέλειο κάταγμα ‖ ~ **interest** *n* ἀνατοκισμός.

comprehend [kɔmpri'hend] *vt* (*understand*) καταλαβαίνω ‖ (*include*) συμπεριλαμβάνω.

comprehension [kɔmpri'henʃən] *n* κατανόησις, ἀντίληψις.

comprehensive [kɔmpri'hensiv] *a* περιεκτικός, νοήμων.

compress [kəm'pres] *vt* συμπιέζω ‖ ['kɔmpres] *n* (*med*) ἐπίθεμα, κομπρέσσα ‖ ~**ion** *n* (συμ)πίεσις, σύμπτυξις.

comprise [kəm'praiz] *vi* ἀποτελοῦμαι ἀπό.

compromise ['kɔmprəmaiz] *n* συμβιβασμός ‖ *vt* (*expose*) ἐκθέτω ‖ *vi* (*agree*) συμβιβάζομαι.

compulsion [kəm'pʌlʃən] *n* βία, καταναγκασμός.

compulsory [kəm'pʌlsəri] *a* (*obligatory*) ὑποχρεωτικός.

computer [kəm'pju:tə*] *n* ὑπολογιστής.

comrade ['kɔmrid] *n* σύντροφος, συνάδελφος ‖ ~**ship** *n* καμαραντερί.

concave ['kɔn'keiv] *a* κοῖλος, βαθουλός.

conceal [kən'si:l] *vt* (ἀπο)κρύπτω.

concede [kən'si:d] *vt* (*admit*) παραδέχομαι ‖ *vi* (*yield*) παραχωρῶ.

conceit [kən'si:t] *n* ματαιοδοξία, ξηπασιά ‖ ~**ed** *a* φαντασμένος, ξηπασμένος.

conceivable [kən'si:vəbl] *a* διανοητός, δυνατός.

conceive [kən'si:v] *vt* (*imagine*) φαντάζομαι ‖ (*child*) συλλαμβάνω.

concentrate ['kɔnsəntreit] *vi* (+*on*) συγκεντρώνομαι ‖ *vt* συγκεντρώνω.

concentration [kɔnsən'treiʃən] *n* συγκέντρωσις ‖ ~ **camp** *n* στρατόπεδον συγκεντρώσεως.

concentric [kən'sentrik] *a* ὁμόκεντρος.

concept ['kɔnsept] *n* ἰδέα, ἔννοια ‖ ~**ion** *n* σύλληψις, ἀντίληψις.

concern [kən'sə:n] *n* (*affair*) ἐνδιαφέρον,

συμφέρον ‖ (*business*) ἐπιχείρησις ‖ (*anxiety*) ἀνησυχία ‖ *vt* ἐνδιαφέρομαι, ἐνδιαφέρω ‖ ~ed *a* (*anxious*) ἀνήσυχος ‖ ~ing *prep* ὅσον ἀφορᾶ.

concert ['kɔnsət] *n* συνεννόησις, συμφωνία ‖ (*mus*) συναυλία ‖ in ~ ἐκ συμφώνου, μαζί ‖ ~ed [kən'sə:tid] *a* συμπεφωνημένος ‖ ~ hall *n* αἴθουσα συναυλιῶν.

concertina [kɔnsə'ti:nə] *n* ἀκορντεόν.

concerto [kən'tʃeətəu] *n* κονσέρτο.

concession [kən'seʃən] *n* παραχώρησις, ἐκχώρησις.

conciliation [kənsili'eiʃən] *n* συμφιλίωσις.

conciliatory [kən'siliətəri] *a* διαλλακτικός.

concise [kən'sais] *a* σύντομος, βραχυλόγος.

conclave ['kɔnkleiv] *n* κογκλάβιον, συμβούλιον.

conclude [kən'klu:d] *vt* (*end*) τελειώνω, περαίνω ‖ (*settle*) συνάπτω, κλείνω ‖ (*decide*) συμπεραίνω, καταλήγω ‖ *vi* τερματίζω.

conclusion [kən'klu:ʒən] *n* συμπέρασμα, τέλος ‖ in ~ ἐν τέλει.

conclusive [kən'klu:siv] *a* ἀποφασιστικός, πειστικός ‖ ~ly *ad* ἀποφασιστικῶς, ἀναμφισβητήτως.

concoct [kən'kɔkt] *vt* (*drink etc*) κατασκευάζω ‖ (*plan etc*) ἐφευρίσκω, καταστρώνω.

concrete ['kɔnkri:t] *n* σκυροκονίαμα, μπετόν ‖ *a* συγκεκριμένος.

concur [kən'kə:*] *vi* συμπίπτω, συμφωνῶ.

concurrently [kən'kʌrəntli] *ad* ἀπό κοινοῦ.

concussion [kən'kʌʃən] *n* τράνταγμα ‖ (*med*) διάσεισις.

condemn [kən'dem] *vt* καταδικάζω ‖ ~ation *n* καταδίκη, μομφή.

condensation [kɔnden'seiʃən] *n* συμπύκνωσις.

condense [kən'dens] *vi* συμπυκνοῦμαι ‖ *vt* συμπυκνώνω ‖ ~d milk *n* συμπεπυκνωμένο γάλα.

condescend [kɔndi'send] *vi* καταδέχομαι ‖ ~ing *a* καταδεκτικός, εὐπροσήγορος.

condition [kən'diʃən] *n* (*state*) κατάστασις, συνθήκη ‖ (*term*) ὅρος ‖ *vt* ρυθμίζω, καθορίζω ‖ on ~ that ὑπό τόν ὅρον νά ‖ ~s *npl* (*circumstances, weather*) συνθῆκες ‖ ~al *a* ὑπό ὅρους, προϋποθετικός.

condolences [kən'dəulənsiz] *npl* συλλυπητήρια.

condone [kən'dəun] *vt* συγχωρῶ, παραβλέπω.

conducive [kən'dju:siv] *a* (+*to*) συντελεστικός.

conduct ['kɔndʌkt] *n* (*behaviour*) διαγωγή ‖ (*management*) διεξαγωγή ‖ [kən'dʌkt] *vt* (*people*) ὁδηγῶ, φέρω ‖ (*affairs*) διευθύνω, ἐκτελῶ ‖ (*mus*) διευθύνω ‖ ~ed tour *n* ξενάγησις ‖ ~or *n* (*orchestra*) μαέστρος ‖ (*bus*) εἰσπράκτωρ ‖ ~ress *n* (*bus*) εἰσπρακτόρισσα.

cone [kəun] *n* (*math*) κῶνος ‖ (*ice cream*)

παγωτό χωνάκι ‖ (*pine*) κουκουνάρι.

confectioner [kən'fekʃənə*] *n* ζαχαροπλάστης ‖ ~'s (*shop*) *n* ζαχαροπλαστεῖον ‖ ~y *n* ζαχαροπλαστεῖον.

confederation [kənfedə'reiʃən] *n* συνομοσπονδία.

confer [kən'fə:*] *vt* (*grant*) ἀπονέμω, παρέχω ‖ *vi* (*consult*) συζητῶ, διασκέπτομαι ‖ ~ence ['kɔnfərəns] *n* (συν)διάσκεψις, συμβούλιον.

confess [kən'fes] *vti* (*admit*) (ἐξ)ὁμολογῶ ‖ (*rel*) ἐξομολογοῦμαι ‖ ~ion *n* ὁμολογία ‖ (*rel*) ἐξομολόγησις ‖ ~ional *n* ἐξομολογητήριον ‖ ~or *n* ὁμολογητής ‖ (*priest*) πνευματικός.

confetti [kən'feti] *n* χαρτοπόλεμος, κονφετί.

confide [kən'faid] *vi*: to ~ in ἐμπιστεύομαι ‖ ~nce ['kɔnfidəns] *n* (*trust*) ἐμπιστοσύνη ‖ (*secret*) μυστικόν ‖ ~nce trick *n* κόλπο, ἀπάτη.

confident ['kɔnfidənt] *a* βέβαιος, μέ θάρρος ‖ ~ial *a* (*secret*) ἐμπιστευτικός ‖ (*trusted*) τῆς ἐμπιστοσύνης.

confine [kən'fain] *vt* περιορίζω ‖ (*shut up*) ἐγκλείω ‖ ~s ['kɔnfainz] *npl* ὅρια ‖ ~d *a* (*space*) περιορισμένος ‖ ~ment *n* (*limiting*) περιορισμός ‖ (*birth*) λοχεία, τοκετός.

confirm [kən'fə:m] *vt* (*report*) ἐπιβεβαιώνω ‖ (*appointment*) ἐπικυρώνω ‖ ~ation *n* (*general*) ἐπιβεβαίωσις ‖ (*rel*) χρῖσμα, μύρωσις ‖ ~ed *a* ἔγκυρος, πείσμων.

confiscate ['kɔnfiskeit] *vt* δημεύω.

confiscation [kɔnfis'keiʃən] *n* δήμευσις.

conflagration [kɔnflə'greiʃən] *n* πυρκαϊά.

conflict ['kɔnflikt] *n* σύγκρουσις, διαμάχη, ἀντίθεσις ‖ [kən'flikt] *vi* συγκρούομαι, διαφέρω, ἀντιμάχομαι ‖ ~ing *a* ἀντιφατικός, συγκρουόμενος.

conform [kən'fɔ:m] *vi* (+*to*) συμμορφώνομαι, προσαρμόζομαι.

confront [kən'frʌnt] *vt* ἀντιμετωπίζω ‖ ~ation *n* ἀντιμετώπισις.

confuse [kən'fju:z] *vt* συγχύζω, ταράσσω.

confusing [kən'fju:ziŋ] *a* συγκεχυμένος.

confusion [kən'fju:ʒən] *n* (*disorder*) σύγχυσις ‖ (*tumult*) ἀναστάτωσις, ἀναμπουμπούλα ‖ (*embarrassment*) σάστισμα.

congeal [kən'dʒi:l] *vi* πήζω.

congenial [kən'dʒi:niəl] *a* ταιριαστός, εὐχάριστος.

congested [kən'dʒestid] *a* (*overcrowded*) συνωστισμένος.

congestion [kən'dʒestʃən] *n* (*of traffic etc*) συμφόρησις, συνωστισμός.

conglomeration [kənglɔmə'reiʃən] *n* σύμφυρμα, συμπήγμα.

congratulate [kən'grætjuleit] *vt* (+*on*) συγχαίρω.

congratulations [kəngrætju'leiʃənz] *npl* συγχαρητήρια.

congregate ['kɔŋgrigeit] *vi* συναθροίζομαι.

congregation [kɔŋgri'geiʃən] *n* συνάθροισις, πλήρωμα ἐκκλησίας.

congress ['kɔŋgres] *n* συνέλευσις, συνέδριον ‖ (*US*) Κογκρέσσον ‖ ~**ional** *a* κοινοβουλευτικός ‖ ~**man** *n* (*US*) μέλος τοῦ Κογκρέσσου.

conical ['kɔnikəl] *a* κωνικός, κωνοειδής.

conifer ['kɔnifə*] *n* κωνοφόρον (δένδρον) ‖ ~**ous** [kə'nifərəs] *a* κωνοφόρος.

conjecture [kən'dʒektʃə*] *n* εἰκασία, συμπερασμός ‖ *vti* εἰκάζω, συμπεραίνω.

conjugal ['kɔndʒugəl] *a* συζυγικός.

conjunction [kən'dʒʌŋkʃən] *n* σύνδεσμος ‖ **in** ~ **with** ἀπό κοινοῦ μέ.

conjure ['kʌndʒə*] *vti* πλέκω, μηχανεύω ‖ **to** ~ **up** *vt* ἐπινοῶ, ἐπικαλοῦμαι ‖ ~**r** *n* ταχυδακτυλουργός.

conjuring ['kʌndʒəriŋ] *n*: ~ **trick** *n* ταχυδακτυλουργία.

conk [kɔŋk]: **to** ~ **out** *vi* (*col*) σβήνω.

connect [kə'nekt] *vti* (*train*) συνδέω, συνδέομαι, συνδυάζω ‖ ~**ion** *n* (*joining*) σύνδεσις, συνάφεια ‖ (*relation*) σχέσις, συσχετισμός ‖ **in** ~**ion with** σχετικῶς μέ.

connexion [kə'nekʃən] *n* = **connection** ‖ *see* **connect**.

connoisseur [kɔnə'sə:*] *n* εἰδήμων, τεχνοκρίτης.

conquer ['kɔŋkə*] *vt* (*overcome*) ὑπερνικῶ, ὑποτάσσω ‖ (*by war*) κατακτῶ, κυριεύω ‖ ~**or** *n* κατακτητής, νικητής.

conquest ['kɔŋkwest] *n* κατάκτησις.

conscience ['kɔnʃəns] *n* συνείδησις.

conscientious [kɔnʃi'enʃəs] *a* εὐσυνείδητος ‖ ~ **objector** *n* ἀντιρρησίας συνειδήσεως.

conscious ['kɔnʃəs] *a* συνειδός, συναισθανόμενος ‖ ~**ness** *n* συναίσθησις.

conscript ['kɔnskript] *n* στρατεύσιμος, κληρωτός ‖ ~**ion** [kən'skripʃən] *n* στρατολογία.

consecrate ['kɔnsikreit] *vt* ἐγκαινιάζω, χειροτονῶ ‖ (*devote*) ἀφιερώνω.

consecutive [kən'sekjutiv] *a* διαδοχικός.

consensus [kən'sensəs] *n* κοινή συναίνεσις, ἐπικρατοῦσα γνώμη.

consent [kən'sent] *n* συγκατάθεσις, συναίνεσις ‖ *vi* (+ *to*) συγκατατίθεμαι.

consequence ['kɔnsikwəns] *n* (*importance*) σπουδαιότης ‖ (*result, effect*) συνέπεια, ἐπακόλουθον.

consequently ['kɔnsikwəntli] *ad* ἑπομένως, συνεπῶς.

conservation [kɔnsə'veiʃən] *n* συντήρησις, διατήρησις.

conservative [kən'sə:vətiv] *a* συντηρητικός, μετριοπαθής ‖ **C**~ *a* (*party*) συντηρητικός ‖ *npl* οἱ Συντηρητικοί.

conservatory [kən'sə:vətri] *n* (*greenhouse*) θερμοκήπιον, σέρρα ‖ (*mus*) ὠδεῖον.

conserve [kən'sə:v] *vt* συντηρῶ, διατηρῶ.

consider [kən'sidə*] *vt* (*think over*) μελετῶ ‖ (*take into account*) λαμβάνω ὑπ'ὄψιν ‖ (*deem*) θεωρῶ ‖ ~**able** *a* σημαντικός,

ἀξιόλογος ‖ ~**ate** *a* διακριτικός, ἁβρόφρων ‖ ~**ation** *n* (*thoughtfulness*) ἁβροφροσύνη, διακριτικότης ‖ (*serious thought*) μελέτη, σκέψις ‖ (*reason*) λόγος ‖ (*reward*) ἀμοιβή ‖ ~**ing** *prep* λαμβανομένου ὑπ'ὄψιν.

consign [kən'sain] *vt* ἀποστέλλω, παραδίδω ‖ ~**ment** *n* ἀποστολή.

consist [kən'sist] *vi* (+ *of*) συνίσταμαι, ἀποτελοῦμαι.

consistency [kən'sistənsi] *n* (*firmness*) συνοχή, συνέπεια, σταθερότης ‖ (*density*) πυκνότης, στερεότης.

consistent [kən'sistənt] *a* σταθερός, συνεπής, σύμφωνος.

consolation [kɔnsə'leiʃən] *n* παρηγοριά ‖ ~ **prize** *n* βραβεῖον παρηγοριᾶς.

console [kən'səul] *vt* παρηγορῶ.

consolidate [kən'sɔlideit] *vt* συγχωνεύω, παγιώνω.

consommé [kən'sɔmei] *n* ζωμός κρέατος κονσομέ.

consonant ['kɔnsənənt] *n* (*gram*) σύμφωνον.

consortium [kən'sɔ:tiəm] *n* κοινοπραξία, κονσόρτιουμ.

conspicuous [kən'spikjuəs] *a* καταφανής περίβλεπτος ‖ (*prominent*) ἀξιοσημείωτος, σημαντικός.

conspiracy [kən'spirəsi] *n* συνωμοσία.

conspire [kən'spaiə*] *vi* συνωμοτῶ, συν εργῶ.

constable ['kʌnstəbl] *n* ἀστυφύλαξ, χωροφύλαξ.

constabulary [kən'stæbjuləri] *n* ἀστυνομία.

constancy ['kɔnstənsi] *n* σταθερότης, εὐστάθεια.

constant ['kɔnstənt] *a* σταθερός, συνεχής ‖ (*math*) σταθερόν ‖ ~**ly** *ad* σταθερῶς συνεχῶς.

constellation [kɔnstə'leiʃən] *n* ἀστερισμός.

consternation [kɔnstə'neiʃən] *n* κατάπληξις.

constipated ['kɔnstipeitid] *a* δυσκοίλιος.

constipation [kɔnsti'peiʃən] *n* δυσκοιλιότης.

constituency [kən'stitjuənsi] *n* ἐκλογική περιφέρεια.

constituent [kən'stitjuənt] *n* (*elector*) ψηφοφόρος ‖ (*essential part*) συστατικόν.

constitute ['kɔnstitju:t] *vt* (*amount to*) συνιστῶ, ἀποτελῶ.

constitution [kɔnsti'tju:ʃən] *n* (*laws*) σύνταγμα ‖ (*health*) κρᾶσις ‖ ~**al** *a* συνταγματικός.

constrain [kən'strein] *vt* ἐξαναγκάζω ‖ ~**t** *n* ἐξαναγκασμός ‖ (*feelings*) ταραχή, τράκ.

constrict [kən'strikt] *vt* συσφίγγω ‖ ~**ion** *n* σύσφιγξις, σφίξιμο.

construct [kən'strʌkt] *vt* κατασκευάζω, οἰκοδομῶ ‖ ~**ion** *n* κατασκευή, οἰκοδόμησις ‖ (*gram*) σύνταξις, ἑρμηνεία ‖ **under** ~**ion** ὑπό κατασκευήν ‖ ~**ive** *a* ἐποικοδομητικός, δημιουργικός.

construe [kən'stru:] *vt* ἑρμηνεύω.

consul ['kɔnsəl] *n* πρόξενος ‖ ~ate ['kɔn-sjulit] *n* προξενεῖον.

consult [kən'sʌlt] *vt* συμβουλεύομαι ‖ ~ant *n* (*med*) συμβουλεύων ἰατρός ‖ (*other specialist*) σύμβουλος ‖ ~ation *n* συμβούλιον, συνδιάσκεψις ‖ ~ing room *n* ἰατρεῖον.

consume [kən'sju:m] *vt* καταναλίσκω ‖ ~r *n* καταναλωτής.

consumption [kən'sʌmpʃən] *n* κατανάλωσις ‖ (*med*) φθίσις, φυματίωσις.

contact ['kɔntækt] *n* ἐπαφή ‖ *vt* ἔρχομαι εἰς ἐπαφήν μέ ‖ ~ lenses *npl* φακοί ἐπαφῆς.

contagious [kən'teidʒəs] *a* μεταδοτικός, κολλητικός.

contain [kən'tein] *vt* περιέχω ‖ to ~ o.s. συγκρατοῦμαι ‖ ~er *n* (*small*) δοχεῖον ‖ (*transport*) (ἐμπορευματικό) κιβώτιον.

contaminate [kən'tæmineit] *vt* μολύνω, μιαίνω.

contamination [kəntæmi'neiʃən] *n* μόλυνσις, μίανσις.

contemplate ['kɔntempleit] *vt* (*look at*) κυττάζω, παρατηρῶ ‖ (*meditate*) μελετῶ, ἀναπολῶ ‖ (*intend*) σχεδιάζω.

contemplation [kɔntem'pleiʃən] *n* σκέψις, συλλογή.

contemporary [kən'tempərəri] *a* σύγχρονος ‖ *n* σύγχρονος, συνομίληκος.

contempt [kən'tempt] *n* περιφρόνησις ‖ ~ible *a* ἀξιοκαταφρόνητος ‖ ~uous *a* περιφρονητικός.

contend [kən'tend] *vt* (*strive*) (συν)ἀγωνίζομαι ‖ (*argue*) ἰσχυρίζομαι ‖ ~er *n* (*competitor*) ἀνταγωνιστής.

content [kən'tent] *a* ἱκανοποιημένος, εὐχαριστημένος ‖ *vt* ἱκανοποιῶ ‖ ['kɔntent] *n* (*of article etc*) περιεχόμενον ‖ ~s *npl* (*of room*) περιεχόμενα ‖ (*of book*) (πίναξ) περιεχομένων ‖ (*of barrel*) περιεκτικότης ‖ ~ed *a* ἱκανοποιημένος.

contention [kən'tenʃən] *n* (*dispute*) ἀγών, διαμάχη ‖ (*opinion*) ἰσχυρισμός.

contentment [kən'tentmənt] *n* ἱκανοποίησις.

contest ['kɔntest] *n* ἀγών, πάλη ‖ [kən'test] *vt* διαμφισβητῶ, διεκδικῶ, ἀγωνίζομαι ‖ ~ant *n* ἀγωνιζόμενος, διεκδικητής.

context ['kɔntekst] *n* συμφραζόμενα.

continent ['kɔntinənt] *n* ἤπειρος ‖ the C~ Εὐρώπη ‖ ~al *a* ἠπειρωτικός.

contingency [kən'tindʒənsi] *n* ἐνδεχόμενον, σύμπτωσις.

contingent [kən'tindʒənt] *n* ἐνδεχόμενος ‖ (*mil*) τμῆμα στρατοῦ ἤ ναυτικοῦ ‖ *a* (+ (*up*)*on*) ἐξηρτημένος ἀπό.

continual [kən'tinjuəl] *a* (*endless*) συνεχής, ἀδιάκοπος ‖ (*often repeated*) συχνά ‖ ~ly *ad* συνεχῶς.

continuation [kəntinju'eiʃən] *n* συνέχεια, συνέχισις.

continue [kən'tinju:] *vi* συνεχίζομαι ‖ (*remain*) (παρα)μένω ‖ *vt* συνεχίζω ‖ (*resume*) ἐξακολουθῶ.

continuity [kɔnti'nju:iti] *n* συνέχεια.

continuous [kən'tinjuəs] *a* συνεχής, ἀδιάκοπος.

contort [kən'tɔ:t] *vt* συστρίβω, παραμορφώνω ‖ ~ion *n* στρίψιμο ‖ (*of face*) μορφασμός ‖ ~ionist *n* ἀκροβάτης.

contour ['kɔntuə*] *n* (*shape*) περίγραμμα ‖ (*of map*) ἰσοΰψεῖς καμπύλαι.

contraband ['kɔntrəbænd] *n* λαθρεμπόριον, κοντραμπάντο.

contraception [kɔntrə'sepʃən] *n* πρόληψις συλλήψεως.

contraceptive [kɔntrə'septiv] *n* ἀντισυλληπτικόν.

contract ['kɔntrækt] *n* συμβόλαιον, συμφωνία ‖ [kən'trækt] *vi* (*to do sth*) συμφωνῶ, συμβάλλομαι ‖ (*become smaller*) συστέλλομαι, στενεύω ‖ ~ion *n* συστολή, μάζεμα ‖ ~or *n* ἐργολάβος, προμηθευτής.

contradict [kɔntrə'dikt] *vt* (*say the opposite*) ἀντιλέγω ‖ (*deny*) διαψεύδω ‖ ~ion *n* (*in terms*) ἀντίφασις ‖ (*denial*) διάψευσις.

contralto [kən'træltəu] *n* μεσόφωνος, κοντράλτο.

contraption [kən'træpʃən] *n* μηχανή, μαραφέτι.

contrary ['kɔntrəri] *a* (*opposite*) ἐνάντιος, ἀντίθετος ‖ (*unfavourable*) ἀντίθετος, δυσμενής ‖ [kən'treəri] (*perverse*) διεστραμμένος ‖ *n* ἀντίθετον ‖ on the ~ τουναντίον ‖ to the ~ ἀντιθέτως.

contrast ['kɔntra:st] *n* σύγκρισις, ἀντίθεσις ‖ [kən'tra:st] *vt* συγκρίνω, ἀντιπαραβάλλω.

contravene [kɔntrə'vi:n] *vt* (*a rule etc*) παραβαίνω, καταπατῶ ‖ (*conflict with*) διαψεύδω, προσκρούω.

contribute [kən'tribju:t] *vi* (*help*) συμβάλλω, βοηθῶ ‖ (*subscribe*) συνεισφέρω ‖ *vt* καταβάλλω.

contribution [kɔntri'bju:ʃən] *n* συνεισφορά, συνεργασία.

contributor [kən'tribjutə*] *n* συνεισφέρων, συνεργάτης.

contrite ['kɔntrait] *a* συντετριμμένος, μετανοῶν.

contrivance [kən'traivəns] *n* τέχνασμα, ἐπινόησις.

contrive [kən'traiv] *vt* (*bring about*) καταφέρνω.

control [kən'trəul] *vt* (*check*) συγκρατῶ, χαλιναγωγῶ ‖ (*direct*) διευθύνω, ἐξουσιάζω ‖ *n* (*check*) ἔλεγχος, ἐπίβλεψις ‖ (*restraint*) χαλινός ‖ ~s *npl* χειριστήριον, ἔλεγχος ‖ ~ point *n* σημεῖον ἐλέγχου ‖ out of ~ ἀκυβέρνητος ‖ under ~ ὑπό ἔλεγχον.

controversial [kɔntrə'və:ʃəl] *a* συζητήσιμος.

controversy [kən'trɔvəsi] *n* συζήτησις, λογομαχία.

convalesce [kɔnvə'les] vi ἀναρρωνύω ‖ ~nce n ἀνάρρωσις ‖ ~nt a,n ἀναρρωνύων.

convene [kən'vi:n] vti συγκαλῶ, συνέρχομαι.

convenience [kən'vi:niəns] n (being convenient) καταλληλότης, συμφωνία ‖ (thing) εὐκολία, ἄνεσις.

convenient [kən'vi:niənt] a κατάλληλος, βολικός, χρήσιμος.

convent ['kɔnvənt] n μονή γυναικῶν.

convention [kən'venʃən] n (assembly) συνέδριον, συνέλευσις ‖ (custom) ἔθιμον, συνήθεια ‖ ~al a (traditional) ἐθιμοτυπικός, συνήθης.

converge [kən'və:dʒ] vi συγκλίνω.

conversant [kən'və:sənt] a (+ with) οἰκεῖος, γνωστός.

conversation [kɔnvə'seiʃən] n συνδιάλεξις, συνομιλία, κουβέντα ‖ ~al a ὁμιλητικός, καθομιλούμενος.

converse [kən'və:s] vi συνομιλῶ, συνδιαλέγομαι ‖ ['kɔnvə:s] a ἀντίθετος ‖ ~ly ad ἀντιστρόφως, ἀντιθέτως.

conversion [kən'və:ʃən] n μετατροπή ‖ (esp rel) προσηλύτισις ‖ ~ table n πίναξ μετατροπῶν.

convert [kən'və:t] vt (change) μετατρέπω ‖ (esp rel) προσηλυτίζω ‖ ['kɔnvə:t] n προσήλυτος ‖ ~ible n (aut) καπριολέ.

convex [kən'veks] a κυρτός.

convey [kən'vei] vt (carry) μεταφέρω ‖ (communicate) μεταβιβάζω, μεταδίδω ‖ ~or belt n μεταφορεύς.

convict [kən'vikt] vt καταδικάζω ‖ ['kɔnvikt] n κατάδικος ‖ ~ion n (verdict) καταδίκη ‖ (belief) πεποίθησις.

convince [kən'vins] vt πείθω.

convincing [kən'vinsiŋ] a πειστικός.

convivial [kən'viviəl] a εὔθυμος, κεφάτος.

convoy ['kɔnvɔi] n συνοδεία, νηοπομπή.

convulse [kən'vʌls] vt (esp with laughter) ξεραίνομαι στά γέλια.

convulsion [kən'vʌlʃən] n σπασμός.

coo [ku:] vi (dove) τερετίζω σάν περιστέρι.

cook [kuk] vt μαγειρεύω ‖ vi ψήνεται ‖ n μάγειρας ‖ ~book n βιβλίον μαγειρικῆς ‖ ~er n συσκευή μαγειρέματος ‖ ~ery n μαγειρική ‖ ~ery book n = cookbook ‖ ~ie n μπισκότο ‖ ~ing n μαγειρική.

cool [ku:l] a (fairly cold) δροσερός ‖ (calm) ψύχραιμος ‖ (unfriendly) ψυχρός, ἀδιάφορος ‖ (impudent) ἀναιδής, θρασύς ‖ vti δροσίζω, κρυώνω ‖ ~ness n ψύχρα, ψυχρότης.

coop [ku:p] n κοττέτσι, κλούβα ‖ vt: to ~ up (fig) περιορίζω, κλείνω.

co-op ['kəu'ɔp] n = cooperative.

cooperate [kəu'ɔpəreit] vi συνεργάζομαι.

cooperation [kəuɔpə'reiʃən] n συνεργασία.

cooperative [kəu'ɔpərətiv] a συνεργατικός ‖ n (farmers) συνεταιρισμός ‖ ~ store n (retail) πρατήριον συνεταιρισμοῦ.

coordinate [kəu'ɔ:dineit] vt συνδυάζω, συντονίζω.

coordination [kəuɔ:di'neiʃən] n συντονισμός.

coot [ku:t] n φαλαρίδα, λούφα.

cope [kəup] vi (+ with) ἀντιμετωπίζω, ἀνταπεξέρχομαι.

co-pilot ['kəu'pailət] n δεύτερος χειριστής.

copper ['kɔpə*] n (of street) χαλκός, μπακίρι ‖ (coin) δεκάρα ‖ (sl: policeman) ἀστυφύλακας.

coppice ['kɔpis] n, copse [kɔps] n δασύλλιον, λόγγος.

copulate ['kɔpjuleit] vi συνουσιάζομαι, γαμῶ.

copy ['kɔpi] n (imitation) ἀντίγραφον, ἀντιγραφή ‖ (of book) ἀντίτυπον ‖ vt ἀντιγράφω, ἀπομιμοῦμαι ‖ ~book n τετράδιον ‖ ~cat n μιμήτρια ‖ ~right n πνευματική ἰδιοκτησία ‖ ~right reserved ἀπαγορεύεται ἡ ἀναδημοσίευσις.

coral ['kɔrəl] n κοράλλιον ‖ ~ reef n κοραλλιογενές νησί.

cord [kɔ:d] n σχοινί, χορδή ‖ see vocal.

cordial ['kɔ:diəl] a ἐγκάρδιος ‖ ~ly ad (invite) ἐγκαρδίως, θερμῶς.

cordon ['kɔ:dn] n (ornamental) κορδόνι ‖ (of police etc) ζώνη.

corduroy ['kɔ:dərɔi] n κοτλέ.

core [kɔ:*] n πυρήν, καρδία ‖ vt ἀφαιρῶ τόν πυρήνα.

cork [kɔ:k] n φελλός ‖ (of bottle) πῶμα ‖ ~screw n τιρ-μπουσόν.

cormorant ['kɔ:mərənt] n φαλακροκόραξ, καλικατζοῦ.

corn [kɔ:n] n σιτηρά, δημητριακά ‖ (US: maize) καλαμπόκι ‖ (on foot) κάλος.

cornea ['kɔ:niə] n κερατοειδής.

corned ['kɔ:nd] ~ beef n εἶδος ἁλιπάστου κρέατος.

corner ['kɔ:nə*] n (of street) γωνία ‖ (of room) γωνία, κώχη ‖ (fig) δύσκολη θέσι ‖ vt φέρω εἰς δύσκολον θέσιν, στριμώχνω ‖ (econ) μονοπωλῶ ‖ vi (turn) παίρνω στροφήν ‖ ~ kick n κόρνερ ‖ ~stone n ἀκρογωνιαῖος λίθος, βάσις.

cornet ['kɔ:nit] n (mus) κορνέττα ‖ (ice cream) χωνάκι.

cornflour ['kɔ:nflauə*] n καλαμποκάλευρο, κορνφλάουερ.

cornice ['kɔ:nis] n κορνίζα.

cornstarch ['kɔ:nsta:tʃ] n (US) = cornflour.

corny ['kɔ:ni] a (joke) σαχλό.

coronary ['kɔrənəri] a στεφανιαῖος ‖ n στεφανιαία ‖ ~ thrombosis n θρόμβωσι τῆς στεφανιαίας.

coronation [kɔrə'neiʃən] n στέψις.

coroner ['kɔrənə*] n ἰατροδικαστής.

corporal ['kɔ:pərəl] n (mil) δεκανέας ‖ (aviat) ὑποσμηνίας ‖ a σωματικός.

corporation [kɔ:pə'reiʃən] n σωματεῖον ‖ (esp business) ἑταιρεία.

corps [kɔ:*] n (στρατιωτικόν) σῶμα.

corpse [kɔ:ps] n πτῶμα, κουφάρι.

corpulent ['kɔ:pjulənt] *a* παχύσαρκος.

corpuscle ['kɔ:pʌsl] *n* σωματίδιον ‖ *(blood corpuscle)* αἱμοσφαίριον.

corral [kə'ra:l] *n* μάνδρα.

correct [kə'rekt] *a (accurate)* ἀκριβής, ὀρθός, διορθωμένος ‖ *(proper)* ἄψογος, ὅπως πρέπει ‖ *vt (papers etc)* διορθώνω ‖ *(make right)* ἐπανορθώνω ‖ ~**ion** *n* διόρθωσις ‖ ~**ly** *ad* ὀρθῶς, σωστά.

correlate ['kɔrileit] *vt* σχετίζομαι, φέρω εἰς σχέσιν.

correlation [kɔri'leiʃən] *n* συσχετισμός, συσχέτισις.

correspond [kɔris'pɔnd] *vi (agree with)* ἀνταποκρίνομαι, ταιριάζω ‖ *(write)* ἀλληλογραφῶ ‖ ~**ence** *n (letters)* ἀλληλογραφία ‖ *(similarity)* ἀντιστοιχία, ἀντιπόκρισις ‖ ~**ence course** *n* μάθημα ἀλληλογραφίας ‖ ~**ent** *n (reporter)* ἀνταποκριτής ‖ ~**ing** *a* ἀντίστοιχος.

corridor ['kɔridɔ:*] *n* διάδρομος.

corroborate [kə'rɔbəreit] *vt* ἐπιβεβαιώνω, ἐνισχύω.

corroboration [kərɔbə'reiʃən] *n* ἐπιβεβαίωσις, ἐπίρρωσις.

corrode [kə'rəud] *vti* διαβιβρώσκω, σκουριάζω.

corrosion [kə'rəuʒən] *n* διάβρωσις, σκωρίασις.

corrugated ['kɔrəgeitid] *a* κυματοειδής ‖ ~ **cardboard** *n* κυματοειδές χαρτόνι ‖ ~ **iron** *n* αὐλακωτόν ἔλασμα.

corrupt [kə'rʌpt] *a* διεφθαρμένος ‖ *vt* διεφθείρω ‖ ~**ion** *n* διαφθορά, δεκασμός.

corset ['kɔ:sit] *n* κορσές.

cortège [kɔ:'te:ʒ] *n* νεκρώσιμος πομπή.

cortisone ['kɔ:tizəun] *n* κορτιζόνη.

cosh [kɔʃ] *n* μαγκούρα, βούρδουλας ‖ *vt* κτυπῶ μέ βούρδουλα.

cosine ['kəusain] *n* συνημίτονον.

cosiness ['kəuzinis] *n* ἄνεσις.

cosmetic [kɔz'metik] *n* καλλυντικόν.

cosmic ['kɔzmik] *a* κοσμικός.

cosmonaut ['kɔzmənɔ:t] *n* ἀστροναύτης, κοσμοναύτης.

cosmopolitan [kɔzmə'pɔlitən] *a* κοσμοπολιτικός.

cosmos ['kɔzmɔs] *n* κόσμος, τό σύμπαν.

cost [kɔst] *(irreg v)* *n* κόστος, τιμή, δαπάνη ‖ *vt* κυστίζω, στοιχίζω ‖ **it** ~**s £5** στοιχίζει πέντε λίρες ‖ **it** ~**s too much** στοιχίζει πολλά ‖ **it** ~ **him his life** τοῦ κόστιζε τήν ζωή ‖ **at all** ~**s** πάση θυσία.

costing ['kɔstiŋ] *n* κοστολόγησις.

costly ['kɔstli] *a (expensive)* δαπανηρος ‖ *(jewellery etc)* πολύτιμος.

cost price ['kɔstprais] *n* τιμή κόστους.

costume ['kɔstju:m] *n (style of dress)* ἔνδυμα, φορεσιά, μόδα ‖ *(woman's outer clothes)* ἐνδυμασία, κοστούμι ‖ *(for bathing)* μπανιερό, μαγιώ ‖ ~ **jewellery** *n* κοσμήματα.

cosy ['kəuzi] *a* ἀναπαυτικός, ζεστός.

cot [kɔt] *n (child's bed)* κρεββατάκι.

cottage ['kɔtidʒ] *n* ἐξοχικό σπιτάκι ‖ ~ **cheese** *n* ἄσπρο τυρί, φέτα.

cotton ['kɔtn] *n* βαμβάκι, μπαμπάκι ‖ *a*: ~ **dress etc** μπαμπακερό ‖ ~ **wool** *n* ἀκατέργαστος βάμβαξ.

couch [kautʃ] *n* ντιβάνι, καναπές ‖ *vt* ἐκφράζω, συγκαλύπτω.

cough [kɔf] *vi* βήχω ‖ *n* βήχας ‖ ~ **drop** *n* παστίλια.

could [kud] *pt of* **can** ‖ ~**n't** = **could not** ‖ *see* **can**.

council ['kaunsl] *n* συμβούλιον ‖ ~**lor** *n* σύμβουλος.

counsel ['kaunsəl] *n (law)* δικηγόρος ‖ *(opinion)* συμβουλή ‖ ~**lor** *n* σύμβουλος.

count [kaunt] *vt (add up)* μετρῶ, ἀριθμῶ ‖ *(include)* ὑπολογίζω, συμπεριλαμβάνω ‖ *vi (be of importance)* ὑπολογίζομαι, στηρίζομαι ‖ *n (reckoning)* ἀρίθμησις, μέτρησις, λογαριασμός ‖ *(nobleman)* κόμης ‖ **to** ~ **on** *vt* ὑπολογίζω, στηρίζομαι εἰς ‖ **to** ~ **up** *vt* μετρῶ ἕως, προσθέτω.

counter ['kauntə*] *n* θυρίς, γκισέ ‖ *(machine that counts)* μετρητής ‖ *vt* ἀντιτίθεμαι, ἀνταπαντῶ ‖ *ad* ἐναντίον, ἀντιθέτως ‖ ~**act** *vt* ἀντιδρῶ, ἐξουδετερώνω ‖ ~**-attack** *n* ἀντεπίθεσις ‖ ~**balance** *vt* ἀντισταθμίζω ‖ ~**clockwise** *ad* ἀριστερόστροφα ‖ ~**espionage** *n* ἀντικατασκοπεία ‖ ~**feit** *a* πλαστός, κίβδηλος ‖ *n* παραποίησις, ἀπάτη ‖ *vt* πλαστογραφῶ ‖ ~**foil** *n* στέλεχος ‖ ~**part** *n* ἀντίστοιχον, ταίρι.

countess ['kauntis] *n* κόμισσα, κοντέσσα.

countless ['kauntlis] *a* ἀναρίθμητος, ἀμέτρητος.

country ['kʌntri] *n (land)* χώρα ‖ *(of birth)* πατρίδα ‖ *(rural district)* ὕπαιθρος, ἐξοχή, ἐπαρχία ‖ *(region)* περιοχή ‖ ~ **dancing** *n* ἐθνικός χορός, λαϊκός χορός ‖ ~ **house** *n* ἐξοχικό σπίτι ‖ ~**man** *n (national)* (συμ)πατριώτης ‖ *(rural)* ἐπαρχιώτης, χωριάτης ‖ ~**side** *n* ὕπαιθρος.

county ['kaunti] *n* κομητεία ‖ ~ **town** *n* πρωτεύουσα κομητείας.

coup [ku:] *n (also* ~ **d'état)** πραξικόπημα.

coupé ['ku:pei] *n* κουπέ.

couple ['kʌpl] *n* ζευγάρι, δύο ‖ *vt* ἐνώνω, ζευγαρώνω.

couplet ['kʌplit] *n* δίστιχον.

coupling ['kʌpliŋ] *n* σύζευξις.

coupon ['ku:pɔn] *n* κουπόνι, ἀπόκομμα.

courage ['kʌridʒ] *n* θάρρος, γενναιότητα ‖ ~**ous** *a* θαρραλέος.

courier ['kuriə*] *n* ἀγγελιαφόρος.

course [kɔ:s] *n (path, track)* διαδρομή ‖ *(line of action)* πορεία, δρόμος ‖ *(series, procedure)* μάθημα, κούρ ‖ *(career, journey)* πορεία ‖ *(part of meal)* φαγητό, πιάτο ‖ *of* ~ φυσικά, καί βέβαια ‖ **in the** ~ **of** κατά τήν διάρκειαν τοῦ ‖ **in due** ~ ἐν καιρῷ τῷ δέοντι ‖ *see* **golf**.

court [kɔːt] *n (attendants of sovereign)* αὐλή ‖ *(residence of sovereign)* (βασιλική) αὐλή ‖ *(of justice)* δικαστήριον ‖ *vt* κορτάρω, προσκαλῶ, ἐπιδιώκω ‖ *see* tennis.
courteous ['kɜːtiəs] *a* εὐγενής.
courtesy ['kɜːtisi] *n* εὐγένεια.
courthouse ['kɔːthaus] *n (US)* δικαστικόν μέγαρον.
courtier ['kɔːtiə*] *n* αὐλικός.
court-martial ['kɔːt'maːʃəl] *n* στρατοδικεῖον.
court room ['kɔːtrum] *n* αἴθουσα δικαστηρίου.
courtyard ['kɔːtjaːd] *n* αὐλή.
cousin ['kʌzn] *n* ξάδελφος, ξαδέλφη.
cove [kəuv] *n* ὅρμος.
cover ['kʌvə*] *vt (place over)* καλύπτω, σκεπάζω ‖ *(shield, screen)* καλύπτω, προστατεύω, κρύβω ‖ *(deal with)* καλύπτω, περιλαμβάνω ‖ *(protect)* προστατεύω ‖ *n* κάλυμμα, σκέπασμα ‖ ~ **age** *n (of news)* ρεπορτάζ ‖ ~ **charge** *n* κουβέρ ‖ ~**ing** *n* κάλυψις, σκέπασμα, ἐπένδυσις ‖ ~**ing letter** *n* ἐπιβεβαιωτική ἐπιστολή.
covet ['kʌvit] *vt* ἐποφθαλμιῶ.
covetous ['kʌvitəs] *a* ἄπληστος.
cow [kau] *n* ἀγελάδα.
coward ['kauəd] *n* ἄνανδρος, δειλός ‖ ~**ice** *n* δειλία ‖ ~**ly** *a* ἄνανδρος, δειλός.
cowboy ['kaubɔi] *n* κάου-μπόϊ.
cower ['kauə*] *vi* μαζεύομαι, τρέμω.
co-worker ['kəu'wɜːkə*] *n* συνεργάτης.
cowshed ['kauʃed] *n* βουστάσιον.
coxswain ['kɔksn] *n (abbr* cox) πηδαλιοῦχος.
coy [kɔi] *a* ντροπαλός, σεμνός.
crab [kræb] *n* κάβουρας ‖ ~ **apple** *n* ἀγριόμηλον.
crack [kræk] *n (sharp noise)* κρότος, τριγμός ‖ *(of whip)* στράκα ‖ *(split)* ρωγμή, σκάσιμο ‖ *vt (noise)* κροτῶ ‖ *(split)* θραύω, ραγίζω ‖ *a* λαμπρός, ἐκλεκτός ‖ ~**er** *n (firework)* βαρελότο, στράκα ‖ *(biscuit)* παξιμαδάκι, μπισκότο ‖ **to ~ up** *vi* κομματιάζω ‖ *(fig)* καταρρέω.
crackling ['krækliŋ] *n* κροταλισμός, τρίξιμο ‖ *(of pig)* πέτσα ψημένου γουρουνιοῦ.
cradle ['kreidl] *n* κοιτίς, λίκνον, κούνια.
craft [kraːft] *n (skill)* τέχνη, χειροτεχνία, ἐπάγγελμα ‖ *(cunning)* πανουργία, δόλος ‖ *(boat)* σκάφος, βάρκα ‖ ~**sman** *n* τεχνίτης ‖ ~**smanship** *n* τέχνη ‖ ~**y** *a* πανούργος, πονηρός, πολυμήχανος.
crag [kræg] *n* κατσάβραχο, γκρεμός ‖ ~**gy** *a* ἀπόκρημνος, βραχώδης.
cram [kræm] *vt* μπάζω, χώνω.
cramp [kræmp] *n* σπασμός, κράμπα ‖ *vt* ἐμποδίζω, περιορίζω.
crane [krein] *n* γερανός, κρένι.
cranium ['kreiniəm] *n* κρανίον.
crank [kræŋk] *n (lever)* (χειρο)στρόφαλος, μανιβέλλα ‖ *(person)* ἰδιότυπος,

ἐκκεντρικός ‖ *vt* βάζω μπρός μέ μανιβέλλα ‖ ~**shaft** *n* στροφαλοφόρος (ἄξων).
cranny ['kræni] *n* σχισμή, ρωγμή.
crap [kræp] *n (nonsense)* τρίχες.
craps [kræps] *n* ζάρι.
crash [kræʃ] *n* κρότος, βρόντος ‖ *(aviat)* συντριβή, πτῶσις ‖ *(aut)* σύγκρουσις ‖ *(econ)* κράχ ‖ *vti* πέφτω, συντρίβομαι ‖ ~ **helmet** *n* προστατευτικόν κράνος ‖ ~ **landing** *n* ἀναγκαστική προσγείωσις.
crate [kreit] *n* κασόνι, κοφίνι, καφάσι.
crater ['kreitə*] *n* κρατήρ.
cravat(e) [krə'væt] *n* γραβάτα.
crave [kreiv] *vi (+for)* ἐκλιπαρῶ, ποθῶ.
craving ['kreiviŋ] *n* πόθος, λαχτάρα.
crawl [krɔːl] *vi* ἕρπω, σέρνομαι ‖ *n* σύρσιμο, βραδυπορία ‖ *(swimming)* κρώουλ.
crayon ['kreiən] *n* κραγιόνι, παστέλ.
craze [kreiz] *n* μανία, λόξα.
crazy ['kreizi] *a (foolish)* ἀνόητος ‖ *(insane)* παράφρων, τρελλός, μουρλός ‖ *(madly eager for)* ἔχω μανία γιά ‖ ~ **paving** *n* ἀκανόνιστο πλακόστρωμα.
creak [kriːk] *n* τριγμός ‖ *vi* τρίζω.
cream [kriːm] *n* καϊμάκι, κρέμα, σαντιγί ‖ *(polish)* ἀλοιφή ‖ *(cosmetic)* κρέμα ‖ *(colour)* ἰβουάρ, μπέίζ ‖ ~ **cake** *n* πάστα, τούρτα ‖ ~**ery** *n* γαλατάδικο ‖ ~**y** *a* καϊμακλίδικος, βουτιράτος.
crease [kriːs] *n* πτυχή, τσάκισμα, τσαλάκωμα ‖ *vti* διπλώνω, ζαρώνω, τσαλακώνω.
create [kriː'eit] *vt (bring into being)* δημιουργῶ ‖ *(cause)* προξενῶ.
creation [kriː'eiʃən] *n* δημιούργημα.
creative [kriː'eitiv] *a* δημιουργικός.
creator [kriː'eitə*] *n* δημιουργός.
creature ['kriːtʃə*] *n* πλάσμα, ὄν.
credentials [kri'denʃəlz] *npl (papers)* διαπιστευτήρια, πιστοποιητικά.
credibility [kredə'biləti] *n* ἀξιοπιστία, (τό) πιστευτόν.
credible ['kredibl] *a* πιστευτός, ἀξιόπιστος.
credit ['kredit] *n* πίστις, πίστωσις ‖ *(recognition)* ἀναγνώρισις ‖ *vt* πιστεύω ‖ **to one's ~** πρός τιμήν τοῦ ‖ ~**able** *a* ἔντιμος, ἀξιέπαινος ‖ ~ **card** *n* κάρτα πιστώσεως ‖ ~**or** *n* πιστωτής.
creed [kriːd] *n* πίστις, θρήσκευμα.
creek [kriːk] *n* κολπίσκος ‖ *(US)* ρέμα.
creep [kriːp] *(irreg v) vi* ἕρπω, σύρομαι ‖ ~**er** *n (animal)* ἑρπετόν ‖ *(plant)* ἀναρριχητικόν ‖ ~**y** *a (frightening)* ἀνατριχιαστικόν.
cremate [kri'meit] *vt* ἀποτεφρώνω (νεκρόν).
cremation [kri'meiʃən] *n* καῦσις (νεκροῦ).
crematorium [kremə'tɔːriəm] *n* κρεματόριον.
crêpe [kreip] *n* κρέπ(ι).
crept [krept] *pt,pp of* creep.
crescent ['kresnt] *n* ἡμισέληνος ‖ *(esp street)* ἡμικυκλικός δρόμος.

cress [kres] n κάρδαμο.

crest [krest] n (tuft) λοφίον, λειρί || (of wave) κορυφή || (badge) κορωνίς, οἰκόσημον || ~ fallen a κατηφής, ἀποθαρρημένος.

Crete [kri:t] n Κρήτη.

cretin ['kretin] n ἠλίθιος || (med) κρετῖνος.

crevasse [kri'væs] n σχισμή.

crevice ['krevis] n ρωγμή, χαραμάδα.

crew [kru:] n πλήρωμα || ~-cut n πολύ κοντό μαλλί.

crib [krib] n (child's bed) παιδικό κρεββάτι || (copy) ἀντιγραφή.

cribbage ['kribidʒ] n κρίμπιτζ.

crick [krik] n πιάσιμο.

cricket ['krikit] n (insect) γρύλλος, τριζόνι || (game) κρίκετ || ~ er n παίκτης τοῦ κρίκετ.

crime [kraim] n (wicked act) κακούργημα || (lawbreaking) ἔγκλημα.

criminal ['kriminl] n ἐγκληματίας, κακοῦργος || a ἐγκληματικός, ἐνοχικός.

crimson ['krimzn] n βαθύ ἐρυθρόν, βυσσινί || a κατακόκκινος.

cringe [krindʒ] vi φέρομαι δουλοπρεπῶς, σκύβω.

crinkle ['kriŋkl] vt ζαρώνω, τσαλακώνω || (rustle) τρίβω.

cripple ['kripl] n ἀνάπηρος, χωλός || vt τραυματίζω, σακατεύω, παραλύω.

crisis ['kraisis] n (time of danger etc) κρίσις.

crisp [krisp] a εὔθρυπτος, ἀφράτος, φρέσκος || n ξεροτηγανισμένη πατάτα.

criss-cross ['kriskrɔs] a σταυρωτός, καφασιτός.

criterion [krai'tiəriən] n κριτήριον.

critic ['kritik] n (theat etc) τεχνοκρίτης, κριτικός || ἐπικριτής || ~al a (like a critic) κριτικός || (danger) κρίσιμος || (severe) αὐστηρός || ~ally ad μέ κριτική διάθεσι, κρίσιμος || ~ism ['kritisizəm] n (judgment) κριτική || (finding fault) ἐπίκρισις || ~ize ['kritisaiz] vt (ἐπι)κρίνω, κατακρίνω.

croak [krəuk] vi (crow) κρώζω || (frog) κοάζω || n (of crow) κρωγμός || (of frog) κοασμός.

crochet ['krəuʃei] n κροσέ.

crockery ['krɔkəri] n πήλινα σκεύη.

crocodile ['krɔkədail] n κροκόδειλος.

crocus ['krəukəs] n κρόκος.

crony ['krəuni] n γέρος, παλιόφιλος.

crook [kruk] n (criminal) λωποδύτης, ἀπατεών || (of shepherd) γκλίτσα || ~ed a ἀγκυλωτός.

crop [krɔp] n συγκομιδή, σοδιά || to ~ up vi (fig) παρουσιάζομαι, προκύπτω.

croquet ['krəukei] n κροκέ.

croquette [krəu'ket] n κροκέτα, κεφτές.

cross [krɔs] n (of Christ) σταυρός || (mark) σταυρό || (breed) διασταύρωσις || (misfortune) ἐμπόδιον, δυσκολία, || vt (pass over) διασχίζω, περνῶ || (make sign) σταυροκοπιέμαι || (place across) σταυρώνω || (mix breeds) διασταυρώνω || (cheque) διαγραμμίζω || a θυμωμένος, κακόκεφος || ~ breed n μιγάς || ~-country (race) n ἀνώμαλος δρόμος || ~-examination n ἐξέτασις κατ'ἀντιπαράστασιν || ~-examine vt ἐξετάζω κατ'ἀντιπαράστασιν || ~-eyed a ἀλλοίθωρος || ~ ing n (road etc) διάβασις, πέρασμα || (sea passage) διάπλους || (place for crossing) διάβασις || ~ at ~-purposes παρεξηγημένοι, σέ ἀντίθεσι || ~-reference n παραπομπή || ~ roads n σταυροδρόμι || ~ section n ἐγκαρσία τομή || ~-wind· n τλάγιος ἄνεμος || ~ word (puzzle) n σταυρόλεξον.

crotch [krɔtʃ] n διακλάδωσις δένδρου, καβάλος τοῦ πανταλονιοῦ.

crotchet ['krɔtʃit] n ἰδιοτροπία, βίδα.

crotchety ['krɔtʃiti] a (person) ἰδιότροπος.

crouch [krautʃ] vi σκύβω, μαζεύομαι, ὀκλάζω.

crow [krəu] n κορώνη, κουρούνα || vi κράζω, λαλῶ || (fig) κομπάζω.

crowbar ['krəuba:*] n λοστός.

crowd [kraud] n πλῆθος, ὄχλος, συρροή || vt (fill) γεμίζω || vi (flock together) συνωθοῦμαι, συνωστίζομαι || ~ ed a γιομάτος.

crown [kraun] n (royal headdress) στέμμα, κορώνα || (of tooth) κορώνα, μύλη || (top of head etc) κορυφή, κορφή || (of flowers) στεφάνι || vt (put crown on) στεφανώνω || (be at top of) πάνω ἀπ'ὅλα, ἀποκορυφώνω || ~ jewels npl κοσμήματα τοῦ Στέμματος || ~ prince n διάδοχος τοῦ θρόνου.

crucial ['kru:ʃəl] a ἀποφασιστικός, κρίσιμος.

crucifix ['kru:sifiks] n ἐσταυρομένος || ~ ion n σταύρωσις.

crucify ['kru:sifai] vt σταυρώνω, βασανίζω.

crude [kru:d] a (unfinished) ἀκατέργαστος || (petroleum) ἀργόν πετρέλαιον || (harsh) ὠμός, ἄξεστος || (humour) χονδρό χιοῦμορ || ~ly ad ὠμῶς, χονδρά, πρόστυχα || ~ness n τραχύτης, σκληρότης a (of thought) χοντροκοπιά.

crudity ['kru:diti] n = crudeness || see crude.

cruel ['kruəl] a (vicious) αἱμοβόρος, ἀμείλικτος || (severe, distressing) σκληρός, ὠμός || (hard-hearted) σκληρόκαρδος || ~ty n σκληρότης, ἀσπλαγχνία || (to wife) κακοποίησις.

cruise [kru:z] n περίπλους, κρουαζιέρα || vi κάνω κρουαζιέρα, περιπλέω || ~ r n καταδρομικόν.

crumb [krʌm] n ψιχίον, ψίχουλο || (fig) ἀπομεινάρι.

crumble ['krʌmbl] vti καταρρέω, θρυμματίζομαι.

crumbly ['krʌmbli] a εὔθρυπτος.

crumpet ['krʌmpit] n εἶδος κέῖκ.

crumple ['krʌmpl] *vt* τσαλακώνω, ζαρώνω.

crunch [krʌntʃ] *n* δαγκωνιά || (*sound*) τρίξιμο || *vt* μασῶ, τραγανίζω || ~y *a* τραγανιστός.

crusade [kru:'seid] *n* σταυροφορία || ~r *n* σταυροφόρος.

crush [krʌʃ] *n* σύνθλιψις, συνωστισμός || *vt* συνθλίβω || (*a rebellion*) συντρίβω, καταβάλλω || *vi* (*material*) τσαλακώνω || ~ing *a* συντριπτικός.

crust [krʌst] *n* (*of bread*) κόρα || (*of cake etc*) κρούστα || (*of earth etc*) φλοιός, κρούστα.

crutch [krʌtʃ] *n* δεκανίκι, πατερίτσα.

crux [krʌks] *n* οὐσία, κεντρικόν σημεῖον.

cry [krai] *vi* (*sell etc*) διαλαλῶ || (*shout*) φωνάζω, βάζω τίς φωνές || (*weep*) κλαίω, θρηνῶ || *n* φωνή, κλάμα || ~ing *a* ἐπείγων, κραυγαλέα.

crypt [kript] *n* κρύπτη.

cryptic ['kriptik] *a* μυστικός, δυσνόητος.

crystal ['kristl] *n* (*natural form*) κρύσταλλος || (*clear glass*) κρύσταλλον || ~-clear *a* κρυστάλλινος || ~lize *vti* (*lit*) (ἀπο)-κρυσταλλώνω || (*fig*) (ἀπο)κρυσταλλοῦμαι.

cub [kʌb] *n* νεογνόν ζῶον.

cube [kju:b] *n* (*figure*) κύβος.

cubic ['kju:bik] *a* κυβικός.

cubicle ['kju:bikəl] *n* θαλαμίσκος.

cubism ['kju:bizəm] *n* κυβισμός.

cuckoo ['kuku:] *n* κοῦκος || (*fig*) χαζός || ~ clock *n* ρολόι κούκου.

cucumber ['kju:kʌmbə*] *n* ἀγγούρι.

cuddle ['kʌdl] *vti* ἀγκαλιάζω, κουκουλώνομαι || *n* ἀγκάλιασμα.

cue [kju:] *n* (*hint*) νύξι, ὑπαινιγμός || (*in billiards*) στέκα.

cuff [kʌf] *n* (*of shirt, coat etc*) μανικέτι || (*US*) = turnup || ~link *n* μανικετόκουμπα.

cuisine [kwi'zi:n] *n* μαγειρική.

cul-de-sac ['kʌldə'sæk] *n* ἀδιέξοδον.

culinary ['kʌlinəri] *a* μαγειρικός.

culminate ['kʌlmineit] *vi* ἀποκορυφώνομαι, μεσουρανῶ.

culmination [kʌlmi'neiʃən] *n* μεσουράνημα, κολοφών.

culprit ['kʌlprit] *n* ἔνοχος.

cult [kʌlt] *n* (*religious*) λατρεία || (*mode*) μόδα, λόξα.

cultivate ['kʌltiveit] *vt* καλλιεργῶ || ~d *a* καλλιεργημένος.

cultivation [kʌlti'veiʃən] *n* καλλιέργεια.

cultural ['kʌltʃərəl] *a* πνευματικός, μορφωτικός.

culture ['kʌltʃə*] *n* (*refinement*) καλλιέργεια || (*intellectual development*) ἀνάπτυξις, κουλτούρα || ~d *a* μορφωμένος, καλλιεργημένος.

cumbersome ['kʌmbəsəm] *a* ἐνοχλητικός, βαρύς, δυσκίνητος.

cumulative ['kju:mjulətiv] *a* ἐπισωρευτικός, ἀθροιστικός.

cunning ['kʌniŋ] *n* πανουργία, καπατσοσύνη || *a* πονηρός, τετραπέρατος.

cup [kʌp] *n* κούπα, φλυτζάνι || (*prize*) κύπελλον || ~board ['kʌbəd] *n* ντουλάπι, ἀρμάρι || ~ final *n* τελικός (πρωταθλήματος) || ~ful *n* φλυτζανιά.

Cupid ['kju:pid] *n* Ἔρως.

cupola ['kju:pələ] *n* θόλος, τροῦλλος.

cup-tie ['kʌptai] *n* ἡμιτελικός (ἀγών).

curable ['kjuərəbl] *a* ἰάσιμος, πού γιατρεύεται.

curator [kjuə'reitə*] *n* ἔφορος (μουσείου).

curb [kə:b] *vt* χαλιναγωγῶ, ἐλέγχω || *n* χαλινός, φραγμός || βλ καί kerb(stone).

curfew ['kə:fju:] *n* σβέσις φώτων.

curiosity [kjuəri'ɔsiti] *n* περιέργεια || (*strange object*) περίεργον ἀντικείμενον.

curious ['kjuəriəs] *a* (*philoperiergos*) (*strange*) περίεργος, παράξενος || ~ly *ad* περιέργως.

curl [kə:l] *n* βόστρυχος, μπούκλα || (*of lips etc*) στρίψιμο || *vti* (*hair etc*) σγουραίνω || (*lips*) στρίβω, στραβώνω || (*wrap*) τυλίγω || ~er *n* ρολλά, μπικουτί.

curlew ['kə:lu:] *n* νουμήνιος.

curling ['kə:liŋ] *n* κατσάρωμα.

curly ['kə:li] *a* κατσαρός, σγουρός.

currant ['kʌrənt] *n* Κορινθιακή σταφίς.

currency ['kʌrənsi] *n* νόμισμα, κυκλοφοροῦν νόμισμα || (*of ideas*) κυκλοφορία, πέραση.

current ['kʌrənt] *n* ρεῦμα, ροή, ρέμα || *a* κυκλοφορῶν, ἐν χρήσει || ~ account *n* τρέχων λογαριασμός || ~ affairs *npl* ἐπίκαιρα || ~ly *ad* γενικῶς, κοινῶς.

curriculum [kə'rikjuləm] *n* κύκλος μαθημάτων || ~ vitae *n* περίληψις προσόντων.

curry ['kʌri] *n* κάρρι || ~ powder *n* σκόνη κάρρι.

curse [kə:s] *vi* βλαστημῶ, ὑβρίζω || *vt* καταριέμαι, ἀναθεματίζω || *n* κατάρα, ἀνάθεμα || (*bad language*) βλαστημιά.

cursory ['kə:səri] *a* γρήγορος, βιαστικός.

curt [kə:t] *a* ἀπότομος, κοφτός.

curtail [kə:'teil] *vt* περικόπτω, περιορίζω.

curtain ['kə:tn] *n* (*esp at window*) κουρτίνα || (*theat*) αὐλαία, παραπέτασμα.

curtsy ['kə:tsi] *n* ὑπόκλισις || *vi* κάνω ὑπόκλισιν.

curve [kə:v] *n* καμπή.

cushion ['kuʃən] *n* μαξιλαράκι.

custard ['kʌstəd] *n* ψημένη κρέμα.

custodian [kʌs'təudiən] *n* φύλακας, ἐπιστάτης.

custody ['kʌstədi] *n* ἐπιτήρησις, κηδεμονία || (*under arrest*) κράτησις.

custom ['kʌstəm] *n* (*fashion*) ἔθιμον, συνήθεια || (*business*) πελατεία || ~s *n* (*taxes*) δασμοί || C~s *n* (*place*) τελωνεῖον || ~ary *a* ἐθιμικός, συνήθης || ~er *n* πελάτης || ~-made *a* καμωμένο ἐπί παραγγελία || ~s officer *n* τελωνειακός ὑπάλληλος.

cut [kʌt] *vt* (*irreg v*) (*divide*) κόβω, χαράζω

‖ (wound) πληγώνω, πονῶ ‖ (reduce)
κατεβάζω (τιμές) ‖ n (sharp stroke) κόψις,
κόψιμο ‖ (wound) τομή, κόψιμο, πληγή
‖ (reduction) περικοπή, μείωσις ‖ (share)
μερίδιον.
cute [kju:t] a χαριτωμένος.
cuticle ['kju:tikl] n (on nail) ἐπιδερμίς.
cutlery ['kʌtləri] n μαχαιροπήρουνα.
cutlet ['kʌtlit] n κοτολέττα.
cutout ['kʌtaut] n (elec) διακόπτης.
cut-price ['kʌtprais] a τιμή ἠλαττωμένη.
cutting ['kʌtiŋ] n αἰχμή, κόψη.
cyanide ['saiənaid] n κυανίδη.
cybernetics [saibə'netiks] n κυβερνητική.
cyclamen ['sikləmən] n κυκλάμινον.
cycle ['saikl] n (bicycle) ποδήλατον ‖ (series)
κύκλος, περίοδος ‖ (of poems etc) κύκλος
‖ vi πηγαίνω μέ ποδήλατο.
cycling ['saikliŋ] n ποδηλατοδρομία, ποδήλατο.
cyclist ['saiklist] n ποδηλατιστής.
cyclone ['saikləun] n κυκλών.
cygnet ['signit] n μικρός κύκνος.
cylinder ['silində*] n κύλινδρος ‖ (of gas etc)
φιάλη, μπουκάλα ‖ ~ block n συγκρότημα κυλίνδρου ‖ ~ capacity n ὄγκος
κυλίνδρου ‖ ~ head n κεφαλή κυλίνδρου.
cymbals ['simbəlz] npl κύμβαλα.
cynic ['sinik] n κυνικός ‖ ~al a κυνικός,
δύσπιστος ‖ ~ism ['sinisizəm] n κυνι-
σμός, χονδροκουβέντα.
cypress ['saipris] n κυπαρίσσι.
Cyprus ['saiprəs] n Κύπρος.
cyst [sist] n κύστις.
czar [za:*] n τσάρος ‖ ~ina n τσαρίνα.
Czech [tʃek] a Τσεχικός ‖ n Τσέχος ‖
~oslovakia n Τσεχοσλοβακία.

D, d

dab [dæb] vt ἐπιψαύω, ἐπαλείφω ‖ n (tap)
ἐλαφρό κτύπημα, φάπα ‖ (smear) μικρή
ποσότης, λίγο.
dad(dy) ['dæd(i)] n μπαμπᾶς, μπαμπάκας ‖
daddy-long-legs n τιπούλη, ἀλογατάκι.
daffodil ['dæfədil] n ἀσφόδελος.
daft [da:ft] a ἀνόητος, τρελλός.
dagger ['dægə*] n ἐγχειρίδιον, στιλέττο.
dahlia ['deiliə] n ντάλια.
daily ['deili] a ἡμερήσιος ‖ n καθημερινή
(ἐφημερίς).
dainty ['deinti] a κομψός, νόστιμος.
dairy ['deəri] n (shop) γαλακτοπωλεῖον,
γαλατάδικο ‖ (on farm) γαλακτοκομεῖον
‖ a γαλακτοκομικό.
daisy ['deizi] n μαργαρίτα.
dally ['dæli] vi χασομερῶ.
dam [dæm] n (for water) φράγμα, ἀνάχωμα
‖ vt φράσσω.
damage ['dæmidʒ] n βλάβη, ζημιά ‖ vt

βλάπτω, ζημιώνω ‖ ~s npl (law) ἀποζημιώσις.
dame [deim] n κυρία, κυρά.
damn [dæm] vt καταδικάζω ‖ a (col)
διαβολο- ‖ ~ it! νά πάρη ὁ διάβολος!, νά
πάρη ἡ εὐχή! ‖ ~ing a καταδικαστικός,
ἐπιβαρυντικός.
damp [dæmp] a ὑγρός, νοτερός ‖ n ὑγρασία, ὑγρότης ‖ vt (also ~en) ὑγραίνω,
μουσκεύω ‖ (discourage) μειώνω, ἐλαττώνω, κόβω ‖ ~ness n ὑγρασία, ὑγρότης.
damson ['dæmzən] n δαμάσκηνον.
dance [da:ns] n χορός ‖ (party) χορευτική
συγκέντρωσις, πάρτυ ‖ vi χορεύω ‖ ~
hall n χορευτικόν κέντρον ‖ ~r n
χορευτής, χορεύτρια.
dancing ['da:nsiŋ] n χορός.
dandelion ['dændilaiən] n ἀγριοραδίκι.
dandruff ['dændrəf] n πιτυρίδα.
dandy ['dændi] n κομψευόμενος, δανδής.
Dane [dein] n Δανός.
danger ['deindʒə*] n κίνδυνος ‖ ~! (sign)
προσοχή! ‖ in ~ διατρέχω κίνδυνον ‖
~ous a ἐπικίνδυνος ‖ ~ously ad ἐπι-
κινδύνως.
dangle ['dæŋgl] vti αἰωροῦμαι, ταλαντεύομαι, κρέμομαι.
Danish ['deiniʃ] a Δανικός ‖ n Δανική
γλῶσσα.
dare [deə*] vt τολμῶ, ἀψηφῶ ‖ vi: to ~
(to) do sth τολμῶ, κοτῶ ‖ I ~ say ἀσφαλῶς, πιθανῶς.
daring ['deəriŋ] a τολμηρός, ἄφοβος.
dark [da:k] a (dim) σκοτεινός, μαῦρος ‖
(gloomy) σκοτεινός, μελαγχολικός ‖
(colour) μελαχροινός, μελαψός ‖ n
σκοτάδι ‖ (ignorance) ἐν πλήρει ἀγνοία ‖
after ~ ἀφοῦ νυχτώσει ‖ D~ Ages npl
Μεσαίων ‖ ~en vti σκοτεινιάζω ‖ ~ness
n σκότος, σκοτάδι ‖ ~ room n σκοτεινός
θάλαμος.
darling ['da:liŋ] n πολυαγαπημένος.
darn [da:n] n μαντάρισμα ‖ vt μπαλώνω,
καρικώνω.
dart [da:t] n (quick move) ὁρμή ‖ (weapon)
βέλος, σαΐτα ‖ vi ἐξακοντίζω, ὁρμῶ ‖ ~s
n σαΐτα ‖ ~board n στόχος σαΐτας.
dash [dæʃ] n (rush) ἐξόρμησις ‖ (waves)
χτύπημα, πλάτς ‖ (mark) παῦλα ‖ vt (lit)
ρίχνω, χτυπῶ, καταστρέφω ‖ vi ἐφορμῶ,
πέφτω ‖ ~board n ταμπλώ ‖ ~ing a
(person) ὁρμητικός, ζωηρός.
data ['deitə] npl δεδομένα, στοιχεῖα ‖ ~
processing n κατεργασία στοιχείων.
date [deit] n (point in time) χρονολογία,
ἡμερομηνία ‖ (with person) ραντεβοῦ ‖
(fruit) χουρμᾶς ‖ vt (letter etc) βάζω
ἡμερομηνία ‖ (person) δίνω ραντεβοῦ ‖
~d a μέ χρονολογίαν . . . ‖ ~line n
γραμμή ἀλλαγῆς ἡμερομηνίας.
dative ['deitiv] a δοτική.
daub [dɔ:b] vt (smear) πασαλείβω, ἀλείφω
‖ (paint badly) μουντζουρώνω.

daughter ['dɔːtə*] *n* θυγατέρα, κόρη ‖ **~-in-law** *n* νύφη.

dawdle ['dɔːdl] *vi* χασομερῶ, κοπροσκυλιάζω.

dawn [dɔːn] *n* αὐγή ‖ *vi* ὑποφώσκω, χαράζω ‖ *(become apparent)* ἀποκαλύπτω.

day [dei] *n* ἡμέρα, μέρα ‖ *(24 hours)* εἰκοσιτετράωρον ‖ *(date, time)* ἡμερομηνία ‖ *(daylight)* φῶς τῆς ἡμέρας ‖ ~ **by** ~ ἡμέρα μέ τήν ἡμέρα ‖ ~**break** *n* αὐγή, χάραμα ‖ ~**dream** *n* ὀνειροπόλημα, ρεμβασμός ‖ *vi* ὀνειροπολῶ, ρεμβάζω ‖ ~**light** *n* φῶς τῆς ἡμέρας ‖ ~**time** *n* ἡμέρα.

daze [deiz] *vt* θαμπώνω, γυαλίζω ‖ *n* θάμβος, ζάλη.

dazzle ['dæzl] *vt* θαμπώνω, τυφλώνω ‖ *n* θάμβωμα, θάμβος.

deacon ['diːkən] *n* διάκονος.

dead [ded] *a* νεκρός, πεθαμένος ‖ *(without feeling)* ἀναίσθητος ‖ *(exact)* πλήρης, ἀκριβής ‖ *ad* τελείως, ἀκριβῶς, ἀπολύτως ‖ **the** ~ *npl* οἱ νεκροί, οἱ πεθαμένοι ‖ ~**en** *vt* νεκρώνω, κατασιγάζω ‖ ~ **end** *n* ἀδιέξοδον ‖ ~ **heat** *n* ἰσοπαλία ‖ ~**line** *n* *(χρονικόν)* ὅριον ‖ ~**lock** *n* ἀδιέξοδον ‖ ~**ly** *a* θανατηφόρος, θανάσιμος ‖ ἀδυσώπητος, ἀφόρητος ‖ ~**pan** *a* (ἠθοποιός) χωρίς ἔκφρασιν ‖ ~**wood** *n* (*fig*) ἄχρηστος, χαραμοφάης.

deaf [def] *a* κουφός ‖ ~**-aid** *n* ἀκουστικόν κωφῶν ‖ ~**en** *vt* (ξε)κουφαίνω ‖ ~**ening** *a* ἐκκωφαντικός ‖ ~**ness** *n* κωφότης, κουφαμάρα ‖ ~**-mute** *n* κωφάλαλος.

deal [diːl] *(irreg v)* *n* συμφωνία, δουλειά ‖ *vti* *(cards)* μοιράζω, δίνω ‖ **a great** ~ **of** ποσότης, πολύ ‖ **to** ~ **with** *vt* ἀντιμετωπίζω, λαμβάνω μέτρα ‖ ~**er** *n* ἔμπορος, ἀντιπρόσωπος ‖ *(cards)* μοιραστής.

dear [diə*] *a* *(beloved)* ἀγαπητός, προσφιλής ‖ *(expensive)* ἀκριβός, δαπανηρός ‖ *n* προσφιλής, ἀγαπημένος ‖ ~ **me!** Θεέ μου! ‖ **D**~ **Sir** ἀξιότιμε, ἀγαπητέ κύριε ‖ **D**~ **John** ἀγαπητέ Γιάννη ‖ ~**ly** *ad* *(love)* πολυαγαπημένος ‖ *(pay)* ἀκριβά.

death [deθ] *n* θάνατος ‖ ~**bed** *n* νεκροκρέββατο ‖ ~ **certificate** *n* πιστοποιητικόν θανάτου ‖ ~ **duties** *npl* *(Brit)* φόρος κληρονομίας ‖ ~**ly** *a* νεκρικός, ὠχρός ‖ ~ **penalty** *n* ποινή θανάτου ‖ ~ **rate** *n* θνησιμότης.

debase [di'beis] *vt* ξεφτελίζω, ὑποβιβάζω.

debatable [di'beitəbl] *a* συζητήσιμος.

debate [di'beit] *n* συζήτησις ‖ *vt* συζητῶ ‖ *(consider)* σκέπτομαι.

debauched [di'bɔːtʃt] *a* διεφθαρμένος, ἀκόλαστος.

debauchery [di'bɔːtʃəri] *n* ἀκολασία.

debit ['debit] *n* δοῦναι, παθητικόν ‖ *vt* χρεώνω.

debris ['debriː] *n* συντρίμματα, μπάζα.

debt [det] *n* χρέος, ὀφειλή ‖ **to be in** ~ χρεωστῶ ‖ ~**or** *n* ὀφειλέτης, χρεώστης.

début ['deibuː] *n* πρώτη ἐμφάνισις, ντεμποῦτο.

decade ['dekeid] *n* δεκαετία.

decadence ['dekədəns] *n* παρακμή.

decanter [di'kæntə*] *n* καράφα.

decay [di'kei] *n* παρακμή, φθορά, κατάπτωσις ‖ *vi* παρακμάζω, μαραίνομαι.

decease [di'siːs] *n* θάνατος ‖ ~**d** *n* μακαρίτης.

deceit [di'siːt] *n* ἀπάτη, δόλος ‖ ~**ful** *a* δόλιος, ἀπατηλός.

deceive [di'siːv] *vt* ἐξαπατῶ, κοροϊδεύω.

decelerate [di:'seləreit] *vti* ἐπιβραδύνω, κόβω ταχύτητα.

December [di'sembə*] *n* Δεκέμβρης.

decency ['diːsənsi] *n* *(fit behaviour)* εὐπρέπεια, σεμνότης ‖ *(respectability)* κοσμιότης.

decent ['diːsənt] *a* *(respectable)* εὐπρεπής, συμμαζεμένος ‖ *(pleasant)* ἀρκετό καλό.

decentralization [diːsentrəlai'zeiʃən] *n* ἀποκέντρωσις.

deception [di'sepʃən] *n* ἐξαπάτησις, τέχνασμα.

deceptive [di'septiv] *a* ἀπατηλός.

decibel ['desibel] *n* ντεσιμπέλ.

decide [di'said] *vt* *(settle)* κρίνω, ἀποφασίζω ‖ *vi* *(determine)* ἀποφασίζω, καταλήγω ‖ **to** ~ **to do** ἀποφασίζω ‖ ~**d** *a* ἀποφασισμένος, ὁριστικός ‖ ~**dly** *ad* ἀποφασιστικά, βεβαίως.

deciduous [di'sidjuəs] *a* φυλλοβόλος.

decimal ['desiməl] *a* δεκαδικός ‖ *n* δεκαδικόν ‖ ~ **point** *n* ὑποδιαστολή ‖ ~ **system** *n* δεκαδικόν σύστημα.

decimate ['desimeit] *vt* ἀποδεκατίζω.

decipher [di'saifə*] *vt* ξεδιαλύνω, βγάζω.

decision [di'siʒən] *n* ἀπόφασις.

decisive [di'saisiv] *a* ἀποφασιστικός.

deck [dek] *n* *(naut)* κατάστρωμα, κουβέρτα ‖ *(of bus)* ὄροφος ‖ *(of cards)* τράπουλα ‖ ~**chair** *n* σαίζ-λόγκ ‖ ~ **hand** *n* ναύτης καταστρώματος.

declaration [deklə'reiʃən] *n* δήλωσις, διακήρυξις.

declare [di'kleə*] *vt* *(state)* δηλώνω ‖ *(war)* κηρύσσω ‖ *(in customs)* δηλώνω.

decline [di'klain] *n* *(decay)* παρακμή, πτῶσις, πέσιμο ‖ *(lessening)* πέσιμο, κατάπτωση ‖ *vt* *(refuse)* ἀρνοῦμαι ‖ *(gram)* κλίνω ‖ *vi* φθίνω, ἐξασθενίζω, ἀδυνατίζω.

declutch [di:'klʌtʃ] *vi* ντεμπραγιάρω.

decode [di:'kəud] *vt* ἀποκρυπτογραφῶ.

decompose [di:kəm'pəuz] *vi* *(rot)* ἀποσυντίθεμαι, σαπίζω.

decomposition [di:kɔmpə'ziʃən] *n* ἀποσύνθεσις.

decontaminate [di:kən'tæmineit] *vt* ἀπολυμαίνω.

décor ['deikɔ:*] *n* διακόσμησις, ντεκόρ.

decorate ['dekəreit] *vt* *(renew paint etc)* χρωματίζω, βάφω ‖ *(adorn)* (δια)κοσμῶ,

D

στολίζω ‖ (*give medal etc*) παρασημοφορῶ.

decoration [dekə'reiʃən] *n* (*of house*) διακόσμησις ‖ παράσημον.

decorative ['dekərətiv] *a* διακοσμητικός.

decorator ['dekəreitə*] *n* διακοσμητής.

decorum [di'kɔ:rəm] *n* εὐπρέπεια.

decoy ['di:kɔi] *n* δέλεαρ, δόλωμα.

decrease [di:'kri:s] *n* μείωσις, ἐλάττωσις ‖
vti μειώνω, ἐλάττοῦμαι.

decree [di'kri:] *n* διάταγμα, βούλευμα.

decrepit [di'krepit] *a* παραγηρασμένος
(*furniture etc*) ξεχαρβαλωμένος.

dedicate ['dedikeit] *vt* ἀφιερώνω.

dedication [dedi'keiʃən] *n* ἀφιέρωσις.

deduce [di'dju:s] *vt* συμπεραίνω.

deduct [di'dʌkt] *vt* ἀφαιρῶ ‖ ~**ion** *n* ἀφαίρεσις, συμπέρασμα ‖ (*in price etc*)
ἔκπτωσις.

deed [di:d] *n* πρᾶξις, ἔργον ‖ (*law*) ἔγγραφον.

deep [di:p] *a* (*water*) βαθύς ‖ (*breath*) βαθεία
‖ (*voice*) βαθειά, βαρειά ‖ **in ~ water** εἰς
μεγάλην δυσκολίαν ‖ ~**en** *vt* ἐκβαθύνω,
βαθαίνω ‖ ~**-freeze** *n* κατάψυξις ‖
~**-seated** *a* βαθειά ριζωμένος.

deer [diə*] *n* ἐλάφι.

deface [di'feis] *vt* παραμορφώνω.

defamation [defə'meiʃən] *n* δυσφήμισις.

default [di'fɔ:lt] *n* παράλειψις, ἀθέτησις ‖
(*law*) ἀπουσία ‖ *vi* παραλείπω καθῆκον,
φυγοδικῶ ‖ **by ~** ἐρήμην ‖ ~**er** *n* φυγόδικος.

defeat [di'fi:t] *n* (*overthrow*) ἀνατροπή,
ματαίωσις ‖ ἦττα, συντριβή ‖ *vt* νικῶ,
ἀνατρέπω ‖ ~**ist** *a* ἡττοπαθής.

defect [di'fekt] *n* ἀτέλεια, ἐλάττωμα ‖
[di'fekt] *vi* λιποτακτῶ ‖ ~**ive** *a* ἐλλιπής,
ἐλαττωματικός.

defence [di'fens] *n* (*mil, sport*) ἄμυνα,
ὑπεράσπισις ‖ δικαιολογία ‖ ~**less** *a*
ἀνυπεράσπιστος.

defend [di'fend] *vt* ὑπερασπίζω ‖ ~**ant** *n*
ἐναγόμενος ‖ ~**er** *n* ὑπερασπιστής,
ὑπέρμαχος.

defensive [di'fensiv] *a* ἀμυντικός ‖ *n* ἄμυνα.

defer [di'fə:*] *vt* ἀναβάλλω ‖ ~**ence**
['defərəns] *n* σεβασμός ‖ ~**ential**
[defə'renʃəl] *a* εὐλαβής, πλήρης σεβα-
σμοῦ.

defiance [di'faiəns] *n* ἀψηφισιά, περιφρόνησις.

defiant [di'faiənt] *a* προκλητικός, ἀψηφῶν.

deficiency [di'fiʃənsi] *n* ἔλλειψις, ἀτέλεια.

deficient [di'fiʃənt] *a* ἀτελής, ἐλλιπής.

deficit ['defisit] *n* ἔλλειμμα.

define [di'fain] *vt* (καθ)ορίζω ‖ (*explain*)
ἐξηγῶ, σαφηνίζω.

definite ['definit] *a* (*fixed*) (καθ)ωρισμένος
‖ (*clear*) σαφής ‖ (*gram*) ὁριστικόν ‖ ~**ly**
ad σαφῶς, ὁριστικῶς.

definition [defi'niʃən] *n* (καθ)ορισμός.

definitive [di'finitiv] *a* ὁριστικός, τελικός

deflate [di:'fleit] *vt* ξεφουσκώνω ‖ (*currency*) ὑποτιμῶ.

deflation [di:'fleiʃən] *n* (*fin*) ὑποτίμησις.

deflect [di'flekt] *vt* ἐκτρέπω, παρεκκλίνω.

deform [di'fɔ:m] *vt* παραμορφώνω, ἀσχη-
μίζω ‖ ~**ed** *a* δύσμορφος, παραμορφωμένος ‖ ~**ity** *n* δυσμορφία, σακατηλίκι.

defraud [di'frɔ:d] *vt* ἐξαπατῶ, κλέβω.

defray [di'frei] *vt* πληρώνω, καταβάλλω.

defrost [di:'frɔst] *vt* (*fridge*) ξεπαγώνω.

deft [deft] *a* ἐπιτήδειος, ἐπιδέξιος.

defunct [di'fʌŋkt] *a* μακαρίτης.

defy [di'fai] *vt* (*challenge*) προκαλῶ ‖
(*ignore*) ἀψηφῶ.

degenerate [di'dʒenəreit] *vi* ἐκφυλίζομαι ‖
[di'dʒenərit] *a* ἐκφυλισμένος.

degradation [degrə'deiʃən] *n* ξεφτελισμός,
ὑποβιβασμός.

degrading [di'greidiŋ] *a* ξεφτελιστικός,
ταπεινωτικός.

degree [di'gri:] *n* (*step, stage*) βαθμός ‖
(*univ*) πτυχίον ‖ (*measurement*) μοῖρα ‖
by ~s βαθμηδόν.

dehydrated [di:hai'dreitid] *a* ἀφυδατω-
μένος.

de-ice [di:'ais] *vt* (*windscreen*) ξεπαγώνω.

deign [dein] *vi* καταδέχομαι, εὐαρεστοῦμαι.

deity ['di:iti] *n* θεότης.

dejected [di'dʒektid] *a* κατηφής, ἄκεφος.

dejection [di'dʒekʃən] *n* κατήφεια, ἀκεφιά.

delay [di'lei] *vt* ἀναβάλλω, καθυστερῶ ‖
vi βραδύνω, ἀργῶ ‖ *n* ἀργοπορία, ἀναβολή, ἐπιβράδυνσις ‖ **without ~** ἄνευ
ἀναβολῆς ‖ ~**ed action** *n* ἐπιβραδυνο-
μένη, καθυστερημένη.

delegate ['deligit] *n* ἀντιπρόσωπος, ἀπεσταλμένος ‖ ['deligeit] *vt* ἐντέλλομαι,
ἐξουσιοδοτῶ.

delegation [deli'geiʃən] *n* ἀντιπροσωπεία.

delete [di'li:t] *vt* ἀφαιρῶ, σβήνω.

deliberate [di'libərit] *a* (*intentional*) ἐσκεμμένος ‖ (*slow*) ἀργός, ἐπιφυλακτικός ‖
[di'libəreit] *vi* διαλογίζομαι, συνδι-
ασκέπτομαι ‖ ~**ly** *ad* ἐσκεμμένως.

delicacy ['delikəsi] *n* (*daintiness*) εὐαισθησία, λεπτότης ‖ (*refinement*) λεπτότης ‖
(*choice food*) λιχουδιές.

delicate ['delikit] *a* (*fine*) λεπτός, ἁπαλός ‖
(*fragile*) λεπτός ‖ (*situation*) λεπτός,
δύσκολος ‖ (*med*) λεπτή, εὐπαθής ‖ ~**ly**
ad μέ λεπτότητα.

delicious [di'liʃəs] *a* νόστιμος, εὐχάριστος.

delight [di'lait] *n* εὐχαρίστησις, τέρψις ‖
vt χαιροποιῶ, τέρπω ‖ ~**ful** *a* γοητευτικός, πολύ εὐχάριστος.

delinquency [di'liŋkwənsi] *n* πλημμέλημα,
ἀδίκημα.

delinquent [di'liŋkwənt] *n* ἐγκληματίας,
παραπτωματίας ‖ *a* παραπτωματικός ‖
(*econ*) ἐκπρόθεσμος.

delirium [di'liriəm] *n* παραλήρημα.

deliver [di'livə*] *vt* (*distribute*) (παρα)δίδω,
διανέμω ‖ (*pronounce*) ἐκφωνῶ, μεταδίδω

|| (*free*) ἀπαλλάσσω, ἐλευθερώνω, σώζω || ~y *n* παράδοσις, διανομή || (*of speech*) παράδοσις, ἐκφώνησις.

delouse ['di:'laus] *vt* ξεψειριάζω.

delta ['deltə] *n* δέλτα.

delude [di'lu:d] *vt* ἐξαπατῶ.

deluge ['delju:dʒ] *n* κακακλυσμός.

delusion [di'lu:ʒən] *n* (αὐτ)ἀπάτη.

de luxe [di'lʌks] *a* ντέ λούξ.

demand [di'ma:nd] *vt* ἀπαιτῶ, ἀξιώνω || *n* ἀξίωσις, ἀπαίτησις || (*call for a commodity*) ζήτησις || in ~ ζητοῦμαι || on ~ ἐπί τῇ ἐμφανίσει || ~ing *a* ἀπαιτητικός, διεκδικητικός.

demarcation [di:ma:'keiʃən] *n* ὁροθεσία.

demented [di'mentid] *a* παράφρων, τρελλός.

demi- ['demi] *prefix* ἡμι-.

demise [di'maiz] *n* ἀποβίωσις.

demobilization ['di:məubilai'zeiʃən] *n* ἀποστράτευσις.

democracy [di'mɔkrəsi] *n* δημοκρατία.

democrat ['deməkræt] *n* δημοκράτης || ~ic *a* δημοκρατικός || ~ically *ad* δημοκρατικῶς.

demolish [di'mɔliʃ] *vt* (*lit*) κατεδαφίζω, κατακρημνίζω || (*fig*) συντρίβω.

demolition [demə'liʃən] *n* κατεδάφισις.

demon ['di:mən] *n* δαίμων.

demonstrate ['demənstreit] *vt* ἀποδεικνύω || (*protest*) διαδηλώνω.

demonstration [demən'streiʃən] *n* ἀπόδειξις, ἐπίδειξις || (*pol*) διαδήλωσις.

demonstrative [di'mɔnstrətiv] *a* ἐκδηλωτικός || (*gram*) δεικτικός.

demonstrator ['demənstreitə*] (*pol*) διαδηλωτής.

demoralize [di'mɔrəlaiz] *vt* ἐξαχρειώνω, ἀποθαρρύνω.

demote [di'məut] *vt* ὑποβιβάζω.

demure [di'mjuə*] *a* σοβαρός, μετριόφρων.

den [den] *n* τρώγλη, φωλιά || (*room*) καμαρούλα.

denationalize [di:'næʃnəlaiz] *vt* ἀπεθνικοποιῶ.

denial [di'naiəl] *n* ἄρνησις.

denigrate ['denigreit] *vt* δυσφημῶ.

Denmark ['denma:k] *n* Δανία.

denomination [dinɔmi'neiʃən] *n* (*name*) ὀνομασία || (*rel*) δόγμα, θρήσκευμα.

denote [di'nəut] *vt* δείχνω, ἐμφαίνω.

denounce [di'nauns] *vt* καταγγέλω.

dense [dens] *a* πυκνός || (*stupid*) βλάκας, ἀμαθής || ~ly *ad* πυκνῶς.

density [i'densiti] *n* πυκνότης.

dent [dent] *n* κοίλωμα, βαθούλωμα || *v* κοιλαίνω, ζουλίζω.

dental ['dentl] *a* (*gram*) ὀδοντόφωνος || ~ surgeon *n* = dentist.

dentist ['dentist] *n* ὀδοντίατρος |, ~ry *n* ὀδοντιατρική.

denture ['dentʃə*] *n* ὀδοντοστοιχία, μασέλα.

denude [di'nju:d] *vt* ἀπογυμνώνω.

deny [di'nai] *vt* (*declare untrue*) διαψεύδω ἀρνοῦμαι || (*disown*) ἀπαρνιέμαι, ἀνακαλῶ || (*refuse*) ἀρνοῦμαι.

deodorant |di:'əudərənt] *n* ἀποσμητικόν.

depart [di'pa:t] *vi* ἀναχωρῶ.

department [di'pa:tmənt] *n* τμῆμα, ὑπηρεσία, κλάδος || (*univ, sch*) τμῆμα || (*pol*) διεύθυνσις, γραφεῖον || (*US*) ὑπουργεῖον || ~al [di:pa:t'mentl] *a* ὑπηρεσιακός | ~ store *n* μεγάλο ἐμπορικό κατάστημα.

departure [di'pa:tʃə*] *n* ἀναχώρησις || new ~ *n* νέα τάσις.

depend [di'pend] *vi*: it ~s ἐξαρτᾶται || to ~ on *vti* ἐξαρτῶμαι ἀπό || ~able *a* ἀξιόπιστος || (*car, machine etc*) ἀπολύτου ἀσφαλείας || ~ent *n* (*person*) προστατευόμενος || *a* (+ *on*) ἐξαρτώμενος ἀπό ~ence *n* ἐξάρτησις || (*trust*) ἐμπιστοσύνη.

depict [di'pikt] *vt* περιγράφω, ἀπεικονίζω.

depleted [di'pli:tid] *a* ἐξηντλημένος.

deplorable [di'plɔ:rəbl] *a* θλιβερός, ἀξιοθρήνητος.

deplore [di'plɔ:*] *vt* θρηνῶ, λυποῦμαι πολύ.

deploy [di'plɔi] *vt* ἀναπτύσσω.

depopulation ['di:pɔpju'leiʃən] *n* ἐλάττωσις πληθυσμοῦ.

deport [di'pɔ:t] *vt* ἐκτοπίζω, ἀπελαύνω || ~ation *n* ἀπέλασις, ἐκτοπισμός || ~ment *n* συμπεριφορά.

depose [di'pəuz] *vt* ἐκθρονίζω.

deposit [di'pɔzit] *n* κατάθεσις || (*down payment*) προκαταβολή, καπάρο || (*chem*) ἵζημα, κατακάθι || *vt* (*bank*) (παρα)καταθέτω, ἀποταμιεύω || (*place*) τοποθετῶ βάζω || ~ account *n* λογαριασμός καταθέσεως || ~or *n* καταθέτης.

depot ['depəu] *n* ἀποθήκη || (*mil*) βάσις ἀνεφοδιασμοῦ || (*US: for buses etc*) σταθμός.

deprave [di'preiv] *vt* διαφθείρω, ἐξαχρειώνω || ~d *a* διεφθαρμένος.

depravity [di'præviti] *n* ἀχρειότης, διαφθορά.

depreciate [di'pri:ʃieit] *vt* ὑποτιμῶ || *vi* ὑποτιμοῦμαι, πέφτω.

depreciation [dipri:ʃi'eiʃən] *n* ὑποτίμησις πέσιμο.

depress [di'pres] *vt* (*make sad*) συντρίβω ἀποθαρρύνω || (*press down*) καταπιέζω κατεβάζω || ~ed *a* (*person*) μελαγχολικός, ἀποκαρδιωμένος || (*area*) φτωχή (συνοικία), ὑποανάπτυκτος || ~ing *a* καταθλιπτικός, ἀποθαρρυντικό || ~ion *n* (*econ*) ὕφεσις, κρίσις || (*hollow*) κοίλωμα, λακούβα || (*meteorology*) βαρομετρική ὕφεσις.

deprivation [depri'veiʃən] *n* στέρησις.

deprive [di'praiv] *vt* (+ *of*) στερῶ τοῦ ~d *a* ἐστερημένος.

depth [depθ] *n* βάθος, πυθμήν, βαθύτης in the ~s of στήν καρδιά τοῦ

deputation [depju'teiʃən] n ἀποστολή, ἐπιτροπή.

deputize ['depjutaiz] vi (+for) ἀναπληρῶ, ἀντιπροσωπεύω.

deputy ['depjuti] a ἀναπληρωτικός, βοηθητικός ‖ n ἀναπληρωτής, ἀντικαταστάτης.

derail [di'reil] vt ἐκτροχιάζω ‖ ~ment n ἐκτροχίασις.

deranged [di'reindʒd] a παράφρων, στριμμένος.

derby ['da:bi] n (US: bowler hat) ἡμίψηλον, μελόν.

derelict ['derilikt] a ἐγκαταλελειμμένος.

deride [di'raid] vt χλευάζω, ἐμπαίζω.

derision [di'riʒən] n ἐμπαιγμός, χλευασμός.

derisory [di'raisəri] a σκωπτικός, εἰρωνικός.

derivation [deri'veiʃən] n καταγωγή ‖ (math etc) παραγωγή.

derivative [di'rivətiv] a παράγωγος.

derive [di'raiv] vt παράγω, ἀποκομίζω ‖ vi κατάγομαι, παράγομαι.

dermatitis [də:mə'taitis] n δερματῖτις.

derogatory [di'rɔgətəri] a ξεφτελιστικός, δυσφημιστικός, μειωτικός.

derrick ['derik] n γερανός ‖ (of oil well) ἱκρίωμα γεωτρήσεως.

desalination [di:sæli'neiʃən] n ἀφαλάτωσις.

descend [di'send] vti κατεβαίνω ‖ (rain etc) πέφτω ‖ vi: to ~ from κατάγομαι ‖ ~ant n ἀπόγονος.

descent [di'sent] n (coming down) κάθοδος, κατέβασμα ‖ (origin) καταγωγή.

describe [dis'kraib] vt περιγράφω.

description [dis'kripʃən] n περιγραφή ‖ (kind, sort) εἶδος, τύπος.

descriptive [dis'kriptiv] a περιγραφικός.

desecrate ['desikreit] vt βεβηλώνω.

desert ['dezət] n ἔρημος ‖ [di'zə:t] vt ἐγκαταλείπω ‖ vi (mil) λιποτακτῶ ‖ ~er n λιποτάκτης ‖ ~ion n λιποταξία.

deserve [di'zə:v] vt ἀξίζω.

deserving [di'zə:viŋ] a ἄξιος, ἀξιόλογος.

design [di'zain] n (plan) σχέδιον, σκοπός, ἐπιδίωξις ‖ (drawing) σχέδιον, τύπος ‖ (the art) σχέδιον ‖ vt (plan) σχεδιάζω ‖ (purpose) προορίζω ‖ to have ~s on ἔχω βλέψεις σέ.

designate ['dezigneit] vt (προ)ὁρίζω, διορίζω ‖ ['dezignit] a ἐκλεγείς.

designation [dezig'neiʃən] n ὁρισμός, τίτλος.

designer [di'zainə*] n (tech) μελετητής ‖ (art) σχεδιαστής.

desirability [dizaiərə'biliti] n τό ἐπιθυμητόν.

desirable [di'zaiərəbl] a ἐπιθυμητός.

desire [di'zaiə*] n ἐπιθυμία, πόθος ‖ vt ἐπιθυμῶ, ποθῶ ‖ (ask for) ζητῶ.

desk [desk] n γραφεῖον ‖ (of student) θρανίον.

desolate ['desəlit] a (barren, dismal) ἔρημος.

desolation [desə'leiʃən] n ἐρήμωσις, καταστροφή

despair [dis'pεə*] n ἀπόγνωσις, ἀπελπισία ‖ vi (+ of) ἀπελπίζομαι διά.

despatch [dis'pætʃ] = dispatch.

desperate ['despərit] a (hopeless) ἀπελπιστικός ‖ (reckless) ἀπεγνωσμένος, σκληρός ‖ ~ly ad ἀπεγνωσμένως.

desperation [despə'reiʃən] n ἀπόγνωσις.

despicable [dis'pikəbl] a ἀηδής, σιχαμερός εὐτελής.

despise [dis'paiz] vt περιφρονῶ.

despite [dis'pait] prep παρά, εἰς πεῖσμα.

despondent [dis'pɔndənt] a ἀπελπισμένος, συντετριμμένος.

dessert [di'zə:t] n ἐπιδόρπιον ‖ ~spoon n κουταλάκι τοῦ γλυκοῦ.

destination [desti'neiʃən] n προορισμός.

destine ['destin] vt προορίζω.

destiny ['destini] n προορισμός ‖ (fate) μοῖρα.

destitute ['destitju:t] a ἄπορος.

destroy [dis'trɔi] vt καταστρέφω ‖ ~er n (naut) ἀντιτορπιλλικόν.

destruction [dis'trʌkʃən] n καταστροφή.

destructive [dis'trʌktiv] a καταστρεπτικός.

detach [di'tætʃ] vt ἀποσπῶ, ἀφαιρῶ ‖ ~able a ἀφαιρούμενον, κινητός ‖ ~ed a (attitude) ἀνεππρέαστος ‖ ~ment n (mil) ἀπόσπασμα ‖ ἀπόσπασις, ἀμεροληψία.

detail ['di:teil] n λεπτομέρεια, ἀπόσπασμα ‖ vt ἐκθέτω λεπτομερῶς ‖ (mil) ὁρίζω, ἀποσπῶ ‖ in ~ λεπτομερῶς.

detain [di'tein] vt κρατῶ, ἐμποδίζω ‖ (imprison) φυλακίζω, κρατῶ.

detect [di'tekt] vt ἀνακαλύπτω, διακρίνω ‖ ~ion n ἀνακάλυψις ‖ ~ive n μυστικός ἀστυνομικός, ντετέκτιβ ‖ ~ive story n ἀστυνομικόν μυθιστόρημα ‖ ~or n ἀνιχνευτής.

detention [di'tenʃən] n κράτησις.

deter [di'tə:*] vt ἀποτρέπω.

detergent [di'tə:dʒənt] n ἀπολυμαντικόν, καθαρτικόν.

deteriorate [di'tiəriəreit] vi ἐπιδεινοῦμαι, χειροτερεύω.

deterioration [ditiəriə'reiʃən] n ἐπιδείνωσις.

determination [ditə:mi'neiʃən] n ἀπόφασις, ἀποφασιστικότης.

determine [di'tə:min] vt (καθ)ὁρίζω, ἀποφασίζω ‖ ~d a ἀποφασιστικός, ἀποφασισμένος.

deterrent [di'terənt] n προληπτικόν ‖ a ἀποτρεπτικός.

detest [di'test] vt ἀπεχθάνομαι, ἀποστρέφομαι, σιχαίνομαι ‖ ~able a ἀπεχθής, σιχαμένος.

detonate ['detəneit] vti ἐκρηγνύω, ἐκπυρσοκροτῶ.

detonator ['detəneitə*] n ἐπικρουστήρ, πυροκροτητής.

detour ['di:tuə*] n ἀπόκλισις, στροφή, λοξοδρόμησις.

detract [di'trækt] vi (+from) δυσφημῶ, μειώνω.

detriment ['detrimənt] n: to the ~ of πρός ζημίαν τοῦ ‖ ~al a ἐπιβλαβής, ἐπιζήμιος.

devaluation [divælju'eiʃən] n ὑποτίμησις.

devalue ['diː'vælju:] vt ὑποτιμῶ.

devastate ['devəsteit] vt ἐρημώνω, καταστρέφω.

devastating ['devəsteitiŋ] a ἐξολοθρευτικός.

develop [di'veləp] vt (make grow) ἀναπτύσσω ‖ (film) ἐμφανίζω ‖ vi (unfold) ἀναπτύσσομαι, ἐκδηλοῦμαι ‖ (grow) ἀναπτύσσομαι ‖ ~er n (phot) ἐμφανιστής ‖ ~ing a (country) ἀναπτυσσομένη ‖ ~ment n ἀνάπτυξις.

deviate ['diːvieit] vi ἐκτρέπομαι, παρεκκλίνω.

deviation [diːvi'eiʃən] n παρέκκλισις.

device [di'vais] n ἐπινόημα, τέχνασμα.

devil ['devl] n διά(β)ολος, δαίμονας ‖ ~ish a διαβολικός.

devious ['diːviəs] a (means) ἔμμεσος, παρεκκλίνων ‖ (person) ἀνέντιμος.

devise [di'vaiz] vt ἐπινοῶ, μηχανεύομαι.

devoid [di'vɔid] a: ~ of ἐστερημένος, ξένοιαστος.

devote [di'vəut] vt ἀφιερώνω ‖ ~d a ἀφοσιωμένος ‖ ~e n λάτρης, ὀπαδός.

devotion [di'vəuʃən] n ἀφοσίωσις, λατρεία.

devour [di'vauə*] vt καταβροχθίζω.

devout [di'vaut] a εὐσεβής, ἔνθερμος.

dew [djuː] n δρόσος, δροσιά.

dexterity [dcks'teriti] n ἐπιδεξιότης.

diabetes [daiə'biːtiːz] n διαβήτης.

diabetic [daiə'betik] a,n διαβητικός.

diagnose ['daiəgnəuz] vt κάνω διάγνωσιν.

diagnosis [daiəg'nəusis] n διάγνωσις.

diagonal [dai'ægənl] a,n διαγώνιος.

diagram ['daiəgræm] n διάγραμμα, σχέδιον.

dial ['daiəl] n (esp tel) δίσκος ἐπιλογῆς, καντράν ‖ vt καλῶ, παίρνω ἕνα νούμερο ‖ ~ling tone n ἔνδειξις ἐλευθέρας γραμμῆς.

dialect ['daiəlekt] n διάλεκτος.

dialogue ['daiələg] n διάλογος.

diameter [dai'æmitə*] n διάμετρος.

diamond ['daiəmənd] n διαμάντι ‖ (cards) καρρό.

diapers ['daiəpəz] npl (US) πάνες.

diaphragm ['daiəfræm] n διάφραγμα.

diarrhoea [daiə'riːə] n διάρροια.

diary ['daiəri] n ἡμερολόγιον.

dice [dais] npl ζάρια ‖ vt (vegetables) κόβω σέ κύβους.

dictate [dik'teit] vt ὑπαγορεύω ‖ (impose) ἐπιβάλλω ‖ ['dikteit] n πρόσταγμα, διαταγή.

dictation [dik'teiʃən] n ὑπαγόρευσις.

dictator [dik'teitə*] n δικτάτωρ.

dictatorship [dik'teitəʃip] n δικτατορία.

diction ['dikʃən] n ὕφος λόγου, λεκτικόν.

dictionary ['dikʃənri] n λεξικόν.

did [did] pt of **do** ‖ ~n't = **did not** ‖ see do.

die [dai] vi πεθαίνω, τά τινάζω ‖ (end) σβήνω ‖ to ~ away vi ἐξασθενίζω, σβήνω ‖ to ~ down vt ἐξασθενίζω, πέφτω to ~ out vi ἀποθνήσκω, σβήνω.

Diesel ['diːzəl] ~ engine n ντῆζελ.

diet ['daiət] n (food) (δια)τροφή ‖ (special course) δίαιτα ‖ vi κάνω δίαιτα.

differ ['difə*] vi διαφέρω, ξεχωρίζω ‖ (disagree) διαφωνῶ ‖ ~ence n διαφορά (disagreement) διαφωνία, διαφορά ‖ ~ent a διάφορος, διαφορετικός ‖ ~ently ad διαφορετικά ‖ ~ential [difə'renʃəl] n (aut) διαφορικόν ‖ (wages) διαφορική ‖ ~entiate vti διαφοροποιῶ, ξεχωρίζω.

difficult ['difikəlt] a δύσκολος ‖ ~y n δυσκολία, δυσχέρεια.

diffidence ['difidəns] n ἐπιφυλακτικότης, ντροπαλότης.

diffident ['difidənt] a διστακτικός, ντροπαλός.

diffuse [di'fjuːs] a διάχυτος ‖ [di'fjuːz] vt διαχέω, σκορπῶ.

dig [dig] (irreg v) vt (hole) σκάβω ‖ (garden) σκάβω ‖ (nails) μπήζω ‖ (delve into) ψάχνω, τρυπῶ ‖ n (prod) κάρφωμα, πείραγμα ‖ (arch) ἐκσκαφή ‖ to ~ up vi ἐκσκάπτω, ξερριζώνω, ξεθάβω.

digest [dai'dʒest] vt χωνεύω ‖ (work over) ἐπεξεργάζομαι ‖ ['daidʒest] n περίληψις, σύνοψις ‖ ~ible [di'dʒestəbl] a εὐκολοχώνευτος ‖ ~ion n χώνευσις.

digit ['didʒit] n (number) ψηφίον, ἀριθμός ‖ (toe, finger) δάκτυλος.

dignified ['dignifaid] a ἀξιοπρεπής.

dignify ['dignifai] vt τιμῶ, ἐξυψώνω.

dignitary ['dignitəri] n ἀξιωματοῦχος.

dignity ['digniti] n ἀξιοπρέπεια.

digress [dai'gres] vi ἐκτρέπομαι, ξεφεύγω ‖ ~ion n ἐκτροπή, παρέκβασις.

digs [digz] npl (Brit col) δωμάτιον

dilapidated [di'læpideitid] a σαραβαλιασμένος.

dilate [dai'leit] vti διαστέλλω, πλαταίνω διαστέλλομαι.

dilemma [dai'lemə] n δίλημμα.

diligence ['dilidʒəns] n ἐπιμέλεια.

diligent ['dilidʒənt] a ἐπιμελής.

dilute [dai'luːt] vt ἀραιώνω, νερώνω ‖ a ἀραιός.

dim [dim] a ἀμυδρός, μουντός, σκοτεινός ‖ (stupid) κουτός ‖ vt χαμηλώνω, θολώνω.

dime [daim] n (US) δέκατον τοῦ δολλαρίου.

dimension [di'menʃən] n διάστασις, ἔκτασις ‖ ~s npl διαστάσεις.

diminish [di'miniʃ] vti ἐλαττώνω, ἐλαττώνομαι.

diminutive [di'minjutiv] a ὑποκοριστικός n ὑποκοριστικόν.

dimly ['dimli] ad ἀμυδρῶς, θαμπά.

dimple ['dimpl] n λακκάκι, λακκίτσα.

dim-witted ['dim'witid] a (col) βλάκας

din [din] n θόρυβος, πάταγος.

dine [dain] vi γευματίζω, τρώγω ‖ ~r n τραπεζαρία τραίνου ‖ (person) γευματίζων.

dinghy ['diŋgi] n μικρά λέμβος.

dingo ['diŋgəu] n ντίγκο.

dingy ['dindʒi] a μαυρισμένος, σκοτεινός.

dining car ['dainiŋkɑ:*] n βαγκόν-ρεστωράν.

dining room ['dainiŋrum] n τραπεζαρία.

dinner ['dinə*] n γεῦμα, φαΐ ‖ (public) ἐπίσημον γεῦμα ‖ ~ jacket n σμόκιν ‖ ~ party n τραπέζι ‖ ~ time n ὥρα φαγητοῦ.

dinosaur ['dainəsɔ:*] n δεινόσαυρος.

diocese ['daiəsis] n ἐπισκοπή.

dip [dip] n (slope) κλίσις, πλαγιά ‖ (bath) βουτιά ‖ vt ἐμβαπτίζω, βουτῶ ‖ (aut) χαμηλώνω ‖ (flag) κατεβάζω ‖ vi (slope) γέρνω, κατηφορίζω, χαμηλώνω.

diphtheria [dif'θiəriə] n διφθερῖτις.

diphthong ['difθɔŋ] n δίφθογγος.

diploma [di'pləumə] n δίπλωμα.

diplomacy [di'pləuməsi] n διπλωματία.

diplomat ['dipləmæt] n διπλωμάτης ‖ ~ic a διπλωματικός ‖ ~ic corps n διπλωματικόν σῶμα.

dipstick ['dipstik] n βυθομετρική ράβδος.

dire [daiə*] a καταστρεπτικός, τρομερός, ἔσχατος.

direct [dai'rekt] a (straight) εὐθύς, ἴσιος ‖ (immediate) ἄμεσος ‖ vt (manage) διευθύνω, διοικῶ ‖ (aim) κατευθύνω, δείχνω ‖ ~ current n συνεχές ρεῦμα ‖ ~ hit n εὐστοχία ‖ ~ion [di'rekʃən] n (control) διεύθυνσις, διαχείρισις ‖ (of traffic) ρύθμισις ‖ (of movement) κατεύθυνσις, φορά ‖ ~ions npl (for use) ὁδηγίες ‖ ~ional a κατά διεύθυνσιν ‖ ~ly ad (in straight line) εὐθέως, ἴσια ‖ (at once) ἀμέσως ‖ ~or n διευθυντής, ὁ γενικός ‖ ~ory n (esp tel) (τηλεφωνικός) κατάλογος.

dirt [dɜ:t] n ἀκαθαρσία, βρωμιά, ρύπος ‖ ~ road n (US) χωματόδρομος ‖ ~y a ρυπαρός, λερωμένος, ἀκάθαρτος ‖ (mean) βρώμικο, πρόστυχο ‖ vt λερώνω, μουντζουρώνω.

dis- [dis] prefix ἀπο-, ξε-, ἐξ-, δυσ-, ἀ-, ἀν-

disability [disə'biliti] n ἀνικανότης ‖ (physical) ἀναπηρία.

disabled [dis'eibld] a ἀνίκανος, σακατεμένος, ἀνάπηρος.

disadvantage [disəd'vɑ:ntidʒ] n μειονέκτημα, ἐλάττωμα ‖ (sell at) ζημία ‖ ~ous [disædvɑ:n'teidʒəs] a ἀσύμφορος, δυσμενής.

disagree [disə'gri:] vi διαφωνῶ ‖ to ~ with vt δέν ταιριάζω, δέν πηγαίνω ‖ (food) πειράζω ‖ ~able a δυσάρεστος, ἀντιπαθής ‖ ~ment n διαφωνία, διάστασις, ἀσυμφωνία.

disallow ['disə'lau] vt ἀρνοῦμαι, ἀπορρίπτω, ἀπαγορεύω.

disappear [disə'piə*] vi ἐξαφανίζομαι ‖ ~ance n ἐξαφάνισις.

disappoint [disə'pɔint] vt ἀπογοητεύω, χαλῶ, στενοχωροῦμαι ‖ ~ing a ἀπογοητευτικός ‖ ~ment n ἀπογοήτευσις, λύπη.

disapproval [disə'pru:vəl] n ἀποδοκιμασία.

disapprove [disə'pru:v] vi (+ of) ἀποδοκιμάζω, ἐπικρίνω.

disarm [dis'ɑ:m] vt ἀφοπλίζω ‖ ~ament n ἀφοπλισμός.

disaster [di'zɑ:stə*] n συμφορά, δυστύχημα.

disastrous [di'zɑ:strəs] a ὀλέθριος, καταστρεπτικός.

disband [dis'bænd] vt ἀπολύω, διαλύω.

disbelief ['disbə'li:f] n δυσπιστία.

disc [disk] n δίσκος.

discard [dis'kɑ:d] vt ἀπορρίπτω, ἀφήνω.

disc brake ['diskbreik] n δισκόφρενο.

discern [di'sɜ:n] vt διακρίνω, ξεχωρίζω ‖ ~ing a ὀξυδερκής, ἀνοιχτομάτης.

discharge [dis'tʃɑ:dʒ] vt (unload ship etc) ξεφορτώνω ‖ (fire a gun) πυροβολῶ ‖ (dismiss) ἀπολύω ‖ (mil) ἀποστρατεύω ‖ (perform duties) ἐκτελῶ, ἐκπληρῶ ‖ n (med) ἀπέκκριμα ‖ (mil) ἀποστράτευσις ‖ (flow) ἐκκένωσις.

disciple [di'saipl] n μαθητής, ὀπαδός.

disciplinary ['disiplinəri] a πειθαρχικός.

discipline ['disiplin] n πειθαρχία ‖ vt πειθαρχῶ, τιμωρῶ.

disclaim [dis'kleim] vt ἀπαρνοῦμαι.

disclose [dis'kləuz] vt ἀποκαλύπτω.

disclosure [dis'kləuʒə*] n ἀποκάλυψις, ἐκδήλωσις.

disco ['diskəu] n abbr of discothèque.

discoloured [dis'kʌləd] a ξεβαμμένο, μουντζουρωμένο.

discomfort [dis'kʌmfət] n (uneasiness) δυσφορία, στενοχωριά ‖ (lack of comfort) ἔλλειψις ἀνέσεως, κακουχία.

disconcert [diskən'sɜ:t] vt ταράσσω, συγχύζω.

disconnect ['diskə'nekt] vt διασπῶ, διαχωρίζω.

discontent ['diskən'tent] n δυσαρέσκεια ‖ ~ed a δυσαρεστημένος.

discontinue ['diskən'tinju:] vti διακόπτω, καταργῶ.

discord ['diskɔ:d] n (quarrelling) διαφωνία, διχόνοια ‖ (mus) παραφωνία ‖ ~ant a ἀσύμφωνος, παράφωνος.

discothèque ['diskəutek] n ντισκοτέκ.

discount ['diskaunt] n ἔκπτωσις, σκόντο ‖ (bank) προεξόφλησις, ὑφαίρεσις ‖ [dis'kaunt] vt (disbelieve) περιφρονῶ, δέν πιστεύω.

discourage [dis'kʌridʒ] vt (take away confidence) ἀποθαρρύνω ‖ (disapprove) ἀποδοκιμάζω, ἀποτρέπω.

discouraging [dis'kʌridʒiŋ] a ἀποθαρρυντικός.

discourteous [dis'kɜ:tiəs] a ἀγενής.

discover 251 dispute

discover [dis'kΛnə*] *vt* ἀνακαλύπτω ‖ ~**y** *n* ἀνακάλυψις.

discredit [dis'kredit] *vt* δυσπιστῶ, ὑποτιμῶ.

discreet [dis'kri:t] *a* νουνεχής, διακριτικός ‖ ~**ly** *ad* συνετῶς, ἐπιφυλακτικά.

discrepancy [dis'krepənsi] *n* διαφορά, ἀσυμφωνία.

discretion [dis'kreʃən] *n* (*prudence*) διακριτικότης, σύνεσις ‖ (*right to decide*) βούλησις, φρόνησις.

discriminate [dis'krimineit] *vi* κάνω διάκρισιν, ξεχωρίζω.

discriminating [dis'krimineitiŋ] *a* διακριτικός, μεροληπτικός.

discrimination [diskrimi'neiʃən] *n* διάκρισις, ὀρθοφροσύνη.

discus ['diskəs] *n* δίσκος.

discuss [dis'kΛs] *vt* συζητῶ ‖ ~**ion** *n* συζήτησις.

disdain [dis'dein] *vt* περιφρονῶ ‖ *n* περιφρόνησις ‖ ~**ful** *a* ὑπεροπτικός, περιφρονητικός.

disease [di'zi:z] *n* νόσημα, ἀσθένεια ‖ ~**d** *a* νοσῶν, ἄρρωστος.

disembark [disim'ba:k] *vti* ἀποβιβάζω, ἀποβιβάζομαι.

disenchanted ['disin'tʃa:ntid] *a* ἀπογοητευμένος, ξεμαγεμένος.

disengage [disin'geidʒ] *vt* (*aut*) ἀποσυμπλέκω.

disentangle ['disin'tæŋgl] *vt* διαχωρίζω, ξεμπλέκω.

disfigure [dis'figə*] *vt* παραμορφώνω.

disgrace [dis'greis] *n* (*general*) δυσμένεια ‖ (*thing*) ὄνειδος, ἐντροπή ‖ *vt* ντροπιάζω, ξεφτελίζω ‖ ~**ful** *a* ἐπονείδιστος.

disgruntled [dis'grΛntld] *a* δυσαρεστημένος, κατσουφιασμένος.

disguise [dis'gaiz] *vt* (*change appearance*) μεταμφιέζω ‖ (*hide*) ἀποκρύπτω ‖ *n* μεταμφίεσις, ἀπόκρυψις.

disgust [dis'gΛst] *n* ἀηδία ‖ *vt* ἀηδιάζω ‖ ~**ing** *a* ἀηδιαστικός, σιχαμερός.

dish [diʃ] *n* πιάτο ‖ (*meal*) φαγητό ‖ **to** ~ **up** *vt* παρουσιάζω, σερβίρω ‖ ~**cloth** *n* πιατόπανο.

dishearten [dis'ha:tn] *vt* ἀποθαρρύνω, ἀπελπίζω.

dishevelled [di'ʃevəld] *a* ξεμαλλιασμένος, ἀνακατωμένος.

dishonest [dis'ɔnist] *a* ἀνέντιμος, κακοήθης, πρόστυχος ‖ ~**y** *n* κακοήθεια, ἀτιμία.

dishonour [dis'ɔnə*] *n* αἶσχος, ἀτιμία.

dishwasher ['diʃwɔʃə*] *n* πλυντήριο πιάτων.

disillusion [disi'lu:ʒən] *vt* ἀπογοητεύω.

disinfect [disin'fekt] *vt* ἀπολυμαίνω ‖ ~**ant** *n* ἀπολυμαντικόν.

disintegrate [dis'intigreit] *vi* ἀποσυντίθεμαι, θρυμματίζομαι.

disinterested [dis'intristid] *a* ἀμερόληπτος, ἀδιάφορος.

disjointed [dis'dʒɔintid] *a* ἀσυνάρτητος, ἐξηρθρωμένος.

disk [disk] *n* = **disc**.

dislike [dis'laik] *n* ἀντιπάθεια, ἀποστροφή ‖ *vt* ἀντιπαθῶ, ἀπεχθάνομαι.

dislocate ['disləukeit] *vt* (*bone*) ἐξαρθρώνω, στραμπουλίζω ‖ ξεχαρβαλώνω, χαλνῶ.

dislodge [dis'lɔdʒ] *vt* ἐκτοπίζω, ἐκδιώκω.

disloyal ['dis'lɔiəl] *a* ἄπιστος.

dismal ['dizməl] *a* ζοφερός, μελαγχολικός.

dismantle [dis'mæntl] *vt* παροπλίζω, λύω.

dismay [dis'mei] *n* κατάπληξις, φόβος ‖ *vt* (*dishearten*) πτοῶ, φοβίζω, ἀπογοητεύω.

dismiss [dis'mis] *vt* (*discharge*) ἀπολύω, παύω ‖ (*out of mind*) βγάζω ‖ (*send away*) ἀπομακρύνω, διώχνω ‖ (*law*) ἀπορρίπτω, ἀπαλλάσσω ‖ ~**al** *n* ἀπόλυσις, παῦσις.

disobedience [disə'bi:diəns] *n* ἀνυπακοή, παρακοή.

disobedient [disə'bi:diənt] *a* ἀνυπάκουος, πεισματάρης.

disobey ['disə'bei] *vt* παρακούω, παραβαίνω.

disorder [dis'ɔ:də*] *n* (*confusion*) ἀκαταστασία, ἀταξία ‖ (*commotion*) ταραχή, φασαρία ‖ (*med*) διαταραχή.

disorderly [dis'ɔ:dəli] *a* (*untidy*) ἀκατάστατος ‖ (*unruly*) ἄτακτος, ἀπείθαρχος.

disown [dis'əun] *vt* ἀπαρνοῦμαι, ἀποκηρύττω.

disparaging [dis'pæridʒiŋ] *a* δυσφημιστικό.

disparity [dis'pæriti] *n* ἀνισότης, διαφορά.

dispassionate [dis'pæʃnit] *a* ψύχραιμος, ἀμερόληπτος.

dispatch [dis'pætʃ] *vt* (*goods*) στέλνω, διεκπεραιώνω ‖ *n* ἀποστολή, διεκπεραίωσις ‖ (*esp mil*) ἀναφορά, μήνυμα.

dispel [dis'pel] *vt* διασκορπίζω.

dispensary [dis'pensəri] *n* θεραπευτήριον.

dispense [dis'pens] *vt* διανέμω, χορηγῶ ‖ **to** ~ **with** *vt* κάνω χωρίς.

dispersal [dis'pə:səl] *n* διασκορπισμός.

disperse [dis'pə:s] *vt* διασκορπίζω ‖ *vi* διασκορπίζομαι.

dispirited [dis'piritid] *a* ἀπελπισμένος.

displace [dis'pleis] *vt* ἐκτοπίζω, μετατοπίζω ‖ ~**d person** *n* πρόσφυγας.

display [dis'plei] *n* (*of goods*) ἔκθεσις, ἐπίδειξις ‖ (*of feeling*) ἐκδήλωσις ‖ (*mil*) ἐπίδειξις ‖ *vt* ἐπιδεικνύω, ἐκθέτω.

displease [dis'pli:z] *vt* δυσαρεστῶ.

displeasure [dis'pleʒə*] *n* δυσαρέσκεια.

disposal [dis'pəuzəl] *n* (*of property*) ἐκχώρησις, διάθεσις ‖ **at one's** ~ στήν διάθεσί.

dispose [dis'pəuz] **to** ~ **of** *vt* ἀπαλλάσσομαι, ξεφορτώνομαι.

disposed [dis'pəuzd] *a* διατεθειμένος.

disposition [dispə'ziʃən] *n* (*character*) προδιάθεσι, χαρακτήρ.

disproportionate [disprə'pɔ:ʃnit] *a* δυσανάλογος.

disprove [dis'pru:v] *vt* ἀναιρῶ, ἀνασκευάζω.

dispute [dis'pju:t] *n* ἀμφισβήτησις, φιλονεικία ‖ *vt* ἀμφισβητῶ, διεκδικῶ.

disqualify [dis'kwɔlifai] *vt* (*sport*) ἀποκλείω | καθιστῶ ἀνίκανον.

disregard ['disri'gaːd] *vt* παραβλέπω, ἀγνοῶ, περιφρονῶ.

disreputable [dis'repjutəbl] *a* ἀνυπόληπτος, κακόφημος.

disrespectful [disris'pektful] *a* ἀσεβής.

disrupt [dis'rʌpt] *vt* διασπῶ, διαλύω | **~ion** *n* διάσπασις.

dissatisfaction ['dissætis'fækʃən] *n* δυσαρέσκεια.

dissatisfied ['dis'sætisfaid] *a* δυσαρεστημένος.

dissect [di'sekt] *vt* κατατέμνω, διαμελίζω.

disseminate [di'semineit] *vt* διασπείρω.

dissent [di'sent] *n* διχογνωμία, διαφωνία ‖ *vi* διαφωνῶ.

dissident ['disidənt] *a* διϊστάμενος, διαφωνῶν.

dissimilar ['di'similə*] *a* ἀνόμοιος, διαφορετικός.

dissipate ['disipeit] *vt* (*waste*) σπαταλῶ, ἀσωτεύω ‖ (δια)σκορπίζω ‖ **~d** *a* ἔκλυτος, ἀκόλαστος.

dissipation [disi'peiʃən] *n* διασκόρπησις, ἀσωτεία.

dissociate [di'səuʃieit] *vt* ἀποσπῶ, διαχωρίζω, ἀπομακρύνω.

dissolute ['disəluːt] *a* ἄσωτος, ἔκλυτος.

dissolve [di'zɔlv] *vt* διαλύω ‖ *vi* διαλύομαι, λυώνω.

dissuade [di'sweid] *vt* ἀποτρέπω, μεταπείθω.

distance ['distəns] *n* ἀπόστασις, διάστημα ‖ **in the ~** μακρυά.

distant ['distənt] *a* (*far away*) μακρυά, μακρυνός ‖ ἀπομεμακρυσμένος, ἐπιφυλακτικός.

distaste ['dis'teist] *n* ἀποστροφή, ἀπέχθεια ‖ **~ful** *a* δυσάρεστος, ἀπεχθής.

distemper [dis'tempə*] *n* (*paint*) ἀσβεστόχρωμα ‖ (*disease*) ἀρρώστεια τῶν σκύλων.

distend [dis'tend] *vti* ἐκτείνω, τεντώνω.

distil [dis'til] *vt* ἀποστάζω, διϋλίζω ‖ **~lery** *n* ποτοποιεῖον.

distinct [dis'tiŋkt] *a* (*different*) διαφορετικός ‖ (*clear*) εὐδιάκριτος, σαφής ‖ **~ion** *n* (*difference*) διαφορά ‖ (*honour etc*) διάκρισις, τιμή ‖ (*medal etc*) παράσημον ‖ **~ive** *a* διακριτικός, χαρακτηριστικός ‖ **~ly** *ad* εὐδιακρίτως, καθαρά.

distinguish [dis'tiŋgwiʃ] *vt* διακρίνω, ξεχωρίζω, διαφοροποιῶ ‖ **~ed** *a* (*eminent*) διακεκριμένος ‖ **~ing** *a* χαρακτηριστικός, διακριτικόν.

distort [dis'tɔːt] *vt* (*out of shape*) διαστρέφω, στραβώνω ‖ διαστρεβλώνω, παραποιῶ ‖ **~ion** *n* παραμόρφωσις, διαστρέβλωσις.

distract [dis'trækt] *vt* ἀποσπῶ, περισπῶ ‖ (*drive mad*) περιπλέκω, τρελλαίνω ‖ **~ing** *a* τρομακτικός, ἐνοχλητικός ‖ **~ion** *n* (*inattention*) περίσπασις, ἀφηρη-

μάδα ‖ (*distress*) διατάραξις, ἀναστάτωσις ‖ (*diversion*) διασκέδασις.

distraught [dis'trɔːt] *a* ταραγμένος, συγχυσμένος.

distress [dis'tres] *n* (*grief*) ἀπελπισία, ἀγωνία, πίκρα ‖ (*suffering*) ἀθλιότης, δυστυχία ‖ (*difficulty*) κίνδυνος, σέ δύσκολη θέσι ‖ *vt* θλίβω, στενοχωρῶ ‖ **~ing** *a* δυσάρεστος, ὀδυνηρός ‖ **~ signal** *n* σῆμα κινδύνου.

distribute [dis'tribjuːt] *vt* (*give out*) διανέμω, μοιράζω ‖ (*spread*) ἐξαπλώνω.

distribution [distri'bjuːʃən] *n* διανομή, κατανομή.

distributor [dis'tribjutə*] *n* (*one who distributes*) διανομεύς, ἀντιπρόσωπος ‖ (*aut etc*) διανομεύς.

district ['distrikt] *n* (*of country*) περιοχή, περιφέρεια ‖ (*of town*) συνοικία ‖ **~ attorney** *n* (*US*) εἰσαγγελεύς ‖ **~ nurse** *n* (*Brit*) ἐπισκέπτρια νοσοκόμος.

distrust [dis'trʌst] *n* δυσπιστία, ὑποψία ‖ *vt* δυσπιστῶ πρός, ὑποπτεύομαι.

disturb [dis'təːb] *vt* (*upset*) ταράσσω, ἐνοχλῶ ‖ (*agitate*) ταράσσω, κλονίζω ‖ **~ance** *n* διατάραξις, φασαρία ‖ **~ing** *a* ἐνοχλητικός, ἀνησυχητικός.

disused [dis'juːzd] *a* ἀχρηστευμένος, ἀπηρχαιωμένος.

ditch [ditʃ] *n* τάφρος, χανδάκι.

ditto ['ditəu] *n* ὁμοίως.

divan [di'væn] *n* (*bed*) ντιβάνι.

dive [daiv] *n* (*into water*) βουτιά ‖ (*aviat*) βύθισις ‖ *vi* βυθίζομαι, βουτῶ ‖ **~r** *n* (*professional*) δύτης.

diverge [dai'vəːdʒ] *vi* διΐσταμαι, ἀποκλίνω.

diverse [dai'vəːs] *a* διάφορος, ποικίλος.

diversification [daivəːsifi'keiʃən] *n* διαφοροποίησις.

diversify [dai'vəːsifai] *vt* διαφοροποιῶ, ποικίλλω.

diversion [dai'vəːʃən] *n* ἀπόκλισις, λοξοδρομία ‖ (*of traffic*) διοχέτευσις ‖ (*pastime*) διασκέδασις.

diversity [dai'vəːsiti] *n* ἀνομοιότης, ποικιλία.

divert [dai'vəːt] *vt* ἀποσπῶ, ἐκτρέπω ‖ (*entertain*) διασκεδάζω.

divide [di'vaid] *vt* διανέμω, (δια)μοιράζω, χωρίζω ‖ *vi* διαιρῶ, χωρίζω.

dividend ['dividend] *n* μέρισμα, τοκομερίδιον ‖ (*math*) διαιρετέος.

divine [di'vain] *a* θεῖος, θεϊκός.

diving board ['daiviŋbɔːd] *n* ἐξέδρα γιά βουτιές.

divinity [di'viniti] *n* θεότης ‖ (*study*) θεολογία.

divisible [di'vizəbl] *a* διαιρετός.

division [di'viʒən] *n* (*dividing*) διανομή, μοιρασιά ‖ (*math*) διαίρεσις ‖ (*mil*) μεραρχία ‖ (*part*) τμῆμα ‖ (*of opinion*) διχόνοια, διαίρεσις.

divorce [di'vɔːs] *n* διαζύγιον, διάζευξις

‖ vt διαζευγνύω ‖ ~**d** a χωρισμένος.
divulge [dai'vʌldʒ] vt ἀποκαλύπτω, φανερώνω.
dizziness ['dizinis] n ἴλιγγος, ζάλη.
dizzy ['dızı] a ζαλισμένος.
do [du:] (irreg v) vt κάνω, ἐκτελῶ, ἐκπληρῶ, τελειώνω, ταιριάζω, ἀρκῶ ‖ vi (act, proceed) κάνω ‖ (be suitable) ταιριάζω, κάνω ‖ n (party) πάρτυ.
docile ['dəusail] a εὐάγωγος, ὑπάκοος.
dock [dɔk] n (naut) νηοδόχη, ντόκος, δεξαμενή ‖ (court) ἐδώλιον ‖ (naut) δεξαμενίζομαι ~**er** n φορτοεκφορτωτής, λιμενεργάτης.
docket ['dɔkit] n περιληπτική ἐπιγραφή.
dockyard ['dɔkja:d] n ναύσταθμος.
doctor ['dɔktə*] n (med) ἰατρός, γιατρός ‖ (univ) διδάκτωρ.
doctrinaire [dɔktri'neə*] a θεωρητικός.
doctrine ['dɔktrin] n δόγμα, θεωρία.
document ['dɔkjument] n ἔγγραφον ‖ ~**ary** [dɔkju'mentəri] n (film) ντοκυμαντέρ.
dodge [dɔdʒ] n ὑπεκφυγή, τέχνασμα ‖ vt ξεφεύγω, ἀποφεύγω ‖ vi ἐκφεύγω, παραμερίζω, κάνω πλάϊ.
dog [dɔg] n σκυλί ‖ (human) παλιάνθρωπος ‖ ~ **biscuit** n μπισκότο γιά σκύλους ‖ ~ **collar** n λαιμοδέτης (σκύλου) ‖ (col) κολλάρο κληρικοῦ ‖ ~-**eared** a τσάκισμα γωνίας τῆς σελίδος ‖ ~**fish** n σκυλόψαρο ‖ ~ **food** n φαγητό γιά σκύλους.
dogged ['dɔgid] a ἰσχυρογνώμων, πεισματάρης.
dogma ['dɔgmə] n δόγμα ‖ ~**tic** [dɔg'mætik] a (stubborn) κατηγορηματικός, δογματικός.
doings ['du:iŋz] npl (activities) πράξεις, ἔργα.
doldrums ['dɔldrəmz] npl: in the ~ ἄκεφος.
dole [dəul] n (Brit: for unemployed) ἐπίδομα ἀνεργίας ‖ on the ~ παίρνω ἐπίδομα ὡς ἄνεργος ‖ to ~ **out** vt ἀπονέμω, μοιράζω.
doleful ['dəulful] a λυπητερός, πένθιμος.
doll [dɔl] n κούκλα ‖ vt: to ~ o.s. up στολίζομαι.
dollar ['dɔlə*] n δολλάριο, τάληρο.
dolphin ['dɔlfin] n δελφίνι.
dome [dəum] n θόλος, τροῦλλος.
domestic [də'mestik] a (of the house) οἰκιακός, τοῦ σπιτιοῦ ‖ (of the country) ἐσωτερικός, ἐγχώριος ‖ (tame: of animal) οἰκιακόν ζῶον ‖ ~**ated** a ἐξημερωμένος.
domicile ['dɔmisail] n διαμονή.
dominant ['dɔminənt] a ἐπικρατῶν, ὑπερισχύων.
dominate ['dɔmineit] vt δεσπόζω, κυριαρχῶ.
domination [dɔmi'neiʃən] n κυριαρχία.
domineering [dɔmi'niəriŋ] a δεσποτικός, αὐταρχικός.
dominion [də'miniən] n (rule) κυριαρχία, ἐξουσία ‖ (land) κτῆσις (ἀποικία).
dominoes ['dɔminəuz] npl ντόμινο.

don [dɔn] n καθηγητής πανεπιστημίου.
donate [dəu'neit] vt δωρίζω.
donation [dəu'neiʃən] n δωρεά.
done [dʌn] pp of did.
donkey ['dɔŋki] n γάϊδαρος, γαϊδούρι.
donor ['dəunə*] n δωρητής.
don't [dəunt] = **do not** ‖ see do.
doom [du:m] n (fate) μοῖρα ‖ (death) θάνατος, καταστροφή ‖ vt: to be ~**ed** εἶμαι καταδικασμένος.
door [dɔ:*] n πόρτα, θύρα ‖ ~**bell** n κουδούνι (τῆς πόρτας) ‖ ~**handle** n πόμολο, (χειρο)λαβή ‖ ~**man** n θυρωρός, πορτιέρης ‖ ~**mat** n ψάθα ἐξώπορτας ‖ ~**step** n σκαλοπάτι ‖ ~**way** n εἴσοδος.
dope [dəup] n (drug) ναρκωτικόν.
dopey ['dəupi] a (col) βλάκας ‖ (doped) χασικλωμένος.
dormant ['dɔ:mənt] a λανθάνων, κοιμώμενος.
dormitory ['dɔ:mitri] n ὑπνοθάλαμος.
dormouse ['dɔ:maus] n μυωξός.
dosage ['dəusidʒ] n δόσις.
dose [dəus] n δόσις ‖ vt δίδω φάρμακον.
dossier ['dɔsiei] n φάκελλος.
dot [dɔt] n στιγμή ‖ **on the** ~ στήν στιγμήν, στήν ὥρα.
dote [dəut] to ~ **on** vt ἀγαπῶ τρελλά.
double ['dʌbl] a διπλός, διπλάσιος ‖ ad διπλά, διπλάσια, δυό-δύο ‖ n (match) σωσίας, ταῖρι ‖ vt διπλασιάζω ‖ (fold in two) διπλώνω ‖ vi διπλασιάζομαι, διπλώνομαι ‖ at the ~ τροχάδην ‖ ~**s** npl (tennis) διπλοῦς (ἀγών) ‖ ~ **bass** n κοντραμπάσσο ‖ ~ **bed** n διπλό κρεββάτι ‖ ~-**breasted** a σταυρωτός ‖ ~-**cross** n προδοσία ‖ vt προδίδω, ἐξαπατῶ ‖ ~-**decker** n διόροφον (λεωφορεῖον) ‖ ~ **room** n δίκλινο.
doubly ['dʌbli] ad διπλασίως.
doubt [daut] n ἀμφιβολία ‖ vt ἀμφιβάλλω, διαμφισβητῶ ‖ **without** ~ χωρίς καμμιά ἀμφιβολίαν ‖ ~**ful** a ἀμφίβολος ‖ ~**less** ad ἀναμφιβόλως.
dough [dəu] n ζυμάρι ‖ ~**nut** n τηγανίτα, λουκουμάς.
dove [dʌv] n περιστέρι ‖ ~**tail** n ψαλιδωτή ἕνωσις ‖ vt ταιριάζω.
dowdy ['daudi] a ἄκομψος, κακοντυμένος.
down [daun] n (fluff) πούπουλο, χνούδι ‖ ad κάτω, χάμω ‖ prep πιό κάτω, πρός τά κάτω, χαμηλότερα ‖ vt καταβιβάζω, καταρρίπτω, νικῶ ‖ ~ **with X!** κάτω ὁ Χ! ‖ ~-**and-out** a κατεστραμμένος, στήν ψάθα ‖ ~-**at-heel** a μπατήρης ‖ ~**cast** a κατηφής ‖ ~**fall** n πτῶσις, παρακμή ‖ ~-**hearted** a ἀποθαρρυμένος, κακόκεφος ‖ ~**hill** ad κατηφορικῶς, πρός τά κάτω ‖ ~**pour** n μπόρα ‖ ~**right** a ἰσχυρός, εἰλικρινής, ἀπόλυτος ‖ ~**stairs** ad κάτω ‖ a κάτω, εἰς τό κάτω πάτωμα ‖ ~**stream** ad μέ τό ρεῦμα ‖ ~**town** ad στήν πόλι ‖

~ward *a* κατηφορικός, κατερχόμενος ‖ **~wards** *ad* πρός τά κάτω, καί κάτω.

dowry ['dauri] *n* προίκα.

doze [dəuz] *vi* λαγοκοιμᾶμαι ‖ *n* ὑπνάκος.

dozen ['dʌzn] *n* δωδεκάδα.

drab [dræb] *a* (*dull*) μονότονος, ἀνιαρός.

drachma ['drækmə] *n* δραχμή.

draft [dra:ft] *n* (*rough copy*) (προ)σχέδιον ‖ (*econ*) γραμμάτιον, συναλλαγματική ‖ (*US mil*) στρατολογία ‖ *vt* συντάσσω, ἑτοιμάζω προσχέδιον ‖ *see* draught.

drag [dræg] *vt* (*pull*) σέρνω ‖ (*naut*) βυθοκορῶ ‖ *vi* βραδυπορῶ, σέρνομαι ‖ *n* (*bore*) φορτικός ἄνθρωπος ‖ **to ~ on** *vi* συνεχίζω ἀνιαρά.

dragon ['drægən] *n* δράκος.

drain [drein] *n* (*lit*) ὀχετός, ἀγωγός, αὐλάκι ‖ (*fig*) φυγή, διαρροή, ἐξάντλησις ‖ *vt* (*water*) ἀποχετεύω ‖ ἀδειάζω, ἀπομυζῶ, μαδῶ ‖ *vi* (*of water*) στάζω, στραγγίζω ‖ **~age** *n* ἀποχέτευσις, ἀποστράγγισις ‖ **~pipe** *n* σωλήν ἀποχετεύσεως, ὑδορρορόη.

dram [dræm] *n* δράμι ‖ (*col*) σταγόνα.

drama ['dra:mə] *n* δρᾶμα ‖ **~tic** [drə'mætik] *a* δραματικός ‖ **~tist** *n* δραματογράφος, δραματουργός.

drank [dræŋk] *pt of* drink.

drape [dreip] *vt* κοσμῶ μέ ὕφασμα, ντύνω ‖ **~s** *npl* (*US*) κουρτίνες ‖ **~r** *n* ὑφασματέμπορος.

drastic ['dræstik] *a* δραστικός, ἀποφασιστικός.

draught [dra:ft] *n* (*air*) ρεῦμα (ἀέρος) ‖ (*naut*) βύθισμα ‖ **~s** *n* (*game*) ντάμα, νταμιέρα ‖ (*beer*) on ~ μπύρα τοῦ βαρελιοῦ ‖ **~board** *n* ἀβάκιον ‖ **~sman** *n* σχεδιαστής ‖ **~y** *a* μέ πολλά ρεύματα.

draw [drɔ:] (*irreg v*) *vt* (*pull*) σέρνω, τραβῶ, σηκώνω ‖ (*attract*) ἑλκύω, τραβῶ ‖ (*a picture*) χαράσσω, σχεδιάζω, ζωγραφίζω ‖ (*take out*) ἐξάγω, βγάζω, τραβάω ‖ *vi* (*sport*) ἔρχομαι ἰσόπαλος ‖ *n* (*sport*) ἰσοφάρησις ‖ (*lottery*) κλήρωσις ‖ **to ~ to a close** πλησιάζω στό τέλος ‖ **to ~ out** *vi* (*train*) ξεκινῶ ‖ (*lengthen*) παρατείνω, τραβῶ σέ μάκρος ‖ *vt* (*take out*) ἀποσύρω, τραβῶ ‖ **to ~ up** *vi* (*stop*) φθάνω ‖ *vt* (*document*) συντάσσω, καταστρώνω ‖ **~back** *n* μειονέκτημα, ἐλάττωμα ‖ **~bridge** *n* κρεμαστή γέφυρα ‖ **~er** *n* συρτάρι ‖ **~ing** *n* σχέδιον, σκίτσο ‖ (*art of drawing*) σχέδιον ‖ **~ing pin** *n* πινέζα ‖ **~ing room** *n* σαλόνι, σάλα.

drawl [drɔ:l] *n* συρτή φωνή ‖ *vi* σέρνω τή φωνή.

dread [dred] *n* τρόμος, φόβος, ἀνησυχία ‖ *vt* φοβοῦμαι, τρέμω ‖ **~ful** *a* φοβερός, τρομερός.

dream [dri:m] (*irreg v*) *n* ὄνειρο ‖ (*fancy*) ὀνειροπόλησις ‖ *vi* ὀνειρεύομαι ‖ *a* ὀνειρώδης ‖ **~er** *n* ὀνειροπόλος ‖ **~y** *a* ὀνειροπόλος, φαντασιόπληκτος, θολός.

dreary ['driəri] *a* μονότονος, πληκτικός.

dredge [dredʒ] *vt* βυθοκορῶ, ἐκβαθύνω ‖ **~r** *n* βυθοκόρος.

dregs [dregz] *npl* κατακάθι, μούργα.

drench [drentʃ] *vt* καταβρέχω, μουσκεύω.

dress [dres] *n* ἐνδυμασία, ροῦχα, ντύσιμο ‖ (*esp woman's*) φόρεμα, φουστάνι ‖ *vt* ντύνω, στολίζω ‖ (*a wound*) ἐπενδύω ‖ (*food*) ἑτοιμάζω γιά μαγείρευμα ‖ **to ~ up** *vi* ντύνομαι ‖ **~ circle** *n* πρῶτος ἐξώστης ‖ **~er** *n* (*person*) πού ντύνεται καλά ‖ (*US*) κομψός ‖ **~ing** *n* (*med*) ἐπίδεσις ‖ (*of food*) ἑτοιμασία, σάλτσα ‖ **~ing gown** *n* ρόμπα ‖ **~ing room** *n* (*theat*) καμαρίνι ‖ **~ing table** *n* τουαλέττα (ἔπιπλον) ‖ δωμάτιον καλλωπισμοῦ ‖ **~maker** *n* ράφτρα, μοδίστρα ‖ **~making** *n* ραπτική ‖ **~ rehearsal** *n* τελευταία πρόβα, γενική δοκιμή.

drew [dru:] *pt of* draw.

dribble ['dribl] *vi* (*trickle*) στάζω ‖ *vt* (*sport*) κάνω τρίπλες.

dried [draid] *a* ξηρός, ἀπεξηραμένος, στεγνός.

drift [drift] *n* (*driven by tide etc*) κατεύθυνσις, διεύθυνσις, ταχύτης ‖ (*mass of snow etc*) χιονοστιβάς, συσσώρευσις ‖ (*meaning*) ἔννοια, νόημα ‖ *vi* (*off course*) παρασύρομαι, ξεπέφτω ‖ (*aimlessly*) περιφέρομαι ἀσκόπως ‖ **~wood** *n* ἐπιπλέον ξύλον.

drill [dril] *n* (*tool*) τρυπάνι, δράπανο ‖ (*mil*) γυμνάσια, ἄσκησις ‖ *vt* (*bore*) τρυπῶ, ἀνοίγω ‖ (*exercise*) ἐκπαιδεύω γυμνάζω ‖ *vi* (+*for*) κάνω γεώτρησι ‖ **~ing** *n* (*of well etc*) διάτρησις, γεώτρησις.

drink [driŋk] (*irreg v*) *n* (*liquid*) ποτόν, ἀναψυκτικόν ‖ (*alcoholic*) ποτό ‖ *vti* (*swallow liquid*) πίνω ‖ **~able** *a* πόσιμος ‖ **~er** *n* πότης ‖ **~ing water** *n* πόσιμο νερό.

drip [drip] *n* στάξιμο, σταλαγματιά ‖ *vi* στάζω, σταλάζω ‖ **~ping** *n* λίπος ψητοῦ ‖ **~ping wet** *a* μουσκεμένος.

drive [draiv] (*irreg v*) *n* (*trip in car*) κούρσα, διαδρομή ‖ (*road*) δρόμος πάρκου ‖ (*campaign*) καμπάνια, ἔρανος ‖ (*energy*) ἐνεργητικότητα, δραστηριότητα ‖ (*sport*) κτήπημα ‖ *vt* (*car etc*) ὁδηγῶ, σωφάρω ‖ (*urge*) διώχνω, σπρώχνω ‖ (*nail etc*) καρφώνω, μπήγω ‖ (*operate*) κινῶ, βάζω μπρός ‖ (*force*) ἀναγκάζω, παρακινῶ ‖ *vi* (*at controls*) ὁδηγῶ, χειρίζομαι ‖ (*travel*) ταξιδεύω, πηγαίνω.

driver ['draivə*] *n* ὁδηγός ‖ **~'s license** *n* (*US*) ἄδεια ὁδηγοῦ.

driving ['draiviŋ] *a* (*rain*) νεροποντή ‖ **~ instructor** *n* δάσκαλος ὁδηγήσεως ‖ **~ lesson** *n* μάθημα ὁδηγήσεως ‖ **~ licence** *n* (*Brit*) ἄδεια ὁδηγοῦ ‖ **~ school** *n* σχολή ὁδηγῶν ‖ **~ test** *n* ἐξέτασις δι'ἄδειαν ὁδηγοῦ.

drizzle ['drizl] *n* ψιχάλισμα ‖ *vi* ψιχαλίζω.

droll [draul] *a* ἀστεῖος, κωμικός.

dromedary ['drɔmidəri] *n* κάμηλος ἡ δρομάς.

drone [draun] *n* (*bee*) κηφήν ‖ (*sound*) βόμβος, βουητό ‖ *vi* σαλιαρίζω, μωρολογῶ.

droop [dru:p] *vi* πέφτω, γέρνω, σκύβω.

drop [drɔp] *n* (*of liquid*) σταγόνα, στάλλα ‖ (*fall*) πτῶσις, πέσιμο ‖ (*med*) σταγών ‖ *vt* (*let fall*) ρίγνω, ἀφήνω νά πέση ‖ (*lower*) κατεβάζω, χαμηλώνω ‖ (*cease*) ἐγκαταλείπω, παρατῶ, ἀφήνω ‖ *vi* (*fall*) πέφτω ‖ **to ~ off** *vi* (*sleep*) ἀποκοιμιέμαι ‖ **to ~ out** *vi* (*withdraw*) ἀποσύρομαι ‖ **~ kick** *n* κλωτσιά ἀπό γκέλι.

dross [drɔs] *n* ἀκαθαρσίες, ἀπορρίμματα.

drought [draut] *n* ξηρασιά.

drove [drəuv] *pt of* **drive** ‖ *n* (*crowd*) πλῆθος ἀνθρώπων, κοπάδι.

drown [draun] *vt* πνίγω ‖ (*flood*) πλημμυρίζω ‖ *vi* πνίγομαι.

drowsy ['drauzi] *a* νυσταλέος, νυσταγμένος.

drudgery ['drʌdʒəri] *n* μόχθος, ἀγγαρεία.

drug [drʌg] *n* (*med*) φάρμακον ‖ (*narcotic*) ναρκωτικόν ‖ *vt* δίδω ναρκωτικόν εἰς, ντοπάρω ‖ **~ addict** *n* τοξικομανής, πρεζάκιας ‖ **~gist** *n* (*US*) φαρμακοποιός ‖ **~store** *n* (*US*) φαρμακεῖον.

drum [drʌm] *n* (*mus*) τύμπανον, τούμπανο ‖ βαρέλι ‖ **~mer** *n* τυμπανιστής.

drunk [drʌŋk] *pp of* **drink** ‖ *n* μέθυσος, μπεκρής ‖ **~ard** *n* μεθύστακας ‖ **~en** *a* μεθυσμένος ‖ **~enness** *n* μέθη, μεθύσι.

dry [drai] *a* (*not wet*) ξηρός, ξερός ‖ (*of well*) στερεμένος ‖ (*rainless*) ἄνυδρος ‖ (*uninteresting*) ξερό, κρύο ‖ (*wine*) μπροῦσκο ‖ *vt* ξηραίνω, στεγνώνω, στίβω ‖ *vi* ξεραίνομαι, στεγνώνω ‖ **to ~ up** *vi* ξεραίνομαι ‖ (*of well*) στερεύω ‖ **~ cleaner** *n* καθαριστήριον ‖ **~er** *n* στεγναστής, στεγνωτήριον ‖ **~ goods** *npl* νεωτερισμοί ‖ **~ness** *n* ξηρασιά, ξηρότης ‖ **~ rot** *n* σαράκι.

dual ['djuəl] *a* διπλός, διττός, δυϊκός ‖ **~ nationality** *n* διπλῆ ὑπηκοότης ‖ **~-purpose** *a* διπλῆς χρήσεως.

dubbed [dʌbd] *a* (*cine*) ντουμπλαρισμένο.

dubious ['dju:biəs] *a* ἀμφίβολος, ἀμφιβάλλων, ἀβέβαιος.

duchess ['dʌtʃis] *n* δούκισσα.

duck [dʌk] *n* πάπια ‖ *vt* βουτῶ, σκύβω ‖ *vi* βουτῶ ‖ **~ling** *n* παπάκι.

duct [dʌkt] *n* ἀγωγός, σωλήν.

dud [dʌd] *n* μή ἐκραγεῖσα ὀβίς ‖ *a* ἄχρηστος, τενεκές, ἀποτυχημένος.

due [dju:] *a* (*owing*) ὀφειλόμενος, λήγων ‖ (*deserved*) δίκαιος, σωστός ‖ (*expected*) ἀναμενόμενος *ad* κατ'εὐθείαν, ἴσια πρός ‖ **~s** *npl* (*debt*) τέλη, δασμός ὀφειλόμενον, ἀνήκον ‖ **~ to** ὀφειλόμενον εἰς, λόγω.

duel ['djuəl] *n* μονομαχία.

duet [dju:'et] *n* δωδία, ντουέτο.

dug [dʌg] *pt,pp of* **dig**.

duke [dju:k] *n* δούξ, δούκας.

dull [dʌl] *a* (*person*) βραδύνους, μπουνταλᾶς ‖ (*boring*) πληκτικός, ἀνιαρός ‖ (*weather*) βαρύς, σκοτεινός ‖ *vt* (*soften, weaken*) ἐξασθενίζω, ξεθωριάζω.

duly ['dju:li] *ad* δεόντως, ἐγκαίρως.

dumb [dʌm] *a* (*lit*) βουβός, μουγγός ‖ (*stupid*) ἀνόητος, κουτός, ἠλίθιος.

dummy ['dʌmi] *n* (*model*) κούκλα, ἀνδρείκελον ‖ (*substitute*) ὁμοίωμα ‖ (*for baby*) πιπιλίστρα ‖ *a* πλαστός, ψεύτικος, εἰκονικός.

dump [dʌmp] *n* σκουπιδότοπος ‖ (*storing place*) ἀποθήκη ‖ *vt* ξεφορτώνω, ἀπορρίπτω ‖ **~ing** *n* (*comm*) ντάμπιγκ ‖ (*rubbish*) ἀνατροπή, ἐκφόρτισις.

dumpling ['dʌmpliŋ] *n* βρασμένη μπουλέττα ‖ (*pie*) πίττα.

dunce [dʌns] *n* ἀμαθής, ντουβάρι.

dune [dju:n] *n* ἀμμόλοφος.

dung [dʌŋ] *n* κοπριά.

dungarees [dʌŋgə'ri:z] *npl* φόρμα ἐργάτου.

dungeon ['dʌndʒən] *n* μπουντρούμι, φυλακή.

duodenal [dju:əu'di:nl] *a* δωδεκαδακτυλικός.

dupe [dju:p] *n* θῦμα, ἀπάτη, κορόϊδο ‖ *v* ἐξαπατῶ, κοροϊδεύω.

duplicate ['dju:plikit] *a* διπλοῦς, διπλάσιος ‖ *n* διπλότυπον ‖ ['dju:plikeit] *vt* ἀντιγράφω ‖ **in ~** εἰς διπλοῦν.

duplicator ['dju:plikeitə*] *n* πολύγραφος.

durability [djuərə'biliti] *n* ἀνθεκτικότης, στερεότης.

durable ['djuərəbl] *a* ἀνθεκτικός, διαρκής.

duration [djuə'reiʃən] *n* διάρκεια.

during ['djuəriŋ] *prep* ἐπί, κατά τήν διάρκειαν.

dusk [dʌsk] *n* σούρουπο.

dust [dʌst] *n* σκόνη, κονιορτός, στάκτη ‖ *vt* ξεσκονίζω, πασπαλίζω ‖ **~bin** *n* (*Brit*) τενεκές σκουπιδιῶν ‖ **~er** *n* ξεσκονόπανο ‖ (*feather*) φτερό ‖ **~man** *n* (*Brit*) ὁδοκαθαριστής, σκουπιδιάρης ‖ **~storm** *n* κονιορτοθύελλα ‖ **~y** *a* σκονισμένος.

Dutch [dʌtʃ] *a* Ὀλλανδικός ‖ *n* (*ling*) ὀλλανδικά ‖ **the ~** *npl* Ὀλλανδοί ‖ **~man** *n* Ὀλλανδέζος ‖ **~woman** *n* Ὀλλανδέζα.

dutiable ['dju:tiəbl] *a* φορολογήσιμος.

duty ['dju:ti] *n* καθῆκον ‖ (*job*) καθήκον(τα), ὑποχρέωσις ‖ (*mil*) ὑπηρεσία ‖ (*tax*) δασμός, φόρος ‖ **on ~** ἐν ὑπηρεσία ‖ **~-free** *a* ἀφορολόγητος ‖ *n* ἀφορολόγητον.

dwarf [dwɔ:f] *n* νάνος.

dwell [dwel] (*irreg v*) *vi* διαμένω, κατοικῶ ‖ **to ~ on** *vt* ἐμμένω εἰς, ἐπιμένω ‖ **~ing** *n* κατοικία.

dwindle ['dwindl] vi ἐλαττώνομαι, μικραίνω.

dye [dai] n βαφή, χρωματισμός ‖ vt βάφω.

dying ['daiiŋ] a (man) ἐτοιμοθάνατος.

dynamic [dai'næmik] a δυναμικός ‖ ~s n δυναμική.

dynamite ['dainəmait] n δυναμῖτις.

dynamo ['dainəməu] n γεννήτρια, δυναμό.

dynasty ['dinəsti] n δυναστεία.

dysentery ['disntri] n δυσεντερία.

dyspepsia [dis'pepsiə] n δυσπεψία.

E, e

each [i:tʃ] a ἕκαστος, πᾶς, καθένας, κάθε ‖ pron ἕκαστος, κάθε ‖ ~ other ὁ ἕνας τόν ἄλλον, ἀλλήλους.

eager ['i:gə*] a ἔνθερμος, ἀνυπόμονος, παθιασμένος ‖ ~ly ad ἐντόνως, ζωηρῶς ‖ ~ness n ζῆλος, ζέσις, ἀνυπομονησία.

eagle ['i:gl] n ἀετός.

ear [iə*] n αὐτί ‖ (for music) λεπτή ἀκοή ‖ (of corn) στάχυς ‖ ~ache n ὠταλγία, αὐτόπονος ‖ ~drum n τύμπανον.

earl [ə:l] n κόμης, κόντες.

early ['ə:li] a (before the season) πρώϊμος, πρόωρος ‖ (in the morning) πρωϊνός ‖ ad (in the morning) πρωΐ ‖ (in time) ἐνωρίς.

earn [ə:n] vt κερδίζω, βγάζω ‖ (acquire) ἀποκτῶ, κατακτῶ.

earnest ['ə:nist] a σοβαρός ‖ (ardent) διάπυρος, ἔνθερμος ‖ in ~ ad στά σοβαρά.

earnings ['ə:niŋz] npl ἀπολαβαί, ἀποδοχαί ‖ (of a firm) κέρδη.

earphones ['iəfəunz] npl ἀκουστικά.

earring ['iəriŋ] n σκουλαρίκι.

earth [ə:θ] n (planet) γῆ, κόσμος ‖ (soil) γῆ, ἔδαφος, χῶμα ‖ (elec) γῆ, προσγείωσις ‖ vt (elec) προσγειώνω ‖ ~enware n πήλινα ‖ ~quake n σεισμός.

earwig ['iəwig] n (insect) φορφικούλη, ψαλλίδα.

ease [i:z] n (facility) εὐχέρεια, εὐκολία, ἄνεσις ‖ (comfort) ἀνάπαυσις, ἄνεσις, ξεκούρασις ‖ vt (reduce pain etc) ἀνακουφίζω, καταπραΰνω ‖ (remove pressure) καθησυχάζω, ξεφορτώνω ‖ at ~ ! ἀνάπαυσις! ‖ to ~ off or up vi ἐλαττώνω, ἐργάζομαι ἀργότερα.

easily ['i:zili] ad ἠρέμως, ἤρεμα, εὔκολα.

east [i:st] n (direction) ἀνατολή ‖ (in direction) ἀνατολικά ‖ a ἀνατολικός ‖ ad πρός ἀνατολάς, ἀνατολικά ‖ the E ~ Ἀνατολή.

Easter ['i:stə*] n Πάσχα, Λαμπρή.

eastern ['i:stən] a (from, of the east) ἀνατολικός.

eastward(s) ['i:stwəd(z)] ad πρός ἀνατολάς.

easy ['i:zi] a (not difficult) εὐχερής, εὔκολος ‖ (life) ξεκούραστη, ἄνετη ‖ (manner) ἄνετος, ἀβίαστος ‖ (yielding) καλόβολος ‖ ad εὔκολα, ἤρεμα, ἥσυχα.

eat [i:t] (irreg v) vt (swallow) τρώγω ‖ (one's words) καταπίνω ‖ (consume) (κατα)-τρώγω, ὑπονομεύω ‖ to ~ away vt κατατρώγω, προσβάλλω ‖ ~able a φαγώσιμος.

eau de Cologne ['əudəkə'ləun] n κολώνια.

eavesdrop ['i:vzdrɔp] vi (+on) κρυφακούω.

ebb [eb] n ἄμπωτις ‖ (fig) παρακμή, πέσιμο ‖ vi κατεβαίνω, πέφτω.

ebony ['ebəni] n ἔβενος, ἀμπανός.

ebullient [i'buliənt] a (enthusiastic) ἐκχειλίζων, ἐνθουσιώδης.

eccentric [ik'sentrik] a (odd) ἐκκεντρικός, παράξενος ‖ n (person) ἰδιότροπος.

ecclesiastical [ikli:zi'æstikl] a ἐκκλησιαστικός.

echo ['ekəu] n ἠχώ, ἀντήχησις, ἀντίλαλος. ‖ vt ἀντηχῶ ‖ vi ἀντηχῶ, ἀπηχῶ, ἀντιλαλῶ.

eclipse [i'klips] n ἔκλειψις ‖ vt προκαλῶ ἔκλειψιν ‖ (fig) ἐπισκιάζω.

economic [i:kə'nɔmik] a οἰκονομικός ‖ ~al a οἰκονομικός ‖ (of person) φειδωλός ‖ ~s npl οἰκονομικά.

economist [i'kɔnəmist] n οἰκονομολόγος.

economize [i'kɔnəmaiz] vi (+on) οἰκονομῶ, κάνω οἰκονομία σέ.

economy [i'kɔnəmi] n (thrift) οἰκονομία ‖ (of country) οἰκονομία.

ecstasy ['ekstəsi] n ἔκστασις, μάγευμα.

ecstatic [ek'stætik] a ἐκστατικός.

ecumenical [i:kju:'menikl] a οἰκουμενικός.

eczema ['eksimə] n ἔκζεμα.

Eden ['i:dn] n Ἐδέμ.

edge [edʒ] n (boundary) ὄχθη, παρυφή, ἄκρη ‖ (of garment) οὔγια ‖ (brink) ἀκμή, χεῖλος, ἄκρη ‖ (of knife) κόψη, ἀκμή ‖ on ~ = edgy.

edging ['edʒiŋ] n: ~ strip n πλαίσιον, μπορντούρα.

edgy ['edʒi] a ἐκνευρισμένος.

edible ['edibl] a φαγώσιμος.

edict ['i:dikt] n ἔδικτον, διάταγμα.

edifice ['edifis] n οἰκοδόμημα, κτίριον.

edit ['edit] vt ἐκδίδω, διευθύνω ‖ ~ion [i'diʃən] n ἔκδοσις ‖ ~or n (of newspaper) (ἀρχι)συντάκτης ‖ (of book) ἐκδότης, ἐπιμελητής ἐκδόσεως ‖ ~orial a ἐκδοτικός, συντακτικός ‖ n (κύριον) ἄρθρον.

educate ['edjukeit] vt ἐκπαιδεύω, σπουδάζω, μαθαίνω.

education [edju'keiʃən] n (system) ἐκπαίδευσις ‖ (schooling) σπουδαί, ἐκπαίδευσις, μόρφωσις ‖ ~al a ἐκπαιδευτικός, μορφωτικός.

eel [i:l] n χέλι.

eerie ['iəri] a μυστηριώδης, παράξενος, τρομακτικός.

efface [i'feis] vt ἐξαλείφω, ἀπαλείφω, σβήνω.

effect [i'fekt] n (result) ἐνέργεια, ἐπίδρασις, ἐπιρροή, ἀποτέλεσμα ‖ (impression) ἐντύπωσις, αἴσθησις ‖ vt πραγματοποιῶ,

επιτυγχάνω ‖ ~s npl (sound, visual)
σκηνικά εφφέ ‖ in ~ πράγματι, πραγματικά ‖ ~ive a αποτελεσματικός, ουσιαστικός.
effeminate [i'feminit] a θηλυπρεπής, γυναικώτος.
effervescent [efə'vesnt] a (ανα)βράζων, αεριούχος ‖ (person) ζωηρός.
efficiency [i'fiʃənsi] n αποτελεσματικότης, δραστικότης ‖ (of machine) απόδοσις.
efficient [i'fiʃnt] a αποτελεσματικός ‖ (person) ικανός, επιδέξιος ‖ ~ly ad αποτελεσματικώς, μέ επιδεξιότητα.
effigy ['efidʒi] n ομοίωμα, εικών.
effort ['efət] n προσπάθεια ‖ ~less a άνευ προσπαθείας, εύκολος.
effrontery [i'frʌntəri] n αυθάδεια, αδιαντροπία.
egalitarian [igæli'teəriən] a ισοπεδωτικός.
egg [eg] n αυγό ‖ boiled ~ n βραστό αυγό ‖ to ~ on vt εξωθώ, παρακινώ, σπρώχνω ‖ ~cup n αυγουλιέρα ‖ ~plant n μελιτζανιά ‖ ~shell n τσόφλι αυγού.
ego ['iːgəu] n τό εγώ.
egotism ['egətizəm] n εγωπάθεια, περιαυτολογία.
egotist ['egətist] n περιαυτολόγος.
Egypt ['iːdʒipt] n Αίγυπτος ‖ ~ian n Αιγύπτιος ‖ a αιγυπτιακός.
eiderdown ['aidədaun] n (quilt) πουπουλένιο πάπλωμα.
eight [eit] num οκτώ, οχτώ ‖ ~een num δέκα οκτώ ‖ ~h a όγδοος ‖ ~y num ογδόντα.
Eire ['eərə] n Ιρλανδία.
either ['aiðə*] a εκάτερος, έκαστος, καθένας ‖ pron ο είς ή ο άλλος, έκαστος ‖ cj ή ... ή, είτε ... είτε ‖ ad ούτε ... ούτε.
eject [i'dʒekt] vt εκβάλλω, βγάζω ‖ (throw out) διώχνω, βγάζω έξω ‖ ~or seat n εκτοξευόμενον κάθισμα.
elaborate [i'læbərit] a επιμελημένος, εξονυχιστικός, περίπλοκος ‖ [i'læbəreit] vt επεξεργάζομαι, δουλεύω, επιμελούμαι ‖ ~ly ad επιμελώς, μετά προσοχής.
elapse [i'læps] vi παρέρχομαι, περνώ.
elastic [i'læstik] n ελαστικόν, λάστιχο ‖ a ελαστικός, εύκαμπτος ‖ ~ band n λαστιχάκι.
elated [i'leitid] a συνεπαρμένος, έξαλλος.
elation [i'leiʃən] n έπαρσις, χαρά, κέφι.
elbow ['elbəu] n αγκώνας, αγκώνας.
elder ['eldə*] a πρεσβύτερος, μεγαλύτερος ‖ n μεγαλύτερος ‖ (tree) ακτή, σαμπούκος ‖ ~ly a ηλικιωμένος.
elect [i'lekt] vt εκλέγω ‖ a εκλεκτός ‖ ~ion n εκλογή ‖ ~ioneering n ψηφοθηρία ‖ ~or n ψηφοφόρος ‖ ~oral a εκλογικός ‖ ~orate n οι ψηφοφόροι.
electric [i'lektrik] a (appliance) ηλεκτρικός ‖ ~al a ηλεκτρικός ‖ ~ blanket n θερμοφόρα κουβέρτα ‖ ~ chair n (US) ηλεκτρική καρέκλα ‖ ~ cooker n η. κουζίνα,

μάτι ‖ ~ current n η. ρεύμα ‖ ~ fire n ηλεκτρική σόμπα ‖ ~ian [ilek'triʃən] n ηλεκτρολόγος ‖ ~ity [ilek'trisiti] n ηλεκτρισμός.
electrification [i'lektrifi'keiʃən] n εξηλεκτρισμός.
electrify [i'lektrifai] vt (εξ)ηλεκτρίζω.
electro- [i'lektrəu] prefix ηλεκτρο-.
electrocute [i'lektrəkju:t] vt θανατώνω δι'ηλεκτρισμού, δι'ηλεκτροπληξίας.
electrocution [ilektrə'kju:ʃən] n ηλεκτροπληξία.
electron [i'lektrən] n ηλεκτρόνιον.
electronic [ilək'trɔnik] a ηλεκτρονικός ‖ ~s n ηλεκτρονική.
elegance ['eligəns] n κομψότης.
elegant ['eləgənt] a κομψός.
element ['eləmənt] n (chem) στοιχείον ‖ (fig) στοιχείον ‖ (elec) στοιχείον ‖ ~ary [eli'mentəri] a στοιχειώδης.
elephant ['elifənt] n ελέφας.
elevate ['eliveit] vt (αν)υψώνω.
elevation [eli'veiʃən] n (height) ύψος ύψωμα.
elevator ['eliveitə*] n ανελκυστήρ, ασανσέρ.
eleven [i'levən] a έντεκα ‖ n (team) ομάς ένδεκα παικτών ‖ ~ses npl κολατσό.
elf [elf] n έλφα, αγερικό, ξωτικό.
elicit [i'lisit] vt εξάγω, αποσπώ, βγάζω.
eligible ['elidʒibl] a εκλέξιμος, κατάλληλος.
eliminate [i'limineit] vt αποβάλλω, διαγράφω ‖ (math) εξαλείφω.
elimination [ilimi'neiʃən] n αποκλεισμός, διαγραφή.
élite [i'liːt] n εκλεκτόν μέρος.
elm [elm] n φτελιά.
elocution [elə'kjuːʃən] n ευγλωττία, απαγγελία.
elongated ['iːlɔŋgeitid] a επιμήκης, μακρύς.
elope [i'ləup] vi απάγομαι, φεύγω (εκουσίως), κλέβομαι ‖ ~ment n εκουσία απαγωγή.
eloquence ['eləkwəns] n ευφράδεια.
eloquent ['eləkwənt] a ευφραδής, εύγλωττος ‖ ~ly ad ευγλώττως.
else [els] ad οποιοσδήποτε άλλος, επί πλέον, αλλού ‖ (otherwise) άλλως, ειδεμή, αλλοιώς ‖ ~where ad αλλαχού αλλού.
elucidate [i'luːsideit] vt διευκρινίζω, διασαφίζω.
elude [i'luːd] vt ξεφεύγω, διαφεύγω.
elusive [i'luːsiv] a άπιαστος, απατηλός.
emaciated [i'meisieitid] a αδυνατισμένος, πετσί καί κόκκαλο.
emanate ['eməneit] vi απορρέω, προέρχομαι, πηγάζω.
emancipate [i'mænsipeit] vt απελευθερώνω ‖ ~d a χειράφετος, ελευθερωθείς.
emancipation [imænsi'peiʃən] n χειραφέτησις, απελευθέρωσις.

E

embalm [im'ba:m] *vt* ταριχεύω, βαλσαμώνω.

embankment [im'bæŋkmənt] *n* ανάχωμα.

embargo [im'ba:gəu] *n* απαγόρευσις, περιορισμός.

embark [im'ba:k] *vt* επιβιβάζω ‖ *vi* επιβιβάζομαι ‖ **to ~ on** *vt* αρχίζω ‖ **~ation** [emba:'keiʃən] *n* μπαρκάρισμα.

embarrass [im'bærəs] *vt* φέρω εις αμηχανίαν, στενοχωρώ ‖ **~ing** *a* (*humiliating*) ενοχλητικός, ξεφτελιστικός ‖ **~ment** *n* στεναχώρια, αμηχανία, μπλέξιμο.

embassy ['embəsi] *n* πρεσβεία.

embed [im'bed] *vt* ενθέτω, χώνω, θάβω.

embellish [im'beliʃ] *vt* καλλωπίζω, γαρνίρω.

embers ['embəz] *npl* θράκα.

embezzle [im'bezl] *vt* καταχρώμαι ‖ **~ment** *n* κατάχρησις, σφετερισμός.

embitter [im'bitə*] *vt* πικραίνω.

emblem ['embləm] *n* (*symbol*) σύμβολον ‖ (*badge etc*) έμβλημα.

embodiment [im'bɔdimənt] *n* ενσάρκωσις, προσωποποίησις.

embody [im'bɔdi] *vt* (*ideas*) ενσαρκώνω, πραγματοποιώ ‖ (*new features*) ενσωματώνω, περιλαμβάνω.

emboss [im'bɔs] *vt* αναγλύφω, χαράσσω αναγλύφως.

embrace [im'breis] *vt* (*clasp*) εναγκαλίζομαι, αγκαλιάζω ‖ (*include*) περιλαμβάνω, περικλείω ‖ *n* εναγκαλισμός, ασπασμός.

embroider [im'brɔidə*] *vt* κεντώ, κάνω κέντημα ‖ **~y** *n* κέντημα.

embryo ['embriəu] *n* (*fig*) έμβρυον.

emerald ['emərld] *n* σμαράγδι.

emerge [i'mə:dʒ] *vi* αναδύομαι, (ξε)βγαίνω, ξεπροβάλλω ‖ **~nce** *n* εμφάνισις ‖ **~ncy** *n* επείγουσα ανάγκη ‖ *a* (*action*) βοηθητικός, έκτακτος ‖ **~ncy exit** *n* έξοδος κινδύνου.

emery ['eməri] *n*: **~ board** *n* γυαλόχαρτο ‖ **~ paper** *n* σμυριδόχαρτον.

emetic [i'metik] *n* εμετικόν.

emigrant ['emigrənt] *n* μετανάστης „ *a* μεταναστευτικός.

emigrate ['emigreit] *vi* μεταναστεύω.

emigration [emi'greiʃən] *n* μετανάστευσις.

eminence ['eminəns] *n* (*distinction*) ανωτερότης, διασημότης ‖ (*eccl*) εξοχότης.

eminent ['eminənt] *a* διακεκριμένος, έξοχος, διάσημος.

emission [i'miʃən] *n* (*of gases*) εκπομπή, αποβολή.

emit [i'mit] *vt* εκπέμπω, αναδίδω.

emotion [i'məuʃən] *n* συγκίνησις, (ψυχική) αναταραχή ‖ **~al** *a* (*person*) ευσυγκίνητος, ευαίσθητος ‖ (*scene*) συγκινητικός ‖ **~ally** *ad* συγκινητικώς, ευαισθήτως.

emotive [i'məutiv] *a* συγκινητικός.

emperor ['empərə*] *n* αυτοκράτορας.

emphasis ['emfəsis] *n* έμφασις.

emphasize ['emfəsaiz] *vt* τονίζω, υπογραμμίζω.

emphatic [im'fætik] *a* εμφατικός ‖ **~ally** *ad* εντόνως, εμφατικώς.

empire ['empaiə*] *n* αυτοκρατορία.

empirical [em'pirikl] *a* εμπειρικός.

employ [em'plɔi] *vt* (*use*) χρησιμοποιώ, εφαρμόζω ‖ (*hire*) απασχολώ, έχω ‖ **~ee** *n* υπάλληλος ‖ **~er** *n* εργοδότης ‖ **~ment** *n* (*job*) απασχόλησις, δουλειά, εργασία ‖ (*jobs collect*) χρήσις, χρησιμοποίησις.

empress ['empris] *n* αυτοκράτειρα.

emptiness ['emptinis] *n* κενότης.

empty ['empti] *a* κενός, άδειος ‖ *vt* (*contents*) κενώνω, αδειάζω ‖ (*container*) αδειάζω ‖ **~-handed** *a* με άδεια χέρια.

emulate ['emjuleit] *vt* αμιλλώμαι, μιμούμαι, ακολουθώ.

emulsion [e'mʌlʃən] *n* γαλάκτωμα.

enable [i'neibl] *vt* καθιστώ ικανόν, διευκολύνω, επιτρέπω.

enamel [i'næml] *n* βερνίκι, σμάλτο, λάκα ‖ (*of teeth*) σμάλτο.

enamoured [i'næməd] *a* (+*of*) ερωτευμένος.

encase [in'keis] *vt* εγκιβωτίζω, καλύπτω.

enchant [in'tʃa:nt] *vt* (*bewitch*) μαγεύω ‖ (*delight*) γοητεύω ‖ **~ing** *a* (*delightful*) γοητευτικός.

encircle [in'sə:kl] *vt* (περι)κυκλώνω, (περι)σφίγγω.

enclose [in'kləuz] *vt* (*shut in*) περικλείω, (περι)μαντρώνω ‖ (*in a letter etc*) εγκλείω, εσωκλείω.

enclosure [in'kləuʒə*] *n* (*space*) φράκτης, μανδρότοιχος ‖ (*in a letter*) συνημμένον εσώκλειστον.

encore ['ɔnkɔ:*] *n* πάλιν, μπίς.

encounter [in'kauntə*] *n* συνάντησις ‖ (*battle*) σύγκρουσις ‖ *vt* (*meet*) συναντώ.

encourage [in'kʌridʒ] *vt* ενθαρρύνω, δίνω κουράγιο ‖ **~ment** *n* εμψύχωσις, ενθάρρυνσις.

encouraging [in'kʌridʒiŋ] *a* ενθαρρυντικός.

encroach [in'krəutʃ] *vi* (+(*up*)*on*) καταπατώ.

encyclop(a)edia [ensaikləu'pi:diə] *n* εγκυκλοπαίδεια.

end [end] *n* (*finish*) τέρμα, τέλος ‖ (*book, day, rope, street, queue*) άκρη, τέλος, ουρά ‖ (*purpose*) σκοπός, επιδίωξις ‖ *a* τελικός, ακραίος ‖ *vt* τερματίζω, τελειώνω ‖ *vi* τερματίζομαι, καταλήγω.

endanger [en'deindʒə*] *vt* διακινδυνεύω, (εκ)θέτω εις κίνδυνον.

endeavour [en'devə*] *n* προσπάθεια ‖ *vi* προσπαθώ, πασχίζω.

ending [in'diŋ] *n* τέλος, κατάληξις.

endive ['endaiv] *n* αντίδι, ραδίκι.

endless ['endlis] *a* ατελείωτος, απέραντος.

endorse [in'dɔs] *vt* (*cheque etc*) οπισθογραφώ, θεωρώ ‖ (*approve*) υποστηρίζω, ἐγκρίνω ‖ ~ment *n* ὀπισθογράφησις ‖ (*of action*) ἔγκρισις.

endow [en'dau] *vt* προικίζω ‖ (*equip*) διωρίζω.

end product ['endprɔdʌkt] *n* τελικὸν προϊόν.

endurable [en'djuərəbl] *a* ἀνεκτός, ὑποφερτός.

endurance [en'djuərəns] *n* ἀντοχή.

endure [en'djuə*] *vt* ὑπομένω, ἀνέχομαι *vi* διαρκῶ, ἀντέχω.

enemy ['enəmi] *n* ἐχθρός ‖ *a* ἐχθρικός.

energetic [enə'dʒetik] *a* ἐνεργητικός, δραστήριος.

energy ['enədʒi] *n* (*of person*) ἐνέργεια, δύναμις ‖ (*phys*) ἐνέργεια.

enforce [en'fɔːs] *vt* ἐπιβάλλω, ἐκτελῶ, ἐφαρμόζω.

engage [en'geidʒ] *vt* (*hire*) προσλαμβάνω, παίρνω ‖ (*take part in*) ἀπασχολῶ, ἐπισύρω, τραβῶ ‖ (*begin fight*) ἐπιτίθεμαι ‖ (*tech*) συνδέω, βάζω ‖ ~d *a* (*to marry*) ἀρραβωνιασμένος ‖ (*tel*) κατειλημμένη, μιλάει ‖ (*in use*) ἀπησχολημένος, πιασμένος ‖ (*person*) εἶμαι προσκεκλημένος, ἔχω κλείσει ‖ ~ment *n* (*appointment*) δέσμευσις, ραντεβοῦ ‖ (*to marry*) μνηστεία, ἀρραβώνιασμα ‖ (*mil*) συμπλοκή, σύγκρουσις ‖ ~ment ring *n* βέρα.

engaging [en'geidʒiŋ] *a* θελκτικός, πού τραβάει.

engender [en'dʒendə*] *vt* γεννῶ, προκαλῶ.

engine ['endʒin] *n* (*aut*) μηχανή, κινητήρ, μοτέρ ‖ (*rail*) ἀτμομηχανή, ὡτομοτρίς ‖ ~er *n* μηχανικός ‖ (*US rail*) μηχανοδηγός ‖ ~ering *n* μηχανολογία ‖ ~ failure *or* trouble *n* βλάβη μηχανῆς ἤ κινητῆρος.

England ['iŋglənd] *n* Ἀγγλία.

English ['iŋgliʃ] *a* ἀγγλικός ‖ *n* (*ling*) (τά) ἀγγλικά ‖ the ~ *npl* οἱ Ἄγγλοι ‖ ~ Channel *n* ἡ Μάγχη ‖ ~man *n* Ἄγγλος, Ἐγγλέζος ‖ ~woman *n* Ἀγγλίδα.

engrave [en'greiv] *vt* χαράσσω.

engraving [en'greiviŋ] *n* χαρακτική.

engrossed [en'grəust] *a* ἀπορροφημένος.

engulf [en'gʌlf] *vt* καταβροχθίζω, καταποντίζω.

enhance [en'haːns] *vt* ἐξαίρω, ἀνυψῶ, ἀνεβάζω.

enigma [e'nigmə] *n* αἴνιγμα ‖ ~tic [enig'mætik] *a* αἰνιγματικός, μυστηριώδης.

enjoy [en'dʒɔi] *vt* μοῦ ἀρέσει, χαίρομαι (κάτι) ‖ (*privileges etc*) ἀπολαμβάνω, κατέχω ‖ ~able *a* ἀπολαυστικός, εὐχάριστος ‖ ~ment *n* ἀπόλαυσις.

enlarge [en'laːdʒ] *vt* μεγεθύνω, ἐπεκτείνω ‖ (*phot*) μεγεθύνω, μεγαλώνω ‖ ~ment *n* μεγέθυνσις.

enlighten [en'laitn] *vt* διαφωτίζω ‖ ~ed *a* φωτισμένος ‖ ~ment *n* διαφώτισις.

enlist [en'list] *vt* στρατολογῶ, προσλαμ-

βάνω ‖ *vi* στρατολογοῦμαι, κατατάσσομαι.

enmity ['enmiti] *n* ἔχθρα, ἐχθρότης.

enormity [i'nɔːmiti] *n* φρικαλεότης, τερατωδία.

enormous [i'nɔːməs] *a* τεράστιος, πελώριος, κολοσσιαῖος ‖ ~ly *ad* κολοσσιαίως, καταπληκτικῶς.

enough [e'nʌf] *n* ἀρκετός, ἐπαρκής, ἱκανός ‖ *a* ἀρκετό ‖ *ad* ἐπαρκῶς, ἀρκετά ‖ ~! ἀρκετά!, φθάνει!, φθάνει πιά!

enquire [en'kwaiə*] = **inquire**.

enrich [en'ritʃ] *vt* (ἐμ)πλουτίζω.

enrol [en'rəul] *vt* (*mil*) στρατολογῶ ‖ *vi* ἐγγράφω, προσλαμβάνω, παίρνω ‖ ~ment *n* στρατολογία ‖ (*sch*) ἀριθμός μαθητῶν.

en route [ɑ̃'ruːt] *ad* καθ'ὁδόν.

ensign [en'sain] *n* (*flag*) σημαία ‖ (*naut*) σημαιοφόρος.

enslave [en'sleiv] *vt* ὑποδουλώνω, σκλαβώνω.

ensue [en'sjuː] *vi* ἕπομαι, ἐπακολουθῶ.

ensuing [en'sjuiŋ] *a* ἑπόμενος, κατοπινός.

ensure [in'ʃuə*] *vt* (*make certain*) (ἐξ)ἀσφαλίζω.

entail [en'tail] *vt* συνεπάγομαι, ἐπιφέρω.

enter ['entə*] *vt* (*go into*) εἰσέρχομαι, μπαίνω ‖ (*join*) εἰσέρχομαι, κατατάσσομαι, γίνομαι ‖ (*write in*) ἐγγράφω, γράφω ‖ *vi* εἰσέρχομαι, μπαίνω ‖ to ~ for *vt* ἐγγράφω ‖ to ~ into *vt* (*agreement*) μπαίνω, συνάπτω, μετέχω ‖ (*argument*) μπαίνω ‖ to ~ upon *vt* ἀναλαμβάνω, ἀρχίζω.

enterprise ['entəpraiz] *n* τόλμη, θάρρος ‖ (*comm*) ἐπιχείρησις.

enterprising ['entəpraiziŋ] *a* τολμηρός.

entertain [entə'tein] *vt* (*as guest*) φιλοξενῶ, περιποιοῦμαι ‖ (*amuse*) διασκεδάζω ‖ ~er *n* ντιτζέρ ‖ ~ing *a* διασκεδαστικός ‖ ~ment *n* (*amusement*) διασκέδασις ‖ (*show*) θέαμα.

enthralled [in'θrɔːld] *a* γοητευμένος, κατακτημένος.

enthusiasm [in'θuːziæzəm] *n* ἐνθουσιασμός.

enthusiast [in'θuːziæst] *n* θαυμαστής, λάτρης ‖ ~ic [inθuːzi'æstik] *a* ἐνθουσιώδης, μανιώδης.

entice [in'tais] *vt* (*tempt*) δελεάζω, ξεμυαλίζω.

entire [en'taiə*] *a* ὁλόκληρος, ὁλάκαιρος, πλήρης ‖ ~ly *ad* ἀκέραια, πλήρως ‖ ~ty *n*: in its ~ty συνολικά.

entitle [en'taitl] *vt* (*allow*) ἐξουσιοδοτῶ, δίδω τό δικαίωμα, ἐπιτρέπω ‖ (*name*) τιτλοφορῶ.

entrance ['entrəns] *n* εἴσοδος, μπάσιμο ‖ [en'traːns] *vt* γοητεύω, μαγεύω ‖ ~ examination *n* εἰσαγωγικές ἐξετάσεις ‖ ~ fee *n* τιμή εἰσητηρίου, τιμή ἐγγραφῆς.

entrancing [in'tra:nsiŋ] *a* γοητευτικός, μαγευτικός.

entrant ['entrənt] *n* ἀρχάριος, μαθητευόμενος.

entrée ['ɔntrei] *n* πρῶτο πιάτο, ἐντράδα.

entrenched [in'trentʃd] *a* ὀχυρωμένος.

entrust [in'trʌst] *vt* (*confide*) ἐμπιστεύομα ‖ (*put in charge*) ἐπιφορτίζω, ἀναθέτω.

entry ['entri] *n* (*place*) εἴσοδος ‖ (*act*) εἴσοδος, ἐμφάνισις ‖ (*in dictionary*) ἐγγραφή, καταχώρισις ‖ 'no ~' 'ἀπαγορεύεται ἡ εἴσοδος' ‖ ~ form *n* αἴτησις ἐγγραφής, δελτίον ἐγγραφῆς.

enunciate [i'nʌnsieit] *vt* προφέρω.

envelop [in'veləp] *vt* (περι)καλύπτω, τυλίγω, σκεπάζω ‖ ~e ['envələup] *n* φάκελλος.

enviable ['enviəbl] *a* ἐπίζηλος, ἀξιοζήλευτος.

envious ['enviəs] *a* ζηλόφθονος, φθονερός, ζηλιάρης.

environment [in'vaiərənmənt] *n* περιβάλλον ‖ ~al *a* τοῦ περιβάλλοντος.

envoy ['envɔi] *n* ἀπεσταλμένος.

envy ['envi] *n* φθόνος, ζήλεια ‖ (*object of envy*) ἀντικείμενον ζήλειας ‖ *vt* φθονῶ, ζηλεύω.

enzyme ['enzaim] *n* ἔνζυμον.

ephemeral [i'femərəl] *a* ἐφήμερος.

epic ['epik] *n* ἔπος, ἐπικόν ποίημα ‖ *a* ἐπικός.

epidemic [epi'demik] *n* ἐπιδημία.

epigram ['epigræm] *n* ἐπίγραμμα.

epilepsy ['epilepsi] *n* ἐπιληψία.

epileptic [epi'leptik] *a,n* ἐπιληπτικός.

epilogue ['epilɔg] *n* ἐπίλογος.

episode ['episəud] *n* ἐπισόδειον.

epistle [i'pisl] *n* ἐπιστολή, γράμμα.

epitaph ['epita:f] *n* ἐπιτάφιον.

epitome [i'pitəmi] *n* ἐπιτομή, περίληψις σύνοψις.

epitomize [i'pitəmaiz] *vt* συνοψίζω, κάνω περίληψιν.

epoch ['i:pɔk] *n* ἐποχή.

equable ['ekwəbl] *a* ὁμοιόμορφος, ἴσος.

equal ['i:kwl] *a* (*same*) ἴσος ‖ (*qualified*) ἀντάξιος, ἀνταποκρίνομαι πρός ‖ *n* ἴσος, ὁμότιμος, ὅμοιος ‖ *vt* ἰσοῦμαι, εἶμαι ἴσος ‖ ~ to ὁμοιό του, ἀνταποκρινόμενος ‖ without ~ ἀσυναγώνιστος ‖ ~ity *n* ἰσότης ‖ ~ize *vt* ἐξισώνω, ἀντισταθμίζω ‖ ~izer *n* ἐξισωτής, ἀντισταθμιστής ‖ ~ly *ad* ἐξ ἴσου, ὁμοίως ‖ ~(s) sign *n* σημεῖον ἰσότητος.

equanimity [ekwə'nimiti] *n* γαλήνη, ἠρεμία.

equate [i'kweit] *vt* ἐξισώνω.

equation [i'kweiʒən] *n* ἐξίσωσις.

equator [i'kweitə*] *n* ἰσημερινός ‖ ~ial [ekwə'tɔ:riəl] *a* ἰσημερινός.

equilibrium [i:kwi'libriəm] *n* ἰσορροπία.

equinox [i'kwinɔks] *n* ἰσημερία.

equip [i'kwip] *vt* ἐφοδιάζω, ἐξοπλίζω ‖ ~ment *n* ἐφόδια, ἐφοδιασμός, ὑλικά.

equitable ['ekwitəbl] *a* δίκαιος.

equity ['ekwiti] *n* δίκαιον, τιμιότης.

equivalent [i'kwivələnt] *a* ἰσότιμος ‖ (*tech*) ἰσοδύναμος ‖ *n* ἰσόποσον.

equivocal [i'kwivəkl] *a* (*doubtful*) διφορούμενος, ἀμφίβολος ‖ (*suspicious*) ὕποπτος.

era ['iərə] *n* ἐποχή.

eradicate [i'rædikeit] *vt* ξερριζώνω.

erase [i'reiz] *vt* ἐξαλείφω, σβήνω ‖ ~r *n* γομολάστιχα, γόμα.

erect [i'rekt] *a* ὀρθός, ὄρθιος, στητός, σηκωμένος ‖ *vt* ὑψώνω, ἀνεγείρω, κτίζω ‖ ~ion *n* ὄρθωσις, σήκωμα, ἀνέργεσις.

ermine ['ə:min] *n* ἐρμίνα.

erode [i'rəud] *vt* διαβιβρώσκω, τρώγω.

erosion [e'rəuʒən] *n* διάβρωσις.

erotic [i'rɔtik] *a* ἐρωτικός ‖ ~ism [i'rɔtisizəm] *n* ἐρωτισμός.

err [ə:*] *vi* (*make mistakes*) σφάλλω, σφάλλομαι ‖ (*sin*) πλανῶμαι, ἁμαρτάνω.

errand ['erənd] *n* παραγγελία, ἀποστολή ‖ ~ boy *n* ὁ μικρός.

erratic [i'rætik] *a* ἄτακτος, ἀκανόνιστος, ἐκκεντρικός.

erroneous [e'rəuniəs] *a* ἐσφαλμένος, λαθεμένος.

error ['erə*] *n* σφάλμα, λάθος.

erudite ['erjudait] *a* πολυμαθής, διαβασμένος.

erupt [i'rʌpt] *vi* ἐκρήγνυμι ‖ ~ion *n* ἔκρηξις, ξέσπασμα.

escalate ['eskəleit] *vt* ἀνεβάζω ‖ *vi* ἀνεβαίνω.

escalator ['eskəleitə*] *n* κυλιωμένη κλῖμαξ.

escapade [eskə'peid] *n* ξέσκασμα, κασκαρίκα.

escape [is'keip] *n* (*getting away*) (δια)φυγή, δραπέτευσις, σκάσιμο ‖ (*leakage*) ἐκφυγή, διαρροή ‖ *vi* (*get free*) δραπετεύω, (δια)σώζομαι ‖ (*unpunished*) ξεφεύγω, γλυτώνω ‖ (*leak*) διαφεύγω, διαρρέω, τρέχω ‖ *vt* (*be forgotten*) διαφεύγω, εἶμαι ἀπαρατήρητος.

escapist [is'keipist] *a* τῆς φυγῆς.

escort ['eskɔ:t] *n* (*mil*) συνοδεία, φρουρά ‖ (*of lady*) συνοδός, καβαλιέρος ‖ [is'kɔ:t] *vt* (*lady*) συνοδεύω ‖ (*mil*) συνοδεύω.

Eskimo ['eskiməu] *n* Ἐσκιμῶος.

especially [is'peʃəli] *ad* εἰδικῶς, ἰδιαιτέρως, κυρίως.

espionage ['espiəna:ʒ] *n* κατασκοπεία.

esplanade ['espləneid] *n* τόπος περιπάτου.

esquire [es'kwaiə*] *n*: J. Brown ε~ (Κύριον).

essay ['esei] *n* (*sch*) ἔκθεσις ‖ (*liter*) δοκίμιον, διατριβή.

essence ['esns] *n* (*quality*) οὐσία ‖ (*perfume*) ἄρωμα, μυρουδιά.

essential [i'senʃl] *a* (*necessary*) οὐσιώδης, οὐσιαστικός ‖ (*basic*) βασικός, ἀπαραίτητος ‖ *n* οὐσία, τό ἀπαραίτητον ‖ ~ly *ad* οὐσιαστικά, κυρίως.

establish [es'tæbliʃ] *vt* (*set up*) ἱδρύω,

θεμελιώνω, ἐγκαθιστῶ ‖ (*prove*) στηρίζω, στερεώνω, ἀποδεικνύω ‖ **~ment** *n* (*setting up*) ἵδρυσις, δημιουργία, ἐπιβολή ‖ (*house of business*) ἵδρυμα, κατάστημα, οἶκος ‖ (*mil*) σύνθεσις (μονάδος) ‖ **the E~ment** τό Κατεστημένον.

estate [es'teit] *n* (*landed property*) κτῆμα, ἀκίνητον ‖ (*property left*) κληρονομία ‖ **~ agent** *n* κτηματομεσίτης ‖ **~ car** *r* (*Brit*) στέϊσον-βάγκον.

esteem [es'ti:m] *n* ἐκτιμῶ, θεωρῶ.

estimate ['estimit] *n* (*opinion*) ἐκτίμησις ‖ (*price quoted*) (προ)ὑπολογισμός, τιμολόγιον ‖ ['estimeit] *vt* ἐκτιμῶ, ὑπολογίζω, λογαριάζω.

estimation [esti'meiʃən] *n* (*judgment*) κρίσις, γνώμη ‖ (*esteem*) ἐκτίμησις, ὑπόληψις.

estuary ['estjuəri] *n* ἐκβολή.

etching ['etʃiŋ] *n* γκραβούρα.

eternal [i'tə:nl] *a* αἰώνιος, ἀτελείωτος ‖ **~ly** *ad* αἰωνίως.

eternity [i'tə:niti] *n* αἰωνιότης.

ether ['i:θə*] *n* αἰθέρας.

ethical ['eθikl] *a* ἠθικός.

ethics ['eθiks] *npl* ἠθική.

ethnic ['eθnik] *a* ἐθνικός.

etiquette ['etiket] *n* ἐθιμοτυπία, ἐτικέττα.

Eucharist ['ju:kərist] *n* Εὐχαριστία, Ἁγία Μετάληψις.

eulogy ['ju:lədʒi] *n* ἐγκώμιον.

eunuch ['ju:nək] *n* εὐνοῦχος, μουνοῦχος.

euphemism ['ju:fəmizəm] *n* εὐφημισμός.

euphoria [ju:'fɔ:riə] *n* εὐφορία.

Europe ['juərəp] *n* Εὐρώπη ‖ **~an** *a* εὐρωπαϊκός.

euthanasia [ju:θə'neiziə] *n* εὐθανασία.

evacuate [i'vækjueit] *vt* ἐκκενώνω, διακομίζω.

evacuation [ivækju'eiʃən] *n* ἐκκένωσις, διακομιδή.

evade [i'veid] *vt* ἀποφεύγω, ξεφεύγω, διαφεύγω.

evaluate [i'væljueit] *vt* ἐκτιμῶ, ὑπολογίζω.

evangelical [i:væn'dʒelikl] *a* εὐαγγελικός.

evangelist [i'vændʒəlist] *n* Εὐαγγελιστής.

evaporate [i'væpəreit] *vi* ἐξατμίζομαι, ξεθυμαίνω ‖ *vt* ἐξατμίζω ‖ **~d milk** *n* γάλα ἔβαπορέ.

evaporation [ivæpə'reiʃən] *n* ἐξάτμισις.

evasion [i'veiʒən] *n* (*avoiding question*) ὑπεκφυγή, πρόφασις.

evasive [i'veisiv] *a* πού ξεφεύγει, πού διαφεύγει.

even ['i:vən] *a* ὁμαλός, ἐπίπεδος, ἴσιος ‖ (*score etc*) ἰσόπαλος, πάτσι ‖ (*number*) ἄρτιος, ζυγός ‖ *vt* σιάζω, ἰσώνω, ἐξισώνω ‖ *ad* ἀκόμη, καί ἄν, ἤ ἀκόμη (*emphasis*) καί ἄν ἀκόμη ‖ **~ if** κάν ‖ **to ~ out** or **up** *vi* πατσίζω, ἀνταποδίδω τά ἴσα.

evening ['i:vniŋ] *n* (*time*) ἑσπέρα, βράδυ ‖ (*event*) ἑσπερίς, βραδυνή συγκέντρωσις ‖ **in the ~** τό βράδυ ‖ **~ class** *n* βραδυνό

μάθημα ‖ **~ dress** *n* (*man's*) φράκο ‖ (*woman's*) βραδυνή τουαλέττα.

evenly ['i:vənli] *ad* ὁμοιομόρφως, ὁμαλῶς, κανονικά.

evensong ['i:vənsɔŋ] *n* (*eccl*) ἑσπερινός.

event [i'vent] *n* (*happening*) γεγονός, περίπτωσις, ἔκβασις ‖ (*sport*) ἄθλημα, ἀγών, μάτς ‖ **in the ~ of** εἰς περίπτωσιν ‖ **~ful** *a* πλήρης γεγονότων, ἀλησμόνητος.

eventual [i'ventʃuəl] *a* (*final*) ὁριστικός, ἀναπόφευκτος, τελικός ‖ **~ity** *n* πιθανότης ‖ **~ly** *ad* (*at last*) τελικά ‖ (*given time*) πιθανῶς.

ever ['evə*] *ad* ποτέ, καμμιά φορά ‖ (*always*) πάντα, πάντοτε ‖ **~ so big** τόσος δά ‖ **~ so many** τόσοι καί τόσοι ‖ **~green** *a* ἀειθαλής ‖ **~lasting** *a* αἰώνιος, διαρκής, ἄφθαρτος.

every ['evri] *a* ἕκαστος, κάθε ‖ **~ other day** μέρα παρά μέρα ‖ **~body** *pron* ὅλοι, ὅλος ὁ κόσμος, καθένας ‖ **~day** *a* (*daily*) κάθε μέρα, καθημερινός ‖ (*commonplace*) συνηθισμένος, κοινός ‖ **~one = ~body** ‖ **~thing** *pron* τά πάντα, ὅλα, κάθε τι ‖ **~where** *ad* πανταχοῦ, παντοῦ.

evict [i'vikt] *vt* ἐκδιώκω, ἐξώνω, διώχνω ‖ **~ion** *n* ἔξωσις, ἐκβολή.

evidence ['evidəns] *n* (*sign*) σημάδι, σημεῖον, ἔνδειξις ‖ (*proof*) ἀπόδειξις, μαρτυρία ‖ **in ~** (*obvious*) διακρινόμαι, ξεχωρίζω.

evident ['evidənt] *a* προφανής, κατάδηλος, φανερός ‖ **~ly** *ad* προφανῶς, ὁλοφάνερα.

evil [i'i:vil] *a* κακός ‖ *n* τό κακόν ‖ (*sin*) κακίᾳ, ἁμαρτία.

evocative [i'vɔkətiv] *a* ἐπικλητικός.

evoke [i'vəuk] *vt* ἐπικαλοῦμαι, ἀναπολῶ.

evolution [i:və'lu:ʃən] *n* ἐξέλιξις, ἀνέλιξις.

evolve [i'vɔlv] *vt* ἀναπτύσσω, συνάγω ‖ *vi* ἐξελίσσομαι, ἀπορρέω.

ewe [ju:] *n* προβατίνα.

ex- [eks] *a* (*former*) πρώην, τέως.

exact [eg'zækt] *a* ἀκριβής, σωστός ‖ *vt* (*obedience etc*) ἀπαιτῶ, ζητῶ ‖ (*payment*) ἀποσπῶ, παίρνω ‖ **~ing** *a* ἀπαιτητικός, κουραστικός ‖ **~itude** *n* ἀκρίβεια ‖ **~ly** *ad* ἀκριβῶς, σωστά ‖ **~ness** *n* ἀκρίβεια.

exaggerate [eg'zædʒəreit] *vti* ὑπερβάλλω, μεγαλοποιῶ, (παρα)φουσκώνω ‖ **~d** *a* ὑπερβολικός, ὑπερβάλλων.

exaggeration [egzædʒə'reiʃən] *n* ὑπερβολή, μεγαλοποίησις.

exalt [eg'zɔ:lt] *vt* ἐξυμνῶ, ἐκθειάζω, ἐπαινῶ.

exam [eg'zæm] *n* (*col, sch, univ*) see **examination**.

examination [egzæmi'neiʃən] *n* (*sch, univ*) ἐξετάσεις, διαγωνισμός ‖ (*med*) (ἰατρική) ἐξέτασις ‖ (*inquiry*) ἀνάκρισις, ἐξέτασις ‖ (*customs*) ἔλεγχος, ἔρευνα.

examine [eg'zæmin] *vt* (*sch*) ἐξετάζω ‖ (*med*) ἐξετάζω ‖ (*consider*) ἐξετάζω, ἐρευνῶ ‖ (*baggage*) ἐρευνῶ, ἐλέγχω ‖ **~r** *n* ἐξεταστής, ἐπιθεωρητής.

example 262 expand

example [ig'za:mpl] *n* (παρά)δειγμα, ὑπόδειγμα ‖ **for** ~ παραδείγματος χάριν, λόγου χάριν.

exasperate [eg'za:spəreit] *vt* ἐξάπτω, ἐξαγριώνω.

exasperating [eg'za:spəreitiŋ] *a* ἐρεθιστικός, ἐξοργιστικός.

exasperation [egza:spə'reiʃən] *n* ἐκνευρισμός, ἔξαψις, ἀπόγνωσις.

excavate ['ekskəveit] *vt* (*hollow out*) σκάπτω, ἀνοίγω, βαθαίνω ‖ (*unearth*) ἀνασκάπτω, κάνω ἀνασκαφές.

excavation [ekskə'veiʃən] *n* ἀνασκαφή.

excavator ['ekskəveitə*] *n* ἐκσκαφεύς.

exceed [ek'si:d] *vt* (*number*) ὑπερβαίνω, (ξε)περνῶ ‖ (*limit*) ὑπερβαίνω ‖ (*powers*) ὑπερβαίνω, ἐξέρχομαι ‖ (*hopes*) ὑπερβάλλω ‖ ~ingly *ad* ὑπερβολικά, πολύ.

excel [ek'sel] *vi* διακρίνομαι, διαπρέπω, ξεχωρίζω ‖ *vt* ὑπερέχω, ὑπερτερῶ, ξεπερνῶ ‖ ~lence ['eksələns] *n* ἀξία, ὑπεροχή, ἀρετή ‖ **His E~lency** *n* ἡ Αὐτοῦ Ἐξοχότης ‖ ~lent *a* ἐξαίρετος, θαυμάσιος, ἐξαίσιος.

except [ek'sept] *prep* (*also* ~ **for**) ἐκτός, ἔξω ἀπό, ἐξαιρουμένου τοῦ ‖ *vt* ἐξαιρῶ, ἀποκλείω ‖ ~ing *prep* = except ‖ ~ion *n* ἐξαίρεσις ‖ **to take** ~ion to προσβάλλομαι, ἀντιλέγω ‖ ~ional *a* ἐξαιρετικός, ἔξοχος, ἀσύγκριτος ‖ ~ionally *ad* ἐξαιρετικά, ὑπερβολικά.

excerpt ['eksə:pt] *n* ἀπόσπασμα.

excess [ek'ses] *n* ὑπερβολή, πληθώρα ‖ *c* (*fare, baggage*) ὑπερβάλλων ‖ ~ive *a* ὑπερβολικός ‖ ~ively *ad* ὑπερβολικά.

exchange [eks'tʃeindʒ] *n* ἀνταλλαγή ‖ (*foreign money*) συνάλλαγμα ‖ (*tel*) κέντρον ‖ *vt* (*goods*) ἀνταλλάσσω, ἀλλάζω ‖ (*greetings*) ἀνταλλάσσω χαιρετισμούς ‖ (*blows*) ἀνταλλάσσω γροθιές ‖ *see* rate.

exchequer [eks'tʃekə*] *n* δημόσιον ταμεῖον, θησαυροφυλάκιον.

excisable [ek'saizəbl] *a* φορολογήσιμος.

excise ['eksaiz] *n* φόρος ‖ [ek'saiz] *vt* φορολογῶ.

excitable [ek'saitəbl] *a* εὐερέθιστος, εὐέξαπτος.

excite [ek'sait] *vt* (ἐξ)ἐρεθίζω, ἐξεγείρω, κεντρίζω ‖ ~d *a* συγκινημένος, ἐκνευρισμένος ‖ **to get** ~d ἐξάπτομαι ‖ ~ment *n* ἔξαψις, ἀναστάτωσις.

exciting [ek'saitiŋ] *a* συναρπαστικός, συγκινητικός.

exclaim [eks'kleim] *vi* φωνάζω, ἀναφωνῶ.

exclamation [eksklə'meiʃən] *n* ἀναφώνησις, κραυγή ‖ ~ **mark** *n* θαυμαστικόν.

exclude [iks'klu:d] *vt* ἀποκλείω.

exclusion [iks'klu:ʒən] *n* ἀπόκλεισις.

exclusive [iks'klu:siv] *a* (*select*) κλειστή, περιορισμένη ‖ (*sole*) ἀποκλειστικότης ‖ μοναδικός ‖ (*news etc*) ἀποκλειστικότης ‖ ~ly *ad* ἀποκλειστικῶς, μόνον.

excommunicate [ekskə'mju:nikeit] *vt* ἀφορίζω, ἀναθεματίζω.

excrement ['ekskrimənt] *n* ἀποπάτημα, σκατά.

excruciating [eks'kru:ʃieitiŋ] *a* φρικτός, ἀνυπόφορος.

excursion [eks'kə:ʃən] *n* ἐκδρομή.

excusable [eks'kju:zəbl] *a* συγχωρητός.

excuse [eks'kju:s] *n* δικαιολογία, πρόφασις ‖ [eks'kju:z] *vt* (*let off*) ἀπαλλάσσω, συγχωρῶ ‖ (*overlook*) δικαιολογῶ ‖ ~ me! συγγνώμη, μέ συγχωρεῖτε.

execute ['eksikju:t] *vt* (*perform*) ἐκτελῶ, ἐκπληρῶ, ἐνεργῶ ‖ (*put to death*) ἐκτελῶ, θανατώνω.

execution [eksi'kju:ʃən] *n* ἐκτέλεσις ‖ ~er *n* δήμιος, μπόγιας.

executive [eg'zekjutiv] *n* (*comm*) διευθυντής ‖ (*pol*) ἐκτελεστική ἐξουσία ‖ *a* ἐκτελεστικός.

executor [eg'zekjutə*] *n* ἐκτελεστής.

exemplary [ig'zempləri] *a* ὑποδειγματικός.

exemplify [ig'zemplifai] *vt* παραδειγματίζω.

exempt [ig'zempt] *a* ἀπηλλαγμένος, ἐξηρημένος ‖ *vt* ἐξαιρῶ, ἀπαλλάσσω ‖ ~ion *n* ἀπαλλαγή.

exercise ['eksəsaiz] *n* (*of duties*) ἄσκησις ‖ (*physical*) γυμναστική ‖ (*sch*) σχολική ἄσκησις, γυμναστική ‖ (*mil*) ἄσκησις, γυμνάσια ‖ *vt* (*muscle*) ἐξασκῶ, γυμνάζω ‖ (*power*) ἐξασκῶ ‖ (*patience*) ἐξαντλῶ ὑπομονήν, κάνω ὑπομονή ‖ ~ **book** *n* τετράδιον (μαθητοῦ).

exhaust [ig'zɔ:st] *n* (*fumes*) ἐξάτμισις, καυσαέρια ‖ (*pipe*) σωλήν ἐξαγωγῆς ‖ *vt* (*weary*) ἐξαντλῶ, κατακουράζω ‖ (*use up*) ἐξαντλῶ, στειρεύω ‖ ~ed *a* ἐξηντλημένος ‖ ~ing *a* ἐξαντλητικός, κουραστικός ‖ ~ion *n* ἐξάντλησις, ἀποκάμωμα, τσάκισμα ‖ ~ive *a* ἐξαντλητικός, πλήρης.

exhibit [ig'zibit] *n* (*art*) ἔκθεμα, ἔκθεσις ‖ (*law*) τεκμήριον ‖ *vt* ἐκθέτω, παρουσιάζω, ἐπιδεικνύω ‖ ~ion [eksi'biʃən] *n* (*art*) ἔκθεσις ‖ (*of temper etc*) ἐπίδειξις, γελοιοποίησις ‖ ~ionist *n* ἐπιδειξίας ‖ ~or *n* ἐκθέτης.

exhilarating [ig'ziləreitiŋ] *a* φαιδρυντικός, εὐχάριστος.

exhilaration [igzilə'reiʃən] *n* χαρά, εὐθυμία, κέφι.

exhort [ig'zɔ:t] *vt* προτρέπω, ἐνθαρρύνω.

exile ['eksail] *n* ἐξορία ‖ (*person*) ἐξόριστος.

exist [ig'zist] *vi* ὑπάρχω, ὑφίσταμαι, εἰμαι, ζῶ ‖ ~ence *n* (*state of being*) ὕπαρξις ‖ (*way of life*) ζωή ‖ ~ing *a* ὑπάρχων, παρών, σημερινός.

exit ['eksit] *n* ἔξοδος.

exorbitant [eg'zɔ:bitənt] *a* ὑπερβολικός, ὑπέρμετρος.

exotic [ig'zɔtik] *a* ἐξωτικός.

expand [iks'pænd] *vt* (*spread*) διαστέλλω,

εὐρύνω, ἁπλώνω ‖ (operations) ἐπεκτείνω, ἀναπτύσσω ‖ vi διαστέλλομαι, φουσκώνω.

expanse [eks'pæns] n ἔκτασις.

expansion [iks'pænʃən] n ἐπέκτασις, ἀνάπτυξις ‖ (phys) διαστολή, ἐκτόνωσις.

expatriate [eks'pætrieit] vt ἐκπατρίζω, ἐκπατρίζομαι.

expect [iks'pekt] vt (anticipate) ἀναμένω, προσδοκῶ, περιμένω ‖ (require) ἀπαιτῶ, ἀναμένω ‖ (suppose) σκέπτομαι, φρονῶ, πιστεύω ‖ (baby) περιμένω ‖ vi: to be ~ing περιμένω παιδί ‖ ~ant a (hopeful) περιμένων, ἀναμένων ‖ (mother) ἐπίτοκος ‖ ~ation [ekspek'teiʃən] n (hope) προσδοκία, ἐλπίδα ‖ ~ations npl ἐλπίδες.

expedience [eks'pi:diəns] n, **expediency** [eks'pi:diənsi] n σκοπιμότης, ὠφελιμότης.

expedient [eks'pi:diənt] a σκόπιμος, πρόσφορος, κατάλληλος ‖ n μέσον, τρόπος, τέχνασμα.

expedite ['ekspidait] vt ἐπισπεύδω, ἐπιταχύνω.

expedition [ekspi'diʃən] n (journey) ἀποστολή, ἐκστρατεία.

expel [eks'pel] vt διώχνω, βγάζω ‖ (alien) ἀπελαύνω.

expend [eks'pend] vt (time) ἀφιερώνω, διαθέτω ‖ (money) δαπανῶ, ξοδεύω ‖ (effort) δαπανῶ, ἐξαντλῶ ‖ ~able a ἀναλώσιμος ‖ ~iture n δαπάνη, κατανάλωσις, ἔξοδα.

expense [eks'pens] n (cost) δαπάνη, ἔξοδα ‖ (high cost) βάρος, ἀκρίβεια ‖ ~s npl ἀποζημιώσεις, δαπάναι ‖ at the ~ of μέ τήν θυσία τοῦ, εἰς βάρος τοῦ ‖ ~ account n ἔξοδα παραστάσεως.

expensive [eks'pensiv] a πολυδάπανος, δαπανηρός, ἀκριβός.

experience [eks'piəriəns] n (happening) δοκιμασία, περιπέτεια ‖ (knowledge) πεῖρα, ἐμπειρία ‖ vt δοκιμάζω, ὑφίσταμαι, αἰσθάνομαι ‖ ~d a πεπειραμένος, ἔμπειρος.

expert ['ekspə:t] n εἰδικός, ἐμπειρογνώμων, πραγματογνώμων ‖ a πεπειραμένος, εἰδικός ‖ ~ise n πραγματογνωμοσύνη.

expiration [ekspi'reiʃən] n ἐκπνοή.

expire [eks'paiə*] vi (end) ἐκπνέω, λήγω, τελειώνω ‖ (die) ἀποθνήσκω, πεθαίνω ‖ (ticket) λήγω.

expiry [eks'paiəri] n ἐκπνοή, λῆξις.

explain [eks'plein] vt (make clear) ἐξηγῶ, λύω, ἑρμηνεύω ‖ (account for) ἐξηγοῦμαι, δικαιολογοῦμαι ‖ to ~ away vt ἐξηγῶ, δικαιολογῶ.

explanation [eksplə'neiʃən] n ἐξήγησις.

explanatory [eks'plænətəri] a ἑρμηνευτικός, ἐξηγητικός.

explicable [eks'plikəbl] a ἐξηγήσιμος.

explicit [eks'plisit] a ῥητός, σαφής, καθα-

ρός, κατηγορηματικός ‖ ~ly ad κατηγορηματικῶς, ῥητῶς.

explode [eks'pləud] vi σκάω, ἀνατινάζομαι.

exploit ['eksplɔit] n κατόρθωμα, ἀνδραγάθημα ‖ [iks'plɔit] vt ἐκμεταλλεύομαι ‖ ~ation n ἐκμετάλλευσις.

exploration [eksplə'reiʃən] n ἐξερεύνησις, ἔρευνα.

exploratory [eks'plɔrətəri] a (fig) δοκιμαστικός.

explore [eks'plɔ:*] vt (for discovery) ἐξερευνῶ ‖ (examine) ἐξετάζω, (ἐξ)ἐρευνῶ ‖ ~r n ἐξερευνητής.

explosion [eks'pləuʒən] n (lit) ἔκρηξις, ἐκτόνωσις ‖ (fig) ξεχείλισμα, ξέσπασμα.

explosive [eks'pləuziv] a ἐκρηκτικός ‖ n ἐκρηκτικόν, ἐκρηκτική ὕλη.

exponent [eks'pəunənt] n ἑρμηνευτής, ὑπέρμαχος ‖ (math) ἐκθέτης.

export [eks'pɔ:t] vt ἐξάγω ‖ ['ekspɔ:t] n ἐξαγωγή ‖ a (trade) ἐξαγωγικός ‖ ~ation n ἐξαγωγή ‖ ~er n ἐξαγωγεύς.

expose [eks'pəuz] vt (uncover) ἐκθέτω, ἀποκαλύπτω, ξεσκεπάζω ‖ (leave unprotected) ἀφήνω ἀπροστάτευτον, ἐκθέτω ‖ (plot) ἀποκαλύπτω.

exposé [eks'pəuzei] n (of scandal) ἀποκάλυψις σκανδάλου.

exposed [eks'pəuzd] a (position) ἐκτεθειμένος.

exposure [eks'pəuʒə*] n τράβηγμα, πόζα, φωτογραφία ‖ (med) ἔκθεσις ‖ ~ meter n φωτόμετρον.

expound [eks'paund] vt ἀναπτύσσω, ἐκθέτω, ἐξηγῶ.

express [eks'pres] a (clearly stated) σαφής, ῥητός ‖ (speedy) ταχύς ‖ n (fast train) ταχεία, ἐξπρές ‖ ad (speedily) γρήγορα, ἄνευ σταθμοῦ ‖ vt (idea) ἐκφράζω, διατυπώνω ‖ (feeling) ἐκφράζω, ἐκδηλώνω ‖ to ~ o.s. ἐκφράζομαι ‖ ~ion n (phrase) (ἐκ)φρασις, τρόπος ἐκφράσεως ‖ (look on face) ἔκφρασις ‖ (showing) ἐκδήλωσις ‖ ~ive a ἐκφραστικός ‖ ~ly ad ῥητῶς, ἐπίτηδες.

expropriate [eks'prəuprieit] vt ἀπαλλοτριῶ.

expulsion [eks'pʌlʃən] n ἀπέλασις, ἀποβολή.

exquisite [eks'kwizit] a ἄριστος, εὐχάριστος, λεπτός ‖ ~ly ad μέ λεπτότητα, ἐξαιρετικά.

extend [eks'tend] vt (visit) παρατείνω ‖ (building) ἐπεκτείνω, μεγαλώνω ‖ (hand) τείνω, δίνω (τό χέρι) ‖ (welcome) εὔχομαι, καλωσορίζω.

extension [eks'tenʃən] n (general) ἔκτασις, ἐπέκτασις, ἅπλωμα ‖ (building) ἐπέκτασις, εὔρυνσις ‖ (tel) ἐσωτερική γραμμή.

extensive [eks'tensiv] a ἐκτεταμένος, ἐκτενής, μεγάλος ‖ ~ly ad (travel) εὐρέως ‖ (use) ἐκτεταμένα.

extent [eks'tent] n ἔκτασις, σημασία, μέγεθος.

extenuating [eks'tenju:eitiŋ] *a* ἐλαφρυντικόν.

exterior [eks'tiəriə*] *a* ἐξωτερικός ‖ *n* ἐξωτερικόν, ἔξω.

exterminate [eks'tə:mineit] *vt* ἐξοντώνω, ἐξολοθρεύω.

extermination [ekstə:mi'neiʃən] *n* ἐξολόθρευσις, ἐκρίζωσις.

external [eks'tə:nl] *a* ἐξωτερικός ‖ ~ly *ad* ἐξωτερικῶς, ἀπέξω.

extinct [eks'tiŋkt] *a* (*animal etc*) ἐκλειπών, ἐξαφανισθείς ‖ ~ion *n* ἐξαφάνισις, σβήσιμο.

extinguish [eks'tiŋgwiʃ] *vt* σβήνω ‖ ~er *n* πυροσβεστήρ.

extort [iks'tɔ:t] *vt* (+*from*) ἀποσπῶ ‖ ~ion [iks'tɔ:ʃən] *n* ἀναγκαστικὴ εἴσπραξις, ἀπόσπασις ‖ ~ionate *a* ὑπερβολικός.

extra ['ekstrə] *a* πρόσθετος, ἔκτακτος, ἔξτρα ‖ *ad* ἄνω τοῦ συνήθους, ἐξαιρετικῶς, πολύ ‖ *n* συμπλήρωμα ‖ (*newspaper*) ἔκτακτος ἔκδοσις ‖ (*theat*) κομπάρσος.

extract [eks'trækt] *vt* (*distil*) ἀποστάζω ‖ (*select*) ἐξάγω, βγάζω, παίρνω ‖ ['ekstrækt] *n* (*liter*) ἀπόσπασμα, ἐκλογὴ ‖ (*cooking*) ἐκχύλισμα ‖ ~ion *n* ἐξαγωγή, βγάλσιμο ‖ (*origin*) καταγωγή, προέλευσις.

extradite ['ekstrədait] *vt* ἐκδίδω (ἐγκληματίαν).

extradition [ekstrə'diʃən] *n* ἔκδοσις (ἐγκληματίου).

extraneous [eks'treiniəs] *a* ξένος, ἄσχετος.

extraordinary [eks'trɔ:dnri] *a* ἔκτακτος, ἐξαιρετικός ‖ (*strange*) παράξενος, ἀλλόκοτος.

extravagance [eks'trævəgəns] *n* (*wasteful spending*) σπατάλη ‖ (*no restraint*) ὑπερβολή, παραλογισμός.

extravagant [eks'trævəgənt] *a* (*lavish*) ὑπερβολικός, παράλογος ‖ (*wasteful*) σπάταλος, ἄσωτος.

extreme [eks'tri:m] *a* (*last*) ἀκραῖος, ἔσχατος, μακρυνός ‖ (*very great*) ὑπερβολικός, μέγιστος ‖ (*not moderate*) τῶν ἄκρων, ἐξαιρετικός ‖ *n* ἄκρον, ἐσχατιά, ἄκρη ‖ ~s *npl* ἄκρα ‖ ~ly *ad* ἄκρως, εἰς τὸ ἔπακρον.

extremist [eks'tri:mist] *a* ἀδιάλλακτος, τῶν ἄκρων ‖ *n* ἐξτρεμιστής.

extremity [eks'tremiti] *n* (*farthest end*) ἄκρον, ἐσχατιά, ἄκρη ‖ (*necessity*) ἐσχάτη ἀνάγκη ‖ (*anat*) τά ἄκρα.

extricate ['ekstrikeit] *vt* ἐξάγω, βγάζω, ξεμπλέκω.

extrovert ['ekstrəuvə:t] *a,n* ἐξώστροφος.

exuberance [ig'zju:bərəns] *n* ὑπερεκχείλισις, διάχυσις.

exuberant [ig'zju:bərənt] *a* διαχυτικός, ὑπερεκχειλίζων.

exude [ig'zju:d] *vt* ἐξιδρῶ, ἐκχύνω.

exult [ig'zʌlt] *vi* χαίρομαι, ἀγάλλομαι,

θριαμβεύω ‖ ~ation [egzʌl'teiʃən] *n* ἀγαλλίασις.

eye [ai] *n* (*anat*) ὀφθαλμός, μάτι ‖ (*of needle*) μάτι, τρύπα ‖ (*for perception*) καλό μάτι, μάτι ζωγράφου κτλ ‖ (*in the public eye*) διάσημος ‖ *vt* ὑποβλέπω, ἐποφθαλμιῶ, κοιτάζω ‖ **to keep an ~ on** προσέχω, ἐπιβλέπω, παρακολουθῶ ‖ **in the ~s of** ἐνώπιον, στὰ μάτια ‖ **up to the ~s in** πνιγμένος στό, φορτωμένος μέ ‖ ~**ball** *n* βολβός ὀφθαλμοῦ ‖ ~**brow** *n* φρύδι ‖ ~**lash** *n* βλεφαρίδα, ματοτσίνουρο ‖ ~**lid** *n* βλέφαρον ‖ ~**-opener** *n* ἔκπληξις, ἀποκάλυψις ‖ ~**shadow** *n* σκιά ματιῶν ‖ ~**sight** *n* ὅρασις ‖ ~**sore** *n* ἀσχημιά ‖ ~**wash** *n* (*lit*) κολλύριον ὑγρόν ‖ (*fig*) ἀπάτη, φούμαρα ‖ ~**witness** *n* αὐτόπτης μάρτυς.

F, f

fable ['feibl] *n* μῦθος, παραμύθι.

fabric ['fæbrik] *n* (*cloth*) ὕφασμα, πανί.

fabulous ['fæbjuləs] *a* (*imaginary*) μυθικός, μυθώδης ‖ (*wonderful*) μυθικός ‖ (*unbelievable*) ὑπερβολική.

façade [fə'sa:d] *n* πρόσοψις.

face [feis] *n* (*anat*) πρόσωπον, φάτσα, μούρη ‖ (*appearance*) φυσιογνωμία ‖ (*grimace*) μορφασμός ‖ (*front*) ὄψις, ἐμφάνισις ‖ (*of clock*) καντράν ‖ *vt* (*look towards*) ἀντικρύζω, γυρίζω ‖ (*bravely*) ἀντιμετωπίζω ‖ **in the ~ of** ἐνώπιον, μπρός ἀπό, εἰς ‖ **to ~ up to** *vt* ἀντιμετωπίζω ‖ ~ **cream** *n* κρέμα (τοῦ προσώπου) ‖ ~ **powder** *n* πούδρα (τοῦ προσώπου).

facet ['fæsit] *n* (*single part*) μέρος, πλευρά ‖ (*of gem*) ἕδρα διαμαντιοῦ.

facetious [fə'si:ʃəs] *a* εὐτράπελος, ἀστεῖος, περιπαικτικός ‖ ~ly *ad* εὐτράπελα, πειραχτά.

face to face ['feistu'feis] *ad* πρόσωπο μέ πρόσωπο, φάτσα μέ φάτσα.

face value ['feis'vælju:] *n* ὀνομαστικὴ ἀξία.

facial ['feiʃəl] *a* τοῦ προσώπου, καθάρσις, μάσκα.

facile ['fæsail] *a* (*US: easy*) εὔκολος.

facilitate [fə'siliteit] *vt* (δι)ευκολύνω.

facility [fə'siliti] *n* (*ease*) εὐχέρεια, εὐκολία ‖ **facilities** *npl* ἀνέσεις, εὐκολίες.

facing ['feisiŋ] *a,prep* ἀπέναντι ἀπό, ἀντίκρυ.

facsimile [fæk'simili] *n* πανομοιότυπον.

fact [fækt] *n* γεγονός, πραγματικότης ‖ *see* matter.

faction ['fækʃən] *n* φατρία, κόμμα.

factor ['fæktə*] *n* παράγων, συντελεστής.

factory ['fæktəri] *n* ἐργοστάσιον.

factual ['fæktjuəl] *a* πραγματικός.

faculty ['fækəlti] *n* (*ability*) ἱκανότης, προσόν ‖ (*univ*) σχολὴ ‖ (*US: teaching staff*) διδακτικὸν προσωπικόν.

fade [feid] *vt* (*cause to fade*) ξεθωριάζω, ξεβάφω ‖ *vi* (*grow dim*) ἐξασθενίζω, ἀδυνατίζω, πέφτω ‖ (*lose colour*) ξασπρίζω, ξεθωριάζω, ξεβάφω ‖ (*wither*) μαραίνομαι ‖ ~**d** *a* ξεβαμμένος, ξεθωριασμένος ‖ (*of flower*) μαραμένος.

fag [fæg] *n* ἀγγαρεία, μόχθος ‖ (*col: cigarette*) τσιγάρο ‖ ~**ged** *a* (*exhausted*) ἐξηντλημένος.

Fahrenheit ['færənhait] *n* Φαρενάϊτ.

fail [feil] *vt* (*exam*) ἀπορρίπτω, ἀποτυγχάνω ‖ *vi* (*run short*) ἐλείπω, λείπω, δέν ὑπάρχω ‖ (*lose. power*) ἐγκαταλείπω, χάνω, ἐξασθενίζω ‖ (*light*) ἐξασθενίζω, πέφτω, σβήνω ‖ (*remedy*) ἀποτυγχάνω ‖ **to ~ to do sth** (*neglect*) παραλείπω, ἐγκαταλείπω ‖ (*be unable*) ἀποτυγχάνω ‖ **without ~** χωρίς ἄλλο ‖ ~**ing** *n* (*shortcoming*) ἐλάττωμα, ἀδυναμία ‖ *prep* ἐλλείψει ‖ ~**ure** *n* (*person*) ἀποτυχημένος ‖ (*mech*) διακοπή, βλάβη.

faint [feint] *a* ἀδύνατος, ἀσθενής, ἀμυδρός, δειλός ‖ *n* λιποθυμία, ἀναισθησία ‖ *vi* λιποθυμῶ ‖ ~**hearted** *a* δειλός, μικρόψυχος, φοβιτσιάρης ‖ ~**ly** *ad* ντροπαλά, ἀδύνατα, ἄτονα, μόλις ‖ ~**ness** *n* (*of voice*) ἀδυναμία ‖ (*of light*) ἀμυδρότης.

fair [fɛə*] *a* (*beautiful*) ὡραῖος, ὅμορφος ‖ (*light*) ξανθός, ἄσπρος ‖ (*weather*) καλός καιρός, καλοκαιριά ‖ (*just, honest*) δίκαιος, ἔντιμος, τίμιος ‖ (*tolerable*) ὑποφερτός ‖ (*conditions*) ἔτσι καί ἔτσι ‖ (*sizeable*) ἀρκετός, μεγάλος ‖ *ad* (*play*) τίμια, δίκαια, ἐντίμως ‖ *n* (*comm*) πανήγυρις, ἔκθεσις ‖ (*fun fair*) λούνα-πάρκ, πανηγύρι ‖ ~**ly** *ad* ἔντιμα, δίκαια ‖ (*rather*) ἀρκετά καλό, σχεδόν, καλούτσικα ‖ ~**ness** *n* τιμιότης, ἐντιμότης ‖ ~**way** *n* (*golf*) κανονική διαδρομή.

fairy ['fɛəri] *n* νεράιδα ‖ ~**land** *n* χώρα τῶν παραμυθιῶν ‖ ~ **tale** *n* παραμύθι.

faith [feiθ] *n* (*trust*) ἐμπιστοσύνη, πίστις ‖ (*rel*) πίστις, θρήσκευμα, θρησκεία ‖ **on good ~** μέ καλή πίστι ‖ ~**ful** *a* πιστός ‖ ~**fully** *ad* πιστῶς, ἐντίμως ‖ (*in letter*) ὑμέτερος.

fake [feik] *n* (*thing*) ψεύτικο εἶδος, ἀπομίμησις ‖ (*person*) ἀπατεών ‖ *a* ψεύτικο, πλαστό ‖ *vt* παραποιῶ, πλαστογραφῶ.

falcon ['fɔ:lkən] *n* γεράκι.

fall [fɔ:l] (*irreg v*) *n* πτῶσις, κατέβασμα ‖ (*drop*) πτῶσις, πέσιμο ‖ (*of snow*) πτῶσις ‖ (*US: autumn*) φθινόπωρον ‖ *vi* πέφτω, πίπτω ‖ ~**s** *npl* (*waterfall*) καταρράκτης ‖ **to ~ down** *vi* (*person*) πέφτω χάμω ‖ (*building*) καταρρέω, γκρεμίζομαι ‖ (*fail*) ἀποτυγχάνω, πέφτω ‖ **to ~ flat** *vi* πάω χαμένο, πέφτω στά κούφια, πέφτω ‖ **to ~ for** *vt* (*trick*) πιάνομαι κορόϊδο, πέφτω στήν παγίδα ‖ **to ~ off** *vi* (*drop off*) πέφτω ‖ (*diminish*) πέφτω, φθίνω, μειώνομαι, ὀλιγοστεύω ‖ **to ~ out** *vi* τσακώνομαι, τά χαλῶ ‖ **to ~ through** *vi* ἀποτυγχάνω,

γκρεμίζομαι ‖ **to ~ under** *vi* ὑπάγομαι εἰς.

fallacy ['fæləsi] *n* σόφισμα, πλάνη.

fallen ['fɔ:lən] *pp of* **fall**.

fallible ['fæləbl] *a* σφαλερός.

fallout ['fɔ:laut] *n* ραδιενεργός κόνις.

fallow ['fæləu] *a* χέρσος, ἀκαλλιέργητος.

false [fɔ:ls] *a* (*untrue*) ψευδής, ψεύτικος, λαθεμένος ‖ (*sham*) πλαστός, τεχνητός, κίβδηλος ‖ **under ~ pretences** δι'ἀπάτης ‖ ~ **alarm** *n* ἀδικαιολόγητος φόβος ‖ ~**ly** *ad* ψεύτικα, ἀπατηλά ‖ ~ **teeth** *npl* μασέλλες.

falter ['fɔ:ltə*] *vi* διστάζω, κοντοστέκω, κομπιάζω ‖ (*in speech*) τραυλίζω, ψευδίζω ‖ ~**ing** *a* διστακτικός, ἀσταθής.

fame [feim] *n* φήμη.

familiar [fə'miliə*] *a* (*well-known*) γνωστός, γνώριμος ‖ (*intimate*) οἰκεῖος, στενός, φιλικός ‖ **to be ~ with** ξαίρω, γνωρίζω ‖ ~**ity** *n* οἰκειότης, ἐξοικείωσις ‖ ~**ize** *vt* ἐξοικειοῦμαι μέ, συνηθίζω.

family ['fæmili] *n* οἰκογένεια, φαμίλια ‖ ~ **allowance** *n* ἐπίδομα οἰκογενείας ‖ ~ **business** *n* οἰκογενειακή ἐπιχείρησις ‖ ~ **doctor** *n* οἰκογενειακός ἰατρός ‖ ~ **life** *n* οἰκογενειακή ζωή.

famine ['fæmin] *n* λιμός, πεῖνα.

famished ['fæmiʃt] *a* πειναμένος.

famous ['feiməs] *a* διάσημος, περίφημος, φημισμένος ‖ ~**ly** *ad* περίφημα, σπουδαῖα.

fan [fæn] *n* (*folding ~*) βεντάλια ‖ (*elec*) ἀνεμιστήρας ‖ (*sport etc*) φανατικός, θαυμαστής, λάτρης ‖ *vt* ἀεριζω, ἀνεμίζω ‖ **to ~ out** *vi* ἀναπτύσσω, ἁπλώνω.

fanatic [fə'nætik] *n* φανατικός ‖ ~**al** *a* φανατικός.

fan belt ['fænbelt] *n* ἱμάς, ταινία, λουρί.

fancied ['fænsid] *a* φανταστικός, φαντασιώδης.

fanciful ['fænsiful] *a* (*odd*) παράξενος, ἰδιότροπος ‖ (*imaginative*) φανταστικός.

fancy ['fænsi] *n* (*liking*) συμπάθεια, ἀγάπη, τσίμπημα ‖ (*imagination*) φαντασία, φανταστικόν πρᾶγμα ‖ *a* φαντασιώδης, φανταχτερός, φαντάζι ‖ *vt* (*like*) συμπαθῶ, μοῦ ἀρέσει ‖ (*imagine*) φαντάζομαι, ὑποθέτω ‖ (*just*) ~ (*that*)! γιά φαντάσου! ‖ ~ **dress** *n* μεταμφίεσις ‖ ~**-dress ball** *n* χορός μεταμφιεσμένων, μπάλ μασκέ.

fanfare ['fænfɛə*] *n* σάλπισμα.

fang [fæŋ] *n* δόντι ‖ (*of snake*) φαρμακερό δόντι.

fantastic [fæn'tæstik] *a* παράξενος, φαντασιώδης, ἀλλόκοτος.

fantasy ['fæntəzi] *n* φαντασία, καπρίτσιο.

far [fɑ:*] *a* μακρυνός, ἀπώτερος ‖ *ad* μακρυά, μακράν ‖ (*very much*) κατά πολύ, τόσο πολύ ‖ ~ **away**, ~ **off** πολύ μακρυά ‖ **by ~** ἀσυγκρίτως, κατά πολύ ‖ **so ~**

ἕως ἐδῶ, μέχρι τοῦδε ‖ ~**away** *a* μακρυνός ‖ the F ~ East ΄Άπω ΄Ανατολή.
farce [fɑːs] *n* κωμωδία, φάρσα.
farcical [ˈfɑːsikəl] *a* γελοῖος, κωμικός, σάν φάρσα.
fare [fɛə*] *n* εἰσητήριον, ναῦλα ‖ (*food*) φαΐ ‖ *vi* τά πάω, πηγαίνω ‖ ~**well** *n* ἀποχαιρετισμός ‖ *excl* ἀντίο!, χαίρετε!, γειά σου! ‖ *a* ἀποχαιρετιστήριος.
far-fetched [ˈfɑːˈfetʃt] *a* ἐξεζητημένος, παρατραβηγμένος.
farm [fɑːm] *n* ἀγρόκτημα, φάρμα ‖ *vt* καλλιεργῶ ‖ ~**er** *n* γεωργός, ἀγρότης, φαρμαδόρος ‖ ~**hand** *n* ἀγροτικός ἐργάτης ‖ ~**house** *n* ἀγροικία ‖ ~**ing** *n* γεωργία, καλλιέργεια ‖ ~**land** *n* ἀγροτική ἔκτασις ‖ ~**yard** *n* περίβολος ἀγροικίας.
far-reaching [ˈfɑːˈriːtʃiŋ] *a* μεγάλης ἐκτάσεως, μεγάλης σημασίας.
far-sighted [ˈfɑːˈsaitid] *a* προνοητικός, διορατικός.
fart [fɑːt] (*col*) *n* πορδή ‖ *vi* πέρδομαι, κλάνω.
farther [ˈfɑːðə*] *a* μακρυνότερος, ἀπώτερος ‖ *ad* μακρύτερα, περαιτέρω.
farthest [ˈfɑːðist] *a* ἀπώτατος, μακρυνότερος ‖ *ad* μακρύτατα, πιὸ μακρυά.
fascinate [ˈfæsineit] *vt* γοητεύω, μαγεύω.
fascinating [ˈfæsineitiŋ] *a* γοητευτικός, μαγευτικός.
fascination [fæsiˈneiʃən] *n* γοητεία, μάγεμα
fascism [ˈfæʃizəm] *n* φασισμός.
fascist [ˈfæʃist] *n* φασιστής, φασίστας ‖ *a* φασιστικός.
fashion [ˈfæʃən] *n* (*custom*) ράψιμο, μόδα ‖ (*manner*) τρόπος, συνήθεια, μορφή ‖ *vt* σχηματίζω, διαμορφώνω, πλάθω ‖ **in ~** τῆς μόδας ‖ **out of ~** ντεμοντέ ‖ **after a ~** ὅπως-ὅπως, ἔτσι κι ἔτσι ‖ ~**able** *a* (*clothes*) τῆς μόδας, μοντέρνος ‖ (*place*) κοσμικός ‖ ~ **show** *n* ἐπίδειξις μόδας.
fast [fɑːst] *a* (*swift*) ταχύς, γρήγορος ‖ (*ahead of time*) πού τρέχει, πού πάει ἐμπρός ‖ (*steady, firm*) σταθερός, στερεός, σφικτός ‖ (*firmly fixed*) στερεός, γερός ‖ *ad* (*rapidly*) ταχέως, γρήγορα ‖ (*firmly*) στερεά, γερά ‖ *n* νηστεία ‖ *vi* νηστεύω.
fasten [ˈfɑːsn] *vt* (*attach*) στερεώνω, σφίγγω ‖ (*with rope*) δένω ‖ (*coat*) κουμπώνω ‖ *vi* δένομαι, κουμπώνομαι ‖ ~**er** *n*, ~**ing** *n* (*on box*) συνδετήρας, ἐνδέτης ‖ (*on clothes*) ἀγκράφα, φερμουάρ.
fastidious [fæsˈtidiəs] *a* δύσκολος, δύστροπος, στριφνός.
fat [fæt] *a* παχύς, χονδρός, εὔσωμος ‖ *n* (*of person*) ξύγγι, πάχος ‖ (*on meat*) λίπος ξύγγι ‖ (*for cooking*) λίπος.
fatal [ˈfeitl] *a* (*ending in death*) θανάσιμος ‖ (*disastrous*) μοιραῖος, καταστρεπτικός, ὀλέθριος ‖ ~**ism** *n* μοιρολατρεία, φαταλισμός ‖ ~**ity** *n* (*road death etc*) θάνατος,

θύμα ‖ ~**ly** *ad* μοιραία, ἀναπόφευκτα, θανάσιμα.
fate [feit] *n* (*destiny*) μοῖρα, πεπρωμένον, τό γραφτό ‖ (*death*) μοῖρα, θάνατος ‖ ~**ful** *a* (*prophetic*) προφητικός ‖ (*important*) ὑψίστης σημασίας, ἀποφασιστικός.
father [ˈfɑːðə*] *n* (*parent*) πατέρας ‖ (*priest*) πάτερ, πατήρ ‖ (*early leader*) πατήρ, δημιουργός ‖ ~**-in-law** *n* πεθερός ‖ ~**ly** *a* πατρικός, σάν πατέρας.
fathom [ˈfæðəm] *n* ὀργυιά ‖ *vt* (*sound*) βυθομετρῶ ‖ (*understand*) βολιδοσκοπῶ, καταλαβαίνω.
fatigue [fəˈtiːg] *n* (*weariness*) κούρασις, κόπωσις, κάματος ‖ *vt* κουράζω, καταπονῶ.
fatness [ˈfætnis] *n* πάχος, πολυσαρκία, χόντρος.
fatten [ˈfætn] *vt* παχαίνω, σιτεύω ‖ *vi* παχαίνω, χοντραίνω.
fatty [ˈfæti] *a* (*food*) παχύς, λιπαρός.
fatuous [ˈfætjuəs] *a* ἀνόητος, ἠλίθιος, χαζός.
faucet [ˈfɔːsit] *n* (*US*) κάνουλα, βρύση.
fault [fɔːlt] *n* (*offence*) σφάλμα, λάθος ‖ (*defect*) ἐλάττωμα ‖ (*blame*) λάθος, φταίξιμο ‖ (*geol*) ρῆγμα, ρωγμή ‖ **at ~** σφάλλω, λαθεύω, εἶμαι πταίστης ‖ ~**less** *a* ἄψογος, τέλειος ‖ ~**y** *a* ἐλαττωματικός, λανθασμένος.
fauna [ˈfɔːnə] *n* πανίς.
favour, (*US*) **favor** [ˈfeivə*] *n* (*approval*) εὔνοια, συμπάθεια ‖ (*kindness*) χάρις, χατήρι ‖ *vt* (*plan*) προτιμῶ, ὑποστηρίζω, μεροληπτῶ ‖ (*in race*) παίζω τό φαβορί ‖ **in ~ of** ὑπέρ ‖ ~**able** *a* εὐνοϊκός ‖ ~**ably** *ad* εὐνοϊκά, συμπαθητικά ‖ ~**ite** *a* εὐνοούμενος, ἀγαπητός ‖ *n* εὐνοούμενος ‖ ~**itism** *n* εὐνοιοκρατία, ρουσφετολογία.
fawn [fɔːn] *a*,*n* (*colour*) πυρόξανθο.
fear [fiə*] *n* φόβος, τρόμος ‖ *vt* φοβοῦμαι, τρέμω, ἀνησυχῶ ‖ **no ~!** μή φοβᾶσαι!, δέν εἶναι πιθανόν! ‖ ~**ful** *a* (*timid*) δειλός, φοβιτσιάρης ‖ (*terrible*) φοβερός, τρομερός ‖ ~**less** *a* ἀτρόμητος, ἄφοβος ‖ ~**lessly** *ad* ἄφοβα, ἀτρόμητα ‖ ~**lessness** *n* ἀφοβία, θάρρος, τόλμη.
feasibility [fiːzəˈbiliti] *n* (τό) πραγματοποιήσιμον.
feasible [ˈfiːzəbl] *a* δυνατός, κατορθωτός.
feast [fiːst] *n* τραπέζι, φαγοπότι, γλέντι ‖ *vi* (+*on*) ἀπολαμβάνω, χορταίνω ‖ ~ **day** *n* (*rel*) γιορτή.
feat [fiːt] *n* κατόρθωμα.
feather [ˈfeðə*] *n* φτερό.
feature [ˈfiːtʃə*] *n* χαρακτηριστικόν ‖ (*article*) κύριον ἄρθρον ‖ (*film*) κυρία ταινία ‖ *vti* χαρακτηρίζω, τονίζω, ἐμφανίζω ‖ ~**less** *a* πλαδαρός, ἀσήμαντος.
February [ˈfebruəri] *n* Φλεβάρης.
fed [fed] *pt*,*pp* of **feed** to be ~ **up** *vi* βαριέμαι, μπουχτώνω, ἀηδιάζω.

federal ['fedərəl] *a* ὁμόσπονδος, ὁμοσπονδιακός.

federation [fedə'reiʃən] *n* ὁμοσπονδία, συνασπισμός.

fee [fi:] *n* (*payment*) ἀμοιβή ‖ (*for entrance*) δίδακτρα, τέλος.

feeble ['fi:bl] *a* (*person*) φιλασθενής, ἀρρωστιάρης ‖ (*excuse*) ἀδύνατος, ἀμφίβολος ‖ ~-minded *a* διανοητικῶς ἀνεπαρκής.

feed [fi:d] (*irreg v*) *n* τροφή, τάϊσμα, τροφοδότησις ‖ *vt* τρέφω, θρέφω ‖ (*machine etc*) τροφοδοτῶ ‖ to ~ on *vt* τρέφω μέ, τρέφομαι μέ ‖ ~ back *n* ἀνάδρασις.

feel [fi:l] (*irreg v*) *n* (*touch*) ἀφή, πιάσιμο ‖ (*feeling*) αἴσθησις, αἴσθημα ‖ *vt* (*touch*) ἀγγίζω, ἄπτομαι ‖ (*examine*) ψηλαφῶ, ψαύω, πιάνω ‖ (*be mentally aware of*) αἰσθάνομαι, νοιώθω ‖ (*think, believe*) νοιώθω ‖ *vi* (*give impression*) αἰσθάνομαι, νοιώθω ‖ ~er *n* βολιδοσκόπησις ‖ ~ing *n* (*sensation*) ἀφή, αἴσθημα ‖ (*emotion*) εὐαισθησία, συγκίνησις ‖ (*opinion*) ἐντύπωσις, γνώμη, αἴσθημα.

feet [fi:t] *npl of* foot.

feign [fein] *vt* προσποιοῦμαι, ὑποκρίνομαι ‖ ~ed *a* προσποιητός, ψεύτικος.

feint [feint] *n* προσποίησις ‖ (*mil*) ψευδεπίθεσις.

fell [fel] *pt of* fall ‖ *vt* (*tree*) κόβω, ρίπτω κάτω ‖ *n* (*hill*) βραχώδης λόφος.

fellow ['felau] *n* (*companion*) σύντροφος, συνάδελφος ‖ (*member of society*) ἑταῖρος, μέλος ‖ (*man or boy*) ἄνθρωπος, βλάμης, παιδί τζιμάνι ‖ ~ citizen *n* συμπολίτης ‖ ~ countryman *n* συμπατριώτης ‖ ~ feeling *n* συναδελφοσύνη ‖ ~ men *npl* συνάνθρωποι ‖ ~ship *n* (*group*) (συν)ἀδελφότης, ἑταιρεία ‖ (*friendliness*) συντροφιά, συντροφικότης ‖ ~ worker *n* συνεργάτης, συνάδελφος.

felony ['feləni] *n* κακούργημα.

felt [felt] *pt,pp of* feel ‖ *n* πίλημα, κετσές.

female ['fi:meil] *n* θῆλυ, γυναίκα ‖ *a* θηλυκός, γυναικεῖος.

feminine ['feminin] *a* (*gram*) θηλυκόν ‖ (*qualities*) θηλυκός, γυναικεῖος.

feminist ['feminist] *n* φεμινιστής, φεμινίστρια.

fence [fens] *n* φράγμα, φράχτης ‖ *vt* (*also* ~ in, ~ off) περιφράσσω, (περι)μαντρώνω ‖ *vi* ξιφομαχῶ.

fencing ['fensiŋ] *n* (*swordplay*) ξιφασκία, ξιφομαχία ‖ (*fences*) περίφραξις, φράκτης.

fend [fend] *vi*: to ~ for o.s. φροντίζω, συντηροῦμαι, καταφέρνω.

fender ['fendə*] *n* κυγκλίδωμα, πυρομάχος ‖ (*US: wing, mudguard*) προφυλακτήρας.

fennel ['fenl] *n* μάραθο.

ferment [fə'ment] *vi* ζημοῦμαι, βράζω ‖ ['fə:ment] *n* ζύμωσις, ἀναβρασμός ‖ ~ation *n* ζύμωσις, βράσιμο.

fern [fə:n] *n* φτέρη.

ferocious [fə'rəuʃəs] *a* ἄγριος, θηριώδης ‖ ~ly *ad* θηριωδῶς, ἄγρια.

ferry ['feri] *n* (*small*) πέραμα, πορθμεῖον ‖ (*large: also* ~boat) φέρρυ-μπότ ‖ *vt* διεκπεραιῶ, διαπορθμεύω, περνῶ.

fertile ['fə:tail] *a* (*agr*) εὔφορος, γόνιμος ‖ (*biol*) γονιμοποιός.

fertility [fə'tiliti] *n* εὐφορία, γονιμότης.

fertilization [fə:tilai'zeiʃən] *n* γονιμοποίησις.

fertilize ['fə:tilaiz] *vt* γονιμοποιῶ ‖ ~r *n* λίπασμα.

fervent ['fə:vənt] *a* θερμός, φλογερός.

festival [festivəl] *n* (*rel etc*) ἑορτή, πανηγύρι ‖ (*art, mus*) φεστιβάλ.

festive ['festiv] *a* γιορταστικός, γιορτάσιμος ‖ (*person*) εὔθυμος, κεφάτος ‖ the ~ season (*Christmas*) ἐποχή γιορτῶν.

festivity [fes'tiviti] *n* γιορτή, γλέντι, festivities *npl* γιορτή.

fetch [fetʃ] *vt* πηγαίνω νά φέρω ‖ (*a price*) ἀποφέρω, πιάνω.

fetching ['fetʃiŋ] *a* γοητευτικός, ἑλκυστικός.

fête [feit] *n* γιορτή, πανηγύρι.

fetters ['fetəz] *npl* δεσμά, ἁλυσίδες.

fetus ['fi:təs] *n* (*US*) = foetus.

feud [fju:d] *n* ἔχθρα, ἔρις, βεντέτα ‖ *vi* εἶμαι στά χέρια μέ ‖ ~al *a* φεουδαλικός, τιμαριωτικός ‖ ~alism *n* φεουδαλισμός.

fever ['fi:və*] *n* πυρετός, θέρμη ‖ ~ish *a* (*med*) ἐμπύρετος ‖ (*fig*) πυρετώδης ‖ ~ishly *ad* (*fig*) πυρετωδῶς, μέ τά μούτρα.

few [fju:] *a* ὀλίγοι, λίγοι, μερικοί ‖ a ~ μερικοί, ὀλίγοι ‖ ~er ὀλιγώτεροι, σπανιώτεροι ‖ ~est ἐλάχιστοι, λιγοστά.

fiancé [fi'ā:nsei] *n* μνηστήρ, ἀρραβωνιαστικός ‖ ~e *n* ἀρραβωνιαστικιά.

fiasco [fi'æskəu] *n* φιάσκο, ἀποτυχία.

fib [fib] *n* ψεμματάκι, μπούρδα ‖ *vi* ψεύδομαι.

fibre, (*US*) fiber ['faibə*] *n* ἴνα, ἴνες ‖ ~glass *n* ὑαλοβάμβαξ.

fickle ['fikl] *a* ἀλλοπρόσαλος, ἀλαφρόμυαλος ‖ ~ness *n* ἀστάθεια, ἄστατος χαρακτήρ.

fiction ['fikʃən] *n* (*invention*) φαντασία ‖ (*novels*) μυθιστορήματα ‖ ~al *a* τῶν μυθιστορημάτων.

fictitious [fik'tiʃəs] *a* φανταστικός.

fiddle ['fidl] *n* (*violin*) βιολί, βιολιστής ‖ (*swindle*) κομπίνα ‖ *vt* (*cheat*) ξεγελῶ ‖ *vi* παίζω, μαστορεύω, χάνω (τόν χρόνο) ‖ to ~ with *vt* παίζω, μαστορεύω ‖ ~r *n* βιολιστής.

fidelity [fi'deliti] *n* πίστις, ἀφοσίωσις, πιστότης.

fidget ['fidʒit] *vi* κάνω νευρικές κινήσεις ‖ ~y *a* ἀεικίνητος, νευρικός, ἀνήσυχος.

field [fi:ld] *n* (*land*) χωράφι, κάμπο, περιοχή ‖ (*sport: ground*) γήπεδον ‖ (*sport: in race*) τά ἄλογα ‖ (*range*) ἔκτασις, πεδίον

|| (*battleground*) πεδίον || ~ **day** n (*gala*) μεγάλη ἡμέρα || ~ **marshal** n στρατάρχης || ~**work** n (*mil*) ἔργον ἐκστρατείας.

fiend [fi:nd] n δαίμονας, τέρας || ~**ish** a διαβολικός.

fierce [fiəs] a θηριώδης, μανιασμένος || ~**ly** ad βιαίως, ἀπότομα, λυσσασμένα || ~**ness** n ἀγριότης, θηριωδία, σκληρότης.

fiery ['faiəri] a (*of fire*) φλογερός, καφτερός, φλεγόμενος || (*person*) ζωηρός, ὁρμητικός, ζωντανός.

fifteen [fif'ti:n] num δέκα πέντε.

fifth [fifθ] a πέμπτος.

fiftieth ['fiftiiθ] a πεντηκοστός.

fifty ['fifti] num πενήντα.

fig [fig] n σῦκο || (*tree*) συκιά.

fight [fait] (*irreg v*) n (*between people*) καυγᾶς, πιάσιμο || (*campaign*) μάχη, ἀγών, πάλη || vt πολεμῶ, μάχομαι || vi (*struggle against*) μάχομαι, ἀγωνίζομαι, παλεύω || ~**er** n πολεμιστής, μαχητής || (*aviat*) καταδιωκτικόν || ~**ing** n μάχη, καυγᾶς || (*sport*) πυγμαχία.

figurative ['figərətiv] a μεταφορικός, παραστατικός.

figure ['figə*] n (*shape*) μορφή, σχῆμα || (*of person*) παράστημα, κορμοστασιά, σιλουέττα || (*picture*) εἰκών, ἀπεικόνισις || (*person*) πρόσωπον, ἄνθρωπος || προσωπικότης || (*math*) σχῆμα || (*cipher*) ἀριθμός, ψηφίον, νούμερο || vt (*US: imagine*) ὑπολογίζω, λογαριάζω || vi (*appear*) ἐμφανίζομαι, φαντάζομαι || to ~ **out** vt ὑπολογίζω, λογαριάζω || ~**head** n (*naut*) ξόανον, γοργόνα || (*fig*) διακοσμητικόν πρόσωπον || ~**-skating** n φιγούρες (τῆς παγοδρομίας).

filament ['filəmənt] n νῆμα.

file [fail] n (*tool*) ρίνη, λίμα || (*dossier*) φάκελλος, ἀρχεῖον || (*folder*) φάκελλος, σεμίζ || (*row*) στοῖχος, γραμμή, ἀράδα || vt (*wood*) λιμάρω || (*nails*) λιμάρω || (*papers*) ταξινομῶ, ἀρχειοθετῶ || (*claim*) καταθέτω, ὑποβάλλω || vi: to ~ **in**, **out** μπαίνω (βγαίνω) ἕνας-ἕνας || **in single** ~ κατ' ἄνδρα.

filing ['failiŋ] n (*of papers*) ταξινόμησις, ἀρχειοθέτησις || ~**s** npl ρινίσματα, λιμαδούρα || ~ **cabinet** n δελτιοθήκη, ἀρχειοθήκη.

fill [fil] vt (*make full*) πληρῶ, γεμίζω || (*occupy completely*) συμπληρώνω, γεμίζω || (*satisfy*) ἱκανοποιῶ, χορταίνω || (*position etc*) κατέχω, γεμίζω || n πλησμονή, κορεσμός, γέμισμα || to the bill (*fig*) ἀνταποκρίνομαι || to ~ **in** vt (*hole*) γεμίζω, βουλώνω || (*form*) συμπληρώνω || to ~ **up** vt (*container*) γεμίζω τελείως || (*form*) συμπληρώνω.

fillet ['filit] n (*food*) φιλέτο || vt χωρίζω τά φιλέτα.

filling ['filiŋ] n (*for cakes, pies etc*) γέμισι ||

(*for tooth*) σφράγισμα, βούλωμα || ~ **station** n πρατήριον βενζίνης, βενζινάδικο.

fillip ['filip] n (*reviver*) ἀναζωογόνησις, τόνωσις.

film [film] n (*thin layer*) ἐλαφρόν στρῶμα, μεμβράνη || (*phot*) (φωτο)ταινία, φίλμ, πλάκα || (*moving picture*) ταινία, φίλμ || vt (*scene*) γυρίζω ταινίαν, φιλμάρω || ~ **script** n σενάριο, σκρίπτ || ~ **star** n ἀστήρ τοῦ κινηματογράφου.

filter ['filtə*] n φίλτρον || (*phot*) φίλτρον || vt διϋλίζω, φιλτράρω, λαμπικάρω || vi (*fig*) διεισδύω, εἰσχωρῶ || ~ **tip** n ἐπιστόμιον φίλτρου || ~**-tipped cigarette** n τσιγάρο φίλτρο.

filth [filθ] n (*lit*) ἀκαθαρσίες, σκουπίδια, βρῶμα || (*fig*) ἠθική φθορά, βρωμιά, αἰσχρολογία || ~**y** a ἀκάθαρτος, ρυπαρός, βρώμικος.

fin [fin] n (*fish*) πτερύγιον, φτερό.

final ['fainl] a τελικός, τελευταῖος, ὁριστικός || n (*sport*) τελικός (ἀγώνας) || ~**s** npl (*univ*) ἀπολυτήριοι ἐξετάσεις || ~**e** [fi'na:li] n (*theat*) φινάλε || (*mus*) φινάλε || ~**ist** n (*sport*) φιναλιστής || ~**ize** vt ὁριστικοποιῶ || ~**ly** ad (*lastly*) τελικῶς || (*eventually*) εἰς τό τέλος || (*irrevocably*) ὁριστικῶς, τελεσιδίκως.

finance [fai'næns] n οἰκονομία || vt χρηματοδοτῶ || ~**s** npl οἰκονομικά.

financial [fai'nænʃəl] a (*policy*) οἰκονομική (πολιτική) || (*year*) οἰκονομικόν (ἔτος) || ~**ly** ad οἰκονομικῶς.

financier [fai'nænsiə*] n κεφαλαιοῦχος, χρηματοδότης.

find [faind] (*irreg v*) vt (*come across*) εὑρίσκω, βρίσκω || (*discover, get*) ἀνακαλύπτω, (ἀνε)βρίσκω || (*learn*) ἀνακαλύπτω, διαπιστώνω || (*declare*) ἀποφαίνομαι, κηρύσσω || n ἀνακάλυψις, εὕρημα || to ~ **out** (**about**) ἀνακαλύπτω, ἀναζητῶ, πληροφορούμαι || ~**ings** npl (*law*) ἀπόφασις, ἐτυμηγορία || (*of report*) διαπίστωσις, συμπέρασμα.

fine [fain] a (*thin, slender*) λεπτός, ψιλός, ψιλόλιγνος || (*delicate*) λεπτός, φίνος || (*handsome*) ὡραῖος, ὄμορφος || (*pure*) καθαρός || (*rainless*) ὡραῖος, καλός || ad (*well*) θαυμάσια, περίφημα || (*small*) λεπτῶς, λεπτομερῶς, ψιλά || n (*law*) ποινική ρήτρα, πρόστιμον || vt (*law*) ἐπιβάλλω πρόστιμον || ~ **arts** n καλαί τέχναι || ~**ness** n λεπτότης, κομψότης || ~**ry** n στολίδια, στόλισμα || ~**sse** [fi'nes] n τέχνασμα, πανουργία, φινέτσα.

finger ['fiŋgə*] n δάκτυλος, δάχτυλο || vt ψαύω, ψηλαφῶ, πιάνω || ~**nail** n νύχι || ~**print** n δακτυλικόν ἀποτύπωμα || ~**stall** n δακτυλήθρα || ~**tip** n ἄκρα τοῦ δακτύλου.

finicky ['finiki] a μικρολόγος, λεπτολόγος.

finish ['finiʃ] n (end) τέλος ‖ (sport) τερματισμός, τέλος, τέρμα ‖ (completion) τελείωμα, ἀποπεράτωσις, συμπλήρωμα ‖ vt (also ~ off, ~ up) τερματίζω, τελειώνω, ἀποτελειώνω ‖ vi (general) τελειώνω, τερματίζομαι, λήγω ‖ (sport) τερματίζω ‖ ~ing line n τέρμα ‖ ~ing school n σχολεῖον γενικῆς μορφώσεως.

finite ['fainait] a πεπερασμένος, περιωρισμένος.

Finland ['finlənd] n Φινλανδία.

Finn [fin] n Φινλανδός ‖ ~ish a φινλανδικός ‖ n (ling) φιννική.

fiord [fjɔ:d] n φιόρδ.

fir [fə:*] n ἔλατο.

fire [faiə*] n (element) πῦρ ‖ (in grate) φωτιά ‖ (damaging) πυρκαϊά ‖ (mil) πῦρ, βολή ‖ vt (cause to burn) ἀνάβω, βάζω φωτιά ‖ (gun etc) πυροδοτῶ, βάλλω, ρίχνω ‖ (fig: imagination) ἐνθουσιάζω, ἐξάπτω ‖ (col: dismiss) ἀπολύω, παύω, διώχνω ‖ vi (gun) πυροβολῶ ‖ on ~ καίομαι, παίρνω φωτιά ‖ ~ alarm n κώδων πυρκαϊᾶς ‖ ~arm n (πυροβόλον) ὅπλον ‖ ~ brigade n πυροσβεστική (ὑπηρεσία) ‖ ~ engine n ἀντλία πυρκαϊᾶς ‖ ~ escape n κλῖμαξ πυρκαϊᾶς ‖ ~ extinguisher n πυροσβεστήρ ‖ ~man n πυροσβέστης ‖ (rail) θερμαστής ‖ ~place n τζάκι ‖ ~proof a πυρίμαχος, ἀλεξίπυρος ‖ ~side n παραστιά, τζάκι ‖ ~ station n πυροσβεστικός σταθμός ‖ ~wood n καυσόξυλα ‖ ~works npl (lit) πυροτεχνήματα.

firing ['faiəriŋ] n (mil) βολή, πυροβολισμός, πῦρ ‖ ~ squad n ἐκτελεστικόν ἀπόσπασμα.

firm [fə:m] a (solid) στεριός, σφιχτός ‖ (determined) ἀμετακίνητος, σταθερός ‖ n οἶκος, ἑταιρεία, φίρμα ‖ ~ly ad σταθερῶς, στερεά, γερά ‖ ~ness n σταθερότης, στερεότης.

first [fə:st] a (time) πρῶτος ‖ (place) πρῶτος ‖ ad (before others) πρῶτος ‖ (firstly = in the first place) πρωτίστως, πρῶτα-πρῶτα ‖ (sooner = before then) στήν ἀρχή, μᾶλλον, καλύτερα ‖ n (person: in race) πρῶτος ‖ (univ) λίαν καλῶς, ἄριστα ‖ (aut) πρώτη (ταχύτητα) ‖ at ~ κατά πρῶτον, στήν ἀρχή ‖ ~ of all πρίν ἀπ᾿ὅλα, κατ᾿ἀρχήν ‖ ~ aid n πρῶται βοήθειαι ‖ ~-aid kit n σακκίδιον πρώτων βοηθειῶν ‖ ~-class a πρώτης τάξεως ‖ ~-hand a ἀπό πρῶτο χέρι ‖ ~ lady n (US) πρώτη κυρία ‖ ~ly ad πρωτίστως, πρῶτα-πρῶτα ‖ ~ name n μικρόν ὄνομα ‖ ~ night n πρώτη, πρεμιέρα ‖ ~-rate a πρώτης τάξεως.

fiscal ['fiskəl] a οἰκονομικός.

fish [fiʃ] n ψάρι ‖ vt ἁλιεύω, ψαρεύω ‖ vi ψαρεύω ‖ to go ~ing πάω γιά ψάρεμα ‖ ~erman n ψαρᾶς ‖ ~ery n ἁλιεία, ψαρική ‖ ~ hook n ἀγκίστρι ‖ ~ing boat n ψαρόβαρκα ‖ ~ing line n ἁρμίδι,

~ing rod n καλάμι ‖ ~ing tackle n σύνεργα ψαρικής ‖ ~ market n ἰχθυαγορά ‖ ~monger n ἰχθυοπώλης ‖ ~y a (suspicious) ὕποπτος, βρώμικος.

fission ['fiʃən] n διάσπασις.

fissure ['fiʃə*] n σχισμή, ρωγμή.

fist [fist] n πυγμή, γροθιά.

fit [fit] a (med, sport) σέ φόρμα, ὑγιής ‖ (suitable) κατάλληλος, ἁρμόζων, καλός ‖ (qualified, worthy) ἱκανός ‖ vt (suit) συμφωνῶ, ταιριάζω ‖ (insert, attach) πηγαίνω, μπαίνω ‖ vi (correspond) ἐφαρμόζω, πιάνω ‖ (of clothes) πηγαίνω, ἔρχεται ‖ n (of clothes) ἐφαρμογή, ταίριασμα ‖ (med: mild, of coughing) παροξυσμός ‖ (med: serious, epilepsy) προσβολή ‖ (of anger) ξέσπασμα, ἔκρηξις ‖ (of laughter) ξέσπασμα ‖ to ~ in vi συμφωνῶ, ταιριάζω ‖ n ἑνώνω, συνδέω ‖ to ~ out vt ἐξαρτίζω, ἐφοδιάζω, ντύνω ‖ to ~ up vt ἐφαρμόζω, ταιριάζω, μοντάρω ‖ ~fully, by ~s and starts ἀκανόνιστα, ἄστατα ‖ ~ness n (suitability) ἱκανότης, καταλληλότης ‖ (med) ὑγεία ‖ ~ter n ἐφαρμοστής ‖ (of clothes) δοκιμαστής ‖ ~ting a κατάλληλος, πρέπον, ταιριαστός ‖ n (of dress) πρόβα, προβάρισμα ‖ (piece of equipment) ἐφαρμογή, μοντάρισμα ‖ ~tings npl ἐπιπλώσεις, ἐξαρτήματα, σύνεργα.

five [faiv] num πέντε ‖ ~r n (Brit) πεντάρι (λίρες).

fix [fiks] vt (fasten) τοποθετῶ, στερεώνω, καρφώνω ‖ (determine) καθορίζω, (προσδι)ὁρίζω, ρυθμίζω ‖ (repair) ἐπισκευάζω, ἐπιδιορθώνω ‖ (drink) ἑτοιμάζω, φτιάχνω ‖ n: in a ~ μπελάδες, μπλέξιμο, σκοτούρες ‖ ~ed a σταθερός, ἀμετάβλητος, στερεωμένος ‖ ~ture n ἀκινητοποιημένο ἔπιπλον, ἐξάρτημα.

fizz [fiz] n σπίθισμα, τσιτσίρισμα ‖ vi σπιθίζω.

fizzle ['fizl] vi ἀφρίζω, τσιρίζω ‖ to ~ out vi βγαίνω τζίφος, ἀποτυγχάνω.

fizzy ['fizi] a ἀεριοῦχος, ἀφρώδης.

fjord [fjɔ:d] n = **fiord**.

flabbergasted ['flæbəga:stid] a κατάπληκτος, ξερός.

flabby ['flæbi] a πλαδαρός, ἄτονος.

flag [flæg] n (banner) σημαία ‖ (also ~stone) πλάκα, πλακόλιθος ‖ vi (strength) ἐξασθενίζω, χαλαρῶμαι ‖ (spirit) κάμπτομαι, πέφτω, σπάω ‖ to ~ down vt σταματῶ.

flagon ['flægən] n καράφα.

flagpole ['flægpəul] n κοντάρι.

flagrant ['fleigrənt] a κατάφωρος, κατάφανής.

flair [fleə*] n ὀξυδέρκεια, ἱκανότης.

flake [fleik] n (of rust) λέπι, τρίμα, φύλλο ‖ (of snow) νιφάς, στούπα ‖ vi (also ~ off) ξελεπίζω, ξεφλουδίζομαι.

flame [fleim] n φλόγα.

flaming ['fleimiŋ] a (col) φλογερός, ἀστραφτερός.

flamingo [fla'miŋgəu] n φλαμίγκος.

flange [flændʒ] n φλάντζα.

flank [flæŋk] n (side) λαγόνα, πλαγιά ‖ (mil) πλευρά ‖ vt εὑρίσκομαι πλάϊ.

flannel ['flænl] n φανέλλα ‖ ~s npl (trousers) φανελλένιο παντελόνι.

flap [flæp] n καπάκι ‖ (of pocket) καπάκι (τσέπης) ‖ (of envelope) κλείσιμο (φακέλλου) ‖ vt (of birds) φτερουγίζω ‖ vi (sail, flag) ἀνεμίζομαι, κυματίζω.

flare [flɛə*] n φωτοβολίς ‖ (in skirt etc) φάρδεμα ‖ to ~ up vi (into flame) ἀστράφτω, ἀνάβω ‖ (in anger) ἀνάβω, ἐξάπτομαι.

flash [flæʃ] n ἀναλαμπή, λάμψις ‖ (news flash) τελευταία εἴδησις ‖ (phot) φλάς ‖ vt (light) κάνω νά λάμψη, ρίχνω ‖ (torch) ρίπτω, ἀνάβω ‖ (message) μεταδίδω ‖ vi ἀστράφτω, γυαλίζω ‖ in a ~ στή στιγμή ‖ to ~ by or past vi περνῶ σάν ἀστραπή ‖ ~back n ἀναδρομή ‖ ~ bulb n λάμπα φλάς ‖ ~er n (aut) φανάρι τοῦ στόπ.

flashy ['flæʃi] a (pej) φανταχτερός, χτυπητός.

flask [fla:sk] n τσότρα, φλασκί ‖ (chem) φιάλη ‖ (vacuum flask) θερμός.

flat [flæt] a (level) ἐπίπεδος, ἴσιος ‖ (dull) ἄνευ προοπτικῆς, θαμπό ‖ (below pitch) σέ ὕφεσι, μπεμόλ ‖ (beer) ξεφουσκωμένο ‖ (tyre) ξεφουσκωμένο, πεσμένο ‖ n (rooms) διαμέρισμα ‖ (mus) ὕφεσις ‖ (aut) ξεφουσκωμένο λάστιχο ‖ ~ broke a ἀπένταρος, πατήρης ‖ ~footed a μέ πλατειά πόδια ‖ ~ly ad σαφῶς, κατηγορηματικῶς ‖ ~ness n ἐπιπεδότης ‖ (of beer) ξεθύμασμα ‖ ~ten vt (also ~ten out) ἐπιπεδώνω, ἰσώνω.

flatter ['flætə*] vt κολακεύω ‖ ~er n κόλακας ‖ ~ing a κολακευτικός ‖ ~y n κολακεία.

flaunt [flɔ:nt] vt ἐπιδεικνύω, δείχνω.

flavour, (US) flavor ['fleivə*] n γεῦσις ‖ vt καρικεύω, ἀρωματίζω ‖ ~ing n καρίκευμα, ἄρωμα.

flaw [flɔ:] n ἐλάττωμα ‖ ~less a ἄψογος, τέλειος.

flax [flæks] n λινάρι ‖ ~en a κυτάξανθος.

flea [fli:] n ψύλλος.

fled [fled] pt,pp of **flee**.

flee [fli:] (irreg v) vi (κατα)φεύγω ‖ vt φεύγω.

fleece [fli:s] n δορά, δέρμα, τομάρι ‖ vt (rob) ληστεύω, γδέρνω, γδύνω.

fleet [fli:t] n (naut) στόλος ‖ (of cars) συνοδεία, πομπή.

fleeting ['fli:tiŋ] a φευγαλέος, περαστικός.

Flemish ['flemiʃ] a φλαμανδικός ‖ n (ling) φλαμανδική.

flesh [fleʃ] n σάρξ, σάρκα ‖ (meat) κρέας ‖ (of fruit) σάρξ ‖ ~ wound n ἐλαφρόν τραῦμα.

flew [flu:] pt of **fly**.

flex [fleks] n εὔκαμπτον καλώδιον ‖ vt κάμπτομαι ‖ ~ibility n εὐκαμψία ‖ ~ible a εὔκαμπτος ‖ (plans) ἐλαστικός.

flick [flik] vt κτυπῶ ἐλαφρά.

flicker ['flikə*] n (of light) τρεμούλιασμα, παίξιμο ‖ vi τρέμω, τρεμοσβύνω.

flier ['flaiə*] n ἱπτάμενος, ἀεροπόρος.

flight [flait] n (flying) πτῆσις, πέταμα ‖ (of squadron) σμῆνος ‖ (journey) διαδρομή ‖ (also ~ of steps) σκαλοπάτια, κλῖμαξ ‖ to take ~ τρέπομαι εἰς φυγήν ‖ to put to ~ τρέπω εἰς φυγήν ‖ ~ deck n κατάστρωμα ἀπογειώσεως ‖ ~y a ἄστατος, κουφιοκέφαλος.

flimsy ['flimzi] a σαθρός, λεπτός, μικρᾶς ἀντοχῆς ‖ (weak) ἀδύνατος, ἀσθενής, πρόχειρος.

flinch [flintʃ] vi ὑποχωρῶ, δειλιάζω.

fling [fliŋ] (irreg v) vt ρίχνω, πετῶ.

flint [flint] n (in lighter) τσακμακόπετρα.

flip [flip] vt δίνω ἐλαφρόν κτύπημα.

flippancy ['flipənsi] n ἀπερισκεψία, ἀφέλεια.

flippant ['flipənt] a ἐλαφρός, ἀφελής.

flirt [flə:t] vi φλερτάρω ‖ n φιλάρεσκη, κοκέττα ‖ ~ation n φλέρτ, φλερτάρισμα.

flit [flit] vi πηγαινοέρχομαι.

float [fləut] n πλωτήρ, φλοτέρ ‖ (esp in procession) ἀποκρίατικο ἅρμα ‖ vi (ἐπι)πλέω ‖ (swimming) κολυμπῶ ἀνάσκελα ‖ (in air) πλέω ‖ vt (company) ἱδρύω ‖ (loan) ἐκδίδω δάνειον ‖ (rumour) διαδίδω, κυκλοφορῶ ‖ ~ing a (lit) ἐπιπλέων ‖ (fig: population) κινητός πληθυσμός.

flock [flɔk] n ποίμνιον, κοπάδι ‖ (of people) πλῆθος, κοπάδι.

flog [flɔg] vt μαστιγώνω, ραβδίζω.

flood [flʌd] n πλημμύρα, κατακλυσμός ‖ vt πλημμυρίζω, κατακλύζω ‖ ~ing n πλημμύρισμα, ὑπερεκχείλισις ‖ ~light n προβολεύς ‖ vt φωτίζω διά προβολέως ‖ ~lighting n φωτισμός διά προβολέως.

floor [flɔ:*] n (of room) δάπεδον, πάτωμα ‖ (storey) ὄροφος, πάτωμα ‖ vt (person) ρίχνω κάτω ‖ ground ~ (Brit), first ~ (US) ἰσόγειον ‖ first ~ (Brit), second ~ (US) πρῶτο πάτωμα ‖ ~board n σανίδα ‖ ~ show n νούμερα.

flop [flɔp] vi (fail) ἀποτυγχάνω, καταρρέω ‖ (fall) κάνω πλάφ, σωριάζομαι.

floppy ['flɔpi] a πλαδαρός.

flora ['flɔ:rə] npl χλωρίς ‖ ~l a ἀνθικός, λουλουδένιος.

florid ['flɔrid] a ἀνθηρός, γεμάτος φιοριτούρες.

florist ['flɔrist] n ἀνθοπώλης ‖ ~'s (shop) n ἀνθοπωλεῖον.

flounce [flauns] n βολλάν ‖ vi: to ~ in, out μπαίνω, βγαίνω ἀπότομα.

flounder ['flaundə*] vi παραπατῶ, σπαρταρῶ, τσαλαβουτῶ.

flour ['flauə*] n ἀλεύρι.

flourish ['flʌrɪʃ] vi (thrive, prosper) προοδεύω, ἀνθῶ, προκόβω ‖ vt κραδαίνω, κουνῶ ‖ n (ornament) ποίκιλμα, κόσμημα, τζίφρα ‖ ἐπίδειξις, φανφάρα ‖ ~ing a (thriving) ἀκμάζον, ἀνθοῦν.

flout [flaut] vt ἐμπαίζω, περιφρονῶ.

flow [fləu] n (movement) ροή, ρεῦμα ‖ (stream: lit, fig) ρους, χύσις, χείμαρρος ‖ (of dress) χυτές γραμμές, ντραπέ ‖ vi ρέω, χύνομαι ‖ κυλῶ ‖ (traffic, supply) κυκλοφορῶ, κινοῦμαι ‖ (robes, hair) χύνομαι, πέφτω.

flower ['flauə*] n ἄνθος, λουλούδι ‖ vi ἀνθίζω ‖ ~ bed n παρτέρι, βραγιά ‖ ~pot n βάζο ‖ ~y a πολυγαρνιρισμένος.

flowing ['fləuiŋ] a (movement) ρέων ‖ (hair) χυτός, μακρυά ‖ (style) ρέων, ἄνετος.

flown [fləun] pp of fly.

flu [flu:] n γρίππη.

fluctuate ['flʌktjueit] vi κυμαίνομαι.

fluctuation [flʌktju'eiʃən] n διακύμανσις.

fluency ['flu:ənsi] n εὐγλωττία, εὐφράδεια.

fluent ['flu:ənt] a εὐφράδης, στρωτός ‖ ~ly ad εὐχερῶς, ἄνετα.

fluff [flʌf] n χνούδι ‖ ~y a χνουδάτος.

fluid ['flu:id] n ρευστόν, ὑγρόν ‖ a (lit) ρευστός, ρέων ‖ (fig: plans) ρευστός, εὐμετάβλητος.

fluke [flu:k] n (col: lucky stroke) κατά τύχην.

flung [flʌŋ] pt, pp of fling.

fluorescent [fluə'resnt] a φθορίζων.

fluoride ['fluəraid] n φθοριοῦχον.

flurry ['flʌri] n (of activity) ἀναστάτωσις, πανικός.

flush [flʌʃ] n (blush) κοκκίνισμα, ἐρύθημα ‖ (of excitement) ξέσπασμα ‖ (cards) χρῶμα, φλός ‖ vt ποτίζω, καθαρίζω, τραβῶ (τό καζανάκι) ‖ vi (blush) κοκκινίζω ‖ a ἐπίπεδος, λεῖος, στό ντουζένι ‖ ~ed a (blushing) κόκκινο, ξαναμμένο ‖ (with anger) κόκκινος.

fluster ['flʌstə*] n ἀναστάτωσις ‖ ~ed a ταραγμένος.

flute [flu:t] n φλογέρα, φλάουτο.

fluted ['flu:tid] a αὐλακωτός.

flutter ['flʌtə*] n (of wings) φτερούγισμα ‖ (of excitement) ἀναστάτωσις, συγκίνησις ‖ vi (of birds) φτερουγίζω, τρέμω, ταράσσομαι.

flux [flʌks] n: in a state of ~ σέ ρευστή κατάστασι.

fly [flai] (irreg v) n (insect) μύγα ‖ (on trousers: also flies) μπροστινό ἄνοιγμα ‖ vt (plane) πετῶ, πιλοτάρω ‖ (passengers) μεταφέρω ἀεροπορικῶς ‖ vi (travel by air) ἵπταμαι, πετῶ ‖ (flee) φεύγω, τρέχω ‖ (of flag) κυματίζω ‖ ~er n = flier ‖ ~ing n (activity) πτῆσις, ἀεροπορία ‖ a (rapid visit) ταχύς, γρήγορος, πεταχτός, σύντομος, βιαστικός ‖ a ~ing saucer n ἱπτάμενος δίσκος ‖ ~ing start n καλή ἀρχή, ταχύ ξεκίνημα ‖ ~over n (Brit)

ἐναέριος διάβασις ‖ ~paper n μυγοπαγίδα ‖ ~past n παρέλασις ἀεροπλάνων ‖ ~swatter n μυγοδιώχτης ‖ ~wheel n σφόνδυλος, βολάν.

foal [fəul] n πουλάρι.

foam [fəum] n ἀφρός ‖ (plastic etc) ἀφρολέξ ‖ vi ἀφρίζω.

fob [fɔb] to ~ off vt πασσάρω, κοροϊδεύω.

focal ['fəukəl] a ἐστιακός.

focus ['fəukəs] n ἐστία ‖ vt συγκεντρώνω, ρυθμίζω ‖ in ~ ρυθμισμένος, εὐκρινής ‖ out of ~ μή ρυθμισμένος, θαμπός.

fodder ['fɔdə*] n φορβή, χόρτο.

foe [fəu] n ἐχθρός, ἀντίπαλος.

foetus ['fi:təs] n ἔμβρυον.

fog [fɔg] n ὁμίχλη ‖ vt (issue) θολώνω, περιπλέκω ‖ ~gy a ὁμιχλώδης.

foible ['fɔibl] n ἀδυναμία.

foil [fɔil] vt ἀνατρέπω, προλαμβάνω ‖ (of metal) ἔλασμα, φύλλον ‖ (person) κοντράστο ‖ (fencing) ξίφος.

fold [fəuld] n (bend, crease) πτυχή, ζάρα, δίπλα ‖ vt διπλώνω, πτυχώνω ‖ to ~ up vi (map etc) τυλίγω, διπλώνω ‖ (business) κλείνω τό μαγαζί, χρεωκοπῶ ‖ ~er n (pamphlet) (πτυσσομένη) διαφήμισις ‖ (portfolio) φάκελλος, σεμίζ ‖ ~ing a (chair, bed etc) πτυσσόμενος, τσακιστός.

foliage ['fəuliidʒ] n φυλλωσιά.

folio ['fəuliəu] n φύλλον, ἵν φόλιο.

folk [fəuk] n ἄνθρωποι ‖ a λαϊκός ‖ ~s npl ἄνθρωποι, συγγενείς, δικοί μου ‖ ~lore n λαογραφία ‖ ~song n δημοτικό τραγούδι.

follow ['fɔləu] vt (come after) (παρ)ἀκολουθῶ ‖ (obey) ἀκολουθῶ ‖ (go along path) ἀκολουθῶ, παίρνω ‖ (profession) ἀκολουθῶ, ἀσκῶ ‖ (understand) καταλαβαίνω, παρακολουθῶ ‖ vi (after) ἀκολουθῶ, συνοδεύω ‖ (result) ἕπομαι, προκύπτω ‖ to ~ up vt συνεχίζω, ἐκμεταλλεύομαι ‖ ~er n ὁπαδός ‖ ~ing a ἀκολουθῶν, ἐπόμενος, n ὁπαδοί, ἀκολουθία.

folly ['fɔli] n ἀνοησία, τρέλλα.

fond [fɔnd] a: to be ~ of (person) εἶμαι ἀφοσιωμένος, συμπαθῶ, ἀγαπῶ ‖ (thing) μοῦ ἀρέσει, τρελλαίνομαι γιά ‖ ~ly ad ἀφελῶς ‖ (with affection) στοργικά ‖ ~ness n (+for) ἀφοσίωσις, συμπάθεια ·σέ ‖ ἀγάπη γιά, τάσι στό.

font [fɔnt] n κολυμβήθρα.

food [fu:d] n τροφή, τρόφιμα, φαΐ, φαγητόν ‖ ~ mixer n μίξερ, ἀνάμικτρον ‖ ~poisoning n δηλητηρίασι ‖ ~stuffs npl εἴδη διατροφῆς.

fool [fu:l] n (silly person) ἠλίθιος, βλάκας, κουτός, χαζός ‖ (clown) παλιάτσος ‖ vt (deceive) ἐξαπατῶ, γελῶ ‖ vi (act like a fool) κάνω τόν βλάκα ‖ ~hardy a παράτολμος, ἀπερίσκεπτος ‖ ~ish a παράλογος, γελοῖος ‖ ~ishly ad παράλογα, ἀνόητα ‖ ~ishness n ἀπερισκεψία, ἀνοησία ‖ ~proof a (plan etc) ἀλάνθαστος.

foot [fut] n (of person) πόδι, ποδάρι ‖ (of animal) πόδι ‖ (base) πέλμα, πόδι, κάτω ἄκρον ‖ (measure) ἀγγλικός πούς, πόδι (0.3μ) ‖ vt (bill) πληρώνω, κάνω τά ἔξοδα ‖ on ~ πεζῆ, μέ τά πόδια ‖ ~ball n (ball) μπάλλα ‖ (game) ποδόσφαιρον ‖ ~baller n ποδοσφαιριστής ‖ ~brake n ποδόφρενο ‖ ~bridge n γέφυρα πεζῶν ‖ ~hills npl χαμηλοί λόφοι ‖ ~hold n πάτημα, στήριγμα ‖ ~ing n (lit) ἀσφαλής θέσις, πάτημα ‖ (fig) θέσις, κατάστασις ‖ ~lights npl ράμπα, προσκήνιον ‖ ~man n (servant) ὑπηρέτης, λακές ‖ ~-and-mouth (disease) n ἀφθώδης πυρετός ‖ ~note n ὑποσημείωσις ‖ ~path n μονοπάτι ‖ ~ sore a μέ πονεμένα πόδια ‖ ~step n βῆμα, πάτημα ‖ (trace) ἴχνος, πατησιά ‖ ~wear n παπούτσι.

for [fɔ:*] prep διά, γιά ‖ (in spite of) μόλον ‖ cj διότι, γιατί ‖ what ~? γιατί;, γιά ποιό λόγο;.

forage ['fɔridʒ] n βοσκή, χορτονομή, χόρτο ‖ vi (col) ψάχνω γιά.

foray ['fɔrei] n ἐπιδρομή, διαρπαγή.

forbearing [fɔ:'bɛəriŋ] a ὑπομονητικός, ἀνεκτικός.

forbid [fə'bid] (irreg v) vt ἀπαγορεύω ‖ ~den a ἀπηγορευμένον ‖ ~ding a ἀποκρουστικός, δυσάρεστος.

force [fɔ:s] n (strength) δύναμις, ἰσχύς ‖ (compulsion) ἐξαναγκασμός, ζόρι ‖ (body of men) δύναμις ‖ vt (compel) ἐξαναγκάζω, ἐκβιάζω ‖ (break open) παραβιάζω ‖ to ~ into vt πιέζω, σπρώχνω, μπάζω ‖ in ~ ἰσχύον ‖ the F~s npl αἱ ἔνοπλες ‖ ~d a (smile) προσποιητό, ψεύτικο ‖ (landing) ἀναγκαστική ‖ ~ful a ἀποφασιστικός, δραστήριος.

forcible ['fɔ:səbl] a ρωμαλέος, βίαιος.

forcibly ['fɔ:səbli] ad μέ τό ζόρι, ἀποφασιστικά.

ford [fɔ:d] n πέραμα ‖ vt περνῶ.

fore [fɔ:*] a πρόσθιος, μπροστινός ‖ n: to the ~ στό προσκήνιον, διαπρέπων.

forearm ['fɔ:a:m] n ἀντιβράχιον.

foreboding [fɔ:'bəudiŋ] n κακόν προαίσθημα, κακός οἰωνός.

forecast ['fɔ:ka:st] n πρόβλεψις, πρόγνωσις ‖ vt προβλέπω.

forecourt ['fɔ:kɔ:t] n προαύλιον.

forefathers ['fɔ:fa:ðəz] npl πρόγονοι.

forefinger ['fɔ:fiŋgə*] n δείκτης.

forefront ['fɔ:frʌnt] n πρόσοψις ‖ (fig) πρώτη σειρά.

forego [fɔ:'gəu] vt προηγοῦμαι ‖ ~ing a προειρημένος ‖ ~ne ['fɔ:gɔn] a (conclusion) προκαθορισμένος.

foreground ['fɔ:graund] n πρῶτο πλάνο.

forehead ['fɔrid] n μέτωπον, κούτελο.

foreign ['fɔrin] a (country) ξένος, ἄσχετος ‖ (trade) ἐξωτερικόν ‖ (accent) ξενική ‖

(body) ξένος ‖ ~er n ξένος, ἀλλοδαπός ‖ ~ exchange n συνάλλαγμα ‖ F~ Minister n ὑπουργός ἐξωτερικῶν.

foreman ['fɔ:mən] n προϊστάμενος, ἐργοδηγός.

foremost ['fɔ:məust] a πρῶτος, πρώτιστος, ἐπί κεφαλῆς.

forensic [fə'rensik] a: ~ medicine n ἰατροδικαστική.

forerunner ['fɔ:rʌnə*] n πρόδρομος.

foresee [fɔ:'si:] vt προβλέπω ‖ ~able a δυνάμενος νά προβλεφθῆ.

foresight ['fɔ:sait] n πρόβλεψις, πρόνοια.

forest ['fɔrist] n δάσος, ρουμάνι.

forestall [fɔ:'stɔ:l] vt προλαμβάνω.

forestry ['fɔristri] n δασοκομία.

foretaste ['fɔ:teist] n προαίσθησις.

foretell [fɔ:'tel] vt προλέγω, προμηνύω.

forever [fə'revə*] ad παντοτεινά, γιά πάντα.

foreword ['fɔ:wə:d] n πρόλογος.

forfeit ['fɔ:fit] n ποινική ρήτρα ‖ vt χάνω (διά κατασχέσεως), χάνω.

forge [fɔ:dʒ] n καμίνι, σιδεράδικο ‖ vt (falsely) πλάθω, πλαστογραφῶ ‖ (shape) σφυρηλατῶ ‖ to ~ ahead vi προηγοῦμαι, προχωρῶ ‖ ~r n (criminal) πλαστογράφος, παραχαράκτης ‖ ~ry n (activity) πλαστογράφησις ‖ (article) πλαστόν, κίβδηλον (ἀντικείμενον).

forget [fə'get] vti λησμονῶ, ξεχνῶ, παραλείπω ‖ ~ful a ξεχασιάρης, ἀπρόσεκτος ‖ ~fulness n ἀπερισκεψία, ἔλλειψι μνήμης.

forgive [fə'giv] vt συγχωρῶ ‖ ~ness n συγχώρηση.

forgo [fɔ:'gəu] vt παραιτοῦμαι, ἀποφεύγω, κάνω χωρίς.

fork [fɔ:k] n (for food) πηρούνι ‖ (farm tool) δικράνα, διχάλα ‖ (branch) διακλάδωσις ‖ vi (road) διχάζομαι, χωρίζομαι ‖ to ~ out vti (col: pay) πληρώνω ‖ ~ed a (lightning) ζίγκ-ζάγκ.

forlorn [fə'lɔ:n] a (person) ἀπελπισμένος, ἐγκαταλελειμμένος ‖ (hope) ἀπελπισμένος, ἄπελπις.

form [fɔ:m] n (structure) μορφή, σχῆμα, φόρμα ‖ (class) τάξις ‖ (bench) μπάγκος ‖ (document) ἔντυπον, τύπος ‖ (also mental, physical condition) κατάστασις, φόρμα ‖ vt (shape) διαμορφώνω, σχηματίζω, φτιάνω ‖ (make part of) συγκροτῶ, σχηματίζω.

formal ['fɔ:məl] a (according to rule) ἐπίσημος, ἐθιμοτυπικός ‖ (stiff) τυπικός ‖ (dress) ἐπίσημος ‖ ~ity n (of occasion) τύπος, τυπικότης ‖ ~ities npl διατυπώσεις, ἐθιμοτυπία ‖ ~ly ad (ceremoniously) τυπικῶς, μέ διατυπώσεις ‖ (officially) ἐπισήμως, τυπικῶς.

format ['fɔ:mæt] n σχῆμα.

formation [fɔ:'meiʃən] n διαμόρφωσις, σχηματισμός ‖ (forming) σχηματισμός, διάπλασις ‖ (group) σχηματισμός, διάταξις, τάξις.

formative ['fɔːmətiv] a (years) διαπλαστικός, μορφωτικός.

former ['fɔːmə*] a παλαιότερος, προγενέστερος, πρώην, τέως ‖ (opposite of latter) πρώτος ‖ ~ly ad άλλοτε, παλαιότερα.

formica [fɔːˈmaikə] n φορμάϊκα.

formidable ['fɔːmidəbl] a φοβερός, τρομερός.

formula ['fɔːmjulə] n τύπος ‖ (fig) τύπος, στερεοτυπία, κλισέ ‖ (math) τύπος ‖ ·~ te ['fɔːmjuleit] vt διατυπώνω.

forsake [fəˈseik] (irreg v) vt έγκαταλείπω, άφήνω, άρνούμαι.

fort [fɔːt] n φρούριον.

forte [fɔːt] n δύναμις, φόρτε.

forth [fɔːθ] ad πρός τά έμπρός, πρός τά έξω ‖ (in space) πρόσω, έμπρός, μπροστά ‖ (in time) άπό τούδε, άπό τώρα καί έμπρός ‖ ~coming a (έπ)ερχόμενος, προσεχής.

fortieth ['fɔːtiiθ] a τεσσαρακοστός.

fortification [fɔːtifiˈkeiʃən] n (walls etc) όχύρωμα, όχύρωσις.

fortify ['fɔːtifai] vt (strengthen) ένισχύω, δυναμώνω, τονώνω ‖ (protect) όχυρώνω.

fortnight ['fɔːtnait] n δεκαπενθήμερον ‖ ~ly a δεκαπενθήμερος ‖ ad άνά δεκαπενθήμερον.

fortress ['fɔːtris] n φρούριον, κάστρο.

fortunate ['fɔːtʃənit] a εύτυχής, τυχερός, εύμενής ‖ ~ly ad εύτυχῶς.

fortune ['fɔːtʃən] n (chance) τύχη, σύμπτωσις, καλοτυχία ‖ (wealth) πλοῦτος, περιουσία ‖ ~teller n μάντις, χαρτορίχτρα.

forty ['fɔːti] num σαράντα.

forward ['fɔːwəd] a (lying ahead) πρόσθιος, μπροστινός ‖ (movement) κίνησις πρός τά πρόσω, προοδευτικός ‖ (advanced) μέ πρόωρον άνάπτυξιν ‖ ad (πρός τά) έμπρός, μπρός ‖ n (sport) κυνηγός ‖ vt (mail etc) άποστέλλω, διεκπεραιώνω ‖ (help) προωθῶ, εύνοῶ, προάγω ‖ ~s ad άπό τώρα καί στό έξῆς.

fossil ['fɔsl] n άπολίθωμα.

foster ['fɔstə*] vt καλλιεργῶ, τρέφω ‖ ~ child n θετόν τέκνον ‖ ~ mother n μητρυιά, ψυχομάννα.

fought [fɔːt] pt,pp of **fight**.

foul [faul] a άκάθαρτος, ρυπαρός, βρωμερός, μολυσμένος ‖ (language) βωμολόχος, πρόστυχος, αίσχρός ‖ (weather) κακοκαιρίας ‖ n (sport) φάουλ ‖ vt (mechanism) φράσσω, μπλέκω, πιάνω ‖ (sport) κάνω φάουλ.

found [faund] pt,pp of **find** ‖ vt (establish) ίδρύω, θεμελιώνω, κτίζω ‖ ~ation n (act) ίδρυσις, θεμελίωσις, θεμελίον ‖ (fig) ίδρυμα, κληροδότημα ‖ ~ations npl (building) θεμέλια.

founder ['faundə*] n ίδρυτής ‖ vi (naut) βυθίζομαι, βουλιάζω.

foundry ['faundri] n χυτήριον.

fount [faunt] n (source) πηγή ‖ ~ain n πηγή ‖ (jet of water) συντριβάνι ‖ ~ain pen n στυλογράφος, στυλό.

four [fɔː*] num τέσσερα ‖ on all ~s μέ τά τέσσερα ‖ ~some n διπλή παρτίδα ‖ ~teen num δέκα τέσσερα ‖ ~teenth a δέκατος τέταρτος ‖ ~th a τέταρτος.

fowl [faul] n πουλί, πουλερικόν.

fox [fɔks] n άλεποῦ ‖ ~hunting n κυνήγι τῆς άλεποῦς ‖ ~trot n φόξ-τρότ.

foyer ['fɔiei] n φουαγιέ.

fraction ['frækʃən] n (part) τεμάχιον, κομμάτι ‖ (math) κλάσμα.

fracture ['fræktʃə*] n (of bone) κάταγμα ‖ vt θραύω, τσακίζω, προκαλῶ κάταγμα,

fragile ['frædʒail] a εὔθραυστος.

fragment ['frægmənt] n θραῦσμα, θρύμμα, σύντριμμα ‖ (part) τεμάχιον, άπόκομμα, άπόσπασμα ‖ ~ary a άποσπασματικός, κλαστικός.

fragrance ['freigrəns] n ἄρωμα, μυρωδιά.

fragrant ['freigrənt] a εὔοσμος, μυρωδάτος.

frail [freil] a εὐπαθής, άσθενικός.

frame [freim] n σκελετός, πλαίσιον ‖ (border) πλαίσιον, κορνίζα ‖ vt (put into frame) πλαισιώνω, κορνιζάρω ‖ (put together) καταστρώνω, διαμορφώνω, κατασκευάζω ‖ (col: incriminate) μηχανορραφῶ, σκηνοθετῶ ‖ ~ of mind n πνευματική κατάστασις, διάθεσις ‖ ~work n σκελετός, πλαίσιον.

France [frɑːns] n Γαλλία.

franchise ['fræntʃaiz] n προνόμιον.

frank [fræŋk] a είλικρινής ‖ ~ly ad είλικρινά, ντόμπρα ‖ ~ness n είλικρίνεια, παρρησία.

frankincense ['fræŋkinsens] n λιβάνι.

frantic ['fræntik] a φρενιτιώδης, μανιώδης ‖ ~ally ad μανιασμένα, τρομερά.

fraternal [frəˈtɜːnl] a άδελφικός.

fraternity [frəˈtɜːniti] n (club) όργάνωσις ‖ (spirit) άδελφότης ‖ (US sch) φοιτητική όργάνωσις.

fraternization [frætənaiˈzeiʃən] n συναδέλφωσις.

fraternize ['frætənaiz] vi (+ with) συναδελφώνομαι μέ.

fraud [frɔːd] n (trickery) δόλος, άπάτη ‖ (trick) κόλπο, άπάτη, παγίδα ‖ (person) άπατεών, κατεργάρης.

fraudulent ['frɔːdjulənt] a δόλιος, άπατηλός.

fray [frei] n σύρραξις, καυγᾶς, σύγκρουσις ‖ vt τρίβω, ταράζω, ξεφτίζω ‖ vi ξεφτίζομαι, τρίβομαι ‖ ~ed a τριμμένος, φαγωμένος.

freak [friːk] n ίδιοτροπία, καπρίτσιο ‖ (col) τέρας ‖ a περίεργον φαινόμενον.

freckle ['frekl] n πανάδα ‖ ~d a μέ πανάδες.

free [friː] a (at liberty) άνεξάρτητος, έλεύθερος ‖ (loose) έλεύθερος ‖ (not

occupied) ἐλεύθερος ‖ *(gratis)* δωρεάν, τζάμπα ‖ *(liberal)* φιλελεύθερος, γενναιόφρων, ἀνοιχτός ‖ *vt (set free)* (ἀπ)ελευθερώνω ‖ *(unblock)* ἀποφράσσω, καθαρίζω ‖ ~dom *n* ἐλευθερία, ἀνεξαρτησία ‖ ~lance *a* ἀνεξάρτητος ‖ ~ly *ad* ἐλευθέρως, ἀβίαστα ‖ ~mason *n* μασῶνος ‖ ~masonry *n* τεκτωνισμός, μασωνία ‖ ~ trade *n* ἐλεύθερον ἐμπόριον ‖ ~way *n (US)* αὐτοκινητόδρομος ‖ ~ wheel *vi* πηγαίνω μέ ἐλεύθερον τροχόν ‖ ~ will *n* ἐλευθέρα θέλησις.

freesia ['fri:ziə] *n* φρισία.

freeze [fri:z] *(irreg v) vi (become ice)* ψύχω, καταψύχω, παγώνω ‖ *(feel cold)* κρυώνω ‖ *vt (lit)* (κατα)ψύχω, παγώνω ‖ *(fig)* δεσμεύω, ἀκινητοποιῶ ‖ *n (lit)* (κατά)ψυξις, παγωνιά ‖ *(fig, econ)* δέσμευσις ‖ ~r *n* παγωτιέρα, ψυγεῖον καταψύξεως.

freezing ['fri:ziŋ] *a:* ~ cold *a* παγερό κρύο ‖ ~ point *n* σημεῖον ψύξεως, πήξεως.

freight [freit] *n (goods)* φορτίον, ἐμπορεύματα ‖ *(money charged)* ναῦλος ‖ ~ car *n (US)* φορτηγόν βαγόνι ‖ ~er *n (naut)* φορτηγόν.

French [frentʃ] *a* γαλλικός ‖ *n (ling)* (τά) γαλλικά ‖ the ~ *npl* οἱ Γάλλοι ‖ ~ fried potatoes *npl* πατάτες τηγανιτές ‖ ~man *n* Γάλλος ‖ ~ window *n* τζαμόπορτα ‖ ~woman *n* Γαλλίδα.

frenzy ['frenzi] *a* φρενῖτις, τρέλλα, παραλήρημα.

frequency ['fri:kwənsi] *n* συχνότης, πυκνότης ‖ *(phys)* συχνότης.

frequent ['fri:kwənt] *a (happening often)* συχνός, διαδεδομένος, συνήθης ‖ *(numerous)* ἄφθονος, πολυάριθμος ‖ [fri:'kwent] *vt* συχνάζω ‖ ~ly *ad* συχνά.

fresco ['freskəu] *n* νωπογραφία, φρέσκο.

fresh [freʃ] *a (new, additional)* νέος, καινούριος, φρέσκος ‖ *(recent)* νέος, πρωτότυπος ‖ *(not stale)* νωπός, φρέσκος ‖ *(not tired)* ρωμαλαίος, ξεκούραστος, φρέσκος ‖ *(cool)* καθαρός, δροσερός ‖ *(cheeky)* ἀναιδής, ζωηρός ‖ ~en *(also* ~ *up) vi* φρεσκάρω, συνέρχομαι ‖ *vt* ἀναζωογονῶ, φρεσκάρω ‖ ~ly *ad* προσφάτως, νεο-, φρεσκο- ‖ ~ness *n* φρεσκάδα, δροσερότης ‖ ~water *a* τοῦ γλυκοῦ νεροῦ.

fret [fret] *vi* ταράσσομαι, ἀνησυχῶ, στεναχωριέμαι.

friar ['fraiə*] *n* μοναχός, καλόγηρος.

friction ['frikʃən] *n (resistance)* τριβή, τρίψιμο ‖ *(disagreement)* προστριβή, τσάκωμα.

Friday ['fraidi] *n* Παρασκευή ‖ see **good**.

fridge [fridʒ] *n* ψυγεῖον.

fried [fraid] *a* τηγανισμένο.

friend [frend] *n* φίλος, γνωστός, γνώριμος ‖ ~liness *n* φιλία, καλωσύνη ‖ ~ly *a (person)* εὐμενής, φιλικός ‖ *(attitude)* φιλικός ‖ ~ship *n* φιλία.

frieze [fri:z] *n (archit)* διάζωμα, ζωφόρος.

frigate ['frigit] *n* φρεγάτα.

fright [frait] *n* τρόμος, φόβος ‖ *(ugly)* ἄσχημος, σχιάχτρο ‖ ~en *vt* (κατα)τρομάζω, φοβίζω ‖ ~ening *a* τρομακτικός, τρομερός ‖ ~ful *a (col)* τρομερός, φρικτός ‖ ~fully *ad* τρομερά, τρομακτικά.

frigid ['fridʒid] *a* ψυχρός, παγερός, κρύος ‖ ~ity *n* ψυχρότης ‖ *(sexual)* ἀναφροδισία.

frill [fril] *n* βολλάν.

fringe [frindʒ] *n (border)* κροσσός, κρόσι ‖ *(fig)* περιθώριον, παρυφή.

frisky ['friski] *a* παιχνιδιάρης, κεφάτος.

fritter ['fritə*] *n* τηγανίτα, σβίγγος ‖ to ~ away *vt* σπαταλῶ.

frivolity [fri'vɔliti] *n* ἐπιπολαιότης.

frivolous ['frivələs] *a* ἐπιπόλαιος.

frizzy ['frizi] *a* σγουρός.

fro [frəu] see **to**.

frock [frɔk] *n (of monk)* ράσο ‖ *(of woman)* φουστάνι.

frog [frɔg] *n* βάτραχος ‖ ~man *n* βατραχάνθρωπος.

frolic ['frɔlik] *n* παιχνίδι, γλέντι ‖ *vi* διασκεδάζω, παιχνιδίζω.

from [frɔm] *prep* ἀπό, ἐκ, ἐξ.

front [frʌnt] *n (of house)* πρόσοψις, μπροστινή, φάτσα ‖ *(mil)* μέτωπον ‖ *(pol)* μέτωπον ‖ *(meteorology)* μέτωπον ‖ *(fig: appearances)* ὄψις, μούτρα, ἀναίδεια ‖ *a (forward)* πρόσθιος, μπροστινός ‖ *(first)* μπροστινός, πρῶτος ‖ *(door)* κυρία εἴσοδος, μπροστινή πόρτα ‖ ~age *n* πρόσοψις ‖ ~al *a* μετωπικός ‖ ~ier *n* σύνορον, μεθόριος ‖ ~-page *a* τῆς πρώτης σελίδος ‖ ~-wheel drive *n* κίνησις στούς προσθίους τροχούς.

frost [frɔst] *n* παγετός, παγωνιά ‖ ~bite *n* κρυοπάγημα ‖ ~ed *a (glass)* μάτ, ἀδιαφανής ‖ ~y *a* παγερός, παγωμένος.

froth [frɔθ] *n* ἀφρός ‖ *(on beer)* κολλάρο ‖ ~y *a* ἀφρισμένος, ἀφρώδης.

frown [fraun] *n* συνοφρύωσις, κατσούφιασμα ‖ *vi* συνοφρυοῦμαι, σκυθρωπάζω ‖ to ~ upon *vt* κάνω μούτρα σέ.

froze [frəuz] *pt of* **freeze** ‖ ~n *pp of* **freeze** ‖ *(comm)* παγωμένος ‖ ~n food *n* κατεψυγμένα.

frugal ['fru:gəl] *a* λιτός, οἰκονομικός.

fruit [fru:t] *n* φροῦτον, καρπόν ‖ ~s *npl* καρποί, κέρδη ‖ ~erer *n* ὀπωροπώλης ‖ ~ful *a* καρποφόρος, γόνιμος ‖ ~ion [fru:'iʃən] *n* ἐκπλήρωσις, ἀπόλαυσις.

frustrate [frʌs'treit] *vt* ματαιώνω, ἐξουδετερώνω, ἐμποδίζω ‖ ~d *a* ἀπογοητευμένος.

frustration [frʌs'treiʃən] *n* ματαίωσις, ἀπογοήτευσις.

fry [frai] *vt* τηγανίζω ‖ small ~ *npl* οἱ ἀνθρωπάκοι, τά κατακάθια ‖ ~ing pan *n* τηγάνι.

fuchsia ['fju:ʃə] *n* φούξια.

fudge [fʌdʒ] *n* ζαχαρωτόν, καραμέλα.

fuel [fjuəl] *n* (*oil*) καύσιμος ὕλη, πετρέλαιον | (*petrol*) καύσιμον, βενζίνη | (*wood*) καυσόξυλα | (*coal*) κάρβουνο | (*gas*) καύσιμον ἀέριον | ~ **oil** *n* (*diesel fuel*) ἀκάθαρτον πετρέλαιον | ~ **tank** *n* ντεπόζιτο βενζίνης.

fugitive [ˈfjuːdʒitiv] *n* φυγάς, δραπέτης.

fulfil [fulˈfil] *vt* (*accomplish*) ἐκπληρώνω | (*obey*) ἐκτελῶ, εἰσακούω | ~**ment** *n* ἐκπλήρωσις, ἐκτέλεσις.

full [ful] *a* (*box, bottle*) πλήρης, γεμᾶτος | (*vehicle*) πλήρης, γεμᾶτος | (*person: satisfied*) χορτᾶτος, μπουκωμένος | (*session*) ὁλομέλεια | (*complete*) ὁλόκληρος | (*moon*) πανσέληνος | (*price*) ὁλόκληρο | (*speed*) ὁλοταχῶς | (*skirt*) φαρδύς, μπουφφάν | in ~ χωρὶς ἔκπτωσιν, ὁλογράφως, ἀκέραιον | ~**back** *n* ὀπισθοφύλαξ | ~**ness** *n* πληρότης, τελειότης | ~ **stop** *n* τελεία | ~-**time** *a* (*work*) μέ πλήρες ὡράριον | *ad* ἀκριβῶς, τελείως | ~**y** *ad* πλήρως, τελείως, ἀπολύτως | ~**y-fledged** *a* ὥριμος.

fumble [ˈfʌmbl] *vti* ψαχουλεύω, χειρίζομαι ἀτζαμίστικα.

fume [fjuːm] *vi* (*smoke*) ἀναδίδομαι, καπνίζω | (*be furious*) ἐξάπτομαι, λυσσάζω | ~**s** *npl* ἀτμοί, ἀναθυμιάσεις, καπνιές.

fumigate [ˈfjuːmigeit] *vt* ἀπολυμαίνω.

fun [fʌn] *n* διασκέδασις, κέφι, ἀστεῖο, χωρατό | **to make** ~ **of** κοροϊδεύω, περιπαίζω.

function [ˈfʌŋkʃən] *n* (*use*) λειτουργία, ἔργον, λειτούργημα | (*public occasion*) τελετή, δεξίωσις | *vi* λειτουργῶ | ~**al** *a* λειτουργικός.

fund [fʌnd] *n* (*capital*) ταμεῖον, κεφάλαιον, παρακαταθήκη | (*store*) ἀπόθεμα, πηγή.

fundamental [fʌndəˈmentl] *a* θεμελιώδης | ~**s** *npl* στοιχεῖα, βασικές ἀρχές | ~**ly** *ad* οὐσιαστικῶς, βασικῶς.

funeral [ˈfjuːnərəl] *n* κηδεία | *a* νεκρώσιμος, πένθιμος.

fun fair [ˈfʌnfɛə*] *n* λούνα-πάρκ.

fungus [ˈfʌŋgəs] *n* μύκης, μανιτάρι.

funnel [ˈfʌnl] *n* χωνί | (*of ship*) φουγάρο.

funnily [ˈfʌnili] *ad* κωμικά, περίεργα | ~ **enough** περίεργως.

funny [ˈfʌni] *a* (*comical*) ἀστεῖος, κωμικός | (*strange*) παράξενος, περίεργος.

fur [fəː*] *n* γούνα, γουναρικό | ~ **coat** *n* γούνινο παλτό.

furious [ˈfjuəriəs] *a* μαινόμενος, λυσσαλέος, ἀγριεμένος | ~**ly** *ad* ἄγρια, λυσσωδῶς.

furlong [ˈfəːlɔŋ] *n* = 220 ὑάρδες (201 μέτρα).

furlough [ˈfəːləu] *n* (*US*) ἄδεια.

furnace [ˈfəːnis] *n* κλίβανος, κάμινος, φοῦρνος.

furnish [ˈfəːniʃ] *vt* (*with furniture*) ἐπιπλώνω | (*supply*) παρέχω, προμηθεύω, προσφέρω | ~**ings** *npl* ἔπιπλα, ἐπίπλωσις.

furniture [ˈfəːnitʃə*] *n* ἔπιπλα.

furrow [ˈfʌrəu] *n* αὐλακώνω.

furry [ˈfəːi] *a* γούνινος.

further [ˈfəːðə*] *comp of* far | *a* (*additional*) νέος, πρόσθετος, μεταγενέστερος | (*more distant*) πιό πέρα | *ad* (*more*) περαιτέρω, περισσότερον | (*moreover*) ἄλλωστε, ἐπὶ πλέον | *vt* προάγω, ὑποστηρίζω | ~**more** *ad* ἐκτός ἀπ'αὐτό ἐξ ἄλλου.

furthest [ˈfəːðist] *superl of* far.

furtive [ˈfəːtiv] *a* λαθραῖος, κρυμμένος, ὕπουλος | ~**ly** *ad* κρυφά, λαθραία.

fury [ˈfjuəri] *n* ὀργή, θυμός, μάνιτα.

fuse [fjuːz] *n* (*elec*) ἀσφάλεια | (*cord*) φυτίλι | *vt* τήκω, λειώνω | *vi* (*elec*) τήκομαι, λιώνω | ~ **box** *n* κιβώτιον ἀσφαλειῶν.

fuselage [ˈfjuːzəlaːʒ] *n* ἄτρακτος, σκελετός.

fusion [ˈfjuːʒən] *n* (*union*) συγχώνευσις, σύμπραξις.

fuss [fʌs] *n* (*dispute*) φασαρία, θόρυβος, ταραχή | (*bustle*) φασαρία, ἀναστάτωσις, μπερδέματα | ~**y** *a* πολυπράγμων, λεπτολόγος, ἰδιότροπος.

futile [ˈfjuːtail] *a* (*useless*) φροῦδος, μάταιος | (*unimportant*) ἀσήμαντος, κούφιος.

futility [fjuːˈtiliti] *n* ματαιότης.

future [ˈfjuːtʃə*] *a* μέλλων, μελλοντικός | *n* μέλλον | **in (the)** ~ στὸ μέλλον.

futuristic [fjuːtʃəˈristik] *a* φουτουριστικός.

fuze [fjuːz] (*US*) = fuse.

fuzzy [ˈfʌzi] *a* (*indistinct*) θαμπός | (*from drink*) σουρωμένος.

G, g

gabble [ˈgæbl] *vi* φλυαρῶ.

gable [ˈgeibl] *n* ἀέτωμα.

gadget [ˈgædʒit] *n* μαραφέτι.

gag [gæg] *n* φίμωτρον | (*funny phrase*) ἀστεῖο, κασκαρίκα | *vt* φιμώνω, ἀποστομώνω.

gaiety [ˈgeiiti] *n* εὐθυμία.

gaily [ˈgeili] *ad* εὔθυμα, χαρούμενα.

gain [gein] *vt* (*obtain*) ἀποκτῶ, κερδίζω | (*win over*) κερδίζω, παίρνω | (*make progress*) προχωρῶ, προηγοῦμαι | *vi* (*improve*) κερδίζω, κατακτῶ | (*clock etc*) τρέχω μπρός | *n* κέρδος, αὔξησις | ~**ful** *a* ἐπικερδής.

gala [ˈgaːlə] *n* γιορτή.

galaxy [ˈgæləksi] *n* (*stars*) γαλαξίας.

gale [geil] *n* θύελλα, φουρτούνα | ~ **warning** *n* ἀναγγελία θυέλλης.

gallant [ˈgælənt] *a* (*fine, brave*) γενναῖος, ἡρωικός | (*to women*) γαλάντης, περιποιητικός | ~**ry** *n* γενναιότης, λεβεντιά | (*to women*) περιποιητικότης.

G

gall-bladder ['gɔ:lblædə*] n χοληδόχος κύστις.

gallery ['gæləri] n (art) πινακοθήκη ‖ (theat) γαλαρία, ἐξώστης.

galley ['gæli] n (of ship) μαγειρεῖον ‖ (vessel) γαλέρα.

gallon ['gælən] n γαλλόνι (04.54 χλγρ.).

gallop ['gæləp] n καλπασμός, γκάλοπ ‖ vi καλπάζω.

gallows ['gæləuz] npl ἀγχόνη, κρεμάλα.

gallstone ['gɔ:lstəun] n χολόλιθος.

gamble ['gæmbl] vi παίζω ‖ vt (risk) ριψοκινδυνεύω ‖ n (τυχηρόν) παιχνίδι ‖ ~r n (χαρτο)παίκτης.

gambling ['gæmbliŋ] n παιχνίδι, παίξιμο.

game [geim] n (play) παιχνίδι, διασκέδασις ‖ (animals) θήραμα, κυνήγι ‖ a θαρραλέος, τολμηρός ‖ ~keeper n φύλαξ κυνηγίου.

gammon ['gæmən] n ὀπίσθια μπούτια, χοιρομέρι.

gang [gæŋ] n συμμορία, σπεῖρα.

gangrene ['gæŋgri:n] n γάγγραινα.

gangster ['gæŋstə*] n γκάγκστερ.

gangway ['gæŋwei] n (of ship) διαβάθρα, μαδέρι ‖ (aisle) διάδρομος.

gaol [dʒeil] n = jail.

gap [gæp] n (opening) τρύπα, ῥῆγμα ‖ (empty space) διάκενον.

gape [geip] vi χάσκω, χασμουριέμαι.

gaping ['geipiŋ] a χαίνων.

garage ['gæra:ʒ] n γκαράζ.

garbage ['ga:bidʒ] n σκουπίδια ‖ ~ can n (US) σκουπιδοτενεκές.

garbled ['ga:bld] a (story) παραμορφωμένος, ἀλλοιωμένος.

garden ['ga:dn] n κῆπος, μπαξές ‖ vi ἀσχολοῦμαι μέ κηπουρικήν ‖ ~er n κηπουρός, περιβολάρης ‖ ~ing n κηπουρική ‖ ~ party n γκάρντεν-πάρτυ.

gargle ['ga:gl] vi γαργαρίζω ‖ n γαργάρα.

gargoyle ['ga:gɔil] n ὑδρορρόη.

garish ['gɛəriʃ] a φανταχτερός, κακόγουστος.

garland ['ga:lənd] n στέφανος, γιρλάντα.

garlic ['ga:lik] n σκόρδο.

garment ['ga:mənt] n φόρεμα.

garnish ['ga:niʃ] vt (food) γαρνίρω ‖ n γαρνιτούρα.

garret ['gærit] n σοφίτα.

garrison ['gærisən] n φρουρά ‖ vt ἐγκαθιστῶ φρουράν.

garrulous ['gæruləs] a φλύαρος, πολυλογάς.

garter ['ga:tə*] n καλτσοδέτα.

gas [gæs] n ἀέριον ‖ (coalgas) φωταέριον, γκάζ ‖ (med) ἀναισθητικόν ‖ (US: gasoline) βενζίνη ‖ vt δηλητηριάζω (δι'ἀερίου) ‖ ~ cooker n κουζίνα ‖ ~ cylinder n φιάλη ἀερίου ‖ ~ fire n σόμπα τοῦ γκαζιοῦ.

gash [gæʃ] n ἐγκοπή, μαχαιριά ‖ vt κόβω, πληγώνω.

gasket ['gæskit] n (tech) παρένθεμα.

gasmask ['gæsma:sk] n προσωπίς ἀερίων, μάσκα.

gas meter ['gæsmi:tə*] n μετρητής τοῦ γκαζιοῦ.

gasoline ['gæsəli:n] n (US) βενζίνη.

gasp [ga:sp] vi ἀσθμαίνω, λαχανιάζω ‖ n κομμένη ἀναπνοή, ῥόγχος.

gas ring ['gæsriŋ] n μάτι τοῦ γκαζιοῦ.

gas station ['gæssteiʃən] n (US) βενζινάδικο.

gas stove ['gæs'stəuv] n κουζίνα τοῦ γκαζιοῦ.

gassy ['gæsi] a (drink) ἀεριοῦχος.

gastric ['gæstrik] a γαστρικός ‖ ~ ulcer n ἕλκος τοῦ στομάχου.

gastronomy [gæs'trɔnəmi] n γαστρονομία.

gate [geit] n πύλη, πόρτα ‖ (of estate etc) καγκελόπορτα, αὐλόπορτα ‖ ~crasher n (party) σελέμης, τζαμπατζῆς ‖ ~way n πύλη, εἴσοδος.

gather ['gæðə*] vt συλλέγω, μαζεύω ‖ (gain) συμπεραίνω, συνάγω ‖ vi (assemble) συγκεντροῦμαι, μαζεύομαι ‖ ~ing n συγκέντρωσις, μάζεμα.

gauche [gəuʃ] a χωρίς τάκτ.

gaudy ['gɔ:di] a ἐπιδεικτικός, φανταχτερός.

gauge [geidʒ] n (of metal) διάμετρος, διαμέτρημα ‖ (rail) πλάτος, μετατρόχιον ‖ (measure) μετρητής, (ἐν)δείκτης ‖ vt (δια)μετρῶ, ἐκτιμῶ.

gaunt [gɔ:nt] a (lean) ἰσχνός, κοκκαλιάρης ‖ (grim) ἄγριος, συντετριμμένος.

gauze [gɔ:z] n γάζα.

gave [geiv] pt of give.

gay [gei] a (merry) εὔθυμος ‖ (brightly coloured) λαμπρός, ζωηρός ‖ (col) τοιοῦτος.

gaze [geiz] n ἀτενές βλέμμα ‖ to ~ at vt ἀτενίζω, καρφώνω.

gazelle [gə'zel] n γαζέλλα.

gazetteer [gæzi'tiə*] n γεωγραφικόν λεξικόν.

gear [giə*] n (equipment) εἴδη ‖ (mech) μηχανισμός, ὀδοντωτός τροχός ‖ (aut) γρανάζι ‖ in ~ κινούμενος, στήν ταχύτητα ‖ out of ~ νεκρό σημεῖον, ἐκτός λειτουργίας ‖ ~box n κιβώτιον ταχυτήτων ‖ ~-lever, (US) ~shift n μοχλός ταχυτήτων.

geese [gi:s] npl of goose.

gelatin(e) ['dʒeləti:n] n ζελατίνη, πηκτή.

gelignite ['dʒelignait] n ζελινίτης.

gem [dʒem] n πολύτιμος λίθος, πέτρα.

gender ['dʒendə*] n γένος.

general ['dʒenərəl] n στρατηγός ‖ a γενικός ‖ ~ election n γενικαί ἐκλογαί ‖ ~ization n γενίκευσις ‖ ~ize vi γενικεύω, ἐκλαϊκεύω ‖ ~ly ad γενικά, κατά κανόνα.

generate ['dʒenəreit] vt παράγω, (ἐπι)φέρω, προκαλῶ ‖ (elec) παράγω.

generation [dʒenə'reiʃən] n (into being) γέννησις, γένεσις ‖ (descent in family) γενεά, γενιά ‖ (of same period) (σημερινή) γενεά ‖· (about 30 years) (μιά) γενεά.

generator ['dʒenəreitə*] n γεννήτρια.

generosity [dʒenə'rɔsiti] n γενναιοδωρία, γενναιοψυχία.

generous ['dʒenərəs] a γενναιόδωρος, μεγαλόψυχος ‖ (col) γενναῖο, πλούσιο ‖ ~ly ad γενναιόδωρα, μεγαλόψυχα.

genetics [dʒi'netiks] npl γενετική.

genial ['dʒi:niəl] a εὔκρατος, ἤπιος, προσηνής.

genitals ['dʒenitlz] npl γεννητικά ὄργανα.

genitive ['dʒenitiv] n γενική (πτῶσις).

genius ['dʒi:niəs] n (person) ἰδιοφυῖα, μεγαλοφυῖα ‖ (ability) πνεῦμα.

genteel [dʒen'ti:l] a εὐγενής, κομψός.

gentile ['dʒentail] n ἐθνικός, μή Ἰουδαίος.

gentle ['dʒentl] a ἤπιος, μαλακός, εὐγενής ‖ ~man n εὐγενής, κύριος, τζέντλεμαν ‖ ~ness n λεπτότης.

gently ['dʒentli] ad ἤρεμα, μαλακά.

gentry ['dʒentri] n ἀρχοντολόϊ.

gents [dʒents] n ἄνδρες, κύριοι.

genuine ['dʒenjuin] a γνήσιος, αὐθεντικός, ἀληθινός ‖ ~ly ad εἰλικρινά, γνησίως.

geographical [dʒiə'græfikəl] a γεωγραφικός.

geography [dʒi'ɔgrəfi] n γεωγραφία.

geological [dʒiə'lɔdʒikəl] a γεωλογικός.

geologist [dʒi'ɔlədʒist] n γεωλόγος.

geology [dʒi'ɔlədʒi] n γεωλογία.

geometric(al) [dʒiə'metrik(əl)] a γεωμετρικός.

geometry [dʒi'ɔmitri] n γεωμετρία.

geranium [dʒi'reiniəm] n γεράνι.

germ [dʒə:m] n (of disease) μικρόβιον ‖ (bud or seed) σπέρμα ‖ (beginning) σπέρμα.

German ['dʒə:mən] a γερμανικός ‖ n (person) Γερμανός ‖ (ling) γερμανικά ‖ ~y n Γερμανία.

germination [dʒə:mi'neiʃən] n βλάστησις, κύησις.

gesticulate [dʒes'tikjuleit] vi χειρονομῶ.

gesticulation [dʒestikju'leiʃən] n χειρονομία.

gesture ['dʒestʃə*] n χειρονομία, νεῦμα.

get [get] (irreg v) vt (fetch) (πηγαίνω νά) φέρω ‖ (become) γίνομαι ‖ (persuade) πείθω, καταφέρνω ‖ (catch) (συλλαμβάνω, πιάνω ‖ vi (reach) πηγαίνω, φθάνω, γίνομαι ‖ to ~ along vi (of people) πηγαίνω καλά ‖ (depart) προχωρῶ, (ὥρα) νά φύγω ‖ to ~ at vt (facts) φθάνω, βρίσκω, πλησιάζω ‖ to ~ away vi (leave) ἀναχωρῶ, ἀποχωρῶ ‖ (escape) φεύγω, τό σκάω ‖ to ~ down vt κατεβάζω, γράφω ‖ to ~ in vi (train) μπαίνω, πιάνω φιλίες ‖ to ~ on vi (well, badly etc) εὐδοκιμῶ, συμφωνῶ, τά πάω καλά ‖ to ~ out vi βγάζω, ἀφαιρῶ, βγαίνω ‖ to ~ over vt (illness) συνέρχομαι, τελειώνω ‖ to ~ up

vi (in morning) σηκώνομαι ‖ ~away ι φυγή, δραπέτευσις.

geyser ['gi:zə*] n θερμοπίδαξ, γκάιζερ ‖ (heater) θερμοσίφων.

ghastly ['gɑ:stli] a φρικιός, τρομερός ‖ (pale) ὠχρός.

gherkin ['gə:kin] n ἀγγουράκι.

ghetto ['getəu] n γκέττο, ὀβριακή.

ghost [gəust] n φάντασμα ‖ ~ly a φαντασματικός.

giant ['dʒaiənt] n γίγας ‖ a γιγαντιαῖος.

gibberish ['dʒibəriʃ] n ἀλαμπουρνέζικα.

gibe [dʒaib] n σκῶμμα, πείραγμα.

giblets ['dʒiblits] npl ἐντόσθια (πουλερικῶν).

giddiness ['gidinis] n ἵλιγγος, ζάλη.

giddy ['gidi] a (dizzy) ζαλισμένος ‖ (frivolous) ἐπιπόλαιος.

gift [gift] n δῶρον ‖ (talent) προσόν, τάλαντον ‖ ~ed a προικισμένος, μέ ταλέντο.

gigantic [dʒai'gæntik] a γιγαντιαῖος.

giggle ['gigl] vi χασκογελῶ ‖ n κακάρισμα.

gild [gild] (irreg v) vt (ἐπι)χρυσώνω.

gill [dʒil] n (measure = ¼ pint) ⅛ τοῦ λίτρου ‖ [gil] n (fish) βράγχιον, σπάραχνο.

gilt [gilt] pp of **gild** ‖ n ἐπιχρύσωσις, χρύσωμα ‖ a (ἐπι)χρυσωμένος.

gin [dʒin] n (liquor) τζίν.

ginger ['dʒindʒə*] n πιπερόρριζα ‖ ~ beer n τζιτζιμπύρα ‖ ~bread n μελόψωμο ‖ ~-haired a κοκκινοτρίχης.

gingerly ['dʒindʒəli] ad προσεκτικά μαλακά.

gipsy ['dʒipsi] n τσιγγάνος, γύφτος.

giraffe [dʒi'rɑ:f] n καμηλοπάρδαλις.

girder ['gə:də*] n δοκός.

girdle ['gə:dl] n ζωνάρι ‖ vt (περι)ζώνω.

girl [gə:l] n (child) κοριτσάκι, κορίτσι ‖ (young woman) νέα, κοπέλα ‖ ~friend (of girl) φιλινάδα ‖ (of boy) φιλινάδα, φίλη ‖ ~ish a κοριτσίστικος.

girth [gə:θ] n (measurement) περιφέρεια, περίμετρος ‖ (strap) ἔποχον, ἵγγλα.

gist [dʒist] n οὐσία, ἔννοια.

give [giv] (irreg v) vt (hand over) δίνω, χαρίζω ‖ (supply) παρέχω, ἀπονέμω ‖ vi (break) ὑποχωρῶ, λυγίζω ‖ to ~ away v' (give free) χαρίζω ‖ (betray) καταδίδω, προδίδω ‖ to ~ back vt ἀποδίδω, ξανα δίδω, γυρίζω ‖ to ~ in vi (yield, agree) ὑποχωρῶ, ὑποκύπτω ‖ vt (hand ir) παραδίδω ‖ to ~ up vi (surrender) παραδίδομαι ‖ vt (post, office) παραιτοῦμαι, ἐγκαταλείπω ‖ to ~ way vi θραύομαι, ὑποχωρῶ, ἀντικαθίσταμαι ‖ ~r n δωρητής, δότης.

glacier ['glæsiə*] n παγετών.

glad [glæd] a εὐχαριστημένος, εὐχάριστο ‖ ~den vt χαροποιῶ.

gladiator ['glædieitə*] n μονομάχος.

gladioli [glædi'əulai] npl γλαδίολες.

gladly ['glædli] ad εὐχαρίστως, μέ χαρά

glamorous ['glæmərəs] *a* γοητευτικός, μαγευτικός.

glamour ['glæmə*] *n* γοητεία, μαγεία.

glance [gla:ns] *n* βλέμμα, ματιά ‖ *vi* (+ *at*) (*look*) ρίχνω ματιά ‖ γλιστρῶ πλαγίως.

glancing ['gla:nsiŋ] *a* (*blow*) πλάγιος.

gland [glænd] *n* ἀδήν ‖ ~**ular** *a* ἀδενικός.

glare [gleə*] *n* (*light*) ἐκτυφλωτική λάμψι ‖ (*fierce stare*) ἄγριο βλέμμα ‖ *vi* ἀπαστράπτω, λάμπω ‖ (*angrily*) ἀγριοκοιτάζω.

glaring ['gleəriŋ] *a* (*mistake*) ἔκδηλος, ὀλοφάνερος.

glass [gla:s] *n* (*substance*) ὕαλος, γυαλί ‖ (*vessel*) ποτήρι ‖ (*mirror*) καθρέπτης ‖ ~**es** *npl* γυαλιά ‖ ~**house** *n* (*agr*) θερμοκήπιον, σέρρα ‖ ~**ware** *n* γυαλικά ‖ ~**y** *a* (*eye*) σάν γυαλί, ἀνέκφραστος.

glaze [gleiz] *vt* (*furnish with glass*) βάζω τζάμια ‖ (*finish*) βερνικώνω, γυαλίζω ‖ *n* βερνίκι.

glazier ['gleiziə*] *n* τζαμτζῆς.

gleam [gli:m] *n* ἀκτίδα, λάμψις ‖ *vi* ἀκτινοβολῶ, λάμπω ‖ ~**ing** *a* ἀπαστράπτων, λάμπων.

glee [gli:] *n* εὐθυμία, χαρά ‖ ~**ful** *a* εὔθυμος, χαρούμενος.

glen [glen] *n* χαράδρα, δερβένι.

glib [glib] *a* εὔγλωττος, ἐπιπόλαιος ‖ ~**ly** *ad* εὔκολα, πονηρά.

glide [glaid] *vi* ὀλισθαίνω, γλυστρῶ, κυλῶ ‖ *n* ὀλίσθησις, βολπλανέ ‖ ~**r** *n* (*aviat*) ἀνεμόπτερον.

gliding ['glaidiŋ] *n* ὀλίσθησις, ἀνεμοπορία.

glimmer ['glimə*] *n* ἀμυδρόν φῶς.

glimpse [glimps] *n* γρήγορη ματιά ‖ *vt* βλέπω φευγαλέα.

glint [glint] *n* λάμψις ‖ *vi* λάμπω, ἀστράπτω.

glisten ['glisn] *vi* ἀπαστράπτω, σπιθίζω.

glitter ['glitə*] *vi* λάμπω, σπινθηροβολῶ ‖ *n* λαμποκόπημα, γυάλισμα ‖ ~**ing** *a* ἀστράπτων, λαμπερός.

gloat [gləut] **to ~ over** *vt* κοιτάζω μέ χαιρεκακίαν.

global ['gləubl] *a* παγκόσμιος.

globe [gləub] *n* (*light*) γλόμπος, λάμπα ‖ (*earth*) σφαίρα, ὑδρόγειος σφαῖρα.

gloom [glu:m] *n* (*also* ~**iness**) (*darkness*) σκότος, σκοτάδι ‖ (*depression*) μελαγχολία, ἀκεφιά ‖ ~**ily** *ad* μελαγχολικά, σκυθρωπά ‖ ~**y** *a* σκοτεινός, βαρύς, μελαγχολικός.

glorification [glɔ:rifi'keiʃən] *n* ἐξύμνησις.

glorify ['glɔ:rifai] *vt* ἐκθειάζω, ἐξυμνῶ, δοξάζω.

glorious ['glɔ:riəs] *a* ἔνδοξος, δοξασμένος, λαμπρός.

glory ['glɔ:ri] *n* (*splendour*) δόξα, μεγαλεῖον ‖ (*fame*) τιμή, φήμη, δόξα.

gloss [glɔs] *n* (*shine*) στιλπνότης, λοῦστρο, γυαλάδα.

glossary ['glɔsəri] *n* λεξιλόγιον, γλωσσάριον.

glossy ['glɔsi] *a* (*surface*) στιλπνός, γυαλιστερός.

glove [glʌv] *n* γάντι.

glow [gləu] *vi* πυρακτοῦμαι, κοκκινίζω ‖ (*look hot*) ζεσταίνομαι, ἀνάβω ‖ (*with emotion*) ἀστράφτω, λάμπω ‖ *n* (*heat*) πυράκτωσις ‖ (*colour*) ροδαλότης, κοκκινάδα ‖ (*feeling*) σφρῖγος, φλόγα.

glower ['glauə*] *vi* στραβοκοιτάζω.

glucose ['glu:kəus] *n* γλυκόζη.

glue [glu:] *n* κόλλα ‖ *vt* κολλῶ.

glum [glʌm] *a* σκυθρωπός, κατσούφης.

glut [glʌt] *n* ὑπεραφθονία ‖ *vt* (*econ*) πλημμυρίζω.

glutton ['glʌtn] *n* λαίμαργος, φαγᾶς ‖ ~**ous** *a* ἀδηφάγος ‖ ~**y** *n* λαιμαργία.

glycerin(e) ['glisəri:n] *n* γλυκερίνη.

gnarled [na:ld] *a* ροζιάρικος.

gnat [næt] *n* σκνίπα.

gnaw [nɔ:] *vt* ροκανίζω, τραγανίζω.

gnome [nəum] *n* (*goblin*) καλικάντζαρος.

go [gəu] (*irreg v*) *vi* (*travel*) πηγαίνω, πάω ‖ (*progress*) κινοῦμαι, πάω ‖ (*function*) πάω, τρέχω, λειτουργῶ ‖ (*depart*) ἀναχωρῶ, φεύγω ‖ (*disappear*) χάνομαι ‖ (*be sold*) (+ *for*) πουλιέται γιά ‖ (*fit, suit*) πηγαίνω, ταιριάζω ‖ (*become*) γίνομαι ‖ (*break etc*) σπάζω, κόβομαι, πωλοῦμαι ‖ *n* (*energy*) δραστηριότης, διάθεσις ‖ (*attempt*) δοκιμή, προσπάθεια, ἀπόπειρα ‖ **to ~ ahead** *vi* (*proceed*) προχωρῶ, προοδεύω ‖ **to ~ along with** *vt* (*agree to support*) συμφωνῶ, ταιριάζω ‖ **to ~ away** *vi* (*depart*) φεύγω ‖ **to ~ back** *vi* (*return*) ἐπιστρέφω ‖ **to ~ back on** *vt* (*promise*) παραβαίνω, προδίδω ‖ **to ~ by** *vi* (*years, time*) περνῶ ‖ **to ~ down** *vi* (*sun*) κατεβαίνω, γέρνω, πέφτω ‖ **to ~ for** *vt* (*fetch*) πάω γιά ‖ (*like*) συμπαθῶ ‖ **to ~ in** *vi* (*enter*) εἰσέρχομαι, μπαίνω ‖ (*fit*) μπαίνω ‖ **to ~ into** *vt* (*enter*) μπαίνω ‖ (*study*) ἐξετάζω, μελετῶ ‖ **to ~ off** *vi* (*depart*) ἐξέρχομαι, φεύγω ‖ (*milk*) ξυνίζω ‖ (*explode*) ἐκπυρσοκροτῶ ‖ *vt* (*dislike*) ξεθυμαίνω, ἀντιπαθῶ ‖ **to ~ on** *vi* (*continue*) συνεχίζω, ἐξακολουθῶ ‖ **to ~ out** *vi* (*fire, light*) σβήνω ‖ (*of house*) βγαίνω ‖ **to ~ over** *vt* (*examine, check*) ἐξετάζω, ἐπαναλαμβάνω ‖ **to ~ up** *vi* (*price*) ἀνεβαίνω ‖ (*explode*) ἀνατινάσσομαι ‖ **to ~ without** *vt* περνῶ χωρίς.

goad [gəud] *vt* κεντρίζω, προκαλῶ ‖ *n* βούκεντρον, κίνητρον.

go-ahead ['gəuəhed] *a* δραστήριος.

goal [gəul] *n* (*purpose*) σκοπός ‖ (*sports field*) τέρμα ‖ (*score*) γκώλ ‖ ~**keeper** *n* τερματοφύλαξ ‖ ~-**post** *n* δοκός.

goat [gəut] *n* κατσίκα, γίδα.

gobble ['gɔbl] *vt* καταβροχθίζω.

go-between ['gəubitwi:n] *n* μεσάζων, μεσολαβητής.

god [gɔd] *n* θεός ‖ **G~** Θεός ‖ ~**child** *n* βαπτησιμιός ‖ ~**dess** *n* θεά ‖ ~**father**

n νουνός ‖ ~**forsaken** *a* ἐγκαταλελειμμένος, καταραμένος ‖ ~**mother** *n* νουνά ‖ ~**send** *n* θεῖον δῶρον, κελεπούρι.

goggle ['gɔgl] *vi* γουρλώνω ‖ ~**s** *npl* προστατευτικά γυαλιά.

going ['gəuiŋ] *n* (*condition of ground*) κατάστασις ἐδάφους ‖ *a* (*rate*) τρέχουσα (τιμή) ‖ (*concern*) δραστήριος ‖ ~**s-on** *npl* συμβάντα, συμπεριφορά.

gold [gəuld] *n* χρυσός, χρυσάφι ‖ ~**en** *a* χρυσοῦς, χρυσαφένια ‖ ~**fish** *n* χρυσόψαρο ‖ ~ **mine** *n* χρυσορυχεῖον.

golf [gɔlf] *n* γκόλφ ‖ ~ **club** *n* (*society*) λέσχη τοῦ γκόλφ ‖ (*stick*) κλώμπ ‖ ~ **course** *n* γήπεδον τοῦ γκόλφ ‖ ~**er** *n* παίκτης τοῦ γκόλφ.

gondola ['gɔndələ] *n* γόνδολα.

gone [gɔn] *pp of* **go.**

gong [gɔŋ] *n* γκόγκ, κώδων.

good [gud] *n* (*well-being*) καλόν, ὄφελος ‖ (*goodness*) ἀρετή, καλόν ‖ *a* (*well-behaved*) καλός, ἔντιμος ‖ (*virtuous*) τίμιος, ἀγαθός, καλός ‖ (*well-done*) ἐξαιρετικός, καλός ‖ (*suitable*) ταιριαστός, πού πάει ‖ (*sound*) σέ καλή κατάσταση ‖ ~**s** *npl* κινητά, ἀγαθά, εἴδη ‖ **a** ~ **deal, a** ~ **many** ἀρκετός, πολύς ‖ ~**bye**! ἀντίο! γειά σου! ‖ στό καλό ‖ **G** ~ **Friday** *n* Μεγάλη Παρασκευή ‖ ~**looking** *a* εὔμορφος ‖ ~ **morning**! καλημέρα! ‖ ~**ness** *n* καλωσύνη, ἀρετή ‖ ~**will** *n* καλή θέλησι, κέφι.

goose [gu:s] *n* χήνα ‖ ~**berry** *n* φραγκοστάφυλο ‖ ~**flesh** *n* ἀνατριχίλα.

gore [gɔ:*] *vt* κερατίζω ‖ *n* πηκτόν αἷμα.

gorge [gɔ:dʒ] *n* στενόν, φαράγγι ‖ *vti* παρατρώγω.

gorgeous ['gɔ:dʒəs] *a* πολύχρωμος, ἐξαίσιος.

gorilla [gə'rilə] *n* γορίλλας.

gorse [gɔ:s] *n* σπάρτο.

gory ['gɔ:ri] *a* (*details*) αἱματοβαφής.

go-slow ['gəu'sləu] *n* ἀπεργία κωλυσιεργίας.

gospel ['gɔspəl] *n* εὐαγγέλιον.

gossip ['gɔsip] *n* (*idle talk*) κουβεντολόϊ ‖ (*person*) κουτσομπόλης ‖ *vi* κουτσομπολεύω, φλυαρώ.

got [gɔt] *pt,pp of* **get** ‖ ~**ten** (*US*) *pp of* **get.**

gout [gaut] *n* ἀρθρῖτις, ποδάγρα.

govern ['gʌvən] *vt* (*general*) κυβερνῶ, διοικῶ, διευθύνω ‖ (*gram*) συντάσσομαι μέ ‖ ~**ess** *n* γκουβερνάντα, νταντά ‖ ~**ing** *a* διευθύνων, διοικῶν, κατευθυντήριος ‖ ~**ment** *n* κυβέρνησις ‖ (*management*) διοίκησις ‖ ~**mental** *a* κυβερνητικός ‖ ~**or** *n* κυβερνήτης, διοικητής.

gown [gaun] *n* φόρεμα, φουστάνι ‖ (*of judge etc*) τήβεννος.

grab [græb] *vt* ἁρπάζω, πιάνω ‖ *n* ἁρπαγή ‖ (*excavator*) ἁρπάγη.

grace [greis] *n* (*charm*) χάρις, χάρη ‖ (*favour, kindness*) εὔνοια, χατήρι ‖ (*God's blessing*) θεία χάριτι ‖ (*short prayer*) προσευχή ‖ *vt* (*honour*) τιμῶ ‖ (*adorn*) στολίζω, ὀμορφαίνω ‖ **5 days'** ~ πενθήμερος χάρις ‖ ~**ful** *a* χαριτωμένος, κομψός ‖ ~**fully** *ad* χαριτωμένα.

gracious ['greiʃəs] *a* (*kind, courteous*) καλός, ἀγαθός, καλόβολος.

gradation [grə'deiʃən] *n* διαβάθμισις.

grade [greid] *n* (*degree, rank*) βαθμός, τάξις, βαθμίδα ‖ (*slope*) κλίσις ‖ *vt* (*classify*) διαβαθμίζω, ταξινομῶ ‖ ~ **crossing** *n* (*US*) ἰσόπεδος διάβασις.

gradient ['greidiənt] *n* κλίσις.

gradual ['grædjuəl] *a* βαθμιαῖος ‖ ~**ly** *ad* βαθμηδόν.

graduate ['grædjuit] *n* πτυχιοῦχος ‖ ['grædjueit] *vi* ἀποφοιτῶ.

graduation [grædju'eiʃən] *n* ἀποφοίτησις ‖ (*grade*) διαβάθμισις.

graft [gra:ft] *n* (*shoot*) μπόλι, κεντρί ‖ (*on humans*) μόσχευμα ‖ (*unfair means*) δωροδοκία, ρεμούλα ‖ *vt* μπολιάζω ‖ ~**ing** *n* μεταμόσχευσις.

grain [grein] *n* (*seed*) κόκκος, σπυρί ‖ (*crop*) δημητριακά ‖ (*small particle*) ψήγμα, κόκκος ‖ (*fibre*) κόκκος, ὑφή, ἴς.

grammar ['græmə*] *n* γραμματική.

grammatical [grə'mætikəl] *a* γραμματικός.

gram(me) [græm] *n* γραμμάριον.

gramophone ['græməfəun] *n* γραμμόφωνον.

granary ['grænəri] *n* σιταποθήκη.

grand [grænd] *a* (*fine, splendid*) μέγας, μεγαλοπρεπής ‖ (*final*) πλήρης, ὁλόκληρος ‖ ~**daughter** *n* ἐγγονή ‖ ~**eur** *n* μεγαλεῖον, μεγαλοπρέπεια ‖ ~**father** *n* πάππος, παπποῦς ‖ ~**iose** *a* (*imposing*) μεγαλοπρεπής ‖ (*pompous*) πομπώδης, φαντασμένος ‖ ~**mother** *n* μάμη, γιαγιά ‖ ~ **piano** *n* πιάνο μέ οὐρά ‖ ~**son** *n* ἐγγονος ‖ ~**stand** *n* ἐξέδρα.

granite ['grænit] *n* γρανίτης.

granny ['græni] *n* (*col*) γιαγιά, γρηούλα.

grant [gra:nt] *vt* (*bestow*) ἀπονέμω, δίδω ‖ (*allow*) (ἀπο)δέχομαι ‖ *n* δωρεά, ἐπιχορήγησις.

granule ['grænju:l] *n* κοκκίδιον, κοκκίον.

grape [greip] *n* σταφύλι, ρώγα ‖ ~**fruit** *n* φράπα, γκρέϊπ-φρούτ ‖ ~ **juice** *n* χυμός σταφυλιοῦ.

graph [gra:f] *n* διάγραμμα, γραφική παράστασις ‖ ~**ic** *a* (*vivid*) ζωηρός, ἐκφραστικός ‖ (*drawing, writing*) γραφικός.

grapple ['græpl] *vi* (+ *with*) πιάνομαι, ἔρχομαι στά χέρια.

grasp [gra:sp] *vt* πιάνω, σφίγγω, ἁρπάζω ‖ (*understand*) συλλαμβάνω, κατανοῶ ‖ *n* (*handgrip*) λαβή, πιάσιμο, σφίξιμο ‖ (*possession*) ἔλεγχος, ἐξουσία ‖ (*understanding*) ἀντίληψις, γνῶσις ‖ ~**ing** *a* ἄπληστος, πλεονέκτης.

grass [grɑːs] *n* χορτάρι, γρασίδι ‖ ~-**hopper** *n* ἀκρίδα ‖ ~**land** *n* λιβάδι ‖ ~ **snake** *n* νερόφιδο ‖ ~**y** *a* χορταριασμένος, πράσινος.

grate [greit] *n* ἐσχάρα, κάγκελο ‖ *vi* (*scrape*) ξύω ‖ (*make harsh sound*) τρίζω ‖ (*irritate*) ἐνοχλῶ ‖ *vt* (*into small pieces*) τρίβω.

grateful ['greitful] *a* εὐγνώμων, εὐχάριστος ‖ ~**ly** *ad* εὐγνωμόνως.

grater ['greitə*] *n* ξύστρα, τρίφτης.

gratification [grætifi'keiʃən] *n* ἱκανοποίησις.

gratify ['grætifai] *vt* εὐχαριστῶ, ἱκανοποιῶ.

gratifying ['grætifaiiŋ] *a* εὐχάριστος.

grating ['greitiŋ] *n* (*iron bars*) κιγκλίδωμα, κάγκελα ‖ *a* (*noise*) κακόηχος, στρίγγλικος.

gratitude ['grætitjuːd] *n* εὐγνωμοσύνη.

gratuitous [grə'tjuːitəs] *a* (*uncalled for*) ἀδικαιολόγητος ‖ (*given free*) δωρεάν, χαριστικός.

gratuity [grə'tjuːiti] *n* φιλοδώρημα, πουρμπουάρ.

grave [greiv] *n* τάφος ‖ *a* βαρύς, σοβαρός, δυσάρεστος ‖ ~**digger** *n* νεκροθάπτης.

gravel ['grævəl] *n* χαλίκι, ἄμμο.

gravely ['greivli] *ad* σοβαρά, βαρειά.

gravestone ['greivstəun] *n* ἐπιτάφιος πλάκα.

graveyard ['greivjɑːd] *n* νεκροταφεῖον.

gravitate ['græviteit] *vi* ἕλκομαι, ρέπω πρός.

gravity ['græviti] *n* βαρύτης, βάρος ‖ (*seriousness*) σοβαρότης.

gravy ['greivi] *n* σάλτσα.

gray [grei] *a* = **grey**.

graze [greiz] *vi* (*feed*) βόσκω ‖ *vt* (*touch*) ψαύω, ἐγγίζω ‖ (*scrape*) ξύνω ‖ *n* (*med*) ξέγδαρμα.

grease [griːs] *n* (*fat*) λίπος, ξύγγι ‖ (*lubricant*) γράσο, λάδι ‖ *vt* λαδώνω, γρασάρω ‖ ~ **gun** *n* γρασαδόρος ‖ ~**proof** *a* μή διαπερατός ἀπό λάδι.

greasy ['griːsi] *a* λιπαρός, λαδωμένος.

great [greit] *a* (*large*) μεγάλος ‖ (*important*) σπουδαῖος ‖ (*distinguished*) μεγάλος ‖ **G~ Britain** *n* Μεγάλη Βρεττανία ‖ ~**-grandfather** *n* πρόπαππος ‖ ~**-grandmother** *n* προμάμμη ‖ ~**ly** *ad* μεγάλως, πολύ ‖ ~**ness** *n* μεγαλεῖον, μέγεθος.

Greece [griːs] *n* Ἑλλάς.

greed [griːd] *n* (*also* ~**iness**) ἀπληστία, πλεονεξία ‖ ~**ily** *ad* ἀπλήστως ‖ ~**y** *a* ἄπληστος, πλεονέκτης ‖ (*gluttonous*) λαίμαργος, ἀδηφάγος.

Greek [griːk] *n* (*person*) Ἕλλην, Ρωμαιός ‖ (*ling*) ἑλληνικά ‖ *a* ἑλληνικός.

green [griːn] *a* πράσινος, ἄγουρος ‖ (*inexperienced*) ἄπειρος ‖ ~**gage** *n* πράσινο δαμάσκηνο ‖ ~**grocer** *n* μανάβης ‖ ~**house** *n* θερμοκήπιον ‖ ~**ish** *a* πρασινωπός

greet [griːt] *vt* χαιρετίζω ‖ ~**ing** *n* χαιρετισμός ‖ ~**ings!** χαιρετισμούς!

gregarious [gri'gɛəriəs] *a* κοινωνικός.

grenade [gri'neid] *n* (χειρο)βομβίδα.

grew [gruː] *pt of* **grow**.

grey [grei] *a* σταχτής, γκρίζος, ψαρός ‖ (*dismal*) σκοτεινός ‖ ~**-haired** *a* γκριζομάλλης, ψαρομάλλης ‖ ~**hound** *n* λαγωνικό ‖ ~**ish** *a* γκριζωπός.

grid [grid] *n* (*of bars*) ἐσχάρα, σχάρα, πλέγμα ‖ (*network*) πλέγμα, δίκτυον ‖ (*of map*) δικτυωτόν, τετραγωνισμός ‖ ~**iron** *n* σχάρα.

grief [griːf] *n* θλῖψις, λύπη, ἀτύχημα.

grievance ['griːvəns] *n* παράπονο.

grieve [griːv] *vi* λυποῦμαι, θλίβομαι ‖ *vt* λυπῶ, πικραίνω.

grill [gril] *n* (*on cooker*) σχάρα, τῆς σχάρας ‖ *vt* ψήνω στή σχάρα ‖ (*interrogate*) ἀνακρίνω.

grille [gril] *n* (*on car etc*) γρίλλιες.

grilled [grild] *a* (*food*) τῆς σχάρας, τῆς ὥρας.

grim [grim] *a* φρικαλέος, ἀπειλητικός, σκληρός.

grimace [gri'meis] *n* γκριμάτσα ‖ *vi* μορφάζω.

grime [graim] *n* ἀκαθαρσία, λέρα, φοῦμο.

grimly ['grimli] *ad* ἀπαίσια, σκληρά, αὐστηρά.

grimy ['graimi] *a* ἀκάθαρτος, βρώμικος.

grin [grin] *n* χαμόγελο, μειδίαμα ‖ *vi* χαμογελῶ, μορφάζω.

grind [graind] (*irreg v*) *vt* (*crush*) τρίβω, ἀλέθω, κοπανίζω ‖ (*sharpen*) τροχίζω, τορνάρω, λειαίνω ‖ (*teeth*) τρίζω ‖ *n* (*bore*) ἀγγαρεία, μαγγανοπήγαδο.

grip [grip] *n* (*firm hold*) σφίξιμο, πιάσιμο, χειραψία ‖ (*handle*) λαβή ‖ (*mastery*) πυγμή, γνῶσις, ἐπιβάλλων ‖ (*suitcase*) βαλιτσάκι ‖ *vt* πιάνω, σφίγγω.

gripes [graips] *npl* (*bowel pains*) κωλικόπονοι.

gripping ['gripiŋ] *a* (*exciting*) συγκινητικό, συναρπαστικό.

grisly ['grizli] *a* φρικιαστικός, τρομακτικός.

gristle ['grisl] *n* χόνδρος, τραγανό.

grit [grit] *n* (*sand*) ἀμμόλιθος, ἀκαθαρσίες ‖ (*courage*) τόλμη, θάρρος ‖ *vt* τρίζω τά δόντια.

groan [grəun] *n* ἀναστεναγμός ‖ *vi* (ἀνα)στενάζω.

grocer ['grəusə*] *n* μπακάλης ‖ ~**ies** *npl* εἴδη μπακαλικῆς.

groggy ['grɔgi] *a* (*dazed, staggering*) κλονιζόμενος, σουρωμένος, ἀσταθής.

groin [grɔin] *n* βουβών.

groom [gruːm] *n* ἱπποκόμος ‖ (*bridegroom*) γαμπρός ‖ *vt* (*o.s.*) προετοιμάζω, ντύνομαι.

groove [gruːv] *n* αὐλάκι, διάξυσμα ‖ (*rut*) ρουτίνα.

grope [grəup] vi ψηλαφῶ, ψάχνω.

gross [grəus] a (coarse) χονδροειδής, σωματώδης ‖ (very bad) χονδρός, καταφανής ‖ (total) ὁλικός, χονδρικός ‖ n γρόσσα, δώδεκα δωδεκάδες ‖ ~ly ad χονδροειδῶς, χονδρά.

grotesque [grəu'tesk] a μασκαρένιος, παράλογος.

grotto ['grɔtəu] n σπηλαιά, κρύπτη.

ground [graund] pt,pp of grind ‖ n (surface) ἔδαφος, γῆ, χῶμα ‖ (piece of land) οἰκόπεδο, γῆ ‖ (generally pl: reason) λόγος, αἰτία, βάσις ‖ ~s npl (dregs) κατακάθι, ἴζημα ‖ (land) περιοχή, κῆποι, πάρκο ‖ vt (run ashore) προσαράσσω, ἐξοκέλλω ‖ (compel to stay) καθηλώνω ‖ (instruct) διδάσκω ἐντατικά ‖ vi ἐξοκέλλω ‖ ~ing n (instruction) οἱ βάσεις ‖ ~sheet n μουσαμᾶς ἐδάφους ‖ ~work n θεμέλια, βάσις.

group [gru:p] n ὁμάδα, παρέα ‖ vt συνδυάζω, συνδέω, συγκεντρώνω.

grouse [graus] n (bird) χαμωτίδα, ἀγριόγαλλος ‖ (complaint) γκρίνια ‖ vi (complain) γκρινιάζω.

grove [grəuv] n ἄλσος, ἀσύλιον.

grovel ['grɔvl] vi (in fear) σέρνομαι, κυλίομαι ‖ (abase o.s.) ταπεινοῦμαι, πέφτω στά πόδια.

grow [grəu] (irreg v) vi (in size) μεγαλώνω, ἀναπτύσσομαι ‖ (be produced) φύομαι ‖ (become) καθίσταμαι, γίνομαι ‖ vt (raise crops etc) καλλιεργῶ ‖ to ~ up vi μεγαλώνω ‖ ~er n καλλιεργητής ‖ ~ing a αὐξανόμενος, πού μεγαλώνει.

growl [graul] vi μουγγρίζω ‖ n μούγγρισμα, βρυχηθμός.

grown-up ['grəun'ʌp] a ὥριμος ‖ n ἐνῆλιξ.

growth [grəuθ] n (development) ἀνάπτυξις ‖ (increase) αὔξησις, μεγάλωμα ‖ (what has grown) καλλιέργεια ‖ (med) σάρκωμα.

grub [grʌb] n (larva) σκουλίκι ‖ (col: food) φαγητό ‖ ~by a ἀκάθαρτος, βρώμικος.

grudge [grʌdʒ] n (μνησι)κακία, ἔχθρα ‖ vt ζηλεύω ὑλα, δεικνύω ἀπροθυμίαν ‖ to bear a ~ κρατάω κακία γιά.

grudging ['grʌdʒiŋ] a ἀπρόθυμος, φειδωλός.

gruelling ['gruəliŋ] a ἐξαντλητικός.

gruesome ['gru:səm] a φρικτός, ἀπαίσιος.

gruff [grʌf] a τραχύς, ἀπότομος.

grumble ['grʌmbl] vi γκρινιάζω, μουγγρίζω ‖ n μουγγρητό, γκρίνια.

grumpy ['grʌmpi] a κατσούφης, γκρινιάρης.

grunt [grʌnt] n γρύλλισμα ‖ vi γρυλλίζω.

guarantee [gærən'ti:] n (of goods) ἐγγύησις ‖ (promise to pay) ἐγγύησις, ἐνέχυρον ‖ vt ἐγγυῶμαι.

guard [ga:d] n (defence) φρουρά, προφύλαξις ‖ (sentry) σκοπός ‖ (official) φύλαξ ‖ vt φυλάσσω, προστατεύω, φρουρῶ ‖ ~ed a ὑπό φρούρησιν ‖ (words etc)

ἐπιφυλακτικός ‖ ~ian n (keeper) φύλαξ, προστάτης ‖ (of child) κηδεμών.

guerilla [gə'rilə] n ἀντάρτης ‖ ~ warfare n ἀνταρτοπόλεμος.

guess [ges] vti μαντεύω ‖ (US) νομίζω ‖ n εἰκασία, γνώμη ‖ ~work n εἰκασία.

guest [gest] n καλεσμένος, ξένος ‖ (of hotel) πελάτης ‖ ~-house n πανσιόν ‖ ~ room n (in private house, for friends) δωμάτιον τῶν ξένων.

guffaw [gʌ'fɔ:] n καγχασμός ‖ vi ξεσπῶ στά γέλια.

guidance ['gaidəns] n (control) καθοδήγησις ‖ (advice) συμβουλές, ὁδηγίες.

guide [gaid] n (person) ὁδηγός, συνοδός, ξεναγός ‖ (book etc) ὁδηγός ‖ vt (καθ)ὁδηγῶ ‖ girl ~ n προσκοπίνα ‖ ~book n ὁδηγός ‖ ~d missile n κατευθυνόμενον βλῆμα ‖ ~ lines npl ὁδηγός.

guild [gild] n (old: company) συντεχνία ‖ (society) ἕνωσις, σωματεῖον ‖ ~hall n (Brit: town hall) δημαρχεῖον.

guile [gail] n τέχνασμα, δόλος ‖ ~less a ἄδολος.

guillotine ['giləti:n] n λαιμητόμος, γκιλοτίνα.

guilt [gilt] n ἐνοχή ‖ ~y a ἔνοχος.

guise [gaiz] n (appearance) μορφή, ἐμφάνισις.

guitar [gi'ta:*] n κιθάρα ‖ ~ist n κιθαριστής.

gulf [gʌlf] n κόλπο, κόρφος ‖ (abyss) χάσμα.

gull [gʌl] n γλάρος.

gullet ['gʌlit] n οἰσοφάγος.

gullible ['gʌlibl] a εὔπιστος, κορόῖδο.

gully ['gʌli] n ρεματιά, στενό, ὑπόνομος.

gulp [gʌlp] vi (hastily) καταπίνω, καταβροχθίζω ‖ (choke) κομπιάζομαι, πνίγομαι ‖ n ρουφηξιά, γουλιά.

gum [gʌm] n (of teeth) οὖλον ‖ (for sticking) γόμα, γόμμι ‖ (for chewing) τσίκλα, μαστίχα ‖ vt κολλῶ, ἀλείφω μέ γόμα ‖ ~boil n ἀπόστημα, φουσκάλα ‖ ~boots npl μπότες ἀπό καουτσούκ.

gum tree ['gʌmtri:] n εὐκάλυπτος.

gun [gʌn] n (cannon) πυροβόλον, κανόνι ‖ (rifle) τυφέκι ‖ (revolver) πιστόλι ‖ ~fire n βολή, πῦρ, κανονιοβολισμός ‖ ~man n ληστής, κακοποιός ‖ ~ner n πυροπολητής ‖ ~powder n πυρῖτις, μπαρούτι ‖ ~shot n τουφεκιά, κανονιά.

gurgle ['gə:gl] n παφλασμός, κελάρισμα.

gush [gʌʃ] n ἐκροή, διάχυσις, ξέσπασμα ‖ vi (out) ἐκχύνομαι, ἀναπηδῶ ‖ (be moved) συγκινοῦμαι, ἀναλύομαι εἰς.

gusset ['gʌsit] n ἐπένθεμα.

gust [gʌst] n ἀνεμορυπή, μπουρίνι.

gut [gʌt] n (intestine) ἔντερον, σπλάχνον ‖ (string) χορδή ‖ ~s npl θάρρος.

gutter ['gʌtə*] n (channel) λούκι, σουγελο ‖ (of street) ρεῖθρον, χαντάκι.

guttural ['gʌtərəl] a λαρυγγικός.

guy [gai] *n* (*naut*) πρόδρομος, γκάγια ‖ (*effigy*) ἀνδρείκελον, σκιάχτρο ‖ (*man, fellow*) τύπος, παιδί.

guzzle ['gʌzl] *vi* καταβροχθίζω, ρουφῶ.

gym(nasium) [dʒim('neiziəm)] *n* γυμναστήριον.

gymnast ['dʒimnæst] *n* γυμναστής ‖ ~ics *n* γυμναστική.

gyn(a)ecologist [gaini'kɔlədʒist] *n* γυναικολόγος.

gypsy ['dʒipsi] *n* = **gipsy**.

gyrate [dʒai'reit] *vi* περιστρέφομαι.

H, h

habit ['hæbit] *n* συνήθεια, ἔθιμον ‖ (*dress*) φόρεμα.

habitable ['hæbitəbl] *a* κατοικήσιμος.

habitation [hæbi'teiʃən] *n* κατοικία, διαμονή.

habitual [hə'bitjuəl] *a* συνήθης, συνηθισμένος ‖ ~ly *ad* συνήθως.

hack [hæk] *vt* κατακόβω, πετσοκόβω ‖ *n* ἀγοραῖον ἄλογον.

hackneyed ['hæknid] *a* ξεφτελισμένος, φθαρμένος.

had ['hæd] *pt,pp* of **have**.

haddock ['hædɔk] *n* βακαλάος.

hadn't ['hædnt] = **had not** ‖ *see* **have**.

haemorrhage, (*US*) **hemo~** ['heməridʒ] *n* αἱμορραγία.

haemorroids, (*US*) **hemo~** ['heməɔidz] *npl* ζοχάδες.

haggard ['hægəd] *a* κάτωχρος, χαμένος.

haggle ['hægl] *vi* κάνω παζάρι.

hail [heil] *n* (*meteorology*) χαλάζι ‖ *vt* (*greet*) χαιρετῶ ‖ *vi* (*meteorology*) ρίχνει χαλάζι ‖ **to ~ from** *vt* προέρχομαι ἀπό ‖ ~**stone** *n* κόκκος χαλάζης.

hair [hɛə*] *n* (*general*) τρίχα, μαλλιά ‖ (*one hair*) τρίχα ‖ ~**'s breadth** *n* παρά τρίχα ‖ ~**brush** *n* βούρτσα μαλλιῶν ‖ ~**cut** *n* κούρεμα ‖ ~**do** *n* κτένισμα ‖ ~**dresser** *n* κομμωτής, κουρέας ‖ ~**-drier** *n* σεσουάρ ‖ ~**net** *n* δίχτυ γιά τά μαλλιά ‖ ~**oil** *n* λάδι γιά τά μαλλιά ‖ ~**pin** *n* (*lit*) φουρκέτα ‖ (*bend*) ἀπότομος στροφή ‖ ~**-raising** *a* τρομακτικός ‖ ~ **style** *n* κόμμωσις, χτενισιά ‖ ~**y** *a* τριχωτός, μαλλιαρός.

half [ha:f] *n* ἥμισυ, μισό ‖ *a* μισός ‖ *ad* κατά τό ἥμισυ, μισό ‖ ~**-breed**, ~**-caste** *n* μιγάς ‖ ~**-hearted** *a* χλιαρός, μέ μισή καρδιά ‖ ~**-hour** *n* ἡμίωρον, μισή (ὥρα) ‖ ~**penny** *n* μισή πέννα ‖ ~**-price** μισή τιμή, μισό εἰσιτήριο ‖ ~**way** *ad* στό ἥμισυ τῆς ἀποστάσεως, μισοστραθῆς.

halibut ['hælibət] *n* ἱππόγλωσσος, εἶδος γλώσσας.

hall [hɔ:l] *n* μεγάλη αἴθουσα ‖ (*building, house*) δημόσιον κτίριον ‖ (*dining*) τραπεζαρία ‖ (*entrance*) εἴσοδος, χώλ.

hallo [hʌ'ləu] *excl* = **hello**.

hallucination [həlu:si'neiʃən] *n* παραίσθησις, αὐταπάτη.

halo ['heiləu] *n* (*of saint*) φωτοστέφανος ‖ (*of sun, moon*) ἅλως, ἁλώνι.

halt [hɔ:lt] *n* στάσις, σταμάτημα ‖ *vt* σταματῶ ‖ *vi* σταθμεύω, σταματῶ.

halve [ha:v] *vt* χωρίζω στά δύο, μοιράζω.

ham [hæm] *n* χοιρομέρι, ζαμπόν ‖ ~**burger** *n* μπιφτέκι ἀπό κιμά.

hamlet ['hæmlət] *n* χωριουδάκι.

hammer ['hæmə*] *n* σφυρί ‖ *vt* κτυπῶ δυνατά, σφυρηλατῶ.

hammock ['hæmək] *n* ἁμάκ, κούνια ‖ (*naut*) αἰώρα, μπράντα.

hamper ['hæmpə*] *n* καλάθι ‖ *vt* ἐμποδίζω, παρακωλύω.

hand [hænd] *n* χέρι ‖ (*of clock*) δείκτης ‖ (*factory*) ἐργάτης ‖ (*help*) βοήθεια ‖ *vt* δίδω ‖ βοηθῶ ‖ ~**s** *npl* (*naut*) πλήρωμα ‖ **to ~ down** *vt* μεταβιβάζω ‖ **to ~ over** *vt* παραδίδω ‖ **at ~** κοντά ‖ **in ~** στήν διάθεσί μου ‖ **ὑπό τόν ἔλεγχό μου** ‖ ~**s up!** ψηλά τά χέρια! ‖ ~**bag** *n* τσάντα ‖ ~**book** *n* ἐγχειρίδιον ‖ (*guide*) ὁδηγός ‖ ~**brake** *n* χειρόφρενο ‖ ~**cuffs** *npl* χειροπέδες ‖ ~**ful** *n* φούχτα, φουχτιά.

handicap ['hændikæp] *n* ἐμπόδιον, μειονέκτημα ‖ (*sport*) χάντικαπ ‖ *vt* παρεμποδίζω, δυσχεραίνω ‖ (*sport*) βάζω χάντικαπ.

handicraft ['hændikra:ft] *n* χειροτεχνία, τέχνη.

handkerchief ['hæŋkətʃif] *n* μαντήλι.

handle ['hændl] *n* (*of door etc*) πόμολο, (χειρο)λαβή ‖ (*of cup etc*) χερούλι ‖ (*for winding*) χειρολαβή, χερούλι ‖ *vt* (*use, treat*) μεταχειρίζομαι ‖ (*manipulate*) χειρίζομαι ‖ (*touch*) πιάνω, πασπατεύω ‖ (*comm*) διεκπεραιώνω, διαχειρίζομαι.

hand-luggage ['hændlʌgidʒ] *n* ἀποσκευαί τοῦ χεριοῦ.

handmade ['hændmeid] *a* χειροποίητος.

handshake ['hændʃeik] *n* χειραψία, σφίξιμο τοῦ χεριοῦ.

handsome ['hænsəm] *a* ὡραῖος, ὄμορφος ‖ (*generous*) σημαντικός, γενναιόδωρος.

handwriting ['hændraitiŋ] *n* γραφή, γράψιμο.

handy ['hændi] *a* ἐπιδέξιος ‖ (*useful*) βολικός, χρήσιμος.

handyman ['hændimən] *n* πολυτεχνίτης.

hang [hæŋ] (*irreg v*) *vt* ἀναρτῶ, κρεμῶ ‖ (*one's head*) σκύβω ‖ (*wallpaper*) κολλῶ ‖ *vi* κρέμομαι ‖ **to ~ about** *vi* περιφέρομαι, τριγυρίζω, τεμπελιάζω.

hangar ['hæŋə*] *n* ὑπόστεγον.

hanger ['hæŋə*] *n* κρεμάστρα.

hanger-on ['hæŋər'ɔn] *n* κολλιτσίδα.

hangover ['hæŋəuvə*] *n* (*med*) πονοκέφαλο (ἀπό μεθύσι).

hanker ['hæŋkə*] *vi*: **to ~ after** ποθῶ διακαῶς, λαχταρῶ.

haphazard [hæp'hæzəd] *a* στήν τύχη, τυχαίως.

happen ['hæpən] *vi* συμβαίνω, τυγχάνω ~ing *n* συμβάν, γεγονός.

happily ['hæpili] *ad* εὐτυχῶς.

happiness ['hæpinis] *n* εὐτυχία.

happy ['hæpi] *a* εὐτυχής, τυχερός, ἐπιτυχημένος | ~-go-lucky *a* ξένοιαστος.

harass ['hærəs] *vt* παρενοχλῶ, βασανίζω.

harbour, (*US*) **harbor** ['ha:bə*] *n* λιμάνι, καταφύγιον | *vt* στεγάζω, παρέχω ἄσυλον.

hard [ha:d] *a* σκληρός, στερεός | (*task*) δύσκολος, δυσχερής | (*person etc*) αὐστηρός, ἀλύπητος | (*work*) ἐπίπονος, σκληρός *ad* δυνατά, σκληρά, δύσκολα ~ by κοντά | ~-boiled *a* (*egg*) σφιχτό (*person*) σκληρός | ~en *vi* σκληραίνω ~-hearted *a* σκληρόκαρδος, ἀλύπητος ~ly *ad* μόλις | ~ship *n* κακουχία, δοκιμασία, ταλαιπωρία | ~ up *a* ἀπένταρος | ~ware *n* σιδηρικά, εἴδη καγκελαρίας.

hardy ['ha:di] *a* σκληραγωγημένος | (*brave*) τολμηρός, θαρραλέος.

hare [hεə*] *n* λαγός.

harem [ha:'ri:m] *n* χαρέμι.

harm [ha:m] *n* κακόν, βλάβη, ζημία | *vt* βλάπτω, θίγω | ~ful *a* ἐπιβλαβής, βλαβερός | ~less *a* ἄκακος, ἀβλαβής, ἀκίνδυνος.

harmonica [ha:'mɔnikə] *n* φυσαρμόνικα.

harmonious [ha:'məuniəs] *a* ἁρμονικός (*mus*) μελωδικός.

harmonize ['ha:mənaiz] *vt* ἐναρμονίζω (*agree*) συμφωνῶ | *vi* ἐναρμονίζομαι, ταιριάζω.

harmony ['ha:məni] *n* (*mus*) ἁρμονία (*agreement*) συμφωνία.

harness ['ha:nis] *n* σαγή, χάμουρα, χαμούρωμα | *vt* (*horse*) χαμουρώνω.

harp [ha:p] *n* ἄρπα | ~ist *n* ἁρπιστής.

harpoon [ha:'pu:n] *n* καμάκι.

harrow ['hærəu] *n* βωλοκόπος, σβάρνα | *vt* βωλοκοπῶ.

harrowing ['hærəuiŋ] *a* θλιβερός, σπαρακτικός.

harsh [ha:ʃ] *a* σκληρός, τραχύς | ~ly *ad* σκληρά, ἀπότομα | ~ness *n* τραχύτης, σκληρότης | (*of taste*) ξυνίλα.

hart [ha:t] *n* ἐλάφι.

harvest ['ha:vist] *n* συγκομιδή, ἐσοδεία | (*season*) θέρος, ἐποχή θερισμοῦ | *vt* θερίζω, μαζεύω.

harvester ['ha:vistə*] *n* θεριστική μηχανή.

has [hæz] *see* **have**.

hash [hæʃ] *n* κιμάς | *vt* κατακόπτω, κάνω κιμά.

hashish ['hæʃi:ʃ] *n* χασίς.

haste [heist] *n* βία, βιασύνη, γρηγοράδα | ~n *vt* σπεύδω, ἐπιταχύνω | *vi* βιάζομαι, κάνω γρήγορα.

hastily ['heistili] *ad* βιαστικά.

hasty ['heisti] *a* βιαστικά, ὀξύθυμος.

hat [hæt] *n* καπέλλο.

hatch [hætʃ] *n* καταπακτή, μπουκαπόρτα | *vi* ἐκκολάπτομαι, βγαίνω, σκάω | *vt* κλοσσῶ.

hatchet ['hætʃit] *n* τσεκούρι.

hate [heit] *vt* μισῶ | *n* μῖσος ~ful *a* μισητός.

hatred ['heitrid] *n* ἔχθρα, μῖσος.

haughty ['hɔ:ti] *a* ὑπεροπτικός, αὐθάδης.

haul [hɔ:l] *n* τράβηγμα | (*fish*) διχτυά | *vt* ἕλκω, τραβῶ, σύρω | ~age *n* μεταφορά ἐμπορευμάτων.

haunch [hɔ:ntʃ] *n* ἰσχίον, γοφός.

haunt [hɔ:nt] *n* λημέρι, στέκι | *vt* συχνάζω εἰς | (*of ghosts*) στοιχειώνω.

have [hæv] (*irreg v*) *vt* ἔχω, κατέχω | (*be obliged*) ἀναγκάζω, ἔχω νά, πρέπει νά | (*meal*) λαμβάνω, παίρνω | (*obtain*) παίρνω | (*children etc*) γεννῶ, κάνω ~ to ~ on *vt* φορῶ.

haven ['heivən] *n* λιμάνι (*refuge*) καταφύγιον, ἄσυλον.

haversack ['hævəsæk] *n* σακκίδιον || (*mil*) γυλιός.

havoc ['hævək] *n* πανωλεθρία, καταστροφή.

hawk [hɔ:k] *n* γεράκι.

hawser ['hɔ:zə*] *n* (*naut*) λαντσάνα, παλαμάρι.

hay [hei] *n* σανός, ἄχυρο || ~ fever *n* φθινοπωρινός κατάρρους || ~stack *n* θημωνιά.

haywire ['haiwaiə*] *a* (*col*) it's gone ~ δέν πάει καλά.

hazard ['hæzəd] *n* (*chance*) τύχη || (*danger*) κίνδυνος || *vt* διακινδυνεύω, ριψοκινδυνεύω || ~ous *a* ριψοκίνδυνος.

haze [heiz] *n* καταχνιά.

hazelnut ['heizlnʌt] *n* φουντούκι.

hazy ['heizi] *a* (*weather*) καταχνιασμένος | (*vague*) ἀμυδρός, ἀόριστος.

he [hi:] *pron* αὐτός, ἐκεῖνος || ἀρσενικός.

head [hed] *n* (*anat*) κεφάλι || (*leader*) ἀρχηγός, προϊστάμενος, διευθυντής | (*top*) ἄκρον || *a* πρωτεύων, κύριος | *vt* ἡγοῦμαι, διευθύνω, διοικῶ || to ~ for *vt* κινοῦμαι πρός, κατευθύνομαι || ~ache *n* κεφαλόπονος, πονοκέφαλος || ~ing *n* ἐπικεφαλίς, τίτλος || ~lamp *n* πρόσθιον φῶς, φανάρι || ~land *n* ἀκρωτήρι || ~light = ~lamp || ~line *n* ἐπικεφαλίς, τίτλος || ~long *ad* μέ τό κεφάλι, ἀπερίσκεπτος || ~master *n* διευθυντής σχολείου || ~mistress *n* διευθύντρια (σχολείου) || ~-on *a* κατά μέτωπον || ~quarters *npl* ἀρχηγεῖον, στρατηγεῖον || ~rest *n* κουμπιστήρι || ~strong *a* ἰσχυρογνώμων, ξεροκέφαλος || ~ waiter *n* ἀρχισερβιτόρος, μαίτρ || ~way *n* πρόοδος || ~wind *n* ἀντίθετος ἄνεμος, ἀέρας κόντρα || ~y *a* ὁρμητικός, φουριόζος || (*drink etc*) πού ζαλίζει, βαράει στό κεφάλι.

heal 284 **hernia**

heal [hi:l] *vt* θεραπεύω, γιατρεύω ‖ *vi* επουλώνομαι, γιατρεύομαι.

health [helθ] *n* υγεία ‖ *(toast)* πρόποσις ‖ ~ *y a* υγιής, εύρωστος, γερός.

heap [hi:p] *n* σωρός ‖ πλῆθος ‖ *vt* γεμίζω, συσσωρεύω.

hear [hiə*] *(irreg v) vt* ακούω ‖ ακροῶμαι ‖ *(learn)* ακούω, μαθαίνω ‖ ~ing *n (sense)* ακοή ‖ ακρόασις ‖ *(law)* (ακροαματική) εξέτασις μαρτύρων ‖ ~ing aid *n* ακουστικά βαρυκοΐας ‖ ~say *n* φήμη, διάδοσις.

hearse [hə:s] *n* νεκροφόρος.

heart [ha:t] *n (anat)* καρδιά ‖ *(centre)* καρδιά ‖ *(courage)* θάρρος ‖ *(emotion)* ψυχή ‖ *(tenderness)* καρδιά, ψυχή ‖ *(cards)* κούπα ‖ ~ attack *n* καρδιακή προσβολή ‖ ~beat *n* παλμός καρδιάς ‖ ~breaking *a* θλιβερός, λυπητερός ‖ ~broken *a* περίλυπος, θλιμμένος ‖ ~burn *n* καρδιαλγία, καούρα (στομάχου) ‖ ~ failure *n* συγκοπή ‖ ~felt *a* εγκάρδιος, καρδιακός.

hearth [ha:θ] *n* τζάκι ‖ πυροστιά.

heartily ['ha:tili] *ad* ειλικρινά, μέ όρεξι, τελείως.

heartless ['ha:tlis] *a* άκαρδος.

hearty ['ha:ti] *a* εγκάρδιος ‖ *(healthy)* εύρωστος ‖ *(meal)* πλούσια, θρεπτικός.

heat [hi:t] *n* θερμότης ‖ *(weather)* ζέστη, κάψα ‖ *(anger)* έξαψις, οργή ‖ *(sport)* αγών δρόμου, κούρσα ‖ *vt* θερμαίνω, ζεσταίνω ‖ to ~ up *vi* ανάβω, (υπερ)θερμαίνομαι ‖ ~ed *a* ζεστός, θερμασμένος ‖ ~er *n* θερμαστής, θερμάστρα, σόμπα.

heath [hi:θ] *n (Brit)* χέρσος γῆ, ρεικιά ‖ ρείκη.

heathen ['hi:ðən] *n* ειδωλολάτρης, εθνικός ‖ *a* ειδωλολατρικός.

heather ['heðə*] *n* (ε)ρείκι.

heating ['hi:tiŋ] *n* θέρμανσις.

heatstroke ['hi:tstrəuk] *n* θερμοπληξία.

heatwave ['hi:tweiv] *n* κῦμα ζέστης, καύσων.

heave [hi:v] *(irreg v) vt* σηκώνω, ανυψώνω ‖ *(throw)* ρίπτω ‖ *vi* ανυψοῦμαι ‖ *(naut)* βιράρω ‖ *n* ανύψωσις, σήκωμα ‖ φούσκωμα.

heaven ['hevən] *n* ουρανός ‖ for ~'s sake! γιά όνομα τοῦ Θεοῦ! ‖ good ~s! Θεέ μου! ‖ ~ly *a* ουράνιος ‖ *(col)* περίφημα.

heavily ['hevili] *ad* βαρειά, δυνατά.

heavy ['hevi] *a* βαρύς ‖ *(difficult)* δύσκολος, δύσβατος ‖ *(abundant)* άφθονος ‖ ~ eater *n* μεγάλος φαγάς.

Hebrew ['hi:bru:] *n (person)* Εβραίος ‖ *(ling)* εβραϊκά ‖ *a* εβραϊκός.

heckle ['hekl] *vt* βομβαρδίζω μέ ενοχλητικές ερωτήσεις.

hectare ['hekta:*] *n* εκτάριον.

hectic ['hektik] *a* πυρετώδης ‖ ταραχώδης.

hedge [hedʒ] *n* φράχτης, φραγμός ‖ *vt (surround)* περιφράσσω, φράττω ‖ *vi* υπεκφεύγω, μασῶ τά λόγια μου.

hedgehog ['hedʒhɔg] *n* σκαντζόχοιρος.

heed [hi:d] *vt* προσέχω ‖ *n* προσοχή ‖ ~ful *a* προσεκτικός ‖ ~less *a* απρόσεκτος, αμέριμνος.

heel [hi:l] *n* φτέρνα ‖ *(of shoe)* τακούνι ‖ *vt (shoe)* βάζω τακούνι εἰς.

hefty ['hefti] *a* δυνατός, ρωμαλέος.

heifer ['hefə*] *n* δάμαλι.

height [hait] *n (of person)* ανάστημα, μπόϊ ‖ *(of object)* ύψος, ύψωμα ‖ ακμή ‖ *(of mountain)* κορυφή ‖ ~en *vt* υψώνω, αυξάνω.

heir [εə*] *n* κληρονόμος ‖ ~ess *n* η κληρονόμος ‖ ~loom *n* οικογενειακόν κειμήλιον.

held [held] *pt,pp* of **hold.**

helicopter ['helikɔptə*] *n* ελικόπτερο.

hell [hel] *n* κόλασις.

he'll [hi:l] = he will, he shall ‖ see **will, shall.**

hellish ['heliʃ] *a* απαίσιος, καταχθόνιος.

hello [hʌ'ləu] *excl (greeting)* γιάσου! ‖ *(tel)* αλλό! ‖ *(surprise)* μπά, μπά!

helm [helm] *n* τιμόνι, δοιάκι.

helmet ['helmit] *n* κράνος, κάσκα ‖ περικεφαλαία.

helmsman ['helmzmən] *n* πηδαλιοῦχος.

help [help] *n* βοήθεια ‖ *vt* βοηθῶ, ενισχύω ‖ *(prevent)* αποφεύγω, εμποδίζω ‖ *(serve food)* σερβίρω ‖ ~er *n* βοηθός ‖ ~ful *a* χρήσιμος ‖ ~ing *n* μερίδα ‖ ~less *a* αβοήθητος, εις αμηχανίαν.

hem [hem] *n* στρίφωμα ‖ to ~ in *vt* περικυκλώνω, στριμώχνω.

hemisphere ['hemisfiə*] *n* ημισφαίριον.

hemp [hemp] *n* κάνναβις, καννάβι.

hen [hen] *n* κότα, θηλυκό πτηνό ‖ ~coop *n* κοτέτσι.

hence [hens] *ad* απ'εδῶ, από τώρα ‖ *(therefore)* απ'αυτό.

henchman ['hentʃmən] *n* πιστός οπαδός, μπράβος.

her [hə:*] *pron* αυτήν ‖ *a* δικός της.

herald ['herəld] *n* κήρυκας, πρόδρομος ‖ *vt* αναγγέλω, προμηνύω, προαγγέλω.

heraldry ['herəldri] *n* οικοσημολογία.

herb [hə:b] *n* βότανο, χόρτο.

herd [hə:d] *n (general)* κοπάδι.

here [hiə*] *ad* εδῶ ‖ εδῶ ‖ ~! ιδού νά! ‖ come ~! έλα (δῶ)! ‖ ~after *ad* στό εξής ‖ *n* μέλλουσα ζωή ‖ ~by *ad* μ'αυτό, διά τοῦ παρόντος.

hereditary [hi'reditri] *a* κληρονομικός.

heredity [hi'rediti] *n* κληρονομικότης.

heresy ['herisi] *n* αίρεσις.

heretic ['herətik] *n* αιρετικός ‖ ~al [hi'retikəl] *a* αιρετικός.

herewith [hiə'wið] *ad* μετ'αυτοῦ, μ'αυτό.

heritage ['heritidʒ] *n* κληρονομία.

hermit ['hə:mit] *n* ερημίτης.

hernia ['hə:niə] *n* κήλη.

hero ['hiərəu] *n* ἥρωας, παληκάρι ‖ (*of a story*) πρωταγωνιστής ‖ ~**ic** *a* ἡρωϊκός.

heroin ['herəuin] *n* ἡρωΐνη.

heroine ['herəuin] *n* ἡρωΐδα, πρωταγωνίστρια.

heroism ['herəuizm] *n* ἡρωϊσμός.

heron ['hern] *n* ἐρωδιός, τσικνιάς.

herring ['heriŋ] *n* ῥέγγα.

hers [hə:z] *pron* αὐτῆς, δικός της.

herself [hə:'self] *pron* ἡ ἴδια, τόν ἑαυτόν της.

he's [hi:z] = **he is, he has** ‖ *see* be, have.

hesitant ['hezitnt] *a* διστακτικός.

hesitate ['heziteit] *vi* διστάζω.

hesitation [hezi'teiʃən] *n* δισταγμός, ἐνδοιασμός.

het up ['het'ʌp] *a* θυμωμένος, στενοχωρημένος.

hew [hju:] (*irreg v*) *vt* κατακόπτω, πελεκῶ.

hexagon ['heksəgən] *n* ἑξάγωνον.

heyday ['heidei] *n* ἀκμή, ἄνθος, καλές μέρες.

hi [hai] *excl* ἔ!, σύ! ‖ (*US*) καλημέρα!, γιάσου!

hibernate ['haibəneit] *vi* διαχειμάζω.

hibernation [haibə'neiʃən] *n* χειμερία νάρκη.

hiccough, hiccup ['hikʌp] *vi* ἔχω λόξυγγα ‖ ~**s** *npl* λόξυγγας.

hid [hid] *pt* of **hide**.

hidden ['hidn] *pp* of **hide**.

hide [haid] (*irreg v*) *n* δέρμα, πετσί, τομάρι ‖ *vt* (ἀπό) κρύβω ‖ *vi* κρύβομαι ‖ ~**-and-seek** *n* κρυφτό.

hideous ['hidiəs] *a* φρικτός, ἀποκρουστικά ἄσχημος ‖ ~**ly** *ad* ἀπαίσια, φρικτά.

hiding ['haidiŋ] *n* (*beating*) σπάσιμο στό ξύλο ‖ **in** ~ (*concealed*) κρυμμένος ‖ ~ **place** *n* κρυψώνας.

hierarchy ['haiəra:ki] *n* ἱεραρχία.

high [hai] *a* (*far up*) ψηλά ‖ (*tall*) ψηλός ‖ (*rank*) ἀνώτερος, σπουδαῖος ‖ (*class*) ἀνώτερος ‖ (*price*) ἀκρίβεια, ψηλή (τιμή) ‖ (*pressure etc*) ὑψηλός, μεγάλος ‖ (*opinion*) μεγάλη ἐκτίμηση σέ ‖ *a* ψηλά, πλούσια ‖ ~**chair** *n* ψηλό καρεκλάκι γιά μωρά ‖ ~**-handed** *a* αὐθαίρετα ‖ ~**-heeled** *a* μέ ψηλά τακούνια ‖ ~**-level** *a* στό ἀνώτερο ἐπίπεδο, σέ μεγάλο ὕψος ‖ ~**light** *n* (*fig*) ἀποκορύφωμα, τό μεγάλο νούμερο ‖ ~**ly** *ad* ἐξαιρετικά, πάρα πολύ ‖ ~**ly strung** *a* εὐερέθιστος, νευρικός ‖ **H~ Mass** *n* μεγάλη λειτουργία (τῶν Καθολικῶν) ‖ ~**ness** *n* (*title*) ὑψηλότης ‖ ~**-pitched** *a* (*voice*) διαπεραστική, ὀξύς ‖ ~ **school** *n* γυμνάσιον ‖ ~**-speed** *a* μεγάλης ταχύτητος ‖ ~ **tide** *n* φουσκονεριά, πλημμυρίδα ‖ ~**way** *n* ἐθνική ὁδός

hijack ['haidʒæk] *vt* κάνω ἀεροπειρατία ‖ ~**er** *n* (*aviat*) ἀεροπειρατής.

hike [haik] *vi* πεζοπορῶ ‖ *n* πεζοπορία ‖ ~**r** *n* πεζοπόρος.

hiking ['haikiŋ] *n* πεζοπορία.

hilarious [hi'leəriəs] *a* ἱλαρός, εὔθυμος.

hilarity [hi'læriti] *n* ἱλαρότης, εὐθυμία.

hill [hil] *n* λόφως ‖ ~**y** *a* λοφώδης.

hilt [hilt] *n* λαβή (ξίφους) ‖ **up to the** ~ τελείως.

him [him] *pron* αὐτόν, σ'αὐτόν.

himself [him'self] *pron* τόν ἑαυτόν του (αὐτός) ὁ ἴδιος.

hind [haind] *a* ὀπίσθιος ‖ *n* ἔλαφος.

hinder ['hində*] *vt* ἐμποδίζω, κωλύω.

hindrance ['hindrəns] *n* ἐμπόδιον.

Hindu ['hin'du:] *n* Ἰνδός.

hinge [hindʒ] *n* ἄρθρωσις, μεντεσές ‖ *vt* κρεμῶ σέ μεντεσέδες ‖ *vi* (*fig*) ἐξαρτῶμαι.

hint [hint] *n* νύξις, ὑπαινιγμός ‖ *vi* ὑπαινίσσομαι.

hip [hip] *n* ἰσχίον, γοφός.

hippopotamus [hipə'pɒtəməs] *n* ἱπποπόταμος.

hire ['haiə*] *n* μίσθωσις, ἐνοικίασις ‖ *vt* (*worker*) μισθώνω, πληρώνω, προσλαμβάνω ‖ (*rent*) ἐνοικιάζω ‖ (*car*) νοικιάζω ‖ **'for** ~' 'ἐλεύθερον', ἐνοικιάζεται ‖ ~ **purchase** *n* μέ δόσεις.

his [hiz] *pron* δικός του ‖ *a* αὐτοῦ, (δικός) του.

hiss [his] *n* σφύριγμα ‖ *vi* ἀποδοκιμάζω, σφυρίζω.

historian [his'tɔ:riən] *n* ἱστορικός.

historic(al) [his'tɔrik(əl)] *a* ἱστορικός.

history ['histəri] *n* ἱστορία.

hit [hit] (*irreg v*) *n* κτύπημα ‖ (*success*) ἐπιτυχία ‖ *vt* κτυπάω, πλήττω ‖ (*target*) εὐστοχῶ.

hitch [hitʃ] *n* τίναγμα, τράβηγμα ‖ (*bend*) θηλειά ‖ (*fig*) ἐμπόδιο ‖ *vt* δένω, προσδένω ‖ (*jerk*) τραντάζω.

hitch-hike ['hitʃhaik] *vi* κάνω ὠτοστόπ ‖ ~**r** *n* ὁ κάνων ὠτοστόπ.

hive [haiv] *n* κυψέλη.

hoard [hɔ:d] *n* θησαυρός, σωρός ‖ *vt* συσσωρεύω, θησαυρίζω, ἀποκρύπτω.

hoarding ['hɔ:diŋ] *n* ἀποθησαυρισμός ἀπόκρυψις.

hoarfrost ['hɔ:'frɒst] *n* πάχνη.

hoarse [hɔ:s] *a* βραχνιασμένος.

hoax [həuks] *n* ἀστεῖο, τέχνασμα, φάρσα.

hobble ['hɒbl] *vi* χωλαίνω, κουτσαίνω.

hobby ['hɒbi] *n* μεράκι, χόμπυ.

hobo ['həubəu] *n* (*US*) ἀλήτης.

hock [hɒk] *n* (*wine*) ἄσπρο κρασί τοῦ Ρήνου.

hockey ['hɒki] *n* χόκεϋ.

hoe [həu] *n* τσάπα ‖ *vt* τσαπίζω.

hog [hɒg] *n* γουρούνι.

hoist [hɔist] *n* ἀνελκυστήρας ‖ τράβηγμα, σπρώξιμο ‖ *vt* ἀνυψώνω.

hold [həuld] (*irreg v*) *n* λαβή, πιάσιμο ‖ (*influence*) ἔχω ἐπιρροήν πάνω σέ ‖ (*naut*) ἀμπάρι ‖ *vt* (*grasp*) κρατῶ ‖ (*keep*) κρατῶ, φέρω ‖ (*contain*) περιέχω ‖ (*keep* *back*) συγκρατῶ, σταματῶ ‖ (*meeting etc*) συγκαλῶ, κάνω ‖ (*title*) κατέχω, ἔχω ‖ **to ~ back** *vt* συγκρατῶ ‖ (*secret*) ἀποκρύβω ‖ (*control*) ἀναχαιτίζω ‖ **to ~ down** *vt* κρατῶ ‖ **to ~ out** *vt* ἐκτείνω ‖ (*resist*) ἀντέχω ‖ **to ~ up** *vt* (*support*) ὑποστηρίζω ‖ (*display*) ἐπιδεικνύω ‖ (*stop*) σταματῶ, καθυστερῶ ‖ (*rob*) ληστεύω ‖ *vi* (*withstand pressure*) ἀντέχω ‖ **~er** *n* κάτοχος ‖ (*handle*) λαβή, σφιγκτήρας ‖ **~ing** *n* (*share*) μετοχή ‖ **~ings** *npl* ἀποθεματικόν ‖ **~up** *n* παρακώλησις ‖ (*robbery*) ληστεία.

hole [houl] *n* τρύπα ‖ *vt* τρυπῶ, ἀνοίγω.

holiday [ˈhɔlidei] *n* γιορτή, ἀργία ‖ (*annual*) διακοπές ‖ **~-maker** *n* γιορταστής ‖ παραθεριστής.

holiness [ˈhəulinis] *n* ἁγιότης.

Holland [ˈhɔlənd] *n* Ὁλλανδία.

hollow [ˈhɔləu] *a* βαθουλός, κοῖλος ‖ (*empty*) κούφιος ‖ (*false*) ψεύτικος ‖ *n* κοίλωμα, βαθούλωμα, γούβα ‖ **to ~ out** *vt* βαθουλώνω, σκάβω.

holly [ˈhɔli] *n* (*tree*) πουρνάρι.

holster [ˈhəulstə*] *n* πιστολιοθήκη.

holy [ˈhəuli] *a* ἅγιος, ἱερός ‖ (*divine*) θεῖος.

homage [ˈhɔmidʒ] *n* ὑποταγή.

home [həum] *n* σπίτι, κατοικία ‖ (*native country*) πατρίδα ‖ (*institution*) ἄσυλον ‖ *a* (*country*) σπιτικό ‖ ἐγχώριος, ἐντόπιος ‖ *ad* στὸ σπίτι, στὴν πατρίδα ‖ **at ~** στὸ σπίτι ‖ (*at ease*) ἄνετα ‖ **~coming** *n* ἐπάνοδος, ἐπαναπατρισμός ‖ **~less** *a* ἄστεγος ‖ **~-made** *a* σπιτήσιος, ντόπιος ‖ **~sick** *a* νοσταλγός ‖ **~ward(s)** *ad* πρός τό σπίτι ‖ **~work** *n* κατ᾽οἶκον ἐργασία.

homicide [ˈhɔmisaid] *n* (*US*) ἀνθρωποκτονία.

homogeneous [hɔməˈdʒiːniəs] *a* ὁμοιογενής.

homosexual [ˈhɔməuˈseksjuəl] *a* ὁμοφυλόφιλος ‖ *n* ὁμοφυλόφιλος, ἀνώμαλος.

hone [həun] *n* ἀκόνι ‖ *vt* ἀκονίζω.

honest [ˈɔnist] *a* τίμιος, ἔντιμος, εὐθύς ‖ **~ly** *ad* τίμια ‖ **~y** *n* ἐντιμότης.

honey [ˈhʌni] *n* μέλι ‖ **~comb** *n* κερήθρα ‖ **~moon** *n* μήνας τοῦ μέλιτος.

honk [hɔŋk] *n* (*aut*) κορνάρισμα ‖ *vi* κορνάρω.

honor [ˈɔnə*] (*US*) = **honour**.

honorary [ˈɔnərəri] *a* τιμητικός ‖ (*degree etc*) ἐπίτιμος.

honour [ˈɔnə*] *n* τιμή, ὑπόληψις ‖ *vt* τιμῶ ‖ (*bill*) ἐξοφλῶ, πληρώνω ‖ **~s** *npl* (*univ*) τίτλοι, τιμητική διάκρισις ‖ **~able** *a* ἔντιμος ‖ (*title*) ἐντιμώτατος.

hood [hud] *n* κουκούλα, σκούφος ‖ (*cover*) κάλυμμα ‖ (*US aut*) καπό ‖ **~wink** *vt* ἐξαπατῶ, κοροϊδεύω.

hoof [huːf] *n* ὀπλή, πέλμα, νύχι.

hook [huk] *n* ἀγκίστρι, γάντζος ‖ *vt* ἀγκιστρώνω, γαντζώνω.

hooligan [ˈhuːligən] *n* ταραξίας, ἀλήτης.

hoop [huːp] *n* στεφάνι, τσέρκι.

hoot [huːt] *n* (*of owl*) γρούξιμο ‖ (*aut*) κορνάρισμα ‖ *vi* γιουχάρω, σφυρίζω ‖ **~er** *n* (*naut*) σειρήνα, σφυρίχτρα ‖ (*aut*) κλάξον, κόρνα.

hop [hɔp] *n* χοροπήδημα, πήδημα ‖ *vi* σκιρτῶ, πηδῶ, χοροπηδῶ.

hope [həup] *n* ἐλπίδα ‖ *vi* ἐλπίζω ‖ **~ful** *a* γεμᾶτος ἐλπίδες, ἐλπιδοφόρος ‖ **~less** *a* (*without hope*) ἀπελπισμένος ‖ (*useless*) μάταιον.

hops [hɔps] *npl* λυκίσκος.

horde [hɔːd] *n* ὀρδή, στῖφος.

horizon [həˈraizn] *n* ὁρίζων ‖ **~tal** [hɔriˈzɔntl] *a* ὁριζόντιος.

hormone [ˈhɔːməun] *n* ὁρμόνη.

horn [hɔːn] *n* κέρατο ‖ (*insect*) κεραία ‖ (*mus*) κέρας, κόρνα ‖ (*aut*) κλάξον ‖ **~ed** *a* μέ κέρατα.

hornet [ˈhɔːnit] *n* σφήκα.

horny [ˈhɔːni] *a* κεράτινος, σκληρός.

horoscope [ˈhɔrəskəup] *n* ὡροσκόπιον.

horrible [ˈhɔribl] *a* φρικτός, φρικώδης, ἀπαίσιος.

horrid [ˈhɔrid] *a* φρικτός, ἀποτρόπαιος ‖ (*col*) κακός.

horrify [ˈhɔrifai] *vt* τρομάζω ‖ (*shock*) σκανδαλίζω.

horror [ˈhɔrə*] *n* φρίκη, τρόμος.

hors d'oeuvres [ɔːˈdəːvr] *npl* ὀρεκτικά, μεζεδάκια, ὀρντέβρ.

horse [hɔːs] *n* ἄλογο ‖ **on ~back** καβάλλα ‖ **~chestnut** *n* ἀγριοκάστανο ‖ **~drawn** *a* ἱπποκίνητο ‖ **~power** *n* ἱπποδύναμις ‖ **~-racing** *n* ἱπποδρομίες ‖ **~shoe** *n* πέταλο.

horticulture [ˈhɔːtikʌltʃə*] *n* κηπουρική.

hose [həuz] *n* (*water*) σωλήνας ποτίσματος ‖ **~pipe** *n* μάνικα, σωλήνας.

hosiery [ˈhəuʒəri] *n* πλεκτά εἴδη.

hospitable [hɔsˈpitəbl] *a* φιλόξενος.

hospital [ˈhɔspitl] *n* νοσοκομεῖο.

hospitality [hɔspiˈtæliti] *n* φιλοξενία.

host [həust] *n* οἰκοδεσπότης ‖ (*hotel*) ξενοδόχος, χανιτζῆς ‖ (*large number*) πλῆθος, στρατιά.

hostage [ˈhɔstidʒ] *n* ὅμηρος.

hostel [ˈhɔstəl] *n* οἰκοτροφεῖον, χάνι.

hostess [ˈhəustes] *n* οἰκοδέσποινα.

hostile [ˈhɔstail] *a* ἐχθρικός.

hostility [hɔsˈtiliti] *n* ἐχθρότης ‖ **hostilities** *npl* ἐχθροπραξίες.

hot [hɔt] *a* θερμός, ζεστός ‖ (*fiery*) ὀξύθυμος, ἀναμμένος ‖ **~dog** *n* λουκάνικο ‖ **~-water bottle** *n* θερμοφόρα.

hotel [həuˈtel] *n* ξενοδοχεῖον ‖ (*residential*) πανσιόν.

hound [haund] *n* σκυλί, λαγωνικό ‖ *vt* καταδιώκω, παροτρύνω.

hour [ˈauə*] *n* ὥρα ‖ **~ly** *a,ad* κάθε ὥρα.

house [haus] *n* σπίτι, κατοικία ‖ (*parl*) βουλή ‖ (*theat*) ἀκροατήριον ‖ [hauz] *vt* στεγάζω ‖ (*store*) ἀποθηκεύω ‖ **~boat** *n* πλωτό σπίτι ‖ ~**breaking** n διάρρηξι σπιτιοῦ ‖ ~**hold** n σπίτι ‖ οἰκογένεια, σπιτικό ‖ ~**keeper** n νοικοκυρά ‖ ~**keeping** n νοικοκυριό, σπιτικό ‖ ~**maid** n ὑπηρέτρια, ὑπηρεσία ‖ ~**wife** n νοικοκυρά ‖ ~**work** n νοικοκυριό.

housing [ˈhauziŋ] n στέγασις.

hovel [ˈhɔvl] n καλύβα.

hover [ˈhɔvə*] vi μετεωρίζομαι, πλανῶμαι ‖ (between) διστάζω, ταλαντεύομαι ‖ ~**craft** n χόβερκραφτ.

how [hau] ad πῶς, μέ ποιό τρόπο ‖ (extent) πόσο ‖ and ~! (US) καί βέβαια!, ἀσφαλῶς! ‖ ~**ever** ad ὁπωσδήποτε, ὅπως κι ἄν ‖ (much) ὁσονδήποτε, ὅσο κι ἄν ‖ (yet) παρά ταῦτα, κι ὅμως.

howl [haul] n οὐρλιασμα, οὐρλιαχτό ‖ vi οὐρλιάζω, σκοΰζω.

howler [ˈhaulə*] n ὠρυόμενος ‖ (mistake) γκάφα, χοντροκοπιά.

hub [hʌb] n (of wheel) ἀφαλός ‖ (of activity) κέντρον.

hubbub [ˈhʌbʌb] n φασαρία, θόρυβος, ὀχλοβοή.

hub cap [ˈhʌbkæp] n καπάκι τῆς ρόδας.

huddle [ˈhʌdl] n σωρός, σωρό κουβάρι ‖ vi συσσωρεύω, συνωθοῦμαι, κουλουριάζω.

hue [hju:] n χροιά, χρῶμα, ἀπόχρωσις.

huff [hʌf] n παραφορά, θυμός.

hug [hʌg] n ἀγκάλιασμα ‖ vt ἀγκαλιάζω, σφίγγω ‖ (naut) παραπλέω, πηγαίνω κόστα-κόστα.

huge [hju:dʒ] a πελώριος, θεόρατος, τεράστιος.

hulk [hʌlk] n (naut) ξαρματωμένο πλοῖο, σαπιοκάραβο ‖ (person) μπατάλης, χοντράνθρωπος ‖ ~**ing** a δυσκίνητος, χοντρός, βαρύς.

hull [hʌl] n σκάφος, γάστρα.

hullo [hʌˈləu] excl = **hello**.

hum [hʌm] n βόμβος, βουητό, ψίθυρος ‖ vi βουΐζω, ψιθυρίζω ‖ vt μουρμουρίζω.

human [ˈhju:mən] a ἀνθρώπινος ‖ n ἄνθρωπος.

humane [hju:ˈmein] a ἀνθρωπιστικός, φιλάνθρωπος.

humanity [hju:ˈmæniti] n ἀνθρωπότης ‖ (kindness) φιλανθρωπία.

humble [ˈhʌmbl] a ταπεινός, ἁπλός ‖ (unimportant) ἀσήμαντος ‖ vt ταπεινώνω, ξευτελίζω.

humbly [ˈhʌmbli] ad ταπεινά, ἁπλά.

humdrum [ˈhʌmdrʌm] a μονότονος, ἀνιαρός, πληκτικός.

humid [ˈhju:mid] a ὑγρός, νοτερός ‖ ~**ity** n ὑγρασία, νότισμα.

humiliate [hju:ˈmilieit] vt ταπεινώνω, ξευτελίζω, κουρελιάζω.

humiliation [hju:miliˈeiʃən] n ταπείνωσις, κουρέλιασμα.

humility [hju:ˈmiliti] n ταπεινότης, μετριοφροσύνη.

humor [ˈhju:mə*] (US) = **humour**.

humorist [ˈhju:mərist] n χιουμορίστας.

humorous [ˈhju:mərəs] a γεμάτος χιοῦμορ, εὔθυμος.

humour [ˈhju:mə*] n χιοῦμορ, κέφι, διάθεσις ‖ vt κάνω τά χατήρια, κάνω τά κέφια.

hump [hʌmp] n καμπούρα.

hunch [hʌntʃ] n ὗβος, καμπούρα ‖ (suspicion) ὑποψία ‖ vt κυρτώνω, καμπουριάζω ‖ ~**back** n καμπούρης.

hundred [ˈhʌndrid] num,n ἑκατόν ‖ ~**weight** n στατήρ (112 λίτρες).

hung [hʌŋ] pt,pp of **hang**.

Hungarian [hʌŋˈgeəriən] a οὐγγρικός ‖ n (person) Οὔγγρος ‖ (ling) οὐγγρική.

Hungary [ˈhʌŋgəri] n Οὐγγαρία.

hunger [ˈhʌŋgə*] n πεῖνα ‖ (desire) σφοδρά ἐπιθυμία ‖ vi πεινῶ, ποθῶ ἐντόνως ‖ ~ **strike** n ἀπεργία πείνης.

hungrily [ˈhʌŋgrili] ad ἄπληστα, ἀχόρταγα, πεινασμένα.

hungry [ˈhʌŋgri] a πεινασμένος.

hunt [hʌnt] n κυνήγι ‖ (seeking) ἀναζήτησις ‖ vt κυνηγῶ ‖ (search) διώχνω ‖ vi κυνηγῶ ‖ (seek) ψάχνω ‖ ~**er** n κυνηγός ‖ ~**ing** n κυνήγι.

hurdle [ˈhə:dl] n (lit) φράκτης ‖ (fig) ἐμπόδιον.

hurl [hə:l] vt ἐκσφενδονίζω, ρίχνω.

hurrah [huˈra:] n, **hurray** [huˈrei] ζητοκραυγή.

hurricane [ˈhʌrikən] n καταιγίδα, λαίλαπας.

hurried [ˈhʌrid] a βιαστικός ‖ ~**ly** ad βιαστικά.

hurry [ˈhʌri] n βία, βιασύνη ‖ vi βιάζομαι, εἶμαι βιαστικός ‖ vt ἐπισπεύδω, βιάζω.

hurt [hə:t] (irreg v) n κακόν ‖ (wound) τραῦμα, πληγή ‖ (damage) βλάβη, ζημία ‖ vt κτυπῶ, τραυματίζω, πληγώνω ‖ (insult) προσβάλλω, πειράζω ‖ vi πονῶ, θίγομαι ‖ ~**ful** a βλαβερός.

hurtle [ˈhə:tl] vt ἐκσφενδονίζω ‖ vi (rush) ἐφορμῶ, ρίχνομαι.

husband [ˈhʌzbənd] n ἄνδρας.

hush [hʌʃ] n σιωπή, σιγή ‖ vt (καθ)ήσυχάζω, καλμάρω ‖ vi σωπαίνω ‖ ~! σιωπή!, σούτ!

husk [hʌsk] n φλοιός, φλούδα, τσόφλι.

husky [ˈhʌski] a (voice) βραχνός ‖ γεροδεμένος ‖ n σκύλος ἐλκύθρου.

hustle [ˈhʌsl] n σπουδή, βιασύνη ‖ (push) σπρωξίδι ‖ vt (push) σπρώχνω ‖ σκουντῶ, βιάζω.

hut [hʌt] n καλύβα ‖ (mil) παράπηγμα.

hutch [hʌtʃ] n κονικλοτροφεῖον.

hyacinth [ˈhaiəsinθ] n ὑάκινθος.

hybrid [ˈhaibrid] n μιγάς, μικτογενή, νόθος ‖ a μιγάς, μπασταρδεμένος.

hydrant [ˈhaidrənt] n σωλήν πυρκαϊᾶς, στόμιον ὑδρολήψιας.

hydraulic [haiˈdrɔ:lik] a ὑδραυλικός.

hydroelectric ['haidrəui'lektrik] *a* ὑδροηλεκτρικός.

nydrogen ['haidrədʒen] *n* ὑδρογόνον.

hyena [hai'i:nə] *n* ὕαινα.

hygiene ['haidʒi:n] *n* ὑγιεινη.

hygienic [hai'dʒi:nik] *a* ὑγιεινός.

hymn [him] *n* ὕμνος, ὑμνωδία.

hyphen ['hǎifən] *n* ἑνωτικόν.

hypnosis [hip'nəusis] *n* ὕπνωσις.

hypnotism ['hipnətizəm] *n* ὑπνωτισμός.

hypnotist ['hipnətist] *n* ὑπνωτιστής.

hypnotize ['hipnətaiz] *vt* ὑπνωτίζω.

hypochondriac [haipə'kɔndriæk] *n* ὑποχόνδριος.

hypocrisy [hi'pɔkrisi] *n* ὑποκρισία.

hypocrite ['hipəkrit] *n* ὑποκριτής.

hypocritical [hipə'kritikl] *a* ὑποκριτικός.

hypothesis [hai'pɔθisis] *n* ὑπόθεσις.

hypothetic(al) [haipə'θetik(əl)] *a* ὑποθετικός.

hysteria [his'tiəriə] *n* ὑστερία.

hysterical [his'terikl] *a* ὑστερικός.

hysterics [his'teriks] *npl* ὑστερία.

I, i

I [ai] *pron* ἐγώ.

ice [ais] *n* πάγος ‖ (*refreshment*) παγωτό ‖ *vt* (*cake*) γκλασάρω ‖ *vi* (*also* ~ **up**) παγώνω ‖ ~ **axe** *n* πέλεκυς πάγου ‖ ~ **berg** *n* παγόβουνο ‖ ~ **box** *n* (*US*) ψυγεῖον ‖ ~ **cream** *n* παγωτό ‖ ~ **cold** *a* παγερός, παγωμένος ‖ ~ **cube** *n* παγάκι ‖ ~ **hockey** *n* χόκεϋ ἐπὶ πάγου.

icicle ['aisikl] *n* σταλακτίτης πάγου.

icing ['aisiŋ] *n* κρούστα γιά κέϊκ, γκλασάρισμα.

icon ['aikɔn] *n* εἰκόνα.

icy ['aisi] *a* (*slippery*) γλιστερός ‖ (*frozen*) παγετώδης, παγωμένος.

I'd [aid] = **I would, I had** ‖ *see* **would, have**.

idea [ai'diə] *n* ἰδέα ‖ (*plan*) σκοπός, ἰδέα.

ideal [ai'diəl] *n* ἰδανικόν, ἰδεῶδες ‖ *a* ἰδανικός, ἰδεώδης ‖ ~ **ism** *n* ἰδεαλισμός ‖ ~ **ist** *n* ἰδεαλιστής ‖ ~ **ly** *ad* ἰδανικῶς, ἰδεωδῶς.

identical [ai'dentikəl] *a* ὅμοιος, ἴδιος, ἀπαράλλακτος.

identification [aidentifi'keiʃən] *n* ἐξακρίβωσις ταυτότητος, συνταύτισις.

identify [ai'dentifai] *vt* (*person*) διαπιστώνω, ἐξακριβώνω ‖ (*regard as same*) ταυτίζω.

identity [ai'dentiti] *n* ταυτότης.

ideology [aidi'ɔlədʒi] *n* ἰδεολογία.

idiocy ['idiəsi] *n* ἠλιθιότης.

idiom ['idiəm] *n* ἰδίωμα ‖ (*dialect*) διάλεκτος.

idiosyncrasy [idiə'siŋkrəsi] *n* ἰδιοσυγκρασία.

idiot ['idiət] *n* ἠλίθιος, ἀνόητος | ~ **ic** [idi'ɔtik] *a* ἠλίθιος.

idle ['aidl] *a* ἀργός ‖ (*lazy*) ὀκνηρός, τεμπέλης ‖ (*useless*) μάταιος, ἀνωφελής ‖ ~ **ness** *n* ἀργία, τεμπελιά ‖ ~ **r** *n* ἀργόσχολος.

idol ['aidl] *n* εἴδωλον ‖ ~ **ize** *vt* λατρεύω, θαυμάζω.

idyllic [i'dilik] *a* εἰδυλλιακός.

if [if] *cj* (*condition*) ἐάν, ἄν, ὅταν ‖ (*whether*) ἄν.

ignite [ig'nait] *vt* ἀναφλέγω, ἀνάβω.

ignition [ig'niʃən] *n* ἀνάφλεξις ‖ ~ **key** *n* (*aut*) κλειδὶ (ξεκινήσεως).

ignorance ['ignərəns] *n* ἄγνοια.

ignorant ['ignərənt] *a* ἀμαθής, ἀγνοῶν.

ignore [ig'nɔ:*] *vt* ἀγνοῶ, ἀψηφῶ.

ikon ['aikɔn] *n* = **icon**.

I'll [ail] = **I will, I shall** ‖ *see* **will, shall**.

ill [il] *a* ἄρρωστος ‖ (*evil*) κακός ‖ *n* κακόν, ἀτυχία ‖ ~ **-advised** *a* ἀσύνετος, ἀπερίσκεπτος ‖ ~ **-at-ease** *a* στενοχωρημένος, ἀνήσυχος.

illegal [i'li:gəl] *a* παράνομος ‖ ~ **ly** *ad* παράνομα.

illegible [i'ledʒəbl] *a* δυσανάγνωστος.

illegitimate [ili'dʒitimit] *a* νόθος.

ill-fated ['il'feitid] *a* κακότυχος.

ill-feeling ['il'fi:liŋ] *n* κακία, ἔχθρα.

illicit [i'lisit] *a* παράνομος, ἀθέμιτος.

illiterate [i'litərit] *a* ἀγράμματος.

ill-mannered ['il'mænəd] *a* κακότροπος, κακομαθημένος.

illness ['ilnis] *n* ἀσθένεια, ἀρρώστεια.

illogical [i'lɔdʒikəl] *a* παράλογος.

ill-treat ['il'tri:t] *vt* κακομεταχειρίζομαι.

illuminate [i'lu:mineit] *vt* φωτίζω, φωταγωγῶ.

illumination [ilu:mi'neiʃən] *n* φωτισμός, φωταγώγησις.

illusion [i'lu:ʒən] *n* αὐταπάτη, πλάνη.

illusive [i'lu:siv] *a*, **illusory** [i'lu:səri] *a* ἀπατηλός.

illustrate ['iləstreit] *vt* εἰκονογραφῶ.

illustration [iləs'treiʃən] *n* εἰκονογράφησις, εἰκόνα.

illustrious [i'lʌstriəs] *a* ἔνδοξος, ἐπιφανής.

ill will ['il'wil] *n* κακοβουλία, κακία.

I'm [aim] = **I am** ‖ *see* **be**.

image ['imidʒ] *n* (*statue*) εἰκών, εἴδωλον ‖ (*likeness*) ὁμοίωμα, ἀναπαράστασις ‖ (*reflection*) εἴδωλον ‖ ~ **ry** *n* ρητορικὰ σχήματα.

imaginable [i'mædʒinəbl] *a* διανοητός.

imaginary [i'mædʒinəri] *a* φανταστικός.

imagination [imædʒi'neiʃən] *n* φαντασία.

imaginative [i'mædʒinətiv] *a* εὐφάνταστος, ἐπινοητικός.

imagine [i'mædʒin] *vt* φαντάζομαι, διανοοῦμαι.

imbalance [im'bæləns] *n* ἀνισότης, ἀνισορροπία.

imbecile ['imbəsi:l] *n* βλάκας, ἠλίθιος.

imbue [im'bju:] *vt* (ἐμ)ποτίζω, διαποτίζω.

imitate ['imiteit] *vt* μιμοῦμαι, ἀντιγράφω.

imitation [imi'teiʃən] n (άπο)μίμησις.
imitator ['imiteitə*] n μιμητής.
immaculate [i'mækjulit] a άσπιλος, άμόλυντος.
immaterial [imə'tiəriəl] a ' ἀσήμαντος, ἄϋλος.
immature [imə'tjuə*] a ἀνώριμος, ἄγουρος.
immediate [i'mi:diət] a (near) ἄμεσος, προσεχές ‖ (present) ἐπείγων, ἄμεσος ‖ (not separated) πλησιέστερος ‖ (instant) ἄμεσος, στιγμιαῖος ‖ ~ly ad (at once) ἀμέσως, στῆ στιγμή.
immense [i'mens] a ἀπέραντος, ἄπειρος ‖ ~ly ad ἀπέραντα.
immerse [i'mə:s] vt ἐμβαπτίζω, βυθίζω, βουτῶ.
immigrant ['imigrənt] n μετανάστης.
immigration [imi'greiʃən] n μετανάστευσις.
imminent ['iminənt] a ἐπικείμενος, ἄμεσος.
immobilize [i'məubilaiz] vt ἀκινητοποιῶ.
immoderate [i'mɔdərit] a ὑπερβολικός, ὑπέρμετρος.
immoral [i'mɔrəl] a ἀνήθικος, κακοήθης ‖ ~ity [imə'ræliti] n ἀνηθικότης.
immortal [i'mɔ:tl] a ἀθάνατος, ἄφθαρτος ‖ n ἀθάνατος ‖ ~ity n ἀθανασία ‖ ~ize vt ἀποθανατίζω.
immune [i'mju:n] a ἀπρόσβλητος.
immunity [i'mju:niti] n ἀπαλλαγή ‖ (med) ἀνοσία.
immunization [imjunai'zeiʃən] n ἀνοσοποίησις.
immunize ['imjunaiz] vt ἀνοσοποιῶ.
impact ['impækt] n (lit) σύγκρουσις, κτύπημα ‖ (fig) ἐπίδρασις.
impair [im'pεə*] vt βλάπτω, ἐξασθενίζω.
impale [im'peil] vt ἀνασκολοπίζω, παλου κώνω.
impartial [im'pɑ:ʃəl] a ἀμερόληπτος ‖ ~ity n ἀμεροληψία.
impassable [im'pɑ:səbl] a ἀδιάβατος.
impassioned [im'pæʃnd] a ἐμπαθής παθιασμένος.
impatience [im'peiʃəns] n ἀνυπομονησία.
impatient [im'peiʃənt] a ἀνυπόμονος ‖ ~ly ad ἀνυπόμονα, βιαστικά.
impeccable [im'pekəbl] a ἄψογος, τέλειος.
impede [im'pi:d] vt ἐμποδίζω, παρακωλύω.
impediment [im'pedimənt] n κώλυμα, ἐμπόδιον.
impending [im'pendiŋ] a ἐπικείμενος.
impenetrable [im'peni̱trəbl] a ἀδιαπέραστος, ἀνεξιχνίαστος.
imperative [im'perətiv] a ἐπιτακτικός ‖ n (gram) προστακτική.
imperceptible [impə'septəbl] a ἀνεπαίσθητος, ἀδιόρατος.
imperfect [im'pɑ:fikt] a ἐλαττωματικός, (incomplete) ἐλλειπής ‖ ~ion n ἀτέλεια, ἐλάττωμα.
imperial [im'piəriəl] a αὐτοκρατορικός ‖

(majestic) μεγαλοπρεπής ‖ ~ism n ἰμπεριαλισμός.
imperil [im'peril] vt διακινδυνεύω, ἐκθέτω εἰς κίνδυνον.
impersonal [im'pə:snl] a ἀπρόσωπος.
impersonate [im'pə:səneit] vt προσωποποιῶ, ὑποδύομαι, παριστάνω.
impersonation [impə:sə'neiʃən] n προσωποποίησις, ἐνσάρκωσις, μίμησις.
impertinence [im'pə:tinəns] n αὐθάδεια.
impertinent [im'pə:tinənt] a αὐθάδης, ἄσχετος.
imperturbable [impə'tə:bəbl] a ἀτάραχος.
impervious [im'pə:viəs] a ἀδιαπέραστος, στεγανός, ἀνεπηρέαστος.
impetuous [im'petjuəs] a ὁρμητικός, βίαιος.
impetus ['impitəs] n ὤθησις, ὁρμή.
impinge [im'pindʒ] to ~ on vt συγκρούομαι, καταπατῶ.
implausible [im'plɔ:zəbl] a ἀπίθανος.
implement ['implimənt] n ὄργανον, ἐργαλεῖον, σύνεργο ‖ ['impliment] vt ἐφαρμόζω.
implicate ['implikeit] vt ἐμπλέκω, ἀναμιγνύω.
implication [impli'keiʃən] n ἐνοχοποίησις, ὑπαινιγμός.
implicit [im'plisit] a ὑπονοούμενος, σιωπηρός ‖ (complete) ἀπόλυτος, ἀμέριστος.
implore [im'plɔ:*] vt ἱκετεύω, ἐκλιπαρῶ
imply [im'plai] vt ὑπονοῶ, ὑπαινίσσομαι, προϋποθέτω.
impolite [impə'lait] a ἀγενής, βάναυσος.
imponderable [im'pondərəbl] a ἀστάθμητος, ἀνεξιχνίαστος.
import [im'pɔ:t] vt εἰσάγω ‖ ['impɔ:t] n εἰσαγωγή ‖ (meaning) σημασία ‖ ~ duty n (εἰσαγωγικός) δασμός ‖ ~ licence n ἄδεια εἰσαγωγής.
importance [im'pɔ:təns] n σπουδαιότης, σοβαρότης ‖ (value) σημασία, ἀξία.
important [im'pɔ:tənt] a σημαντικός, σπουδαῖος.
importation [impɔ:'teiʃən] n εἰσαγωγή.
importer [im'pɔ:tə*] n εἰσαγωγεύς.
impose [im'pəuz] vt ἐπιβάλλω, ἐπιτάσσω ‖ (on s.o.) ἐπωφελοῦμαι.
imposing [im'pəuziŋ] a ἐπιβλητικός.
imposition [impə'ziʃən] n (burden) φόρος, φορολογία ‖ (punishment) ποινή.
impossibility [impɔsə'biliti] n (τό) ἀδύνατον.
impossible [im'pɔsəbl] a ἀδύνατος, ἀκατόρθωτος, ἀνυπόφορος.
impostor [im'pɔstə*] n ἀγύρτης, λαοπλάνος.
impotence ['impətəns] n (esp sexual) ἀνικανότης.
impotent ['impətənt] a ἀνίκανος, ἀνίσχυρος.
impound [im'paund] vt κατάσχω.
impoverished [im'pɔvəriʃt] a πάμπτωχος, ἐξηντλημένος.

impracticable [im'præktikəbl] *a* ἀκατόρ-θωτος, ἀπραγματοποίητος.

impractical [im'præktikəl] *a* οὐχί πρακτι-κόν.

impregnable [im'pregnəbl] *a* ἀπόρθητος.

impregnate ['impregneit] *vt* γονιμοποιῶ, ἐμποτίζω.

impress [im'pres] *vt* (*influence*) κάνω ἐντύπωσιν ‖ (*imprint*) ἐντυπώνω, ἐγχα-ράσσω ‖ ~**ion** *n* (*mark*) ἀποτύπωσις, ἀποτύπωμα ‖ (*printed copy*) ἔκδοσις ‖ (*effect*) ἐντύπωσις, αἴσθησις ‖ (*belief*) ἰδέα, ἐντύπωσις, γνώμη ‖ ~**ionable** *a* εὐαίσθητος, εὐσυγκίνητος ‖ ~**ionist** *n* ἰμπρεσσιονιστής ‖ ~**ive** *a* ἐντυπωσι-ακός, συγκινητικός.

imprison [im'prizn] *vt* φυλακίζω ‖ ~**ment** *n* φυλάκισις.

improbable [im'prɔbəbl] *a* ἀπίθανος.

impromptu [im'prɔmptju:] *a* αὐτοσχέδιος, ἐκ τοῦ προχείρου ‖ *ad* ἐκ τοῦ προχείρου.

improper [im'prɔpə*] *a* (*wrong*) ἐσφαλμέ-νος ‖ (*unsuitable*) ἀνάρμοστος ‖ (*indecent*) ἀπρεπής.

impropriety [imprə'praiəti] *n* ἀπρέπεια, ἀκαταλληλότης.

improve [im'pru:v] *vt* βελτιώνω, κάνω καλύτερον ‖ *vi* (*become better*) βελτι-οῦμαι, καλυτερεύω ‖ ~**ment** *n* βελτίωσις, πρόοδος.

improvisation [imprəvai'zeiʃən] *n* αὐτο-σχεδιασμός.

improvise ['imprəvaiz] *vi* αὐτοσχεδιάζω ‖ *vt* κάνω ἐκ τοῦ προχείρου.

imprudence [im'pru:dəns] *n* ἀφροσύνη, ἀπερισκεψία.

imprudent [im'pru:dənt] *a* ἀσύνετος, ἀστόχαστος.

impudence ['impjudəns] *n* ἀναίδεια, θράσος.

impudent ['impjudənt] *a* ἀναιδής, ἀναίσχυν-τος.

impulse ['impʌls] *n* (*sudden desire*) ὁρμή, ὁρμέμφυτον ‖ ὤθησις, πρόωσις.

impulsive [im'pʌlsiv] *a* αὐθόρμητος, ὁρμέμφυτος.

impunity [im'pju:niti] *n* ἀτιμωρησία.

impure [im'pjuə*] *a* ἀκάθαρτος ‖ (*bad*) μιαρός, αἰσχρός.

impurity [im'pjuəriti] *n* ἀκαθαρσία, ξένο σῶμα.

in [in] *prep* εἰς, ἐν, ἐντός, σέ ‖ (*made of*) σέ ‖ (*expressed in*) εἰς, μέ ‖ (*dressed in*) μέ ‖ *ad* ἐντός, μέσα ‖ ~**s and outs** *npl* τά μέσα καί τά ἔξω.

inability [inə'biliti] *n* ἀνικανότης, ἀδυνα-μία.

inaccessible [inæk'sesəbl] *a* ἀπρόσιτος, ἀπλησίαστος.

inaccuracy [in'ækjurəsi] *n* ἀνακρίβεια.

inaccurate [in'ækjurit] *a* ἀνακριβής, ἐσφαλμένος.

inaction [in'ækʃən] *n* ἀδράνεια, ἀπραξία.

inactivity [inæk'tiviti] *n* ἀδράνεια, ἀργία.

inadequacy [in'ædikwəsi] *n* ἀνεπάρκεια, ἀτέλεια.

inadequate [in'ædikwit] *a* ἀνεπαρκής, ἀτελής.

inadvertently [inəd'və:təntli] *ad* ἀπρόσεκτα, ἐξ ἀμελείας.

inadvisable [inəd'vaizəbl] *a* ἀσύμφορος.

inane [i'nein] *a* κενός, ἀνόητος.

inanimate [in'ænimit] *a* ἄψυχος.

inapplicable [in'æplikəbl] *a* ἀνεφάρμοστος.

inappropriate [inə'prəupriit] *a* ἀκατάλ-ληλος, ἀνάρμοστος.

inapt [in'æpt] *a* ἀνεπιτήδειος, ἀδέξιος ‖ ~**itude** *n* ἀνικανότης, ἀδεξιότης.

inarticulate [ina:'tikjulit] *a* ἄναρθρος, βουβός, ἀσύνδετος.

inartistic [ina:'tistik] *a* ἀφιλόκαλος.

inasmuch [inəz'mʌtʃ] ~ **as** ἐπειδή, ἐφ' ὅσον.

inattention [inə'tenʃən] *n* ἀπροσεξία, ἀφηρημάδα.

inattentive [inə'tentiv] *a* ἀπρόσεκτος, ἀμελής.

inaudible [in'ɔ:dəbl] *a* ἀνεπαίσθητος, ἀσθενής.

inaugural [i'nɔ:gjurəl] *a* ἐναρκτήριος.

inaugurate [i'nɔ:gjureit] *vt* ἐγκαινιάζω.

inauguration [inɔ:gju'reiʃən] *n* ἐγκαινι-ασμός, ἐγκαίνια.

inborn ['in'bɔ:n] *a* ἔμφυτος.

inbred ['in'bred] *a* ἔμφυτος, φυσικός.

incalculable [in'kælkjuləbl] *a* ἀνυπολόγι στος.

incapability [inkeipə'biliti] *n* ἀνικανότης.

incapable [in'keipəbl] *a* ἀνίκανος.

incapacitate [inkə'pæsiteit] *vt* καθιστῶ ἀνίκανον.

incapacity [inkə'pæsiti] *n* ἀνικανότης, ἀναρμοδιότης.

incarcerate [in'ka:səreit] *vt* φυλακίζω.

incarnate [in'ka:nit] *a* ἐνσαρκωμένος.

incarnation [inka:'neiʃən] *n* ἐνσάρκωσις.

incendiary [in'sendiəri] *a* ἐμπρηστικός ‖ *n* ἐμπρηστής.

incense ['insens] *n* θυμίαμα, λιβάνι ‖ [in'sens] *vt* ἐξοργίζω, ἐξαγριώνω.

incentive [in'sentiv] *n* κίνητρον, ἐλατήριον, τονωτικόν.

incessant [in'sesnt] *a* ἀδιάκοπος ‖ ~**ly** *ad* ἀδιάκοπα.

incest ['insest] *n* αἱμομιξία.

inch [intʃ] *n* ἴντσα (.0254 μ.).

incidence ['insidəns] *n* πρόσπτωσις, περίπτωσις.

incident ['insidənt] *n* ἐπεισόδιον, περιπέ-τεια ‖ ~**al** *a* τυχαῖος, συμπτωματικός ‖ ~**ally** *ad* παρεμπιπτόντως.

incinerator [in'sinəreitə*] *n* ἀποτεφρωτήρ.

incision [in'siʒən] *n* ἐντομή, χαραματιά.

incisive [in'saisiv] *a* κοφτερός ‖ (*cutting*) δηκτικός.

incite [in'sait] *vt* ὑποκινῶ, παροτρύνω.

inclement [in'klemənt] a δριμύς, κακός.

inclination [inkli'neiʃən] n κλίσις, τάσις, διάθεσις.

incline ['inklain] n κλίσις ‖ [in'klain] vi κλίνω, γέρνω ‖ (be disposed) ρέπω, τείνω.

include [in'klu:d] vt (συμ)περιλαμβάνω, περιέχω.

inclusion [in'klu:ʒən] n συμπερίληψις.

inclusive [in'klu:siv] a συμπεριλαμβάνων, περιέχων.

incognito [in'kɔgnitəu] ad ἰνκόγνιτο.

incoherent [inkəu'hiərənt] a ἀσυνάρτητος.

income ['inkʌm] n εἰσόδημα ‖ ~ tax n φόρος εἰσοδήματος.

incoming ['inkʌmiŋ] a (tide) ἀνερχόμενος, εἰσερχόμενος.

incomparable [in'kɔmpərəbl] a ἀσύγκριτος, ἀπαράμιλλος.

incompatible [inkəm'pætəbl] a ἀσυμβίβαστος..

incompetence [in'kɔmpitəns] n ἀναρμοδιότης, ἀνικανότης.

incompetent [in'kɔmpitənt] a ἀνίκανος, ἀναρμόδιος.

incomplete [inkəm'pli:t] a ἀτελής.

incomprehensible [inkɔmpri'hensəbl] a ἀκατανόητος, ἀκατάληπτος.

inconceivable [inkən'si:vəbl] a ἀσύλληπτος, ἀπίστευτος.

inconclusive [inkən'klu:siv] a μή πειστικός.

incongruity [inkɔŋ'gru:iti] n ἀσυνέπεια, ἀσυναρτησία.

incongruous [in'kɔŋgruəs] a ἀσύμφωνος, ἀνάρμοστος.

inconsequential [inkɔnsi'kwenʃəl] a ἀνακόλουθος, ἀσήμαντος.

inconsiderable [inkən'sidərəbl] a ἀσήμαντος.

inconsiderate [inkən'sidərit] a ἀπερίσκεπτος, ἀδιάκριτος.

inconsistency [inkən'sistənsi] n ἀσυνέπεια, ἀντίφασις.

inconsistent [inkən'sistənt] a ἀσυνεπής, ἀντιφατικός.

inconspicuous [inkən'spikjuəs] a ἀφανής, ὄχι κτυπητός.

inconstancy [in'kɔnstənsi] n ἀστάθεια.

inconstant [in'kɔnstənt] a εὐμετάβολος, ἄσταθής.

incontinence [in'kɔntinəns] n ἀκολασία, ἀκράτεια.

incontinent [in'kɔntinənt] a ἀκόλαστος, ἀκρατής.

inconvenience [inkən'vi:niəns] n δυσχέρεια, ἐνόχλησις, μπελάς.

inconvenient [inkən'vi:niənt] a στενόχωρος, ἐνοχλητικός, ἀκατάλληλος.

incorporate [in'kɔ:pəreit] vt ἐνσωματώνω, συγχωνεύω.

incorporated [in'kɔ:pəreitid] a ἐνσωματωμένος, συγχωνευμένος ‖ (US) ἀνώνυμος (ἑταιρεία)

incorrect [inkə'rekt] a ἐσφαλμένος, ἀνακριβής.

incorrigible [in'kɔridʒəbl] a ἀδιόρθωτος.

incorruptible [inkə'rʌptəbl] a ἀδιάφθορος, ἀκέραιος, ἀδέκαστος.

increase ['inkri:s] n αὔξησις ‖ [in'kri:s] vt αὐξάνω, μεγαλώνω ‖ vi αὐξάνομαι.

increasingly [in'kri:siŋli] ad διαρκῶς περισσότερον.

incredible [in'kredəbl] a ἀπίστευτος.

incredibly [in'kredəbli] ad ἀπίστευτα.

incredulity [inkri'dju:liti] n δυσπιστία, ὀλιγοπιστία.

incredulous [in'kredjuləs] a δύσπιστος.

increment ['inkrimənt] n αὔξησις.

incriminate [in'krimineit] vt ἐνοχοποιῶ.

incubation [inkju'beiʃən] n ἐπώασις, κλώσημα.

incubator ['inkjubeitə*] n κλωσσομηχανή.

incur [in'kə:*] vt ὑφίσταμαι, διατρέχω, προκαλῶ.

incurable [ink'juərəbl] a ἀνίατος, ἀγιάτρευτος.

incursion [in'kə:ʃən] n ἐπιδρομή.

indebted [in'detid] a ὑποχρεωμένος, ὑπόχρεως.

indecency [in'di:snsi] n ἀπρέπεια.

indecent [in'di:snt] a ἀπρεπής, ἄσεμνος.

indecision [indi'siʒən] n ἀναποφασιστικότης, ἀοριστία.

indecisive [indi'saisiv] a μή ἀποφασιστικός.

indeed [in'di:d] ad πράγματι, πραγματικά, ἀληθινά.

indefinable [indi'fainəbl] a ἀπροσδιόριστος.

indefinite [in'definit] a ἀόριστος ‖ ~ly ad ἀορίστως.

indelible [in'deləbl] a ἀνεξίτηλος.

indemnify [in'demnifai] vt ἀποζημιώνω, ἐξασφαλίζω.

indentation [inden'teiʃən] n (typing) ὀδόντωσις, δόντιασμα.

independence [indi'pendəns] n ἀνεξαρτησία.

independent [indi'pendənt] a ἀνεξάρτητος.

indescribable [indis'kraibəbl] a ἀπερίγραπτος.

index ['indeks] n εὑρετήριον ‖ ~ finger n δείκτης.

India ['indiə] n 'Ινδία ‖ ~n n 'Ινδός ‖ (of America) ἐρυθρόδερμος ‖ a ἰνδικός, ἰνδιάνικος.

indicate ['indikeit] vt δεικνύω, ἐμφαίνω, δηλῶ.

indication [indi'keiʃən] n ἔνδειξις, σημεῖον.

indicative [in'dikətiv] a (gram) ὁριστική (ἔγκλισις).

indicator ['indikeitə*] n (sign) δείκτης.

indict [in'dait] vt μηνύω, ἐνάγω, καταγγέλλω ‖ ~able a ἐνακτέος ‖ ~ment n μήνυσις, κατηγορία.

indifference [in'difrəns] n ἀδιαφορία.

indifferent [in'difrənt] *a* (*not caring*) ἀδιάφορος | (*unimportant*) ἀδιάφορος ‖ (*neither good nor bad*) συνηθισμένος, ἔτσι καί ἔτσι ‖ (*moderate*) μέτριος, οὐδέτερος ‖ (*impartial*) ἀμερόληπτος.

indigenous [in'didʒinəs] *a* γηγενής, ἰθαγενής, ντόπιος.

indigestible [indi'dʒestəbl] *a* δυσκολοχώνευτος.

indigestion [indi'dʒestʃən] *n* δυσπεψία.

indignant [in'dignənt] *a* ἀγανακτισμένος.

indignation [indig'neiʃən] *n* ἀγανάκτησις.

indignity [in'digniti] *n* προσβολή, ταπείνωσις, ὕβρις.

indigo ['indigəu] *n* λουλάκι ‖ *a* ἰνδικόν.

indirect [indi'rekt] *a* πλάγιος, ἔμμεσος ‖ ~ly *ad* ἐμμέσως.

indiscernible [indi'sə:nəbl] *a* δυσδιάκριτος.

indiscreet [indis'kri:t] *a* ἀδιάκριτος, ἀπρόσεκτος.

indiscretion [indis'kreʃən] *n* ἀδιακρισία, ἀκριτομυθία.

indiscriminate [indis'kriminit] *a* χωρίς διακρίσεις, τυφλός.

indispensable [indis'pensəbl] *a* ἀπαραίτητος.

indisposed [indis'pəuzd] *a* ἀδιάθετος, ἀπρόθυμος.

indisposition [indispə'ziʃən] *n* ἀδιαθεσία, ἀπροθυμία.

indisputable [indis'pju:təbl] *a* ἀναμφισβήτητος, ἀναμφίβολος.

indistinct [indis'tiŋkt] *a* ἀδιόρατος, συγκεχυμένος, ἀμυδρός.

indistinguishable [indis'tiŋgwiʃəbl] *a* δυσδιάκριτος, ἀνεπαίσθητος.

individual [indi'vidjuəl] *n* ἄτομον, πρόσωπο ‖ *a* ἰδιαίτερος, ἰδιωτικός, ἀτομικός ‖ ~ist *n* ἀτομικιστής ‖ ~ity *n* ἀτομικότης, προσωπικότης ‖ ~ly *ad* προσωπικῶς, ἀτομικῶς.

indoctrinate [in'dɔktrineit] *vt* διδάσκω, κατηχῶ, ἐμποτίζω.

indoctrination [indɔktri'neiʃən] *n* ἐμποτισμός, διδασκαλία.

indolence ['indələns] *n* νωθρότης, τεμπελιά, βαρεμάρα.

indolent ['indələnt] *a* νωθρός, τεμπέλης.

indoor ['indɔ:*] *a* τοῦ σπιτιοῦ, κατ'οἶκον ‖ ~s *ad* στό σπίτι.

indubitable [in'dju:bitəbl] *a* ἀναμφίβολος, βέβαιος.

induce [in'dju:s] *vt* πείθω, προτρέπω, προκαλῶ ‖ ~ment *n* προτροπή, κίνητρον.

induct [in'dʌkt] *vt* ἐγκαθιστῶ, εἰσάγω, μυῶ.

indulge [in'dʌldʒ] *vt* ἱκανοποιῶ ‖ (*allow pleasure*) ἐντρυφῶ, παραδίδομαι ‖ ~nce *n* ἐπιείκια, διασκέδασις, ἐντρύφησις ‖ ~nt *a* ἐπιεικής, συγκαταβατικός.

industrial [in'dʌstriəl] *a* βιομηχανικός ‖ ~ist *n* βιομήχανος ‖ ~ize *vt* ἐκβιομηχανίζω.

industrious [in'dʌstriəs] *a* φιλόπονος, ἐπιμελής.

industry ['indəstri] *n* βιομηχανία ‖ (*diligence*) φιλοπονία.

inebriated [i'ni:brieitid] *a* μεθυσμένος.

inedible [in'edibl] *a* ἀκατάλληλος πρός βρῶσιν.

ineffective [ini'fektiv] *a*, **ineffectual** [ini'fektjuəl] *a* ἀτελέσφορος, μάταιος.

inefficiency [ini'fiʃənsi] *n* ἀνικανότης ἀνεπάρκεια.

inefficient [ini'fiʃənt] *a* ἀνίκανος, ἀτελέσφορος.

inelegant [in'eligənt] *a* ἄκομψος, ἄγαρμπος.

ineligible [in'elidʒəbl] *a* μή ἐκλέξιμος, ἀκατάλληλος.

inept [i'nept] *a* ἄτοπος, ἀνόητος.

inequality [ini'kwɔliti] *n* ἀνισότης.

ineradicable [ini'rædikəbl] *a* ἀξερρίζωτος.

inert [i'nə:t] *a* ἀδρανής.

inertia [i'nə:ʃə] *n* ἀδράνεια.

inescapable [inis'keipəbl] *a* ἀναπόφευκτος.

inessential ['ini'senʃəl] *a* μή ἀπαραίτητος.

inestimable [in'estiməbl] *a* ἀνεκτίμητος.

inevitability [inevitə'biliti] *n* (τό) ἀναπόφευκτον.

inevitable [in'evitəbl] *a* ἀναπόφευκτος.

inexact [inig'zækt] *a* ἀνακριβής.

inexcusable [iniks'kju:zəbl] *a* ἀσυγχώρητος.

inexhaustible [inig'zɔ:stəbl] *a* ἀνεξάντλητος.

inexorable [in'eksərəbl] *a* ἀδυσώπητος, ἀμείλικτος.

inexpensive [iniks'pensiv] *a* φθηνός, ἀνέξοδος.

inexperience [iniks'piəriəns] *n* ἀπειρία ‖ ~d *a* ἄπειρος.

inexplicable [iniks'plikəbl] *a* ἀνεξήγητος.

inexpressible [iniks'presəbl] *a* ἀνέκφραστος.

inextricable [iniks'trikəbl] *a* ἀδιέξοδος, ἄλυτος.

infallibility [infælə'biliti] *n* (τό) ἀλάνθαστον.

infallible [in'fæləbl] *a* ἀλάνθαστος, σίγουρος.

infamous ['infəməs] *a* ἐπονείδιστος, κακοήθης.

infamy ['infəmi] *n* ἀτιμία, κακοήθεια.

infancy ['infənsi] *n* νηπιότης ‖ (*early stages*) ἀπαρχαί, πρώτη περίοδος.

infant ['infənt] *n* νήπιον, βρέφος ‖ ~ile *a* παιδικός, παιδιάστικος ‖ ~ school *n* νηπιαγωγεῖον.

infantry ['infəntri] *n* πεζικόν ‖ ~man *n* στρατιώτης, φαντάρος.

infatuated [in'fætjueitid] *a* ξεμυαλισμένος συνεπαρμένος.

infatuation [infætju'eiʃən] *n* ξεμυάλισμα, τρέλλα.

infect [in'fekt] *vt* μολύνω, μιαίνω, βρωμίζω ‖ (*influence*) ἐπηρεάζω ‖ ~ion *n* μόλυνσις, ἐπίδρασις ‖ ~ious *a* μολυσματικός, μεταδοτικός.

infer [inˈfəː*] vt συνάγω, συμπεραίνω, ὑπονοῶ ‖ ~**ence** [ˈinfərəns] n συμπέρασμα, πόρισμα.

inferior [inˈfiəriə*] a κατώτερος, ὑποδεέστερος ‖ n κατώτερος, ὑφιστάμενος ‖ ~**ity** n κατωτερότης, μειονεκτικότης ‖ ~**ity complex** n (σύμ)πλέγμα κατωτερότητος.

infernal [inˈfəːnl] a καταχθόνιος, διαβολικός, ἀπαίσιος.

inferno [inˈfəːnəu] n κόλασις.

infertile [inˈfəːtail] a ἄγονος, ἄκαρπος.

infertility [infəˈtiliti] n (τό) ἄγονον, στειρότης.

infest [inˈfest] vt λυμαίνομαι, κατακλύζω.

infidel [ˈinfidəl] n ἄπιστος.

infidelity [infiˈdeliti] n ἀπιστία.

infiltrate [ˈinfiltreit] vti (δι)εἰσδύω, εἰσχωρῶ.

infinite [ˈinfinit] a ἄπειρος, ἀπέραντος.

infinitive [inˈfinitiv] n ἀπαρέμφατον.

infinity [inˈfiniti] n ἄπειρον, ἀπεραντοσύνη.

infirm [inˈfəːm] a ἀσθενής, ἀδύνατος ‖ (*irresolute*) ἀσταθής, ταλαντευόμενος.

infirmary [inˈfəːməri] n νοσοκομεῖον, θεραπευτήριον.

infirmity [inˈfəːmiti] n ἀδυναμία, ἀναπηρία.

inflame [inˈfleim] vt (*excite*) ἐξάπτω, ἐρεθίζω.

inflammable [inˈflæməbl] a εὔφλεκτος.

inflammation [infləˈmeiʃən] n φλόγωσις, ἐρεθισμός.

inflate [inˈfleit] vt φουσκώνω ‖ (*econ*) προκαλῶ πληθωρισμόν.

inflation [inˈfleiʃən] n πληθωρισμός.

inflexible [inˈfleksəbl] a ἄκαμπτος, ἀλύγιστος.

inflict [inˈflikt] vt καταφέρω, δίνω, ἐπιβάλλω ‖ ~**ion** n ἐπιβολή, βάρος, τιμωρία.

inflow [ˈinfləu] n εἰσροή.

influence [ˈinfluəns] n ἐπίδρασις, ἐπιρροή ‖ vt ἐπηρεάζω, ἐπιδρῶ.

influential [influˈenʃəl] a σημαίνων, μέ ἐπιρροήν.

influenza [influˈenzə] n γρίππη.

influx [ˈinflʌks] n εἰσροή, διείσδυσις.

inform [inˈfɔːm] vt πληροφορῶ, εἰδοποιῶ.

informal [inˈfɔːməl] a ἀνεπίσημος, παράτυπος ‖ ~**ity** n ἀνεπισημότης.

information [infəˈmeiʃən] n πληροφορίες, εἰδήσεις.

informative [inˈfɔːmətiv] a κατατοπιστικος, πληροφοριακός.

informer [inˈfɔːmə*] n καταδότης, χαφιές.

infrared [infrəˈred] a ὑπέρυθρος.

infrequent [inˈfriːkwənt] a σπάνιος.

infringe [inˈfrindʒ] vt παραβαίνω, παραβιάζω ‖ vi καταπατῶ ‖ ~**ment** n παράβασις.

infuriate [inˈfjuərieit] vt ἐξαγριώνω.

infuriating [inˈfjuərieitiŋ] a ἐξοργιστικό.

ingenious [inˈdʒiːniəs] a ὀξύνους, πολυμήχανος.

ingenuity [indʒiˈnjuːiti] n εὐφυΐα, ὀξύνοια.

ingot [ˈiŋgət] n ράβδος, χελώνα.

ingratiate [inˈgreiʃieit] vt ἀποκτῶ εὔνοιαν.

ingratitude [inˈgrætitjuːd] n ἀγνωμοσύνη.

ingredient [inˈgriːdiənt] n συστατικόν.

inhabit [inˈhæbit] vt κατοικῶ, μένω ‖ ~**ant** n κάτοικος.

inhale [inˈheil] vt εἰσπνέω, ρουφῶ.

inherent [inˈhiərənt] a (+ *in*) συμφυής, ἔμφυτος.

inherit [inˈherit] vt κληρονομῶ ‖ ~**ance** n κληρονομία.

inhibit [inˈhibit] vt ἐμποδίζω, ἀναχαιτίζω, ἀπαγορεύω ‖ ~**ion** n ἀπαγόρευσις, ἀναχαίτισις.

inhospitable [inhɔsˈpitəbl] a ἀφιλόξενος.

inhuman [inˈhjuːmən] a ἀπάνθρωπος.

inimitable [iˈnimitəbl] a ἀμίμητος.

iniquity [iˈnikwiti] n ἀδικία, κακοήθεια.

initial [iˈniʃəl] a ἀρχικός, πρῶτος ‖ n ἀρχικόν ‖ vt μονογράφω ‖ ~**ly** ad ἀρχικῶς, κατ' ἀρχήν.

initiate [iˈniʃieit] vt ἀρχίζω, εἰσάγω ‖ (*in a society*) μυῶ.

initiation [iniʃiˈeiʃən] n μύησις.

initiative [iˈniʃətiv] n πρωτοβουλία.

inject [inˈdʒekt] vt ἐγχέω, εἰσάγω, κάνω ἔνεσιν ‖ ~**ion** n ἔγχυσις, ἔνεσις.

injure [ˈindʒə*] vt βλάπτω, ζημιώνω, πληγώνω.

injury [ˈindʒəri] n βλάβη, τραῦμα, ζημία.

injustice [inˈdʒʌstis] n ἀδικία.

ink [iŋk] n μελάνι.

inkling [ˈiŋkliŋ] n ὑποψία, ὑπόνοια.

inky [ˈiŋki] a μελανωμένος, μαῦρος.

inlaid [ˈinˈleid] a ἐμπαιστός.

inland [ˈinlænd] a ἐσωτερικός, μεσόγειος ‖ ad στό ἐσωτερικό, στά ἐνδότερα ‖ ~ **revenue** n (*Brit*) φορολογία.

in-laws [ˈinlɔːz] npl πεθερικά.

inlet [ˈinlet] n ὁρμίσκος, εἴσοδος.

inmate [ˈinmeit] n ἔνοικος.

inn [in] n πανδοχεῖον, ξενοδοχεῖον.

innate [iˈneit] a ἔμφυτος.

inner [ˈinə*] a ἐσωτερικός.

innocence [ˈinəsns] n ἀθωότης, ἀφέλεια.

innocent [ˈinəsnt] a ἀθῶος, ἁγνός, ἀφελής.

innocuous [iˈnɔkjuəs] a ἀβλαβής.

innovation [inəuˈveiʃən] n καινοτομία, νεωτερισμός.

innuendo [injuˈendəu] n ὑπαινιγμός.

innumerable [iˈnjuːmərəbl] a ἀναρίθμητος.

inoculation [inɔkjuˈleiʃən] n ἐμβολιασμός.

inopportune [inˈɔpətjuːn] a ἄκαιρος, ἄτοπος.

inordinately [iˈnɔːdinitli] ad ὑπερβολικά.

inorganic [inɔːˈgænik] a ἀνόργανος.

in-patient [ˈinpeiʃənt] n ἐσωτερικός (ἀσθενής).

input [ˈinput] n εἰσαγωγή.

inquest [ˈinkwest] n ἀνάκρισις, ἔρευνα.

inquire [inˈkwaiə*] vi ρωτῶ, ζητῶ ‖ vt (*price*) ρωτῶ τήν τιμήν ‖ **to ~ into** vt ἐρευνῶ, ἐξετάζω.

inquiring [in'kwaiəriŋ] *a* (*mind*) ἐρευνητικός.

inquiry [in'kwaiəri] *n* ἐρώτησις ‖ (*search*) ἔρευνα, ἀνάκρισις ‖ ~ office *n* ὑπηρεσία πληροφοριῶν.

inquisitive [in'kwizitiv] *a* περίεργος, ἀδιάκριτος.

inroad ['inrəud] *n* εἰσβολή, ἐπιδρομή.

insane [in'sein] *a* παράφρων, τρελλός.

insanitary [in'sænitəri] *a* ἀνθυγιεινός.

insanity [in'sæniti] *n* παραφροσύνη, τρέλλα.

insatiable [in'seiʃəbl] *a* ἀκόρεστος, ἄπληστος.

inscription [in'skripʃən] *n* ἐπιγραφή, ἀφιέρωσις.

inscrutable [in'skru:təbl] *a* ἀνεξιχνίαστος, μυστηριώδης.

insect ['insekt] *n* ἔντομον, ζουζούνι ‖ ~icide *n* ἐντομοκτόνον.

insecure [insi'kjuə*] *a* ἐπισφαλής.

insecurity [insi'kjuəriti] *n* ἀνασφάλεια, (τό) ἐπισφαλές.

insensible [in'sensəbl] *a* ἀνεπαίσθητος, ἀναίσθητος.

insensitive [in'sensitiv] *a* ἀναίσθητος, χωρίς ντροπή.

inseparable [in'sepərəbl] *a* ἀχώριστος, ἀναπόσπαστος.

insert [in'sə:t] *vt* παρεμβάλλω, καταχωρῶ, εἰσάγω ‖ ['insə:t] *n* παρεμβολή, ἔνθεμα ‖ ~ion *n* παρεμβολή, καταχώρησις, βάλσιμο.

inshore ['in'ʃɔ:*] *a,ad* κοντά στήν ἀκτή.

inside ['in'said] *n* (τό) μέσα, ἐσωτερικόν (μέρος) ‖ *a* ἐσωτερικός ‖ *ad* ἐσωτερικά, μέσα ‖ *prep* ἐντός, μέσα ‖ ~-forward *n* (*sport*) μέσος κυνηγός ‖ ~ out *ad* ἀνάποδα, τό μέσα ἔξω ‖ ~r *n* μεμυημένος, γνώστης.

insidious [in'sidiəs] *a* ὕπουλος, δόλιος.

insight ['insait] *n* διορατικότης, ὀξύνοια.

insignificant [insig'nifikənt] *a* ἀσήμαντος, τιποτένιος.

insincere [insin'siə*] *a* ἀνειλικρινής.

insincerity [insin'seriti] *n* ἀνειλικρίνεια.

insinuate [in'sinjueit] *vt* παρεισάγω, ὑπαινίσσομαι.

insinuation [insinju'eiʃən] *n* ὑπαινιγμός, παρεισαγωγή.

insipid [in'sipid] *a* ἀνούσιος, σαχλός.

insist [in'sist] *vi* (+ *on*) ἐπιμένω, ἐμμένω ‖ ~ence *n* ἐπιμονή ‖ ~ent *a* ἐπίμονος, ἐπείγων.

insolence ['insələns] *n* ἀναίδεια, θρασύτης.

insolent ['insələnt] *a* ἀναιδής, θρασύς.

insoluble [in'sɔljubl] *a* ἄλυτος, ἀδιάλυτος.

insolvent [in'sɔlvənt] *a* ἀφερέγγυος, ἀναξιόχρεος.

insomnia [in'sɔmniə] *n* ἀϋπνία.

inspect [in'spekt] *vt* ἐπιθεωρῶ, ἐπιτηρῶ, ἐπιβλέπω ‖ ~ion *n* ἐπιθεώρησις,

ἐπιτήρησις ‖ ~or *n* ἐπιθεωρητής ‖ (*rail*) ἐπιστάτης, ἐπόπτης.

inspiration [inspə'reiʃən] *n* ἔμπνευσις.

inspire [in'spaiə*] *vt* ἐμπνέω.

inspiring [in'spaiəriŋ] *a* ἐμπνέων.

instability [instə'biliti] *n* ἀστάθεια.

install [in'stɔ:l] *vt* ἐγκαθιστῶ, μοντάρω ‖ (*in office*) ἐγκαθιστῶ ‖ ~ation *n* ἐγκατάστασις, τοποθέτησις.

instalment, (*US*) **installment** [in'stɔ:lmənt] *n* δόσις, παρτίδα.

instance ['instəns] *n* περίπτωσις, παράδειγμα ‖ for ~ παραδείγματος χάριν.

instant ['instənt] *n* στιγμή ‖ *a* ἄμεσος, ἐπείγων ‖ ~ coffee *n* καφέ τῆς στιγμῆς ‖ ~ly *ad* ἀμέσως, στή στιγμή.

instead [in'sted] *ad* ἀντ'αὐτοῦ ‖ ~ of ἀντί.

instigation [insti'geiʃən] *n* παρακίνησις, ὑποκίνησις.

instil [in'stil] *vt* ἐμποτίζω, βάζω.

instinct ['instiŋkt] *n* ἔνστικτον, ὁρμέμφυτον ‖ ~ive *a* ἐνστικτώδης ‖ ~ively *ad* ἐνστικτωδῶς.

institute ['institju:t] *n* ἴδρυμα, ἰνστιτοῦτον ‖ *vt* θεσπίζω, ἱδρύω, ἐγκαθιστῶ.

institution [insti'tju:ʃən] *n* (*custom*) θεσμός, θέσμιον ‖ (*organization*) ἵδρυμα, ὀργάνωσις ‖ (*beginning*) ἵδρυσις, σύστασις.

instruct [in'strʌkt] *vt* (*order*) παραγγέλλω, διατάσσω ‖ (*teach*) διδάσκω, μαθαίνω ‖ ~ion *n* διδασκαλία ‖ (*direction*) ὁδηγία ‖ ~ions *npl* ἐντολές, ὁδηγίες ‖ ~ive *a* διδακτικός, ἐνημερωτικός ‖ ~or *,n* διδάσκαλος, ἐκπαιδευτής ‖ (*US*) ἐπιμελητής.

instrument ['instrumənt] *n* (*implement*) ἐργαλεῖον, ὄργανον ‖ (*mus*) ὄργανον ‖ ~al *a* ἐνόργανος ‖ (*helpful*) συντελεστικός, συμβάλλων ‖ ~alist *n* ὀργανοπαίκτης ‖ ~ panel *n* ταμπλώ.

insubordinate [insə'bɔ:dənit] *a* ἀνυπότακτος, ἀνυπάκουος.

insubordination ['insəbɔ:di'neiʃən] *n* ἀνυπακουή, ἀνυποταξία.

insufferable [in'sʌfərəbl] *a* ἀνυπόφορος, ἀφόρητος.

insufficient [insə'fiʃənt] *a* ἀνεπαρκής, λειψός ‖ ~ly *ad* ἀνεπαρκῶς.

insular ['insjələ*] *a* (*narrow-minded*) μέ στενές ἀντιλήψεις ‖ ~ity *n* στενές ἀντιλήψεις.

insulate ['insjuleit] *vt* μονώνω ‖ (*set apart*) ἀπομονώνω.

insulating ['insjuleitiŋ] ~ tape *n* μονωτική ταινία.

insulation [insju'leiʃən] *n* (*elec*) μόνωσις.

insulin ['insjulin] *n* (*for diabetic*) ἰνσουλίνη.

insult [in'sʌlt] *n* προσβολή, ὕβρις ‖ [in'sʌlt] *vt* ὑβρίζω, προσβάλλω ‖ ~ing *a* προσβλητικός.

insuperable [in'su:pərəbl] *a* ἀνυπέρβλητος.

insurance [in'ʃurəns] *n* ἀσφάλεια ‖ ~

agent n πράκτωρ ἀσφαλειῶν ‖ ~ **policy** n ἀσφαλιστήριον.

insure [in'ʃuə*] vt (ἐξ)ἀσφαλίζω.

insurmountable [insə'mauntəbl] a ἀνυπέρβλητος.

insurrection [insə'rekʃən] n ἐπανάστασις, ἐξέγερσις.

intact [in'tækt] a ἄθικτος, ἀπείραχτος.

intake ['inteik] n (mech) εἰσαγωγή.

intangible [in'tændʒəbl] a (difficult) δυσνόητος.

integral ['intigrəl] a (essential) ἀναπόσπαστος ‖ (complete) ὁλοκληρωτικός.

integrate ['intigreit] vti ὁλοκληρώνω.

integration [inti'greiʃən] n ὁλοκλήρωσις.

integrity [in'tegriti] n ἀκεραιότης, ἐντιμότης.

intellect ['intilekt] n διάνοια, νόησις, μυαλό ‖ ~**ual** a διανοητικός, πνευματικός ‖ n διανοούμενος.

intelligence [in'telidʒəns] n νοημοσύνη ‖ (information) πληροφορία.

intelligent [in'telidʒənt] a εὐφυής, νοήμων, μυαλωμένος ‖ ~**ly** ad εὐφυῶς, ἔξυπνα.

intelligible [in'telidʒəbl] a (κατα)νοητός, καταληπτός.

intemperate [in'tempərit] a ἀκρατής, μέθυσος.

intend [in'tend] vt (mean) προτίθεμαι ‖ **to ~ to do sth** σκοπεύω.

intense [in'tens] a ἔντονος, ἰσχυρός ‖ ~**ly** ad ὑπερβολικά, ἐντόνως.

intensify [in'tensifai] vt ἐντείνω, ἐπιτείνω.

intensity [in'tensiti] n ἔντασις, σφοδρότης, ὁρμή.

intensive [in'tensiv] a ἐντατικός ‖ ~**ly** ad ἐντόνως, ἐντατικά.

intent [in'tent] n = **intention** ‖ see below ‖ **to all** ~**s and purposes** οὐσιαστικά, πραγματικά ‖ ~**ion** n πρόθεσις ‖ (plan) τελικός σκοπός ‖ ~**ional** a σκόπιμος, ἐσκεμμένος ‖ ~**ionally** ad ἠθελημένως, σκοπίμως ‖ ~**ly** ad προσεκτικά, ἔντονα.

inter [in'tə:*] vt ἐνταφιάζω, θάβω.

inter- ['intə*] prefix διά-, μεσ(ο)-, μεταξύ.

interact [intər'ækt] vi ἀλληλεπιδρῶ ‖ ~**ion** n ἀλληλεπίδρασις.

intercede [intə'si:d] vi ἐπεμβαίνω, μεσολαβῶ, μεσιτεύω.

intercept [intə'sept] vt ἀνακόπτω, συλλαμβάνω, πιάνω ‖ ~**ion** n σύλληψις, ὑποκλοπή.

interchange ['intə'tʃeindʒ] n (exchange) ἀνταλλαγή † (roads) μεταλλαγή ‖ [intə'tʃeindʒ] vt ἀνταλλάσσω ‖ ~**able** a ἀνταλλάξιμος, ἐναλλάξιμος.

intercom ['intəkɔm] n ἐνδοσυνεννόησις.

interconnect [intəkə'nekt] vi ἀλληλοσυνδέω.

intercontinental ['intəkɔnti'nentl] a διηπειρωτικός

intercourse ['intəkɔ:s] n συναλλαγή, σχέσεις ‖ (sexual) συνουσία, γαμήσι.

interdependence [intədi'pendəns] n ἀλληλεξάρτησις.

interest ['intrist] n (curiosity) ἐνδιαφέρον ‖ (advantage) συμφέρον ‖ (money paid) τόκος ‖ (comm: stake) συμφέροντα, συμμετοχή ‖ vt ἐνδιαφέρω, προσελκύω ‖ ~**ed** a ἐνδιαφερόμενος ‖ (attentive) μὲ ἐνδιαφέρον ‖ **to be** ~**ed in** ἐνδιαφέρομαι γιά ‖ ~**ing** a ἐνδιαφέρον.

interfere [intə'fiə*] vi ἐπεμβαίνω ‖ (+ with) συγκρούομαι μέ, ἀνακατεύομαι ‖ ~**nce** n (general) ἐπέμβασις, ἀνάμιξις ‖ (TV) παράσιτα.

interim ['intərim] a προσωρινός ‖ n: **in the** ~ στὸ μεταξύ.

interior [in'tiəriə*] n ἐσωτερικόν ‖ (inland) ἐνδοχώρα ‖ a ἐσωτερικός.

interjection [intə'dʒekʃən] n (gram) ἐπιφώνημα.

interlock [intə'lɔk] vi συνδέομαι, διασταυρώνομαι ‖ vt συνδέω, συμπλέκω.

interloper ['intələupə*] n παρείσακτος.

interlude ['intəlu:d] n διάλειμμα ‖ (theat) ἰντερμέτζο.

intermarriage [intə'mæridʒ] n ἐπιγαμία, ἐπιμιξία.

intermarry [intə'mæri] vi ἐπιμιγνύομαι.

intermediary [intə'mi:diəri] n μεσάζων, μεσίτης.

intermediate [intə'mi:diət] a μεσολαβῶν, ἐνδιάμεσος.

interminable [in'tə:minəbl] a ἀτελείωτος.

intermission [intə'miʃən] n διάλειμμα, διακοπή.

intermittent [intə'mitənt] a διαλείπων ‖ ~**ly** ad διακεκομμένα.

intern [in'tə:n] vt ἡ θέτω ὑπὸ περιορισμόν ‖ ['intə:n] n (US) ἐσωτερικός ἰατρός.

internal [in'tə:nl] a ἐσωτερικός ‖ ~**ly** ad (med) ἐσωτερικῶς ‖ ~ **revenue** n (US) φορολογία.

international [intə'næʃnəl] a διεθνής ‖ n (sport) διεθνής (παίκτης).

internment [in'tə:nmənt] n ἐγκάθειρξις, περιορισμός.

interplanetary [intə'plænitəri] a διαπλανητικός.

interplay ['intəplei] n ἀλληλεπίδρασις.

Interpol ['intəpɔl] n Ἰντερπόλ.

interpret [in'tə:prit] vt ἐξηγῶ ‖ (translate) μεταφράζω ‖ (theat) ἑρμηνεύω ‖ ~**ation** n ἑρμηνεία, ἐξήγησις ‖ ~**er** n διερμηνεύς.

interrelated [intəri'leitid] a ἀλληλένδετος.

interrogate [in'terəgeit] vt ἐρωτῶ, ἀνακρίνω.

interrogation [intərə'geiʃən] n ἀνάκρισις, ἐξέτασις.

interrogative [intə'rɔgətiv] a ἐρωτηματικός.

interrogator [in'terəgeitə*] n ἀνακριτής.

interrupt [intə'rʌpt] vt διακόπτω, ἐμποδίζω ‖ ~**ion** n διακοπή.

intersect [intə'sekt] vt τέμνω, διακόπτω,

κόβω ‖ *vi* (*roads*) διασταυροῦμαι ‖ ~**ion**
n (*roads*) διασταύρωσις, σταυροδρόμι.

intersperse [intəˈspəːs] *vt* διασπείρω,
ἀναμιγνύω.

interval [ˈintəvəl] *n* διάλειμμα, διάστημα ‖
(*mus*) διάστημα ‖ **at ~s** κατὰ διαστήματα.

intervene [intəˈviːn] *vi* μεσολαβῶ, παρεμβαίνω, ἐπεμβαίνω.

intervening [intəˈviːniŋ] *a* παρεμβαίνων,
μεσολαβῶν.

intervention [intəˈvenʃən] *n* μεσολάβησις,
παρέμβασις.

interview [ˈintəvjuː] *n* (*press etc*) συνέντευξις ‖ (*for job*) συνάντησις, ραντεβοῦ ‖
vt παίρνω συνέντευξιν ‖ ~**er** *n* ὁ
λαμβάνων συνέντευξιν.

intestate [inˈtestit] *a* χωρὶς διαθήκην.

intestinal [intesˈtainl] *a* ἐντερικός.

intestine [inˈtestin] *n* ἔντερον.

intimacy [ˈintiməsi] *n* οἰκειότης ‖ (*sexual*)
συνουσία.

intimate [ˈintimit] *a* ἐνδόμυχος, ἰδιαίτερος
‖ (*familiar*) οἰκεῖος, στενός ‖ [ˈintimeit]
vt ὑποδηλῶ, ἐκδηλώνω, ὑπαινίσσομαι ‖
~**ly** *ad* στενά, κατὰ βάθος.

intimidate [inˈtimideit] *vt* (ἐκ)φοβίζω,
φοβερίζω.

intimidation [intimiˈdeiʃən] *n* ἐκφοβισμός.

into [ˈintu] *prep* (*movement*) εἰς, ἐντός,
μέσα ‖ (*change*) εἰς.

intolerable [inˈtɔlərəbl] *a* ἀνυπόφορος,
ἀφόρητος.

intolerance [inˈtɔlərəns] *n* μισαλλοδοξία.

intolerant [inˈtɔlərənt] *a* μισαλλόδοξος,
ἀδιάλλακτος.

intonation [intəuˈneiʃən] *n* διακύμανσις
τῆς φωνῆς.

intoxicate [inˈtɔksikeit] *vt* μεθῶ, ζαλίζω ‖
~**d** *a* μεθυσμένος.

intoxication [intɔksiˈkeiʃən] *n* μέθυσι,
παραζάλη.

intractable [inˈtræktəbl] *a* ἀνυπάκουος,
ἀτίθασος.

intransigent [inˈtrænsidʒənt] *a* ἀδιάλλακτος.

intransitive [inˈtrænsitiv] *a* ἀμετάβατος.

intravenous [intrəˈviːnəs] *a* ἐνδοφλέβιος.

intrepid [inˈtrepid] *a* ἀτρόμητος, ἄφοβος.

intricacy [ˈintrikəsi] *n* περιπλοκή, (τὸ)
περίπλοκον.

intricate [ˈintrikit] *a* περίπλοκος ‖ (*of
thoughts*) συγκεχυμένος.

intrigue [inˈtriːɡ] *n* μηχανορραφία ‖ *vt*
(*make curious*) προσελκύω, μαγεύω.

intriguing [inˈtriːɡiŋ] *a* (*fascinating*)
περίεργος, μυστηριώδης.

intrinsic [inˈtrinsik] *a* οὐσιαστικός,
πραγματικός.

introduce [intrəˈdjuːs] *vt* (*person*) συνιστῶ,
συστήνω ‖ (*sth new*) παρουσιάζω, μπάζω
(*subject*) εἰσάγω.

introduction [intrəˈdʌkʃən] *n* παρουσίασις,
σύστασις ‖ (*book*) εἰσαγωγή, πρόλογος.

introductory [intrəˈdʌktəri] *a* εἰσαγωγικός.

introspective [intrəuˈspektiv] *a* ἐνδοσκο-
πικός.

introvert [ˈintrəuvəːt] *a,n* ἐνδόστροφος.

intrude [inˈtruːd] *vi* (+ *on*) ἐπιβάλλω,
ἐπεμβαίνω ‖ ~**r** *n* παρείσακτος.

intrusion [inˈtruːʒən] *n* ἐπέμβασις, διείσδυσις.

intrusive [inˈtruːsiv] *a* παρείσακτος,
ἐνοχλητικός.

intuition [intjuːˈiʃən] *n* διαίσθησις, ἐνόρασις.

intuitive [inˈtjuːitiv] *a* διαισθητικός,
ἐνστικτώδης ‖ ~**ly** *ad* ἐνστικτωδῶς.

inundate [ˈinʌndeit] *vt* (*fig*) κατακλύζω,
πλημμυρίζω.

invade [inˈveid] *vt* εἰσβάλλω, καταπατῶ ‖
~**r** *n* ἐπιδρομεύς, εἰσβολεύς.

invalid [ˈinvəlid] *n* ἀσθενής, ἀνάπηρος ‖
[inˈvælid] *a* (*not valid*) ἄκυρος ‖ ~**ate**
vt ἀκυρώνω, ἀναιρῶ.

invaluable [inˈvæljuəbl] *a* ἀνεκτίμητος.

invariable [inˈvɛəriəbl] *a* ἀμετάβλητος.

invariably [inˈvɛəriəbli] *ad* ἀμεταβλήτως.

invasion [inˈveiʒən] *n* εἰσβολή, ἐπιδρομή.

invective [inˈvektiv] *n* βρισιά, λοιδωρία.

invent [inˈvent] *vt* ἐφευρίσκω ‖ (*make up*)
πλάθω ‖ ~**ion** *n* ἐφεύρεσις ‖ ~**ive**
a ἐφευρετικός, δημιουργικός ‖ ~**iveness**
n ἐφευρετικότης ‖ ~**or** *n* ἐφευρέτης.

inventory [ˈinvəntri] *n* ἀπογραφή, κατάλογος.

inverse [ˈinvəːs] *n* ἀντίστροφος, ἀνάστρο-
φος ‖ ~**ly** *ad* ἀντιστρόφως.

invert [inˈvəːt] *vt* ἀντιστρέφω ‖ ~**ed
commas** *npl* εἰσαγωγικά.

invertebrate [inˈvəːtibrit] *n* ἀσπόνδυλον.

invest [inˈvest] *vt* (*econ*) ἐπενδύω ‖ (*control*)
παρέχω, ἀναθέτω.

investigate [inˈvestigeit] *vt* ἐρευνῶ, ἐξετάζω.

investigation [investiˈgeiʃən] *n* ἔρευνα,
ἐξέτασις.

investigator [inˈvestigeitə*] *n* ἐρευνητής,
ἀναζητητής.

investiture [inˈvestitʃə*] *n* ἐγκαθίδρυσις.

investment [inˈvestmənt] *n* ἐπένδυσις.

investor [inˈvestə*] *n* κεφαλαιοῦχος,
ἐπενδύτης.

inveterate [inˈvetərit] *a* (*habitual*) φανατικός, ἀδιόρθωτος.

invigorating [inˈviɡəreitiŋ] *a* ἀναζωογονη-
τικός, τονωτικός.

invincible [inˈvinsəbl] *a* ἀήττητος.

inviolate [inˈvaiəlit] *a* ἀπαραβίαστος,
ἀπαράβατος.

invisible [inˈvizəbl] *a* (*general*) ἀόρατος,
ἄδηλος ‖ (*ink*) συμπαθητικὴ μελάνι.

invitation [inviˈteiʃən] *n* πρόσκλησις.

invite [inˈvait] *vt* (προσ)καλῶ ‖ (*attract*)
ἑλκύω, προκαλῶ.

inviting [inˈvaitiŋ] *a* δελεαστικός, ἑλκυστικός.

invoice ['invɔis] *n* τιμολόγιον ‖ *vt* τιμολογῶ.

invoke [in'vəuk] *vt* ἐπικαλοῦμαι, ἀπαιτῶ.

involuntarily [in'vɔləntərili] *ad* ἀκουσίως, ἀθέλητα.

involuntary [in'vɔləntəri] *a* ἀκούσιος, ἀθέλητα.

involve [in'vɔlv] *vt* (*include*) συνεπάγομαι ‖ (*entangle*) (περι)πλέκω, ἀνακατώνω ‖ ~d *a* περιπεπλεγμένος ‖ ~ment *n* ἀνάμιξις, μπλέξιμο.

invulnerable [in'vʌlnərəbl] *a* ἄτρωτος.

inward ['inwəd] *a* ἐσωτερικός, πρός τά μέσα ‖ ~(s) *ad* πρός τά ἔσω ‖ ~ly *ad* ἐσωτερικῶς, μέσα.

iodine ['aiədi:n] *n* ἰώδιον.

iota [ai'əutə] *n* (*fig*) γιώτα, τίποτε, ἐλάχιστη ποσότης.

Iran [i'ra:n] *n* Ἰράν, Περσία.

Iraq [i'ra:k] *n* Ἰράκ.

irascible [i'ræsibl] *a* εὐέξαπτος, ὀξύθυμος.

irate [ai'reit] *a* θυμωμένος, ἐξηγριωμένος.

Ireland ['aiələnd] *n* Ἰρλανδία.

iris ['aiəris] *n* (*anat*) ἴρις ‖ (*bot*) ἴρις, ρίδι.

Irish ['aiəriʃ] *a* Ἰρλανδικός ‖ the ~ *npl* οἱ Ἰρλανδοί ‖ ~man *n* Ἰρλανδός ‖ ~woman *n* Ἰρλανδή.

irk [ə:k] *vt* ἐνοχλῶ, στενοχωρῶ.

iron ['aiən] *n* σίδηρος ‖ (*flat iron*) σίδερο ‖ (*golf club*) ρόπαλον τοῦ γκόλφ ‖ *a* σιδερένιος ‖ *vt* σιδερώνω ‖ ~s *npl* (*chains*) ἁλυσίδες, δεσμά ‖ to ~ out *vt* (*crease*) σιδερώνω ‖ (*difficulties*) ἐξομαλύνω ‖ ~ curtain *n* σιδηροῦν παραπέτασμα.

ironic(al) [ai'rɔnik(əl)] *a* εἰρωνικός ‖ ~ally *ad* εἰρωνικά.

ironing ['aiəniŋ] *n* σιδέρωμα ‖ ~ board *n* σιδερώστρα, τάβλα.

ironmonger ['aiənmʌŋgə*] *n* σιδηροπώλης ‖ ~'s (shop) *n* σιδηροπωλεῖο.

iron ore ['aiənɔ:*] *n* σιδηρομετάλλευμα.

ironworks ['aiənwə:ks] *n* σιδηρουργεῖον.

irony ['aiərəni] *n* εἰρωνεία.

irrational [i'ræʃənl] *a* παράλογος.

irreconcilable [irekən'sailəbl] *a* ἀδιάλλακτος, ἀσυμβίβαστος.

irredeemable [iri'di:məbl] *a* (*comm*) ἀνεξαγόραστος.

irrefutable [iri'fju:təbl] *a* ἀκαταμάχητος, ἀδιάψευστος.

irregular [i'regjulə*] *a* (*not regular*) ἀκανόνιστος, ἄτακτος ‖ (*not smooth*) ἀνώμαλος ‖ (*against rule*) ἀντικανονικός, ἀντίθετος ‖ ~ity *n* ἀνωμαλία.

irrelevance [i'reləvəns] *n* (τό) ἄσχετον.

irrelevant [i'reləvənt] *a* ἄσχετος, ξεκάρφωτος.

irreligious [iri'lidʒəs] *a* ἄθρησκος, ἀσεβής.

irreparable [i'repərəbl] *a* ἀνεπανόρθωτος, ἀγιάτρευτος.

irreplaceable [iri'pleisəbl] *a* ἀναντικατάστατος.

irrepressible [iri'presəbl] *a* ἀκατάσχετος, ἀκάθεκτος.

irreproachable [iri'prəutʃəbl] *a* ἄμεμπτος, ἄψογος.

irresistible [iri'zistəbl] *a* ἀσυγκράτητος, ἀκαταμάχητος.

irresolute [i'rezəlu:t] *a* ἀναποφάσιστος, διστακτικός.

irrespective [iri'spektiv] ~ of *prep* ἀνεξάρτητα ἀπό.

irresponsibility ['irispɔnsə'biliti] *n* (τό) ἀνεύθυνον, ἀμυαλιά.

irresponsible [iris'pɔnsəbl] *a* ἀπερίσκεπτος, ἐλαφρόμυαλος.

irretrievably [iri'tri:vəbli] *ad* ἀνεπανορθώτως, ὁριστικά.

irreverence [i'revərəns] *n* ἀνευλάβεια, ἀσέβεια.

irreverent [i'revərənt] *a* ἀσεβής, ἀναιδής.

irrevocable [i'revəkəbl] *a* ἀμετάκλητος, ἀνέκκλητος.

irrigate ['irigeit] *vt* ἀρδεύω, ποτίζω.

irrigation [iri'geiʃən] *n* ἄρδευσις, πότισμα.

irritability [iritə'biliti] *n* ὀξυθυμία, (τό) εὐέξαπτον.

irritable ['iritəbl] *a* ὀξύθυμος, εὐέξαπτος.

irritant ['iritənt] *n* ἐρεθιστικόν.

irritate ['iriteit] *vt* (*annoy*) (ἐξ)ἐρεθίζω, ἐκνευρίζω ‖ (*skin etc*) ἐρεθίζω.

irritating ['iriteitiŋ] *a* ἐρεθιστικός, ἐκνευριστικός.

irritation [iri'teiʃən] *n* ἐρεθισμός, θυμός.

is [iz] *see* be.

Islam ['izla:m] *n* Ἰσλάμ.

island ['ailənd] *n* νησί ‖ ~er *n* νησιώτης.

isle [ail] *n* νησί, νησάκι.

isn't ['iznt] = is not ‖ *see* be.

isobar ['aisəuba:*] *n* ἰσοβαρής.

isolate ['aisəuleit] *vt* (ἀπο)μονώνω ‖ ~d *a* ἀπομονωμένος, ἀπόμερος.

isolation [aisəu'leiʃən] *n* ἀπομόνωσις.

isotope ['aisəutəup] *n* ἰσότοπον.

Israel ['izreil] *n* Ἰσραήλ ‖ ~i *n* Ἰσραηλινός.

issue ['iʃu:] *n* (*question*) ὑπόθεσις, ζήτημα ‖ (*giving out*) ἔκδοσις, διανομή, χορήγησις ‖ (*copy*) τεῦχος, φύλλον ‖ (*offspring*) ἀπόγονοι ‖ *vt* (*rations*) διανέμω ‖ (*orders*) ἐκδίδω, δημοσιεύω ‖ (*equipment*) διανέμω, ἐκδίδω ‖ at ~ ὑπό συζήτησιν.

isthmus ['isməs] *n* ἰσθμός.

it [it] *pron* τόν, τήν, τό, αὐτό.

Italian [i'tæliən] *a* ἰταλικός ‖ *n* (*person*) Ἰταλός ‖ (*ling*) ἰταλικά.

italic [i'tælik] *a* κυρτός, πλάγιος ‖ ~s *npl* πλάγια γραφή.

Italy [i'təli] *n* Ἰταλία.

itch [itʃ] *n* (*fig*) πόθος, ὄρεξι ‖ (*med*) φαγούρα, ψώρα ‖ *vi* ἔχω φαγούρα ‖ ~ing *n* φαγούρα.

it'd ['itd] = it would, it had ‖ *see* would, have.

item ['aitəm] *n* (*on list*) εἶδος, κονδύλιον,

ἐγγραφή ‖ (in programme) νούμερο ‖ (in agenda) θέμα ‖ (in newspaper) εἴδησις ‖ ~ize vt ἀναλύω.
itinerant [i'tinərənt] a περιοδεύων.
itinerary [ai'tinərəri] n δρομολόγιον.
it'll ['itl] = it will, it shall ‖ see will, shall.
its [its] poss a του ‖ poss pron ἰδικός του.
it's [its] = it is, it has ‖ see be, have.
itself [it'self] pron τόν ἑαυτόν του.
I've [aiv] = I have ‖ see have.
ivory ['aivəri] n ἐλεφαντοστοῦν ‖ ~ tower n (fig) τόπος μονώσεως.
ivy ['aivi] n κισσός.

J, j

jab [dʒæb] vti κτυπῶ, κεντῶ, μπήζω.
jabber ['dʒæbə*] vi φλυαρῶ, τραυλίζω.
jack [dʒæk] n (mech) γρύλλος ‖ (cards) βαλές, φάντης ‖ to ~ up vt σηκώνω μέ γρύλλο.
jackdaw ['dʒækdɔ:] n κολοιός, καλιακούδα.
jacket ['dʒækit] n ζακέττα, σακκάκι ‖ (mech) χιτώνιον, πουκάμισο.
jack-knife ['dʒæknaif] n μεγάλος σουγιάς, κολοκοτρώνης.
jade [dʒeid] n (stone) νεφρίτης.
jaded ['dʒeidid] a κουρασμένος, τσακισμένος.
jagged ['dʒægid] a ἀνώμαλος, ὀδοντωτός, μυτερός.
jail [dʒeil] n φυλακή ‖ ~break n δραπέτευσις ‖ ~er n δεσμοφύλαξ.
jam [dʒæm] n (fruit) μαρμελάδα ‖ (stoppage) ἐμπλοκή, φρακάρισμα, στρίμωγμα ‖ vt ἐνσφηνώνω, σφίγγω, στριμώχνω ‖ vi σφίγγομαι, φρακάρω, κολλῶ.
jangle ['dʒæŋgl] vti ἠχῶ κακόηχα, κουδουνίζω.
janitor ['dʒænitə*] n (caretaker) θυρωρός, ἐπιστάτης.
January ['dʒænjuəri] n Γενάρης.
Japan [dʒə'pæn] n `Ιαπωνία ‖ ~ese a `Ιαπωνικός ‖ n (ling) ἰαπωνική.
jar [dʒɑ:*] n (glass) βάζο, λαγήνι, στάμνα ‖ vi τραντάζω, συγκρούομαι.
jargon ['dʒɑ:gən] n ἀλαμπουρνέζικα.
jarring ['dʒɑːriŋ] a (sound) κακόηχος, σοκάρων, ἐνοχλητικός.
jasmin(e) ['dʒæzmin] n γιασεμί.
jaundice ['dʒɔ:ndis] n ἴκτερος, χρυσή ‖ ~d a (attitude) κακόβουλος, φθονερός.
jaunt [dʒɔ:nt] n βόλτα, περίπατος ‖ ~y a ζωηρός, ξένοιαστος.
javelin ['dʒævlin] n ἀκόντιον, κοντάρι.
jaw [dʒɔ:] n σαγόνι, μασέλα ‖ ~s npl (fig) στόμα.
jazz [dʒæz] n τζάζ ‖ to ~ up vt ζωηρεύω, ἐπιταχύνω ‖ ~band n τζάζ-μπάντ.
jealous ['dʒeləs] a (envious) ζηλιάρης ‖ (watchful) ζηλότυπος, προσεκτικός ‖

~ly ad ζηλοτύπως, ἐπιμελῶς ‖ ~y n ζήλεια.
jeans [dʒi:nz] npl ντρίλινο παντελόνι.
jeep [dʒi:p] n τζίπ.
jeer [dʒiə*] vi (+ at) κοροϊδεύω, χλευάζω, γιουχαΐζω ‖ n ἐμπαιγμός, γιούχα ‖ ~ing a σκωπτικός.
jelly ['dʒeli] n ζελέ(ς) ‖ ~fish n μέδουσα, τσούχτρα.
jeopardize ['dʒepədaiz] vt διακινδυνεύω.
jeopardy ['dʒepədi] n: in ~ ἐν κινδύνω.
jerk [dʒə:k] n τίναγμα, τράνταγμα ‖ (US: idiot) χαζός ‖ vti τινάζω, τραντάζω.
jerkin ['dʒə:kin] n πέτσινο σακκάκι.
jerky ['dʒə:ki] a ἀπότομος, κοφτός.
jersey ['dʒə:zi] n φανέλλα.
jest [dʒest] n ἀστεϊσμός, χωρατό, ἀστεῖο ‖ vi κάνω ἀστεῖα, ἀστειεύομαι.
jet [dʒet] n (stream) ἐκροή, ἀναπήδησις ‖ (spout) στόμιον, μπέκ ‖ (aviat) τζέτ ‖ ~-black a κατάμαυρος ‖ ~ engine n κινητήρ τζέτ.
jettison ['dʒetisn] vt ἀπορρίπτω.
jetty ['dʒeti] n μῶλος, λιμενοβραχίων.
Jew [dʒu:] n `Εβραῖος.
jewel ['dʒu:əl] n κόσμημα ‖ (fig) διαμάντι χρυσός ‖ ~ler, (US) ~er n κοσμηματοπώλης ‖ ~(l)er's (shop) n κοσμηματοπωλεῖον ‖ ~(le)ry n κοσμήματα, διαμαντικά.
Jewess ['dʒu:is] n `Εβραία.
Jewish ['dʒu:iʃ] a ἑβραϊκός.
jib [dʒib] n (naut) ἀρτέμων, φλόκος ‖ vi ἀρνοῦμαι, κωλώνω, κλωτσῶ.
jibe [dʒaib] n πείραγμα, ἀστεῖο.
jiffy ['dʒifi] n (col) in a ~ στή στιγμή, ἀμέσως.
jigsaw ['dʒigsɔ:] n (also ~ puzzle) (παιχνίδι) συναρμολογήσεως.
jilt [dʒilt] vt διώχνω, στρίβω.
jingle ['dʒiŋgl] n κουδούνισμα, γκλίνγκλίν ‖ vti κουδουνίζω.
jinx [dʒiŋks] n (col) γρουσούζης.
jitters ['dʒitəz] npl (col) to get the ~ τρέμω, φοβᾶμαι.
jittery ['dʒitəri] a (col) φοβιτσιάρικος, ἐκνευριστικός.
jiujitsu [dʒu:'dʒitsu:] n ζίου-ζίτσου.
job [dʒɔb] n ἔργον, ἐργασία ‖ (position) θέσις, δουλειά ‖ (difficult task) ἀγγαρεία, χαμαλήκι ‖ ~bing a μέ τό κομμάτι, κατ' ἀποκοπήν ‖ ~less a ἄνεργος.
jockey ['dʒɔki] n τζόκεϋ ‖ vi ἑλίσσομαι, μανουβράρω.
jocular ['dʒɔkjulə*] a ἀστεῖος, εὔθυμος.
jog [dʒɔg] vt σπρώχνω, σκουντῶ ‖ vi (move jerkily) κλυδωνίζω, τραντάζω.
john [dʒɔn] n (US col: loo) ἀποχωρητήριο.
join [dʒɔin] vt (fasten) ἑνώνω, συνδέω, ματίζω ‖ (club) ἐγγράφομαι, γίνομαι μέλος ‖ vi (the army) κατατάσσομαι ‖ n ἕνωσις, ραφή ‖ ~er n μαραγκός ‖ ~ery n ξυλουργική ‖ ~t n (tech) ἁρμός,

ἄρθρωσις) (of meat) τεμάχιον κρέατος | (col: place) καταγώγιον, τρώγλη | ~tly ad ὁμοῦ, μαζί.

joist [dʒɔist] n δοκάρι, πατερό.

joke [dʒəuk] n ἀστεῖο, χωρατό, καλαμπούρι | vi ἀστεῖζομαι || ~r n ἀστειολόγος | (cards) μπαλλαντέρ.

joking ['dʒəukiŋ] a ἀστεῖος, ἀστειευόμενος | ~ly ad ἀστεῖα.

jollity ['dʒɔliti] n εὐθυμία, χαρά, γιορτή.

jolly ['dʒɔli] a εὔθυμος, χαρούμενος, κεφάτος | ad (col) ἐξαιρετικά, πολύ | to ~ s.o. along διασκεδάζω κάποιον.

jolt [dʒəult] n τίναγμα, τράνταγμα | (col) ξάφνιασμα | vt τινάζω, κουνῶ.

jostle ['dʒɔsl] vt σπρώχνω.

jot [dʒɔt] n: not one ~ οὔτε ἴχνος, οὐδέ κατά κεραίαν | to ~ down vt σημειώνω, γράφω | ~ter n σημειωματάριον.

journal ['dʒə:nl] n ἐφημερίδα, περιοδικόν | ~ese n δημοσιογραφικόν ὕφος | ~ism n δημοσιογραφία | ~ist n δημοσιο-γράφος.

journey ['dʒə:ni] n ταξίδι, διαδρομή.

jovial ['dʒəuviəl] a εὔθυμος, κεφάτος, φαιδρός.

joy [dʒɔi] n χαρά, εὐθυμία | ~ful a περι-χαρής, χαρμόσυνος | ~fully ad χαρού-μενα, ~ous a εὔθυμος | ~ ride n περίπατος μέ αὐτοκίνητο.

jubilant ['dʒu:bilənt] a χαρούμενος, πανηγυρίζων.

jubilation [dʒu:bi'leiʃən] n ἀγαλλίασις, χαρά.

jubilee ['dʒu:bili:] n γιορτή.

judge [dʒʌdʒ] n (in court) δικαστής) (race-track) κριτής | (in dispute) πραγματο-γνώμων, κριτής | vt δικάζω, κρίνω | vi (estimate) ὑπολογίζω, θεωρῶ | ~ment, **judgment** n (sentence) δικαστική ἀπόφασις | (opinion) κρίσις, γνώμη.

judicial [dʒu:'diʃəl] a (law) δικαστικός | (discerning) κριτικός, δίκαιος.

judicious [dʒu:'diʃəs] a συνετός, σώφρων, φρόνιμος.

judo ['dʒu:dəu] n τζούντο.

jug [dʒʌg] n κανάτι, στάμνα.

juggle ['dʒʌgl] vi ταχυδακτυλουργῶ, ἐξαπατῶ | ~r n ταχυδακτυλουργός.

Jugoslav ['ju:gəu'sla:v] = **Yugoslav.**

jugular ['dʒʌgjulə*] a (vein) σφαγῖτις.

juice [dʒu:s] n χημός, ζουμί.

juiciness ['dʒu:sinis] n ζουμεράδα.

juicy ['dʒu:si] a χυμώδης, ζουμερός.

jukebox ['dʒu:kbɔks] n τζούκ μπόξ.

July [dʒu:'lai] n Ἰούλιος.

jumble ['dʒʌmbl] n ἀνακάτεμα, κυκεών, μπέρδεμα | vt (also ~ up) ἀνακατεύω, μπερδεύω.

jumbo ['dʒʌmbəu] attr: ~ jet n τζάμπο τζέτ.

jump [dʒʌmp] vi/vt πηδῶ, πηδῶ πάνω ἀπό, ὑπερπηδῶ | n πήδημα, ἅλμα | ~ed-up a (col) νεόπλουτος | ~er n μπλούζα,

ριχτή ζακέττα | ~y a νευρικός.

junction ['dʒʌŋkʃən] n (road) διασταύρωσις | (rail) διακλάδωσις.

juncture ['dʒʌŋktiʃə*] n: at this ~ στό σημεῖο αὐτό.

June [dʒu:n] n Ἰούνιος.

jungle ['dʒʌŋgl] n (tropical) ζούγκλα.

junior ['dʒu:niə*] a (in age) νεώτερος | (in rank) κατώτερος, ὑφιστάμενος | n (US: school) προτελειόφοιτος.

junk [dʒʌŋk] n (rubbish) σκουπίδια, παλιοπράγματα | (ship) τζόγκα | ~shop n παλιατζίδικο.

junta ['dʒʌntə] n χούντα.

jurisdiction [dʒuəris'dikʃən] n δικαιοδοσία.

jurisprudence [dʒuəris'pru:dəns] n νομο-λογία, νομομάθεια.

juror ['dʒuərə*] n ἔνορκος.

jury ['dʒuəri] n ἔνορκοι | (of contest) κριτική ἐπιτροπή | ~man n = **juror.**

just [dʒʌst] a (fair, right) δίκαιος, σωστός | (exact) ἀκριβής | ad (exactly) ἀκριβῶς | (barely) μόλις | ~ as I arrived μόλις ἔφθασα | I have ~ arrived μόλις ἦλθα | ~ a little τόσο δά, ὀλίγο | ~ now πρό λίγου, μόλις τώρα | ~ you and me ἐμεῖς μόνον, σύ κι ἐγώ.

justice ['dʒʌstis] n (fairness) δικαιοσύνη | (magistrate) δικαστικός, δικαστής.

justifiable ['dʒʌstifaiəbl] a δικαιολογή-σιμος, εὔλογος.

justifiably ['dʒʌstifaiəbli] ad δικαιολογη-μένα.

justification [dʒʌstifi'keiʃən] n δικαίωσις, δικαιολογία.

justify ['dʒʌstifai] vt (prove right) αἰτιολογῶ | (defend etc) δικαιώνω, δικαιολογῶ.

justly ['dʒʌstli] ad δίκαια, ὀρθῶς.

justness ['dʒʌstnis] n ὀρθότης, τό δίκαιον.

jut [dʒʌt] vi (also ~ out) προεξέχω.

juvenile ['dʒu:vənail] a νεανικός, παιδικός | n νέος, νεανίας.

juxtapose ['dʒʌkstəpəuz] vt (ἀντι)παρα-θέτω.

juxtaposition [dʒʌkstəpə'ziʃən] n (ἀντι)-παράθεσις.

K, k

kaleidoscope [kə'laidəskəup] n καλειδο-σκόπιον.

kangaroo [kæŋgə'ru:] n καγκουρώ.

keel [ki:l] n τρόπις, καρίνα.

keen [ki:n] a (sharp) ὀξύς, ἐπιμελής, θερμός | ~ly ad ἔντονα, βαθειά, σφόδρα | ~ness n ζῆλος, ἐνθουσιασμός.

keep [ki:p] (irreg v) vt (have) ἔχω, κρατῶ, συντηρῶ | (take care of) φυλάω, συντηρῶ, τρέφω | (detain) (κατα)κρατῶ, καθυστερῶ || (be faithful) τηρῶ, σέβομαι | μένω πιστός εἰς | vi (continue) συνεχίζω, ἐξακολουθῶ | (of food) διατηρούμαι,

J
K

krατῶ ‖ (remain: quiet etc) μένω, στέκομαι ‖ n τροφή, συντήρησις, ἔξοδα συντηρήσεως ‖ (tower) (ἀκρό)πύργος ‖ to ~ back vti κρατῶ πίσω, ἀπομακρύνομαι, κρύπτω ‖ to ~ on vi συνεχίζω, ἐξακολουθῶ νά φορῶ ‖ to ~ out vt μένω ἔξω, ἀπέχω ‖ '~ out!' 'ἀπαγορεύεται ἡ εἴσοδος!' ‖ to ~ up vi (+ with) διατηρῶ, καλλιεργῶ ‖ ~ing n (care) φύλαξις, συντήρησις ‖ in ~ing with σύμφωνος μέ, ἀνάλογα μέ.

keg [keg] n βαρελάκι.

kennel ['kenl] n σπιτάκι σκύλου.

kept [kept] pt,pp of **keep**.

kerb(stone) ['kə:b(stəun)] n κράσπεδον πεζοδρομίου.

kernel ['kə:nl] n πυρήν, κόκκος, ψύχα.

kerosene ['kerəsi:n] n φωτιστικόν πετρέλαιον, παραφίνη.

kestrel ['kestrəl] n γεράκι, κιρκινέζι.

ketchup ['ketʃəp] n κετσάπ, σάλτσα τομάτας.

kettle ['ketl] n χύτρα, τσαγιέρα ‖ ~ **drum** n εἶδος τυμπάνου.

key [ki:] n κλειδί ‖ (of problem) κλείς ‖ (set of answers) κλείς, λύσις ‖ (lever) πλῆκτρον ‖ (mus) τόνος ‖ a (position etc) βασικός, καίριος ‖ ~**board** n πλῆκτρον, κλαβιέ ‖ ~**hole** n κλειδαρότρυπα ‖ ~**note** n κυρία ἰδέα, γνώμων ‖ ~ **ring** n κρίκος κλειδιῶν.

khaki ['ka:ki] n,a χακί.

kibbutz [ki'buts] n κιμπούτς.

kick [kik] vt λακτίζω, κλωτσῶ ‖ vi (col) παραπονιέμαι, ἀντιδρῶ ‖ n λάκτισμα, κλωτσιά ‖ (thrill) συγκίνησις ‖ to ~ **around** vi (col) σέρνομαι, χαζεύω ‖ to ~ **off** vi (sport) δίνω τή πρώτη κλωτσιά ‖ to ~ **up** vi (col) κάνω φασαρία ‖ ~**off** n (sport) ἐναρκτήριον λάκτισμα.

kid [kid] n (child) πιτσιρίκος, παιδάκι ‖ (goat) κατσικάκι, ρίφι ‖ (leather) σεβρό.

kidnap ['kidnæp] vt ἀπάγω, κλέβω ‖ ~**per** n ἀπαγωγεύς ‖ ~**ping** n ἀπαγωγή.

kidney ['kidni] n νεφρόν.

kill [kil] vt (murder) φονεύω, σκοτώνω ‖ (destroy) ξερριζώνω, ἀφανίζω ‖ n κυνήγι ‖ ~**er** n φονέας, φονιάς.

kiln [kiln] n καμίνι, κλίβανος.

kilo ['ki:ləu] n κιλό ‖ ~**gramme**, (US) ~**gram** n χιλιόγραμμον ‖ ~**metre**, (US) ~**meter** n χιλιόμετρον ‖ ~**watt** n κιλοβάτ.

kilt [kilt] n φουστανέλλα.

kimono [ki'məunəu] n κιμονό.

kin [kin] n συγγενείς, συγγενολόϊ.

kind [kaind] a καλός, καλοκάγαθος, καλόβολος ‖ n εἶδος ‖ **a ~ of** ἄς τόν ποῦμε, κάποιος ‖ (two) **of a ~** τοῦ ἰδίου φυράματος ‖ **in ~** (merchandise) εἰς εἶδος ‖ (same way) μέ τό ἴδιο νόμισμα.

kindergarten ['kindəga:tn] n νηπιαγωγεῖον.

kind-hearted ['kaind'ha:tid] a καλόκαρδος.

kindle ['kindl] vt ἀνάβω ‖ (rouse) ἐξάπτω, προκαλῶ.

kindliness ['kaindlinis] n καλωσύνη.

kindly ['kaindli] a καλός, εὐγενικός ‖ ad εὐγενικά, μαλακά, φιλικά.

kindness ['kaindnis] n ἀγαθότης, καλωσύνη.

kindred ['kindrid] a συγγενής, συγγενικός.

kinetic [ki'netik] a (energy) κινητικός.

king [kiŋ] n βασιλιᾶς ‖ (cards) ρήγας ‖ ~**dom** n βασίλειον ‖ ~**fisher** n ψαροφάγος, μπιρμπίλι ‖ ~**pin** n (of game) κεντρικός πασσαλίσκος ‖ (indispensable person) κινητήριος μοχλός.

kink [kiŋk] n ζάρα, στράβωμα ‖ ~**y** a (fig) ἰδιότροπος ‖ (hair) σγουρός.

kiosk ['ki:ɔsk] n (tel) θάλαμος ‖ (shop) κιόσκι, περίπτερον.

kipper ['kipə*] n καπνιστή ρέγγα.

kiss [kis] n φιλί, φίλημα ‖ vt φιλῶ ‖ vi **they** ~**ed** φιλήθηκαν.

kit [kit] n σύνεργα, ἀτομικά εἴδη ‖ ~**bag** n σάκκος.

kitchen ['kitʃin] n κουζίνα ‖ ~ **garden** n λαχανόκηπος ‖ ~ **sink** n νεροχύτης.

kite [kait] n (χαρτ)ἀετός ‖ (bird) τσίφτης

kith [kiθ] n: ~ **and kin** φίλοι καί συγ γενείς.

kitten ['kitn] n γατάκι.

kitty ['kiti] n (pool of money) γκανιότα βιδάνιο.

kleptomaniac [kleptəu'meiniæk] n κλεπτο μανής.

knack [næk] n ἐπιδεξιότης, κόλπο.

knapsack ['næpsæk] n δισάκκι, γυλιός.

knave [neiv] n (cards) βαλές, φάντης.

knead [ni:d] vt ζυμώνω.

knee [ni:] n γόνατο ‖ ~**cap** n ἐπιγονατίς ‖ ~**deep** a ὡς τό γόνατο.

kneel [ni:l] (irreg v) vi γονατίζω.

knell [nel] n καμπάνισμα, κωδωνοκρουσία

knelt [nelt] pt,pp of **kneel**.

knew [nju:] pt of **know**.

knickers ['nikəz] npl κυλόττα.

knife [naif] n μαχαίρι ‖ vt μαχαιρώνω.

knight [nait] n ἱππότης ‖ (chess) ἄλογο ‖ ~**hood** n ἱπποτισμός, ἱπποσύνη.

knit [nit] vt πλέκω ‖ vi συγκολλῶ ‖ ~**ting** n πλέξιμο, πλεκτική ‖ ~**ting machine** n πλεκτομηχανή ‖ ~**ting needle** n βελόνα (τοῦ πλεξίματος) ‖ ~**wear** n πλεκτό τρικό.

knives [naivz] npl of **knife**.

knob [nɔb] n (of door) πόμολο ‖ (butter etc) κομμάτι.

knock [nɔk] vt (criticize) βρίζω, κακολογῶ ‖ vi προσκρούω, κτυπῶ ‖ n κτύπημα ‖ to ~ **off** vi (finish) σταματῶ ‖ to ~ **out** vt βγάζω, τινάζω ‖ (sport) βγάζω νόκ-ἄουτ ‖ ~**er** n (on door) κτυπητήρι ‖ ~**-kneed** a στραβοπόδης, στραβοκάνης ‖ ~**out** n (lit) νόκ-ἄουτ ‖ (fig) σπουδαῖο πρᾶγμα.

knot [nɔt] n (of rope etc) κόμπος, δεσμός ‖

(σ; *ribbon*) κόμπος (*lump*) ρόζος (*measure*) κόμβος vt δένω κόμπο ~ted a κομπιασμένος.

know [nəu] (*irreg v*) vti (*be aware of*) ξέρω (*recognize*) γνωρίζω, διακρίνω, ξέρω **to ~ how to do** ξέρω πώς ~-**how** *n* μέθοδος, τέχνη ~**ing** *a* νοήμων, ἔξυπνος, πονηρός ~**ingly** *ad* σκοπίμως, πονηρά ‖ ~-(**it**-)**all** *n* παντογνώστης.

knowledge ['nɔlidʒ] *n* (*what one knows*) γνῶσις, μάθησις (*information*) εἴδησις, πληροφορίες ‖ ~-**able** *a* καλῶς πληροφορημένος, μορφωμένος.

known [nəun] *pp of* **know**.

knuckle ['nʌkl] *n* φάλαγξ, κλείδωσις (*of meat*) κότσι.

Koran [kɔ'ra:n] *n* Κοράνιον.

L, l

lab [læb] *n* (*col*) ἐργαστήριον.

label ['leibl] *n* ἐτικέττα vt ἐπιγράφω, κολλῶ ἐτικέττα.

labor ['leibə*] *n* (*US*) = **labour**.

laboratory [lə'bɔrətəri] *n* ἐργαστήριον.

laborious [lə'bɔ:riəs] *a* κοπιώδης, ἐπίπονος.

labour ['leibə*] *n* ἐργασία, μόχθος (*workmen*) ἐργάτες ‖ ~**er** *n* ἐργάτης ‖ **L~ Party** *n* Ἐργατικόν Κόμμα.

laburnum [lə'bɔ:nəm] *n* κύτισος, λαβούρνον, λιβόρνο.

labyrinth ['læbərinθ] *n* λαβύρινθος.

lace [leis] *n* δαντέλλα (*braid*) σειρήτι (*cord*) κορδόνι vt δένω, πλέκω, βάζω δαντέλλες.

lacerate ['læsəreit] vt ξεσχίζω.

lack [læk] vt στεροῦμαι *n* ἔλλειψις **for ~ of** λόγω ἐλλείψεως.

lackadaisical [lækə'deizikəl] *a* ἄτονος νωθρός.

laconic [lə'kɔnik] *a* λακωνικός.

lacquer ['lækə*] *n* βερνίκι, λάκα.

lad [læd] *n* (*boy*) ἀγόρι (*young man*) παλληκάρι.

ladder ['lædə*] *n* (*lit*) σκάλα, ἀνεμόσκαλα (*fig*) (κοινωνική) κλῖμαξ.

laden ['leidn] *a* φορτωμένος.

ladle ['leidl] *n* κουτάλα.

lady ['leidi] *n* κυρία ‖ (*title*) λαίδη ‖ '**Ladies**' (*lavatory*) 'Κυριῶν', 'Γυναικῶν' ‖ ~**bird**, (*US*) ~**bug** *n* λαμπρίτσα, πασχαλίτσα ‖ ~-**in-waiting** *n* Κυρία τῶν Τιμῶν ‖ ~**like** *a* ἀρχοντική, εὐγενική ‖ ~**ship** *n* κυρία, ἡ εὐγενία της.

lag [læg] *n* (*delay*) ὑστέρησις, ἐπιβράδυνσις ‖ vi (*also* ~ **behind**) βραδυπορῶ ‖ vt (*pipes*) ἐπενδύω, φασκιώνω.

lager ['la:gə*] *n* ἐλαφρά μπύρα, λάγκερ.

lagging ['lægiŋ] *n* μονωτική ἐπένδυσις.

lagoon [lə'gu:n] *n* λιμνοθάλασσα.

laid [leid] *pt,pp of* **lay** ‖ **to be ~ up** εἶμαι κρεβατωμένος.

lair [lɛə*] *n* φωλιά, ἄντρον.

laity ['leiiti] *n* οἱ λαϊκοί, οἱ κοσμικοί.

lake [leik] *n* λίμνη.

lamb [læm] *n* ἀρνάκι (*meat*) ἀρνί ~ **chop** *n* παϊδάκι.

lame [leim] *a* κουτσός (*excuse*) μή πειστικός.

lament [lə'ment] *n* θρῆνος vt θρηνῶ, ὀδύρομαι ‖ ~**able** *a* ἀξιοθρήνητος ~**ation** *n* θρῆνος.

laminated ['læmineitid] *a* φυλλωτός.

lamp [læmp] *n* λύχνος, λυχνάρι (*globe*) λάμπα (*in street*) φανάρι ~**post** *n* φανοστάτης ~**shade** *n* ἀμπαζούρ.

lance [la:ns] *n* λόγχη vt ἐγχειρίζω, ἀνοίγω ~ **corporal** *n* ὑποδεκανεύς.

lancet ['la:nsit] *n* νυστέρι.

land [lænd] *n* γῆ, στερεά (*ground*) γῆ, ἔδαφος (*country*) γῆ, χώρα (*estate*) κτῆμα vi (*from ship*) ἀποβιβάζομαι (*aviat*) προσγειοῦμαι (*fig: arrive, fall*) πέφτω vt (*obtain*) πιάνω, λαμβάνω (*passengers, goods*) ἀποβιβάζω, ξεφορτώνω ‖ ~**ed** *a* κτηματικός ‖ ~**ing** *n* ἀπο(βί)βασις (*aviat*) προσγείωσις (*platform*) πλατύσκαλον ~**ing craft** *n* ἀποβατικόν σκάφος ~**ing stage** *n* ἀποβάθρα ~**ing strip** *n* λωρίδα προσγειώσεως ~**lady** *n* σπιτονοικοκυρά ‖ ~**locked** *a* μεσόγειος ‖ ~**lord** *n* σπιτονοικοκύρης (*innkeeper*) ξενοδόχος ~**lubber** *n* στεριανός ‖ ~**mark** *n* ὁρόσημον ‖ ~**owner** *n* γαιοκτήμων ‖ ~**scape** *n* τοπίον (*painting*) ζωγραφική τοπίων ~**slide** *n* (*geog*) (κατ)ὀλίσθησις (*pol*) ἐντυπωσιακή στροφή.

lane [lein] *n* δρομίσκος, μονοπάτι (*of road*) λωρίδα, διάδρομος (*sport*) ἀτομική πίστα, λωρίδα.

language ['læŋgwidʒ] *n* γλῶσσα (*national*) γλῶσσα, διάλεκτος (*style*) γλῶσσα ὁμιλία.

languid ['læŋgwid] *a* νωθρός, ἀδρανής.

languish ['læŋgwiʃ] *vi* κυττάζω τρυφερά, λιγώνω.

lank [læŋk] *a* μακριά καί ἴσια ~**y** *a* μακρύς καί λεπτός.

lanolin ['lænəulin] *n* λανολίνη.

lantern ['læntən] *n* φανάρι.

lanyard ['lænjəd] *n* κορδόνι.

lap [læp] *n* ἀγκαλιά (*sport*) γύρος, βόλτα vt γλείφω vi (*of waves*) παφλάζω ~**dog** *n* χαϊδεμένο σκυλάκι.

lapel [lə'pel] *n* πέτο.

lapse [læps] *n* σφάλμα (*fall from virtue*) παράβασις (*of time*) παρέλευσις ἐκπνοή.

larceny ['la:səni] *n* κλοπή.

lard [la:d] *n* λαρδί.

larder ['la:də*] *n* ἀποθήκη τροφίμων, κελλάρι.

large [la:dʒ] *a* (*broad*) εὐρύχωρος, ἐκτενής (*big, numerous*) μεγάλος **at ~** (*free*) ἐλεύθερος ‖ (*extensively*) γενικά ‖ **by and** ~ γενικά ‖ **~ly** *ad* μεγάλως, σέ μεγάλο βαθμό ‖ **~-scale** *a* εἰς μεγάλη κλίμακα, μεγάλος ‖ **~sse** *n* (*generosity*) γενναιοδωρία.

lark [la:k] *n* (*bird*) κορυδαλλός ‖ (*joke*) ἀστεῖο, φάρσα ‖ **to** ~ **about** *vi* (*col*) ἀστιεύομαι, κάνω φάρσες.

larva ['la:və] *n* νύμφη.

laryngitis [lærin'dʒaitis] *n* λαρυγγῖτις.

larynx ['læriŋks] *n* λαρύγγι.

lash [læʃ] *a* (*stroke*) καμτσικιά ‖ *vt* (*beat against*) δέρνω, ξεσπῶ, κτυπῶ ‖ (*whip*) μαστιγώνω ‖ (*bind*) (προσ)δένω ‖ **to** ~ **out** *vi* (*with fists*) ἐπιτίθεμαι, ἐφορμῶ ‖ (*spend money*) κάνω σπατάλες ‖ **~ing** *n* (*beating*) μαστίγωσις ‖ (*tie*) πρόσδεσις, δέσιμο ‖ **~ings of** (*col*) ἀφθονία.

lass [læs] *n* κορίτσι, κοπέλλα.

lasso [læ'su:] *n* λάσσο ‖ *vt* πιάνω μέ λάσσο.

last [la:st] *a* τελευταῖος, τελικός ‖ *ad* τελευταῖον ‖ *n* (*person or thing*) τελευταῖος, ὕστατον ‖ (*for shoe*) καλαπόδι ‖ *vi* (*continue, hold out*) διαρκῶ, παραμένω ‖ (*remain*) συντηροῦμαι, διατηροῦμαι ‖ **at** ~ ἐπί τέλους ‖ ~ **night** χθές τό βράδυ ‖ ~ **week** τήν περασμένη βδομάδα ‖ **~ing** *a* διαρκείας, πού κρατᾶ ‖ **~-minute** *a* τῆς τελευταίας στιγμῆς ‖ **the** ~ **straw** *n* (*fig*) τό τελειωτικόν κτύπημα.

latch [lætʃ] *n* μάνταλο, σύρτης ‖ (*yale lock*) λουκέτο ‖ **~key** *n* ἁπλό κλειδί, ἀντικλείδι.

late [leit] *a* καθυστερημένος, ἀργοπορημένος ‖ (*not early*) ἀργά ‖ (*recent*) παλαιός, πρώην, τέως ‖ (*recently dead*) μακαρίτης ‖ *ad* ἐν καθυστερήσει, ἀργά ‖ (*late hour*) ἀργά ‖ **of** ~ προσφάτως ‖ ~ **in the day** ἀργά τό βραδάκι ‖ **~comer** *n* ἀργοπορημένος ‖ **~ly** *ad* ἐσχάτως, τελευταία.

lateness ['leitnis] *n* (*of person*) ἀργοπορία ‖ (*of hour*) ἡ προχωρημένη ὥρα.

latent ['leitənt] *a* ἀφανής, κρυφός ‖ (*existing*) λανθάνων.

later ['leitə*] *comp a*, *comp ad of* late.

lateral ['lætərəl] *a* πλάγιος, πλευρικός.

latest ['leitist] *sup a*, *sup ad of* late ‖ *n* (*news*) τό νεώτερον ‖ **at the** ~ τό ἀργότερον.

lathe [leið] *n* τόρνος.

lather ['læðə*] *n* σαπουνάδα ‖ *vt* σαπουνίζω ‖ *vi* κάνω ἀφρό.

Latin ['lætin] *n* λατινική (γλῶσσα) ‖ *a* λατινικός ‖ **~ America** *n* Λατινοαμερική ‖ **~-American** *a* λατινοαμερικανικός ‖ *n* Λατινοαμερικανός.

latitude ['lætitju:d] *n* γεωγραφικόν πλάτος ‖ (*freedom*) εὐρυχωρία, περιθώριο.

latrine [lə'tri:n] *n* ἀποχωρητήριον, μέρος.

latter ['lætə*] *a* (*more recent*) ὁ δεύτερος, ἕτερος ‖ (*later*) τελευταῖος, πρόσφατος ‖ *n* (*opposite of* former) ὁ δεύτερος, ἕτερος ‖ **~ly** *ad* τώρα τελευταία, ἀργότερα.

lattice work ['lætiswə:k] *n* δικτυωτόν, καφάσι.

laudible ['lɔ:dəbl] *a* ἀξιέπαινος.

laugh [la:f] *n* γέλιο ‖ *vi* γελῶ ‖ **to** ~ **at** *vt* διασκεδάζω, περιγελῶ, γελῶ γιά ‖ **to** ~ **off** *vt* γελοιοποιῶ ‖ **~able** *a* γελοῖος, ἀστεῖος, διασκεδαστικός ‖ **~ing** *a* γελαστός ‖ **~ing stock** *n* περίγελως, κορόϊδο ‖ **~ter** *n* γέλιο.

launch [lɔ:ntʃ] *n* (*of ship*) καθέλκυσις ‖ (*of rocket*) ἐκτόξευσις ‖ (*ship*) σκαμπαβία ‖ (*motor*) βενζινάκατος ‖ *vt* (*ship*) καθελκύω ‖ προβάλλω, βάζω ἐμπρός ‖ **~ing** *n* καθέλκυσις, ἐκτόξευσις ‖ **~(ing) pad** *n* πλατφόρμα ἐκτοξεύσεως.

launder ['lɔ:ndə*] *vt* πλένω καί σιδερώνω ‖ **~ette** *n* πλυντήριον αὐτοεξυπηρετήσεως.

laundry ['lɔ:ndri] *n* (*place*) πλυντήριον ‖ (*clothes*) ροῦχα γιά πλύσιμο.

laureate ['lɔ:riit] *a see* poet.

laurel ['lɔrəl] *n* δάφνη.

lava ['la:və] *n* λάβα.

lavatory ['lævətri] *n* ἀποχωρητήριον, τουαλέτα.

lavender ['lævində*] *n* λεβάντα.

lavish ['læviʃ] *a* γενναιόδωρος, σπάταλος ‖ (*abundant*) ἄφθονος, πλούσιος ‖ *vt* κατασπαταλῶ, διασπαθίζω ‖ **~ly** *ad* ἄφθονα, σπάταλα.

law [lɔ:] *n* νόμος, νομικά ‖ (*system of laws*) δίκαιον ‖ (*of game etc*) κανόνες ‖ **~-abiding** *a* νομοταγής ‖ **~breaker** *n* παραβάτης τοῦ νόμου ‖ ~ **court** *n* δικαστήριον ‖ **~ful** *a* νόμιμος ‖ **~fully** *ad* νομίμως ‖ **~less** *a* ἄνομος, παράνομος.

lawn [lɔ:n] *n* πρασιά, γρασίδι ‖ **~mower** *n* χορτοκόπτης ‖ ~ **tennis** *n* τέννις.

law school ['lɔ:sku:l] *n* σχολή νομικῆς.

law student ['lɔ:stju:dənt] *n* φοιτητής νομικῆς.

lawsuit ['lɔ:su:t] *n* δίκη.

lawyer ['lɔ:jə*] *n* νομικός, δικηγόρος.

lax [læks] *a* χαλαρός ‖ (*morals etc*) ἔκλυτος, ἄτακτος.

laxative ['læksətiv] *n* καθάρσιον.

laxity ['læksiti] *n* χαλαρότης.

lay [lei] (*irreg v*) *pt of* lie ‖ *a* λαϊκός, μή εἰδικός ‖ *vt* (*put down*) τυποθετῶ, θέτω, βάζω ‖ (*lay low*) ξαπλώνω, σωριάζω ‖ (*prepare*) βάζω, στρώνω ‖ (*eggs*) γεννῶ, κάνω ‖ **to** ~ **aside** *vt* θέτω κατά μέρος, βάζω ‖ **to** ~ **by** *vt* ἀποταμιεύω, οἰκονομῶ ‖ **to** ~ **down** *vt* παραδίδω ‖ (*plan*) σχεδιάζω ‖ **to** ~ **off** *vt* (*workers*) ἀπολύω ‖ **to** ~ **on** *vt* ἐπιβάλλω, ἐπιθέτω ‖ **to** ~ **out** *vt* ἁπλώνω ‖ (*spend*) ξοδεύω ‖ (*plan*) σχεδιάζω ‖ **to** ~ **up** *vt* (*store*) ἀποθηκεύω ‖ (*ship*) παροπλίζω ‖ **~-by** *n* πλάτυσμα σταθμεύσεως ‖ **~er** *n* στρῶμα ‖ **~ette** *n* τά μωρουδιακά ‖ **~man** *n* λαϊκός ‖ **~out** *n* σχέδιον.

laze [leiz] *vi* τεμπελιάζω, χασομερῶ.

lazily ['leizili] *ad* τεμπέλικα.

laziness ['leizinis] *n* τεμπελιά, χάζεμα.

lazy ['leizi] *a* όκνηρός, τεμπέλης.

lead [led] *n* μόλυβδος ‖ *(of pencil)* μολυβδίς, γραφίτης ‖ *a* μολύβδινος.

lead [li:d] *(irreg v) n (front position)* πρώτη θέσις, ἀρχηγία ‖ *(distance, time ahead)* προπορεία ‖ *(example)* καθοδήγησις, παράδειγμα ‖ *(clue)* ὑπαινιγμός ‖ *(theat)* πρωταγωνιστής ‖ *vt* όδηγῶ, καθοδηγῶ ‖ *(group etc)* ήγοῦμαι, διευθύνω ‖ *vi* ἄγω, καταλήγω, πηγαίνω ‖ **to ~ astray** *vt* παραπλανῶ ‖ **to ~ away** *vt* (παρα)σύρω ‖ **to ~ back** *vt* ἐπαναφέρω ‖ **to ~ on** *vt* προτρέπω, κεντρίζω ‖ **to ~ to** *vi (street)* όδηγῶ εἰς, πηγαίνω εἰς ‖ *(result in)* καταλήγω ‖ **to ~ up to** *vt* όδηγῶ εἰς ‖ **~er** *n* ἀρχηγός, ἡγέτης ‖ *(newspaper)* κύριον ἄρθρον ‖ **~ership** *n* ἡγεσία, ἀρχηγία ‖ **~ing** *a* κύριος, ἡγετικός, σημαίνων ‖ **~ing lady** *n (theat)* πρωταγωνίστρια ‖ **~ing light** *n (person)* ἡγετική φυσιογνωμία ‖ **~ing man** *n (theat)* πρωταγωνιστής.

leaf [li:f] *n* φύλλον ‖ *(thin sheet)* φύλλον ‖ *(table)* φύλλο (τραπεζιοῦ) ‖ **~let** *n* φυλλάδιον ‖ **~y** *a* φυλλωτός, φυλλώδης.

league [li:g] *n* σύνδεσμος, ἔνωσις, συμμαχία ‖ *(measure)* λεύγα.

leak [li:k] *n* διαφυγή, διαρροή ‖ *(hole)* τρύπα ‖ *vt (liquid etc)* διαρρέω, (δια)φεύγω ‖ *(naut)* κάνω νερά ‖ *vi (of pipe etc)* διαρρέω, τρέχω ‖ **to ~ out** *vi (liquid etc)* διαρρέω ‖ *(information)* διαδίδομαι.

lean [li:n] *(irreg v) a (thin)* λιγνός ‖ *(meat)* ἄπαχος ‖ *(poor)* ἰσχνός, φτωχός ‖ *n* ἄπαχο κρέας ‖ *vi* κλίνω, γέρνω ‖ *vt* ἀκουμπῶ, στηρίζομαι ‖ **to ~ back** *vi* γέρνω πρός τά πίσω ‖ **to ~ forward** *vi* γέρνω πρός τά ἐμπρός ‖ **to ~ on** *vi* στηρίζομαι, ἀκουμπῶ ‖ **to ~ over** *vi* κύπτω ‖ **~ing** *n* κλίσις, τάσις ‖ **~t** [lent] *pt,pp of* lean ‖ **~to** *n* ὑπόστεγον.

leap [li:p] *(irreg v) n* πήδημα ‖ *vi* πηδῶ ‖ **by ~s and bounds** ἁλματωδῶς, καλπάζων ‖ **~frog** *n* καβάλες, τά βαρελάκια ‖ **~t** [lept] *pt,pp of* leap ‖ **~ year** *n* δίσεκτον ἔτος.

learn [lə:n] *(irreg v) vti* μαθαίνω ‖ **~ed** *a* μορφωμένος, πολυμαθής ‖ **~er** *n (also aut)* μαθητευόμενος, ἀρχάριος ‖ **~ing** *n* (ἐκ)μάθησις, μόρφωσις.

lease [li:s] *n* ἐκμίσθωσις, ἐνοικίασις, συμβόλαιον ‖ *vt* ἐκμισθώνω, ἐνοικιάζω.

leash [li:ʃ] *n* λουρί, ἁλυσίδα.

least [li:st] *a* ἐλάχιστος, μικρότατος, ὁλίγιστος ‖ *n* (τό) λιγώτερον, (τό) μικρότερον ‖ **at ~** τουλάχιστον ‖ **not in the ~** καθόλου, ποτέ.

leather ['leðə*] *n* δέρμα, πετσί ‖ *a* δερμάτινο, πέτσινο ‖ **~y** *a* σάν πετσί, σάν δέρμα.

leave [li:v] *(irreg v) vt (go away from)* φεύγω,

ἐγκαταλείπω ‖ *(go without taking)* ἀφήνω ‖ *(let stay)* ἀφήνω ‖ *(give by will)* ἀφήνω ‖ *vi (depart)* φεύγω ‖ *n* ἄδεια ‖ *(mil)* ἄδεια ‖ **on ~** σέ ἄδεια ‖ **to take one's ~ of** ἀποχαιρετῶ, φεύγω ‖ **to ~ off** *vi* ἐγκαταλείπω, σταματῶ, κόβω ‖ **to ~ out** *vt* παραλείπω.

leaves [li:vz] *npl of* leaf.

Lebanon ['lebənən] **the ~** τό Λίβανον.

lecherous ['letʃərəs] *a* λάγνος, ἀσελγής.

lectern ['lektə(:)n] *n* ἀναγνωστήριον, ἀναλόγιον.

lecture ['lektʃə*] *n* διάλεξις, μάθημα ‖ *vi* κάνω διάλεξιν, κάνω μάθημα ‖ **~r** *n* ὁμιλητής, ὑφηγητής.

led [led] *pt,pp of* lead.

ledge [ledʒ] *n* ἄκρον, χεῖλος, ράφι ‖ *(of rock)* ὕφαλος, ξέρα.

ledger ['ledʒə*] *n* καθολικόν (κατάστιχον).

lee [li:] *n (from wind)* προκάλυμμα.

leech [li:tʃ] *n* βδέλλα.

leek [li:k] *n* πράσο.

leer [liə*] *n* λοξό βλέμμα, στραβοκοίταγμα ‖ *vi* στραβοκοιτάζω.

leeway ['li:wei] *n (fig)* χαμός χρόνου, κενόν.

left [left] *pt,pp of* leave ‖ *a* ἀριστερός ‖ *n* (τό) ἀριστερόν, ἡ ἀριστερά ‖ **the L ~** *(pol)* ἡ ἀριστερά ‖ **~-hand drive** *n* ἀριστερό τιμόνι ‖ **~-handed** *a* ζερβός, ἀριστερός ‖ **~-luggage (office)** *n* γραφεῖον καταθέσεως ἀποσκευῶν ‖ **~-overs** *npl* πλεονάσματα, ὑπολείμματα ‖ **~-wing** *n (pol)* ἀριστερός.

leg [leg] *n* πόδι, γάμπα ‖ *(of table etc)* πόδι ‖ *(on trouser etc)* γάμπα.

legacy ['legəsi] *n* κληροδότημα ‖ *(from ancestors)* κληρονομία.

legal ['li:gəl] *a* νομικός ‖ *(allowed)* νόμιμος ‖ **~ize** *vt* νομιμοποιῶ ‖ **~ly** *ad* νομίμως, νομικῶς ‖ **~ tender** *n* νόμισμα (ὑποχρεωτικῶς δεκτόν).

legation [li'geiʃən] *n* πρεσβεία.

legend ['ledʒənd] *n* θρύλος, μύθος ‖ **~ary** *a* θρυλικός, μυθικός.

-legged ['legid] *a* μέ πόδια.

leggings ['leginz] *npl* γκέτες.

legibility [ledʒi'biliti] *n* τό εὐανάγνωστον.

legible ['ledʒəbl] *a* εὐανάγνωστος.

legibly ['ledʒəbli] *ad* εὐανάγνωστα.

legion ['li:dʒən] *n* λεγεών ‖ *a (countless)* ἀναρίθμητος.

legislate ['ledʒisleit] *vi* νομοθετῶ.

legislation [ledʒis'leiʃən] *n* νομοθεσία.

legislative ['ledʒislətiv] *a* νομοθετικός.

legislator ['ledʒisleitə*] *n* νομοθέτης.

legislature ['ledʒislətʃə*] *n* νομοθετικόν σῶμα.

legitimacy [li'dʒitiməsi] *n* νομιμότης, γνησιότης.

legitimate [li'dʒitimit] *a* νομικός, λογικός.

leisure ['leʒə*] *n* σχόλη, ἀργία, ἄνεσις, ἐλεύθερες ὧρες ‖ *a* τῆς σχόλης, τῆς ἀργίας ‖ at ~ ἐλεύθερος, ἔχων καιρό ‖ ~ly a ἀβίαστα, ἀργά, ἄνετα.

lemon ['lemən] n λεμόνι ‖ (colour) λεμονής ‖ ~ade n λεμονάδα.

lend [lend] (irreg v) vt δανείζω ‖ (dignity etc) (προσ)δίδω ‖ it ~s itself to προσφέρεται, κάνει γιά ‖ ~er n δανειστής ‖ ~ing library n δανειστική βιβλιοθήκη.

length [leŋθ] n μήκος, μάκρος ‖ (of road, pipe etc) μῆκος ‖ (of material) τεμάχιον ‖ at ~ (finally) ἐπί τέλους ‖ (time) γιά πολλήν ὥραν ‖ (extent) ἐν ἐκτάσει ‖ ~en vt μακραίνω, ἐπιμηκύνω ‖ vi ἐπεκτείνομαι, παρατείνομαι ‖ ~ways ad κατά μῆκος, στό μάκρος ‖ ~y a μακρόσκελής, ἐκτενής.

leniency ['li:niənsi] n ἠπιότης, ἐπιείκεια.

lenient ['li:niənt] a ἤπιος, ἐπιεικής ‖ ~ly ad ἐπιεικῶς.

lens [lenz] n φακός.

lent [lent] pt,pp of **lend** ‖ **L** ~ n Σαρακοστή.

lentil ['lentl] n φακή.

leopard ['lepəd] n λεοπάρδαλις.

leper ['lepə*] n λεπρός.

leprosy ['leprəsi] n λέπρα.

lesbian ['lezbiən] a λεσβιακός ‖ n λεσβία.

less [les] a comp of **little** ‖ (ὀ)λιγώτερος ‖ ad (ὀ)λιγώτερον ‖ n λιγώτερον.

lessen ['lesn] vi μειοῦμαι, μικραίνω, λιγοστεύω ‖ vt μειώνω, ἐλαττώνω, μικραίνω.

lesson ['lesn] n μάθημα.

lest [lest] cj μήπως, μή τυχόν.

let [let] (irreg v) vt (allow) ἀφήνω, ἐπιτρέπω ‖ (lease) ἐνοικιάζω, ἐκμισθώνω ‖ n: without ~ or hindrance ἄνευ κωλύματος, ἐλεύθερα ‖ ~ us pray ἅς προσευχηθῶμε ‖ ~'s go ἅς πᾶμε ‖ 'to ~' 'ἐνοικιάζεται' ‖ to ~ down vt κατεβάζω ‖ (disappoint) ἀπογοητεύω, ἐγκαταλείπω ‖ to ~ go vti ἐλευθερώνω, χαλαρώνω ‖ to ~ off vt ἀπαλλάσσω, ἀφήνω, συγχωρῶ, ἀπολύω ‖ to ~ out vt ἀφήνω ‖ (garment) ἀνοίγω ‖ (scream) ἀφήνω (κραυγήν) ‖ to ~ up vi μειοῦμαι, ἐλαττοῦμαι ‖ ~-down n ἀπογοήτευσις.

lethal ['li:θəl] a θανατηφόρος.

lethargic [le'θɑ:dʒik] a ληθαργικός, νυσταλέος.

lethargy ['leθədʒi] n λήθαργος, ἀτονία.

letter ['letə*] n (sign) γράμμα, στοιχεῖον ‖ ἐπιστολή, γράμμα ‖ ~s npl (literature) γράμματα, φιλολογία ‖ ~box n γραμματοκιβώτιον ‖ ~ing n γράμματα, μαρκάρισμα.

lettuce ['letis] n μαρούλι.

let-up ['letʌp] n (col) μείωσις, χαλάρωσις.

leukaemia, (US) **leukemia** [lu:'ki:miə] n λευχαιμία.

Levant [li'vænt] the ~ n ή Ἀνατολή.

level ['levl] n a ἐπίπεδος, ὁριζόντιος ‖ ad ὁριζοντίως ‖ n ἐπίπεδον, ἐπίπεδος ἐπιφάνεια ‖ (height) στάθμη ‖ vt ἰσοπε-

δώνω, ὁριζοντιώνω ‖ on the ~ (lit) ἐπίπεδος, στό ἀλφάδι ‖ (fig: honest) τίμια, ἐν τάξει ‖ to ~ off or out vi ἐξισῶνω ‖ ~ crossing n ἐπίπεδος διάβασις ‖ ~-headed a ἰσορροπημένος, ψύχραιμος.

lever ['li:və*] n μοχλός ‖ vt κινῶ μοχλόν ‖ ~age n ἐνέργεια μοχλοῦ, μόχλευσις.

levity ['leviti] n ἐλαφρότης, ἔλλειψις σοβαρότητος.

levy ['levi] n (taxes) εἴσπραξις ‖ (mil) στρατολογία ‖ vt εἰσπράττω, ἐπιβάλλω ‖ (mil) στρατολογῶ.

lewd [lu:d] a λάγνος, ἀσελγής.

liability [laiə'biliti] n (being liable) εὐθύνη, ὑποχρέωσις ‖ (debt) ὑποχρέωσις, ὀφειλή ‖ (disadvantage) προδιάθεσις, τάσις.

liable ['laiəbl] a (responsible) ὑπεύθυνος ‖ (likely) ὑποκείμενος.

liaison [li:'eizɔn] n (coordination) σύνδεσμος.

liar ['laiə*] n ψεύτης.

libel ['laibəl] n λίβελλος, δυσφήμισις ‖ vt διασύρω, δυσφημῶ ‖ ~lous, (US) ~ous a δυσφημιστικός.

liberal ['libərəl] a (generous) γενναιόδωρος ‖ (open-minded) φιλελεύθερος ‖ n φιλελεύθερος ‖ **L** ~ **Party** Φιλελεύθερον Κόμμα ‖ ~ly ad (abundantly) γενναιόδωρα, πλούσια.

liberate ['libəreit] vt ἀπελευθερώνω.

liberation [libə'reiʃən] n ἀπελευθέρωσις.

liberty ['libəti] n ἐλευθερία ‖ at ~ ἐλεύθερος, εὔκαιρος ‖ to take liberties with παίρνω θάρρος, γίνομαι ἀναιδής.

librarian [lai'brɛəriən] n βιβλιοθηκάριος.

library ['laibrəri] n βιβλιοθήκη.

libretto [li'bretəu] n λιμπρέττο.

Libya ['libiə] n Λιβύη ‖ ~n a᾽ λιβυκός ‖ n (person) ἐκ Λιβύης.

lice [lais] npl of **louse**.

licence, (US) **license** ['laisəns] n (permit) ἄδεια, ἔγκρισις, προνόμιον ‖ (lack of control) κατάχρησις ‖ ~ plate n (US aut) πινακίδα.

license ['laisəns] vt δίνω ἄδειαν, παρέχω ἄδειαν ‖ ~d a (for alcohol: premises) μέ ἄδεια πωλήσεως ποτοῦ ‖ ~e n προνομιοῦχος.

licentious [lai'senʃəs] a ἀκόλαστος.

lichen ['laikən] n λειχήνα.

lick [lik] vt γλείφω ‖ (of flames etc) παίζω μέ, ἐγγίζω, καταβροχθίζω ‖ n γλείψιμο ‖ (small amount) μικρά ποσότης.

licorice ['likəris] n γλυκόρριζα.

lid [lid] n κάλυμμα, καπάκι.

lido ['li:dəu] n (for swimming) δημοσία πισίνα.

lie [lai] (irreg v) n ψέμμα ‖ vi (speak) ψεύδομαι ‖ (rest) εἶμαι ξαπλωμένος, μένω ‖ (of object: be situated) κεῖμαι, εὑρίσκομαι ‖ to ~ idle μένω ἀκίνητος ‖ ~ detector n ἀνιχνευτής ψεύδους.

lieu [lu:] *n*: **in ~ of** ἀντί του, εἰς θέσιν τοῦ.

lieutenant [lef'tenənt] *n* (*army*) ὑπολοχαγός ‖ [lu:'tenənt] (*US*) ὑποσμηναγός.

life [laif] *n* (*being alive*) ζωή ‖ (*way of living*) τρόπος ζωῆς, ζωή ‖ (*time of life*) ζωή, διάρκεια ζωῆς, βίος ‖ (*story*) βίος, βιογραφία ‖ (*energy, vigour*) ζωηρότης, ζωή, κίνησις ‖ **~ assurance** *n* ἀσφάλεια ζωῆς ‖ **~belt** *n* σωσίβιος ‖ **~boat** *n* ναυαγοσωστική λέμβος ‖ **~guard** *n* ναυαγοσώστης ‖ **~ jacket** *n* σωσίβιος χιτών ‖ **~less** *a* (*dead*) νεκρός, χωρίς ζωή, χωρίς κέφι ‖ **~like** *a* ρεαλιστικός, ζωντανός ‖ **~line** *n* (*lit*) σωσίβιον σχοινί ‖ **~long** *a* ἰσόβιος, ὁλοκλήρου ζωῆς ‖ **~ preserver** *n* σωσίβιον ‖ **~ raft** *n* σωσίβιος σχεδία ‖ **~-sized** *a* φυσικοῦ μεγέθους ‖ **~ span** *n* διάρκεια ζωῆς, μέσος ὅρος ζωῆς ‖ **~time** *n* ζωή.

lift [lift] *vt* (ἀν)ὑψώνω, σηκώνω ‖ (*col: steal*) κλέβω ‖ *vi* ὑψοῦμαι, σηκώνομαι ‖ *n* ἀνύψωσις, σήκωμα ‖ (*aviat*) ἄνωσις ‖ (*machine, elevator*) ἀνελκυστήρ, ἀσανσέρ ‖ (*free ride*) παίρνω στό αὐτοκίνητο.

ligament ['ligəmənt] *n* σύνδεσμος.

light [lait] (*irreg v*) *n* φῶς ‖ (*giving light*) φῶς, φωτισμός ‖ (*for cigarette*) φωτιά ‖ (*lamp*) φῶς, λάμπα ‖ (*brightness*) λάμψις ‖ (*of dawn*) λάμψις ‖ (*information*) διαφώτισις ‖ (*aspect*) φῶς, ὄψις, ἄποψις ‖ *vt* ἀνάβω ‖ (*set burning*) ἀνάβω ‖ (*brighten*) φωτίζω, φέγγω ‖ *a* (*bright*) φωτεινός ‖ (*colour*) ἀνοιχτόχρωμος, ξανθός ‖ (*not heavy*) ἐλαφρός ‖ (*easy to do*) εὔκολος ‖ (*delicate*) ἐλαφρός, ἁπαλός ‖ (*cheerful*) εὔθυμος ‖ **to ~ up** *vi* (*lamps*) ἀνάβω, φωτίζω ‖ (*face*) ἀστράφτω, λάμπω ‖ *vt* (*illuminate*) (δια)φωτίζω ‖ **~ bulb** *n* λάμπα, λαμπτήρ ‖ **~en** *vi* (*brighten*) φωτίζομαι ‖ (*flash lightning*) ἀστράπτω ‖ *vt* (*give light to*) φωτίζω ‖ (*make less heavy*) ἐλαφρώνω ‖ **~er** *n* (*cigarette lighter*) ἀναπτήρας ‖ (*boat*) φορτηγίδα ‖ **~-headed** *a* ζαλισμένος ‖ (*thoughtless*) ἐπιπόλαιος, ἀπερίσκεπτος ‖ **~-hearted** *a* εὔθυμος, χαρούμενος ‖ **~house** *n* φάρος ‖ **~ing** *n* (*on road*) φωτισμός ‖ (*in theatre*) φωτισμός ‖ **~ing-up time** *n* ὥρα ἀφῆς φώτων ‖ **~ly** *ad* ἐλαφρῶς, ἐλαφρά ‖ **~ meter** *n* (*phot*) μετρητής φωτός ‖ **~ness** *n* ἐλαφρότης ‖ **~ning** *n* ἀστραπή, κεραυνός ‖ **~ning conductor** *n* ἀλεξικέραυνον ‖ **~ship** *n* φαρόπλοιον ‖ **~-year** *n* ἔτος φωτός.

ignite ['lignait] *n* λιγνίτης.

ike [laik] *vt* μοῦ ἀρέσει, συμπαθῶ, προτιμῶ ‖ *prep* σάν, ὅπως, ὡς ‖ *a* (*similar*) ὅμοιος, ὁμοιάζων ‖ (*equal*) τά ἴσα, παρόμοια ‖ *ad* ὅπως, σάν ‖ *n* ὅμοιος ‖ **~able** *a* ἀγαπητός, συμπαθής ‖ **~lihood** *n* πιθανότης ‖ **~ly** *a* πιθανός, πού μπορεῖ νά ‖ *ad* πιθανόν, ἴσως ‖ **~-minded** *a* μέ τήν αὐτήν γνώμην ‖ **~n**

vt συγκρίνω, παρομοιάζω ‖ **~wise** *ad* ὁμοίως, ἐπίσης, ἐπί πλέον.

liking ['laikiŋ] *n* κλίσις, τάσις, συμπάθεια, γοῦστο.

lilac ['lailək] *n* πασχαλιά.

lilting ['liltiŋ] *a* ρυθμικός, μουσικός.

lily ['lili] *n* κρίνον.

limb [lim] *n* μέλος, ἄκρον ‖ (*of tree*) κλάδος.

limber ['limbə*] **to ~ up** *vi* γίνομαι εὐλύγιστος.

limbo ['limbəu] *n*: **to be in ~** (*fig*) εἶμαι στή φυλακή, στό φρέσκο.

lime [laim] *n* (*tree*) γλυκολεμονιά, κίτριον ‖ (*fruit*) γλυκολέμονο, κίτρο ‖ (*geol*) ἀσβέστης ‖ **~ juice** *n* χυμός γλυκολεμονιοῦ ‖ **~light** *n* (*fig*) τό προσκήνιον, δημοσιότης.

limestone ['laimstəun] *n* ἀσβεστόλιθος.

limit ['limit] *n* ὅριον, σύνορον, πέρας ‖ *vt* περιορίζω ‖ **~ation** *n* περιορισμός, ἀνικανότης ‖ **~ed** *a* περιωρισμένος, στενός ‖ **~ed company** *n* ἑταιρεία περιωρισμένης εὐθύνης.

limousine ['liməzi:n] *n* λιμουζίνα.

limp [limp] *n* χωλότης ‖ *vi* χωλαίνω, κουτσαίνω ‖ *a* ἀπαλός, πλαδαρός, μαλακός ‖ (*without energy*) λυωμένος, τσακισμένος.

limpet ['limpit] *n* πεταλίδα.

line [lain] *n* (*cord, wire, string*) σχοινί, γραμμή, σύρμα ‖ (*narrow mark*) γραμμή ‖ (*row, series*) σειρά, γραμμή ‖ (*course, direction*) κατεύθυνσις, τρόπος, πορεία ‖ (*class of goods*) σειρά, συλλογή, εἶδος ‖ (*poetry etc*) στίχος, γραμμή ‖ *vt* (*coat etc*) φοδράρω ‖ (*border*) χαράσσω ‖ **in ~ with** σύμφωνα μέ ‖ **to ~ up** *vi* μπαίνω στή γραμμή ‖ σχηματίζω οὐράν ‖ *vt* παρατάσσω, βάζω στή γραμμή.

linear ['liniə*] *a* (*of length*) τοῦ μήκους γραμμικά.

linen ['linin] *n* λινόν ὕφασμα ‖ (*articles*) ἀσπρόρουχα.

liner ['lainə*] *n* πλοῖον γραμμῆς.

linesman ['lainzmən] *n* (*sport*) λάϊνσμαν.

line-up ['lainʌp] *n* παράταξις.

linger ['liŋgə*] *vi* (*remain long*) χρονοτριβῶ, παρατείνομαι ‖ (*delay*) ἀργοπορῶ, βραδύνω.

lingerie ['lænʒəri:] *n* γυναικεῖα ἐσώρρουχα.

lingering ['liŋgəriŋ] *a* παρατεταμένος, βραδύς, ἀνιαρός.

lingo ['liŋgəu] *n* (*col*) γλῶσσα, διάλεκτος.

linguist ['liŋgwist] *n* γλωσσολόγος, γλωσσομαθής.

linguistic [liŋ'gwistik] *a* γλωσσολογικός ‖ **~s** *n* γλωσσολογία.

liniment ['linimənt] *n* ὑγρόν ἐντριβῆς, ἐπάλειψις.

lining ['lainiŋ] *n* φόδρα.

link [liŋk] *n* (*of chain*) κρίκος ‖ δεσμός, σύνδεσμος ‖ *vt* συνδέω, ἑνώνω ‖ **~s** *npl* γήπεδον γκόλφ ‖ ~-up n (communication) σύνδεσις.

linoleum [li'nəuliəm] n λινοτάπης, λινόλεουμ.

linseed oil ['linsi:d'ɔil] n λινέλαιον.

lint [lint] n ξαντόν.

lion ['laiən] n λιοντάρι ‖ ~ess n λέαινα.

lip [lip] n χείλι, χεῖλος ‖ (to pay) ~ service (+ to) κάνω ψεύτικες ὑποσχέσεις ‖ ~stick n κραγιόν.

liquefy ['likwifai] vt ὑγροποιῶ.

liqueur [li'kjuə*] n λικέρ.

liquid ['likwid] n ὑγρόν ‖ a (substance) ὑγρός, ρευστός ‖ (asset) ρευστός, διαθέσιμος ‖ ~ate vt διαλύω, ξεκαθαρίζω, χρεωκοπῶ ‖ ~ation n διάλυσις, ἐξόφλησις, χρεωκόπησις.

liquor ['likə*] n (strong drink) οἰνοπνευματώδες ποτόν.

lisp [lisp] n τραυλισμός, ψεύδισμα.

list [list] n (of names etc) κατάλογος ‖ (on ship) κλίσις, γέρσιμο ‖ vt (write down) ἐγγράφω, καταγράφω ‖ vi (of ship) κλίνω, γέρνω.

listen ['lisn] vi ἀκούω, προσέχω ‖ to ~ to vt ἀκούω ‖ ~er n ἀκροατής.

listless ['listlis] a ἄτονος, νωθρός, ἀδιάφορος ‖ ~ly ad ἀδιάφορα, ἀπαθῶς ‖ ~ness n ἀδιαφορία, ἀπάθεια.

lit [lit] pt,pp of light.

litany ['litəni] n λιτανεία.

liter ['li:tə*] n (US) = litre.

literacy ['litərəsi] n βαθμός μορφώσεως.

literal ['litərəl] a (word for word) κατά λέξιν ‖ (usual meaning) κατά κυριολεξίαν ‖ ~ly ad κυριολεκτικά.

literary ['litərəri] a λογοτεχνικός, φιλολογικός.

literate ['litərit] a ἐγγράμματος.

literature ['litəritʃə*] n φιλολογία, λογοτεχνία.

lithograph ['liθəugra:f] n λιθόγραφον, λιθογραφία.

litigate ['litigeit] vi βρίσκομαι εἰς δίκην, διεκδικῶ.

litmus ['litməs] n: ~ paper χάρτης ἡλιοτροπίου.

litre ['li:tə*] n λίτρον.

litter ['litə*] n (untidy bits) σκουπίδια ‖ (young animals) γέννα, νεογνά ‖ vt κάνω ἄνω-κάτω, βρωμίζω μέ σκουπίδια.

little ['litl] a (small) μικρός, ὀλίγος, κοντός ‖ (unimportant) ἀσήμαντος ‖ ad ἐλάχιστα, λίγο ‖ n ὀλίγον, λίγο.

liturgy ['litədʒi] n λειτουργία.

live [liv] vi ζῶ ‖ (pass one's life) ζῶ ‖ (last) ζῶ, διαρκῶ ‖ (dwell) κατοικῶ, διαμένω, ζῶ ‖ to ~ down vt κάνω νά ξεχασθῆ, ὑπερνικῶ ‖ to ~ on vt τρέφομαι μέ, συντηρούμαι μέ ‖ to ~ up to vt ἐφαρμόζω, τιμῶ, ἐκπληρώνω.

live [laiv] a (living) ζωντανός ‖ (burning) ἀναμμένος ‖ (wire) ἠλεκτρισμένον, μέ

ρεῦμα ‖ (broadcast) ζωντανόν πρόγραμμα.

livelihood ['laivlihud] n τά πρός τό ζῆν.

liveliness ['laivlinis] n ζωηρότης, ζωτικότης.

lively ['laivli] a ζωηρός.

liver ['livə*] n (anat) σηκότι ‖ ~ish a ἡπατικός, εὐερέθιστος.

livery ['livəri] n στολή ὑπηρέτου.

lives [laivz] npl of life.

livestock ['laivstɔk] n ζῶα, κτήνη.

livid ['livid] a (lit) πελιδνός, ὠχρός ‖ (furious) φουριόζος.

living ['liviŋ] n τά πρός τό ζῆν, βίος ‖ a ζωντανός, ζῶν ‖ (wage) βασικός μισθός ‖ ~ room n καθημερινόν δωμάτιον.

lizard ['lizəd] n σαύρα.

load [ləud] n φορτίον, φόρτωμα ‖ vt φορτώνω, γεμίζω.

loaf [ləuf] n καρβέλι ‖ vi χαζεύω, τεμπελιάζω.

loan [ləun] n δάνειον, δανεισμός ‖ vt δανείζω ‖ on ~ ἀπεσπασμένος.

loathe [ləuð] vt σιχαίνομαι.

loathing ['ləuðiŋ] n σιχαμός, ἀηδία.

loaves [ləuvz] npl of loaf.

lobby ['lɔbi] n προθάλαμος, εἴσοδος ‖ vt ἐπηρεάζω βουλευτάς.

lobe [ləub] n λοβός.

lobster ['lɔbstə*] n ἀστακός.

local ['ləukəl] a τοπικός, ἐπιτόπιος ‖ n (pub) ταβέρνα ‖ the ~s npl ντόπιοι ‖ ~ colour n τοπικόν χρῶμα ‖ ~ity n θέσις, μέρος, τοποθεσία ‖ ~ly ad τοπικῶς, ἐπιτοπίως.

locate [ləu'keit] vt ἐντοπίζω ‖ (establish) τοποθετῶ.

location [ləu'keiʃən] n τοποθεσία.

loch [lɔx] n λίμνη.

lock [lɔk] n (of door) κλειδαριά ‖ (of canal etc) ὑδροφράκτης, φράγμα ‖ (of hair) βόστρυχος, μπούκλα ‖ vt κλειδώνω σφίγγω, στερεώνω ‖ vi (door etc) ἀσφαλίζομαι ‖ (wheels) σφηνώνω, μπλοκάρομαι.

locker ['lɔkə*] n ἁρμάρι, ντουλάπι, ἀποθήκη.

locket ['lɔkit] n μενταγιόν.

locomotive [ləukə'məutiv] n ἀτμάμαξα, ἀτμομηχανή.

locust ['ləukəst] n ἀκρίδα.

lodge [lɔdʒ] n ἐξοχική οἰκία ‖ (at gate) οἰκίσκος τοῦ φύλακος ‖ (meeting place) στοά ‖ vi φιλοξενοῦμαι, διαμένω ‖ (rent a room) εἶμαι νοικάρης ‖ (stick) ἐνσφηνοῦμαι, πιάνομαι ‖ vt καταθέτω, ὑποβάλλω ‖ ~r n ἔνοικος.

lodgings ['lɔdʒiŋz] npl δωμάτια.

loft [lɔft] n ὑπερῷον, σοφίτα.

lofty ['lɔfti] a ὑψηλός ‖ (proud) ὑπεροπτικός, ἀγέρωχος.

log [lɔg] n (of wood) κούτσουρο ‖ (of ship etc) ἡμερολόγιον.

logarithm ['lɔgəriθəm] *n* λογάριθμος.

logbook ['lɔgbuk] *n* ἡμερολόγιον (πλοίου).

loggerheads ['lɔgəhədz] *n*: at ~ τσακωμένος, στά μαχαίρια.

logic ['lɔdʒik] *n* λογική ‖ ~al *a* λογικός ‖, ~ally *ad* λογικά.

loin [lɔin] *n* ὀσφύς, λαγών.

loiter ['lɔitə*] *vi* χρονοτριβῶ, χαζεύω.

loll [lɔl] *vi* ξαπλώνω, χουζουρεύω.

lollipop ['lɔlipɔp] *n* γλειφιτζούρι.

London ['lʌndən] *n* Λονδῖνον ‖ ~er *n* (*person*) Λονδρέζος.

one [ləun] *a* (*solitary*) μόνος, μοναχικός ‖ ~liness *n* μοναξιά, ἐρημιά ‖ ~ly *a* (*sad*) μελαγχολικός, ἔρημος, ἀκατοίκητος.

long [lɔŋ] *a* μακρύς, μακρά, ἐκτενής ‖ (*length*) μάκρος ‖ *ad* (*time*) ἐπί μακρόν, πολλή ὥρα ‖ (*during*) ὅλη, σ' ὅλη ‖ *vi* (+ *for*) ποθῶ, λαχταρῶ ‖ ~ ago πρό πολλοῦ, τοῦ παλαιοῦ καιροῦ ‖ **before** ~ ἐντός ὀλίγου, σύντομα ‖ **as** ~ **as** ἐφ' ὅσον ‖ **in the** ~ **run** στό τέλος, τελικά ‖ ~-distance *a* (*tel*) ὑπεραστικόν ‖ (*sport*) μεγάλων δρόμων ‖ ~-haired *a* μακρυμάλλης ‖ ~hand *n* συνήθης γραφή ‖ ~ing *n* πόθος, λαχτάρα ‖ *a* λαχταρῶν, ποθῶν ‖ ~ish *a* μακρούτσικος ‖ ~itude *n* μῆκος ‖ ~ jump *n* ἅλμα εἰς μῆκος ‖ ~-lost *a* χαμένος πρό πολλοῦ ‖ ~-playing **record** *n* δίσκος μακρᾶς διαρκείας ‖ ~-range *a* μεγάλης διαρκείας, μεγάλης ἀκτίνος ‖ ~-sighted *a* πρεσβύωψ, ὀξυδερκής ‖ ~-standing *a* παλαιός, μακροχρόνιος ‖ ~-suffering *a* ὑπομονητικός, μακρόθυμος ‖ ~-term *a* μακροπρόθεσμος, μακροχρόνιος ‖ ~ wave *n* μακρόν κῦμα ‖ ~-winded *a* ἀτελείωτος, φλύαρος.

loo [luː] *n* μέρος.

loofah ['luːfə] *n* (ἐλ.)λύφι.

look [luk] *vi* (*see*) κοιτάζω, βλέπω ‖ (*seem*) φαίνομαι ‖ (*face*) βλέπω, ἀντικρύζω ‖ *n* βλέμμα, ματιά ‖ ~s *npl* ὄψις, ἐμφάνισις ‖ **to** ~ **after** *vt* φροντίζω γιά ‖ **to** ~ **down on** *vt* (*fig*) περιφρονῶ ‖ **to** ~ **for** *vt* ψάχνω, ζητῶ ‖ (*expect*) προσδοκῶ ‖ **to** ~ **forward to** *vt* προσδοκῶ ‖ **to** ~ **out for** *vt* ἀναζητῶ, ψάχνω, προσέχω ‖ **to** ~ **to** *vt* φροντίζω γιά, βασίζομαι εἰς ‖ **to** ~ **up** *vi* βελτιοῦμαι ‖ *vt* ἐπισκέπτομαι, ψάχνω (εἰς βιβλίον) ‖ **to** ~ **up to** *vt* σέβομαι ‖ ~-out *n* (*watch*) προσοχή ‖ (*view*) θέα ‖ (*mil*) φρούρησις, φρουρός.

loom [luːm] *n* ἀργαλειός ‖ *vi* διαφαίνομαι, διακρίνομαι ἀσαφῶς.

loop [luːp] *n* βρόχος, θηλιά ‖ *vt* κάνω θηλιά, δένω μέ θηλιά ‖ ~hole *n* (*for escape*) ὑπεκφυγή, διέξοδος.

loose [luːs] *a* χαλαρός ‖ (*free*) ἐλεύθερος, λυμένος ‖ (*slack*) ἀπρόσεκτος, ἅπαλός ‖ *vt* λύνω, λασκάρω, χαλαρώνω ‖ **at a** ~ **end** χωρίς ἀπασχόλησιν ‖ ~ly *ad*

χαλαρά, ἀσαφῶς ‖ ~n *vt* λύνω, λασκάρω ‖ ~ness *n* χαλαρότης.

loot [luːt] *n* λάφυρον, λεία, πλιάτσικο ‖ *vt* λαφυραγωγῶ, λεηλατῶ ‖ ~ing *n* λεηλασία.

lop [lɔp] **to** ~ **off** *vt* (ἀπο)κόπτω, κλαδεύω.

lop-sided ['lɔp'saidid] *a* ἑτεροβαρής, πού γέρνει.

lord [lɔːd] *n* ἄρχων, ἀφέντης ‖ (*Brit*) λόρδος ‖ **the L~** ὁ Κύριος ‖ ~ly *a* μεγαλοπρεπής, ἀγέρωχος ‖ ~ship *n* (*title*) ἐξοχότης.

lore [lɔː*] *n* εἰδική γνῶσις, παραδόσεις.

lorry ['lɔri] *n* φορτηγόν (αὐτοκίνητον), καμιόνι ‖ ~ **driver** *n* ὁδηγός φορτηγοῦ.

lose [luːz] (*irreg v*) *vt* χάνω ‖ (*be robbed of*) χάνω ‖ (*waste*) σπαταλῶ, χάνω ‖ (*miss*) χάνω ‖ (*be defeated*) χάνω ‖ *vi* χάνω ‖ ~r *n* ἡττημένος, χαμένος.

losing ['luːziŋ] *a* χάνων.

loss [lɔs] *n* ἀπώλεια, χάσιμο ‖ (*what is lost*) ἀπώλεια ‖ (*harm*) ζημία ‖ **at a** ~ ἔχω χαμένα, βρίσκομαι εἰς ἀμηχανίαν.

lost [lɔst] *pt,pp* of **lose** ‖ *a* ἀπολεσθείς, χαμένος ‖ ~ **cause** *n* χαμένη ὑπόθεσις ‖ ~ **property** *n* (γραφεῖον) ἀπολεσθέντων ἀντικειμένων.

lot [lɔt] *n* (*large quantity*) πολύ ‖ (*for prize*) κλῆρος ‖ (*group of objects*) σύνολον, σέ παρτίδες ‖ **a** ~ **of** ἕνα σωρό, πολύ ‖ ~s **of** πλῆθος, ἕνα σωρό.

lotion ['ləuʃən] *n* λοσιόν.

lottery ['lɔtəri] *n* λαχεῖον.

loud [laud] *a* βροντερός, θορυβώδης, μεγαλόφωνος ‖ (*showy*) κτυπητός ‖ *ad* δυνατά, μεγαλοφώνως ‖ ~ly *ad* δυνατά, θορυβωδῶς ‖ ~ness *n* ἠχηρότης, δύναμις θορύβου ‖ ~speaker *n* μεγάφωνον.

lounge [laundʒ] *n* μικρό σαλόνι, χώλ ξενοδοχείου ‖ *vi* περιφέρομαι ἀσκόπως, χαζεύω ‖ ~ **suit** *n* καθημερινό κοστούμι.

louse [laus] *n* ψείρα.

lousy ['lauzi] *a* (*lit*) ψειριάρης ‖ (*fig*) βρωμερός, ἄθλιος.

lout [laut] *n* ἄξεστος, ντουβάρι.

lovable ['lʌvəbl] *a* ἀξιαγάπητος.

love [lʌv] *n* ἀγάπη, ἔρως, στοργή ‖ (*person loved*) ἀγαπημένος, ἐρωμένη ‖ (*sport*) μηδέν ‖ *vt* (*person*) ἀγαπῶ ‖ (*activity*) λατρεύω, ἀγαπῶ ‖ **to** ~ **to do** μοῦ ἀρέσει νά κάνω ‖ **to make** ~ κάνω ἔρωτα, φλερτάρω ‖ ~ **affair** *n* ἐρωτική ὑπόθεσι ‖ ~ **letter** *n* ἐρωτικό γράμμα ‖ ~ **life** *n* ἐρωτική ζωή ‖ ~ly *a* ὡραῖος, χαριτωμένος, εὐχάριστος ‖ ~-making *n* ἐρωτοτροπία, κόρτε ‖ ~r *n* (*general*) φιλο- ‖ (*man*) ἐραστής, φίλος ‖ ~song *n* ἐρωτικό τραγούδι.

loving ['lʌviŋ] *a* τρυφερός, στοργικός ‖ ~ly *ad* στοργικά, μέ ἀγάπη.

low [ləu] *a* (*not tall*) χαμηλός ‖ (*rank*) ταπεινός, κατώτερος ‖ (*common*) χυδαῖος, ἄξεστος ‖ (*not loud*) ἀδύνατος.

χαμηλός ‖ (weak) κακόκεφος ‖ (tide) ἄμπωτις ‖ ad χαμηλά ‖ (not loudly) χαμηλόφωνα, χαμηλά ‖ n (low point) ναδίρ ‖ (meteorology) βαρομετρικόν χαμηλόν ‖ ~-cut a (dress) ντεκολτέ.

lower ['ləuə*] vt κατεβάζω, χαμηλώνω ‖ (make less) ἐλαττώνω.

lowly ['ləuli] a ταπεινός, μετριόφρων.

loyal ['lɔiəl] a πιστός, ἀφοσιωμένος ‖ ~ly ad πιστῶς, πιστά ‖ ~ty n πίστις, ἀφοσίωσις.

lozenge ['lɔzindʒ] n παστίλια.

lubricant ['lu:brikənt] n λιπαντικόν, γράσο.

lubricate ['lu:brikeit] vt λιπαίνω, λαδώνω, γρασάρω.

lubrication [lu:bri'keiʃən] n λίπανσις, γρασάρισμα.

lucid ['lu:sid] a σαφής, διαυγής ‖ ~ity n σαφήνεια, διαύγεια ‖ ~ly ad σαφῶς, καθαρά.

luck [lʌk] n τύχη ‖ ~ily ad εὐτυχῶς ‖ ~y a τυχερός.

lucrative ['lu:krətiv] a ἐπικερδής.

ludicrous ['lu:dikrəs] a ἀλλόκοτος, γελοῖος, ἀστεῖος.

lug [lʌg] vt σέρνω μέ δυσκολία.

luggage ['lʌgidʒ] n ἀποσκευές ‖ ~ rack n (in train etc) σκευοθέσιον, δίχτυ γιά βαλίτσες.

lugubrious [lu:'gu:briəs] a πένθιμος, λυπητερός.

lukewarm ['lu:kwɔ:m] a χλιαρός ‖ (indifferent) ἀδιάφορος.

lull [lʌl] n ἀνάπαυλα, κόπασις ‖ vt νανουρίζω ‖ (calm) καθησυχάζω, καταπραΰνω ‖ ~aby n νανούρισμα.

lumbago [lʌm'beigəu] n ὀσφυαλγία.

lumber ['lʌmbə*] n (old articles) παλιατσούρες ‖ (wood) ξυλεία ‖ ~jack n ξυλοκόπος.

luminous ['lu:minəs] a φωτεινός, λάμπων.

lump [lʌmp] n (σ)βῶλος, μεγάλο τεμάχιον ‖ (swelling) ἐξόγκωμα, καρούμπαλο ‖ (of sugar) κομμάτι ζάχαρι ‖ vt σβωλιάζω, συσσωρεύω ‖ a ~ sum στρογγυλόν ποσόν, ὁλική τιμή ‖ ~y a σβωλιασμένος.

lunacy ['lu:nəsi] n παραφροσύνη.

lunar ['lu:nə*] a σεληνιακός.

lunatic ['lu:nətik] n παράφρων ‖ a παράφρων, τρελλός.

lunch [lʌntʃ] n (also ~eon) γεῦμα ‖ ~ hour n μεσημβρινή διακοπή ‖ ~time n = ~ hour.

lung [lʌŋ] n πνευμόνι ‖ ~ cancer n καρκίνος πνευμονιοῦ.

lunge [lʌndʒ] vi μπήζω, κτυπῶ ξαφνικά, ἐφορμῶ.

lupin ['lu:pin] n λούπινον.

lurch [lə:tʃ] vi τρικλίζω, μποτζάρω ‖ n κλυδώνισμα, μπότζι.

lure [ljuə*] n δέλεαρ, δόλωμα, ἕλξις ‖ vt δελεάζω, θέλγω.

lurid ['ljuərid] a (shocking) τρομερός.

lurk [lə:k] vi παραμονεύω, κρύβομαι.

luscious ['lʌʃəs] a γευστικός, χυμώδης, γλυκύτατος.

lush [lʌʃ] a γεμάτος χυμούς ‖ (countryside) πλούσιο εἰς βλάστησι.

lust [lʌst] n σαρκική ἐπιθυμία ‖ vi (+ after) ἐποφθαλμιῶ, ὀρέγομαι ‖ ~ful a λάγνος.

lustre, (US) **luster** ['lʌstə*] n λάμψις, στιλπνότης.

lusty ['lʌsti] a εὔρωστος, σφριγηλός.

lute [lu:t] n λαοῦτο.

luxuriant [lʌg'zjuəriənt] a ἄφθονος, πλούσιος.

luxurious [lʌg'zjuəriəs] a πολυτελής, πλούσιος.

luxury ['lʌkʃəri] n πολυτέλεια, λοῦσο.

lying ['laiiŋ] n κείμενος ‖ (not truthful) ψευδόμενος ‖ a ψεύτικος.

lynch [lintʃ] vt λυντσάρω.

lyre ['laiə*] n λύρα.

lyric ['lirik] n λόγια τραγουδιοῦ ‖ a λυρικός ‖ ~al a (fig) ἐνθουσιώδης, πομπώδης.

M, m

mac [mæk] n (raincoat) ἀδιάβροχο.

macaroni [mækə'rəuni] n μακαρόνια.

macaroon [mækə'ru:n] n ἐργολάβος.

mace [meis] n κηρύκειον ‖ (spice) μοσχοκάρυδο.

machine [mə'ʃi:n] n (general) μηχανή, μηχάνημα ‖ vt (dress etc) ἐπεξεργάζομαι, κατεργάζομαι ‖ ~ gun n πολυβόλον ‖ ~ry n μηχανές ‖ (parts) μηχανήματα ‖ (of government) μηχανισμός ‖ ~ tool n ἐργαλειομηχανή.

machinist [mə'ʃi:nist] n μηχανουργός.

mackerel ['mækrəl] n σκουμπρί.

mackintosh ['mækintɔʃ] n ἀδιάβροχο.

macro- ['mækrəu] prefix μακρο-.

mad [mæd] a παράφρων, τρελλός ‖ (foolish) παράλογος ‖ ~ about ξετρελλαμένος ‖ (very angry) ἐξαγριωμένος.

madam ['mædəm] n κυρία.

madden ['mædn] vt τρελλαίνω ‖ ~ing a ἐκνευριστικός, τρομερός.

made [meid] pt,pp of **make** ‖ ~-to-measure a κατασκευασθέν ἐπί παραγγελία ‖ ~-up a τεχνητός, φτιαστός.

madly ['mædli] ad τρελλά, ἄγριως.

madman ['mædmən] n (maniac) φρενοβλαβής, τρελλός.

madness ['mædnis] n παραφροσύνη, τρέλλα.

Madonna [mə'dɔnə] n Παναγία.

magazine [mægə'zi:n] n περιοδικόν.

maggot ['mægət] n σκουλίκι.

magic ['mædʒik] n μαγεία ‖ a μαγικός, μαγεμένος ‖ ~al a μαγικός ‖ ~ian n μάγος.

magistrate ['mædʒistreit] *n* δικαστικός ὑπάλληλος ‖ (*judge*) δικαστής.

magnanimity [mægnə'nimiti] *n* μεγαλοψυχία, γενναιοφροσύνη.

magnanimous [mæg'næniməs] *a* μεγαλόψυχος.

magnate ['mægneit] *n* μεγιστάν.

magnet ['mægnit] *n* μαγνήτης ‖ ~ic *a* μαγνητικός ‖ ~ism *n* μαγνητισμός.

magnification [mægnifi'keiʃən] *n* μεγέθυνσις.

magnificence [mæg'nifisəns] *n* μεγαλοπρέπεια.

magnificent [mæg'nifisənt] *a* μεγαλοπρεπής ‖ ~ly *ad* μεγαλοπρεπῶς.

magnify ['mægnifai] *vt* μεγεθύνω, ὑπερβάλλω ‖ ~ing glass *n* μεγεθυντικός φακός.

magnitude ['mægnitju:d] *n* μέγεθος, σπουδαιότης.

magnolia [mæg'nəulia] *n* μανόλια.

magpie ['mægpai] *n* καρακάξα.

maharajah [ma:hə'ra:dʒə] *n* μαχαραγιάς.

mahogany [mə'hɔgəni] *n* μαόνι.

maid [meid] *n* (*servant*) ὑπηρέτρια ‖ ~en *r.* κορίτσι, παρθένος ‖ *a* (*lady*) ἄγαμος ‖ ~en name *n* οἰκογενειακόν ὄνομα ‖ ~en speech *n* παρθενικός λόγος ‖ ~en voyage *n* παρθενικόν ταξίδι.

mail [meil] *n* ἐπιστολές, ταχυδρομεῖον ‖ (*system*) ταχυδρομεῖον ‖ *vt* (*US*) ταχυδρομῶ ‖ ~box *n* (*US*) γραμματοκιβώτιον ‖ ~order *n* ταχυδρομική ἐντολή.

maim [meim] *vt* ἀκρωτηριάζω, σακατεύω.

main [mein] *a* κύριος, πρωτεύων ‖ *n* (*pipe*) κεντρικός ἀγωγός ‖ in the ~ γενικά, ὡς ἐπί τό πλεῖστον ‖ ~land *n* στερεά, ἠπειρωτική χώρα ‖ ~ road *n* κεντρική ὁδός ‖ ~stay *n* (*fig*) κύριον ἔρεισμα, στήριγμα.

maintain [mein'tein] *vt* (*machine*) διατηρῶ, συντηρῶ ‖ (*support*) συντηρῶ, τρέφω ‖ (*traditions*) συντηρῶ, συνεχίζω ‖ (*an opinion*) ὑποστηρίζω.

maintenance ['meintinəns] *n* (*tech*) συντήρησις.

maisonette [meizə'net] *n* διαμέρισμα, μονοκατοικία.

maize [meiz] *n* ἀραποσίτι, καλαμπόκι.

majestic [mə'dʒestik] *a* μεγαλοπρεπής.

majesty ['mædʒisti] *n* μεγαλεῖον ‖ His, Her M~ ή Αὐτοῦ Μεγαλειότης, ή Αὐτή Μεγαλειότης ‖ Your M~ ή Μεγαλειότης σας.

major ['meidʒə*] *n* (*mil*) ταγματάρχης ‖ *a* (*mus*) μείζων.

majority [mə'dʒɔriti] *n* πλειοψηφία (*number*) πλειονότης.

make [meik] (*irreg v*) *vt* (*build, shape, produce*) κάνω, φτιάχνω, δημιουργῶ ‖ (*appoint*) κάνω, ὁρίζω (*cause to do*) ἀναγκάζω, κάνω, ὑποχρεώνω (*reach*) φθάνω ‖ (*earn*) κάνω, ἀποκτῶ, κερδίζω

βγάζω ‖ (*do, perform*) κάνω ‖ (*amount to*) κάνω ‖ (*prepare*) φτιάνω ‖ *n* (*style*) κατασκευή, τύπος ‖ (*kind*) μάρκα ‖ to ~ for *vt* (*place*) κατευθύνομαι, πηγαίνω ‖ to ~ out *vi* ἐπιτυγχάνω, καταφέρνω ‖ *vt* (*write out*) συντάσσω, βγάζω, ἐτοιμάζω ‖ (*understand*) καταλήγω, καταλαμβάνω (*pretend*) προσποιοῦμαι, παριστάνω ‖ to ~ up *vt* (*make*) συντάσσω, φτιάνω. πλάθω ‖ (*face*) βάφομαι, μακιγιάρομαι. φτιάνομαι ‖ (*settle*) ρυθμίζω, συμφιλιώνω, διευθετῶ ‖ to ~ up for *vt* ἀνακτῶ, καλύπτω ‖ ~-believe *n* προσποίησις, ὑπόκρισις ‖ *a* προσποιητός, ψεύτικος ‖ ~r *n* κατασκευαστής, δημιουργός ‖ ~shift *a* προσωρινή λύσις ‖ ~-up *n* (*cosmetics*) μακιγιάζ, ψιμύθιον ‖ (*theat*) μακιγιάζ, βάψιμο.

making ['meikin] *n*: in the ~ ἐν ἐξελίξει

maladjusted ['mælə'dʒʌstid] *a* ἀπροσάρμοστος.

malaise [mæ'leiz] *n* ἀδιαθεσία.

malaria [mə'leəriə] *n* ἐλονοσία.

Malaysia [mə'leiziə] *n* Μαλαισία.

male [meil] *n* ἄρρην, ἄνδρας ‖ *a* ἀρσενικός.

malevolence [mə'levələns] *n* κακοβουλία, μοχθηρία.

malevolent [mə'levələnt] *a* κακόβουλος.

malfunction [mæl'fʌŋkʃən] *vi* λειτουργῶ ἐλαττωματικῶς.

malice ['mælis] *n* κακεντρέχεια, ἐχθρα.

malicious [mə'liʃəs] *a* κακόβουλος, μοχθηρός ‖ ~ly *ad* μοχθηρά, μέ κακίαν.

malign [mə'lain] *vt* δυσφημίζω, κακολογῶ.

malignant [mə'lignənt] *a* (*tumour*) κακοήθης.

malleable ['mæliəbl] *a* ἐλάσιμος, μαλακός.

mallet ['mælit] *n* ξύλινο σφυρί, κόπανος.

malnutrition ['mælnju'triʃən] *n* ὑποσιτισμός.

malpractice ['mæl'præktis] *n* ἀδίκημα, κατάχρησις.

malt [mɔ:lt] *n* βύνη.

Malta ['mɔ:ltə] *n* Μάλτα.

maltreat [mæl'tri:t] *vt* κακομεταχειρίζομαι.

mammal ['mæməl] *n* θηλαστικόν, μαστοφόρον.

mammoth ['mæməθ] *a* γιγαντιαῖος, πελώριος.

man [mæn] *n* ἄνθρωπος ‖ (*male*) ἀνήρ, ἄνδρας ‖ (*race*) ἀνθρωπότης *vt* ἐπανδρώνω.

manage ['mænidʒ] *vi* (*succeed*) καταφέρνω *vt* χειρίζομαι, διευθύνω, διοικῶ ‖ ~able *a* εὐχείριστος ‖ (*person*) εὔκολος ~ment *n* χειρισμός, διαχείρισις ‖ (*directors*) διεύθυνσις, διοίκησις ‖ ~r *n* διευθυντής ‖ ~ress *n* διευθύντρια ‖ ~rial *a* διευθυντικός, τεχνοκρατικός.

managing ['mænidʒiŋ] *a*: ~ director *n* γενικός διευθυντής.

mandarin ['mændərin] *n* (*orange*) μανταρίνι ‖ μανδαρῖνος.

mandate ['mændeit] n (*instruction*) ἐντολή || (*commission*) ἐντολή.

mandatory ['mændətəri] a ἐπιτακτικός.

mandolin(e) ['mændəlin] n μαντολίνο.

mane [mein] n χαίτη.

maneuver [mə'nu:və*] (*US*) = manoeuvre.

manful ['mænful] a ρωμαλέος, θαρραλέος || ~ly ad παλληκαρίσια.

mangle ['mæŋgl] vt καταξεσκίζω, κατακόπτω.

mango ['mæŋgəu] n μάγγο.

manhandle ['mænhændl] vt ξυλοφορτώνω, κακομεταχειρίζομαι.

manhole ['mænhəul] n ἀνθρωποθυρίς, εἴσοδος ὑπονόμου.

manhood ['mænhud] n ἀνδρικότης, ἀνδρική ἡλικία.

man-hour ['mæn'auə*] n ὡριαία ἐργασία.

manhunt ['mænhʌnt] n ἀνθρωποκηνύγι.

mania ['meiniə] n (*craze*) μανία, πάθος || τρέλλα || ~c n μανιακός.

manicure ['mænikjuə*] n μανικιούρ || vt φτιάχνω τά νύχια || ~ set n κασετίνα τοῦ μανικιούρ.

manifest ['mænifest] vt ἐπιδεικνύω, ἐκδηλώνω || a ἔκδηλος, προφανής || ~ation n ἐκδήλωσις || ~ly ad προφανῶς || ~o n διακήρυξις, μανιφέστο.

manipulate [mə'nipjuleit] vt χειρίζομαι, μανουβράρω.

manipulation [mənipju'leiʃən] n χειρισμός, τέχνασμα.

mankind [mæn'kaind] n ἀνθρωπότης, οἱ ἄνδρες.

manliness ['mænlinis] n ἀνδρικότης, ἀνδρισμός.

manly ['mænli] a ἀνδρικός, ἀνδροπρεπής, ἀντρίκιος.

manner ['mænə*] n τρόπος || (*custom*) συμπεριφορά, εἶδος || ~s npl συμπεριφορά, τρόποι || ~ism n (*of person*) ἰδιορρυθμία, ἰδιοτροπία.

manoeuvrable [mə'nu:vrəbl] a εὐέλικτος, εὐχείριστος.

manoeuvre [mə'nu:və*] vti ἑλίσσομαι, μανουβράρω || n (*mil*) ἑλιγμός, ἄσκησις || ἑλιγμός, μηχανορραφίες, μανοῦβρες || ~s npl γυμνάσια.

manor ['mænə*] n τιμάριον, κτῆμα || ~ house n ἀρχοντικό σπίτι.

manpower ['mænpauə*] n δύναμις εἰς ἄνδρας.

manservant ['mænsə:vənt] n ὑπηρέτης, καμαριέρης.

mansion ['mænʃən] n μέγαρον.

manslaughter ['mænslɔ:tə*] n ἀνθρωποκτονία.

mantelpiece ['mæntlpi:s] n γείσωμα τζακιοῦ.

mantle ['mæntl] n μανδύας.

manual ['mænjuəl] a χειρωνακτικός || n ἐγχειρίδιον.

manufacture [mænju'fæktʃə*] vt κατασκευ-άζω, βιομηχανοποιῶ || n κατασκευή, βιομηχανία || ~r n βιομήχανος.

manure [mə'njuə*] n κοπριά, λίπασμα.

manuscript ['mænjuskript] n χειρόγραφον.

many ['meni] a πολλοί, ἀρκετοί || n ἀρκετοί, πολλοί, ὅσοι.

map [mæp] n χάρτης || vt χαρτογραφῶ || to ~ out vt χαράσσω, καθορίζω, κανονίζω.

maple ['meipl] n σφεντάμι.

mar [mɑ:*] vt βλάπτω, χαλῶ, παραμορφώνω.

marathon ['mærəθən] n μαραθώνιος.

marauder [mə'rɔ:də*] n λεηλάτης, ληστής.

marble ['mɑ:bl] n μάρμαρον || pl (*game*) βῶλος, μπίλια.

March [mɑ:tʃ] n Μάρτης.

march [mɑ:tʃ] vi βαδίζω, βηματίζω, ὁδηγῶ || n (*tune*) ἐμβατήριον || πορεία, βάδισμα || ~-past n παρέλασις.

mare [mεə*] n φοράδα.

margarine [mɑ:dʒə'ri:n] n μαργαρίνη.

margin ['mɑ:dʒin] n (*page*) περιθώριον || (*extra amount*) περιθώριον || ~al a περιθωριακός.

marigold ['mærigəuld] n χρυσάνθεμο.

marijuana [mæri'hwa:nə] n μαριχουάνα.

marina [mə'ri:nə] n (*for boats*) μαρίνα.

marine [mə'ri:n] a θαλάσσιος, ναυτικός, πεζοναυτικός || n πεζοναύτης || ~r ['mærinə*] n ναύτης, ναυτιλόμενος.

marionette [mæriə'net] n μαριονέττα.

marital ['mæritl] a συζυγικός.

maritime ['mæritaim] a θαλασσινός, ναυτικός || (*power*) ναυτική (δύναμις).

marjoram ['mɑ:dʒərəm] n μαντζουράνα.

mark [mɑ:k] n (*coin*) μάρκα || (*scar etc*) σημάδι, ἴχνος, στίγμα || (*sign*) σημεῖον, ἔνδειξις || (*target*) στόχος, σημάδι || (*grade*) βαθμός || vt (*make a mark*) μαρκάρω, σημαδεύω || (*indicate*) δεικνύω, ἐκδηλώνω, δείχνω || (*watch etc*) προσέχω, κοιτάζω || (*exam*) διορθώνω, βαθμολογῶ || to ~ time κάνω βῆμα σημειωτόν || (*make no progress*) δέν προχωρῶ || to ~ out vt σημαδεύω || ~ed a ἔντονος, σαφής, φανερός, ἐμφανής || ~edly ad ἐντόνως, σαφῶς, καταφανῶς || ~er n (*sign*) δείκτης.

market ['mɑ:kit] n ἀγορά || (*overseas*) ἀγορά || (*demand*) ζήτησις || vt (*comm: new product*) πωλῶ || (*project*) προβάλλω || ~ day n ἡμέρα ἀγορᾶς || ~ garden n (*Brit*) περιβόλι (κηπουρικῶν) || ~ing n ἀγορά, πώλησις || ~ place n ἀγορά, παζάρι.

marksman ['mɑ:ksmən] n σκοπευτής || ~ship n σκοπευτική ἱκανότης.

marmalade ['mɑ:məleid] n μαρμελάδα.

maroon [mə'ru:n] vt (*usually passive*) ἐγκαταλείπω εἰς ἔρημον ἀκτήν || a (*colour*) ἐρυθρόφαιος.

marquee [mɑ:'ki:] n μεγάλη τέντα.

marquess. marquis ['mɑːkwis] n μαρκήσιος.

marriage ['mæridʒ] n (institution) παντρειά || (wedding) γάμος.

married ['mærid] a (person) ἔγγαμος || (life) ἔγγαμος βίος, παντρειά.

marrow ['mærəu] n μυελός, μεδούλι || (vegetable) κολοκύθι.

marry ['mæri] vt νυμφεύω, παντρεύω || vi (also get married) νυμφεύομαι, παντρεύομαι.

Mars [mɑːz] n ῎Αρης.

marsh [mɑːʃ] n ἕλος, βάλτος.

marshal ['mɑːʃəl] n (US) σερίφης || vt παρατάσσω, συγκεντρώνω || see field.

marshy ['mɑːʃi] a ἑλώδης.

martial ['mɑːʃəl] a πολεμικός, στρατιωτικός || ~ law n στρατιωτικός νόμος.

martyr ['mɑːtə*] n μάρτυρας || (fig) βασανιζόμενος, πάσχων ἀπό || ~dom n μαρτύριον.

marvel ['mɑːvəl] n θαῦμα || vi (+ at) ἐκπλήσσομαι, ξαφνίζομαι || ~lous, (US) ~ous a θαυμάσιος, καταπληκτικός || ~lously, (US) ~ously ad θαυμάσια, ὑπέροχα.

Marxism ['mɑːksizəm] n μαρξισμός.

Marxist ['mɑːksist] n μαρξιστής.

mascara [mæs'kɑːrə] n μάσκαρα.

mascot ['mæskət] n μασκώτ.

masculine ['mæskjulin] a ἄρρην, ἀρσενικός || (manly) ἀνδροπρεπής, ρωμαλέος || (gram) ἀρσενικός || n τό ἀρσενικόν.

masculinity [mæskju'liniti] n ἀρρενότης, ἀνδρικόν ὕφος.

mashed [mæʃt] a: ~ potatoes npl πατάτες πουρέ.

mask [mɑːsk] n προσωπίς, μάσκα || (pretence) προσωπεῖον || vt καλύπτω, ἀποκρύπτω.

masochist ['mæzəukist] n μαζοχιστής.

mason ['meisn] n (stonemason) κτίστης || (freemason) τέκτων || ~ic [mə'sɔnik] a τεκτονικός, μασονικός || ~ry ['meisnri] n λιθοδομή, κτίσιμο.

masquerade [mæskə'reid] n μεταμφίεσις || vi μεταμφιέζομαι.

mass [mæs] n (phys) μάζα || (information, people) ὄγκος, μάζα, πλῆθος || τό μεγαλύτερον μέρος, ἡ πλειοψηφία || (rel) λειτουργία || vi συγκεντρώνω, ἀθροίζω, μαζεύω || vi συγκεντροῦμαι, μαζεύομαι.

massacre ['mæsəkə*] n σφαγή, μακελειό || vt σφάζω.

massage ['mæsɑːʒ] n μάλαξις, μασσάζ || vt μαλάσσω, κάνω μασσάζ.

masseur [mæ'sɔː*] n μασσέρ.

masseuse [mæ'səːz] n μασέζ.

massive ['mæsiv] a ὀγκώδης, δυνατός.

mass media ['mæs'miːdiə] npl μέσα μαζικῆς ἐπικοινωνίας.

mass-produce ['mæsprə'djuːs] vi παράγω μαζικῶς.

mass production ['mæsprə'dʌkʃən] n μαζική παραγωγή.

mast [mɑːst] n ἱστός, κατάρτι || (pole) στήλη, στῦλος.

master ['mɑːstə*] n κύριος, ἀφεντικό || (teacher) δάσκαλος, καθηγητής || (head) ἀρχηγός || (of ship) καπετάνιος || (artist) μεγάλος καλλιτέχνης || vt ἐξουσιάζω, ἐλέγχω || (learn) μαθαίνω τέλεια || ~ly a ἔντεχνος, ἀριστοτεχνικός || ~mind n ἰθύνων νοῦς || vt συλλαμβάνω, πραγματοποιῶ || M~ of Arts n πτυχιοῦχος φιλολογίας || ~piece n ἀριστούργημα || ~ stroke n ἀριστοτεχνικόν κτύπημα || ~y n ἐξουσία, ὑπεροχή, μαεστρία.

masturbate ['mæstəbeit] vi μαλακίζομαι.

masturbation [mæstə'beiʃən] n μαλακία.

mat [mæt] n ψάθα, χαλάκι || (material for table) στρωσίδι τραπεζιοῦ || (tangled mass) μπλεγμένα νήματα κτλ || vti μπλέκω, μπερδεύομαι.

matador ['mætədə*] n ταυρομάχος.

match [mætʃ] n (matchstick) σπίρτο || (game) ἀγών || (equal) ταίρι || (marriage) συνοικέσιον || vt (be like) ἐναρμονίζω, ταιριάζω || (equal strength etc) ἐξισοῦμαι μέ, φθάνω || vi συμβιβάζομαι, συμφωνῶ, ταιριάζω || ~box n κουτί σπίρτα || ~ing a προσαρμογή, ταίριασμα || ~less a ἀπαράμιλλος.

mate [meit] n σύντροφος, συνάδελφος || (husband, wife) σύζυγος, ταίρι || (naut) ὑποπλοίαρχος || vi (chess) κάνω μάτ || (of animal) ζευγαρώνομαι.

material [mə'tiəriəl] n ὕλη, ὑλικόν || a σημαντικός, οὐσιώδης || (of matter) ὑλικός || (opposite of spirit) ὑλικός || ~s npl ὑλικά, ἐφόδια || ~istic a ὑλιστικός || ~ize vi πραγματοποιοῦμαι, γίνομαι || ~ly ad ὑλικῶς, οὐσιαστικά.

maternal [mə'tɜːnl] a μητρικός || (relatives) ἀπό τήν μητέρα.

maternity [mə'tɜːniti] n (dress) φόρεμα ἐγγύου || μητρότης || (hospital) μαιευτήριον.

matey ['meiti] a (col) φιλικός.

mathematical [mæθə'mætikəl] a μαθηματικός || (exact) μαθηματική (ἀκρίβεια) || ~ly ad μαθηματικῶς.

mathematician [mæθəmə'tiʃən] n μαθηματικός.

mathematics [mæθə'mætiks] n (also maths) μαθηματικά.

matinée ['mætinei] n παράστασις (ἀπογευματινή).

mating ['meitiŋ] n ζευγάρωμα, βάτεμα.

matins ['mætinz] npl ὄρθρος.

matriarchal [meitri'ɑːkl] a μητριαρχικός.

matrimonial [mætri'məuniəl] a γαμήλιος, συζυγικός.

matrimony ['mætriməni] n γάμος, ἔγγαμος βίος.

matron ['meitrən] n (med) προϊσταμένη ||

(sch) ἐπιμελήτρια, οἰκονόμος ‖ ~ly a
σεβάσμιος, ἀτάραχος.

matt [mæt] a (paint) μουντός, μάτ.

matter ['mætə*] n οὐσία, ὕλη ‖ (affair)
ὑπόθεσις, θέμα, πρᾶγμα ‖ (question,
issue etc) ζήτημα ‖ (discharge) πύον,
ἔμπυον ‖ vi ἔχω σημασίαν, ἐνδιαφέρω ‖
what is the ~? τί συμβαίνει; ‖ as a ~ of
fact τῷ ὄντι ‖ ~-of-fact a πεζός,
πρακτικός.

matting ['mætiŋ] n ψάθα, πλέγμα.

mattress ['mætris] n στρῶμα.

mature [mə'tjuə*] a ὥριμος ‖ vi ὡριμάζω.

maturity [mə'tjuəriti] n (fin) λῆξις.

maul [mɔːl] vt κακοποιῶ, κοπανίζω.

mausoleum [mɔːsə'liːəm] n μαυσωλεῖον.

mauve [məuv] a (colour) μώβ.

mawkish [mɔːkiʃ] a ἀνούσιος, ἀηδής.

maxim ['mæksim] n ἀπόφθεγμα, γνωμικόν.

maximize ['mæksimaiz] vt φέρω εἰς
μέγιστον.

maximum ['mæksiməm] a ἀνώτατος,
μέγιστος ‖ n μέγιστον, μάξιμουμ.

May [mei] n Μάης.

may [mei] (irreg v) vi (be possible) ἐνδέχεται
νά, ἴσως νά ‖ (have permission) ἔχω τήν
ἄδειαν νά, μπορῶ νά ‖ ~be ad ἴσως,
δυνατόν.

May Day ['meidei] n Πρωτομαγιά.

mayonnaise [meiə'neiz] n μαγιονέζα.

mayor [mεə*] n δήμαρχος ‖ ~ess n (wife)
κυρία δημάρχου ‖ (lady mayor) ἡ
δήμαρχος.

maze [meiz] n (network) λαβύρινθος ‖
(confused state) κυκεών.

me [miː] pron (after prep) (ἐ)μέ, σ' ἐμένα.

meadow ['mεdəu] n λειβάδι.

meagre, (US) meager ['miːgə*] a ἰσχνός,
πενιχρός.

meal [miːl] n φαγητό ‖ (grain) χονδράλευ-
ρον ‖ ~time n ὥρα φαγητοῦ ‖ ~y-
mouthed a γλυκομίλητος, μέ παχειά
λόγια.

mean [miːn] (irreg v) a ἄθλιος, φτωχός,
ταπεινός ‖ (stingy) φιλάργυρος, τσιγκούνης ‖ (average) μέσος, μεσαῖος ‖ vt
(signify) ἐννοῶ, σημαίνω, θέλω νά πῶ ‖
(intend) προτίθεμαι, σκοπεύω ‖ (be
resolved) προορίζω ‖ n (average) μέσος
ὅρος, μέσον ‖ ~s npl μέσα, τρόποι ‖
(wealth) πόροι, μέσα, περιουσία ‖ by
~s of διά, μέ τήν βοήθειαν τοῦ ‖ by all
~s ὁπωσδήποτε.

meander [mi'ændə*] vi ἑλίσσομαι, σχηματίζω μαιάνδρους.

meaning ['miːniŋ] n (intention) λόγος,
σκοπός ‖ (sense of word) ἔννοια, σημασία, νόημα ‖ ~ful a μέ σημασία, πού
λέει πολλά ‖ ~less a χωρίς νόημα.

meanness ['miːnnis] n μικρότης, μικροπρέ-
πεια.

meant [mεnt] pt,pp of mean.

meantime ['miːntaim] ad, meanwhile

['miːn'wail] ad ἐν τῷ μεταξύ, στό μεταξύ.

measles ['miːzlz] n ἱλαρά ‖ German ~ n
ἐρυθρά.

measly ['miːzli] a (col) ἀσήμαντος, ἀνάξιος,
τιποτένιος.

measurable ['mεʒərəbl] a καταμετρητός,
μετρήσιμος.

measure ['mεʒə*] vt (find size) μετρῶ ‖
(test) δοκιμάζω, ἀναμετρῶμαι ‖ vi (be
certain size) εἶναι, ἔχει διαστάσεις . . . ‖
n (unit) μέτρον ‖ (tape measure) μεζούρα,
μέτρον ‖ (plan) μέτρον, ἐνέργεια,
πρᾶξις ‖ (a law) μέτρον ‖ ~d a μετρημένος ‖ ~ment n (way of measuring)
μέτρησις, μέτρημα ‖ (amount measured)
μέτρα, διαστάσεις.

meat [miːt] n (flesh) κρέας ‖ ~ pie n
κρεατόπιττα ‖ ~y a (lit) σαρκώδης ‖
(fig) οὐσιαστικός, δεμένος, ζουμερός.

Mecca ['mεkə] n Μέκκα ‖ (fig) Μέκκα.

mechanic [mi'kænik] n τεχνίτης, μηχανικός ‖ ~s n μηχανική ‖ ~al a μηχανικός
‖ (automatically) μηχανικός, αὐτόματος.

mechanism ['mεkənizəm] n μηχανισμός.

mechanization [mεkənai'zeiʃən] n μηχανο-
ποίησις.

mechanize ['mεkənaiz] vt μηχανοποιῶ,
κάνω μηχανοκίνητο.

medal ['mεdl] n μετάλλιον ‖ ~lion
[mi'dæljən] n μενταγιόν ‖ ~list, (US)
~ist n κάτοχος μεταλλίου.

meddle ['mεdl] vi (+ with) ἀνακατεύομαι,
ἐπεμβαίνω ‖ ~some a πολυπράγμων,
ἀνακατωσούρης.

media ['miːdiə] npl (of communication)
μέσα.

mediate ['miːdieit] vi μεσολαβῶ.

mediation [miːdi'eiʃən] n μεσολάβησις.

mediator ['miːdieitə*] n μεσολαβητής.

medical ['mεdikəl] a (science) ἰατρικός ‖
(student) (φοιτητής) ἰατρικῆς ‖ ~ly ad
ἰατρικῶς.

medicated ['mεdikeitid] a ἐμποτισμένος μέ
φάρμακον.

medicinal [mε'disinl] a φαρμακευτικός,
ἰατρικός, θεραπευτικός.

medicine ['mεdsin] n ἰατρική ‖ (drugs)
φάρμακα, ἰατρικό ‖ ~ chest n φαρμακεῖο.

medieval [mεdi'iːvəl] a μεσαιωνικός.

mediocre [miːdi'əukə*] a μέτριος, τῆς
ἀράδας.

mediocrity [miːdi'ɔkriti] n μετριότης.

meditate ['mεditeit] vi (+ on) μελετῶ,
σκέπτομαι, συλλογίζομαι.

meditation [mεdi'teiʃən] n συλλογισμός,
διαλογισμός.

Mediterranean (Sea) [mεditə'reiniən(siː)] n
Μεσόγειος (θάλασσα).

medium ['miːdiəm] a μεσαῖος, μέτριος ‖ n
μέσον, μέσος ὅρος ‖ (means) μέσον, διά
τοῦ.

medley ['mεdli] n σύμφυρμα, κυκεών,
μίγμα.

meek [mi:k] *a* πρᾶος, ἥρεμος, πειθήνιος ‖ ~**ly** *ad* ἤρεμα, μαλακά.

meet [mi:t] (*irreg v*) *a* (*old*) πρέπων, σωστός, ποὺ ταιριάζει ‖ *vt* συναντῶ, ἀπαντῶ, ἀνταμώνω ‖ (*come across*) βρίσκω, ἀπαντῶ, διασταυροῦμαι ‖ (*go towards*) προχωρῶ πρός συνάντησιν, πηγαίνω ‖ (*pay, satisfy*) ἐκπληρώνω, ἀνταποκρίνομαι, τιμῶ ‖ *vi* (*by arrangement*) συναντῶμαι, βλέπομαι ‖ (*fight*) ἀντιμετωπίζω ‖ (*join*) συναντῶμαι, συναθροίζομαι, συνέρχομαι ‖ **to** ~ **with** *vt* (*problems*) συναντῶ, ἀντιμετωπίζω ‖ (*US: people*) συναντῶ, γνωρίζω ‖ ~**ing** *n* συνάντησις, συνάθροισις, συνέλευσις ‖ ~ **ing place** *n* τόπος συναντήσεως.

megaphone ['megəfəun] *n* μεγάφωνον.

melancholy ['melənkəli] *n* μελαγχολία, κατήφεια ‖ *a* μελαγχολικός.

mellow ['meləu] *a* ὤριμος ‖ (*delicate*) ἁπαλός, γλυκός ‖ (*aged*) ἁπαλός ‖ *vi* ὡριμάζω, ἀπαλύνομαι.

melodious [mi'ləudiəs] *a* μελωδικός.

melodrama ['melɔudra:mə] *n* μελόδραμα ‖ ~**tic** *a* μελοδραματικός.

melody ['melɔdi] *n* μελωδία.

melon ['melən] *n* πεπόνι.

melt [melt] *vi* τήκομαι, λυώνω ‖ (*disappear*) χάνομαι, διαλύομαι ‖ *vt* τήκω, λυώνω ‖ **to** ~ **away** *vi* λυώνω, διαλύομαι ‖ **to** ~ **down** *vt* λυώνω, τήκω ‖ ~**ing point** *n* σημεῖον τήξεως ‖ ~**ing pot** *n* (*fig*) χωνευτήριον, ρευστή κατάστασις.

member ['membə*] *n* μέλος ‖ (*part*) βουλευτής ‖ ~**ship** *n* ἰδιότης μέλους ‖ τά μέλη, ἀριθμός μελῶν.

membrane ['membrein] *n* μεμβράνη.

memento [mə'mentəu] *n* ἐνθύμιον, ἐνθύμησις.

memo ['meməu] *n* (*comm*) ὑπόμνημα, σημείωσις.

memoir ['memwa:*] *n* ὑπόμνημα ‖ ~**s** *npl* ἀπομνημονεύματα.

memorable ['memərəbl] *a* ἀξιομνημόνευτος, ἀξέχαστος.

memorandum [memə'rændəm] *n* (*comm*) ὑπόμνημα, σημείωσις.

memorial [mi'mɔ:riəl] *n* μνημεῖον ‖ *a* ἀναμνηστικός, ἐπιμνημόσυνος.

memorize ['meməraiz] *vt* ἀποστηθίζω, μαθαίνω ἀπ' ἔξω.

memory ['meməri] *n* μνήμη, μνημονικό, θυμητικό ‖ (*thing recalled*) ἀνάμνησις, θύμηση ‖ **in** ~ **of** εἰς μνήμην τοῦ, εἰς ἀνάμνησιν τοῦ.

men [men] *npl of* **man**.

menace ['menis] *n* ἀπειλή, φοβέρα ‖ *vt* ἀπειλῶ, φοβερίζω.

menacing ['menisiŋ] *a* ἀπειλητικός ‖ ~**ly** *ad* ἀπειλητικά.

ménage [me'na:ʒ] *n* νοικοκυριό.

menagerie [mi'nædʒəri] *n* θηριοτροφεῖον.

mend [mend] *vt* (ἐπι)διορθώνω, βελτιώνω ‖

vi ἀναρρωνύω ‖ *n* ἐπιδιόρθωσις, ἐπισκευή ‖ **on the** ~ συνέρχομαι, πάω καλύτερα.

menial ['mi:niəl] *a* ταπεινός, δουλοπρεπής.

meningitis [menin'dʒaitis] *n* μηνιγγῖτις.

menopause ['menɔupɔ:z] *n* ἐμμηνόπαυσις.

menstrual ['menstruəl] *a* καταμήνιος, ἔμμηνος.

menstruation [menstru'eiʃən] *n* ἔμμηνα, περίοδος.

mental ['mentl] *a* διανοητικός, νοερός, πνευματικός ‖ (*col: abnormal*) τρελλός ‖ ~**ity** *n* νοοτροπία ‖ ~**ly** *ad* πνευματικώς.

mentholated ['menθəleitid] *a* περιέχον μινθόλην.

mention ['menʃən] *n* μνεία ‖ *vt* ἀναφέρω ‖ **don't** ~ **it!** παρακαλῶ!

menu ['menju:] *n* μενού.

mercantile ['mə:kəntail] *a* ἐμπορικός.

mercenary ['mə:sinəri] *a* φιλοχρήματος, πλεονέκτης ‖ *n* μισθοφόρος.

merchandise ['mə:tʃəndaiz] *n* ἐμπορεύματα.

merchant ['mɔ:tʃənt] *n* ἔμπορος ‖ *a* ἐμπορικός ‖ ~ **navy** *n* ἐμπορικόν ναυτικόν.

merciful ['mɔ:siful] *a* εὔσπλαχνος ‖ ~**ly** *ad* σπλαχνικά.

merciless ['mə:silis] *a* ἀνηλεής, ἄσπλαχνος ‖ ~**ly** *ad* ἀνηλεῶς, ἀλύπητα.

mercurial [mə:'kjuəriəl] *a* ὑδραργυρικός, ζωηρός.

mercury ['mə:kjuri] *n* ὑδράργυρος.

mercy ['mə:si] *n* εὐσπλαχνία, ἔλεος ‖ (*blessing*) εὐλογία ‖ **at the** ~ **of** στό ἔλεός τοῦ.

mere [miə*] *a* ἁπλός, τίποτε ἄλλο ἀπό ‖ ~**ly** *ad* ἁπλῶς, μόνον.

merge [mə:dʒ] *vt* ἀπορροφῶ, συγχωνεύω ‖ *vi* (*become absorbed*) ἀπορροφοῦμαι, συγχωνεύομαι ‖ ~**r** *n* (*comm*) συγχώνευσις.

meridian [mə'ridiən] *n* μεσημβρινός.

meringue [mə'ræŋ] *n* μαρέγγα.

merit ['merit] *n* ἀξία, προσόν ‖ *vt* ἀξίζω.

mermaid ['mə:meid] *n* γοργόνα.

merrily ['merili] *ad* εὔθυμα, χαρούμενα.

merriment ['merimənt] *n* εὐθυμία, διασκέδασις.

merry ['meri] *a* εὔθυμος, φαιδρός, χαρωπός ‖ (*col: after drink*) στό κέφι, πιωμένος.

mesh [meʃ] *n* θηλειά (δικτύου) ‖ *vti* (*gears*) ἐμπλέκω, ἐμπλέκομαι.

mesmerize ['mezməraiz] *vt* μαγνητίζω, ὑπνωτίζω.

mess [mes] *n* σαλάτα, θάλασσα ‖ (*untidy state*) ἀκαθαρσία, ἄνω-κάτω ‖ (*mil*) συσσίτιον, τραπέζι ‖ (*officers' mess*) λέσχη ἀξιωματικῶν ‖ **to** ~ **about** *vi* χασομερῶ ‖ **to** ~ **about with** *vt* πασπατεύω, σαχλαμαρίζω ‖ **to** ~ **up** *vt* χαλῶ, μπλέκω, περιπλέκω.

message ['mesidʒ] *n* μήνυμα, διάγγελμα εἴδησις.

messenger ['mesindʒə*] *n* ἀγγελιαφόρος.

messy ['mesi] *a* ἀκάθαρτος, φύρδην-μύγδην.

met [met] *pt,pp of* **meet**.

metabolism [me'tæbəlizəm] *n* μεταβολισμός.

metal ['metl] *n* μέταλλον || **~lic** *a* μεταλλικός || **~lurgy** *n* μεταλλουργία.

metamorphosis [metə'mɔ:fəsis] *n* μεταμόρφωσις.

metaphor ['metəfɔ:*] *n* μεταφορά || **~ical** *a* μεταφορικός.

metaphysics [metə'fiziks] *n* μεταφυσική.

meteor ['mi:tiə*] *n* μετέωρον || **~ic** *a* μετεωρικός, λαμπρός || **~ite** *n* μετεωρίτης || **~ological** *a* μετεωρολογικός || **~ology** *n* μετεωρολογία.

meter ['mi:tə*] *n* (*instrument*) μετρητής || (*US*) = **metre**.

method ['meθəd] *n* μέθοδος || **~ical** *a* μεθοδικός.

Methodist ['meθədist] *a,n* μεθοδιστής.

methodology [meθə'dɔlədʒi] *n* μεθοδολογία.

methylated spirit ['meθileitid'spirit] *n* (*also* **meths**) μεθυλικόν οἰνόπνευμα.

meticulous [mi'tikjuləs] *a* λεπτολόγος, λεπτομερειακός.

metre ['mi:tə*] *n* μέτρον.

metric(al) ['metrik(əl)] *a* μετρικός || **~ system** *n* μετρικόν σύστημα.

metronome ['metrənəum] *n* μετρονόμος.

metropolis [mi'trɔpəlis] *n* μητρόπολις.

mews [mju:z] *n* ἀδιέξοδος.

Mexican ['meksikən] *a* μεξικανικός || *n* Μεξικανός.

Mexico ['meksikəu] *n* Μεξικόν.

mezzanine ['mezəni:n] *n* μετζοπάτωμα, μέτζο.

miaow [mi:'au] *vi* νιαουρίζω.

mice [mais] *npl of* **mouse**.

mickey ['miki] *n* (*col*) **to take the ~ out of s.o.** κοροϊδεύω, τῇ σκάω.

microbe ['maikrəub] *n* μικρόβιον.

microfilm ['maikrəufilm] *n* μικροφίλμ.

microphone ['maikrəfəun] *n* μικρόφωνον.

microscope ['maikrəskəup] *n* μικροσκόπιον.

microscopic [maikrə'skɔpik] *a* μικροσκοπικός.

mid [mid] *a* μέσος, μεσαῖος || **in ~ course** στό μέσον, στήν ἀκμήν.

midday ['mid'dei] *n* μεσημέρι.

middle ['midl] *n* μέσον || *a* μέσος, μεσαῖος || **~-aged** *a* μεσῆλιξ || **the M~ Ages** *npl* ὁ Μεσαίων || **~ class** *n* μεσαία τάξις, ἀστική τάξις || **~-class** *a* ἀστικός || **M~ East** *n* Μέση Ἀνατολή || **~man** *n* μεταπωλητής, μεσίτης || **~ name** *n* ὄνομα πατρός.

middling ['midliŋ] *ad* μέτρια, καλούτσικα.

midge [midʒ] *n* σκνίπα.

midget ['midʒit] *n* νάνος, ἀνθρωπάκι || *a* μικρός, μικροσκοπικός.

Midlands ['midləndz] *n* (*of England*) κεντρικές κομητεῖες (τῆς Ἀγγλίας).

midnight ['midnait] *n* μεσάνυκτα.

midst [midst] *n*: **in the ~ of** στό μέσον.

midsummer ['mid'sʌmə*] *n* μεσοκαλόκαιρο.

midway ['mid'wei] *ad* (+ *between*) στό μέσον || *a* μέσος.

midweek ['mid'wi:k] *ad* στά μέσα τῆς ἑβδομάδος.

midwife ['midwaif] *n* μαία, μαμμή || **~ry** ['midwifəri] *n* μαιευτική.

midwinter ['mid'wintə*] *n* στό μέσον τοῦ χειμῶνος, μεσοχείμωνο.

might [mait] *pt of* **may** || *n* ἰσχύς, δύναμις || **~ily** *ad* (*very*) πάρα πολύ, περίφημα || ἰσχυρός, μέ δύναμιν || **~n't** = **might not**, *see* **may** || **~y** *a* ἰσχυρός, δυνατός || *ad* (*col*) πολύ, τρομερά.

migraine ['mi:grein] *n* ἡμικρανία.

migrant ['maigrənt] *n* μεταναστευτικός, περαστικός || *a* ἀποδημητικός, μεταναστευτικός.

migrate [mai'greit] *vi* (*birds*) ἀποδημῶ.

migration [mai'greiʃən] *n* μετανάστευσις.

mike [maik] *n* (*microphone*) μικρόφωνον.

mild [maild] *a* (*rebuke*) ἐπιεικής, μαλακός || (*warm*) ἤπιος, εὔκρατος || (*not sour*) ἐλαφρό || (*slight*) ἐλαφρό || *n* (*beer*) ἐλαφριά μπύρα.

mildew ['mildju:] *n* μούχλα, σείρηκας.

mildly ['maildli] *ad* ἤρεμα, μαλακά.

mildness ['maildnis] *n* ἡπιότης, γλύκα, ἐπιείκεια.

mile [mail] *n* μίλι (1609 μ) || **~age** *n* ἀπόστασις εἰς μίλια || **~stone** *n* μιλιοδείκτης || (*fig*) ἱστορικός σταθμός.

militant ['militənt] *n* ὀπαδός τῆς ἀμέσου δράσεως || *a* μαχητικός.

militarism ['militərizəm] *n* μιλιταρισμός.

military ['militəri] *a* στρατιωτικός || *n* οἱ στρατιωτικοί, στρατός.

militate ['militeit] *vi* (+ *against*) ἀντιστρατεύομαι, ἀντιμάχομαι.

militia [mi'liʃə] *n* ἐθνοφυλακή.

milk [milk] *n* γάλα || *vt* (*cow*) ἀρμέγω || (*fig*) ἐκμεταλλεύομαι, μαδῶ || **~ chocolate** *n* σοκολάτα γάλακτος || **~ing** *n* ἄρμεγμα || **~man** *n* γαλατάς || **M~y Way** *n* Γαλαξίας.

mill [mil] *n* μύλος || (*building*) μύλος || (*factory*) ἐργοστάσιον || *vt* (*grind*) ἀλέθω || *vi* (*move around*) στριφογυρίζω || **~ed** *a* ὀδοντωτός, μέ ῥαβδώσεις.

millenium [mi'leniəm] *n* χιλιετηρίς.

miller ['milə*] *n* μυλωνάς.

millet ['milit] *n* κεχρί, σόργον.

milligram(me) ['miligræm] *n* χιλιοστόγραμμον.

millilitre, (*US*) **~liter** ['milili:tə*] *n* χιλιοστόλιτρον.

millimetre, (*US*) **~meter** [milimi:tə*] *n* χιλιοστόμετρον.

milliner ['milinə*] *n* καπελοῦ || **~y** *n* γυναικεῖα καπέλλα || ἐμπόριον γυναικείων καπέλλων.

million ['miljən] *n* ἑκατομμύριον ‖ ~**aire** *n* ἑκατομμυριοῦχος ‖ ~**th** *a* ἑκατομμυριοστός.

mime [maim] *n* μῖμος, μιμόδραμα ‖ *vti* μιμοῦμαι, παίζω μέ μιμικήν.

mimic ['mimik] *n* μῖμος, μιμητής ‖ *vti* μιμοῦμαι, κοροϊδεύω, ἀντιγράφω ‖ ~**ry** *n* μίμησις, μιμική.

mince [mins] *vt* ψιλοκόβω, κάνω κιμᾶ ‖ (*words*) μασῶ ‖ *vi* βαδίζω μέ προσποιητήν χάριν ‖ *n* (*meat*) κιμᾶς ‖ ~**meat** *n* κομπόστα ‖ ~ **pie** *n* σκαλτσούνι, κρεατόπιττα ‖ ~**r** *n* κρεατομηχανή.

mincing ['minsiŋ] *a* (*manner*) προσποιητός, φτιαστός, ψεύτικος.

mind [maind] *n* νοῦς, μυαλό ‖ (*intelligence*) σκέψις, γνώμη, ἰδέα ‖ (*memory*) μνήμη, ἀνάμνησις, θύμησις ‖ *vti* φροντίζω, προσέχω ‖ (*be careful*) προσέχω ‖ (*object to*) ἀντιτίθεμαι πρός, ἐνοχλοῦμαι, πειράζομαι ‖ **on my** ~ στή σκέψι μου, ἀνησυχῶ ‖ **to my** ~ κατά τήν γνώμην μου ‖ **out of one's** ~ τρελλός ‖ **never** ~ !, δέν πειράζει, ἄστο, μήν ἀνησυχεῖς ‖ **to bear or keep in** ~ δέν ξεχνῶ, λαμβάνω ὑπ' ὄψιν ‖ **to make up one's** ~ ἀποφασίζω ‖ '~ **the step'** 'πρόσεχε τήν σκάλα' ‖ ~**ed** *a* διατεθειμένος, μέ πνεῦμα ‖ ~**ful** *a* προσεκτικός ‖ ~**less** *a* ἀπερίσκεπτος, ἀδιάφορος, ἐπιλήσμων.

mine [main] *poss pron* δικός μου, δική μου, δικό μου ‖ *n* ὀρυχεῖον, μεταλλεῖον ‖ (*naut*) νάρκη ‖ (*source*) πηγή ‖ *vt* ἐξορύσσω ‖ (*naut*) ναρκοθετῶ ‖ *vi* ἐκμεταλλεύομαι ‖ ~**field** *n* ναρκοπέδιον ‖ ~**r** *n* μεταλλορύχος, ἀνθρακορύχος.

mineral ['minərəl] *a* ὀρυκτός, μεταλλευτικός ‖ *n* ὀρυκτόν, μετάλλευμα ‖ ~**ogy** *n* ὀρυκτολογία ‖ ~ **water** *n* ἀεριοῦχο ποτό, μεταλλικόν ὕδωρ.

minesweeper ['mainswi:pə*] *n* ναρκαλιευτικόν.

mingle ['miŋgl] *vt* ἀναμιγνύω ‖ *vi* (+ **with**) ἀναμιγνύομαι.

mingy ['mindʒi] *a* (*col*) στριμμένος, γύφτος, μίζερος.

mini- ['mini] *prefix* μικρο-.

miniature ['minitʃə*] *a* μικρογραφικός ‖ *n* μικρογραφία, μινιατούρα ‖ (*model*) μακέτα ‖ **in** ~ μικρό σχήματος.

minibus ['minibʌs] *n* μικρό λεωφορεῖο.

minicab ['minikæb] *n* μικρό ταξί.

minimal ['miniml] *a* ἐλάχιστος.

minimize ['minimaiz] *vt* ἐλαττώνω, μικραίνω, περιορίζω.

minimum ['miniməm] *n* ἐλάχιστον, κατώτατον ὅριον, μίνιμουμ ‖ *a* κατώτατος, ἐλάχιστος.

mining ['mainiŋ] *n* ἐξόρυξις ‖ (*naut*) ναρκοθέτησις ‖ *a* μεταλλευτική, ὀρυκτική.

minion ['minjən] *n* (*pej*) εὐνοούμενος, δοῦλος.

miniskirt ['miniskə:t] *n* κοντή φοῦστα, μίνι.

minister ['ministə*] *n* ὑπουργός ‖ (*eccl*) ἱερεύς ‖ ~**ial** [minis'tiəriəl] *a* ὑπουργικός, κυβερνητικός.

ministry ['ministri] *n* (*government*) ὑπουργεῖον, κυβέρνησις ‖ (*eccl*) τό ἱερατεῖον, κλῆρος.

mink [miŋk] *n* εἶδος νιφίτσας ‖ *a*: ~ **coat** *n* παλτό ἀπό μίνκ.

minor ['mainə*] *a* μικρότερος, μικρός ‖ (*mus*) ἐλάσσων ‖ *n* (*under 18: Brit*) ἀνήλικος ‖ ~**ity** [mai'nɔriti] *n* μειοψηφία, μειονότης.

minster ['minstə*] *n* καθεδρικός ναός ‖ (*of monastery*) ἐκκλησία μονῆς.

minstrel ['minstrəl] *n* ψωμαδός, τραγουδιστής.

mint [mint] *n* (*plant*) δυόσμος ‖ (*sweet*) μέντα ‖ (*for coins*) νομισματοκοπεῖον ¶ (*large amount*) μέ τό τσουβάλι ‖ *a* (*condition*) καινούργιος, κατακαίνουργος ‖ ~ **sauce** *n* σάλτσα μέ δυόσμο.

minuet [minju'et] *n* μενουέτο.

minus ['mainəs] *n* σημεῖον τοῦ πλήν ‖ *prep* πλήν, μεῖον.

minute [mai'nju:t] *a* μικροσκοπικός, ἐλάχιστος ‖ (*detailed*) λεπτομερής ‖ ['minit] *n* λεπτόν (τῆς ὥρας) ‖ (*moment*) στιγμή ‖ ~**s** *npl* πρακτικά ‖ ~**ly** *ad* ἐπιμελῶς, λεπτομερειακῶς.

miracle ['mirəkl] *n* (*esp rel*) θαῦμα ‖ ~ **play** *n* θρησκευτικόν δρᾶμα.

miraculous [mi'rækjuləs] *a* θαυματουργός, ὑπερφυσικός, θαυμαστός ‖ ~**ly** *ad* ὡς ἐκ θαύματος.

mirage ['mira:ʒ] *n* ἀντικατοπτρισμός, ὀπτική ἀπάτη.

mirror ['mirə*] *n* καθρέπτης, κάτοπτρον ‖ *vt* ἀντικατοπτρίζω, ἀντανακλῶ.

mirth [mə:θ] *n* εὐθυμία, χαρά, κέφι.

misadventure [misəd'ventʃə*] *n* κακοτυχία, ἀτύχημα.

misanthropist [mi'zænθrəpist] *n* μισάνθρωπος.

misapply ['misə'plai] *vt* ἐφαρμόζω κακῶς.

misapprehension ['misæpri'henʃən] *n* (*misunderstanding*) παρεξήγησις.

misappropriate ['misə'prəuprieit] *vt* (*take dishonestly*) καταχρῶμαι.

misappropriation ['misəprəupri'eiʃən] *n* κατάχρησις, διασπάθισις.

misbehave ['misbi'heiv] *vi* φέρομαι ἄσχημα.

miscalculate ['mis'kælkjuleit] *vt* ὑπολογίζω ἐσφαλμένα.

miscalculation ['miskælkju'leiʃən] *n* ἐσφαλμένος ὑπολογισμός.

miscarriage ['miskæridʒ] *n* ἀποτυχία ‖ (*of justice*) δικαστικόν λάθος ‖ (*med*) ἀποβολή.

miscellaneous [misi'leiniəs] *a* ποικίλος, ἀνάμικτος.

mischance [mis'tʃa:ns] *n* ἀποτυχία, ἀτυχημα.

mischief ['mistʃif] n σκανταλιά, κατεργαριά.

mischievous ['mistʃivəs] a κατεργάρης, σκανταλιάρης ‖ ~ly ad βλαβερά, κατεργάρικα.

misconception ['miskən'sepʃən] n ἐσφαλμένη ἀντίληψις.

misconduct [mis'kɔndʌkt] n παράπτωμα, κακή διαγωγή.

misconstrue ['miskən'stru:] vt (misunderstand) παρερμηνεύω.

miscount ['mis'kaunt] vt μετρῶ ἐσφαλμένα.

misdemeanour, (US) **misdemeanor** [misdi'mi:nə*] n (less important offence) πταῖσμα, πλημμέλημα.

misdirect ['misdi'rekt] vt (person, letter) κατευθύνω ἐσφαλμένα, διευθύνω κακῶς.

miser ['maizə*] n φιλάργυρος, τσιγκούνης.

miserable ['mizərəbl] a δυστυχής, θλιβερός ‖ (poor) ἄθλιος, ἐλεεινός, φτωχός.

miserably ['mizərəbli] ad θλιβερά, ἄθλια.

miserly ['maizəli] a τσιγκούνικος.

misery ['mizəri] n δυστυχία, βάσανον ‖ (poverty) ἀθλιότης, φτώχια.

misfire ['mis'faiə*] vi ρετάρω, παθαίνω ἀφλογιστίαν ‖ (plan) πέφτω στό κενό.

misfit ['misfit] n (person) ἀπροσάρμοστος.

misfortune [mis'fɔ:tʃən] n ἀτυχία, ἀτύχημα.

misgiving [mis'giviŋ] n (often pl) ἀνησυχία, ἀμφιβολία, φόβος.

misguided ['mis'gaidid] a πλανόμενος, παρασυρόμενος.

mishandle ['mis'hændl] vt (manage badly) κακομεταχειρίζομαι.

mishap ['mishæp] n ἀτυχία, ἀναποδιά.

mishear ['mis'hiə*] vt (hear wrongly) παρακούω.

misinform ['misin'fɔ:m] vt πληροφορῶ κακῶς.

misinterpret ['misin'tə:prit] vt παρερμηνεύω ‖ ~ation n παρερμηνεία.

misjudge ['mis'dʒʌdʒ] vt κρίνω ἐσφαλμένα.

mislay [mis'lei] vt (misplace, lose) παραπετῶ, χάνω.

mislead [mis'li:d] vt (deceive) παραπλανῶ, ἐξαπατῶ ‖ ~ing a παραπλανητικός.

misnomer ['mis'nəumə*] n ἐσφαλμένη ὀνομασία.

misogynist [mi'sɔdʒinist] n μισογύνης.

misplace ['mis'pleis] vt (mislay) τοποθετῶ κατά λάθος, χάνω.

misprint ['misprint] n τυπογραφικόν λάθος.

mispronounce ['misprə'nauns] vt προφέρω ἐσφαλμένα.

misread ['mis'ri:d] vt κακοδιαβάζω, παρερμηνεύω.

misrepresent ['misrepri'zent] vt διαστρέφω, παριστάνω κακῶς.

miss [mis] vt ἀστοχῶ, ἀποτυγχάνω ‖ (not notice) δέν βλέπω, χάνω ‖ (train etc) χάνω ‖ (omit) παραλείπω ‖ (regret absence) μοῦ λείπει, ἀποζητῶ ‖ vi ἀντιλαμβάνομαι ‖ n (shot) ἀστοχία ‖ (failure) ἀποτυχία ‖

(title) δεσποινίδα ‖ to ~ the bus or boat (fig) χάνω εὐκαιρίαν ‖ M~ Smith Δεσποινίδα Σμίθ, Δις Σμίθ.

misshapen ['mis'ʃeipən] a παραμορφωμένος.

missile ['misail] n (esp nuclear) βλῆμα.

missing ['misiŋ] a (person) ἀπών, ἀγνοούμενος ‖ (thing) χαμένος.

mission ['miʃən] n ἀποστολή ‖ (church) ἱεραποστολή ‖ ~ary n ἱεραπόστολος.

misspent ['mis'spent] a (youth) χαμένα (νειάτα).

mist [mist] n ὀμίχλη, καταχνιά ‖ vi (also ~ over, ~ up) σκεπάζω μέ ὀμίχλην, θαμπώνω.

mistake [mis'teik] n σφάλμα, λάθος ‖ vt παρανοῶ, παρερμηνεύω ‖ (for another) παίρνω γιά ἄλλον, παραγνωρίζω ‖ ~n a (person) σφάλλω, κάνω λάθος ‖ (identity) σφάλλω περί τό πρόσωπον.

mister ['mistə*] n (abbr Mr) κύριος (Κος) ‖ Mr Smith Κος Σμίθ.

mistletoe ['misltəu] n ἱξός, γκί.

mistranslation ['mistræns'leiʃən] n ἀνακριβής μετάφρασις.

mistreat [mis'tri:t] vt κακομεταχειρίζομαι.

mistress ['mistris] n (teacher) δασκάλα ‖ (of house) κυρία, οἰκοδέσποινα ‖ (lover) ἐρωμένη, μαιτρέσσα ‖ (abbr Mrs) κυρία (Κα) ‖ Mrs Smith Κα Σμίθ.

mistrust ['mis'trʌst] vt δυσπιστῶ πρός, ὑποπτεύομαι.

misty ['misti] a ὀμιχλώδης, θαμπός, σκοτεινιασμένος.

misunderstand ['misʌndə'stænd] vti παρανοῶ, παρεξηγῶ ‖ ~ing n παρανόησις, παρεξήγησις.

misunderstood ['misʌndə'stud] a (person) παρεξηγημένος.

misuse ['mis'ju:s] n κακή χρῆσις ‖ ['mis'ju:z] vt κάνω κατάχρησιν, χρησιμοποιῶ ἐσφαλμένως.

mite [mait] n (insect) σκουλήκι.

miter ['maitə*] n (US) = **mitre**.

mitigate ['mitigeit] vt μετριάζω, καταπραΰνω.

mitre ['maitə*] n λοξή ἕνωσις, ὀνυχωτή ἕνωσις ‖ (eccl) μίτρα.

mitt(en) ['mit(n)] n εἶδος γαντιοῦ.

mix [miks] vt ἀναμιγνύω, ἀνακατώνω ‖ vi ἀναμιγνύομαι, ταιριάζω ‖ n (mixture) μῖξις, μῖγμα ‖ to ~ up vt ἀνακατεύω ‖ (confuse) μπερδεύω ‖ ~ed a (assorted) ἀνάμικτος ‖ (school etc) μικτός ‖ ~ed grill n μίξτ γκρίλλ ‖ ~ed-up a (confused) ζαλισμένος, ἄνω-κάτω ‖ ~r n (for food) μίξερ ‖ (person) κοινωνικός ‖ ~ture n (assortment) ἀμάλγαμα, ἀνακάτεμα ‖ (med) μῖγμα ‖ ~-up n (confusion) σύγχυσις, ἀνακατωσούρα.

moan [məun] n (groan) γογγυσμός, βογγητό ‖ (complaint) γκρίνια, μουρμουρητό

|| vi στενάζω, βογγῶ, γογγύζω || ~ing n βογγητό, κλάμα.

moat [məʊt] n τάφρος.

mob [mɔb] n ὄχλος, τό πλῆθος || vt (star etc) πολιορκῶ, κυκλώνω.

mobile ['məʊbail] a εὐκίνητος, κινητός, εὐμετάβολος.

mobility [məʊ'biliti] n εὐκινησία, κινητικότης.

mock [mɔk] vt ἐμπαίζω, κοροϊδεύω, περιπαίζω || a ψεύτικος, φτιαστός || ~ery n (derision) ἐμπαιγμός, κοροϊδία || (object) περίγελας, κοροῖδο || ~ing a (tone) εἰρωνικός, σαρκαστικός || ~-up n ὑπόδειγμα, μακέττα.

model ['mɔdl] n ὁμοίωμα, μοντέλλο || (example) πρότυπον, ὑπόδειγμα || (person) μοντέλλο || (of clothes) μανεκκέν || vt (δια)πλάθω, διαμορφώνω, σχεδιάζω || (display clothes) κάνω ἐπίδειξι (ρούχων) || a (railway: toy) τραινάκι || (child) πρότυπον, ἰδεώδης || ~ling, (US) ~ing n σχέδιασμα, πλάσιμο || (of styles) ἐπίδειξις μόδας.

moderate ['mɔdərit] a μέτριος, μέσος || (fairly good) μέτριος, τῆς σειρᾶς || n (pol) μετριοπαθής || ['mɔdəreit] vi προΐσταμαι, προεδρεύω || vt μετριάζω, περιορίζω || ~ly ad μετρημένα, συγκρατημένα, μέτρια.

moderation [mɔdə'reiʃən] n μετριασμός, μετριοπάθεια.

modern ['mɔdən] a σύγχρονος, μοντέρνος || ~ization n (ἐκ)συγχρονισμός || ~ize vt συγχρονίζω, ἀνανεώνω.

modest ['mɔdist] a (attitude) μετριόφρων, σεμνός || (meal, home) ταπεινός, μέτριος || ~ly ad μετριοπαθῶς, σεμνά, ντροπαλά || ~y n μετριοφροσύνη, σεμνότης, ταπεινότης.

modicum ['mɔdikəm] n: with a ~ of μέ ἐλάχιστο, μέ λίγο.

modification [mɔdifi'keiʃən] n τροποποίησις, μετριασμός.

modify ['mɔdifai] vt τροποποιῶ, μετριάζω.

module ['mɔdju:l] n (space) σεληνάκατος.

mohair ['məʊhɛə*] n μαλλί μοχαίρ.

moist [mɔist] a ὑγρός, νοτισμένος || ~en vt ὑγραίνω, μουσκεύω || ~ure n ὑγρασία.

molar ['məʊlə*] n γομφίος, μυλίτης, τραπεζίτης.

mold [məʊld] (US) = mould.

mole [məʊl] n (spot) κρεατοελιά || (animal) τυφλοπόντικας || (pier) κυματοθραύστης, μῶλος.

molecular [mə'lekjulə*] a μοριακός.

molecule ['mɔlikju:l] n μόριον.

molest [məʊ'lest] vt (παρ)ενοχλῶ, πειράζω.

molt [məʊlt] (US) = moult.

molten ['məʊltən] a τετηγμένος, λυωμένος.

moment ['məʊmənt] n στιγμή || (importance) βαρύτης, σπουδαιότης || ~arily ad σέ μιά στιγμή || ~arv a στιγμιαίος, προσω-

ρινός || ~ous a βαρυσήμαντος, σημαντικός || ~um n ὁρμή, φορά.

monarch ['mɔnək] n μονάρχης || ~ist n μοναρχικός || ~y n μοναρχία.

monastery ['mɔnəstri] n μοναστήρι.

monastic [mə'næstik] a μοναχικός, μοναστικός.

Monday ['mʌndi] n Δευτέρα.

monetary ['mʌnitəri] a νομισματικός, χρηματικός.

money ['mʌni] n χρῆμα, νόμισμα, παράς || (wealth) χρήματα, πλούτη || ~ed a πλούσιος || ~lender n τοκιστής, τοκογλύφος || ~making a ἐπικερδής, κερδοφόρος || n ἀπόκτησις χρημάτων || ~order n ταχυδρομική ἐπιταγή.

mongol ['mɔŋgəl] n (child) πάσχων ἐκ μογγολισμοῦ || a μογγολικός.

mongrel ['mʌŋgrəl] n μιγάς || a μιγαδικός μιξιγενής.

monitor ['mɔnitə*] n παρεναίτης, ἐπιμελητής || (television monitor) ἐλεγκτής || vt (broadcasts) ἐλέγχω.

monk [mʌŋk] n καλόγηρος, μοναχός.

monkey ['mʌŋki] n πίθηκος, μαϊμοῦ || ~nut n ἀραποφύστικο || ~ wrench n γαλλικό κλειδί.

mono- ['mɔnəʊ] prefix μον(ο)-.

monochrome ['mɔnəkrəʊm] a (TV) μονόχρωμος.

monocle ['mɔnəkl] n μονύαλος, μονόκλ.

monogram ['mɔnəgræm] n μονόγραμμα, μονογραφή.

monolithic [mɔnəʊ'liθik] a μονολιθικός.

monologue ['mɔnələg] n μονόλογος.

monopolize [mə'nɔpəlaiz] vt μονοπωλῶ.

monopoly [mə'nɔpəli] n μονοπώλιον.

monorail ['mɔnəʊreil] n μονόραβδος.

monosyllabic ['mɔnəʊsi'læbik] a (person) μονοσυλλαβικός.

monotone ['mɔnətəʊn] n μονοτονία ἤχου, μονότονος ὁμιλία.

monotonous [mə'nɔtənəs] a μονότονος.

monotony [mə'nɔtəni] n μονοτονία.

monsoon [mɔn'su:n] n (with rains) θερινός μουσών.

monster ['mɔnstə*] n (huge animal) τέρας, τερατούργημα || (wicked person) τέρας || a (col) κολοσσιαῖος, πελώριος.

monstrosity [mɔns'trɔsiti] n τερατωδία, κτηνωδία.

monstrous ['mɔnstrəs] a τερατώδης, ἐκτρωματικός.

montage [mɔn'ta:ʒ] n (picture) μοντάζ, μοντάρισμα.

month [mʌnθ] n μήν, μήνας || ~ly a μηνιαῖος, μηνιάτικος || ad μηνιαίως, κάθε μήνα || n (magazine) μηνιαίον περιοδικόν || monthlies npl ἔμμηνα.

monument ['mɔnjumənt] n μνημεῖον || ~al a μνημειακός || (work etc) μνημειώδης.

moo [mu:] vi (cow) μηκώμαι, μουγκρίζω.

mood [mu:d] n διάθεσις, κέφι || (gram)

ἔγκλισις ‖ in the ~ καλόκεφος, ἔχω ὄρεξι γιά ‖ ~ily ad κακόκεφα, σκυθρωπά ‖ ~iness n σκυθρωπότης, κακοκεφιά ‖ ~y a κακόκεφος, κατσούφης, σκυθρωπός, ἰδιότροπος.

moon [mu:n] n σελήνη, φεγγάρι ‖ ~less a χωρίς φεγγάρι ‖ ~light n σεληνόφως, φεγγάρι ‖ ~lit a φεγγαρόλουστος.

moor [muə*] n (Brit: heath) ἕλος, βάλτος, ρεικότοπος ‖ vt (ship) πρυμνοδετῶ, δένω (πλοῖον) ‖ vi πλευρίζω, πέφτω δίπλα ‖ M~ n (person) Μαυριτανός, `Ἀράπης ‖ ~ings npl πρυμνήσια, πρυμάτσες, ναύδετα ‖ M~ish a μαυριτανικός ‖ ~land n ἕλος, βάλτος, ρεικότοπος.

moose [mu:s] n ἄλκη ἡ Ἀμερικανική.

moot [mu:t] vt ἀνακοινῶ, φέρω πρός συζήτησιν ‖ a: ~ point n συζητήσιμον ζήτημα.

mop [mɔp] n πατσαβούρα ‖ (duster) ξεσκονιστήρι ‖ vt σφουγγαρίζω ‖ ~ of hair n ξεχτένιστα μαλλιά.

mope [məup] vi μελαγχολῶ, πλήττω.

moping ['məupiŋ] n κατήφεια, ἀθυμία.

moral ['mɔrəl] a ἠθικός, ψυχικός ‖ n ἐπιμύθιον, ἠθικόν δίδαγμα ‖ ~s npl ἤθη ‖ ~e n ἠθικόν ‖ ~ity n ἠθικότης, ἠθικόν αἴσθημα ‖ ~ly ad ἠθικῶς.

morass [mə'ræs] n ἕλος ‖ (fig) βόρβορος.

morbid ['mɔ:bid] a νοσηρός, ἀρρωστιάρικος.

more [mɔ:*] a περισσότερος ‖ ad περισσότερον, πλέον, πιό ‖ ~ or less σχεδόν, πάνω κάτω ‖ ~ than ever περισσότερον παρά ποτέ ‖ ~over ad ἐπί πλέον, ἐκτός τούτου.

morgue [mɔ:g] n νεκροτομεῖον.

moribund ['mɔribʌnd] a ἑτοιμοθάνατος.

morning ['mɔ:niŋ] n πρωΐ ‖ a πρωϊνός ‖ in the ~ τό πρωΐ ‖ ~ sickness n πρωϊνή ἀδιαθεσία.

Moroccan [mə'rɔkən] a,n Μαροκινός.

Morocco [mə'rɔkəu] n Μαρόκον.

moron ['mɔ:rɔn] n καθυστερημένος ‖ (col) ἠλίθιος, βλάκας ‖ ~ic [mə'rɔnik] a ἠλίθιος, βλακώδης.

morose [mə'rəus] a κακότροπος, σκυθρωπός.

morphine ['mɔ:fi:n] n μορφίνη.

Morse [mɔ:s] ~ code n μορσικός κώδιξ.

morsel ['mɔ:sl] n (of food) μπουκιά, κομματάκι.

mortal ['mɔ:tl] a θνητός ‖ (deadly) θανάσιμος, θανατηφόρος ‖ (very great) τρομερός ‖ n (human being) θνητός (ἄνθρωπος) ‖ ~ity n θνητότης ‖ (death rate) θνησιμότης ‖ ~ly ad (wounded) θανάσιμα ‖ (offended) θανάσιμα.

mortar ['mɔ:tə*] n ἀσβεστοκονίαμα, πηλός, λάσπη ‖ (bowl) γουδί ‖ (weapon) ὅλμος.

mortgage ['mɔ:gidʒ] n ὑποθήκη.

mortified ['mɔ:tifaid] a ντροπιασμένος, ταπεινωμένος.

mortuary ['mɔ:tjuəri] n νεκροθάλαμος.

mosaic [məu'zeiik] n μωσαϊκόν, ψηφιδωτόν.

Moscow ['mɔskəu] n Μόσχα.

Moslem ['mɔzlem] n Μουσουλμάνος ‖ a μουσουλμανικός.

mosque [mɔsk] n τέμενος, τζαμί.

mosquito [mɔs'ki:təu] n κουνούπι ‖ ~ net n κουνουπιέρα.

moss [mɔs] n βρύον ‖ ~y a βρυώδης, βρυόφυτος.

most [məust] a πλεῖστος, περισσότερος ‖ πιό πολύς ‖ ad πλέον, πιό, πιό πολύ, πάρα πολύ ‖ n οἱ περισσότεροι ‖ at the (very) ~ τό πιό πολύ ‖ to make the ~ of ἐπωφελοῦμαι ‖ ~ly ad ὡς ἐπί τό πλεῖστον, κυρίως, συνήθως.

motel [məu'tel] n μοτέλ.

moth [mɔθ] n βότριδα, σκῶρος ‖ ~ball n ναφθαλίνη (σέ μπάλλες) ‖ ~eaten a σκωροφαγωμένος.

mother ['mʌðə*] n μητέρα, μάννα ‖ vt (spoil) χαϊδεύω, κανακεύω ‖ a (tongue; country) μητρική (γλῶσσα) ‖ ~hood n μητρότης ‖ ~in-law n πεθερά ‖ ~ly a μητρικά, σάν μάννα ‖ ~to-be n σέ ἐνδιαφέρουσα.

motif [məu'ti:f] n μοτίφ, θέμα, μοτίβο.

motion ['məuʃən] n κίνησις ‖ (proposal) πρότασις ‖ vi κάνω νόημα, νεύω ‖ ~less a ἀκίνητος ‖ ~ picture n ταινία, φίλμ.

motivated ['məutiveitid] a αἰτιολογούμενος, κινητήριος.

motivation [məuti'veiʃən] n κίνητρον, ἐλατήριον.

motive ['məutiv] n κίνητρον, αἴτιον, ἐλατήριον ‖ a κινητήριος.

motley ['mɔtli] a (heterogeneous) πολύχρωμος, ἑτερογενής.

motor ['məutə*] n κινητήρ, μηχανή ‖ (automobile) αὐτοκίνητο ‖ vi ταξιδεύω μέ αὐτοκίνητον ‖ ~bike n μοτοσυκλέτα ‖ ~boat n βενζινάκατος ‖ ~car n αὐτοκίνητον ‖ ~cycle n = ~bike ‖ ~cyclist n μοτοσυκλετιστής ‖ ~ing n χρῆσις τοῦ αὐτοκινήτου, ὁδήγησις ‖ a τοῦ αὐτοκινήτου, τῆς ὁδηγήσεως ‖ ~ist n αὐτοκινητιστής ‖ ~ oil n ἔλαιον κινητήρων ‖ ~ racing n αὐτοκινητοδρομία ‖ ~ scooter n σκούτερ, βέσπα ‖ ~ vehicle n αὐτοκίνητον ‖ ~way n (Brit) αὐτοκινητόδρομος.

mottled ['mɔtld] a διάστικτος, μέ νερά.

motto ['mɔtəu] n ρητόν, μόττο, ἀρχή.

mould [məuld] n τύπος, μήτρα, καλούπι ‖ (shape) τύπωμα, πρότυπον ‖ (mildew) εὐρώς, μούχλα ‖ vt χύνω σέ τύπους ‖ (fig) διαπλάθω, διαμορφώνω ‖ ~er vi (decay) σαπίζω, φθείρομαι ‖ ~ing n (in plaster) τυποποιία, χυτόν ἀντικείμενον ‖ (in wood) κορνίζα ‖ ~y a (food etc) μουχλιασμένος.

moult [məult] vi μαδῶ.

mound [maund] *n* ἀνάχωμα, λοφίσκος, πρόχωμα.

mount [maunt] *n* (*high hill*) ὄρος, βουνό ‖ (*horse*) ἄλογο ‖ (*for jewel etc*) κορνίζα, ὑποστήριγμα, σκελετός ‖ *vt* (*get on horse*) ἀνεβάζω, ἀνεβαίνω στό ‖ (*put in setting*) μοντάρω, δένω, κορνιζάρω ‖ (*exhibition*) ἀνεβάζω ‖ (*attack*) ὀργανώνω ἐπίθεσιν ‖ *vi* (*also ~ up*) ἀνέρχομαι, ἀνεβαίνω ‖ **~ain** *n* ὄρος, βουνό ‖ (*pile*) σωρός, πλῆθος ‖ **~aineer** *n* (*climber*) ὀρειβάτης ‖ **~aineering** *n* ὀρειβασία ‖ **to go ~aineering** κάνω ὀρειβασίαν ‖ **~ainous** *a* ὀρεινός ‖ **~ainside** *n* πλευρά βουνοῦ.

mourn [mɔːn] *vt* πενθῶ, θρηνῶ ‖ *vi* (+ *for*) θρηνῶ, κλαίω ‖ **~er** *n* πενθῶν, πενθοφορῶν ‖ **~ful** *a* πένθιμος ‖ **~ing** *n* πένθος ‖ **in ~ing** (*period etc*) ἔχω πένθος ‖ (*dress*) πένθιμα ροῦχα, μαῦρα.

mouse [maus] *n* ποντικός ‖ **~trap** *n* ποντικοπαγίδα, φάκα.

moustache [məs'taːʃ] *n* μουστάκι.

mouth [mauθ] *n* (*anat*) στόμα ‖ (*opening*) στόμιον ‖ (*entrance*) ἐκβολή, στόμιον ‖ [mauð] *vt* (*words*) λέγω πομπωδῶς, ὁμιλῶ μέ στόμφον ‖ **down in the ~** τσακισμένος, χαμένα ‖ **~ful** *n* μπουκιά ‖ **~ organ** *n* φυσαρμόνικα ‖ **~piece** *n* ἐπιστόμιον ‖ (*speaker*) ὄργανον, φερέφωνον, ἐκπρόσωπος ‖ **~wash** *n* γαργάρα ‖ **~-watering** *a* γαργαλιστικός.

movable ['muːvəbl] *a* κινητός.

move [muːv] *n* (*movement*) κίνησις ‖ (*in game*) κίνησις ‖ (*step*) ἐνέργεια, βῆμα ‖ (*from house*) μετακόμισις ‖ *vt* (*meta*)κινῶ, μετατοπίζω ‖ (*stir, rouse*) συγκινῶ, γίνομαι (ἐξωφρενῶν κλ) ‖ *vi* (*general*) κινοῦμαι, κουνιέμαι ‖ (*ravel*) μετακινοῦμαι, φεύγομαι ‖ (*take action*) ἐνεργῶ ‖ (*go elsewhere*) μετακομίζω ‖ **to get a ~ on** σπεύδομαι, κάνω γρήγορα ‖ **to ~ house** μετοικῶ, μετακομίζω ‖ **to ~ about** *vi* περιφέρομαι, τριγυρίζω ‖ **to ~ away** *vi* ἀπομακρύνομαι, φεύγω ‖ **to ~ back** *vi* ὑποχωρῶ, ξαναγυρίζω πίσω ‖ **to ~ forward** *vi* προχωρῶ ‖ *vt* κινῶ πρός τά ἐμπρός ‖ **to ~ in** *vi* (*house*) μετακομίζω (στό νέο σπίτι), ἐγκαθίσταμαι ‖ **to ~ on** *vi* προχωρῶ, τραβῶ τόν δρόμο μου ‖ *vt* κάνω νά κυκλοφορῇ ‖ **to ~ out** *vi* (*house*) μετακομίζω (ἀλλοῦ), ἀδειάζω ‖ **~ment** *n* κίνησις, μετακίνησις ‖ (*social etc*) κίνημα, κίνησις ‖ (*mus*) μέρος.

movie ['muːvi] *n* (*film*) φίλμ ‖ **the ~s** (*cinema*) σινεμά ‖ **~ camera** *n* (*amateur*) κινηματογραφική μηχανή.

moving ['muːviŋ] *a* (*lit*) κινούμενος, κινητός ‖ (*stirring*) συνταρακτικός, συγκινητικός ‖ (*touching*) συγκινητικός.

mow [məu] (*irreg*) *vt* θερίζω ‖ **to ~ down** *vt* θερίζω ‖ **~er** *n* (*machine*) θεριστική μηχανή.

Mr ['mistə•] *see* **mister**.

Mrs ['misiz] *see* **mistress**.

much [mʌtʃ] *a* πολύς ‖ *ad* πολύ, μεγάλως, καλή, συχνά, σχεδόν ‖ *n* πολλά, πολύ ‖ **how ~ is it?** πόσον κάνει; ‖ **too ~** πάραπολυ.

muck [mʌk] *n* (*lit*) κοπριά, βρωμιά ‖ (*fig*) σύγχυσις, καταστροφή ‖ **to ~ about** *vi* (*col*) περιφέρομαι ἀσκόπως, χαζεύω ‖ *vt* (*col*) λασπώνω, βρωμίζω ‖ **to ~ up** *vt* (*col*) (*ruin*) χαλάω μιά δουλειά ‖ **~y** *a* (*dirty*) βρώμικος, βρωμερός.

mud [mʌd] *n* λάσπη.

muddle ['mʌdl] *n* ἀκαταστασία, σαλάτα, μπέρδεμα ‖ *vt* (*also ~ up*) μπερδεύω ‖ κάνω ἄνω-κάτω ‖ **to ~ through** *vi* καταφέρνω κουτσά-στραβά.

muddy ['mʌdi] *a* λασπώδης, λασπωμένος ‖

mud flats ['mʌdflæts] *npl* παραλία μέ λάσπη.

mudguard ['mʌdgaːd] *n* φτερό (αὐτοκινήτου).

mudpack ['mʌdpæk] *n* μάσκα (ἀπό πηλό).

mud-slinging ['mʌdsliŋiŋ] *n* συκοφαντία κακογλωσσιά.

muff [mʌf] *n* (*for hands*) μανσόν.

muffle ['mʌfl] *vt* πνίγω (ἦχον) ‖ (*wrap up*) κουκουλώνω, σκεπάζω ‖ **~d** *a* ὑπόκουφος, πνιγμένος.

mug [mʌg] *n* (*cup*) μεγάλο φλυτζάνι, φλυτζάνα ‖ (*col: face*) μοῦτρο, φάτσα ‖ (*col: dupe*) χαζός, κορόϊδο ‖ *vt* (*assault*) κτυπῶ ἀπό πίσω ‖ **~ging** *n* (*assault*) ἐπίθεσι ἀπό πίσω.

muggy ['mʌgi] *a* (*weather*) βαρύς (καιρός), ὑγρός.

mulatto [mju:'lætəu] *n* μιγάς, μουλάτος.

mule [mju:l] *n* ἡμίονος, μουλάρι.

mull [mʌl] **to ~ over** *vt* γυροφέρνω στό μυαλό.

mulled [mʌld] *a* (*wine*) ζεστό κρασί με κανέλλα.

multi- ['mʌlti] *prefix* πολύ-.

multicoloured, (*US*) **multicolored** ['mʌltiˈkʌləd] *a* πολύχρωμος.

multilateral ['mʌlti'lætərəl] *a* πολύπλευρος

multiple ['mʌltipl] *n* πολλαπλάσιον ‖ *a* πολλαπλός ‖ **~ store** *n* κατάστημα μέ πολλά ὑποκαταστήματα.

multiplication [mʌltipli'keiʃən] *n* πολλαπλασιασμός.

multiply ['mʌltiplai] *vt* πολλαπλασιάζω ‖ *vi* πολλαπλασιάζομαι.

multiracial ['mʌlti'reiʃəl] *a* πολλῶν φυλῶν.

multitude ['mʌltitjuːd] *n* πλῆθος.

mum [mʌm] *n* (*col*) μαμά.

mumble ['mʌmbl] *vti* μουρμουρίζω, μασῶ ‖ *n* περδεμένα λόγια, μουρμούρα.

mummy ['mʌmi] *n* μούμια ‖ (*col*) μαμά.

mumps [mʌmps] *n* παρωτῖτις.

munch [mʌntʃ] *vti* μασουλίζω, τραγανίζω.

mundane ['mʌn'dein] *a* ἐγκόσμιος, γήϊνος

municipal [mju:'nisipəl] *a* δημοτικός.

munificence [mju:'nifisns] n γενναιοδωρία.

munitions [mju:'niʃənz] npl πολεμοφόδια.

mural ['mjuərəl] n τοιχογραφία.

murder ['mə:də*] n φόνος, δολοφονία ‖ (fig: col) φονικό ‖ vt φονεύω, σκοτώνω, δολοφονῶ ‖ ~er n φονιᾶς, δολοφόνος ‖ ~ess n φόνισσα ‖ ~erous a (δολο)-φονικός.

murky ['mə:ki] a σκοτεινός, ζοφερός.

murmur ['mə:mə*] n ψίθυρος, μουρμου-ρητό ‖ vi ψιθυρίζω, μουρμουρίζω, παραπονοῦμαι.

muscle ['mʌsl] n μῦς.

muscular ['mʌskjulə*] a μυϊκός, γεροδε-μένος.

Muse [mju:z] n Μοῦσα.

muse [mju:z] vi ρεμβάζω, ὀνειροπολῶ.

museum [mju:'ziəm] n μουσεῖον.

mush [mʌʃ] n πολτός ‖ ~room n μανιτάρι ‖ a ἐφήμερος.

mushy [mʌʃi] a πολτώδης, μαλακός.

music ['mju:zik] n μουσική ‖ to face the ~ ἀκούω ἐξάψαλμον ‖ ~ stand n ἀναλόγιον μουσικοῦ ‖ ~al n μουσική παράστασις ‖ a μουσικός, φιλόμουσος ‖ ~ian n μουσικός.

musk [mʌsk] n μόσχος.

musket ['mʌskit] n τουφέκι ‖ ~eer n σωματοφύλαξ.

musky ['mʌski] a μοσχοβολῶν.

muslin ['mʌzlin] n μουσελίνα.

mussel ['mʌsl] n μύδι.

must [mʌst] auxiliary v (obligation) I ~ do it πρέπει νά τό κάνω ‖ I ~ not do it δέν πρέπει νά τό κάνω ‖ (probability) he ~ be there now πρέπει νά εἶναι ἐκεῖ τώρα ‖ n γλῦκος, μοῦστος ‖ it is a ~ εἶναι ἀναγκαῖον.

mustache ['mʌstæf] n (US) = moustache.

mustard ['mʌstəd] n (condiment) μουστάρ-δα.

mustiness ['mʌstinis] n μοῦχλα, ὑγρασία.

mustn't ['mʌsnt] = must not ‖ see must.

musty ['mʌsti] a τῆς μούχλας ‖ (col) παλιατσούρα, μπαγιάτικος.

mute [mju:t] a βουβός, μουγγός ‖ (gram) ἄφωνος ‖ n βουβός, μουγγός ‖ (on instrument) σουρντίνα.

mutilate ['mju:tileit] vt ἀκρωτηριάζω, σακατεύω.

mutilation [mju:ti'leiʃən] n ἀκρωτηρια-σμός, σακάτεμα.

mutinous ['mju:tinəs] a στασιαστικός, ἀνταρτικός.

mutiny ['mju:tini] n στάσις, ἀνταρσία ‖ vi στασιάζω.

mutter ['mʌtə*] vti μουρμουρίζω.

mutton ['mʌtn] n ἀρνήσιον κρέας.

mutual ['mju:tjuəl] a ἀμοιβαῖος, κοινός ‖ ~ly ad ἀμοιβαίως.

muzzle ['mʌzl] n (mouth and nose) ρύγχος, μουσούδα ‖ (straps) φίμωτρον ‖ (of gun) στόμιον, στόμα ‖ vt φιμώνω.

my [mai] poss a ἰδικός μου, μου.

myopic [mai'ɔpik] a μυωπικός.

myrrh [mə:*] n σμύρνα, μύρρα.

myself [mai'self] pron ἐγώ ὁ ἴδιος τόν ἑαυτόν μου.

mysterious [mis'tiəriəs] a μυστηριώδης ‖ ~ly ad μυστηριωδῶς.

mystery ['mistəri] n μυστήριον ‖ ~ play n μυστήριον.

mystic ['mistik] n μυστικός, ἐσωτερικός ‖ ~al a μυστικιστικός; μυστηριώδης ‖ ~ism n μυστικισμός, μυστικοπάθεια.

mystification [mistifi'keiʃən] n παραζάλη, συσκότισις, ἀπάτη.

mystify ['mistifai] vt ἐξαπατῶ, ζαλίζω.

myth [miθ] n μῦθος ‖ ~ical a μυθικός ‖ ~ological a μυθολογικός ‖ ~ology n μυθολογία.

N, n

nab [næb] vt ἁρπάζω, συλλαμβάνω.

nadir ['neidiə*] n ναδίρ.

nag [næg] n (horse) μικρό ἄλογο (ἱππασίας) ‖ (person) γρινιάρης, καυγατζῆς ‖ vti γρινιάζω, καυγαδίζω ‖ ~ging a (doubt) σαράκι (ἀμφιβολίας) ‖ n καυγάς, φασαρία.

nail [neil] n νύχι ‖ (spike) καρφί, πρόκα ‖ vt καρφώνω ‖ to ~ down vt (fig) δεσμεύω ‖ ~brush n βούρτσα τῶν νυχιῶν ‖ ~file n λίμα (γιά νύχια) ‖ ~ polish n βερνίκι τῶν νυχιῶν, μανόν ‖ ~ scissors npl ψαλιδάκι (γιά νύχια) ‖ ~ varnish n βερνίκι γιά τά νύχια.

naive [nai'i:v] a ἀφελής ‖ ~ly ad ἀφελῶς.

naked ['neikid] a γυμνός ‖ (uncovered) ἐκτεθειμένος, καθαρός ‖ ~ness n γυμνότης.

name [neim] n ὄνομα ‖ (reputation) φήμη, ὑπόληψις ‖ vt ὀνομάζω ‖ (call by name) ἀναφέρω, κατονομάζω ‖ (appoint) ὁρίζω, διορίζω ‖ in the ~ of ἐξ ὀνόματός του ‖ (authority of) ἐν ὀνόματι ‖ ~less a ἄγνωστος, ἀνώνυμος ‖ ~ly ad δηλαδή ‖ ~sake n ὁμώνυμος, συνωνόματος.

nanny ['næni] n (for child) νταντά.

nap [næp] n (sleep) ὑπνάκος ‖ to have a ~ τόν παίρνω λιγάκι.

nape [neip] n αὐχήν, σβέρκος.

napkin ['næpkin] n πετσέτα φαγητοῦ ‖ (Brit) χαρτοπετσέτα, πάνα (βρέφους).

nappy ['næpi] n (for baby) πάνα.

narcissus [na:'sisəs] n νάρκισσος, ζαμπάκι.

narcotic [na:'kɔtik] n ναρκωτικόν.

nark [na:k] vt (col: annoy) ἐξερεθίζω, ἐξαγριώνω.

narrate [nə'reit] vt διηγοῦμαι.

narration [nə'reiʃən] n διήγησις.

narrative ['nærətiv] n διήγημα, ἀφήγησις ‖ a ἀφηγηματικός.

narrator [nə'reitə*] n ἀφηγητής.

narrow ['nærəu] *a* στενός, στενόχωρος ‖ *vi* στενεύω ‖ **to ~ sth down to** περιορίζω ‖ **~ly** *ad* (*miss*) μόλις, ὀλίγον νά ‖ **~-minded** *a* στενοκέφαλος ‖ **~-mindedness** *n* στενοκεφαλιά.

nasal ['neizəl] *a* ἔνρινος, ρινικός, τῆς μύτης.

nastily ['nɑ:stili] *ad* δυσάρεστα, πρόστυχα, χυδαῖα.

nastiness ['nɑ:stinis] *n* κακία, ἀχρειότης, προστυχιά.

nasty ['nɑ:sti] *a* (*mess*) δυσάρεστος, βρώμικος ‖ (*business*) δύσκολος, ἐπικίνδυνος, φοβερός ‖ (*person*) πρόστυχος, ρεμάλι, κακός.

nation ['neiʃən] *n* ἔθνος ‖ **~al** ['næʃənl] *a* ἐθνικός ‖ *n* ὑπήκοος, πολίτης ‖ **~al anthem** *n* ἐθνικός ὕμνος ‖ **~alism** *n* ἐθνικισμός ‖ **~alist** *a,n* ἐθνικιστής, ἐθνικόφρων ‖ **~ality** *n* ἐθνικότης ‖ **~alization** *n* ἐθνικοποίησις ‖ **~alize** *vt* ἐθνικοποιῶ ‖ **~ally** *ad* ἀπὸ ἐθνικῆς ἀπόψεως ‖ **~wide** *a* πανεθνικόν ‖ *ad* καθ' ὁλόκληρον τὴν χώραν.

native ['neitiv] *n* ἐντόπιος ‖ (*non-European*) ἰθαγενής ‖ *a* ἐγχώριος ‖ (*country etc*) γενέθλιος, μητρικός ‖ (*inborn*) ἔμφυτος, φυσικός.

natter ['nætə*] *vi* (*col: chat*) κουβεντιάζω.

natural ['nætʃrəl] *a* φυσικός ‖ (*inborn*) ἔμφυτος, φυσικός ‖ **~ist** *n* φυσιοδίφης ‖ **~ize** *vt* πολιτογραφῶ ‖ (*plant etc*) ἐγκλιματίζω ‖ **~ly** *ad* φυσικά, βέβαια ‖ **~ness** *n* φυσικότης.

nature ['neitʃə*] *n* φύσις ‖ (*sort, kind*) εἶδος, χαρακτήρ ‖ **by ~** ἐκ φύσεως.

naught [nɔ:t] *n* τίποτε, μηδενικόν.

naughtily ['nɔ:tili] *ad* ἄτακτα, κακά.

naughtiness ['nɔ:tinis] *n* κακή συμπεριφορά, ἀνυπακοή.

naughty ['nɔ:ti] *a* (*child*) ἄτακτος, κακός.

nausea ['nɔ:siə] *n* ναυτία, ἀναγούλα ‖ (*disgust*) ἀηδία, ἀποστροφή ‖ **~te** *vt* ἀηδιάζω (κάτι), προξενῶ ναυτίαν.

nauseating ['nɔ:sieitiŋ] *a* ἀηδιαστικός, σιχαμερός.

nautical ['nɔ:tikəl] *a* ναυτικός.

naval ['neivəl] *a* ναυτικός.

nave [neiv] *n* κλίτος, νάρθηξ.

navel ['neivəl] *n* ὀμφαλός, ἀφαλός.

navigable ['nævigəbl] *a* πλωτός.

navigate ['nævigeit] *vt* (*ship etc*) κυβερνῶ, διευθύνω ‖ *vi* ναυσιπλοῶ, πλέω, ταξιδεύω.

navigation [nævi'geiʃən] *n* ναυτιλία, πλοῦς, διάπλους.

navigator ['nævigeitə*] *n* ναυτίλος, πλοηγός ‖ (*explorer*) θαλασσοπόρος ‖ (*aviat*) ἀεροναυτίλος.

navvy ['nævi] *n* ἀνειδίκευτος ἐργάτης, σκαφτιᾶς.

navy ['neivi] *n* ναυτικόν ‖ **~ blue** *n* (*colour*) σκοῦρος μπλέ, μπλέ μαρίν.

nay [nei] *ad* (*no*) ὄχι ‖ (*also*) τί λέω, ἤ καλύτερα.

Nazi ['nɑ:tsi] *n* Ναζιστής.

neap [ni:p] *a* (*tide*) ἄμπωτις.

near [niə*] *a* (*close*) ἐγγύς, πλησίον ‖ κοντά ‖ (*related*) πλησίον, στενός ‖ *ad* (*space*) κοντά, πλησίον ‖ (*time*) περί, ἐγγύς, κοντά ‖ *prep* (*also ~ to*) κοντά σέ, παρά, πλησίον ‖ (*space*) παρά, πλησίον ‖ (*time*) περί, κοντά ‖ *vt* πλησιάζω ‖ **~by** *a* κοντινός, πλαϊνός ‖ *ad* πολύ κοντά, ἐγγύτατα ‖ **N~ East** *n* Μέση Ἀνατολή, Ἐγγὺς Ἀνατολή ‖ **~ly** *ad* σχεδόν, περίπου ‖ **~ miss** *n* λίγο ἔλειψε (νά), παρ' ὀλίγο (νά) ‖ **~ness** *n* ἐγγύτης, στενότης ‖ **~side** *n* (*aut*) ἀριστερά πλευρά.

neat [ni:t] *a* (*tidy*) καθαρός, καλοβαλμένος, κομψός ‖ (*clever*) καλοβαλμένος, ἐπιτυχής, κομψός ‖ (*pure*) καθαρός, ἄγνός, χωρίς νερό ‖ **~ly** *ad* μέ τάξιν, περιποιημένα ‖ **~ness** *n* ἁπλότης, κομψότης, τάξις, καθαρότης.

nebulous ['nebjuləs] *a* νεφελώδης.

necessarily ['nesisərili] *ad* ἀπαραιτήτως, κατ' ἀνάγκην.

necessary ['nesisəri] *a* ἀναγκαῖος, ἀπαραίτητος.

necessitate [ni'sesiteit] *vt* κάνω ἀναγκαῖο ὑποχρεώνω.

necessity [ni'sesiti] *n* ἀνάγκη.

neck [nek] *n* λαιμός, αὐχήν, τράχηλος, σβέρκος ‖ (*narrow part*) λαιμός, στένωμα ‖ **~ and ~** στά ἴσια, ἰσόπαλος, πλάϊ-πλάϊ ‖ **~lace** *n* περιδέραιον, κολλιέ ‖ **~line** *n* λαιμός, ντεκολτέ ‖ **~tie** *n* γραβάτα.

née [nei] *a* τό γένος.

need [ni:d] *n* ἀνάγκη, χρειά ‖ (*poverty*) ἔνδεια, φτώχια ‖ *vt* (*of person*) χρειάζομαι ‖ (*of thing*) ἀπαιτῶ, ζητῶ (κάτι). ἀπαιτεῖται ‖ **to ~ to do** ἔχω ἀνάγκην νά κάνω (κάτι).

needle ['ni:dl] *n* βελόνι ‖ (*knitting*) βελόνα ‖ (*compass etc*) βελόνη.

needless ['ni:dlis] *a* ἄχρηστος, περιττός ‖ **~ly** *ad* ἀνωφελῶς, χωρίς ἀνάγκην.

needlework ['ni:dlwə:k] *n* ἐργόχειρον.

needy ['ni:di] *n* ἐνδεής, ἄπορος.

negation [ni'geiʃən] *n* ἄρνησις.

negative ['negativ] *n* (*phot*) ἀρνητικόν ‖ *a* ἀρνητικός.

neglect [ni'glekt] *vt* παραμελῶ ‖ *n* ἀμέλεια, παραμέλησις.

negligée ['neglizei] *n* νυχτικό.

negligence ['neglidʒəns] *n* ἀμέλεια.

negligent ['neglidʒənt] *a* ἀμελής, ἀπρόσεκτος ‖ **~ly** *ad* ἀπρόσεκτα, ἀμελῶς.

negligible ['neglidʒəbl] *a* ἀμελητέος.

negotiable [ni'gəuʃiəbl] *a* (*cheque*) ἐμπορεύσιμος, μετατρεπτός, μεταβιβάσιμος.

negotiate [ni'gəuʃieit] *vi* διαπραγματεύομαι ‖ *vt* (*treaty*) διαπραγματεύομαι ‖

N

(*difficulty*) διαβαίνω, ξεπερνῶ.

negotiation [nigəuʃi'eiʃən] *n* διαπραγμάτευσις.

negotiator [ni'gəuʃieitə*] *n* διαπραγματευτής.

Negress ['ni:grɛs] *n* νέγρα, μαύρη.

Negro ['ni:grəu] *n* νέγρος, μαῦρος.

neighbour, (*US*) **neighbor** ['neibə*] *n* γείτων, γείτονας ‖ ~**hood** *n* γειτονιά, περιοχή ‖ ~**ing** *a* γειτονικός ‖ ~**ly** *a* καλὸς γείτονας, γειτονικός.

neither ['naiðə*] *a* οὔτε ὁ ἕνας οὔτε ὁ ἄλλος, κανένας ‖ *cj* οὔτε . . . οὔτε, οὔτε (καί) ‖ *pron* κανένας.

neo- ['ni:əu] *prefix* νεο-.

neon ['ni:ɔn] *n* νέον ‖ ~ **light** *n* φῶς μὲ νέον.

nephew ['nevju:] *n* ἀνεψιός.

nerve [nəːv] *n* νεῦρον ‖ (*courage*) σθένος, θάρρος ‖ (*impudence*) θράσος ‖ ~-**racking** *a* ἐκνευριστικός.

nervous ['nəːvəs] *a* νευρικός ‖ (*timid*) ντροπαλός, νευρικός, δειλός ‖ ~ **breakdown** *n* νευρικὸς κλονισμός ‖ ~**ly** *ad* δειλά, φοβισμένα ‖ ~**ness** *n* νευρικότης, δειλία.

nest [nest] *n* φωλιά.

nestle ['nesl] *vi* φωλιάζω, κουλουριάζομαι.

net [net] *n* δίκτυον, δίχτυ ‖ (*hair*) φιλές, δίχτυ ‖ *a* καθαρός, νέτος.

Netherlands ['neðələndz] *npl* Ὁλλανδία.

netting ['netiŋ] *n* δικτύωμα, πλέγμα.

network ['netwəːk] *n* δίκτυον.

neurosis [njuə'rəusis] *n* νεύρωσις.

neurotic [njuə'rɔtik] *a* νευρωτικός ‖ *n* νευροπαθής.

neuter ['njuːtə*] *a* οὐδέτερος ‖ *n* οὐδέτερον.

neutral ['njuːtrəl] *a* οὐδέτερος ‖ ~**ity** *n* οὐδετερότης.

never ['nevə*] *ad* ποτέ ‖ ~-**ending** *a* ἀτελείωτος ‖ ~**theless** *ad* οὐχ ἧττον, μόλον τοῦτο, κι' ὅμως.

new [njuː] *a* νέος, καινούργιος ‖ (*clothes etc*) καινουργής, καινούργιος ‖ (*modern*) σύγχρονος, μοντέρνος ‖ (*at work etc*) ἀρχάριος, ἄπειρος ‖ ~-**born** *a* νεογέννητος ‖ ~**comer** *n* φρεσκοφερμένος, ἄρτι ἀφιχθείς ‖ ~**ly** *ad* νεωστί, προσφάτως ‖ ~ **moon** *n* καινούργιο φεγγάρι ‖ ~**ness** *n* νεότης, φρεσκάδα.

news [njuːz] *n* νέα, εἰδήσεις ‖ ~**agent** *n* πράκτωρ ἐφημερίδων ‖ ~ **flash** *n* ἔκτακτος εἴδησις ‖ ~**letter** *n* δελτίον εἰδήσεων ‖ ~**paper** *n* ἐφημερίδα ‖ ~**reel** *n* ταινία ἐπικαίρων.

New Year [njuː'jiə*] *n* νέον ἔτος ‖ ~'**s Day** *n* Πρωτοχρονιά ‖ ~'**s Eve** *n* παραμονή τῆς Πρωτοχρονιᾶς.

New Zealand [njuː'ziːlənd] *n* Νέα Ζηλανδία.

next [nekst] *a* πλησιέστερος, γειτονικός, πλαϊνός ‖ (*in time*) προσεχής, ἐπόμενος

‖ *ad* ἔπειτα, κατόπιν, μετά ‖ *prep*: ~ **to** κοντά εἰς, σχεδὸν ‖ **the** ~ **day** τὴν ἄλλην ἡμέραν, ἡ ἐπομένη ‖ ~ **year** ἑπόμενον ἔτος, ἄλλος χρόνος, τοῦ χρόνου ‖ ~ **of kin** *n* πλησιέστερος συγγενής.

nibble ['nibl] *vt* δαγκώνω, μασουλίζω, τρώγω σιγά-σιγά.

nice [nais] *a* εὐχάριστος, καλός, ὡραῖος ‖ (*exact*) λεπτός, εὐαίσθητος ‖ ~-**looking** *a* ὡραῖος, ὄμορφος ‖ ~**ly** *ad* ὡραία, εὐχάριστα.

nick [nik] *n* χαραγή, ἐγκοπή ‖ κατάλληλος στιγμή.

nickel ['nikl] *n* νικέλιον ‖ (*US*) πεντάρα (5 σέντς).

nickname ['nikneim] *n* παρατσούκλι.

nicotine ['nikətiːn] *n* νικοτίνη.

niece [niːs] *n* ἀνεψιά.

niggardly ['nigədli] *a* φιλάργυρος, τσιγγούνης.

niggling ['nigliŋ] *a* ἀσημαντολόγος.

night [nait] *n* νύχτα, βράδυ, σκότος ‖ **good** ~! καλή νύχτα! ‖ **at** *or* **by** ~ τὴν νύκτα ‖ ~**cap** *n* (*drink*) νυκτερινὸ ρόφημα ‖ ~ **club** *n* νυκτερινὸν κέντρον ‖ ~**dress** *n* νυχτικό ‖ ~**fall** *n* σούρουπο ‖ ~**ingale** *n* ἀηδόνι ‖ ~ **life** *n* νυχτερινὴ ζωή ‖ ~**ly** *a* νυκτερινός, βραδυνός ‖ *ad* κάθε νύχτα, κάθε βράδυ ‖ ~**mare** *n* ἐφιάλτης ‖ ~ **school** *n* βραδυνὴ σχολή ‖ ~-**time** *n* νύχτα ‖ ~ **watchman** *n* νυκτοφύλαξ.

nil [nil] *n* μηδέν, τίποτε.

nimble ['nimbl] *a* εὔστροφος, εὐκίνητος.

nine [nain] *num* ἐννέα, ἐνιά ‖ ~**teen** *num* δεκαεννιά ‖ ~**ty** *num* ἐνενήντα.

ninth [nainθ] *a* ἔνατος.

nip [nip] *vt* (*pinch etc*) τσιμπῶ, δαγκώνω ‖ *n* τσίμπημα, δάγκωμα.

nipple ['nipl] *n* (*anat*) θηλή, ρώγα.

nippy ['nipi] *a* (*person*) ζωηρός, ξύπνιος, σβέλτος.

nitrogen ['naitrədʒən] *n* ἄζωτον.

no [nəu] *a* κανείς, κανένας, οὐδείς, καθόλου, μή ‖ *n* ἄρνησις, ἀρνητικὴ ψῆφος.

nobility [nəu'biliti] *n* (*social class*) εὐγένεις.

noble ['nəubl] *a* εὐγενής, μεγαλοπρεπής ‖ (*splendid*) θαυμαστός ‖ *n* εὐγενής, εὐπατρίδης.

nobly ['nəubli] *ad* εὐγενικά, μεγαλοπρεπῶς.

nobody ['nəubədi] *pron* κανείς, κανένας, οὐδείς ‖ *n* (*unimportant person*) μηδαμινότης, τιποτένιος.

nod [nɔd] *vi* νεύω, νέφω, κάνω νόημα ‖ (*droop with sleep*) νυστάζω, κουτουλῶ ‖ *n* νεῦμα, νόημα, κουτούλισμα.

noise [nɔiz] *n* κρότος, βοή ‖ (*unpleasant*) θόρυβος.

noisily ['nɔizili] *ad* θορυβωδῶς, μὲ φασαρία.

noisy ['nɔizi] *a* θορυβώδης.

nomad ['nəumæd] n νομάς ‖ ~ic a νομαδικός.

nominal ['nɔminl] a ὀνομαστικός, μή πραγματικός.

nominate ['nɔmineit] vt προτείνω, ὀνομάζω ‖ (appoint) διορίζω.

nomination [nɔmi'neiʃən] n πρότασις, ὑποψηφιότης, διορισμός.

nominee [nɔmi'ni:] n ὑποψήφιος.

non- [nɔn] prefix μή-, ἀντι-, ἀν-, ἀ- ‖ ~- **alcoholic** a ἄνευ οἰνοπνεύματος.

nonchalant ['nɔnʃələnt] a ψύχραιμος, ἀδιάφορος.

nondescript ['nɔndiskript] a ἀκαθόριστος, ἀχαρακτήριστος.

none [nʌn] a κανείς ‖ pron κανείς, καμμία, κανέν ‖ ad καθόλου.

nonentity [nɔ'nentiti] n μηδαμινότης, ἀσήμαντος ἄνθρωπος.

nonplussed ['nɔn'plʌst] a (τά ἔχω) χαμένα, (εἶμαι) ζαλισμένος.

nonsense ['nɔnsəns] n ἀνοησία, παραλογισμός.

non-stop ['nɔn'stɔp] a ἄνευ σταθμοῦ.

noodles ['nu:dlz] npl χυλοπῆτες.

noon [nu:n] n μεσημέρι.

no one ['nəuwʌn] pron = **nobody**.

noose [nu:s] n βρόχος, θηλειά.

nor [nɔ:*] cj οὔτε, μήτε.

norm [nɔ:m] n κανών, τύπος, μέτρον.

normal ['nɔ:məl] a κανονικός, συνήθης, ὁμαλός ‖ ~ly ad κανονικῶς.

north [nɔ:θ] n βορρᾶς, βοριᾶς ‖ (of country etc) ἰά βόρεια ‖ a βόρειος ‖ ad βορείως, πρός βοράν ‖ ~-east n βορειοανατολικόν ‖ ~ern a βόρειος, βορεινός ‖ N~ Pole n Βόρειος Πόλος ‖ N~ Sea n Βόρειος Θάλασσα ‖ ~ward(s) ad πρός βορράν ‖ ~-west n βορειοδυτικόν.

Norway ['nɔ:wei] n Νορβηγία.

Norwegian [nɔ:'wi:dʒən] a νορβηγικός ‖ n Νορβηγός.

nose [nəuz] n μύτη ‖ (smell) ὄσφρησις, μύτη ‖ ~bleed n ρινορραγία, μάτωμα τῆς μύτης ‖ ~-dive n κάθετος ἐφόρμησις ‖ ~y a περίεργος, ἀδιάκριτος.

nostalgia [nɔs'tældʒiə] n νοσταλγία.

nostalgic [nɔs'tældʒik] a νοσταλγικός.

nostril ['nɔstril] n ρουθούνι.

not [nɔt] ad δέν, μή, ὄχι.

notable ['nəutəbl] a ἀξιοσημείωτος, σημαντικός.

notably ['nəutəbli] ad ἰδιαιτέρως, εἰδικῶς.

notch [nɔtʃ] n ἐγκοπή, χαραγή, ὀδόντωσις.

note [nəut] n νότα, τόνος, πλῆκτρον ‖ (short letter) γραμματάκι, σημείωμα ‖ (remark) σημείωσις, ὑπόμνημα ‖ (reputation) φήμη, διάκρισις ‖ vt σημειώνω, παρατηρῶ ‖ (write down) σημειώνω, (κατα)γράφω ‖ ~book n σημειωματάριον, καρνέ ‖ ~-case n πορτοφόλι ‖ ~d a σημαίνων, διακεκριμένος, διάσημος ‖ ~paper n χαρτί ἀλληλογραφίας.

nothing ['nʌθiŋ] n μηδέν, τίποτε ‖ for ~ (free) δωρεάν, τζάμπα.

notice ['nəutis] n (announcement) ἀγγελία, ἀναγγελία ‖ (attention) προσοχή, παρατήρησις ‖ (warning) εἰδοποίησις, προειδοποίησις ‖ vt (observe) παρατηρῶ, ἀντιλαμβάνομαι, προσέχω ‖ ~able a ἀξιοσημείωτος, ἀξιοπρόσεκτος ‖ ~board n (Brit) ἐνοικιαστήριον, πίναξ ἀνακοινώσεων.

notification [nəutifi'keiʃən] n (ἀν)ἀγγελία, ἀνακοίνωσις, δήλωσις, γνωστοποίησις.

notify ['nəutifai] vt πληροφορῶ, εἰδοποιῶ, γνωστοποιῶ.

notion ['nəuʃən] n ἀντίληψις, ἰδέα ‖ (fancy) γνώμη, ἰδέα, σκέψις.

notorious [nəu'tɔ:riəs] a περιβόητος, πασίγνωστος.

notwithstanding [nɔtwið'stændiŋ] ad παρ' ὅλα ταῦτα, ἐν τούτοις, παρ' ὅλον.

nougat ['nu:ga:] n χαλβαδόπητα.

nought [nɔ:t] n (zero) μηδέν ‖ τίποτε, μηδέν.

noun [naun] n ὄνομα, οὐσιαστικόν.

nourish ['nʌriʃ] vt (δια)τρέφω ‖ ~ing a θρεπτικός ‖ ~ment n (δια)τροφή, θρέψις.

novel ['nɔvəl] n μυθιστόρημα ‖ a νέος, πρωτότυπος ‖ ~ist n μυθιστοριογράφος ‖ ~ty n νεωτερισμός.

November [nəu'vembə*] n Νοέμβρης.

novice ['nɔvis] n ἀρχάμιος, μαθητευόμενος.

now [nau] ad τώρα, λοιπόν ‖ right ~ ἀμέσως, στή στιγμή ‖ ~ and then, ~ and again κάπου-κάπου, κάθε τόσο, καμμιά φορά, μερικές φορές, ποῦ καί ποῦ ‖ ~adays ad σήμερα.

nowhere ['nəuwɛə*] ad πουθενά.

nozzle ['nɔzl] n στόμιον (σωλῆνος), προφύσιον, ἀκροφύσιον.

nuance ['nju:ã:ns] n ἀπόχρωσις.

nuclear ['nju:kliə*] a (energy etc) πυρηνικός.

nucleus ['nju:kliəs] n πυρήν ‖ (of atom) πυρήν.

nude [nju:d] a γυμνός, γδυτός ‖ n (art) γυμνόν.

nudge [nʌdʒ] vt ἀγκωνίζω, σκουντῶ.

nudist ['nju:dist] n γυμνιστής.

nudity ['nju:diti] n γυμνότης.

nuisance ['nju:sns] n ἐνόχλησις, μπελάς.

null [nʌl] a ἄκυρος ‖ ~ify vt ἀκυρώνω.

numb [nʌm] a ναρκωμένος, μουδιασμένος ‖ vt ναρκώνω, μουδιάζω.

number ['nʌmbə*] n ἀριθμός, ψηφίον, νούμερο ‖ (sum) ἀριθμός, σύνολον, ἄθροισμα ‖ (quantity) πολλοί, πλῆθος ‖ (gram) ἀριθμός ‖ (issue) ἀριθμός (τεύχους) ‖ vt (ἀπ)ἀριθμῶ, μετρῶ ‖ (amount to) ἀνέρχομαι, φθάνω, ἀριθμῶ ‖ ~ plate n (Brit aut) πίναξ (αὐτοκινήτου).

numbness ['nʌmnis] n νάρκωσις, μούδιασμα,

numeral ['nju:mərəl] *n* ἀριθμός.
numerical [nju:'merikəl] *a* (*order*) ἀριθμητικός.
numerous ['nju:mərəs] *a* πολυάριθμος.
nun [nʌn] *n* μοναχή, καλόγρηα.
nurse [nɜ:s] *n* νοσοκόμος ‖ (*for children*) παραμάννα, τροφός ‖ *vt* (*patient, invalid*) περιποιοῦμαι, νοσηλεύω ‖ (*fig*) φροντίζω, ἐπιμελοῦμαι, συγκρατῶ ‖ ~**ry** *n* παιδικός σταθμός, βρεφοκομεῖον ‖ (*plants*) φυτώριον ‖ ~**ry rhyme** *n* παιδικό τραγουδάκι ‖ ~**ry school** *n* νηπιαγωγεῖον.
nursing ['nɜ:siŋ] *n* (*profession*) ἐπάγγελμα νοσοκόμου ‖ ~ **home** *n* (ἰδιωτική) κλινική.
nut [nʌt] *n* περικόχλιον, παξιμάδι ‖ (*fruit*) καρύδι, ξηρός καρπός ‖ ~**s** *a* (*col: crazy*) τρελλός.
nutcrackers ['nʌtkrækəz] *npl* καρυοθραύστης.
nutmeg ['nʌtmeg] *n* μοσχοκάρυδο.
nutrient ['nju:triənt] *n* θρεπτικόν, τρόφιμον.
nutrition [nju:'triʃən] *n* θρέψις, διατροφή.
nutritious [nju:'triʃəs] *a* θρεπτικός.
nutshell ['nʌtʃel] *n*: **in a** ~ σύντομος, μέ λίγα λόγια.
nylon ['nailon] *a,n* νάϋλον.

O, o

O, o [əu] *excl* = **oh**.
oaf [əuf] *n* ἀδέξιος, ἄξεστος.
oak [əuk] *n* δρῦς, βαλανιδιά ‖ *a* δρύϊνος.
oar [ɔ:*] *n* κώπη, κουπί.
oasis [əu'eisis] *n* ὄασις.
oath [əuθ] *n* ὅρκος ‖ (*swearword*) βλαστήμια.
oats [əuts] *npl* βρώμη.
obedience [ə'bi:diəns] *n* ὑπακοή, εὐπείθεια.
obedient [ə'bi:diənt] *a* ὑπάκους.
obelisk ['ɔbilisk] *n* ὀβελίσκος.
obesity [əu'bi:siti] *n* παχυσαρκία.
obey [ə'bei] *vti* ὑπακούω.
obituary [ə'bitjuəri] *n* νεκρολογία.
object ['ɔbdʒikt] *n* ἀντικείμενον ‖ (*target*) στόχος, σκοπός, ἀντικείμενον ‖ (*gram*) ἀντικείμενον ‖ [əb'dʒekt] *vi* (+ *to*) (*proposal*) ἀντιτίθεμαι, ἀποδοκιμάζω ‖ (*a noise etc*) ἀποκρούω, ἐπικρίνω ‖ ~**ion** *n* ἀντίρρησις, ἀντιλογία ‖ (*obstacle*) ἐμπόδιον, δυσκολία ‖ ~**ionable** *a* ἀπαράδεκτος, ἀνεπιθύμητος ‖ ~**ive** *n* ἀντικειμενικός σκοπός ‖ *a* (*impartial*) ἀντικειμενικός ‖ ~**ively** *ad* ἀντικειμενικά ‖ ~**ivity** *n* ἀντικειμενικότης ‖ ~**or** *n* ἀντιρρησίας, ἀντιλέγων.
obligation [ɔbli'geiʃən] *n* ὑποχρέωσις.
obligatory [ɔ'bligətəri] *a* ὑποχρεωτικός.
oblige [ə'blaidʒ] *vt* ὑποχρεώνω, ἐπιβάλλω ‖ (*do a favour*) ἐξυπηρετῶ, ὑποχρεώνω.

obliging [ə'blaidʒiŋ] *a* ὑποχρεωτικός, ἐξυπηρετικός.
oblique [ə'bli:k] *a* λοξός, πλάγιος.
obliterate [ə'blitəreit] *vt* ἐξαλείφω, σβήνω, καταστρέφω.
oblivion [ə'bliviən] *n* λήθη.
oblivious [ə'bliviəs] *a* (+ *of*) ἐπιλήσμων, ξεχασιάρης.
oblong ['ɔblɔŋ] *n* ἐπίμηκες σχῆμα, ὀρθογώνιον ‖ *a* ἐπιμήκης, μακρουλός.
obnoxious [əb'nɔkʃəs] *a* ἀπεχθής, δυσάρεστος.
oboe ['əubəu] *n* ὄμπος.
obscene [əb'si:n] *a* αἰσχρός, πρόστυχος.
obscenity [əb'seniti] *n* αἰσχρότης, ἀχρειότης.
obscure [əb'skjuə*] *a* σκοτεινός, σκοῦρος ‖ (*unnoticed*) ἄσημος, ταπεινός ‖ *vt* συσκοτίζω, σκεπάζω.
obscurity [əb'skjuəriti] *n* σκοτάδι, ἀφάνεια.
obsequious [əb'si:kwiəs] *a* δουλοπρεπής.
observable [əb'zə:vəbl] *a* ὁρατός, εὐδιάκριτος.
observance [əb'zə:vəns] *n* τήρησις, ἑορτασμός.
observant [əb'zə:vənt] *a* παρατηρητικός, προσεκτικός.
observation [ɔbzə'veiʃən] *n* παρατήρησις, παρακολούθησις.
observatory [əb'zə:vətri] *n* ἀστεροσκοπεῖον.
observe [əb'zə:v] *vt* (*the law etc*) τηρῶ, κρατῶ ‖ (*study*) παρατηρῶ, κοιτάζω ‖ (*understand*) διακρίνω, ἀντιλαμβάνομαι ‖ ~**r** *n* παρατηρητής, τηρητής.
obsess [əb'ses] *vt* κατέχω, βασανίζω ‖ ~**ion** *n* ἔμμονος ἰδέα ‖ ~**ive** *a* καταθλιπτικός, βασανιστικός.
obsolescence [ɔbsə'lesns] *n* τάσις πρός ἀχρηστίαν, παλαίωμα.
obsolete ['ɔbsəli:t] *a* ἀπηρχαιωμένος.
obstacle ['ɔbstəkl] *n* ἐμπόδιον, πρόσκομμα ‖ ~ **race** *n* δρόμος μετ' ἐμποδίων.
obstetrics [əb'stetriks] *n* μαιευτική.
obstinacy ['ɔbstinəsi] *n* ἰσχυρογνωμοσύνη, ἐπιμονή.
obstinate ['ɔbstinit] *a* ἐπίμονος, πείσμων ‖ ~**ly** *ad* ἐπίμονα.
obstreperous [əb'strepərəs] *a* φασαρίας, ταραχοποιός.
obstruct [əb'strʌkt] *vt* φράσσω, ἐμποδίζω ‖ ~**ion** *n* κωλυσιεργία, ἐμπόδιον ‖ ~**ive** *a* κωλυσιεργός.
obtain [əb'tein] *vt* παίρνω, ἀποκτῶ, ἐπιτυγχάνω ‖ ~**able** *a* ἐπιτευκτός, εὐαπόκτητος.
obtrusive [əb'tru:siv] *a* ἐνοχλητικός, φορτικός.
obtuse [əb'tju:s] *a* (*person*) ἀμβλύνους.
obvious ['ɔbviəs] *a* προφανής, εὐνόητος ‖ ~**ly** *ad* προφανώς, φανερά.
occasion [ə'keiʒən] *n* (*time*) εὐκαιρία, φορά ‖ (*event*) ἀφορμή, περίστασις ‖ (*reason*)

λόγος, αἰτία ‖ vt προξενῶ ‖ ~al a σποραδικός, τυχαῖος ‖ (drink) πού καί πού ‖ ~ally ad κάπου-κάπου.

occult [ɔ'kʌlt] n: the ~ οἱ ἀπόκρυφοι ἐπιστῆμες.

occupant ['ɔkjupənt] n κάτοχος ‖ (of house) ἔνοικος.

occupation [ɔkju'peiʃən] n ἀπασχόλησις, ἀσχολία, ἐπάγγελμα ‖ (of country) κατάληψις, κτῆσις ‖ ~al a (hazard) ἐπαγγελματικός.

occupier ['ɔkjupaiə*] n (of house) ἔνοικος.

occupy ['ɔkjupai] vt (take possession) κατέχω, κατακτῶ ‖ (live in) κατοικῶ ‖ (hold) κατέχω ‖ (employ) ἀπασχολῶ.

occur [ə'kə:*] vi συμβαίνω, γίνομαι, λαμβάνω χώραν ‖ (be found) συναντῶμαι, ἐμφανίζομαι ‖ (+ to) παρουσιάζομαι στήν σκέψιν, μοῦ ἔρχεται ‖ ~rence n γεγονός, συμβάν.

ocean ['əuʃən] n ὠκεανός ‖ ~-going a ὑπερωκεάνειος.

ochre ['əukə*] n ὤχρα.

o'clock [ə'klɔk] ad: it is 5 ~ εἶναι πέντε (ὥρα).

octagonal [ɔk'tægənl] a ὀκταγώνιος.

octane ['ɔktein] n ὀκτάνιον.

octave ['ɔktiv] n ὀχτάβα.

October [ɔk'təubə*] n Ὀκτώβρης.

octopus ['ɔktəpəs] n χταπόδι.

odd [ɔd] a (number) περιττός, μονός ‖ (not part of set) μονό, παράταιρος ‖ (with some left over) περισσεύκων, τόσα, καί κάτι ‖ (strange) περίεργος, παράξενος ‖ (casual) τυχαῖος ‖ ~ity n παραδοξότης ‖ παράξενος ἄνθρωπος ‖ ~ly ad περιέργως, περίεργα ‖ ~ly enough τό περίεργον εἶναι ‖ ~ments npl ὑπολείμματα ‖ ~s npl ἀνισότης, διαφορά ‖ (balance of advantage) πλεονέκτημα, πιθανότητες ‖ (chances) πιθανότητες ‖ (at racetrack) στοίχημα, ποντάρισμα ‖ at ~s διαφωνῶ, εἶμαι τσακωμένος ‖ ~s and ends npl ρετάλια, μικροπράγματα.

ode [əud] n ὠδή.

odious ['əudiəs] a ἀπεχθής, μισητός.

odour, (US) **odor** ['əudə*] n ὀσμή, μυρουδιά ‖ ~less a ἄοσμος.

of [ɔv, əv] prep ἀπό, περί, ὡς πρός.

off [ɔf] ad (absent) μακρυά ‖ (of switch) 'κλειστόν' ‖ (milk) ὄχι φρέσκο, χαλασμένη ‖ prep ἀπό, μακρυά ἀπό, ὀλιγώτερον ἀπό.

offal ['ɔfəl] n ἐντόσθια.

off-colour, (US) **off-color** ['ɔf'kʌlə*] a (ill) χλωμός.

offence [ə'fens] n (crime) παράπτωμα, πταῖσμα ‖ (insult) προσβολή.

offend [ə'fend] vt προσβάλλω ‖ ~er n παραβάτης ‖ ~ing a προσβλητικός, πειρακτικός.

offense [ə'fens] n (US) = **offence**.

offensive [ə'fensiv] a προσβλητικός, δυσάρεστος ‖ (weapon) ἐπιθετικός.

offer ['ɔfə*] n προσφορά ‖ vt προσφέρω, προτείνω ‖ ~ing n (esp rel) θυσία, προσφορά.

offhand ['ɔf'hænd] a αὐθόρμητος, ἀπότομος ‖ ad στή στιγμή, ἀπότομα.

office ['ɔfis] n (position) γραφεῖον ‖ ~r n (mil) ἀξιωματικός ‖ δημόσιος ὑπάλληλος, ἀξιωματοῦχος ‖ ~ work n ἐργασία γραφείου.

official [ə'fiʃəl] a (authorized) ἐπίσημος, ὑπηρεσιακός ‖ n ὑπάλληλος (δημόσιος) ‖ ~ly ad ἐπισήμως.

officious [ə'fiʃəs] a ἐπεμβαίνων, ἐνοχλητικός.

offing ['ɔfiŋ] n: in the ~ ἐν ὄψει, στά ἀνοιχτά.

off-season ['ɔfsi:zn] a μή ἐποχιακός, ἐκτός ἐποχῆς, νεκρά ἐποχή.

offset ['ɔfset] vt ἀντισταθμίζω, ἀποζημιώνω.

offshore ['ɔf'ʃɔ:*] ad στά ἀνοιχτά a χερσαῖος, στεριανός ‖ ἀπόγειος.

offside ['ɔf'said] a (aut) ἔξω πλευρά, δεξιά πλευρά ‖ n (sport) ὄφ-σάϊντ.

offspring ['ɔfspriŋ] n ἀπόγονος, βλαστός ‖ ἀποτέλεσμα.

often ['ɔfən] ad συχνά, πολλές φορές.

ogle ['əugl] vt γλυκοκοιτάζω.

oh [əu] excl ὤ!, ἄχ!

oil [ɔil] n ἔλαιον ‖ πετρέλαιον, λάδι ‖ vt λαδώνω ‖ ~can n λπδωτήρι ‖ ~field n πετρελαιοφόρος περιοχή ‖ ~-fired a καίων πετρέλαιον ‖ ~ level n στάθμη ἐλαίου ‖ ~ painting n ἐλαιογραφία ‖ ~ refinery n διυλιστήριον ‖ ~skins npl μουσαμᾶς ‖ ~ tanker n δεξαμενόπλοιον ‖ ~ well n πετρελαιοπηγή ‖ ~y a ἐλαιώδης, λαδερός.

ointment ['ɔintmənt] n ἀλοιφή.

O.K., **okay** ['əu'kei] excl πολύ καλά!, ἐν τάξει! ‖ n ἔγκρισις ‖ vt ἐγκρίνω.

old [əuld] a γέρων, γέρος, ἡλικιωμένος ‖ (of age) τῆς ἡλικίας, χρονῶν ‖ (worn) παλαιός, σαραβαλωμένος ‖ (former) παλαιός, πρώην, τέως ‖ (friend) παλαιός (σύντροφος) ‖ ~ age n (βαθειά) γηράματα ‖ ~en a (old) παλιό, τοῦ παλιοῦ ‖ ~-fashioned a ὀπαδός τοῦ παλιοῦ καιροῦ ‖ (out of date) ἀπηρχαιωμένος, παλαιάς μόδας ‖ ~ maid n γεροντοκόρη.

olive ['ɔliv] n (fruit) ἐλαία, ἐλιά ‖ a (colour) λαδής, ἐλαιόχρους ‖ ~ oil n ἐλαιόλαδον, λάδι.

Olympic [əu'limpik] a Ὀλυμπιακός ‖ ~ Games npl (also ~s) Ὀλυμπιακοί Ἀγῶνες.

omelet(te) ['ɔmlit] n ὀμελέττα.

omen ['əumen] n οἰωνός, σημάδι.

ominous ['ɔminəs] a δυσοίωνος, δυσμενής.

omission [əu'miʃən] n παράλειψις, παραδρομή.

omit [əu'mit] vt παραλείπω.

on [ɔn] prep ἐπί, πάνω σέ, εἰς, κατά, περί ‖ ad ἐμπρός, πρός τά ἐμπρός, ἐν λειτουργία ‖ ~ and off ἐνίοτε, κάπου-κάπου ‖ ~ the left ἀριστερά, στ' ἀριστερά ‖ ~ Friday τήν Παρασκευή.

once [wʌns] ad μιά φορά, ἅπαξ, ἄλλοτε, κάποτε ‖ cj μόλις, ἀπό τή στιγμή που, μιά καί ‖ at ~ ἀμέσως, στή στιγμή ‖ (same time) ταυτοχρόνως, συγχρόνως ‖ all at ~ ὅλως αἰφνιδίως ‖ ὅλοι μαζί ‖ ~ more ἀκόμη μιά φορά ‖ more than ~ πολλές φορές ‖ ~ and for all μιά καί καλή ‖ ~ upon a time μιά φορά (καί ἕναν καιρό).

oncoming ['ɔnkʌmiŋ] a (traffic) ἐπερχόμενος, προσεγγίζων.

one [wʌn] a ἕνας, μία, ἕνα ‖ (united) ἕνας, μιά, ἕνα ‖ (only) μόνος, μοναδικός ‖ n ἕνα, ἕνας, μιά ‖ pron ἕνα, αὐτός, κανείς, τέτοιος ‖ this ~ αὐτός ἐδῶ ‖ that ~ αὐτός ἐκεῖ ‖ ~ by ~ ἕνας-ἕνας ‖ ~ never knows ποτέ δέν ξέρει κανείς ‖ ~ another ἀλλήλους ‖ ~-man a (business) (δουλειά) γιά ἕνα ἄνθρωπο ‖ ~self pron ἑαυτόν ‖ ~-way a (street, traffic) μονῆς κατευθύνσεως.

onion ['ʌnjən] n κρομμύδι.

onlooker ['ɔnlukə*] n θεατής.

only ['əunli] ad μόνον ‖ a μόνος.

onset ['ɔnset] n (beginning) ἀπαρχή.

onshore ['ɔnʃɔ:*] a,ad πρός τήν ἀκτήν.

onslaught ['ɔnslɔ:t] n ἐφόρμησις, ἐπίθεσις.

onto ['ɔntu] prep = on to.

onus ['əunəs] n βάρος, εὐθύνη, καθῆκον.

onwards ['ɔnwədz] ad (place) πρός τά ἐμπρός, καί πέραν ‖ (time) καί εἰς τό ἑξῆς.

ooze [uz] vi (liquid) στάζω, ἐκρέω, διεισδύω.

opacity [əu'pæsiti] n ἀδιαφάνεια, θολότης.

opaque [əu'peik] a ἀδιαφανής, θαμπός.

open ['əupən] a ἀνοιχτός ‖ (unlimited) ἀνοικτός, ἀπεριόριστος ‖ (without cover) ἀκάλυπτος, ξέσκεπος ‖ (clear) φανερός, ἔκδηλος ‖ (question) φανερός, ἔκδηλος ‖ (free) ἐλεύθερος, ἀνοιχτός ‖ (sincere) εἰλικρινής, ἀπροκάλυπτος ‖ vt (mouth) ἀνοίγω ‖ (letter) ἀποσφραγίζω, ἀνοίγω ‖ (box) λύνω, ἀνοίγω ‖ (door) ἀνοίγω ‖ (account) ἀνοίγω ‖ vi ἀρχίζω, ἀνοίγω ‖ (shop) ἀνοίγω ‖ (play) ἀρχίζω ‖ to ~ out vt ἀνοίγω, ξεδιπλώνω ‖ to ~ up vt (route) ἀνοίγω, χαράσσω, διανοίγω ‖ ~-air a ὑπαίθριος ‖ ~er n (for cans) ἀνοικτήρι ‖ ~ing n ἄνοιγμα, ῥωγμή ‖ (beginning) ἔναρξις ‖ (good chance) εὐκαιρία ‖ ~ly ad φανερά, εἰλικρινή, δημοσία ‖ ~-minded a εὐρύνους, μέ ἀνοιχτό μυαλό ‖ ~-necked a ἀνοιχτό ‖ (φόρεμα) ντεκολτέ.

opera ['ɔpərə] n μελόδραμα, ὄπερα ‖ ~ house n λυρική σκηνή, ὄπερα.

operate ['ɔpəreit] vt (machine) ἐνεργῶ, κινῶ, διευθύνω ‖ vi λειτουργῶ, δρῶ, ἐνεργῶ ‖ (med) (+ on) χειρουργῶ, ἐγχειρίζω.

operatic [ɔpə'rætik] a μελοδραματικός.

operation [ɔpə'reiʃən] n λειτουργία, δρᾶσις ‖ (med) ἐγχείρησις ‖ (mil) ἐπιχείρησις ‖ ~al a τῆς ἐπιχειρήσεως.

operative ['ɔpərətiv] a ἐνεργός, ἰσχύων ‖ χειρουργικός ‖ n ἐργάτης, τεχνίτης.

operator ['ɔpəreitə*] n (of machine) χειριστής, ὀπεράτερ ‖ (tel) τηλεφωνήτρια.

operetta [ɔpə'retə] n ὀπερέττα.

opinion [ə'pinjən] n γνώμη, ἰδέα, δοξασία.

opium ['əupiəm] n ὄπιον.

opponent [ə'pəunənt] n ἀντίπαλος.

opportune ['ɔpətju:n] a ἐπίκαιρος, εὔθετος, κατάλληλος.

opportunist [ɔpə'tju:nist] n καιροσκόπος.

opportunity [ɔpə'tju:niti] n εὐκαιρία.

oppose [ə'pəuz] vt ἀντιτάσσω, ἀντικρούω, καταπολεμῶ ‖ ~d a (+ to) ἀντίθετο (πρός), ἀντιτιθέμενος.

opposing [ə'pəuziŋ] a (side) ἀντίθετος, ἀντίπαλος.

opposite ['ɔpəzit] a ἀντίθετος, ἀντικρυνός ‖ (direction) ἀντίθετος ‖ ad ἔναντι, ἀπέναντι, ἀντίκρυ ‖ prep ἔναντι, ἀπέναντι ‖ n ἀντίστοιχον, ἀντίθετον ‖ ~ number n (person) ἀντίστοιχος.

opposition [ɔpə'ziʃən] n ἀντίστασις, ἀντίθεσις ‖ (party) ἀντιπολίτευσις.

oppress [ə'pres] vt καταπιέζω, καταδυναστεύω ‖ (heat etc) καταθλίβω, βασανίζω ‖ ~ion n καταπίεσις, στενοχώρια ‖ ~ive a καταθλιπτικός, πνιγηρός.

opt [ɔpt] vi: to ~ for sth διαλέγω, ἐπιλέγω.

optical ['ɔptikal] a ὀπτικός.

optician [ɔp'tiʃən] n ὀπτικός.

optimism ['ɔptimizəm] n αἰσιοδοξία.

optimist ['ɔptimist] n αἰσιόδοξος ‖ ~ic a αἰσιόδοξος.

optimum ['ɔptiməm] a εὐνοϊκός, ἄριστος.

option ['ɔpʃən] n ἐκλογή ‖ δικαίωμα ἐκλογῆς ‖ ~al a προαιρετικός.

opulence ['ɔpjuləns] n πλοῦτος, ἀφθονία.

opulent ['ɔpjulənt] a πλούσιος, ἄφθονος.

opus ['əupəs] n μουσική σύνθεσις, ἔργον.

or [ɔ:*] cj ἤ.

oracle ['ɔrəkl] n χρησμός, μαντεῖον.

oral ['ɔ:rəl] a προφορικός ‖ n (exam) προφορικαί (ἐξετάσεις).

orange ['ɔrindʒ] n πορτοκάλι ‖ (colour) πορτοκαλλί.

oration [ɔ:'reiʃən] n λόγος.

orator ['ɔrətə*] n ῥήτωρ.

oratorio [ɔrə'tɔ:riəu] n ὀρατόριον.

orbit ['ɔ:bit] n τροχιά ‖ vt (earth) περιστρέφομαι.

orchard ['ɔ:tʃəd] n ὀπωρόκηπος, περιβόλι.

orchestra ['ɔ:kistrə] n ὀρχήστρα ‖ ~l [ɔ:'kestrəl] a ὀρχηστρικός.

orchid ['ɔ:kid] n ὀρχεοειδές φυτόν.

ordain [ɔːˈdein] vt (προ)ορίζω, θεσπίζω, διορίζω ‖ (eccl) χειροτονῶ.

ordeal [ɔːˈdiːl] n βασανιστήριον.

order [ˈɔːdə*] n (arrangement) τάξις, σειρά, διαδοχή ‖ (instruction) διαταγή, ἐντολή, διάταγμα ‖ (rank, class) τάξις ‖ (eccl) βαθμός ἱερωσύνης ‖ τάγμα ‖ (decoration) παράσημον ‖ (comm) ἐπιταγή, παραγγελία ‖ vt διατάσσω ‖ διευθετῶ, ταξινομῶ ‖ (comm) παραγγέλλω ‖ ~ form n ἔντυπον ἐντολῆς ‖ ~ly n ἀγγελιαφόρος, ὀρτινάντσα ‖ a φρόνιμος, τακτικός, ἥσυχος ‖ (tidy) συγυρισμένος, τακτικός.

ordinal [ˈɔːdinl] a (number) τακτικός.

ordinarily [ɔːˈdnrili] ad συνήθως, κανονικά.

ordinary [ˈɔːdnri] a συνήθης, συνηθισμένος ‖ (commonplace) τῆς ἀράδας, κοινός ‖ ordination [ɔːdiˈneiʃən] n χειροτονία.

ordnance [ˈɔːdnəns] n ὑλικοῦ πολέμου, τηλεβόλα, πυροβόλα.

ore [ɔː*] n ὀρυκτόν, μετάλλευμα.

organ [ˈɔːgən] n (mus) ὄργανον ‖ (of sight etc) ὄργανον ‖ (means of action) ὄργανον ‖ ~ic [ɔːˈgænik] a ὀργανικός, ἐνόργανος ‖ ~ism n ὀργανισμός ‖ ~ist n ὀργανοπαίκτης.

organization [ɔːgənaiˈzeiʃən] n ὀργάνωσις, ὀργανισμός.

organize [ˈɔːgənaiz] vt ὀργανώνω ‖ ~r n (δι)ὀργανωτής.

orgasm [ˈɔːgæzəm] n ὀργασμός, παροξυσμός.

orgy [ˈɔːdʒi] n ὄργιον.

Orient [ˈɔːriənt] n: the ~ Ἀνατολή, Ἄπω Ἀνατολή.

oriental [ɔːriˈentəl] a ἀνατολικός, ἀσιατικός ‖ n Ἀσιάτης.

orientate [ˈɔːrienteit] vt προσανατολίζω.

origin [ˈɔridʒin] n ἀρχή, γένεσις, καταγωγή.

original [əˈridʒinl] a (first) ἀρχικός ‖ (new) πρωτότυπος ‖ (individual) ἰδιότυπος, πρωτότυπος ‖ n πρωτότυπον ‖ ~ity [ɔridʒiˈnæliti] n πρωτοτυπία ‖ ~ly ad ἀρχικῶς ‖ ἐξ ἀρχῆς.

originate [əˈridʒineit] vi κατάγομαι, προέρχομαι ‖ vt γεννῶ, δημιουργῶ.

originator [əˈridʒineitə*] n δημιουργός, ἐγκαινιαστής.

Orlon [ˈɔːlɔn] n ℝ ὀρλόν.

ornament [ˈɔːnəmənt] n κόσμημα, στολίδι ‖ ~al a (δια)κοσμητικός ‖ ~ation n διακόσμησις.

ornate [ɔːˈneit] a κεκοσμημένος, φανταχτερός.

ornithologist [ɔːniˈθɔlədʒist] n ὀρνιθολόγος.

ornithology [ɔːniˈθɔlədʒi] n ὀρνιθολογία.

orphan [ˈɔːfən] n ὀρφανός ‖ vt ἀπορφανίζω ‖ ~age n ὀρφανοτροφεῖον.

orthodox [ˈɔːθədɔks] a ὀρθόδοξος ‖ (conventional) καθιερωμένος.

orthopaedic, (US) ~pedic [ɔːθəuˈpiːdik] a ὀρθοπεδικός.

oscillation [ɔsiˈleiʃən] n αἰώρησις, ταλάντευσις.

ostensible [ɔsˈtensəbl] a προφανής, φαινομενικός, δῆθεν.

ostensibly [ɔsˈtensəbli] ad κατά τά φαινόμενα, δῆθεν.

ostentation [ɔstenˈteiʃən] n ἐπίδειξις, φιγούρα.

ostentatious [ɔstenˈteiʃəs] a ἐπιδεικτικός, φιγουρατζῆς, φανταχτερός.

ostracize [ˈɔstrəsaiz] vt ἐξοστρακίζω.

ostrich [ˈɔstritʃ] n στρουθοκάμηλος.

other [ˈʌðə*] a ἄλλος ‖ (additional) ἄλλος, ἐπιπρόσθετος ‖ (opposite) ἄλλος, ἀπέναντι ‖ pron ἄλλος ‖ ad: ~ than διαφορετικός ἀπό, ἐκτός ἀπό ‖ ~wise ad ἄλλως, ἀλλοιώτικα ‖ (in other ways) κατά τά ἄλλα ‖ (or else) διαφορετικά, ἀλλοιῶς, εἰδεμή.

otter [ˈɔtə*] n ἐνίδρυς, βύδρα.

ought [ɔːt] auxiliary v πρέπει, θέ ἔπρεπε ‖ I ~ to do it πρέπει νά τό κάνω ‖ you ~ to go πρέπει νά φύγης ‖ he ~ to win πρέπει νά κερδίση.

ounce [auns] n οὐγγιά.

our [auə*] poss a ἰδικός μας ‖ ~s poss pron ἰδικός μας ‖ ~selves pron ἐμεῖς οἱ ἴδιοι.

oust [aust] vt ἐκβάλλω, ἐκτοπίζω.

out [aut] ad ἔξω ‖ (not indoors) ἐκτός ‖ (not alight) σβησμένος ‖ (open) πού βγῆκαν, βγαλμένα ‖ (made known) γνωστον, πού ἀπεκαλύφθη ‖ (in reckoning) εἰς λάθος, ἔξω ‖ ~ of prep ἔξω ἀπό ‖ (from among) ἀπό ‖ (without) χωρίς ‖ made ~ of wood καμωμένο ἀπό ξύλο ‖ ~-of-bounds a ἀπαγορευμένος ‖ ~-of-date a ξεπερασμένος ‖ ~ of doors ad ἔξω, στό ὕπαιθρον ‖ ~ of order a βεβλαμένος, χαλασμένος ‖ ~-of-theway a παράμερος, ἀπόμερος ‖ (unusual) ἀσυνήθης, ἀσυνήθιστος.

outback [ˈautbæk] n τό ἐσωτερικόν.

outboard (motor) [ˈautbɔːd(ˈməutə*)] n ἐξωλέμβιος (κινητήρ).

outbreak [ˈautbreik] n ἔκρηξις, ξέσπασμα, ἔναρξις.

outbuilding [ˈautbildiŋ] n παράρτημα οἰκοδομῆς.

outburst [ˈautbəːst] n ἔκρηξις, ξέσπασμα.

outcast [ˈautkaːst] n ἀπόβλητος.

outclass [autˈklaːs] vt ὑπερτερῶ, ὑπερβαίνω.

outcome [ˈautkʌm] n ἔκβασις, πέρας.

outcry [ˈautkrai] n (κατα)κραυγή.

outdated [ˈautˈdeitid] a παλιωμένος, ξεπερασμένος.

outdo [autˈduː] vt ὑπερβαίνω, ὑπερέχω.

outdoor [ˈautdɔː*] a ὑπαίθριος, ἐξωτερικός.

outdoors [autˈdɔːz] ad στό ὕπαιθρον.

outer [ˈautə*] a ἐξωτερικός ‖ ~ space n διάστημα.

outfit ['autfit] n ἐξοπλισμός, ἐργαλεῖα, ἀπαιτούμενα ‖ ~ters npl (of clothes) ἔμπορος ἀνδρικῶν ἐνδυμάτων.

outgoings ['autgəuiŋz] npl (expenses) ἔξοδα, πληρωμές.

outgrow [aut'grəu] vt γίνομαι ὑψηλότερος ἀπό, ξεπερνῶ ‖ ἀπαλλάσσομαι.

outing ['autiŋ] n ἐκδρομή.

outlandish [aut'lændiʃ] a παράξενος, ἀσυνήθιστος

outlaw ['autlɔ] n ληστής, παράνομος ‖ vt προγράφω.

outlay ['autlei] n δαπάνη, ἔξοδα.

outlet ['autlet] n διέξοδος, ἄνοιγμα.

outline [autlain] n περίμετρος, περίγραμμα ‖ περίληψις.

outlive [aut'liv] vt ἐπιζῶ.

outlook ['autluk] n (prospect) πρόβλεψις.

outlying ['autlaiiŋ] a ἀπόκεντρος, ἀπόμερος.

outmoded [aut'məudid] a ντεμοντέ.

outnumber [aut'nʌmbə*] vt ὑπερτερῶ ἀριθμητικῶς.

outpatient ['autpeiʃənt] n ἐξωτερικός ἀσθενής.

outpost ['autpəust] n (people, also place) προφυλακή, φυλάκιον.

output ['autput] n παραγωγή, ἀπόδοσις, προϊόν.

outrage ['autreidʒ] n προσβολή, κατάφωρον ἀδίκημα ‖ vt προσβάλλω, πληγώνω, ταράζω ‖ ~ous a σκανδαλώδης, τερατώδης, ἀχρεῖος.

outright ['autrait] ad ἀπεριφράστως, ὠμά, ξάστερα ‖ (once for all) τελείως, ἐντελῶς ‖ a τέλειος, ὁριστικός.

outset ['autset] n ἀρχή, ξεκίνημα.

outside ['aut'said] n ἐξωτερικόν ‖ a ἐξωτερικός, πιθανός ‖ ad ἀπ' ἔξω, ἔξω ‖ prep ἔξω ἀπό, ἐκτός ἀπό, πέραν τοῦ ‖ ~-forward n ἔξω κυνηγός ‖ ~r n (in race etc) χωρίς πιθανότητες ‖ (independent) ξένος, θεατής.

outsize ['autsaiz] a μεγάλων διαστάσεων.

outskirts ['autskəts] npl προάστια, περίχωρα.

outspoken [aut'spəukən] a εἰλικρινής, ντόμπρος.

outstanding [aut'stændiŋ] a προέχων, κύριος, σημαντικός ‖ (person) διακεκριμένος, σπουδαῖος, διαπρεπής ‖ (unsettled) ἐκκρεμής, ἀπλήρωτος.

outstay [aut'stei] vt (welcome) μένω περισσότερον ἀπό.

outstretched ['autstretʃt] a (hand) ἀπλωμένος, μέ ἀνοιχτάς ἀγκάλας.

outward ['autwəd] a (sign) ἐξωτερικός ‖ (journey) πρός τά ἔξω, ἔξω, ἔξω ‖ ~ly ad ἐξωτερικῶς, φαινομενικῶς.

outweigh [aut'wei] vt (in importance) βαρύνω περισσότερον, ὑπερτερῶ.

outwit [aut'wit] vt ξεγελῶ.

outworn [aut'wɔn] a (dated) παλιωμένος.

oval ['əuvəl] a ὠοειδής, ἐλλειψοειδής ‖ n ὠοειδές σχῆμα.

ovary ['əuvəri] n ὠοθήκη.

ovation [əu'veiʃən] n ἐπευφημία.

oven ['ʌvn] n κλίβανος, φοῦρνος.

over ['əuvə*] ad (above) ἄνωθεν, πάνω ἀπό ‖ (across) ἀπέναντι, πέραν ‖ (finished) περασμένος, τελειωμένος ‖ (too much) πέραν τοῦ δέοντος, ἐπί πλέον ‖ (again) φορές (συνέχεια), πάλι ‖ prep (above) ἄνωθεν, ἀπό πάνω, πάνω ‖ (across) ἀπέναντι ‖ (in rank) ὑπεράνω, ὑψηλότερος, ἀνώτερος ‖ (about) περί, γιά ‖ all ~ (everywhere) παντοῦ, σ' ὅλο ‖ (finished) τελειωμένος, τετέλεσται, περασμένα ‖ ~ and ~ πολλές φορές, ἐπανειλημμένως ‖ ~ and above πέραν ἀπό.

over- ['əuvə*] prefix ὑπέρ-, παρά-.

overact [əuvər'ækt] vi ὑπερβάλλω, παρακάνω.

overall ['əuvərɔl] n (Brit) (coat for woman etc) μπλούζα, ποδιά ‖ ~s npl (including trousers, for man) φόρμα.

overawe [əuvər'ɔ] vt ἐκφοβίζω, τρομοκρατῶ, ἐπιβάλλομαι (εἰς).

overbalance [əuvə'bæləns] vi ἀνατρέπω, ὑπερέχω.

overbearing [əuvə'beəriŋ] a αὐταρχικός, δεσποτικός, ὑπεροπτικός.

overboard ['əuvəbɔd] ad στή θάλασσα (ἀπό πλοῖον).

overcast ['əuvəkɑst] a συννεφιασμένος, σκοτεινιασμένος.

overcharge ['əuvə'tʃɑdʒ] vt (price) παίρνω πολλά, γδύνω, ἐπιβαρύνω.

overcoat ['əuvəkəut] n ἐπανωφόρι, παλτό.

overcome [əuvə'kʌm] vt νικῶ, καταβάλλω.

overcrowded [əuvə'kraudid] a ὑπερπλήρες, παραγεμισμένο.

overcrowding [əuvə'kraudiŋ] n ὑπερπλήρωσις, ὑπερπληθυσμός.

overdo [əuvə'du] vt (cook) παραψήνω ‖ (exaggerate) ὑπερβάλλω, μεγαλοποιῶ, παρακάνω.

overdose ['əuvədəus] n ὑπερβολική δόσις.

overdraft ['əuvədrɑft] n ἀκάλυπτος λογαριασμός.

overdrawn ['əuvə'drɔn] a (account) see **overdraft**.

overdrive ['əuvədraiv] n (aut) πολλαπλασιασμένη ταχύτης.

overdue ['əuvə'dju] a καθυστερημένος, ἐκπρόθεσμος.

overestimate ['əuvər'estimeit] vt ὑπερεκτιμῶ, ὑπερτιμῶ.

overexcited ['əuvərik'saitid] a ὑπερδιεγειρόμενος.

overexertion ['əuvərig'zəʃən] n ὑπερκόπωσις, ξεθέωσια.

overexpose ['əuvəriks'pəuz] vt (phot) ὑπερεκθέτω, ὑπερφωτίζω.

overflow [əuvə'fləu] vi ξεχειλίζω ‖ ['əuvəfləu] n ὑπερχείλησις, ξεχείλισμα.

overgrown ['əuvə'grəun] a (garden) κατάφυτος, γεμάτο ἀπό, σκεπασμένο μέ.

overhaul ['əuvə'hɔːl] vt (repair) ἐξετάζω, ἐπιθεωρῶ, ἐλέγχω ‖ ['əuvəhɔːl] n προσεκτική ἐξέτασις, ἐπιθεώρησις, ἐπισκευή.

overhead ['əuvəhed] a ἐναέριος, γενικός ‖ ['əuvə'hed] ad ἐπάνω, ὑπεράνω, ψηλά ‖ ~s npl γενικά ἔξοδα.

overhear ['əuvə'hiə*] vt ἀκούω τυχαία, κρυφακούω.

overjoyed ['əuvə'dʒɔid] a περιχαρής, γεμάτος χαρά.

overland ['əuvələænd] a χερσαῖος, στεριανός ‖ ['əuvə'lænd] ad (journey) διά ξηρᾶς.

overlap ['əuvə'læp] vi καβαλικεύω, σκεπάζω μερικῶς ‖ ['əuvələæp] n ἐπικάλυψις, καβαλίκεμα.

overleaf ['əuvə'liːf] ad ὄπισθεν (τῆς σελίδος).

overload ['əuvə'ləud] vt παραφορτώνω, ὑπερφορτίζω.

overlook ['əuvə'luk] vt κοιτάζω ἐπάνω ἀπό, δεσπόζω ‖ (not notice) παραβλέπω, παραμελῶ ‖ (pardon) παραβλέπω, συγχωρῶ.

overlord ['əuvələːd] n ἀνώτατος ἄρχων, ἐπικυρίαρχος.

overnight ['əuvə'nait] a ὁλονύκτιος, ξενυχτισμένος ‖ ad ὅλην τήν νύκτα, ξενύχτι.

overpass ['əuvəpɑːs] n (road) ἀνυψωμένη διάβασις.

overpower ['əuvə'pauə*] vt καταβάλλω, συντρίβω, καταπνίγω ‖ ~ing a συντριπτικός, ἀποπνικτικός.

overrate ['əuvə'reit] vt ὑπερτιμῶ.

override ['əuvə'raid] vt (invalidate) ὑπερβαίνω, ἀνατρέπω.

overriding ['əuvə'raidiŋ] a πρωταρχικός, δεσπόζων.

overrule ['əuvə'ruːl] vt ἀνατρέπω, ἀγνοῶ, ἀναιρῶ.

overseas ['əuvə'siːz] ad στό ἐξωτερικόν a (trade) ἐξωτερικός.

overseer ['əuvəsiə*] n ἐπιτηρητής, ἐπιστάτης.

overshadow ['əuvə'ʃædəu] vt ἐπισκιάζω.

overshoot ['əuvə'ʃuːt] vt (runway) προσγειώνομαι μακρυά.

oversight ['əuvəsait] n παράβλεψις, παραδρομή.

oversimplify ['əuvə'simplifai] vt ὑπεραπλοποιῶ.

oversleep ['əuvə'sliːp] vi παρακοιμᾶμαι.

overstate ['əuvə'steit] vt (case) μεγαλοποιῶ, ὑπερβάλλω ‖ ~ment n ὑπερβολή, μεγαλοποίησις.

overt ['əu'vəːt] a ἔκδηλος, καταφανής, ἐμφανής.

overtake ['əuvə'teik] vt (κατα)φθάνω, ξεπερνῶ ‖ vi συμβαίνω εἰς, τυχαίνω εἰς.

overtaking ['əuvə'teikiŋ] n ξεπέρασμα.

overthrow ['əuvə'θrəu] vt (vanquish) συντρίβω, ἀνατρέπω, τσακίζω.

overtime ['əuvətaim] n ὑπερωρίες.

overtone ['əuvətəun] n (mus) ἁρμονική.

overture ['əuvətjuə*] n (mus) εἰσαγωγή, 'οὐβερτούρα.

overturn ['əuvə'təːn] vt ἀνατρέπω, ἀναποδογυρίζω ‖ vi ἀνατρέπομαι.

overweight ['əuvə'weit] a μέ βάρος ἀνώτερον τοῦ κανονικοῦ.

overwhelm ['əuvə'welm] vt συντρίβω, κατακλύζω, καταβάλλω ‖ ~ing a συντριπτικός, ἀκαταμάχητος.

overwork ['əuvə'wəːk] n καταπόνησις, ὑπερκόπωσις ‖ vt παραφορτώνω, παρακουράζω ‖ vi ἐργάζομαι ὑπερβολικά, παρακουράζομαι.

overwrought ['əuvə'rɔːt] a πολυδουλεμένος, πολυκουρασμένος.

owe [əu] vt ὀφείλω, χρεωστῶ, χρωστῶ.

owing ['əuiŋ] ~ to prep λόγω, ἕνεκα, συνεπεία, ἐξ αἰτίας.

owl [aul] n κουκουβάγια.

own [əun] vt (κατ)ἔχω, κέκτημαι ‖ ὁμολογῶ ‖ a ἴδιος, δικός (μου) ‖ n δικός (μου), ἰδιαίτερος ‖ all my ~ μοῦ ἀνήκει, ὅλο δικό μου ‖ on one's ~ ἀνεξάρτητα, μόνος (μου) ‖ to ~ up vi (confess) ὁμολογῶ ‖ ~er n ἰδιοκτήτης, κύριος, ‖ ~ership n κυριότης, ἰδιοκτησία.

ox [ɔks] n βόδι, βοῦς.

oxide ['ɔksaid] n ὀξείδιον.

oxyacetylene ['ɔksiə'setiliːn] a ὀξυακετυλενικός.

oxygen ['ɔksidʒən] n ὀξυγόνον ‖ ~ mask n μάσκα ὀξυγόνου ‖ ~ tent n ἀσκός ὀξυγόνου.

oyster ['ɔistə*] n στρείδι.

ozone ['əuzəun] n ὄζον.

P, p

pa [pɑː] n (col: father) πατέρας, μπαμπᾶς.

pace [peis] n βῆμα, βάδισμα ‖ (speed) ταχύτης ‖ vi βαδίζω, βηματίζω, περπατῶ ‖ to keep ~ with συμβαδίζω ‖ ~maker n προπονητής ‖ (med) βηματοδότης.

pacification [pæsifi'keiʃən] n εἰρήνευσις.

Pacific (Ocean) [pə'sifik('əuʃən)] n Εἰρηνικός ('Ωκεανός).

pacifism ['pæsifizəm] n εἰρηνοφιλία, πα(τ)σιφισμός.

pacifist ['pæsifist] n εἰρηνόφιλος.

pacify ['pæsifai] vt εἰρηνεύω, καθησυχάζω.

pack [pæk] n (bundle) δέμα, πακέτο ‖ (wolves) ἀγέλη, κοπάδι ‖ (cards) δεσμίς, τράπουλα ‖ (gang) συμμορία ‖ vt (case) συσκευάζω, πακετάρω, κάνω δέμα ‖ (clothes) μαζεύω (τά ροῦχα μου) ‖ ~age n δέμα ‖ ~et n δεματάκι, πακέτο ‖ ~ice n σωρός πάγων, ὀγκόπαγοι ‖ ~ing n (action) πακετάρισμα ‖ (material) συσκευασία ‖ ~ing case *n* κιβώτιον συσκευασίας, κασόνι.

pact [pækt] *n* συμφωνία, συνθήκη.

pad [pæd] *n* μαξιλαράκι ‖ μπλόκ ‖ (*for inking*) ταμπόν ‖ *vt* (παρα)γεμίζω.

paddle ['pædl] *n* (*oar*) κουπί, ἀναδευτήρ ‖ *vt* (*boat*) κωπηλατῶ, τραβῶ κουπί ‖ *vi* (*in sea*) κωπηλατῶ ἤρεμα, τσαλαβουτῶ.

paddling pool ['pædliŋpu:l] *n* λιμνούλα (γιά παιδιά).

paddock ['pædək] *n* περίβολος, μάνδρα (γιά ἄλογα).

paddy ['pædi] ~ field *n* ὀρυζοφυτεία.

padlock ['pædlɔk] *n* λουκέτο.

padre ['pɑ:dri] *n* παπᾶς.

paediatrics [pi:di'ætriks] *n* παιδιατρική.

pagan ['peigən] *a* εἰδωλολατρικός.

page [peidʒ] *n* (*of book*) σελίδα ‖ (*boy servant*) νεαρός ὑπηρέτης, γκρούμ ‖ (*wedding*) ἀκόλουθος, παράνυμφος ‖ *vt* (*in hotel etc*) στέλνω μικρόν νά φωνάξη (κάποιον).

pageant ['pædʒənt] *n* φαντασμαγορικόν θέαμα, ἐπιβλητική πομπή ‖ ~ry *n* ἐπίδειξις, θεαματικότης, πομπή.

pagoda [pə'gəudə] *n* παγόδα.

paid [peid] *pt,pp* of pay.

pail [peil] *n* κάδος, κουβάς.

pain [pein] *n* πόνος ‖ ~s *npl* (*efforts*) κόπος ‖ ~ed *a* (*expression*) θλιμμένος, πικραμένος, πονεμένος ‖ ~ful *a* (*physically*) πού πονεῖ ‖ (*difficult*) ἐπίπονος ‖ ὀδυνηρός ‖ ~killing drug *n* παυσίπονον ‖ ~less *a* ἀνώδυνος ‖ ~staking *a* φιλόπονος, προσεκτικός.

paint [peint] *n* χρῶμα, μπογιά ‖ *vt* ζωγραφίζω, ἀπεικονίζω ‖ (*house etc*) μπογιατίζω, χρωματίζω ‖ ~brush *n* χρωστήρ, πινέλλο ‖ ~er *n* (*art*) ζωγράφος ‖ (*decorator*) χρωματιστής, μπογιατζῆς ‖ ~ing *n* (*action*) ζωγραφική ‖ (*picture*) πίναξ, ζωγραφιά.

pair [pεə*] *n* (*of shoes*) ζεύγος, ζευγάρι ‖ ~ of scissors *n* ψαλίδι ‖ ~ of trousers *n* πανταλόνι.

pajamas [pə'dʒɑ:məz] *npl* (*US*) πυτζάμες.

pal [pæl] *n* (*col*) βλάμης, μακαντάσης, φίλος.

palace ['pælis] *n* ἀνάκτορον, παλάτι.

palatable ['pælətəbl] *a* εὔγευστος, νόστιμος.

palate ['pælit] *n* ὑπερώα, οὐρανίσκος ‖ (*taste*) γεῦσις.

pale [peil] *a* (*face*) ὠχρός, χλωμός ‖ (*colour*) ἀνοιχτό ‖ ~ness *n* ὠχρότης, χλωμάδα.

palette ['pælit] *n* παλέττα.

palisade [pæli'seid] *n* φράκτης ἀπό πασσάλους.

pall [pɔ:l] *n* (*of smoke*) σύννεφο ‖ *vi* ξεθυμαίνω, μπουχτίζω.

pally ['pæli] *a* (*col*) πού πιάνει εὔκολα φιλίες.

palm [pɑ:m] *n* (*tree*) φοῖνιξ, βάϊον ‖ (*of hand*) παλάμη ‖ ~ist *n* χειρομάντης ‖

P~ Sunday *n* Κυριακή τῶν Βαΐων ‖ ~ tree *n* φοῖνιξ, χουρμαδιά.

palpable ['pælpəbl] *a* (*obvious*) φανερός, καταφανής.

palpitation [pælpi'teiʃən] *n* παλμός, σπαρτάρισμα.

paltry ['pɔ:ltri] *a* μηδαμινός, τιποτένιος, ἄθλιος.

pamper ['pæmpə*] *vt* (παρα)χαϊδεύω.

pamphlet ['pæmflit] *n* φυλλάδιον.

pan [pæn] *n* τηγάνι, κατσαρόλα ‖ *vi* (+ *out*) ἐπιτυγχάνω, ἀποδίδω.

pan- [pæn] *prefix* παν-.

panacea [pænə'siə] *n* (*fig*) πανάκεια.

pancake ['pænkeik] *n* τηγανίτα.

panda ['pændə] *n* πάνδα.

pandemonium [pændi'məuniəm] *n* πανδαιμόνιον.

pander ['pændə*] *vi* (+ *to*) κάνω τόν ρουφιάνο, κολακεύω πρόστυχα.

pane [pein] *n* τζάμι.

panel ['pænl] *n* (*of wood*) φάτνωμα, φύλλο ‖ (*of people*) ἐπιτροπή ‖ ~ling, (*US*) ~ing *n* ξυλεπένδυσις.

pang [pæŋ] *n* δυνατός πόνος ‖ ἀγωνία.

panic ['pænik] *n* πανικός ‖ *a* (*reaction*) πανικόβλητος ‖ *vi* πανικοβάλλομαι ‖ ~ky *a* (*person*) πανικόβλητος, ἔντρομος, φοβισμένος.

pannier ['pæniə*] *n* κοφίνι, πανέρι.

panorama [pænə'rɑ:mə] *n* πανόραμα.

panoramic [pænə'ræmik] *a* πανοραματικός.

pansy ['pænzi] *n* (*flower*) πανσές.

pant [pænt] *vi* λαχανιάζω.

panther ['pænθə*] *n* πάνθηρ.

panties ['pæntiz] *npl* (*woman's*) κυλότα.

pantomime ['pæntəmaim] *n* παντομίμα.

pantry ['pæntri] *n* κελλάρι ‖ (*butler's*) κάβα.

pants [pænts] *npl* (*woman's*) κυλότα ‖ (*man's*) σώβρακο ‖ (*US: trousers*) πανταλόνι.

papal ['peipəl] *a* παπικός.

paper ['peipə*] *n* (*material*) χαρτί ‖ (*newspaper*) ἐφημερίδα ‖ (*essay*) μελέτη, διατριβή, ὑπόμνημα ‖ *a* χάρτινος ‖ *vt* σκεπάζω μέ χαρτί, στολίζω μέ χαρτί ‖ ~s *npl* (*identity*) πιστοποιητικά ‖ ἔγγραφα ‖ ~back *n* χαρτόδετον (βιβλίον) ‖ ~ bag *n* χαρτοσακκούλα ‖ ~ clip *n* συνδετήρας ‖ ~weight *n* πρές-παπιέ ‖ ~ work *n* γραφικὴ ἐργασία.

papier-mâché ['pæpiei'mæʃei] *n* πεπιεσμένος χάρτης.

par [pɑ:*] *n* (*comm*) ἰσοτιμία, ἄρτιον, ἰσότης ‖ on a ~ with ἴσον μέ, ἴση ἀξία μέ.

parable ['pærəbl] *n* παραβολή.

parachute ['pærəʃu:t] *n* ἀλεξίπτωτον ‖ *vi* κατέρχομαι δι' ἀλεξιπτώτου ‖ ~ jump *n* πτῶσις μέ ἀλεξίπτωτον.

parade [pə'reid] *n* (*procession*) παρέλασις ‖ (*review*) παράταξις, παρέλασις ‖ *vt* ἐπιδεικνύω, κάνω παρέλασιν ‖ *vi* παρελαύνω.

paradise ['pærədais] n παράδεισος.

paradox ['pærədɔks] n παράδοξον, παραδοξολογία ‖ ~ical a παράδοξος ‖ ~ically ad παραδόξως.

paraffin ['pærəfin] n παραφίνη.

paragraph ['pærəgrɑ:f] n παράγραφος.

parallel ['pærəlel] a παράλληλος ‖ (similar) ὅμοιος, παράλληλος, ἀνάλογος ‖ n παράλληλος.

paralysis [pə'ræləsis] n παράλυσις.

paralyze ['pærəlaiz] vt παραλύω.

paramount ['pærəmaunt] a ὕψιστος, ὑπέρτατος, ἐξαίρετος.

paranoia [pærə'nɔiə] n παράνοια.

parapet ['pærəpit] n στηθαῖον, παραπέτο, πρόχωμα.

paraphernalia [pærəfə'neiliə] n διάφορα, καλαμπαλίκια.

paraphrase ['pærəfreiz] vt παραφράζω.

paraplegic [pærə'pli:dʒik] a παραπληγικός.

parasite ['pærəsait] n παράσιτον.

parasol [pærə'sɔl] n ὀμπρέλλα ἡλίου.

paratrooper ['pærətru:pə*] n ἀλεξιπτωτιστής.

parcel ['pɑ:sl] n δέμα, πακέτο ‖ vt (also ~ up) πακετάρω.

parch [pɑ:tʃ] vt ξηραίνω, καψαλίζω, ψήνω ‖ ~ed a ξηρός, στεγνός, ἄνυδρος.

parchment ['pɑ:tʃmənt] n περγαμηνή.

pardon ['pɑ:dn] n συγγνώμη, συγχώρησις ‖ vt (free from punishment) δίδω χάριν εἰς ‖ ~! συγγνώμη! ‖ ~ me! μέ συγχωρεῖτε! ‖ I beg your ~! συγγνώμη! ‖ I beg your ~? παρακαλῶ;.

parent ['pεərənt] n γονεύς ‖ ~al a πατρικός, μητρικός.

parenthesis [pə'renθisis] n παρένθεσις.

parish ['pæriʃ] n ἐνορία, κοινότης ‖ ~ioner n ἐνορίτης.

parity ['pæriti] n (fin) ἰσότης, ἰσοτιμία, παριτέ.

park [pɑ:k] n πάρκο ‖ (cars) χῶρος σταθμεύσεως ‖ vti σταθμεύω, παρκάρω ‖ ~ing n στάθμευσις, παρκάρισμα, πάρκιν ‖ 'no ~ing' 'ἀπαγορεύεται ἡ στάθμευσις' ‖ ~ing lot n (US) χῶρος σταθμεύσεως ‖ ~ing meter n παρκόμετρον ‖ ~ing place n θέσις σταθμεύσεως.

parliament ['pɑ:ləmənt] n κοινοβούλιον ‖ (in Britain) κοινοβούλιον, Βουλή ‖ ~ary a κοινοβουλευτικός.

parochial [pə'rəukiəl] a ἐνοριακός, κοινοτικός ‖ (narrow-minded) περιωρισμένος, τοπιστικός.

parody ['pærədi] n παρωδία.

parole [pə'rəul] n: on ~ ἐλεύθερος (προσωρινός) ἐπί λόγου.

parquet [pɑ:'kei] n παρκέτο.

parrot ['pærət] n παπαγάλος ‖ ~ fashion ad (learn) παπαγαλίστικα.

parry ['pæri] vt ἀποκρούω, ἀποφεύγω, ξεφεύγω.

parsimonious [pɑ:si'məuniəs] a φειδωλός,

σφιχτός, τσιγγούνης ‖ ~ly ad μετά φειδούς, μετρημένα.

parsley ['pɑ:sli] n μαϊντανός.

parsnip ['pɑ:snip] n δαυκί.

parson ['pɑ:sn] n ἐφημέριος, παπᾶς.

part [pɑ:t] n μέρος, κομμάτι ‖ (in play) ρόλος ‖ (of machine) τμῆμα, μέρος, ἐξάρτημα, τεμάχιον ‖ a μερικό, ἡμι-, μισο- ‖ ad = partly ‖ vt χωρίζω, διαιρῶ, κόβω ‖ vi (people) χωρίζουμε, χωρίζομαι ‖ (roads) παρεκκλίνω, χωρίζομαι ‖ for my ~ ὅσο γιά μένα ‖ for the most ~ ὡς ἐπί τό πλεῖστον ‖ to ~ with vt ἐγκαταλείπω, παραδίδω ‖ ~ial ['pɑ:ʃəl] a μερικός ‖ (favouring) μεροληπτικός ‖ (+ to) ἔχω συμπάθειαν πρός, ἔχω κλῆσιν ‖ ~ially ad μερικῶς, ἐν μέρει.

participate [pɑ:'tisipeit] vi (+ in) συμμετέχω, παίρνω μέρος.

participation [pɑ:tisi'peiʃən] n συμμετοχή.

participle ['pɑ:tisipl] n μετοχή.

particular [pə'tikjulə*] a συγκεκριμένος ‖ (single) ἰδιαίτερος ‖ (hard to please) ἰδιότροπος, ἀκριβολόγος ‖ n λεπτομέρεια, ἰδιομορφία ‖ ~s npl (details) χαρακτηριστικά, περιγραφή ‖ ~ly ad ἰδιαιτέρως, εἰδικῶς, συγκεκριμένως.

parting ['pɑ:tiŋ] n (separation) ἀναχώρησις, χωρισμός ‖ (of hair) χωρίστρα ‖ a ἀποχαιρετιστήριος ‖ διαχωριστικός.

partisan [pɑ:ti'zæn] n ὀπαδός, παρτιζάνος ‖ a μεροληπτικός.

partition [pɑ:'tiʃən] n διαχωρισμός, διαίρεσις ‖ (wall) χώρισμα, μεσότοιχος.

partly ['pɑ:tli] ad ἐν μέρει.

partner ['pɑ:tnə*] n ἐταῖρος, συνέταιρος ‖ (in dance etc) καβαλιέρος, ντάμα ‖ vt συνεταιρίζομαι, συμπράττω ‖ ~ship n συνεταιρισμός, συνεργασία ‖ ἑταιρεία.

partridge ['pɑ:tridʒ] n πέρδικα.

part-time ['pɑ:t'taim] ad γιά λίγες ὧρες, μερικῶς ἄνεργος.

party ['pɑ:ti] n (pol) κόμμα ‖ (group) ὁμάς, συντροφιά ‖ (lawsuit, agreement) διάδικος ‖ μέτοχος, πρόσωπον ‖ (celebration) πάρτυ ‖ a (dress) τοῦ πάρτυ, τῆς διασκεδάσεως ‖ (pol) τοῦ κόμματος, κομματικός.

pass [pɑ:s] vt περνῶ, διέρχομαι, παρέρχομαι ‖ διαβαίνω ‖ (surpass) ὑπερβαίνω, ξεπερνῶ, προσπερνῶ ‖ (move one to another) μεταβιβάζω, διαβιβάζω, δίνω ‖ (spend time) περνῶ ‖ (be successful) ἐπιτυγχάνω, περνῶ ‖ (approve) ἐγκρίνω ‖ vi μεταβαίνω, διαβαίνω, διέρχομαι ‖ n (passage) στενόν, πέρασμα, δερβένι ‖ (permission) ἄδεια ‖ (success) περνῶ (ἴσα-ἴσα) ‖ (sport) πάσσα ‖ to ~ away vi (die) πεθαίνω ‖ ἐξαφανίζομαι ‖ to ~ by vi (ἀντι)παρέρχομαι ‖ παραμελῶ ‖ to ~ for vt θεωροῦμαι ὡς, περνῶ γιά ‖ to ~ out vi (faint) λιποθυμῶ ‖ ~able a διαβατός ‖ (fairly good) ὑποφερτός, καλούτσικος ‖ ~ably ad ὑποφερτά, μέτρια ‖ ~age n (corridor) διάδρομος ‖ (part of book etc) χωρίον, ἀπόσπασμα, κομμάτι ‖ (crossing) διάβασις, δίοδος, διάβα ‖ ~ageway n δίοδος, πέρασμα ‖ πάροδος.

passenger ['pæsindʒə*] n ἐπιβάτης.

passer-by ['pa:sə'bai] n διαβάτης, περαστικός.

passing ['pɑ:siŋ] n (death) θάνατος ‖ a (car) διερχόμενος, διαβατικός ‖ in ~ παρεμπιπτόντως.

passion ['pæʃən] n πάθος, θέρμη, μανία ‖ (love) Ἔρως, πάθος ‖ ~ate a σφοδρός, φλογερός, βίαιος ‖ ~ately ad περιπαθῶς, θερμά.

passive ['pæsiv] a (gram) παθητικός.

Passover ['pɑ:səuvə*] n Λαμπρή, Πάσχα.

passport ['pɑ:spɔ:t] n διαβατήριον.

password ['pɑ:swɔ:d] n σύνθημα, παρασύνθημα.

past [pɑ:st] ad,prep (beyond) πέραν, πέρα ἀπό, ἐκεῖθεν ‖ (with numbers) περασμένος ‖ (with time) παρωχημένος, περασμένα ‖ a (years) περασμένος, τόν παλιό καιρό ‖ (president etc) τέως, πρώην.

paste [peist] n (for paper) κόλλα ‖ (for cooking) πάστα, ζυμάρι.

pastel ['pæstəl] a (colour) παστέλ.

pasteurized ['pæstəraizd] a παστεριωμένον.

pastille ['pæstil] n παστίλλια.

pastime ['pɑ:staim] n διασκέδασις, παιχνίδι.

pastor ['pɑ:stə*] n πάστωρ, παπᾶς.

pastoral ['pɑ:stərəl] a ποιμενικός, βουκολικός.

pastry ['peistri] n ζύμη, πάστα ‖ (pies, tarts etc) γλυκό.

pasture ['pɑ:stʃə*] n (ground) βοσκοτόπι.

pasty ['pæsti] n κρεατόπιττα ‖ ['peisti] a ζυμώδης, ὠχρός.

pat [pæt] n ἐλαφρόν κτύπημα, χάδι ‖ vt κτυπῶ ἐλαφρά, χαϊδεύω.

patch [pætʃ] n ἐπίραμμα, μπάλωμα ‖ τσιρότο ‖ (stain) λεκές ‖ vt μπαλώνω ‖ ~work n σύρραμα, συνονθύλευμα ‖ ~y a (irregular) ἀνομοιόμορφος.

pate [peit] n κεφάλι, κούτρα.

patent ['peitənt] n προνόμιον, δίπλωμα εὑρεσιτεχνίας, πατέντα ‖ vt πατεντάρω ‖ a προφανής, ἁπλός, προνομιακός, πρωτότυπος ‖ ~ leather n λουστρίνι ‖ ~ly ad φανερά, ὁλοφάνερα ‖ ~ medicine n εἰδικόν φάρμακον, ἰδιοσκεύασμα.

paternal [pə'tə:nl] a πατρικός.

paternity [pə'tə:niti] n πατρότης.

path [pɑ:θ] n δρομάκος, μονοπάτι ‖ (of su etc) διαδρομή, πορεία, γραμμή, ἴχνος.

pathetic [pə'θetik] a συγκινητικός, περιπαθής ‖ ~ally ad παθητικά, συγκινητικά.

pathological [pæθə'lɔdʒikəl] a παθολογικός

pathologist [pə'θɔlədʒist] n παθολόγος.

pathology [pə'θɔlədʒi] n παθολογία.

pathos ['pciθɔs] n πάθος, συγκινητικότης.

pathway ['pɑ:θwei] n μονοπάτι, ἀτραπός.

patience ['peiʃəns] n ὑπομονή.

patient ['peiʃənt] n νοσηλευόμενος, ἄρρωστος ‖ a ὑπομονητικός ‖ ~ly ad ὑπομονετικά.

patio ['pætiəu] n πλακόστρωτος αὐλή.

patriarch ['peitria:k] n πατριάρχης.

patriotic [pætri'ɔtik] a πατριωτικός.

patriotism ['pætriətizəm] n πατριωτισμός.

patrol [pə'trəul] n περίπολος, περιπολία ‖ vti περιπολῶ ‖ on ~ εἰς περιπολίαν ‖ ~ car n περιπολικόν ‖ ~man n (US) ἀστυφύλαξ.

patron ['peitrən] n πάτρων, προστάτης, ὑποστηρικτής ‖ (comm) τακτικός πελάτης ‖ ~age ['pætrənidʒ] n προστασία, πατρονάρισμα ‖ ~ize ['pætrənaiz] vt πατρονάρω ‖ (manner) μεταχειρίζομαι συγκαταβατικά ‖ ~izing a (attitude) συγκαταβατικός ‖ ~ saint n προστάτης ἅγιος.

patter ['pætə*] n (sound) ἐλαφρά συνεχῆ χτυπήματα ‖ (sales talk) φλυαρία, κορακίστικα ‖ vi χτυπῶ ἐλαφρά καί συνεχῶς.

pattern ['pætən] n ὑπόδειγμα, πρότυπον, μοντέλο ‖ (design) σχέδιον, τύπος, μοντέλο.

paunch [pɔ:ntʃ] n κοιλιά.

pauper ['pɔ:pə*] n ἄπορος, πτωχός.

pause [pɔ:z] n παῦσις, διακοπή, ἀνάπαυλα, διάλειμμα ‖ vi σταματῶ, διστάζω, κοντοστέκομαι.

pave [peiv] vt ἐπιστρώνω ‖ to ~ the way for ἀνοίγω τόν δρόμον, προετοιμάζω τό ἔδαφος ‖ ~ment n (Brit) πεζοδρόμιον.

pavilion [pə'viliən] n (building) περίπτερον, ὑπόστεγον.

paving ['peiviŋ] n στρώσιμο.

paw [pɔ:] n πέλμα ζώου, πόδι ‖ vt χτυπῶ μέ τό πόδι ‖ (person) πασπατεύω.

pawn [pɔ:n] n ἐνέχυρον ‖ vt ἐνεχυριάζω, βάζω ἐνέχυρον ‖ ~broker n ἐνεχυροδανειστής ‖ ~shop n ἐνεχυροδανειστήριον.

pay [pei] (irreg v) n πληρωμή, μισθός ‖ vt πληρώνω, καταβάλλω, ξοδεύω ‖ (be profitable to) συμφέρω, ἀποδίδω ‖ vi πληρώνομαι, εἶναι συμφέρον ‖ to ~ attention (to) προσέχω ‖ to ~ for vt πληρώνω, κερνῶ ‖ to ~ up vi ἐξοφλῶ ‖ ~able a πληρωτέος ‖ ~day n ἡμέρα πληρωμῆς ‖ ~ee n πληρωόμενος ‖ ~ing a ἐπικερδής, ἀποδοτικός ‖ ~ment n πληρωμή ‖ (compensation) ἀποζημίωσις, ἀνταπόδοσις ‖ ~roll n μισθοδοτική κατάστασις.

pea [pi:] n (seed) μπιζέλι.

peace [pi:s] n εἰρήνη, ἡσυχία ‖ ~ably ad εἰρηνικά, ἥσυχα, ἥρεμα ‖ ~ful a γαλή-

νιος, ήσυχος, εἰρηνόφιλος ‖ ~ **offering**
n δῶρον συμφιλιώσεως.

peach [pi:tʃ] *n* ροδάκινον.

peacock ['pi:kɔk] *n* παγώνι.

peak [pi:k] *n* κορυφή ‖ (*of cap*) γεῖσος.

peal [pi:l] *n* κωδωνοκρουσία, κτύπημα.

peanut ['pi:nʌt] *n* ἀράπικο φυστίκι.

pear [pɛə*] *n* ἀπίδι, ἀχλάδι.

pearl [pɔ:l] *n* μαργαριτάρι.

peasant ['pezənt] *n* χωρικός, χωριάτης, ἀγρότης.

peat [pi:t] *n* τύρφη, πόανθραξ.

pebble ['pebl] *n* χαλίκι.

peck [pek] *vti* ραμφίζω, τσιμπῶ ‖ *n* (*with beak*) ραμφισμός, τσίμπημα ‖ (*kiss*) φιλάκι.

peckish ['pekiʃ] *a* (*col*) to feel ~ νοιώθω τό στομάχι ἄδειο.

peculiar [pi'kju:liə*] *a* (*interest*) εἰδικός, ἰδιαίτερος ‖ (+ *to*) τελείως δικό (του), χαρακτηριστικόν, ἰδιάζων ‖ ~**ity** *n* ἰδιάζων χαρακτήρ, ἰδιορρυθμία ‖ (*oddness*) παραξενιά ‖ ~**ly** *ad* ἰδιαίτερα, περίεργα.

pedal ['pedl] *n* ποδωστήριον, πετάλι ‖ *vti* κάνω πετάλι ‖ ποδηλατῶ.

pedantic [pi'dæntik] *a* σχολαστικός.

peddle ['pedl] *vt* κάνω τόν μικροπωλητήν, πωλῶ στούς δρόμους.

pedestal ['pedistl] *n* βάθρον, βάσις ἀγάλματος.

pedestrian [pi'destriən] *n* πεζός, διαβάτης ‖ *a* μέ τά πόδια, πεζός ‖ (*humdrum*) μονότονος, πεζός ‖ ~ **crossing** *n* διάβασις πεζῶν.

pediatrics [pi:di'ætriks] *n* (*US*) = **paediatrics**.

pedigree ['pedigri:] *n* γενεαλογικόν δένδρον, καταγωγή ‖ *a* (*animal*) καθαρόαιμος.

pee [pi:] (*col*) *n* οὖρα ‖ *vi* κατουρῶ, κάνω πιπί.

peek [pi:k] *n* ματιά ‖ *vi* κρυφοκοιτάζω, ξεπροβάλλω.

peel [pi:l] *n* φλούδα ‖ *vi* (*paint etc*) ξεφλουδίζομαι, φεύγω ‖ ~**ings** *npl* φλοῦδες, φλούδια.

peep [pi:p] *n* (*look*) φευγαλέον βλέμμα, ματιά ‖ (*sound*) τιτίβισμα, σκούξιμο, τσίριγμα ‖ *vi* (*look*) κρυφοκοιτάζω.

peer [piə*] *vi* κοιτάζω ἐπισταμένως ‖ (+ *at*) κοιτάζω προσεκτικά ‖ (*peep*) κρυφοκοιτάζω ‖ *n* (*nobleman*) λόρδος, εὐγενής ‖ (*equal*) ἰσάξιος, ἴσος, ταίρι ‖ ~**age** *n* τάξις εὐγενῶν ‖ ~**less** *a* ἀπαράμιλλος, ἀσύγκριτος.

peeve [pi:v] *vt* (*col*) ἐκνευρίζω ‖ ~**d** *a* ἐκνευρισμένος.

peevish ['pi:viʃ] *a* εὐερέθιστος, δύστροπος ‖ ~**ness** *n* ὀξυθυμία, γκρίνια.

peg [peg] *n* γόμφος, πάσσαλος, κρεμάστρα ‖ off the ~ στά στραβά, μέ κλειστά μάτια.

pekinese [pi:ki'ni:z] *n* πεκινουά.

pelican ['pelikən] *n* πελεκάνος.

pellet ['pelit] *n* (*of paper, bread etc*) σφαιρίδιον, σκάγιον ‖ δισκίον.

pelt [pelt] *vt* πετροβολῶ, πετῶ, κτυπῶ ‖ *vi* (*fall heavily*) πίπτω καταρρακτωδῶς ‖ *n* δορά, δέρμα, προβειά.

pelvis ['pelvis] *n* λεκάνη.

pen [pen] *n* (*for writing*) γραφίς, πέννα, στυλό ‖ (*for sheep*) μάντρα.

penal ['pi:nl] *a* ποινικός ‖ ~**ize** *vt* ἐπιβάλλω ποινήν εἰς, τιμωρῶ ‖ ~**ty** ['penəlti] *n* ποινή, τιμωρία ‖ ~**ty kick** *n* πέναλτυ.

penance ['penəns] *n* αὐτοτιμωρία, μετάνοια.

pence [pens] *npl* πέννες.

penchant ['pɑ:ŋʃɑ:n] *n* (+ *for*) κλίσις (γιά).

pencil ['pensl] *n* μολύβι ‖ (*of light*) δέσμη ‖ ~ **sharpener** *n* ξύστρα.

pendant ['pendənt] *n* κρεμαστόν κόσμημα.

pending ['pendiŋ] *prep* κατά τήν διάρκειαν τοῦ, μέχρι ‖ *a* ἐκκρεμής.

pendulum ['pendjuləm] *n* ἐκκρεμές.

penetrate ['penitreit] *vt* εἰσχωρῶ εἰς, διεισδύω ‖ (*pierce*) διαπερνῶ, τρυπῶ ‖ **penetrating** *a* διαπεραστικός, ὀξύς.

penetration [peni'treiʃən] *n* (*lit*) διείσδυσις.

penfriend ['penfrend] *n* φίλος ἐξ ἀλληλογραφίας.

penguin ['peŋgwin] *n* πιγκουῖνος.

penicillin [peni'silin] *n* πενικιλλίνη.

peninsula [pi'ninsjulə] *n* χερσόνησος.

penis ['pi:nis] *n* πέος.

penitence ['penitəns] *n* μετάνοια.

penitent ['penitənt] *a* μετανοημένος ‖ ~**iary** *n* (*US*) σωφρονιστήριον.

penknife ['pennaif] *n* σουγιάς.

pen name ['penneim] *n* ψευδώνυμον (φιλολογικόν).

pennant ['penənt] *n* ἐπισείων, φλάμπουλα.

penniless ['penilis] *a* ἀπένταρος.

penny ['peni] *n* πέννα.

pension ['penʃən] *n* (*from job*) σύνταξις ‖ ~**able** *a* δικαιούμενος σύνταξιν ‖ ~**er** *n* συνταξιούχος.

pensive ['pensiv] *a* ἔμφροντις, σκεπτικός, συλλογισμένος.

pentagon ['pentəgən] *n* πεντάγωνον.

Pentecost ['pentikɔst] *n* Πεντηκοστή.

penthouse ['penthaus] *n* πρόστεγον, ὑπόστεγον.

pent-up ['pentʌp] *a* (*feelings*) συγκρατουμένη συγκίνησις.

penultimate [pi'nʌltimit] *a* προτελευταῖος.

people ['pi:pl] *n* ἄνθρωποι, κόσμος ‖ (*nation*) λαός, ἔθνος ‖ *vt* κατοικῶ, οἰκίζω.

pep [pep] *n* (*col*) κέφη, ζωή ‖ to ~ up *vt* ἐνθαρρύνω, δίνω κέφι εἰς.

pepper ['pepə*] *n* πιπέρι ‖ (*green*) πιπεριά ‖ *vt* (*pelt*) πιπερώνω, βομβαρδίζω ‖ ~**mint** *n* (*plant*) ἡδύοσμος, μέντα ‖ (*sweet*) μέντα (καραμέλα).

per [pɔ:*] *prep* κατά, ἀνά, διά ‖ ~ **cent*** τοῖς ἑκατόν.

perceive [pə'si:v] *vt* διακρίνω, βλέπω ‖

(understand) ἀντιλαμβάνομαι, καταλαβαίνω.

percentage [pə'sentidʒ] n ποσοστόν, τοῖς ἑκατόν.

perceptible [pə'septəbl] a αἰσθητός.

perception [pə'sepʃən] n ἀντίληψις, αἴσθησις.

perceptive [pə'septiv] a ἀντιληπτικός.

perch [pə:tʃ] n κούρνια, ξύλο || (fish) πέρκα || νί κουρνιάζω, τοποθετῶ ψηλά.

percolator ['pə:kəleitə*] n σουρωτήρι, φίλτρο.

percussion [pə:'kʌʃən] n (mus) κρουστά ὄργανα.

peremptory [pə'remptəri] a τελικός, ἀμετάκλητος, ἀποφασιστικός.

perennial [pə'reniəl] a αἰώνιος, χρόνιος, ἀέναος || n πολυετές φυτόν.

perfect ['pə:fikt] a τέλειος, πλήρης, τελειωμένος || (gram) τετελεσμένος || n (gram) παρακείμενος || [pə'fekt] νt τελειοποιῶ, συμπληρώνων || ~ion [pə'fekʃən] n τελειότης, ἐντέλεια, τελειοποίησις || ~ly ad ἐντελῶς, τέλεια.

perforate ['pə:fəreit] νt διατρυπῶ, διεισδύω || ~d a διάτρητος.

perforation [pə:fə'reiʃən] n διάτρησις, τρυπούλα.

perform [pə'fɔ:m] νt ἐκτελῶ, ἐκπληρῶ, ἐπιτελῶ || (theat) παριστάνω, παίζω || νi (theat) παίζεται, παίζω || ~ance n ἐκτέλεσις, κατόρθωμα || (theat) παράστασις || ~er n ἐκτελεστής, ἠθοποιός || ~ing a (animal) γυμνασμένο (ζῷο).

perfume ['pə:fju:m] n ὀσμή, μυρωδιά || (scent) ἄρωμα, μυρωδικό.

perhaps [pə'hæps] ad ἴσως.

peril ['peril] n κίνδυνος || ~ous a ἐπικίνδυνος || ~ously ad ἐπικινδύνως.

perimeter [pə'rimitə*] n περίμετρος.

period ['piəriəd] n ἐποχή, περίοδος || (stop) τελεία || (med) στάδιον, φάσις, περίοδος || a (costume) τῆς ἐποχῆς || ~ic a περιοδικός || ~ical a περιοδικός || n περιοδικόν || ~ically ad κατά περιόδους.

peripheral [pə'rifərəl] a περιφερειακός, περιμετρικός.

periphery [pə'rifəri] n περιφέρεια, περίμετρος.

periscope ['periskəup] n περισκόπιον.

perish ['periʃ] νi χάνομαι, ἀφανίζομαι, πεθαίνω || ~ the thought! μακράν ἐμοῦ ἡ σκέψις || ~able a φθαρτός || ~ing a (col: cold) τρομερό, ψῶφο.

perjury ['pə:dʒəri] n ἐπιορκία, ψευδομαρτυρία.

perk [pə:k] to ~ up νi ξανακάνω κέφι, ξαναζωντανεύω || ~y a (cheerful) ζωηρός, εὔθυμος.

perm [pə:m] n περμανάντ.

permanence ['pə:mənəns] n μονιμότης.

permanent ['pə:mənənt] a μόνιμος, διαρκής || ~ly ad μονίμως.

permissible [pə'misəbl] a ἐπιτρεπόμενος, ἀνεκτός.

permission [pə'miʃən] n ἄδεια, ἔγκρισις.

permissive [pə'misiv] a ἐπιτρέπων.

permit ['pə:mit] n (ἔγγραφος) ἄδεια || [pə'mit] νt ἐπιτρέπω.

permutation [pə:mju'teiʃən] n (ἀντι)μετάθεσις, ἀντιμετάταξις.

pernicious [pə:'niʃəs] a ὀλέθριος, καταστρεπτικός.

perpendicular [pə:pən'dikjulə*] a κάθετος, κατακόρυφος.

perpetrate ['pə:pitreit] νt διαπράττω.

perpetual [pə'petjuəl] a διηνεκής, συνεχής, παντοτεινός || ~ly ad παντοτεινά, ἀδιάκοπα.

perpetuate [pə'petjueit] νt διαιωνίζω, ἀποθανατίζω.

perplex [pə'pleks] νt περιπλέκω, φέρω εἰς ἀμηχανίαν, μπερδεύω || ~ed a εἰς ἀμηχανίαν || ~ing a στενόχωρος, σκοτεινός || ~ity n ἀμηχανία, παραζάλη, δίλημμα.

persecute ['pə:sikju:t] νt (oppress) καταδιώκω, διώκω.

persecution [pə:si'kju:ʃən] n διωγμός, καταδίωξις.

perseverance [pə:si'viərəns] n καρτερία, ἐμμονή, ἐπιμονή.

persevere [pə:si'viə*] νi ἐμμένω, ἐπιμένω.

Persia ['pə:ʃə] n Περσία || ~n a περσικός || n (person) Πέρσης || (ling) περσικά || ~n Gulf n Περσικός Κόλπος.

persist [pə'sist] νi ἐξακολουθῶ, διαρκῶ, συνεχίζομαι || (keep saying) ἐπιμένω, ἐμμένω || ~ence n ἐπιμονή, ἐμμονή || ~ent a ἐπίμονος, διαρκής || ~ently ad ἐπιμόνως.

person ['pə:sn] n πρόσωπον, ἄνθρωπος, ἄτομον || ~able a εὐπαρουσίαστος, ὡραῖος || ~al a προσωπικός, ἀτομικός || (of body) σωματικός || ~ality n προσωπικότης || ~ally ad προσωπικῶς || ~ify νt προσωποποιῶ.

personnel [pə:sə'nel] n προσωπικόν || ~ manager n διευθυντής προσωπικοῦ.

perspective [pə'spektiv] n προοπτική || (view) ἄποψις, θέα.

Perspex ['pə:speks] n ® ἄθραυστος ὕαλος, περσπέξ.

perspiration [pə:spə'reiʃən] n ἐφίδρωσις, ἱδρώτας.

perspire [pəs'paiə*] νi ἱδρώνω.

persuade [pə'sweid] νt πείθω, καταφέρνω.

persuasion [pə'sweiʒən] n πειθώ, πειστικότης || (belief) πεποίθησις, θρήσκευμα.

persuasive [pə'sweisiv] a πειστικός || ~ly ad πειστικά.

pert [pə:t] a ἀναιδής, αὐθάδης, τσαχπίνης.

pertaining [pə:'teiniŋ] ~ to σχετικά μέ.

pertinent ['pə:tinənt] a σχετικός, κατάλληλος, σωστό.

perturb [pə'tə:b] vt διαταράσσω, άναστατώνω.

perusal [pə'ru:zəl] n άνάγνωσις, διάβασμα.

pervade [pə:'veid] vt ἐμποτίζω, διαπερῶ, ἐπικρατῶ.

perverse [pə'və:s] a διεστραμμένος, κακότροπος ‖ ~ly ad διεστραμμένα ‖ ~ness n διαστροφή, κακία.

perversion [pə'və:ʃən] n διαστροφή, άνωμαλία.

perversity [pə'və:siti] n διαστροφή, δυστροπία.

pervert ['pə:və:t] n διεστραμμένος, άνώμαλος τύπος, ἐκφυλισμένος ‖ [pə'və:t] vt διαστρέφω, στρεβλώνω, διαφθείρω.

pessimism ['pesimizəm] n άπαισιοδοξία.

pessimist ['pesimist] n άπαισιόδοξος ‖ ~ic a άπαισιόδοξος.

pest [pest] n ἐπιβλαβές φυτόν (ἤ ἔντομον) ‖ (fig: person, thing) ἐνοχλητικός, πληγή.

pester ['pestə*] vt ἐνοχλῶ, πειράζω.

pestle ['pesl] n κόπανος, γουδοχέρι.

pet [pet] n ἀγαπημένος, εὐνοούμενος, χαϊδεμένος ‖ vt χαϊδεύω.

petal ['petl] n πέταλον.

peter ['pi:tə*] to ~ out vi ἐξαφανίζομαι, σβήνω.

petite [pə'ti:t] a μικροκαμωμένη.

petition [pə'tiʃən] n αἴτησις, άναφορά.

petrified ['petrifaid] a άπολιθωμένος.

petrol ['petrəl] n (Brit) βενζίνη ‖ ~ engine n βενζινομηχανή ‖ ~eum [pi'trəuliəm] n πετρέλαιον ‖ ~ pump n (in car) άντλία βενζίνης ‖ (at garage) πρατήριον βενζίνης ‖ ~ station n πρατήριον βενζίνης ‖ ~ tank n δεξαμενή, ντεπόζιτο βενζίνης.

petticoat ['petikəut] n μισοφόρι.

pettifogging ['petifɔgiŋ] a στρεψόδικος, τιποτένιος.

pettiness ['petinis] n σμικρότης.

petty ['peti] a μικρός, άσήμαντος, κατώτερος ‖ (mean) μικρόνους, στενοκέφαλος ‖ ~ cash n μικροέξοδα, πρόχειρον ταμεῖον ‖ ~ officer n ὑπαξιωματικός, ὑποκελευστής.

petulant ['petjulənt] a ὀξύθυμος, εὐερέθιστος.

pew [pju:] n στασίδι.

pewter ['pju:tə*] n κρᾶμα κασσιτέρου καί μολύβδου.

phantom ['fæntəm] n φάντασμα.

Pharaoh ['fɛərəu] n Φαραώ.

pharmacist ['fɑ:məsist] n φαρμακοποιός.

pharmacy ['fɑ:məsi] n (shop) φαρμακεῖον ‖ φαρμακευτική.

phase [feiz] n φάσις.

pheasant ['feznt] n φασιανός.

phenomenal [fi'nɔminl] a φαινομενικός, ἐξαιρετικός ‖ ~ly ad ἐξαιρετικά, θαυμάσια.

phenomenon [fi'nɔminən] n φαινόμενον.

phew [fju:] excl οὔφ! ‖ Πφ!

phial ['faiəl] n φιαλίδιον.

philanthropic [filən'θrɔpik] a φιλάνθρωπος, φιλανθρωπικός.

philanthropist [fi'lænθrəpist] n φιλάνθρωπος.

philatelist [fi'lætəlist] n φιλοτελιστής.

philately [fi'lætəli] n φιλοτελισμός.

philosopher [fi'lɔsəfə*] n φιλόσοφος.

philosophical [filə'sɔfikəl] a φιλοσοφικός.

philosophy [fi'lɔsəfi] n φιλοσοφία.

phlegm [flem] n φλέγμα ‖ (calmness) ἠρεμία, ἀδιαφορία ‖ ~atic [fleg'mætik] a φλεγματικός, ἤρεμος.

phobia ['fəubiə] n φοβία, φοβοπάθεια.

phoenix ['fi:niks] n φοῖνιξ.

phone [fəun] (abbr of telephone) n τηλέφωνον ‖ vt τηλεφωνῶ.

phonetics [fəu'netiks] n φωνολογία, φωνητική γραφή.

phon(e)y ['fəuni] (col) a ψευδής, ψεύτικος ‖ n άπατεώνας.

phonograph ['fəunəgrɑ:f] n (US) φωνογράφος.

phonology [fəu'nɔlədʒi] n φωνολογία.

phosphate ['fɔsfeit] n φωσφορικόν ἄλας.

phosphorus ['fɔsfərəs] n φωσφόρος.

photo ['fəutəu] n abbr of **photograph**.

photocopier ['fəutəu'kɔpiə*] n φωτοτυπική μηχανή.

photocopy ['fəutəukɔpi] n φωτοαντίτυπον, φωτοτυπία ‖ vt κάνω φωτοτυπία.

photoelectric ['fəutəui'lektrik] a φωτοηλεκτρικόν.

photogenic [fəutəu'dʒenik] a φωτογενής.

photograph ['fəutəugræf] n φωτογραφία ‖ vt φωτογραφίζω, βγάζω φωτογραφίες ‖ ~er [fə'tɔgrəfə*] n φωτογράφος ‖ ~ic a φωτογραφικός ‖ ~y n φωτογραφική τέχνη, φωτογράφισις.

photostat ['fəutəustæt] n φωτοστατικόν άντίτυπον.

phrase [freiz] n φράσις ‖ vt διατυπώνω ‖ ~book n συλλογή ἐκφράσεων.

physical ['fizikəl] a φυσικός ‖ (of the body) σωματικός ‖ ~ly ad φυσικῶς, σωματικῶς.

physician [fi'ziʃən] n ἰατρός.

physicist ['fizisist] n φυσικός.

physics ['fiziks] n φυσική.

physiology [fizi'ɔlədʒi] n φυσιολογία.

physiotherapist [fiziə'θerəpist] n φυσιοθεραπευτής.

physiotherapy [fiziə'θerəpi] n φυσιοθεραπεία.

physique [fi'zi:k] n σωματική διάπλασις.

pianist ['piənist] n πιανίστας.

piano ['pjɑ:nəu] n πιάνο.

pick [pik] n (tool) άξίνα, κασμᾶς, σκαπάνη ‖ (choice) ἐκλογή ‖ (best) ὅ, τι ἐκλεκτόν, άφρόκρεμα ‖ vti μαζεύω, κόβω, συλλέγω ‖ (choose) ἐκλέγω, διαλέγω ‖ to ~ s.o.'s pocket βουτῶ ἀπό τήν τσέπη, κλέβω τό πορτοφόλι ‖ to ~ out vt διαλέγω ‖ to ~ up vi (improve) ἀποκτῶ πάλιν, ἀνακτῶ ‖

vt (*arrest*) συλλαμβάνω, πιάνω ‖ (*from ground*) σηκώνω, μαζεύω ‖ (*in car etc*) παίρνω ‖ ~ **axe** *n* σκαπάνη, κασμᾶς.

picket ['pikit] *n* (*stake*) πάσσαλος, παλούκι ‖ (*strikers*) σκοπός ἀπεργῶν, ἀπεργός φρουρῶν ‖ *vt* βάζω σκοπούς.

pickle ['pikl] *n* (*also* ~**s**: *as condiment*) τουρσί, ἄλμη ‖ *vt* διατηρῶ εἰς ἄλμην, παστώνω.

pick-me-up ['pikmi:ʌp] *n* στυλωτικό, πού δυναμώνει.

pickpocket ['pikpokit] *n* πορτοφολᾶς.

pickup ['pikʌp] *n* (*on record player*) φωνολήπτης, πικάπ ‖ (*small truck*) μικρό φορτηγό ‖ (*casual acquaintance*) ψάρεμα, τσίμπημα πελάτου.

picnic ['piknik] *n* ἐκδρομή, πικνίκ ‖ *vi* τρώγω στήν ἐξοχή ‖ ~ **ker** *n* ἐκδρομεύς.

pictorial [pik'tɔ:riəl] *a* εἰκονογραφικός ‖ γραφικός ‖ (*illustrated*) εἰκονογραφημένον.

picture ['piktʃə*] *n* εἰκών, ζωγραφιά, προσωποποίησις ‖ *vt* ζωγραφίζω, ἀπεικονίζω, φαντάζομαι ‖ **the** ~**s** *npl* κινηματογράφος ‖ ~ **book** *n* βιβλίον μέ εἰκόνες ‖ ~**sque** *a* γραφικός.

pidgin ['pidʒin] *a*: ~ **English** *n* παρεφθαρμένα Ἀγγλικά.

pie [pai] *n* πίττα.

piece [pi:s] *n* τεμάχιον, κομμάτι ‖ **in** ~**s** (*broken*) (σέ) κομμάτια ‖ (*taken apart*) σέ τεμάχια ‖ ~**meal** *ad* λίγο-λίγο, κατά τεμάχια ‖ ~**work** *n* ἐργασία μέ τό κομμάτι.

pier [piə*] *n* (*landing place*) προβλής, ἀποβάθρα.

pierce [piəs] *vt* τρυπῶ, διεισδύω, εἰσχωρῶ.

piercing ['piəsiŋ] *a* (*cry*) διαπεραστικός.

piety ['paiəti] *n* εὐσέβεια, θρησκοληψία.

piffling ['pifliŋ] *a* ἀσήμαντος, τιποτένιος.

pig [pig] *n* γουρούνι ‖ (*person*) παλιάνθρωπος, γουρούνι.

pigeon ['pidʒən] *n* περιστέρι ‖ ~**hole** *n* (*compartment*) θυρίδα, γραμματοθήκη ‖ *vt* βάζω στό χρονοντούλαπο.

piggy bank ['pigibæŋk] *n* κουμπαρᾶς.

pigheaded ['pig'hedid] *a* πείσμων, ξεροκέφαλος.

piglet ['piglit] *n* γουρουνόπουλο.

pigment ['pigmənt] *n* χρῶμα, βαφή ‖ ~**ation** *n* σχηματισμός τοῦ χρωμοφόρου.

pigmy ['pigmi] *n* = **pygmy**.

pigskin ['pigskin] *n* γουρουνόδερμα.

pigsty ['pigstai] *n* χοιροστάσιον.

pigtail ['pigteil] *n* κοτσίδα.

pilchard ['piltʃəd] *n* μεγάλη σαρδέλλα.

pile [pail] *n* (*of books*) σωρός, στοίβα ‖ (*in ground*) πάσσαλος, παλούκι, κολώνα ‖ (*on carpet*) τρίχα, χνούδι, μαλλί ‖ *vti* (*also* ~ **up**) συσσωρεύω, στοιβάζομαι.

piles [pailz] *npl* αἱμορροΐδες, ζοχάδες.

pilfer ['pilfə*] *vt* ὑπεξαιρῶ, βουτῶ, σουφρώνω ‖ ~**ing** *n* μικροκλοπή, σούφρωμα.

pilgrim ['pilgrim] *n* προσκυνητής ‖ ~**age** *n* προσκύνημα.

pill [pil] *n* χάπι ‖ **the P** ~ *n* χάπι ἀντισυλληπτικό.

pillage ['pilidʒ] *vt* λεηλατῶ.

pillar ['pilə*] *n* κίων, κολώνα, στύλος ‖ (*fig*) στύλος ‖ ~ **box** *n* (*Brit*) γραμματοκιβώτιον.

pillion ['piljən] *n* ὀπίσθιον κάθισμα ‖ ~ **passenger** *n* ἐπιβάτης (ἀπό πίσω).

pillory ['piləri] *n* κυφών, γεβεντιστήρι ‖ *vt* διαπομπεύω, στηλιτεύω.

pillow ['piləu] *n* προσκέφαλο, μαξιλάρι ‖ ~**case** *n* μαξιλαροθήκη.

pilot ['pailət] *n* πλοηγός, πιλότος ‖ (*aviat*) χειριστής, πιλότος ‖ *vt* (*aviat*) ὁδηγῶ, πιλοτάρω ‖ ~ **light** *n* καυστήρ (θερμάστρας φωταερίου).

pimp [pimp] *n* μαστρωπός, ρουφιάνος.

pimple ['pimpl] *n* ἐξάνθημα, σπυρί.

pimply ['pimpli] *a* σπυριάρης.

pin [pin] *n* καρφίτσα ‖ (*peg*) περόνη ‖ *vt* καρφιτσώνω ‖ (*hold fast*) καρφώνω, πλακώνομαι ‖ (*on*) ~**s and needles** 'στά κάρβουνα' ‖ **to** ~ **down** *vt* (*fig: person*) καθηλώνω.

pinafore ['pinəfɔ:*] *n* ποδιά.

pincers ['pinsəz] *npl* τανάλια.

pinch [pintʃ] *n* μικρά ποσότης, πρέζα ‖ (*nip*) τσίμπημα, τσιμπιά ‖ *vt* (*with fingers*) τσιμπῶ ‖ (*col: steal*) ἀποσπῶ, σουφρώνω, βουτῶ ‖ *vi* (*shoe*) στενεύω, κτυπῶ, σφίγγω ‖ **at a** ~ στήν ἀνάγκη, εἰς ὥραν ἀνάγκης.

pincushion ['pinkuʃən] *n* μαξιλαράκι γιά καρφίτσες.

pine [pain] *n* (*also* ~ **tree**) πεύκο ‖ *vi*: **to** ~ **for** ποθῶ, φθίνω, μαραζώνω.

pineapple ['painæpl] *n* ἀνανᾶς.

ping [piŋ] *n* (*noise*) σφύριγμα, κουδούνισμα ‖ ~**-pong** *n* (*US*) πίγκ-πόγκ.

pink [piŋk] *n* (*plant*) γαρουφαλλιά ‖ (*pale red*) ροδόχρουν χρῶμα, ρόζ ‖ *a* ροδόχρους, ρόζ, ρόδινος.

pin money ['pinmʌni] *n* χαρτζιλίκι.

pinnacle ['pinəkl] *n* (*highest point*) κορυφή, κολοφών.

pinpoint ['pinpoint] *vi* ὑποδεικνύω ἐπακριβῶς.

pint [paint] *n* πίντα (.567 λ.), μπουκάλι.

pioneer [paiə'niə*] *n* πρωτοπόρος.

pious ['paiəs] *a* εὐσεβής, θρήσκος.

pip [pip] *n* (*seed*) κουκούτσι ‖ (*on uniform*) ἄστρον (ἐπωμίδος).

pipe [paip] *n* σωλήνας ‖ ὀχετός ‖ (*smoking*) πίπα, τσιμπούκι ‖ (*instrument*) αὐλός ‖ (*of bird*) κελάδημα ‖ **to** ~ **down** *vi* (*be quiet*) τό βουλώνω ‖ ~ **dream** *n* ματαία ἐλπίς ‖ ~**line** *n* ἀγωγός ‖ ~**r** *n* αὐλητής, παίκτης γκάϊντας ‖ ~ **tobacco** *n* καπνό πίπας.

piping ['paipiŋ] *ad*: ~ **hot** καυτερός, ζεματιστός, ἀχνιστό.

piquant ['pi:kənt] *a* πικάντικος.

pique [pi:k] *n* μνησικακία, φούρκα.

piracy ['paiərəsi] *n* πειρατεία.

pirate ['paiərit] *n* πειρατής ‖ ~ **radio** *n* πειρατικός σταθμός.

pirouette [piru'et] *n* πιρουέτα ‖ *vi* κάνω πιρουέτες, περιστρέφομαι.

pissed [pist] *a* (col) μεθυσμένος.

pistol ['pistil] *n* πιστόλι.

piston ['pistən] *n* έμβολον, πιστόνι.

pit [pit] *n* λάκκος, ἀνθρακωρυχεῖον ‖ *vt* σημαδεύω, κόβω ‖ (put to test) ἔχω κάποιον ὡς ἀντίπαλον.

pitch [pitʃ] *n* (way of throwing) βολή, ῥιξιά ‖ (ground) γήπεδον ‖ (degree) βαθμός, κλίσις ‖ (of note) ὕψος τόνου, διαπασσῶν ‖ (tar) πίσσα, κατράμι ‖ *vt* (throw) πετῶ ‖ (tent) στήνω (σκηνήν) ‖ *vi* (fall head-long) πέφτω ‖ (of ship) σκαμπανεβάζω ‖ ~**-black** *a* μαῦρος σάν κατράμι ‖ ~**ed battle** *n* μάχη ἐκ τοῦ συστάδην.

pitcher ['pitʃə*] *n* στάμνα, κανάτα.

pitchfork ['pitʃfɔ:k] *n* δίκρανον, τσουγκράνα, φούρκα ‖ *vt* φορτώνω μέ δικράνι.

pitfall ['pitfɔ:l] *n* (trap) παγίδα.

pith [piθ] *n* (essence) οὐσία, σθένος.

pithead ['pithed] *n* στόμιον φρέατος.

pithy ['piθi] *a* (concise) μέ οὐσίαν, οὐσιαστικός.

pitiable ['pitiəbl] *a* ἀξιολύπητος, ἀξιοθρήνητος, οἰκτρός.

pitiful ['pitiful] *a* ἀξιολύπητος ‖ (mean) ἐλεεινός ‖ ~**ly** *ad* ἀθλιβερά, ἐλεεινά.

pitiless ['pitilis] *a* ἀνηλεής, ἄσπλαγχνος, ἄκαρδος ‖ ~**ly** *ad* σκληρά, ἀνηλεῶς.

pittance ['pitəns] *n* γλίσχρος μισθός, ἐξευτελιστικός μισθός.

pity ['piti] *n* ἔλεος, οἶκτος, λύπησι ‖ (of regret) κρίμα ‖ **what a ~**! τί κρίμα! ‖ ~**ing** *a* συμπονετικός.

pivot ['pivət] *n* ἄξων, κέντρον περιστροφῆς, κεντρικόν σημεῖον ‖ *vi* (turn) περιστρέφομαι.

pixie ['piksi] *n* ξωτικό, νεράιδα.

placard ['plækɑ:d] *n* τοιχοκόλλησις, ταμπέλλα, πλακάρ.

placate [plə'keit] *vt* κατευνάζω.

place [pleis] *n* τόπος, μέρος, τοποθεσία ‖ (position) σημεῖον, μέρος ‖ θέσις ‖ τοποθεσία ‖ (town etc) τόπος ‖ (employment, rank) θέσις, ὑπηρεσία, βαθμός ‖ (seat) θέσις, κάθισμα ‖ *vt* (object) τοποθετῶ, θέτω, βάζω ‖ (order) τοποθετῶ, πωλῶ ‖ (in race) ἔρχομαι πλασέ ‖ **in ~** ἁρμόζων, ἐντάξει ‖ **out of ~** ἄτοπος ‖ **in the first ~** ἐν πρώτοις.

placid ['plæsid] *a* γαλήνιος, ἤρεμος, ἀτάραχος ‖ ~**ity** *n* πραότης, γαλήνη, ἀταραξία.

plagiarism ['pleidʒiərizəm] *n* λογοκλοπή, λογοκλοπία.

plague [pleig] *n* πληγή, μάστιξ, λοιμός, πανούκλα.

plaice [pleis] *n* γλῶσσα (ψάρι).

plaid [plæd] *n* καρῶ.

plain [plein] *a* (clear) σαφής, φανερός ‖ (simple) ἁπλός, λιτός ‖ (not beautiful) κοινός, ὄχι ὡραῖος ‖ *ad* σαφῶς, καθαρά, εὐδιακρίτως, εἰλικρινῶς ‖ *n* πεδιάς, κάμπος ‖ **in ~ clothes** (police) μέ πολιτικά ‖ ~**ly** *ad* προφανῶς, ὁλοφάνερα ‖ ἁπλά ‖ ~**ness** *n* ἁπλότης, σαφήνεια.

plaintiff ['pleintif] *n* ἐνάγων, μηνυτής.

plait [plæt] *n* πλόκαμος, πλεξούδα ‖ *vt* πλέκω.

plan [plæn] *n* σχέδιον, προσχέδιον, πρόγραμμα ‖ (of house etc) σχέδιο, πλάνο, σχεδιάγραμμα ‖ (pol, econ) σχέδιον ‖ *vt* (holiday etc) σχεδιάζω ‖ *vi* (make a plan) καταστρώνω, σχεδιαγραφῶ.

plane [plein] *n* (tree) πλάτανος ‖ (tool) πλάνη, ροκάνι, πλάνια ‖ (level) ἐπίπεδον, ἐπίπεδος (ἐπιφάνεια) ‖ (aviat) ἀεροπλάνον ‖ *a* ἐπίπεδος ‖ *vt* (with tool) ροκανίζω, πλανίζω, ἰσιάζω.

planet ['plænit] *n* πλανήτης.

plank [plæŋk] *n* σανίδα, μαδέρι.

plankton ['plæŋktən] *n* πλαγκτόν.

planner ['plænə*] *n* προγραμματιστής, σχεδιαστής.

planning ['plæniŋ] *n* χάραξις (σχεδίου), κατάστρωσις, προγραμματισμός.

plant [plɑ:nt] *n* φυτόν ‖ (factory) ἐγκατάστασις, ἐργοστάσιον, μηχανήματα ‖ *vt* φυτεύω ‖ (set firmly) ἐμπηγνύω, καρφώνω, ἐγκαθιστῶ.

plantain ['plæntin] *n* ἀρνόγλωσσον.

plantation [plæn'teiʃən] *n* φυτεία.

plaque [plæk] *n* (on wall) πλάκα (ἀναμνηστική).

plasma ['plæzmə] *n* πλάσμα, πρωτόπλασμα.

plaster ['plɑ:stə*] *n* σουβάς, κονία, γύψος ‖ (for wounds) ἔμπλαστρον, τσιρότο ‖ *vt* σοβατίζω ‖ φορτώνω, γεμίζω, σκεπάζω ‖ ~ **in** ~ (leg etc) σέ γύψο ‖ ~**ed** *a* (col) μεθυσμένος ‖ ~**er** *n* σουβατζής.

plastic ['plæstik] *n* πλαστική ὕλη ‖ *a* πλαστικός ‖ (easily shaped) εὔπλαστος ‖ **P~ine** *n* ® πλαστιλίνη ‖ ~ **surgery** *n* πλαστική ἐγχείρησις.

plate [pleit] *n* πιάτο, δίσκος, σκεύη ‖ (table utensils) χρυσά ἤ ἀργυρά ἐπιτραπέζια σκεύη, ἀσημικά ‖ (flat sheet) πλάκα, λάμα, φύλλον.

plateau ['plætəu] *n* ὑψίπεδον, ὀροπέδιον.

plateful ['pleitful] *n* πιάτο γεμάτο.

plate glass ['pleit'glɑ:s] *n* κρύσταλλον, ὑαλοπίναξ.

platform ['plætfɔ:m] *n* (at meeting) ἐξέδρα, βῆμα ‖ (rail) ἀποβάθρα, ἐξέδρα.

platinum ['plætinəm] *n* λευκόχρυσος, πλατίνη.

platitude ['plætitju:d] *n* κοινοτοπία, πλαδαρότης.

platoon [plə'tu:n] *n* διμοιρία, οὐλαμός.

platter ['plætə*] *n* καραβάνα, πινάκιον.

plausibility [plɔːzəˈbiliti] *n* εὐλογοφάνεια.

plausible [ˈplɔːzəbl] *a* εὔλογος, εὐλογοφανής.

plausibly [ˈplɔːzəbli] *ad* ἀληθοφανῶς, εὐλογοφανῶς.

play [plei] *n* παιχνίδι, διασκέδασις ‖ *(stage)* ἔργον ‖ *(of shadows etc)* παίξιμο, λαμποκόπημα ‖ *(mech)* ἀνοχή, παίξιμο, τζόγος ‖ *vt* παίζω, διασκεδάζω ‖ *(trick)* παιχνιδιάζω, κάνω ἀστεῖο ‖ *(part)* παίζω, ὑποδύομαι ρόλον, ἑρμηνεύω ‖ *(instrument)* παίζω ‖ *vi (amuse o.s.)* διασκεδάζω, παίζω ‖ *(of light etc)* σπιθοβολῶ, παίζω, χοροπηδῶ ‖ ~**boy** *n* γλεντζές, ἔκλυτος νέος ‖ ~**ed-out** *a* ἐξηντλημένος, ἀποκαμωμένος ‖ ~**er** *n* παίκτης, ἠθοποιός ‖ ~**ful** *a* παιχνιδιάρικος, παιχνιδιάρης ‖ ~**goer** *n* θεατρόφιλος ‖ ~**ground** *n* προαύλιον, τόπος διασκεδάσεως ‖ ~**ing card** *n* τραπουλόχαρτο ‖ ~**ing field** *n* γήπεδον ‖ ~**mate** *n* συμπαίκτης, σύντροφος στό παιχνίδι ‖ ~**thing** *n* παιχνίδι, παιχνιδάκι ‖ ~**wright** *n* θεατρικός συγγραφεύς

plea [pliː] *n* (*law*) ἔκκλησις, ἀγωγή, ἔνστασις.

plead [pliːd] *vt* ἐπικαλοῦμαι, προβάλλω ‖ *vi* παρακαλῶ, ἱκετεύω ‖ *(law)* ὑποστηρίζω, ὑπερασπίζω, ἀπολογοῦμαι.

pleasant [ˈpleznt] *a* εὐχάριστος ‖ ~**ly** *ad* εὐχάριστα ‖ ~**ness** *n* χάρις, θέλγητρον, καλωσύνη ‖ ~**ry** *n* εὐθυμία, κέφι, χιούμορ.

please [pliːz] *vt* ἀρέσκω εἰς, ἀρέσω, εὐχαριστῶ ‖ ~! παρακαλῶ! ‖ **my bill**, ~ τόν λογαριασμόν, παρακαλῶ ‖ ~ **yourself**! κάνε τό κέφι σου! ‖ ~**d** *a (happy, glad)* εὐχαριστημένος, ἱκανοποιημένος.

pleasing [ˈpliːziŋ] *a* εὐχάριστος.

pleasurable [ˈpleʒərəbl] *a* εὐχάριστος, τερπνός.

pleasurably [ˈpleʒərəbli] *ad* εὐχάριστα, τερπνά.

pleasure [ˈpleʒə*] *n* τέρψις, εὐχαρίστησις, χαρά ‖ *(amusement)* ἀπολαύσεις, ἡδοναί, χαρές ‖ **it's a** ~! χαίρομαι!, παρακαλῶ!

pleat [pliːt] *n* πτυχή, πιέτα.

plebiscite [ˈplebisit] *n* δημοψήφισμα.

plebs [plebz] *npl* λαουτζίκος.

plectrum [ˈplektrəm] *n* πλῆκτρον.

pledge [pledʒ] *n* ἐνέχυρον, δεσμευτική ὑπόσχεσις, ἐχέγγυον ‖ *vt* ἐγγυῶμαι, ὑπόσχομαι.

plentiful [ˈplentiful] *a* ἄφθονος, πλουσιοπάροχος.

plenty [ˈplenti] *n* ἀφθονία, πλῆθος ‖ *(enough)* ἀρκετόν ‖ *ad (col)* πάραπολυ ‖ ~ **of** ἄφθονα, μέ τό τσουβάλι.

plethora [ˈpleθərə] *n* πληθώρα.

pleurisy [ˈpluərisi] *n* πλευρίτις.

pliability [plaiəˈbiliti] *n* εὐκαμψία, εὐστροφία.

pliable [ˈplaiəbl] *a* εὔκαμπτος, εὐλύγιστος.

pliers [ˈplaiəz] *npl* τανάλια, λαβίς.

plight [plait] *n* κατάστασις, θέσις.

plinth [plinθ] *n* πλίνθος, πλινθίον.

plod [plɔd] *vi* περπατῶ βαρειά, σέρνομαι ‖ ~**der** *n* φιλόπονος, εὐσυνείδητος ‖ ~**ding** *a* (βῆμα) συρτό ‖ πού μοχθεῖ, ἀργός καί ἐπίπονος.

plot [plɔt] *n (conspiracy)* συνωμοσία ‖ *(of story)* πλοκή, ὑπόθεσις ‖ *(land)* οἰκόπεδον, χωράφι ‖ *vt* χαράσσω, σχεδιάζω ‖ *vt (plan secretly)* συνωμοτῶ, μηχανορραφῶ ‖ ~**ter** *n* συνωμότης ‖ ~**ting** *n* γραφική παράστασις.

plough, (*US*) **plow** [plau] *n* ἄροτρον, ἀλέτρι ‖ *vt (earth)* ἀροτριῶ, ἀλετρίζω ‖ *(col: exam candidate)* ἀπορρίπτω (μαθητήν) ‖ **to** ~ **back** *vt (comm)* ἐπενδύω (τά κέρδη) ἐκ νέου ‖ **to** ~ **through** *vt (book)* διαβάζω μέ κόπο ‖ ~**ing** *n* ἄροσις, ἀλέτρισμα.

pluck [plʌk] *vt (fruit)* κόβω ‖ *(feathers)* μαδῶ ‖ *n (col)* κουράγιο, θάρρος ‖ **to** ~ **up courage** παίρνω κουράγιο ‖ ~**y** *a* θαρραλέος, παλ ηκάρι.

plug [plʌg] *n (for hole)* πῶμα, βούλωμα, τάπα ‖ *(wall socket)* πρίζα ‖ *(col: publicity)* διαφήμισις, προβολή ‖ *(aut)* μπουζί ‖ *vt (hole)* βουλώνω, ταπώνω ‖ *(col: advertise)* διαφημίζω, προβάλλω.

plum [plʌm] *n (fruit)* δαμάσκηνο ‖ *a* ἐκλεκτό πρᾶμα ‖ καλύτερη θέσις.

plumage [ˈpluːmidʒ] *n* πτέρωμα, φτερά.

plumb [plʌm] *a* κατακόρυφος ‖ πλήρης, ἀληθής ‖ *ad (exactly)* ἀκριβῶς ‖ τελείως ‖ *vt* βυθομετρῶ, βολίζω.

plumber [ˈplʌmə*] *n* ὑδραυλικός.

plumbing [ˈplʌmiŋ] *n (craft)* ὑδραυλική τέχνη ‖ *(piping)* σωληνώσεις, ὑδραυλικά.

plume [pluːm] *n* λοφίον, φτερόν.

plump [plʌmp] *a* στρογγυλός, παχουλός, ἀφράτος ‖ *vi* σωριάζομαι, κάνω πλάφ ‖ *vt* πετῶ ἀπότομα ‖ **to** ~ **for** *vt (col: choose)* ὑποστηρίζω, ψηφίζω ὑπέρ ‖ ~**ness** *n* πολυσαρκία, πάχος.

plunder [ˈplʌndə*] *n* λεία, λεηλασία, πλιάτσικο ‖ *vt* λεηλατῶ, λαφυραγωγῶ.

plunge [plʌndʒ] *n* κατάδυσις, βουτιά ‖ *vt* (κατα)βυθίζω, βουτῶ, χώνω ‖ *vi* καταδύομαι, βουτῶ, πέφτω.

plunging [ˈplʌndʒiŋ] *a (neckline)* μεγάλο (ντεκολτέ).

pluperfect [ˈpluːˈpəːfikt] *n* ὑπερσυντέλικον.

plural [ˈpluərəl] *a* πληθυντικός, πολλαπλός ‖ *n* πληθυντικός.

plus [plʌs] *prep* πλέον, σύν, μαζί μέ ‖ *a* θετικός.

plush [plʌʃ] *a (col: luxurious)* πολυτελής, πλούσιος ‖ *n* βελοῦδο.

ply [plai] *n as in* three-~ *(wood)* φύλλον, φλοίωμα ‖ *(wool)* πτυχή, δίπλα ‖ *vt (a trade)* ἀσκῶ ἐπάγγελμα ‖ *(with questions)* ταλαιπωρῶ (μέ ἐρωτήσεις) ‖ *vi* ταξιδεύω, ἐκτελῶ γραμμήν ‖ ~wood n κόντρα-πλακέ.

pneumatic [nju:'mætik] a πνευματικός, τοῦ πεπιεσμένου ἀέρος.

pneumonia [nju:'məuniə] n πνευμονία.

poach [pəutʃ] vt (cook) βράζω ξεφλουδι-σμένο αὐγό, ποσάρω ‖ (steal) κλέβω ‖ vi λαθροθηρῶ ‖ ~ed a (egg) (αὐγό) ποσέ ‖ ~er n λαθροθήρας ‖ ~ing n λαθροθη-ρία, κλοπή.

pocket ['pokit] n τσέπη ‖ (hollow) θύλαξ, λάκκος ‖ (of resistance) νησίς ἀντιστά-.σεως ‖ vt τσεπώνω, βάζω στὴν τσέπη ‖ out of ~ ζημιωμένος, βγαίνω χαμένος ‖ ~book n πορτοφόλι ‖ σημειωματάριον (τῆς τσέπης) ‖ βιβλίον τσέπης ‖ ~ful n (ὅσο χωρεῖ μιά) τσέπη ‖ ~ knife n σουγιᾶς (τῆς τσέπης) ‖ ~ money n χαρτζι-λίκι.

pockmarked ['pokma:kt] a (face) βλογι-οκομμένος.

pod [pod] n περικάρπιον.

podgy ['podʒi] a κοντόχονδρος, χοντρός.

poem ['pəuim] n ποίημα.

poet ['pəuit] n ποιητής ‖ ~ic [pəu'etik] a ποιητικός ‖ ~ laureate n ἐπίσημος ποιητής ‖ ~ry n ποίησις.

poignant ['poinjənt] a ὀξύς, δριμύς, τσου-χτερός, δυνατός ‖ ~ly ad πικάντικα, σπαρακτικά.

point [point] n (sharp end) ἀκίς, ἄκρα, αἰχμή, μύτη ‖ (dot) στίξις, σημεῖον ‖ (moment) στιγμή, σημεῖον ‖ (detail) λεπτομέρεια, στοιχεῖον, σημεῖον ‖ (headland) ἀκρωτήριον ‖ (rail) κλειδί, διασταύρωσις ‖ (of compass) ρόμβος πυξίδος, κάρτα ‖ (degree) βαθμός, σημεῖον ‖ (decimal point) κόμμα ‖ vt στρέφω, κατευθύνω, δείχνω ‖ (gun etc) σκοπεύω μέ, σημαδεύω ‖ vi δείχνω, δακτυλοδεικτῶ ‖ ~s npl κλειδί ‖ ~ of view n ἄποψις, ἔποψις ‖ what's the ~? τί τό ὄφελος; ‖ to ~ out vt δείχνω, ἐπισύρω τήν προσοχήν, ὑπογραμμίζω ‖ to ~ to vt δείχνω, δακτυλοδεικτῶ, ἐμφαίνω ‖ ~-blank ad κατ' εὐθεῖαν, ἀπερίστροφος ‖ ~ duty n ὑπηρεσία τροχαίας ‖ ~ed a (shape) αἰχμηρός, μυτερός ‖ (remark) δηκτικός, καυστικός, τσουχτερός ‖ ~edly ad ὁλοκάθαρα, ὠμά ‖ σαρκα-στικά ‖ ~er n δείκτης ‖ ~less a ἄσκοπος, ξεκάρφωτος ‖ ~lessly ad ἄσκοπα, ἄσχετα ‖ ~lessness n ἀσημαντότης ‖ ἀστοχία.

poise [poiz] n παρουσιαστικό, κορμοστασιά ‖ vti ἰσορροπῶ, σταθμίζω ‖ περιίπταμαι.

poison ['poizn] n δηλητήριον ‖ vt δηλητηρι-άζω, μολύνω ‖ ~ing n δηλητηρίασις ‖ ~ous a δηλητηριώδης, φαρμακερός.

poke [pəuk] vt (stick into sth) κτυπῶ, χώνω ‖ (fire) ἀναζωπυρῶ, σκαλίζω ‖ n (jab) κτύπημα, σπρωξιά ‖ to ~ one's nose into ἀνακατεύομαι ‖ to ~ about vi ψηλαφῶ,

ψάχνω ‖ ~r n σκαλιστήρι ‖ (cards) πόκερ ‖ ~r-faced a μέ ἀνέκφραστο πρόσωπο, ἀπαθές πρόσωπο.

poky ['pəuki] a μικρός, στενάχωρος.

Poland ['pəulənd] n Πολωνία.

polar ['pəulə*] a πολικός ‖ ~ bear n πολική ἄρκτος ‖ ~ize vt πολώνω ‖ vi πολοῦμαι.

pole [pəul] n (of wood) στῦλος, ἱστός, κοντάρι ‖ (elec) στῦλος ‖ (geog) πόλος ‖ ~cat n (US) εἶδος νυφίτσας ‖ ~ star n πολικός ἀστήρ ‖ ~ vault n ἅλμα ἐπί κοντῶ.

police [pə'li:s] n ἀστυνομία ‖ vt ἀστυνο-μεύω, ἐλέγχω, τηρῶ (τήν τάξιν) ‖ ~ car n ἀστυνομικόν (αὐτοκίνητον) ‖ ~man n ἀστυφύλαξ, ἀστυνόμος, πολισμάνος ‖ ~ state n ἀστυνομικόν κράτος ‖ ~ station n ἀστυνομικόν τμῆμα ‖ ~woman n ἡ ἀστυνόμος.

policy ['polisi] n πολιτική ‖ (prudence) φρόνησις ‖ (insurance) ἀσφαλιστήριον.

polio ['pəuliəu] n πολυομυελῖτις.

Polish ['pəuliʃ] a πολωνικός ‖ n (ling) πολωνικά.

polish ['poliʃ] n βερνίκι ‖ (surface) γυαλάδα, στιλπνότης, λοῦστρο ‖ (fig: refinement) εὐγένεια, καλοί τρόποι ‖ vt στιλβώνω, γυαλίζω, λουστράρω ‖ (refine) ἐξευγε-νίζω ‖ to ~ off vi (work) τελειώνω βιαστικά ‖ (food) ἀδειάζω, κατεβάζω, καθαρίζω ‖ ~ed a (fig) εὐγενικός, λεπτός ‖ ἐκλεπτισμένο.

polite [pə'lait] a εὐγενής, φιλόφρων ‖ ~ly ad εὐγενικά ‖ ~ness n εὐγένεια, λεπτό-της.

politic ['politik] a (wise) συνετός, προνο-ητικός ‖ ~al [pə'litikəl] a πολιτικός ‖ ~ally ad πολιτικῶς ‖ ~ian [poli'tiʃən] n πολιτικός, πολιτικάντης ‖ ~s npl (ἡ) πολιτική ‖ (US) πολιτικολογία.

polka ['polkə] n πόλκα ‖ ~ dot (φόρεμα) μέ πίκες, μέ βούλες, πουαντιγιέ.

poll [pəul] n ψηφοφορία, ἀριθμός ψήφων ‖ vt λαμβάνω ψήφους, δίνω ψήφους.

pollen ['polən] n γύρις (λουλουδιοῦ).

pollination [poli'neiʃən] n ἐπικονίασις, γονιμοποίησις.

polling booth ['pəuliŋbu:θ] n ἀπομονωτή-ριον ἐκλογικοῦ τμήματος.

polling day ['pəuliŋdei] n ἡμέρα ἐκλογῶν.

polling station ['pəuliŋsteiʃən] n ἐκλογικόν τμῆμα.

pollute [pə'lu:t] vt μολύνω, βρωμίζω.

pollution [pə'lu:ʃən] n μίανσις, μόλυνσις.

polo ['pəuləu] n πόλο.

poly- ['poli] prefix πολυ-.

polygamy [po'ligəmi] n πολυγαμία.

polytechnic [poli'teknik] n (college) τεχνική σχολή, πολυτεχνεῖον.

polythene ['poliθi:n] n πολυθένιον.

pomegranate ['poməgrænit] n ρόδι.

pommel ['poml] vt γρονθοκοπῶ, κοπανίζω.

pomp [pɔmp] *n* λαμπρότης, πομπή, ἐπί-δειξις.

pompous ['pɔmpəs] *a* πομπώδης, φανφαρόνος ‖ ~**ly** *ad* πομπωδῶς, μέ στόμφον.

ponce [pɔns] *n* (*col*) σωματέμπορος.

pond [pɔnd] *n* λιμνοστάσιον, νερόλακκος, λιμνούλα.

ponder ['pɔndə*] *vti* σταθμίζω, ξανασκέπτομαι, μελετῶ, ζυγίζω ‖ ~**ous** *a* βαρύς, στιβαρός, βραδύς, ἀνιαρός.

pontiff ['pɔntif] *n* ποντίφηξ, πάπας.

pontificate [pɔn'tifikeit] *vi* (*fig*) τά λέω μέ ὕφος ποντίφηκος.

pontoon [pɔn'tu:n] *n* ἐπιπλέων στήριγμα γέφυρας ‖ (*cards*) εἴκοσι-ἕνα (περίπου 31).

pony ['pəuni] *n* ἀλογάκι ‖ ~ **tail** *n* ἀλογοουρά.

poodle ['pu:dl] *n* μαλλιαρό σκυλάκι.

pooh-pooh [pu:'pu:] *vt* γελοιοποιῶ, κοροϊδεύω, ἀδιαφορῶ.

pool [pu:l] *n* (*of liquid*) λιμνούλα, νερόλακκος, δεξαμενή ‖ (*at cards*) πόστα, πότ ‖ (*football*) προ-πό ‖ (*billiards*) μπάτσικα ‖ *vt* (*money etc*) ἐνώνω, συγκεντρώνω ‖ σχηματίζω κοινοπραξίαν.

poor [puə*] *a* πτωχός, δυστυχής ‖ (*feeble*) ἀδύνατος, ἄθλιος ‖ (*pitied*) κακόμοιρος, ἀξιολύπητος ‖ *n*: the ~ οἱ φτωχοί ‖ ~**ly** *ad* φτωχικά, ἄθλια ‖ *a* ἀδιάθετος.

pop [pɔp] *n* (*noise*) ξηρός κρότος ‖ (*mus*) μουσική πόπ ‖ (*col US: father*) μπαμπάς ‖ *vt* (*put suddenly*) θέτω ἀπότομα ‖ *vi* (*explode*) κάνω πόπ, κροτῶ ‖ (*come suddenly*) μπαίνω ξαφνικά, βγαίνω ‖ ~ **concert** *n* λαϊκή συναυλία (πόπ) ‖ ~**corn** *n* ψημένο καλαμπόκι, πόπ-κόρν.

Pope [pəup] *n* Πάπας.

poplar ['pɔplə*] *n* λεύκη.

poplin ['pɔplin] *n* ποπλίνα.

poppy ['pɔpi] *n* παπαρούνα ‖ ~**cock** *n* (*col*) κουταμάρα, μπούρδα.

populace ['pɔpjuləs] *n* λαός, τό πλῆθος.

popular ['pɔpjulə*] *a* δημοφιλής, κοσμοαγάπητος ‖ (*of the people*) λαϊκός ‖ ~**ity** *n* δημοτικότης, δημοφιλία ‖ ~**ize** *vt* ἐκλαϊκεύω ‖ ἐπιβάλλω μόδαν, καθιστῶ δημοφιλή ‖ ~**ly** *ad* λαϊκῶς ‖ κοινῶς.

populate ['pɔpjuleit] *vt* (συν)οικίζω, κατοικῶ.

population [pɔpju'leiʃən] *n* πληθυσμός.

populous ['pɔpjuləs] *a* πολυάνθρωπος, πυκνοκατοικημένος.

porcelain ['pɔ:slin] *n* πορσελάνη.

porch [pɔ:tʃ] *n* πρόστεγον ‖ (*US*) βεράνδα.

porcupine ['pɔ:kjupain] *n* σκαντζόχοιρος.

pore [pɔ:*] *n* ὁ πόρος ‖ to ~ over *vt* ἀπορροφῶμαι ἀπό.

pork [pɔ:k] *n* χοιρινό.

pornographic [pɔ:nə'græfik] *a* πορνογραφικός.

pornography [pɔ:'nɔgrəfi] *n* πορνογραφία.

porous ['pɔ:rəs] *a* πορώδης.

porpoise ['pɔ:pəs] *n* φώκαινα.

porridge ['pɔridʒ] *n* χυλός (βρώμης).

port [pɔ:t] *n* λιμήν, λιμάνι ‖ (*town*) πόρτο ‖ (*naut: left side*) ἀριστερά πλευρά ‖ (*wine*) πορτό, οἶνος Πορτογαλίας.

portable ['pɔ:təbl] *a* φορητός.

portal ['pɔ:tl] *n* πυλών, πύλη.

portcullis [pɔ:'kʌlis] *n* καταρρακτή θύρα, καταρραχτή.

portend [pɔ:'tend] *vt* προοιωνίζομαι, προμηνύω.

portent [pɔ:'tent] *n* κακός οἰωνός ‖ (*good*) θαυμάσιον πρᾶγμα, οἰωνός.

porter ['pɔ:tə*] *n* ἀχθοφόρος, χαμάλης ‖ μικρός ὑπηρέτης (ξενοδοχείου) ‖ (*door-keeper*) θυρωρός, πορτιέρης.

porthole ['pɔ:thəul] *n* (*naut*) φινιστρίνι.

portico ['pɔ:tikəu] *n* πρόστωον, στοά.

portion ['pɔ:ʃən] *n* μερίς, μερίδιον.

portly ['pɔ:tli] *a* παχύς, θεωρητικός.

portrait ['pɔ:trit] *n* προσωπογραφία, πορτραῖτο, φωτογραφία.

portray [pɔ:'trei] *vt* (*describe*) περιγράφω ‖ ~**al** *n* ἀπεικόνισις, περιγραφή.

Portugal ['pɔ:tjugəl] *n* Πορτογαλία.

Portuguese [pɔ:tju'gi:z] *a* πορτογαλικός ‖ *n* (*person*) Πορτογάλος ‖ (*ling*) πορτογαλικά.

pose [pəuz] *n* (*position*) στάσις ‖ (*affectation*) προσποίησις, πόζα ‖ *vi* (*take up attitude*) ποζάρω ‖ (*assume false pose*) ἐμφανίζομαι, παριστάνω ‖ *vt* (*put question*) θέτω ‖ ~**r** *n* (*problem*) δύσκολον πρόβλημα ‖ ~**ur** [pəu'zɔ:*] *n* (*person*) ἄνθρωπος πού κάνει καμώματα.

posh [pɔʃ] *a* (*col*) ὡραῖος, κομψός, φίνος, μοντέρνος.

position [pə'ziʃən] *n* θέσις, στάσις ‖ (*place*) θέσις, σειρά ‖ τοποθεσία ‖ (*attitude*) θέσις, πρότασις ‖ (*rank*) θέσις, βαθμός ‖ (*job*) θέσις, ἐργασία.

positive ['pɔzitiv] *a* θετικός, καταφατικός ‖ (*confident*) πεπεισμένος, βέβαιος, σίγουρος ‖ (*real*) πραγματικός, ἀληθινός ‖ (*character*) θετικός, κατηγορηματικός ‖ ~**ly** *ad* κατηγορηματικά, θετικά.

posse ['pɔsi] *n* (*US*) ἀπόσπασμα (ἀστυνομικῶν).

possess [pə'zes] *vt* (κατ)έχω, διατηρῶ ‖ ~**ion** *n* κατοχή, κτῆσις, κτῆμα ‖ (*owning*) κατοχή ‖ ~**ive** *a* κτητικός, παθολογικά στοργικός ‖ (*gram*) κτητικόν ‖ ~**or** *n* κάτοχος, κύριος, κτήτωρ.

possibility [pɔsə'biliti] *n* (*chance*) πιθανότης ‖ (*event*) δυνατότης.

possible ['pɔsəbl] *a* δυνατός, ἐνδεχόμενος, λογικός ‖ if ~ ἄν μπορῶ, εἰ δυνατόν.

possibly ['pɔsəbli] *ad* κατά τό δυνατόν, πιθανόν, ἴσως, πιθανῶς.

post [pəust] *n* (*pole*) στύλος, πάσσαλος, κολώνα ‖ (*mail*) ταχυδρομεῖον ‖ (*delivery*) ταχυδρόμος, ταχυδρομεῖον ‖ (*station*) θέσις, φυλακή, πόστο ‖ (*job*) θέσις, πόστο ‖ vt (notice) τοιχοκολλῶ ‖ (letters) ταχυδρομῶ, ρίχνω (στό κουτί) ‖ (station) ἐγκαθιστῶ, τοποθετῶ ‖ ~**age** n ταχυδρομικά, γραμματόσημα ‖ ~**al** a ταχυδρομικός ‖ ~**al order** n ταχυδρομική ἐπιταγή ‖ ~**box** n γραμματοκιβώτιον ‖ ~**card** n κάρτ-ποστάλ, κάρτα ‖ ~**date** vt (cheque) μεταχρονολογῶ, ἐπιχρονολογῶ ‖ ~**er** n διαφήμισις, ἀφίσα ‖ ~**e restante** n πόστ-ρεστάντ.

posterior [pɔs'tiəriə*] n (col) ὁ πισινός, κῶλος.

posterity [pɔs'teriti] n (οἱ) μεταγενέστεροι.

postgraduate ['pəust'grædjuit] n πτυχιοῦχος συνεχίζων σπουδάς.

posthumous ['pɔstjuməs] a (works) κατάλοιπα ‖ ~**ly** ad μετά τόν θάνατον (τοῦ συγγραφέως).

postman ['pəustmən] n ταχυδρόμος.

postmark ['pəustma:k] n ταχυδρομική σφραγίς.

postmaster ['pəustma:stə*] n διευθυντής ταχυδρομείου.

post-mortem ['pəust'mɔ:tem] n (examination) νεκροψία.

post office ['pəustɔfis] n ταχυδρομεῖον.

postpone [pəust'pəun] vt ἀναβάλλω ‖ ~**ment** n ἀναβολή.

postscript ['pəusskript] n ὑστερόγραφον.

postulate ['pɔstjuleit] vt ἀπαιτῶ, ἀξιώνω ‖ ὑποθέτω.

posture ['pɔstʃə*] n στάσις, θέσις, κατάστασις ‖ vi τοποθετῶ, στήνω, ποζάρω.

postwar ['pəust'wɔ:*] a μεταπολεμικός.

posy ['pəuzi] n μπουκέτο (ἀπό λουλούδια), ἀνθοδέσμη.

pot [pɔt] n (for cooking) χύτρα, δοχεῖον, γλάστρα ‖ (sl: marijuana) ναρκωτικά ‖ vt (plant) βάζω σέ γλάστρα, φυτεύω εἰς γλάστρα.

potash ['pɔtæʃ] n ποτάσσα, κάλιον.

potato [pə'teitəu] n πατάτα.

potency ['pəutənsi] n δύναμις, ἰσχύς, ἱκανότης.

potent ['pəutənt] a ἰσχυρός, πειστικός, ἱκανός.

potentate ['pəutənteit] n ἡγεμών, δυνάστης.

potential [pəu'tenʃəl] a δυνητικός, λανθάνων, δυναμικός ‖ n δυναμικόν, πιθανός δυνατός ‖ ~**ly** ad δυνάμει.

pothole ['pɔthəul] n φρέαρ, σπήλαιον ‖ (in road) λακκούβα, λάκκος ‖ ~**r** n σπηλαιολόγος.

potholing ['pɔthəuliŋ] n σπηλαιολογία.

potion ['pəuʃən] n δόσις (φαρμάκου).

potshot ['pɔtʃɔt] n πυροβόλισι στήν τύχη.

potted ['pɔtid] a (food) διατηρημένον ‖ (plant) στήν γλάστρα, τῆς γλάστρας.

potter ['pɔtə*] n κεραμοποιός, τσουκαλᾶς vi χασομερῶ, ψευδοδουλεύω ‖ ~**y** n ἀγγειοπλαστική, κεραμεική ‖ (place) κεραμοποιεῖον.

potty ['pɔti] a (mad) λοξός, παράφρων ‖ n (child's potty) δοχεῖον (μωροῦ).

pouch [pautʃ] n (zool) θύλακος ‖ (tobacco) ταμπακιέρα.

poultice ['pəultis] n κατάπλασμα.

poultry ['pəultri] n πουλερικά ‖ ~ **farm** n ὀρνιθοτροφεῖον.

pounce [pauns] vi (+ on) ἐφορμῶ, ἐπιπίπτω, χυμῶ ‖ n πήδημα, ἐφόρμησις.

pound [paund] n (weight) λίμπρα (435 γρ), λίβρα, λίτρα ‖ (sterling) λίρα (Ἀγγλίας) ‖ (area) περίβολος, μάντρα ‖ vt κτυπῶ, κοπανίζω ‖ (crush to powder) λειοτριβῶ, κονιοποιῶ, κοπανίζω ‖ ~**ing** n σφυροκόπημα ‖ γδοῦπος.

pour [pɔ:*] vt (cause) χύνω ‖ vi μπαίνω σάν ποτάμι, τρέχω, χύνομαι ‖ **to ~ away** or **off** vt χύνω (ἔξω), ἐκχέω ‖ **to ~ in** vi (people) μπαίνω κατά κύματα ‖ ~**ing rain** n βροχή μέ τό τουλούμι, καταρρακτώδης βροχή.

pout [paut] n κατσούφιασμα ‖ vi κατσουφιάζω, στραβομουριάζω.

poverty ['pɔvəti] n φτώχεια, ἔνδεια ‖ ~**-stricken** a ἐξαθλιωμένος, ἄπορος.

powder ['paudə*] n κόνις, σκόνη ‖ (medicine) κόνις ‖ (cosmetic) πούδρα ‖ vt (make into powder) κονιοποιῶ, τρίβω ‖ (put on powder) πουδράρω μέ ‖ **to ~ one's nose** πουδράρομαι ‖ πάω στό μέρος ‖ ~ **room** n τουαλέττα ‖ ~**y** a κονιώδης, σάν σκόνη.

power [pauə*] n (ability to act) ἐξουσία, δύναμις, μπόρεση ‖ (strength) δύναμις, μέσα ‖ (mighty nation) (μεγάλη) δύναμις ‖ (mental) ἱκανότης, ἰδιοφυΐα, ταλέντο ‖ (elec) ἐνέργεια, δύναμις ‖ (pol: of party or leader) ἐξουσία, ἐπιρροή, ἰσχύς ‖ vt παρέχω ἐνέργειαν εἰς, κινῶ ‖ ~ **cut** n κοπή ρεύματος ‖ ~**ful** a (person) ρωμαλέος, μεγάλος, δυνατός ‖ (government) ἰσχυρός ‖ (engine) ἰσχυρός, ἀποδοτικός, μέ δύναμιν ‖ ~**less** a ἀνίσχυρος, ἀδύναμος ‖ ~ **line** n γραμμή μεταφορᾶς ‖ ~ **station** n ἐργοστάσιον παραγωγῆς ρεύματος.

powwow ['pauwau] n συνέδριον, συγκέντρωσις ‖ vi ὀργανώνω συνέδριον, συζητῶ.

practicability [præktikə'biliti] n (τό) δυνατόν (γενέσθαι), ἐπιτευκτόν.

practicable ['præktikəbl] a δυνατός, κατορθωτός, ἐφαρμόσιμος.

practical ['præktikəl] a πρακτικός, ἔμπειρος, ἐφαρμόσιμος ‖ ~ **joke** n βαρύ ἀστεῖο, φάρσα ‖ ~**ly** ad (almost) σχεδόν οὐσιαστικῶς.

practice ['præktis] n ἄσκησις, ἐξάσκησις, γυμναστική ‖ (habit) συνήθεια, ἔθιμον, ἕξις ‖ (business) ἄσκησις, ἐξάσκησις, πελατεία ‖ **in ~** (in reality) στήν πραγματικότητα ‖ **out of ~** (sport) ξεσυνηθίζω, δέν εἶμαι σέ φόρμα.

practicing ['præktisiŋ] *a (US)* = **practising**.
practise, *(US)* **practice** ['præktis] *vt* ἀσκῶ, ἐφαρμόζω, ἀκολουθῶ, συνηθίζω ‖ *(sport)* ἐκγυμνάζω ‖ *(piano)* μελετῶ, κάνω ἀσκήσεις ‖ *(profession)* ἐπαγγέλομαι, (ἐξ)ἀσκῶ.
practising ['præktisiŋ] *a (Christian etc)* ἄσκησις.
practitioner [præk'tiʃənə*] *n* ἀσκῶν, ἐπαγγελματίας.
pragmatic [præg'mætik] *a* πρακτικός, πραγματικός.
pragmatism ['prægmətizəm] *n* πραγματισμός, σχολαστικότης.
prairie ['preəri] *n* λιβάδι, κάμπος, στέππα.
praise [preiz] *n* ἔπαινος, ἐγκώμιον ‖ *vt* ἐπαινῶ, ἐξυμνῶ ‖ *(worship)* λατρεύω, δοξάζω ‖ ~**worthy** *a* ἀξιέπαινος.
pram [præm] *n* καροτσάκι μωροῦ.
prance [pra:ns] *vi* ἀνασκιρτῶ, ἀναπηδῶ ‖ *(strut)* κορδώνομαι, κοκορεύομαι.
prank [præŋk] *n* τρέλλα, κατεργαριά, κόλπο.
prattle ['prætl] *vi* φλυαρῶ, λογοκοπανῶ.
prawn [prɔ:n] *n* εἶδος γαρίδας.
pray [prei] *vi* προσεύχομαι, παρακαλῶ ‖ ~**er** *n* προσευχή ‖ *(praying)* παράκλησις ‖ ~**er book** *n* εὐχολόγιον, προσευχητήριον.
pre- [pri:] *prefix* προ-.
preach [pri:tʃ] *vi* κηρύττω ‖ προτρέπω, νουθετῶ ‖ ~**er** *n* ἱεροκῆρυξ, παπᾶς.
preamble [pri:'æmbl] *n* προοίμιον, εἰσαγωγή.
prearranged ['pri:ə'reindʒd] *a* προκαθωρισμένος, προσυμπεφωνημένος.
precarious [pri'kεəriəs] *a* ἐπισφαλής, ἐπικίνδυνος, ἀβέβαιος ‖ ~**ly** *ad* ἐπισφαλῶς, ἀβέβαια.
precaution [pri'kɔ:ʃən] *n* προφύλαξις ‖ ~**ary** *a (measure)* προφυλακτικός, προληπτικός.
precede [pri'si:d] *vti* προηγοῦμαι, προπορεύομαι ‖ ~**nce** ['presidəns] *n (of position)* πρωτεῖα ‖ ~**nt** *n* προηγούμενον.
preceding [pri'si:diŋ] *a* προηγούμενος.
precept ['pri:sept] *n* κανών, δίδαγμα, διαταγή.
precinct ['pri:siŋkt] *n* περίβολος, περιοχή.
precious ['preʃəs] *a* πολύτιμος ‖ *(affected)* μέ ἐπιτήδευσιν, προσποιητός.
precipice ['presipis] *n* κρημνός.
precipitate [pri'sipitit] *a (hasty)* βιαστικός, ἐσπευσμένος ‖ ~**ly** *ad* βιαστικά.
precipitation [prisipi'teiʃən] *n (rainfall)* ὄμβρος, βροχόπτωσις.
precipitous [pri'sipitəs] *a (steep)* κρημνώδης ‖ ~**ly** *ad* ἀπότομα.
précis ['preisi:] *n* περίληψις, ἐπιτομή, σύνοψις.
precise [pri'sais] *a* ἀκριβός, ὡρισμένος, συγκεκριμένος ‖ *(careful)* ἀκριβολόγος, τυπικός ‖ ~**ly** *ad* ἀκριβῶς, σωστά.

preclude [pri'klu:d] *vt* ἀποκλείω, προλαμβάνω, ἐμποδίζω.
precocious [pri'kəuʃəs] *a* πρόωρος.
preconceived ['pri:kən'si:vd] *a (idea)* προκαταληπτικός.
precondition [pri:kən'diʃən] *n* προϋπόθεσις.
precursor [pri:'kə:sə*] *n* πρόδρομος.
predator ['predətə*] *n* ληστής, διαγουμιστής ‖ ~**y** *a (of animals)* ἁρπακτικός.
predecessor ['pri:disesə*] *n* προκάτοχος.
predestination [pri:desti'neiʃən] *n* προκαθορισμός, μοιρολατρεία.
predetermine ['pri:di'tə:min] *vt* προκαθορίζω, προαποφασίζω.
predicament [pri'dikəmənt] *n* δύσκολη θέσις, δυσχέρεια, ἀμηχανία.
predicate [predikit] *n* βεβαιώνω, ὑποδηλῶ, βεβαιῶ.
predict [pri'dikt] *vt* προλέγω, προφητεύω ‖ ~**ion** *n* πρόρρησις, προφητεία.
predominance [pri'dɔminəns] *n* ἐπικράτησις, ὑπεροχή.
predominant [pri'dɔminənt] *a* ὑπερισχύων, ἐπικρατῶν ‖ ~**ly** *ad* κυρίως, ἐπί τό πλεῖστον, κατά τό ἐπικρατέστερον.
predominate [pri'dɔmineit] *vi* ἐπικρατῶ, ὑπερισχύω.
pre-eminent [pri:'eminənt] *a* ἐξέχων, ὑπερέχων, ἀνώτερος.
pre-empt [pri:'empt] *vt* ἀποκτῶ πρῶτος.
preen [pri:n] *vt*: **to ~ o.s.** σιάζομαι, κορδώνομαι.
prefabricated ['pri:'fæbrikeitid] *a* προκατασκευασμένος.
preface ['prefis] *n* πρόλογος, εἰσαγωγή, προοίμιον.
prefect ['pri:fekt] *n (of school)* ἐπιμελητής.
prefer [pri'fə:*] *vt* προτιμῶ, ὑποβάλλω, προάγω ‖ ~**able** ['prefərəbl] *a (+ to)* προτιμώτερος, καλύτερος (ἀπό) ‖ ~**ably** *ad* προτιμώτερα, καλύτερα ‖ ~**ence** *n* προτίμησις ‖ ~**ential** *a* προνομιακός, προνομιούχος.
prefix ['pri:fiks] *n* πρόθεμα.
pregnancy ['pregnənsi] *n* ἐγκυμοσύνη, γκάστρωμα.
pregnant ['pregnənt] *a* ἔγκυος, γκαστρωμένη ‖ *(of ideas)* γόνιμος (εἰς), γεμᾶτος συνέπειες.
prehistoric ['pri:his'tɔrik] *a* προϊστορικός.
prehistory ['pri:'histəri] *n* προϊστορία.
prejudice ['predʒudis] *n* προκατάληψις, πρόληψις ‖ *(harm)* ζημία, βλάβη ‖ *vt* ζημιώνω, ἐπηρεάζω ‖ ~**d** *a* προκατειλημμένος, προδιατεθειμένος.
prelate ['prelit] *n* ἱεράρχης.
preliminary [pri'liminəri] *a* προκαταρκτικός ‖ **the preliminaries** *npl* προεισαγωγικά, προκαταρκτικά.
prelude ['prelju:d] *n* πρόλογος, προοίμιον ‖ *(mus)* προανάκρουσμα, πρελούντιο.
premarital ['pri:'mæritl] *a* προγαμιαῖος.

premature ['prematʃuə*] *a* πρόωρος ‖ ~**ly**
ad πρόωρα.

premeditated [pri:'mediteitid] *a* προεσκεμ-
μένος, ἐκ προμελέτης.

premeditation [pri:medi'teiʃən] *n* προμε-
λέτη.

premier ['premiə*] *a* πρῶτος, κύριος ‖ *n*
πρωθυπουργός ‖ ~**e** [premi'εə*] *n*
πρεμιέρα.

premise ['premis] *n* πρότασις ‖ ~**s** *npl*
οἴκημα, κτίριον, κατάστημα.

premium ['pri:miəm] *n* (*insurance*) ἀσφάλιστρον.

premonition [pri:mə'niʃən] *n* προειδοποίησις, προαίσθημα.

preoccupation [pri:ɔkju'peiʃən] *n* προκατάληψις, ἀφηρημάδα, ἀπορρόφησις.

preoccupied [pri:'ɔkjupaid] *a* ἀπορροφημένος, ἀφηρημένος.

prep [prep] *n* (*sch: study*) ὥρα μελέτης ‖
φροντιστήριον.

preparation [prepə'reiʃən] *n* προπαρα-
σκευή, προετοιμασία.

preparatory [pri'pærətəri] *a* (*sch*) προπαρα-
σκευαστικός, προεισαγωγικός.

prepare [pri'peə*] *vt* προετοιμάζω, προπα-
ρασκευάζω ‖ *vi* προετοιμάζομαι, προπα
ρασκευάζομαι ‖ ~**d for** εἶμαι ἕτοιμος
γιά ‖ ~**d to** εἶμαι διατεθειμένος νά.

preponderance [pri'pondərəns] *n* ὑπεροχή,
ἐπικράτησις.

preposition [prepə'ziʃən] *n* πρόθεσις.

preposterous [pri'pɔstərəs] *a* παράλογος,
γελοῖος.

prerequisite ['pri:'rekwizit] *n* προϋπόθεσις,
ἀναγκαῖος ὅρος.

prerogative [pri'rɔgətiv] *n* προνόμιον.

Presbyterian [prezbi'tiəriən] *a,n* πρεσβυτε-
ριανός.

presbytery ['prezbitəri] *n* (*house*) κατοικία
ἱερέως.

preschool ['pri:'sku:l] *a* προσχολικός.

prescribe [pris'kraib] *vt* ὁρίζω, παραγγέλλω ‖ (*medicine*) δίνω συνταγήν.

prescription [pris'kripʃən] *n* (*for medicine*)
συνταγή.

prescriptive [pris'kriptiv] *a* ὁριζόμενος ὑπὸ
τοῦ νόμου, διατακτικός.

presence ['prezns] *n* παρουσία ‖ (*bearing*)
ὕφος, παρουσιαστικό, ἐμφάνισις ‖ ~ **of
mind** *n* ψυχραιμία, ἑτοιμότης πνεύματος.

present ['preznt] *a* παρών ‖ (*time*) σημερινός ‖ *n* (*time*) παρόν, τά τωρινά, τό
σήμερα ‖ (*gift*) δῶρον ‖ (*gram*) ἐνεστώς
‖ [pri'zent] *vt* παρουσιάζω, παρουσιάζομαι ‖ (*introduce*) συστήνω, παρουσιάζω ‖ (*offer, give*) καταθέτω, προσφέρω,
δίνω ‖ **at** ~ τώρα, πρός τό παρόν ‖ ~**able**
a παρουσιάσιμος ‖ ~**ation** *n* παρουσίασις, παράστασις ‖ ~**day** *a* σημερινός
‖ ~**ly** *ad* (*soon*) σέ λίγο, ἀμέσως, εὐθύς ‖
(*at present*) τώρα ‖ ~ **participle** *n* μετοχή
ἐνεστῶτος ‖ ~ **tense** *n* ἐνεστώς.

preservation [prezə'veiʃən] *n* διατήρησις,
διαφύλαξις.

preservative [pri'zə:nətiv] *n* προφυλακτι-
κόν, ἀντισηπτικόν.

preserve [pri'zə:v] *vt* διαφυλάσσω ‖ (*keep
up*) συντηρῶ, διατηρῶ ‖ *n* μέρος διατη-
ρήσεως ζώων ‖ (*jam*) γλυκό κουταλιοῦ,
μαρμελάδα.

preside [pri'zaid] *vi* προεδρεύω.

presidency ['prezidənsi] *n* προεδρεία.

president ['prezidənt] *n* διευθυντής, πρύτανις, πρόεδρος ‖ (*of a country*) πρόεδρος ‖ ~**ial** *a* προεδρικός.

press [pres] *n* (*machine*) πιεστήριον
πρέσσα ‖ (*printing house*) (τυπογραφικόν) πιεστήριον, τυπογραφεῖον ‖ (*news-
papers*) τύπος, ἐφημερίδες ‖ (*journalists*)
τύπος, δημοσιογράφοι ‖ *vt* πιέζω, σθῶ.
συνθλίβω ‖ (*urge*) πιέζω, ἐπιμένω
(*clothes*) σιδερώνω ‖ *vi* πιέζομαι, σφίγγομαι ‖ **to be** ~**ed** for χρειάζομαι, εἶμαι
στενοχωρημένος, πιέζομαι ἀπό ‖ **to** ~
for sth κινηγῶ, ἐπιμένω εἰς, ἀσκῶ πίεσιν
γιά ‖ **to** ~ **on** *vi* σπεύδω, ἐπιταχύνω,
συνεχίζω ‖ ~ **agency** *n* πρακτορεῖον
εἰδήσεων ‖ ~ **conference** *n* συνέντευξις
δημοσιογραφική ‖ ~ **cutting** *n* ἀπόκομμα
ἐφημερίδος ‖ ~**ing** *a* ἐπείγων, ἐπίμονος,
πιεστικός ‖ ~ **stud** *n* κουμπί μέ πίεσιν.

pressure ['preʃə*] *n* πίεσις ‖ ~ **cooker** *n*
χύτρα ταχύτητος, κατσαρόλα ταχύτητος
‖ ~ **gauge** *n* θλιβόμετρον, πιεζόμετρον,
μανόμετρον ‖ ~ **group** *n* ὁμάς μέ ἰσχυράν
ἐπιρροήν.

pressurized ['preʃəraizd] *a* πιεζόμενος, ὑπό
πίεσιν.

prestige [pres'ti:ʒ] *n* γόητρον.

presumably [pri'zju:məbli] *ad* κατά τό
φαινόμενον, πιθανῶς.

presume [pri'zju:m] *vti* ὑποθέτω, προϋποθέτω ‖ (*venture*) τολμῶ, λαμβάνω τό
θάρρος.

presumption [pri'zʌmpʃən] *n* ὑπόθεσις,
παραδοχή ‖ (*impudence*) ἀλαζονεία,
ἀναίδεια.

presumptuous [pri'zʌmptjuəs] *a* ἀναιδής.

presuppose [pri:sə'pəuz] *vt* προϋποθέτω.

pretence [pri'tens] *n* προσποίησις ‖ (*false
excuse*) πρόσχημα, πρόφασις.

pretend [pri'tend] *vt* (*feign*) προσποιοῦμαι,
ὑποκρίνομαι ‖ *vi* προσποιοῦμαι.

pretense [pri'tens] *n* (*US*) = **pretence**.

pretension [pri'tenʃən] *n* (*claim to merit*)
ἀξίωσις, ἀπαίτησις.

pretentious [pri'tenʃəs] *a* ἀπαιτητικός,
ἐπιδεικτικός.

pretext ['pri:tekst] *n* πρόφασις, πρόσχημα.

prettily ['pritili] *ad* ὄμορφα, μέ χάριν.

pretty ['priti] *a* χαριτωμένος, ἑλκυστικός.

prevail [pri'veil] *vi* ἐπικρατῶ, ὑπερισχύω
(*succeed*) ἐπιβάλλω, πείθω ‖ ~**ing** *a*
(*current*) ἐπικρατῶν, ἰσχύων.

prevalent ['prevələnt] *a* διαδεδομένος, ἐπικρατῶν.

prevarication [priværi'keiʃən] *n* ὑπεκφυγή, στρίψιμο, ψεῦδος.

prevent [pri'vent] *vt* ἀποτρέπω, προλαμβάνω, προφυλάσσω ἀπό ‖ (*hinder*) ἐμποδίζω, (παρα)κωλύω ‖ **~able** *a* ἀποφεύξιμος ‖ **~ative** *n* προληπτικόν (φάρμακον) ‖ **~ion** *n* πρόληψις, ἐμπόδισις ‖ **~ive** *a* προληπτικός, προφυλακτικός.

preview ['pri:vju:] *n* προκαταρκτική προβολή, δοκιμαστική προβολή.

previous ['pri:viəs] *a* προηγούμενος ‖ **~ly** *ad* προηγουμένως, προτύτερα.

prewar ['pri:'wɔ:*] *a* προπολεμικός.

prey [prei] *n* λεία, βορά, θῦμα ‖ **to ~ on** *vt* καταδιώκω, κινηγῶ, τρώγω ‖ (*mind*) βασανίζω.

price [prais] *n* τιμή, τίμημα ‖ (*value*) ἀξία ‖ *vt* διατιμῶ, καθορίζω τιμήν ‖ **~less** *a* ἀνεκτίμητος ‖ **~ list** *n* τιμοκατάλογος, τιμολόγιον.

prick [prik] *n* τσίμπημα ‖ *vt* τσιμπῶ, κεντρῶ, τρυπῶ.

prickle ['prikl] *n* ἀγκάδι.

prickly ['prikli] *a* (*lit*) ἀκανθῶδες, τσουχτερός ‖ (*fig: person*) δύσκολος.

pride [praid] *n* (*self-respect*) φιλότιμο ‖ (*something to be proud of*) ὑπερηφάνεια, καμάρι ‖ (*conceit*) ἀλαζονεία, ὑπεροψία ‖ **to ~ o.s. on sth** ὑπερηφανεύομαι, καυχῶμαι.

priest [pri:st] *n* ἱερεύς, παπᾶς ‖ **~ess** *n* ἱέρεια ‖ **~hood** *n* ἱερωσύνη, (οἱ) ἱερεῖς.

prig [prig] *n* φαντασμένος, ξιππασμένος.

prim [prim] *a* ἀκριβής, τυπικός, μαξεμένος.

primarily ['praimərili] *ad* πρωτίστως, κυρίως ‖ (*at first*) ἀρχικά, πρῶτα-πρῶτα.

primary ['praiməri] *a* πρῶτος, ἀρχικός, ἀρχέτυπος ‖ (*first in importance*) πρωτεύων, κύριος, οὐσιώδης ‖ (*education*) στοιχειώδης ‖ (*election*) προκριματική ἐκλογή κόμματος ‖ **~ colours** *npl* πρωτεύοντα χρώματα ‖ **~ school** *n* δημοτικόν σχολεῖον.

primate ['praimit] *n* ἀρχιεπίσκοπος, πριμᾶτος ‖ ['praimeit] (*zool*) πρωτεύων.

prime [praim] *a* πρῶτος, πρώτιστος, κύριος ‖ (*excellent*) ἐξαίρετος, πρώτης ποιότητος ‖ *vt* κατηχῶ, δασκαλεύω ‖ (*gun, pump*) γεμίζω, γομῶ ‖ **~ minister** *n* πρωθυπουργός ‖ **~r** *n* ἀλφαβητάριον, πρῶτον βιβλίον ‖ **~val** [prai'mi:vəl] *a* πρωτόγονος, ἀρχέγονος, προϊστορικός.

primitive ['primitiv] *a* πρωτόγονος, ἀρχικός, ἁπλός.

primrose ['primrəuz] *n* ἠράνθεμο, δακράκι, πασχαλούδα.

primula ['primjulə] *n* πριμούλη.

primus (stove) ['praiməs(stəuv)] *n* ® γκαζιέρα.

prince [prins] *n* ἠγεμών, μεγιστάν ‖ (*of royal family*) πρίγκηψ, βασιλόπαις ‖ **~ss** *n* πριγκήπισσα.

principal ['prinsipəl] *a* κύριος, κυριώτερος ‖ *n* (*capital*) κεφάλαιον ‖ (*of school*) προϊστάμενος, διευθυντής ‖ **~ity** *n* πριγκηπᾶτον ‖ **~ly** *ad* κυρίως, πρό παντός, κατά τό πλεῖστον.

principle ['prinsəpl] *n* ἀρχή, τιμιότης.

print [print] *n* σφραγίς, τύπος, ἀποτύπωμα ‖ (*phot*) ἀντίτυπον, κόπια ‖ (*picture*) εἰκών, γραβούρα ‖ (*pattern*) ἐμπριμέ ‖ *vt* τυπώνω, ἐκτυπώνω ‖ **~ed matter** *n* ἔντυπα ‖ **~er** *n* τυπογράφος ‖ **~ing** *n* (ἐκ)τύπωσις, τυπογραφία ‖ **~ing press** *n* πιεστήριον (τυπογραφείου).

prior ['praiə*] *a* προγενέστερος, προηγούμενος ‖ *n* ἡγούμενος ‖ **~ity** *n* προτεραιότης ‖ **~y** *n* μοναστήρι, κοινόβιον.

prise [praiz] *vt*: **to ~ open** ἀνοίγω μέ μοχλό.

prism ['prizəm] *n* πρίσμα.

prison ['prizn] *n* φυλακή ‖ **~er** *n* φυλακισμένος, ὑπόδικος, κατάδικος ‖ (*of war*) αἰχμάλωτος.

prissy ['prisi] *a* (*col*) λεπτολόγος, μικρολόγος.

pristine ['pristain] *a* πρωτόγονος, ἀρχικός.

privacy ['privəsi] *n* μοναξιά ‖ μυστικότης.

private ['praivit] *a* ἰδιωτικός, ἰδιαίτερος, μυστικός ‖ *n* φαντάρος ‖ '**~**' (*sign*) 'ἰδιωτικόν', 'ἰδιαίτερον' ‖ **in ~** ἰδιαιτέρως, μυστικά ‖ **~ eye** *n* ἰδιωτικός ἀστυνομικός ‖ **~ly** *ad* ἰδιωτικῶς, ἀτομικῶς.

privet ['privit] *n* λιγοῦστρον, ἀγριομυρτιά.

privilege ['privilidʒ] *n* προνόμιον ‖ **~d** *a* προνομιοῦχος.

privy ['privi] *a*: **~ council** ἀνακτοβούλιον.

prize [praiz] *n* βραβεῖον, ἔπαθλον ‖ *a* (*example*) λαμπρόν (ὑπο)δείγματος ‖ (*idiot*) ὑποδείγματος ἠλιθίου ‖ *vt* ἐκτιμῶ, τιμῶ ‖ **~ fight** *n* πυγμαχικός ἀγών ‖ **~ giving** *n* βράβευσις ‖ **~winner** *n* βραβευθείς.

pro- [prəu] *prefix* (*in favour*) ὑπέρ-, ἀντί- ‖ **the pros and cons** τά ὑπέρ καί τά κατά.

pro [prəu] *n* (*professional*) ἐπαγγελματίας.

probability [prɔbə'biliti] *n* πιθανότης.

probable ['prɔbəbl] *a* ἐνδεχόμενος, πιθανός.

probably ['prɔbəbli] *ad* πιθανῶς, πιθανόν.

probation [prə'beiʃən] *n* δοκιμασία ‖ (*in court etc*) ἀστυνομική ἐπιτήρησις ‖ **on ~** ὑπό δοκιμασίαν ‖ **~ary** *a* (περίοδος) δοκιμασίας ‖ **~er** *n* δόκιμος.

probe [prəub] *n* (*med*) καθετήρ, μήλη ‖ (*enquiry*) ἐξερεύνησις, διερεύνησις ‖ *vti* (ἐξ)ερευνῶ, διερευνῶ.

probity ['prəubiti] *n* χρηστότης, τιμιότης, ἀκεραιότης.

problem ['prɔbləm] *n* πρόβλημα ‖ **~atic** *a* προβληματικός.

procedure [prə'si:dʒə*] *n* διαδικασία, μέθοδος, πορεία.

proceed [prə'si:d] *vi* προχωρῶ, συνεχίζω, τραβῶ ‖ *(begin)* προβαίνω, ἀρχίζω ‖ **~ings** *npl* συζητήσεις, πρακτικά ‖ *(law)* δικαστική ἐνέργεια, δίκη ‖ **~s** ['prəusi:dz] *npl* εἰσπραχθέν ποσόν, εἰσπράξεις.

process ['prəuses] *n* πορεία, ἐξέλιξις ‖ *(method)* μέθοδος, τρόπος ‖ *vt* ἐπεξεργάζω, κατεργάζω.

procession [prə'seʃən] *n* πομπή, παρέλασις ‖ *(orderly progress)* παράταξις, σειρά, συνοδεία.

proclaim [prə'kleim] *vt* κηρύττω, ἀνακηρύσσω, ἀναγορεύω ‖ *(show)* φανερώνω, δείχνω.

proclamation [proklə'meiʃən] *n* (προ)κήρυξις, ἀνακήρυξις.

procrastination [prəukræsti'neiʃən] *n* ἀναβολή, χρονοτριβή, χασομέρι.

procreation [prəukri'eiʃən] *n* γέννησις, τεκνοποιΐα.

procure [prə'kjuə*] *vt* προμηθεύω, προμηθεύομαι, ἐξευρίσκω.

prod [prɔd] *vt* σκαλίζω, κεντρίζω, ἐξάπτω ‖ *n* *(push, jab)* μπήξιμο, κέντρισμα.

prodigal ['prɔdigəl] *a* ἄσωτος, σπάταλος.

prodigious [prə'didʒəs] *a* τεράστιος, καταπληκτικός, θαυμάσιος.

prodigy ['prɔdidʒi] *n* φαινόμενον, θαῦμα.

produce ['prɔdju:s] *n* *(agr)* προϊόν, καρπός ‖ [prə'dju:s] *vt* *(show)* παρουσιάζω, ἐπιδεικνύω ‖ *(make)* παράγω, γεννῶ, προξενῶ ‖ *(play)* ἀνεβάζω, παρουσιάζω ‖ **~r** *n* παραγωγός ‖ *(theat)* σκηνοθέτης, παραγωγός.

product ['prɔdʌkt] *n* προϊόν, ἀποτέλεσμα ‖ **~ion** *n* παραγωγή, κατασκευή, γένεσις ‖ προϊόντα, παραγωγή ‖ *(theat)* σκηνοθέτησις, παράστασις, ἀνέβασμα ‖ **~ion line** *n* γραμμή παραγωγῆς ‖ **~ive** *a* παραγωγικός ‖ *(fertile)* γόνιμος.

productivity [prɔdʌk'tiviti] *n* παραγωγικότης, γονιμότης.

profane [prə'fein] *a* βέβηλος ‖ *(language)* βλάσφημος.

profess [prə'fes] *vt* διακηρύττω, ὁμολογῶ ‖ *(claim)* προσποιοῦμαι ‖ **~ion** *n* ἐπάγγελμα ‖ *(declaration)* ὁμολογία, διακήρυξις ‖ **~ional** *a* ἐπαγγελματίας ‖ *a* ἐπαγγελματικός ‖ **~ionalism** *n* ἐπαγγελματισμός ‖ **~or** *n* καθηγητής.

proficiency [prə'fiʃənsi] *n* εἰδικότης, ἐπιδεξιότης, ἱκανότης.

proficient [prə'fiʃənt] *a* ἱκανός, εἰδικός, ἐγκρατής.

profile ['prəufail] *n* *(of face)* κατατομή, προφίλ ‖ *(fig: report)* σύντομος βιογραφία.

profit ['prɔfit] *n* κέρδος, ὄφελος, ὠφέλεια ‖ *vi* (+ *by, from*) ὠφελοῦμαι (ἀπό), ἐπωφελοῦμαι ‖ **~able** *a* ἐπικερδής, ἐπωφελής ‖ **~ably** *ad* ἐπωφελῶς, ἐπικερδῶς, ὠφέλιμα ‖ **~eering** *n* κερδοσκοπία.

profound [prə'faund] *a* βαθύς, μυστηριώδης ‖ **~ly** *ad* βαθέως, βαθύτατα.

profuse [prə'fju:s] *a* ἄφθονος, γενναιόδωρος ‖ **~ly** *ad* ἀφθόνως, ἄφθονα.

profusion [prə'fju:ʒən] *n* ἀφθονία.

progeny ['prɔdʒini] *n* ἀπόγονοι, νεογνά, παιδιά.

programing ['prəugræmiŋ] *n* (*US*) = **programming.**

programme, (*US*) **program** ['prəugræm] *n* πρόγραμμα.

programming ['prəugræmiŋ] *n* προγραμματισμός.

progress ['prəugres] *n* πρόοδος, ἐξέλιξις ‖ [prə'gres] *vi* προοδεύω, προχωρῶ, ἐξελίσσομαι ‖ **to make ~** σημειώνω πρόοδον, προκόβω ‖ **~ion** *n* πρόοδος ‖ **~ive** *a* προοδευτικός ‖ **~ively** *ad* προοδευτικῶς, βαθμηδόν.

prohibit [prə'hibit] *vt* ἀπαγορεύω ‖ **~ion** *n* (*US*) ἀπαγόρευσις, ποταπαγόρευσις ‖ **~ive** *a* *(price etc)* ἀπαγορευτικός, ἀπλησίαστος.

project ['prɔdʒekt] *n* *(plan)* σχέδιον ‖ *(final project)* μελέτη ‖ [prə'dʒekt] *vt* *(throw)* ρίπτω, ἐξακοντίζω ‖ *(extend)* προεκτείνω ‖ *(film etc)* προβάλλω ‖ *vi* (προ)ἐξέχω, προβάλλω ‖ **~ile** *n* βλήμα ‖ **~ion** *n* προεξοχή, προβολή ‖ **~or** *n* *(film)* προβολεύς, μηχάνημα προβολῆς.

proletarian [prəulə'teəriən] *a* προλεταριακός ‖ *n* προλετάριος.

proletariat [prəulə'teəriət] *n* προλεταριάτον.

proliferate [prə'lifəreit] *vi* πολλαπλασιάζομαι.

proliferation [prəlifə'reiʃən] *n* πολλαπλασιασμός.

prolific [prə'lifik] *a* γόνιμος, ἄφθονος.

prologue ['prəulɔg] *n* πρόλογος.

prolong [prə'lɔŋ] *vt* παρατείνω, προεκτείνω.

prom [prɔm] *n abbr of* **promenade** ‖ *abbr of* **promenade concert** ‖ (*US: college ball*) φοιτητικός χορός.

promenade [prɔmi'na:d] *n* περίπατος, τόπος περιπάτου ‖ **~ concert** *n* συναυλία ‖ **~ deck** *n* *(naut)* κατάστρωμα περιπάτου.

prominence ['prɔminəns] *n* ὑπεροχή, προεξοχή.

prominent ['prɔminənt] *a* προεξέχων περίβλεπτος, διακεκριμένος.

promiscuity [prɔmis'kju:iti] *n* συγχρονισμός, σμίξιμο, ἀνακάτεμα.

promise ['prɔmis] *n* ὑπόσχεσις, τάξιμο ‖ *(hope)* ὑπόσχεσις ‖ *vti* ὑπόσχομαι, παρέχω ὑποσχέσεις, φαίνομαι καλά.

promising ['prɔmisiŋ] *a* γεμᾶτος ὑποσχέσεις, παρέχων ἐλπίδας.

promontory ['prɔməntri] *n* ἀκρωτήριον.

promote [prə'məut] *vt* προάγω, προβιβάζω ‖ *(help on)* ὑποστηρίζω, ὑποκινῶ ‖ **~r** *n* ὑποστηρικτής, ὑποκινητής, διοργανωτής.

promotion [prə'məuʃən] *n (of sales etc)* διαφήμισις, προαγωγή ‖ *(in rank)* προαγωγή, προβιβασμός.

prompt [prɔmpt] *a* ἄμεσος, σύντομος, πρόθυμος, ταχύς ‖ *ad (punctually)* στήν ὥρα ‖ *vt* παρακινῶ, ἐμπνέω ‖ *(remind)* ὑποβάλλω ‖ ~**er** *n (theat)* ὑποβολεύς ‖ ~**ly** *ad* ταχέως, γρήγορα, γοργά ‖ ~**ness** *n* ταχύτης, ἑτοιμότης, προθυμία.

prone [prəun] *a* πρηνής, μπρουμιτισμένος ‖ *(inclined)* (+ *to*) ἐπιρρεπής, ἔχων κλίσιν.

prong [prɔŋ] *n* δόντι πηρουνιοῦ, πηρούνα, διχάλα.

pronoun ['prəunaun] *n* ἀντωνυμία.

pronounce [prə'nauns] *vt (gram)* προφέρω ‖ *(law)* ἐκδίδω, ἐπιβάλλω, ἀπαγγέλλω, γνωματεύω ‖ ~**d** *a (marked)* ἔντονος, ζωηρός ‖ ~**ment** *n* δήλωσις, διακήρυξις.

pronto ['prɔntəu] *ad (col)* ἀμέσως, γρήγορα.

pronunciation [prənʌnsi'eiʃən] *n* προφορά.

proof [pru:f] *n* ἀπόδειξις, τεκμήριον ‖ *(test)* δοκιμή, δοκιμασία ‖ *(copy)* δοκίμιον ‖ *a* ἀδιαπέραστος, στεγανός, ἀνθιστάμενος εἰς.

prop [prɔp] *n* στήριγμα, ἔρεισμα, ὑποστήριγμα ‖ *(theat)* βοηθητικά, ἀξεσουάρ ‖ *vt (also ~ up)* (ὑπο)στηρίζω, στηλώνω.

propaganda [prɔpə'gændə] *n* προπαγάνδα.

propagation [prɔpə'geiʃən] *n (of plants)* ἀναπαραγωγή, πολλαπλασιασμός ‖ *(of knowledge)* διάδοσις.

propel [prə'pel] *vt* προωθῶ, δίδω ὤθησιν εἰς ‖ ~**ler** *n* ἕλιξ, προπέλλα.

proper ['prɔpə*] *a* πρέπον, ἁρμόζων ‖ ~**ly** *ad* πρεπόντως, δεόντως, καταλλήλως, σωστά ‖ ~ **noun** *n* κύριον ὄνομα.

property ['prɔpəti] *n* ἰδιοκτησία, περιουσία ‖ *(quality)* ἰδιότης, χαρακτηριστικόν ‖ *(theat)* βοηθητικόν, ἀξεσουάρ ‖ *(land)* κτῆμα, ἀκίνητον ‖ ~ **owner** *n* ἰδιοκτήτης.

prophecy ['prɔfisi] *n (prediction)* προφητεία.

prophesy ['prɔfisai] *vt* προφητεύω, προλέγω.

prophet ['prɔfit] *n* προφήτης ‖ ~**ic** *a* προφητικός.

proportion [prə'pɔ:ʃən] *n* σχέσις, ἀναλογία ‖ *(share)* μέρος, τμῆμα ‖ *vt* ρυθμίζω, μοιράζω κατ' ἀναλογίαν ‖ ~**al** *a* ἀνάλογος, συμμετρικός, ἀναλογικός ‖ ~**ate** *a* ἀνάλογος, σύμμετρος, ρυθμισμένος ‖ ~**ed** *a* μέ καλές ἀναλογίες.

proposal [prə'pəuzl] *n* πρότασις, σχέδιον, εἰσήγησις ‖ *(of marriage)* πρότασις γάμου.

propose [prə'pəuz] *vt* προτείνω, σκοπεύω ‖ *vi (marriage)* κάνω πρότασιν γάμου ‖ ~**r** *n* ὁ προτείνων, ὁ ὑποβάλλων (πρότασιν).

proposition [prɔpə'ziʃən] *n* πρότασις, σχέδιον, ὑπόθεσις.

propound [prə'paund] *vt (theory)* προτείνω, ἀναπτύσσω.

proprietary [prə'praiətəri] *a* τῆς ἰδιοκτησίας, τῆς κυριότητος.

proprietor [prə'praiətə*] *n* ἰδιοκτήτης.

propulsion [prə'pʌlʃən] *n* (προ)ώθησις.

pro-rata ['prəu'ra:tə] *ad* κατ' ἀναλογίαν.

prosaic [prəu'zeiik] *a (ordinary)* πεζός.

prose [prəuz] *n* πεζός λόγος, πεζογραφία, πρόζα.

prosecute ['prɔsikju:t] *vt* ὑποβάλλω μήνυσιν.

prosecution [prɔsi'kju:ʃən] *n* (ποινική) δίωξις ‖ *(people bringing action)* κατηγορία, μηνυτής.

prosecutor ['prɔsikju:tə*] *n* εἰσαγγελεύς.

prospect ['prɔspekt] *n (expectation)* προσδοκία, ἐλπίς ‖ ~**ing** *n (for minerals)* ἀναζήτησις (μεταλλευμάτων) ‖ ~**ive** *a* προσδοκόμενος, μελλοντικός ‖ ~**or** *n* μεταλλοδίφης ‖ *(for gold)* χρυσοθήρας ‖ ~**us** *n* ἀγγελία, πρόγραμμα.

prosper ['prɔspə*] *vi* εὐδοκιμῶ, ἀκμάζω, προκόπτω ‖ ~**ity** *n* εὐημερία, εὐδαιμονία ‖ ~**ous** *a* εὐημερῶν, ἀκμάζων, ἐπιτυχής.

prostitute ['prɔstitju:t] *n* πόρνη, πουτάνα.

prostrate ['prɔstreit] *a (lying flat)* πρηνής, μπρούμυτος.

protagonist [prəu'tægənist] *n* πρωταγωνιστής.

protect [prə'tekt] *vt* προστατεύω, προφυλάσσω, ὑπερασπίζω, καλύπτω ‖ ~**ion** *n* προστασία, ὑπεράσπισις, ἄμυνα ‖ *(shelter)* σκέπαστρον, προστατευτικόν μέσον ‖ ~**ive** *a* προστατευτικός ‖ ~**or** *n* προστάτης, προφυλακτήρ.

protégé ['prɔteʒei] *n* προστατευόμενος.

protein ['prəuti:n] *n* πρωτεΐνη.

protest [prəutest] *n* διαμαρτυρία, διαμαρτύρησις ‖ [prə'test] *vi* (+ *against*) διαμαρτύρομαι ‖ **P**~**ant** *a,n* διαμαρτυρόμενος, προτεστάντης.

protocol ['prəutəkɔl] *n* πρωτόκολλον.

prototype ['prəutəutaip] *n* πρωτότυπον, μοντέλλο.

protracted [prə'træktid] *a* παρατεταμένος.

protractor [prə'træktə*] *n* μοιρογνωμόνιον.

protrude [prə'tru:d] *vt* προεξέχω, ξεβγαίνω.

protuberance [prə'tju:bərəns] *n* (ἐξ)όγκωμα, πρήξιμο.

proud [praud] *a* περήφανος ‖ φαντασμένος ‖ ἀκατάδεκτος.

prove [pru:v] *vt (show)* ἀποδεικνύω, ἐπαληθεύω ‖ *(turn out)* δείχνομαι.

proverb ['prɔvə:b] *n* παροιμία.

provide [prə'vaid] *vt* προμηθεύω ‖ χορηγῶ ‖ ~**d** *cj* ἐφ' ὅσον, ἀρκεῖ νά.

province ['prɔvins] *n* ἐπαρχία ‖ ἁρμοδιότης.

provincial [prə'vinʃəl] *a* ἐπαρχιακός, τοπικιστικός.

provision [prə'viʒən] *n (supply)* προμήθεια ‖ *(condition)* ὅρος ‖ ~**s** *npl (food)* τρόφιμα, έφόδια ‖ ~ **al** *a* προσωρινός.

provocation [prɔvəˈkeiʃən] *n* πρόκλησις.

provocative [prəˈvɔkətiv] *a* προκλητικός, ἐρεθιστικός.

provoke [prəˈvəuk] *vt* προκαλῶ, διεγείρω, ἐξερεθίζω.

prow [prau] *n* πρώρα, πλώρη ‖ ~**ess** *n* ἐπιδεξιότης ‖ (*bravery*) ἀνδρεία, παλη-καριά.

prowl [praul] *vi* (*streets*) περιφέρομαι, τριγυρίζω ‖ *n*: on the ~ ψάχνω διαρκῶς ‖ ~**er** *n* νυχτοπάτης, τριγυριστής, σουρτούκης.

proximity [prɔkˈsimiti] *n* ἐγγύτης, γειτνί-ασις.

proxy [ˈprɔksi] *n* πληρεξούσιος, πληρε-ξούσιον, ἀντιπρόσωπος ‖ **by** ~ δι’ ἀντιπροσώπου.

prudence [ˈpruːdəns] *n* φρόνησις, σύνεσις, φροντίς.

prudent [ˈpruːdənt] *a* συνετός, φρόνιμος ‖ ~**ly** *ad* σωφρόνως, συνετά, φρόνιμα.

prudish [ˈpruːdiʃ] *a* σεμνότυφος ‖ ~**ness** *n* σεμνοτυφία.

prune [pruːn] *n* ξερό δαμάσκηνο ‖ *vt* κλαδεύω.

pry [prai] *vi* (+ *into*) ψάχνω, χώνω τή μύτη (σέ).

psalm [saːm] *n* ψαλμός.

pseudo [ˈsjuːdəu] *a* ψεύτικος, κίβδηλος ‖ (*in compds*) ψευδο- ‖ ~**nym** *n* ψευδώ-νυμον.

psyche [ˈsaiki] *n* (*soul, mind, intelligence*) ψυχή.

psychiatric [saikiˈætrik] *a* ψυχιατρικός.

psychiatrist [saiˈkaiətrist] *n* ψυχίατρος.

psychiatry [saiˈkaiətri] *n* ψυχιατρική.

psychic(al) [ˈsaikik(əl)] *a* ψυχικός.

psychoanalyse [saikəuˈænəlaiz] *vt* ψυχανα-λύω (κάποιον).

psychoanalysis [saikəuəˈnælisis] *n* ψυχανά-λυσις.

psychoanalyst [saikəuˈænəlist] *n* ψυχανα-λυτής.

psychoanalyze [saikəuˈænəlaiz] *vt* (*US*) = **psychoanalyse**.

psychological [saikəˈlɔdʒikəl] *a* ψυχολο-γικός ‖ ~**ly** *ad* ψυχολογικῶς.

psychologist [saiˈkɔlədʒist] *n* ψυχολόγος.

psychology [saiˈkɔlədʒi] *n* ψυχολογία.

psychopath [ˈsaikəupæθ] *n* ψυχοπαθής.

psychosomatic [ˈsaikəusəuˈmætik] *a* ψυχο-σωματικός.

psychotherapy [ˈsaikəuˈθerəpi] *n* ψυχοθε-ραπεία.

psychotic [saiˈkɔtik] *a,n* ψυχοπαθής.

pub [pʌb] *n* (*Brit*) = **public house** ‖ *see* **public**.

puberty [ˈpjuːbəti] *n* ἥβη, ἐφηβεία.

public [ˈpʌblik] *a* δημόσιος ‖ (*generally known*) πασίγνωστος ‖ *n* (*also* the general ~) κοινόν ‖ ~**an** *n* (*innkeeper*) ταβερνι-άρης, κάπελλας ‖ ~**ation** *n* (*something*

published) δημοσίευσις, ἔκδοσις ‖ (*making known*) κοινοποίησις, δημοσί-ευσις ‖ ~ **house** *n* ταβέρνα ‖ ~**ity** *n* δημοσιότης, διαφήμισις ‖ ~**ly** *ad* δημοσία, ὁλοφάνερα ‖ ~ **opinion** *n* κοινή γνώμη ‖ ~ **relations** *n* δημόσιες σχέσεις, διαφήμισις ‖ ~ **school** *n* (*Brit*) ἰδιωτικόν σχολεῖον (᾽Αγγλίας) ‖ ~- **spirited** *a* ἐνδιαφερόμενος γιά τό κοινόν καλόν, φιλόπατρις.

publish [ˈpʌbliʃ] *vt* ἐκδίδω, δημοσιεύω ‖ (*figures etc*) ἀναγγέλλω, δημοσιεύω ‖ ~**er** *n* ἐκδότης ‖ ~**ing** *n* ἔκδοσις, δημο-σίευσις.

pucker [ˈpʌkə*] *vt* ζαρώνω.

pudding [ˈpudin] *n* πουτίγγα.

puddle [ˈpʌdl] *n* (*pool*) νερόλακκος, λιμνούλα.

puerile [ˈpjuərail] *a* παιδαριώδης.

puff [pʌf] *n* ξεφύσημα, φύσημα, ρουφηξιά ‖ (*pad*) πομπόν ‖ *vt* ξεφυσῶ, βγάζω, ἐκπέμπω ‖ *vi* φυσῶ, τραβῶ, λαχανιάζω ‖ ~**ed** *a* (*col: out of breath*) λαχανιασμέ-νος.

puff pastry [ˈpʌfˈpeistri] *n*, (*US*) **puff paste** [ˈpʌfˈpeist] *n* πάτ-φεγιετέ.

puffy [ˈpʌfi] *a* φουσκωμένος, φουσκω-τός.

pull [pul] *n* (*tug*) ἕλξις, τράβηγμα ‖ (*fig*) ἐπιρροή, μέσον ‖ *vt* (*trolley*) σύρω, ἕλκω, τραβῶ, σέρνω ‖ (*hair*) τραβῶ ‖ (*trigger*) πατῶ, τραβῶ ‖ *vi* (*on rope etc*) τραβῶ, σύρω ‖ ‘~’ (*sign*) ᾽τράβηξε’, ᾽ἡηήρετε’ ‖ **to** ~ **a face** κάνω μούτρα, μορφάζω ‖ **to** ~ **to pieces** τραβῶ καί κομματιάζω, κριτικάρω δυσμενῶς ‖ **to** ~ **o.s. together** συνέρχομαι ‖ **to** ~ **apart** *vt* (*break*) σχίζω στά δύο, ἀποχωρίζω ‖ (*dismantle*) λυώνω ‖ **to** ~ **down** *vt* (*house*) κατεδαφίζω, γκρεμίζω ‖ **to** ~ **in** *vi* (*rail*) εἰσέρχομαι (στό σταθμό) ‖ **to** ~ **off** *vt* (*deal etc*) ἐπιτυγχάνω (κάτι) ‖ **to** ~ **out** *vi* ἐξέρχομαι, ξεκινῶ, ἀναχωρῶ ‖ (*vehicle*) βγαίνω ἀπό τήν λωρίδα ‖ *vt* ἀφαιρῶ, βγάζω, τραβῶ ‖ **to** ~ **round** *or* **through** *vi* συνέρχομαι, γλυτώνω, ἀναρ-ρωνύω ‖ **to** ~ **up** *vi* σταματῶ.

pulley [ˈpuli] *n* τροχαλία.

pullover [ˈpuləuvə*] *n* πουλόβερ.

pulp [pʌlp] *n* πολτός, σάρκωμα.

pulpit [ˈpulpit] *n* ἄμβων.

pulsate [pʌlˈseit] *vi* πάλλομαι, πάλλω, σφύζω.

pulse [pʌls] *n* σφυγμός, παλμός ‖ (*vegetable*) ὄσπρια.

pulverize [ˈpʌlvəraiz] *vt* λειοτριβῶ, κονι-οποιῶ.

pummel [ˈpʌml] *vt* γρονθοκοπῶ.

pump [pʌmp] *n* ἀντλία, τρούμπα, πόμπα ‖ *vt* ἀντλῶ ‖ **to** ~ **up** *vt* (*tyre*) φουσκώνω (λάστιχο).

pumpkin [ˈpʌmpkin] *n* κολοκύθα.

pun [pʌn] *n* λογοπαίγνιον.

punch [pʌntʃ] n τρυπητήρι, ζουμπάς ‖ (blow) γροθιά ‖ (drink) πώντς, πόντσι ‖ vt γρονθοκοπῶ, δίνω μία γροθιά ‖ (a hole) τρυπῶ, ἀνοίγω ‖ ~-drunk a τύφλα στό μεθύσι.

punctual [ˈpʌŋktjuəl] a ἀκριβής, τακτικός ‖ ~ity n ἀκρίβεια, τάξις.

punctuate [ˈpʌŋktjueit] vt στίζω ‖ (fig) τονίζω, ὑπογραμμίζω.

punctuation [pʌŋktjuˈeiʃən] n στίξις.

puncture [ˈpʌŋktʃə*] n (παρα)κέντησις, τρύπα ‖ vt παρακεντῶ, τρυπῶ, σπάζω.

pundit [ˈpʌndit] n (σοφο)λογιώτατος.

pungent [ˈpʌndʒənt] a δριμύς, σουβλερός, ὀξύς.

punish [ˈpʌniʃ] vt τιμωρῶ, δέρνω ‖ (in boxing etc) τρώγω ἄγριο ξύλο, μαστιγώνω ‖ ~able a ἀξιόποινος, τιμωρητέος ‖ ~ment n τιμωρία ‖ κτυπήματα.

punitive [ˈpjuːnitiv] a ποινικός ‖ (mil) ἀντιποίνων.

punt [pʌnt] n πλοιάρι, ρηχή λέμβος.

punter [ˈpʌntə*] n (gambler) παίκτης.

puny [ˈpjuːni] a μικροκαμωμένος, ἀδύνατος, ἀσήμαντος.

pup [pʌp] n σκυλάκι, κουτάβι.

pupil [ˈpjuːpil] n μαθητής ‖ (of eye) κόρη (ὀφθαλμοῦ).

puppet [ˈpʌpit] n μαριονέττα ‖ (person) ἀνδρείκελον.

puppy [ˈpʌpi] n σκυλάκι.

purchase [ˈpəːtʃis] n ψώνισμα, ψώνιο ‖ (buying) ἀγορά, ψώνισμα ‖ vt ἀγοράζω, ψωνίζω ‖ ~r n ἀγοραστής.

pure [pjuə*] a καθαρός ‖ (innocent) ἄδολος, ἁγνός ‖ (unmixed) ἀμιγής, ἄκρατος, ἀνόθευτος.

purée [ˈpjuərei] n πουρέ(ς).

purely [ˈpjuəli] ad καθαρῶς.

purge [pəːdʒ] n καθάρσιον ‖ (pol) ἐκκαθάρισις ‖ vt (ἐκ)καθαρίζω.

purification [pjuərifiˈkeiʃən] n καθαρισμός, ἐξυγίανσις.

purify [ˈpjuərifai] vt καθαρίζω, ἐξαγνίζω.

purist [ˈpjuərist] n καθαρευουσιάνος.

puritan [ˈpjuəritən] n πουριτανός ‖ ~ical a πουριτανικός.

purity [ˈpjuəriti] n καθαρότης ‖ (unmixed) καθαρότης, γνησιότης.

purl [pəːl] n ἀνάποδη βελονιά ‖ vt πλέκω ἀνάποδες.

purple [ˈpəːpl] (colour) a πορφυροῦς ‖ n πορφύρα, πορφυροῦν (χρῶμα).

purpose [ˈpəːpəs] n σκοπός, πρόθεσις ‖ on ~ σκόπιμα ‖ ~ful a (προ)ἐσκεμμένος, σκόπιμος ‖ ~ly ad ἐπίτηδες, σκόπιμα.

purr [pəː*] vi (of cat) ρουθουνίζω, κάνω ρονρόν ‖ n χουρχούρισμα, ροχάλισμα.

purse [pəːs] n πορτοφόλι ‖ vt ζαρώνω.

purser [ˈpəːsə*] n λογιστής (πλοίου).

pursue [pəˈsjuː] vt (καταδιώκω, κυνηγῶ ‖ (carry on) συνεχίζω, ἀκολουθῶ, τραβῶ ‖ ~r n διώκτης.

pursuit [pəˈsjuːt] n (κατα)δίωξις, κυνήγημα ‖ (occupation) ἐπιδίωξις, ἐπάγγελμα.

purveyor [pəːˈveiə*] n προμηθευτής (τροφίμων).

pus [pʌs] n πύον.

push [puʃ] n ὤθησις, σκούντημα, σπρωξιά ‖ (mil) προώθησις ‖ vt σπρώχνω, σκουντῶ ‖ (forward) προχωρῶ, προοδεύω ‖ vi σπρώχνω, ὠθῶ, ἀσκῶ πίεσιν ‖ (make one's way) προχωρῶ (μέ δυσκολίαν) ‖ '~' (sign) 'ὠθήσετε' ‖ at a ~ (if necessary) ἐν ἀνάγκη, στήν ἀνάγκη ‖ to ~ aside vt ἀπωθῶ, παραμερίζω ‖ to ~ off vi (col) φεύγω, ξεκινῶ ‖ to ~ on vi (continue) προχωρῶ, συνεχίζω, ἐπισπεύδω ‖ to ~ through vt (measure) περνῶ (νομοσχέδιον κτλ) ‖ ~ chair n καρροτσάκι ‖ παιδικό ἁμαξάκι ‖ ~ing a ἐνεργητικός, ρέκτης ‖ ~over n (col) εὔκολο πρᾶμα, εὔκολη κατάκτησι.

puss [pus] n γατάκι, ψιψίνα.

put [put] (irreg v) vt θέτω, τοποθετῶ, βάζω ‖ (express) ἐκφράζω, ἐξηγῶ, ὑποβάλλω ‖ to ~ about vt στρέφομαι, ἀναστρέφω ‖ vt διαδίδω, θέτω εἰς κυκλοφορίαν ‖ to ~ across vt (succeed) ἐπιτυγχάνω, βγάζω πέρα ‖ (meaning) δίνω νά καταλάβη ‖ to ~ away vt (store) βάζω κατά μέρος, φυλάσσω ‖ to ~ back vt (replace) βάζω πίσω ‖ (postpone) ἐπιβραδύνω, ἀναβάλλω ‖ to ~ by (money) ἀποταμιεύω ‖ to ~ down vt (lit) κατεβάζω ‖ (in writing) γράφω, σημειώνω ‖ to ~ forward vt (idea) ἀναπτύσσω, εἰσηγοῦμαι, προτείνω ‖ (date) ἀναβάλλω ‖ to ~ off vt (postpone) ἀναβάλλω ‖ (discourage) μεταπείθω, ἐμποδίζω, ἀποθαρρύνω ‖ to ~ on vt (clothes etc) φορῶ ‖ (light etc) ἀνάβω ‖ (play etc) ἀνεβάζω ‖ (brake) φρενάρω ‖ (false air) προσποιοῦμαι ‖ to ~ out vt (hand etc) ἐκτείνω, ἁπλώνω ‖ (news, rumour) διαδίδω ‖ (light etc) σβήνω ‖ (person: inconvenience) στενοχωρῶ, ἐνοχλῶ ‖ to ~ up vt (raise) σηκώνω, ὑψώνω, ἀνεγείρω ‖ (guest) παρέχω τροφή καί κατάλυμα, φιλοξενῶ ‖ to ~ up with vt ἀνέχομαι.

putrid [ˈpjuːtrid] a σαπρός, σάπιος.

putt [pʌt] vt σέρνω (τή μπάλλα) ‖ n συρτό χτύπημα, πάτιγκ.

putty [ˈpʌti] n στόκος.

put-up [ˈputʌp] a: ~ job δουλειά σκαρωμένη, στημένη μηχανή.

puzzle [ˈpʌzl] n αἴνιγμα, δύσλυτον πρόβλημα, μπέρδεμα ‖ (toy) παιχνίδι συναρμολογήσεως, γρῖφος ‖ vt (perplex) περιπλέκω, συγχίζω, ζαλίζω ‖ vi σπάζω τό κεφάλι μου.

puzzling [ˈpʌzliŋ] a πολύπλοκος, δύσλυτος, μπλεγμένος.

pygmy [ˈpigmi] n πυγμαῖος.

pyjamas [piˈdʒaːməz] npl πυζάμες.

pylon [ˈpailən] n στύλος.

pyramid ['pirəmid] *n* πυραμίς.
python ['paiθən] *n* πύθων.

Q, q

quack [kwæk] *n* κραυγή πάπιας | (*dishonest person*) κομπογιαννίτης, τσαρλατάνος.
quad [kwɔd] *n abbr of* quadrangle, quadruple, quadruplet.
quadrangle ['kwɔdræŋgl] *n* (*court*) τετράγωνος αὐλή.
quadruped ['kwɔdruped] *n* τετράποδον.
quadruple ['kwɔdrupl] *a* τετραπλός, τετραπλάσιος, τετράδιπλος || ['kwɔ'dru:pl] *vti* τετραπλασιάζω, τετραπλασιάζομαι.
quadruplet [kwɔ'dru:plit] *n* τετράδυμο.
quagmire ['kwægmaiə*] *n* ἕλος, τέλμα, βάλτος.
quaint [kweint] *a* παράξενος, ἀλλόκοτος |
~ly *ad* παράξενα, ἀλλόκοτα, πρωτότυπα
~ness *n* πρωτοτυπία, ἰδιοτροπία, παραξενιά.
quake [kweik] *vi* τρέμω, σείομαι || **Q~r** *n* Κουάκερος.
qualification [kwɔlifi'keiʃən] *n* ἱκανότης, προσόν || (*reservation*) ἐπιφύλαξις, ὅρος, περιορισμός.
qualified ['kwɔlifaid] *a* ἔχων τά προσόντα, κατάλληλος || (*reserved*) ἐπιφυλακτικός, περιωρισμένος, μετριασμένος.
qualify ['kwɔlifai] *vt* καθιστῶ κατάλληλον, ἀποκτῶ τά προσόντα || (*limit*) τροποποιῶ, προσδιορίζω || *vi* (*acquire degree*) λαμβάνω δίπλωμα.
qualitative ['kwɔlitətiv] *a* ποιοτικός.
quality ['kwɔliti] *n* (*kind*) ποιότης || (*of person*) ἰδιότης, χαρακτηριστικόν, ἱκανότης || *a* καλῆς ποιότητος.
qualm [kwa:m] *n* (*misgiving*) τύψις, ἐνδοιασμός.
quandary ['kwɔndəri] *n* ἀμηχανία, δίλημμα.
quantitative ['kwɔntitətiv] *a* ποσοτικός.
quantity ['kwɔntiti] *n* ποσότης || (*large amount*) μεγάλη ποσότης, πολύ, μέ τό σωρό.
quarantine ['kwɔrənti:n] *n* κάθαρσις, καραντίνα.
quarrel ['kwɔrəl] *n* (*argument*) φιλονεικία, διένεξις, καυγάς, τσακωμός || *vi* (*argue*) φιλονεικῶ, τσακώνομαι || ~**some** *a* εὐέξαπτος, καυγατζῆς.
quarry ['kwɔri] *n* (*of stone*) λατομεῖον |
(*animal*) θήραμα, κυνήγι.
quart [kwɔ:t] *n* τέταρτον τοῦ γαλλονιοῦ.
quarter ['kwɔ:tə*] *n* τέταρτον || (*of year*) τριμηνία || *vt* κόβω εἰς τά τέσσερα |
(*mil*) στρατωνίζω || ~**s** *npl* (*esp mil*) κατάλυμα, στρατών | στέγασις || ~ **of an hour** ἕνα τέταρτον (τῆς ὥρας) |
past three τρεῖς καί τέταρτον || ~ **to three** τρεῖς παρά τέταρτο || ~**-deck** *n*

πρυμναῖον κατάστρωμα, κάσαρο | ~**ly** *a* τριμηναῖος | ~**master** *n* (*naut*) ὑποναύκληρος || (*mil*) ἐπιμελητής.
quartet(te) [kwɔ:'tet] *n* τετραφωνία κουαρτέτο.
quartz [kwɔ:ts] *n* χαλαζίας.
quash [kwɔʃ] *vt* (*verdict*) ἀναιρῶ, ἀκυρώνω.
quasi ['kwa:zi] *a* σάν, σχεδόν, τρόπον τινά.
quaver ['kweivə*] *n* (*mus*) ὄγδοον || *vi* τρέμω, κάνω τρίλιες.
quay [ki:] *n* ἀποβάθρα, προκυμαία.
queasiness ['kwi:zinis] *n* εὐαισθησία, ἀηδία, δισταγμοί.
queasy ['kwi:zi] *a* εὐαίσθητος, ἀηδής, δύσκολος.
queen [kwi:n] *n* βασίλισσα || (*cards*) ντάμα
|| ~ **mother** *n* βασιλομήτωρ.
queer [kwiə*] *a* ἀλλόκοτος, παράξενος *n* (*col: homosexual*) 'τοιοῦτος'.
quell [kwel] *vt* καταπνίγω, καταβάλλω, κατευνάζω.
quench [kwentʃ] *vt* κόβω (τήν δίψα μου), κατευνάζω | (*fire etc*) σβήνω.
query ['kwiəri] *n* ἐρώτησις, ἐρώτημα *vt* ἐρωτῶ, ἐρευνῶ.
quest [kwest] *n* ἀναζήτησις, ἔρευνα.
question ['kwestʃən] *n* ἐρώτησις, ἐρώτημα
|| (*problem*) ζήτημα, θέμα || (*doubt*) ἀμφιβολία, ἀμφισβήτησις || *vt* ἐρωτῶ, ἐξετάζω || (*doubt*) ἀμφισβητῶ || **beyond** ~ ἀναμφισβητήτως || **out of the** ~ ἐκτός συζητήσεως, ἀπαράδεκτος || ~**able** *a* ἀμφίβολος, ἀμφισβητήσιμος || ~**er** *n* ἐξεταστής, ἀνακριτής || **-ing** *a* ὁ ρώτη σις, ἀνάκρισις || ~ **mark** *n* ἐρωτηματολογικόν || ~**naire** *n* ἐρωτηματολόγιον.
queue [kju:] *n* (*line*) οὐρά || *vi* μπαίνω στήν οὐρά, σχηματίζω οὐρά.
quibble ['kwibl] *n* (*petty objection*) ὑπεκφυγή.
quick [kwik] *a* (*fast*) ταχύς, γρήγορος, γοργός || (*impatient*) βιαστικός, εὐέξαπτος || (*keen*) ζωηρός, ζωντανός, ἔξυπνος || *ad* γρήγορα, ταχέως || *n* (*anat*) εὐαίσθητον σημεῖον, σάρκα, κρέας || (*old: the living*) οἱ ζῶντες || ~**en** *vt* (*hasten*) ἐπιταχύνω || (*rouse*) (ἀνα)ζωογονῶ, ζωντανεύω || *vi* (ξανα)ζωντανεύω, ἀναζωπυροῦμαι || ~**ly** *ad* ταχέως, γρήγορα || ~**ness** *n* ταχύτης, ὀξύτης, σβελτάδα || ~**sand** *n* κινητή ἄμμος || ~**step** *n* (*music*) ταχύς ρυθμός || ~**-witted** *a* ἀγχίνους, ξύπνιος, ἀτσίδα.
quid [kwid] *n* (*Brit col: £1*) λίρα ('Αγγλίας).
quiet ['kwaiət] *a* (*without noise*) σιωπηλός, σιγαλός, ἀθόρυβος || (*still*) ἤρεμος, γαλήνιος, ἥσυχος || (*peaceful*) ἤρεμος, ἀτάραχος || *n* ἡσυχία, ἠρεμία || ~**en** *vti* (*also* ~**en down**) (κ̣αθ)ησυχάζω, καλμάρω || ~**ly** *ad* ἤρεμα, ἀπαλά, σιγαλά, σιωπηλά || ~**ness** *n* ἠρεμία, γαλήνη, κάλμα.
quill [kwil] *n* (*pen*) πέννα ἀπό φτερό.

quilt [kwilt] *n* πάπλωμα, ἐφάπλωμα ‖ ~**ing** *n* φοδράρισμα, καπιτονάρισμα.

quin [kwin] *n abbr of* **quintuplet.**

quince [kwins] *n* κυδώνι.

quinine [kwi'ni:n] *n* κινίνη.

quinquennial [kwiŋ'kweniəl] *a* πενταετής.

quinquennium [kwiŋ'kweniəm] *n* πενταετία.

quinsy ['kwinzi] *n* πυώδης ἀμυγδαλῖτις, πονόλαιμος.

quintett(te) [kwin'tet] *n* κουΐντέτο.

quintuplet [kwin'tju:plit] *n* πεντάδυμον.

quip [kwip] *n* εὐφυολόγημα, σκῶμα, σαρκασμός ‖ *vi* εὐφυολογῶ.

quit [kwit] (*irreg v*) *vt* ἐγκαταλείπω, ἀναχωρῶ, φεύγω ‖ *vi* (*give up*) παραιτοῦμαι, ἐγκαταλείπω.

quite [kwait] *ad* τελείως, ἐξ ὁλοκλήρου, ἐντελῶς ‖ (*fairly*) μᾶλλον, πολύ ‖ ~ (*so*)! σωστά!, σύμφωνοι!

quits [kwits] *ad* στά ἴσια, πάτσι.

quiver ['kwivə*] *vi* τρέμω, τρεμουλιάζω, πάλλομαι ‖ *n* (*for arrows*) φαρέτρα, σαϊτοθήκη.

quiz [kwiz] *n* στραβοκοίταγμα ‖ (*test*) προφορική ἐξέτασις ‖ *vt* (*question*) ἐξετάζω ‖ ~**zical** *a* αἰνιγματώδης, πειραχτικός, ἐρωτηματικός.

quoit [kwɔit] *n* ἀμάδα.

quorum ['kwɔ:rəm] *n* ἀπαρτία.

quota ['kwəutə] *n* ἀνάλογον μερίδιον, μερίδα.

quotation [kwəu'teiʃən] *n* (*marks*) εἰσαγωγικά ‖ (*from book*) χωρίον, ἀπόσπασμα ‖ (*price*) τιμή, τιμολόγιον.

quote [kwəut] *n* (*quotation*) ἀπόσπασμα ‖ *vti* (*price*) καθορίζω, δίνω τιμήν, προσφέρω τιμήν ‖ (*cite*) παραθέτω, ἀναφέρω.

quotient ['kwəuʃənt] *n* πηλίκον.

R, ɪ

rabbi ['ræbai] *n* ραββῖνος.

rabbit ['ræbit] *n* κουνέλι ‖ ~ **hole** *n* φωλιά κουνελιοῦ, τρύπα ‖ ~ **hutch** *n* κλουβί κουνελιοῦ.

rabble ['ræbl] *n* ὄχλος.

rabid ['ræbid] *a* (*fig*) μανιασμένος, ἀδιάλλακτος.

rabies ['reibi:z] *n* λύσσα.

race [reis] *n* (*people*) ράτσα, φυλή, γενιά ‖ (*animals*) ράτσα ‖ (*competition*) δρόμος, ἀγών δρόμου ‖ (*rush*) βία, γρηγοράδα ‖ *vt* κάνω ἀγών δρόμου ‖ *vi* τρέχω ‖ (*compete*) συναγωνίζομαι ‖ ~**course** *n* (*for horses*) ἱππόδρομος ‖ ~**horse** *n* ἵππος ἀγώνων ‖ ~ **meeting** *n* (*for horses*) ἱπποδρομία ‖ ~ **relations** *npl* φυλετικές σχέσεις ‖ ~**track** *n* (*for cars etc*) πίστα (ἀγώνων).

racial ['reiʃəl] *a* φυλετικός ‖ ~ **discrimination** *n* φυλετική διάκρισις ‖ ~**ism** *n* φυλετισμός, ρα(τ)σισμός ‖ ~**ist** *a* ρα(τ)σιστικός ‖ *n* ὀπαδός τοῦ ρα(τ)σισμοῦ.

racing ['reisiŋ] *n* ἀγώνες, συμμετοχή εἰς ἀγώνες ‖ ~ **car** *n* αὐτοκίνητον ἀγώνων ‖ ~ **driver** *n* ὁδηγός αὐτοκινήτου ἀγώνων.

racist ['reisist] *a* ρατσιστής.

rack [ræk] *n* (*clothes etc*) κρεμάστρα ‖ *vt* βασανίζω ‖ ~ **and ruin** καταστροφή, κατά διαβόλου.

racket ['rækit] *n* θόρυβος, φασαρία, πατιρντί ‖ (*dishonest scheme*) κομπίνα ‖ λοβιτούρα ‖ (*for tennis*) ρακέττα.

racquet ['rækit] *n* ρακέττα.

racy ['reisi] *a* (*spirited*) ζωηρός, κεφάτος.

radar ['reidɑ:*] *n* ραδιοεντοπισμός, ραντάρ.

radiance ['reidiəns] *n* ἀκτινοβολία, λάμψις.

radiant ['reidiənt] *a* λαμπερός ‖ (*giving out rays*) ἀκτινοβόλος.

radiate ['reidieit] *vt* (*of heat*) ἀκτινοβολῶ, ἐκπέμπω ‖ *vi* (*lines*) ἐκτείνω ἀκτινοειδῶς.

radiation [reidi'eiʃən] *n* ἀκτινοβολία.

radiator ['reidieitə*] *n* σῶμα καλοριφέρ ‖ (*aut*) ψυγεῖον ‖ ~ **cap** *n* πῶμα τοῦ ψυγείου.

radical ['rædikəl] *a* ριζικός ‖ (*pol*) ριζοσπαστικός ‖ ~**ly** *ad* ριζικῶς.

radio ['reidiəu] *n* ἀσύρματος ‖ (*set*) ραδιόφωνον ‖ ~**active** *a* ραδιενεργός ‖ ~**activity** *n* ραδιενέργεια ‖ ~**grapher** *n* ἀκτινογράφος ‖ ~**graphy** *n* ραδιογραφία, ἀκτινογραφία ‖ ~ **station** *n* σταθμός ραδιοφώνου ‖ ~**telephone** *n* ἀσύρματον τηλέφωνον ‖ ~ **telescope** *n* ἀσύρματον τηλεσκόπιον ‖ ~**therapist** *n* ἀκτινολόγος ἰατρός.

radish ['rædiʃ] *n* ρεπανάκι.

radium ['reidiəm] *n* ράδιον.

radius ['reidiəs] *n* ἀκτίς.

raffia ['ræfiə] *n* ραφία.

raffish ['ræfiʃ] *a* (ψευτο)παλληκαρᾶς, ἀνυπόληπτος.

raffle ['ræfl] *n* λαχεῖον, λοταρία.

raft [rɑ:ft] *n* σχεδία, σάλι.

rafter ['rɑ:ftə*] *n* δοκάρι, καδρόνι.

rag [ræg] *n* (*of cloth*) ράκος, κουρέλι ‖ (*col: newspaper*) ἐφημερίδα ‖ *vt* κάνω φάρσα, κάνω καζούρα ‖ ~**bag** *n* (*fig*) κακοντυμένη γυναίκα.

rage [reidʒ] *n* (*fury*) λύσσα, μανία, ἔξαψις ‖ (*fashion*) μανία, τῆς μόδας ‖ *vi* (*person*) μαίνομαι, εἶμαι ἔξω φρενῶν ‖ (*storm*) μαίνομαι, εἶμαι ἀγριεμένος.

ragged ['rægid] *a* (*edge*) τραχύς, ἀπότομος.

raging ['reidʒiŋ] *a* μαινόμενος, ἀγριεμένος.

raid [reid] *n* (*mil*) ἐπιδρομή, ἔφοδος, αἰφνιδιασμός ‖ (*criminal*) ἐπιδρομή, γιουρούσι ‖ (*by police*) ἐπιδρομή, μπλόκος ‖ *vt* εἰσβάλλω εἰς, κάνω μπλόκο ‖ ~**er** *n* ἐπιδρομεύς.

rail [reil] *n* (*on stair*) κάγκελο, κιγκλίδωμα ‖ (*of ship*) σταθμίς, δρύφρακτον ‖ (*rail*) σιδηροτροχιά, γραμμή ‖ ~s npl (rail) τροχιά, γραμμές ‖ by ~ σιδηροδρομικῶς, μέ τραῖνο ‖ ~ing(s) n(pl) κάγκελλα, φράχτης ‖ ~road n (US), ~way n (Brit) σιδηρόδρομος, σιδηροδρομική γραμμή ‖ ~road or ~way station n σιδηροδρομικός σταθμός.

rain [rein] n βροχή ‖ vti βρέχω ‖ πέφτω σάν βροχή ‖ the ~s npl (ἐποχή) τῶν βροχῶν ‖ ~bow n οὐράνιον τόξον ‖ ~coat n ἀδιάβροχο ‖ ~drop n σταγόνα βροχῆς, σταλαματιά ‖ ~fall n βροχόπτωσις ‖ ~storm n καταιγίδα, κατακλυσμός ‖ ~y a (region) βροχερή (περιοχή) ‖ (day) βροχερή (ἡμέρα) ‖ (fig) ὥρα ἀνάγκης ‖ (season) ἐποχή τῶν βροχῶν.

raise [reiz] n (esp US: increase) αὔξησις (μισθοῦ) ‖ vt (build) (ἀν)ἐγείρω, στήνω ‖ (lift) σηκώνω, ὑψώνω, ἀνεβάζω ‖ (a question) προβάλλω, θέτω ‖ (doubts) ἐγείρω, προκαλῶ, γεννῶ ‖ (collect) ἐξευρίσκω, μαζεύω, συλλέγω ‖ (bring up) ἀνατρέφω, τρέφω.

raisin ['reizən] n σταφίδα.

rake [reik] n τσουγκράνα ‖ (dissolute person) ἔκλυτος, ἀκόλαστος ‖ vt (agr) μαζεύω μέ τσουγκράνα, σκαλίζω ‖ (with shot) καταπυροβολῶ, πλευροκοπῶ ‖ (search keenly) ἐξετάζω, ἐρευνῶ ‖ to ~ in, together etc vt μαζεύω.

rakish ['reikiʃ] a κομψός, ἐπιδεικτικός.

rally ['ræli] n (pol etc) συγκέντρωσις, συναγερμός ‖ (aut) ράλλυ ‖ (improvement) ἀνάκτησις, βελτίωσις ‖ vt συναθροίζω, συγκεντρώνω, συνάζω ‖ vi (health) συνέρχομαι, ἀναρρωνύω ‖ to ~ round vti συσπειρόμαι.

ram [ræm] n κριάρι ‖ (beam) ἔμβολον, κριός ‖ vt ἐμβολίζω, μπήζω, κτυπῶ ‖ (stuff) παραγεμίζω, χώνω.

ramble ['ræmbl] n περίπατος, περιπλάνησις ‖ vi κάνω βόλτες, περιφέρομαι ‖ (be delirious) μιλῶ ἀσυνάρτητα ‖ ~r n πλάνης, σουλατσαδόρος ‖ (plant) ἀναρριχομένη τριανταφυλλιά.

rambling ['ræmbliŋ] a (plant) ἀναρρηχιτικός, ἕρπων ‖ (speech) ἀσύνδετος, ἀσυνάρτητος.

ramification [ræmifi'keiʃən] n διακλάδωσις.

ramp [ræmp] n (incline) κλιτύς, πρανές, ἀνωφέρεια.

rampage [ræm'peidʒ] n: to be on the ~ vi (also ~) τά βάζω μέ ὅλο τόν κόσμο.

rampant ['ræmpənt] a (unchecked) ἀχαλίνωτος, ἐξαπλωμένος ‖ (on hind legs) ὄρθιος, συσπειρώμενος.

rampart ['ræmpɑːt] n ἔπαλξις, προμαχών, ντάπια.

ramshackle ['ræmʃækl] a ἑτοιμόρροπος, ἐρειπωμένος, ρημάδι.

ran [ræn] pt of run.

ranch [rɑːntʃ] n ἀγρόκτημα, ράντσο ‖ ~er n κτηματίας ‖ ἐργάτης σέ ράντσο.

rancid ['rænsid] a ταγγός, τσαγγός.

rancour, (US) rancor ['ræŋkə*] n μνησικακία, ἔχθρα.

random ['rændəm] a τυχαῖος ‖ n: at ~ στήν τύχη, στά κουτουρού.

randy ['rændi] a (lustful) ἀσελγής, λάγνος.

rang [ræŋ] pt of ring.

range [reindʒ] n (row, line) σειρά, ὁροσειρά ‖ (extent, series) ἔκτασις, σειρά, περιοχή ‖ (of gun) βεληνεκές, ἐμβέλεια ‖ (for shooting) πεδίον βολῆς, σκοπευτήριον ‖ (cooking stove) κουζίνα, μαγειρική συσκευή ‖ vt παρατάσσω, βάζω στή σειρά ‖ (roam) περιπλανῶμαι, περιφέρομαι ‖ vi (extend) ἐκτείνομαι, ἁπλώνομαι ‖ ~r n (of forest) δασάρχης, δασονόμος.

rank [ræŋk] n (row, line) στοῖχος, γραμμή ‖ (social position) (κοινωνική) τάξις ‖ (high position) ἀνωτέρα θέσις, βαθμός ‖ vi (of place) κατατάσσομαι, ἔρχομαι ‖ a (strong-smelling) κάκοσμος, τσαγγός ‖ (extreme) πλήρης, τέλειος, ἀπόλυτος ‖ the ~s npl (mil) οἱ στρατιῶτες, φαντάροι ‖ the ~ and file (fig) ὁ ἁπλός λαός.

rankle ['ræŋkl] vi (cause pain) μένω στό μυαλό, μένω στήν καρδιά.

ransack ['rænsæk] vt λεηλατῶ, κάνω ἄνω κάτω, ψάχνω καλά.

ransom ['rænsəm] n λύτρα ‖ to hold s.o. to ~ ζητῶ λύτρα, χαρατσώνω (κάποιον).

rant [rænt] vi φωνασκῶ, οὐρλιάζω ‖ ~ing n στόμφος, φωνασκία.

rap [ræp] n κτύπημα, κτύπος, κρότος ‖ vt κρούω, κτυπῶ.

rape [reip] n (lit) βιασμός ‖ (fig) ἀπαγωγή, κλέψιμο ‖ vt (woman) βιάζω.

rapid ['ræpid] a ταχύς, γρήγορος ‖ ~s npl μικρός καταρράκτης ‖ ~ity n ταχύτης ‖ ~ly ad ταχέως, γρήγορα, γοργά.

rapist ['reipist] n (esp US) βιαστής.

rapport [ræ'pɔː*] n (sympathy) συμπάθεια.

rapprochement [ræ'prɔʃmɑ̃ːŋ] n προσέγγισις.

rapt [ræpt] a ἐκστατικός, ἀπορροφημένος.

rapture ['ræptʃə*] n ἔκστασις, μεγάλη χαρά.

rapturous ['ræptʃərəs] a ἐκστατικος, ἐνθουσιώδης.

rare [reə*] a σπάνιος, ἀσυνήθης, ἀραιός ‖ (especially good) θαυμάσιος, σπουδαῖος ‖ (in cooking) μισοψημένος, σαινιάν ‖ ~fied a (air, atmosphere) ἀραιός, ἀραιωμένος ‖ ~ly ad σπάνια, σπανίως.

rarity ['reəriti] n σπάνιον πρᾶγμα ‖ (scarcity) σπανιότης.

rascal ['rɑːskəl] n παλιάνθρωπος, μασκαράς, μαγκάκι.

rash [ræʃ] a παράτολμος, ἀπερίσκεπτος ‖ n ἐξάνθημα.

rasher ['ræʃə*] n ψιλή φέτα μπέϊκον.

rashly ['ræʃli] ad ἀπερίσκεπτα, ἀσυλλόγιστα.

rashness ['ræʃnis] n ἀπερισκεψία, ἀμυαλιά.

raspberry ['ra:zbəri] n σμέουρο, φραμπουάζ, βατόμουρο.

rasping ['ra:spiŋ] a (noise) (ἦχος) λίμας, ὀξύς, στριγγιά.

rat [ræt] n (animal) ἀρουραῖος, ποντικός.

ratable ['reitəbl] a: ~ **value** φορολογήσιμον τεκμαρτὸν ἐνοίκιον (ἀκινήτου).

ratchet ['rætʃit] n δνυξ, ἀναστολεύς, κασπάνια.

rate [reit] n (proportion) ἀναλογία, ἀνάλογον ποσόν, ἀνάλογος ἀριθμός ‖ (price) ποσοστόν, τόκος, ὕψος, τιμή ‖ (speed) ρυθμός, ταχύτης ‖ vt ἐκτιμῶ, ταξινομῶ ‖ ~s npl (Brit) τοπικὸς φόρος, εἰσφορά ‖ at any ~ ὁπωσδήποτε, ἐν πάσει περιπτώσει ‖ at this ~ ἔτσι ‖ ~ of exchange n τιμὴ συναλλάγματος ‖ ~payer n φορολογούμενος ‖ see first.

rather ['ra:ðə*] ad μᾶλλον (ἤ), καλύτερα (παρά) ‖ (somewhat) λίγο, κάπως, μᾶλλον, σχετικά.

ratification [rætifi'keiʃən] n (ἐπι)κύρωσις.

ratify ['rætifai] vt (ἐπι)κυρῶ, ἐγκρίνω.

rating ['reitiŋ] n (classification) ἐκτίμησις, τάξις ‖ (naut) μέλος πληρώματος, εἰδικότης.

ratio ['reiʃiəu] n λόγος, ἀναλογία.

ration ['ræʃən] n (usually pl) μερίς, σιτηρέσιον, τροφή ‖ vt περιορίζω, ἐπιβάλλω μερίδες.

rational ['ræʃənl] a λογικός ‖ ~e [ræʃə'na:l] n λογικὴ ἐξήγησις, λογικὴ βάσις ‖ ~ization n ὀρθολογισμός ‖ ~ize vt ὀρθολογίζομαι, ὀργανώνω ὀρθολογικῶς ‖ ~ly ad λογικῶς, λογικά.

rationing ['ræʃniŋ] n καθορισμὸς μερίδων, διανομὴ διὰ δελτίου.

rattle ['rætl] n κρότος, κροταλισμός ‖ (toy) ροκάνα, κρόταλον ‖ vi κροταλίζω, κροτῶ ‖ ~snake n κροταλίας.

raucous ['rɔ:kəs] a βραχνός ‖ ~ly ad βραχνά.

ravage ['rævidʒ] vt ἐρημώνω, ἀφανίζω, ρημάζω ‖ ~s npl (of time etc) φθορὰ τοῦ χρόνου.

rave [reiv] vi παραληρῶ, παραμιλῶ ‖ (rage) μαίνομαι, οὐρλιάζω.

raven ['reivn] n κοράκι, κόρακας.

ravenous ['rævənəs] a (hungry) πεινασμένος, λιμασμένος.

ravine [rə'vi:n] n φαράγγι

raving ['reiviŋ] a: ~ **lunatic** μανιακός, παράφρων.

ravioli [rævi'əuli] n ραβιόλια.

ravish ['ræviʃ] vt ἀπάγω, κλέβω, βιάζω ‖ ~ing a γοητευτικός, μαγευτικός.

raw [rɔ:] a (uncooked) ὠμός, ἄψητος ‖ (not manufactured) ἀκατέργαστος ‖ (tender) εὐαίσθητος, ματωμένος ‖ (inexperienced) ἄξεστος, ἀτζαμής ‖ ~ **material** n πρῶτες ὕλες.

ray [rei] n ἀκτίς, ἀχτίδα.

rayon ['reiɔn] n ρεγιόν, τεχνητὴ μέταξα.

raze [reiz] vt ἰσοπεδώνω, κατεδαφίζω, γκρεμίζω.

razor ['reizə*] n ξυράφι ‖ ~ **blade** n ξυριστικὴ λεπίδα.

re- [ri:] prefix ἀντι-, ἀνά-, ξανά-.

reach [ri:tʃ] n ἔκτασις, ἄπλωμα, τέντωμα (χειρός) ‖ (distance) ἐντὸς βολῆς, κοντά, πλησίον ‖ vt (ἐκ)τείνω, ἁπλώνω, τεντώνω ‖ φθάνω, ἐγγίζω ‖ vi (ἐπ)εκτείνομαι ‖ to ~ **out** vi ἁπλώνω (τὸ χέρι).

react [ri:'ækt] vi ἀντιδρῶ ‖ ~**ion** n ἀντίδρασις ‖ ~**ionary** a ἀντιδραστικός ‖ ~**or** n ἀντιδραστήρ.

read [ri:d] (irreg v) n ἀνάγνωσις, διάβασμα ‖ vti διαβάζω, ἀναγιγνώσκω ‖ (aloud) διαβάζω δυνατά ‖ (understand) ἑρμηνεύω, δεικνύω ‖ (find in book) διαβάζομαι ‖ ~**able** a ἀναγνώσιμος, ποὺ διαβάζεται ‖ ~**er** n ἀναγνώστης ‖ (book) ἀναγνωστικόν ‖ ~**ership** n (of newspaper etc) σύνολον ἀναγνωστῶν.

readily ['redili] ad πρόθυμα, ἀδίστακτα, εὔκολα.

readiness ['redinis] n προθυμία ‖ (being ready) ἑτοιμότης.

reading ['ri:diŋ] n ἀνάγνωσις, διάβασμα ‖ ~ **lamp** n λάμπα τοῦ τραπεζιοῦ ‖ ~ **room** n ἀναγνωστήριον.

readjust ['ri:ə'dʒʌst] vt ἀναπροσαρμόζω, διορθώνω, σιάζω ‖ ~**ment** n διόρθωσις, σιάξιμο.

ready ['redi] a ἕτοιμος ‖ (willing) πρόθυμος, διατεθειμένος ‖ (condition) ἕτοιμος, γινόμενος ‖ (quick, facile) ταχύς, γρήγορος, εὔκολος ‖ (available) πρόχειρος ‖ ad τελείως ‖ n: at the ~ ἕτοιμος νά ‖ ~-**made** a ἕτοιμος ‖ ~ **reckoner** n πίνακες λογιστικῶν ὑπολογισμῶν.

real [riəl] a πραγματικός, ἀληθινός ‖ ~ **estate** n ἀκίνητος περιουσία, οἰκόπεδα ‖ ~**ism** n πραγματισμός, ρεαλισμός ‖ ~**ist** n πραγματιστής, ρεαλιστής ‖ ~**istic** a ρεαλιστικός ‖ ~**istically** ad ρεαλιστικά ‖ ~**ity** [ri:'æliti] n πραγματικότης, ἀλήθεια ‖ **in** ~**ity** πράγματι, πραγματικά ‖ ~**ization** n κατανόησις, σαφὴς ἀντίληψις ‖ (fulfilment) πραγματοποίησις ‖ ~**ize** vt (understand) κατανοῶ, ἀντιλαμβάνομαι, καταλαβαίνω ‖ (bring about) πραγματοποιῶ ‖ ~**ly** ad πραγματικά, ἀληθινά, ὄχι δά.

realm [relm] n σφαίρα, δικαιοδοσία ‖ (kingdom) βασίλειον.

ream [ri:m] n δεσμὶς χάρτου γραφῆς.

reap [ri:p] vt θερίζω ‖ (harvest) συγκομίζω, μαζεύω ‖ ~**er** n (machine) θεριστικὴ μηχανή.

reappear ['ri:ə'piə*] vi ἐπανεμφανίζομαι, ξαναφαίνομαι ‖ ~**ance** n ἐπανεμφάνισις, ἐπάνοδος.

reapply ['ri:ə'plai] vi (+ to, for) ξαναϋποβάλλω (αἴτησιν).

reappoint ['riːə'pɔint] *vt* ἐπαναδιορίζω.

reappraisal ['riːə'preizəl] *n* ἐπανεκτίμησις.

rear [riə*] *a* ὀπίσθιος, πισινός ‖ *n* νῶτα, ὀπίσθια, ὀπισθοφυλακή ‖ *vt* (bring up) (ἀνα)τρέφω ‖ *vi* ἀνορθοῦμαι, σηκώνομαι σούζα ‖ ~-engined *a* (aut) μέ μηχανή πίσω ‖ ~guard *n* ὀπισθοφυλακή.

rearm ['riˈaːm] *vti* ἐπανεξοπλίζω, ἐπανεξοπλίζομαι ‖ ~ament *n* ἐπανεξοπλισμός.

rearrange ['riːə'reindʒ] *vt* τακτοποιῶ πάλιν, ξανασιάζω.

rear-view ['riəvjuː] *a*: ~ **mirror** κάτοπτρον ὁδηγήσεως.

reason ['riːzn] *n* (cause) λόγος, αἰτία ‖ (ability to think) λογικόν, λογική ‖ (judgment) κρίσις ‖ *vi* σκέπτομαι, συλλογίζομαι, συμπεραίνω ‖ ~able *a* λογικός, δίκαιος ‖ (fair) μετριοπαθής, μέτριος ‖ ~ably *ad* λογικά ‖ ~ed *a* (argument) αἰτιολογημένος, δικαιολογημένος ‖ ~ing *n* συλλογισμός, ἐπιχειρήματα.

reassemble ['riːə'sembl] *vt* ξανασυγκεντρώνω, συγκαλῶ ἐκ νέου ‖ (engine) ξαναμοντάρω.

reassert ['riːə'səːt] *vt* βεβαιῶ ἐκ νέου, ἐπιβεβαιῶ.

reassurance ['riːə'ʃuərəns] *n* ἐξασφάλισις, καθησύχασις, ἐνθάρρυνσις.

reassure ['riːə'ʃuə*] *vt* διαβεβαιώνω, ἀναθαρρύνω, καθησυχάζω.

reassuring ['riːə'ʃuəriŋ] *a* καθησυχαστικός, ἐνθαρρυντικός.

reawakening ['riːə'weikniŋ] *n* ἀφύπνισις, ξαναζωντάνεμα.

rebate ['riːbeit] *n* ἔκπτωσις.

rebel ['rebl] *n* ἀντάρτης, ἐπαναστάτης ‖ *a* ἐπαναστατημένος, ἀνταρτικός ‖ ~lion [ri'beliən] *n* ἀνταρσία, ρεμπελιό ‖ ~lious *a* ἀνταρτικός, ἀνυπότακτος.

rebirth ['riː'bəːθ] *n* ἀναγέννησις.

rebound [ri'baund] *vi* ἀναπηδῶ ‖ ['riːbaund] *n* ἀναπήδησις.

rebuff [ri'bʌf] *n* ἀπόκρουσις, ἄρνησις ‖ *vt* ἀποκρούω, ἀρνοῦμαι.

rebuild ['riː'bild] *vt* ἀνοικοδομῶ ‖ ~ing *n* ἀνοικοδόμησις.

rebuke [ri'bjuːk] *n* ἐπίπληξις, μομφή ‖ *vt* ἐπιπλήττω, ἐπιτιμῶ.

recalcitrant [ri'kælsitrənt] *a* ἀνυπάκουος, δυστροπῶν.

recall [ri'kɔːl] *vt* (call back) ἀνακαλῶ ‖ (remember) ξαναθυμίζω, ξαναθυμᾶμε ‖ (withdraw) ἀνακαλῶ.

recant [ri'kænt] *vi* ἀνακαλῶ, ἀναιρῶ, ἀναθεωρῶ.

recap ['riːkæp] *vti* ξαναβουλώνω.

recapture ['riː'kæptʃə*] *vt* ἀνακτῶ, ἀνακαταλαμβάνω, ξαναπιάνω.

recede [ri'siːd] *vi* ἀποσύρομαι, ὑποχωρῶ, τραβιέμαι.

receipt [ri'siːt] *n* ἀπόδειξις παραλαβῆς ‖

(receiving) λῆψις, παραλαβή ‖ ~s *npl* εἰσπράξεις, ἔσοδα.

receive [ri'siːv] *vt* λαμβάνω ‖ (welcome) (ὑπο)δέχομαι ‖ ~r *n* (tel) ἀκουστικόν.

recent ['riːsnt] *a* πρόσφατος, νέος ‖ ~ly *ad* προσφάτως, πρόσφατα.

receptacle [ri'septəkl] *n* δοχεῖον.

reception [ri'sepʃən] *n* (welcome) ὑποδοχή ‖ (party) δεξίωσις ‖ (at hotel etc) γραφεῖον ὑποδοχῆς ‖ ~ist *n* ὑπάλληλος ἐπὶ τῆς ὑποδοχῆς.

receptive [ri'septiv] *a* (ἐπι)δεικτικός.

recess [ri'ses] *n* (interval) διακοπή, διάλειμμα ‖ (in wall) κοίλωμα, ἐσοχή, βαθούλωμα ‖ (inner place) μυχός, μυστικόν μέρος.

recharge ['riː'tʃaːdʒ] *vt* (battery) ἀναφορτίζω, ξαναγεμίζω.

recipe ['resipi] *n* συνταγή.

recipient [ri'sipiənt] *n* δέκτης, λήπτης, παραλήπτης.

reciprocal [ri'siprəkəl] *a* ἀμοιβαῖος, ἀντίστροφος.

reciprocate [ri'siprəkeit] *vt* ἀνταποδίδω, ἐναλλάσσω.

recital [ri'saitl] *n* (mus) ρεσιτάλ.

recitation [resi'teiʃən] *n* ἀπαγγελία.

recite [ri'sait] *vt* ἀπαγγέλλω, ἀποστηθίζω ‖ (tell one by one) ἐξιστορῶ, ἀπαριθμῶ.

reckless ['reklis] *a* ἀδιάφορος, ἀπρόσεκτος, ἀπερίσκεπτος ‖ ~ly *ad* ἀπερισκέπτως, παράτολμα ‖ ~ness *n* τολμηρότης, ἀπερισκεψία.

reckon ['rekən] *vt* (count) ὑπολογίζω, λογαριάζω, μετρῶ ‖ (consider) ἐκτιμῶ, λογαριάζω ‖ *vi* στηρίζομαι, ὑπολογίζω ‖ to ~ on *vt* στηρίζομαι σέ, ὑπολογίζω ‖ ~ing *n* ὑπολογισμός.

reclaim [ri'kleim] *vt* (land) ἐκχερσώνω, ἀποξηραίνω.

reclamation [reklə'meiʃən] *n* ἐγγειοβελτίωσις, ἀποξήρανσις.

recline [ri'klain] *vi* ξαπλώνω, πλαγιάζω, ἀκουμπῶ.

reclining [ri'klainiŋ] *a* πλαγιαστός, ξαπλωμένος, κεκλιμένος.

recluse [ri'kluːs] *n* ἐρημίτης.

recognition [rekəg'niʃən] *n* ἀναγνώρισις.

recognizable ['rekəgnaizəbl] *a* ἀναγνωρίσιμος.

recognize ['rekəgnaiz] *vt* ἀναγνωρίζω ‖ (admit) ὁμολογῶ, παραδέχομαι.

recoil [ri'kɔil] *n* ἀναπήδησις, ὀπισθοδρόμησις ‖ *vi* ἀποστρέφομαι, μαζεύομαι, ἐξανίσταμαι ‖ ἀναπηδῶ, ὀπισθοδρομῶ, κλωτσῶ.

recollect [rekə'lekt] *vt* ἐνθυμοῦμαι, ἀναπολῶ ‖ ~ion *n* ἀνάμνησις, μνημονικόν.

recommend [rekə'mend] *vt* συνιστῶ, ἐμπιστεύομαι ‖ ~ation *n* (advice) σύστασις ‖ προσόν.

recompense ['rekəmpens] *n* (ἀντ)ἀμοιβή,

ἀποζημιώσις ‖ *vt* ανταμείβω, ἀποζημιώνω.

reconcilable ['rekənsailəbl] *a* εὐσυμβίβαστος, διαλλακτικός.

reconcile ['rekənsail] *vt* (*make agree*) συμβιβάζω ‖ (*make friendly*) συμφιλιώνω.

reconciliation [rekənsili'eiʃən] *n* συμφιλίωσις, συμβιβασμός.

reconditioned ['ri:kən'diʃənd] *a* ἐπισκευασμένος, ἀνακαινισθείς.

reconnaissance [ri'kɔnisəns] *n* κατόπτευσις, ἀναγνώρισις, ἐξερεύνησις.

reconnoitre, (*US*) **reconnoiter** [rekə'nɔitə*] *vti* κατοπτεύω, ἀναγνωρίζω, ἐξερευνῶ.

reconsider ['ri:kən'sidə*] *vti* ἀναθεωρῶ, ἐπανεξετάζω.

reconstitute ['ri:'kɔnstitju:t] *vt* ἀναπαριστῶ.

reconstruct ['ri:kən'strʌkt] *vt* ἀνοικοδομῶ, ἀνασυγκροτῶ ‖ ~ion *n* ἀνοικοδόμησις, ἀνασυγκρότησις.

record ['rekɔ:d] *n* ἀναγραφή, καταγραφή, σημείωσις ‖ (*disc*) δίσκος, πλάκα ‖ (*best performance*) πρωτάθλημα, ρεκόρ, ἐπίδοσις ‖ *a* (*time*) μέ μεγάλη ταχύτητα, σημειώνουσα ρεκόρ ‖ [ri'kɔ:d] *vt* (*set down*) καταγράφω, ἀναγράφω ‖ (*music etc*) ἠχογραφῶ, ἐγγράφω ‖ ~ed *a* (*music*) ἠχογραφημένος ‖ ~er *n* μηχάνημα ἐγγραφῆς, μαγνητόγραφο ‖ ~ holder *n* (*sport*) πρωταθλητής ‖ ~ing *n* (*music*) ἠχογράφησις ‖ ~ player *n* πικάπ.

recount ['ri:kaunt] *n* νέα καταμέτρησις ‖ [ri'kaunt] *vt* ξαναμετρῶ ‖ (*tell in detail*) ἀφηγοῦμαι, ἐξιστορῶ.

recoup [ri'ku:p] *vt* ἀποζημιώνω, ξαναπέρνω.

recourse [ri'kɔ:s] *n* καταφύγιον, ἔκκλησις.

recover [ri'kʌvə*] *vt* (ἐπ)ανακτῶ, ξαναβρίσκω ‖ *vi* ἀνακτῶ (τήν ὑγείαν μου), θεραπεύομαι ‖ ~y *n* ἀνάκτησις, ἀνεύρεσις, βρέσιμο ‖ ἀνάρρωσις.

recreate ['ri:krieit] *vt* διασκεδάζω.

recreation [rekri'eiʃən] *n* ἀναψυχή, διασκέδασις ‖ ~al *a* διασκεδαστικός.

recrimination [rikrimi'neiʃən] *n* ἀντέγκλησις, ἀντικατηγορία.

recruit [ri'kru:t] *n* νεοσύλλεκτος ‖ *vt* στρατολογῶ ‖ ~ing office *n* γραφεῖον στρατολογικόν ‖ ~ment *n* στρατολογία.

rectangle ['rektæŋgl] *n* ὀρθογώνιον.

rectangular [rek'tæŋgjulə*] *a* ὀρθογώνιος.

rectify ['rektifai] *vt* ἐπανορθώνω, διορθώνω.

rectory ['rektəri] *n* (*eccl*) πρεσβυτέριον, ἐφημερεῖον.

recuperate [ri'ku:pəreit] *vi* ἀναλαμβάνω, ἀναρρωνύω.

recur [ri'kə:*] *vi* ἐπανέρχομαι, συμβαίνω πάλιν ‖ ~rence *n* ἐπανάληψις ‖ ~rent *a* περιοδικός, ἐπαναλαμβανόμενος.

red [red] *n* (*colour*) κόκκινο ‖ (*Communist*) κομμουνιστής, ἀριστερός ‖ *a* κόκκινος, ἐρυθρός ‖ in the ~ ἔλλειμα ‖ R~ Cross

n 'Ερυθρός Σταυρός ‖ ~den *vti* κοκκινίζω ‖ ~dish *a* κοκκινωπός.

redecorate ['ri:'dekəreit] *vt* κάνω καινούργια διακόσμησι.

redecoration ['ri:dekə'reiʃən] *n* καινούργια διακόσμησις.

redeeming [ri'di:miŋ] *a* (*virtue, feature*) ἀντισταθμίζων, καλύπτων.

red-haired ['red'hɛəd] *a* κοκκινομάλλης.

red-handed ['red'hændid] *a* ἐπ' αὐτοφώρω στά πράσα.

redhead ['redhed] *n* κοκκινομάλλα.

red herring ['red'heriŋ] *n* (*fig*) ξεγέλασμα ἀλλαγή κουβέντας.

red-hot ['red'hɔt] *a* ἐρυθροπυρωμένος ‖ (*fig*) φανατικός, ἔνθερμος.

redirect ['ri:dai'rekt] *vt* (*mail*) ἀπευθύνω εἰς νέαν διεύθυνσιν.

rediscovery ['ri:dis'kʌvəri] *n* ἐκ νέου ἀνακάλυψις.

redistribute ['ri:dis'tribju:t] *vt* ἀνακατα-'έμω.

red-letter ['red'letə*] *a*: ~ day ἡμέρα εὐτυχῶν γεγονότων, ἀξιομνημόνευτος ἡμέρα.

redness ['rednis] *n* κοκκινίλα ‖ κοκκινάδα.

redo ['ri:'du:] *vt* ξανακάνω.

redouble [ri:'dʌbl] *vt* (ἀνα)διπλασιάζω.

red tape ['red'teip] *n* γραφειοκρατία.

reduce [ri'dju:s] *vt* (*decrease*) ἐλαττώνω, μικραίνω, περιορίζω, ἀδυνατίζω ‖ (*lower*) ὑποβιβάζω, κατεβάζω ‖ (*change state*) μεταβάλλω, σχηματίζω, ἀπλοποιῶ ‖ ~d *a* (*price*) μειωμένη (τιμή).

reduction [ri'dʌkʃən] *n* ἐλάττωσις, σμίκρυνσις ‖ (*in price*) ἔκπτωσις.

redundancy [ri'dʌndənsi] *n* περίσσεια, πλεόνασμα.

redundant [ri'dʌndənt] *a* πλεονάζων, περιττός.

reed [ri:d] *n* καλάμι ‖ (*of clarinet etc*) γλωττίς, γλωσσίδι.

reef [ri:f] *n* (*at sea*) ὕφαλος, ξέρα.

reek [ri:k] *vi* ἀναδίδω κακήν ὀσμήν, βρομάω.

reel [ri:l] *n* (*for rope*) ἀνέμη ‖ (*for cotton, film etc*) πηνίον, καρούλι, μασούρι ‖ (*dance*) ζωηρός (σκωτικός) χορός ‖ *vi* τυλίγω ‖ (*stagger*) τρικλίζω, ζαλίζομαι.

re-election ['ri:i'lekʃən] *n* ἐπανεκλογή.

re-engage ['ri:in'geidʒ] *vt* ξανασυμπλέκω ‖ ἀναπροσλαμβάνω.

re-enter ['ri:'entə*] *vi* ξαναμπαίνω.

re-entry ['ri:'entri] *n* ἐπάνοδος, ξαναμπάσιμο.

re-examine ['ri:ig'zæmin] *vt* ἐπανεξετάζω.

re-export ['ri:'ekspɔ:t] *vt* ἐπανεξάγω.

ref [ref] *n* (*col: abbr of referee*) διαιτητής.

refectory [ri'fektəri] *n* τραπεζαρία (μοναστηρίου).

refer [ri'fə:*] *vt* παραπέμπω ‖ to ~ to *vt* ἀναφέρομαι εἰς ‖ συμβουλεύομαι.

referee [refə'ri:] *n* διαιτητής ‖ (*for job*

application) ὑπέγγυος, ἐγγυητής | *vt*
(*sport*) διαιτητεύω.

reference ['refrəns] *n* ἀναφορά | (*in book
etc*) παραπομπή | (*of character*) πιστο-
ποιητικόν, σύστασις | (*person referred
to*) ὁ δίδων τήν σύστασίν, ὁ ἐγγυητής |
(*allusion*) μνεία, ὑπαινιγμός | ~ **book** *n*
βιβλίον ὁδηγός, σύμβουλος.

referendum [refə'rendəm] *n* δημοψήφισμα.

refill ['ri:fil] *n* (*for pen etc*) ἀνταλλακτικόν.

refine [ri'fain] *vt* καθαρίζω, διυλίζω,
ραφινάρω | (*make finer*) ἐκλεπτύνω,
ἐξευγενίζω | ~**d** *a* (*person*) λεπτός,
καλλιεργημένος | ~**ment** *n* ἐξευγενι-
σμός, λεπτή διάκρισις | ~**ry** *n* διϋλι-
στήριον.

reflect [ri'flekt] *vt* ἀντανακλῶ | *vi* (*medi-
tate*) σκέπτομαι, συλλογίζομαι, μελετῶ
| ~**ion** *n* (ἀντ)ἀνάκλασις | (*thought*)
σκέψις | ~**or** *n* ἀνακλαστήρ, ἀνταυγα-
στής, κάτοπτρον.

reflex ['ri:fleks] *a* (*involuntary*) (ἀντ)ἀνα-
κλαστικός | ~**ive** *a* (*gram*) αὐτοπαθής.

reform [ri'fo:m] *n* μεταρρύθμισις, ἀποκατά-
στασις, ἀνασχηματισμός | *vt* μεταρ-
ρυθμίζω, σχηματίζω ἐκ νέου, ἀποκα-
θιστῶ, ἀναμορφώνω | **the R~ation** *n*
ἡ Μεταρρύθμισις | ~**er** *n* ἀναμορφωτής,
μεταρρυθμιστής.

refrain [ri'frein] *vi* (+ *from*) ἀπέχω, συγκρατοῦμαι.

refresh [ri'fref] *vt* ἀναζωογονῶ, δροσίζω,
ὀνθυμίζω | ~ **er course** *n* ἐπανάλιψις,
μετεκπαίδευσις | ~**ing** *a* ἀναψυκτικός,
ἀναζωογονητικός, δροσιστικός | ~-
ments *npl* (*food, drink*) ἀναψυκτικά.

refrigeration [rifridʒə'reiʃən] *n* (κατά)-
ψυξις.

refrigerator [ri'fridʒəreitə*] *n* ψυγεῖον.

refuel ['ri:'fjuəl] *vti* ἀνεφοδιάζομαι (μέ
καύσιμα) | ~**ling** *n* ἀνεφοδιασμός εἰς
καύσιμα.

refuge ['refju:dʒ] *n* καταφύγιον, καταφυγή,
προστασία | ~**e** [refju'dʒi:] *n* πρόσφυγας.

refund ['ri:fʌnd] *n* ἐπιστροφή, ἀπόδοσις |
[ri'fʌnd] *vt* ἐπιστρέφω (χρήματα).

refurbish ['ri:'fə:biʃ] *vt* (*decorate*) ἀνακαινίζω, φρεσκάρω.

refurnish ['ri:'fə:niʃ] *vt* ἐπιπλώνω ἐκ νέου.

refusal [ri'fju:zəl] *n* ἄρνησις, ἀποποίησις.

refuse ['refju:s] *n* ἀπορρίμματα, σκουπίδια |
[ri'fju:z] *vti* ἀρνοῦμαι, ἀποποιοῦμαι,
ἀπορρίπτω.

refute [ri'fju:t] *vt* ἀνασκευάζω, ἀνατρέπω.

regain [ri'gein] *vt* ἐπανακτῶ.

regal ['ri:gəl] *a* βασιλικός | ~**ia** [ri'geiliə]
n (*royal*) βασιλικά κειμήλια.

regard [ri'ga:d] *n* (*respect*) ἐκτίμησις,
σεβασμός | *vt* (*consider*) θεωρῶ | ~**s** *npl*
(*greetings*) χαιρετισμοί, χαιρετίσματα |
~**ing, as** ~**s** ὅσον ἀφορᾷ, σχετικά μέ |
as ~**s, with** ~ **to** ὡς πρός, ὅσο γιά |

regatta [ri'gætə] *n* λεμβοδρομία.

regency ['ri:dʒənsi] *n* ἀντιβασιλεία.

regent ['ri:dʒənt] *n* ἀντιβασιλεύς.

régime [rei'ʒi:m] *n* καθεστώς.

regiment ['redʒimənt] *n* σύνταγμα | ~**al** *a*
τοῦ συντάγματος | ~**ation** *n* ὀργάνωσις
εἰς πειθαρχημένα τμήματα.

region ['ri:dʒən] *n* περιοχή | ~**al** *a* τοπικός,
περιφερειακός] ~**al development** *n*
περιφερειακή ἀνάπτυξις.

register ['redʒistə*] *n* κατάλογος, ληξι-
αρχικόν βιβλίον, μητρῶον , *vt* κατα-
γράφω, ἐγγράφω | (*write down*) σημει-
ώνω | *vi* (*at hotel*) ἐγγράφομαι | (*make
impression*) δεικνύω | ~**ed** *a* (*design*)
κατατεθειμένον | (*letter*) συστημένον
γράμμα.

registrar [redʒis'tra:*] *n* ληξίαρχος,
γραμματεύς.

registration [redʒis'treiʃən] *n* (*act*) καταγραφή, ἐγγραφή . (*number*) ἀριθμός
ἐγγραφῆς.

registry ['redʒistri] *n* ληξιαρχεῖον | ~
office *n* (*for civil marriage*) ληξιαρχεῖον.

regret [ri'gret] *n* λύπη, μετάνοια | *vt*
λυποῦμαι, μετανοῶ | ~**fully** *ad* μέ
λύπην, μέ πόνον | ~**table** *a* ἀξιοθρήνη-
τος, ἀξιολύπητος, λυπηρός.

regroup ['ri:'gru:p] *vti* ἀνασυγκροτῶ,
ἀνακατατάσσω.

regular ['regjulə*] *a* τακτικός, κανονικός,
συνήθης | (*not varying*) ὁμαλός | *n*
(*client etc*) τακτικός (πελάτης) | ~**ity** *n*
κανονικότης, ὁμαλότης | ~**ly** *ad* τα-
κτικά, κανονικά.

regulate ['regjuleit] *vt* κανονίζω, τακτοποιῶ, ρυθμίζω.

regulation [regju'leiʃən] *n* (δια)κανονισμός
| (*control*) ρύθμισις.

rehabilitation ['ri:əbili'teiʃən] *n* ἀποκατάστασις, παλινόρθωσις.

rehash ['ri:'hæʃ] *vt* (*col*) ξαναδουλεύω,
διασκευάζω.

rehearsal [ri'hə:səl] *n* δοκιμή, πρόβα.

rehearse [ri'hə:s] *vt* (*practise*) κάνω δοκιμές,
προβάρω.

reign [rein] *n* (*period*) βασιλεία | *vi* βασι-
λεύω, ἄρχω | ~**ing** *a* (*monarch*) βασι-
λεύων | (*champion*) ἐπικρατῶν.

reimburse [ri:im'bə:s] *vt* ἐπιστρέφω
(χρήματα), ἀποζημιώνω.

rein [rein] *n* ἡνία, χαλινός.

reindeer ['reindiə*] *n* τάρανδος.

reinforce [ri:in'fo:s] *vt* ἐνισχύω, δυναμώνω
| ~**d** *a* (*concrete*) ὡπλισμένον σκυροκο-
νίαμα, μπετόν ἀρμέ | ~**ment** *n* ἐνίσχυσις
| ~**ments** *npl* (*mil*) ἐνισχύσεις.

reinstate ['ri:in'steit] *vt* παλινορθῶ, ἀποκαθιστῶ, ἐπανεγκαθιστῶ.

reissue ['ri:'ifju:] *vt* ἐπανεκδίδω.

reiterate [ri:'itəreit] *vt* ἐπαναλαμβάνω.

reject [ri'dʒekt] vt ἀπορρίπτω, ἀποκρούω ‖ ['ri:dʒekt] n ἀπόρριμα, σκάρτο ‖ ~ion n ἀπόρριψις.

rejoice [ri'dʒɔis] vi χαίρομαι, χαίρω.

relapse [ri'læps] n ὑποτροπή.

relate [ri'leit] vt διηγοῦμαι, ἐξιστορῶ ‖ (connect) συσχετίζω ‖ ~d a (subjects) σχετιζόμενος, σχετικῶς μέ ‖ (people) (+ to) συγγενής.

relating [ri'leitiŋ] prep: ~ to σχετικός μέ, ἀφορῶν (εἰς).

relation [ri'leiʃən] n (of family) συγγενής ‖ (connection) σχέσις, συγγένεια ‖ ~ship n συγγένεια, σχέσις.

relative ['relətiv] n συγγενής ‖ a ἀναφορικός, σχετικός ‖ ~ly ad σχετικά ‖ ~ pronoun n ἀναφορική ἀντωνυμία.

relax [ri'læks] vi χαλαρώνω, λασκάρω ‖ (rest) ἀνακουφίζω ‖ vt χαλαρούμαι, ἀναπαύομαι, ξεκουράζομαι ‖ ~ation n ἀναψυχή, διασκέδασις ‖ ~ed a χαλαρός, λάσκος ‖ ~ing a ξεκουραστικός.

relay ['ri:lei] n (sport) σκυταλοδρομία ‖ vt (message) ἀναμεταδίδω.

release [ri'li:s] n (relief) ἀπαλλαγή, ἀπόλυσις, ἀποφυλάκισις ‖ (device) διακόπτης ‖ vt ἀπελευθερώνω ‖ (prisoner) ἀπολύω, ἀποφυλακίζω ‖ (grip) χαλαρῶ, λασκάρω, ἀπεμπλέκω ‖ (report, news) θέτω εἰς κυκλοφορίαν, ἐπιτρέπω δημοσίευσιν.

relegate ['religeit] vt (put down) ὑποβιβάζω.

relent [ri'lent] vi κάμπτομαι, μαλακώνω ‖ ~less a ἀδιάλλακτος, ἀμείλικτος, ἀνηλεής ‖ ~lessly ad ἀλύπητα, σκληρά, ἀδιάκοπα.

relevance ['relɔvəns] n σχετικότης, ὀρθότης, καταλληλότης.

relevant ['relɔvənt] a σχετικός, ἔχων σχέσιν.

reliability [rilaiɔ'biliti] n ἀξιοπιστία.

reliable [ri'laiəbl] a ἀξιόπιστος.

reliably [ri'laiəbli] ad ἀσφαλῶς, σίγουρα.

reliance [ri'laiəns] n ἐμπιστοσύνη, πεποίθησις.

relic ['relik] n ἀπομεινάρι, ἐνθύμιον ‖ (of saint) λείψανον.

relief [ri'li:f] n (from pain etc) ἀνακούφισις, ξελάφρωμα ‖ (help) περίθαλψις, βοήθεια, ἐνίσχυσις ‖ (from duty) ἀντικατάστασις, ἀλλαγή ‖ (design) ἀνάγλυφον ‖ (distinctness) προβολή, εὐδιακρισία.

relieve [ri'li:v] vt (pain etc) ἀνακουφίζω, ξελαφρώνω ‖ (bring help) βοηθῶ, περιθάλπω ‖ (take place of) ἀντικαθιστῶ, ἀπαλλάσσω ‖ to ~ s.o. of sth παίρνω, ἀπαλλάσσω.

religion [ri'lidʒən] n θρησκεία, θρήσκευμα.

religious [ri'lidʒəs] a θρησκευτικός, εὐσεβής ‖ ~ly ad μέ εὐσέβειαν ‖ μέ ἀκρίβειαν.

reline ['ri:'lain] vt (brakes) ἐπενδύω ἐκ νέου.

relinquish [ri'liŋkwiʃ] vt παραιτοῦμαι, ἐγκαταλείπω.

relish ['reliʃ] n (sauce) καρύκευμα, σάλτσα ‖ vt ἀπολαμβάνω, τρώγω εὐχάριστα.

relive ['ri:'liv] vt ξαναζῶ.

reload ['ri:'lɔud] vt ξαναγεμίζω.

reluctance [ri'lʌktəns] n ἀπροθυμία, ἀκουσιότης.

reluctant [ri'lʌktənt] a ἀπρόθυμος ‖ ~ly ad μέ τό ζόρι, μέ τό στανιό.

rely [ri'lai] to ~ on vt βασίζομαι, στηρίζομαι, ἐμπιστεύομαι.

remain [ri'mein] vi (be left) ἀπομένω, ἀπολείπομαι ‖ (stay) παραμένω, (δια)μένω ‖ ~der n ὑπόλοιπον ‖ ~ing a (ἀπο)μένων, ὑπόλοιπος ‖ ~s npl ὑπολείμματα, ἐρείπια, λείψανα.

remand [ri'ma:nd] n: on ~ παραπομπή (κατηγορουμένου) ‖ vt: to ~ in custody προφυλακίζω.

remark [ri'ma:k] n παρατήρησις, σημείωσις ‖ vt (say) λέγω ‖ (notice) παρατηρῶ ‖ ~able a ἀξιοσημείωτος, ἀσυνήθης ‖ ~ably ad ἀξιόλογα, ἐξαιρετικά.

remarry ['ri:'mæri] vi ξαναπαντρεύομαι.

remedial [ri'mi:diɔl] a θεραπευτικός.

remedy ['remɔdi] n θεραπεία, φάρμακον, γιατρικό ‖ vt θεραπεύω, διορθώνω.

remember [ri'membɔ*] vt ἐνθυμοῦμαι, θυμᾶμαι ‖ (give regards) δίνω χαιρετισμούς εἰς.

remembrance [ri'membrəns] n ἀνάμνησις, μνήμη.

remind [ri'maind] vt ὑπενθυμίζω, θυμίζω ‖ ~er n κάτι πού θυμίζει, ἐνθύμημα.

reminisce [remi'nis] vi ἀναπολῶ, ξαναθυμᾶμαι ‖ ~nces npl ἀναμνήσεις, ἀπομνημονεύματα ‖ ~nt a (+ of) πού θυμίζει κάτι, ἐνθυμίζων.

remission [ri'miʃən] n ἄφεσις, ἐλάττωσις ‖ (release) χάρις, μείωσις (ποινῆς).

remit [ri'mit] vt (send money) ἐμβάζω, μεταβιβάζω ‖ ~tance n ἔμβασμα (χρηματικόν).

remnant ['remnɔnt] n ὑπόλειμμα, λείψανον.

remorse [ri'mɔ:s] n τύψις, μεταμέλεια ‖ ~ful a γεμᾶτος τύψεις, μετανοιωμένος ‖ ~less a ἄσπλαγχνος, ἀνηλεής ‖ ~lessly ad ἀλύπητα, ἄσπλαγχνα.

remote [ri'mɔut] a μακρυνός, ἀπομονωμένος, ἀπόμερος ‖ (slight) ἀμυδρός, ἐλαφρός, ἀόριστος ‖ ~ control n τηλερρυθμιστής ‖ ~ly ad ἀόριστως, μακρινά.

remould ['ri:'mɔuld] vt (tyre) ξαναφορμάρω.

removable [ri'mu:vɔbl] a μεταθέσιμος, κινητός, φορητός.

removal [ri'mu:vɔl] n ἀφαίρεσις, βγάλσιμο, μετακόμισις, μετακίνησις ‖ (from office) ἀπόλυσις, ἀνάκλησις, ἔκπτωσις ‖ ~ van n φορτηγόν μετακομίσεως.

remove [ri'mu:v] vt ἀφαιρῶ, βγάζω, μεταφέρω ‖ (dismiss) ἀπολύω, ἀπομακρύνω ‖

~τ (for paint etc) ἐξαλειπτικόν μέσον ‖ ~rs npl (company) ἑταιρεία μεταφορῶν οἰκοσκευῶν.

remuneration [rimju:nə'reiʃən] n ἀμοιβή, πληρωμή.

Renaissance [rə'neisā:ns] the ~ n ἡ Ἀναγέννησις.

rename ['ri:'neim] vt μετονομάζω.

rend [rend] (irreg v) vt σχίζω, ἀποσπῶ.

render ['rendə*] vt (make) καθιστῶ, κάνω ‖ (translate) μεταφράζω ‖ ~ing n (mus) ἑρμηνεία, ἀπόδοσις.

rendezvous ['rɔndivu:] n συνάντησις, ραντεβοῦ.

renew [ri'nju:] vt (make new) ἀνανεώνω ‖ (begin again) ἀνασυνδέω, ξαναπιάνω ‖ (negotiations) ἐπαναλαμβάνω ‖ ~al n ἀνανέωσις, ἀνασύνδεσις.

renounce [ri'nauns] vt (give up) ἐγκαταλείπω, ἀποκηρύσσω ‖ (disown) ἀρνοῦμαι, ἀποποιοῦμαι.

renovate ['renəuveit] vt ἀνακαινίζω, ἐπισκευάζω.

renovation [renəu'veiʃən] n ἀνακαίνισις, ἐπισκευή.

renown [ri'naun] n φήμη ‖ ~ed a φημισμένος, ὀνομαστός.

rent [rent] n (of dwelling) ἐνοίκιον, μίσθωμα, νοίκι ‖ vt μισθώνω, ἐνοικιάζω ‖ (aut etc) ἐνοικιάζω (αὐτοκίνητον) ‖ ~al n μίσθωμα, νοίκι.

renunciation [rinʌnsi'eiʃən] n ἀπάρνησις.

reopen ['ri:'əupən] vt ξαναανοίγω.

reorder ['ri:'ɔ:də*] vt κάνω νέαν παραγγελίαν.

reorganization ['ri:ɔ:gənai'zeiʃən] n ἀναδιοργάνωσις.

reorganize ['ri:'ɔ:gənaiz] vt ἀναδιοργανώνω.

rep [rep] n (comm: representative) ἀντιπρόσωπος ‖ (theat: repertory) ρεπερτόριο.

repair [ri'pεə*] n ἐπισκευή, ἐπιδιόρθωσις ‖ (good condition) σέ καλή κατάσταση ‖ vt ἐπισκευάζω, (ἐπι)διορθώνω ‖ ~ kit n σύνεργα ἐπισκευῆς ‖ ~man n ἐπισκευαστής, ἐπιδιορθωτής ‖ ~ shop n (aut etc) συνεργεῖον (αὐτοκινήτου).

repartee [repa:'ti:] n ἑτοιμολογία, (εὔστοχος) ἀπάντησις.

repay [ri:'pei] vt (pay back) ἀνταποδίδω ‖ (money) ξεπληρώνω ‖ ~ment n ἀνταπόδοσις.

repeal [ri'pi:l] n ἀνάκλησις, ἀκύρωσις ‖ vt ἀνακαλῶ, ἀκυρώνω.

repeat [ri'pi:t] n (rad, TV) ἐπανάληψις ‖ vt ἐπαναλαμβάνω ‖ ~edly ad ἐπανειλημμένως, πολλές φορές.

repel [ri'pel] vt ἀποκρούω, ἀπωθῶ ‖ ~lent a ἀποκρουστικός, ἀπωθητικός ‖ n: insect ~lent ἀπωθητικόν ἐντόμων.

repent [ri'pent] vi μετανοιώνω, μεταμελοῦμαι ‖ ~ance n μετάνοια, μεταμέλεια.

repercussion [ri:pə'kʌʃən] n (effect) ἀντίδρασις, ἀντίκτυπος.

repertoire ['repətwa:*] n δραματολόγιον, ρεπερτόριον.

repertory ['repətəri] n (theat) ρεπερτόριον.

repetition [repi'tiʃən] n ἐπανάληψις.

repetitive [ri'petitiv] a ἐπαναληπτικός.

replace [ri'pleis] vt ἀντικαθιστῶ ‖ (put back) ἐπαναθέτω ‖ ~ment n ἀντικατάστασις ‖ (person) ἀντικαταστάτης.

replenish [ri'pleniʃ] vt ξαναγεμίζω, συμπληρώνω.

replete [ri'pli:t] a γεμᾶτος, πλήρης, παραγεμισμένος.

replica ['replikə] n πανομοιότυπον, ἀντίγραφον ἔργου τέχνης.

reply [ri'plai] n ἀπάντησις ‖ vi ἀπαντῶ, ἀποκρίνομαι.

report [ri'pɔ:t] n (account) ἔκθεσις, ἐξιστόρησις, ἀναφορά ‖ (bang) κρότος, πυροβολισμός ‖ vt ἀναφέρω ‖ (give account of) ἐξιστορῶ ‖ (news) κάνω ρεπορτάζ ‖ vi (make a report) ἐκθέτω, ἀναφέρω, κάνω ἀναφορὰν ‖ (present o.s.) παρουσιάζομαι ‖ ~er n δημοσιογράφος.

reprehensible [repri'hensibl] a ἀξιόμεμπτος.

represent [repri'zent] vt (describe) παριστάνω, παρουσιάζω ‖ (act) ἀντιπροσωπεύω ‖ ~ation n παράστασις, ἀναπαράστασις ‖ (in parliament) ἀντιπροσώπευσις, ἀντιπροσωπεία ‖ ~ative n ἀντιπρόσωπος ‖ a ἀντιπροσωπευτικός, παραστατικός.

repress [ri'pres] vt καταβάλλω, καταστέλλω, καταπνίγω ‖ ~ion n καταστολή, κατάπνιξις ‖ ~ive a κατασταλτικός, καταθλιπτικός.

reprieve [ri'pri:v] n ἀναστολή (θανατικῆς ποινῆς), ἀναβολή ‖ vt ἀναστέλλω, ἀνακουφίζω.

reprimand ['reprima:nd] n ἐπιτίμησις, ἐπίπληξις ‖ vt ἐπιτιμῶ, ἐπιπλήττω.

reprint ['ri:print] n ἀνατύπωσις ‖ ['ri:'print] vt ἀνατυπώνω.

reprisal [ri'praizəl] n ἀντεκδίκησις, ἀντίποινον.

reproach [ri'prəutʃ] n ἐπίπληξις, μομφή ‖ (disgrace) ὄνειδος ‖ vt ἐπιπλήττω, μέμφομαι, ψέγω ‖ ~ful a ἐπιπληκτικός, ὑβριστικός, ἐπονείδιστος.

reproduce [ri:prə'dju:s] vt ἀναπαράγω ‖ (make copy) ἀνατυπώνω ‖ vi ἀναπαράγομαι, πολλαπλασιάζομαι.

reproduction [ri:prə'dʌkʃən] n (copy) ἀναπαράστασις, ἀντίγραφον ‖ (breeding) γένεσις, πολλαπλασιασμός.

reproductive [ri:prə'dʌktiv] a ἀναπαραγωγικός.

reprove [ri'pru:v] vt ἐπιπλήττω.

reproving [ri'pru:viŋ] a ἐπικριτικός, ὕφος ἐπικρίσεως.

reptile ['reptail] n ἑρπετόν.

republic [ri'pʌblik] n δημοκρατία ‖ ~an a

δημοκρατικός ‖ *(party: US)* ρεπουμπλι-
κανικός ‖ *n* δημοκράτης, ρεπουμπλι-
κάνος.
repudiate [ri'pju:dieit] *vt* (ἀπ)ἀρνοῦμαι,
ἀποκρούω, ἀπορρίπτω.
repugnance [ri'pʌgnəns] *n* ἀπέχθεια,
ἀποστροφή.
repugnant [ri'pʌgnənt] *a* ἀπεχθής, ἀηδής,
σιχαμερός.
repulse [ri'pʌls] *vt* ἀπωθῶ, ἀποκρούω
(reject) ἀποκρούω, ἀπορρίπτω.
repulsion [ri'pʌlʃən] *n* ἀποστροφή, ἄπωσις
repulsive [ri'pʌlsiv] *a* ἀποκρουστικός,
ἀντιπαθής, ἀηδής.
repurchase ['ri:'pə:tʃis] *vt* ξαναγοραζω ‖ *r*
ἀγορά ἐκ νέου.
reputable ['repjutəbl] *a* ἔντιμος, ἀξιοπρεπής.
reputation [repju'teiʃən] *n* φήμη, ὑπόληψις,
ὄνομα.
repute [ri'pju:t] *n* ἐκτίμησις, ὑπόληψις
~**d** *a* φημισμένος, ὑποτιθέμενος ‖
~**dly** *ad* κατά τήν κοινήν γνώμην.
request [ri'kwest] *n* αἴτησις, παράκλησις ‖
(demand) ζήτησις, μόδα ‖ *vt* ζητῶ,
παρακαλῶ.
requiem ['rekwiem] *n* μνημόσυνον.
require [ri'kwaiə*] *vt* ζητῶ, ἀπαιτῶ
(oblige) χρειάζομαι ‖ ~**ment** *n* ἀπαίτησις,
ἀνάγκη.
requisite ['rekwizit] *n* ἀπαιτούμενον
πρᾶγμα, χρειῶδες ‖ *a* ἀπαιτούμενος.
requisition [rekwi'ziʃən] *n* ἐπίταξις, ἀπαίτησις ‖ *vt* ἀπαιτῶ, ἐπιτάσσω.
reroute ['ri:'ru:t] *vt* χαράσσω νέα πορεία,
κάνω ἄλλο δρόμο.
resale ['ri:'seil] *n* μεταπώλησις, ξαναπού-
λημα.
rescind [ri'sind] *vt* ἀκυρῶ, καταργῶ,
ἀνακαλῶ.
rescue ['reskju:] *n* διάσωσις, ἀπολύτρωσις
‖ *vt (save)* σώζω, λυτρώνω ‖ ~**r** *n* σωτήρας, λυτρωτής.
research [ri'sə:tʃ] *n* ἔρευνα ‖ *vi (+ into)*
ἐνεργῶ ἔρευνας ‖ *vt* ἐρευνῶ ‖ ~**er** *n*
ἐρευνητής ‖ ~ **work** *n* ἔρευνες, μελέτες
‖ ~ **worker** *n* ἐρευνητής.
resell ['ri:'sel] *vt* ξαναπουλῶ.
resemblance [ri'zembləns] *n* ὁμοιότης.
resemble [ri'zembl] *vt* ὁμοιάζω, μοιάζω.
resent [ri'zent] *vt* φέρω βαρέως, θίγομαι
ἀπό ‖ ~**ful** *a* μνησίκακος, πειραγμένος
‖ ~**ment** *n* μνησικακία, ἔχθρα, πίκα.
reservation [rezə'veiʃən] *n* ἐπιφύλαξις,
περιορισμός ‖ *(place)* ἐξασφάλισις,
κλείσιμο ‖ *(doubt)* ἐπιφύλαξις.
reserve [ri'zə:v] *n* ἀπόθεμα, ἀποθεματικόν
‖ *(self-restraint)* ἐπιφύλαξις, συντηρη-
τικότης ‖ *(area of land)* ἐπιφυλασσομένη
περιοχή ‖ *(sport)* ἐφεδρικός παίκτης ‖
vt (seats etc) κρατῶ, ἀγκαζάρω, κλείνω
~**s** *npl (mil)* ἐφεδρεῖες ‖ **in** ~ κατά
μέρος, ρεζέρβα ‖ ~**d** *a* ἐπιφυλακτικός,

συγκρατημένος ‖ '~**d**' *(notice)* 'κλεισμέ-
νος', 'κρατημένος'.
reservist [ri'zə:vist] *n* ἔφεδρος.
reservoir ['rezəvwa:*] *n* δεξαμενή, ντεπόζιτο, ρεζερβουάρ ‖ *(store)* ἀπόθεμα.
reshape ['ri:'ʃeip] *vt* μεταπλάθω, τροποποιῶ, ἀναπλάθω.
reshuffle ['ri:'ʃʌfl] *n (pol)* ἀνασχηματισμός.
reside [ri'zaid] *vi* διαμένω, ἐνυπάρχω ‖
~**nce** ['rezidəns] *n* κατοικία, σπίτι ‖
(living) διαμονή, παραμονή ‖ ~**nt** *n*
κάτοικος ‖ *a* ἐγκατεστημένος ‖ ~**ntial**
a τῆς μονίμου διαμονῆς, μέ ἰδιωτικές
κατοικίες.
residue ['rezidju:] *n* ὑπόλοιπον, ὑπόλειμμα,
κατάλοιπον.
resign [ri'zain] *vt* παραιτοῦμαι ‖ *(submit)*
ὑποτάσσομαι, ἐγκαταλείπομαι ‖ ~**ation**
[rezig'neiʃən] *n* παραίτησις ‖ *(submission)*
ὑποταγή, ὑπομονή ‖ ~**ed** *a* ἀνεχόμενος,
ὑποτακτικός.
resilience [ri'ziliəns] *n* ἐλαστικότης,
ἀναπήδησις.
resilient [ri'ziliənt] *a* ἐλαστικός.
resin ['rezin] *n* ρητίνη, ρετσίνα.
resist [ri'zist] *vt* ἀνθίσταμαι εἰς, ἀντιδρῶ
κατά ‖ ~**ance** *n* ἀντίστασις ‖ ~**ant** *a*
(to stains etc) ἀνθεκτικός, ἀντέχων.
resolute ['rezəlu:t] *a* ἀποφασιστικός,
σταθερός ‖ ~**ly** *ad* ἀποφασιστικά, μέ
ἀπόφασιν.
resolution [rezə'lu:ʃən] *n* ἀποφασιστικότης
‖ *(decision)* ἀπόφασις.
resolve [ri'zɔlv] *n* ἀπόφασις ‖ *vt* ἀναλύω,
διαλύω, λύω ‖ *vi* διαλύομαι, ἀναλύομαι ‖
(decide) ἀποφασίζω ‖ ~**d** *a* ἀποφασισμένος.
resonant ['rezənənt] *a* ἀντηχῶν, ἀντηχη-
τικός.
resort [ri'zɔ:t] *n* τόπος διαμονῆς, θέρετρον
‖ *(help)* καταφυγή, μέσον, βοήθεια ‖ *vi*
(+ to) προσφεύγω, καταφεύγω (εἰς) ‖ **in
the last** ~ σάν τελευταία λύση.
resound [ri'zaund] *vi* ἀντηχῶ, ἀπηχῶ ‖
~**ing** *a* (ἀπ)ηχῶν, ἠχηρός.
resource [ri'sɔ:s] *n* καταφύγιον, μέσον,
βοήθημα ‖ ~**s** *npl (of fuel)* πλοῦτος (εἰς
καύσιμα) ‖ *(of a country etc)* οἱ πόροι,
πλοῦτος ‖ ~**ful** *a* ἐφευρετικός ‖ ~**fulness** *n* ἐφευρετικότης, (τό) πολυμήχανον.
respect [ris'pekt] *n* σεβασμός ‖ *(way)*
ἀναφορά ‖ *vt* σέβομαι ‖ *(treat with consideration)* προσέχω ‖ ~**s** *npl (greetings)*
σέβη, χαιρετίσματα ‖ **with** ~ **to** ὅσον
ἀφορᾶ ‖ **in** ~ **of** ἐν σχέσει πρός ‖ **in
this** ~ ὡς πρός αὐτό τό σημεῖον ‖
~**ability** *n* ἐντιμότης ‖ ~**able** *a* ἔντιμος,
εὐϋπόληπτος ‖ *(fairly good)* ὑποφερτός,
ἀρκετά καλός ‖ ~**ed** *a* σεβαστός ‖ ~**ful**
a γεμᾶτος σεβασμόν ‖ ~**fully** *ad* εὐσεβά-
στως ‖ ~**ing** *prep* σχετικά μέ, ὅσον
ἀφορᾶ εἰς ‖ ~**ive** *a* σχετικός, ἀμοιβαῖος,
ἀντίστοιχος ‖ ~**ively** *ad* ἀντιστοίχως.

respiration [respi'reiʃən] n ἀναπνοή.

respiratory [res'paiərətəri] a ἀναπνευστικός.

respite ['respait] n ἀνάπαυλα, διακοπή.

resplendent [ris'plendənt] a λαμπρός, λάμπων ‖ μεγαλοπρεπής.

respond [ris'pond] vi ἀπαντῶ, ἀποκρίνομαι ‖ (act in answer) ἀνταποκρίνομαι, ἀνταποδίδω.

response [ris'pons] n ἀπάντησις, ἀνταπόκρισις.

responsibility [risponsə'biliti] n εὐθύνη.

responsible [ris'ponsəbl] a ὑπεύθυνος, ὑπόλογος ‖ (reliable) ἀξιόπιστος.

responsibly [ris'ponsəbli] ad ὑπευθύνως.

responsive [ris'ponsiv] a εὐσυγκίνητος, εὐαίσθητος.

rest [rest] n ἀνάπαυσις, ξεκούρασις ‖ (pause) πτῶσις, ἀνάπαυλα ‖ (remainder) ὑπόλοιπον ‖ vi ἀναπαύομαι, ξεκουράζομαι ‖ (be supported) στηρίζομαι, ἀκουμπῶ ‖ (remain) στηρίζομαι, βασίζομαι ‖ the ~ of them οἱ ὑπόλοιποι.

restaurant ['restərɔ̃:ŋ] n ἐστιατόριον ‖ ~ car n βαγκόν-ρεστωράν.

rest cure ['restkjuə*] n θεραπεία ἀναπαύσεως.

restful ['restful] a ξεκούραστος, ἥσυχος, ἀναπαυτικός.

rest home ['resthəum] n πρεβαντόριο, ἀναρρωτήριον.

restitution [resti'tju:ʃən] n ἀποκατάστασις, ἀπόδοσις.

restive ['restiv] a ἀτίθασος, ἀνήσυχος.

restless ['restlis] a ἀνήσυχος, ἀεικίνητος, ἄϋπνος ‖ ~ly ad ἀνήσυχα, νευρικά, ταραγμένα ‖ ~ness n ἀνησυχία, νευρικότης.

restock ['ri:'stɔk] vt ἀνεφοδιάζω.

restoration [restə'reiʃən] n ἀποκατάστασις, παλινόρθωσις ‖ (of building etc) ἐπισκευή, ἀναστήλωσις.

restore [ris'tɔ:*] vt ἐπιστρέφω, ἀποκαθιστῶ ‖ (repair) ἐπισκευάζω, ἀναστηλώνω.

restrain [ris'trein] vt ἀναχαιτίζω, συγκρατῶ ‖ ~ed (style etc) ἤρεμος, συγκρατημένος, μετρημένος ‖ ~t n περιορισμός, περιστολή ‖ (self-control) συγκράτησις.

restrict [ris'trikt] vt περιορίζω ‖ ~ed a περιωρισμένος ‖ ~ion n περιορισμός ‖ ~ive a περιοριστικός.

rest room ['restrum] n (US) ἀποχωρητήριον, τουαλέτα.

result [ri'zʌlt] n ἀποτέλεσμα, συνέπεια ‖ (of test) ἀποτελέσματα ‖ vi (+ in) καταλήγω, ἀπολήγω ‖ ~ant a προκύπτων.

resume [ri'zju:m] vt ἐπαναρχίζω, ξαναρχίζω.

résumé ['reizju:mei] n περίληψις.

resumption [ri'zʌmpʃən] n (ἐπ)ἀνάληψις, συνέχισις.

resurgence [ri'sɔ:dʒəns] n ἀναζωογόνησις, ἀνάνεωσις, ξεσήκωμα.

resurrection [rezə'rekʃən] n ἀνάστασις, ἀνάνεωσις.

resuscitate [ri'sʌsiteit] vt ἀνασταίνω, ἐπαναφέρω εἰς τήν ζωήν.

resuscitation [risʌsi'teiʃən] n ἀναζωογόνησις, ἀνάστασις.

retail ['ri:teil] n λιανική πώλησις ‖ a λιανικός ‖ [ri:'teil] vt πωλῶ λιανικῶς ‖ ~er n μεταπωλητής, λιανέμπορος ‖ ~ price n τιμή λιανικῆς πωλήσεως.

retain [ri'tein] vt διατηρῶ, συγκρατῶ, κρατῶ ‖ ~er n ὑπηρέτης ‖ (fee) προκαταβολή δικηγόρου.

retaliate [ri'tælieit] vi ἀντεκδικοῦμαι, ἀνταποδίδω.

retaliation [ritæli'eiʃən] n ἀντεκδίκησις, ἀνταπόδοσις, ἀντίποινα.

retarded [ri'ta:did] a καθυστερημένος.

retention [ri'tenʃən] n διατήρησις, συγκράτησις.

retentive [ri'tentiv] a συνεκτικός, ἰσχυρός.

rethink ['ri:'θiŋk] vt ξανασκέπτομαι.

reticence ['retisəns] n παρασιώπησις, ἀποσιώπησις.

reticent ['retisənt] a σιωπηλός, λιγομίλητος, κλειστός.

retina ['retinə] n ἀμφιβληστροειδής (χιτών).

retinue ['retinju:] n ἀκολουθία, συνοδεία.

retire [ri'taiə*] vi ἀποχωρῶ, γίνομαι συνταξιοῦχος ‖ (withdraw, retreat) ὑποχωρῶ, ἀποσύρομαι ‖ (go to bed) πάω γιά ὕπνο ‖ ~d a (person) συνταξιοῦχος ‖ ~ment n ἀποχώρησις, σύνταξις.

retiring [ri'taiəriŋ] a ἐπιφυλακτικός, ἀκοινώνητος, ντροπαλός.

retort [ri'tɔ:t] n (reply) ὀξεῖα ἀπάντησις, ἐξυπνη ἀπάντησις ‖ vi ἀνταπαντῶ, ἀποκρίνομαι.

retrace [ri'treis] vt ἀνατρέχω, ξαναγυρίζω.

retract [ri'trækt] vti ἀνακαλῶ, μαζεύω, παίρνω πίσω (κάτι) ‖ ~able a (aerial) εἰσελκόμενος.

retread ['ri:tred] vt (aut: tyre) ἀνεπιστρώνω, ξαναφορμάρω.

retreat [ri'tri:t] n ὑποχώρησις, ὀπισθοχώρησις ‖ (escape) καταφύγιον ‖ vi ὑποχωρῶ, ὀπισθοχωρῶ.

retrial ['ri:'traiəl] n νέα δίκη.

retribution [retri'bju:ʃən] n τιμωρία, ἀνταπόδοσις, ἐκδίκησις.

retrieval [ri'tri:vəl] n ἐπανάκτησις, ἐπανόρθωσις.

retrieve [ri'tri:v] vt ἐπανακτῶ, ἀποδίδω (rescue) ἐπανορθώνω, σώζω ‖ ~r n κυνηγετικός κύων, ριτρίβερ.

retrograde ['retrəugreid] a (step, action) ὀπισθοδρομικός, παλινδρομικός.

retrospect ['retrəuspekt] n: in ~ σέ ἀνασκόπηση, ὅταν τό σκέπτομαι ‖ ~ive a (law) ἀναδρομικός.

return [ri'tɔ:ŋ] n ἐπιστροφή, ἐπάνοδος, γύρισμα, ἐρχομός ‖ (profits) κέρδος, εἰσπράξεις ‖ (official report) ἔκθεσις, στατιστική, ἀπογραφή ‖ (rail ticket etc) εἰσιτήριον μετ' ἐπιστροφῆς ‖ (journey) ταξίδιον ἐπιστροφῆς ‖ (match) ἀγών ἀνταποδόσεως, ρεβάνς ‖ vi ἐπιστρέφω, γυρίζω, ἐπανέρχομαι ‖ vt (give back) ἐπιστρέφω, δίνω πίσω, γυρίζω ‖ (pay back) ἐπιστρέφω, πληρώνω ‖ (elect) ἐκλέγω ‖ ~able a (bottle etc) ἐπιστρεφόμενον, ἐπιστρεπτός.

reunion [ri:'ju:njən] n συνάντησις, συγκέντρωσις.

reunite ['ri:ju:'nait] vt ἑνώνω πάλιν, συναντῶμαι.

rev [rev] n (aut) στροφές ‖ vti (also ~ up) φουλάρω.

revamp ['ri:'væmp] vt ἐπιδιορθώνω, ἀνορθώνω.

reveal [ri'vi:l] vt ἀποκαλύπτω, φανερώνω ‖ ~ing a ἀποκαλυπτικός.

reveille [ri'væli] n ἐγερτήριον σάλπισμα.

revel ['revl] vi (+ in) ἐντρυφῶ εἰς, γλεντῶ.

revelation [revə'leiʃən] n ἀποκάλυψις.

reveller ['revlə*] n γλεντζές.

revelry ['revlri] n διασκέδασις, γλέντι.

revenge [ri'vendʒ] n ἐκδίκησις ‖ vt ἐκδικοῦμαι ‖ ~ful a ἐκδικητικός.

revenue ['revənju:] n πρόσοδος, ἔσοδα, εἰσόδημα.

reverberate [ri'və:bəreit] vi ἀντηχῶ, ἀντανακλῶμαι.

reverberation [rivə:bə'reiʃən] n ἀντήχησις, ἀντανάκλασις.

revere [ri'viə*] vt σέβομαι, εὐλαβοῦμαι ‖ ~nce ['revərəns] n σέβας, σεβασμός ‖ the R~nd Smith ὁ αἰδεσιμώτατος Σμίθ ‖ ~nt a εὐσεβής.

reverie ['revəri] n ὀνειροπόλησις, ρεμβασμός.

reversal [ri'və:səl] n ἀντιστροφή, ἀναστροφή.

reverse [ri'və:s] n ἀντίστροφον ‖ (defeat) ἧττα, ἀτυχία ‖ (aut: gear) ὄπισθεν ‖ a (order, direction) ἀντίθετος, ἀντίστροφος ‖ vt (put upside down) ἀναστρέφω ‖ (change) ἀντιστρέφω ‖ vi βάζω τήν ὄπισθεν.

reversion [ri'və:ʃən] n ἐπιστροφή, ἐπάνοδος.

revert [ri'və:t] vi ἐπανέρχομαι, ἐπιστρέφω.

review [ri'vju:] n ἐπιθεώρησις ‖ (of critic) κριτική (βιβλίου) ‖ (magazine) ἐπιθεώρησις, περιοδικόν ‖ vt (look back on) ἀνασκοπῶ, ἐξετάζω ‖ (troops) ἐπιθεωρῶ ‖ (a book) γράφω κριτικήν ‖ ~er n (critic) κριτικογράφος, κριτικός.

revise [ri'vaiz] vt ἀναθεωρῶ, ξανακοιτάζω, διορθώνω.

revision [ri'viʒən] n ἀναθεώρησις, ἐπανεξέτασις.

revisit ['ri:'vizit] vt ξαναεπισκέπτομαι.

revitalize ['ri:'vaitəlaiz] vt ἀναζωογονῶ.

revival [ri'vaivəl] n ἀναγέννησις ‖ (of play) ἐπανάληψις.

revive [ri'vaiv] vt ἀναζωογονῶ, ἀναστείνω, ξαναζωντανεύω ‖ vi ἀναζωογονοῦμαι, ξαναζωντανεύω, ἀναζωπυροῦμαι.

revoke [ri'vəuk] vt ἀνακαλῶ, ἀκυρώνω.

revolt [ri'vəult] n στάσις, ἐπανάστασις ‖ vi ἐπαναστατῶ ‖ ~ing a ἀηδιαστικόν, σκανδαλώδης.

revolution [revə'lu:ʃən] n (of wheel) περιστροφή ‖ (change) ἐπανάστασις ‖ ~ary a ἐπαναστατικός, ἀνατρεπτικός ‖ n ἐπανάστασις, περιστροφή ‖ ~ize vt ἀνατρέπω ἄρδην, ἀλλάζω τελείως.

revolve [ri'vɔlv] vi περιστρέφομαι ‖ ~r n περίστροφον.

revue [ri'vju:] n ἐπιθεώρησις (θεατρική).

revulsion [ri'vʌlʃən] n μεταστροφή.

reward [ri'wɔ:d] n (ἀντ)ἀμοιβή ‖ vt ἀνταμείβω ‖ ~ing a ἀνταμειπτικός ‖ (fig) πού ἀξίζει τόν κόπο.

rewind ['ri:'waind] vt ξανατυλίγω, ξανακουρδίζω.

rewire [ri:'waiə*] vt (house) ἀλλάζω τά σύρματα (σπιτιοῦ).

reword ['ri:'wə:d] vt ἀνασυντάσσω, ξαναγράφω μέ ἄλλες λέξεις.

rewrite ['ri:'rait] vt ξαναγράφω.

rhapsody ['ræpsədi] n ραψωδία.

rhetoric ['retərik] n ρητορική, ρητορία ‖ ~al a ρητορικός.

rheumatic [ru:'mætik] a ρευματικός.

rheumatism ['ru:mətizəm] n ρευματισμός.

rhinoceros [rai'nɔsərəs] n ρινόκερως.

Rhodesia [rəu'di:zə] n Ροδεσία ‖ ~n a ἐκ Ροδεσίας ‖ n (person) ἐκ Ροδεσίας.

rhododendron [rəudə'dendrən] n ροδόδενδρον.

rhubarb ['ru:ba:b] n ραβέντι, ρουμπάρμπαρο.

rhyme [raim] n ὁμοιοκαταληξία, ρίμα.

rhythm ['riðəm] n ρυθμός, μέτρον ‖ ~ic(al) a ρυθμικός ‖ ~ically ad ρυθμικά, μέ ρυθμό.

rib [rib] n πλευρά, πλευρό ‖ vt (mock) ἐμπαίζω, κοροϊδεύω.

ribald ['ribəld] a αἰσχρός, πρόστυχος, σόκιν.

ribbed [ribd] a ραβδωτός, μέ νευρώσεις.

ribbon ['ribən] n ταινία, κορδέλλα.

rice [rais] n ρύζι ‖ ~ pudding n ρυζόγαλο.

rich [ritʃ] a πλούσιος ‖ (fertile) εὔφορος, πλούσιος, γόνιμος ‖ (splendid) πολυτελής, λαμπρός, ὑπέροχος ‖ (of food) παχύς, ἀπό ἐκλεκτά συστατικά ‖ the ~ οἱ πλούσιοι ‖ ~es npl πλούτη, ἀφθονία ‖ ~ly ad πλούσια ‖ ~ness n πλοῦτος, ἀφθονία.

rick [rik] n θημωνιά.

rickety ['rikiti] a (unsteady) πού τρέμει, σαθρός, σαραβαλιασμένος.

rickshaw ['rikʃɔ:] n δίτροχος ἅμαξα συρομένη ἀπό ἄνθρωπον.

ricochet [ˈrikəʃei] *n* ἐποστρακισμός ‖ *vi* ἐποστρακίζω, ἀναπηδῶ.

rid [rid] (*irreg v*) *vt* ἀπαλλάσσω, ἐλευθερώνω ‖ **to get ~ of** ἀπαλλάσσομαι ἀπό ‖ **good ~ dance!** καλά ξεκουμπίδια!, ἂς πάη στό καλό!

riddle [ˈridl] *n* (*puzzle*) αἴνιγμα ‖ *vt* (*esp passive*) κάνω κόσκινο.

ride [raid] (*irreg v*) *n* διαδρομή, περίπατος, ταξίδι ‖ *vt* τρέχω, διασχίζω ‖ (*horse, bicycle*) καβαλικεύω ‖ *vi* πάω καβάλα, καβαλικεύω, πηγαίνω μέ ἁμάξι ‖ (*naut*) εἶμαι ἀγκυροβολημένος ‖ **~r** *n* ἱππεύς, καβαλάρης ‖ (*in contract etc*) προσθήκη, παράρτημα, συμπληρωματική διάταξις.

ridge [ridʒ] *n* (*hill*) κορυφογραμμή, ράχη ‖ (*of roof*) κολοφών, καβελαριά, κορφιάς ‖ (*narrow raised strip*) πτυχή, ζάρα, προεξοχή.

ridicule [ˈridikju:l] *n* περίγελως, ἐμπαιγμός, κοροϊδία ‖ *vt* κοροϊδεύω, γελοποιῶ.

ridiculous [riˈdikjuləs] *a* γελοῖος ‖ **~ly** *ad* γελοῖα.

riding [ˈraidiŋ] *n*: **to go ~** πηγαίνω ἱππασία ‖ **~ habit** *n* ἀμαζών ‖ **~ school** *n* σχολή ἱππασίας.

rife [raif] *a*: **~ with** μεστός, γεμᾶτος ἀπό.

riffraff [ˈrifræf] *n* ἀληθεία, σκυλολόϊ.

rifle [ˈraifl] *n* ὅπλον, τουφέκι ‖ *vt* (*rob*) ἀδειάζω, διαρπάζω ‖ **~ range** *n* πεδίον βολῆς, σκοπευτήριον.

rift [rift] *n* σχισμή, ρωγμή.

rig [rig] *n* (*outfit*) φορεσιά, στόλισμα ‖ (*oil rig*) γεωτρύπανον ‖ *vt* (*election etc*) νοθεύω τάς ἐκλογάς ‖ **~ging** *n* ξάρτια ‖ **to ~ out** *vt* ντύνω, στολίζω ‖ **to ~ up** *vt* στήνω, μαντάρω.

right [rait] *a* (*correct, proper*) ὀρθός, σωστός, κανονικός ‖ (*just, good*) εὐθύς, δίκαιος, ἔντιμος ‖ (*on right side*) δεξιός, δεξιά ‖ *n* (*what is just, true*) τό δίκαιον, ἡ δικαιοσύνη, τό καλόν ‖ (*title, claim*) δικαίωμα, προνόμιον ‖ (*not left*) δεξιά (πλευρά), τό δεξιόν ‖ (*pol*) ἡ Δεξιά ‖ *ad* (*straight*) εὐθέως, ἴσια, ντρίτα ‖ (*completely, thoroughly*) ἀκριβῶς, κατ' εὐθείαν, τελείως, δεξιά ‖ *vt* ἀνορθῶ, ἰσορροπῶ, ξαναφέρνω στά ἴσια ‖ *excl* σωστά!, σύμφωνοι!, ἔχεις δίκιο! ‖ **to be ~** ἔχω δίκαιον ‖ **all ~!** ἐν τάξει! ‖ **~ now** ἀμέσως ‖ **by ~s** δικαιωματικῶς, νομίμως ‖ **on the ~** στά δεξιά ‖ **~ angle** *n* ὀρθή γωνία ‖ **~eous** *a* εὐθύς, ἠθικός, δίκαιος ‖ **~eousness** *n* δικαιοσύνη, ὀρθότης, τιμιότης ‖ **~ful** *a* νόμιμος, δίκαιος ‖ **~fully** *ad* δικαίως, νομίμως ‖ **~hand drive** *a* μέ δεξιό τιμόνι ‖ **~handed** *a* δεξιόχειρ, δεξιόστροφος ‖ **~hand man** *n* τό δεξί χέρι ‖ **~hand side** *n* (πρός) τά δεξιά ‖ **~ly** *ad* δικαίως, ὀρθῶς ‖ **~minded** *a* λογικός, ὀρθοφρονῶν ‖ **~ of way** *n* ἡ προτεραιότης ‖ **~winger** *n* δεξιός.

rigid [ˈridʒid] *a* ἄκαμπτος, ἀλύγιστος ‖ (*strict*) αὐστηρός ‖ **~ity** *n* ἀκαμψία, ἀλυγισία ‖ **~ly** *ad* ἄκαμπτα, ἀλύγιστα. αὐστηρά.

rigmarole [ˈrigmərəul] *n* ἀσυναρτησίες, κουραφέξαλα.

rigor [ˈrigə*] *n* (*US*) = **rigour**.

rigor mortis [ˈrigəˈmɔːtis] *n* πτωματική ἀκαμψία.

rigorous [ˈrigərəs] *a* αὐστηρός, δριμύς, τραχύς ‖ **~ly** *ad* αὐστηρά, σκληρά.

rigour [ˈrigə*] *n* αὐστηρότης, δριμύτης.

rig-out [ˈrigaut] *n* (*col*) ντύσιμο, στόλισμα.

rile [rail] *vt* (*annoy, infuriate*) ἐκνευρίζω, ἐξαγριώνω, ἀγριεύω.

rim [rim] *n* στεφάνη, χεῖλος ‖ (*of wheel*) σῶτρον, στεφάνη, ζάντα ‖ **~less** *a* χωρίς σκελετό, χωρίς γεῖσον ‖ **~med** *a* μέ στεφάνην, μέ σκελετόν.

rind [raind] *n* φλοιός, φλούδα.

ring [riŋ] (*irreg v*) *n* δακτύλιος, δακτυλίδι ‖ (*of people*) συντροφιά, φατρία, συμμορία ‖ (*arena*) παλαίστρα, στῖβος, πίστα, ἀρένα, ρίγκ ‖ (*tel*) τηλεφώνημα, κτύπημα τηλεφώνου ‖ *vt* κτυπῶ τό κουδούνι ‖ *vi* (*tel*) (*also ~ up*) τηλεφωνῶ ‖ (*resound*) ἀντηχῶ, κτυπῶ, κουδουνίζω ‖ **to ~ off** *vi* διακόπτω τήν συνομιλίαν, κλείνω τηλέφωνον ‖ **~ binder** *n* κλασέρ ‖ **~ leader** *n* (*of gang*) ἀρχηγός συμμορίας ‖ **~lets** *npl* (*hair*) μπούκλες ‖ **~ road** *n* περιφερειακή ὁδός.

rink [riŋk] *n* πίστα πατινάζ.

rinse [rins] *n* ξέπλυμα ‖ *vt* ξεπλένω, ξεβγάζω.

riot [ˈraiət] *n* στάσις, ὀχλαγωγία ‖ *vi* ὀχλαγωγῶ, θορυβῶ ‖ **~er** *n* ταραξίας, ὀχλαγωγός ‖ **~ous** *a* ταραχώδης, ὀχλαγωγικός, ὀργιαστικός ‖ **~ously** *ad* στασιαστικῶς, ἐκλύτως.

rip [rip] *n* σχισμή, σχίσιμο ‖ *vti* (δια)σχίζω, ξεσχίζω.

ripcord [ˈripkɔːd] *n* σχοινίον ἀνοίγματος.

ripe [raip] *a* ὥριμος, γενομένο ‖ **~n** *vti* ὡριμάζω, γίνομαι ‖ **~ness** *n* ὡριμότης.

ripple [ˈripl] *n* κυμάτιον, κυματιστός, ρυτίδα ‖ *vti* κυματίζω, ρυτιδοῦμαι.

rise [raiz] (*irreg v*) *n* ὕψωμα, ἀνήφορος, κλίσις ‖ (*esp in wages*) αὔξησις, ἀνύψωσις ‖ ἄνοδος ‖ ἀνέβασμα, αὔξησις, σήκωμα (ἀέρος) ‖ *vi* (*from chair*) σηκώνομαι ὄρθιος ‖ (*from bed*) ξυπνῶ, σηκώνομαι ‖ (*sun*) ἀνατέλλω, βγαίνω ‖ (*smoke*) ὑψοῦμαι, ἀνεβαίνω ‖ (*mountain*) ὑψοῦμαι ‖ (*ground*) ἀνηφορίζω, ὑψοῦμαι ‖ (*prices*) ἀνέρχομαι, ὑψοῦμαι, ἀνεβαίνω ‖ (*revolt*) ἐξεγείρομαι, ξεσηκώνομαι, ἐπαναστατῶ ‖ **to give ~ to** προκαλῶ ‖ **to ~ to the occasion** αἴρομαι εἰς τό ὕψος τῶν περιστάσεων.

risk [risk] *n* κίνδυνος, ριψοκινδύνευσις ‖ *vt* ριψοκινδυνεύω ‖ **~y** *a* ἐπικίνδυνος, ριψοκίνδυνος.

risqué ['ri:skei] a τολμηρό.

rissole ['risəul] n κεφτές, κροκέττα.

rite [rait] n ίεροτελεστία, ἐκκλησιαστική τελετή.

ritual ['ritjuəl] n τυπικόν, λειτουργικόν || a τυπικός, καθιερωμένος.

rival ['raivəl] n,a ἀντίπαλος, ἀντίζηλος, ἀνταγωνιστής || vt ἀνταγωνίζομαι, συναγωνίζομαι || ~ry n ἀνταγωνισμός, συναγωνισμός.

river ['rivə*] n ποταμός, ποτάμι || ~bank n ὄχθη (ποταμοῦ) || ~bed n κοίτη ποταμοῦ || ~side n ὄχθη || a τῆς ὄχθης.

rivet ['rivit] n ἧλος, κοινωμάτιον, καρφί || vt καθηλώνω, καρφώνω, πριτσιλίζω || (fix) προσηλώνω, καρφώνω.

Riviera [rivi'eərə] n: the ~ ἡ Ριβιέρα.

road [rəud] n ὁδός, δρόμος || ~block n ὁδόφραγμα || ~hog n κακός ὁδηγός || ~map n ὁδικός χάρτης || ~side n παρυφή δρόμου, δίπλα στὸ δρόμο || a στὸ δρόμο, τοῦ δρόμου || ~sign n ταμπέλα δρόμου || ~way n ἁμαξιτή ὁδός || ~worthy a κατάλληλος γιὰ τὸν δρόμο.

roam [rəum] vi περιπλανῶμαι, περιφέρομαι || vt διασχίζω, διατρέχω, τριγυρίζω.

roar [rɔ:*] n βρυχηθμός, μουγγρητό || vi βρυχῶμαι, ὠρύομαι || ~ing a (fire) γερή (φωτιά), δυνατή (φωτιά) || (trade) ἀκμάζον (ἐμπόριον), καλές (δουλειές).

roast [rəust] n ψητὸν κρέας, ψητό || vt ψήνω, καβουρντίζω.

rob [rɔb] vt κλέβω, ληστεύω, ἀποστερῶ || ~ber n ληστής, κλέφτης || ~bery n ληστεία.

robe [rəub] n ρόμπα, φόρεμα || (of office) στολή, τήβεννος || vt ἐνδύω, περιβάλλω, ντύνω.

robin ['rɔbin] n κοκκινολαίμης, κομπογιάννης.

robot ['rəubɔt] n αὐτόματον, ρομπότ.

robust [rəu'bʌst] a εὔρωστος, ρωμαλέος.

rock [rɔk] n βράχος || (geol) πέτρωμα || (candy) εἶδος καραμέλλας || vti λικνίζω, κουνῶ, κουνιέμαι || on the ~s (drink) μέ πάγο χωρίς νερό || (ship) (πέφτω) στὰ βράχια || (marriage etc) ὑπὸ διάλυσιν, σέ δύσκολη θέσι || ~-bottom n (fig) κατώτερον σημεῖον || ~ climber n ὀρειβάτης (βράχων) || to go ~ climbing πηγαίνω ὀρειβασία σέ βράχους || ~ery n τεχνητοί βράχοι.

rocket ['rɔkit] n ρουκέττα, πύραυλος, βολίς.

rock fall ['rɔkfɔ:l] n πτῶσις βράχων.

rocking chair ['rɔkiŋtʃeə*] n κουνιστή πολυθρόνα.

rocking horse ['rɔkiŋhɔ:s] n ἀλογάκι (παιδικό).

rocky ['rɔki] a βραχώδης.

rococo [rəu'kəukəu] a,n ροκοκό.

rod [rɔd] n (bar) ράβδος, βέργα.

rode [rəud] pt of ride.

rodent ['rəudənt] n τρωκτικόν.

rodeo ['rəudiəu] n διαγωνισμός (καουμπόηδων).

roe [rəu] n (deer) δορκάς, ζαρκάδι || (of fish) αὐγά ψαριῶν.

rogue [rəug] n παλιάνθρωπος || (mischievous) κατεργάρης, πειραχτήριο, πονηρός.

roguish ['rəugiʃ] a (playful) κατεργάρικος, τσαχπίνικος || (cheating) δόλιος, πανοῦργος.

rôle [rəul] n ρόλος.

roll [rəul] n (paper, meat etc) κύλινδρος, ρολό, τόπι || (bread) φραντζολάκι, κουλουράκι || (list) κατάλογος, λίστα || (of drum) συνεχής τυμπανόκρουσία || vt (over) κυλινδρῶ, κυλιῶ, τσουλάω || (wind round) τυλίγω, κάνω ρολό || (smooth out) ἰσοπεδώνω, πατῶ, στρώνω || vi (swing) στριφογυρίζω, διατοιχίζομαι, μποτζάρω || (make deep sound) ἠχῶ, βροντῶ || to ~ by vi (time) περνῶ (κυλῶντας) || to ~ in vi (mail) μπαίνω κυλῶντας || συρρέω || to ~ over vi ἀνατρέπομαι, κυλιέμαι || to ~ up vi (arrive) φθάνω, κουβαλιέμαι || vt (carpet) τυλίγω, διπλώνω || ~ call n ὀνομαστικὴ κλῆσις, προσκλητήριον || ~ed a (umbrella) τυλιγμένος || ~er n κύλινδρος, τροχός || ~er skates npl πατίνια μέ ρόδες.

rollicking ['rɔlikiŋ] a εὔθυμος, γλεντζέδικος, χαρούμενος.

rolling ['rəuliŋ] a (landscape) ἀνώμαλον ἔδαφος || ~ pin n πλάστης (γιά ἄνοιγμα φύλλου) || ~ stock n τροχαῖον ὑλικόν.

roly-poly ['rəuli'pəuli] n (pudding) πουτίγκα ρολό μέ φροῦτα.

Roman ['rəumən] a ρωμαϊκός || n Ρωμαῖος || ~ Catholic a,n ρωμαιοκαθολικός.

romance [rəu'mæns] n ρομάντζο || ρομαντική ἱστορία, μῦθος, θρῦλος || vi ὑπερβάλλω, φαντασιολογῶ || ~r n παραμυθᾶς, μυθοπλάστης.

Romanesque [rəumə'nesk] a ρωμανικός (ρυθμός).

Roman numerals ['rəumən'nju:mərəlz] npl λατινικοί ἀριθμοί.

romantic [rəu'mæntik] a ρομαντικός.

romp [rɔmp] n εὔθυμον παιχνίδι, φασαρία || vi (also ~ about) θορυβῶ, κάνω φασαρία, ἀτακτῶ || ~ers npl μπλούζα, ποδιά παιδιῶν, φοφούλια.

rondo ['rɔndəu] n (mus) ρονττό, ρόντο.

roof [ru:f] n στέγη, σκεπή || (of car etc) σκεπή || (of mouth) οὐρανίσκος || vt στεγάζω, σκεπάζω || ~ garden n κῆπος μέ ταράτσα || ~ing n στέγασις, ταβάνωμα.

rook [ruk] n (bird) κορώνη, κουρούνα, χαβαρῶνι || (thief) κλέφτης, λωποδύτης || vt (cheat) κλέβω, χαρτοκλέβω.

room [rum] n (in house) δωμάτιον, κάμαρα || (space) χῶρος, τόπος || (opportunity) περιθώριον, λόγος ‖ **~s** npl (flat) δωμάτια, διαμέρισμα ‖ (lodgings) δωμάτια μετά φαγητοῦ ‖ **~iness** n εὐρυχωρία ‖ **~ing house** n οἰκία ἐνοικιάζουσα ἐπιπλωμένα δωμάτια ‖ **~mate** n συγκάτοικος, σύνοικος ‖ **~ service** n ὑπηρεσία ‖ **~y** a εὐρύχωρος.

roost [ru:st] n κούρνια, κοτέτσι ‖ vi κουρνιάζω.

root [ru:t] n ρίζα ‖ (source) πηγή, αἰτία, ρίζα ‖ vt ριζώνω ‖ **to ~ about** vi (fig) ψάχνω ‖ **to ~ for** vt ὑποστηρίζω, ἐνθαρρύνω ‖ **to ~ out** vt ἐκριζώνω.

rope [roup] n σχοινί ‖ vt δένω μέ σχοινί ‖ **to ~ in** περικλείω, προσηλυτίζω, παρασύρω ‖ **to know the ~s** ξαίρω τήν δουλειά μου, εἶμαι μπασμένος ‖ **~ ladder** n ἀνεμόσκαλα.

rosary ['rəuzəri] n κομβολόγι.

rose [rəuz] pt of **rise** ‖ (flower) n τριαντάφυλλον, ρόδον ‖ a ροδόχρωμος, ρόζ.

rosé ['rəuzei] n (wine) κοκκινέλι.

rosebed ['rəuzbed] n ροδωνιά, συστάδα ρόδων.

rosebud ['rəuzbʌd] n μπουμπούκι τριανταφύλλου.

rosebush ['rəuzbuʃ] n τριανταφυλλιά.

rosemary ['rəuzməri] n δενδρολίβανον.

rosette [rəu'zet] n ροζέττα.

roster ['rɔstə*] n κατάλογος, κατάστασις.

rostrum ['rɔstrəm] n ἄμβων, βῆμα.

rosy ['rəuzi] a (colour) ροδόχρους, ρόδινος, ρόζ ‖ (hopeful) ρόδινα.

rot [rɔt] n σῆψις, σαπίλα, σάπισμα ‖ (nonsense) ἀνοησία, μπούρδα ‖ vti σήπομαι, ἀποσυντίθεμαι, σαπίζω.

rota ['rəutə] n κατάλογος, πίναξ.

rotary ['rəutəri] a περιστροφικός.

rotate [rəu'teit] vt (two or more things in order) ἐναλλάσσω, ἐκτελῶ ἐκ περιτροπῆς ‖ vi περιστρέφομαι, γυρίζω (γύρω ἀπό).

rotating [rəu'teitiŋ] a περιστρεφόμενος, περιστροφικός.

rotation [rəu'teiʃən] n περιστροφή ‖ **in ~** ἐκ περιτροπῆς.

rotor ['rəutə*] n στροφεῖον, ρώτωρ, ρότορ.

rotten ['rɔtn] a σαθρός, σάπιος, σαπισμένος ‖ (dishonest) πρόστυχος, κακῆς ποιότητος.

rotting ['rɔtiŋ] a πού σαπίζει.

rotund [rəu'tʌnd] a στρογγυλός, παχουλός.

rouble ['ru:bl] n ρούβλι(ον).

rouge [ru:ʒ] n κοκκινάδι, βαφή.

rough [rʌf] a (uneven) ἀνώμαλος, τραχύς ‖ (violent, coarse) χονδροειδής, πρόστυχος, τραχύς, ἀπότομος ‖ (stormy, wild) ἄγριος, σφοδρός, τρικυμιώδης ‖ (without comforts) πρόχειρος, στοιχειώδης ‖ (unfinished) πρόχειρο (σκίτσο), τοῦ προσχεδίου, ἀκατέργαστος ‖ (make-shift) βιαστικό, πρόχειρος ‖ (approximate) κατά προσέγγισιν, χονδρικός ‖ n

(uncut grass) ψηλό χορτάρι ‖ (violent person) μάγκας, κουτσαβάκης ‖ vt: **to ~ it** στεροῦμαι τίς ἀνέσεις, ἀντιμετωπίζω δυσκολίες ‖ **to play ~** παίζω σκληρό παιχνίδι ‖ **to ~ out** vt (draft) προσχεδιάζω, κάνω πρόχειρα ‖ **~en** vt τραχύνω ‖ **~ly** ad χονδροειδῶς, πρόχειρα ‖ κατά προσέγγισιν, περίπου, γενικά ‖ **~ness** n τραχύτης, σκληρότης.

roulette [ru:'let] n ρουλέττα.

Roumania [ru:'meiniə] n Ρουμανία ‖ **~n** n (person) Ρουμάνος ‖ a ρουμανικός.

round [raund] a στρογγυλός, σφαιρικός, κυκλικός ‖ (rough) στρογγυλός ‖ ad πέριξ, γύρω, τριγύρω ‖ prep γύρω ἀπό, περί ‖ n κύκλος, γῦρος ‖ (duty) γῦρος, βόλτα, περιοδεία, καθημερινή δουλειά ‖ (sport) γῦρος ‖ vt (corner) κάμπτω, στρίβω, κάνω στροφήν, παίρνω τήν στροφήν ‖ **to ~ off** vt στρογγυλεύω, τελειώνω ‖ **to ~ up** vt συγκεντρώνω, μαζεύω, πιάνω, περικυκλώνω ‖ **~ of ammunition** n φυσίγγιον ‖ **~ of applause** n ὁμοβροντία χειροκροτημάτων ‖ **~ of drinks** n ἕνα γῦρο ποτῶν, μιά βόλτα ‖ **~about** n παρακαμπτήριος ὁδός ‖ στρογγυλή μάντρα ‖ (merry-go-round) περιστρεφόμενα ξύλινα ἀλογάκια ‖ a κυκλικός, περιφερειακός ‖ **~ed** a στρογγυλευμένος ‖ **~ers** n (game) μπάλλα (εἶδος παιγνιδιοῦ) ‖ **~ly** ad (fig) τέλεια, ὁλοσχερῶς, πλήρως ‖ **~-shouldered** a μέ κυρτούς ὤμους, σκυφτός ‖ **~sman** n περιοδεύων μεταφορεύς, διανομεύς ‖ **~up** n περιμάζεμα, μπλόκο.

rouse [rauz] vt ξηκώνω ‖ (stir up) προκαλῶ, διεγείρω, ξεσηκώνω.

rousing ['rauziŋ] a (welcome) θορυβώδης, ζωηρός.

rout [raut] n φυγή, ἥττα, ἄτακτος φυγή ‖ vt κατατροπώνω, τρέπω εἰς φυγήν.

route [ru:t] n δρομολόγιον, δρόμος, πορεία ‖ **~ map** n ὁδικός χάρτης.

routine [ru:'ti:n] n ρουτίνα, στερεότυπος πορεία ‖ a τρέχων, κανονικός, τακτικός.

rover ['rəuvə*] n πλάνης, ἀλήτης, σουρτούκης.

roving ['rəuviŋ] a διατρέχων, περιπλανώμενος, πλάνης.

row [rəu] n (line) σειρά, στοῖχος, γραμμή, ἀράδα ‖ vt (boat) κινῶ μέ κουπί, μεταφέρω μέ τά κουπιά ‖ vi (in boat) κωπηλατῶ, τραβῶ κουπί.

row [rau] n (noise) θόρυβος, φασαρία, σαματάς ‖ (dispute) φιλονικία, καυγᾶς ‖ (scolding) ἐπίπληξις, κατσάδα, λούσιμο ‖ vi φιλονεικῶ, καυγαδίζω, ἁρπάζομαι.

rowboat ['rəubəut] n (US) λέμβος κωπηλασίας, βάρκα μέ κουπιά.

rowdiness ['raudinis] n θόρυβος, φασαρία.

rowdy ['raudi] a θορυβώδης, πού κάνει

σαματά ‖ n (person) θορυβοποιός, καυγαντζῆς, νταῆς.

rowing ['rəuiŋ] n κωπηλασία, κουπί ‖ ~ **boat** n βάρκα μέ κουπιά.

rowlock ['rɔlək] n σκαλμοί.

royal ['rɔiəl] a βασιλικός ‖ ~**ist** n βασιλόφρων, βασιλικός ‖ a βασιλικός ‖ ~**ty** n (family) βασιλική οἰκογένεια ‖ (payment) (to inventor) δικαιώματα ἐφευρέτου ‖ (to author) συγγραφικά δικαιώματα.

rub [rʌb] n (polish, with cloth) τρίψιμο, σφούγγισμα ‖ vt τρίβω, ἐπαλείφω, προστρίβω ‖ (clean) στεγνώνω, σκουπίζω ‖ **to** ~ **off** vi ἀφαιρῶ διά τριβῆς, φεύγω.

rubber ['rʌbə*] n (substance) καουτσούκ, κόμμι ‖ (Brit) γομμολάστιχα ‖ ~ **band** n λάστιχο ‖ ~ **stamp** n ἐβέα, δένδρον καουτσούκ ‖ ~ **stamp** n (lit) σφραγίδα ‖ (fig) ὁ ἐγκρίνων τυφλῶς ‖ ~**y** a κομμιώδης.

rubbish ['rʌbiʃ] n σκουπίδια, ἀπορρίμματα ‖ (nonsense) ἀνοησίες, κολοκύθια ‖ ~ **dump** n τόπος ἀπορρίψεως σκουπιδιῶν ‖ ~**y** a τιποτένιος, τῆς πεντάρας.

rubble ['rʌbl] n χαλίκι, σκύρα.

ruble ['ru:bl] n (US) = **rouble**.

ruby ['ru:bi] n ρουμπίνι ‖ a κόκκινο, ρουμπινί.

rucksack ['rʌksæk] n σακκίδιον.

ructions ['rʌkʃənz] npl (old) καυγᾶς, κατσάδα.

rudder ['rʌdə*] n πηδάλιον, τιμόνι.

ruddy ['rʌdi] a (colour) ροδοκόκκινος, ἐρυθρωπός ‖ (col: bloody) τρομερός, βρωμο-, παλιο-.

rude [ru:d] a (vulgar) πρόστυχος ‖ (impolite) βάναυσος, ἀπολίτιστος, ἀγενής ‖ (rough) τραχύς, πρωτόγονος ‖ ~**ly** ad πρωτόγονα, ἀπότομα, ἀπρεπῶς ‖ ~**ness** n χοντροκοπιά, ἀποτομότης.

rudiment ['ru:dimənt] n στοιχεῖον, ὑποτυπώδης ἀρχή ‖ ~**ary** a στοιχειώδης.

ruff [rʌf] n τραχηλιά.

ruffian ['rʌfiən] n παλιάνθρωπος, μαχαιροβγάλτης.

ruffle ['rʌfl] vt ρυτιδώνω, τσαλακώνω, ἀνακατεύω.

rug [rʌg] n τάπης, χαλί ‖ (for knees) σάλι, χράμι.

rugby ['rʌgbi] n ράγκμπυ.

rugged ['rʌgid] a τραχύς, ἀνώμαλος.

rugger ['rʌgə*] n ράγκμπυ.

ruin ['ru:in] n καταστροφή, συμφορά, ἀφανισμός ‖ vt καταστρέφω, ἀφανίζω ‖ ~**s** npl ἐρείπια ‖ ~**ation** n καταστροφή, ὄλεθρος, ρήμαγμα.

rule [ru:l] n (guide) κανόνας ‖ (what is usual) τό σύνηθες, τό κανονικόν ‖ (government) ἐξουσία, ἀρχή, κυριαρχία ‖ (stick) κανόνας, χάρακας, ρίγα, μέτρον ‖ vt κυβερνῶ, διοικῶ ‖ (pervade) διέπω ‖ (lines) χαρακώνω ‖ **as a** ~ κατά κανόνα,

συνήθως ‖ ~**d** a (paper) ρίγωτός, χαρακωμένος ‖ ~**r** n κυβερνήτης, ἄρχων ‖ (straight edge) χάρακας.

ruling ['ru:liŋ] a (party) ἄρχων, διευθύνων, κρατῶν ‖ (class) ἄρχουσα (τάξις).

rum [rʌm] n ροῦμι ‖ a (col) παράξενος, ἀλλόκοτος.

rumble ['rʌmbl] n ὑπόκωφος βοή, βροντή ‖ vi μυκῶμαι, βροντῶ, βουΐζω, γουργουρίζω.

ruminate ['ru:mineit] vi (think over) διαλογίζομαι, σκέπτομαι διά, μελετῶ.

rummage ['rʌmidʒ] n ἔρευνα, ψάξιμο ‖ vi ἐρευνῶ, ψάχνω.

rumour, (US) **rumor** ['ru:mə*] n φήμη, διάδοσις ‖ vt: **it is** ~**ed that** λέγεται ὅτι, διαδίδεται ὅτι, φημολογεῖται ὅτι.

rump [rʌmp] n γλουτός, ὀπίσθια ‖ ~**steak** n κόντρα φιλέτο.

rumpus ['rʌmpəs] n θόρυβος, ταραχή ‖ (col) καυγᾶς, σαματᾶς.

run [rʌn] (irreg v) n (running) δρόμος, τρέξιμο ‖ (aut) διαδρομή, βόλτα ‖ (series) σειρά, ἀλληλουχία, συνέχεια ‖ (sudden demand) συρροή, ζήτησις ‖ (enclosed space) βοσκότοπος, χῶρος κλειστός ‖ (ski run) πίστα τοῦ σκί, κατήφορος γιά σκί ‖ vt (cause to run) κατευθύνω, λειτουργῶ, γυρίζω ‖ (train, bus) κυκλοφορῶ, κινῶ, λειτουργῶ, κάνω διαδρομή ‖ (manage) διευθύνω ‖ (compete in race) τρέχω εἰς ἀγῶνα, βάζω ὑποψηφιότητα ‖ (force) περνῶ, κάνω νά περάση, καρφώνω ‖ (pass: hand, eye) περνῶ ‖ vi (move quickly) τρέχω, τό βάζω στό πόδι, στρίβω ‖ (compete) θέτω ὑποψηφιότητα, τρέχω εἰς ἀγῶνας ‖ (machine) λειτουργῶ, κινοῦμαι, δουλεύω ‖ (flow) ρέω, κυλῶ, τρέχω ‖ (colours) ξεβάφω, βγαίνω, τρέχω ‖ **on the** ~ εἰς φυγήν, πολυάσχολος ‖ **to** ~ **riot** ὀργιάζω, ἀπειθαρχῶ ‖ **to** ~ **a risk** ριψοκινδυνεύω ‖ **to** ~ **about** vi (children) τρέχω ἐδῶ καί κεῖ ‖ **to** ~ **across** vt (find) συναντῶ τυχαία ‖ **to** ~ **away** vi δραπετεύω, διαφεύγω ‖ **to** ~ **down** vi (clock) ξεκουρδίζω ‖ vt (run over) κτυπῶ, πατῶ (κάποιον), πλακώνω ‖ (talk against) δυσφημῶ, κατηγορῶ, ἐξυβρίζω ‖ **to be** ~**down** εἶμαι ἐξηντλημένος, εἶμαι τσακισμένος ‖ **to** ~ **off** vi φεύγω, τρέπομαι εἰς φυγήν, τό σκάω ‖ **to** ~ **out** vi (person) βγαίνω τρέχοντας ‖ (liquid) χύνομαι, τρέχω, στάζω ‖ (lease) παρέρχομαι, λήγω, περνῶ, ἐκπνέω ‖ (money) τελειώνω, ἐξαντλοῦμαι ‖ **to** ~ **out of** vt ἐξαντλῶ, τελειώνω, μένω ἀπό ‖ **to** ~ **over** vt κτυπῶ, πλακώνω, πολτοποιῶ ‖ (read) ρίχνω μιά ματιά ‖ **to** ~ **through** vt (instructions) διαβάζω γρήγορα, ἐξετάζω βιαστικά ‖ **to** ~ **up** vt (debt) ἀφήνω νά ἀνεβῆ, χρεώνομαι περισσότερα ‖ (dress) ράβω γρήγορα-γρήγορα ‖ **to** ~ **up against** vt (*difficulties*) συναντώ, ἀντιμετωπίζω ‖ **~about** n (*small car*) αὐτοκίνητο δύο θέσεων ‖ **~away** a (*horse*) ἀφηνιασμένο (ἄλογο) ‖ (*truck*) ἀποσπασθέν (ὄχημα).

rung [rʌŋ] *pp of* **ring** ‖ n βαθμίς, σκαλί ἀνεμόσκαλας.

runner ['rʌnə*] n (*messenger*) ἀγγελιαφόρος ‖ (*of sleigh*) πατίνι ‖ **~-up** n ὁ ἐπίλαχών, ὁ δεύτερος (νικητής).

running ['rʌniŋ] n (*of business*) διεύθυνσις, ἐκμετάλλευσις ‖ (*of machine*) λειτουργία, κίνησις ‖ a (*water*) ρέων, τρεχούμενος ‖ **~ commentary** n σχολιασμένη ἔκδοσις, (ραδιο)ρεπορτάζ.

run-of-the-mill ['rʌnəndə'mil] a κοινός, συνηθισμένος.

runt [rʌnt] n κοντοστούμπης.

run-through ['rʌnθru:] n γρήγορο διάβασμα, γρήγορη ἐπανάληψις.

runway ['rʌnwei] n διάδρομος ἀπογειώσεως.

rupture ['rʌptʃə*] n (*med*) ρῆξις, διάρρηξις ‖ vt: **to ~ o.s.** πάσχω ἐκ κήλης.

rural ['ruərəl] a ἀγροτικός, ὑπαίθριος.

ruse [ru:z] n τέχνασμα, πανουργία, κόλπο.

rush [rʌʃ] n (*dash*) σπουδή, τρέξιμο, βιασύνη ‖ (*sudden demand*) μεγάλη ζήτησις ‖ (*current*) ἐκτόξευσις, εἰσροή ‖ vt ὁρμῶ, τρέχω ἐπειγόντως, φέρω ἐπειγόντως ‖ (*attack*) ἐνεργῶ ἔφοδον ‖ (col: *overcharge*) γδέρνω ‖ vi (*dash*) (ἐξ)ὁρμῶ, ἐφορμῶ, σπεύδω, τρέχω ‖ **~es** npl (*bot*) βούρλον, σπάρτο ‖ **~ hour** n ὥρα συνωστισμοῦ, ὥρα πολλῆς δουλειᾶς.

rusk [rʌsk] n παξιμάδι.

Russia ['rʌʃə] n Ρωσία ‖ **~n** n Ρῶσος ‖ a ρωσικός, ρούσικος.

rust [rʌst] n σκωρία, σκουριά ‖ vi σκουριάζω.

rustic ['rʌstik] a (*of the country*) ἀγροτικός, χωριάτικος ‖ (*roughly made*) χοντροκαμωμένο.

rustle ['rʌsl] n ψίθυρος, τρίξιμο, μουρμούρισμα ‖ vi θροΐζω, μουρμουρίζω ‖ vt (US) κλέβω, εἶμαι ζωοκλέπτης.

rustproof ['rʌstpru:f] a ἀνοξείδωτος.

rusty ['rʌsti] a σκουριασμένος.

rut [rʌt] n (*track*) αὐλάκι, τροχιά, ροδιά ‖ (*routine*) ρουτίνα, μονοτονία.

ruthless ['ru:θlis] a ἀνηλεής, ἄσπλαγχνος, ὠμός ‖ **~ly** ad ἄνευ οἴκτου, ἀλύπητα ‖ **~ness** n ἀσπλαγχνία, σκληρότης.

rye [rai] n σίκαλις ‖ **~ bread** n ψωμί ἀπό σίκαλη.

S, s

sabbath ['sæbəθ] n (*Jewish*) Σάββατον ‖ (*Christian*) Κυριακή.

sabbatical [sə'bætikəl] a: **~ year** ἄδεια ἑνός ἔτους (καθηγητοῦ).

saber ['seibə*] n (US) = **sabre**.

sabotage ['sæbətɑ:ʒ] n δολιοφθορά.

sabre ['seibə*] n σπαθί.

saccharin(e) ['sækərin] n σακχαρίνη.

sachet ['sæʃei] n σακκουλάκι (μέ ἀρώματα).

sack [sæk] n σάκκος, τσουβάλι ‖ (*dismissal*) ἀπόλυσις ‖ vt ἀπολύω ‖ (*town*) λεηλατῶ ‖ **~ful** n σακκιά, τσουβάλι ‖ **~ing** n (*material*) σακκόπανον ‖ (*dismissal*) ἀπόλυσις, παῦσις.

sacrament ['sækrəmənt] n μυστήριον, μετάληψις.

sacred ['seikrid] a ἱερός, ἅγιος ‖ (*duty etc*) ἀπαραβίαστος.

sacrifice ['sækrifais] n θυσία ‖ vt θυσιάζω.

sacrilege ['sækrilidʒ] n ἱεροσυλία, βεβήλωσις.

sacrosanct ['sækrəusæŋkt] a ἱερός καί ἀπαραβίαστος.

sad [sæd] a λυπημένος, θλιμένος ‖ (*dull*) θλιβερός, ἐλεεινός ‖ **~den** vt λυπῶ, θλίβω.

saddle ['sædl] n σέλλα ‖ vt (*burden*) φορτώνω ‖ **~bag** n δισάκκι.

sadism ['seidizəm] n σαδισμός.

sadist ['seidist] n σαδιστής ‖ **~ic** [sə'distik] a σαδιστικός.

sadly ['sædli] ad λυπηρά, θλιβερά ‖ (*much*) πολύ.

sadness ['sædnis] n θλῖψις, μελαγχολία.

safari [sə'fɑ:ri] n σαφάρι.

safe [seif] a ἀσφαλής, σῶος ‖ (*cautious*) προσεκτικός, σίγουρος ‖ (*sure*) ἀσφαλής, ἀκίνδυνος ‖ n χρηματοκιβώτιον ‖ **~guard** n ἐξασφάλισις, προστασία ‖ vt προστατεύω ‖ **~ keeping** n ἀσφάλεια ‖ **~ly** ad ἀσφαλῶς, σίγουρα ‖ **~ness** n ἀσφάλεια, σιγουριά ‖ **~ty** n ἀσφάλεια, σιγουριά ‖ **~ty belt** n ζώνη ἀσφαλείας ‖ **~ty curtain** n αὐλαία ἀσφαλείας ‖ **~ty pin** n παραμάνα.

sag [sæg] vi κάμπτομαι, βουλιάζω.

saga ['sɑ:gə] n ἔπος, σάγκα.

sage [seidʒ] n (*herb*) φασκομηλιά, ἀλιφασκιά ‖ (*man*) σοφός.

sago ['seigəu] n (*food*) σάγος, σαγοῦ.

said [sed] pt,pp of **say** ‖ a λεγόμενος, λεχθείς.

sail [seil] n ἱστίον, πανί ‖ (*trip*) πλοῦς, ταξίδι, ἀπόπλους ‖ vt κυβερνῶ (πλοῖον) ‖ vi πλέω, πάω μέ τό πανί ‖ (*depart*) ἀποπλέω ‖ (*fig: cloud etc*) τρέχω, περνῶ ‖ **~boat** n (US) βάρκα μέ πανί ‖ **~ing** n (*sport*) ἱστιοδρομία ‖ **to go ~ing** κάνω ἱστιοδρομίες ‖ **~ing ship** n ἱστιοφόρον (πλοῖον) ‖ **~or** n ναύτης, ναυτικός.

saint [seint] n ἅγιος ‖ **~liness** n ἁγιότης ‖ **~ly** a ἁγίου.

sake [seik] n: **for the ~ of** πρός χάριν τοῦ ‖ **for your ~** γιά τό καλό σου.

salad ['sæləd] n σαλάτα ‖ **~ dressing** n εἶδος μαγιονέζας ‖ **~ oil** n λάδι γιά σαλάτα.

S

salami [sə'la:mi] *n* σαλάμι.

salaried ['sælərid] *a* (*staff*) ἔμμισθος, μισθωτός.

salary ['sæləri] *n* μισθός.

sale [seil] *n* πώλησις, πούλημα ‖ (*for short periods*) ξεπούλημα, ἐκπτώσεις ‖ ~room *n* δημοπρατήριον ‖ ~sman *n* πωλητής ‖ ~smanship *n* τέχνη τοῦ πωλεῖν ‖ ~swoman *n* πωλήτρια.

salient ['seiliənt] *a* προεξέχων, περίοπτος.

saliva [sə'laivə] *n* σάλιο.

sallow ['sæləu] *a* ὠχρός, χλωμός.

salmon ['sæmən] *n* σολομός.

salon ['sælɔ:ŋ] *n* κομμωτήριον.

saloon [sə'lu:n] *n* (*aut*) κλειστόν (αὐτοκίνητον) ‖ (*ship's lounge*) σαλόνι.

salt [sɔ:lt] *n* ἅλας, ἁλάτι ‖ (*chem*) ἅλας ‖ *vt* (*cure*) ἁλατίζω, παστώνω ‖ (*flavour*) ἁλατίζω ‖ ~cellar *n* ἁλατιέρα ‖ ~ mine *n* ἁλατορυχεῖον ‖ ~y *a* ἁλμυρός.

salutary ['sæljutəri] *a* σωστικός, σωτήριος.

salute [sə'lu:t] *n* (*mil*) χαιρετισμός ‖ *vt* (*mil*) χαιρετίζω, ἀποδίδω χαιρετισμόν.

salvage ['sælvidʒ] *n* διάσωσις ‖ (*property saved*) ὑλικὸν ἐκ περισυλλογῆς ‖ *vt* διασώζω.

salvation [sæl'veiʃən] *n* σωτηρία ‖ S~ Army *n* ὁ Στρατὸς τῆς Σωτηρίας.

salver ['sælvə*] *n* δίσκος.

salvo ['sælvəu] *n* κανονιοβολισμός, ὁμοβροντία.

same [seim] *a* ἴδιος ‖ all the ~ παρ' ὅλα ταῦτα.

sample ['sa:mpl] *n* δεῖγμα ‖ *vt* (*test*) δοκιμάζω.

sanatorium [sænə'tɔ:riəm] *n* σανατόριον.

sanctify ['sæŋktifai] *vt* ἁγιάζω, καθαγιάζω ‖ (*establish*) καθιερώνω.

sanctimonious [sæŋkti'məuniəs] *a* ψευτοθεοφοβούμενος, ὑποκριτής.

sanction ['sæŋkʃən] *n* (*pol, econ*) (ἐπι)κύρωσις.

sanctity ['sæŋktiti] *n* ἁγιότης, ἁγιοσύνη ‖ (*sacredness*) ἱερότης, ἀπαραβίαστον.

sanctuary ['sæŋktjuəri] *n* ἱερόν, ἄδυτον ‖ (*for fugitive*) ἄσυλον ‖ (*refuge*) καταφύγιον.

sand [sænd] *n* ἄμμος ‖ *vt* στρώνω μὲ ἄμμο ‖ ~s *npl* ἀμμουδιά.

sandal ['sændl] *n* σανδάλι, πέδιλον.

sandbag ['sændbæg] *n* σάκκος ἄμμου.

sand dune ['sænddju:n] *n* ἀμμόλοφος.

sandpaper ['sændpeipə*] *n* γυαλόχαρτο.

sandpit ['sændpit] *n* (*for children*) ἀμμόκουτο.

sandstone ['sændstəun] *n* ψαμμίτης, ψαμμόλιθος.

sandwich ['sænwidʒ] *n* σάντουϊτς ‖ *vt* παρεμβάλλω, στριμώχνω.

sandy ['sændi] *a* (*with sand*) ἀμμώδης, ἀμμιουδερός ‖ (*colour*) πυρόξανθος.

sane [sein] *a* ἐχέφρων, σώφρων ‖ (*sensible*) λογικός.

sang [sæŋ] *pt of* sing.

sanguine ['sæŋgwin] *a* (*hopeful*) αἰσιόδοξος.

sanitarium [sæni'teəriəm] *n* (*US*) = sanatorium.

sanitary ['sænitəri] *a* ὑγιεινός ‖ (*protective*) ὑγιεινομικός ‖ ~ napkin (*US*), ~ towel *n* πετσέτα ὑγιεινῆς.

sanitation [sæni'teiʃən] *n* ὑγιεινή, καθαριότης.

sanity ['sæniti] *n* πνευματικὴ ὑγεία, ὑγιὴς νοῦς ‖ (*good sense*) μετριοπάθεια, λογική.

sank [sæŋk] *pt of* sink.

Santa Claus [sæntə'klɔ:z] *n* ῾Ἅη Βασίλης.

sap [sæp] *n* (*of plants*) χυμός, ὀπός ‖ *vt* (*wear away*) ὑπονομεύω, ὑποσκάπτω.

sapling ['sæpliŋ] *n* δενδρύλλιον.

sapphire ['sæfaiə*] *n* σάπφειρος.

sarcasm ['sa:kæzəm] *n* σαρκασμός.

sarcastic [sa:'kæstik] *a* σαρκαστικός.

sarcophagus [sa:'kɔfəgəs] *n* σαρκοφάγος.

sardine [sa:'di:n] *n* σαρδέλλα.

sardonic [sa:'dɔnik] *a* σαρδόνιος, κοροϊδευτικός.

sartorial [sa:'tɔ:riəl] *a* τοῦ ράφτη, τῶν ραφτικῶν.

sash [sæʃ] *n* (*mil*) ζώνη ἀξιωματικῶν.

sat [sæt] *pt,pp of* sit.

Satan ['seitn] *n* Σατανᾶς ‖ ~ic [sə'tænik] *a* σατανικός.

satchel ['sætʃəl] *n* (*sch*) τσάντα, σάκκα.

satellite ['sætəlait] *n* δορυφόρος ‖ *a* δορυφορικός, ὑπόκεντρος.

satin ['sætin] *n* σατέν ‖ *a* σατινέ ἀπὸ σατέν.

satire ['sætaiə*] *n* σάτυρα.

satirical [sə'tirikəl] *a* σατυρικός.

satirize ['sætəraiz] *vt* σατυρίζω, διακωμῳδῶ.

satisfaction [sætis'fækʃən] *n* ἱκανοποίησις, εὐχαρίστησις.

satisfactorily [sætis'fæktərili] *ad* ἱκανοποιητικά.

satisfactory [sætis'fæktəri] *a* ἱκανοποιητικός.

satisfy ['sætisfai] *vt* ἱκανοποιῶ ‖ (*convince*) πείθω, διαβεβαιῶ ‖ ~ing *a* ἱκανοποιητικός.

saturate ['sætʃəreit] *vt* διαβρέχω, διαποτίζω, μουσκεύω.

saturation [sætʃə'reiʃən] *n* διάβρεξις, κορεσμός.

Saturday ['sætədi] *n* Σάββατον.

sauce [sɔ:s] *n* σάλτσα ‖ ~pan *n* κατσαρόλα τέντζερες ‖ ~r *n* πιατάκι.

saucily ['sɔ:sili] *ad* ἀναιδῶς, μόρτικα τσαχπίνικα.

sauciness ['sɔ:sinis] *n* ἀναίδεια, ἀδιαντροπιά.

saucy ['sɔ:si] *a* ἀναιδής, αὐθάδης.

saunter ['sɔ:ntə*] *vi* σουλατσάρω, περπατῶ ἄσκοπα ‖ *n* βόλτα, χάζεμα.

sausage ['sɔsidʒ] *n* λουκάνικο ‖ ~ **roll** *n* λουκάνικο μέ ζύμη.

savage ['sævidʒ] *a* ἄγριος, θηριώδης ‖ (*uncivilized*) ἀπολίτιστος, βάρβαρος ‖ *n* ἄγριος ‖ *vt* δαγκώνω, ἐπιτίθεμαι ἀγρίως ‖ ~**ly** *ad* μέ ἀγριότητα ‖ ~**ry** *n* ἀγριότης, βαρβαρότης.

save [seiv] *vt* σώζω, γλυτώνω ‖ (*store up*) (ἐξ)οἰκονομῶ, ἀποταμιεύω, μαζεύω ‖ (*avoid using up*) φειδωλεύομαι, ἀποφεύγω ‖ *n* οἰκονομία ‖ *prep,cj* πλήν, ἐκτός, ἐξαιρουμένου.

saving ['seiviŋ] *a* (*redeeming*) σωτήριος ‖ *n* οἰκονομία ‖ ~**s** *npl* ἀποταμιεύσεις, καταθέσεις, οἰκονομίες ‖ ~**s bank** *n* ταμιευτήριον.

saviour ['seivjə*] *n* σωτήρας.

savoir-faire ['sævwɑ:'feə*] *n* ἐπιδεξιότης, τάκτ.

savour, (*US*) **savor** ['seivə*] *n* οὐσία, γεῦσις, γοῦστο ‖ *vt* γεύομαι ‖ (+ *of*) ὄζω, μυρίζω ἀπό ‖ ~**y** *a* γευστικός, νόστιμος, ὀρεκτικός.

savvy ['sævi] *n* (*col*) καταλαβαίνω.

saw [sɔ:] (*irreg v*) *n* (*tool*) πριόνι ‖ *vt* πριονίζω ‖ *pt of* see ‖ ~**dust** *n* πριονίδια ‖ ~**mill** *n* πριονιστήριον.

Saxon ['sæksn] *n* Σάξων.

saxophone ['sæksəfəun] *n* σαξόφωνον.

say [sei] (*irreg v*) *n* λόγος, κουβέντα ‖ *vt* (*tell*) λέγω ‖ (*repeat*) (ξανα)λέγω ‖ (*suppose*) ὑποθέτω ‖ ~**ing** *n* ρητόν.

scab [skæb] *n* κάρκαδο ‖ (*pej: industry*) ἀπεργοσπάστης.

scabby ['skæbi] *a* καρκαδιασμένος.

scaffold ['skæfəld] *n* ἱκρίωμα ‖ ~**ing** *r.* σκαλωσιά.

scald [skɔ:ld] *n* ζεμάτισμα ‖ *vt* ζεματίζω ‖ ~**ing** *a* (*hot*) ζεματιστός.

scale [skeil] *n* (*of fish*) λέπι ‖ (*mus*) κλῖμαξ, σκάλα ‖ (*for measuring*) κλῖμαξ, διαβάθμισις ‖ (*on map*) κλῖμαξ ‖ (*size*) κλίμακα ‖ *vt* (*climb*) ἀναρριχῶμαι, σκαρφαλώνω ‖ ~**s** *npl* (*balance*) ζυγός, ζυγαριά ‖ **on a large** ~ σέ μεγάλη κλίμακα ‖ ~ **drawing** *n* σχέδιον ὑπό κλίμακα.

scallop ['skɔləp] *n* (*shellfish*) χτένι.

scalp [skælp] *n* τριχωτόν δέρμα κεφαλῆς ‖ *vt* γδέρνω τό κρανίον.

scalpel ['skælpəl] *n* νυστέρι.

scamp [skæmp] *vt* κακοφτιάνω, πασα λείβω.

scamper ['skæmpə*] *vi* τρέχω τρελλά, τό στρίβω.

scan [skæn] *vt* ἐξονυχίζω, διερευνῶ ‖ (*poet*) διαβάζω ἐμμέτρως.

scandal ['skændl] *n* σκάνδαλον ‖ (*gossip*) κακολογία, κουτσομπολιό ‖ ~**ize** *vt* σκανδαλίζω, ταράσσω ‖ ~**ous** *a* σκανδαλώδης.

Scandinavia [skændi'neiviə] *n* Σκανδιναβία ‖ ~**n** *a,n* Σκανδιναβικός.

scant [skænt] *a* πενιχρός, ἀνεπαρκής,

λιγοστός ‖ ~**ily** *ad* ἀνεπαρκῶς, ἐλαφρά, λιγοστά ‖ ~**iness** *n* σπάνις, ἀνεπάρκεια, ἀραιότης ‖ ~**y** *a* ἀνεπαρκής, λιγοστός, πρόχειρος.

scapegoat ['skeipgəut] *n* ἀποδιοπομπαῖος τράγος.

scar [skɑ:*] *n* οὐλή, σημάδι ‖ *vt* ἀφήνω σημάδι.

scarce [skeəs] *a* σπάνιος, σπανίζω ‖ ~**ly** *ad* μόλις, σχεδόν καθόλου ‖ ~**ness** *n* σπανιότης, ἔλλειψις.

scarcity ['skeəsiti] *n* σπάνις, ἔλλειψις.

scare [skeə*] *n* ἐκφόβισις, τρομάρα ‖ *vt* φοβίζω, τρομάζω ‖ ~**crow** *n* φόβητρον, σκιάχτρο.

scarf [skɑ:f] *n* σάρπα, κασκόλ.

scarlet ['skɑ:lit] *a* (*colour*) κατακόκκινος ‖ *n* κτυπητό κόκκινο ‖ ~ **fever** *n* ὀστρακιά, σκαρλατίνα.

scarves [skɑ:vz] *npl of* scarf.

scary ['skeəri] *a* (*col*) τρομακτικός, τρομερός.

scathing ['skeidiŋ] *a* καυστικός, δηκτικός.

scatter ['skætə*] *n* διασπορά, σκόρπισμα ‖ *vt* (*sprinkle*) σκορπίζω ‖ (*an enemy*) διασκορπίζω ‖ *vi* διαλύομαι, σκορπίζω ‖ ~**brained** *a* ἄμυαλος, ξεμυαλισμένος ‖ ~**ing** *n* μικρά ποσότης, σκόρπισμα.

scavenger ['skævindʒə*] *n* (ὁδο)καθαριστής, σκουπιδιάρης.

scene [si:n] *n* (*of accident etc*) τόπος, θέατρον ‖ (*of play*) σκηνή ‖ (*division of play*) σκηνή ‖ (*view*) τοπεῖον, ἄποψις, θέα ‖ (*fuss*) σκηνή, φασαρία, ἐπεισόδιον ‖ (*incident*) σκηνή, συμβάν ‖ **on the** ~ ἐπί τόπω, ἐπί σκηνῆς ‖ ~**ry** *n* σκηνικόν, σκηνογραφία, σκηνή ‖ (*view*) τοπίον, θέα, ἄποψις.

scenic ['si:nik] *a* σκηνικός, θεαματικός.

scent [sent] *n* ὀσμή, ἄρωμα, μυρουδιά ‖ (*sense of smell*) ὄσφρησις ‖ *vt* (*make fragrant*) ἀρωματίζω, μοσχοβολῶ.

scepter ['septə*] *n* (*US*) = **sceptre**.

sceptic ['skeptik] *n* σκεπτικιστής ‖ ~**al** *a* σκεπτικός, δύσπιστος ‖ ~**ism** *n* σκεπτικισμός.

sceptre ['septə*] *n* σκῆπτρον.

schedule ['fedju:l, (*US*)'skedju:l] *n* κατάλογος, πρόγραμμα, δρομολόγιον ‖ *vt* καταγράφω, προγραμματίζω ‖ **on** ~ στήν ὥρα ‖ σύμφωνα μέ τό πρόγραμμα ‖ **behind** ~ καθυστερημένος.

scheme [ski:m] *n* διάταξις, συνδυασμός ‖ (*plan*) σχέδιον ‖ (*plot*) μηχανορραφία, δολοπλοκία ‖ *vi* μηχανορραφῶ, σχεδιάζω.

scheming ['ski:miŋ] *a* δολοπλόκος, κόμπιναδόρος.

schism ['sizəm] *n* σχίσμα.

schizophrenic [skitsəu'frenik] *a* σχιζοφρενικός.

scholar ['skɔlə*] *n* μελετητής, μορφωμένος ‖ (*with scholarship*) ὑπότροφος ‖ ~**ly** *ad* μορφωμένος ‖ ~**ship** n ὑποτροφία ‖ (*learning*) μόρφωσις.

school [sku:l] n σχολεῖον, σκολειό ‖ (*group*) σχολή ‖ (*department*) σχολή attr a σχολικό, τοῦ σχολείου ‖ vt διδάσκω, γυμνάζω, μορφώνω ‖ ~**book** n σχολικόν βιβλίον ‖ ~**boy** n μαθητής ‖ ~**days** npl σχολικά χρόνια ‖ ~**girl** n μαθήτρια ‖ ~**ing** n ἐκπαίδευσις, μόρφωσις ‖ ~**master** n (δι)δάσκαλος, καθηγητής ‖ διευθυντής ‖ ~**mistress** n δασκάλα, καθηγήτρια ‖ ~**room** n αἴθουσα διδασκαλίας ‖ ~**teacher** n δημοδιδάσκαλος.

schooner ['sku:nə*] n (*ship*) σκούνα ‖ (*glass for sherry etc*) ποτηράκι.

sciatica [sai'ætikə] n ἰσχιαλγία.

science ['saiəns] n ἐπιστήμη.

scientific [saiən'tifik] a ἐπιστημονικός.

scientist ['saiəntist] n ἐπιστήμων.

scintillating ['sintileitiŋ] a σπινθοβόλος, ἀστραφτερός.

scissors ['sizəz] npl ψαλίδι ‖ **a pair of** ~ ψαλίδι.

scoff [skɔf] vt (*eat*) τρώγω, καταβροχθίζω ‖ vi (*mock*) (+ *at*) σκόπτω, κοροϊδεύω.

scold [skəuld] vt ἐπιπλήττω, μαλώνω.

scone [skɔn] n εἶδος κέϊκ.

scoop [sku:p] n φτυάρι, σέσουλα ‖ vt (*also* ~ **out** *or* **up**) ἀδειάζω ‖ ἀνασκάπτω.

scooter ['sku:tə*] n (*motorcycle*) βέσπα ‖ (*child's toy*) πατίνι.

scope [skəup] n ἀντίληψις, γνῶσις ‖ (*opportunity*) ὁρίζων, εὐκαιρία, περιθώριον.

scorch [skɔ:tʃ] n καψάλισμα, κάψιμο ‖ vt καψαλίζω, τσουρουφλίζω ‖ (*wither*) ψήνω, ξεραίνω ‖ ~**er** n (*col: hot day*) πολύ ζεστή ἡμέρα, κάψα ‖ ~**ing** a καφτερός, καυστική.

score [skɔ:*] n (*points*) σκόρ ‖ (*mus*) παρτιτούρα ‖ (*reason*) θέμα, σημεῖον, ζήτημα ‖ (*twenty*) εἰκοσάς, εἰκοσαριά ‖ vt (*win points*) σημειώνω, κάνω (πόντους) ‖ (*mark*) χαράσσω, χαρακώνω ‖ vi (*keep record*) κρατῶ σκόρ ‖ ~**board** n πίνακα τῶν σκόρ ‖ ~**r** n (*player*) ὁ ἐπιτυχών τέρμα ‖ (*recorder*) μαρκαδόρος.

scorn ['skɔ:n] n περιφρόνησις ‖ vt περιφρονῶ ‖ ~**ful** a περιφρονητικός ‖ ~**fully** ad περιφρονητικά.

scorpion ['skɔ:piən] n σκορπιός.

Scot [skɔt] n Σκῶτος, Σκωτσέζος ‖ ~**ch** n (*whisky*) (σκωτσέζικο) οὐΐσκυ.

scotch [skɔtʃ] vt (*terminate*) ἀποτρέπω, καταπνίγω.

Scotland ['skɔtlənd] n Σκωτία.

Scots [skɔts] npl Σκωτσέζοι ‖ a σκωτσέζος ‖ ~**man** n Σκωτσέζος ‖ ~**woman** n Σκωτίς, Σκωτσέζα.

Scottish ['skɔtiʃ] a σκωτικός, σκωτσέζικος.

scoundrel ['skaundrəl] n παλιάνθρωπος.

scour ['skauə*] vt (*search*) διατρέχω, ἐρευνῶ ‖ (*clean*) καθαρίζω, παστρεύω,

γυαλίζω, τρίβω ‖ ~**er** n (*for pans*) σύρμα, μπρίλλο.

scourge [skə:dʒ] n (*plague*) πληγή.

scout [skaut] n ἀνιχνευτής ‖ (*boy scout*) πρόσκοπος ‖ vi (*reconnoitre*) ἀνιχνεύω, κατοπτεύω.

scowl [skaul] n συνοφρύωσις, σκυθρωπότης ‖ vi συνοφρυοῦμαι, κατσουφιάζω.

scraggy ['skrægi] a ἰσχνός, κοκκαλιάρης.

scram [skræm] vi (*col*) στρίβω, τό βάζω στά πόδια ‖ ~! στρίβε!, δίνε του!

scramble ['skræmbl] n σκαρφάλωμα ‖ ἀγών, πάλη ‖ vi ἀνεβαίνω, κατεβαίνω, μπουσουλῶ ‖ συνωστίζομαι, σπρώχνομαι ‖ ~**d eggs** npl (αὐγά) σφουγγάτο.

scrap [skræp] n κομματάκι, ἀπόρριμμα, ψίχουλο ‖ (*fight*) συμπλοκή, καυγᾶς ‖ (*scrap iron*) παλιοσίδερα ‖ a γιά πέταμα, ἄχρηστος ‖ vt πετῶ ὡς ἄχρηστον, ἀπορρίπτω ‖ vi (*fight*) πιάνομαι στά χέρια ‖ ~**s** npl (*waste*) ἀπομεινάρια, ἀπορρίμματα ‖ ~**book** n λεύκωμα ἀποκομμάτων.

scrape [skreip] n (*ἀπό*)ξέσις, ξύσιμο ‖ (*awkward position*) ἀμηχανία, μπελάς ‖ vt (*ἀπο*)ξέω, ξύνω, ξεγδέρνω ‖ (*clean*) ξύνω, τρίβω ‖ vi τρίζω, στριγγλίζω, ξύνω ‖ ~**r** n ξύστρα, ξέστρα.

scrap heap ['skræphi:p] n σωρός παλιοσιδερικῶν.

scrap merchant ['skræpmə:tʃənt] n ἔμπορος παλιοσιδερικῶν.

scrappy ['skræpi] a ἀσύνδετος, ἀσυνάρτητος, ἀνακατεμένος.

scratch ['skrætʃ] n νυχιά, ἀμυχή, γρατσουνιά ‖ (*itch*) ξύσιμο ‖ a ἐκ τοῦ προχείρου ‖ vt ξύνω, τρίβω ‖ (*wound*) γρατσουνίζω, ξεγδέρνω ‖ vi (*rub*) ξύνομαι.

scrawl [skrɔ:l] n ὀρνιθοσκαλίσματα ‖ vti κακογραφῶ, ὀρνιθοσκαλίζω.

scream [skri:m] n κραυγή, ξεφωνητό, στριγγλιά ‖ vi ξεφωνάζω ‖ (*speak loudly*) στριγγλίζω.

scree [skri:] n λιθῶν.

screech [skri:tʃ] n κραυγή, σκούξιμο, στριγγλιά ‖ vi σκούζω, στριγγλίζω, οὐρλιάζω.

screen [skri:n] n παραπέτασμα, προπέτασμα, παραβάν ‖ (*for films*) ὀθόνη, πανί ‖ (*church*) κιγκλίδωμα ‖ vt προφυλάσσω, προστατεύω ‖ (*film*) κινηματογραφῶ, γυρίζω.

screw [skru:] n κοχλίας, βίδα ‖ (*naut*) ἕλιξ, προπέλλα ‖ vt βιδώνω, σφίγγω ‖ (*col*) καταπιέζω, ξεζουμίζω ‖ ~**driver** n κατσαβίδι ‖ ~**y** a (*col*) μουρλός, ξεβιδωμένος.

scribble ['skribl] n κακογραφία ‖ vt γράφω βιαστικά, ὀρνιθοσκαλίζω.

scribe [skraib] n γραφεύς, γραφιᾶς.

script [skript] n χειρόγραφον ‖ (*of play*) κείμενον, σενάριο.

Scripture ['skriptʃə*] n Ἁγία Γραφή.

scriptwriter ['skriptraitə*] n σεναριογράφος.

scroll [skrəul] n κύλινδρος, ρόλλος (περγαμηνῆς).

scrounge [skraundʒ] vt (col) βουτῶ, τρακάρω, σελεμίζω ‖ n: on the ~ πάω τσάρκα.

scrub [skrʌb] n (clean) τριβή, τρίψιμο, βούρτσισμα ‖ (countryside) χαμόκλαδα, ἀγριμιά ‖ vt πλένω, βουρτσίζω, τρίβω ‖ (erase) ἀπορρίπτω, σβήνω.

scruff [skrʌf] n σβέρκο.

scrum(mage) ['skrʌm(idʒ)] n συμπλοκή, συνωστισμός.

scruple ['skru:pl] n συνείδησις, ἐνδοιασμός, δισταγμός.

scrupulous ['skru:pjuləs] a εὐσυνείδητος ~ly ad εὐσυνείδητα.

scrutinize ['skru:tinaiz] vt ἐξετάζω προσεκτικά, διερευνῶ.

scrutiny ['skru:tini] n (αὐστηρός) ἔλεγχος, διερεύνησις.

scuff [skʌf] vt (shoes) σέρνω τά πόδια, τρίβω, φθείρω.

scuffle ['skʌfl] n συμπλοκή, καυγᾶς.

scull [skʌl] vi κωπηλατῶ.

scullery ['skʌləri] n πλυντήριον μαγειρίου, λάντσα.

sculptor ['skʌlptə*] n γλύπτης.

sculpture ['skʌlptʃə*] n γλυπτική ‖ (statue) γλυπτόν.

scum [skʌm] n ἀφρός, βρωμιά ‖ (people) κατακάθια, ἀποβράσματα.

scurrilous ['skʌriləs] a ὑβριστικός, ἀχρεῖος, βρώμικος.

scurry ['skʌri] vi τρέχω, σπεύδω.

scurvy ['skə:vi] n σκορβοῦτον.

scuttle ['skʌtl] vt (plans) ἐγκαταλείπω, ὑποχωρῶ ‖ vi (scamper) τρέχω βιαστικά, τό στρίβω.

scythe [saið] n δρεπάνι.

sea [si:] n θάλασσα ‖ (broad stretch) ὠκεανός, θάλασσα ‖ a θαλασσινός, τῆς θάλασσας ‖ ~ bird n θαλασσοπούλι ‖ ~board n ἀκτή, παραλία ‖ ~ breeze n θαλασσία αὔρα, μπάτης ‖ ~farer n θαλασσινός, θαλασσοπόρος ‖ ~faring a θαλασσοπόρος, θαλασσινός ‖ ~food n θαλασσινά ‖ ~ front n παραλία, προκυμαία ‖ ~going a ποντοπόρος ‖ ~gull n γλάρος.

seal [si:l] n (animal) φώκια ‖ (stamp) σφραγίδα, βούλα ‖ (impression) σφραγίδα ‖ vt σφραγίζω ‖ (close) κλείνω, σφραγίζω, βουλώνω.

sea level ['si:levl] n ἐπιφάνεια θαλάσσης.

sealing wax ['si:liŋwæks] n βουλοκέρι.

sea lion ['si:laiən] n εἶδος φώκιας.

seam [si:m] n ραφή ‖ (joining) ἕνωσις, ραφή ‖ (of coal etc) φλέβα.

seaman ['si:mən] n ναυτικός, ναύτης.

seamless ['si:mlis] a χωρίς ραφήν.

seamy ['si:mi] a ἀνάποδος, ἄσχημος.

seaport ['si:pɔ:t] n λιμάνι.

search [sə:tʃ] n ἔρευνα, ἀναζήτησις ‖ vt ἐρευνῶ, ἀναζητῶ, ψάχνω ‖ κάνω ἔρευνες ‖ ~ing a ἐρευνητικός, προσεκτικός ‖ ~light n προβολεύς ‖ ~ party n ἀπόσπασμα ἐρεύνης.

seashore ['si:ʃɔ:*] n ἀκτή, παραλία.

seasick ['si:sik] a ναυτιῶν ‖ ~ness n ναυτία.

seaside ['si:said] n παραλία, γιαλό.

season ['si:zn] n ἐποχή ‖ vt ἀρτύω, καρυκεύω, ὡριμάζω ‖ ~al a ἐποχιακός ‖ ~ed a (food) καρυκευμένος, πικάντικο ‖ ~ing n καρύκευσις, ἄρτυμα, μπαχαρικό ‖ ~ ticket n διαρκές εἰσιτήριον.

sea water ['si:wɔ:tə*] n θαλασσινό νερό.

seaweed ['si:wi:d] n φύκι, φύκια.

seaworthy ['si:wə:ði] a πλόϊμος, ἱκανός νά πλεύση.

secede [si'si:d] vi ἀποχωρῶ, ἀποσπῶμαι.

secluded [si'klu:did] a παράμερος, ἀπομονωμένος, μοναχικός.

seclusion [si'klu:ʒən] n ἀπομόνωσις.

second ['sekənd] a δεύτερος ‖ ad (in second position) δεύτερος ‖ (rail) δευτέρα (θέσι) ‖ n (of time) δευτερόλεπτο ‖ ὁ δεύτερος ‖ (comm: imperfect) δεύτερο (χέρι) ‖ vt ὑποστηρίζω, βοηθῶ ‖ ~ary a δευτερεύων, ἀσήμαντος ‖ (education) μέση (ἐκπαίδευσις) ‖ ~ary school n γυμνάσιον ‖ ~er n ὑποστηρικτής ‖ ~hand a μεταχειρισμένος, δεύτερο χέρι ‖ (not original) μή πρωτότυπος, ἐμμέσως ‖ ~ly ad κατά δεύτερον λόγον ‖ ~ nature n δευτέρα φύσις ‖ ~-rate a μέτριος, δευτέρας ποιότητος ‖ ~ thoughts npl δεύτερες σκέψεις.

secrecy ['si:krəsi] n μυστικότης, ἐχεμύθεια.

secret ['si:krit] n μυστικόν ‖ a μυστικός, κρυφός, ἀπόρρητος.

secretarial [sekrə'teəriəl] a τοῦ γραμματέως.

secretariat [sekrə'teəriət] n γραμματεία.

secretary ['sekrətri] n γραμματεύς ‖ (minister etc) ὑπουργός.

secretive ['si:krətiv] a κρυψίνους.

secretly ['si:kritli] ad μυστικά, κρυφά.

sect [sekt] n αἵρεσις ‖ ~arian a αἱρετικός, στενοκέφαλος, κομματικός.

section ['sekʃən] n χωρισμός, τμῆσις, κόψιμο ‖ (piece) τμῆμα, μέρος, τομή ‖ ~al a τμηματικός, τοπικός.

sector ['sektə*] n (private or public sector) τομεύς.

secular ['sekjulə*] a λαϊκός, κοσμικός ‖ μακροχρόνιος.

secure [si'kjuə*] a βέβαιος, ἥσυχος,

ἀκίνδυνος ‖ (*fixed*) ἀσφαλής ‖ *vt* (*fix*)
στερεώνω, σφίγγω ‖ (*obtain*) ἐξασφαλίζω ‖ **~ly** *ad* ἀσφαλῶς, σίγουρα ‖
στερεά.

security [si'kjuəriti] *n* ἀσφάλεια, σιγουριά
‖ (*bond*) ἐγγύησις, χρεώγραφον ‖
(*national security*) ἀσφάλεια ‖ *see*
social.

sedate [si'deit] *a* ἀτάραχος, ἤρεμος.

sedation [si'deiʃən] *n* (*med*) καταπράϋνσις.

sedative ['sedətiv] *n* καταπραϋντικόν ‖ *a*
καταπραϋντικός.

sedentary ['sedntri] *a* ἀδρανής, καθιστικός.

sediment ['sedimənt] *n* ὑποστάθμη, κατακάθι, ἵζημα ‖ **~ary** *a* (*geol*) ἱζηματογε-
νής.

seduce [si'dju:s] *vt* (*general*) δελεάζω,
παρασύρω ‖ (*sexually*) διαφθείρω,
ἀποπλανῶ.

seduction [si'dʌkʃən] *n* ἀποπλάνησις,
δελεασμός.

seductive [si'dʌktiv] *a* γοητευτικός,
ἀποπλανητικός.

see [si:] (*irreg v*) *vt* βλέπω ‖ (*find out*)
φροντίζω, κοιτάζω ‖ (*understand*) καταλαβαίνω ‖ (*make sure*) φροντίζω ‖
(*accompany*) συνοδεύω ‖ (*visit*) πηγαίνω,
βλέπω, ἐπισκέπτομαι ‖ *vi* ἀντιλαμβάνομαι, συλλαμβάνω ‖ φροντίζω, ἐξετάζω
‖ *n* (*bishop's*) ἐπισκοπή ‖ **to ~ through**
φροντίζω μέχρι τέλους, παρακολουθῶ ‖
to ~ to φροντίζω γιά ‖ **to ~ off** προπέμπω, ξεπροβοδίζω.

seed [si:d] *n* σπόρος ‖ (*grain*) κόκκος,
σπειρί ‖ **~ling** *n* δενδρύλλιον, νεαρόν
φυτόν ‖ **~y** *a* (*ill*) ἀδιάθετος, τσακισμένος ‖ (*shabby*) κουρελιασμένος.

seeing ['si:iŋ] *cj* ἐφόσον, ἀφοῦ, δεδομένου
ὅτι.

seek [si:k] (*irreg v*) *vt* ἀναζητῶ, ψάχνω,
ζητῶ.

seem [si:m] *vi* φαίνομαι, μοιάζω ‖ **~ingly**
ad φαινομενικά, κατά τά φαινόμενα ‖
~ly *a* κόσμιος, καθώς πρέπει.

seen [si:n] *pp of* **see**.

seep [si:p] *vi* διαρρέω, περνῶ ἀπό.

seer [siə*] *n* προφήτης.

seesaw ['si:sɔ:] *n* (*plank*) τραμπάλα.

seethe [si:ð] *vi* (*be agitated*) ἀναταράσσο-
μαι, βράζω.

see-through ['si:θru:] *a* (*dress*) διαφανής,
ση-θρού.

segment ['segmənt] *n* τμῆμα.

segregate ['segrigeit] *vt* ἀπομονώνω,
χωρίζω.

segregation [segri'geiʃən] *n* ἀπομόνωσις,
χωρισμός.

seismic ['saizmik] *a* σεισμικός.

seize [si:z] *vt* ἁρπάζω, πιάνω ‖ (*take possession*) κατάσχω ‖ καταλαμβάνω ‖ (*understand*) ἀντιλαμβάνω, συλλαμβάνω ‖ **to
~ up** *vi* (*mech*) σφηνώνομαι, μαγκώνω,
κολλῶ.

seizure ['si:ʒə*] *n* (*illness*) ἀπότομη προσβολή.

seldom ['seldəm] *ad* σπανίως, σπάνια.

select [si'lekt] *a* ἐκλεκτός, διαλεχτός ‖ *vt*
ἐκλέγω, διαλέγω ‖ **~ion** *n* ἐκλογή,
διαλογή, ἐπιλογή ‖ **~ive** *a* ἐκλεκτικός ‖
~or *n* (*person*) ἐκλέγων, ἐκλέκτωρ ‖
(*tech*) ἐπιλογεύς.

self [self] *n* ἑαυτός, τό πρόσωπον, τό
ἄτομον ‖ **~-appointed** *a* αὐτοδιορισμένος
‖ **~-assurance** *n* αὐτοπεποίθησις ‖
~-assured *a* ἐπηρμένος, φαντασμένος ‖
~-confidence *n* αὐτοπεποίθησις ‖
~-confident *a* γεμάτος αὐτοπεποίθησιν
‖ **~-conscious** *a* δειλός, ἔχων τράκ ‖
~-contained *a* αὐτοτελής, ἀνεξάρτητος
‖ (*reserved*) ἐπιφυλακτικός ‖ **~-defence**
n αὐτοάμυνα ‖ **~-evident** *a* αὐταπόδεικτος
‖ **~-explanatory** *a* αὐτεξήγητος ‖
~-indulgent *a* αὐτεντρύφητος, συβαρίτης ‖ **~-interest** *n* ἰδιοτέλεια ‖ **~-ish**
a ἐγωϊστικός, ἰδιοτελής ‖ **~-ishly** *ad*
ἐγωϊστικά ‖ **~-ishness** *n* ἐγωϊσμός,
ἰδιοτέλεια ‖ **~-lessly** *ad* ἀλτρουϊστικά ‖
~-made *a* αὐτοδημιούργητος ‖ **~-
portrait** *n* αὐτοπροσωπογραφία ‖ **~-
propelled** *a* αὐτοκινούμενος ‖ **~-reliant**
a ἀνεξάρτητος ‖ **~-respect** *n* αὐτοσεβα-
σμός ‖ **~-respecting** *a* σεβόμενος τόν
ἑαυτόν του ‖ **~-righteous** *a* ὑποκριτικός
‖ **~-satisfied** *a* ἔχων αὐταρέσκειαν,
καμαρωτός ‖ **~-service** *a* αὐτοσερβίρισμα
‖ **~-sufficient** *a* αὐτάρκης ‖ **~-supporting**
a (*fin*) αὐτοσυντήρητος, αὐτάρκης.

sell [sel] (*irreg v*) *vt* πωλῶ, πουλῶ ‖ *vi*
(*comm*) πωλοῦμαι ‖ **~er** *n* πωλητής ‖
~ing price *n* τιμή πωλήσεως.

selves [selvz] *pl of* **self**.

semantic [si'mæntik] *a* σημασιολογικός ‖
~s *n* σημασιολογία.

semaphore ['seməfɔ:*] *n* (*system*) σηματοφόρος.

semi ['semi] *prefix* ἡμι- ‖ **~circle** *n* ἡμικύ-
κλιον ‖ **~colon** *n* ἄνω τελεία ‖ **~-
conscious** *a* ἡμιαναίσθητος ‖ **~-detached
house** *n* διζόντιος διπλοκατοικία ‖
~final *n* ἡμιτελικός.

seminar ['semina:*] *n* σεμινάριον.

semiquaver ['semikweivə*] *n* (*mus*) δέκατον
ἕκτον.

semiskilled ['semi'skild] *a* ἡμιεκπαιδευ-
μένος.

semitone ['semitəun] *n* (*mus*) ἡμιτόνιον.

semolina [semə'li:nə] *n* σιμιγδάλι.

senate ['senit] *n* σύγκλητος ‖ (*US*) γερουσία.

senator ['senitə*] *n* γερουσιαστής.

send [send] (*irreg v*) *vt* πέμπω, στέλνω,
ἀποστέλλω ‖ (*col: inspire*) ἐνθουσιάζω,
τρελλαίνω ‖ **to ~ away** *vt* ἀπολύω,
διώχνω ‖ **to ~ back** *vt* στέλνω πίσω,
ἐπιστρέφω ‖ **to ~ for** *vt* στέλνω νά
φωνάξω, καλῶ ‖ **to ~ off** *vt* (*goods*)

ἀποστέλνω, στέλνω ‖ *(player)* ἀποβάλλω ‖ **to ~ out** *vt (invitation)* στέλνω ‖ **to ~ up** *vt (general)* ἀνεβάζω, στέλνω, ἀνυψώνω ‖ **~er** *n* ἀποστολεύς ‖ **~-off** *n* ἀποχαιρετισμός.

senile ['si:nail] *a* γεροντικός.

senility [si'niliti] *n* γεράματα, ξεμωράματα.

senior ['si:niə*] *a* μεγαλύτερος, πρεσβύτερος ‖ *(rank)* ἀρχαιότερος, ἀνώτερος ‖ *n* πρεσβύτερος, γηραιότερος, μεγαλύτερος ‖ *(US)* τελειόφοιτος ‖ **~ity** *n* ἀρχαιότης (βαθμοῦ).

sensation [sen'seiʃən] *n* αἴσθησις, αἴσθημα ‖ *(state of excitement)* αἴσθησις, ἐντύπωσις ‖ **~al** *a* ἐντυπωσιακός.

sense [sens] *n* αἴσθησις ‖ *(understanding)* λογική, λογικόν ‖ *(meaning)* ἔννοια, νόημα ‖ *(feeling)* (συν)αἴσθημα ‖ *vi* (δι)αἰσθάνομαι ‖ **~less** *a* ἀνόητος, παράλογος ‖ *(unconscious)* ἀναίσθητος ‖ **~lessly** *ad (stupidly)* ἀνόητα, βλακωδῶς.

sensibility [sensi'biliti] *n* εὐαισθησία, εὐπάθεια.

sensible ['sensəbl] *a* λογικός, αἰσθητός, συνειδός.

sensibly ['sensəbli] *ad* αἰσθητά ‖ συνετά.

sensitive ['sensitiv] *a* (+ *to*) εὐαίσθητος, εὐπαθής ‖ *(easily hurt)* εὐσυγκίνητος, εὔθικτος.

sensitivity [sensi'tiviti] *n* εὐαισθησία, εὐπάθεια.

sensual ['sensjuəl] *a* αἰσθησιακός, σαρκικός, φιλήδονος.

sensuous ['sensjuəs] *a* ἡδονοπαθής, τέρπων τάς αἰσθήσεις.

sent [sent] *pt,pp of* **send**.

sentence ['sentəns] *n (gram)* πρότασις ‖ *(law)* ἀπόφασις, ποινή.

sentiment ['sentimənt] *n* αἴσθημα, αἰσθηματικότης ‖ *(thought)* γνώμη, ἄποψις ‖ **~al** *a* αἰσθηματικός ‖ **~ality** *n* αἰσθηματισμός.

sentinel ['sentinl] *n* σκοπός, φρουρός.

sentry ['sentri] *n* σκοπός, φρουρός.

separable ['sepərəbl] *a* διαιρετός, διαχωριστός.

separate ['seprit] *a* χωριστός ‖ ['sepəreit] *vt* χωρίζω, ξεχωρίζω ‖ *vi* χωρίζομαι, ἀπομακρύνομαι ‖ **~ly** *ad* ξεχωριστά.

separation [sepə'reiʃən] *n* χωρισμός, διαχώρισις.

September [sep'tembə*] *n* Σεπτέμβρης.

septic ['septik] *a* σηπτικός.

sequel ['si:kwəl] *n* συνέπεια, ἀποτέλεσμα ‖ *(continuation)* συνέχεια.

sequence ['si:kwəns] *n* διαδοχή, συνέχεια, ἀκολουθία.

sequin ['si:kwin] *n* πούλι(α).

serenade [serə'neid] *n* σερενάτα ‖ *vt* κάνω σερενάτα.

serene [sə'ri:n] *a* γαλήνιος, ἀτάραχος ‖ **~ly** *ad* ἤρεμα, γαλήνια.

serenity [si'reniti] *n* γαλήνη, ἠρεμία.

C.G.D.—N

serf [sə:f] *n* δουλοπάροικος, κολλήγος.

serge [sə:dʒ] *n* σέρζ.

sergeant ['sa:dʒənt] *n* λοχίας ‖ *(police)* ἐνωμοτάρχης.

serial ['siəriəl] *n* ἱστορία σέ συνέχειες ‖ *a (number)* τεῦχος, αὔξων (ἀριθμός) ‖ **~ize** *vt* δημοσιεύω εἰς συνεχείας.

series ['siəriz] *n* σειρά.

serious ['siəriəs] *a* σοβαρός ‖ **~ly** *ad* σοβαρά ‖ **~ness** *n* σοβαρότης.

sermon ['sə:mən] *n* κήρυγμα, ὁμιλία.

serpent ['sə:pənt] *n* ὄφις, φίδι.

serrated [se'reitid] *a* ὀδοντωτός, πριονωτός.

serum ['siərəm] *n* ὀρός.

servant ['sə:vənt] *n* ὑπηρέτης ‖ *see* **civil**.

serve [sə:v] *vt* ὑπηρετῶ ‖ *(do work of)* ἐξυπηρετῶ, ἐκτελῶ ‖ *(supply)* προμηθεύω ‖ *vi (be useful)* χρησιμεύω γιά ‖ *(in army)* ὑπηρετῶ ‖ *(wait at table)* σερβίρω ‖ *(tennis)* σερβίρω ‖ *n (tennis)* σερβίρισμα ‖ **it ~ s him right** καλά νά πάθη ‖ **to ~ out** *or* **up** *vt (food)* σερβίρω, διανέμω.

service ['sə:vis] *n* ὑπηρεσία ‖ *(work done)* ἐξυπηρέτησις ‖ *(government department)* ὑπηρεσία ‖ *(civil etc)* ὑπηρεσία, ἐργασία ‖ *(help)* διάθεσις, χρησιμότης ‖ *(rel)* λειτουργία ‖ *(set of dishes)* σερβίτσιο ‖ *(tennis)* σερβίς ‖ *(aut: maintenance)* συντήρησις, ἐπισκευή ‖ *vt (aut, mech)* συντηρῶ, ἐπισκευάζω ‖ **the S~s** *npl (armed forces)* τά ὅπλα, στρατός ‖ **~able** *a* εὔχρηστος, ἀνθεκτικός, χρήσιμος ‖ **~man** *n (soldier etc)* στρατιώτης ‖ **~ station** *n* γκαράζ.

serviette [sə:vi'et] *n* πετσέτα (φαγητοῦ).

servile ['sə:vail] *a* δουλικός, δουλοπρεπής.

session ['seʃən] *n* συνεδρίασις, συνεδρία.

set [set] *(irreg v) n (of things)* σειρά, συλλογή, τακίμι ‖ *(rad, TV)* συσκευή ‖ *(tennis)* γῦρος, σέτ ‖ *(group of people)* ὁμάς, κατηγορία, συντροφιά, κόσμος ‖ *(cine)* συσκευή ‖ *(theat)* διάκοσμος, σκηνικόν ‖ *a* καθωρισμένος, ἄκαμπτος ‖ *a (subject)* ὑποχρεωτικός ‖ *(ready)* ἀποφασισμένος ‖ καθωρισμένος ‖ *vt* θέτω, τοποθετῶ, βάζω ‖ *(arrange)* κανονίζω ‖ *(adjust)* ρυθμίζω, βάζω, κανονίζω ‖ *(exam)* δίδω τά θέματα ‖ *vi (of sun)* δύω, βασιλεύω ‖ *(fix)* σκληρύνομαι, σφίγγω, πιάνω ‖ **to ~ on fire** καίω, πυρπολῶ, βάζω φωτιά ‖ **to ~ free** ἐλευθερώνω ‖ **to ~ sth going** ξεκινῶ ‖ **to ~ sail** ἀποπλέω ‖ **to ~ about** *vt (task)* ἀρχίζω ‖ **to ~ aside** *vt* ξεχωρίζω, βάζω κατά μέρος, ἀπορρίπτω ‖ **to ~ back** *vt (in time)* ἐπιβραδύνω, καθυστερῶ ‖ *(cost)* κοστίζω ‖ **to ~ off** *vi* ξεκινῶ, φεύγω ‖ *vi (explode)* ἐκτοξεύω, ρίχνω, ἐκρηγνύω ‖ *(show up well)* ἐξαίρω, ἀναδεικνύω, τονίζω, ὑπογραμμίζω ‖ **to ~ out** *vi* ξεκινῶ, φεύγω ‖ *vt (arrange)* ρυθμίζω, κανονίζω, σιάζω ‖ *(state)* (καθ)ὁρίζω ‖ **to ~ up** *vt* (*organization*) ἱδρύω, ὀργανώνω ‖ ~back n (*reverse*) ἀποτυχία, ἀτυχία, ἀναποδιά.

settee [se'ti:] n καναπές.

setting ['setiŋ] n (*scenery*) τοποθεσία, πλαίσιον ‖ (*mus*) μελοποίησις, μουσική τραγουδιοῦ.

settle ['setl] vt (*med: calm*) καθησυχάζω, καταπραΰνω ‖ (*pay*) ἐξοφλῶ, πληρώνω ‖ (*agree*) ῥυθμίζω, κανονίζω ‖ vi (*also ~ down*) ἐγκαθίσταμαι ‖ καθίζω ‖ σοβαρεύω ‖ (*come to rest*) ἐγκαθίσταμαι ‖ ~ment n (*payment*) ἐξόφλησις ‖ (*colony*) ἐποικισμός ‖ ἀποκατάστασις ‖ ~r n ἄποικος, μετανάστης.

setup ['setʌp] n (*arrangement*) τοποθέτησις, ὀργάνωσις ‖ (*situation*) κατάστασις.

seven ['sevn] num ἑπτά ‖ ~teen num δεκαεπτά ‖ ~th a ἕβδομος ‖ ~ty num ἑβδομήκοντα.

sever ['sevə*] vt κόβω, διακόπτω.

several ['sevrəl] a διάφορος, ξεχωριστός ‖ pron μερικοί.

severance ['sevərəns] n διαχωρισμός, (δια)κοπή.

severe [si'viə*] a αὐστηρός, σκληρός ‖ (*serious*) σοβαρός ‖ (*hard, rigorous*) δριμύς, σκληρός, ἄγριος ‖ (*unadorned*) αὐστηρός, ἀπέριττος, λιτός ‖ ~ly ad αὐστηρά, σκληρά.

severity [si'veriti] n αὐστηρότης, σκληρότης, δριμύτης.

sew [səu] (*irreg v*) vti ράβω ‖ to ~ up vt ἐπιρράπτω, ράβω.

sewage ['sju:idʒ] n ἀκαθαρσίες ὑπονόμων, βρωμόνερα.

sewer ['sjuə*] n ὀχετός, ὑπόνομος.

sewing ['səuiŋ] n ράψιμο ‖ ~ machine n ραπτομηχανή.

sewn [səun] pp of sew.

sex [seks] n φῦλον, σέξ ‖ (*activity*) γενετήσιος ὁρμή ‖ ~ act n συνουσία, γαμήσι.

sextant ['sekstənt] n ἑξάς.

sexual ['seksjuəl] a γενετήσιος, σεξουαλικός ‖ ~ly ad σεξουαλικά.

sexy ['seksi] a ἑλκυστικός, σεξουαλικός.

shabbily ['ʃæbili] ad ἄθλια, φτωχικά.

shabbiness ['ʃæbinis] n κουρέλιασμα ‖ πενιχρότης, φτήνεια.

shabby ['ʃæbi] a κουρελιασμένος, σαραβαλιασμένο ‖ (*mean*) μικροπρεπής, τσιγγούνης.

shack [ʃæk] n καλύβα.

shackle ['ʃækl] vt δεσμεύω, βάζω τά σίδερα σέ ‖ ~s npl δεσμά, χειροπέδες.

shade [ʃeid] n σκιά, ἴσκιος ‖ (*for lamp*) ἀμπαζούρ ‖ (*of colour*) ἀπόχρωσις ‖ (*small quantity*) ἴχνος, μικρά ποσότης ‖ vt σκιάζω.

shadow ['ʃædəu] n σκιά, σκοτάδι ‖ vt (*follow*) παρακολουθῶ ‖ ~y a σκιερός, σκιασμένος ‖ (*dim*) ἀσαφής, θαμπός.

shady ['ʃeidi] a σκιερός ‖ (*dubious*) ὑποπτος

shaft [ʃɑ:ft] n κοντάρι, στέλεχος, λαβή ‖ (*of mine*) φρέαρ ‖ (*of machine*) ἄξων, ἄτρακτος ‖ (*of light*) ἀχτίδα.

shaggy ['ʃægi] a τραχύς, τριχωτός.

shake [ʃeik] (*irreg v*) vt σείω, κουνῶ, τινάζω ‖ (*fist etc*) ἀπειλῶ μέ τή γροθιά μου ‖ (*rock*) (συγ)κλονίζω, κουνῶ, τραντάζω ‖ (*weaken*) κλονίζω ‖ (*alarm*) συγκλονίζω, ἀναστατώνω ‖ vi τρέμω, κλονίζομαι, τραντάζομαι ‖ n τίναγμα, κούνημα, δόνησις ‖ to ~ off vt τινάζω, ἀπαλλάσσομαι ἀπό ‖ to ~ up vt (*lit*) ταράζω, κουνῶ, κουρταλῶ ‖ (*fig*) ξυπνῶ, τονώνω, κουνῶ ‖ ~-up n πρόχειρο πρᾶμα ‖ μεγάλη μεταβολή.

shakily ['ʃeikili] ad ἀσταθῶς, τρέμοντας.

shakiness ['ʃeikinis] n ἀστάθεια, τρεμούλιασμα.

shaky ['ʃeiki] a ἀσταθής, τρεμουλιαστός ‖ (*weak*) κλονισμένος, ἀδύνατος.

shale [ʃeil] n σχιστόλιθος.

shall [ʃæl] auxiliary v: I ~ go θά φύγω, θά πάω ‖ you ~ do it! θά τό κάμης!

shallot [ʃə'lɔt] n κρόμμυον τό ἀσκαλωνικόν.

shallow ['ʃæləu] a (*lit*) ῥηχός ‖ (*fig*) ἐπιπόλαιος.

sham [ʃæm] n προσποίησις, ἀπομίμησις, ψευτιά ‖ a προσποιητός, ψεύτικος, πλαστός.

shambles ['ʃæmblz] n sing μακελιό, σφαγεῖον.

shame [ʃeim] n ἐντροπή, ντροπή ‖ (*disgrace*) (κατ)αισχύνη, αἶσχος ‖ (*pity*) ντροπή, ἁμαρτία, κρῖμα ‖ vt (*humiliate*) ντροπιάζω ‖ what a ~! τί κρῖμα! ‖ ~faced a κατησχυμένος, ντροπιασμένος ‖ ~ful a ἐπαίσχυντος, ντροπιασμένος ‖ ~fully ad αἰσχρά, ἀπαίσια, πρόστυχα ‖ ~less a ἀναίσχυντος, ξετσίπωτος.

shampoo [ʃæm'pu:] n λούσιμο, σαμπουάν ‖ vt λούζω (τά μαλλιά μου) ‖ ~ and set n λούσιμο καί κτένισμα.

shamrock ['ʃæmrɔk] n τριφύλλι.

shandy ['ʃændi] n (*beer and lemonade*) μπύρα μέ λεμονάδα.

shan't [ʃɑ:nt] = shall not ‖ see shall.

shanty ['ʃænti] n καλύβα, παράγγα ‖ ~town n παραγγούπολις.

shape [ʃeip] n σχῆμα, μορφή, φόρμα, καλούπι ‖ vt σχηματίζω, διαμορφώνω, διαπλάθω ‖ to take ~ διαμορφοῦμαι, παίρνω μορφήν ‖ ~less a ἄμορφος, ἀκανόνιστος ‖ ~ly a καλοσχηματισμένος, ὄμορφος.

share [ʃɛə*] n (*thing received*) μερίδιον, μερδικό ‖ (*contribution*) μετοχή, μερίδιον ‖ (*fin*) μετοχή, τίτλος, ἀξία ‖ vt μοιράζω, διανέμω ‖ (*in common*) (συμ)μετέχω ‖ ~holder n μέτοχος.

shark [ʃɑ:k] n (*fish*) σκυλόψαρο, καρχαρίας.

sharp [ʃɑ:p] a ὀξύς, αἰχμηρός, μυτερός,

κοφτερός ‖ (distinct) ξεχωριστός, έντονος, καθαρός ‖ (biting) δριμύς, διαπεραστικός ‖ (quick-witted) όξύνους, έξυπνος, πού κόβει ‖ (unscrupulous) πονηρός, κατεργάρης ‖ n δίεσις ‖ ad άκριβῶς, έντονα, καθαρά ‖ look ~! κάνε γρήγορα! ‖ κουνήσου! ‖ ~en vt άκονίζω, τροχίζω, ξεμυτίζω ‖ ~ener n ξύστρα ‖ ~eyed a πού κόβει τό μάτι του ‖ ~ness n κόψη, όξύτης, μυτεράδα ‖ ξινίλα ‖ ~-witted a όξύνους, εὐφυής.

shatter ['ʃætə*] vt θρυμματίζω, θραύω, κάνω κομμάτια ‖ (fig) συντρίβω, κλονίζω ‖ vi συντρίβομαι, σπάω ‖ ~ing a (experience) συντριπτικός.

shave [ʃeiv] (irreg v) n ξύρισμα ‖ vt ξυρίζω ‖ περνῶ ξυστά ‖ vi ξυρίζομαι ‖ ~n a (head) ξυρισμένος ‖ ~r n (elec) ξυριστική μηχανή.

shaving ['ʃeiviŋ] n (action) ξύρισμα, πλανίδρισμα ‖ ~s npl (of wood etc) ροκανίδια, ρινίσματα ‖ ~ brush n πινέλο τοῦ ξυρίσματος ‖ ~ cream n κρέμα ξυρίσματος ‖ ~ soap n σαπούνι ξυρίσματος.

shawl [ʃɔ:l] n σάλι.

she [ʃi:] pron αὐτή ‖ a θήλυς, θηλυκός.

sheaf [ʃi:f] n δέσμη, δεμάτι.

shear [ʃiə*] (irreg v) vt (sheep etc) κείρω, κουρεύω ‖ to ~ off vt κόβω ‖ ~s npl (for hedge) ψαλίδια.

sheath [ʃi:θ] n θήκη, κολεός, θηκάρι ‖ ~e [ʃi:ð] vt βάζω σέ θήκη, περικαλύπτω, ἐπενδύω.

shed [ʃed] (irreg v) n ὑπόστεγον ‖ vt ἀποβάλλω, βγάζω, ρίχνω ‖ (pour out) χύνω.

she'd [ʃi:d] = she had, she would ‖ see have, would.

sheep [ʃi:p] n πρόβατον ‖ ~dog n τσοπανόσκυλο ‖ ~ish a δειλός, ντροπαλός ‖ ~skin n προβιά.

sheer [ʃiə*] a καθαρός, πραγματικός, γνήσιος ‖ (steep) κατακόρυφος, ἀπότομος ‖ (almost transparent) διαφανής, λεπτός ‖ ad τελείως, πλήρως, ἀπολύτως.

sheet [ʃi:t] n σεντόνι ‖ (thin piece) ἔλασμα, φύλλον, λαμαρίνα ‖ (paper) φύλλον, κόλλα ‖ ~ing n ὕφασμα γιά σεντόνια ‖ (metal etc) θωράκισις, λαμαρίνα ‖ ~ lightning n διάχυτες ἀστραπές.

sheik(h) [ʃeik] n σείχης.

shelf [ʃelf] n ράφι.

she'll [ʃi:l] = she will, she shall ‖ see will, shall.

shell [ʃel] n κέλυφος, τσόφλι, φλοιός ‖ (explosive) ὀβίδα, βλῆμα ‖ (of building) σκελετός, καραγιαπί ‖ vt ξεφλουδίζω ‖ (mil) βομβαρδίζω ‖ ~fish n (zool) ὀστρακοειδές ‖ (as food) θαλασσινά.

shelter ['ʃeltə*] n σκέπαστρον, καταφύγιον ‖ (protection) προστασία ‖ vt προφυλάσσω, προστατεύω, στεγάζω ‖ vi προφυλάσσομαι, φυλάγομαι ‖ ~ed a

(life) ἀποτραβηγμένος, περιωρισμένος ‖ (spot) προφυλαγμένος, προστατευμένος.

shelve [ʃelv] vt (put aside) βάζω στό ράφι ‖ ~s npl of shelf.

shelving ['ʃelviŋ] n (shelves etc) ράφια.

shepherd ['ʃepəd] n ποιμήν, βοσκός ‖ vt (guide) ὁδηγῶ, συνοδεύω ‖ ~ess n βοσκοπούλα ‖ ~'s pie n κρέας ἀ-λα-χασάπα.

sheriff ['ʃerif] n σερίφης.

sherry ['ʃeri] n σέρι.

she's [ʃi:z] = she is, she has ‖ see be, have.

shield [ʃi:ld] n ἀσπίδα, σκουτάρι ‖ (protection) προστατευτικόν κάλυμμα ‖ vt προασπίζω, προστατεύω ‖ καλύπτω.

shift [ʃift] n (time) βάρδια ‖ συνεργεῖον, ὀμάδα, βάρδια ‖ vt μετατοπίζω, μετα-θέτω, μετακινῶ ‖ (remove) ἀλλάζω, μεταβάλλω ‖ vi μετακινοῦμαι, μετατοπίζομαι ‖ ~y a πολυμήχανος, πονηρός, ὕπουλος.

shilling ['ʃiliŋ] n (old) σελλίνι.

shilly-shally ['ʃiliʃæli] vi διστάζω, κοντοστέκω, δέν ἀποφασίζω.

shimmer ['ʃimə*] n ἀνταύγεια, μαρμαρυγή, γυάλισμα ‖ vi ἀπαστράπτω, λαμποκοπῶ γυαλίζω.

shin [ʃin] n ἀντικνήμιον, καλάμι (ποδιοῦ).

shine [ʃain] (irreg v) n (gleam) γυάλισμα, στιλπνότης, γυαλάδα ‖ vt (polish) στίλβω, λουστράρω, γυαλίζω ‖ (torch) ἀκτινοβολῶ, λάμπω ‖ vi λάμπω, ἀστράφτω, γυαλίζω ‖ (excel) διακρίνομαι, ξεπροβάλλω.

shingle ['ʃingl] n ξυλοκέραμος, ταβανοσάνιδο ‖ (on beach) βότσαλα, κροκάλαι ‖ ~s npl (med) ἕρπης, ζωστήρ.

shining ['ʃainiŋ] a (light) ἀπαστράπτων, λαμπερός, γυαλιστερός.

shiny ['ʃaini] a λαμπερός, γυαλιστερός.

ship [ʃip] n πλοῖον, σκάφος ‖ vt ἐπιβιβάζω. μπαρκάρω ‖ (transport as cargo) φορτώνω, ἀποστέλλω ‖ ~building n ναυπηγική ‖ ~ canal n πλωτή διώρυξ ‖ ~ment n φόρτωσις ‖ (goods) φορτίον, ἐμπόρευμα ‖ ~per n (sender) ἀποστολεύς ‖ ~ping n (act) φόρτωσις ‖ (ships) πλοῖα, ναυτιλία ‖ (ships of country) ἐμπορική ναυτιλία ‖ ~shape a τακτικος, ἐξαιρετικός ‖ ~wreck n ναυάγιον ‖ ~yard n ναυπηγεῖον.

shire ['ʃaiə*] n κομητεία.

shirk [ʃə:k] vt ὑπεκφεύγω, ἀποφεύγω, ξεφεύγω, φυγοπονῶ.

shirt [ʃə:t] n (man's shirt) πουκάμισο ‖ ~y a (col) εὐερέθιστος, εὐέξαπτος.

shiver ['ʃivə*] n θραῦσμα, θρύμμα ‖ ρῖγος, τρεμούλα ‖ vi (with cold) τρέμω, τουρτουρίζω.

shoal [ʃəul] n (of fish) κοπάδι (ψαριῶν).

shock [ʃɔk] n δόνησις, σύγκρουσις, τίναγμα ‖ (elec) ἠλεκτρικόν σόκ, ἠλεκτροπληξία ‖ (emotional) συγκλονισμός, ταραχή ‖ (*med*) κατάπληξία, σόκ ‖ *vt* σκανδαλίζω, σοκάρω ‖ ~ **absorber** *n* αποσβεστήρ κρούσεων, αμορτισέρ ‖ ~**ing** *a* σκανδαλώδης ‖ συγκλονιστικός ‖ ~**proof** *a* (*watch*) προφυλαγμένος από δονήσεις.

shod [ʃɔd] *pt,pp* of **shoe**.

shoddiness [ʃɔdinis] *n* κακή ποιότης.

shoddy [ʃɔdi] *a* κακής ποιότητος, τῆς πεντάρας.

shoe [ʃuː] (*irreg v*) *n* ὑπόδημα, παπούτσι ‖ (*of horse*) πέταλον ‖ *vt* ὑποδέω, πεταλώνω (ἄλογον) ‖ ~**brush** *n* βούρτσα τῶν παπουτσιῶν ‖ ~**horn** *n* κόκκαλο τῶν παπουτσιῶν ‖ ~**lace** *n* κορδόνι ‖ ~**shop** *n* παπουτσάδικο.

shone [ʃɔn] *pt,pp* of **shine**.

shook [ʃuk] *pt* of **shake**.

shoot [ʃuːt] (*irreg v*) *n* (*branch*) βλαστός, βλαστάρι ‖ *vt* (*gun*) πυροβολῶ, ἐκκενῶ ‖ (*kill*) σκοτώνω ‖ (*film*) τραβῶ, γυρίζω (ταινία) ‖ *vi* (*move swiftly*) (ἐξ)ὁρμῶ, τρέχω, πετῶ ‖ (*let off gun*) πυροβολῶ, κτυπῶ ‖ **don't** ~ ! μή ρίχνετε!, μή βαράτε! ‖ **to** ~ **down** *a* (*plane*) καταρρίπτω ‖ ~**ing** *n* (*shots*) πυροβολισμός, πόλεμος ‖ (*hunting*) κυνήγι ‖ ~**ing star** *n* διάττων ἀστήρ.

shop [ʃɔp] *n* κατάστημα, μαγαζί ‖ (*workshop*) ἐργαστήριον, μαγαζί ‖ *vi* (*also go* ~**ping**) ψωνίζω ‖ ~ **assistant** *n* ὑπάλληλος καταστήματος ‖ ~**keeper** *n* καταστηματάρχης, μικρέμπορος ‖ ~**lifter** *n* κλέπτης καταστημάτων ‖ ~**lifting** *n* κλοπή καταστημάτων ‖ ~**per** *n* πελάτης, ἀγοραστής ‖ ~**ping** *n* ἀγοραί, ψώνια ‖ ~**ping bag** *n* τσάντα γιά τά ψώνια ‖ ~**ping centre**, (*US*) ~**ping center** *n* ἀγορά, ἐμπορικόν κέντρον ‖ ~**soiled** *a* σταραπατσαρισμένο ‖ ~ **steward** *n* (*industry*) ἀντιπρόσωπος τοῦ συνδικάτου ‖ ~ **window** *n* προθήκη, βιτρίνα ‖ *see* **talk**.

shore [ʃɔː*] *n* (*of sea, lake*) ἀκτή, παραλία ‖ ὄχθη ‖ *vt*: **to** ~ **up** ὑποστηρίζω, (ἀντι)στηρίζω.

shorn [ʃɔːn] *pp* of **shear**.

short [ʃɔːt] *a* βραχύς, κοντός ‖ (*not tall*) κοντός ‖ (*soon finished*) βραχύς, σύντομος ‖ (*curt*) ἀπότομος, ξηρός, κοφτός ‖ (*in measure*) λιποβαρής, ἐλλειπής, λειψός ‖ (*elec: short-circuit*) βραχύς (βραχυκύκλωμα) ‖ *ad* ἀπότόμως, ἀπότομα ‖ ἐντεύθεν τοῦ στόχου, κοντά ‖ *vti* (*elec*) βραχυκυκλώνω, βραχυκυκλοῦμαι ‖ **to cut** ~ τερματίζω ἀπότόμως, συντομεύω, διακόπτω ‖ **to fall** ~ πέφτω κοντά, δέν πετυχαίνω ‖ **to stop** ~ σταματῶ ξαφνικά ‖ ~**age** *n* ἀνεπάρκεια, ἔλλειψις, στενότης ‖ ~**bread** *n* εἶδος κέϊκ ‖ ~**circuit** *n* βραχυκύκλωμα ‖ *vi* βραχυκυκλοῦμαι ‖ ~**coming** *n* ἐλάττωμα, ἀτέλεια, μειονέκτημα ‖ ~ **cut** *n* συντομώτερος δρόμος, κοφτό ‖ ~**en** *vt*

βραχύνω, κονταίνω ‖ ~**hand** *n* στενογραφία ‖ ~**hand typist** *n* στενοδακτυλογράφος ‖ ~**lived** *a* βραχύβιος, ἐφήμερος ‖ ~**ly** *ad* (*soon*) προσεχῶς, σύντομα, σέ λίγο ‖ ~**ness** *n* βραχύτης, συντομία ‖ ~**sighted** *a* (*lit*) μύωψ ‖ (*fig*) μή προνοητικός, κοντόφθαλμος ‖ ~**-sightedness** *n* μυωπία ‖ (*fig*) ἀπερισκεψία ‖ ~ **story** *n* διήγημα ‖ ~**-tempered** *a* ἀπότομος, εὐέξαπτος ‖ ~**-term** *a* (*fin*) βραχυπρόθεσμος ‖ ~**wave** *n* (*rad*) βραχύ κῦμα.

shot [ʃɔt] *pt,pp* of **shoot** ‖ *n* (*firing etc*) πυροβολισμός, τουφεκιά ‖ (*person*) σκοπευτής ‖ (*attempt*) δοκιμή, προσπάθεια, ἀπόπειρα ‖ (*injection*) ἔνεσις ‖ (*phot*) λῆψις φωτογραφίας ‖ **like a** ~ (*very readily*) ἀμέσως, πρόθυμα ‖ ~**gun** *n* κυνηγετικόν ὅπλον.

should [ʃud] *auxiliary v*: **I** ~ **go now** πρέπει νά φύγω (τώρα) ‖ **he** ~ **be there now** πρέπει νά ἔχη φθάση (τώρα) ‖ **I** ~ **like to** θά ἤθελα.

shoulder [ʃəuldə*] *n* ὦμος ‖ *vt* ἐπωμίζομαι ‖ ~ **blade** *n* ὠμοπλάτη, κουτάλα.

shouldn't [ʃudnt] = **should not** ‖ *see* **should**.

shout [ʃaut] *n* κραυγή, φωνή ‖ *vt* κραυγάζω ‖ *vi* κραυγάζω, φωνάζω ‖ ~**ing** *n* φωνές, κραυγές.

shove [ʃʌv] *n* ὤθησις, σπρωξιά, σπρώξιμο ‖ *vt* σπρώχνω ‖ **to** ~ **off** *vi* (*naut*) ἀπωθῶ, ἀβαράρω ‖ (*fig, col*) φεύγω, ξεκινῶ.

shovel [ʃʌvl] *n* φτυάρι ‖ *vt* φτυαρίζω.

show [ʃəu] (*irreg v*) *n* ἐπίδειξις, προβολή ‖ (*appearance*) ἐμφάνισις, ὄψις, προσποίησις ‖ (*exhibition*) ἔκθεσις, θέαμα ‖ (*theat, cine*) θέατρον, σινεμά, παράστασις ‖ *vt* δεικνύω, δείχνω, ὁδηγῶ ‖ (*demonstrate*) παρουσιάζω, ἀποδεικνύω ‖ (*explain*) δεικνύω, ἐξηγῶ ‖ (*give*) δεικνύω ‖ *vi* (*be visible*) δεικνύομαι, φαίνομαι, ξεπροβάλλω ‖ **to** ~ **in** πές νά μπῆ ‖ **to** ~ **out** συνοδεύω ὡς τήν ἔξοδο ‖ **to** ~ **off** *vi* (*pej*) ἐπιδεικνύομαι, κορδώνομαι, καμαρώνω ‖ *vt* (*display*) ἀποδεικνύω, δείχνω, διαφημίζω ‖ **to** ~ **up** *vi* (*stand out*) διακρίνομαι, ξεχωρίζω ‖ *vt* ἐμφανίζομαι, παρουσιάζομαι ‖ ἀποκαλύπτομαι, βγαίνω στήν φόρα ‖ ~**down** *n* ἀναμέτρησις, διακήρυξις προθέσεων.

shower [ʃauə*] *n* μπόρα ‖ (*stones etc*) βροχή ἀπό πέτρες κτλ ‖ (*shower bath*) ντούς ‖ *vt* (*fig only*) δίδω ἄφθονα ‖ ~**y** *a* (*weather*) βροχερός.

showground [ʃəugraund] *n* χῶρος ἐκθέσεως.

showing [ʃəuiŋ] *n* (*of film*) ἐμφάνισις, προβολή.

showmanship [ʃəumənʃip] *n* ἱκανότης ἐπιδείξεως.

shown [ʃəun] *pp* of **show**.

show-off [ʃəuɔf] *n* (*col: person*) κορδωμένος.

showroom [ʃəurum] *n* αἴθουσα ἐκθέσεως,

shrank [ʃræŋk] pt of shrink.

shrapnel ['ʃræpnl] n βολιδοφόρον βλῆμα.

shred [ʃred] n (generally pl) κομμάτι, λουρίδα, κουρέλι ‖ vt κομματιάζω, σχίζω σέ λουρίδες ‖ in ~s ξεσχισμένος, κουρελιασμένος.

shrewd [ʃru:d] a ἀγχίνους, διορατικός, ἐπιδέξιος ‖ ~ly ad μέ ἐξυπνάδα, ἔξυπνα ‖ ~ness n εὐφυΐα, ἐξυπνάδα.

shriek [ʃri:k] n ξεφωνητό, στριγγλιά ‖ vti ξεφωνίζω, στριγγλίζω.

shrill [ʃril] a ὀξύς, διαπεραστικός.

shrimp [ʃrimp] n γαρίδα.

shrine [ʃrain] n λειψανοθήκη, βωμός, ἱερός τόπος.

shrink [ʃriŋk] (irreg v) vi συστέλλομαι, μαζεύομαι ‖ vt (make smaller) ρικνῶ, συστέλλω, κάνω νά μαζέψῃ ‖ ~age n συστολή, μπάσιμο, μάζεμα.

shrivel ['ʃrivl] vti (also ~ up) συρρικνώνω, ζαρώνω, ξεραίνομαι.

shroud [ʃraud] n σάβανον ‖ vt σαβανώνω ‖ σκεπάζω, καλύπτω.

Shrove Tuesday ['ʃrəuv'tju:zdi] n Καθαρά Τρίτη.

shrub [ʃrʌb] n θάμνος, χαμόκλαδο ‖ ~bery n θαμνών, λόγγος.

shrug [ʃrʌg] n σήκωμα τῶν ὤμων ‖ to ~ off vt ἀνασηκώνω τούς ὤμους.

shrunk [ʃrʌŋk] pp of shrink ‖ ~en a πού μπῆκε, πού μάζεψε ‖ ζαρωμένος.

shudder ['ʃʌdə*] n ρίγος, φρικίασις, τρεμούλα ‖ vi τρέμω.

shuffle ['ʃʌfl] n (cards) ἀνακάτεμα (τράπουλας) ‖ vt ἀνακατεύω ‖ vi σέρνω τά πόδια.

shun [ʃʌn] vt ἀποφεύγω.

shush [ʃuʃ] excl (col) σούτ! ‖

shut [ʃʌt] (irreg v) vt κλείνω ‖ vi κλείομαι, κλείνω ‖ to ~ down vti κλείνω, σταματῶ ἐργασίες ‖ to ~ off vt (supply) διακόπτω, ἀποκόπτω, ἀποκλείω ‖ to ~ up vi (keep quiet) σωπαίνω, βουλώνω ‖ vt (close) κλείνω καλά, κλειδώνω ‖ (silence) ἀποστομώνω, κλείνω τό στόμα ‖ ~ up! σκασμός! ‖ ~ter n παραθυρόφυλλον, παντζούρι ‖ (of camera) φωτοφράκτης.

shuttlecock ['ʃʌtlkɔk] n φτερωτή σφαίρα, βολάν.

shy [ʃai] a ντροπαλός, δειλός ‖ ~ly ad ντροπαλά, δειλά ‖ ~ness n δειλία, ντροπαλότητα.

Siamese [saiə'mi:z] a: ~ cat Σιαμαία γάτα.

sick [sik] a ἀσθενής, ἄρρωστος ‖ (inclined to vomit) ἔχω τάσιν πρός ἐμετόν ‖ (disgusting) ἀηδιαστικός, σιχαμερός ‖ ~ bay n νοσοκομεῖον πλοίου ‖ ~bed n κλίνη ἀσθενοῦς ‖ ~en vi ἀρρωσταίνω, ἀηδιάζω ‖ vi ἀηδιάζω ‖ ~ening a (fig) ἀηδιαστικός.

sickle ['sikl] n δρεπάνι.

sick leave ['sikli:v] n ἀναρρωτική ἄδεια.

sick list ['siklist] n κατάλογος ἀσθενῶν.

sickly ['sikli] a ἀρρωστιάρης, ὠχρός,

ἀσθενικός ‖ (nauseating) πού προκαλεῖ ἀναγούλα.

sickness ['siknis] n ἀσθένεια, ἀρρώστεια, νόσος ‖ (vomiting) ναυτία, ἀναγούλα, ἐμμετός.

sick pay ['sikpei] n ἐπίδομα ἀσθενείας.

side [said] n πλευρά, πλευρόν, μέρος, μεριά ‖ (of body) πλευρά, μεριά ‖ (of lake) ὄχθη ‖ (aspect) πλευρά, ὄψι, ἄποψις ‖ a (door, entrance) πλάγια (εἴσοδος), πλαϊνή (εἴσοδος) ‖ vi: to with πάω μέ, παίρνω τό μέρος τοῦ ‖ by the ~ of στό πλευρό τοῦ, ἐν συγκρίσει μέ ‖ on all ~s ἀπό παντοῦ ‖ to take ~s (with) ὑποστηρίζω, μεροληπτῶ ‖ ~board n μπουφές ‖ ~boards, ~burns npl (whiskers) φαβορίτες ‖ ~ effect n (med) παρενέργεια ‖ ~light n (aut) πλευρικός φανός ‖ ~line n (rail) δευτερεύουσα γραμμή ‖ (fig: hobby) πάρεργον ‖ ~road n πάροδος ‖ ~show n δευτερεῦον θέαμα ‖ ~track vt (fig) περισπῶ ‖ ~walk n (US) πεζοδρόμιον ‖ ~ways ad πλαγίως, πλάγια, πολλά.

siding ['saidiŋ] n πλευρική διακλάδωσις.

sidle ['saidl] vi: to ~ up πλησιάζω δειλά καί πλάγια.

siege [si:dʒ] n πολιορκία.

siesta [si'estə] n μεσημβρινός ὕπνος.

sieve [siv] n κόσκινο ‖ vt κοσκινίζω.

sift [sift] vt κοσκινίζω ‖ (examine) ξεχωρίζω, ἐξονυχίζω.

sigh [sai] n ἀναστεναγμός ‖ vi (ἀνα)στενάζω.

sight [sait] n ὅρασις ‖ (scene) θέα, θέαμα ‖ (of rifle) κλισιοσκόπιον ‖ στόχαστρον ‖ vt ἀντικρύζω, βλέπω, παρατηρῶ ‖ in ~ φαίνομαι, γίνομαι ὁρατός ‖ out of ~ δέν φαίνομαι ‖ ~seeing n ἐπίσκεψις ἀξιοθεάτων ‖ to go ~seeing περιέρχομαι τά ἀξιοθέατα ‖ ~seer n περιηγητής, τουρίστας.

sign [sain] n (with hand) νεῦμα, νόημα ‖ (indication) ἔνδειξις, σημάδι ‖ (notice, road etc) σῆμα, ταμπέλα, πινακίς ‖ (written symbol) σημεῖον, σημάδι ‖ vt ὑπογράφω ‖ to ~ off vi ξεμπαρκάρω ‖ to ~ up vti (mil) κατατάσσομαι.

signal ['signl] n σύνθημα, σημεῖον, σῆμα ‖ vt σηματοδοτῶ, στέλνω μέ σήματα.

signature ['signətʃə*] n ὑπογραφή ‖ ~ tune n μουσικόν χαρακτηριστικόν (σταθμοῦ).

significance [sig'nifikəns] n σημασία, ἔννοια, νόημα ‖ (importance) σπουδαιότης, σημαντικότης.

significant [sig'nifikənt] a μέ σημασίαν, σημαντικός ‖ (important) σημαντικός, σπουδαῖος, σημαίνων ‖ ~ly ad μέ ἔννοιαν, μέ σημασίαν.

signify ['signifai] vt σημαίνω, ἐννοῶ ‖ (express) εἶμαι ἔνδειξις, (ἐκ)δηλώνω.

sign language ['sainlæŋgwidʒ] n δακτυλολογία.

signpost ['sainpəust] n σήμα κυκλοφορίας, οδοδείκτης.

silence ['sailəns] n σιγή, σιωπή, ησυχία ‖ vt σωπαίνω, ησυχάζω ‖ καταπνίγω ‖ ~r n σιγαστήρ, σιλανσιέ.

silent ['sailənt] a σιωπηλός, αθόρυβος, σιγαλός ‖ (saying nothing) άφωνος, αμίλητος ‖ ~ly ad σιωπηλά, σιγαλά, αθόρυβα.

silhouette [silu:'et] n (outline) σιλουέττα ‖ vt διαγράφομαι σάν σιλουέττα.

silk [silk] n μετάξι ‖ a μεταξωτός ‖ ~y a μεταξένιος, απαλός, προσποιητός.

silliness ['silinis] n μωρία, ανοησία, χαζομάρα.

silly ['sili] a ανόητος, μωρός.

silo ['sailəu] n σιλό.

silt [silt] n ιλύς, λάσπη.

silver ['silvə*] n άργυρος, ασήμι ‖ (coins) αργυρά νομίσματα ‖ (objects) ασημικά ‖ a αργυρούς, ασημένιος ‖ ~ paper n ασημόχαρτο ‖ ~-plate n ασημικά ‖ ~smith n αργυροχόος ‖ ~ware n ασημικά ‖ ~y a ασημένιος.

similar ['similə*] a (+ to) όμοιος (μέ) ‖ ~ity n ομοιότης ‖ ~ly ad ομοίως, όμοια.

simile ['simili] n παρομοίωσις.

simmer ['simə*] vi σιγοβράζω.

simple ['simpl] a (easy) απλός, εύκολος ‖ (natural) απλός, απλοϊκός ‖ (plain) απλός, απλοϊκός ‖ (of one kind) απλός ‖ (weak-minded) αφελής, μωρόπιστος ‖ ~-minded a αφελής, απλοϊκός.

simplicity [sim'plisiti] n απλότης, λιτότης, ειλικρίνεια.

simplification [simplifi'keiʃən] n απλοποίησις, απλούστευσις.

simplify ['simplifai] vt απλουστεύω, απλοποιώ.

simply ['simpli] ad απλώς, απλά, μόνον.

simulation [simju'leiʃən] n (imitation) απομίμησις, προσποίησις.

simultaneous [siməl'teiniəs] a ταυτόχρονος ‖ ~ly ad ταυτόχρονα, σύγχρονα μέ.

sin [sin] n αμάρτημα, αμαρτία ‖ vi αμαρτάνω.

since [sins] ad έκτοτε, από τότε ‖ prep από ‖ cj (time) αφ' ότου, από τότε πού ‖ (because) αφού, εφ' όσον.

sincere [sin'siə*] a ειλικρινής ‖ ~ly ad ειλικρινώς.

sincerity [sin'seriti] n ειλικρίνεια.

sinecure ['sainikjuə*] n αργομισθία.

sinew ['sinju:] n τένων, νεύρο.

sinful ['sinful] a αμαρτωλός.

sing [siŋ] (irreg v) vt (song) τραγουδώ ‖ vi σφυρίζω, βουΐζω.

singe [sindʒ] vt τσουρουφλίζω, καψαλίζω.

singer ['siŋə*] n αοιδός, τραγουδιστής.

singing ['siŋiŋ] n τραγούδι.

single ['siŋgl] a μόνος, μοναδικός ‖ (bed, room) μονό (κρεββάτι, δωμάτιο) ‖ (unmarried) άγαμος ‖ (ticket) απλούν

(εισητήριον) ‖ (one part) απλός, ένας ‖ n (ticket) απλούν εισητήριον ‖ ~s npl (tennis) απλό παιχνίδι, σίγκλ ‖ to ~ out vt διαλέγω, επιλέγω, ξεχωρίζω ‖ ~-breasted a μονός, μονόπετος ‖ in ~ file κατ' άνδρα, στήν αράδα, ένας-ένας ‖ ~-handed a ολομόναχος, αβοήθητος, μόνος ‖ ~-minded a πού έχει ένα μόνον σκοπόν.

singlet ['siŋglit] n φανελλίτσα.

singly ['siŋgli] ad ξεχωριστά, ένα-ένα χωρίς βοήθειαν.

singular ['siŋgjulə*] a ενικός ‖ (odd) παράξενος, σπάνιος, μοναδικός ‖ n (gram) ενικός αριθμός ‖ ~ly ad μοναδικά, εξαιρετικά.

sinister [sinistə*] a απαίσιος, κακός.

sink [siŋk] (irreg v) n νεροχύτης ‖ vt (put under) καταβυθίζω, βουλιάζω ‖ (dig) σκάπτω, ανοίγω ‖ vi (fall slowly) καταβυθίζομαι, βουλιάζω, καθίζω ‖ to ~ in vi (news etc) χαράσσομαι στό μυαλό ‖ ~ing a (feeling) απογοητευτικός ‖ with ~ing heart μέ σφιγμένη καρδιά.

sinner ['sinə*] n αμαρτωλός.

Sino- ['sainəu] prefix Σινο-, Κινεζο-.

sinuous ['sinjuəs] a ελικοειδής, κυματοειδής, στριστός.

sinus ['sainəs] n (anat) κόλπος.

sip [sip] n ρουφηξιά, γουλιά ‖ vt πίνω γουλιά-γουλιά, ρουφώ.

siphon ['saifən] n σιφόνι(ον) ‖ to ~ off vt αναρροφώ, σιφωνίζω.

sir [sə:*] n κύριος, κύριε ‖ σέρ, τίτλος ευγενείας ‖ yes S~ μάλιστα, κύριε.

siren ['saiərən] n σειρήνα.

sirloin ['sə:lɔin] n κόντρα φιλέττο.

sirocco [si'rɔkəu] n σιρόκκος.

sissy ['sisi] n (col: coward) δειλός.

sister ['sistə*] n αδελφή ‖ προϊσταμένη, αρχινοσοκόμος ‖ (nun) μοναχή, καλογριά, αδελφή ‖ ~-in-law n κουνιάδα, νύφη.

sit [sit] (irreg v) vi κάθομαι ‖ (at session) συνεδριάζω ‖ vt (exam) δίδω εξετάσεις, εξετάζομαι ‖ to ~ tight δέν τό κουνώ, βάζω τά δυνατά μου ‖ to ~ down vi κάθομαι ‖ to ~ up vi (after lying) ανασηκώνομαι ‖ (at night) αγρυπνώ, ξενυχτώ.

site [sait] n τοποθεσία, θέσις ‖ vt τοποθετώ, εγκαθιστώ.

sit-in ['sitin] n (demonstration) διαδήλωσις.

siting ['saitiŋ] n (location) τοποθέτησις.

sitting ['sitiŋ] n συνεδρίασις ‖ ~ room n αίθουσα διαμονής.

situated ['sitjueitid] a κείμενος, ευρισκόμενος.

situation [sitju'eiʃən] n (state of affairs) κατάστασις ‖ (place) τοποθεσία, θέσις ‖ (post) θέσις, εργασία, δουλειά.

six [siks] num έξι(η) ‖ ~teen num δεκαέξ ‖ ~th a έκτος ‖ ~ty num εξήντα.

size [saiz] n μέγεθος, διάστασις, έκτασις

ὄγκος ‖ (*glue*) κόλλα ‖ (*of clothing*) νούμερο ‖ **to ~ up** *vt* (*assess*) ἐκτιμῶ (τό μέγεθος), σχηματίζω γνώμην γιά ‖ **~able** *a* εὐμεγέθης, μεγαλούτσικος.

sizzle ['sizl] *n* τριγμός, σφύριγμα, τσιγάρισμα ‖ *vi* τσιτσιρίζω, σφυρίζω, τσιγαρίζω.

skate [skeit] *n* πέδιλον, πατίνι ‖ *vi* πατινάρω, παγοδρομῶ ‖ **~r** *n* πατινέρ, παγοδρόμος.

skating ['skeitiŋ] *n*: **to go ~** πηγαίνω γιά πατινάζ ‖ **~ rink** *n* παγοδρόμιον, πατινάζ.

skeleton ['skelitn] *n* σκελετός.

skeptic ['skeptik] *n* (*US*) = sceptic.

sketch [sketʃ] *n* σκαρίφημα, σκιαγραφία ‖ (*play*) σκίτσο, σκέτς ‖ *vt* σκιαγραφῶ, σκιτσάρω ‖ **~ book** *n* συλλογή σκίτσων ‖ σημειωματάριον ‖ **~ing** *n* σκιτσάρισμα ‖ **~ pad** *n* καρνέ γιά σκίτσα ‖ **~y** *a* ἀτελής, ἀσαφής, ἀκαθόριστος.

skew [skju:] *n*: **on the ~** λοξά.

skewer ['skjuə*] *n* σούβλα.

ski [ski:] *n* σκί ‖ *vi* κάνω σκί ‖ **~ boot** *n* παπούτσι τοῦ σκί.

skid [skid] *n* (*skid-pan*) τροχοπεδωτικόν πέδιλον ‖ *vi* γλυστρῶ πλαγίως, ντεραπάρω.

skidmark ['skidma:k] *n* ἴχνη ντεραπαρίσματος.

skier ['ski:ə*] *n* σκιέρ.

skiing ['ski:iŋ] *n*: **to go ~** πάω γιά σκί.

skijump ['ski:dʒʌmp] *n* πήδημα μέ σκί.

skilful ['skilful] *a* ἱκανός, ἐπιδέξιος, ἐπιτήδειος ‖ **~ly** *ad* μέ ἐπιδεξιότητα.

skill [skil] *n* ἱκανότης, ἐπιδεξιότης ‖ **~ed** *a* ἐπιδέξιος, εἰδικευμένος.

skim [skim] *vt* ξαφρίζω, βγάζω ‖ (*read*) ξεφυλλίζω ‖ (*glide over*) ψαύω, περνῶ ξυστά.

skimp [skimp] *vt* (*do carelessly*) ψευτοφτιάνω, τσαπατσουλεύω ‖ **~y** *a* (*work, dress*) ἀνεπαρκής, στενό.

skin [skin] *n* δέρμα, πετσί, τομάρι ‖ (*peel, rind*) φλοιός, φλούδα ‖ (*on milk*) πέτσα ‖ *vt* γδέρνω, ξεφλουδίζω ‖ **~-deep** *a* ἐπιπόλαιος, ἐπιφανειακός ‖ **~ diving** *n* ὑποβρύχιον κολύμπι ‖ **~ny** *a* ἀδύνατος, κοκκαλιάρης, τσίρος ‖ **~tight** *a* (*dress etc*) ἐφαρμοστό.

skip [skip] *n* (ἀνα)πήδημα, σκίρτημα ‖ *vi* σκιρτῶ, πηδῶ, πετάγομαι ‖ *vt* παραλείπω, πηδῶ.

ski pants ['ski:'pænts] *npl* πανταλόνι τοῦ σκί.

skipper ['skipə*] *n* (*naut, sport*) πλοιοκτήτης ‖ καπετάνιος ‖ ἀρχηγός (ὁμάδος).

skipping rope ['skipiŋrəup] *n* σχοινάκι.

skirmish ['skə:miʃ] *n* ἀψιμαχία.

skirt [skə:t] *n* φούστα ‖ *vt* περιτρέχω, φέρνω βόλτα.

ski run ['ski:rʌn] *n* διάδρομος τοῦ σκί.

skit [skit] *n* εὐθυμογράφημα, παρωδία, νούμερο.

ski tow ['ski:'təu] *n* κρεμαστός σιδηρόδρομος γιά σκί.

skittle ['skitl] *n* (*one pin*) τσούνι ‖ **~s** *n* (*game*) τσούνια.

skulk [skʌlk] *vi* κρύβομαι, φυγοπονῶ.

skull [skʌl] *n* κρανίον.

skunk [skʌŋk] *n* μεφῖτις, εἶδος ἀσβοῦ.

sky [skai] *n* οὐρανός ‖ **~-blue** *a* ἀνοιχτό μπλέ ‖ **~ blue** *n* οὐρανί (χρῶμα) ‖ **~light** *n* φεγγίτις, ἀναφωτίς ‖ **~scraper** *n* οὐρανοξύστης.

slab [slæb] *n* πλάξ, πλάκα.

slack [slæk] *a* χαλαρός, λάσκος ‖ (*slow, dull*) πεσμένος, νεκρά (ἐποχή) ‖ (*careless*) ἀμελής, ἀδρανής, πλαδαρός ‖ *vi* ἀτονῶ, τεμπελιάζω ‖ *n* (*in rope etc*) χαλαρότης, τά μπόσικα ‖ **~s** *npl* (ναυτικό) πανταλόνι, φαρδύ πανταλόνι ‖ **~en** (*also* **~en off**) *vi* χαλαρούμαι, μειοδμαι, πέφτω ‖ *vt* χαλαρώνω, μετριάζω, ἐπιβραδύνω, λασκάρω ‖ **~ness** *n* νωθρότης, ἀτονία ‖ κάμψις.

slag [slæg] *n* σκωρία, ἐκβολάς μετάλλου ‖ **~ heap** *n* σωρός σκωριῶν.

slam [slæm] *n* κρότος, κτύπημα πόρτας ‖ *vt* (*door*) κλείνω ἀπότομα, κτυπῶ ‖ (*throw down*) πετάω μέ δύναμιν ‖ *vi* κλείνω μέ κρότον.

slander ['sla:ndə*] *n* κακολογία, διαβολή, συκοφαντία ‖ *vt* συκοφαντῶ, κακολογῶ, διαβάλλω ‖ **~ous** *a* συκοφαντικός.

slang [slæŋ] *n* μάγκικη γλῶσσα, ἀργκό, σλάγκ.

slant [sla:nt] *n* (*lit*) κλίσις, γέρσιμο ‖ (*fig*) ἄποψις, ἀντίληψις ‖ *vti* κλίνω, γέρνω ‖ **~ing** *a* κεκλιμένος, πλάγιος.

slap [slæp] *n* κτύπημα, ράπισμα, μπάτσο, φάπα ‖ *vt* ραπίζω, μπατσίζω, καρπαζώνω ‖ *ad* (*directly*) κατ' εὐθεῖαν ‖ **~dash** *ad* ξέννοιαστα, ἀπρόσεκτα ‖ **~stick** *n* (*comedy*) φάρσα ‖ **~-up** *a* (*meal*) ἐξαίσιος, φίνος.

slash [slæʃ] *n* δυνατό κτύπημα, σχίσιμο ‖ *vt* κόβω, σχίζω, πετσοκόβω.

slate [sleit] *n* σχιστόλιθος ‖ (*piece of slate*) ἀβάκιον, πλάκα ‖ *vt* (*criticize*) ἐπικρίνω, κουρελιάζω.

slaughter ['slɔ:tə*] *n* σφαγή, σφάξιμο ‖ *vt* σφάζω.

Slav [slɑːv] *n* (*person*) Σλάβος ‖ *a* Σλαυικός.

slave [sleiv] *n* σκλάβος, δοῦλος ‖ *vi* δουλεύω σκληρά, μοχθῶ ‖ **~ry** *n* δουλεία, σκλαβιά.

slavish ['sleiviʃ] *a* δουλικός ‖ **~ly** *ad* δουλικά.

sledge [sledʒ] *n* ἕλκηθρον ‖ **~hammer** *n* βαρειά, μεγάλο σφυρί.

sleek [sli:k] *a* λεῖος, ἀπαλός, προσποιητός.

sleep [sli:p] (*irreg v*) *n* ὕπνος ‖ *vi* κοιμούμαι, πλαγιάζω ‖ **to go to ~** ἀποκοιμούμαι ‖ **to ~ in** *vi* (*late*) ξυπνῶ ἀργά ‖ **~er** *n* ὑπναράς ‖ (*beam*) δοκός, τραβέρσα κλινάμαξα ‖ **~ily** *ad* κοιμισμένα ‖

~iness n ὑπνηλία, νυσταγμός, νύστα ‖ **~ing** attr a κοιμώμενος, κοιμισμένος ‖ **~ing bag** n σάκκος ὕπνου ‖ **~ing car** n κλινάμαξα, βαγκόν-λί ‖ **~ing pill** n ὑπνωτικὸ χάπι ‖ **~less** a (night) ἄϋπνος, ἄγρυπνος ‖ **~lessness** n ἀϋπνία, ἀγρυπνία ‖ **~walker** n ὑπνοβάτης ‖ **~y** a νυσταλέος, νυστάζων.

sleet [sli:t] n χιονόνερο.

sleeve [sli:v] n μανίκι ‖ **~less** a (garment) χωρὶς μανίκια.

sleigh [slei] n ἔλκηθρον.

sleight [slait] n: ~ **of hand** ταχυδακτυλουργία.

slender ['slendə*] a λεπτός, λιγνός ‖ (small) ἰσχνός, ἀσθενής.

slept [slept] pt,pp of sleep.

slice [slais] n κομμάτι, μερίς, φέτα ‖ vt τεμαχίζω, κόβω σὲ φέτες.

slick [slik] a (smart) γλυστερός, δόλιος. προσποιητός.

slid [slid] pt,pp of slide.

slide [slaid] (irreg v) n τσουλήθρα, ὀλισθητήριον, στίβος ‖ (phot: transparency) διαφανὴς φωτογραφία, σλάϊντ ‖ (brooch) τσιμπιδάκι ‖ (fall in prices) πτῶσις τιμῶν ‖ vt παρακάμπτω, ξεφεύγω ‖ vi ὀλισθαίνω, γλυστρῶ, τσουλῶ ‖ **to let** ~ ἀδιαφορῶ, ἀφήνω στὴν τύχη ‖ ~ **rule** n λογαριθμικὸς κανών, ρέγουλα.

sliding ['slaidiŋ] a (door) συρτή (πόρτα).

slight [slait] a λεπτός, ἰσχνός ‖ (trivial) ἐλαφρός, μικρός ‖ (small) μικροκαμωμένος, μικρούλης ‖ n ὑποτίμησις, περιφρόνησις ‖ vt (offend) προσβάλλω, θίγω ‖ **~ly** ad ἐλαφρά, κάπως, λιγάκι.

slim [slim] a λεπτός, ἀνεπαρκής, μικρός ‖ vi ἀδυνατίζω, λεπτύνω, κάνω δίαιτα.

slime [slaim] n λάσπη, βοῦρκος, ἰλύς.

slimming ['slimiŋ] n ἀδυνάτισμα.

slimness ['slimnis] n λεπτότης, λυγεράδα, σβελτάδα.

slimy ['slaimi] a βορβορώδης, γλοιώδης.

sling [sliŋ] (irreg v) n (bandage) ἀνωμίτης, κρεμαστάρι ‖ vt ἐκσφενδονίζω, ρίχνω, κρεμῶ.

slip [slip] n (slipping) ὀλίσθημα, γλύστρημα ‖ (petticoat) μισοφόρι ‖ (of paper) φύλλο χαρτί ‖ vt γλυστρῶ ἀθορύβως, εἰσέρχομαι, μπαίνω ‖ (escape from) ξεφεύγω ἀπὸ ‖ vi (lose balance) ὀλισθαίνω, γλυστρῶ ‖ (move smoothly) κινοῦμαι ἀθορύβως ‖ (make mistake) κάνω γκάφα, σφάλλω ‖ (decline) παρεκτρέπομαι, παραστρατῶ ‖ **to ~ away** vi στρίβω, τὸ σκάω στὴ ζούλα ‖ **to ~ in** vt βάζω, χώνω ‖ **to ~ out** vi ἐξέρχομαι, βγαίνω (κρυφά) ‖ **~per** n παντούφλα ‖ **~pery** a ὀλισθηρός, γλυστερός ‖ (tricky) πανοῦργος, πονηρός ‖ **~shod** a (untidy) ἀκατάστατος, ἀπρόσεκτος ‖ **~-up** n (mistake) σφάλμα, γκάφα ‖ **~way** n ναυπηγικὴ κλίνη.

slit [slit] (irreg v) n σχίσιμο, σχισμή ‖ vt κόβω, σχίζω, σχίζομαι.

slither ['sliðə*] vi ὀλισθαίνω, γλυστρῶ.

slob [slɔb] n (col: unpleasant person) ἀντιπαθής, ἀτζαμής.

slog [slɔg] n (great effort) ἀγγαρεία, βαρειὰ δουλειά ‖ vi (work hard) δουλεύω σκληρά.

slogan ['sləugən] n (catchword) σύνθημα.

slop [slɔp] vi ξεχειλίζω, χύνομαι ‖ vt χύνω.

slope [sləup] n κλιτύς, πλαγιά ‖ (slant) κλίσις ‖ vi: **to ~ down** κατηφορίζω ‖ **to ~ up** vi ἀνηφορίζω.

sloping ['sləupiŋ] a λοξός, ἐπικλινής, κεκλιμένος.

sloppily ['slɔpili] ad ἀκατάστατα, τσαπατσούλικα.

sloppiness ['slɔpinis] n τσαπατσουλιά.

sloppy ['slɔpi] a λασπωμένος, λασπώδης ‖ (untidy) μπατάλικος, ἀκατάστατος ‖ (weak, silly) ἄνοστος, σαχλός.

slot [slɔt] n σχισμή, χαραμάδα, τρύπα ‖ vt: **to ~ in** αὐλακώνω, χαράσσω (κάτι) ‖ ~ **machine** n αὐτόματος πωλητής ‖ μηχάνημα τυχερῶν παιχνιδιῶν.

slouch [slautʃ] vi κινοῦμαι ἀδέξια.

slovenly ['slʌvnli] a ἀκατάστατος, ἀπρόσεκτος.

slow [sləu] a βραδύς, ἀργός ‖ (of clock) ἐν καθυστερήσει, πίσω ‖ (stupid) βραδύνους, χοντροκέφαλος ‖ ad σιγά, ἀργά ‖ '~' (roadsign) 'ἀργά' ‖ **to ~ down** vi ἐπιβραδύνω, μειώνω, κόβω (ταχύτητα) ‖ vt ἐπιβραδύνω ‖ **to ~ up** vi σταματῶ, φρενάρω ‖ vt ἐπιβραδύνω ‖ **~ly** ad βραδέως, ἀργά ‖ **in ~ motion** εἰς ἀργὸν ρυθμόν, ραλαντί.

sludge [slʌdʒ] n λάσπη, βοῦρκος.

slug [slʌg] n γυμνοσάλιαγκας ‖ (bullet) μικρὴ σφαίρα ‖ **~gish** a ἀδρανής, τεμπέλης, νωθρός ‖ **~gishly** ad νωθρά, ὀκνά, τεμπέλικα ‖ **~gishness** n νωθρότης, τεμπελιά ‖ βραδύτης.

sluice [slu:s] n ὑδροφράκτης, φράγμα ‖ βάνα.

slum [slʌm] n πτωχογειτονιά, χαμόσπιτο.

slumber ['slʌmbə*] n γαλήνιος ὕπνος.

slump [slʌmp] n πτῶσις, ἐλάττωσις ζητήσεως ‖ vi πέφτω ἀπότομα.

slung [slʌŋ] pt,pp of sling.

slur [slə:*] n βιαστικὴ προφορά, τραύλισμα ‖ (insult) ὕβρις, προσβολή ‖ vt (also ~ over) κακοπροφέρω, τραυλίζω ‖ **~red** a (pronunciation) κακῆς ἀρθρώσεως.

slush [slʌʃ] n λασπωμένο χιόνι ‖ **~y** a (lit) λασπωμένος ‖ (fig: sentimental) σαχλός, γλυκανάλατος.

slut [slʌt] n τσούλα, παλιοθήλυκο.

sly [slai] a πονηρός, πανοῦργος, ὕπουλος ‖ **~ly** ad ὕπουλα, πονηρά, μπαμπέσικα ‖ **~ness** n πανουργία, πονηριά, κατεργαριά.

smack [smæk] n (slap) κτύπημα, ράπισμα

μπάτσος ‖ *vt* (*slap*) ραπίζω, καρπαζώνω ‖
to ~ one's lips κτυπῶ τά χείλη.

small [smɔ:l] *a* μικρός, ὀλίγος ‖ **~ change**
n ψιλά ‖ **~holding** *n* μικρό κτῆμα ‖ **~
hours** *npl* πολύ πρωϊνές ὧρες ‖ **~ish** *a*
μᾶλλον μικρός, μικρούτσικος ‖ **~ness** *n*
μικρότης, στενότης ‖ **~pox** *n* εὐλογία,
βλογιά ‖ **~-scale** *a* μικρᾶς κλίμακος ‖
~ talk *n* φλυαρία.

smarmy ['sma:mi] *a* (*col*) γλοιώδης, κωλογλείφτης.

smart [sma:t] *a* (*well-dressed*) κομψός,
μοντέρνος ‖ (*clever*) ἔξυπνος, ἐπιδέξιος
‖ (*sharp, quick*) δριμύς, ταχύς, ζωηρός ‖
vi πονῶ, τσούζω, ὑποφέρω ‖ **to ~en up**
vi ζωηρεύω, κάνω κέφι ‖ ξυπνῶ ‖ *vt*
ἐπισπεύδω, ἐπιταχύνω ‖ **~ly** *ad* ζωηρά,
σβέλτα ‖ κομψά ‖ **~ness** *n* εὐφυΐα,
κατατσοσύνη ‖ κομψότης.

smash [smæʃ] *n* (*collision*) σύγκρουσις ‖
vt τσακίζω, θρυμματίζω, κομματιάζω ‖
(*destroy*) καταστρέφω, συντρίβω ‖ *vi*
θραύομαι, κομματιάζομαι ‖ **~ing** *a*
(*col*) σπουδαῖος, περίφημος.

smattering ['smætəriŋ] *n* ἐπιπολαία γνῶσις,
πασάλειμμα.

smear [smiə*] *n* κηλίς, λεκές ‖ ἐπίχρισμα ‖
vt ἀλείφω, πασαλείφω ‖ λερώνω,
μουντζουρώνω.

smell [smel] (*irreg v*) *n* ὄσφρησις ‖ (*odour*)
ὀσμή, μυρωδιά ‖ *vt* (*breathe in*) ὀσφραίνομαι, μυρίζω ‖ *vi* μυρίζω, παίρνω
μυρωδιά ‖ (*give out smell*) μυρίζω,
βρωμάω ‖ **~y** *a* (*unpleasant*) κάκοσμος,
βρωμερός.

smile [smail] *n* χαμόγελο ‖ *vi* χαμογελῶ.

smiling ['smailiŋ] *a* χαμογελαστός, γελαστός.

smirk [smə:k] *n* ψεύτικο χαμόγελο ‖ *vi*
χαμογελῶ ψεύτικα.

smith [smiθ] *n* σιδηρουργός, σιδεράς ‖
~y ['smiði] *n* σιδηρουργεῖον, σιδεράδικο.

smock [smɔk] *n* μπλούζα, φόρμα.

smog [smɔg] *n* μολυσμένη ὁμίχλη.

smoke [smauk] *n* καπνός, καπνίλα ‖
(*tobacco*) κάπνισμα, τσιγάρο ‖ *vt* (*puff*)
καπνίζω ‖ (*dry food*) καπνίζω ‖ *vi* ἀναδίδω καπνούς, καπνίζω ‖ (*of cigarette*)
καπνίζω ‖ **~d** *a* (*bacon etc*) καπνιστός ‖
~r *n* (*person*) καπνιστής ‖ (*rail*) βαγόνι
καπνιστῶν ‖ **~room** *n* (*in pub*) καπνι-
στήριον.

smoking ['smaukiŋ] *n* κάπνισμα ‖ **'no ~'**
(*sign*) 'ἀπαγορεύεται τό κάπνισμα'.

smoky ['smauki] *a* γεμάτος καπνό, καπνι-
σμένος.

smolder ['smauldə*] *vi* (*US*) = smoulder.

smooth [smu:ð] *a* (*in consistency*) ἀπαλός,
γλυκόπιοτο ‖ (*movement*) ὁμαλός,
μαλακός, ἀθόρυβος ‖ (*person*) γλυκομίλητος, γαλήνης ‖ *vt* (*also ~ out*) λειαίνω,
ἐξομαλύνω, ἰσιάζω ‖ **~ly** *ad* ὁμαλά,

ἤρεμα, στρωτά ‖ **~ness** *n* ὁμαλότης,
ἀπαλότης.

smother ['smʌðə*] *vt* πνίγω, σβήνω ‖
καταπνίγω, σκεπάζω.

smoulder ['smauldə*] *vi* ὑποβόσκω, σιγο-
καίω.

smudge [smʌdʒ] *n* κηλίς, λεκές, βρωμιά ‖
vt λεκιάζω, λερώνω, βρωμίζω.

smug [smʌg] *a* αὐτάρεσκος, καμαρωτός,
ἐπηρμένος.

smuggle ['smʌgl] *vt* κάνω λαθρεμπόριο,
περνῶ λαθραία ‖ **~r** *n* λαθρέμπορος,
κοντραμπαντζῆς.

smuggling ['smʌgliŋ] *n* λαθρεμπόριο,
κοντραμπάντο.

smugly ['smʌgli] *ad* ἐπηρμένα, καμαρωτά

smugness ['smʌgnis] *n* ὑπεροψία, ἔπαρσις,
αὐταρέσκεια.

smutty ['smʌti] *a* (*fig: obscene*) αἰσχρός,
βρώμικος, πρόστυχος.

snack [snæk] *n* ἐλαφρό φαγητό, κολατσό
‖ **~ bar** *n* σνάκ-μπάρ.

snag [snæg] *n* (*obstacle*) ἐμπόδιο, κώλυμα
‖ (*in stocking*) τράβηγμα κλωστῆς.

snail [sneil] *n* σαλιγκάρι.

snake [sneik] *n* ὄφις, φίδι.

snap [snæp] *n* δάγκωμα, ἅρπαγμα, δαγκω-
ματιά ‖ (*sound*) ψαλιδιά, κράκ, στράκα,
ξηρός κρότος ‖ (*photograph*) στιγμιότυπον, ἐνσταντανέ, φωτογραφία ‖ *a*
βιαστικός, ἀπροσδόκητος ‖ *vt* (*make
sound*) κροταλίζω, κάνω στράκα ‖
(*break*) θραύω, σπάζω, τσακίζω ‖ (*photograph*) φωτογραφίζω, τραβῶ, πέρνω ‖ *vi*
(*break*) σπάω ‖ **to ~ off** *vt* (*break*) σπάω
‖ **to ~ up** *vt* ἀρπάζω, βουτάω, ψάχνω ‖
~py *a* δηκτικός, ἀπότομος, ζωηρός ‖
~shot *n* φωτογραφία ἐνσταντανέ.

snare [snɛə*] *n* παγίδα ‖ *vt* παγιδεύω,
πιάνω.

snarl [sna:l] *n* γρυλισμός, μούγγρισμα ‖ *vi*
(*also person*) γρυλίζω ‖ βρίζω.

snatch [snætʃ] *n* ἅρπαγμα ‖ (*small amount*)
τεμάχιον, κομμάτι ‖ *vt* ἀρπάζω, τσακώνω.

sneak [sni:k] *vi* κινοῦμαι κρυφά.

sneakers ['sni:kəz] *npl* παπούτσια γυμνα-
στικῆς.

sneer [sniə*] *n* καγχασμός, σαρκασμός ‖
vi κοροϊδεύω, σαρκάζω, περιφρονῶ.

sneeze [sni:z] *n* φτέρνισμα ‖ *vi* φτερνίζομαι.

snide [snaid] *a* ψεύτικος, σαρκαστικός.

sniff [snif] *n* εἰσπνοή, ρούφηγμα, μύρισμα
‖ *vi* ξεφυσῶ, εἶμαι συναχωμένος ‖ *vt*
(*smell*) ὀσφραίνομαι, μυρίζω, ρουφῶ.

snigger ['snigə*] *n* πνιχτό γέλιο, πονηρό
γέλιο ‖ *vi* κρυφογελῶ, ξεργελῶ.

snip [snip] *n* ψαλίδισμα, κομματάκι ‖
(*bargain*) εὐκαιρία, καλή δουλειά ‖ *vt*
ψαλιδίζω, ἀποκόβω.

snipe [snaip] *n* μπεκάτσα.

sniper ['snaipə*] *n* (*marksman*) ἐλεύθερος
σκοπευτής.

snippet ['snipit] n κομματάκι, απόσπασμα.

saivelling ['snivliŋ] a (whimpering) κλαψι-άρικος.

snob [snɔb] n σνόμπ, ψωροπερήφανος, κορδωμένος ‖ ~bery n σνομπισμός ‖ ~bish a σνόμπ, φαντασμένος, ποζάτος ‖ ~bishness n σνομπισμός, πόζα.

snooker ['snu:kə*] n είδος μπιλλιάρδο.

snoop [snu:p] vi: to ~ about χώνω τήν μύτη, ψαχουλεύω.

snooty ['snu:ti] a (col: snobbish) υπερόπτης, ψηλομύτης.

snooze [snu:z] n υπνάκος ‖ vi παίρνω ένα υπνάκο, μισοκοιμάμαι.

snore [snɔ:*] vi ροχαλίζω.

snoring ['snɔ:riŋ] n ροχαλητό.

snorkel ['snɔ:kl] n αναπνευστήρας.

snort [snɔ:t] n φρίμασμα, ξεφύσημα, ρουθούνισμα ‖ vi ρουθουνίζω, φριμάζω, ξεφυσώ.

snotty ['snɔti] a (col: snobbish) ψηλομύτης.

snout [snaut] n ρύγχος, μουσούδα, μύτη.

snow [snəu] n χιόνι ‖ vi χιονίζω, ρίχνω χιόνι ‖ ~ball n μπάλλα χιόνι, χιονό-σφαιρα ‖ ~bound a (απο)κλεισμένος από τά χιόνια ‖ ~drift n χιονοστιβάς ‖ ~drop n γάλανθος ὁ χιονώδης ‖ ~fall n χιονόπτωσις ‖ ~flake n νιφάς ‖ ~man n χιονάνθρωπος ‖ ~plough, (US) ~ plow n άροτρον γιά τά χιόνια ‖ ~storm n χιονοθύελλα.

snub [snʌb] vt αποκρούω, προσβάλλω, κόβω ‖ n επίπληξις, προσβολή, κατσάδα ‖ ~-nosed a μέ ανασηκωμένη μύτη.

snuff [snʌf] n ταμπάκο, πρέζα ‖ ~box n ταμπακέρα.

snug [snʌg] a άνετος, βολικός, ζεστός, αναπαυτικός.

so [səu] ad (extent) τόσο(ν) ‖ (in such manner) έτσι ‖ (thus) ούτω(ς), τοιουτο-τρόπως ‖ (to such an extent) τόσο ‖ cj επομένως, γι' αυτό, έτσι λοιπόν ‖ or ~ περίπου, πάνω κάτω ‖ ~ long! (goodbye) γειά σου!, αντίο! ‖ ~ many, ~ much τόσος ‖ ~ that ούτως ώστε.

soak [səuk] vt διαβρέχω, μουσκεύω ‖ (leave in liquid) διαποτίζω, μουσκεύω ‖ to ~ in vi διεισδύω, διαποτίζω, ποτίζω ‖ ~ing n διάβρεξις, εμποτισμός, κατά-βρεγμα.

soap [səup] n σαπούνι ‖ ~flakes npl τριμμένο σαπούνι ‖ ~ powder n σαπούνι σέ σκόνη ‖ ~y a γεμάτος σαπούνι.

soar [sɔ:*] vi πετώ ψηλά, ανυψούμαι.

sob [sɔb] n λυγμός, αναφυλλητό ‖ vi κλαίω μέ αναφυλλητά.

sober ['səubə*] a νηφάλιος, ξεμέθυστος ‖ (calm) ψύχραιμος, εγκρατής, ήρεμος ‖ to ~ up vi συνέρχομαι, ξεμεθάω ‖ ~ly ad σοβαρά, μετρημένα, λιτά.

so-called ['səu'kɔ:ld] a δήθεν, λεγόμενος.

soccer ['sɔkə*] n ποδόσφαιρον.

sociability [səuʃə'biliti] n κοινωνικότης.

sociable ['səuʃəbl] a κοινωνικός, φιλικός, ομιλητικός.

social ['səuʃəl] a κοινωνικός ‖ ~ism n σοσιαλισμός ‖ ~ist n σοσιαλιστής ‖ a σοσιαλιστικός ‖ ~ly ad κοινωνικώς ‖ ~ science n κοινωνική επιστήμη ‖ ~ security n κοινωνική ασφάλεια ‖ ~ welfare n κοινωνική πρόνοια ‖ ~ work n κοινωνική εργασία ‖ ~ worker n κοινωνικός λειτουργός.

society [sə'saiəti] n (people and customs) κοινωνία ‖ (club) εταιρεία ‖ (fashionable life) κοσμική ζωή, καλός κόσμος.

sociological [səusiə'lɔdʒikəl] a κοινωνιολο-γικός.

sociologist [səusi'ɔlədʒist] n κοινωνιολό-γος.

sociology [səusi'ɔlədʒi] n κοινωνιολογία.

sock [sɔk] n (κοντή) κάλτσα ‖ vt (hit) δίνω γροθιά.

socket ['sɔkit] n ντουΐ, μπρίζα.

sod [sɔd] n (of earth) χορταριασμένος βώλος ‖ (col: term of abuse) παλιάνθρω-πος.

soda ['səudə] n (chem) νάτριον, σόδα ‖ (drink) σόδα ‖ ~ water n αεριούχον ύδωρ, σόδα.

sodden ['sɔdn] a διάβροχος, μουσκεμένος ‖ (moist and heavy) λασπωμένος.

sofa ['səufə] n σοφάς, καναπές.

soft [sɔft] a μαλακός, απαλός ‖ (not loud) απαλός, γλυκός, ελαφρός ‖ (kind) τρυφερός, καλός ‖ (weak, silly) ανόητος, χαζός ‖ ~ drink a αναψυκτικόν ‖ ~en vt μαλακώνω ‖ vi μαλακώνω, γίνομαι μαλακός ‖ ~-hearted a ευαίσθητος, μέ τρυφερή καρδιά ‖ ~ly ad απαλά, μαλακά, αθόρυβα ‖ ~ness n μαλακότης, απαλό-της.

soggy ['sɔgi] a υδαρής, μουσκεμένος.

soil [sɔil] n (earth) έδαφος, χώμα ‖ vt λερώνω ‖ ~ed a λερωμένος, ακάθαρτος.

solar ['səulə*] a ηλιακός ‖ ~ system n ηλιακόν σύστημα.

sold [səuld] pt,pp of sell.

solder ['səuldə*] vt (συγ)κολλῶ ‖ n καλάϊ, κόλλησι.

soldier ['səuldʒə*] n στρατιώτης.

sole [səul] n πέλμα, πατούσα ‖ πέλμα, σόλα ‖ (fish) γλώσσα ‖ a μόνος, μονα-δικός ‖ ~ly ad (only) μόνον, μοναδικά.

solemn ['sɔləm] a σοβαρός ‖ (formal) επίσημος, σεμνός.

solicitor [sə'lisitə*] n δικηγόρος, σύμβου-λος, συνήγορος.

solid ['sɔlid] a στερεός, συμπαγής ‖ (hard) στερεός, γερός, σκληρός ‖ (reliable) σοβαρός, βάσιμος ‖ (meal) γερός, ολόκληρος ‖ n στερεόν ‖ ~arity n ενότης, αλληλεγγύη ‖ ~ify [sə'lidifai] vi στερεοποιούμαι, πήζω ‖ vt στερεοποιώ, πήζω, παγώνω ‖ ~ity n στερεότης ‖ ~ly ad στερεά, γερά.

soliloquy [sə'liləkwi] n μονόλογος, μονολογία.

solitaire [sɔli'teə*] n (game) πασιέντσα ‖ (gem) μονό διαμάντι, μονόπετρο.

solitary ['sɔlitəri] a μόνος ‖ (lonely) ὁλομόναχος, μοναχικός.

solitude ['sɔlitju:d] n μοναξιά, ἐρημιά, ἀπομόνωσις.

solo ['səuləu] n σόλο ‖ ~ist n σολίστας.

solstice ['sɔlstis] n ἡλιοστάσιον.

soluble ['sɔljubl] a διαλυτός, εὐδιάλυτος ‖ (able to be solved) ἐπιδεικτικός λύσεως.

solution [sə'lu:ʃən] n λύσις, λύσιμο ‖ (explanation) λύσις, ἐξήγησις ‖ (in liquid) διάλυσις, διάλυμα.

solve [sɔlv] vt λύω, ἐξηγῶ.

solvent ['sɔlvənt] a ἀξιόχρεος.

sombre, (US) **somber** ['sɔmbə*] a σκοτεινός, μελαγχολικός ‖ ~ly ad σκοτεινά ‖ μελαγχολικά.

some [sʌm] a (uncertain number) ὀλίγος, ὀλίγοι, μερικοί ‖ (indefinite) κάποιος, τίς ‖ (remarkable) σπουδαῖος, περίφημος ‖ (partitive) μερικός, τι ‖ pron μερικοί, κάτι ‖ ad περίπου ‖ ~ body pron κάποιος ‖ n κάποιος, προσωπικότης ‖ ~day ad (μιά) κάποια μέρα ‖ ~how ad κάπως, κατά κάποιον τρόπον ‖ ~one pron = somebody ‖ ~place ad (US) = somewhere.

somersault ['sʌməsɔːlt] n τούμπα, κουτρουβάλα ‖ vi κάνω τούμπα.

something ['sʌmθiŋ] pron κάτι, ὁτιδήποτε.

sometime ['sʌmtaim] ad κάποτε ‖ ~s ad ἐνίοτε, κάπου-κάπου.

somewhat ['sʌmwɔt] ad κάπως.

somewhere ['sʌmweə*] ad κάπου.

son [sʌn] n υἱός, γιός.

sonata [sə'nɑːtə] n σονάτα.

song [sɔŋ] n τραγούδι ‖ ~ writer n (μουσικο)συνθέτης.

sonic ['sɔnik] a ἠχητικός.

son-in-law ['sʌninlɔ:] n γαμβρός.

sonnet ['sɔnit] n σονέττο.

sonny ['sʌni] n (col) μικρέ μου, ἀγόρι μου.

soon [su:n] ad ταχέως, γρήγορα ‖ (early) σύντομα, ἐνωρίς ‖ as ~ as possible τό συντομώτερο ‖ ~er ad (time) γρηγορώτερα ‖ (of preference) καλύτερα, κάλιο.

soot [sut] n αἰθάλη, φοῦμο, καπνιά.

soothe [su:ð] vt καταπραΰνω, παρηγορῶ.

soothing ['su:ðiŋ] a καταπραϋντικός.

sop [sɔp] n (bribe) δωροδοκία, φιλοδώρημα.

sophisticated [sə'fistikeitid] a (person) κοσμικός, μοντέρνος ‖ (machinery) πιό σύγχρονος, τελευταίας λέξεως.

sophistication [səfisti'keiʃən] n ἐξεζητημένα γοῦστα.

sophomore ['sɔfəmɔ:*] n (US) δευτεροετής φοιτητής.

soporific [sɔpə'rifik] a ὑπνωτικός, ναρκωτικός.

sopping ['sɔpiŋ] a (very wet) καταβρεγμένος, μουσκεμένος.

soppy ['sɔpi] a (col: sentimental) δακρύβρεκτος, σαχλός.

soprano [sə'prɑːnəu] n ὑψίφωνος, σοπράνο.

sordid ['sɔːdid] a ἀκάθαρτος, ρυπαρός ‖ (mean) ἄθλιος, χυδαῖος, τσιγγούνης.

sore [sɔ:*] a πονῶν, πού πονεῖ, ἐρεθισμένος ‖ (offended) πειραγμένος, θυμωμένος ‖ n πληγή, τραῦμα ‖ ~ly ad (tempted) βαθειά, σφοδρῶς ‖ ~ness n πόνος, ἐρεθισμός, ὀδυνηρότης.

sorrow ['sɔrəu] n λύπη, θλίψις, μετάνοια ‖ ~ful a θλιμμένος, λυπημένος ‖ ~fully ad θλιβερά, θλιμμένα.

sorry ['sɔri] a λυπημένος, πονεμένος ‖ (pitiable) ἄθλιος, φτωχικός, κακός.

sort [sɔ:t] n εἶδος, τάξις, λογή ‖ vt (also ~ out) (papers) ταξινομῶ, ξεκαθαρίζω ‖ (problems) τακτοποιῶ, (ξε)χωρίζω.

so-so ['səusəu] ad ἔτσι καί ἔτσι, μετρίως ὑποφερτά.

soufflé ['su:flei] n σουφλέ.

sought [sɔ:t] pt,pp of seek.

soul [səul] n ψυχή ‖ ~-destroying a ψυχοφθόρος, ἀποκτηνωτικός ‖ ~ful a αἰσθηματικός, συγκινητικός ‖ ~less a ἄψυχος, ἄκαρδος.

sound [saund] a (healthy) ὑγιής, γερός ‖ (safe) στερεός, ἀσφαλής, σίγουρος ‖ (reasonable) ὀρθός, ἰσχυρός, λογικός ‖ (deep, hearty) γερός, ἄγριος ‖ n (noise) ἦχος, θόρυβος ‖ (geog) στενόν, πορθμός ‖ vt (alarm) κτυπῶ ‖ vi (find depth) βυθομετρῶ ‖ (seem) φαίνομαι, μοιάζω ‖ to ~ out vi (opinions) βυλιδυσκοπῶ ‖ ~ barrier n φράγμα τοῦ ἤχου ‖ ~ing n (naut etc) βυθομέτρησις, βολιδοσκόπησις ‖ ~ly ad (sleep) βαθειά, καλά, ἥσυχα ‖ (beat) γερά, τελείως ‖ ~ness n βασιμότης, ὀρθότης ‖ ~proof a (room) ἠχομονωτικός ‖ vt κάνω ἀδιαπέραστο ἀπό ἦχον ‖ ~ track n (of film) ἠχητική ζώνη (ταινίας).

soup [su:p] n σούπα, ζωμός ‖ in the ~ στή λούμπα ‖ ~spoon n κουτάλι τῆς σούπας.

sour [sauə*] a ξινός, ἄγουρος, πράσινος ‖ (milk) ξυνός ‖ (bad-tempered) στριφνός, γκρινιάρης.

source [sɔ:s] n πηγή, προέλευσις.

sourness ['sauənis] n ὀξύτης, ξινίλα.

south [sauθ] n νότος ‖ a νότιος ‖ ad πρός νότον, νοτίως ‖ ~-east n τό νοτιοανατολικόν ‖ ~-easterly a νοτιοανατολικός ‖ ~ern a νότιος, μεσημβρινός ‖ S-Pole n Νότιος Πόλος ‖ ~ward(s) ad πρός νότον ‖ ~-west n τό νοτιοδυτικόν.

souvenir [su:və'niə*] n ἐνθύμιον, σουβενίρ.

sovereign ['sɔvrin] n ἡγεμών, βασιλεύς ‖ a (independent) κυρίαρχος ‖ ~ty n ἡγεμονία, κυριαρχία, ἀνεξαρτησία.

soviet ['sauviət] a σοβιετικός.

sow [sau] n γουρούνα ‖ [səu] (irreg v) vt σπείρω, σπέρνω ‖ [spread abroad] (ἐν)σπείρω.

soya bean [ˈsɔiəˈbiːn] n σόγια.

spa [spɑː] n ἰαματική πηγή ‖ (place) λουτρόπολις.

space [speis] n χῶρος, θέσις, τόπος ‖ (distance) ἀπόστασις ‖ (length of time) διάστημα ‖ (universe) διάστημα ‖ to ~ out vt ἀραιώνω, τοποθετῶ κατ' ἀποστάσεις ‖ ~craft n διαστημόπλοιον ‖ ~man n κοσμοναύτης.

spacing [ˈspeisiŋ] n ἀραίωσις, κλιμάκωσις.

spacious [ˈspeiʃəs] a εὐρύς, εὐρύχωρος, ἄπλόχωρος.

spade [speid] n (tool) φτυάρι, τσάπα, τσαπί ‖ ~s npl (cards) μπαστούνι, πίκα ‖ ~work n (preliminary work) προκαταρκτική ἐργασία.

spaghetti [spəˈgeti] n σπαγέτο, μακαρονάδα.

Spain [spein] n Ἰσπανία.

span [spæn] n (of arch) ἄνοιγμα, ἀπόστασις ‖ (of time) διάρκεια (ζωῆς) ‖ vt ζευγνύω, καλύπτω ‖ pt of spin.

Spaniard [ˈspænjəd] n Ἰσπανός.

spaniel [ˈspænjəl] n σπάνιελ.

Spanish [ˈspæniʃ] n (ling) ἰσπανικά ‖ a ἰσπανικός.

spank [spæŋk] vt δέρνω (στόν πισινό).

spanner [ˈspænə*] n κλειδί (ὑδραυλικοῦ).

spare [spɛə*] a περίσσιος, λιτός, ἰσχνός ‖ n = ~ part ‖ see below ‖ vt (do without) οἰκονομῶ, φυλάγω, κάνω δίχως ‖ (save from hurt) λυποῦμαι, χαρίζω, φείδομαι ‖ (lend, give) περισσεύω, δίνω, παραχωρῶ, διαθέτω ‖ to ~ περισσεύω ‖ ~ part n ἀνταλλακτικόν, ἐξάρτημα, ρεζέρβα ‖ ~ time n ἐλεύθερες ὧρες.

spark [spɑːk] n σπινθήρ, σπίθα ‖ (fig) ἴχνος, σπίθα ‖ ~ plug n σπινθηριστής, μπουζί.

sparkle [ˈspɑːkl] n σπινθήρ, σπίθα, λάμψις ‖ (gaiety) σπιρτάδα ‖ vi σπινθηρίζω, σπιθοβολῶ, ἀστράφτω.

sparkling [ˈspɑːkliŋ] a (lit) ἀστραφτερός, λάμπων ‖ (wine) ἀφρώδης ‖ (conversation) πνευματώδης (ὁμιλία).

sparrow [ˈspærəu] n σπουργίτης.

sparse [spɑːs] a ἀραιός, σποραδικός ‖ ~ly ad ἀραιά.

spasm [ˈspæzəm] n σπασμός, σπαρτάρισμα ‖ (short spell) κρίσις, ἔξαψις, μικρῆς διαρκείας ‖ ~odic a σπασμωδικός, σπαστικός.

spastic [ˈspæstik] n σπαστικός.

spat [spæt] pt,pp of spit.

spate [speit] n (fig) πλημμύρα, πλημμύρισμα ‖ in ~ (river) φουσκωμένος, πλημμυρισμένος.

spatter [ˈspætə*] n πιτσίλισμα, ράντισμα ‖ vt πιτσιλίζω, ραντίζω ‖ vi ἀναπηδῶ, (ξε)πετιέμαι, στάζω.

spatula [ˈspætjulə] n σπάτουλα.

spawn [spɔːn] vt ἀφήνω αὐγά ‖ γεννῶ.

speak [spiːk] (irreg v) vt λέγω, προφέρω,

ἐκφράζω ‖ (truth) λέγω, λέω ‖ (language) ὁμιλῶ, μιλῶ ‖ vi (+ to) ὁμιλῶ, μιλῶ στόν ‖ μιλῶ, συζητῶ ‖ (make speech) ἀγορεύω, μιλῶ ‖ to ~ for vt συνηγορῶ, μιλῶ γιά κάποιον ‖ to ~ up vi ὑψώνω τήν φωνήν, μιλῶ γιά κάποιον ‖ ~er n ὁμιλητής, συνομιλητής ‖ (chairman) πρόεδρος ‖ (loudspeaker: on record player) μεγάφωνον ‖ on ~ing terms γνώριμοι, πού μιλιοῦνται.

spear [spiə*] n ἀκόντιον, δόρυ, κοντάρι ‖ vt τρυπῶ μέ κοντάρι, πιάνω μέ κοντάρι.

spec [spek] n (col) τύχη, κερδοσκοπία ‖ on ~ στήν τύχη, γιά σπέκουλα.

special [ˈspeʃəl] a εἰδικός, ἴδιος ‖ (particular kind) ἐξαιρετικός, ἀσυνήθης ‖ (particular purpose) ἰδιαίτερος, ξεχωριστός ‖ n (rail) εἰδική ἁμαξοστοιχία ‖ (cooking) εἰδικός, ἰδιαίτερος ‖ ~ist n εἰδικός ‖ ~ity n εἰδικότης ‖ σπεσιαλιτέ ‖ ~ize vi (+ in) εἰδικεύομαι εἰς ‖ ~ly ad εἰδικά, ἰδιαίτερα, πρό παντός, πάνω ἀπ' ὅλα.

species [ˈspiːʃiːz] n εἶδος.

specific [spəˈsifik] a. εἰδικός, ὡρισμένος, ἀκριβής, σαφής ‖ ~ally ad εἰδικά, συγκεκριμένως ‖ ~ation n περιγραφή, καθορισμός, προδιαγραφή.

specify [ˈspesifai] vt καθορίζω, προσδιορίζω, διευκρινίζω.

specimen [ˈspesimin] n δεῖγμα, τύπος.

speck [spek] n κηλίς, λεκές, σταγόνα ‖ (particle) κόκκος, ψῆγμα, μόριον ‖ ~led a διάστικτος, πιτσιλισμένος.

specs [speks] npl (col) γυαλιά.

spectacle [ˈspektəkl] n θέαμα ‖ ~s npl ματογυάλια, γυαλιά.

spectacular [spekˈtækjulə*] a θεαματικός.

spectator [spekˈteitə*] n θεατής.

spectre, (US) specter [ˈspektə*] n φάντασμα, σκιάχτρο.

spectrum [ˈspektrəm] n φάσμα.

speculate [ˈspekjuleit] vi σκέπτομαι, διαλογίζομαι ‖ (fin) κερδοσκοπῶ, σπεκουλάρω.

speculation [spekjuˈleiʃən] n (fin) κερδοσκοπία, σπέκουλα.

speculative [ˈspekjulətiv] a (fin) κερδοσκοπικός.

sped [sped] pt,pp of speed.

speech [spiːtʃ] n λόγος, λαλιά ‖ (talk) λόγος, ἀγόρευσις, ὁμιλία ‖ (manner) ἄρθρωσις, εὐγλωττία, γλῶσσα ‖ ~ day n (sch) ἀπονομή τῶν πτυχίων ‖ ~less a ἄλαλος, βουβός, ἄφωνος ‖ ~ therapy n θεραπευτική ἀγωγή λόγου.

speed [spiːd] (irreg v) n ταχύτης, σπουδή ‖ (gear) ταχύτης ‖ vi σπεύδω, κάνω γρήγορα, τρέχω ‖ to ~ up vi ἐπιταχύνω ‖ vt ἐπισπεύδω, ἐπιταχύνω ‖ ~boat n ἐξωλέμβιος ‖ ~ily ad ταχέως, ἐσπευσμένα, βιαστικά ‖ ~ing n ὑπερβολική ταχύτης ‖ ~ limit n ὅριον ταχύτητος ‖

~ometer n ἐνδείκτης ταχύτητος, κοντέρ ‖ **~way** n αὐτοκινητόδρομος ‖ **~y** a ταχύς, γρήγορος.

spell [spel] (irreg v) n (magic) γοητεία, μαγεία, μάγια ‖ (period of time) διάστημα, χρονική περίοδος ‖ vt ὀρθογραφῶ, γραμματίζω ‖ συλλαβίζω ‖ (mean) σημαίνω ‖ **~bound** a γοητευμένος, μαγεμένος ‖ **~ing** n συλλαβισμός, ὀρθογραφία.

spelt [spelt] pt,pp of **spell**.

spend [spend] (irreg v) vt ξοδεύω, καταναλίσκω, δαπανῶ ‖ (use up) ἐξαντλῶ, περνῶ, χρησιμοποιῶ ‖ **~ing money** n χαρτζιλίκι.

spent [spent] pt,pp of **spend** ‖ a (patience) ἐξηντλημένος.

sperm [spə:m] n (biol) σπέρμα.

spew [spju:] vt ξερνῶ, κάνω ἐμετό.

sphere [sfiə*] n σφαίρα, ὑδρόγειος.

spherical ['sferikəl] a σφαιρικός.

sphinx [sfiŋks] n σφίγξ, σφίγγα.

spice [spais] n καρύκευμα, μπαχαρικό, ἄρωμα ‖ vt καρυκεύω, ἀρτύω, ἀρωματίζω.

spiciness ['spaisinis] n πικάντικη γεῦσις, νοστιμιά.

spick-and-span ['spikən'spæn] a φρέσκος, καθαρός, κομψός.

spicy ['spaisi] a ἀρωματισμένος, πικάντικος.

spider ['spaidə*] n ἀράχνη ‖ **~y** a ἀράχνινος.

spike [spaik] n αἰχμή, καρφί, στάχυ, πάσσαλος.

spill [spil] (irreg v) vt (upset) ἀνατρέπω, ἀναποδογυρίζω ‖ (pour out) χύνω ‖ vi (flow over) χύνομαι.

spin [spin] (irreg v) n (revolution of wheel) περιστροφή, συστροφή ‖ (trip in car) περίπατος, βόλτα ‖ (aviat) περιδίνησις, σπινάρισμα ‖ vt (wool etc) κλώθω, νέθω ‖ γυρίζω, παίζω σβούρα ‖ vi περιστρέφομαι, (στριφο)γυρίζω ‖ **to ~ out** vi (of money etc) οἰκονομῶ (τά λεφτά μου) ‖ vt παρατείνω, παρατραβῶ, ξεντώνω.

spinach ['spinidʒ] n σπανάκι.

spinal ['spainl] a νωτιαῖος, ραχιαῖος, σπονδυλικός ‖ **~ cord** n νωτιαῖος μυελός.

spindly ['spindli] a λιγνός.

spin-drier ['spin'draiə*] n στεγνωτήριον.

spine [spain] n σπονδυλική στήλη, ραχοκοκκαλιά ‖ (thorn) ἀγκάθι ‖ **~less** a δειλός, λαπάς.

spinner ['spinə*] n (of thread) κλώστης, κλώστρια.

spinning ['spiniŋ] n (of thread) κλώσιμο, στρίψιμο ‖ **~ wheel** n ροδάνι, ἀνέμη.

spinster ['spinstə*] n γεροντοκόρη.

spiral ['spaiərəl] n σπεῖρα, ἕλιξ ‖ a ἑλικοειδής, σπειροειδής ‖ vi κινοῦμαι σπειροειδῶς ‖ **~ staircase** n γυριστή σκάλα, στριφτή σκάλα.

spire ['spaiə*] n κορυφή κωδωνοστασίου.

spirit ['spirit] n πνεῦμα, ψυχή ‖ (ghost) φάντασμα ‖ (humour, mood) διάθεσις, κέφι ‖ (courage) σθένος, κουράγιο, θάρρος ‖ (alcoholic) οἰνοπνευματῶδες ποτό, σπίρτο ‖ **in good ~s** κεφάτος, καλόκεφος ‖ **~ed** a ζωηρός, ἔντονος, θαρραλέος ‖ **~ level** n ἀλφάδι ‖ **~ual** a πνευματικός, ψυχικός ‖ n θρησκευτικό τραγούδι ‖ **~ualism** n πνευματισμός.

spit [spit] (irreg v) n (for roasting) σούβλα ‖ (saliva) πτύελον, σάλιο ‖ vi φτύνω ‖ (of motor) ρετάρω.

spite [spait] n μῖσος, ἔχθρα, κακία ‖ vt ἐνοχλῶ, πεισμώνω, φουρκίζω ‖ **in ~ of** παρά τό, παρ' ὅλα ‖ **~ful** a μοχθηρός, ἐκδικητικός.

splash [splæʃ] n πιτσίλισμα, πλατσούλισμα, λεκές ‖ (of colour) πολυχρωμία ‖ vti πλατσουλίζω, πιτσιλίζω ‖ **~down** n προσθαλάσσωσις.

spleen [spli:n] n σπλήνα.

splendid ['splendid] a λαμπρός, μεγαλοπρεπής ‖ (fine) ἐξαίσιος, περίφημος ‖ **~ly** ad λαμπρά, ὑπέροχα, περίφημα.

splendour, (US) **splendor** ['splendə*] n λαμπρότης, λάμψις ‖ (glory) μεγαλοπρέπεια.

splice [splais] vt ἁματίζω, συνδέω.

splint [splint] n νάρθηξ.

splinter ['splintə*] n θραῦσμα, σχίζα ‖ vi θραύομαι, σπάζω.

split [split] (irreg v) n σχισμή, σχίσιμο, ρωγμή, διαίρεσις ‖ vt σχίζω, θρύψω, σπάζω ‖ vi (divide) διασπῶ ‖ (col: depart) ἀναχωρῶ ‖ **to ~ up** vi διαιροῦμαι ‖ vt διαιρῶ, χωρίζω, διασπῶ ‖ **~ting** a (headache) πού πονάει, πού σπάει.

splutter ['splʌtə*] vi λειτουργῶ κακῶς, ρετάρω.

spoil [spoil] (irreg v) vt χαλῶ ‖ **~s** npl λεία, λάφυρα ‖ **~sport** n αὐτός πού χαλάει τό κέφι.

spoke [spəuk] n ἀκτίνα (τροχοῦ) ‖ pt of **speak** ‖ **~n** pp of **speak** ‖ **~sman** n ἐκπρόσωπος.

sponge [spʌndʒ] n σφουγγάρι ‖ vt πλένω, σφουγγίζω ‖ vi (+ on) σελεμίζω, τρακάρω ‖ **~ bag** n σάκκος γιά σφουγγάρι ‖ **~ cake** n παντεσπάνι ‖ **~r** n (col) σελέμης, τρακαδόρος.

spongy ['spʌndʒi] a σπογγώδης.

sponsor ['sponsə*] n ἀνάδοχος, ἐγγυητής, εἰσηγητής ‖ vt ὑποστηρίζω, εἰσηγοῦμαι ‖ **~ship** n ὑποστήριξις.

spontaneity [spontə'neiiti] n αὐθορμητισμός.

spontaneous [spon'teiniəs] a αὐτόματος ‖ (natural) αὐθόρμητος ‖ **~ly** ad αὐθόρμητα.

spooky ['spu:ki] a (col) μέ φαντάσματα, στοιχειωμένος.

spool [spu:l] n καρούλα, μασούρι.

spoon [spu:n] *n* κουτάλι ‖ **~-feed** *vt* (*lit*) ταΐζω μέ τό κουτάλι ‖ (*fig*) ἐπιχορηγῶ ‖ **~ful** *n* κουταλιά.

sporadic [spɔ'rædik] *a* σποραδικός.

sport [spɔ:t] *n* (*games*) ἀθλητισμός, σπόρ ‖ (*fun*) διασκέδασις, παιδιά ‖ (*good-humoured person*) καλός ἄνθρωπος ‖ **~ing** *a* (*fair*) τίμιος ‖ **~s car** *n* αὐτοκίνητον σπόρ ‖ **~(s) coat** *n*, **~(s) jacket** *n* σακκάκι σπόρ ‖ **~sman** *n* φίλαθλος, τίμιος παίκτης ‖ **~smanship** *n* τιμιότης στό σπόρ ‖ **~s page** *n* σελίδα ἀθλητικῶν νέων ‖ **~swear** *n* εἴδη ἀθλητισμοῦ ‖ **~swoman** *n* ἀθλήτρια ‖ **~y** *a* εὐγενικό, πολύ λεπτό.

spot [spɔt] *n* στίγμα, κηλίδα, λεκές ‖ (*place*) τόπος, μέρος, τοποθεσία ‖ (*small amount*) στάλα, λίγο ‖ *vt* (*notice*) διακρίνω, σημειώνω ‖ (*make spots on*) λεκιάζω ‖ (*med*) κηλιδῶ, γεμίζω σπειριά, ἔχω πανάδες ‖ **~ check** *n* ταχύς ἔλεγχος ‖ **~less** *a* ἄσπιλος, ἀκηλίδωτος, καθαρός ‖ **~lessly** *ad* (κατ)ἄσπρο, (πεντα)κάθαρα ‖ **~light** *n* προβολεύς θεάτρου ‖ (*position*) περίοπτος θέσις, κέντρον ‖ **~ted** *a* διάστικτος, πιτσιλωτός ‖ **~ty** *a* (*face*) μέ πανάδες, μέ σπειριά.

spouse [spauz] *n* σύζυγος.

spout [spaut] *n* στόμιον, σωλήν, λούκι ‖ (*jet*) ἐκροή, πίδαξ ‖ *vi* ξεπηδῶ, ἀναπηδῶ, ξεχύνομαι.

sprain [sprein] *n* διάστρεμμα, στραμπούλισμα ‖ *vt* στραμπουλίζω.

sprang [spræŋ] *pt of* spring.

sprawl [sprɔ:l] *vi* ἐκτείνομαι, ξαπλώνομαι.

spray [sprei] *n* (*sprinkle*) ψεκάδες, πιτσιλίσματα ‖ (*instrument*) ψεκαστήρ, βαποριζατέρ ‖ (*branch*) κλωνάρι ‖ *vt* ψεκάζω, καταβρέχω.

spread [spred] (*irreg v*) *n* (*extent*) ἐπέκτασις, διάδοσις ‖ (*col*) τραπέζι, πλούσιο γεῦμα ‖ *vt* ἁπλώνω, στρώνω ‖ (*scatter*) σκορπίζω, στρώνω, διαδίδω ‖ (*smear*) ἀλείφω, χύνω.

spree [spri:] *n* διασκέδασις, ξεφάντωμα, γλέντι.

sprig [sprig] *n* κλωνάρι, βλαστός.

sprightly ['spraitli] *a* ζωηρός, κεφάτος.

spring [spriŋ] (*irreg v*) *n* (*leap*) πήδημα ‖ (*of water*) πηγή ‖ (*coil*) ἐλατήριον ‖ (*season*) ἄνοιξις ‖ *vi* (ἀνα)πηδῶ, ξεπετάγομαι ‖ **to ~ up** *vi* (*problem*) δημιουργοῦμαι, ἐμφανίζομαι ‖ **~board** *n* βατήρ, τραμπλέν ‖ **~-clean** *n* γενικός καθαρισμός ‖ *vt* κάνω γενικόν καθαρισμό ‖ **~-cleaning** *n* γενικός καθαρισμός (ἀνοιξιάτικος) ‖ **~iness** *n* ἐλαστικότης ‖ **~time** *n* ἄνοιξη ‖ **~y** *a* ἐλαστικός, εὔκαμπτος.

sprinkle ['spriŋkl] *n* ράντισμα ‖ *vt* ραντίζω, ραίνω.

sprinkling ['spriŋkliŋ] *n* μικρά ποσότης.

sprint [sprint] *n* δρόμος ταχύτητος ‖ *vi* τρέχω δρόμον ταχύτητος ‖ **~er** *n* δρομεύς ταχύτητος.

sprite [sprait] *n* νεράϊδα.

sprout [spraut] *vi* βλαστάνω, φυτρώνω ‖ *see* **Brussels sprout**.

spruce [spru:s] *n* ἔλατο ‖ *a* κομψός, τακτικός.

sprung [sprʌŋ] *pp of* spring.

spry [sprai] *a* ζωηρός, ἐνεργητικός.

spud [spʌd] *n* (*col: potato*) πατάτα.

spun [spʌn] *pt,pp of* spin.

spur [spɔ:*] *n* πτερνιστήρ, σπηρούνι ‖ (*fig*) κίνητρον, ἐλατήριον ‖ *vt* (*also* **~ on**) κεντρίζω, παρακινῶ ‖ **on the ~ of the moment** χωρίς σκέψι, αὐθόρμητα.

spurious ['spjuəriəs] *a* κίβδηλος, ψεύτικος.

spurn [spə:n] *vt* περιφρονῶ, ἀποκρούω.

spurt [spə:t] *n* (*effort*) σφίξιμο, φουλάρισμα, ξέσπασμα ‖ (*jet*) ἀνάβλυσις, πίδαξ ‖ *vti* ξεχύνομαι, φουλάρω.

spy [spai] *n* κατάσκοπος ‖ *vt* κατασκοπεύω ‖ *vt* διακρίνω, βλέπω, παρατηρῶ ‖ **~ing** *n* (*espionage*) κατασκοπεία.

squabble ['skwɔbl] *n* φιλονεικία, καυγᾶς ‖ *vi* φιλονεικῶ, καυγαδίζω, πιάνομαι (μέ).

squabbling ['skwɔbliŋ] *n* φιλονεικία, καυγᾶς.

squad [skwɔd] *n* (*mil*) ἀπόσπασμα, οὐλαμός ‖ (*police*) ὑπηρεσία διώξεως.

squadron ['skwɔdrən] *n* μοῖρα.

squalid ['skwɔlid] *a* βρώμικος, βρωμερός, ἄθλιος.

squall [skwɔ:l] *n* (*scream*) κραυγή, στριγγλιά ‖ **~y** *a* (*weather*) μέ μπόρες.

squalor ['skwɔlə*] *n* ἀκαθαρσία, βρώμα, ἀθλιότης.

squander ['skwɔndə*] *vt* σπαταλῶ.

square [skweə*] *n* (*figure*) τετράγωνον ‖ (*of town*) πλατεία ‖ (*instrument*) γωνία, γνώμων ‖ (*product*) τετράγωνον ‖ (*col: person*) ἀνιαρός, ἀταίριαστος ‖ *a* τετραγωνικός ‖ (*honest*) τίμιος, καθαρός, δίκαιος ‖ (*ample*) ἱκανοποιητικός, ἄφθονος ‖ (*even*) πάτσι ‖ *ad* (*exactly*) ἀκριβῶς, καθέτως ‖ *vt* (*arrange*) ρυθμίζω, κανονίζω, τακτοποιῶ ‖ (*math*) τετραγωνίζω ‖ *vi* (*agree*) (+ *with*) συμφωνῶ, συμβιβάζομαι ‖ **all ~** στά ἴσια, πάτσι ‖ **2 metres ~** 4 τετραγωνικά μέτρα ‖ **1 ~ metre** 1 τετραγωνικόν μέτρόν ‖ **~ly** *ad* γερά ‖ τίμια, ντόμπρα.

squash [skwɔʃ] *n*⁰(*drink*) χυμός (φρούτων) ‖ *vt* συνθλίβω, ζουλῶ, στίβω.

squat [skwɔt] *a* κοντόχοντρος ‖ *vi* κάθομαι σταυροπόδι ‖ **~ter** *n* σφετεριστής γῆς.

squawk [skwɔ:k] *n* κράξιμο, βραχνή κραυγή ‖ *vi* κράζω, φωνάζω, κραυγάζω.

squeak [skwi:k] *n* ὀξεῖα κραυγή, σκούξιμο ‖ *vi* σκούζω, τσιρίζω, τρίζω ‖ **~y** *a* πού τρίζει, πού σκούζει.

squeal [skwi:l] *n* ὀξεῖα κραυγή, στριγγλιά ‖ *vi* στριγγλίζω, σκούζω.

squeamish ['skwi:miʃ] *a* εὐαίσθητος, ἔχων

ἀναγούλες ‖ (*easily shocked*) σιχασιάρης, δύστροπος ‖ **~ness** *n* δύσκολα γούστα, ὑπερβολική λεπτότης.

squeeze [skwi:z] *n* (*lit*) σύνθλιψις, σφίξιμο, στρίμωγμα ‖ (*econ*) πίεσις ‖ *vt* συνθλίβω, σφίγγω, στύβω ‖ **to ~ out** *vt* στύβω, ἐκθλίβω.

squid [skwid] *n* σουπιά.

squint [skwint] *n* ἀλλοιθωρισμός, στραβισμός ‖ *vi* ἀλλοιθωρίζω, στραβοκοιτάζω.

squire ['skwaiə*] *n* πυργοδεσπότης, προύχων.

squirm [skwə:m] *vi* συστρέφω τό σῶμα, στενοχωριέμαι, ντρέπομαι.

squirrel ['skwirəl] *n* σκίουρος.

squirt [skwə:t] *n* ἐκτόξευσις, πιτσίλισμα, ριπή ‖ *vi* ἀναβλύζω, πετάγομαι, ἐκτοξεύω.

stab [stæb] *n* (*blow*) κτύπημα, μπαμπεσιά ‖ (*col: try*) δοκιμάζω ‖ **~bing** *n* (*incident*) μαχαίρωμα.

stability [stə'biliti] *n* σταθερότης.

stabilization [steibəlai'zeiʃən] *n* σταθεροποίησις.

stabilize ['steibəlaiz] *vt* σταθεροποιῶ ‖ **~r** *n* ζυγοσταθμιστής, σταθεροποιητής.

stable ['steibl] *n* στάβλος ‖ *vt* σταβλίζω ‖ *a* σταθερός, μόνιμος.

staccato [stə'ka:təu] *a* κοφτό, νευρικό, στακκάτο.

stack [stæk] *n* θημωνιά, σωρός ‖ *vt* συσσωρεύω, στοιβάζω.

stadium ['steidiəm] *n* στάδιον.

staff [sta:f] *n* (*stick*) ῥάβδος, μπαστούνι, κοντάκι ‖ (*people*) προσωπικόν, ἐπιτελεῖον ‖ *vt* (*with people*) καταρτίζω προσωπικόν.

stag [stæg] *n* ἔλαφι.

stage [steidʒ] *n* (*theatre*) σκηνή ‖ (*actors*) θέατρον ‖ (*degree*) στάδιον ‖ *vt* (*play*) ἀνεβάζω, σκηνοθετῶ ‖ (*demonstration*) ὀργανώνω, σκηνοθετῶ ‖ **in ~s** βαθμηδόν, κατά στάδια ‖ **~coach** *n* ταχυδρομική ἅμαξα ‖ **~ door** *n* εἴσοδος ἠθοποιῶν ‖ **~ manager** *n* σκηνοθέτης.

stagger ['stægə*] *vi* κλονίζομαι, τρικλίζω, παραπατῶ ‖ *vt* (*person*) ζαλίζω, συγκλονίζω, κάνω νά χάση ‖ (*hours*) κλιμακώνω (τίς ὥρες) ‖ **~ing** *a* (*amazing*) καταπληκτικός, συγκλονιστικός.

stagnant ['stægnənt] *a* στάσιμος, λιμνάζων ‖ (*dull*) ἀδρανής, ἄγονος.

stagnate [stæg'neit] *vi* εἶμαι στάσιμος, ἀδρανῶ.

stagnation [stæg'neiʃən] *n* στασιμότης, νέκρωσις.

staid [steid] *a* θετικός, σοβαρός.

stain [stein] *n* λεκές, μουντζούρα ‖ (*colouring*) χρῶμα, βαφή, μπογιά ‖ *vt* λεκιάζω, λερώνω ‖ **~ed glass** *n* καθεδρική ὕαλος ‖ **~less** *a* (*steel*) ἀνοξείδωτος ‖ **~ remover** *n* καθαριστικόν λεκέδων.

stair [steə*] *n* κλῖμαξ, σκάλα ‖ (*one step*)

σκαλοπάτι, σκαλί ‖ **~case** *n* κλῖμαξ, σκάλα ‖ **~s** *npl* σκάλα ‖ **~way** *n* σκάλα.

stake [steik] *n* πάσσαλος, παλούκι ‖ (*gambling*) στοίχημα, μίζα, ποντάρισμα ‖ *vt* ποντάρω, παίζω, διακυβεύω.

stalactite ['stæləktait] *n* σταλακτίτης.

stalagmite ['stæləgmait] *n* σταλαγμίτης.

stale [steil] *a* μπαγιάτικος ‖ **~mate** *n* ἀδιέξοδον.

stalk [stɔ:k] *n* κοτσάνι, στέλεχος, μίσχος ‖ *vt* παρακολουθῶ ἀθέατος ‖ (*walk stiffly*) βαδίζω μέ μεγάλα βήματα.

stall [stɔ:l] *n* παράπηγμα στάβλου, παχνί ‖ (*stand*) πάγκος, περίπτερον ‖ *vt* (*aut*) κολλῶ, μπλοκάρω ‖ *vi* (*aut*) κολλῶ ‖ (*delay*) ἀναβάλλω, χρονοτριβῶ ‖ **~s** *npl* (*theat*) κάθισμα (ὀρχήστρας).

stallion ['stæliən] *n* ἐπιβήτωρ, κήλων.

stalwart ['stɔ:lwət] *a* ῥωμαλέος, σθεναρός ‖ *n* πρωτοπαλλήκαρο, ἡρακλῆς.

stamina ['stæminə] *n* σφρῖγος, ζωτική δύναμις.

stammer ['stæmə*] *n* τραύλισμα, τσέβδισμα ‖ *vi* τραυλίζω, ψευδίζω, ψελλίζω.

stamp [stæmp] *n* (*postage*) γραμματόσημον ‖ ἔνσημον ‖ (*of foot*) κτύπημα ποδός, ποδοβολητό ‖ (*on document*) σφραγίδα, βούλλα, στάμπα ‖ *vi* χτυπῶ τό πόδι, περπατῶ βαρειά ‖ *vt* (*make mark*) σφραγίζω, μαρκάρω, σταμπάρω ‖ (*fix postage*) κολλῶ γραμματόσημα ‖ **~ album** *n* συλλογή γραμματοσήμων ‖ **~ collecting** *n* φιλοτελισμός.

stampede [stæm'pi:d] *n* ἐσπευσμένη φυγή, πανικός.

stance [stæns] *n* (*posture*) στάσις.

stand [stænd] (*irreg v*) *n* (*position*) στάσις ‖ (*mil*) ἀντίστασις ‖ (*rest*) ὑποστήριγμα, πόδι, στήριγμα ‖ (*seats*) ἐξέδρα ‖ *vi* (*erect*) ἵσταμαι, στέκομαι ‖ (*rise*) σηκώνομαι ‖ (*place, set*) κεῖμαι, βρίσκομαι, εἶμαι ‖ (*halt, stop*) σταματῶ, στέκομαι ‖ *vt* (*place*) τοποθετῶ, βάζω, κουμπῶ (ὄρθιο) ‖ (*endure*) ὑποφέρω, ἀντέχω, ὑπομένω εἰς ‖ **to make a ~** ἀνθίσταμαι, κρατῶ τίς θέσεις μου ‖ **it ~s to reason** εἶναι λογικόν ‖ **to ~ by** *vi* (*be ready*) (εἶμαι) ἕτοιμος, εἶμαι εἰς ἐπιφυλακήν ‖ *vt* (*opinion*) μένω πιστός εἰς ‖ **to ~ for** *vt* (*defend*) ὑπερασπίζομαι, ὑποστηρίζω ‖ (*signify*) ἀντιπροσωπεύω ‖ (*permit, tolerate*) ὑπομένω, ἀνέχομαι ‖ **to ~ in for** *vt* ἀντικαθιστῶ ‖ **to ~ out** *vi* (*be prominent*) (προ)ἐξέχω, ξεχωρίζω ‖ **to ~ up** *vi* (*rise*) ἐγείρομαι, σηκώνομαι ‖ **to ~ up for** *vt* ὑποστηρίζω.

standard ['stændəd] *n* (*measure*) ὑπόδειγμα, κανών, μέτρον ‖ (*flag*) σημαία, λάβαρον ‖ *a* (*size etc*) πρότυπος, κανονικός, συνήθης ‖ **~ization** *n* τυποποίησις, καθιέρωσις, κανόνισις ‖ **~ize** *vt* τυποποιῶ, καθιερῶ ‖ **~ of living** *n* ἐπίπεδον ζωῆς.

stand-by ['stændbai] *n* στήριγμα.

stand-in ['stændin] *n* ἀντικαταστάτης, ἀναπληρωτής.

standing ['stændiŋ] *a* ὄρθιος ‖ (*lasting*) μόνιμος, διαρκής ‖ *n* διάρκεια ‖ (*reputation*) κοινωνική θέσις, ὑπόληψις ‖ ~ **orders** *npl* (*mil*) μόνιμαι διατάξεις, κανονισμοί ‖ ~ **room** only μόνον ὄρθιοι.

stand-offish ['stænd'ɔfiʃ] *a* ὑπεροπτικός.

standpoint ['stændpɔint] *n* ἄποψις, σκοπιά.

standstill ['stændstil] *n*: **at a** ~ στασιμότης, νεκρόν σημεῖον ‖ **to come to a** ~ καταλήγω εἰς ἐδιέξοδον, σταματῶ.

stank [stæŋk] *pt of* stink.

stanza ['stænzə] *n* στροφή, στάντσα.

staple ['steipl] *n* ἄγκιστρον, συνδετήρας ‖ (*product*) κύριον προϊόν. ‖ *a* κύριος, πρωτεύων ‖ *vt* στερεώνω, συνδέω ‖ ~ **r** *n* συνδετήρας.

star [sta:*] *n* ἀστήρ, ἄστρο, ἀστέρι ‖ (*actor*) ἀστήρ, πρωταγωνιστής, στάρ ‖ (*shape*) ἀστέρι ‖ *vi* (*in film*) πρωταγωνιστῶ, παίζω σέ ταινία ‖ *vt* (*to star an actor*) παρουσιάζω ὡς πρωταγωνιστήν.

starboard ['sta:bəd] *n* δεξιά πλευρά, δεξιόν ‖ *a* δεξιά.

starch [sta:tʃ] *n* ἄμυλον ‖ ~**ed** *a* (*collar*) κολλαριστός ‖ ~**y** *a* ἀμυλώδης, ἀμυλοῦχος ‖ (*formal*) ὑπεροπτικός, ποζάτος.

stardom ['sta:dəm] *n* θέσις ἀστέρος.

stare [stɛə*] *n* ἀτενές βλέμμα, καρφωτή ματιά ‖ *vi* (+ *at*) ἀτενίζω, καρφώνω μέ τό μάτι.

starfish ['sta:fiʃ] *n* ἀστερίας.

staring ['stɛəriŋ] *a* (*eyes*) ἁπλανή (ματιά), γουρλωμένα (μάτια).

stark [sta:k] *a* ψυχρός, σκληρός, γυμνός ‖ *ad*: ~ **naked** ὁλόγυμνος, θεόγυμνος, τσίτσιδος.

starless ['sta:lis] *a* (*night*) ἄναστρος, χωρίς ἄστρα.

starlight ['sta:lait] *n* ἀστροφεγγιά.

starling ['sta:liŋ] *n* ψαρώνι, καραβέλι.

starlit ['sta:lit] *a* ἀστρόφεγγος.

starry ['sta:ri] *a* ἔναστρος, ἀστερόφεγγος, λάμπων ‖ ~**-eyed** *a* (*innocent*) λάμπων, ἀθῷος.

start [sta:t] *n* ἀρχή, σημεῖον ἐκκινήσεως, ἐκκίνησις ‖ (*beginning*) ἀρχή, ἀρχίνισμα ‖ (*sudden movement*) ξάφνιασμα, ἀνατίναγμα ‖ *vt* (*set going*) ἀρχίζω, ἀνοίγω, βγάζω ‖ *vi* (*begin journey*) ἀρχίζω, ξεκινῶ ‖ (*make sudden movement*) ἀναπηδῶ, ξαφνίζομαι ‖ **to** ~ **doing sth** ἀρχίζω μέ, πιάνομαι μέ ‖ **to** ~ **off** *vi* (*begin*) ἀρχίζω, ξεκινῶ ‖ **to** ~ **over** *vi* (*begin again*) ξαναρχίζω ‖ **to** ~ **up** *vi* βάζω μπρός ‖ ~**er** *n* (*aut*) ἐκκινητήρ, στάρτερ ‖ (*for race*) ἀφέτης, στάρτερ ‖ ~**ing handle** *n* μανιβέλλα ‖ ~**ing point** *n* ἀφετηρία, σημεῖον ἐκκινήσεως.

startle ['sta:tl] *vt* ξαφνιάζω, φοβίζω, ἐκπλήσσω.

startling ['sta:tliŋ] *a* καταπληκτικός, ἐντυπωσιακός, χτυπητός.

starvation [sta:'veiʃən] *n* λιμός, λιμοκτονία, ἀσιτία, πεῖνα.

starve [sta:v] *vi* (*die of hunger*) πεθαίνω ἀπό πεῖνα ‖ (*suffer from hunger*) ψοφῶ τῆς πείνας, πεινῶ ‖ *vt* (*keep without food*) στερῶ τῆς τροφῆς.

starving ['sta:viŋ] *a* πεινῶν, λιμασμένος, ψόφιος τῆς πείνας.

state [steit] *n* κατάστασις, θέσις ‖ (*government*) κράτος, πολιτεία ‖ ὑπουργεῖον ‖ (*anxiety*) ἀναστατωμένος ‖ *vt* δηλώνω, λέγω, ἀνακοινῶ ‖ ~ **control** *n* κρατικός ἔλεγχος ‖ ~**d** *a* λεχθείς, ὡρισμένος, τακτός ‖ ~**liness** *n* μεγαλοπρέπεια, ἐπιβλητικότης ‖ ~**ly** *a* μεγαλοπρεπής, ἀξιοπρεπής ‖ ~**ment** *n* δήλωσις, ἔκθεσις ‖ ~ **secret** *n* κρατικόν μυστικόν, ἀπόρρητον ‖ ~**sman** *n* πολιτικός.

static ['stætik] *n* στατική, διαταραχή ‖ *a* ἀκίνητος, ἀδρανής ‖ (*phys*) στατικός ‖ ~ **electricity** *n* στατικός ἠλεκτρισμός.

station ['steiʃən] *n* (*rail*) σταθμός ‖ (*post*) σταθμός, θέσις ‖ (*position in life*) κοινωνική θέσις, βαθμός ‖ *vt* (τοπο)θετῶ, βάζω.

stationary ['steiʃənəri] *a* στάσιμος, ἀκίνητος.

stationer ['steiʃənə*] *n* χαρτοπώλης ‖ ~'s (**shop**) *n* χαρτοπωλεῖον ‖ ~**y** *n* χαρτικά εἴδη.

station master ['steiʃənma:stə*] *n* σταθμάρχης.

station wagon ['steiʃənwægən] *n* (*US aut*) στέϊσον-βάγκον.

statistic [stə'tistik] *n* στατιστικόν (στοιχεῖον) ‖ ~**al** *a* στατιστικός ‖ ~**s** *npl* στατιστική.

statue ['stætju:] *n* ἄγαλμα.

stature ['stætʃə*] *n* ἀνάστημα, ὕψος, μέγεθος.

status ['steitəs] *n* θέσις, κατάστασις ‖ **the** ~ **quo** *n* καθεστώς, στάτους κβό.

statute ['stætju:t] *n* νόμος, θέσπισμα.

statutory ['stætjutəri] *a* νομοθετημένος, θεσπισμένος.

staunch [stɔ:ntʃ] *a* ἀξιόπιστος, πιστός, δυνατός ‖ ~**ly** *ad* σταθερῶς, πιστῶς.

stave [steiv] *vi*: ~ **off** *vt* (*attack*) ἀποκρούω, ἀπωθῶ ‖ (*threat*) ἀποτρέπω, ἀποφεύγω.

stay [stei] *n* διαμονή, παραμονή ‖ ἀναβολή ‖ *vi* (*παρα*)μένω ‖ (*at place*) μένω ‖ **to** ~ **put** μένω ἀδιάβλητος, δέν ἀλλάζω πιά ‖ **to** ~ **with friends** μένω μέ φίλους ‖ **to** ~ **the night** μένω τό βράδυ ‖ **to** ~ **behind** *vi* παρακολουθῶ ἀπό πίσω ‖ παραμένω ‖ **to** ~ **in** *vi* (*at home*) μένω (στό σπίτι) ‖ **to** ~ **on** *vi* (*continue*) μένω ‖ **to** ~ **out** *vi* (*of house*) μένω ἔξω, δέν ἐπιστρέφω ‖ **to** ~ **up** *vi* (*at night*) ἀγρυπνῶ, ξενυχτῶ.

steadfast ['stedfəst] *a* σταθερός.

steadily ['stedili] *ad* σταθερά, στέρεα ‖ συνεχῶς, ἐπίμονα.

steadiness ['stedinis] *n* σταθερότης.

steady ['stedi] *a* σταθερός, στερεός ‖ (*regular*) κανονικός, συνεχής, σταθερός ‖ (*reliable*) σταθερός, συνεπής, τακτικός ‖ *vt* σταθεροποιῶ, στερεώνω ‖ to ~ o.s. σταθεροποιοῦμαι, καθησυχάζω.

steak [steik] *n* (*meat*) μπριζόλα, μπιφτέκι ‖ (*fish*) φέτα.

steal [sti:l] (*irreg v*) *vt* κλέβω, βουτῶ, σουφρώνω ‖ *vi* φεύγω κλεφτά, βγαίνω στὴν ζούλα ‖ ~th ['stelθ] *n*: by ~ κρυφά, κλεφτά, στὴ ζούλα ‖ ~thy *a* κρυφός, φευγαλέος, προσεκτικός.

steam [sti:m] *n* ἀτμός ‖ *vt* βράζω στὸν ἀτμό ‖ *vi* ἀναδίδω ἀτμόν, ἀχνίζω ‖ (*ship*) κινοῦμαι, πλέω (δι' ἀτμοῦ) ‖ ~ engine *n* ἀτμομηχανή ‖ ~er *n* ἀτμόπλοιον, βαπόρι ‖ ~roller *n* ὁδοστρωτήρ ‖ ~y *a* ἀτμώδης, γεμᾶτος ἀτμούς.

steel [sti:l] *n* χάλυψ, ἀτσάλι ‖ *a* χαλύβδινος, ἀτσάλινος ‖ ~works *n* χαλυβδουργεῖον.

steep [sti:p] *a* ἀπότομος, ἀπόκρημνος ‖ (*price*) ἐξωφρενικὴ τιμή ‖ *vt* ἐμβαπτίζω, μουσκεύω, βουτῶ.

steeple ['sti:pl] *n* κωδωνοστάσιον ‖ ~chase *n* ἱπποδρομία μετ' ἐμποδίων ‖ ~jack *n* ἐπιδιορθωτὴς καπνοδόχων.

steeply ['sti:pli] *ad* ἀπότομα, κατηφορικά.

steepness ['sti:pnis] *n* τὸ ἀπότομον, τὸ ἀπόκρημνον.

steer [stiə*] *n* μικρό βώδι ‖ *vt* κυβερνῶ, ὁδηγῶ, πηδαλιουχῶ ‖ *vi* κατευθύνομαι, βάζω πλώρη γιά ‖ ~ing *n* (*aut*) ὁδήγησις ‖ ~ing column *n* κίων στηρίξεως τιμονιοῦ ‖ ~ing wheel *n* βολάν, τιμόνι.

stem [stem] *n* στέλεχος, κορμός ‖ *vt* σταματῶ, ἀνακόπτω ‖ to ~ from *vt* προέρχομαι ἀπό.

stench [stentʃ] *n* δυσοσμία, μπόχας.

stencil ['stensl] *n* μεμβράνη ‖ *vt* γράφω μεμβράνες, πολυγραφῶ.

stenographer [ste'nɔgrəfə*] *n* στενογράφος.

step [step] *n* βῆμα, πάτημα ‖ (*stair*) βαθμίς, σκαλοπάτι, σκαλί ‖ (*action*) διάβημα, ἐνέργεια ‖ (*sound*) βῆμα, βάδισμα ‖ *vi* βηματίζω, βαδίζω ‖ ~s *npl* = stepladder *see below* ‖ to ~ down *vi* (*fig*) παραιτοῦμαι ‖ to ~ up *vt* αὐξάνω, ἀνεβάζω ‖ ~brother *n* ἑτεροθαλής ἀδελφός ‖ ~child *n* προγονός, προγονή ‖ ~father *n* πατρυιός ‖ ~ladder *n* σκάλα (φορητή) ‖ ~mother *n* μητρυιά.

steppe [step] *n* στέππα.

stepping stone ['stepiŋstəun] *n* σκαλοπάτι, ἐνδιάμεσος σταθμός.

stereo ['stiəriəu] *n* (*rad*) στερεοφωνικό ραδιόφωνο ‖ ~phonic *a* στερεοφωνικός ‖ ~type *n* στερεοτυπία ‖ *vt* τυπώνω διά στερεοτυπίας.

sterile ['sterail] *a* στεῖρος, ἄγονος, ἄκαρπος ‖ (*free from germs*) ἀποστειρωμένος.

sterility [ste'riliti] *n* στειρότης, ἀγονία.

sterilization [sterilai'zeiʃən] *n* ἀποστείρωσις.

sterilize ['sterilaiz] *vt* στειρώνω ‖ (*from germs*) ἀποστειρώνω.

sterling ['stə:liŋ] *a* στερλίνας ‖ ἀμιγής, καλῆς ποιότητος ‖ (*silver*) ἀσημικά ‖ (*service*) ἐξαιρετικῆς ἐξυπηρετήσεως ‖ ~ area *n* περιοχή στερλίνας.

stern [stə:n] *a* αὐστηρός, βλοσυρός ‖ *n* πρύμνη, πρύμη ‖ ~ly *ad* αὐστηρά, σκληρά ‖ ~ness *n* αὐστηρότης, σκληρότης.

stethoscope ['steθəskəup] *n* στηθοσκόπιον.

stevedore ['sti:vidɔ:*] *n* φορτοεκφορτωτής.

stew [stju:] *n* κρέας μὲ χορταρικά ‖ *vt* κάνω κρέας στὴ κατσαρόλα ‖ *vi* σιγοβράζω.

steward ['stju:əd] *n* (*aviat, naut, rail, in club etc*) φροντιστής, οἰκονόμος, καμαρότος ‖ ~ess *n* (*aviat*) ἀεροσυνοδός.

stick [stik] (*irreg v*) *n* βέργα, ράβδος ‖ (*cane*) μπαστούνι ‖ *vt* ἐμπηγνύω, μπήγω, χώνω, καρφώνω ‖ (*gum*) κολλῶ ‖ (*col: tolerate*) ἀνέχομαι, ὑποφέρω ‖ *vi* (*stop*) πιάνομαι, κολλιέμαι, φρακάρω ‖ (*hold fast*) κολλιέμαι, κολλῶ ‖ to ~ out *vi* (*project*) κρατῶ μέχρι τέλους, ἐπιμένω ‖ to ~ up *vi* (*project*) ὑψοῦμαι, στήνω ‖ to ~ up for *vt* (*defend*) ὑπερασπίζομαι, παίρνω τὸ μέρος ‖ ~er *n* ἐτικέττα.

stickler ['stiklə*] *n* (+ *for*) ἄκαμπτος, στενοκέφαλος (εἰς).

stick-up ['stikʌp] *n* (*col: robbery*) ληστεία.

sticky ['stiki] *a* κολλώδης, γλοιώδης.

stiff [stif] *a* δύσκαμπτος, σκληρός, ντοῦρος ‖ (*examination etc*) δύσκολος ‖ (*paste*) σκληρός, σφιχτός ‖ (*formal*) ἐπιτηδευμένος, τυπικός, ψυχρός ‖ (*strong*) ἰσχυρός, δυνατός ‖ ~en *vt* σκληρύνω, δυναμώνω ‖ *vi* σκληρύνομαι, γίνομαι ἄκαμπτος ‖ ~ness *n* σκληρότης, ἀκαμψία.

stifle ['staifl] *vt* (*keep back*) καταπνίγω, συγκρατῶ.

stifling ['staifliŋ] *a* (*atmosphere*) ἀποπνυκτικός, ἀσφυκτικός.

stigma ['stigmə] *n* στίγμα, κηλίς.

stile [stail] *n* σκάλα, σκάλα.

still [stil] *a* ἀκίνητος, ἀθόρυβος, σιωπηλός ‖ *ad* (*yet*) ἀκόμη ‖ (*even*) ἀκόμη (περισσότερα) ‖ ~born *a* θνησιγενής ‖ ~ life *n* νεκρά φύσις ‖ ~ness *n* ἠρεμία, γαλήνη, κάλμα.

stilt [stilt] *n* ξυλοπόδαρο.

stilted ['stiltid] *a* ἄκαμπτος, τυπικός, τεχνητός.

stimulant ['stimjulənt] *n* διεγερτικόν, τονωτικόν.

stimulate ['stimjuleit] *vt* διεγείρω, ἐξάπτω.

stimulating ['stimjuleitiŋ] a διεγερτικός, τονωτικός.

stimulation [stimju'leifən] n διέγερσις, ὑποκίνησις, τόνωσις.

stimulus ['stimjuləs] n κίνητρον.

sting [stiŋ] (irreg v) n δῆγμα, κέντρισμα ‖ vi κεντρίζω, τσιμπῶ.

stingily ['stindʒili] ad φιλάργυρα, τσιγγούνικα, σφιχτά.

stinginess ['stindʒinis] n φιλαργυρία, τσιγγουνιά.

stingy ['stindʒi] a φιλάργυρος, τσιγγούνης, σφιχτοχέρης.

stink [stiŋk] (irreg v) n δυσοσμία, βρῶμα ‖ vi βρωμῶ, βρωμάω ‖ ~er n (col) (person) ἀντιπαθής, παλιάνθρωπος ‖ (problem) δύσκολο, τρομερό ‖ ~ing a (fig) τρομερός.

stint [stint] n ὅριον, καθῆκον ‖ vt στερῶ, περιορίζω.

stipend ['staipend] n (to vicar etc) μισθός, ἐπίδομα.

stipulate ['stipjuleit] vt ἀποφαίνομαι διά, συμφωνῶ, συνομολογῶ.

stipulation [stipju'leifən] n ὅρος, διάταξις, συμφωνία.

stir [stə:*] n ταραχή, σάλεμα, κούνημα, κίνησις ‖ vt (mix) ἀνακατώνω, ἀναδεύω ‖ vi (move) κουνιέμαι, σαλεύω ‖ to ~ up vt ὑποκινῶ, ὑποδαυλίζω ‖ ~ring a συγκλονιστικός, συγκινητικός.

stirrup ['stirəp] n ἀναβολεύς, σκάλα, ζεγκί.

stitch [stitʃ] n βελονιά, ραφή ‖ (sudden pain) δριμύς πόνος, σουβλιά ‖ vt ράβω, κάνω βελονιές.

stock [stɔk] n (supply) ἀπόθεμα, στόκ, προμήθεια ‖ (trader's goods) ἐμπορεύματα, στόκ ‖ (farm animals) κτήνη, ζῶα ‖ (liquid) ζωμός, κονσομέ ‖ (econ) χρεώγραφον, τίτλος, ἀξία ‖ a τῆς σειράς, κανονικός, συνήθης ‖ vt ἐφοδιάζω, ἔχω παρακαταθήκην ἀπό ‖ to take ~ κάνω ἀπογραφήν ‖ (+ of) κρίνω, ἐκτιμῶ ‖ to ~ up with vt ἀποθηκεύω ‖ ~ade n πασσαλόπηγμα, φράκτης ‖ ~broker n χρηματομεσίτης, χρηματιστής ‖ ~ exchange n χρηματιστήριον.

stocking ['stɔkiŋ] n κάλτσα.

stockist ['stɔkist] n (comm: supplier, distributor) χονδρέμπορος.

stock market ['stɔkma:kit] n ἀγορά χρεωγράφων.

stockpile ['stɔkpail] n ἀποθέματα ‖ vt δημιουργῶ ἀποθέματα.

stocktaking ['stɔkteikiŋ] n (comm) ἀπογραφή.

stocky ['stɔki] a κοντόχοντρος.

stodgy ['stɔdʒi] a βαρύς, ἀνιαρός.

stoic ['stəuik] n στωικός ‖ ~al a στωϊκός ‖ ~ism ['stəuisizəm] n στωϊκισμός.

stoke [stəuk] vt τροφοδοτῶ φωτιάν, διατηρῶ φωτιάν ‖ ~r n θερμαστής.

stole [stəul] pt of steal ‖ n (fur) γούνα,

σάρπα ‖ ~n pp of steal ‖ a κλεμμένος.

stolid ['stɔlid] a ἀπαθής, βαρύς, φλεγματικός.

stomach ['stʌmək] n στομάχι ‖ (inclination) ὄρεξις, διάθεσις ‖ vt ἀνέχομαι, χωνεύω ‖ ~ ache n κοιλόπονος, στομαχόπονος.

stone [stəun] n λίθος, πέτρα ‖ (gem) πολύτιμος λίθος, πετράδι, κόσμημα ‖ (of fruit) πυρήν, κουκούτσι ‖ (weight) βάρος 14 λιβρῶν ‖ a ἀπό λίθους, πέτρινος ‖ vt βγάζω κουκούτσια ἀπό ‖ ~-cold a κρύος σάν μάρμαρο ‖ ~-deaf a θεόκουφος ‖ ~mason n κτίστης, λιθοξόος ‖ ~work n λιθοδομή.

stony ['stəuni] a πετρώδης, γεμάτος πέτρες.

stood [stud] pt,pp of stand.

stool [stu:l] n σκαμνί.

stoop [stu:p] vi σκύβω.

stop [stɔp] n στάσις, τέρμα ‖ (punctuation) σημεῖον στίξεως ‖ vt (prevent) σταματῶ ‖ (bring to end) διακόπτω, σταματῶ ‖ vi (cease) παύω, σταματῶ, διακόπτομαι ‖ (remain) παραμένω, πηγαίνω ‖ to ~ doing sth παύω νά κάνω κάτι, σταματῶ ‖ ~ it! σταμάτα!, φθάνει! ‖ to ~ dead vi σταματῶ ἀπότομα ‖ to ~ in vi (at home) περνῶ ἀπό, ἐπισκέπτομαι ‖ to ~ off vi κατεβαίνω, διακόπτω τό ταξίδι μου ‖ to ~ (hole) φράζω, βουλώνω, κλείνω ‖ ~lights npl (aut) κόκκινα φανάρια, κόκκινα φῶτα ‖ ~over n (on journey) σταθμός, στάθμευσις ‖ ~page n σταμάτημα, παῦσις, διακοπή ‖ ~per n πῶμα, βούλωμα ‖ ~-press n τελευταῖα νέα ‖ ~watch n χρονόμετρον.

storage ['stɔ:ridʒ] n (ἐν)ἀποθήκευσις, ἀποθήκη.

store [stɔ:*] n παρακαταθήκη, ἐφόδιον ‖ (place) ἀποθήκη ‖ (large shop) κατάστημα, μαγαζί ‖ vt ἐφοδιάζω, ἀποθηκεύω ‖ to ~ up vt συσσωρεύω, συγκεντρώνω, μαζεύω ‖ ~room n ἀποθήκη, κελάρι.

storey ['stɔ:ri] n (Brit) ὄροφος, πάτωμα.

stork [stɔ:k] n πελαργός, λελέκι.

storm [stɔ:m] n θύελλα, καταιγίδα, φουρτούνα ‖ (disturbance) θύελλα, καταιγισμός ‖ vi μαίνομαι ‖ vt (attack) ἐξαπολύω ἔφοδον ‖ to take by ~ (lit) καταλαμβάνω ἐξ ἐφόδου ‖ (fig) κατακτῶ, παρασύρω ‖ ~ cloud n μαῦρο σύννεφο ‖ ~y a (weather) θυελλώδης.

story ['stɔ:ri] n (account) ἱστορία, ἀφήγησις, διήγημα ‖ (lie) παραμύθι, ψέμα ‖ (US: storey) ὄροφος, πάτωμα ‖ ~book n βιβλίον διηγημάτων ‖ ~teller n ἀφηγητής, παραμυθᾶς.

stout [staut] a (bold) δυνατός, γερός, θαρραλέος ‖ (too fat) χονδρός, σωματώδης, παχύς ‖ n εἶδος μπύρας ‖ ~ness n παχύτης, πάχος.

stove [stəuv] n (for cooking) κουζίνα,

συσκευή μαγειρεύματος ‖ (for heating) θερμάστρα, σόμπα.

stow [stəu] vt στοιβάζω, ἀποθηκεύω ‖ ~**away** n λαθρεπιβάτης.

straddle ['strædl] vt κάθομαι καβαλικευτά, καβαλικεύω.

strafe [strɑ:f] vt πολυβολῶ.

straggle ['strægl] vi σκορπίζω, βραδυπορῶ ‖ ~**r** n παραπλανημένος, ὁ βραδυπορῶν.

straight [streit] a εὐθύς, εὐθύγραμμος, ἴσιος ‖ (honest) δίκαιος, εὐθύς, τίμιος, ντόμπρος ‖ (in order) τακτικός, τακτοποιημένος, σιαγμένος ‖ ad ἴσια, κατ' εὐθεῖαν, ἀμέσως ‖ (drink) σχέτο ‖ n εὐθεία ‖ ~**away** ad (at once) ἀμέσως ‖ ~ **off** ad (without stopping) στή στιγμή, αὐτοστιγμεί ‖ ~**en** vt (also ~ out) ἰσιώνω, σιάζω, τακτοποιῶ ‖ ~**forward** a (simple) χωρίς περιστροφές, ντόμπρα, εἰλικρινής.

strain [strein] n (mental) ἔντασις, κούρασις ‖ (streak, trace) φυσική διάθεσις, κλίσις, τάσις ‖ vt (stretch) ἐντείνω, τεντώνω, τεζάρω ‖ (filter) διυλίζω, φιλτράρω, στραγγίζω ‖ vi (make effort) μοχθῶ, κοπιάζω, ἐντείνω ‖ ~**s** npl (mus) τόνος, ὕφος ‖ ~**ed** a (laugh) βιασμένο γέλιο, ψεύτικο γέλιο ‖ (relations) τεταμένος ‖ ~**er** n σουρωτήρι, φίλτρον, τρυπητό.

strait [streit] n (geog) στενόν, πορθμός ‖ ~**ened** a (circumstances) σέ οἰκονομικές δυσχέρειες ‖ ~ **jacket** n ζουρλομανδύας ‖ ~**-laced** a ἠθικολόγος, σεμνότυφος.

strand [strænd] n (thread) κλῶνος, κλωνί, σπάγος, κλωστή ‖ vt ἐξοκέλλω ‖ ~**ed** a ἐγκαταλειφθείς, ἀφισμένος πίσω.

strange [streindʒ] a ξένος ‖ (unusual) ἀσυνήθης, ἀσυνήθιστος, παράξενος ‖ ~**ly** ad περίεργα, παράξενα ‖ ~**ness** n τό περίεργον, παράξενον ‖ ~**r** n ξένος, ἄγνωστος ‖ (new to a place) νεοαφιχθείς, καινούργιος.

strangle ['stræŋgl] vt στραγγαλίζω, πνίγω, καταπνίγω.

strangulation [stræŋgju'leiʃən] n στραγγαλισμός.

strap [stræp] n λωρίς, λουρί ‖ vt δένω μέ λουρί ‖ (beat) δέρνω μέ λουρί ‖ ~**less** a (dress) ἔξωμον ‖ ~**ping** a γεροδεμένος.

strata ['strɑ:tə] npl of **stratum**.

stratagem ['strætidʒəm] n στρατήγημα, κόλπο.

strategic [strə'ti:dʒik] a στρατηγικός ‖ ~**ally** ad στρατηγικῶς.

strategist ['strætidʒist] n στρατηγικός, εἰδικός στήν στρατηγικήν.

strategy ['strætidʒi] n στρατηγική, τέχνασμα.

stratosphere ['strætəusfiə*] n στρατόσφαιρα.

stratum ['strɑ:təm] n στρῶμα.

straw [strɔ:] n (agr) ἄχυρον, ψάθα ‖ (drinking straw) καλάμι, καλαμάκι ‖ a (hat,

basket) ψάθινος, ἀχυρόχρους ‖ ~**berry** n φράουλα.

stray [strei] n χαμένος, περιπλανηθέν ζῶον ‖ vi περιπλανῶμαι, ἀπομακρύνομαι ‖ a (animal) περιπλανώμενος, ἀδέσποτος ‖ (thought) ξεκάρφωτος, σκόρπιος, ξεκόλλητος.

streak [stri:k] n γραμμή, λωρίδα, ρίγα ‖ (strain) δόσις ‖ vt χαράσσω, ριγώνω, σχηματίζω ραβδώσεις ‖ ~**y** a ραβδωτός, γραμμωτός, ριγωτός.

stream [stri:m] n ποτάμι, ρυάκι, ρέμα ‖ (flow) ροή, ροῦς, χείμαρρος ‖ (crowd) κύματα, ἀδιάκοπος σειρά ‖ vi ρέω, τρέχω, κυλῶ ‖ ~**er** n ἐπισείων, ταινία. σημαία ‖ ~**lined** a ἀεροδυναμικός.

street [stri:t] n ὁδός, δρόμος ‖ ~**car** n (US: tram) τράμ ‖ ~ **lamp** n φανοστάτης.

strength [streŋθ] n (lit) δύναμις, ἰσχύς ‖ (fig) βασιζόμενος εἰς, στηριζόμενος στό ‖ ~**en** vt ἐνισχύω, δυναμώνω.

strenuous ['strenjuəs] a σθεναρός, δραστήριος ‖ (requiring effort) ἐπίπονος, σκληρός ‖ ~**ly** ad ἐπίπονως, σκληρά.

stress [stres] n (force, pressure) πίεσις, καταναγκασμός ‖ (mental strain) ἔντασις ‖ (accent) τόνος ‖ vt τονίζω.

stretch [stretʃ] n τέντωμα, ἔκτασις, ἅπλωμα ‖ vt τεντώνω, ἁπλώνω ‖ vi ἐκτείνομαι, πλαταίνω ‖ **at a ~** (continuously) χωρίς διακοπή ‖ **to ~ out** vt ἐπεκτείνομαι, ἀραιώνω ‖ vt τείνω, ἁπλώνω ‖ ~**er** n φορεῖον.

stricken ['strikən] a (person) προσβεβλημένος, θλιμμένος ‖ (city, country) πληγείσα.

strict [strikt] a ἀκριβής, αὐστηρός ‖ δριμύς ‖ ~**ly** ad αὐστηρῶς, ἀκριβῶς ‖ ~**ly** speaking κυριολεκτικῶς, γιά νά ποῦμε τήν ἀλήθεια ‖ ~**ness** n αὐστηρότης.

stride [straid] (irreg v) n μεγάλο βῆμα, δρασκελιά ‖ vi δρασκελίζω, βηματίζω.

strident ['straidənt] a ὀξύς, στριγγός, στρίγγλικος.

strife [straif] n ἀγών, πάλη, σύγκρουσις.

strike [straik] (irreg v) n ἀπεργία ‖ (discovery) εὕρησις, συνάντησις ‖ (attack) ἐπιχείρησις, πλήγμα ‖ vt κτυπῶ, προσκρούω, σκουντῶ ‖ (come into mind) μ' ἔρχεται (στό μυαλό), μοῦ φαίνεται ‖ (find gold) ἀνακαλύπτω, βρίσκω ‖ vi (stop work) κηρύσσω ἀπεργίαν, ἀπεργῶ ‖ (attack) χτυπῶ ‖ (clock) ἠχῶ, χτυπῶ, σημαίνω ‖ **to ~ down** vt (lay low) ρίχνω χάμω ‖ **to ~ out** vt (cross out) ἐξαλείφω, διαγράφω, σβήνω ‖ **to ~ up** vt (music) ἀρχίζω (νά παίζω) ‖ (friendship) πιάνω φιλίαν ‖ ~ **pay** n ἐπίδομα ἀπεργίας ‖ ~**r** n ἀπεργός.

striking ['straikiŋ] a κτυπητός, ἑλκυστικός, ἐνδιαφέρων ‖ ~**ly** ad ἐντυπωσιακῶς, χτυπητά.

string [striŋ] *n* σπάγγος, κορδόνι ‖ (*series*) σειρά, άλυσος ‖ (*mus*) χορδή ‖ ~ **bean** *n* φρέσκο φασολάκι.

stringency ['strindʒənsi] *n* αὐστηρότης, στενότης.

stringent ['strindʒənt] *a* αὐστηρός, στενός.

strip [strip] *n* λουρίδα, ταινία ‖ *vt* γυμνώνω, γδύνω, βγάζω ‖ (*machine etc*) ἀποσυνδέω, ξεμαρτώνω ‖ *vi* γδύνομαι, γυμνώνομαι ‖ ~ **cartoon** *n* σειρά εὐθύμων σκίτσων.

stripe [straip] *n* γραμμή, λουρίδα, ράβδωσις ‖ ~**d** *a* ραβδωτός, ριγωτός.

stripper ['stripə*] *n* στριπτηζοῦ.

striptease ['stripti:z] *n* στριπτήζ.

strive [straiv] (*irreg v*) *vi* (+ *for*) ἀγωνίζομαι (γιά), προσπαθῶ ‖ ~**n** ['strivn] *pp of* **strive.**

strode [strəud] *pt,pp of* **stride.**

stroke [strəuk] *n* κτύπημα, πλῆγμα ‖ (*tech*) κίνησις, διαδρομή, ρυθμός ‖ (*sudden attack*) προσβολή ‖ (*caress*) θωπεία, χάδι, χάΐδεμα ‖ *vt* χαϊδεύω, τρίβω, σιάζω ‖ **at a ~** μ' ἕνα κτύπημα, μέ μιᾶς ‖ **on the ~ of 5** στίς 5 ἀκριβῶς.

stroll [strəul] *n* περίπατος, βόλτα ‖ *vi* κάνω περίπατο, κάνω βόλτες.

strong [strɔŋ] *a* δυνατός, ἰσχυρός, γερός ‖ (*firm*) στερεός, γερός ‖ (*flavour*) δυνατός, ἔντονος ‖ (*protest*) ἔντονος ‖ (*wind*) ἰσχυρός, δυνατός ‖ **they are 50 ~** δυνάμεως 50 ἀνδρῶν ‖ ~**hold** *n* φρούριον, ὀχυρόν, προπύργιον ‖ ~**ly** *ad* ἰσχυρῶς, δυνατά, γερά ‖ ~**room** *n* αἴθουσα χρηματοκιβωτίων.

strove [strəuv] *pt of* **strive.**

struck [strʌk] *pt,pp of* **strike.**

structural ['strʌktʃərəl] *a* οἰκοδομικός, κατασκευαστικός, δομικός ‖ ~**ly** *ad* δομικός.

structure ['strʌktʃə*] *n* κατασκευή, δομή ‖ (*building*) οἰκοδόμημα, κτίριον, κτίσμα.

struggle ['strʌgl] *n* ἀγών, πάλη, σκληρή προσπάθεια ‖ *vi* (+ *to*) ἀγωνίζομαι, παλεύω.

strum [strʌm] *vt* (*guitar*) παίζω ἀδέξια, παίζω ἄτεχνα.

strung [strʌŋ] **highly ~** *a* see **high.**

strut [strʌt] *n* (*support*) στήριγμα, ἀντέρεισμα ‖ *vi* περιφέρομαι καμαρωτός, κορδώνομαι.

strychnine ['strikni:n] *n* στρυχνίνη.

stub [stʌb] *n* (*cigarette etc*) ὑπόλειμμα, γόπα.

stubble ['stʌbl] *n* καλαμιά, ρίζες ‖ (*on face*) γένια ἡμερῶν, ἀξουρισία.

stubbly ['stʌbli] *a* γεμᾶτο καλάμια, κοντοκομμένα (γένια).

stubborn ['stʌbən] *a* ἐπίμονος, πείσμων, ξεροκέφαλος ‖ ~**ly** *ad* πεισματικά, ἐπίμονος ‖ ~**ness** *n* πεῖσμα, ξεροκεφαλιά.

stubby ['stʌbi] *a* κοντόχοντρος.

stuck [stʌk] *pt,pp of* **stick** ‖ ~**-up** *a* ὑπεροπτικός, ἀλαζών.

stud [stʌd] *n* πλατυκέφαλο, καρφί ‖ (*of shirt*) κουμπί, ξενόκουμπο ‖ (*of horses*) σταῦλος ἵππων, ἱπποστάσιον ‖ *vt* διαστίζω, κοσμῶ μέ καρφιά.

student ['stju:dənt] *n* φοιτητής, σπουδαστής, μελετητής.

studied ['stʌdid] *a* μελετημένος, ἐσκεμμένος, θελματικός.

studio ['stju:diəu] *n* ἐργαστήριον, ἀτελιέ ‖ (*also TV*) στούντιο.

studious ['stju:diəs] *a* μελετηρός, φιλομαθής ‖ (*careful*) προσεκτικός ‖ ~**ly** *ad* (*carefully*) ἐπιμελῶς.

study ['stʌdi] *n* σπουδή, μελέτη ‖ (*something studied*) μελέτη, ἔρευνα ‖ (*room*) σπουδαστήριον, ἀναγνωστήριον, γραφεῖον ‖ *vt* σπουδάζω, μελετῶ ‖ (*examine*) μελετῶ, παρατηρῶ ‖ *vi* ἐπιμελοῦμαι, μελετῶ.

stuff [stʌf] *n* ὕλη, ὑλικόν, οὐσία ‖ *vt* (παρα)γεμίζω ‖ ~**iness** *n* ἔλλειψις ἀέρος, κλεισούρα ‖ ~**ing** *n* παραγέμισμα, γέμισι ‖ (*of fowl etc*) γέμισμα ‖ ~**y** *a* (*room*) πνιγηρός, χωρίς ἀέρα ‖ (*ideas: old-fashioned*) σεμνότυπος.

stumble ['stʌmbl] *vi* σκοντάφτω, προσκρούω ‖ **to ~ on** *vt* ἀνακαλύπτω ἀναπάντεχα.

stumbling block ['stʌmbliŋblɔk] *n* ἐμπόδιον.

stump [stʌmp] *n* κούτσουρο, στέλεχος ‖ *vt* (*puzzle*) μπερδεύω, τά χάνω.

stun [stʌn] *vt* ζαλίζω, ταράζω.

stung [stʌŋ] *pt,pp of* **sting.**

stunk [stʌŋk] *pp of* **stink.**

stunning ['stʌniŋ] *a* ἐξαίσιος, ὡραῖος.

stunt [stʌnt] *n* ἐκπληκτική παράστασις, ἄθλος ‖ *vt* περιστέλλω, ἐμποδίζω, κολοβώνω ‖ ~**ed** *a* κατσιασμένος.

stupefy ['stju:pifai] *vt* καταπλήσσω, ναρκώνω, ζαλίζω ‖ ~**ing** *a* ναρκωτικός.

stupendous [stju:'pendəs] *a* τεράστιος, πελώριος, καταπληκτικός ‖ ~**ly** *ad* καταπληκτικά.

stupid ['stju:pid] *a* ἠλίθιος, βλάκας, κουτός ‖ ~**ity** *n* βλακεία, κουταμάρα ‖ ~**ly** *ad* ἠλίθια, βλακωδῶς.

stupor ['stju:pə*] *n* νάρκη, λήθαργος, ζάλισμα.

sturdily ['stə:dili] *ad* μέ δύναμιν, γερά, θαρραλέα.

sturdiness ['stə:dinis] *n* ρώμη, δύναμις, λεβεντιά.

sturdy ['stə:di] *a* δυνατός, σθεναρός, γεροδεμένος.

stutter ['stʌtə*] *n* ψέλλισμα, τραύλισμα ‖ *vi* τραυλίζω, τσεβδίζω.

sty [stai] *n* χοιροστάσιον, γουρνοστάσι.

stye [stai] *n* χαλάζιον, κριθαράκι.

style [stail] *n* στύλ, τεχνοτροπία, ὕφος ‖ (*fashion*) ρυθμός, στύλ, μόδα ‖ (*distinction*) ἐπιδεξιότης, μεγαλοπρέπεια.

styling ['stailiŋ] n (of car etc) πλαίσιον, καλούπι.

stylish ['stailiʃ] a μοντέρνος, κομψός ‖ ~ly ad κομψά, μέ σίκ.

stylized ['stailaizd] a στυλιζαρισμένος.

stylus ['stailəs] n στύλος, γραφίς.

styptic ['stiptik] a: ~ pencil στυπτικόν.

suave [swɑːv] a εὐγενής, ἁπαλός, γλυκανάλατος.

sub- [sʌb] prefix ὑπο-.

subconscious ['sʌb'kɔnʃəs] a ὑποσυνείδητος ‖ n: the ~ τό ὑποσυνείδητον.

subdivide ['sʌbdi'vaid] vt ὑποδιαιρῶ.

subdivision ['sʌbdiviʒən] n ὑποδιαίρεσις.

subdue [səb'djuː] vt κατακτῶ, ὑποτάσσω, μαλακώνω ‖ ~d a συντετριμένος, μαλακωμένος.

subject ['sʌbdʒikt] n ὑπήκοος ‖ (theme) θέμα, ἀντικείμενον ‖ (gram) ὑποκείμενον ‖ [səb'dʒekt] vt ὑποτάσσω, ὑποδουλώνω ‖ ὑποβάλλω, ἐκθέτω ‖ to be ~ to ὑπόκειμαι εἰς, ἐξαρτῶμαι ἀπό ‖ ~ion n καθυπόταξις, ὑποταγή ‖ ὑποτέλεια ‖ ~ive a ὑποκειμενικός ‖ ~ively ad ὑποκειμενικῶς ‖ ~ matter n θέμα, περιεχόμενον.

sub judice [sʌb'juːdisi] a ἐκκρεμής, μή ἐκδικασθείς.

subjunctive [səb'dʒʌŋktiv] n ὑποτακτική (ἔγκλισις) ‖ a ὑποτακτικός.

sublet [sʌb'let] vt ὑπεκμισθῶ, ὑπενοικιάζω.

sublime [sə'blaim] a ὑψηλός, ἀνώτερος, ὑπέροχος, ἔξοχος ‖ ~ly ad ὑπερόχως, ἐξαιρετικά.

submarine [sʌbmə'riːn] n ὑποβρύχιον.

submerge [səb'məːdʒ] vt ἐμβαπτίζω, βυθίζω, χώνω στό νερό ‖ vi καταδύομαι, βυθίζομαι, βουλιάζω.

submission [səb'miʃən] n ὑποταγή, ὑπακοή ‖ (presentation) ὑποβολή.

submit [səb'mit] vt ὑποβάλλω ‖ vi ὑποτάσσομαι, ὑποβάλλομαι.

subnormal ['sʌb'nɔːməl] a κάτω τοῦ κανονικοῦ.

subordinate [sə'bɔːdnit] a κατώτερος, ἐξηρτημένος, δευτερεύων ‖ n ὑφιστάμενος.

subpoena [səb'piːnə] n κλῆσις (μαρτύρων) ‖ vt καλῶ, ἀποστέλλω κλῆσιν.

subscribe [səb'skraib] vi (pay contribution) ἐγγράφομαι, συνεισφέρω ‖ (+ to) ἐπιδοκιμάζω, ἀποδέχομαι, παραδέχομαι ‖ ~r n (to periodical) συνδρομητής ‖ (tel) συνδρομητής.

subscription [səb'skripʃən] n συνεισφορά, συνδρομή.

subsequent ['sʌbsikwənt] a ἐπακόλουθος, μεταγενέστερος ‖ ~ly ad ἔπειτα, ἀργότερα.

subside [səb'said] vi κατακαθίζω, καθιζάνω, κοπάζω ‖ ~nce n καθίζησις, κόπασις.

subsidiary [səb'sidiəri] a βοηθητικός, δευτερεύων ‖ n θυγάτηρ ἑταιρεία.

subsidize ['sʌbsidaiz] vt ἐπιχορηγῶ, ἐπιδοτῶ.

subsidy ['sʌbsidi] n ἐπιχορήγησις, βοήθημα, ἐπίδομα.

subsistence [səb'sistəns] n ὕπαρξις, διατήρησις, τά πρός τό ζῆν.

substance ['sʌbstəns] n οὐσία ‖ (matter) περιεχόμενον, οὐσία, ἔννοια ‖ (wealth) περιουσία, ἀξία.

substandard ['sʌb'stændəd] a κάτω τοῦ μέσου ὅρου, κακῆς ποιότητος.

substantial [səb'stænʃəl] a (strong) στερεός, γερός ‖ (important) σημαντικός, οὐσιώδης ‖ ~ly ad οὐσιαστικά, πραγματικά.

substantiate [səb'stænʃieit] vt ἐπαληθεύω, ἀποδεικνύω, αἰτιολογῶ.

substation ['sʌbsteiʃən] n (elec) ὑποσταθμός.

substitute ['sʌbstitjuːt] n ἀντικαταστάτης, ὑποκατάστατον ‖ vt ὑποκαθιστῶ, ἀντικαθιστῶ.

substitution [sʌbsti'tjuːʃən] n ἀντικατάστασις, ὑποκατάστασις.

subterfuge ['sʌbtəfjuːdʒ] n ὑπεκφυγή, τέχνασμα, πρόφασις.

subterranean [sʌbtə'reiniən] a ὑπόγειος.

subtitle ['sʌbtaitl] n (cine) ὑπότιτλος.

subtle ['sʌtl] a (faint) λεπτός, ραφινάτος ‖ (clever, sly) ξέμυτος, πανοῦργος ‖ ~ty n λεπτότης, λεπτολογία, πονηρία.

subtly ['sʌtli] ad λεπτῶς, μέ λεπτότητα.

subtract [səb'trækt] vt ἀφαιρῶ ‖ ~ion n ἀφαίρεσις.

subtropical ['sʌb'trɔpikəl] a ὑποτροπικός.

suburb ['sʌbəːb] n προάστειον ‖ ~an a τῶν προαστείων ‖ ~ia n προάστεια.

subversive [səb'vəːsiv] a ἀνατρεπτικός.

subway ['sʌbwei] n (US) ὑπόγειος σιδηρόδρομος.

sub-zero ['sʌb'ziərəu] a κάτω τοῦ μηδενός.

succeed [sək'siːd] vi ἐπιτυγχάνω, πετυχαίνω ‖ vt διαδέχομαι ‖ ~ing a (following) ἑπόμενος, μελλοντικός.

success [sək'ses] n ἐπιτυχία, εὐτυχής ἔκβασις ‖ ἐπιτυχημένος ἄνθρωπος ‖ ~ful a ἐπιτυχής, ἐπιτυχημένος ‖ ~fully ad ἐπιτυχῶς, μέ ἐπιτυχίαν ‖ ~ion n συνέπεια, διαδοχή ‖ (to throne) διαδοχή ‖ ~ive a διαδοχικός, συνεχής, ἀλλεπάλληλος ‖ ~or n διάδοχος, ἑπόμενος.

succinct [sək'siŋkt] a σύντομος καί σαφής.

succulent ['sʌkjulənt] a εὔχυμος, ζουμερός νόστιμος.

succumb [sə'kʌm] vi (+ to) ὑποκύπτω, ὑποτάσσομαι, ἐνδίδω.

such [sʌtʃ] a (of that kind) τέτοιος, τοιούτου εἴδους ‖ (so great etc) τόσος ‖ pron αὐτός, αὐτοί, τοιοῦτος ‖ ~like a παρόμοιος, τέτοιος ‖ pron παρόμοιος, τοῦ ἰδίου εἴδους.

suck [sʌk] vt (ice cream) γλείφω ‖ (toffee) πιπιλίζω ‖ ~er n (col) κορόιδο.

suction ['sʌkʃən] n ἀναρρόφησις, ἐκμύζησις, τράβηγμα.

Sudan [su'dɑːn] n Σουδάν ‖ ~ese a σουδανικός ‖ n Σουδανέζος.

sudden ['sʌdn] a ξαφνικός, αἰφνίδιος ‖ all of a ~ αἰφνιδίως, ξαφνικά ‖ ~ly ad ξαφνικά ‖ ~ness n (τό) αἰφνίδιον, (τό) ἀπότομον.

sue [suː] vt ἐνάγω, κάνω ἀγωγή σέ.

suède [sweid] n καστόρι, σουέντ.

suet [suit] n λῖπος, ξύγγι.

Suez Canal ['suːizkə'næl] n διώρυξ τοῦ Σουέζ.

suffer ['sʌfə*] vt (death) θανατοῦμαι, ἐκτελοῦμαι ‖ (permit) ὑποφέρω, ἀνέχομαι, δέχομαι ‖ vi ὑποφέρω, πάσχω ‖ ~er n ὑποφέρων, παθών ‖ ~ing n πόνος, βάσανα, πάθη.

suffice [sə'fais] vi (ἐπ)αρκῶ, φθάνω.

sufficient [sə'fiʃənt] a ἐπαρκής, ἀρκετός ‖ ~ly ad ἐπαρκῶς, ἀρκετά.

suffix ['sʌfiks] n κατάληξις, πρόσφυμα.

suffocate ['sʌfəkeit] vi πνίγομαι, ἀσφυκτιῶ.

suffocation [sʌfə'keiʃən] n ἀσφυξία, πνιγμονή, πνίξιμο.

sugar ['ʃugə*] n σάκχαρις, ζάχαρη ‖ vt ζαχαρώνω, βάζω ζάχαρη σέ ‖ ~ beet n τεῦτλον ζαχαροποιΐας ‖ ~ cane n ζαχαροκάλαμο ‖ ~y a ζαχαρένιος, ζαχαρωμένος, γλυκύτατος.

suggest [sə'dʒest] vt εἰσηγοῦμαι, προτείνω ‖ (show indirectly) ὑπαινίσσομαι, ὑπονοῶ ‖ (propose) προτείνω, ὑποβάλλω, ὑποδεικνύω ‖ ~ion n πρότασις, ὑποβολή ‖ ~ive a ὑπενθυμίζων, ὑποβλητικός, μέ ὑπονοούμενα.

suicidal [sui'saidl] a τῆς αὐτοκτονίας.

suicide ['suisaid] n αὐτοκτονία, αὐτόχειρ.

suit [suːt] n (of clothes) κοστούμι ‖ (in cards) τά τέσσαρα χρώματα ‖ vt ταιριάζω, πηγαίνω ‖ (satisfy) ἱκανοποιῶ, βολεύω ‖ (adapt) προσαρμόζω ‖ ~ability n καταλληλότης ‖ ~able a κατάλληλος, ἁρμόζων, ταιριαστός ‖ ~ably ad καταλλήλως, πρεπόντως, ὅπως πρέπει ‖ ~case n βαλίτσα.

suite [swiːt] n (of rooms) διαμέρισμα, ἀπαρτία ‖ (mus) σουΐτα.

sulfur ['sʌlfə*] n (US) = sulphur.

sulk [sʌlk] vi σκυθρωπιάζω, κατσουφιάζω ‖ ~y a κακόκεφος, κατσούφης.

sullen ['sʌlən] a (gloomy) κατηφής, μελαγχολικός ‖ (bad-tempered) κακόκεφος, κατσούφης.

sulphur ['sʌlfə*] n θεῖον, θειάφι.

sulphuric [sʌl'fjuərik] a: ~ acid θειϊκόν ὀξύ, βιτριόλι.

sultan ['sʌltən] n σουλτάνος ‖ ~a n σουλτάνα ‖ (raisin) σουλτανίνα.

sultry ['sʌltri] a ἀσφυκτικός, πνιγηρός.

sum [sʌm] n ἄθροισμα, σύνολον, ποσόν,

σούμα ‖ (problem) ἄθροισμα ‖ (of money) ποσόν (χρημάτων) ‖ to ~ up vt συνοψίζω, ἀνακεφαλαιώνω ‖ vi κρίνω, ἐκτιμῶ ‖ ~marize vt συνοψίζω, συγκεφαλαιώνω ‖ ~mary n (συνοπτική) περίληψις, σύνοψις.

summer ['sʌmə*] n θέρος, καλοκαίρι ‖ attr a (clothing) καλοκαιρινός ‖ ~house n (in garden) περίπτερον κήπου ‖ ~time n καλοκαίρι, θερινή ὥρα.

summing-up ['sʌmiŋ'ʌp] n ἀνακεφαλαίωσις, ἐκτίμησις.

summit ['sʌmit] n κορυφή ‖ ~ conference n συνεδρίασις κορυφῆς.

summon ['sʌmən] vt (συγ)καλῶ, προσκαλῶ ‖ (gather up) συγκεντρώνω, μαζεύω ‖ ~s n κλῆσις ‖ vt κλητεύω, καλῶ.

sump [sʌmp] n φρεάτιον ἀποστραγγίσεως ‖ κάρτερ.

sumptuous ['sʌmptjuəs] a πολυτελής, πολυδάπανος ‖ ~ly ad πολυτελῶς, μεγαλοπρεπῶς ‖ ~ness n μεγαλοπρέπεια, πλοῦτος.

sun [sʌn] n ἥλιος ‖ (rays) λιακάδα ‖ ~bathe vi κάνω ἡλιοθεραπείαν ‖ ~bathing n ἡλιοθεραπεία ‖ ~burn n μαύρισμα ἀπό τόν ἥλιο ‖ ~burnt a ἡλιοκαμμένος, μαυρισμένος.

Sunday ['sʌndi] n Κυριακή.

sundial ['sʌndaiəl] n ἡλιακόν ὡρολόγιον.

sundown ['sʌndaun] n (sunset) ἡλιοβασίλεμα.

sundry ['sʌndri] a διάφορος ‖ **sundries** npl διάφορα εἴδη.

sunflower ['sʌnflauə*] n ἥλιος, ἡλίανθος.

sung [sʌŋ] pp of sing.

sunglasses ['sʌngloːsiz] npl γυαλιά τοῦ ἡλίου.

sunk [sʌŋk] pp of sink ‖ ~en a βυθισμένος, βαθουλωμένος.

sunlight ['sʌnlait] n ἡλιακόν φῶς, λιακάδα.

sunlit ['sʌnlit] a ἡλιόλουστος.

sunny ['sʌni] a εὔηλιος, ἡλιόλουστος ‖ (cheerful) χαρωπός, γελαστός.

sunrise ['sʌnraiz] n ἀνατολή τοῦ ἡλίου.

sunset ['sʌnset] n ἡλιοβασίλεμα.

sunshade ['sʌnʃeid] n (over table) ἀλεξήλιον, ὀμπρέλλα ἡλίου.

sunshine ['sʌnʃain] n λιακάδα.

sunspot ['sʌnspɔt] n ἡλιακή κηλίδα.

sunstroke ['sʌnstrəuk] n ἡλίασις.

suntan ['sʌntæn] n μαύρισμα ἀπό τόν ἥλιο.

sunup ['sʌnʌp] n (sunrise) ἀνατολή τοῦ ἡλίου.

super ['suːpə*] a (col) ὑπέροχος, περίφημος, σπουδαῖος ‖ prefix ὑπερ-.

superannuation [suːpərænju'eiʃən] n (employers' contribution) εἰσφορά ἐργοδότου.

superb [suː'pəːb] a ὑπέροχος, ἔξοχος, ἐξαίσιος ‖ ~ly ad ὑπέροχα, ἔξοχα, λαμπρά.

supercilious [su:pə'siliəs] *a* ἀγέρωχος, ὑπεροπτικός.

superficial [su:pə'fiʃəl] *a* ἐπιφανειακός || (*shallow*) ἐπιπόλαιος, ἐπιφανειακός || ~**ly** *ad* ἐπιφανειακά, ἐπιπολαίως.

superfluous [su'pə:fluəs] *a* περιττός.

superhuman [su:pə'hju:mən] *a* (*effort*) ὑπεράνθρωπος.

superimpose ['su:pərim'pəuz] *vt* ὑπερεπιθέτω, ὑπερθέτω.

superintendent [su:pərin'tendənt] *n* (*police*) ἀξιωματικός τῆς ἀστυνομίας.

superior [su'piəriə*] *a* ἀνώτερος, ὑπέρτερος, ἐξαιρετικός || (*proud*) ὑπεροπτικός, ἀκατάδεχτος || *n* προϊστάμενος, ἀνώτερος || ~**ity** *n* ὑπεροχή, ἀνωτερότης.

superlative [su'pə:lətiv] *a* ἀνώτατος, ὑπερθετικός || *n* (τὸ) ὑπερθετικόν.

superman ['su:pəmæn] *n* ὑπεράνθρωπος.

supermarket ['su:pəma:kit] *n* σουπερμάρκετ.

supernatural [su:pə'nætʃərəl] *a* ὑπερφυσικός.

superpower ['su:pəpauə*] *n* (*eg USA, USSR*) ὑπερδύναμις.

supersede [su:pə'si:d] *vt* ἀντικαθιστῶ, παραμερίζω.

supersonic ['su:pə'sɔnik] *a* ὑπερηχητικός.

superstition [su:pə'stiʃən] *n* δεισιδαιμονία, πρόληψις.

superstitious [su:pə'stiʃəs] *a* δεισιδαίμων, προληπτικός.

supertanker ['su:pətæŋkə*] *n* ὑπερδεξαμενόπλοιον.

supervise ['su:pəvaiz] *vt* ἐπιβλέπω, ἐποπτεύω, διευθύνω.

supervision [su:pə'viʒən] *n* ἐποπτεία, ἐπιθεώρησις, διεύθυνσις.

supervisor ['su:pəvaizə*] *n* ἐπιθεωρητής, ἐπόπτης, ἐπιστάτης || ~**y** *a* τῆς ἐποπτείας, ἐποπτικός.

supper ['sʌpə*] *n* δεῖπνον.

supple ['sʌpl] *a* εὐέλικτος, εὐλύγιστος, λυγερός.

supplement ['sʌplimənt] *n* συμπλήρωμα, παράρτημα || [sʌpli'ment] *vt* συμπληρώνω || ~**ary** *a* συμπληρωματικός, πρόσθετος.

supplier [sə'plaiə*] *n* προμηθευτής.

supply [sə'plai] *vt* παρέχω, ἐφοδιάζω, προμηθεύω || *n* ἐφόδιον, ἀπόθεμα, προμήθεια || (*supplying*) ἐφοδιασμός, τροφοδότησις || **supplies** *npl* (*food*) τρόφιμα || (*mil*) ἐφόδια || ~ **and demand** προσφορά καί ζήτησις.

support [sə'pɔ:t] *n* (*moral, financial etc*) ὑποστήριξις, ἐνίσχυσις || (*tech*) στήριγμα, ὑποστήριγμα, ἔρεισμα || *vt* (ὑπο)στηρίζω, ἐνισχύω || (*provide for*) συντηρῶ, κρατῶ || (*speak for*) ὑποστηρίζω, ἐνισχύω || (*endure*) ὑπομένω, ὑποφέρω || ~**er** *n* (*pol etc*) ὀπαδός, ὑπερασπιστής || (*sport*) ὀπαδός, ὑποστη-

ρικτής || ~**ing** *a* (*programme, role*) βοηθητικός, δευτερεύων.

suppose [sə'pəuz] *vti* ὑποθέτω, προϋποθέτω || (*think, imagine*) φαντάζομαι, νομίζω || ~ **he comes** . . . ἄν ἔρθη . . . || ~**dly** *ad* ὑποθετικῶς, δῆθεν.

supposing [sə'pəuziŋ] *cj* ἐάν, ἄς ὑποθέσουμε ὅτι.

supposition [sʌpə'ziʃən] *n* ὑπόθεσις, γνώμη.

suppress [sə'pres] *vt* καταπνίγω, καταστέλλω || (*hold back*) συγκρατῶ, σκεπάζω || ~**ion** *n* κατάπνιξις, συγκράτησις, ἀπόκρυψις || ~**or** *n* (*mech*) καταστολεύς, ἀναστολεύς.

supra- ['su:prə] *prefix* ὑπέρ-.

supremacy [su'preməsi] *n* ὑπεροχή, ἀνωτάτη ἐξουσία.

supreme [su'pri:m] *a* ὑπέρτατος, ἀνώτατος, ὕψιστος || ~**ly** *ad* στόν ὑπέρτατον βαθμόν, ἐξαιρετικά.

surcharge ['sə:tʃa:dʒ] *n* ἐπιβάρυνσις, πρόσθετος φόρος.

sure [ʃuə*] *a* βέβαιος, ἀσφαλής, σίγουρος || *ad* βεβαίως, ἀσφαλῶς || ~! || (*of course*) βέβαια!, ἀσφαλῶς! || **to make** ~ **of** βεβαιώνω || ~**-footed** *a* μέ σίγουρο πόδι || ~**ly** *ad* ἀσφαλῶς, βεβαίως || (*firmly*) ἀναμφιβόλως || (*gladly*) βεβαίως, μετά χαρᾶς.

surf [sə:f] *n* κῦμα, ἀφρός.

surface ['sə:fis] *n* (*top side*) ἐπιφάνεια || (*outward appearance*) ἐξωτερικόν, ἐμφάνισις || *vt* (*roadway*) ἐπιστρώνω, στρώνω || *vi* βγαίνω στήν ἐπιφάνεια || ~ **mail** *n* τακτικόν ταχυδρομεῖον.

surfboard ['sə:fbɔ:d] *n* σανίδα κολυμπίσεως.

surfeit ['sə:fit] *n* ὑπεραφθονία, πληθώρα, κόρος.

surge [sə:dʒ] *n* μεγάλο κῦμα, σάλος, ἀνύψωσις || *vi* ὁρμῶ, ξεχύνομαι, κυμαίνομαι.

surgeon ['sə:dʒən] *n* χειρουργός.

surgery ['sə:dʒəri] *n* χειρουργική || (*room*) ἰατρεῖον, χειρουργεῖον.

surgical ['sə:dʒikəl] *a* χειρουργικός.

surly ['sə:li] *a* ἀγροῖκος, κατσούφης, ἀγενής.

surmise [sə:'maiz] *vt* εἰκάζω, ὑποθέτω, μαντεύω.

surmount [sə:'maunt] *vt* (*difficulty*) ὑπερνικῶ, ξεπερνῶ.

surname ['sə:neim] *n* ἐπώνυμον.

surpass [sə:'pa:s] *vt* ὑπερτερῶ, ὑπερβαίνω, ξεπερνῶ.

surplus ['sə:pləs] *n* περίσσευμα, πλεόνασμα || *a* πλεονάζων, ὑπεράριθμος.

surprise [sə'praiz] *n* ἔκπληξις, κατάπληξις, ξάφνισμα || *vt* αἰφνιδιάζω || (*astonish*) ἐκπλήσσω, καταπλήσσω, ξαφνίζω.

surprising [sə'praiziŋ] *a* ἐκπληκτικός, καταπληκτικός || ~**ly** *ad* καταπληκτικά, ἐκπληκτικῶς.

surrealism [sə'riəlizəm] *n* σουρρεαλισμός.

surrealist [sə'riəlist] *a* σουρρεαλιστικός ‖ *n* σουρρεαλιστής.

surrender [sə'rendə*] *n* παράδοσις, έγκατάλειψις, έκχώρησις ‖ *vi* παραδίδομαι, παραδίδω, έκχωρῶ.

surreptitious [sʌrəp'tiʃəs] *a* λαθραῖος, κρυφός ‖ **~ly** *ad* λαθραία, στή ζούλα.

surround [sə'raund] *vt* περιβάλλω, περικυκλώνω ‖ **~ing** *a* (*countryside*) περιβάλλων, έξοχικός ‖ **~ings** *npl* περιβάλλον, πλαίσιον.

surveillance [sɔː'veiləns] *n* (*observation*) έπιτήρησις, έποπτεία.

survey ['sɔːvei] *n* έπισκόπησις ‖ χωρογράφησις, τοπογράφησις ‖ [sɔː'vei] *vt* έπισκοπῶ, έξετάζω ‖ (*measure land*) χωρογραφῶ, τοπογραφῶ ‖ **~ing** *n* (*of land*) χωρογράφησις, τοπογραφία ‖ **~or** *n* (*of land*) τοπογράφος.

survival [sə'vaivəl] *n* έπιβίωσις ‖ (*from past*) ὑπόλειμμα, έπιβίωμα.

survive [sə'vaiv] *vi* έπιζῶ ‖ *vt* έπιζῶ ‖ (*a shipwreck etc*) σώζομαι, γλυτώνω.

survivor [sə'vaivə*] *n* έπιζῶν, διασωθείς.

susceptible [sə'septəbl] *a* (+ *to*) έπιδεκτικός, εὐεπηρέαστος.

suspect [sʌspekt] *n* ὕποπτος ‖ *a* ὕποπτος ‖ [səs'pekt] *vt* ὑποπτεύομαι, ὑποψιάζομαι ‖ (*think likely*) ὑποψιάζομαι, φαντάζομαι.

suspend [səs'pend] *vt* άναστέλλω, διακόπτω ‖ (*hang up*) άναρτῶ, κρεμῶ ‖ **~ers** *npl* καλτσοδέτες ‖ (*US*) τιράντες.

suspense [səs'pens] *n* έκκρεμότης, άνησυχία, άβεβαιότης.

suspension [səs'penʃən] *n* άναστολή, άνακοπή ‖ (*being suspended*) άπόλυσις ‖ (*aut*) άνάρτησις ‖ **~ bridge** *n* κρεμαστή γέφυρα.

suspicion [səs'piʃən] *n* ὑποψία, ὑπόνοια ‖ (*small amount*) μικρή δόσις.

suspicious [səs'piʃəs] *a* ὕποπτος, καχύποπτος ‖ **~ly** *ad* ὕποπτα, δύσπιστα.

sustain [səs'tein] *vt* ὑποστηρίζω, στηρίζω, βαστάζω ‖ (*confirm*) άποδέχομαι ‖ (*injury*) ὑφίσταμαι, ζημιοῦμαι, δέχομαι ‖ **~ed** *a* (*effort*) έπίμονος, συνεχής.

sustenance ['sʌstinəns] *n* συντήρησις, τροφή.

swab [swɔb] *n* (*pad*) ξέστρον.

swagger ['swægə*] *vi* κομπάζω, έπιδεικνύομαι, καμαρώνω.

swallow ['swɔləu] *n* (*bird*) χελιδών, χελιδόνι ‖ (*of food etc*) μπουκιά, χαψιά, γουλιά ‖ *vt* καταπίνω, χάφτω ‖ **to ~ up** *vt* καταπίνω, καλύπτω, χάνομαι.

swam [swæm] *pt of* swim.

swamp [swɔmp] *n* ἕλος, βάλτος ‖ *vt* (*overwhelm*) συντρίβω, σαρώνω ‖ **~y** *a* έλώδης, βαλτώδης.

swan [swɔn] *n* κύκνος ‖ **~.song** *n* κύκνειον ᾆσμα.

swap [swɔp] *n* (*exchange*) άνταλλαγή ‖ *vt* (+ *for*) άνταλλάσσω, άλλάζω.

swarm [swɔːm] *n* (*of bees*) σμῆνος, σμάρι ‖ (*of insects*) σύννεφο ‖ (*people*) μπουλούκι, τσοῦρμο ‖ *vi* (*crowd*) συρρέω, συγκεντρώνομαι, γέμω.

swarthy ['swɔːδi] *a* μελαψός, μελαχροινός.

swastika ['swɔstikə] *n* άγκυλωτός σταυρός.

swat [swɔt] *vt* κτυπῶ, βαρῶ.

sway [swei] *vi* ταλαντεύομαι, κουνιέμαι, τρικλίζω ‖ *vt* ταλαντεύω, κουνῶ ‖ (*influence*) διευθύνω, έπηρεάζω, παρασύρω.

swear [swɛə*] (*irreg v*) *vi* ὁρκίζομαι, ὀμνύω ‖ (*curse*) βλαστημῶ, βλασφημῶ, ὑβρίζω ‖ **to ~ to sth** ὁρκίζομαι στό, βεβαιῶ ‖ **~word** *n* βλαστήμια, χοντροκουβέντα.

sweat [swet] *n* ἱδρώτας ‖ (*med*) ἱδρωσία, ἱδρωμα ‖ *vi* ἱδρώνω ‖ (*toil*) μοχθῶ, σπάω στή δουλειά ‖ **~er** *n* πουλόβερ, φανέλλα ‖ **~y** *a* ἱδρωμένος.

Swede [swiːd] *n* Σουηδός.

swede [swiːd] *n* (*turnip*) ραπίτσα.

Sweden ['swiːdn] *n* Σουηδία.

Swedish ['swiːdiʃ] *a* σουηδικός ‖ *n* (*ling*) σουηδικά.

sweep [swiːp] (*irreg v*) *n* σκούπισμα, σάρωμα ‖ (*wide curve*) κυκλική κίνησις, καμπή ‖ (*range*) άνοιγμα, εὐρύτης, έμβέλεια ‖ (*of chimney*) καπνοδοχοκαθαριστής ‖ *vt* σκουπίζω, καθαρίζω, σαρώνω ‖ *vi* (*move in curve*) έκτείνομαι, άπλώνομαι ‖ προχωρῶ μεγαλοπρεπῶς ‖ **to ~ away** *vt* σκουπίζω, σαρώνω ‖ **to ~ past** *vi* περνῶ γρήγορα, άντιπαρέρχομαι ‖ **to ~ up** *vi* φθάνω, άνεβαίνω ‖ *vt* σκουπίζω, μαζεύω ‖ **~ing** *a* (*gesture*) πλατειά (χειρονομία) ‖ (*statement*) γενικός, ριζικός, πλήρης ‖ **~stake** *n* σουηπστέικ.

sweet [swiːt] *n* γλυκό ‖ (*candy*) ζαχαρωτό, καραμέλα ‖ *a* γλυκός ‖ (*fresh*) δροσερός, φρέσκος ‖ (*gentle, pretty*) χαριτωμένος, γλυκός, συμπαθητικός ‖ **~breads** *npl* γλυκάδια ‖ **~en** *vt* γλυκαίνω ‖ **~heart** *n* άγαπητικός, άγαπημένος, άγάπη μου ‖ **~ly** *ad* γλυκά, μελωδικά, εὐχάριστα ‖ **~ness** *n* γλυκύτης, γλύκα ‖ **~ pea** *n* λάθυρος, μοσχομπίζελο ‖ **~ tooth** *n* άδυναμία γιά γλυκά.

swell [swel] (*irreg v*) *n* (*wave*) μεγάλο κῦμα ‖ *a* (*col: excellent*) έξαιρετικός, πρώτης τάξεως ‖ *vt* (*numbers*) έξογκώνω, αὐξάνω ‖ *vi* (*also ~ up*) έξογκοῦμαι, φουσκώνω ‖ (*become louder*) δυναμώνω ‖ (*med*) πρήσκομαι, πρήζομαι ‖ **~ing** *n* έξόγκωσις, πρήξιμο.

sweltering ['sweltəriŋ] *a* ἱδρωμένος, άποπνυκτικός.

swept [swept] *pt, pp of* sweep.

swerve [swɔːv] *n* παρέκκλισις, παρατιμονιά ‖ *vti* παρεκκλίνω, παραστρατίζω, στρίβω.

swift [swift] *n* κλαδευτήρα, σταχτάρα ‖ *a* ταχύς, γρήγορος, ἄμεσος ‖ **~ly** *ad* ταχέως, γρήγορα, γοργά ‖ ~ness *n* ταχύτης, γοργότης, γρηγοράδα.

swig [swig] *n* (*col: of drink*) μεγάλη ρουφηξιά.

swill [swil] *n* (*for pigs*) τροφή χοίρων ‖ *vt* (*pour liquid*) ξεπλένω.

swim [swim] (*irreg v*) *n* κολύμπι ‖ *vi* (*person*) κολυμπῶ ‖ (*be flooded*) πλημμυρίζω, εἶμαι πλημμυρισμένος ‖ (*feel dizzy*) ἰλιγγιῶ, γυρίζω, ζαλίζω ‖ *vt* (*cross by swimming*) περνῶ κολυμπῶντας ‖ ~**mer** *n* κολυμβητής ‖ ~**ming** *n* κολύμπι ‖ to go ~**ming** πάω κολύμπι ‖ ~**ming baths** *npl* κολυμβητικές δεξαμενές ‖ ~**ming cap** *n* σκουφί ‖ ~**ming costume** *n* μαγιό ‖ ~**ming pool** *n* πισίνα ‖ ~**suit** *n* μαγιό.

swindle ['swindl] *n* ἀπάτη ‖ *vt* (ἐξ)ἀπατῶ ‖ ~**r** *n* ἀπατεών, κατεργάρης.

swine [swain] *n* χοῖρος, γουρούνι ‖ (*person*) γουρούνι, παλιάνθρωπος.

swing [swiŋ] (*irreg v*) *n* κούνια ‖ (*swinging*) αἰώρησις, ταλάντευσις ‖ (*music*) ρυθμός, σουίγκ ‖ *vt* ταλαντεύω, κουνῶ ‖ (*move round*) περιστρέφω, στρέφω ‖ *vi* αἰωροῦμαι, κουνιέμαι ‖ (*move round*) περιστρέφομαι, στρέφομαι, κάνω μεταβολήν ‖ **in full** ~ ἐν πλήρει ὀργασμῷ ‖ ~ **bridge** *n* περιστρεφόμενη γέφυρα ‖ ~ **door** *n* πτερυγωτή θύρα.

swipe [swaip] *n* δυνατόν κτύπημα ‖ *vt* (*hit*) κτυπῶ δυνατά ‖ (*col: steal*) κλέβω, βουτῶ.

swish [swiʃ] *a* (*col: smart*) κομψός, μοντέρνος ‖ *vt* θροΐζω, συρίζω, μαστιγώνω.

Swiss [swis] *a* ἐλβετικός ‖ *n* (*person*) Ἐλβετός.

switch [switʃ] *n* (*for light, radio etc*) διακόπτης ‖ (*change*) ἀλλαγή ‖ *vti* διακόπτω ‖ (*turn*) γυρίζω ἀπότομα ‖ **to ~ off** *vt* διακόπτω, σβήνω ‖ **to ~ on** *vt* ἀνάβω, ἀνοίγω ‖ ~**back** *n* (*at fair*) ρωσικά βουνά ‖ ~**board** *n* πίναξ διανομῆς, ταμπλό.

Switzerland ['switsələnd] *n* Ἑλβετία.

swivel ['swivl] *vti* (*also* ~ round) (περι)στρέφομαι, στρέφω.

swollen ['swəulən] *pp* of **swell** ‖ *a* (*ankle etc*) πρησμένος, διογκωμένος.

swoon [swu:n] *vi* λιγοθυμῶ, λαγγεύω.

swoop [swu:p] *n* (*esp by police*) ξαφνική ἐπίθεσις, ἐφόρμησις ‖ *vi* (*also* ~ **down**) ἐφορμῶ, ἐπιπίπτω, πέφτω.

swop [swɔp] = **swap**.

sword [sɔ:d] *n* ξίφος, σπαθί ‖ ~**fish** *n* ξιφίας ‖ ~**sman** *n* ξιφομάχος.

swore [swɔ:*] *pt* of **swear**.

sworn [swɔ:n] *pp* of **swear**.

swum [swʌm] *pp* of **swim**.

swung [swʌŋ] *pt,pp* of **swing**.

sycamore ['sikəmɔ:*] *n* συκομουριά.

sycophantic [sikə'fæntik] *a* συκοφαντικός.

syllable ['siləbl] *n* συλλαβή.

syllabus ['siləbəs] *n* πρόγραμμα.

symbol ['simbəl] *n* σύμβολον, σημεῖον ‖

~**ic(al)** [sim'bɔlik(əl)] *a* συμβολικός ‖ ~**ism** *n* συμβολισμός ‖ ~**ize** *vt* συμβολίζω, παριστάνω.

symmetrical [si'metrikəl] *a* συμμετρικός ‖ ~**ly** *ad* συμμετρικῶς.

symmetry ['simitri] *n* συμμετρία.

sympathetic [simpə'θetik] *a* συμπαθητικός ‖ (*agreeing*) συμπαθής, εὐνοϊκός ‖ ~**ally** *ad* ἐκ συμπαθείας, συμπονετικά.

sympathize ['simpəθaiz] *vi* (+ *with*) συμπάσχω μέ, συμπονῶ, συμπαθῶ ‖ ~**r** *n* συμπαθῶν, ὀπαδός.

sympathy ['simpəθi] *n* συμπάθεια, συμπόνια, οἶκτος.

symphonic [sim'fɔnik] *a* συμφωνικός.

symphony ['simfəni] *n* (*composition*) συμφωνία ‖ ~ **orchestra** *n* συμφωνική ὀρχήστρα.

symposium [sim'pəuziəm] *n* (*meeting for discussion*) συγκέντρωσις, συμπόσιον.

symptom ['simptəm] *n* σύμπτωμα ‖ ~**atic** *a* συμπτωματικός.

synagogue ['sinəgɔg] *n* συναγωγή.

synchromesh ['siŋkrəu'meʃ] *n* συγχρονισμένη ἐμπλοκή.

synchronize ['siŋkrənaiz] *vt* συγχρονίζω ‖ *vi* (+ *with*) γίνομαι ταυτοχρόνως συμφωνῶ.

syndicate ['sindikit] *n* συνδικάτον.

syndrome ['sindrəum] *n* (*med*) σύνδρομον.

synonym ['sinənim] *n* συνώνυμον ‖ ~**ous** [si'nɔniməs] *a* συνώνυμος.

synopsis [si'nɔpsis] *n* σύνοψις, περίληψις.

syntax ['sintæks] *n* σύνταξις, συντακτικόν.

synthesis ['sinθəsis] *n* σύνθεσις.

synthetic [sin'θetik] *a* (*artificial*) συνθετικός ‖ ~**ally** *ad* συνθετικῶς.

syphilis ['sifilis] *n* σύφιλις.

syphon ['saifən] = **siphon**.

syringe [si'rindʒ] *n* σύριγγα.

syrup ['sirəp] *n* σιρόπι ‖ ~**y** *a* σιροπιώδης.

system ['sistəm] *n* σύστημα ‖ (*railway etc*) δίκτυον ‖ (*method*) σύστημα, μέθοδος ‖ ~**atic** *a* συστηματικός, μεθοδικός ‖ ~**atically** *ad* συστηματικῶς, μέ μέθοδον.

T, t

tab [tæb] *n* θηλίτσα, πάτ, αὐτί.

tabby ['tæbi] *n* (*cat*) γάτα ‖ *a* μουαρέ.

tabernacle ['tæbənækl] *n* (*in R.C. Church*) ἱεροφυλάκειον, ἀρτοφόριον.

table ['teibl] *n* τραπέζι ‖ (*list*) πίνακας.

tableau ['tæbləu] *n* (*representation*) ταμπλώ, δραματική σκηνή.

tablecloth ['teiblklɔθ] *n* τραπεζομάντηλο.

table d'hote ['ta:bl'dəut] *a* τάμπλ-ντότ.

table lamp ['teibllæmp] *n* πορτατίφ.

tablemat ['teiblmæt] *n* καρέ, σεμέν.

tablespoon ['teiblspu:n] *n* κουτάλι τῆς σούπας ‖ ~**ful** *n* κουταλιά τῆς σούπας.

T

tablet ['tæblit] n πλάκα, σημειωματάριον ‖ (*pellet*) δισκίον, ταμπλέττα, χάπι.

table tennis ['teibltenis] n πίγκ-πόγκ.

table wine ['teiblwain] n ἐπιτραπέζιο κρασί.

taboo [tə'bu:] n ταμπού ‖ a ἀπηγορευμένος, ταμπού.

tacit ['tæsit] a σιωπηρός, ὑπονοούμενος ‖ ~ly ad σιωπηρῶς ‖ ~urn a σιωπηλός, λιγόλογος.

tack [tæk] n πινέζα ‖ (*stitch*) μεγάλη βελονιά, τρύπωμα ‖ (*naut*) ἀναστροφή, διαδρομή ‖ (*course*) πορεία.

tackle ['tækl] n (*for lifting*) σύσπαστον, παλάγκο ‖ (*sport*) τάκελ ‖ vt ἀντιμετωπίζω, καταπιάνομαι μέ ‖ (*a player*) κάνω τάκελ.

tacky ['tæki] a κολλώδης.

tact [tækt] n τάκτ, λεπτότης ‖ ~ful a μέ τάκτ, λεπτότης ‖ ~fully ad μέ λεπτότητα, λεπτά.

tactical ['tæktikəl] a τακτικός.

tactics ['tæktiks] npl τακτική.

tactless ['tæktlis] a στερούμενος τάκτ, ἀδέξιος ‖ ~ly ad χωρίς τάκτ, ἀδιάκριτα.

tadpole ['tædpəul] n γυρίνος, γύρινος.

taffeta ['tæfitə] n ταφτάς.

tag [tæg] n (*label*) ἐτικέττα.

tail [teil] n οὐρά ‖ to ~ off vi (*in size, quality etc*) ἐλαττώνομαι, λεπτύνω ‖ ~end n ὀπίσθιον ἄκρον, οὐρά, τέλος.

tailor ['teilə*] n ράπτης ‖ ~ing n ραπτική ‖ ~-made a καμωμένο εἰδικῶς.

tailwind ['teilwind] n οὔριος ἄνεμος.

tainted ['teintid] a μολυσμένος, χαλασμένος.

take [teik] (*irreg v*) vt παίρνω, βγάζω ‖ (*seize*) πιάνω, παίρνω, καταλαμβάνω ‖ (*require*) ἀπαιτῶ, χρειάζομαι ‖ (*hire*) παίρνω, νοικιάζω ‖ (*understand*) δέχομαι, παραδέχομαι, συμπεραίνω ‖ (*choose*) διαλέγω ‖ (*phot*) φωτογραφίζω, φωτογραφίζομαι ‖ to ~ part in συμμετέχω ‖ to ~ place συμβαίνω ‖ to ~ after vt μοιάζω ‖ to ~ back vt (*return*) φέρνω πίσω, παίρνω πίσω ‖ to ~ down vt κατεβάζω, ξεκρεμῶ, κατεδαφίζω ‖ (*write*) σημειώνω, καταγράφω ‖ to ~ in vt (*deceive*) ἐξαπατῶ, ξεγελῶ ‖ (*understand*) καταλαβαίνω, ἀντιλαμβάνομαι ‖ (*include*) περιλαμβάνω ‖ to ~ off vi (*aeroplane*) ἀπογειοῦμαι, ξεκινῶ ‖ vt (*remove*) ἀφαιρῶ, βγάζω, παίρνω ‖ (*imitate*) μιμοῦμαι, παρωδῶ ‖ to ~ on vt (*undertake*) ἀναλαμβάνω ‖ (*engage*) μισθώνω, προσλαμβάνω ‖ (*accept as opponent*) δέχομαι τήν πρόσκλησιν ‖ to ~ out vt (*licence etc*) λαμβάνω, παίρνω ‖ (*stain*) βγάζω ‖ to ~ over vt ἀναλαμβάνω, διαδέχομαι ‖ to ~ to vt συμπαθῶ, ἐπιδίδομαι εἰς, μ' ἀρέσει νά ‖ to ~ up vt (*raise*) στήνω, σηκώνω, μαζεύω ‖ (*occupy*) καταλαμβάνω, πιάνω ‖ (*absorb*) ἀπορροφῶ, τραβῶ ‖ (*engage in*) ἀπασχολοῦμαι

εἰς ‖ ~off n (*aviat*) ἀπογείωσις ‖ (*imitation*) μίμησις ‖ ~over n (*comm*) ἀνάληψις ἐπιχειρήσεως, κτῆσις.

takings ['teikiŋz] npl (*comm*) εἰσπράξεις.

talc [tælk] n (*also* ~um powder) τάλκ.

tale [teil] n ἀφήγησις, παραμύθι, ἰστορία.

talent ['tælənt] n ταλέντο ‖ ~ed a μέ ταλέντο.

talk [tɔ:k] n συζήτησις, συνομιλία, κουβέντα ‖ (*rumour*) φλυαρία, διάδοσις ‖ (*speech*) λόγος, ὁμιλία ‖ to ~ shop συζητῶ γιά τήν ἐργασία μου ‖ to ~ over vt συζητῶ ‖ ~ative a φλύαρος ‖ ~er n ὁμιλητής, συζητητής, λογᾶς.

tall [tɔ:l] a ὑψηλός, ψηλός ‖ ~boy n (*furniture*) ψηλό κομμό, ψηλός καθρέπτης ‖ ~ness n ἀνάστημα, ὕψος ‖ ~ story n μπούρδα, ἀρλούμπα.

tally ['tæli] n (*account*) λογαριασμός, ὑπολογισμός.

tambourine [tæmbə'ri:n] n ντέφι.

tame [teim] a ἥμερος ‖ (*dull*) ἄτονος, πλαδαρός ‖ ~ness ν ἡμερότης.

tamper ['tæmpə*] to ~ with vt μαστορεύω, ἀνακατεύομαι μέ.

tan [tæn] n (*colour*) χρῶμα πίτυκα-καφέ, φαιοκίτρινον ‖ (*of sun*) μελαχροινόν χρῶμα, μαύρισμα ‖ a (*colour*) φαιοκίτρινος, καφέ.

tandem ['tændəm] n (ποδήλατο) τάντεμ.

tang [tæŋ] n ὀξεῖα γεῦσις, δυνατή ὀσμή.

tangent ['tændʒənt] n ἐφαπτομένη.

tangerine [tændʒə'ri:n] n μανταρίνι.

tangible ['tændʒəbl] a ἁπτός, ψηλαφητός ‖ (*real*) πραγματικός, αἰσθητός.

tangle ['tæŋgl] n μπέρδεμα, ἀνακάτωμα, περιπλοκή ‖ vti περιπλέκω, μπερδεύομαι.

tango ['tæŋgəu] n ταγκό.

tank [tæŋk] n δεξαμενή, ντεπόζιτο ‖ (*mil*) τάνκ, ἅρμα.

tankard ['tæŋkəd] n κύπελλον, μαστραπᾶς, κούπα.

tanker ['tæŋkə*] n (*ship*) δεξαμενόπλοιον, τάνκερ ‖ (*truck for carrying bulk liquids*) βυτιοφόρον.

tankful ['tæŋkful] n γεμᾶτο δοχεῖο.

tanned [tænd] a (*skin*) κατειργασμένος, ἀργασμένος.

tantalizing ['tæntəlaiziŋ] a προκλητικός, βασανιστικός.

tantrum ['tæntrəm] n ἔκρηξις ὀργῆς, ξέσπασμα, παραφορά.

tap [tæp] n κάνουλα, βρύση, στρόφιγξ ‖ (*gentle blow*) ἐλαφρόν κτύπημα ‖ vt (*strike*) κτυπῶ ἐλαφρά ‖ (*supply*) παίρνω, τροφοδοτῶ, ἀνοίγω.

tap-dance ['tæpdɑ:ns] vi χορεύω μέ κλακέτες.

tape [teip] ´n (*also* magnetic ~) ταινία, μαγνητοταινία ‖ vt (*to record*) μαγνητογραφῶ, ἠχογραφῶ ‖ ~ measure n μετρική ταινία.

taper ['teipə*] *n* λαμπάς, κερί ‖ *vi* λεπτύνομαι, μειοῦμαι, μπαίνω.

tape recorder ['teiprikɔ:də*] *n* μαγνητόφωνον.

tapered ['teipəd] *a*, **tapering** ['teipəriŋ] *a* κωνικός, μυτερός, μειουμένος.

tapestry ['tæpistri] *n* τάπης, ταπέτο, ταπετσαρία.

tappet ['tæpit] *n* ὠστήριον, πλῆκτρον.

taproom ['tæprum] *n* καπελιό.

tar [ta:*] *n* πίσσα.

tardy ['ta:di] *a* βραδύς, ἀργός.

target ['ta:git] *n* στόχος.

tariff ['tærif] *n* (*list of charges*) τιμολόγιον ‖ (*duty*) δασμός, δασμολόγιον.

tarmac ['ta:mæk] *n* (*aviat*) διάδρομος ἀπογειώσεως.

tarn [ta:n] *n* λιμνούλα (τῶν βουνῶν).

tarnish ['ta:niʃ] *vt* (*lit*) θαμπώνω, σκοτεινιάζω ‖ (*fig*) ἀμαυρῶ, κηλιδώνω.

tarpaulin [ta:'pɔ:lin] *n* κηρόπανον, μουσαμᾶς.

tarragon ['tærəgən] *n* τράχος, τραχούρι.

tart [ta:t] *n* (*pie*) τούρτα, τάρτα ‖ (*col: low woman*) τσούλα ‖ *a* ξυνός, ὀξύς, δριμύς.

tartan ['ta:tən] *n* σκωτσέζικο ὕφασμα.

tartar ['ta:tə*] *n* τρύξ, πουρί.

tartly ['ta:tli] *ad* δηκτικά, ἀπότομα.

task [ta:sk] *n* καθῆκον, ἔργον, δουλειά, ἀποστολή.

tassel ['tæsəl] *n* θύσανος, φούντα.

taste [teist] *n* γεῦσις, γοῦστο, προτίμησις ‖ *vti* γεύομαι, δοκιμάζω ‖ ~**ful** *a* κομψός, μέ γοῦστο, καλαίσθητος ‖ ~**fully** *ad* νόστιμα, κομψά, μέ γοῦστο ‖ ~**less** *a* ἄγευστος, ἄνοστος ‖ (*bad taste*) χωρίς γοῦστο, κακόγουστος ‖ ~**lessly** *ad* χωρίς γοῦστο.

tastily ['teistili] *ad* κομψά, μέ γοῦστο.

tastiness ['teistinis] *n* γευστικότης, νοστιμιά.

tasty ['teisti] *a* γευστικός, νόστιμος.

tata ['tæ'ta:] *excl* (*Brit col: goodbye*) γειά, ἀντίο, ὡρεβουάρ.

tattered ['tætəd] *a* κουρελιασμένος, κουρελής.

tatters ['tætəz] *npl*: **in** ~ κουρελιασμένος.

tattoo [tə'tu:] *n* (νυκτερινή) στρατιωτική ἐπίδειξις ‖ (*on skin*) δερματοστιξία, τατουάζ ‖ *vt* διαστίζω, τατουάρω.

tatty ['tæti] *a* (*col: cheap, of poor quality*) φτηνός, πρόστυχος.

taught [tɔ:t] *pt, pp of* **teach**.

taunt [tɔ:nt] *n* χλευασμός, λοιδορία, κοροϊδία ‖ *vt* χλευάζω, κοροϊδεύω.

taut [tɔ:t] *a* τεντωμένος, τεταμένος.

tavern ['tævən] *n* ταβέρνα.

tawdry ['tɔ:dri] *a* φανταχτερός, φτηνός, τιποτένιος.

tawny ['tɔ:ni] *a* φαιοκίτρινος.

tax [tæks] *n* φόρος ‖ *vt* φορολογῶ ‖ (*burden*) ἐξαντλῶ, θέτω ὑπό δοκιμασίαν ‖ ~**ation** *n* φορολογία ‖ ~ **collector** *n* εἰσπράκτωρ

φόρων ‖ ~-**free** *a* ἀτελής, ἀφορολόγητος.

taxi ['tæksi] *n* ταξί ‖ *vi* (*aviat*) τροχοδρομῶ.

taxidermist ['tæksidə:mist] *n* ταριχευτής, βαλσαμωτής.

taxi driver ['tæksidraivə*] *n* ὁδηγός ταξί, ταξιτζῆς.

taxi rank ['tæksiræŋk] *n*, **taxi stand** ['tæksistænd] *n* στάσις ταξί, πιάτσα.

taxpayer ['tækspeiə*] *n* φορολογούμενος.

tea [ti:] *n* τέϊον, τσάϊ ‖ (*drink*) τσάϊ ‖ (*meal*) ἀπογευματικό τσάϊ, γεῦμα μέ τσάϊ ‖ ~ **bag** *n* σακκουλάκι τσαγιοῦ ‖ ~ **break** *n* διάλειμμα γιά τσάϊ ‖ ~**cake** *n* (*small bun*) εἶδος κουλουράκι.

teach [ti:tʃ] (*irreg v*) *vti* διδάσκω, μαθαίνω ‖ ~**er** *n* διδάσκαλος, δασκάλα ‖ ~**ing** *n* διδασκαλία ‖ (*what is taught*) δίδαγμα, μάθημα.

tea cosy ['ti:kəuzi] *n* σκέπασμα τσαγιέρας.

teacup ['ti:kʌp] *n* φλυτζάνι τσαγιοῦ.

teak [ti:k] *n* τίκ, τέκ ‖ *a* ἀπό τίκ.

tea leaves ['ti:li:vz] *npl* φύλλα τσαγιοῦ.

team [ti:m] *n* ὁμάδα, συνεργεῖον ‖ (*of animals*) ζευγάρι ‖ ~ **spirit** *n* πνεῦμα συνεργασίας ‖ ~**work** *n* ὁμαδικό παίξιμο συνεργασία.

tea party ['ti:pa:ti] *n* δεξίωσις μέ τσάϊ.

teapot ['ti:pɔt] *n* τσαγιέρα.

tear [teə*] (*irreg v*) *n* σχίσιμο, σχισμή ‖ *vt* ἀνοίγω τρύπα ‖ (*pull apart*) σχίζω, σπαράσσω ‖ *vi* (*become torn*) σχίζομαι ‖ (*rush*) τρέχω, ὁρμῶ.

tear [tiə*] *n* δάκρυ ‖ **in** ~**s** δακρυσμένος, βουτηγμένος στά δάκρυα ‖ ~**ful** *a* δακρυσμένος, κλαμμένος ‖ ~**gas** *a* δακρυγόνον ἀέριον.

tearing ['teəriŋ] *a* (*hurry*) μέ ἐξωφρενική ταχύτητα.

tearoom ['ti:rum] *n* αἴθουσα τεΐου.

tease [ti:z] *n* πειραχτήριο, πείραγμα ‖ *vt* πειράζω, κοροϊδεύω.

tea set ['ti:set] *n* σερβίτσιο τσαγιοῦ.

teashop ['ti:ʃɔp] *n* τεϊοποτεῖον.

teaspoon ['ti:spu:n] *n* κουταλάκι τοῦ τσαγιοῦ ‖ ~**ful** *n* κουταλιά τοῦ τσαγιοῦ.

tea strainer ['ti:streinə*] *n* σουρωτήρι τοῦ τσαγιοῦ.

teat [ti:t] *n* θηλή, ρώγα.

teatime ['ti:taim] *n* ὥρα τοῦ τσαγιοῦ.

technical ['teknikəl] *a* τεχνικός ‖ ~**ity** *n* τεχνικός χαρακτήρ, τεχνική λεπτομέρεια ‖ ~**ly** *ad* τεχνικῶς.

technician [tek'niʃən] *n* τεχνίτης, τεχνικός, εἰδικός.

technique [tek'ni:k] *n* τεχνική, εἰδική μέθοδος.

technological [teknə'lɔdʒikəl] *a* τεχνολογικός.

technologist [tek'nɔlədʒist] *n* τεχνικός, τεχνολόγος.

technology [tek'nɔlədʒi] *n* τεχνολογία.

teddy (bear) ['tedi(beə*)] *n* ἀρκουδάκι (παιχνίδι).

tedious ['ti:diəs] *a* ἀνιαρός, βαρετός ‖ **~ly** *ad* ἀνιαρά, πληκτικά, βαρετά.

tedium ['ti:diəm] *n* ἀνιαρότης, μονοτονία, ἀνία.

tee [ti:] *n* ὑψωματάκι, σωρός (ἄμμου).

teem [ti:m] *vi* βρίθω, ἀφθονῶ ‖ (*pour*) πέφτω καταρρακτωδῶς.

teenage ['ti:neidʒ] *a* ἐφηβικός, μεταξύ 13 καί 20 ‖ **~r** *n* ἔφηβος.

teens [ti:nz] *npl* ἡλικία μεταξύ 13 καί 20 ἐτῶν.

teeth [ti:θ] *npl of* tooth.

teethe [ti:ð] *vi* βγάζω δόντια.

teething ring ['ti:ðiŋriŋ] *n* ροδέλα μωροῦ (διά ὀδοντοφυῖαν).

teetotal ['ti:'təutl] *a* ἀντιαλκοολικός ‖ **~ler**, (*US*) **~er** *n* ἀπέχων ἀπό οἰνοπνευματώδη ποτά.

telecommunication ['telikəmju:ni'keiʃən] *n* τηλεπικοινωνία.

telegram ['teligræm] *n* τηλεγράφημα.

telegraph ['teligra:f] *n* τηλέγραφος ‖ **~ic** *a* (*address*) τηλεγραφικῆ (διεύθυνσις) ‖ **~ pole** *n* τηλεγραφικός στύλος.

telepathic [teli'pæθik] *a* τηλεπαθητικός.

telepathy [ti'lepəθi] *n* τηλεπάθεια.

telephone ['telifəun] *n* τηλέφωνον ‖ *vt* τηλεφωνῶ ‖ **~ booth**, **~ box** *n* τηλεφωνικός θάλαμος ‖ **~ call** *n* τηλεφώνημα, κλῆσις ‖ **~ directory** *n* τηλεφωνικός κατάλογος ‖ **~ exchange** *n* κέντρον ‖ **~ number** *n* ἀριθμός τηλεφώνου.

telephonist [ti'lefənist] *n* τηλεφωνήτρια.

telephoto ['teli'fəutəu] *a:* **~ lens** τηλεφακός.

teleprinter ['teliprintə*] *n* τηλέτυπον.

telescope ['teliskəup] *n* τηλεσκόπιον ‖ *vt* (*compress*) συμπτύσσω.

telescopic [telis'kɔpik] *a* τηλεσκοπικός.

televiewer ['telivju:ə*] *n* θεατής τηλεοράσεως.

televise ['telivaiz] *vt* μεταβιβάζω διά τῆς τηλεοράσεως.

television ['teliviʒən] *n* τηλεόρασις ‖ **~ set** *n* δέκτης τηλεοράσεως.

tell [tel] (*irreg v*) *vt* λέγω, λέω ‖ (*make known*) ἀφηγοῦμαι, γνωστοποιῶ ‖ (*order*) διατάσσω, παραγγέλλω, λέω σέ ‖ (*person of sth*) λέω κάτι, ἀνακοινώνω ‖ *vi* (*have effect*) ἀποφέρω, συνεπάγομαι, ἔχω ‖ **to ~ on** *vi* (*inform against*) καταδίδω, προδίδω ‖ **to ~ off** *vi* μαλώνω, κατσαδιάζω, περιλούζω ‖ **~er** *n* (*in bank*) ταμίας ‖ **~ing** *a* ἀποτελεσματικός ‖ **~tale** *a* μαρτυριάρης, κουτσομπόλης.

telly ['teli] *n* (*col*) τηλεόρασις.

temerity [ti'meriti] *n* θάρρος, τόλμη.

temper ['tempə*] *n* (*disposition*) διάθεσις, τεμπεραμέντο ‖ (*burst of anger*) ὀργή, θυμός ‖ *vt* (*moderate*) ἀπαλύνω, μαλακώνω, συγκρατῶ ‖ **~ament** *n* διάθε-

σις, ἰδιοσυγκρασία, τεμπεραμέντο ‖ **~amental** *a* (*moody*) ἰδιότροπος, γεμᾶτος βίδες.

temperance ['tempərəns] *n* (*in drinking*) ἀποφυγή οἰνοπνευματωδῶν ποτῶν ‖ (*moderation*) ἐγκράτεια, μετριοπάθεια ‖ **~ hotel** *n* ξενοδοχεῖον ὅπου ἀπαγορεύεται πώλησις τῶν οἰνοπνευματωδῶν ποτῶν.

temperate ['tempərit] *a* μετριοπαθής, εὔκρατος.

temperature ['tempritʃə*] *n* θερμοκρασία.

tempered ['tempəd] *a* (*steel*) ἐσκληρυμένος, βαμμένος.

tempest ['tempist] *n* θύελλα, τρικυμία, φουρτούνα ‖ **~uous** *a* φουρτουνιασμένος.

template ['templit] *n* πρότυπον, ἰχνάριον, φόρμα.

temple ['templ] *n* (*building*) ναός ‖ (*anat*) κρόταφος, μηλίγγι.

tempo ['tempəu] *n* ρυθμός, τέμπο ‖ (*of movement*) ρυθμός, μέτρον.

temporal ['tempərəl] *a* (*of time*) χρονικός, τοῦ χρόνου ‖ (*worldly*) ἐγκόσμιος, κοσμικός.

temporarily ['tempərərili] *ad* προσωρινῶς, γιά λίγο.

temporary ['tempərəri] *a* προσωρινός, πρόσκαιρος.

tempt [tempt] *vt* (*persuade*) παροτρύνω, προτρέπω ‖ (*attract*) δελεάζω ‖ **~ation** *n* πειρασμός, δελεασμός ‖ **~ing** *a* δελεαστικός.

ten [ten] *num* δέκα.

tenable ['tenəbl] *a* ὑπερασπίσιμος, ὑποστηρίξιμος, λογικός.

tenacious [ti'neiʃəs] *a* ἐμμένων, ἐπιμένων ‖ **~ly** *ad* ἐμμένω, μέ ἐπιμονήν.

tenacity [ti'næsiti] *n* ἐμμονή, ἐπιμονή.

tenancy ['tenənsi] *n* ἐνοικίασις, μίσθωσις.

tenant ['tenənt] *n* ἐνοικιαστής, μισθωτής, νοικάτορας.

tend [tend] *vt* (*look after*) περιποιοῦμαι ‖ *vi* τείνω, ρέπω, κλίνω ‖ **~ency** *n* τάσις, κλίσις, ροπή.

tender ['tendə*] *a* τρυφερός, μαλακός ‖ (*delicate*) λεπτός, εὐπαθής, τρυφερός ‖ (*loving*) στοργικός, εὐαίσθητος, πονετικός ‖ *n* (*comm: offer*) προσφορά ‖ **~ly** *ad* ἀπαλά, τρυφερά, μέ στοργή ‖ **~ness** *n* τρυφερότης, λεπτότης, στοργικότης.

tendon ['tendən] *n* τένων.

tenement ['tenimənt] *n* λαϊκή πολυκατοικία.

tenet ['tenət] *n* ἀρχή, ἀξίωμα, γνώμη.

tennis ['tenis] *n* τέννις, ἀντισφαίρισις ‖ **~ ball** *n* μπάλλα τοῦ τέννις ‖ **~ court** *n* γήπεδον τοῦ τέννις ‖ **~ racket** *n* ρακέτα τοῦ τέννις.

tenor ['tenə*] *n* (*male voice*) ὀξύφωνος, τενόρος ‖ (*singer*) τενόρος ‖ (*general meaning*) νόημα, ἔννοια, σημασία.

tense [tens] *a* (*fig*) είς ὑπερέντασιν, τεταμένος ‖ (*taut*) τεντωμένος ‖ *n* χρόνος ‖ ~ly *ad* τεταμένως, τέζα, είς ὑπερέντασιν ‖ ~ness *n* ἔντασις, τεταμένη κατάστασις.

tension ['tenʃən] *n* ἔντασις ‖ (*stretching*) τάσις, τέντωμα, τεζάρισμα.

tent [tent] *n* σκηνή, τέντα.

tentacle ['tentəkl] *n* κεραία, πλόκαμος.

tentative ['tentətiv] *a* δοκιμαστικός, προσωρινός ‖ ~ly *ad* πειραματικώς, δοκιμαστικῶς.

tenterhooks ['tentəhuks] *npl*: on ~ ἀνήσυχος, ἀνυπομονῶν.

tenth [tenθ] *a* δέκατος, δέκατον.

tent peg ['tentpeg] *n* πάσσαλος σκηνής.

tent pole ['tentpəul] *n* ὀρθοστάτης σκηνής.

tenuous ['tenjuəs] *a* λεπτός, ἀραιός, ἐλαφρός.

tenure ['tenjuə*] *n* κατοχή, κτῆσις.

tepid ['tepid] *a* χλιαρός.

term [tə:m] *n* τέρμα, ὅριον, τέλος ‖ (*fixed time*) περίοδος, διάρκεια, χρόνος ‖ (*word*) ὅρος, ἔκφρασις, λέξις ‖ *vt* ὀνομάζω, καλῶ ‖ ~s *npl* ὅροι, διατάξεις ‖ (*relationship*) σχέσεις ‖ ~inal *a* τελικός, ἄκρος, τριμηνιαῖος ‖ *n* (*elec*) ἀκροδέκτης, πόλος ‖ (*for oil, ore etc*) ἀκραῖος σταθμός ‖ ~inate *vi* (+*in*) (κατα)λήγω, τελειώνω, τερματίζομαι ‖ ~ination *n* τερματισμός, περάτωσις, κατάληξις ‖ ~inology *n* ὁρολογία ‖ ~inus *n* ἀκραῖος σταθμός, τέρμα.

termite ['tə:mait] *n* τερμίτης.

terrace ['terəs] *n* σειρά οίκιῶν ‖ (*in garden etc*) ἐπιπέδωμα, ταράτσα ‖ ~d *a* (*garden*) είς βαθμίδας, κλιμακωτός ‖ (*house*) ὁμοίου ρυθμοῦ.

terracotta ['terə'kɔtə] *n* ὀπτή γῆ, τερρακότα.

terrain [te'rain] *n* ἔδαφος, πεδίον, ἔκτασις.

terrible ['terəbl] *a* (*causing fear*) τρομερός, τρομακτικός, φοβερός ‖ (*inferior*) φοβερός, κατώτερος ‖ (*very great*) ἀπερίγραπτος, ὑπερβολικός.

terribly ['terəbli] *ad* τρομερά, φρικτά, τρομακτικά.

terrier ['teriə*] *n* τερριέ.

terrific [tə'rifik] *a* τρομερός, πελώριος ‖ ~ally *ad* τρομακτικά, τρομερά.

terrify ['terifai] *vt* τρομάζω, τρομοκρατῶ ‖ ~ing *a* τρομακτικός, τρομερός.

territorial [teri'tɔ:riəl] *a* ἐδαφικός, τοπικός, κτηματικός ‖ ~ waters *npl* χωρικά ὕδατα.

territory ['teritəri] *n* γῆ, χώρα, περιοχή, ἔδαφος.

terror ['terə*] *n* τρόμος, φρίκη, φόβος, τρομάρα ‖ ~ism *n* τρομοκρατία ‖ ~ist *n* τρομοκράτης ‖ ~ize *vt* τρομοκρατῶ.

terse [tə:s] *a* σύντομος, βραχύς, περιληπτικός.

Terylene ['terəli:n] *n* ® τερυλήνη.

test [test] *n* δοκιμή, δοκιμασία, ἐξέτασις, ἀνάλυσις ‖ *vt* δοκιμάζω, ἐξετάζω.

testament ['testəmənt] *n* διαθήκη.

test flight ['testflait] *n* δοκιμαστική πτῆσις.

testicle ['testikl] *n* ὄρχις, ἀρχίδι.

testify ['testifai] *vi* καταθέτω (ἐνόρκως).

testimonial [testi'məuniəl] *n* πιστοποιητικόν, βεβαίωσις ‖ (*gift*) δῶρον εὐγνωμοσύνης.

testimony ['testiməni] *n* μαρτυρία, κατάθεσις, ἀπόδειξις.

test match ['testmætʃ] *n* (*cricket, rugby*) μεγάλη διεθνής συνάντησις.

test paper ['testpeipə*] *n* (*in exam*) ἐρωτήσεις, δοκιμαστική ἐξέτασις.

test pilot ['testpailət] *n* πιλότος δοκιμῶν.

test tube ['testtju:b] *n* δοκιμαστικός σωλήν.

testy ['testi] *a* (*short-tempered*) εὐέξαπτος, δύστροπος.

tetanus ['tetənəs] *n* τέτανος.

tether ['teðə*] *vt* δένω.

text [tekst] *n* κείμενον ‖ ~book *n* ἐγχειρίδιον, διδακτικόν βιβλίον.

textile ['tekstail] *n* ὕφασμα, ὕφασμα ‖ ~s *npl* ὑφαντά, ὑφάσματα.

texture ['tekstʃə*] *n* (*of surface*) ὑφή.

than [ðæn] *prep,cj* ἤ, παρά, ἀπό.

thank [θæŋk] *vt* εὐχαριστῶ ‖ ~ful *a* εὐγνώμων ‖ ~fully *ad* μέ εὐγνωμοσύνην, εὐγνωμόνως ‖ ~less *a* ἀγνώμων, ἀχάριστος, ἄχαρις ‖ ~s *excl* εὐχαριστῶ ‖ (*gratitude*) εὐγνωμοσύνη, εὐχαριστίαι ‖ T~sgiving *n* (*US: festival*) Ἡμέρα τῶν Εὐχαριστιῶν.

that [ðæt] *a* αὐτός, ἐκεῖνος ‖ *pron* ἐκεῖνος, ὁ ὁποῖος, πού ‖ *cj* ὅτι, ὥστε, διότι, νά ‖ *ad* τόσον, ἔτσι.

thatched [θætʃt] *a* (*cottage*) ἀχυροστρωμένος.

thaw [θɔ:] *n* τῆξις, λυώσιμο ‖ *vi* τήκομαι, λυώνω.

the [ði:, ðə] *definite article* ὁ, ἡ, τό, οἱ, αἱ, τά.

theater (*US*), **theatre** ['θiətə*] *n* θέατρον ‖ (*cinema*) σινεμά ‖ (*drama*) θεατρική τέχνη, δραματική τέχνη ‖ (*med*) ἀμφιθέατρον ‖ ~goer *n* θεατρόφιλος.

theatrical [θi'ætrikəl] *a* θεατρικός, θεαματικός ‖ (*showy*) θεατρινίστικος, προσποιητός.

theft [θeft] *n* κλοπή, κλεψιά.

their [ðeə*] *poss a* δικός τους, δική τους ‖ ~s *poss pron* ἰδικός τους, δικοί τους.

them [ðem, ðəm] *pron* αὐτούς, αὐτές, αὐτά.

theme [θi:m] *n* θέμα, ὑπόθεσις ‖ (*melody*) θέμα, μοτίβο ‖ ~ song *n* (*of film etc*) κυρία μελωδία.

themselves [ðəm'selvz] *pl pron* τούς ἑαυτούς των ‖ αὐτοί οἱ ἴδιοι.

then [ðen] *ad* τότε, ἐκείνην τήν στιγμήν ‖ (*next*) κατόπιν, ἔπειτα, ἀκολούθως ‖ *cj* λοιπόν, τότε, στήν περίπτωσιν αὐτήν ‖ ἐπί πλέον ‖ ἀπ' ἐκείνη ἡ ἐποχή, ἐκεῖ.

theologian [θiə'ləudʒiən] *n* θεολόγος.

theological [θiə'lɔdʒikəl] *a* θεολογικός.

theology [θɪ'ɔlədʒi] n θεολογία.

theorem ['θɪərəm] n θεώρημα.

theoretical [θɪə'retikəl] a θεωρητικός ‖ ~**ly** ad θεωρητικῶς.

theorize ['θɪəraiz] vi κάνω θεωρίες.

theory ['θɪəri] n θεωρία ‖ (idea) ἰδέα.

therapeutic(al) [θerə'pju:tik(əl)] a θεραπευτικός.

therapist ['θerəpist] n θεραπευτής.

therapy ['θerəpi] n θεραπεία.

there [δɛə*] ad ἐκεῖ, νά, ἔλα ‖ n ἐκεῖνος ἐκεῖ ‖ (interj) ἰδού, νά ‖ (never mind) ἔλα, ἔλα ‖ ~ **is** ὑπάρχει ‖ ~ **are** ὑπάρχουν ‖ ~**abouts** ad ἐκεῖ κοντά, περίπου ‖ ~**after** ad μετά ταῦτα, κατόπιν ‖ ~**fore** ad γι'αὐτό τό λόγο, ἐπομένως ‖ ~'**s** = there is ‖ see above.

thermal ['θɜ:məl] a θερμικός.

thermodynamics ['θɜ:məudai'næmiks] n θερμοδυναμική.

thermonuclear ['θɜ:məu'nju:kliə*] a θερμοπυρηνικός.

Thermos ['θɜ:məs] n ℝ (flask) θέρμο(ς).

thermostat ['θɜ:məstæt] n θερμοστάτης.

thesaurus [θɪ'sɔ:rəs] n θησαυρός, συλλογή λέξεων.

these [δi:z] pl pron αὐτοί, αὐτές, αὐτά.

thesis ['θi:sis] n θέμα, θέσις ‖ (univ) διατριβή.

they [δei] pl pron αὐτοί, αὐτές, αὐτά ‖ ~'**d** = they had, they would, see have, would ‖ ~'**ll** = they shall, they will, see shall, will ‖ ~'**re** = they are, see be ‖ ~'**ve** = they have, see have.

thick [θik] a χονδρός, παχύς, πυκνός, πηχτός ‖ (person: slow, stupid) κουτός, χονδροκέφαλος ‖ n: **in the** ~ **of** στῆ φούρια, στό δξύτερο σημεῖον ‖ ~**en** vi (fog) πυκνώνω, γίνομαι πυκνότερον ‖ vt (sauce etc) πήζω, πηχτώνω, δένω ‖ ~**ness** n (of object) πάχος, πυκνότης ‖ (of voice) βραχνάδα ‖ ~**set** a κοντόχοντρος ‖ ~**skinned** a παχύδερμος, χοντρόπετσος.

thief [θi:f] n κλέφτης, λωποδύτης.

thieves [θi:vz] npl of thief.

thieving ['θi:viŋ] n κλοπή, κλεψιά.

thigh [θai] n μηρός, μπούτι ‖ ~**bone** n μηριαῖον ὀστοῦν.

thimble ['θimbl] n δακτυλήθρα.

thin [θin] a λεπτός, ψηλός, ἀδύνατος ‖ (not abundant) ἀραιός, διεσπαρμένος ‖ (person) ἰσχνός, λιγνός, ἀδύνατος ‖ (crowd) ἀραιός, λιγοστός.

thing [θiŋ] n πράγμα, ἀντικείμενον.

think [θiŋk] (irreg v) vi σκέπτομαι ‖ (believe) νομίζω ‖ (have in mind) σκοπεύω ‖ **to** ~ **over** vt σκέπτομαι, συλλογίζομαι ‖ **to** ~ **up** vt σκέπτομαι, καταστρώνω.

thinly ['θinli] ad (disguised) μόλις.

thinness ['θinnis] n λεπτότης, ἀδυναμία, ἀραιότης, ρευστότης.

third [θɜ:d] a τρίτος ‖ n τρίτος, τρίτον ‖ ~**ly** ad κατά τρίτον λόγον, τρίτον ‖

~**party insurance** n ἀσφάλισις τρίτων ‖ ~**rate** a τρίτης τάξεως, κακῆς ποιότητος.

thirst [θɜ:st] n δίψα ‖ (strong desire) δυνατή ἐπιθυμία, πόθος ‖ ~**y** a διψασμένος.

thirteen ['θɜ:'ti:n] num δεκατρία.

thirty ['θɜ:ti] num τριάντα.

this [δis] pron.a αὐτός, αὐτή, αὐτό ‖ τόσος.

thistle ['θisl] n γαϊδουράγκαθο.

thorn [θɔ:n] n ἀγκάθι ‖ (plant) ἀκανθώδης θάμνος, ἀγκάθι ‖ ~**y** a ἀγκαθωτός ‖ (problem) ἀκανθώδης.

thorough ['θʌrə] a πλήρης, τέλειος ‖ (accurate) λεπτομερής, ἐξονυχιστικός ‖ ~**bred** n καθαράαιμος, ἀπό ράτσα ‖ a καθαρόαιμος ‖ ~**fare** n ὁδός, διάβασις, ἀρτηρία ‖ (main street) κεντρικός λεωφόρος, ἀρτηριακός ‖ ~**ly** ad τελείως, πλήρως, κατά βάθος ‖ ~**ness** n ἐπιμέλεια, τελειότης.

those [δəuz] pl pron αὐτές, αὐτοί, αὐτά ‖ a τοῦτοι, ἐκεῖνοι.

though [δəu] cj καίτοι, ἄν καί, μολονότι, ἀγκαλά καί ‖ ad παρά ταῦτα, μολοντοῦτο, κι'ὅμως.

thought [θɔ:t] n ἰδέα, σκέψις ‖ (thinking) σκέψις, συλλογισμός ‖ pt, pp of think ‖ ~**ful** a σοβαρός, σκεπτικός ‖ (also kind) διακριτικός, εὐγενικός ‖ ~**less** a ἀπερίσκεπτος, ἀπρόσεκτος, ἀδιάκριτος.

thousand ['θauzənd] num χίλιοι, χίλια ‖ ~**th** a χιλιοστόν.

thrash [θræʃ] vt (lit) κτυπῶ, δέρνω, ξυλοφορτώνω ‖ (fig) νικῶ.

thread [θred] n (of cotton, silk etc) νῆμα, κλωστή ‖ (of screw) σπείρωμα, βῆμα, πάσο ‖ (of story) συνέχεια, εἱρμός ‖ vt (needle) βάζω κλωστή σέ, περνῶ ‖ vt (pick one's way) περνῶ μέ δυσκολία ‖ ~**bare** a ξεφτισμένος, παλιός.

threat [θret] n φοβέρα, φοβέρισμα ‖ (sign of danger) ἀπειλή ‖ ~**en** vti (person) ἀπειλῶ, φοβερίζω ‖ (storm) ἀπειλεῖται ‖ ~**ening** a ἀπειλητικός.

three [θri:] num τρεῖς, τρία ‖ ~**-dimensional** a τρισδιάστατος ‖ ~**fold** a τριπλός, τρίδιπλος ‖ ~**-piece suit** n (clothes) τρουάπιές ‖ ~**-ply** a (wool) τρίκλωνος ‖ ~**-wheeler** n (car) τρίτροχον (αὐτοκίνητον).

thresh [θreʃ] vt ἁλωνίζω ‖ ~**ing machine** n ἁλωνιστική μηχανή.

threshold ['θreʃhəuld] n (beginning) κατώφλι, ἀρχή ‖ (doorway) κατώφλι.

threw [θru:] pt of throw.

thrift [θrift] n (economy) οἰκονομία, ἀποταμίευσις ‖ ~**y** a οἰκονόμος, μετρημένος.

thrill [θril] n ρίγος, ἀνατριχίλα, σύγκρυο, τρεμούλα ‖ vt προκαλῶ ρῖγος εἰς, συγκινῶ, ἠλεκτρίζω ‖ vi φρικιῶ, ριγῶ, τρέμω, ἀγωνιῶ ‖ ~**er** n μυθιστόρημα

αγωνίας ‖ ~ing a συναρπαστικός, συγκλονιστικός, συγκινητικός.
thrive [θraiv] vi (+on) εὐδοκιμῶ, εὐημερῶ, ἀναπτύσσομαι.
thriving ['θraiviŋ] a ἀκμαῖος, ρωμαλέος, ἀκμάζων, ἐπιτυχής.
throat [θrəut] n λαιμός ‖ (internal passages) φάρυγξ, λάρυγξ, λαρύγγι.
throb [θrɔb] n κτύπημα, παλμός, δόνησις ‖ vi κτυπῶ, πάλλομαι.
throes [θrəuz] npl: in the ~ of ἀγωνιζόμενος μέ, παλαίων μέ.
thrombosis [θrɔm'bəusis] n θρόμβωσις.
throne [θrəun] n θρόνος.
throttle ['θrɔtl] n ρυθμιστική βαλβίς μηχανῆς, δικλείδα ‖ vt (choke) στραγγαλίζω.
through [θru:] prep διά μέσου, καθ'ὅλην τήν διάρκειαν τοῦ ‖ (because of) λόγω τοῦ, ἐξ αἰτίας τοῦ ‖ ad ἐξ ὁλοκλήρου, κατ'εὐθεῖαν, ἀπό τήν ἀρχήν μέχρι τό τέλος ‖ a (without a stop) κατ'εὐθεῖαν ‖ (end to end) πέρα γιά πέρα ‖ (ticket) ὁλοκλήρου διαδρομῆς (εἰσιτήριον) ‖ (finished) τελειωμένος ‖ ~out prep εἰς ὁλόκληρον, εἰς ὅλον, παντοῦ εἰς ‖ ad παντοῦ, ὁλόκληρα.
throw [θrəu] (irreg v) n ρῖξις, ρίξιμο, πέταγμα, βολή ‖ vt ρίπτω, πετῶ ‖ to ~ out vt (lit) ρίπτω, ρίχνω, πετῶ ἔξω ‖ (reject) ἀπορρίπτω, ἀποκρούω ‖ to ~ up vi (vomit) ἐξεμῶ, ξερνῶ, κάνω ἐμετό ‖ ~-in n (sport) ἐπανάληψις τοῦ παιγνιδιοῦ.
thru [θru:] (US) = through.
thrush [θrʌʃ] n κίχλη, τσίχλα.
thrust [θrʌst] (irreg v) n (tech) ὤθησις, ὦσις ‖ vti σπρώχνω, μπήγω ‖ (push one's way) διαπερνῶ, διασχίζω, περνῶ.
thud [θʌd] n γδοῦπος.
thug [θʌg] n γκάγκστερ, μπράβος.
thumb [θʌm] n ἀντίχειρ ‖ vt φυλλομετρῶ (βιβλίον), χειρίζομαι ἀδεξίως ‖ to ~ a lift κάνω ὦτο-στόπ ‖ ~ index n (on book) εὑρετήριον ‖ ~nail n νύχι τοῦ ἀντίχειρος ‖ ~tack n (US) πινέζα.
thump [θʌmp] n βαρύ κτύπημα, γροθιά ‖ vti κτυπῶ δυνατά, γρονθοκοπῶ.
thunder ['θʌndə*] n βροντή ‖ vi βροντῶ, βροντοφωνῶ ‖ ~ous a βροντώδης, θυελλώδης ‖ ~storm n καταιγίδα, θύελλα ‖ ~struck a ἐμβρόντητος, κατάπληκτος ‖ ~y a (weather, sky) θυελλώδης.
Thursday ['θə:zdi] n Πέμπτη.
thus [θʌs] ad οὕτω, τοιουτοτρόπως, ἔτσι ‖ (therefore) ἔτσι, λοιπόν.
thwart [θwɔ:t] vt ματαιώνω, ἀνατρέπω, ἐμποδίζω.
thyme [taim] n θυμάρι.
thyroid ['θairɔid] n θυρεοειδής (ἀδήν).
tiara [ti'a:rə] n διάδημα, τιάρα.
tic [tik] n (nervous) τίκ, σπάσμα, σπασμός.
tick [tik] n τίκ (ὡρολογιοῦ), λεπτόν ‖ (small

mark) σημεῖον ἐλέγχου, τσεκάρισμα ‖ vi κτυπῶ, κάνω τίκ ‖ vt σημειώνω, τσεκάρω.
ticket ['tikit] n (for travel etc) εἰσιτήριον, δελτίον ‖ (label) σημείωσις, ἐτικέττα ‖ ~ collector n ἐλεγκτής, εἰσπράκτωρ ‖ ~ holder n κάτοχος εἰσιτηρίου ‖ ~ office n γραφεῖον ἐκδόσεως εἰσιτηρίων.
ticking-off ['tikiŋ'ɔf] n (col) ἐπίπληξις κατσάδα.
tickle ['tikl] n γαργάλισμα ‖ vt γαργαλίζω γαργαλῶ ‖ (amuse) διασκεδάζω.
ticklish ['tikliʃ] a πού γαργαλιέται εὔκολα ‖ (difficult) λεπτός, δύσκολος.
tidal ['taidl] a παλιρροιακός.
tidbit ['tidbit] n (US) μεζές.
tide [taid] n παλίρροια, ρεῦμα ‖ (season) ἐποχή.
tidily ['taidili] ad μέ τάξιν, καθαρά, τακτικά.
tidiness ['taidinis] n τάξις, εὐπρέπεια.
tidy ['taidi] a συγυρισμένος, τακτοποιημένος, σιαγμένος ‖ vt τακτοποιῶ, σιάζω συγυρίζω.
tie [tai] n λαιμοδέτης, γραβάτα ‖ (connection) δεσμός, δέσιμο ‖ (sport) ἰσοπαλία ‖ vt προσδένω, δένω ‖ (into knot) δένω, κάνω κόμπο ‖ vi ἔρχομαι ἰσόπαλος, ἰσοψηφῶ ‖ to ~ down vt (lit) προσδένω, δένω καλά ‖ (fig) δεσμεύω ‖ to ~ up vt (dog) προσδένω, δένω ‖ (boat) δένω.
tier [tiə*] n στοῖχος, σειρά.
tiff [tif] n μικροτσακωμός, καυγαδάκι.
tiger ['taigə*] n τίγρις.
tight [tait] a σφικτός, στερεός ‖ (stretched) τεντωμένος, τεζαρισμένος ‖ (close) στεγανός, ἑρμητικός ‖ (col) πιωμένος, σκνίπα ‖ (miserly) τσιγγούνης ‖ ~s npl ἐφαρμοστή κυλότα, μαγιό ‖ ~en vti σφίγγω, σφίγγομαι, τεζάρω ‖ ~-fisted a σφιχτοχερής, σπαγγοραμμένος ‖ ~ly ad σφιχτοκλεισμένα, σφιχτά, γερά ‖ ~ness n στεγανότης, τέντωμα, στενότης ‖ ~rope n τεντωμένο σχοινί.
tile [tail] n (in roof) κεραμίδι ‖ (on wall or floor) πλακάκι ‖ ~d a (roof) μέ κεραμίδια.
till [til] n συρτάρι ταμείου ‖ vt καλλιεργῶ ‖ prep ἕως, ὥς, μέχρι ‖ cj ἕως ὅτου, ὥς πού.
tilt [tilt] vti γέρνω, κλίνω.
timber ['timbə*] n ξυλεία ‖ (trees) δάσος, ὑψηλά δένδρα.
time [taim] n χρόνος ‖ (period) καιρός ‖ (hour) ὥρα ‖ (point in time) στιγμή, ὀλίγος, φορά ‖ (occasion) καιρός, ἐποχή ‖ (rhythm, speed) χρόνος, ρυθμός ‖ vt ρυθμίζω, χρονομετρῶ ‖ in ~ ἐγκαίρως, ἐν καιρῷ ‖ (mus) ρυθμός, χρόνος ‖ on ~ στήν ὥρα ‖ five ~s πέντε φορές ‖ local ~ τοπική ὥρα ‖ what ~ is it? τί ὥρα εἶναι; ‖ ~keeper n (sport) χρονομετρητής ‖ ~-lag n (in travel) διαφορά ὥρας ‖ ~less a (beauty) αἰώνιος, ἄφθαρτος ‖ ~ limit n

χρονικόν ὅριον, προθεσμία ‖ ~ly a ἔγκαιρος, ἐπίκαιρος ‖ ~-saving a πού γλυτώνει χρόνον ‖ ~ switch n χρονοδιακόπτης ‖ ~table n δρομολόγιον, ὡρολόγιον πρόγραμμα ‖ ~ zone n ἄτρακτος χρόνου, ὡριαία ζώνη.

timid ['timid] a δειλός, φοβιτσιάρης ‖ ~ity n δειλία, ντροπαλότης ‖ ~ly ad δειλά, ντροπαλά.

timing ['taimiŋ] n ῥύθμισις, χρονισμός, χρονομέτρησις.

timpani ['timpəni] npl τύμπανα.

tin [tin] n κασσίτερος, καλάϊ ‖ (container) τενεκές, κουτί κονσέρβας ‖ ~foil n ἀσημόχαρτο, ἀλουμινόχαρτο, χρυσόχαρτο.

tinge [tindʒ] n χροιά, ἀπόχρωσις, δόσις ‖ vt χρωματίζω, βάφω.

tingle ['tiŋgl] n τσούξιμο, ἔξαψις, διέγερσις ‖ vi τσούζω, διεγείρομαι, τσιμπῶ.

tinker ['tiŋkə*] n γανωματᾶς ‖ to ~ with vt σκαλίζω, φτιάχνω ἀδέξια.

tinkle ['tiŋkl] n κουδούνισμα ‖ (col: phone call) τηλεφώνημα ‖ vi κουδουνίζω, ἠχῶ.

tinned [tind] a (food) κονσέρβα, τοῦ κουτιοῦ.

tin opener ['tinəupnə*] n ἀνοιχτήρι.

tinsel ['tinsəl] n γυαλιστερές κορδέλλες μετάλλου, ἀσημένια βροχή.

tint [tint] n χροιά, ἀπόχρωσις.

tiny ['taini] a μικροσκοπικός, μικρούτσικο.

tip [tip] n ἄκρη, ἄκρον, μύτη ‖ (for protection) σιδηρά ἄκρα, σίδερο, πετσάκι ‖ (of money) φιλοδώρημα, πουρμπουάρ ‖ (useful hint) ὑπαινιγμός, μυστική πληροφορία ‖ vt (put end on) προσθέτω ἄκρην εἰς ‖ γέρνω, ἀναποδογυρίζω ‖ (waiter) φιλοδωρῶ, δίνω πουρμπουάρ ‖ ~-off n (hint) πληροφορία, ὑπαινιγμός ‖ ~ped a (cigarette) μέ φίλτρο.

tipple ['tipl] n (drink) ποτόν.

tipsy ['tipsi] a μεθυσμένος, πιωμένος.

tiptoe ['tiptəu] n: on ~ ἀκροποδητί, στά νύχια.

tiptop ['tip'tɔp] a: in ~ condition σέ καλή φόρμα, πρώτης τάξεως.

tire ['taiə*] n (US) = tyre ‖ vti κουράζω, ἐξαντλῶ, κουράζομαι, βαριέμαι ‖ ~d a κουρασμένος, μπουχτισμένος, ἐξηντλημένος ‖ ~d of βαριέμαι, βαρέθηκα ἀπό ‖ ~dness n κόπωσις, κούρασι ‖ ~less a ἀκούραστος, ἀκαταπόνητος ‖ ~lessly ad ἀκαταπόνητα, δραστήρια ‖ ~some a κουραστικός, βαρετός, ἐνοχλητικός.

tiring ['taiəriŋ] a κουραστικός, πληκτικός, ἀνιαρός.

tissue ['tiʃu:] n (biol) ἱστός, ὑφή ‖ (collection) σύμπλεγμα, δίκτυον ‖ (paper handkerchief) χαρτομάντηλο ‖ ~ paper n τσιγαρόχαρτο.

tit [tit] n (bird) αἰγίθαλος, καλόγηρο ‖ (col: breast) βυζί, μαστός ‖ ~ for tat ὀφθαλμόν ἀντί ὀφθαλμοῦ.

titbit ['titbit] n μεζές.

title ['taitl] n τίτλος, ἐπικεφαλίς ‖ (rank etc) τίτλος ‖ (legal) τίτλος, δικαίωμα ‖ (sport) (παγκόσμιος) τίτλος ‖ ~ deed n τίτλος κυριότητος, τίτλος ἰδιοκτησίας ‖ ~ rôle n πρῶτος ρόλος, ρόλος πού δίνει τόν τίτλον τοῦ ἔργου.

titter ['titə*] vi γελῶ ἀνόητα, κρυφογελῶ.

titular ['titjulə*] a ἐπίτιμος.

tizzy ['tizi] n: in a ~ χαμένα, σέ ἔξαψι, θυμωμένος.

to [tu:, tə] prep (towards) πρός, στό, σ' ‖ (as far as) μέχρι ‖ (comparison) πρός τό, ἔναντι ‖ (for infin) ἵνα, διά νά, γιά νά ‖ ~ and fro πάνω κάτω, πηγαινοέλα, ἀνεβοκατέβασμα.

toad [təud] n φρῦνος, βάτραχος, μποῦφος ‖ ~stool n βωλήτης ὁ δηλητηριώδης (μανιτάρι) ‖ ~y n κωλογλείφτης, γαλίφης.

toast [təust] n φρυγανιά ‖ (drink) πρόποσις ‖ vt (drink) κάνω πρόποσιν ‖ (brown) ψήνω, φρυγανίζω ‖ (warm) ζεσταίνω ‖ ~er n φρυγανιέρα ‖ ~master n προῖστάμενος τῶν προπόσεων ‖ ~ rack n δίσκος γιά τίς φρυγανιές.

tobacco [tə'bækəu] n καπνός ‖ ~nist n καπνοπώλης ‖ ~nist's (shop) n καπνοπωλεῖον.

toboggan [tə'bɔgən] n ἕλκηθρον, τόμπογκαν.

today [tə'dei] n (ή) σήμερον, (τό) σήμερα ‖ ad σήμερα ‖ (present time) σήμερα, τώρα.

toddle ['tɔdl] vi στρατουλίζω.

toddy ['tɔdi] n (warm, alcoholic drink) ζεστό γκρόγκ.

to-do [tə'du:] n (fuss) φασαρία, σαματάς.

toe [təu] n δάκτυλος τοῦ ποδός ‖ vt: to ~ the line (fig) ὑπακούω, ὑποτάσσομαι ‖ ~nail n νύχι τοῦ ποδιοῦ.

toffee ['tɔfi] n καραμέλλα μέ βούτυρο ‖ ~ apple n ζαχαρωμένο μῆλο.

together [tə'geðə*] ad μαζί, μόνοι, ὁ ἕνας μέ τόν ἄλλον ‖ (at the same time) ὁμοῦ, μαζί, συγχρόνως ‖ ~ness n πνεῦμα συνεργασίας.

toil [tɔil] n μόχθος, κόπος, σκληρή δουλειά ‖ vi μοχθῶ, ἐργάζομαι σκληρά.

toilet ['tɔilit] n (lavatory) ἀποχωρητήριον, μέρος ‖ a τῆς τουαλέττας ‖ ~ paper n χαρτί καμπινέτου, χάρτης ὑγείας ‖ ~ries npl εἴδη τουαλέττας ‖ ~ roll n ρολλό χαρτιοῦ καμπινέτου ‖ ~ soap n σαπούνι τουαλέττας ‖ ~ water n κολώνια, ὀ-ντέ-κολόν.

token ['təukən] n ἔνδειξις, τεκμήριον, σημεῖον.

told [təuld] pt, pp of tell.

tolerable ['tɔlərəbl] a ἀνεκτός, ὑποφερτός ‖ (moderate) καλούτσικος.

tolerably ['tɔlərəbli] ad ἀνεκτά, ὑποφερτά.

tolerance ['tɔlərəns] n ἀνοχή, ἀνεκτικότης ‖ (engineering) ἀνοχή.

tolerant ['tɔlərənt] *a* ἀνεκτικός ‖ **~ly** *ad* ἀνεκτικά.

tolerate ['tɔləreit] *vt* ἀνέχομαι, ὑποφέρω.

toleration [tɔlə'reiʃən] *n* ἀνοχή, ἀνεκτικότης.

toll [təul] *n* (*tax, charge*) διόδια, φόρος ‖ (*bell*) κτυπῶ (καμπάνα), καμπανίζω ‖ **~bridge** *n* γέφυρα μέ διόδια ‖ **~ road** *n* ὁδός μέ διόδια.

tomato [tə'mɑːtəu] *n* ντομάτα.

tomb [tuːm] *n* τύμβος, τάφος.

tomboy ['tɔmbɔi] *n* ἀγοροκόριτσο.

tombstone ['tuːmstəun] *n* ἐπιτύμβιος λίθος.

tomcat ['tɔmkæt] *n* γάτος.

tomorrow [tə'mɔrəu] *n* αὔριον, αὐριανή ἡμέρα ‖ *ad* αὔριον.

ton [tʌn] *n* τόννος (2240 λίμπρες) ‖ (*US*) τόννος (2000 λίμπρες) ‖ **~s of** (*col*) μεγάλη ποσότης, πολλές φορές.

tonal ['təunl] *a* τονικός.

tone [təun] *n* τόνος, ἦχος ‖ (*character*) τόνος, πνεῦμα, τάσις ‖ (*colour*) τόνος, ἀπόχρωσις ‖ *vi* συντονίζομαι, ταιριάζω ‖ *vt* τονίζω, τονώνω, ρυθμίζω ‖ **to ~ down** *vt* ἀπαλύνω, μαλακώνω, μετριάζω.

tongs [tɔŋz] *npl* λαβίδα, τσιμπίδα, μασιά.

tongue [tʌŋ] *n* γλῶσσα ‖ (*ox tongue: food*) βοδινή γλῶσσα ‖ **with ~ in cheek** εἰρωνικά ‖ **~-tied** *a* σιωπῶν, βωβός (ἀπό κατάπληξιν) ‖ **~ twister** *n* γλωσσοδέτης.

tonic ['tɔnik] *n* τονωτικόν, δυναμωτικόν ‖ (*mus*) τονική, βασική νότα ‖ **~ water** *n* τόνικ (σόδα).

tonight [tə'nait] *n* σήμερα τό βράδυ ‖ *ad* ἀπόψε.

tonnage ['tʌnidʒ] *n* χωρητικότης, τοννάζ.

tonne [tʌn] *n* (*metric ton*) μετρικός τόννος.

tonsil ['tɔnsl] *n* ἀμυγδαλῆ ‖ **~itis** *n* ἀμυγδαλῖτις.

too [tuː] *ad* πολύ, πάρα πολύ, ὑπερβολικά ‖ (*also*) ἐπίσης, ὡσαύτως, ὁμοίως.

took [tuk] *pt of* **take**.

tool [tuːl] *n* ἐργαλεῖον ‖ **~box** *n* κιβώτιον ἐργαλείων ‖ **~kit** *n* ἐργαλειοθήκη, κιβώτιον ἐργαλείων.

toot [tuːt] *n* κορνάρισμα ‖ *vi* κορνάρω.

tooth [tuːθ] *n* δόντι ‖ (*on gearwheel*) δόντι ‖ **~ache** *n* πονόδοντος, ὀδοντόπονος ‖ **~brush** *n* ὀδοντόβουρτσα ‖ **~paste** *n* ὀδοντόπαστα ‖ **~pick** *n* ὀδοντογλυφίδα ‖ **~ powder** *n* σκόνη γιά τά δόντια.

top [tɔp] *n* κορυφή, κορφή, ἀπάνω (μέρος) ‖ (*at school*) πρῶτος, καλύτερος ‖ (*spinning toy*) σβούρα ‖ *a* ἀνώτερος, ψηλότερος ‖ *vt* (*list*) εἶμαι ἐπί κεφαλῆς, εἶμαι πρῶτος ‖ **from ~ to toe** ἀπό κορυφῆς μέχρις ὀνύχων ‖ **~coat** *n* παλτό ‖ **~flight** *a* (*first-class*) ἀνώτερος, κορυφαῖος ‖ **~ hat** *n* ὑψηλό καπέλλο ‖ **~-heavy** *a* ἀσταθής, βαρύς στήν κορυφήν.

topic ['tɔpik] *n* θέμα, ζήτημα ‖ **~al** *a* ἐπίκαιρος.

top-level ['tɔp'levl] *a* ὑψηλοῦ ἐπιπέδου.

topmost ['tɔpməust] *a* ὑψηλότατος, κορυφαῖος, ὕψιστος.

topple ['tɔpl] *vti* κλονίζομαι, πέφτω, ἀναποδογυρίζω.

top-secret ['tɔp'siːkrit] *a* αὐστηρῶς ἀπόρρητον.

topsy-turvy ['tɔpsi'təːvi] *a,ad* ἄνω-κάτω, κουλουβάχατα.

torch [tɔːtʃ] *n* (*electric*) φακός, φανάρι ‖ (*Olympic*) πυρσός, λαμπάδα, δαυλί.

tore ['tɔː*] *pt of* **tear**.

torment ['tɔːment] *n* βασανιστήριον, μαρτύριον ‖ [tɔː'ment] *vt* ἐνοχλῶ, πειράζω ‖ (*distress*) βασανίζω, τυραννῶ.

torn [tɔːn] *pp of* **tear** ‖ *a* (*undecided*) (**+ between**) ταλαντευόμενος, ἀναποφάσιστος.

tornado [tɔː'neidəu] *n* ἀνεμοστρόβιλος, λαῖλαψ.

torpedo [tɔː'piːdəu] *n* τορπίλλη.

torpor ['tɔːpə*] *n* νάρκη, νωθρότης, ἀδράνεια.

torrent ['tɔrənt] *n* χείμαρρος ‖ **~ial** *a* χειμαρρώδης.

torso ['tɔːsəu] *n* κορμός, τόρσο.

tortoise ['tɔːtəs] *n* χελώνα.

tortuous ['tɔːtjuəs] *a* ἑλικοειδής, στρεβλός ‖ (*deceitful*) ἀνέντιμος, δόλιος.

torture ['tɔːtʃə*] *n* βασανιστήριον, βασανισμός, μαρτύριον ‖ *vt* βασανίζω.

Tory ['tɔːri] *n* συντηρητικός ‖ *a* συντηρητικός, δεξιός.

toss [tɔs] *vt* πετῶ, τραντάζω ‖ (*in the air*) ρίχνω, πετῶ ‖ *n* (*of coin to decide*) στρίψιμο ‖ **to ~ a coin**, **to ~ up for sth** ρίχνω κορώνα-γράμματα.

tot [tɔt] *n* ποτηράκι, γουλιά ‖ (*child*) παιδάκι, μωρό, μπέμπης.

total ['təutl] *n* σύνολον, ὅλον, ἄθροισμα, σούμα ‖ *a* (συν)ολικός, ὁλόκληρος, τέλειος ‖ *vt* προσθέτω, ἀθροίζω ‖ (*amount to*) συμποσοῦμαι εἰς, φθάνω ‖ **~ity** *n* σύνολον, ὁλότης ‖ **~ly** *ad* συνολικῶς, πλήρως, τελείως.

totem pole ['təutəmpəul] *n* στήλη τοῦ τοτέμ.

totter ['tɔtə*] *vi* παραπαίω, τρικλίζω.

touch [tʌtʃ] *n* ἀφή, ἐπαφή, ἄγγισμα, γγίξιμο ‖ (*sense*) ἐπαφή, ἀφή ‖ (*small amount*) μικρά δόσις, ἴχνος, ὑποψία ‖ (*style*) πινελιά, μολυβιά, ὕφος ‖ *vt* ἅπτομαι, ψαύω, ἀγγίζω ‖ (*come against*) ἐφάπτομαι, ἀκουμπῶ ‖ (*move*) θίγω, συγκινῶ ‖ **in ~ with** σ'ἐπαφή μέ, (διατηρῶ) ἐπαφήν, παρακολούθησις ‖ **to ~ on** *vt* (*topic*) θίγω (θέμα) ‖ **to ~ up** *vt* (*paint*) ρετουσάρω, τονίζω ‖ **~-and-go** *a* ἐπικίνδυνος, ἀβέβαιος, ἐπισφαλής ‖ **~down** *n* προσγείωσις ‖ **~iness** *n* εὐθιξία ‖ **~ing** *a* συγκινητικός, παθητικός ‖ **~line** *n* γραμμή τοῦ τέρματος ‖ **~y** *a* (ὑπερ)ευαίσθητος, εὔθικτος.

tough [tʌf] *a* σκληρός, στερεός, ἀλύγιστος ‖ *(difficult)* δυσχερής, σκληρός, δύσκολος ‖ *(meat)* σκληρός ‖ *n (gangster etc)* κακοποιός, μπράβος ‖ **~en** *vti* σκληραίνω, σκληρύνομαι ‖ **~ness** *n* σκληρότης, ἀντοχή.

toupee ['tu:peɪ] *n (wig)* περούκα.

tour ['tuə*] *n* περιοδεία, περιήγησις ‖ *vi* περιηγοῦμαι, περιοδεύω ‖ **~ing** *n* τουρισμός, περιοδεία ‖ **~ism** *n* τουρισμός ‖ **~ist** *n* τουρίστας, περιηγητής ‖ **~ist office** *n* τουριστικόν γραφεῖον.

tournament ['tuənəmənt] *n* πρωτάθλημα, τουρνουά.

tousled ['tauzld] *a (hair)* ἀναστατωμένα, ξεχτένιστα.

tow [təu] *n (pull)* ρυμούλκησις ‖ *vt (pull)* ρυμουλκῶ.

toward(s) [tə'wɔ:d(z)] *prep* πρός, κατά, διά, γιά.

towel ['tauəl] *n* πρόσοψι, πετσέτα.

tower ['tauə*] *n* πύργος ‖ **~ing** *a* πανύψηλος ‖ *(rage)* βίαιος, ἄγριος.

towline ['təulaɪn] *n* ρυμούλκιον, γεντέκι.

town [taun] *n* πόλις, πολιτεία, χώρα ‖ **~ clerk** *n* γραμματεύς δημαρχίας ‖ **~ hall** *n* δημαρχεῖον ‖ **~ planner** *n* πολεοδόμος ‖ **~ planning** *n* πολεοδομία.

towpath ['təupa:θ] *n (along canal)* δρομάκος ρυμουλκήσεως ποταμοπλοίων.

towrope ['təurəup] *n* ρυμούλκιον, γεντέκι.

toxic ['tɔksɪk] *a* τοξικός.

toy [tɔɪ] *n* παιχνίδι, παιχνιδάκι ‖ **to ~ with** *vt* παίζω μέ ‖ σκέπτομαι νά.

trace [treɪs] *n* ἴχνος ‖ *(small amount)* ἴχνος, ὑπόλειμμα, τεκμήριον ‖ *vt* παρακολουθῶ ‖ *(find out)* ἀνιχνεύω, διακρίνω ‖ *(copy)* χαράσσω, ἀντιγράφω, ξεσηκώνω.

track [træk] *n* ἴχνη, πέρασμα, πατημασιές ‖ *(road, path)* ἀτραπός, μονοπάτι, δρομάκος ‖ *(racing)* διάδρομος ἀγώνων, στίβος, πίστα ‖ *(rail)* (σιδηροδρομική) γραμμή ‖ *vt* παρακολουθῶ, καταδιώκω ‖ **to keep ~ of** παρακολουθῶ, βρίσκομαι εἰς ἐπαφήν μέ ‖ **to make ~s for** κατευθύνομαι, πηγαίνω βιαστικά ‖ **to ~ down** *vt* ἀνακαλύπτω, βρίσκω ‖ **~er dog** *n* κυνηγόσκυλο ‖ **~less** *a* ἀδιάβατος, χωρίς μονοπάτια.

tract [trækt] *n* περιοχή, ἔκτασις ‖ *(book)* φυλλάδιον.

tractor ['træktə*] *n* ἑλκυστήρ, τρακτέρ.

trade [treɪd] *n* ἐμπόριον ‖ *(business)* ἐπάγγελμα, δουλειά ‖ *(people)* συντεχνία, κλάδος, συνάφι ‖ *vi (+in)* ἐμπορεύομαι, συναλλάσσομαι, κάνω δουλειές ‖ **~mark** *n* σῆμα (κατατεθέν) ‖ **~ name** *n* ἐμπορική ἐπωνυμία, φίρμα ‖ **~r** *n* ἔμπορος ‖ **~sman** *n* καταστηματάρχης, προμηθευτής, ἐπαγγελματίας ‖ *(skilled workman)* τεχνίτης ‖ **~ union** *n* ἐργατική ἔνωσις, συνδικάτον ‖ **~ unionist** *n* συνδικαλιστής.

trading ['treɪdɪŋ] *n* ἐμποριον ‖ **~ stamp** *n* δελτίον ἐκπτώσεως.

tradition [trə'dɪʃən] *n* παράδοσις ‖ **~s** *npl* παραδόσεις ‖ **~al** *a* ἐκ παραδόσεως, πατροπαράδοτος ‖ **~ally** *ad* κατά παράδοσιν.

traffic ['træfɪk] *n* κίνησις, κυκλοφορία ‖ *(esp in drugs)* ἐμπόριον, συναλλαγή, δοσοληψία ‖ *vt (esp drugs)* ἐμπορεύομαι (κάτι) ‖ **~ circle** *n (US: roundabout)* κυκλοφοριακός δρόμος ‖ **~ jam** *n* συνωστισμός ‖ **~ lights** *npl* φανάρια, φῶτα κυκλοφορίας.

tragedy ['trædʒɪdɪ] *n* τραγωδία, δράμα.

tragic ['trædʒɪk] *a* τραγικός ‖ **~ally** *ad* τραγικά.

trail [treɪl] *n* ἴχνος, πατήματα ‖ *(something trailing)* γραμμή (καπνοῦ), οὐρά ‖ *(rough road)* μονοπάτι ‖ *vi (follow)* σέρνομαι πίσω ‖ *(hang loosely)* σέρνομαι, σέρνω ‖ **on the ~** ἐπί τά ἴχνη ‖ **to ~ behind** *vi* σέρνομαι πίσω ‖ **~er** *n (truck)* ρυμουλκούμενον ὄχημα ‖ *(film)* ἀπόσπασμα ταινίας ‖ *(US: caravan)* τροχόσπιτο.

train [treɪn] *n* συρμός ἁμαξοστοιχίας, τραῖνο ‖ *(of gown)* οὐρά ‖ *(series)* σειρά, ἀλληλουχία, εἱρμός ‖ *vt* ἐκπαιδεύω, διδάσκω, μαθαίνω ‖ *(plant)* κατευθύνω, ὁδηγῶ ‖ *(point gun)* σκοπεύω, διευθύνω ‖ *vi (exercise)* προπονῶ, προγυμνάζω ‖ **~ed** *a* ἐκγυμνασμένος, ἐξησκημένος ‖ **~ee** *n* ἀσκούμενος μαθητής ‖ **~er** *n* ἐκπαιδευτής, προπονητής, γυμναστής ‖ **~ing** *n* ἐκπαίδευσις, ἐξάσκησις, προπόνησις ‖ **in ~ing** σέ φόρμα ‖ **~ing college** *n* ἐπαγγελματική σχολή, διδασκαλεῖον.

traipse [treɪps] *vi (wander)* σέρνομαι ἐδῶ καί κεῖ, σουρτουκεύω.

trait [treɪt] *n* χαρακτηριστικόν.

traitor ['treɪtə*] *n* προδότης.

tram(car) ['træm(ka:*)] *n* τράμ ‖ **~ line** *n* τροχιοδρομική γραμμή, γραμμή τράμ.

tramp [træmp] *n (vagabond)* ἀλήτης ‖ *vi* περπατῶ βαρειά, βηματίζω βαρειά ‖ *(by foot)* πεζοπορῶ, πηγαίνω πεζῆ ‖ *vt (ποδο)πατῶ, καταπατῶ ‖ **~line** *n* τραμπολίνο.

trance [tra:ns] *n* ἔκστασις, ὕπνωσις, ὅραμα.

tranquil ['træŋkwɪl] *a* ἤρεμος, ἥσυχος ‖ **~ity** *n* ἠρεμία ‖ **~lizer** *n (drug)* καταπραϋντικόν.

trans- [trænz] *prefix* διά μέσου, πέραν, στήν ἄλλη πλευράν.

transact [træn'zækt] *vt* ἐκτελῶ, διεξάγω, διεκπεραιώνω ‖ **~ion** *n* διεκπεραίωσις, διεξαγωγή, συναλλαγή.

transatlantic ['trænzət'læntɪk] *a* ὑπερατλαντικός.

transcend [træn'send] *vt* ὑπερέχω, ὑπερβαίνω.

transcript ['trænskrɪpt] *n* ἀντίγραφον, ἀντιγραφή ‖ **~ion** *n* ἀντιγραφή, ἀντίγραφον.

transept ['trænsept] *n* πτέριξ ναοῦ, ἐγκάρσιον κλίτος.

transfer ['trænsfə*] *n* μεταφορά, μετάθεσις || (*legal*) μεταβίβασις, ἐκχώρησις, μεταγραφή || (*design*) χαλκομανία, στάμπα, ἀντιγραφή || (*sport*) μεταβίβασις, μεταφορά || [træns'fə:*] *vt* μεταφέρω, μεταθέτω, ἀλλάζω || ~**able** *a* μεταβιβάσιμος, μεταφερτός || '**not** ~**able**' (*on ticket*) 'προσωπικόν'.

transform [træns'fɔ:m] *vt* μετασχηματίζω, μεταβάλλω, μεταμορφώνω || ~**ation** *n* μετασχηματισμός, μεταβολή, μεταμόρφωσις || ~**er** *n* (*elec*) μετασχηματιστής.

transfusion [træns'fju:ʒən] *n* μετάγγισις.

transient ['trænziənt] *a* παροδικός.

transistor [træn'zistə*] *n* κρυσταλλικός πολλαπλασιαστής || (*radio*) τρανσίστορ, φορητό ραδιόφωνο.

transit ['trænzit] *n*: **in** ~ (κατά) τήν μεταφοράν, ὑπό μεταφοράν.

transition [træn'ziʃən] *n* μετάβασις, μεταβολή, ἀλλαγή || ~**al** *a* μεταβατικός.

transitive ['trænzitiv] *a* μεταβατικόν (ρῆμα) || ~**ly** *ad* μεταβατικῶς.

transitory ['trænzitəri] *a* παροδικός, βραχύς, ἐφήμερος.

translate [trænz'leit] *vt* μεταφράζω.

translation [trænz'leiʃən] *n* μετάφρασις.

translator [trænz'leitə*] *n* μεταφραστής.

transmission [trænz'miʃən] *n* (*of information*) μεταβίβασις, διαβίβασις, μετάδοσις || (*aut*) μετάδοσις || (*rad*) ἐκπομπή, μετάδοσις, διάδοσις.

transmit [trænz'mit] *vt* μεταδίδω, μεταβιβάζω, διαβιβάζω || ~**ter** *n* πομπός.

transparency [træns'pɛərənsi] *n* (*phot*: *slide*) πλάξ προβολῆς, σλάϊντ.

transparent [træns'pɛərənt] *a* διαφανής, διαυγής, καθαρός.

transplant [træns'plɑ:nt] *vt* μεταφυτεύω, μεταφέρω || ['trænsplɑ:nt] *n* (*also med*) μεταφύτευσις, μεταμόσχευσις.

transport ['trænspɔ:t] *n* μεταφορά || [træns'pɔ:t] *vt* μεταφέρω || **means of** ~ μέσα συγκοινωνίας || ~**able** *a* μετακομιστός, φορητός || ~**ation** *n* μεταφορά, συγκοινωνία.

transverse ['trænzvɔ:s] *a* ἐγκάρσιος.

trap [træp] *n* (*trick*) παγίδα, ἀπάτη || (*snare*) παγίδα, φάκα || (*carriage*) δίτροχος ἄμαξα, σούστα || (*col: mouth*) στόμα || *vt* παγιδεύω, πιάνω στήν παγίδα || ~**door** *n* καταπακτή.

trapeze [trə'pi:z] *n* τραπέζιον.

trapper ['træpə*] *n* κυνηγός, παγιδευτής.

trappings ['træpiŋz] *npl* διακόσμησις, στολίδια.

trash [træʃ] *n* σκουπίδια, φτηνολόϊ || (*nonsense*) μπούρδες, τρίχες || ~ **can** *n* (*US*) σκουπιδοτενεκές || ~**y** *a* μηδαμινός, τῆς πεντάρας.

trauma ['trɔ:mə] *n* τραῦμα || ~**tic** *a* τραυματικός.

travel ['trævl] *n* ταξίδι, περιήγησις || *vi* ταξιδεύω, κάνω ταξίδια || *vt* (*distance*) πηγαίνω, βαδίζω, προχωρῶ, μετακινοῦμαι || ~**ler**, (*US*) ~**er** *n* ταξιδιώτης || (*salesman*) πλασιέ, ἀντιπρόσωπος || ~**ler's cheque**, (*US*) ~**er's check** *n* ταξιδιωτική ἐπιταγή, τράβελλερς τσέκ || ~**ling**, (*US*) ~**ing** *n* τά ταξίδια || *attr a* ταξιδιωτικός, τοῦ ταξιδίου || ~ **sickness** *n* ναυτία, ἀναγούλα.

traverse ['trævəs] *vt* διασχίζω, διαβαίνω, περνῶ.

travesty ['trævisti] *n* διακωμώδησις, παρωδία.

trawler ['trɔ:lə*] *n* ἁλιευτικόν, τράτα.

tray [trei] *n* δίσκος.

treacherous ['tretʃərəs] *a* (*person*) δόλιος, ὕπουλος || (*road: dangerous, icy etc*) ἐπικίνδυνος, ἄστατος.

treachery ['tretʃəri] *n* δολιότης, προδοσία, ἀπιστία.

treacle ['tri:kl] *n* μελάσσα, πετιμέζι.

tread [tred] (*irreg v*) *n* περπάτημα || (*way of walking*) βῆμα, βηματισμός || (*stair, tyre*) βαθμίς, πάτημα, πέλμα ἐλαστικοῦ || *vi* βαδίζω, περπατῶ || **to** ~ **on** *vt* (ποδο)πατῶ.

treason ['tri:zn] *n* προδοσία.

treasure ['treʒə*] *n* θησαυρός, χρῆμα, πλούτη || *vt* ἀποθησαυρίζω || (*value highly*) ἐκτιμῶ, θεωρῶ πολύτιμον || ~ **hunt** *n* θησαυροθηρία || ~**r** *n* ταμίας.

treasury ['treʒəri] *n* θησαυροφυλάκειον, ταμεῖον.

treat [tri:t] *n* εὐχαρίστησις, ἀπόλαυσις || *vt* μεταχειρίζομαι, φέρομαι || (*entertain*) κερνῶ, προσφέρω.

treatise ['tri:tiz] *n* πραγματεία, διατριβή.

treatment ['tri:tmənt] *n* μεταχείρησις, περιποίησις, κούρα, θεραπεία.

treaty ['tri:ti] *n* συνθήκη.

treble ['trebl] *a* τριπλός, τριπλάσιος || *vt* τριπλασιάζω || *n* πρίμο || (*voice*) ὑψίφωνος, σοπράνο || ~ **clef** *n* κλειδί τοῦ σόλ.

tree [tri:] *n* δένδρον, δέντρο || ~ **trunk** *n* κορμός δένδρου.

trek [trek] *n* ταξίδι, μετανάστευσις || *vi* (*migrate*) μετοικῶ, μεταναστεύω.

trellis ['trelis] *n* δικτυωτόν πλέγμα, καφασωτόν πλαίσιον.

tremble ['trembl] *vi* τρέμω, δονοῦμαι.

trembling ['trembliŋ] *n* τρόμος, τρεμούλα || *a* τρέμων, τρεμουλιάρης.

tremendous [trə'mendəs] *a* (*vast*) πελώριος, τρομερός || ~**ly** *ad* τρομερά, ὑπερβολικά, ἀφάνταστα.

tremor ['tremə*] *n* τρεμούλιασμα.

trench [trentʃ] *n* τάφρος, αὐλάκι, χαντάκι || (*of war*) χαράκωμα.

trend [trend] *n* τάσις, πορεία || *vi* τείνω.

trepidation [trepi'deiʃən] *n* φόβος, τρόμος, τρεμούλα.

trespass ['trespəs] vi καταπατῶ | '~ers will be prosecuted' 'ἀπαγορεύεται ἡ εἴσοδος'.

tress [tres] n βόστρυχος, πλεξούδα, κοτσίδα, μπούκλα.

trestle ['tresl] n ὑποβάτης, βάσταξ, καβαλέτο | ~ table n τραπέζι σέ καβαλέτο.

tri- [trai] prefix τρι-.

trial ['traiəl] n (in court) δίκη, κρίσις | (test) δοκιμή | (hardship) δοκιμασία, βάσανο | by ~ and error διά δοκιμῆς καί πλάνης, ψαχτά.

triangle ['traiæŋgl] n τρίγωνον.

triangular [trai'æŋgjulə*] a τριγωνικός.

tribal ['traibəl] a φυλετικός.

tribe [traib] n φυλή | ~sman n μέλος φυλῆς.

tribulation [tribju'leiʃən] n δοκιμασία, συμφορά, πάθημα.

tribunal [trai'bju:nl] n δικαστήριον.

tributary ['tribjutəri] n παραπόταμος.

tribute ['tribju:t] n (respect) φόρος τιμῆς.

trice [trais] n: in a ~ στή στιγμή.

trick [trik] n τέχνασμα, κόλπο, κατεργαριά (clever act) δεξιοτεχνία, ταχυδακτυλουργία | (habit) συνήθεια | (cards) κόλπο, πιάσιμο, λεβέ | vt ἐξαπατῶ | ~ery n ἀπάτη, κοροϊδία.

trickle ['trikl] n λεπτή ροή, στάξιμο, στάλα (νερού) | vi σταλάζω, στάζω.

tricky ['triki] a (problem, situation) περίπλοκος, δύσκολος.

tricycle ['traisikl] n τρίκυκλον.

tried [traid] pt, pp of try | a δοκιμασμένος, ἀξιόπιστος.

trier ['traiə*] n (person who tries hard) ὁ δοκιμάζων ἐπίμονα.

trifle ['traifl] n εἶδος τούρτας | (of little importance) μικροπρᾶγμα, ἀσήμαντον γεγονός, μηδαμινόν ποσόν.

trifling ['traifliŋ] a ἀσήμαντος, τιποτένιος.

trigger ['trigə*] n σκανδάλη.

trigonometry [trigə'nɔmitri] n τριγωνομετρία.

trilby ['trilbi] n μαλακό καπέλλο, ρεπούμπλικα.

trim [trim] a τακτικός, κομψός, εὐπρεπής | n τάξις, φόρμα, εὐπρεπής κατάστασις | (haircut etc) κόψιμο, φρεσκάρισμα (μαλλιῶν) | vt κόβω, κουρεύω, κλαδεύω | (decorate) γαρνίρω | ~mings npl γαρνιτούρες.

Trinity ['triniti] n: the ~ (rel) Ἁγία Τριάς.

trinket ['triŋkit] n μικρόν κόσμημα, μπρελόκ, μπιμπελό.

trio ['triəu] n τριάδα | (mus) τρίο.

trip [trip] n ἐκδρομή, ταξίδι | (stumble) παραπάτημα, τρικλοποδιά | vi περπατῶ ἐλαφρά, ἀλαφροπατῶ | (stumble) σκοντάφτω, παραπατῶ | to ~ over vi σκοντάφτω σέ | to ~ up vi ἀναβάλλω ἐλαφροπατόντας | vi βάζω τρικλοποδιά σέ.

tripe [traip] n (food) πατσᾶς | (rubbish) ἀνοησίες, μποῦρδες.

triple ['tripl] a τριπλός, τρίδιπλος | ~ts npl τρίδυμα.

triplicate ['triplikit] n: in ~ εἰς τριπλοῦν.

tripod ['traipɔd] n τρίπους, τρίποδο.

tripper ['tripə*] n ἐκδρομεύς.

trite [trait] a τετριμμένος, κοινός, κοινοτοπικός.

triumph ['traiʌmf] n θρίαμβος | vi θριαμβεύω | ~al a θριαμβικός | ~ant a θριαμβευτικός | ~antly ad θριαμβευτικά.

trivial ['triviəl] a ἀσήμαντος, τιποτένιος | ~ity n ἀσημαντότης, κοινοτοπία.

trod [trɔd] pt of tread | ~den pp of tread.

trolley ['trɔli] n (small truck) καρροτσάκι | ~ bus n τρόλλεϋ.

trombone [trɔm'bəun] n τρομπόνι.

troop [tru:p] n ὁμάς, ἴλη, παρέα | ~s npl στρατεύματα | to ~ in, out vi εἰσέρχομαι, ἐξέρχομαι ὁμαδικῶς | ~er n ἱππεύς, ἔφιππος ἀστυνομικός | ~ship n μεταγωγικόν (πλοῖον).

trophy ['trəufi] n τρόπαιον, ἔπαθλον.

tropic ['trɔpik] n τροπικός | the ~s npl τροπικαί (χῶραι) | T~ of Cancer n Τροπικός τοῦ Καρκίνου | T~ of Capricorn n Τροπικός τοῦ Αἰγόκερω | ~al a τροπικός.

trot [trɔt] n τριποδισμός, ἐλαφρό τρέξιμο | vi τρέχω σιγά.

trouble ['trʌbl] n στενοχώρια, ἀνησυχία, σκοτούρα | (effort, care) κόπος | vt ἐνοχλῶ, ἀνησυχῶ | ~d a ἀνήσυχος, ταραγμένος | ~-free a χωρίς σκοτούρες | ~maker n ταραχοποιός, ταραξίας | ~some a ὀχληρός, ἀνιαρός, δύσκολος.

trough [trɔf] n σκάφη, ποτίστρα | (channel) αὐλών, τάφρος | (meteorology) σφήν ὑφέσεως.

trounce [trauns] vt (esp sport) συντρίβω, τσακίζω.

troupe [tru:p] n θίασος.

trousers ['trauzəz] npl πανταλόνι.

trousseau ['tru:səu] n προῖκα (ἀσπρόρ ρουχα καί φορέματα).

trout [traut] n πέστροφα.

trowel ['trauəl] n μυστρί.

truant ['truənt] n: to play ~ τό σκάω, ἀπουσιάζω ἀδικαιολόγητα.

truce [tru:s] n ἀνακωχή.

truck [trʌk] n φορτηγό ἁμάξι, καμιόνι | (rail) φορεῖον | (barrow) χειράμαξα ἀχθοφόρου | ~driver n ὁδηγός φορτηγοῦ | ~ farm n (US) ἀγρόκτημα λαχανικῶν, περιβόλι.

truculent ['trʌkjulənt] a βίαιος, ἄγριος, ἐπιθετικός.

trudge [trʌdʒ] vi βαδίζω μέ δυσκολίαν, σέρνομαι.

true [tru:] a ἀληθής, ἀληθινός, ἀκριβής | (genuine) πραγματικός, αὐθεντικός, γνήσιος | (friend) πιστός, τίμιος, ἀληθινός.

truffle ['trʌfl] n ὕχνο, τερφεζία.

truly ['tru:li] ad εἰλικρινά, πιστά, γνήσια,

ἀληθῶς ‖ (*exactly*) μέ ἀκρίβειαν, ἀκριβῶς, ὀρθῶς ‖ **yours** ~ ὅλος ὑμέτερος.

trump [trʌmp] *n* (*cards*) ἀτοῦ ‖ ~ **ed-up** *a* ψευδής, σκαρωμένο.

trumpet ['trʌmpit] *n* σάλπιγξ, τρουμπέτα.

truncated [trʌŋ'keitid] *a* κολοβωμένος, κόλουρος.

truncheon ['trʌntʃən] *n* ρόπαλον, ἀστυνομικόν γκλόμπ.

trundle ['trʌndl] *vti:* **to** ~ **along** κυλῶ, τρέχω, τσουλῶ.

trunk [trʌŋk] *n* κορμός, κούτσουρο ‖ (*body*) κορμός, τόρσο ‖ (*box*) κιβώτιον, μπαοῦλο ‖ (*of elephant*) προβοσκίς ‖ ~ **s** *npl* μαγιό, κυλοτίτσα ‖ ~ **call** *n* ὑπεραστική κλήσις.

truss [trʌs] *n* (*med*) κοιλεπίδεσμος, ζώνη.

trust [trʌst] *n* πίστις, ἐμπιστοσύνη ‖ (*property*) καταπίστευμα ‖ *vt* ἐμπιστεύομαι εἰς ‖ ~ **ed** *a* ἔμπιστος, τῆς ἐμπιστοσύνης ‖ ~ **ee** *n* ἐπίτροπος, κηδεμών, ἔφορος ‖ ~ **ful** *a* γεμάτος ἐμπιστοσύνην, εὐκολόπιστος ‖ ~ **ing** *a* πλήρης ἐμπιστοσύνης ‖ ~ **worthy** *a* ἀξιόπιστος ‖ ~ **y** *a* πιστός, ἀξιόπιστος.

truth [truːθ] *n* ἀλήθεια ‖ ~ **ful** *a* φιλαλήθης, ἀληθής ‖ ~ **fully** *ad* ἀληθινά, εἰλικρινῶς, πιστά ‖ ~ **fulness** *n* φιλαλήθεια, εἰλικρίνεια.

try [trai] (*irreg v*) *n* προσπάθεια ‖ (*test*) δοκιμή, ἀπόπειρα ‖ *vt* δοκιμάζω, κάνω δοκιμήν ‖ (*in court*) δικάζω ‖ (*strain*) κουράζω ‖ *vi* (*attempt*) προσπαθῶ, ζητῶ νά ‖ **to** ~ **on** *vt* δοκιμάζω, προβάρω ‖ **to** ~ **out** *vt* δοκιμάζω (πλήρως) ‖ ~ **ing** *a* δυσχερής, κουραστικός, σκληρός, ἐντατικός.

tsar [zaː*] *n* Τσάρος.

T-shirt ['tiːʃəːt] *n* φανέλλα (ἀθλητική).

T-square ['tiːskwɛə*] *n* Ταῦ σχεδιάσεως.

tub [tʌb] *n* μεγάλη λεκάνη, σκάφη, κάδος, μαστέλο, μπάνιο.

tuba ['tjuːbə] *n* μεγάλη κορνέτα, κοντραμπάσο.

tubby ['tʌbi] *a* (*fat*) στρογγυλός σάν βαρέλι, κοντοπύθαρος.

tube [tjuːb] *n* σωλήν, ἀγωγός, αὐλός ‖ (*also for toothpaste etc*) σωληνάριον ‖ (*in London*) ὑπόγειος σιδηρόδρομος ‖ (*aut: for tyre*) σαμπρέλλα ‖ ~ **less** *a* (*aut*) χωρίς σαμπρέλλα.

tuber ['tjuːbə*] *n* βολβός, γογγύλι.

tuberculosis [tjubəːkjuˈləusis] *n* φυματίωσις.

tube station ['tjuːbsteiʃən] *n* σταθμός τοῦ ὑπογείου τραίνου.

tubing ['tjuːbiŋ] *n* σωλήν(ωσις).

tubular ['tjuːbjulə*] *a* (*steel, furniture*) σωληνοειδής, σωληνωτός.

tuck [tʌk] *n* πιέτα ‖ γλυκά ‖ *vt* (*gather*) διπλώνω, μαζεύω ‖ **to** ~ **away** *vi* χώνω ‖ **to** ~ **in** *vt* μαζεύω, χώνω ‖ *vi* (*food*) πέφτω μέ τά μούτρα στό φαΐ ‖ **to** ~ **up** *vt* (*child*) σκεπάζω, τακτοποιῶ ‖ ~ **-shop** *n* ζαχαροπλαστεῖον.

Tuesday ['tʃuːzdi] *n* Τρίτη.

tuft [tʌft] *n* θύσανος, φούντα.

tug [tʌg] *n* ἀπότομο τράβηγμα ‖ (*steamship*) ρυμουλκόν (πλοῖον) ‖ *vti* σύρω, τραβῶ δυνατά ‖ ~ **-of-war** *n* διελκυστίνδα.

tuition [tjuˈiʃən] *n* διδασκαλία, δίδακτρα.

tulip ['tjuːlip] *n* τουλίπα.

tumble ['tʌmbl] *n* πέσιμο, τούμπα, κουτρουβάλα ‖ *vi* πέφτω, τουμπάρω ‖ (*somersault*) κάνω τούμπες, ἀναποδογυρίζω ‖ *vt* (*toss about*) κατρακυλῶ, σωριάζομαι ‖ **to** ~ **to** *vt* συλλαμβάνω, ἀντιλαμβάνομαι ‖ ~ **down** *a* ἑτοιμόρροπος, σαραβαλιασμένος ‖ ~ **r** *n* (*acrobat*) ἀκροβάτης ‖ (*glass*) ποτήρι.

tummy ['tʌmi] *n* (*col: stomach, belly*) στομάχι, κοιλιά.

tumour ['tjuːmə*] *n* ὄγκος.

tumult ['tjuːmʌlt] *n* θόρυβος, σαματᾶς, φασαρία ‖ ~ **uous** *a* θορυβώδης, ταραχώδης, θυελλώδης.

tumulus ['tjuːmjuləs] *n* τύμβος.

tuna ['tjuːnə] *n* τόννος.

tundra ['tʌndrə] *n* τούντρα.

tune [tjuːn] *n* μελωδία, σκοπός ‖ (*pitch*) τόνος, συντονισμός ‖ *vt* κουρδίζω, συντονίζω ‖ (*motorcar*) ρυθμίζω, ἐναρμονίζω, συντονίζω ‖ **in** ~ ἐν ἁρμονία, συντονισμένος ‖ **out of** ~ παραφωνή, ἔξω ἀπό τόν τόνο ‖ **to** ~ **in** *vi* πιάνω σταθμό ‖ **to** ~ **up** *vi* (*mus*) συντονίζομαι, βρίσκω τόν τόνο ‖ ~ **ful** *a* μελωδικός, ἁρμονικός.

tungsten ['tʌŋstən] *n* βολφράμιον, τουγκστένιον.

tunic ['tjuːnik] *n* χιτώνιον, ἀμπέχονο.

tuning ['tjuːniŋ] *n* (*rad*) συντονισμός ‖ (*aut*) ρύθμισις.

tunnel ['tʌnl] *n* σῆραγξ, τουνέλι ‖ *vi* ἀνοίγω σήραγγα.

tunny ['tʌni] *n* τόννος.

turban ['təːbən] *n* σαρίκι, τουρμπάνι.

turbid ['təːbid] *a* θολός, λασπώδης, βρόμικος.

turbine ['təːbain] *n* στρόβιλος, τουρμπίνα.

turbulence ['təːbjuləns] *n* (*aviat*) στροβιλισμός, ρεμού.

turbulent ['təːbjulənt] *a* ταραχώδης, βίαιος, ἄτακτος.

turf [təːf] *n* χλόη, γρασίδι ‖ (*sod*) χορταριασμένος βῶλος ‖ **the T** ~ *n* ὁ ἱππόδρομος.

turgid ['təːdʒid] *a* (*pompous*) στομφώδης, πομπώδης.

Turk [təːk] *n* Τοῦρκος.

turkey ['təːki] *n* γαλλοπούλα, ἰνδιάνος ‖ **T** ~ *n* Τουρκία.

Turkish ['təːkiʃ] *a* τουρκικός ‖ *n* (*ling*) τουρκική ‖ ~ **bath** *n* χαμάμ ‖ ~ **delight** *n* λουκούμι.

turmoil ['təːmɔil] *n* ἀναταραχή, ἀναστάτωσις, πατιρντί.

turn [təːn] *n* περιστροφή, γύρισμα ‖ (*turning*) στροφή ‖ (*performance*) σειρά ‖ (*shape, manner*) νοοτροπία, διάθεσις ‖ (*chance*) σειρά ‖ (*med*) κρίσις ‖ *vt* (περι)στρέφω, γυρίζω, στρίβω ‖ (*change position*) ἀλλάζω, γυρίζω ‖ (*of colour*) ἀλλάζω χρῶμα ‖ *vi* περιστρέφομαι, γυρίζω ‖ (*change direction*) στρέφομαι, κατευθύνομαι, στρίβω ‖ (*become sour*) ξυνίζω ‖ **to ~ back** *vti* γυρίζω πίσω ‖ **to ~ down** *vt* (*refuse*) ἀπορρίπτω ‖ (*fold down*) διπλώνω, τσάκίζω ‖ **to ~ in** *vi* (*go to bed*) πάω γιά ὕπνο ‖ *vt* (*fold*) γυρίζω (μέσα), στριφώνω ‖ **to ~ off** *vi* (*from road*) ἀλλάζω δρόμο, στρίβω ‖ *vt* (*light*) κλείνω, σβήνω ‖ (*rad*) κλείνω, σβήνω ‖ **to ~ on** *vt* (*light*) ἀνοίγω, ἀνάβω ‖ (*rad*) ἀνοίγω ‖ **to ~ out** *vt* ἐξελίσσομαι, πάω ‖ (*extinguish*) κλείνω, σβήνω ‖ **to ~ up** *vi* (*person*) ἐμφανίζομαι, φθάνω αἰφνιδίως ‖ (*lost object*) ξαναβρίσκω ‖ *vt* (*collar*) σηκώνω, ἀνασηκώνω ‖ (*rad: increase volume*) ἀνεβάζω, δυναμώνω ‖ **~around** *n* (*reversal*) γύρισμα, μεταβολή ‖ **~ed-up** *a* (*nose*) ἀνασηκωτή (μύτη) ‖ **~ing** *n* (*in road*) καμπή, στροφή ‖ **~ing point** *n* κρίσιμον σημεῖον, ἀποφασιστικὸν σημεῖον.

turnip ['təːnip] *n* γογγύλι.

turnout ['təːnaut] *n* συνάθροισις, ἀκροατήριον.

turnover ['təːnəuvə*] *n* κεφάλαιον, τζίρος.

turnpike ['təːnpaik] *n* (*US: toll highway*) ὁδὸς μὲ διόδια.

turnstile ['təːnstail] *n* περιστροφικὴ εἴσοδος.

turntable ['təːnteibl] *n* περιστροφικὴ ἐξέδρα, περιστροφικὴ βάσις.

turn-up ['təːnʌp] *n* (*on trousers*) ρεβέρ.

turpentine ['təːpəntain] *n* νέφτι.

turquoise ['təːkwɔiz] *n* τουρκουάζ ‖ *a* (*colour*) κυανοπράσινος.

turret ['tʌrit] *n* πυργίσκος.

turtle ['təːtl] *n* χελώνα.

tusk [tʌsk] *n* χαυλιόδους.

tussle ['tʌsl] *n* τσακωμός, καυγᾶς.

tutor ['tjuːtə*] *n* ἰδιαίτερος καθηγητής, οἰκοδιδάσκαλος ‖ (*at college*) ὑφηγητὴς ‖ **~ial** *n* (*univ*) ἰδιαίτερον μάθημα ἀπὸ καθηγητήν.

tuxedo [tʌk'siːdəu] *n* (*US*) σμόκιν.

twaddle ['twɔdl] *n* (*col*) μωρολογία, φλυαρία, μποῦρδες.

twang [twæŋ] *n* ὀξύς ἦχος χορδῆς, ἔνρινος τόνος, σβούρισμα ‖ *vti* ἀφήνω τεταμένην χορδήν, ἀντηχῶ, σβουρίζω.

tweed [twiːd] *n* τουήντ.

tweezers ['twizəz] *npl* τσιμπίδα.

twelfth [twelfθ] *a* δωδέκατος ‖ **T~ Night** *n* παραμονὴ τῶν Φώτων.

twelve [twelv] *num* δώδεκα.

twentieth ['twentiiθ] *a* εἰκοστός.

twenty ['twenti] *num* εἴκοσι.

twerp [twəːp] *n* (*col: fool*) βλάκας.

twice [twais] *ad* δίς, δύο φορές, διπλάσιος.

twig [twig] *n* κλαδί, κλωνάρι ‖ *vt* (*understand, realize*) ἀντιλαμβάνομαι, μπαίνω, πιάνω.

twilight ['twailait] *n* λυκόφως, λυκαυγές.

twill [twil] *n* (ὕφασμα) καρρωτό.

twin [twin] *n* δίδυμος ‖ *a* δίδυμος.

twine [twain] *n* σπάγγος, χονδρὴ κλωστὴ ‖ *vi* τυλίγομαι.

twinge [twindʒ] *n* δυνατὸς πόνος, σουβλιά.

twinkle ['twiŋkl] *n* σπινθηρισμός, σπίθισμα ‖ *vi* σπινθηροβολῶ, σπιθίζω, τρεμοσβήνω.

twin town ['twin'taun] *n* δίδυμη πόλις.

twirl [twəːl] *n* περιστροφή, στρίψιμο ‖ *vti* περιστρέφω, στρίβω.

twist [twist] *n* συστροφή, στρίψιμο, στράμπούληγμα ‖ *vt* συστρέφω, πλέκω, στρίβω ‖ (*distort*) στρεβλώνω, στραβώνω ‖ (*cheat*) ἐξαπατῶ ‖ *vi* συστρέφομαι, στρίβομαι ‖ (*curve*) στρίβω.

twit [twit] *n* (*col: fool*) κορόιδο, βλάκας.

twitch [twitʃ] *n* σύσπασις, τίναγμα ‖ *vi* συσπῶμαι νευρικά.

two [tuː] *num* δύο ‖ **~-door** *a* (*aut*) μὲ δύο πόρτες ‖ **~-faced** *a* (*pej: person*) διπρόσωπος ‖ **~-fold** *ad* δίς, δύο φορές, διπλά ‖ *a* διπλός ‖ **~-piece** *a* (*suit*) ντεπιές (*swimsuit*) κοστούμι μπάνιου ντεπιές ‖ **~-seater** *n* (*plane*) διθέσιον ‖ (*car*) διθέσιον ‖ **~-some** *n* ζευγάρι ‖ **~-way** *a* (*traffic*) διπλῆς κυκλοφορίας.

tycoon [tai'kuːn] *n* μεγιστὰν τῶν ἐπιχειρήσεων.

type [taip] *n* τύπος ‖ (*example*) εἶδος, τάξις ‖ (*printing*) χαρακτῆρες, στοιχεῖα ‖ *vt* δακτυλογραφῶ ‖ **~script** *n* δακτυλογραφημένον κείμενον ‖ **~writer** *n* γραφομηχανὴ ‖ **~written** *a* δακτυλογραφημένον.

typhoid ['taifɔid] *n* τυφοειδής.

typhoon [tai'fuːn] *n* τυφών.

typhus ['taifəs] *n* τύφος.

typical ['tipikəl] *a* τυπικός, χαρακτηριστικός ‖ **~ly** *ad* τυπικῶς.

typify ['tipifai] *vt* ἀντιπροσωπεύω, συμβολίζω.

typing ['taipiŋ] *n* δακτυλογράφησις.

typist ['taipist] *n* δακτυλογράφος.

tyranny ['tirəni] *n* τυραννία.

tyrant ['taiərənt] *n* τύραννος.

tyre ['taiə*] *n* (*aut*) ρόδα, λάστιχο.

U, u

udder ['ʌdə*] *n* μαστός, μαστάρι.

ugh [əːh] *excl* πφ!, οὔφ!

ugliness ['ʌglinis] *n* ἀσχήμια.

ugly ['ʌgli] *a* ἄσχημος, ἄσχημος ‖ (*bad*) ἄσχημος, κακός ‖ (*dangerous*) δυσάρεστος, ἐπικίνδυνος, ἄσχημος.

ukulele [juːkəˈleili] *n* οὐκελελέ.

ulcer [ˈʌlsə*] *n* (*in mouth, stomach*) ἕλκος.

ulterior [ʌlˈtiəriə*] *a* (*hidden*) ὑστερόβουλος, κρυφός.

ultimate [ˈʌltimit] *a* τελευταῖος, τελικός, ὕστατος, βασικός ‖ ~**ly** *ad* τελικῶς, τελικά, βασικῶς.

ultimatum [ʌltiˈmeitəm] *n* τελεσίγραφον.

ultra- [ˈʌltrə] *prefix* ὑπερ-.

ultraviolet [ˈʌltrəˈvaiəlit] *a*: ~ light ὑπεριῶδες φῶς.

umbilical [ʌmbiˈlaikəl] *a*: ~ cord ὀμφάλιος λῶρος, ὀμφαλίς.

umbrage [ˈʌmbridʒ] *n* : to take ~ πειράζομαι ἀπό, δυσφορῶ.

umbrella [ʌmˈbrelə] *n* ὀμπρέλλα.

umpire [ˈʌmpaiə*] *n* διαιτητής ‖ *vi* διαιτητεύω.

umpteen [ˈʌmptiːn] *num* (*col*) ἕνα σωρό, δέν ξέρω πόσοι.

un- [ʌn] *prefix* ἀ-, ἐκ-, ξε-, ἀντι-, μή-.

unabashed [ˈʌnəˈbæʃt] *a* ἀτάραχος, ἀκλόνητος.

unabated [ˈʌnəˈbeitid] *a* ἀμείωτος, ἀδιάπτωτος.

unable [ʌnˈeibl] *a* ἀνίκανος, μή δυνάμενος.

unaccompanied [ˈʌnəˈkʌmpənid] *a* (*child, lady*) ἀσυνόδευτος, μόνος.

unaccountably [ˈʌnəˈkauntəbli] *ad* ἀνεξηγήτως.

unaccustomed [ˈʌnəˈkʌstəmd] *a* ἀσυνήθης ‖ (+ *to*) ἀσυνήθιστος (σέ, νά).

unadulterated [ˈʌnəˈdʌltəreitid] *a* ἀνόθευτος, ἀγνός.

unaided [ʌnˈeidid] *a* χωρίς βοήθειαν, ἀβοήθητος.

unanimity [juːnəˈnimiti] *n* ὁμοφωνία.

unanimous [juːˈnæniməs] *a* ὁμόθυμος, ὁμόφωνος ‖ ~**ly** *ad* ὁμοφώνως, παμψηφεί.

unattached [ˈʌnəˈtætʃt] *a* (*single*) ἐλεύθερος, ἐργένης.

unattended [ˈʌnəˈtendid] *a* χωρίς συνοδείαν, ἀπεριποίητος.

unattractive [ˈʌnəˈtræktiv] *a* μή συμπαθητικός.

unauthorized [ˈʌnˈɔːθəraizd] *a* ἄνευ ἀδείας, μή ἐξουσιοδοτημένος.

unavoidable [ˈʌnəˈvɔidəbl] *a* ἀναπόφευκτος.

unavoidably [ˈʌnəˈvɔidəbli] *ad* ἀναποφεύκτως.

unaware [ˈʌnəˈwɛə*] *a* ἀνίδεος, μή γνωρίζων, ἀγνοῶν ‖ ~**s** *ad* ἐξ ἀπίνης, χωρίς προειδοποίησιν.

unbalanced [ˈʌnˈbælənst] *a* μή ἰσορροπημένος, ἀνισόρροπος.

unbearable [ʌnˈbɛərəbl] *a* ἀνυπόφορος, ἀφόρητος.

unbeatable [ˈʌnˈbiːtəbl] *a* (*team*) ἀήττητος, ἀκατανίκητος.

unbeaten [ˈʌnˈbiːtn] *a* (*team, record*) ἀήττητος, οὐδέποτε καταρριφθείς.

unbecoming [ˈʌnbiˈkʌmiŋ] *a* ἀνάρμοστος, ἀπρεπής, πού δέν πηγαίνει.

unbeknown [ˈʌnbiˈnəun] *ad* (+ *to*) ἐν ἀγνοίᾳ τοῦ.

unbelief [ˈʌnbiˈliːf] *n* ἀπιστία, δυσπιστία.

unbelievable [ʌnbiˈliːvəbl] *a* ἀπίστευτος.

unbend [ʌnˈbend] *vi* εὐθυγραμμίζομαι σιάζω ‖ *vt* χαλαρώνω, ξετεντώνω.

unbounded [ʌnˈbaundid] *a* ἀπεριόριστος ἀπέραντος.

unbreakable [ʌnˈbreikəbl] *a* ἄθραυστος.

unbridled [ʌnˈbraidld] *a* ἀχαλίνωτος, ἀσυγκράτητος.

unbroken [ˈʌnˈbrəukən] *a* ἄθραυστος, ἄσπαστος, ἀπαράβατος, ἀδιατάρακτος.

unburden [ʌnˈbəːdn] *vt*: to ~ o.s. ἀνακουφίζω, ξαλαφρώνω.

unbutton [ʌnˈbʌtn] *vt* ξεκουμπώνω.

uncalled-for [ʌnˈkɔːldfɔː*] *a* ἄκαιρος, ἀδικαιολόγητος.

uncanny [ʌnˈkæni] *a* παράξενος, ἀφύσικος μυστηριώδης.

unceasing [ʌnˈsiːsiŋ] *a* ἀκατάπαυστος.

uncertain [ʌnˈsəːtn] *a* ἀβέβαιος, ἀμφίβολος ‖ (*weather etc*) ἀσταθής ‖ (*vague*) ἀκαθόριστος ‖ ~**ty** *n* ἀβεβαιότης, ἀμφιβολία, ἀστάθεια.

unchanged [ʌnˈtʃeindʒd] *a* ἀμετάβλητος.

uncharitable [ʌnˈtʃæritəbl] *a* ἄσπλαγχνος, αὐστηρός, ἀφιλάνθρωπος.

uncharted [ʌnˈtʃɑːtid] *a* ἀνεξερεύνητος.

unchecked [ˈʌnˈtʃekt] *a* ἀνεμπόδιστος, ἀσταμάτητος, ἀνεξέλεγκτος.

uncivil [ˈʌnˈsivil] *a* ἀγενής, ἄξεστος, κακότροπος.

uncle [ˈʌŋkl] *n* θεῖος, μπάρμπας.

uncomfortable [ʌnˈkʌmfətəbl] *a* (*uneasy*) ἀνήσυχος, δυσάρεστος.

uncompromising [ʌnˈkɔmprəmaiziŋ] *a* ἀδιάλλακτος, ἄκαμπτος.

uncongenial [ʌnkənˈdʒiːniəl] *a* δυσάρεστος, μή εὐνοϊκός, ἀσυμπαθής.

unconscious [ʌnˈkɔnʃəs] *a* ἀσυνείδητος ‖ (*not aware*) μή ἔχων συνείδησιν τοῦ, ἀγνοῶν ‖ *n*: the ~ τό ἀσυνείδητον ‖ ~**ly** *ad* ἀσυνειδήτως, χωρίς νά τό καταλάβω ‖ ~**ness** *n* (τό) ἀσυνείδητον, ἀναισθησία.

uncontrollable [ˈʌnkənˈtrəuləbl] *a* ἀχαλίνωτος, ἀκατάσχετος, ἀσυγκράτητος.

uncork [ˈʌnˈkɔːk] *vt* ἐκπωματίζω ξεβουλώνω.

uncouth [ʌnˈkuːθ] *a* ἀδέξιος, ἄξεστος.

uncover [ʌnˈkʌvə*] *vt* ξεσκεπάζω ‖ (*expose*) ἀποκαλύπτω, ἐκθέτω.

unctuous [ˈʌŋktjuəs] *a* (*too smooth*) ἀνειλικρινής, γλυκανάλατος.

undaunted [ʌnˈdɔːntid] *a* ἀτρόμητος, ἀπτόητος, ἄφοβος.

undecided [ˈʌndiˈsaidid] *a* ἀναποφάσιστος, ἐκκρεμῶν.

undeniable [ʌndiˈnaiəbl] *a* ἀναμβισβήτητος.

undeniably [ʌndiˈnaiəbli] *ad* ἀναντιρρήτως, ἀναμφισβητήτως.

under [ˈʌndə*] *prep* ὑπό, κάτω ἀπό ‖ (*in time*

of) ἐπί, στήν ἐποχή τοῦ ‖ *ad* κάτω, ὑποκάτω ‖ ~ **age** *a* ἀνήλιξ ‖ ~ **repair** ὑπό ἐπισκευήν.

undercarriage ['ʌndəkæridʒ] *n,* **undercart** ['ʌndəka:t] *n* σύστημα προσγειώσεως.

underclothes ['ʌndəkləuðz] *npl* ἐσώρρουχα.

underclothing ['ʌndəkləuðiŋ] *n* ἐσώρρουχα.

undercoat ['ʌndəkəut] *n* (*paint*) βασικόν χρῶμα.

undercover ['ʌndəklʌvə*] *a* μυστικός, κρυφός.·

undercurrent ['ʌndəklʌrənt] *n* ρεῦμα κάτω ἀπό τήν ἐπιφάνειαν.

undercut ['ʌndəklʌt] *n* (*cooking*) φιλέττο κρέατος ‖ *vt* πουλῶ φθηνότερα ἀπό.

underdeveloped ['ʌndədi'veləpt] *a* (*country*) ὑποανάπτυκτος.

underdog ['ʌndədɔg] *n* ὁ ἡττημένος, ὁ πιό ἀδύνατος.

underdone ['ʌndə'dʌn] *a* (*cooking*) ἄψητος, σαινιάν.

underestimate ['ʌndər'estimeit] *vt* ὑποτιμῶ.

underexpose ['ʌndəriks'pəuz] *vt* ἐκθέτω ὀλιγώτερον τοῦ δέοντος.

underfed ['ʌndə'fed] *a* ὑποσιτιζόμενος.

underfoot ['ʌndə'fut] *ad* κάτω ἀπό τά πόδια.

undergo ['ʌndə'gəu] *vt* ὑφίσταμαι, παθαίνω.

undergraduate ['ʌndə'grædjuit] *n* φοιτητής.

underground ['ʌndəgraund] *n* ὑπόγειος σιδηρόδρομος ‖ *a* (*press etc*) μυστικός, κρυφός, τῆς ἀντιστάσεως.

undergrowth ['ʌndəgrəuθ] *n* θάμνοι, χαμόκλαδα.

underhand ['ʌndəhænd] *a* πανοῦργος, ὕπουλος.

underlie [ʌndə'lai] *vt* ὑπόκειμαι, εἶμαι ἡ βάσις τοῦ.

underline [ʌndə'lain] *vt* ὑπογραμμίζω ‖ (*draw attention to*) ὑπογραμμίζω, τονίζω.

underling ['ʌndəliŋ] *n* ὑφιστάμενος, παραγιός, κολαοῦζος.

undermine [ʌndə'main] *vt* ὑπονομεύω, ὑποσκάπτω, τρώγω.

underneath [ʌndə'ni:θ] *ad* κάτωθεν, ἀπό κάτω ‖ *prep* κάτωθεν, (ὑπο)κάτω ἀπό, ὑπό.

underpaid [ʌndə'peid] *a* κακῶς ἀμειβόμενος.

underpass ['ʌndəpa:s] *n* ὑπόγειος διάβασις.

underprivileged ['ʌndə'privilidʒd] *a* μέ μειωμένα προνόμοια, πτωχός.

underrate [ʌndə'reit] *vt* ὑποτιμῶ.

underside ['ʌndəsaid] *n* κάτω πλευρά, τό ἀποκάτω.

underskirt ['ʌndəskə:t] *n* κομπιναιζόν, μεσοφόρι.

understand [ʌndə'stænd] *vt* ἀντιλαμβάνομαι ‖ (*know*) γνωρίζω, καταλαβαίνω ‖ (*hear, believe*) μαθαίνω, πιστεύω, νομίζω ‖ (*gram*) ὑπονοῶ ‖ ~**able** *a* (κατα)νοητός, καταληπτός, εὐνόητος ‖ ~**ing** *n* συνεννόησις, συμφωνία, κατανόησις.

understatement ['ʌndəsteitmənt] *n* δήλωσις κάτω τῆς πραγματικότητος.

understudy ['ʌndəstʌdi] *n* ἀντικαταστάτης.

undertake [ʌndə'teik] *vt* ἀναλαμβάνω ‖ ~**r** *n* ἐργολάβος κηδειῶν.

undertaking [ʌndə'teikiŋ] *n* ἐπιχείρησις ‖ (*promise*)·δέσμευσις, ὑποχρέωσις.

underwater ['ʌndə'wɔ:tə*] *ad* ὑποβρυχίως ‖ *a* ὑποβρύχιος.

underwear ['ʌndəwɛə*] *n* ἐσώρρουχα.

underweight [ʌndə'weit] *a* λιποβαρής, ἀδύνατος.

underworld ['ʌndəwə:ld] *n* (*of crime*) ὑπόκοσμος.

underwriter ['ʌndəraitə*] *n* (*insurance*) ἀσφαλιστής.

undesirable ['ʌndi'zaiərəbl] *a* ἀνεπιθύμητος.

undies ['ʌndiz] *npl* (*col*) ἐσώρρουχα (γυναικεῖα).

undiscovered ['ʌndis'klʌvəd] *a* μή ἀνακαλυφθείς.

undisputed ['ʌndis'pju:tid] *a* ἀδιαφιλονίκητος, ἀδιαμφισβήτητος.

undistinguished ['ʌndis'tiŋgwiʃt] *a* μέτριος, κοινός, ἀσήμαντος.

undo [ʌn'du:] *vt* λύνω, ξεκουμπώνω, ἀνοίγω ‖ (*work*) καταστρέφω, χαλνῶ ‖ ~**ing** *n* καταστροφή, ἀφανισμός.

undoubted [ʌn'dautid] *a* ἀναμφισβήτητος, ἀναμφίβολος ‖ ~**ly** *ad* ἀναμφισβητήτως.

undress ['ʌn'dres] *vti* γδύνομαι, γδύνω.

undue ['ʌn'dju:] *a* ὑπερβολικός, ἀδικαιολόγητος.

undulating ['ʌndjuleitiŋ] *a* κυμαινόμενος, ταλαντευόμενος.

unduly ['ʌn'dju:li] *ad* ὑπερβολικά, ἀπρεπῶς.

unearth ['ʌn'ə:θ] *vt* ἀνασκάπτω, ἀνακαλύπτω ‖ ~**ly** *a* ὑπερφυσικός, ἀπίθανος.

unease ['ʌn'i:z] *n* ἀνησυχία, στενοχώρια, ταραχή.

uneasy [ʌn'i:zi] *a* ἀνήσυχος, στενοχωρημένος.

uneconomic(al) ['ʌni:kə'nɔmik(əl)] *a* ἀνοικονομικός, σπάταλος, ἀσύμφορος.

uneducated ['ʌn'edjukeitid] *a* ἀπαίδευτος, ἀσπούδαστος, ἀμόρφωτος.

unemployed ['ʌnim'plɔid] *a* ἄνεργος, ἀχρησιμοποίητος ‖ *npl:* **the** ~ οἱ ἄνεργοι.

unemployment ['ʌnim'plɔimənt] *n* ἀνεργία.

unending [ʌn'endiŋ] *a* ἀτελείωτος, διαρκής.

unenviable ['ʌn'enviəbl] *a* ἀζήλευτος, ἀνεπιθύμητος.

unerring ['ʌn'ə:riŋ] *a* ἀλάνθαστος, ἀκριβής.

uneven ['ʌn'i:vən] *a* (*surface*) ἀνώμαλος, ὀρεινός ‖ (*quality*) ἄνισος, ἀκανόνιστος.

unexploded ['ʌniks'pləudid] *a* (*bomb*) μή ἐκραγείς.

unfailing [ʌn'feiliŋ] *a* ἀλάνθαστος, ἀτελείωτος, διαρκής, πιστός.

unfair ['ʌn'fɛə*] *a* (*unkind, unreasonable*) ἄδικος, μή ὀρθός, ἄνισος ‖ ~**ly** *ad* ἄδικα, ἄτιμα, πρόστυχα.

unfaithful [ʌnˈfeiθful] a (to spouse) ἄπιστος.

unfasten [ʌnˈfɑːsn] vt λύνω, ξεκουμπώνω, ξεκλειδώνω.

unfavourable, (US) unfavorable [ʌnˈfeivərəbl] a δυσμενής, δυσοίωνος.

unfeeling [ʌnˈfiːliŋ] a σκληρόκαρδος, ἀναίσθητος.

unfinished [ʌnˈfiniʃt] a ἡμιτελής, ἀτελής.

unfit [ʌnˈfit] a (in health) ἀνίκανος, ἀδιάθετος || (+for) ἀκατάλληλος (γιά).

unflagging [ʌnˈflægiŋ] a ἀκλόνητος, ἀκατάπαυστος, ἀλύγιστος.

unflinching [ʌnˈflintʃiŋ] a σταθερός, ἀποφασιστικός.

unfold [ʌnˈfəuld] vt ξεδιπλώνω, ξετυλίγω, ἁπλώνω || (reveal) ἀποκαλύπτω, ἀναπτύσσω, ἐξηγῶ || vi (develop) ἀναπτύσσομαι, ἐκτυλίσσομαι.

unforeseen [ˈʌnfɔːˈsiːn] a ἀπρόβλεπτος, ἀπροσδόκητος.

unforgivable [ˈʌnfəˈgivəbl] a ἀσυγχώρητος.

unfortunate [ʌnˈfɔːtʃnit] a ἀτυχής, δυστυχής, ἄστοχος || ~ly ad δυστυχῶς, ἄτυχος.

unfounded [ʌnˈfaundid] a (rumour) ἀβάσιμος, ψευδής.

unfriendly [ʌnˈfrendli] a ἀφιλόφρων, ἐχθρικός.

unfurnished [ˈʌnˈfəːniʃt] a (flat) ἄνευ ἐπίπλων.

ungainly [ʌnˈgeinli] a ἀδέξιος.

ungodly [ʌnˈgɔdli] a (col: hour) ἀθεόφοβος, ἀκατάλληλος, παράλογος.

unguarded [ˈʌnˈgɑːdid] a (moment) ἀπρόσεκτος, ἀπερίσκεπτος.

unhappiness [ʌnˈhæpinis] n θλῖψις, στενοχώρια.

unhappy [ʌnˈhæpi] a δυστυχής, δυστυχισμένος, στενοχωρημένος.

unharmed [ʌnˈhɑːmd] a σῶος, ἀβλαβής, ἀπείραχτος.

unhealthy [ʌnˈhelθi] a (lit) ἀνθυγιεινός, ἀρρωστιάρης || (fig) νοσηρός.

unheard-off [ʌnˈhəːdəv] a πρωτάκουστος, ἀνήκουστος.

unhurt [ˈʌnˈhəːt] a χωρίς τραῦμα, σῶος καί ἀβλαβής.

unicorn [ˈjuːnikɔːn] n μονόκερως.

unidentified [ˈʌnaiˈdentifaid] a μή ἀναγνωρισθείς, ἄγνωστος.

unification [juːnifiˈkeiʃən] n ἑνοποίησις.

uniform [ˈjuːnifɔːm] n στολή || a ὁμοιόμορφος, ἴδιος || ~ity n ὁμοιομορφία.

unify [ˈjuːnifai] vt ἑνοποιῶ.

unilateral [ˈjuːniˈlætərəl] a μονόπλευρος.

unimaginable [ʌniˈmædʒinəbl] a ἀδιανόητος, ἀφαντάστος.

uninjured [ˈʌnˈindʒəd] a σῶος καί ἀβλαβής, ἄθικτος.

unintentional [ˈʌninˈtenʃənl] a ἀκούσιος, ἀθέλητος.

union [ˈjuːnjən] n ἕνωσις, συγκόλλησις || (alliance) ἕνωσις, συμφωνία || (of workers)

ἐργατικόν σωματεῖον, συνδικάτον || U~ Jack n Ἀγγλική σημαία.

unique [juːˈniːk] a μοναδικός, ἰδιόρρυθμος, ἀσυνήθης.

unison [ˈjuːnisn] n: in ~ ἐν ὁμοφωνία, ἐν συμφωνία || (mus) ἁρμονία, μονοφωνία, ὁμοηχία.

unit [ˈjuːnit] n μονάς || (team, squad) ὁμάδα, συγκρότημα.

unite [juːˈnait] vt ἑνώνω || vi ἑνώνομαι (μέ) || ~d a ἡνωμένος, ἑνωμένος, συνδεδυασμένος || U~d Kingdom n Ἡνωμένον Βασίλειον || U~d Nations npl Ἡνωμένα Ἔθνη || U~d States (of America) npl Ἡνωμέναι Πολιτεῖαι.

unit trust [ˈjuːnitˈtrʌst] n (Brit) σύστημα ἐπενδύσεων εἰς μετοχάς.

unity [ˈjuːniti] n ἑνότης, ἁρμονία, σύμπνοια, μονάς.

universal [juːniˈvəːsəl] a γενικός, καθολικός, πάγκοινος || (of the world) παγκόσμιος || ~ly ad καθολικῶς, παγκοσμίως.

universe [ˈjuːnivəːs] n σύμπαν, οἰκουμένη.

university [juːniˈvəːsiti] n πανεπιστήμιον.

unjust [ʌnˈdʒʌst] a ἄδικος.

unjustifiable [ʌnˈdʒʌstifaiəbl] a ἀδικαιολόγητος.

unkempt [ˈʌnˈkempt] a ἀκατάστατος, ἀκτένιστος.

unkind [ʌnˈkaind] a ἀφιλόφρων, ἄστοργος, σκληρός.

unknown [ˈʌnˈnəun] a (+to) ἄγνωστος (εἰς), ἀγνοούμενος ἀπό.

unladen [ˈʌnˈleidn] a (col: weight) ἄνευ φορτίου, κενός.

unleash [ˈʌnˈliːʃ] vt λύνω, ἐλευθερώνω.

unleavened [ˈʌnˈlevnd] a ἄζυμος.

unless [ənˈles] cj ἐκτός ἐάν, ἐκτός ἄν.

unlicensed [ˈʌnˈlaisənst] a (to sell alcohol) ἄνευ ἀδείας, μή ἐπιτρεπόμενος.

unlike [ˈʌnˈlaik] a ἀνόμοιος, διάφορος ἀπό.

unlimited [ʌnˈlimitid] a ἀπεριόριστος.

unload [ˈʌnˈləud] vt ἐκφορτώνω, ξεφορτώνω.

unlock [ˈʌnˈlɔk] vt ξεκλειδώνω.

unmarried [ˈʌnˈmærid] a ἄγαμος.

unmask [ˈʌnˈmɑːsk] vt (expose) ἀποκαλύπτω || ἀφαιρῶ προσωπεῖον ἀπό.

unmistakable [ˈʌnmisˈteikəbl] a προφανής, καταφανής, σαφής.

unmistakably [ˈʌnmisˈteikəbli] ad σαφῶς, καταφανῶς, καθαρά.

unmitigated [ʌnˈmitigeitid] a ἀμετρίαστος, ἄκρος, ἀπόλυτος.

unnecessary [ʌnˈnesisəri] a περιττός, ἄσκοπος, μάταιος.

unobtainable [ˈʌnəbˈteinəbl] a ἀνεπίτευκτος.

unoccupied [ˈʌnˈɔkjupaid] a (seat etc) ἐλεύθερος, διαθέσιμος.

unopened [ˈʌnˈəupənd] a (letter etc) κλειστός, πού δέν ἀνοίχθηκε.

unorthodox ['ʌn'ɔ:θədɔks] *a* ἀνορθόδοξος.

unpack ['ʌn'pæk] *vti* ἀδειάζω ἀποσκευές, βγάζω ἀπό βαλίτσες.

unparalleled [ʌn'pærəleld] *a* ἀπαράμιλλος.

unpleasant [ʌn'plezənt] *a* δυσάρεστος.

unplug ['ʌn'plʌg] *vt* ξεβουλώνω, βγάζω τήν πρίζα.

unpopular ['ʌn'pɔpjulə*] *a* ἀντιδημοτικός.

unprecedented [ʌn'presidəntid] *a* ἄνευ προηγουμένου.

unqualified ['ʌn'kwɔlifaid] *a* ἀναρμόδιος, ἀκατάλληλος ‖ (*success*) ἀμετρίαστος, ἀπόλυτος.

unravel [ʌn'rænəl] *vt* ξεφτῶ, ξηλώνω, ξετυλίγω ‖ (*solve*) διευκρινίζω, λύνω, διαλύω.

unreal ['ʌn'riəl] *a* ἀπατηλός, φανταστικός.

unreasonable [ʌn'riznəbl] *a* (*unfair*) παράλογος.

unrelenting ['ʌnri'lentiŋ] *a* ἀδυσώπητος, ἀνηλεής.

unrelieved ['ʌnri'li:vd] *a* (*monotony*) χωρίς ποικιλίαν, μονότονος.

unrepeatable ['ʌnri'pi:təbl] *a* (*offer*) πού δέν ἐπαναλαμβάνεται.

unreserved ['ʌnri'zə:vd] *a* (*seat*) θέσις ὄχι κρατημένη, ἐλεύθερη θέσι.

unrest [ʌn'rest] *n* (*discontent, trouble*) ἀνησυχία, ταραχή.

unroll ['ʌn'rəul] *vt* ξετυλίγω.

unruly [ʌn'ru:li] *a* ἀνυπότακτος, ταραχώδης, ἄτακτος.

unsafe ['ʌn'seif] *a* ἐπικίνδυνος, ἀνασφαλής.

unsaid ['ʌn'sed] *a*: **to leave sth ~** ἀποσιωπῶ κάτι.

unsatisfactory ['ʌnsætis'fæktəri] *a* μή ἱκανοποιητικός, ἀνεπαρκής.

unsavoury, (*US*) **unsavory** ['ʌn'seivəri] *a* (*of bad character*) ὑποπτος, σκοτεινός.

unscrew ['ʌn'skru:] *vt* ξεβιδώνω.

unscrupulous [ʌn'skru:pjuləs] *a* ἀσυνείδητος, ἀνενδοίαστος.

unselfish ['ʌn'selfiʃ] *a* ἀφιλοκερδής, ἀλτρουϊστικός.

unsettled ['ʌn'setld] *a* ἀνήσυχος, ἀβέβαιος, ἀσταθής ‖ (*weather*) εὐμετάβλητος, ἀβέβαιος.

unshaven ['ʌn'ʃeivn] *a* ἀξύριστος, ἀξούριστος.

unsightly [ʌn'saitli] *a* ἄσχημος, δυσειδής.

unskilled ['ʌn'skild] *a* (*workman*) ἀνειδίκευτος.

unsophisticated ['ʌnsə'fistikeitid] *a* ἀφελής, ἀπλός, ἄδωος, ἀγνός.

unsound ['ʌn'saund] *a* (*ideas*) ἐπισφαλής, ἐσφαλμένος.

unspeakable [ʌn'spi:kəbl] *a* ἀπερίγραπτος, ἀνείπωτος, ἀνέκφραστος ‖ (*very bad*) ἀποκρουστικός, ἀηδής, σιχαμερός.

unstuck ['ʌn'stʌk] *a*: **to come ~** ξεκολλῶ ‖ (*lit*) ξεκολλᾶ, ξεκολλιέμαι ‖ (*fig*) καταρρέω, γκρεμίζομαι.

unsuccessful ['ʌnsək'sesful] *a* ἀνεπιτυχής.

unsuitable ['ʌn'su:təbl] *a* ἀκατάλληλος.

unsuspecting ['ʌnsəs'pektiŋ] *a* πού δέν ὑποπτεύεται.

unswerving [ʌn'swə:viŋ] *a* (*loyalty*) σταθερός, πιστός.

untangle ['ʌn'tæŋgl] *vt* ξεχωρίζω, ξεμπλέκω.

untapped ['ʌn'tæpt] *a* (*resources*) μή χρησιμοποιηθείς, ἀνεκμετάλλευτος.

unthinkable [ʌn'θiŋkəbl] *a* ἀσύλληπτος, πολύ ἀπίθανος.

untidy [ʌn'taidi] *a* ἀκατάστατος.

untie ['ʌn'tai] *vt* λύνω, ξεκουμπώνω.

until [ən'til] *prep* μέχρις, ἕως ‖ *cj* μέχρις ὅτου, ἕως ὅτου.

untimely [ʌn'taimli] *a* (*death*) πρόωρος.

untold ['ʌn'təuld] *a* (*countless*) ἀμέτρητος, ἀνυπολόγιστος.

untoward [ʌntə'wɔ:d] *a* δυσάρεστος, ἀτυχής.

untranslatable ['ʌntræns'leitəbl] *a* ἀμετάφραστος.

untried ['ʌn'traid] *a* (*plan*) ἀδοκίμαστος.

unused ['ʌn'ju:zd] *a* ἀσυνήθιστος, μή συνηθισμένος (εἰς).

unusual [ʌn'ju:ʒuəl] *a* ἀσυνήθης, σπάνιος, ἀξιοσημείωτος ‖ **~ly** *ad* ἐξαιρετικά, ἀφάνταστα, ἀσυνήθιστα.

unveil [ʌn'veil] *vt* ἀποκαλύπτω, ξεσκεπάζω.

unwary [ʌn'weəri] *a* ἀπρόσεκτος, ἀμέριμνος.

unwavering [ʌn'weivəriŋ] *a* ἀσάλευτος, σταθερός.

unwell ['ʌn'wel] *a* ἀδιάθετος, ἄρρωστος.

unwieldy [ʌn'wi:ldi] *a* δυσκίνητος, βαρύς, ἀδέξιος.

unwilling ['ʌn'wiliŋ] *a* ἀπρόθυμος, ἀκούσιος.

unwind ['ʌn'waind] *vt* (*lit*) ἐκτυλίσσω, ξεκουρδίζω ‖ *vi* (*relax*) χαλαρώνομαι.

unwitting [ʌn'witiŋ] *a* ἀγνοῶν, ἀκούσιος.

unwrap ['ʌn'ræp] *vt* ξετυλίγω.

unwritten ['ʌn'ritn] *a* (*law*) ἄγραφος, πατροπαράδοτος, προφορικός.

up [ʌp] *prep* πρός τά ἄνω, ἀντίθετα μέ τό ρεῦμα ‖ *ad* ἐπάνω, ἄνω, τελείως ‖ **it is ~ to you** ἐξαρτᾶται ἀπό σένα ‖ **what is he ~ to?** τί ἐπιδιώκει; τί θέλει; ‖ **he is not ~ to it** δέν ἔχει τήν ἱκανότητα (νά) ‖ **~-and-coming** *a* ἐξαιρετικά δραστήριος, ἀναπτυσσόμενος ‖ *n*: **the ~s and downs of** διακυμάνσεις, μεταβολές τῆς τύχης.

upbringing ['ʌpbriŋiŋ] *n* ἀνατροφή.

update [ʌp'deit] *vt* συντομεύω ἡμερομηνίαν (σύγχρονίζω), ἀναταραχή.

upend [ʌp'end] *vt* (*lift up*) σηκώνω.

upheaval [ʌp'hi:vəl] *n* (*violent disturbance*) ἀναστάτωσις, ἀναταραχή.

uphill ['ʌp'hil] *a* ἀνηφορικός ‖ *ad* πρός τά ἄνω.

uphold [ʌp'həuld] *vt* (*maintain*) ὑποστηρίζω.

upholstery [ʌp'həulstəri] *n* ταπετσαρία.

upkeep ['ʌpki:p] *n* συντήρησις, ἔξοδα συντηρήσεως.

upon [ə'pɔn] *prep* ἐπί, εἰς.

upper ['ʌpə*] *a* ἀνώτερος, ἄνω, ἀπό πάνω ‖ the ~ class *n* ἡ ἀνωτέρα τάξις, ἡ καλή κοινωνία ‖ ~-class *a* τῆς ἀ..ωτέρας τάξεως ‖ ~most *a* ὑψηλότερος, πιό πάνω, πάνω-πάνω, ἀνώτατος.

upright ['ʌprait] *a* ὄρθιος, κατακόρυφος, κάθετος ‖ (*honest*) εὐθύς, δίκαιος, τίμιος ‖ *n* ὀρθοστάτης.

uprising [ʌp'raiziŋ] *n* ἐξέγερσις, ξεσήκωμα.

uproar ['ʌprɔː*] *n* θόρυβος, πάταγος, φασαρία, ἀναστάτωσις.

uproot [ʌp'ruːt] *vt* ξερριζώνω.

upset [ʌp'set] *n* ἀναστάτωσις, ἀνατροπή, ἀναποδογύρισμα ‖ [ʌp'set] *vt* ἀνατρέπω, ἀναποδογυρίζω ‖ (*distress*) ταράσσω, ἀναστατῶνω, συγκινῶ ‖ ~ting *a* συνταρακτικός, ἀνησυχητικός.

upshot ['ʌpʃɔt] *n* ἀποτέλεσμα, ἔκβασις, κατάληξις.

upside ['ʌpsaid] ~ down *ad* ἄνω-κάτω, ἀνάποδα, φύρδην-μύγδην.

upstairs ['ʌp'steəz] *ad* στό ἐπάνω πάτωμα ‖ *a* (*room*) ἐπάνω, τοῦ ἄνω ὀρόφου ‖ *n* ἐπάνω.

upstart ['ʌpstaːt] *n* νεόπλουτος, ἀναιδής ἄνθρωπος.

upstream ['ʌp'striːm] *ad* ἀντίθετα μέ τό ρεῦμα.

uptake ['ʌpteik] *n*: quick, (slow) on the ~ (δέν) παίρνω, (δέν) ἁρπάζω.

up-to-date ['ʌptə'deit] *a* σύγχρονος, μοντέρνος, τῆς μόδας.

upturn ['ʌptəːn] *n* (*in luck*) βελτίωσις, ἄνοδος.

upward ['ʌpwəd] *a* πρός τά ἄνω ‖ ~(s) *ad* πρός τά ἄνω.

uranium [ju'reiniəm] *n* οὐράνιον.

urban ['əːbən] *a* ἀστικός.

urbane [əː'bein] *a* εὐγενής, ἁβρόφρων, ραφιναρισμένος.

urchin ['əːtʃin] *n* (*boy*) ἀλητάκι ‖ (*also* sea ~) ἐχῖνος, ἀχινός.

urge [əːdʒ] *n* (*desire*) ἐπίμονος ἐπιθυμία, ὤθησις ‖ *vt* (*entreat*) παροτρύνω, συνιστῶ ‖ to ~ on *vt* παρορμῶ, παρακινῶ, ἐνθαρρύνω.

urgency ['əːdʒənsi] *n* ἐπείγουσα ἀνάγκη, ἐπιμονή, πίεσις.

urgent ['əːdʒənt] *a* ἐπείγων, πιεστικός, ἄμεσος ‖ ~ly *ad* ἐπειγόντως.

uri al ['juərinl] *n* οὐρητήριον, οὐροδοχε ον.

urinate ['juərineit] *vi* (κατ)οὐρῶ.

urine ['juərin] *n* οὖρα.

urn [əːn] *n* ὑδρία, δοχεῖον, ἀγγεῖον ‖ (*teapot*) σαμοβάρι.

us [ʌs] *pron* ἡμᾶς, ἐμᾶς, μας.

usage ['juːzidʒ] *n* μεταχείρησις, ἔθιμον, συνήθειο ‖ (*esp ling*) χρῆσις.

use [juːs] *n* χρῆσις ‖ (*custom*) συνήθεια, ἔθιμον ‖ (*employment*) χρῆσις, χρησιμο-

ποίησις ‖ (*value*) χρησιμότης ‖ [juːz] *vt* χρησιμοποιῶ, μεταχειρίζομαι ‖ (*make most of*) χρησιμεύω ‖ in ~ ἐν χρήσει ‖ out of ~ ἄχρηστος ‖ ~d to συνηθίζω νά ‖ she ~d to do it συνήθιζε νά τό κ νει ‖ to ~ up *vt* καταναλίσκω, ἐξαντλῶ ‖ ~d *a* (*car*) μεταχειρισμένο, δεύτερου χεριοῦ ‖ ~ful *a* χρήσιμος, πρακτικός ‖ ~fulness *n* χρησιμότης, ὠφελιμότης ‖ ~less *a* ἄχρηστος, μάταιος, ἄκαρπος ‖ ~lessly *ad* ματαίως, ἀνωφελῶς, μάταια ‖ ~lessness *n* Ελλειψι; ὠφελιμότητος ‖ ~r *n* χρησιμοποιῶν.

usher ['ʌʃə*] *n* (*at wedding*) παράνυμφος ‖ ~ette *n* (*at cinema*) ταξιθέτρια.

usual ['juːʒuəl] *a* συνήθης, συνηθισμένος ‖ ~ly *ad* συνήθως.

usurp [juː'zəːp] *vt* σφετερίζομαι, ἁρπάζω ‖ ~er *n* σφετεριστής.

usury ['juːʒuri] *n* τοκογλυφία.

utensil [juː'tensl] *n* σκεῦος, ἐργαλεῖον.

uterus ['juːtərəs] *n* μήτρα.

utilitarian [juːtili'tɛəriən] *a* κοινωφελής, ὠφελιμιστικός.

utility [juː'tiliti] *n* χρησιμότης, εὐχρηστία ‖ (*useful thing*) χρήσιμον πρᾶγμα ‖ (*also public utility: electricity supply industry*) δημοσία ὑπηρεσία, κοινωφελής ἐπιχείρησις.

utilization [juːtilai'zeiʃən] *n* χρησιμοποίησις.

utilize ['juːtilaiz] *vt* χρησιμοποιῶ, ἐκμεταλλεύομαι.

utmost ['ʌtməust] *a* ἀκρότατος, ἀπώτατος, ἔσχατος ‖ *n*: to do one's ~ κάνω ὅ,τι μπορῶ.

utter ['ʌtə*] *a* πλήρης, ὁλοσχερής ‖ *vt* ἀρθρώνω, ἐκστομίζω, προφέρω, λέω ‖ ~ance *n* ἔκφρασις, γνώμη ‖ ~ly *ad* τελείως, ἐξ ὁλοκλήρου.

U-turn ['juː'təːn] *n* (*aut*) στροφή 180 μοιρῶν.

V, v

vacancy ['veikənsi] *n* κενόν, κενή θέσις, δωμάτιον.

vacant ['veikənt] *a* κενός ‖ (*not occupied*) ἄδειος, χηρεύων ‖ (*stupid*) ἀφηρημένος, ἀνέκφραστος ‖ '~' (*on door*) 'δωμάτια'.

vacate [və'keit] *vt* ἐκκενώνω, ἀδειάζω, ἐγκαταλείπω.

vacation [və'keiʃən] *n* διακοπή, ἀργία ‖ ~ist *n* (*US*) ἀδειοῦχος, παραθεριστής.

vaccinate ['væksineit] *vt* ἐμβολιάζω, μπολιάζω.

vaccination [væksi'neiʃən] *n* δαμαλισμός, μπόλιασμα.

vaccine ['væksiːn] *n* δαμαλίς, ἐμβόλιον, βατσίνα.

vacuum ['vækjum] *n* κενόν ‖ ~ bottle *n* (*US*) φιάλη κενοῦ, θερμός ‖ ~ cleaner *n* ἠλεκτρική σκούπα ‖ ~ flask *n* (*Brit*) φιάλη κενοῦ, θερμός.

vagary ['veigəri] *n* ἰδιοτροπία, φαντασιοπληξία, βίδα.

vagina [və'dʒainə] *n* κόλπος (γυναικός).

vagrant ['veigrənt] *n* τυχωδιώκτης, ἀλήτης.

vague [veig] *a* ἀσαφής, ἀμυδρός, ἀκαθόριστος ‖ ~**ly** *ad* ἀορίστως, ἀσαφῶς ‖ ~**ness** *n* ἀσάφεια, ἀοριστία.

vain [vein] *a* μάταιος, ἄκαρπος, κενός ‖ (*conceited*) ματαιόδοξος, καμαρωτός ‖ **in** ~ ματαίως, μάταια ‖ ~**ly** *ad* μάταια, ἀνωφελῶς, ἄσκοπα.

vale [veil] *n* κοιλάδα, λαγκαδιά.

valeting ['vælitiŋ] *a*: ~ **service** ὑπηρεσία σιδηρώματος ἀνδρικῶν ἐνδυμάτων.

valiant ['væliənt] *a* γενναῖος ‖ ~**ly** *ad* ἀνδρείως, παλληκαρίσια.

valid ['vælid] *a* ἔγκυρος, βάσιμος, νόμιμος, λογικός ‖ ~**ity** *n* ἐγκυρότης, ἰσχύς.

valise [və'li:z] *n* (*suitcase*) βαλίτσα.

valley ['væli] *n* κοιλάδα, λαγκάδι.

valuable ['væljuəbl] *a* πολύτιμος ‖ ~**s** *npl* ἀντικείμενα ἀξίας.

valuation [vælju'eiʃən] *n* ἐκτίμησις, ἀξία.

value ['vælju:] *n* ἀξία, τιμή, σημασία, ἔννοια ‖ *vt* ἐκτιμῶ ‖ ~**d** *a* (*appreciated*) ἐκτιμώμενος ‖ ~**less** *a* ἄνευ ἀξίας, εὐτελής ‖ ~**r** *n* ἐκτιμητής.

valve [vælv] *n* βαλβίς, βαλβίδα, δικλείς, λυχνία.

vampire ['væmpaiə*] *n* βρυκόλακας.

van [væn] *n* φορτηγόν, σκευοφόρος.

vandal ['vændəl] *n* βάνδαλος ‖ ~**ism** *n* βανδαλισμός.

vanilla [və'nilə] *n* βανίλλη, βανίλλια ‖ *attr a* (*ice cream*) κρέμα.

vanish ['væniʃ] *vi* ἐξαφανίζομαι, ἐκλείπω, χάνομαι.

vanity ['væniti] *n* ματαιοδοξία, ἐγωϊσμός ‖ (*worthless display*) ματαιότης, τό μάταιον ‖ ~ **case** *n* πουντριέρα.

vantage ['va:ntidʒ] *n*: ~ **point** (*good viewpoint*) πλεονεκτική θέσις.

vapour, (*US*) **vapor** ['veipə*] *n* ἀχνός, πάχνη ‖ (*gas*) ἀτμός, ὑδρατμός.

variable ['vɛəriəbl] *a* μεταβλητός, εὐμετάβλητος.

variance ['vɛəriəns] *n*: **at** ~ εἰς διάστασιν, εἰς διαφωνίαν.

variant ['vɛəriənt] *n* διάφορος μορφή, μεταβλητή.

variation [vɛəri'eiʃən] *n* παραλλαγή, παρέκκλισις, μεταβολή.

varicose ['værikəus] *a*: ~ **veins** κιρσώδεις φλέβες.

varied ['vɛərid] *a* διάφορος, ποικίλος, μεταβαλλόμενος.

variety [və'raiəti] *n* ποικιλία, διαφορά ‖ (*varied collection*) ποικιλία, πολλά καί διάφορα ‖ (*kind*) ποικιλία ‖ ~ **show** *n* (*theat*) παράστασις ποικιλιῶν, ἐπιθεώρησις.

various ['vɛəriəs] *a* ποικίλος, πολυειδής.

varnish ['va:niʃ] *n* βερνίκι, στιλβωμένη ἐπιφάνεια ‖ *vt* βερνικώνω, στιλβώνω.

vary ['vɛəri] *vt* διαφοροποιῶ, ποικίλω ‖ *vi* ἀλλάζω, μεταβάλλομαι, παρεκκλίνω ‖ ~**ing** *a* μεταβαλλόμενος, μεταβλητός, ποικίλος.

vase [va:z] *n* βάζο, ἀγγεῖον.

vast [va:st] *a* πελώριος, ἐκτεταμένος, μεγάλος, ἀπέραντος ‖ ~**ly** *ad* ἀπεράντως, ἀπέραντα ‖ ~**ness** *n* ἀπεραντοσύνη, ἀπέραντος ἔκτασις.

vat [væt] *n* κάδος, βούτα, ξυλοβάρελον.

Vatican ['vætikən] *n*: **the** ~ τό Βατικανόν.

vault [vɔ:lt] *n* θόλος, καμάρα ‖ (*cellar*) ὑπόγειον, θολωτός τάφος ‖ (*leap*) πήδημα, ἅλμα ‖ *vt* πηδῶ, κάνω ἅλμα ἐπί κοντῶ.

veal [vi:l] *n* μοσχάρι.

veer [viə*] *vi* στρέφω, μεταπίπτω, γυρίζω.

vegetable ['vedʒitəbl] *n* φυτόν, λαχανικόν, χορταρικό.

vegetarian [vedʒi'tɛəriən] *a,n* χορτοφάγος, φυτοφάγος.

vegetate ['vedʒiteit] *vi* φυτοζωῶ.

vegetation [vedʒi'teiʃən] *n* βλάστησις.

vehemence ['vi:iməns] *n* βιαιότης, βία, ὁρμή.

vehement ['vi:imənt] *a* βίαιος, ὁρμητικός, σφοδρός.

vehicle ['vi:ikl] *n* ὄχημα, ἁμάξι.

vehicular [vi'hikjulə*] *a* (*traffic*) τοῦ ὀχήματος.

veil [veil] *n* πέπλος, βέλο ‖ (*fig*) κάλυμμα, συγκάλυψις ‖ *vt* καλύπτω, ἀποκρύπτω.

vein [vein] *n* φλέψ, φλέβα ‖ (*of ore*) φλέβα, στρῶμα ‖ (*streak*) φλέβα, διάθεσις, ταλέντο ‖ (*mood*) πνεῦμα, διάθεσις, κέφι.

velocity [vi'lɔsiti] *n* ταχύτης.

velvet ['velvit] *n* βελοῦδο.

vendetta [ven'detə] *n* βεντέττα, ἐκδίκησις.

vending machine ['vendiŋməʃi:n] *n* μηχάνημα πωλήσεως.

vendor ['vendɔ:*] *n* πωλητής.

veneer [və'niə*] *n* (*lit*) καπλαμᾶς, ἐπίστρωσις, ἐπένδυσις ‖ (*fig*) ἐπίχρισμα, ἐπίστρωμα, λοῦστρο.

venerable ['venərəbl] *a* ἀξιοσέβαστος, σεβάσμιος.

venereal [vi'niəriəl] *a* (*disease*) ἀφροδίσιος.

venetian [vi'ni:ʃən] *a*: ~ **blind** περσίδες.

vengeance ['vendʒəns] *n* ἐκδίκησις.

venison ['venisn] *n* κρέας ἐλαφιοῦ, κρέας ἀγρίου ζώου.

venom ['venəm] *n* δηλητήριον, φαρμάκι ‖ ~**ous** *a* φαρμακερός ‖ ~**ously** *ad* φαρμακερά.

vent [vent] *n* ὀπή ἐξαερισμοῦ, διέξοδος, ἄνοιγμα ‖ *vt* ξεσπῶ, ξεθυμαίνω.

ventilate ['ventileit] *vt* ἀερίζω.

ventilation [venti'leiʃən] *n* (ἐξ)αερισμός.

ventilator ['ventileitə*] *n* ἐξαεριστήρ, ἀνεμιστήρ.

ventriloquist [ven'triləkwist] *n* ἐγγαστρίμυθος.

venture ['ventʃə*] *n* τόλμημα, ἐγχείρημα, ἐπιχείρησις ‖ *vt* ριψοκινδυνεύω, ρισκάρω ‖ *vi* ἀποτολμῶ, τολμῶ.

venue ['venju:] *n* τόπος συναντήσεως, τόπος δίκης.

veranda(h) [və'rændə] *n* βεράντα.

verb [və:b] *n* ῥῆμα ‖ ~al *a* λεκτικός, προφορικός ‖ (*of a verb*) ῥηματικός ‖ ~ally *ad* προφορικῶς ‖ ~atim *ad* κατά λέξιν, καταλεκτικῶς.

verbose [və:'bəus] *a* πολύλογος, μακροσκελής.

verdict ['və:dikt] *n* κρίσις, γνώμη ‖ (*of jury*) ἐτυμηγορία, ἀπόφασις.

verge [və:dʒ] *n* (*of road*) ἄκρη (τοῦ δρόμου) ‖ on the ~ of doing ἕτοιμος νά ‖ *vi*: to ~ on πλησιάζω, τείνω πρός, γγίζω μέ.

verger ['və:dʒə*] *n* νεωκόρος.

verification [verifi'keiʃən] *n* ἐπιβεβαίωσις, ἐπικύρωσις, ἀπόδειξις.

verify ['verifai] *vt* ἐπιβεβαιώνω, ἐλέγχω, ἀποδεικνύω.

vermin ['və:min] *npl* βλαβερά ζωύφια

vermouth ['və:məθ] *n* βερμούτ.

vernacular [və'nækjulə*] *n* τοπική διάλεκτος, ντοπολαλιά, κοινή γλῶσσα.

versatile ['və:sətail] *a* πολύπλευρος, εὔστροφος.

versatility [və:sə'tiliti] *n* τό πολύπλευρον, εὐστροφία.

verse [və:s] *n* ποίησις, ποιήματα ‖ (*line*) στίχος ‖ (*of poem, song*) στροφή ‖ (*of Bible*) ἐδάφιον ‖ ~d *a* (*+in*) ἐπιδέξιος, πεπειραμένος, μορφωμένος.

version ['və:ʃən] *n* (*account*) ἔκδοσις, ἑρμηνεία.

versus ['və:səs] *prep* κατά, ἐναντίον.

vertebra ['və:tibrə] *n* σπόνδυλος, ραχοκόκκαλο.

vertebrate ['və:tibrit] *a* σπονδυλωτός.

vertical ['və:tikəl] *a* κάθετος, κατακόρυφος, τῆς κορυφῆς ‖ *n*: the ~ κάθετος ‖ ~ly *ad* καθέτως, κατακορύφως.

vertigo ['və:tigəu] *n* ἴλιγγος, ζάλη.

verve [və:v] *n* ἔμπνευσις, ἐνθουσιασμός, κέφι.

very ['veri] *ad* πολύ, ἀκριβῶς ‖ *a* (*identical*) ἴδιος, αὐτός οὗτος ‖ (*mere*) καί μόνη, καί πού.

vespers ['vespəz] *npl* ἑσπερινός.

vessel ['vesl] *n* πλοῖον, σκάφος ‖ (*container*) ἀγγεῖον, σκεῦος.

vest [vest] *n* φανελλάκι ‖ (*US: waistcoat*) γιαλέκο ‖ *vt* περιβάλλω, παραχωρῶ, παρέχω, ἐνδύω ‖ ~ed *a* (*interest*) κεκτημένος, ἐπενδεδυμένος.

vestibule ['vestibju:l] *n* (*of house*) προθάλαμος, χώλ, ἀντρέ.

vestige ['vestidʒ] *n* ὑπόλειμμα, ἴχνος.

vestry ['vestri] *n* ἱεροφυλάκειον, σκευοφυλάκιον, βεστιάριον.

vet [vet] *n* κτηνίατρος ‖ *vt* ἐξετάζω.

veteran ['vetərən] *n* παλαίμαχος, βετεράνος ‖ *a* τοῦ παλαιμάχου, πεπειραμένος.

veterinary ['vetərinəri] *a* κτηνιατρικός ‖ ~ surgeon *n* κτηνίατρος.

veto ['vi:təu] *n* δικαίωμα ἀρνησικυρίας, βέτο ‖ (*prohibition*) ἀπαγόρευσις ‖ *vt* προβάλλω βέτο (εἰς).

vex [veks] *vt* ἐνοχλῶ, ἐρεθίζω, ταράσσω ‖ ~ed *a* θυμωμένος, πειραγμένος.

via ['vaiə] *prep* διά, διά μέσου.

viability [vaiə'biliti] *n* βιωσιμότης.

viable ['vaiəbl] *a* βιώσιμος, βατός.

viaduct ['vaiədʌkt] *n* ὀδογέφυρα, κοιλαδογέφυρα, ἀψιδωτή γέφυρα.

vibrate [vai'breit] *vi* πάλλομαι, δονοῦμαι, ταλαντεύομαι ‖ (*resound*) ἠχῶ.

vibration [vai'breiʃən] *n* ταλάντευσις, δόνησις, κούνημα.

vicar ['vikə*] *n* ἐφημέριος, βικάριος ‖ ~age *n* πρεσβυτέριον, οἰκία ἐφημερίου.

vice [vais] *n* (*evil*) ἐκφυλισμός, ἀκολασία, ἁμάρτημα ‖ (*tech*) συνδήκτωρ, μέγγενη ‖ **vice-** *prefix* ἀντί-, ὑπό ‖ ~-chairman *n* ἀντιπρόεδρος ‖ ~-president *n* ἀντιπρόεδρος ‖ ~ versa *ad* τανάπαλιν.

vicinity [vi'siniti] *n* γειτονιά, ἐγγύτης, περιοχή.

vicious ['viʃəs] *a* (*also cruel*) κακός, κακοήθης, στρυφνός ‖ ~ness *n* κακία.

vicissitudes [vi'sisitju:dz] *npl* περιπέτειες, μεταβολές, γυρίσματα τῆς τύχης.

victim ['viktim] *n* θῦμα ‖ ~ization *n* καταπίεσις, ἀντίποινα ‖ ~ize *vt* λαμβάνω ὡς θῦμα, θυσιάζω.

victor ['viktə*] *n* νικητής.

Victorian [vik'tɔ:riən] *a* βικτωριανός.

victorious [vik'tɔ:riəs] *a* νικηφόρος, θριαμβευτής.

victory ['viktəri] *n* νίκη.

video ['vidəiəu] *a* τῆς εἰκόνος.

vie [vai] *vi* (*compete*) (*+with*) ἁμιλλῶμαι, ἀνταγωνίζομαι.

view [vju:] *n* ὄψις, ματιά, βλέμμα ‖ (*scene*) θέα, προοπτική, ὄψις ‖ (*opinion*) ἄποψις, ἔποψις, ἔκθεσις ‖ (*intention*) πρόθεσις, βλέψις, σκοπός ‖ *vt* (*situation*) κυττάζω, ἐπίθεωρῶ, ἐξετάζω ‖ ~er *n* (*viewfinder*) σκόπευτρον ‖ (*phot: small projector*) μικρό μηχάνημα προβολῆς ‖ (*TV*) θεατής ‖ ~finder *n* στόχαστρον, εἰκονοσκόπιον ‖ ~point *n* σημεῖον μέ καλήν θέαν ‖ (*attitude*) ἄποψις.

vigil ['vidʒil] *n* ἀγρυπνία, ξενύχτι, ὁλονυχτία ‖ ~ance *n* ἀγρυπνία, προσοχή ‖ ~ant *a* ἄγρυπνος, προσεκτικός ‖ ~antly *ad* ἄγρυπνος.

vigor ['vigə*] *n* (*US*) = vigour.

vigorous ['vigərəs] *a* ρωμαλέος, σθεναρός, ζωηρός ‖ ~ly *ad* γερά, δυνατά.

vigour ['vigə*] *n* σθένος, σφρῖγος, ζωτικότης, ζωηρότης.

vile [vail] *a* ἀνήθικος, ἀχρεῖος, αἰσχρός ‖

(foul) ἀκάθαρτος, βρωμερός, σιχαμερός.

villa ['vilə] *n* ἔπαυλις, βίλλα.

village ['vilidʒ] *n* χωριό || ~**r** *n* χωριάτης.

villain ['vilən] *n* ὁ κακός, παλιάνθρωπος.

vindicate ['vindikeit] *vt* δικαιώνω, ὑπερασπίζω, δικαιολογῶ.

vindication [vindi'keiʃən] *n* δικαίωσις, ὑπεράσπισις.

vindictive [vin'diktiv] *a* ἐκδικητικός.

vine [vain] *n* ἄμπελος, κλῆμα.

vinegar ['vinigə*] *n* ὄξος, ξύδι.

vineyard ['vinjəd] *n* ἀμπελών, ἀμπέλι.

vintage ['vintidʒ] *n* (wine) κρασί ὡρισμένου ἔτους || (gathering) τρυγητός, τρύγος.

vinyl ['vainl] *n* βινύλιον.

viola [vi'əulə] *n* (mus) βιόλα.

violate ['vaiəleit] *vt* (break promise) ἀθετῶ, καταπατῶ || (disturb) παραβιάζω || (desecrate) βεβηλώνω.

violation [vaiə'leiʃən] *n* παραβίασις, παράβασις, ἀθέτησις.

violence ['vaiələns] *n* σφοδρότης, ἔντασις || (rough treatment) βία, βιαιότης.

violent ['vaiələnt] *a* βίαιος, σφοδρός, ὁρμητικός || (extreme) ζωηρός, ἔντονος, ὀξύς, ἰσχυρός || ~**ly** *ad* βίαια, ἀπότομα, ἐξαιρετικά, πολύ.

violet ['vaiəlit] *n* βιολέττα, μενεξές || *a* ἰώδης, μώβ.

violin [vaiə'lin] *n* βιολί.

viper ['vaipə*] *n* ἔχιδνα, ὀχιά.

virgin ['və:dʒin] *n* παρθένος || *a* παρθένος, παρθενικός, καθαρός || ~**ity** *n* παρθενία.

virile ['virail] *a* ἀνδρικός, δυνατός, σθεναρός.

virility [vi'riliti] *n* ἀνδρισμός, ἀνδροπρέπεια, δύναμις.

virtual ['və:tjuəl] *a* οὐσιαστικός, πραγματικός || ~**ly** *ad* (in fact) κατ'οὐσίαν, οὐσιαστικῶς || (almost) σχεδόν.

virtue ['və:tju:] *n* ἀρετή || (good quality) ἱκανότης, δραστικότης || **by** ~ **of** δυνάμει, συνεπεία, λόγω, ἐξ αἰτίας τοῦ.

virtuoso [və:tju'əuzəu] *n* δεξιοτέχνης μουσικός, βιρτουόζος.

virtuous ['və:tjuəs] *a* ἐνάρετος.

virulence ['viruləns] *n* φαρμακερότης || (hatred) κακεντρέχεια.

virulent ['virulənt] *a* δηλητηριώδης, θανατηφόρος || (bitter) ἐχθρικός, κακεντρεχής, φαρμακερός.

virus ['vaiərəs] *n* ἰός, μικρόβιον.

visa ['vi:zə] *n* θεώρησις, βίζα.

vis-à-vis ['vi:zəvi:] *prep* ἀπέναντι, ἀντίκρυ, καρσί.

viscount ['vaikaunt] *n* ὑποκόμης.

visibility [vizi'biliti] *n* ὁρατότης.

visible ['vizəbl] *a* ὁρατός, ἐμφανής, προφανής.

visibly ['vizəbli] *ad* καταφανῶς, προφανῶς, ὁλοφάνερα.

vision ['viʒən] *n* ὅρασις || (imagination) διορατικότης || (dream) ὅραμα, ὀπτασία

|| ~**ary** *n* φαντασιοκόπος, οὐτοπιστής, ὀνειροπόλος || *a* (unpractical) οὐτοπικός, φανταστικός.

visit ['vizit] *n* ἐπίσκεψις || *vt* ἐπισκέπτομαι || (stay with) κάνω βίζιτα, φιλοξενοῦμαι || ~**ing** *a* (professor) ἐπισκέπτης καθηγητής || ~**ing card** *n* ἐπισκεπτήριον, μπιλιέτο || ~**or** *n* ἐπισκέπτης || ~**ors' book** *n* βιβλίον ἐπισκεπτῶν.

visor ['vaizə*] *n* προσωπίς.

vista ['vistə] *n* θέα, ἄνοιγμα, προοπτική, ἄποψις.

visual ['vizjuəl] *a* ὀπτικός, ὁρατός, πραγματικός || ~ **aid** *n* ὀπτικό βοήθημα || ~**ize** *vt* κάνω ὁρατόν, ὁραματίζομαι || ~**ly** *ad* ὀπτικῶς.

vital ['vaitl] *a* ὀργανικός, κεφαλαιώδης, ζωτικός || (necessary to life) ζωτικός, οὐσιώδης || ~**ity** *n* ζωτικότης, ἀνθεκτικότης, ζωή || ~**ly** *ad* ζωτικῶς.

vitamin ['vitəmin] *n* βιταμίνη.

vitiate ['viʃieit] *vt* (make ineffective) φθείρω, διαστρέφω.

vivacious [vi'veiʃəs] *a* ζωηρός, εὔθυμος, κεφάτος.

vivacity [vi'væsiti] *n* ζωηρότης, εὐθυμία.

vivid ['vivid] *a* ζωντανός, ζωηρός, σαφής || (bright, clear) ζωηρός, λαμπρός || ~**ly** *ad* ζωηρά, λαμπρά.

vivisection [vivi'sekʃən] *n* ζωοτομία.

vocabulary [vəu'kæbjuləri] *n* λεξιλόγιον.

vocal ['vəukəl] *a* φωνητικός, ἠχητικός || ~ **cord** *n* φωνητική χορδή || ~**ist** *n* ἀοιδός, τραγουδιστής.

vocation [vəu'keiʃən] *n* (calling) προορισμός, κλῆσις || (profession) ἐπάγγελμα, τέχνη.

vociferous [vəu'sifərəs] *a* κραυγαλέος, κραυγάζων, φωνακλάς || ~**ly** *ad* φωνάζοντας, φωνακλάδικα.

vodka ['vɔdkə] *n* βότκα.

vogue [vəug] *n* μόδα, δημοτικότης.

voice [vɔis] *n* φωνή || (right of opinion) ψῆφος, γνώμη || (gram) φωνή (τοῦ ρήματος) || *vt* ἐκφράζω || **with one** ~ ὁμοφώνως.

void [vɔid] *n* κενόν || *a* (of meaning) παράλογος, στερούμενος.

volatile ['vɔlətail] *a* κεφάτος, εὐμετάβολος, παιχνιδιάρικος || (evaporating quickly) πτητικός.

volcanic [vɔl'kænik] *a* ἡφαιστειώδης, ἐκρηκτικός.

volcano [vɔl'keinəu] *n* ἡφαίστειον.

volition [və'liʃən] *n*: **of one's own** ~ μέ τήν θελήσί μου.

volley ['vɔli] *n* ὁμοβροντία || (shower) χείμαρρος, καταιγισμός, θύελλα || (tennis) βολλέ, κατ'εὐθεῖαν κτύπημα || ~ **ball** *n* χειροσφαίρησις, βόλλεϋ-μπώλ.

volt [vəult] *n* βόλτ || ~**age** *n* τάσις, βολτάζ.

volte-face ['vɔlt'fɑ:s] *n* πλήρης στροφή, ἀλλαγή γνώμης.

voluble ['vɔljubl] a εὐφραδής, εὔγλωττος.

volume ['vɔlju:m] n τόμος βιβλίων ‖ (amount) μεγάλη ποσότης ‖ (space) ὄγκος ‖ (loudness of sound) ἔντασις, ὄγκος.

voluntarily ['vɔləntərili] ad ἑκουσίως, αὐθορμήτως, ἐθελοντικῶς.

voluntary ['vɔləntəri] a ἐθελοντικός, ἑκούσιος, ἐθελοντής.

volunteer [vɔlən'tiə*] n ἐθελοντής ‖ vi προσφέρομαι.

voluptuous [və'lʌptjuəs] a φιλήδονος, ἡδυπαθής.

vomit ['vɔmit] n ἐμετός, ξέρασμα ‖ vti ἐξεμῶ, ξερνῶ.

vote [vəut] n ψηφοφορία, ψῆφος ‖ (right) δικαίωμα ψήφου ‖ (result) ἀποτέλεσμα ψηφοφορίας ‖ vt ψηφίζω, ἐγκρίνω ‖ vi ψηφίζω ‖ ~r n ψηφοφόρος, ἐκλογεύς.

voting ['vəutiŋ] n ψηφοφορία.

vouch [vautʃ] to ~ for vt ὑποστηρίζω, ἐγγυῶμαι γιά.

voucher ['vautʃə*] n ἀπόδειξις πληρωμῆς, δικαιολογητικόν.

vow [vau] n εὐχή, ὅρκος, τάξιμο, τάμα ‖ vi ὁρκίζομαι, διακηρύττω.

vowel ['vauəl] n φωνῆεν.

voyage ['vɔiidʒ] n ταξίδι.

vulgar ['vʌlgə*] a χυδαῖος, πρόστυχος, ἄξεστος ‖ (of common people) κοινός, λαϊκός ‖ ~ity n χυδαιότης, προστυχιά.

vulnerability [vʌlnərə'biliti] n τό τρωτόν, τρωτότης, εὐπάθεια.

vulnerable ['vʌlnərəbl] a τρωτός, εὔτρωτος, εὐπρόσβλητος.

vulture ['vʌltʃə*] n γύψ, ὄρνιο.

W, w

wad [wɔd] n (bundle) δέσμη, μάτσο.

wade [weid] vi βαδίζω στό νερό, περνῶ πεζῇ.

wafer ['weifə*] n γκωφρέτα, λεπτό μπισκότο.

waffle ['wɔfl] n (food) εἶδος τηγανίτα ‖ (col: empty talk) φλυαρία, μποῦρδες ‖ vi (col) φλυαρῶ.

waft [wɑ:ft] vti μεταφέρω, σκορπίζω.

wag [wæg] vti κινῶ, κουνῶ, κινοῦμαι.

wage [weidʒ] n ἡμερομίσθιον, μισθός, ἀμοιβή, μεροκάματο ‖ vt διεξάγω, διενεργῶ ‖ ~s npl μισθός ‖ ~ earner n μισθωτός ‖ ~ freeze n παγίωσις μισθῶν.

wager ['weidʒə*] n στοίχημα.

waggle ['wægl] vti (tail) κουνῶ, ταλαντεύομαι.

wag(g)on ['wægən] n (road, rail) ἅμαξα, βαγόνι.

wail [weil] n θρῆνος, ὀλοφυρμός ‖ vi θρηνῶ, κλαίω, ὀλοφύρομαι.

waist [weist] n ὀσφύς, μέση, ζώνη ‖ ~coat n γιλέκο ‖ ~line n μέση, τάγια.

wait [weit] n ἀναμονή, στάσις ‖ vi περι-

μένω, ἀναμμένω, σερβίρω ‖ to ~ for vt περιμένω, ἀναμένω, καρτερῶ ‖ ~er n σερβιτόρος, γκαρσόνι ‖ ~ing room n αἴθουσα ἀναμονῆς, προθάλαμος ‖ ~ress n σερβιτόρα.

wake [weik] (irreg v) vt ἐξυπνῶ ‖ vi ἀγρυπνῶ, εἶμαι ἄϋπνος ‖ n ξενύχτι νεκροῦ ‖ ~n vt ἀφυπνίζω, ξυπνῶ.

Wales [weilz] n Οὐαλλία.

walk [wɔ:k] n πορεία, περπάτημα, βόλτα, περίπατος ‖ (way of walking) βάδισμα, περπατησιά ‖ (path, route) περίπατος, λεωφόρος, δρόμος, πεζοδρόμιον ‖ (occupation) ἐπάγγελμα ‖ vi περπατῶ, βαδίζω ‖ ~er n πεζοπόρος, περπατητής ‖ ~ie-talkie n πομποδέκτης, φορητὸς ἀσύρματος ‖ ~ing n πεζοπορία, περπάτημα ‖ attr a (holiday) μὲ τὰ πόδια, βυδίζων ‖ (shoes) (παπούτσια) πεζοπορίας ‖ ~ing stick n μπαστούνι ‖ ~out n (of workers) ἀπεργία ‖ ~over n (col) εὔκολος νίκη, εὔκολη δουλειά.

wall [wɔ:l] n τοῖχος, τεῖχος ‖ ~ed a (city) περιτειχισμένος.

wallet ['wɔlit] n πορτοφόλι.

wallop ['wɔləp] vt (col: thrash) σπάω στό ξύλο.

wallow ['wɔləu] vi (+ in) κυλιομαι (εἰς), πλέω (εἰς), κολυμπῶ (στό).

wallpaper ['wɔ:lpeipə*] n τοιχόχαρτον, χαρτί ταπετσαρίας.

walnut ['wɔ:lnʌt] n καρύδι ‖ (tree) καρυδιά

walrus ['wɔ:lrəs] n θαλάσσιος ἵππος.

waltz [wɔ:lts] n βάλς ‖ vi χορεύω βάλς.

wand [wɔnd] n ράβδος, ραβδί.

wander ['wɔndə*] vi περιπλανῶμαι, περιφέρομαι, τριγυρίζω ‖ ~er n περιπλανώμενος, σουρτούκης ‖ ~ing a πλανώδιος, περιπλανώμενος.

want [wɔnt] vt θέλω, ἐπιθυμῶ ‖ (need) χρειάζομαι, ἔχω ἀνάγκη, ἐλλείπω ‖ n. for ~ of ἐλλείψει ‖ ~s npl (needs) ἀνάγκες.

wanton ['wɔntən] a ἀχαλίνωτος, ἀκόλαστος, ἐσκεμμένος.

war [wɔ:*] n πόλεμος.

ward [wɔ:d] n (division) περιφέρεια, συνοικία ‖ (hospital) θάλαμος ‖ vt: to ~ off ἀποκρούω, ἀποφεύγω.

warden ['wɔ:dn] n διευθυντής, φύλακας

warder ['wɔ:də*] n φύλαξ, δεσμοφύλαξ.

wardrobe ['wɔ:drəub] n ντουλάπα ‖ (clothing) γκαρταρόμπα, τά ροῦχα.

ware [weə*] n κατασκευασμένα εἴδη ‖ ~s npl ἐμπορεύματα ‖ ~house n ἀποθήκη.

warfare ['wɔ:feə*] n πόλεμος.

warhead ['wɔ:hed] n κῶνος βλήματος.

warily ['wɛərili] ad προσεκτικά ἐπιφυλακτικά.

warlike ['wɔ:laik] a πολεμικός, πολεμοχαρής, φιλοπόλεμος

warm [wɔ:m] a θερμός ‖ (fire) ζεστός ‖ (welcome) ἔνθερμος, ζωηρός ‖ to ~ up *vti* ζεσταίνω ‖ ζωηρεύω, ἐνθουσιάζομαι ‖ ~-hearted *a* μὲ ζεστὴ καρδιά, συμπονετικός ‖ ~ly *ad* θερμά, ἐνθουσιωδῶς ‖ ~th *n* θερμότης, ζεστασιά, ἐνθουσιασμός.

warn [wɔːn] *vt* προειδοποιῶ ‖ ~ing *n* προειδοποίησις ‖ (*caution*) εἰδοποίησις ‖ ~ing light *n* προειδοποιητικὸν φῶς.

warp [wɔːp] *vt* στήμων, στημόνι.

warrant ['wɔrənt] *n* (*police*) ἔνταλμα.

warranty ['wɔrənti] *n* ἐξουσιοδότησις, δικαιολογία, ἐγγύησις.

warrior ['wɔriə*] *n* πολεμιστής.

warship ['wɔːʃip] *n* πολεμικὸν (πλοῖον).

wart [wɔːt] *n* κρεατοελιά.

wartime ['wɔːtaim] *n* πολεμικὴ ἐποχή, πολεμικὴ περίοδος.

wary ['wɛəri] *a* προσεκτικός, πονηρός, ἐπιφυλακτικός.

was [wɔz, wəz] *pt of* be.

wash [wɔʃ] *n* πλύσις, πλύσιμο, νίψιμο ‖ (*clothes*) ροῦχα, μπουγάδα ‖ *vt* πλένω, πλύνω ‖ *vi* πλύνομαι, πλένομαι ‖ to ~ away *vt* παρασύρω, παίρνω ‖ ~able *a* ποὺ πλένεται ‖ ~basin *n* λεκάνη (νιπτήρος) ‖ ~er *n* παράκυκλος, ροδέλλα ‖ (*person, machine*) πλύστρα, πλυντήριον ‖ ~ing *n* (*linen etc*) ροῦχα γιὰ πλύσιμο, πλύση, πλύσιμο ‖ ~ing machine *n* πλυντήριον ‖ ~ing powder *n* σκόνη πλυσίματος ‖ ~ing-up *n* πλύσιμο τῶν πιάτων ‖ ~out *n* (*col*) ἀποτυχία, φιάσκο ‖ ~room *n* τουαλέττα.

wasn't ['wɔznt] = was not ‖ *see* be.

wasp [wɔsp] *n* σφήκα.

wastage ['weistidʒ] *n* σπατάλη.

waste [weist] *n* σπατάλη ‖ (*what is wasted*) ἄχρηστα ὑλικά, σκουπίδια ‖ ἀπορρίμματα, σκάρτα ‖ (*wilderness*) ἔρημος, λόγγος ‖ *a* ἄχρηστος ‖ (*land*) χέρσος, ἐρημωμένος ‖ *vt* (*object*) καταναλίσκω, καταστρέφω, φθείρω ‖ (*time*) σπαταλῶ, χάνω ‖ *vi*: to ~ away φθίνω, ἀδυνατίζω ‖ ~ful *a* σπάταλος, ἄσωτος, σκορποχέρης ‖ ~fully *ad* σπάταλα, ἄσωτα, ἄσκοπα ‖ ~paper basket *n* κάλαθος ἀχρήστων.

watch [wɔtʃ] *n* ἐπίβλεψις, ἐπιτήρησις, ἐπαγρύπνησις ‖ (*guard*) φυλακή, φρουρός ‖ (*naut*) φυλακή, βάρδια ‖ (*timepiece*) ὡρολόγιον, ρολόϊ ‖ *vt* παρατηρῶ, παρακολουθῶ ‖ *vi* ἀγρυπνῶ, προσέχω, φυλάσσω ‖ ~dog *n* (*fig*) ἐπιστάτης, φύλακας ‖ ~ful *a* ἄγρυπνος, προσεκτικός ‖ ~maker *n* ὡρολογοποιός, ρολογάς ‖ ~man *n* (νυκτο)φύλαξ ‖ ~ strap *n* λουρίδα ὡρολογιοῦ.

water ['wɔːtə*] *n* ὕδωρ, νερό ‖ *vt* ποτίζω, βρέχω, καταβρέχω, διαβρέχω ‖ to ~ down *vt* ἀλλοιώνω (ἔκφρασιν), ἐξασθενίζω, συγκαλύπτω ‖ ~closet *n* ἀποχωρητήριον, ἀπόπατος, μέρος ‖ ~colour, (*US*) ~color *n* πίναξ μὲ νερομπογιά,

ἀκουαρέλα ‖ (*paint*) ὑδρόχρωμα, νερομπογιά ‖ ~cress *n* νεροκάρδαμο ‖ ~fall *n* ὑδατόπτωσις, καταρράκτης ‖ ~hole *n* νερόλακκος ‖ ~ing can *n* ποτιστήρι ‖ ~ level *n* (*in radiator*) ὑδροστάτης ‖ ~lily *n* νούφαρο ‖ ~line *n* ἴσαλος (γραμμή) ‖ ~logged *a* πλημμυρισμένος, διάβροχος, μουσκεμμένος ‖ ~melon *n* καρπούζι ‖ ~ polo *n* ὑδρόσφαιρον ‖ ~proof *a* ἀδιάβροχος, ὑδατοστεγής ‖ ~shed *n* γραμμὴ διαχωρισμοῦ ὑδάτων ‖ ~skiing *n* θαλάσσιον σκί ‖ to go ~skiing κάνω θαλάσσιο σκί ‖ ~tight *a* ὑδατοστεγής, στεγανός, ἀδιάβροχος ‖ ~works *npl* μηχανοστάσιον ὑδρεύσεως ‖ ~y *a* (*colour*) ὠχρός, ἄτονος.

watt [wɔt] *n* βάτ(τ).

wave [weiv] *n* κῦμα ‖ (*of hand*) κούνημα τοῦ χεριοῦ ‖ (*rad*) κῦμα ‖ (*in hair*) κυμάτωσις, κατσάρωμα ‖ *vt* (*hand*) χαιρετῶ μὲ τὸ χέρι, κουνῶ τὸ χέρι ‖ (*shape in curves*) κατσαρώνω, ὀντουλάρω ‖ *vi* (*flag*) κυματίζω, ἀνεμίζω ‖ ~length *n* μῆκος κύματος.

waver ['weivə*] *vi* ταλαντεύομαι, κυμαίνομαι ‖ (*weaken*) κλονίζομαι, ἀμφιρρέπω.

wavy ['weivi] *a* κυματώδης, κυματιστός.

wax [wæks] *n* κηρός, κερί ‖ *vt* (*floors*) κερώνω, παρκετάρω ‖ *vi* (*moon*) μεγαλώνω, γίνομαι.

way [wei] *n* ὁδός, δρόμος ‖ (*manner*) τρόπος ‖ (*direction*) κατεύθυνσις, μεριά, δρόμος ‖ (*habit*) τρόπος, συνήθεια, ἔθιμο ‖ in the ~ φράζω, ἐμποδίζω, κόβω (τὸν δρόμο) ‖ by the ~ παρεμπιπτόντως, καθ' ὁδόν, μὲ τὴν εὐκαιρία ‖ '~ in' 'εἴσοδος' ‖ '~ out' 'ἔξοδος' ‖ ~lay *vt* ἐνεδρεύω, καιροφυλακτῶ ‖ ~ward *a* δύστροπος, διεστραμμένος.

we [wiː] *pl pron* ἡμεῖς, ἐμεῖς.

weak [wiːk] *a* ἀδύνατος, ἀσθενής ‖ (*not powerful*) ἀνίσχυρος ‖ (*diluted*) ἀδύνατος, ἐλαφρός ‖ ~en *vti* ἐξασθενίζω, ἀδυνατίζω, ἐξασθενῶ ‖ ~ling *n* ἀδύνατος ἄνθρωπος, ἀσθενὲς πλάσμα ‖ ~ly *ad* ἀδύνατα ‖ ~ness *n* ἀδυναμία ‖ (*fault*) ἐλάττωμα ‖ (*fondness*) προτίμησις, ἀδυναμία.

wealth [welθ] *n* πλοῦτος ‖ (*abundance*) ἀφθονία ‖ (*things having value*) περιουσία ‖ ~y *a* πλούσιος.

wean [wiːn] *vt* ἀπογαλακτίζω, ἀποκόβω.

weapon ['wepən] *n* ὅπλον.

wear [wɛə*] (*irreg v*) *n* ροῦχα, ρουχισμός, φόρεμα ‖ (*use*) χρῆσις, φθορά ‖ *vt* φέρω, φορῶ ‖ (*show*) δείχνω, κρατιέμαι ‖ (*use*) φθείρω, τρώω, τρίβω, λυώνω ‖ *vi* (*last long*) ἀντέχω, διατηροῦμαι ‖ ~ and tear φθορά ‖ to ~ away *vti* φθείρω, φθείρομαι, τρώγω, τρίβω ‖ to ~ down *vt* φθείρω, τρώγω ‖ to ~ off *vi* ἐξαλείφομαι, σβήνομαι, σβήνω ‖ to ~ out *vt* φθείρω, τρίβω, λυώνω ‖ ~er *n* φορῶν.

wearily ['wiərili] *ad* κουρασμένα, κοπιαστικά.

weariness ['wiərinis] *n* κόπωσις, κούρασι.

weary ['wiəri] *a* κουρασμένος, άποκαμωμένος ‖ *(tiring)* κουραστικός, πληκτικός, άνιαρός ‖ *vti* κοπιῶ, κουράζω, κουράζομαι.

weasel ['wi:zl] *n* νυφίτσα, κουνάβι.

weather ['weðə*] *n* καιρός ‖ *vt* διέρχομαι, περνῶ ἐπιτυχῶς ‖ *(season)* ἐκθέτω στόν καιρό ‖ ~-**beaten** *a* άνεμοδαρμένος, ἠλιοκαμμένος, μαυρισμένος ‖ ~**cock** *n* άνεμοδείκτης ‖ ~ **forecast** *n* πρόβλεψις καιροῦ.

weave [wi:v] *(irreg v) vt* ὑφαίνω, πλέκω, συνθέτω ‖ ~**r** *n* ὑφαντής.

weaving ['wi:viŋ] *n* ὕφανσις, πλέξιμο.

web [web] *n* ὕφασμα, μεμβράνη ‖ *(of spider)* ἱστός άράχνης, άράχνη ‖ ~**bed** *a* μεμβρανώδης ‖ ~**bing** *n* ὕφασμα λωρίδων, ἐνισχυτική ταινία.

wed [wed] *vt* νυμφεύω, νυμφεύομαι, παντρεύομαι.

we'd [wi:d] = **we had, we would** ‖ *see* **have, would**.

wedding ['wediŋ] *n* γάμος, παντρειά, στεφάνωμα ‖ ~ **day** *n* ἡμέρα τῶν γάμων, ἐπέτειος τῶν γάμων ‖ ~ **present** *n* γαμήλιον δῶρον ‖ ~ **ring** *n* άρραβών, βέρα.

wedge [wedʒ] *n* σφήν(α) ‖ *vt* ἐνσφηνώνω, χώνω, μπήγω ‖ *(pack tightly)* σφηνώνω, στριμώγνω.

Wednesday ['wenzdi] *n* Τετάρτη.

wee [wi:] *a (Scottish col)* μικρούλης, λιγάκι, τόσο δά.

weed [wi:d] *n* ζιζάνιον, άγριόχορτο ‖ *vt* ξεχορταριάζω, σκαλίζω, βγάζω, καθαρίζω ‖ ~-**killer** *n* ζιζανιοκτόνον.

week [wi:k] *n* ἑβδομάς, βδομάδα ‖ ~**day** *n* καθημερινή ‖ ~**end** *n* Σαββατοκύριακο ‖ ~**ly** *ad* ἑβδομαδιαίως, καθ' ἑβδομάδα ‖ *a* ἑβδομαδιαῖος.

weep [wi:p] *(irreg v) vi* κλαίω, χύνω δάκρυα, δακρύζω.

weigh [wei] *vt* σταθμίζω, ζυγίζω ‖ *(have weight)* ζυγίζω ‖ *vi (be important)* βαραίνω, ζυγίζω ‖ **to ~ down** *vt* (ὑπερ)φορτώνω, βαραίνω, πιέζω ‖ **to ~ up** *vt* ἐκτιμῶ, ζυγίζω ‖ ~**bridge** *n* γεφυροπλάστιγξ.

weight [weit] *n* βαρύτης ‖ *(something used on scales)* σταθμόν, μέτρον, ζύγι ‖ *(load)* βάρος, φορτίον ‖ *(importance)* κῦρος, ἐπιρροή, άξία ‖ ~**lessness** *n* τό άβαρές ‖ ~ **lifting** *n* ἄρσις βαρῶν ‖ ~**y** *a* βαρύς, σπουδαῖος, πειστικός.

weir [wiə*] *n* κλεισιάς, ὑδατοφράκτης.

weird [wiəd] *a* ὑπερφυσικός, παράξενος.

welcome ['welkəm] *n* ὑποδοχή, δεξίωσις ‖ *vt* καλωσορίζω, (ὑπο)δέχομαι.

welcoming ['welkəmiŋ] *a* καλής ὑποδοχής.

weld [weld] *n* συγκόλλησις, κόλλησι ‖ *vt* (συγ)κολλῶ, ἑνώνω ‖ ~**er** *n* συγκολλητής ‖ ~**ing** *n* συγκόλλησις, κόλλησι.

welfare ['welfeə*] *n* εὐημερία, κοινωνική πρόνοια ‖ ~ **state** *n* κράτος προνοίας, κράτος σοσιαλιστικό.

well [wel] *n* φρέαρ, πηγάδι, πηγή, πετρελαιοπηγή ‖ *ad* καλῶς, καλά ‖ *(to considerable extent)* άρκετά, σχεδόν ‖ *(thoroughly)* καλά, τελείως ‖ *a* ὑγιής, καλά ‖ *(satisfactory)* καλόν, καλά ‖ *interj (beginning conversation)* λοιπόν, ἴσως, καλά ‖ *(surprise)* άδύνατον, μπά ‖ **as** ~ *(also)* ἐπίσης, ὁμοίως.

we'll [wi:l] = **we will, we shall** ‖ *see* **will, shall**.

well-behaved ['welbi'heivd] *a* φρόνιμος, πειθαρχημένος.

well-being ['welbi:iŋ] *n* εὐημερία.

well-built ['wel'bilt] *a* καλοφτιαγμένος.

well-developed ['weldi'veləpt] *a (girl)* άναπτυγμένη, γεμάτη.

well-earned ['wel'ə:nd] *a (rest)* δίκαιος, καλοκερδισμένος.

well-heeled ['wel'hi:ld] *a (col: wealthy)* πλούσιος, εὔπορος.

wellingtons ['weliŋtənz] *npl* ψιλές μπότες.

well-known ['wel'nəun] *a (person)* πασίγνωστος, φημισμένος.

well-meaning ['wel'mi:niŋ] *a* καλοπροαίρετος.

well-off ['wel'ɔf] *a* εὔπορος, πλούσιος, τυχερός.

well-read ['wel'red] *a* μορφωμένος, πολυδιαβασμένος.

well-to-do ['weltə'du:] *a* εὔπορος.

well-wisher ['welwiʃə*] *n* καλοθελητής.

Welsh [welʃ] *a* οὐαλλικός ‖ *n (ling)* οὐαλλικά ‖ ~**man** *n* Οὐαλλός.

wench [wentʃ] *n (old)* κορίτσι, κοκότα, τσούλα.

went [went] *pt of* **go**.

wept [wept] *pt,pp of* **weep**.

were [wə:*] *pt of* **be**.

we're [wiə*] = **we are** ‖ *see* **be**.

weren't ['wə:nt] = **were not** ‖ *see* **be**.

west [west] *n* δύσις ‖ *(country)* δυσμαί, δύσις, δυτικά ‖ *a* δυτικός ‖ *ad* δυτικά, πρός δυσμάς ‖ **the W~** *n* ἡ Δύσις ‖ ~**erly** *a* δυτικός (άνεμος), πρός δυσμάς ‖ ~**ern** *a* δυτικός ‖ *n (cine)* ταινία μέ κάου-μπόϋς ‖ **W~ Indies** *npl* Οἱ Άντίλλες ‖ ~**ward(s)** *ad* πρός δυσμάς, δυτικῶς.

wet [wet] *a* ὑγρός, βρε(γ)μένος, μουσκεμένος ‖ *(rainy)* βροχερός ‖ '~ **paint**' 'προσοχή χρῶμα' ‖ ~ **blanket** *n (fig)* ἄνθρωπος πού χαλάει τό κέφι, κρύος ‖ ~**ness** *n* ὑγρότης, ὑγρασία.

we've [wi:v] = **we have** ‖ *see* **have**.

whack [wæk] *n* μπάτσος, γερό κτύπημα ‖ *vt* κτυπῶ, δέρνω στά ψαχνά, συντρίβω.

whale [weil] *n* φάλαινα.

wharf [wɔ:f] *n* άποβάθρα, προκυμαία.

what [wɔt] *a (relative)* ὅτι, ὅσος ‖ *(quantity)* ὅσος, πόσον ‖ *(interrogative)* τί; πῶς;

ποιός; || *interj* τί, πῶς || ~ **ever** *a* ὁποιος...
καί, ὁ, τι . . . καί, ὁποιοσδήποτε.
wheat [wi:t] *n* σῖτος, σιτάρι, στάρι.
wheel [wi:l] *n* τροχός, ρόδα || *vt* (περι)-
στρέφω, σπρώχνω || *vi* περιστρέφομαι,
γυρίζω γύρω-γύρω || ~ **barrow** *n* χειρά-
μαξα || ~ **chair** *n* ἀναπηρική καρέκλα.
wheeze [wiːz] *n* φύσημα, σφύριγμα, λαχά-
νιασμα || *vi* ἀναπνέω δύσκολα, ἀσθμαίνω,
σφυρίζω.
when [wen] *ad* πότε || (*relative*) ὅταν || *cj*
ὅταν, ὅτε, πού || ~ **ever** *ad* ὁποτεδήποτε.
where [wɛə*] *ad* ποῦ || (*relative*) (ἐκεῖ) πού,
ὅπου || ~ **abouts** *ad* ποῦ || (λοιπόν) || ποῦ
περίπου || *n* θέσις, διαμονή, κατατόπια ||
~ **as** *cj* ἐφ' ὅσον, ἐνῶ || ~ **ver** *ad* ὁπουδή-
ποτε, ἀπ'ὅπου.
whet [wet] *vt* (*appetite*) διεγείρω, ἀνοίγω
(τήν ὄρεξι).
whether ['weðə*] *cj* ἐάν, ἄν, εἴτε.
which [witʃ] *a* ποῖος || *pron* (*interrogative*)
ποῖον; || (*relative*) ὁ ὁποῖος, στόν ὁποῖον,
τοῦ ὁποίου || ~ **ever** *a* ὅποιος, ἀπ'ὅπου ||
pron οἱοσδήποτε.
whiff [wif] *n* πνοή, φύσημα, ρουφηξιά.
while [wail] *n* χρονική περίοδος, καιρός,
χρόνος || *cj* ἐνῶ || **for a** ~ γιά λίγη ὥρα,
κάμποσο, γιά λίγο καιρό.
whim [wim] *n* παραξενιά, ἰδιοτροπία,
καπρίτσιο.
whimper ['wimpə*] *n* κλαυθμηρισμός,
κλάψα || *vi* κλαυθμηρίζω, βογγῶ.
whimsical ['wimzikəl] *a* ἰδιότροπος,
παράξενος, βιδάτος.
whine [wain] *n* κλάψιμο, κλάμα, τσίριγμα ||
vi κλαυθμηρίζω, μεμψιμοιρῶ.
whip [wip] *n* μαστίγιον, καμτσίκι || (*parl*)
κοινοβουλευτικός ἡγέτης || *vt* μαστι-
γώνω, δέρνω, κτυπῶ || (*snatch*) κινῶ
ἀπότομα, ἁρπάζω || ~ **-round** *n* ἔρανος,
συνεισφορά.
whirl [wə:l] *n* στροβιλισμός, στριφογύρι-
σμα, γύρισμα || *vti* στροβιλίζω, στριφο-
γυρίζω, περιστρέφομαι || ~ **pool** *n* δίνη,
ρουφήχτρα || ~ **wind** *n* ἀνεμοστρόβιλος.
whirr [wə:*] *vi* βουΐζω, σβουρίζω.
whisk [wisk] *n* (*for eggs*) χτυπητήρι || *vt*
(*cream etc*) κτυπῶ, ἀνακατεύω.
whisker ['wiskə*] *n* φαβορίτες || (*of cat*)
μουστάκι.
whisk(e)y ['wiski] *n* οὐίσκυ.
whisper ['wispə*] *n* ψίθυρος, θρόϊσμα,
ψιθύρισμα || *vi* ψιθυρίζω, μουρμουρίζω ||
(*leaves*) θροΐζω, ψιθυρίζω || *vt* (*secretly*)
ψιθυρίζω, λέγω, σφυρίζω.
whist [wist] *n* οὐίστ.
whistle ['wisl] *n* σφύριγμα || (*instrument*)
σφυρίχτρα || *vi* συρίζω, σφυρίζω.
white [wait] *n* (*for eggs*) λευκόν || (*of egg*,
eye) λεύκωμα, ἀσπράδι || *a* λευκός,
ἄσπρος || (*with fear*) ἄσπρος, κίτρινος,
χλωμός || ~ **-collar worker** *n* δημόσιος
ὑπάλληλος || ~ **lie** *n* ἀθῶο ψέμμα ||

~ **ness** *n* ἀσπρίλα, ἀσπράδα, χλωμάδα ||
~ **wash** *n* (*paint*) ἀσβεστόνερο, ἀσβεστό-
χρωμα || *vt* ἀσβεστώνω, ἀσπρίζω || (*fig*)
ἀποκαθιστῶ, δικαιολογῶ.
Whitsun ['witsn] *n* (*also Whit Sunday*)
Πεντηκοστή.
whittle ['witl] *vt*: **to** ~ **away, down** ἐλαττώνω, περιορίζω, λεπταίνω.
whizz [wiz] *vi* συρίζω, σφυρίζω, περνῶ
ὁλοταχῶς || ~ **kid** *n* (*col*) σπουδαῖο
παιδί.
who [hu:] *pron* ποῖος, ποιός || (*relative*)
ὁποῖος, ὅστις, πού || ~ **ever** *pron* ὁποι-
οσδήποτε, οἱοσδήποτε.
whole [həul] *a* (*complete*) ὁλόκληρος, ὅλος,
πλήρης || (*uninjured*) ἀβλαβής, σῶος || *n*
(τό) ὅλον, σύνολον || (*not broken*)
σύνολον, ἀκέραιον || ~ **hearted** *a* ὁλό-
ψυχος || ~ **heartedly** *ad* ὁλοψύχως ||
~ **sale** *n* χονδρική πώλησις, χονδρεμπό-
ριον || *attr* *a* (*trade*) χονδρικός || (*destruc-
tion*) ὁλοκληρωτικός || ~ **saler** *n* χονδρέμ-
πορος, κατάστημα χονδρικῆς πωλή-
σεως || ~ **some** *a* ὑγιεινός, ὑγιής.
wholly ['həuli] *ad* πλήρως, τελείως.
whom [hu:m] *pron* (*object*) ποῖον || ποιόν
whooping cough [hu:piŋkɔf] *n* κοκκύτης.
whore ['hɔ:*] *n* πόρνη, πουτάνα.
whose [huːz] *pron* ποίου || τίνος || ποιανοῦ
|| τοῦ ὁποίου.
why [wai] *ad* διατί; || γιατί; || (*relative*) πού,
γιατί || *interj* μπά || ἔ || ἄς.
wick [wik] *n* θρυαλλίς, φυτίλι.
wicked ['wikid] *a* κακός, διεστραμμένος
κακοήθης || (*mischievous*) πειρακτικός,
κατεργάρης || ~ **ly** *ad* μέ κακίαν,
αἰσχρῶς, πονηρά || ~ **ness** *n* κακία
ἀχρειότης, κακοήθεια.
wicker ['wikə*] *n* λυγαριά, πλέγμα.
wicket ['wikit] *n* (*cricket*) φράκτης, στυλί-
σκοι τοῦ κρίκετ.
wide [waid] *a* εὐρύς, πλατύς, φαρδύς,
ἐκτενής || (*mouth*) ὀρθάνοιχτος || (*in
firing*) ἔξω (τοῦ στόχου), ἄστοχος || *aa*
(*opening*) διάπλατα || ~ **-angle** *a* (*lens*)
εὐρυγώνιος φακός || ~ **-awake** *a* ἐντελῶς
ξύπνιος, ἄγρυπνος || ~ **ly** *ad* εὐρέως,
πλατειά, κατά πολύ || ~ **n** *vt* (*road*)
εὐρύνω, πλαταίνω, διευρύνω || ~ **ness** *n*
εὐρύτης || ~ **open** *a* (*lit*) ὀρθάνοιχτος,
ἀκάλυπτος || ~ **spread** *a* ἐκτεταμένος,
πλατύς || (*rumour etc*) διαδεδομένος
γενικός.
widow ['widəu] *n* χήρα || ~ **ed** *a* χηρεύσας,
χηρεύσασα || ~ **er** *n* χῆρος, χηρευάμενος
width [widθ] *n* εὖρος, πλάτος, φάρδος.
wield [wi:ld] *vt* χειρίζομαι, ἐλέγχω
ἐξασκῶ.
wife [waif] *n* ἡ σύζυγος, γυναίκα.
wig [wig] *n* περούκα.
wiggle ['wigl] *vti* κινῶ νευρικά, κινῶ
παλινδρομικά.
wild [waild] *a* ἄγριος || (*not cultivated*) εἰς

ἀγρίαν κατάστασιν ‖ (excited) ἀχαλίνωτος, ξετρελλαμένος, τρελλός ‖ the ~s npl ἀκαλλιέργητος ἔκτασις, ζούγκλα ‖ ~erness ['wildənis] n ἔρημος, ἀγριότοπος ‖ ~-goose chase n ματαία ἀναζήτησις, ἄσκοπος ἐπιχείρησις ‖ ~life n ἄγρια ζῶα ‖ ~ly ad παράξενα, σάν τρελλός, μανιωδῶς, ἀπερίσκεπτα.

wilful ['wilful] a ἐσκεμμένος, ἐκ προμελέτης ‖ (obstinate) πείσμων, ἰσχυρογνώμων.

will [wil] auxiliary v: he ~ come θά ἔρθη ‖ I ~ do it! θά τό κάνω! ‖ n βούλησις, θέλησις ‖ (purpose) ἀπόφασις, βούλησις, θέλημα ‖ (inheritance) διαθήκη ‖ vt θέλω, ἀποφασίζω ‖ ~ing a πρόθυμος ‖ ~ingly ad πρόθυμα, εὐχαρίστως ‖ ~ingness n προθυμία.

willow ['wiləu] n ἰτέα, ἰτιά.

will power ['wilpauə*] n θέλησις, αὐτοέλεγχος.

wilt [wilt] vi μαραίνομαι.

wily ['waili] a πανοῦργος.

win [win] (irreg v) n νίκη, ἐπιτυχία ‖ vt νικῶ, κερδίζω ‖ vi ἐπιτυγχάνω ‖ to ~ over vt κατακτῶ, ἀποκτῶ.

wince [wins] n σύσπασις, τρεμούλιασμα ‖ vi μορφάζω, σφίγγομαι.

winch [wintʃ] n βαρούλκον, βίντσι.

wind [waind] (irreg v) vt (wrap) περιελίσσω, τυλίγω ‖ (tighten) σφίγγω, κουρδίζω ‖ vi στρέφω, στρέφομαι, ἑλίσσομαι, τυλίγομαι ‖ to ~ up vt (clock) κουρδίζω ‖ (debate) κλείνω, τερματίζω, διαλύω.

wind [wind] n ἄνεμος, ἀέρας ‖ (med) ἀέρια, τυμπανισμός ‖ ~fall n (good luck) κελεπούρι.

winding ['waindiŋ] a (road) ἑλισσόμενος, φιδίσιος, μέ κορδέλλες, στριφτός.

wind instrument ['windinstrumənt] n (mus) πνευστόν (ὄργανον).

windmill ['windmil] n ἀνεμόμυλος.

window ['windəu] n παράθυρον, βιτρίνα ‖ ~ box n κιβώτιον λουλουδιῶν, γάστρα ‖ ~ cleaner n (man) καθαριστής παραθύρων ‖ ~ frame n πλαίσιον παραθύρου, κούφωμα ‖ ~ ledge n περβάζι παραθύρου ‖ ~ pane n τζάμι ‖ ~sill n περβάζι παραθύρου.

windpipe ['windpaip] n τραχεῖα, λαρύγγι.

windscreen ['windskri:n], (US) windshield ['windʃi:ld] n ἀλεξήνεμον, παρμπρίζ ‖ ~ wiper n ὑαλοκαθαριστήρ.

windswept ['windswept] a ἀνεμοδαρμένος.

windy ['windi] a ἀνεμώδης, ἐκτεθειμένος στούς ἀνέμους.

wine [wain] n οἶνος, κρασί ‖ ~ cellar n κάβα ‖ ~glass n ποτήρι τοῦ κρασιοῦ ‖ ~ list n κατάλογος κρασιῶν ‖ ~ merchant n κρασέμπορος ‖ ~ tasting n δοκιμή κρασιῶν ‖ ~ waiter n σερβιτόρος γιά τά κρασιά.

wing [wiŋ] n πτέρυξ, φτερούγα, φτερό ‖

(of building) πτέρυξ (κτιρίου) ‖ (mil) πτέρυξ ‖ ~s npl (theat) παρασκήνια ‖ ~er n (sport) (ὁ) Ἔξω.

wink [wiŋk] n ἀνοιγοκλείσιμο τοῦ ματιοῦ, νεῦμα ‖ vi κλείνω τό μάτι, νεύω ‖ forty ~s ὑπνάκο.

winner ['winə*] n κερδίσας, νικητής.

winning ['winiŋ] a (team) κερδίζων, νικήτρια (ὁμάδα) ‖ (goal) κερδίζων γκόλ ‖ ~s npl κέρδη ‖ ~ post n ἄφιξις, τέρμα.

winter ['wintə*] n χειμών, χειμώνας ‖ attr a (clothes) χειμωνιάτικα ‖ vi περνῶ τό χειμῶνα (εἰς) ‖ ~ sports npl χειμωνιάτικα σπόρ.

wintry ['wintri] a χειμωνιάτικος, ψυχρός, θυελλώδης.

wipe [waip] n σκούπισμα, στέγνωμα, σφούγγισμα ‖ vt σκουπίζω, στεγνώνω, σφουγγίζω ‖ to ~ out vt (debt) ἀποσβενύω, ἐξοφλῶ ‖ (destroy) ἐξολοθρεύω, σαρώνω.

wire ['waiə*] n σύρμα ‖ (cable) τηλεγράφημα ‖ vt ἐνώνω μέ σύρμα, τοποθετῶ τά καλώδια ‖ ~less n ἀσύρματος ‖ (radio) ραδιόφωνον.

wiry ['waiəri] a σάν σύρμα, νευρώδης, δυνατός.

wisdom ['wizdəm] n σοφία, φρόνησις ‖ (good judgment) σωφροσύνη ‖ (prudence) φρονιμάδα, γνῶση ‖ ~ tooth n φρονιμίτης.

wise [waiz] a σοφός, φρόνιμος, συνετός ‖ ~wise suffix κατά κάποιον τρόπο, σάν ‖ ~crack n εὐφυολόγημα, καλαμπούρι ‖ ~ly ad σοφῶς, φρόνιμα, γνωστικά.

wish [wiʃ] n (desire) ἐπιθυμία, εὐχή ‖ vt (desire) εὔχομαι, ἐπιθυμῶ ‖ with best ~es μέ τίς καλύτερες εὐχές ‖ to ~ s.o. goodbye εὔχομαι καλό ταξίδι ‖ to ~ to do ἐπιθυμῶ, θέλω νά ‖ ~ful thinking n εὐσεβεῖς πόθοι.

wisp [wisp] n (of hair) τσουλούφι, τολύπη.

wistful ['wistful] a ποθῶν, λαχταρῶν, πικραμένος.

wit [wit] n (sense) ἀντίληψις, κατανόησις, νοῦς, μυαλό ‖ (cleverness) πνεῦμα, εὐφυΐα ‖ (person) πνευματώδης ἄνθρωπος, εὐφυής, σπίρτο ‖ ~s npl μυαλό, σκέψι.

witch [witʃ] n μάγισσα ‖ ~craft n μαγεία.

with [wið, wiθ] prep μετά, σύν, μαζί, μέ ‖ (by means of) μέ, ἀπό ‖ (concerning) μαζί μέ, μετά ‖ (notwithstanding) παρά, παρ' ὅλον.

withdraw [wið'drɔ:] vt ἀποσύρω, σύρω, τραβῶ, σέρνω ‖ vi ἀποσύρομαι, ἀποτραβιέμαι, τραβιέμαι ‖ ~al n ἀποχώρησις, ἀνάκλησις.

wither ['wiðə*] vi μαραίνομαι, ξεραίνομαι ‖ ~ed a μαραμένος.

withhold [wið'həuld] vt ἀναστέλλω, κατακρατῶ.

within [wið'in] prep ἐντός, μέσα σέ, ἐν.

without [wið'aut] *prep* ἐκτός, ἄνευ, χωρίς, δίχως.

withstand [wið'stænd] *vt* ἀνθίσταμαι εἰς, ἀντέχω εἰς.

witness ['witnis] *n* μαρτυρία ‖ (*law*) μάρτυς, μάρτυρας ‖ *vt* (*see*) παρίσταμαι μάρτυς, βλέπω ‖ (*sign documents*) ἐπικυρώνω, βεβαιῶ, ὑπογράφω ‖ ~ **box**, (*US*) ~ **stand** *n* θέσις τοῦ ἐξεταζομένου μάρτυρος.

witticism ['witisizəm] *n* εὐφυολογία, εὐφυολόγημα, ἐξυπνάδα, ἀστεῖον.

wittily ['witili] *ad* πνευματωδῶς, ἔξυπνα, σπιρτόζικα.

witty ['witi] *a* πνευματώδης, σπιρτόζικος, ἔξυπνος.

wives [waivz] *npl of* wife.

wizard ['wizəd] *n* μάγος.

wobble ['wɔbl] *vi* παραπατῶ, ταλαντεύομαι, τρέμω.

woe [wəu] *n* συμφορά, δυστυχία, λύπη, θλῖψις.

woke [wəuk] *pt,pp of* wake.

wolf [wulf] *n* λύκος.

wolves [wulvz] *npl of* wolf.

woman ['wumən] *n* γυνή, γυναίκα ‖ *attr a* (*doctor*) (ἡ) ἰατρός, γιατρίνα.

womb [wu:m] *n* μήτρα.

women ['wimin] *npl of* woman.

won [wʌn] *pt,pp of* win.

wonder ['wʌndə*] *n* θαῦμα ‖ (*feeling*) θαυμασμός, κατάπληξις ‖ *vi* (*want to know*) ἀπορῶ, διερωτῶμαι, μήπως ‖ ~**ful** *a* θαυμάσιος, ἐκπληκτικός ‖ ~**fully** *ad* θαυμάσια, ὑπέροχα, περίφημα.

won't [wəunt] = will not ‖ *see* will.

wood [wud] *n* ξύλον, ξυλεία ‖ (*forest*) δάσος, δρυμός, ἄλσος ‖ ~ **carving** *n* ξυλογλυπτική ‖ ~**ed** *a* δασώδης, δασωμένος ‖ ~**en** *a* ξύλινος ‖ (*stiff*) ἀδέξιος, ἄκαμπτος ‖ ~**pecker** *n* δρυοκολάπτης ‖ ~**wind** *n* ξύλινα πνευστά ‖ ~**work** *n* ξυλουργική ‖ ~**worm** *n* σκουλήκι τοῦ ξύλου.

wool [wul] *n* ἔριον, μαλλί ‖ (*material*) μάλλινον ὕφασμα ‖ ~**len**, (*US*) ~**en** *a* μάλλινος ‖ (*industry*) ὑφαντουργική ‖ ~**ly**, (*US*) ~**y** *a* σάν μαλλί, σκεπασμένος μέ μαλλί.

word [wɜːd] *n* λέξις ‖ (*talk, speech*) λόγος, παρατήρησις ‖ (*news*) εἴδησις, εἰδοποίησις, μήνυμα, νέο ‖ (*promise*) λόγος ‖ *vt* διατυπώνω, ἐκφράζω μέ λέξεις ‖ ~**ing** *n* διατύπωσις, φρασεολογία.

wore [wɔː*] *pt of* wear.

work [wɜːk] *n* ἔργον ‖ (*task*) ἐργασία, δουλειά, ἀπασχόλησις ‖ (*art, liter*) ἔργον, προϊόν ἐργασίας ‖ *vi* ἐργάζομαι, δουλεύω ‖ (*have occupation*) ἐργάζομαι, ἀσχολοῦμαι μέ, δουλεύω ‖ *vt* (*cause to act*) λειτουργῶ, ἐπιτυγχάνω ‖ ~**s** *n* (*factory*) ἐργοστάσιον ‖ **to** ~ **on** *vt* συνεχίζω ‖ ἐπηρεάζω ‖ **to** ~ **out** *vi* (*sum*)

ὑπολογίζομαι, ἀνέρχομαι εἰς ‖ *vt* (*problem*) λύνω, ἀναπτύσσω ‖ (*plan*) ἐπεξεργάζομαι ‖ **to** ~ **up to** *vt* ἀνέρχομαι, παράγω ‖ **to get** ~**ed up** ἐξάπτομαι, θυμώνω ‖ ~**able** *a* ἐπεξεργάσιμος, ἐκμεταλλεύσιμος, ἐφαρμόσιμος ‖ ~**er** *n* ἐργάτης, ἐργαζόμενος ‖ ~**ing class** *n* ἐργατική τάξις, ἐργαζόμενοι ‖ ~**ing-class** *a* τῆς ἐργατικῆς τάξεως ‖ ~**ing man** *n* ἐργάτης, δουλευτής ‖ ~**man** *n* ἐργάτης, τεχνίτης ‖ ~**manship** *n* ἐκτέλεσις, δούλεμα, ἐπεξεργασία ‖ ~**shop** *n* ἐργαστήριον.

world [wɜːld] *n* σύμπαν, ὑφήλιος, κόσμος ‖ (*the earth*) γῆ, κόσμος ‖ (*mankind*) κόσμος, ἀνθρωπότης ‖ (*society*) κοινωνία, κόσμος ‖ (*sphere*) κόσμος ‖ *attr a* (*champion*) παγκόσμιος, διεθνής ‖ **out of this** ~ ἀπίστευτος, περίφημος ‖ ~**-famous** *a* παγκοσμίου φήμης ‖ ~**ly** *a* ἐγκόσμιος, τοῦ κόσμου ‖ ~**-wide** *a* παγκόσμιος, διεθνής.

worm [wɜːm] *n* σκουλήκι.

worn [wɔːn] *pp of* wear ‖ *a* ἐφθαρμένος, φορεμένος ‖ ~**-out** *a* (*object*) τριμμένος, φαγωμένος ‖ (*person*) ἐξηντλημένος, τσακισμένος.

worried ['wʌrid] *a* στενοχωρημένος, ἀνήσυχος.

worrier ['wʌriə*] *n* (*person who worries*) ὁ πάντα στενοχωρημένος, ἀνήσυχος.

worry ['wʌri] *n* ἀνησυχία, σκοτούρα, μπελᾶς, βάσανο ‖ *vt* (*trouble*) βασανίζω, στενοχωρῶ ‖ *vi* (*feel uneasy*) ἀνησυχῶ, στενοχωροῦμαι ‖ ~**ing** *a* ἐνοχλητικός, βασανιστικός, πληκτικός.

worse [wɜːs] *a comparative of* bad ‖ *ad comparative of* badly ‖ *n* κάτι χειρότερο, πιό κακό ‖ ~ *n* vt ἐπιδεινώνω, χειροτερεύω ‖ *vi* ἐπιδεινοῦμαι.

worship ['wɜːʃip] *n* λατρεία, προσκύνησις ‖ (*religious service*) λατρεία, ἐκκλησίασμα ‖ (*title*) ἡ αὐτοῦ ἐντιμότης ‖ *vt* λατρεύω ‖ (*adore*) ἀγαπῶ, λατρεύω ‖ ~**per** *n* πιστός.

worst [wɜːst] *a superlative of* bad ‖ *ad superlative of* badly ‖ *n* ὁ χειρότερος, ὁ πιό κακός, χείριστος.

worsted ['wustid] *n* ὑφάσματα πενιέ, μαλλί πενιέ.

worth [wɜːθ] *n* ἀξία ‖ *a* ἀξίζων ‖ ~**less** *a* χωρίς ἀξίαν, ἄχρηστος ‖ ~**while** *a* ἀξίζων τόν κόπον ‖ ~**y** ['wɜːði] *a* ἀξίζων, ἄξιος ‖ (+ *of*) ἀντάξιος.

would [wud] *auxiliary v*: she ~ come ἐρχόταν ‖ if you asked he ~ come ἄν παρακαλοῦσες θ᾿ ἀρχότανε ‖ ~ **you like a drink?** θέλεις κανένα ποτό; ‖ ~**-be** *a* δῆθεν ‖ ~**n't** = ~ **not**.

wound [waund] *pt,pp of* wind ‖ [wu:nd] *n* τραῦμα, πληγή ‖ *vt* τραυματίζω, πληγώνω.

wove [wəuv] *pt of* weave ‖ ~**n** *pp of* weave

wrangle ['ræŋgl] *n* διαπληκτισμός, .σακω-μός, λογομαχία ‖ *vi* διαπληκτίζομαι, λογομαχώ, τσακώνομαι.

wrap [ræp] *n* πανωφόρι, σάλι ‖ *vt* (*also* ~ **up**) τυλίσσω, περιβάλλω, καλύπτω ‖ ~**per** *n* περιτύλιγμα, κάλυμμα, ρόμπα ‖ ~**ping paper** *n* χαρτί περιτυλίγμα-τος.

wreath [ri:θ] *n* στέφανος.

wreck [rek] *n* ερείπιον, καταστροφή (*naut*) ναυάγιον ‖ (*ruin*) καταστροφή ‖ *vt* καταστρέφω, προκαλώ ναυάγιον ‖ ~**age** *n* ναυάγιον, συντρίμματα.

wren [ren] *n* τρόχιλος, τρυποκαρύδα.

wrench [rentʃ] *n* (γαλλικό) κλειδί (*violent twist*) βιαία κίνησις στρέψεως, στρέβλωσις ‖ *vt* στρεβλώνω, στραμπου-λίζω.

wrestle ['resl] *vi* (+ *with*) αγωνίζομαι (*sport*) παλαίω, παλεύω.

wrestling ['resliŋ] *n* πάλη, πάλεμα ‖ ~ **match** *n* αγώνισμα πάλης.

wretched ['retʃid] *a* πολύ δυστυχής, άθλιος, δυστυχής ‖ (*bad, poor*) άθλιος, θλιβερός, αξιοθρήνητος.

wriggle ['rigl] *n* συστροφή, σκωληκοειδής κίνησις ‖ *vi* συστρέφομαι, σπαρταρώ, περνώ συρτά, γλιστρώ.

wring [riŋ] (*irreg v*) *vt* συστρέφω, στρίβω.

wrinkle ['riŋkl] *n* ρυτίδα, πτυχή ‖ *vt* ρυτιδώνω, ζαρώνω ‖ *vi* ρυτιδούμαι, ζαρώνω.

wrist [rist] *n* καρπός (του χεριού) ‖ ~ **watch** *n* ρολόϊ του χεριού.

writ [rit] *n* (*law*) δικαστική πράξις, έν-ταλμα.

write [rait] (*irreg v*) *vt* γράφω ‖ (*book*) συντάσσω, γράφω ‖ *vi* (*send letter*) γράφω, στέλνω γράμμα ‖ **to** ~ **down** *vt* διατυπώνω, (κατα)γράφω, σημειώνω, περιγράφω ‖ **to** ~ **off** *vt* (*dismiss*) άκυ-ρώνω, διαγράφω, ξεγράφω ‖ **to** ~ **out** *vt* καθαρογράφω, γράφω εν εκτάσει, συντάσσω ‖ **to** ~ **up** *vt* (*report*) συντάσσω, γράφω ‖ ~**-off** *n* (*smashed car*) τελείως κατεστραμένο ‖ ~**r** *n* συγγραφεύς, συντάκτης, γράψας.

writing ['raitiŋ] *n* γράψιμο, γραφή ‖ (*books etc*) λογοτεχνικόν έργον ‖ ~ **paper** *n* κόλλα, χαρτί γραψίματος.

written ['ritn] *pp* of **write**.

wrong [roŋ] *a* κακός, άδικος ‖ (*incorrect*) εσφαλμένος, ανακριβής, λαθεμένος ‖ (*mistaken*) λάθος ‖ ~**ful** *a* άδικος, αδικαιολόγητος ‖ ~**ly** *ad* άδικως, εσφαλμένως, λαθεμένα.

wrote [rout] *pt* of **write**.

wrought [rɔ:t] *a*: ~ **iron** κατειργασμένος σίδηρος.

wrung [rʌŋ] *pt,pp* of **wring**.

wry [rai] *a* στρεβλός, στριμμένος, στρα-βός.

X, x

Xmas ['eksməs] *n* (*col: Christmas*) Χρι-στούγεννα.

X-ray ['eks'rei] *n* ακτινογραφία, ακτινο σκόπησις.

xylophone ['zailəfəun] *n* ξυλόφωνον.

Y, y

yacht [jɔt] *n* θαλαμηγός, γιωτ, κότερο ~ **club** *n* ιστιοπλοϊκός όμιλος ~**ing** *n* ενασχόλησις μέ γιώτ, γιώτιγκ ~**sman** *n* άνθρωπος ασχολούμενος μέ γιώτ.

Yank [jænk] *n* (*col: American*) Αμερικα-νός, Γιάγκης.

yap [jæp] *vi* (*dog*) γαυγίζω.

yard [ja:d] *n* (*of house etc*) αυλή, προαύλιον, μάνδρα (*measure*) υάρδα (0.914 μ) ~**stick** *n* (*for comparing*) μέτρον συγκρί-σεως.

yarn [ja:n] *n* νήμα, κλωστή ‖ (*tale*) ιστορία φανταστική.

yawn [jɔ:n] *n* χασμούρημα, χασμουρητό *vi* χασμουριέμαι ‖ ~**ing** *a* (*gap*) χάσκων, ανοικτός.

year ['jiə*] *n* έτος, χρόνος ‖ ~**ly** *a* ετήσιος ‖ *ad* ετησίως, κάθε χρόνος.

yearn [jɔ:n] *vi* (+ *for*) ποθώ, λαχταρώ ~**ing** *n* πόθος, λαχτάρα.

yeast [ji:st] *n* ζύμι, προζύμι, μαγιά.

yell [jel] *n* ωρυγή, κραυγή, σκούξιμο *v* ωρύομαι, φωνάζω δυνατά, σκούξω.

yellow ['jeləu] (*colour*) *a* κίτρινος *n* κίτρινον ‖ ~ **fever** *n* κίτρινος πυρετός.

yelp [jelp] *n* υλακή, γαύγισμα, ουρλιασμα *vi* γαυγίζω, υλακτώ.

yes [jes] *ad* ναί, μάλιστα, ασφαλώς ‖ *n* καταφατική απάντησις, ναί ‖ ~ **man** *n* τυφλός οπαδός, δουλοπρεπής.

yesterday ['jestədei] *n* χθές, ψές ‖ *ad* χθές, χτές, ψές.

yet [jet] *ad* (*by now*) ακόμη, τώρα ‖ (*still*) ακόμη ‖ (*by that time*) κι όμως, παρ' όλα ταύτα ‖ *cj* παρά ταύτα, κι όμως, εν τού-τοις.

yew [ju:] *n* σμίλαξ.

Yiddish ['jidiʃ] *n* (*ling*) γερμανοεβραϊκά.

yield [ji:ld] *n* παραγωγή, απόδοσις ‖ *vt* αποδίδω, αποφέρω, παράγω, δίνω (*surrender*) παραδίδω, παραχωρώ ‖ *vi* (*surrender*) υποτάσσομαι, παραδίδομαι, υποκύπτω.

yodel ['jəudl] *vi* τραγουδώ (τυρολέζικα).

yoga ['jəugə] *n* γιόγκα.

yogourt ['jəugət] *n* γιαούρτι.

yoke [jəuk] *n* ζυγός, ζευγάρι ‖ (*servitude*) ζυγός.

yolk [jəuk] *n* κρόκος, κροκάδι.

you [ju:] *pron* (ε)σείς, (ε)σύ.

X

Y

Z, z

you'd [ju:d] = you had, you would ‖ *see* have, would.

you'll [ju:l] = you will, you shall ‖ *see* will, shall.

young [jʌŋ] *a* νέος, νεαρός, μικρός ‖ *npl* οἱ νέοι, ἡ νεολαία ‖ ~ish *a* μᾶλλον νέος, νεούτσικος ‖ ~ster *n* νεαρός, νέος, ἀγόρι, παιδάκι.

your [ˈjuɔ*] *poss a* σου, σας, ὑμέτερος.

you're [ˈjuɔ*] = you are ‖ *see* be.

yours [ˈjuɔz] *poss pron* (δικός) σου, (δικός) σας, ὑμέτερος ‖ ~ faithfully ὑμέτερος ‖ ~ sincerely ὅλως ὑμέτερος.

yourself [jɔˈself] *pron* σύ (ὁ ἴδιος), τόν ἑαυτόν σας, χωρίς βοήθειαν.

yourselves [jɔˈselvz] *pron pl* σεῖς (οἱ ἴδιοι), μόνοι σας.

youth [ju:θ] *n* νεότης, νειᾶτα, νειότη ‖ (*young man*) νέος, νεαρός, ἔφηβος ‖ (*young people*) νέοι, νεολαία ‖ ~ful *a* νέος, νεανικός, νεαρός ‖ ~ hostel *n* πανδοχεῖον νεότητος.

you've [ju:v] = you have ‖ *see* have.

Yugoslav [ˈju:gɔuˈslɑ:v] *a* γιουγκοσλαβικός ‖ *n* (*person*) Γιουγκοσλάβος ‖ (*ling*) γιουγκοσλαβικά ‖ ~ia *n* Γιουγκοσλαβία.

zany [ˈzeini] *a* ἠλίθιος, βλάκας.

zeal [zi:l] *n* ζῆλος ‖ ~ous *a* γεμᾶτος ζῆλον, ἔνθερμος, φλογερός.

zebra [ˈzi:brə] *n* ζέβρα ‖ ~ crossing *n* διάβασις (πεζῶν).

zenith [ˈzeniθ] *n* ζενίθ.

zero [ˈziərəu] *n* μηδέν, μηδενικόν ‖ ~ hour *n* ὥρα μηδέν, ὥρα (ἐπιθέσεως).

zest [zest] *n* ζέσις, ἐνθουσιασμός, ὄρεξι.

zigzag [ˈzigzæg] *n* ζίγκ-ζάγκ ‖ *vi* κάνω ζίγκ-ζάγκ.

zinc [ziŋk] *n* ψευδάργυρος, τσίγκος.

Zionism [ˈzaiənizəm] *n* σιωνισμός.

zip [zip] *n* (*also* ~ fastener, ~per) φερμουάρ, ἐκλαίρ ‖ *vt* (*also* ~ up) κλείνω (μέ φερμουάρ).

zither [ˈziðə*] *n* σαντούρι.

zodiac [ˈzɔudiæk] *n* ζωδιακός κύκλος.

zone [zɔun] *n* ζώνη.

zoo [zu:] *n* ζωολογικός κῆπος ‖ ~logical *a* ζωολογικός ‖ ~logist *n* ζωολόγος ‖ ~logy *n* ζωολογία.

zoom [zu:m] *vi* βομβῶ, βουίζω ‖ (*rise sharply*) ἀνυψοῦμαι κατακορύφως ‖ ~ lens *n* φακός μεταβλητῆς ἑστιακῆς ἀποστάσεως ζούμ.

English Strong and Irregular Verbs

Ἰσχυρά καί Ἀνώμαλα Ρήματα

Ἐνεστώς	Ἀόριστος	Παθ. Μετοχή
abide	abode	abode
arise	arose	arisen
awake	awoke, awaked	awakened, awoke
be	was	been
bear	bore	born(e)
beat	beat	beaten
begin	began	begun
bend	bent	bent
beseech	besought	besought
bet	bet	bet
bid	bade, bid	bidden
bid	bid	bid
bind	bound	bound
bite	bit	bitten
bleed	bled	bled
blow	blew	blown
break	broke	broken
breed	bred	bred
bring	brought	brought
build	built	built
burn	burned, burnt	burned, burnt
burst	burst	burst
buy	bought	bought
cast	cast	cast
catch	caught	caught
choose	chose	chosen
cling	clung	clung
come	came	come
cost	cost	cost
creep	crept	crept
cut	cut	cut
deal	dealt	dealt
dig	dug	dug
do	did	done
draw	drew	drawn
dream	dreamed, dreamt	dreamed, dreamt
drink	drank	drunk
drive	drove	driven
dwell	dwelt, dwelled	dwelt dwelled
eat	ate	eaten

Z

fall	fell	fallen
feed	fed	fed
feel	felt	felt
fight	fought	fought
find	found	found
flee, fly	fled	fled
fling	flung	flung
fly	flew	flown
forbid	forbade	forbidden
forsake	forsook	forsaken
freeze	froze	frozen
get	got	got, gotten
gild	gilded	gilded, gilt
give	gave	given
go	went	gone
grind	ground	ground
grow	grew	grown
hang	hung	hung
have	had	had
hear	heard	heard
heave (*naut*)	hove	hove
hew	hewed	hewn
hide	hid	hid(den)
hit	hit	hit
hold	held	held
hurt	hurt	hurt
keep	kept	kept
kneel	knelt, kneeled	knelt, kneeled
know	knew	known
lay	laid	laid
lead	led	led
lean	leant, leaned	leant, leaned
leap	leaped, leapt	leaped, leapt
learn	learnt, learned	learnt, learned
leave	left	left
lend	lent	lent
let	let	let
lie	lay	lain
light	lighted, lit	lighted, lit
lose	lost	lost
make	made	made
may	might	—
mean	meant	meant
meet	met	met
mow	mowed	mown
pay	paid	paid
put	put	put
quit	quit	quit
read	read	read
rend	rent	rent
rid	rid	rid
ride	rode	ridden
ring	rang	rung
rise	rose	risen
run	ran	run

saw	sawed	sawn, sawed
say	said	said
see	saw	seen
seek	sought	sought
sell	sold	sold
send	sent	sent
set	set	set
sew	sewed	sewn, sewed
shake	shook	shaken
shall	should	—
shave	shaved	shaved, shaven
shear	sheared	shorn, sheared
shed	shed	shed
shine	shone	shone
shoe	shod	shod
shoot	shot	shot
show	showed	shown
shrink	shrank	shrunk
shut	shut	shut
sing	sang, sung	sung
sink	sank, sunk	sunk
sit	sat	sat
sleep	slept	slept
slide	slid	slid
sling	slung	slung
slit	slit	slit
smell	smelled, smelt	smelled, smelt
sow	sowed	sown
speak	spoke	spoken
speed	sped, speeded	sped, speeded
spell	spelt, spelled	spelt, spelled
spend	spent	spent
spill	spilt	spilt
spin	spun, span	spun
spit	spat, spit	spat, spit
split	split	split
spoil	spoiled, spoilt	spoiled, spoilt
spread	spread	spread
spring	sprang	sprung
stand	stood	stood
steal	stole	stolen
stick	stuck	stuck
sting	stung	stung
stink	stank, stunk	stunk
stride	strode	stridden, strode
strike	struck	struck
strive	strove	striven
swear	swore	sworn
sweep	swept	swept
swell	swelled	swollen
swim	swam	swum
swing	swung	swung
take	took	taken
teach	taught	taught
tear	tore	torn

427

tell	told	told
think	thought	thought
throw	threw	thrown
thrust	thrust	thrust
tread	trod	trodden
try	tried	tried
wake	woke, waked	woken, waked
wear	wore	worn
weave	wove	woven, wove
weep	wept	wept
will	would	—
win	won	won
wind	wound	wound
wring	wrung	wrung
write	wrote	written

Numerals

Ἀριθμητικά

ἈΠΟ´ΛΥΤΑ		CARDINAL NUMBERS
μηδέν	0	zero
ἕνας, μία, ἕνα	1	one
δύο	2	two
τρεῖς, τρία	3	three
τέσσερες, τέσσερα	4	four
πέντε	5	five
ἕξι	6	six
ἑπτά, ἐφτά	7	seven
ὀκτώ, ὀχτό	8	eight
ἐννιά	9	nine
δέκα	10	ten
ἕντεκα	11	eleven
δώδεκα	12	twelve
δεκατρεῖς, δεκατρία	13	thirteen
δεκατέσσερες, δεκατέσσερα	14	fourteen
δεκαπέντε	15	fifteen
δεκαέξι	16	sixteen
δεκαεφτά	17	seventeen
δεκαοχτό	18	eighteen
δεκαννιά	19	nineteen
εἴκοσι	20	twenty
εἴκοσι-ἕνα	21	twenty-one
εἴκοσι-δύο	22	twenty-two
εἴκοσι-τρία	23	twenty-three
τριάντα	30	thirty
σαράντα	40	forty
πενῆντα	50	fifty
ἑξῆντα	60	sixty
ἑβδομῆντα	70	seventy
ὀγδόντα	80	eighty
ἐνενῆντα	90	ninety
ἐνενῆντα-πέντε	95	ninety-five
ἑκατό	100	one hundred
ἑκατό-ἕνα	101	hundred and one
ἑκατό-δέκα	110	hundred and ten
διακόσια	200	two hundred

πεντακόσια σαράντα	540	five hundred and forty
χίλια	1,000	one thousand
ἑβδομῆντα χιλιάδες διακόσια ὀγδόντα	70,280	seventy thousand two hundred and eighty
πεντακόσιες χιλιάδες	500,000	five hundred thousand
ἕνα ἑκατομμύριο	1,000,000	one million
ἕνα δίσεκατομμύριο	1,000,000,000	one billion

TAKTIKA′		ORDINAL NUMBERS
πρῶτος, πρώτη, πρῶτο	1st	first
δεύτερος	2nd	second
τρίτος	3rd	third
τέταρτος	4th	fourth
πέμπτος	5th	fifth
ἕκτος	6th	sixth
ἕβδομος	7th	seventh
ὄγδοος	8th	eighth
ἕνατος	9th	ninth
δέκατος	10th	tenth
ἑνδέκατος	11th	eleventh
δωδέκατος	12th	twelfth
δέκατος τρίτος	13th	thirteenth
δέκατος τέταρτος	14th	fourteenth
δέκατος πέμπτος	15th	fifteenth
δέκατος ἕκτος	16th	sixteenth
δέκατος ἕβδομος	17th	seventeenth
δέκατος ὄγδοος	18th	eighteenth
δέκατος ἕνατος	19th	nineteenth
εἰκοστός	20th	twentieth
εἰκοστός πρῶτος	21st	twenty-first
εἰκοστός δεύτερος	22nd	twenty-second
εἰκοστός τρίτος	23rd	twenty-third
τριακοστός	30th	thirtieth
τεσσερακοστός	40th	fortieth
πεντηκοστός	50th	fiftieth
ἑξηκοστός	60th	sixtieth
ἑβδομηκοστός	70th	seventieth
ὀγδοηκοστός	80th	eightieth
ἐνενηκοστός	90th	ninetieth
ἐνενηκοστός πέμπτος	95th	ninety-fifth
ἑκατοστός	100th	(one) hundredth
διακοσιοστός	200th	two hundredth
χιλιοστός	1,000th	(one) thousandth
ἑκατομμυριοστός	1,000,000th	millionth

430